THE POETRY NOTEBOOKS OF

RALPH WALDO EMERSON

# The Poetry Notebooks
## of
## Ralph Waldo Emerson

EDITED BY
RALPH H. ORTH, ALBERT J. VON FRANK,
LINDA ALLARDT, AND DAVID W. HILL

UNIVERSITY OF MISSOURI PRESS

COLUMBIA, 1986

The preparation and publication of this volume were made possible
in part by grants from the Programs for Editions and Publications
of the National Endowment for the Humanities, an independent
Federal agency.

Library of Congress Cataloging in Publication Data

Emerson, Ralph Waldo, 1803–1882.
    The poetry notebooks of Ralph Waldo Emerson.

    Includes index.
    1. Emerson, Ralph Waldo, 1803–1882—Manuscripts.
2. Emerson, Ralph Waldo, 1803–1882—Poetic works.
I. Orth, Ralph H.  II. Title.
PS1624.A1 1984    811'.3    84–2184
ISBN 0–8262–0444–9

Frontispiece: Engraving of Emerson in 1874.

To David Emerson

For his unfailing support
of Emerson scholarship during
the past thirty years

# Preface

This volume has been a collaborative effort. Ralph H. Orth was responsible for the preparation of notebooks P and Charleston, S.C., St. Augustine, Fla., and of the Additional Manuscripts section; Albert J. von Frank prepared notebooks X and Rhymer; and Linda Allardt and David Hill worked together on notebooks EF, EL, NP, KL[A], and ETE Verses. They have all, however, reviewed and commented upon each other's work at all stages of preparation. Each editor had a hand in the writing of the poetry analyses, and in seeing the volume through the press. Ralph H. Orth is primarily responsible for the introduction, and Linda Allardt for the appendix.

Mr. von Frank, because of his proximity for several years to the manuscripts and the wealth of Emerson material in the Houghton Library, became the central figure of this edition. He did most of the initial research, wrote many of the analyses and reviewed all the others, and came to be regarded as the authority of last resort because of his unmatched knowledge of Emerson's published and unpublished poetry. The other editors acknowledge their debt to him for his dedication and unflagging energy.

The Ralph Waldo Emerson Memorial Association granted the right to publish these notebooks and supported the work of the editors with regular grants-in-aid. The University of Vermont and Harvard University granted Mr. Orth and Mr. von Frank, respectively, sabbatical leaves to devote uninterrupted time to this project. Generous, continuing, and indispensable financial support was provided by the National Endowment for the Humanities.

In the Additional Manuscripts section, the texts of several poems have been reproduced with the permission of the following institutions: "Boston," the Cambridge Public Library; "Boston," the Massachusetts Historical Society; "Fate" ("That you are fair"), the Barrett Library (Ralph Waldo Emerson Collection), University of Virginia Library; "From the Persian of Hafiz" and "Saadi," the Henry W. and Albert A. Berg Collection, New York Public Library, Astor, Lenox, and Tilden Foundations; "Terminus," the Beinecke Rare Book and Manuscript Library (Collection of American Literature), Yale University.

Thanks are due to past and present members of the staff of Houghton Library of Harvard University, especially Professor William H. Bond, Curator of Manuscripts Rodney G. Dennis, Marte Shaw, F. Thomas Noonan, and Suzanne Currier. We also express our gratitude to Mr.

Edward B. Doctoroff and the staff of the Widener Library at Harvard, and the staffs of the Pierpont Morgan Library, the Bailey-Howe Library of the University of Vermont, and the Rush Rhees Library of the University of Rochester.

Our debt to fellow Emerson scholars is especially large. We thank in particular Ronald A. Bosco, Glen M. Johnson, and Susan Sutton Smith, editors of Emerson's topical notebooks; Joseph Slater and Douglas E. Wilson, editors of the *Collected Works* of Emerson; Wallace E. Williams, editor of Emerson's lectures; Eleanor M. Tilton, editor of Emerson's letters; Thomas Wortham, editor of Emerson's published poetry; and Joel Myerson and Robert E. Burkholder, Emerson's bibliographers. Of these individuals, several gave of their time and energy to read manuscripts in libraries the editors were not able to visit: Robert E. Burkholder, Lehigh University Library; Glen M. Johnson, the Library of Congress and the University of Virginia Library; Wallace E. Williams, Lilly Library, Indiana University; and Thomas Wortham, the Huntington Library.

Among individuals who helped in the preparation of these volumes were Mary Steele Cabrera, who made the original transcriptions of the manuscripts, J. J. Fruehwirth, Robert Gallasch, Bradley T. Hughes, David Mycoff, Ghita Orth, Hilary Shadroui, and Barbara Tallon.

Finally, special thanks are due to the early editors of Emerson's poetry manuscripts, James Elliot Cabot and Edward Emerson, and to Carl F. Strauch, who forty years ago undertook the first significant modern research into the tangled skein of the poetry notebooks and showed the way to the present volume.

R. H. O.
Burlington, Vermont
February 1985

# Contents

Preface, *vii*

Introduction, *xi*

Works Frequently Cited, *xviii*

The Poetry Notebooks, *1*

    Charleston, S.C.,
        St. Augustine, Fla., *3*

    P, *16*

    X, *109*

    EF, *264*

    EL, *323*

    Rhymer, *424*

    NP, *468*

    KL[A], *564*

    ETE Verses, *580*

Additional Manuscripts, *607*

Analysis of Poems, *720*

Appendix: Emerson's Indexes, *980*

Index, *984*

# Introduction

Ralph Waldo Emerson, despite his modest opinion of his capacities as a poet—an opinion later generations have chosen not to share—could not resist turning his hand to verse. As early as the age of nine, when he wrote the pious and conventional hymn "The Sabbath," he was regarded as the incipient poet of the family;[1] at the critical moments of his life, such as the deaths of his first wife Ellen and of his son Waldo, he sought to deal with his feelings in poetry; and in the late years of his mental decline, he continued to versify even though his mind no longer could offer up the words he sought.

Emerson's regular journals and miscellaneous notebooks attest to his love of the poetic craft. Almost all of them contain drafts, fragments, and fair copies of poems amid the steady stream of the prose passages. Additional hundreds of pages of loose manuscripts bear further drafts and fair copies. And as the greatest indication of this ongoing commitment, Emerson kept a number of notebooks devoted solely to poetry at various times in his life. These notebooks, containing over thirteen hundred inscribed pages, form the basis of this edition.

Despite the existence of this mass of material, little has ever been done to study the genesis and development of Emerson's poems. His early editors, James Elliot Cabot and Edward Emerson, mined the notebooks for poetic material for their respective editions of Emerson's works, sometimes stringing together series of related fragments to make new poems, but their efforts were not directed toward close or extended analysis. Only Carl F. Strauch, in his doctoral dissertation and a series of incisive articles, has shown how individual poems developed from specific events or flashes of insight, went through successive drafts and reorderings, and emerged as finished entities.[2] Most of Emerson's published poems have not been analyzed in that way. Moreover, scores of unpublished poems, and thousands of additional lines in notebooks and loose manuscripts that never crystallized into finished poems, have barely been studied at all.

The reason for this neglect is not far to seek. An orderly man in many things, Emerson neglected order when the poetic spirit was upon him. In

1. For the texts of poems Emerson wrote between the ages of nine and eighteen, and an extended commentary, see Albert J. von Frank, "Emerson's Boyhood and Collegiate Verse," in *Studies in the American Renaissance 1983*, ed. Joel Myerson (Charlottesville, Va.: University Press of Virginia, 1983), pp. 1-56.

2. *A Critical and Variorum Edition of the Poems of Ralph Waldo Emerson* (Ph.D. diss., Yale University, 1946).

his journals and notebooks, pencil and ink drafts of poems can appear at any point, with little regard for chronology or context; prose passages make their way around them as best they can. The pencil drafts are often erased and the lines written elsewhere, frequently with adjustments and transpositions. Drafts and fair copies of unrelated poems are often superimposed upon one another, so that as many as four successive layers of erased, unerased, canceled, or superseded versions of the same or different poems appear on the same page.

Until this tangle of material was unraveled, no coherent picture of Emerson's poetic practices could be developed. Only when the layers had been separated, the erased pencil drafts recovered to the extent possible, the relationships between the pencil and ink versions determined, the transfers of material from one page to another shown, and an analysis of the resulting evidence made, could the trail of Emerson's creative process be followed. A portion of this task was accomplished with the publication of Emerson's regular journals and miscellaneous notebooks, which made available the poetic passages contained in them.[3] But until Emerson's poetry notebooks and their ancillary manuscripts were subjected to the same editorial scrutiny and published in full, as they are here, a comprehensive study of Emerson as poet was substantially hindered.[4]

A thorough examination of what these notebooks reveal is beyond the scope of this introduction. An analysis of each poem and fragment printed here can be found in the latter part of this volume; these analyses present all of the information necessary for an understanding of the genesis, growth, transformation, significance, and ultimate fate (publication or nonpublication) of each distinct poetic entity, and refer the reader to relevant discussions elsewhere. More far-ranging interpretations of Emerson's poetry, especially as it relates to his inner life, his creative practices, his prose writings, and his public role as seer and bard, will be the province of scholars working with these materials in the years ahead.

## What Is Included

The nine poetry notebooks in this edition, all of which are in the Houghton Library of Harvard University, are printed in chronological order, insofar as that can be determined. Considerable overlap exists between several of the notebooks.

The first, untitled by Emerson, is given the title Charleston, S.C., St. Augustine, Fla. (drawn from Emerson's heading and herein abbreviated CSA), since it grew out of Emerson's sojourn in those two cities in the

3. *The Journals and Miscellaneous Notebooks of Ralph Waldo Emerson*, ed. William H. Gilman et al., 16 vols. (Cambridge, Mass.: Harvard University Press, 1960-1982).
4. A vital contribution to the study of Emerson's poetry will be the new edition of the published poems being prepared by Douglas E. Wilson and Thomas Wortham as vol. 9 of *The Collected Works of Ralph Waldo Emerson*, ed. Alfred R. Ferguson, Joseph Slater et al., 3 vols. to date (Cambridge, Mass.: Harvard University Press, 1971- ).

winter of 1826-1827. Seven succeeding poetry notebooks were titled by Emerson P (for Poetry), X, EF, EL, Rhymer, NP (for New Poetry), and ETE Verses; these span almost fifty years of Emerson's life. Finally, a segment of journal KL containing an uninterrupted version of most of "May-Day" forms an independent poetry unit (it is written upside down and from front to back relative to KL) and is here printed as notebook KL[A] between NP and ETE Verses.[5]

Omitted from this group of notebooks is one called Orientalist, which contains dozens of pages of Emerson's translations from Hafiz and other Persian poets; its main purpose is not poetic but as a repository for material relevant to the East.[6]

Substantial collections of manuscripts of individual poems are in the Houghton Library (especially in a file called Poems folders in this edition), the New York Public Library, the Huntington Library, and the libraries of Yale University and the University of Virginia. Drafts and fair copies of poems in these collections and in others are printed in a section of Additional Manuscripts if they are significantly different versions of any of the poems that appear in the nine poetry notebooks.

## What Is Not Included

Three kinds of manuscript poetry material are noted but not printed in this edition:

(1) those texts already printed in *The Journals and Miscellaneous Notebooks of Ralph Waldo Emerson* (JMN);

(2) those texts to be printed in the forthcoming edition of *The Topical Notebooks of Ralph Waldo Emerson* (TopN);[7] and

(3) those texts in separate manuscripts that do not differ appreciably from other texts printed in this volume.

Neither noted nor printed are drafts and fair copies of poems and poetic fragments no portion of which appears in any of the poetry notebooks that form the core of this edition. Since the notebooks were Emerson's main repositories for his verse, the number of such poems and fragments is small and of relatively little importance.

---

5. The Houghton call number for the Emerson journals and notebooks is MS Am 1280, with the individual notebooks numbered as follows: CSA 19; P 136; X 132; EF 127; EL 126; Rhymer 133; NP 92; KL[A] 80.1; ETE Verses 144.

6. Orientalist is scheduled to be published as part of *The Topical Notebooks of Ralph Waldo Emerson* (University of Missouri Press, forthcoming).

7. Of these notebooks, eighteen deal with individual topics such as Intellect and Art, six are devoted to notes on people, and three were used in the preparation of lectures. Other Emerson notebooks survive: three are indexes and eighteen are of a miscellaneous character, ranging from collections of anecdotes and lists of preaching dates to queries on literature and poems by other people copied for inclusion in Emerson's anthology *Parnassus*, 1874. A number of Emerson's account books also survive. See the Editorial Title List in JMN 1:403-12 and the list of published journals and notebooks in JMN 16:537-41.

## Treatment of the Text

The notebooks are presented in a genetic text, with all of Emerson's deletions, insertions, alternate readings, and other changes retained. A clear-text version, while superficially easier to read, would not give a satisfactory idea of the way in which Emerson's poems developed through their various drafts, and the reconstruction of that development through the use of textual appendixes would be almost impossibly difficult.

Thus, with a very few exceptions, the text is printed exactly as Emerson wrote it. Apostrophes in contractions and possessives are not supplied, nor are closing quotation marks, closing parentheses, or terminal or interior punctuation. Ampersands are retained, as are misspellings and such characteristic Emerson abbreviations as *shd* for *should, wh* for *which,* and *tho't* for *thought.*

However, abbreviations that include superscript letters are silently normalized ($y^e$ and $y^m$ are expanded to *the* and *them*), and lapses of orthography (*tehre* for *there*) are corrected, with the original reading given in a note. Some regularization of indenting is also made.

Emerson occasionally indicated a reversal of word order by subscript numbers, e.g. "destiny$_2$ or fate$_1$." Words and passages so numbered are reversed in the text ("fate or destiny") with the original situation described in a note. Lines indicated for transposition are also printed as Emerson intended.

Material written in the margin or on a facing page but intended for insertion in the text is placed where Emerson desired it, with the situation described in a note.

Various symbols currently in use in genetic transcriptions are used to show recurrent situations in the text:

(1) canceled material is placed within angle brackets: ⟨destiny⟩

(2) inserted or added material is placed within arrows: ↑fate↓

(3) alternate readings are indicated by slashes, with the readings in the order of inscription: /destiny/fate/

(4) material that has not been recovered is indicated by pairs of vertical bars ‖ . . . ‖, with the number of ellipsis points between the bars varying to show the approximate length of the unrecovered passage. Unrecovered material on pages either cut or torn out is delineated by only one set of vertical bars, since the amount of unrecovered matter cannot be known.

When a word or phrase has been canceled in whole or in part by another word or phrase written directly on it, the canceled matter is shown in angle brackets and the substituted matter printed immediately after it: dest⟨roy⟩iny; ⟨fate⟩destiny.

All canceled lines of poetry are shown canceled individually, and all inserted lines of poetry are shown inserted individually. When an inserted line has been written by Emerson above a canceled line, it is here printed below the canceled line to retain the proper sequence of inscription.

When sections of poems or whole pages have been struck through with vertical or diagonal lines to indicate use, revision, or cancellation, no attempt is made to present the situation typographically; it is described in a note.

All material in pencil is indicated as being in pencil. Pencil punctuation in ink writing is assumed to be Emerson's and printed in insert arrows.

Any material inserted by the editors in the text for clarification (to expand abbreviations, names of persons, book titles, or the like) is put in square brackets: [ ]. Editorial omissions are shown by [ . . . ] or more specifically by such statements as [arithmetic omitted].

Brackets by Emerson are printed thus: ⟦ ⟧; his symbol of authorship (see JMN 1, plate VII) is indicated by [R.W.E.].

Omitted are Emerson's practice penmanship, isolated and irrelevant words and letters, stray rules, ink blots, and other random markings. Material not in Emerson's handwriting—usually notes by James Elliot Cabot or Edward Emerson—is also omitted, although information so provided is used in the analyses when helpful.

Emerson's own indexes to notebooks P, X, EF, EL, Rhymer, NP, and ETE Verses are printed in an appendix.

## Page Numbers

Page numbers are supplied throughout, whether Emerson actually inscribed them or not. They are enclosed in special brackets: [52]. Unnumbered front flyleaves are given roman numerals: i, ii, iii. Unnumbered back flyleaves are included in the regular pagination. Occasionally Emerson repeated page numbers; these are indicated thus: 52.1, 52.2. Added unnumbered leaves, or loose sheets laid in between pages, are given subscript letters: $52_a$, $52_b$, $52_c$, and so on.

## Mutilations

Leaves torn or cut out are indicated in the text by the phrase [leaf torn out] or [leaf cut out]. If the leaf stubs bear writing, whatever has been recovered is given in a note or, if the recovered amount is substantial, in the text.

## Levels of Inscription

The various layers of pencil and/or ink writing on a page are indicated by subscript numbers, with 1 the earliest: $52_1$, $52_2$, $52_3$. The layers on a page are printed in sequence, even if this interrupts the flow of a poem on successive pages; for example, $52_1$, $52_2$, $52_3$, $53_1$, $53_2$, $54_1$, $54_2$, $54_3$.

## Erased Pencil Writing

Erased pencil writing is printed when enough has been recovered to make a coherent entry. Unrecovered portions are indicated by pairs of vertical bars ‖ . . . ‖, with the number of ellipsis points between the bars varying to show the approximate amount of unrecovered material. Beginnings and endings of lines where opening and closing words have not been recovered are also indicated by vertical bars.

When successive lines are not recoverable, they are indicated thus: [four lines of erased pencil writing]. Individual recovered words and phrases in such entries are given in a note.

When an entry was written first in pencil, then overwritten in ink, the pencil version is not usually printed; significant differences between the two versions are described in a note.

## Indenting of Poetry

All units of verse are set at a standard poetry indentation unless some other indentation can be shown to have significance. Further indentations are set in accordance with the manuscript.

## Poetry Line Numbers

To facilitate reference to individual lines of poetry in the notes, the lines on each page of the manuscripts, including canceled ones, are numbered by fives. The numbers, in parentheses, are printed in the left margin. Titles, dates, prose passages, long and short rules, and other nonpoetic material are omitted in this numbering. (These numbers do *not* refer to lines of individual poems, but to lines on the manuscript pages, and are *always* enclosed in parentheses.)

## Headnotes

Each notebook is prefaced by two notes. One gives the initial date of the notebook, insofar as that can be determined, its years of primary use, and a general statement of its contents. The other deals with the notebook as a physical object, describing the size and number of its pages, its pagination, any mutilations and peculiarities it may have, and any written or printed enclosures it contains.

## Footnotes

The notebooks are also annotated by individual pages. The key for each note is the manuscript page, which is printed in boldface in the note.

The first part of each note gives the title or first line of poems, parts of poems, or poetic fragments on the page, with (where less than an entire poem is inscribed) the line numbers of the poem as first published or as finally abandoned. When a line in the manuscripts contains elements of two printed lines, the situation is handled thus: 5/6. Short forms of titles and first lines are used when possible; ellipsis points are used in condensed titles ("Hymn Sung at . . . the Ordination of . . . Robbins") but not in shortened first lines. Titles and first lines of unpublished or incomplete poems are cited in the form established in the analyses of poems and poetic fragments (see next section).

Lines of published poems as cited always refer to the poem as first published, not as subsequently revised, since manuscript drafts are considered to have as their natural end the initial publication of the poem. Thus the text of "Each and All" is cited from *The Western Messenger* for February 1839, where it is fifty-three lines long, rather than from *Poems*, 1847, where lines 29-30 are cut, leaving a poem of fifty-one lines. Titles of poems, however, are given in their final authorial form: "To Ellen, at the South" (1847) rather than "To Eva at the South" (1843).

Lines that do not appear in poems as first published (or in the latest forms of unpublished poems or poetic fragments) are indicated by the letter "x" or, in the rare case where lines present in the manuscript were *added* in an edition subsequent to the first, by reference to that later edition. More than three consecutive unused lines are indicated by the phrase "four [or five, etc.] unused lines." The notation "x?" means that not enough of the line has been recovered to determine whether it appears in the poem as published.

Manuscript page line numbers are regularly provided in parentheses where needed for clarification.

Thus the note for page 265 of notebook P, which reads " 'Ode to Beauty,' 80-82, x, 84-88, 90, 92-93, x, x (1-14); 'A pair of crystal eyes,' 1-2 (15-16)" indicates that eleven nonconsecutive lines of "Ode to Beauty," plus three unused lines, occupy the first fourteen lines on the page, and the first two lines of the unpublished five-line poem beginning "A pair of crystal eyes will lead me" occupy lines 15 and 16.

The second part of each note indicates such matters as passages in pencil or erased pencil; lapses of orthography; vertical or diagonal lines showing use, revision, or cancellation of material; recovered portions of erased and mutilated passages; pencil versions of lines overwritten in ink; identification of persons or books in prose passages; and any other information needed for full comprehension.

## Analysis of Poems

Each poem, poetic fragment, and translation in Emerson's poetry notebooks is discussed in an individual analysis following the text of the notebooks and the Additional Manuscripts. A full description of the procedures used in these analyses, which constitute the interpretive heart of this edition, is given at the beginning of the analyses section.

# Works Frequently Cited

Cabot, *Memoir*
James Elliot Cabot. *A Memoir of Ralph Waldo Emerson.* Boston and New York: Houghton Mifflin, 1887. 2 vols.

Channing, *Thoreau*
William Ellery Channing. *Thoreau: The Poet-Naturalist.* Boston: Roberts Brothers, 1873.

*Early Lectures*
*The Early Lectures of Ralph Waldo Emerson.* Edited by Stephen E. Whicher, Robert E. Spiller, and Wallace E. Williams. Cambridge, Mass.: Harvard University Press, 1959-1972. 3 vols.

Furness, *Records*
Horace Howard Furness, ed. *Records of a Lifelong Friendship 1807-1882: Ralph Waldo Emerson and William Henry Furness.* Boston and New York: Houghton Mifflin, 1910.

*Geschichte*
Joseph von Hammer-Purgstall. *Geschichte der schönen Redekünste Persiens, mit einer Blüthenlese aus zweyhundert persischen Dichtern.* Vienna, 1818.

Hafiz, *Diwan*
*Der Diwan von Mohammed Schemsed-din Hafis.* Trans. Joseph von Hammer-Purgstall. Stuttgart and Tübingen, 1812-1813. 2 vols.

Holmes, *Emerson*
Oliver Wendell Holmes. *Ralph Waldo Emerson.* Boston and New York: Houghton Mifflin, 1884.

J
*Journals of Ralph Waldo Emerson.* Edited by Edward Waldo Emerson and Waldo Emerson Forbes. Boston and New York: Houghton Mifflin, 1909-1914. 10 vols.

JMN
*The Journals and Miscellaneous Notebooks of Ralph Waldo Emerson.* William H. Gilman and Ralph H. Orth, chief editors; Alfred R. Ferguson, senior editor; Linda Allardt, Ronald A. Bosco, George P. Clark, Merrell R. Davis, Harrison Hayford, David W. Hill, Glen M. Johnson, J. E. Parsons, A. W. Plumstead, Merton M. Sealts, Jr., Susan Sutton Smith, editors; Ruth H. Bennett, associate editor. Cambridge, Mass.: Harvard University Press, 1960-1982. 16 vols.

L
*The Letters of Ralph Waldo Emerson.* Edited by Ralph L. Rusk. New York: Columbia University Press, 1939. 6 vols.

*May-Day,* 1867
Ralph Waldo Emerson. *May-Day and Other Pieces.* Boston: Ticknor and Fields, 1867.

*One First Love*
*One First Love: The Letters of Ellen Louisa Tucker to Ralph Waldo Emerson.* Edited by Edith W. Gregg. Cambridge, Mass.: Harvard University Press, 1962.

"Persian Poetry," 1858
Ralph Waldo Emerson. "Persian Poetry." *Atlantic Monthly Magazine* 1 (April 1858): 724-34.

*Poems,* 1847 (Boston)
Ralph Waldo Emerson. *Poems.* Boston: James Munroe, 1847.

*Poems,* 1847 (London)
Ralph Waldo Emerson. *Poems.* London: Chapman, Brothers, 1847.

*Poems,* 1884
Ralph Waldo Emerson. *Poems.* Vol. 9 of *Emerson's Complete Works.* Riverside edition. Boston and New York: Houghton Mifflin, 1883-1893. 12 vols.

Poems folders 1-172
Houghton MS Am 1280.235 (1-172)

Rusk, *Life*
Ralph L. Rusk. *The Life of Ralph Waldo Emerson.* New York: Charles Scribner's Sons, 1949.

*Selected Poems,* 1876
Ralph Waldo Emerson. *Selected Poems.* New and rev. ed. Boston: James R. Osgood, 1876.

Strauch diss.
Carl F. Strauch. *A Critical and Variorum Edition of the Poems of Ralph Waldo Emerson.* Ph.D. diss., Yale University, 1946.

*Uncollected Writings,* 1912
Ralph Waldo Emerson. *Uncollected Writings: Essays, Addresses, Poems, Reviews and Letters.* New York: Lamb Publishing Co., 1912.

W
*The Complete Works of Ralph Waldo Emerson.* With a biographical introduction and notes, by Edward Waldo Emerson. Centenary edition. Boston and New York: Houghton Mifflin, 1903-1904. 12 vols.

## Journal Abbreviations

| | |
|---|---|
| AL | American Literature |
| ATQ | American Transcendental Quarterly |
| ESQ | Emerson Society Quarterly |
| HLB | Harvard Library Bulletin |
| MLN | Modern Language Notes |
| MLQ | Modern Language Quarterly |
| NEQ | New England Quarterly |
| PMLA | Publications of the Modern Language Association of America |
| PQ | Philological Quarterly |
| SRom | Studies in Romanticism |

St. Augustine.

For fifteen winter days
I sailed upon the deep, & turned my back
Upon the Northern star, & burning Bear,
And the cold orbs that hang by them in heaven,
Till star by star they sank into the sea.
Full swelled the sail before the driving wind,
Till the stout pilot turned his prow to land,
Where peered, mid orange groves & citron boughs,
The little city of Saint Augustine.

Slow slid the vessel to the fragrant shore,
Loitering along Matanza's sunny waves,
And under Anastasia's verdant isle.
I saw Saint Mark's grim bastions, piles of stone
Planting their deep foundations in the sea,
And speaking to the eye a thousand things
Of Spain, a thousand heavy histories.
Under these bleached walls of old renown
Our ship was moored.
— An hour of busy noise,

Notebook Charleston, S.C., St. Augustine, Fla., page 11.
By permission of the Houghton Library, Harvard University.

Yet not of these I muse
In this familiar place,
But of a kindred face
That never joy or hope shall here diffuse.

Ah Brother
I grudge not these their bed of death
But thanks to these who never wronged
The poorest that drew breath

All inborn power that could
Consist with homage to the good
Flamed from his martial eye

His from youth the leader's look,
gave thy law, took,
And never poor beseeching glance
Shamed that sculptured countenance

Notebook P, page 241. By permission of the
Houghton Library, Harvard University.

68

I am the Muse who sang always
I stood by Jove, at the first day
dawn of
glare of my        puts out
I have a torle that & eclipses the Sun
Though men of health & wealth
If all else is bereft
All have
make amends if I am left
nature was blockish & brute
all way I plastic only all was mute
my wrought

To quicken the stagnant lump with thought
At last the electric heat prevails
Wolves shed their fangs & snakes
snake & dragon shed their scales
Earth smiled with flowers & man is born
Then Asia spawned her Shepherd race
And Thebes substructs her granite base,
Tented Tartary, columned Nile,
Last by from vines on rocky isle
Or the windblown sea-marge bleak
Forward stepped the Perfect Greek

Notebook X, page 68. By permission of the
Houghton Library, Harvard University.

Notebook EF, pages 20-21. By permission of the
Houghton Library, Harvard University.

132  Teacher of man

There is no orator
Can beckon or persuade
Like thee the youth or maid
Nor morn, nor eve this music fails
Thy birds thy songs thy brooks thy gales,
Thy blooms thy kinds
Thy echoes in the wilderness
Heal age & Pain & loves distrust,
~~And fire~~ ~~& nourish minds~~
Thou fair ~~& virtuous~~ ~~that~~ ~~nerve~~ heroic:
Fire fainting Will ~~& nourish mind~~
Soothsayer of the eldest gods.
Revealer of the inmost powers
Promethean proffered love denied.
Disclosing treasures more than true,
Or me what say tomorrow due
Speaking by the tongues of flowers
By the lily's    tongues Why speaking
Singing by the small birds lays
Heart of bird the man's heart seeking

Notebook EL, page 132. By permission of the
Houghton Library, Harvard University.

00                                   00

There are beggars in Iran and Araby,
Seyd was hungrier than all ;
Hafiz said, he was a fly

00   That came to every festival.             00
He came a pilgrim to the mosque,
On trail of camel and caravan,

88   Knew every temple and kiosk          88
Out from Mecca to Ispahan :
Northward he went to the snowy hills,
t Court, he sat in the grave Divan.

77   Was never form and never face       88
So sweet to him as only grace
Which did not slumber like a stone,
But hovered gleaming and was gone.

99   Beauty chased he everywhere,        55
In flame, in storm, in clouds of air.
He smote the lake to feed his eye
With the beryl beam of the broken wave,

44   He flung in pebbles well to hear      44
The moment's music which they gave ;
Loved harebells nodding on a rock,
A cabin topped with curling smoke,

44   Ring of axe, or hum of wheel,        44
Or gleam which Use will paint on steel.
And huts and tents ; nor loved he less
Stately dukes in palaces,
Princely women hard to please,

44   Fenced by form and ceremony,       11
With etiquette and heraldry,
And more revered in mountain land,
Men built with power and grace to stand
Like castles.

44                                 44
Oft pealed for him a lofty tone,
From nodding pole and belting zone,
He heard a voice none else could hear,

14   From centred and from errant sphere,  44
The quaking earth did quake in rhyme,
Seas ebbed and flowed in epic chime ;
In dens of passion and pits of woe,

77   He saw strong Eros struggling through,  47
To sun the dark and solve the curse,
And beam to the bounds of the Universe.
While thus to love he gave his days

Notebook Rhymer, proofsheet between pages 16-17. By permission of the Houghton Library, Harvard University.

44   In loyal worship, scorning praise,   44
How spread their lures for him in vain,
Thieving Ambition and paltering Gain!
He thought it happier to be dead,
To die for Beauty, than live for bread.

Saadi answered, I ̶f̶e̶a̶r̶e̶d̶ this,
That of goods I could not miss,
If I fell into the line,
45   Once a member, all was mine,
Houses, banquets, gardens, fountains,
Fortune's delectable mountains,
But, if I would walk alone,
Was neither cloak nor crumb my own.  44
And thus the high Muse treated me,—
Directly never greeted me,
But, when she spread her dearest spells,
Feigned to speak to some one else;
I was free to overhear,
Or was welcome to forbear;
But that idle word
44   Thus at random overheard,   44
Was the anthem of the spheres,
And proverb of a thousand years;
The light with which all planets shine,
44   The livery all events put on,
It fell in rain, it grew in grain,
It wore flesh in friendly form,
44   It frowned in foes, and growled in storm;
It spoke in Publius Cicero,
In Milton, and in Angelo,
I travelled, and found it in Rome;
Eastward it filled all Christendom,
And it lay on my heart when I came home.
                          44

Mask thy wisdom with delight,
Toy with the bow, yet hit the white.
He loved to round a verse and play  44
Without remoter hope or fear,
Or purpose, than to please his ear.
Meantime every cunning word,  44
Tribes and sages overheard,
Those idle catches told the laws
Holding nature to her cause.   47

Notebook Rhymer, proofsheet between pages 16-17. By permission of the Houghton Library, Harvard University.

The bard has reached the middle date:
Stars to-night that culminate
Shed beams fair and fortunate:               44
Go, inquire his horoscope,
Half of memory, half of hope.               444

What said the sibyl?
What was the fortune
She sung for him?
*Strength for the hour!*               444

Man of marrow, man of mark,
Virtue lodged in sinew stark,
Rich supplies and never stinted,
More behind at need is hinted,               44
Never cumbered with the morrow,
Never knew corroding sorrow,
Too well gifted to have found
Yet his opulence's bound;               44
Most at home in mounting fun,
Beaming joke and luckiest pun,
Masking in the mantling tones
Of his rich laugh-loving voice,               4 44
In speeding troops of social joys,
And in volleys of wild mirth,
Purer metal, rarest worth,               45
Logic, passion, cordial zeal,
Such as bard and hero feel.               44

Strength for the hour!
For the day sufficient power;
Well-advised, too easily great
His large fleece to antedate.               44
But, if another temper come,
If on the sun shall creep a gloom,
A time and tide more exigent,
When the old mounds are torn and rent,
More proud, more strong competitors     44
Marshal the lists for emperors,
Then the pleasant bard will know
To put the frolic mask behind him,               44
Like an old summer-cloak,
And in sky-born mail to bind him,
And single-handed cope with Time,
And parry and deal the thunderstroke.     33

*John Holmes.*

With these there came a humorist,
Kind-hearted, gentle, gay,
Caressing his infirmities
As cossets for his play;
As gentle as a maid,
Yet with a bold address,
Which still surprised to lead
Such masked tenderness.
And he had skill to give
To his walking-stick or chair,
Or to his least affair,
A price superlative.
He was there to lend a grace
To a rude and savage place;
Such his proper merits shone,
That it needed not be known,
He was twin in mind and blood
To the man of merriest mood,
And of keenest point and edge,
And of the Muses' privilege, —
Skilled to show the fair and fit,
Who fills all Saxon minds
With his redundant fancy and his

Notebook Rhymer, proofsheets pasted to page 60. By
permission of the Houghton Library, Harvard University.

## SUPPLENDA.

THE yesterday doth never smile,
  To-day goes drudging through the while,
Yet, in the name of Godhead, I
The morrow front, and can defy :
Though I am weak, yet God, when prayed,
Cannot withhold his conquering aid.                67
Ah, me ! it was my childhood's thought,
If he should make my web a blot
On life's fair picture of delight,
My heart's content would find it right.
45ç                                                664
  In my garden three ways meet,
  Thrice the spot is blest ;
  Hermit thrush comes there to build
  Carrier doves to rest.
66                                                 65ç
  These broad-armed oaks, the copses maze
  The cold sea-wind detain ;
  Here sultry summer overstays
  When autumn chills the plain.
99                                                 55
  Self-sown my stately garden grows,
  The winds and wind-blown seed,
  Cold April rain, and colder snows
  My hedges plant and feed.
55                                                 55
  From mountains far and valleys near,
  The harvests sown to-day,
  Thrive in all weathers without fear, —
  Wild planters plant away !
54                                                 77
  In cities high the careful crowd
  Of woe-worn mortals darkling go,
  But in these sunny solitudes
  My quiet roses blow.
44                                                444
  Methought the sky looked scornful down
  On all was base in man,
  And airy tongues did taunt the town,
  Achieve our peace who can !
444                                               442
  What need I holier dew
  Than Walden's haunted wave,

  Distilled from heaven's alembic blue,
  Steeped in each forest cave.
44                                                444
  If Thought unlock her mysteries,
  If Friendship on me smile,
  I walk in marble galleries,
  I talk with kings the while.
55                                                989
  And chiefest thou, whom Genius loved,
  Daughter of sounding seas,
  Whom Nature pampered in these groves,
  And lavished all to please.
444                                               444
  What wealth of mornings in her year,
  What planets in her sky !
  She chose her best thy heart to cheer,
  Thy beauty to supply.
44                                                777
  Now younger pilgrims find the stream,
  The willows and the vine,
  But also to me the happiest seem
  To draw the dregs of wine.

Notebook ETE Verses, pages 178-79. By permission
of the Houghton Library, Harvard University.

*The Poetry Notebooks*

# Notebook
## Charleston, S.C., St. Augustine, Fla.

Emerson's notation on the front cover implies that he kept this notebook during his recuperative trip to Charleston and St. Augustine from November 1826 to April 1827. In all likelihood, however, it was not begun until after his return to Concord in June: drafts and fair copies of portions of the first three poems occur in journal 1826–1828, which Emerson is known to have taken with him to the South, and the fourth poem celebrates his return to Concord. Other poems, all fair copies, were added at intervals until 1834.

The dark blue paper covers of this notebook and its unlined, hand-sewn pages measure 17 x 19.7 cm. The forty-eight pages are unpaginated by Emerson; twenty-one of them are blank, as are the front cover verso and the inside back cover.

[front cover]                                          R. Waldo Emerson
                                                              1827—
                              1827
                                              Charleston South Carolina.
                                              Saint Augustine, Florida.

[front cover verso] [blank]
[1]        This cup of life is not so shallow
                 That we have drained the best
           That all the wine at once we swallow
                 And lees make all the rest.

(5)        Maids of as soft a bloom shall marry
                 As Hymen yet hath blessed
           And fairer forms are in the quarry
                 Than Phidias eer released.


[2] [blank]
[3]              He must have
           Droll fancies sometimes cross his quiet thoughts,
           Who in my vagrant verse shall look to find
           A holiday from study or from toil,
(5)        And consolation to his mortal care.
           Such idler will not be a man of name,
           But must be, & therein resembles me,
           A little liable to ridicule,
           Because he cares a particle too much
(10)       For the opinion of the fickle world;
           And notes how Merit does not swim to place
           In th' tides of this world,— & feels the scandal oft
           Of low salute to men of meaner mould;
           And yet has felt, albeit with scorn the while,
(15)       A kind of justice in the Seneschal,
           The uncivil fate, that made his fortunes vile.
           I am frank, my friend, your eye has found
           A gipsy muse that reads your lineaments
           To tell the faithful fortunes of your life.
(20)       Go to, I'll feed my humour to the full,
           And still expand the pleasant commentary.
                 Who loves my verse is one whose roving eye
[4]        Detects more beauty than his tongue will own
           In art & nature. Nay his traitor tongue
           Sometimes consenting to the coxcomb's jest,

fc  "R. Waldo Emerson" is written in dark ink over faded ink; "1827—" is in faded ink only.
1   "This cup of life."
3   "He must have / Droll fancies," 1–22.
4   "He must have / Droll fancies," 23–42.

Derides the beauty which delights his soul.
(5) He is a man, who, though he told it not,
Mourned in the hour of manhood whilst he saw
The rich imagination which had tinged
Each earthly thing with hues from paradise
Forsake forever his instructed eye,
(10) Bewailed its loss & felt how dearly bought
Is wisdom at the price of happiness.
Ah me, sometimes in
And sometimes when the dainty southwind blew
Its soft luxurious airs, & called the clouds
(15) Mustering their hosts from all the sunny bays,—
Then when the piping wind & sounding sea
And tossing boughs combined their cadences,
The sweet & solemn melody they made
Enticed him oft in heady wantonness
(20) To scoff at knowledge, mock the forms of life,
[5] Cast off his years & be a boy again.
Then has he left his books, & vulgar cares,
And sallied forth across the freshened fields
With all the heart of highborn cavalier
(5) In quest of forest glades hid from the sun,
And dim enchantments that therein abide.

I had rather follow him than talk to him;
Fast fast he leaves the villages behind,
As one who loathed them, yet he loathes them not,
(10) And snuffs the scents which on the dallying gale
The woods send out as gentle harbingers
Bro't from their inmost glens to lure the step
Of the pleased pilgrim to their alleys green.
I know the pleasures of this humour well
(15) And, please you, reader, I'll remember them.
First the glad sense of solitude, the sure
The absolute deliverance from the yoke
Of social forms, that are as tedious
[6] ⟨To⟩Oft to a fretful & romantic man
As a musquito's song at summer eve.
In the wood he is alone, & for the hollow chat
Of men that do not love, & will not think,
(5) He has the unpretending company
Of birds & squirrels & the fine race of flowers.

5 "He must have / Droll fancies," 43–60. At the left bottom of the page is written "Charleston S.C. 182⟨7⟩6".
6 "He must have / Droll fancies," 61–77.

↑16 Aug.↓   He forms his friendships with the flowers
Whose habits or whose hue ↑may↓ please him best,
Goes by the red & yellow populace

(10)    That with their vulgar beauty spot the plain
To find the honoured orchis—seldom seen,
The low pyrola with a lilac's smell,
Or the small cinque-foil, the wild strawberry's friend.
He speculates with love on Natures forms

(15)    Admires a calyx much as Winkelmann
The architecture of a Doric Pile
Not more he doated on the ‖ . . ‖

[7]    ⟨o⟩Of frieze or triglyph or on architrave,
Than doth this dreamer, on the slender shaft
⟨w⟩With awns & stipules graced, that lifts in air
The lily or the loosestrife, tapestried with leaves.

(5)    And close below
The ⟨sure provision⟩ faithful capsule to transmit its race
Li⟨f⟩ke from its like to another year of flowers,
Once more to be the food of tuneful bird
Low stooping on swift wing, or busy bee,

(10)    Or the small nameless eaters that can find
A country in a leaf.—

[8]–[9] [blank]
[10] [ . . . ]
[11]                 St. Augustine.
For fifteen winter days
I sailed upon the deep, & turned my back
Upon the Northern ⟨star⟩ ↑lights↓, & burning Bear,
↑On the twin Bears fast tethered to the Pole↓

(5)    And the cold orbs that hang by them in heaven,
Till star by star they sank into the sea.
Full swelled the sail before the driving wind,
Till the stout pilot turned his prow to land,
Where peered, mid orange groves & citron boughs,

(10)    The little city of S⟨t⟩aint Augustine.

Slow slid the vessel to the fragrant shore,
Loitering along Matanzas' sunny waves,
And under Anastasia's verdant isle.
I saw Saint Mark's grim bastions, piles of stone

---

7 "He must have / Droll fancies," 78–88.

10 "On the twin Bears fast tethered to the Pole" is written in pencil, bracketed, and indicated for insertion on p. [11] by an arrow.

11 "St. Augustine," 1–20. In line (3), "star" is cancelled and "lights" inserted in pencil. This page is reproduced in Plate 1.

(15)    Planting their deep foundations in the sea,
And speaking to the eye a thousand things
Of Spain, a thousand heavy histories.
Under these bleached walls of old renown
Our ship was moored.
(20)              —An hour of busy noise,
[12]    And I was made a quiet citizen,
Pacing my chamber in a Spanish street.
An exile's bread is salt, his heart is sad,—
Happy, he saith, the eye that never saw
(5)    The smoke ascending from a stranger's fire!

        Yet much is here
Than can beguile the months of banishment
To the pale travellers whom Disease hath sent
Hither for genial air from Northern homes.
(10)    Oh many a tragic story can be read,—
⟨And the dim traces⟩ ↑Dim vestiges↓ of ↑a↓ romantic
    ⟨things⟩ ↑past,↓
Within the small peninsula of sand.
Here is the old land of America
And in this sea-girt nook, the infant steps
(15)    ⟨The⟩ ↑First↓ foot-prints of that Genius giant-grown
That daunt↑s↓ the nations with his power today.

Inquisitive of such, I walk alone
Along the narrow streets, unpaved & old,
Among few dwellers, and the jealous doors
(20)    And windows barred upon the public way.
[13]             I explored
The castle & the ruined monastery
Unpeopled town, ruins of streets of stone,
Pillars upon the margin of the sea,
(5)    With worn inscriptions oft explored in vain,
Then with ↑a↓ keener scrutiny, I marked
The motley population. Hither come
The forest families, timid & tame
Not now as once with stained tomahawk
(10)    The restless red man left his council fire,
Or when, with Mexique art, he pa↑i↓nted haughtily
On canvas woven in his boundless woods
His simple symbols for his foes to read.
Not such an one is ⟨this⟩ ↑yon↓ poor vagabond

---

12 "St. Augustine," 21–40. In line (15), "The" is cancelled and "First" inserted in both pencil and ink.
13 "St. Augustine," 41–62.

(15)        Who in unclean & sloven apathy
                Brings venison from the forest,—silly trade.
                Alas! red men are few, red men are feeble,
                They are few & feeble, & must pass away.—
                       — — And here,
(20)        The dark Minorcan, sad & separate,
                Wrapt in his cloak, strolls with unsocial eye:
                By day, basks idle in the sun, then seeks his food
[14]        All night upon the waters, stilly plying
                His hook & line in all the moonlit bays.
                Here steals the sick man with uncertain gait
                Looks with a feeble spirit at things around
(5)         As if he sighing said, "What is't to me?
                "I dwell afar;— far from this cheerless ⟨beach⟩ ↑fen↓
                "My wife, my children strain their eyes ⟨for⟩to me
                "And oh! in vain. Wo, wo is me! I feel
                "In spite of hope, these wishful eyes no more
(10)        "Shall see New England's ⟨hil⟩wood-crowned hills again."
               x   x   x   x   x
(Here is a chasm very much to be regretted in the original manuscript.)
               x   x   x   x   x   x
[15]        There liest thou, little city of the deep,
                And alway hearest the unceasing sound
                B⟨oth⟩y day & night in summer & in frost,
                ⟨The sea loud lashing thy resounding shore⟩
(5)         The roar of waters on thy coral shore.
                 But softening southward in thy gentle clime
                Even the rude sea relents to clemency,
                Feels the ⟨warm⟩ ↑kind↓ ray of that benignant sun
                And pours warm billows ⟨o⟩up the beach of shells.
(10)        Farewell; & fair befall thee, gentle town!
                The prayer of those who thank thee for their life,
                The benison of those thy fragrant airs,
                And simple hospitality hath blest,
                Be to thee ever as the rich perfume
(15)        Of a good name, & pleasant memory!

[16]–[18] [blank]
[19]                                 Concord, Mass—
                                    June 1827
              Awed I behold once more

14 "St. Augustine," 63–72. The two rows of x's and the statement between them are in pencil.
15 "St. Augustine," 73–87.
19 "Awed I behold once more," 1–20.

My old familiar haunts; here the blue river
The same blue wonder that my infant eye
Admired, sage doubting whence the traveller came,—
(5)      Whence brought his sunny bubbles ere he washed
The fragrant flag roots in my father's fields,
And where thereafter in the world he went.
Look, here he is unaltered, save that now
He hath broke his banks & flooded all the vales
(10)     With his redundant waves.

Here is the rock where yet a simple child
I caught with bended pin my earliest fish,
Much triumphing,— And these the fields
Over whose flowers I chased the butterfly,
(15)     A blooming hunter of a fairy fine.
And hark! where overhead the ancient crows
Hold their sour conversation in the sky.
           These are the same, but I am not the same
But wiser than I was, & wise enough
(20)     Not to regret ⟨my⟩ the changes, tho' they cost
[20]      Me many a sigh. Oh call not Nature dumb;
These trees & stones are audible to me,
These idle flowers, that tremble in the wind,
I understand their faery syllables,
(5)      And all their sad significance. This wind,
That rustles down the well-known forest road—
It hath a sound more eloquent than speech.
The stream, the trees, the grass, the sighing wind,
All of them utter sounds of ↑(↓ad↑)↓monishment
(10)     And grave parental love.

They are not of our race, they seem to say,
And yet have knowledge of our moral race,
And somewhat of majestic sympathy,
Something of pity for the puny clay,
(15)     That holds & boasts the immeasureable mind.

I feel as I were welcome to these trees
After long months of weary wandering,
Acknowledged by their hospitable boughs;
They know me as their son, for side by side,
(20)     They were coeval with my ancestors,
[21]      Adorned with them my country's primitive times,
And soon may give my dust their funeral shade.

20 "Awed I behold once more," 21–40.
21 "Awed I behold once more," 41–42.

[22] [blank]

[23]     In May when seawinds pierced our solitudes
           The red Rhodora blossomed in the woods
           Spreading its leafless blooms in a damp nook
           To please the desert & the sluggish brook
(5)      The purple petals fallen in the pool
           Made the black water with their beauty gay
           Young Raphael might covet such a school
           The lively show beguiled me to delay
           Rhodora! if the sages ask thee why
(10)    This charm is wasted on the marsh & sky
           Tell them, dear, that if eyes are made for seeing
           Then beauty is its own excuse for being
           Why thou wert there o rival of the rose
           I never thought to ask—I never knew—
(15)    But in my simple ignorance suppose
           The selfsame power that bro't me there, bro't you.

Newton 1834

[24] [blank]

[25]     Dear Ellen, many a golden year
           May ripe, then dim, thy beauty's bloom
           But never shall the hour appear
           In sunny joy, in sorrow's gloom,
(5)      When aught shall hinder me from telling
           My ardent love, all loves excelling.

           The spot is not in the ⟨cro⟩rounded earth,
           In cities vast, in islands lone,
           Where I will not proclaim thy worth,
(10)    And glory that thou art mine own;
           Will you, nill you, I'll say I love thee,
           Be the moon of June or of March above thee.

           And when this porcelain clay of thine
           Is laid beneath the cold earth's flowers,
(15)    And close beside reposes mine,
           Prey to the sun & air & showers,
           I'll find thy soul in the upper sphere,
           And say I love thee in Paradise here.

Pepperell Sept. 1829—

[26]     I call her beautif⟨y⟩ul;—she says
           Go to; your words are idle;

23 "The Rhodora." In pencil.
25 "Dear Ellen, many a golden year."
26 "I call her beautiful;—she says."

My lips began to speak her praise,
My lips she tried to bridle.
(5) But, Ellen, I must tell you this,
Your prohibition wasted is,
Unless among your things you find
A little jail to hold the mind;
If you should dazzle out mine eyes,
(10) As dimmer suns sometimes have done,
My sleepless ears, those judges wise,
Would say, ⟨t⟩Tis the *voice* of the Peerless one.
And if your witchery decree
That my five senses closed should be,
(15) The little image in my soul
Is Ellen out of Ellen's controul,
And whilst I live in the Universe
I will say tis my beauty, for better, for worse.

Pepperell, Sept. 1829—

[27]–[30] [blank]
[31]                          Written in Sickness
                    ────────────────

I bear in youth the sad infirmities
That use to undo the limb & eye of age;
It hath pleased Heaven to break the dream of bliss,
That lit my onward way with bright presage;
(5) And my unserviceable limbs forego
The sweet delights I found in fields & farms,
On windy hills, whose tops with morning glow,
And lakes ⟨dim⟩ ↑lone↓ mirrors of ⟨a⟩Aurora's charms;
Yet I think on them in the sleepless night,
(10) Still breaks that morn tho' dim on memory's eye,
And the firm soul doth the ⟨f⟩ grim train defy
Of ⟨disease⟩ pale Disease, that wd. her peace affright.
Please God, I'll wrap me in mine innocence,
And bid each awful muse drive the dark Harpies hence.

[32] [blank]
[33]      I spread my gorgeous sail
Upon a starless sea
And oer the deep with a chilly gale
My painted bark sailed fast & free—

(5)      Old Ocean shook his waves
Beneath the roaring wind,

31 "Written in Sickness." In line (14), "dark" is in both pencil and ink.
33 "I spread my gorgeous sail."

11

But the little keel of the mariner braves
The foaming abyss, & the midnight blind.

The firmament darkened overhead,
(10) Below, the surges swelled,—
My bark ran low in the watery bed,
As the tempest breath its course compelled.

I took my silver lyre,
And waked its voice on high;—
(15) The wild blasts were hushed to admire,
And the stars looked out from the charmed sky.

Bear me then, ye wild waters,
To Apollo's Delphian isle,
My name is *Music,* in Castalie known,
(20) Where bowers of joy the Nine beguile.—

1822

[34] [blank]
[35]                    Oil & Wine,
Sparkling gems, & rich attire,
House & lands that men desire,
—Ye may seek at Plutus' shrine.
                ———

(5)                    High renown,
Plaudits from desiring throngs,
Echoed far by poets ⟨tongues⟩songs
Are dowry to the Victors crown.
                ———

Royal state,
(10) Diamond star, & cap of gold,
Bedizened throne, ↑(↓how hard to hold!↑)↓
—Are got by force, or fraud, or fate.
                ———

Man must learn—.
In haunts of care, in fields of strife,
(15) Are bought the glittering goods of life,
These to ashes turn.
                ———

But go thou home,
Home to the mansion of the mind,
If solid good thy search would find,
(20)       In the bright bower of Joy, & Thought's immortal dome.

35 "Oil & Wine."

[36]     I wear no badge, no tinsel star
          Glitters upon my breast,
          Nor jewelled crown nor victor's car
            Rob me of rest.

(5)     I am not poor, but I am proud
          Of one inalienable right,
          Above the clamor of the crowd
          Thought's holy light.

          Better it is than gems & gold,
(10)    And oh! it cannot die,
          For Thought will glow when the sun grows cold,
           And mix with Deity.

  1823.

[37]↑Canterbury↓
     Goodbye, proud world, I'm going home,
     I am not thy friend, nor art thou mine;
     Long through thy weary crowds I roam,
     Long I've been tossed like the salt sea foam,—
(5)      But now, proud world, I'm going home.

     Goodbye to Flattery's fawning face,
     To Grandeur, with his wise grimace,
     To upstart Wealth's averted eye,
     To supple Office, low & high,
(10)    To crowded halls, to court & street,
     To frozen hearts, & ⟨faint⟩ hasting feet,
     To those who go, & those who come,—
     Goodbye, proud world, Im going home.

     I'm going to my own hearthstone
(15)    Bosomed in yon green hills alone
     A secret ⟨shrine⟩ ↑nook↓ in a pleasant land
     Whose groves the frolic fairies planned,
     Green arches there, the livelong day,
     Echo the blackbird's roundelay,
[38]    And vulgar feet have never trod
     A spot that is sacred to thought & God.

      Oh when I am safe in my sylvan home,
     I ⟨laugh⟩scoff at the pride of Greece & Rome,

36  "I wear no badge."
37  "Good-Bye," 1–3, 5–20. In the bottom right corner of the page "And," is written as a catchword.
38  "Good-Bye," 21–30.

(5) And when I am stretched beneath the pines,
  Where the evening star so holy shines,
  I laugh at the lore & the pride of man,
  At the sophist schools, & the learned clan,
  For what are they all in their high conceit,
(10) When man in the *bush* with God may meet?

[39] An ancient lady who dwelt in Rome
  Bro't Tarquin the King her Album from home
  Nine ponderous volumes conveyed in a cart
  And mentioned that this was only a part
(5) And requested the monarch to buy the nine tomes
  At a price he thought might b⟨y⟩uy nine Romes.
  The unmannerly king refused to buy
  A lady's Album appraised so high,
  And she, to show her honest ire,
(10) Threw the three first volumes into the fire,
  And offered the king the rest of her lore
  At the price she had fixed for the nine before.
  The king was amazed at the lady's story,
  But the argument now was an *a fortiori,*
(15) And he flatly refused to redeem the volumes,
  Whatever might be or might not in their columns.
  The lady departed, & straightway burned
  Three more of the six, & then returned

   x x x x x x x x

[40]–[42] [blank]
[43] All the great & good,
  And all the fair,
  As if in a disdainful mood,
  Forsake the world, & to the grave repair.

(5) Is there a sage
  Needed to curb the unruly times;—
  He hastes to quit the stage,
  And blushing leaves his country to its crimes.

  Is there an angel drest
(10) In weeds of mortal beauty, whom high Heaven
  With all sweet perfections doth invest;—
  It hastes to take what it hath given.

  And, as the delicate snow
  Which latest fell, the thieving wind first takes

39 "An ancient lady." The row of *x*'s at the bottom of the page is in pencil.
43 "All the great & good."

(15)      So thou, dear wife, must go,
         As frail, as spotless, as those new fallen flakes.

         Let me not fear to die,
         But let me live so well,
         As to win this mark of death from on high,
(20)      That I with God, & thee, dear heart, may dwell.

   6 July 1831

[44] [blank]
[45]      The winds are cold↑,↓ the days are dark↑,↓
         In this unlovely land
         The East wind rises with the tide
         To chill the populous strand

(5)       Above me shines no Syrian moon
         With warm luxurious glow↑,↓
         Nor golden orange groves at noon
         Perfume the world below↑.↓

         Yet more I prize this frozen land↑,↓
(10)      This iron soil of ours↑,↓
         Than fields by Indian breezes fanned
         And crimsoned oer with flowers

[46]–[48] [blank]
[inside back cover] [blank]

---

45  "The winds are cold." The added punctuation is in pencil.

# Notebook P

An erased pencil entry in journal A, overwritten by material of December 1834, appears to refer to the start of P: "Let me save my ⟨live⟩ verse" (JMN 4:353, n. 298). The notebook was Emerson's major repository for working drafts and fair copies of poems through 1845 at least.

The covers of notebook P, green and brown marbled paper over boards, measure 16.9 x 20.7 cm. The spine strip, of brown leather, bears eight pairs of horizontal gold lines. Protective corners on the front and back covers are also of brown leather. "P" is written on the spine and the front cover.

Single flyleaves occur at the front and back (pp. i–ii and 333–34). Pages total 336, of which pp. iii–vi and 329–32 are unlined; the rest are lined with 27 lines to a page. The leaf bearing pp. 55–56 is torn out, and the bottom half of the leaf bearing pp. 131–32 is torn off. All leaves measure 16.2 x 20.1 cm.

One hundred and eighty-four pages are numbered in pencil, seventeen in ink, eight in pencil and ink, and 129 are not numbered at all. About one-third of the pages (113 in all) are blank.

The notebook contains the following enclosures:

(1) inside the front cover, a single sheet with pencil notations by Edward Emerson, and three paper strips once used as page markers;

(2) between pp. 52–53, a fragment of a tree leaf;

(3) between pp. 70–71, two tree leaves, one fragmentary, and page proof for pp. 402–4 (numbered 403–5) of *The Dial* ("Ethnical Scriptures. Hermes Trismegistus") for January 1844;

(4) between pp. 90–91, a clipping from a Boston newspaper of early 1842 bearing the poem "The Antiquity of Freedom" by William Cullen Bryant;

(5) between pp. 142–43, a small piece of paper with a notation by Edward Emerson; and

(6) between pp. 196–97, two newspaper clippings, one bearing the poem "The Lost at Sea" by James Otis Rockwell, the other an unidentified twelve-stanza poem (apparently translated from French) beginning "S[lowly?] with measured tread."

[front cover verso] [blank]
[i]—[ii] [blank]
[iii]                                                                    R. W. Emerson.

# P

[iv]—[vi] [blank]
[1]                                    Fame.
                                    =====

        Ah Fate! Cannot a man
          Be wise without a beard?
        East, West, from Beor to Dan,
          Say was it never heard
(5)      That wisdom might in youth be gotten
        Or wit be ripe before t'was rotten?

        He pays too high a price
          For knowledge & for fame
        Who sells his sinews to be wise
(10)     His teeth & bones to buy a name
        And crawls through life a paralytic
        To earn the praise of bard & critic.

        Were it not better done,
          To dine & sleep through forty years;
(15)     Be loved by few; be feared by none;
          Laugh life away; have wine for tears;
        And take the mortal leap undaunted,
        Content that all we asked was granted?

        But Fate will not permit
(20)     The seed of gods to die,
        Nor suffer sense to win from wit
          Its guerdon in the sky,
        Nor let us hide, whateer our pleasure,
        The world's light underneath a measure

[2]      Go then, sad youth! and shine;
          Go, sacrifice to Fame!
        Put youth, joy, health, upon the Shrine
          And life to fan the flame;
(5)      Being for Seeming, bravely barter,
        And die to Fame a happy martyr!
        1826
            =====

1 "Fame," 1–24.
2 "Fame," 25–30.

[3]                      *Written in Naples, March, 1833.*
                   We are what we are made; each following day
             Is the Creator of our human mould
             Not less than was the first; the all wise God
             Gilds a few points in every several life
(5)             And as each flower upon the fresh hill-side,
             And every coloured petal of each flower,
             Is sketched and dyed each with a new design,
             Its spot of purple, ⟨or⟩& its streak of brown,
             So each man's life shall have its proper lights,
(10)           And a few joys, a few peculiar charms,
             For him round in the melancholy hours,
             And reconcile him to the common days.
             Not many men see beauty in the fogs
             Of close low pine-woods in a river town:
(15)           Yet unto me not morn's magnificence,
             Nor the red rainbow of a summer eve,
             Nor Rome, nor joyful Paris, nor the halls
             Of rich men blazing hospitable light,
             Nor wit, nor eloquence, no, nor even the song
(20)           Of any woman that is now alive,
             Hath such a soul, such divine influence,
             Such resurrection of the happy past,
             As is to me when I behold the morn
             Ope in such low moist road-side, & beneath
(25)           Peep the blue violets out of the black loam,
             Pathetic silent poets that sing to me
             Thine elegy, sweet singer, sainted wife!

[4]         The rain has spoiled the farmer's day;
             Shall sorrow put my books away?
             Thereby are two days lost.
             Nature shall mind her own affairs,
(5)             I will attend my proper cares,
             In rain, or sun, or frost.
                     Newton, 1834

[5]         Good bye, proud world! I'm going home
             Thou art not my friend, and I'm not thine;
             Long through thy weary crowds I roam
             ↑A river ark on the ocean brine↓
(5)             Long I've been tossed like the ⟨salt sea⟩ ↑driven↓ foam
             But now, proud world, Im going home.

3 "Written in Naples, March, 1833."
4 "Suum Cuique" ("The rain has spoiled").
5 "Good-Bye," 1–22.

Goodbye to Flattery's fawning face
To Grandeur with his wise grimace
To upstart Wealth's averted eye
(10) To supple Office, low & high,
To crowded halls, to court, & street,
To frozen hearts, & hasting feet,
To those who go, & those who come,
Goodbye, proud world, I'm going home.

(15) I am going to my own hearth stone⟨,⟩
Bosomed in yon green hills alone,
A secret shrine in a pleasant land
Whose groves the frolic fairies planned
Where arches green the livelong day
(20) Echo the blackbirds roundelay
And vulgar ⟨crowds⟩feet have never trod
A spot that is sacred to Thought & God

[6]       O when I am safe in my sylvan home
I laugh at the pride of Greece & Rome
And when I am stretched beneath the pines
Where the evening star so holy shines
(5) I laugh at the lore & the pride of man
At the sophist schools & the learned clan
For what are they all in their high conceit
When man in the bush with God may meet.

[7]         *Shakspeare.*
I see all human wits
Are measured but a few:
Unmeasured still my Shakspeare sits,
Lone as the blessed Jew.

========

[8] [blank]
[9]         Compensation.
========

Why should I keep holiday
When other men have none?
Why but because when these are gay,
I sit and mourn alone.

(5) And why when mirth unseals all tongues
Should mine alone be dumb?

---

6 "Good-Bye," 23–30.
7 "Shakspeare."
9 "Compensation" ("Why should I"). In line (7), "the" is cancelled in pencil.

Ah! late I spoke to ⟨the⟩ silent throngs,
And now their hour is come.

———

New York
Nov. 1834.

[10] [blank]
[11]                               Each in all.
              Little thinks in the field yon red cloaked clown
              Of thee from the hill top looking down
              And the heifer that lows in the upland farm
              Far-heard lows not thine ear to charm
(5)           The sexton tolling his bell at noon
              Dreams not that great Napoleon
              Stops his horse and lists with delight
              Whilst his files sweep round yon Alpine height
              Nor knowest thou what argument
(10)          Thy life to thy neighbor's creed has lent.
              All are needed by each one
              Nothing is fair or good alone.
              I thought the sparrow's note from heaven
              Singing at dawn on the alder bough
(15)          I brought him home in his nest at even
              He sings the song but it pleases not now
              For I did not bring home the river & sky
              He sang to my ear, these sang to my eye.
              The delicate shells lay on the shore
(20)          The bubbles of the latest wave
              Fresh pearls to their enamel gave
              And the bellowing of the savage sea
              Greeted their safe escape to me
[12]          I wiped away the weeds & foam
              I fetched my sea born treasures home
              But the poor unsightly noisome things
              Had left their beauty on the shore
(5)           With the sun & the sand & the wild uproar.
              Nor rose, nor stream, nor bird is fair;
              Their concord is beyond compare.
              The lover watched his graceful maid
              As 'mid the virgin train she strayed
(10)          Nor knew her beauty's best attire
              Was woven still by that snow-white quire.
              At last, she came to his hermitage,

11 "Each and All," 1–23.
12 "Each and All," 24–49.

20

Like ⟨a⟩the bird from the woodlands to the cage;
The gay enchantment was undone,—
(15)    A gentle wife, but fairy none.
Then I said,—'I covet truth;
Beauty is unripe childhoods cheat:
I leave it behind with the games of youth';—
—As I spoke, beneath my feet
(20)    The ground pine curled its pretty wreath
Running over the clubmoss burs.
I inhaled the violet's breath
Around me stood the oaks & firs
Pine cones and acorns lay on the ground
(25)    Over me soared the eternal sky
Full of light and of deity;

[13₁]    Ah strange strange strange
The Dualism of man
That he can enlist
But half his being in his act
(5)    S

Roger Rain
Come again

Ann is spotless
Nell is not less

[13₂]    Again I saw—again I heard—
The rolling river the morning bird:
Beauty through my senses stole,—
I yielded myself to the perfect Whole.

[14]             *Dirge.*          *1838*
I reached the middle of the mount
Up which the incarnate soul must climb,
And paused for them, and looked around,
With me who walked through Space & time.

(5)    Five rosy boys with morning light
Had leaped from one fair mother's arms,
Fronted the sun with hope as bright,
And greeted God with childhood's psalms.

═══════

Knows he who tills this lonely field

13₁ "Ah strange strange strange" (1–5); "Roger rain" (6–7); "Ann is spotless" (8–9). In pencil. In the left margin beside line (2) is written "to" in pencil, followed by an erased word in pencil.
    13₂ "Each and All," 50–53.
    14 "Dirge," eight unused lines, 1–12.

(10)     To reap its scanty corn,
         What mystic fruit his acres yield
         At midnight & at morn?

         In the long sunny afternoon
         The plain was full of ghosts:
(15)     I wandered up, I wandered down,
         Beset by pensive hosts.

         The winding Concord gleamed below
         Pouring as wide a flood
         As when my brothers long ago
(20)     Came with me to the wood.

[15]     But they are gone,—the holy ones
         Who trod with me this lonely vale,
         The strong, star-bright companions
         Are silent, low, & pale.

(5)      My good, my noble, in their prime,
         Who made this world the feast it was,
         Who learned with me the lore of time,
         Who loved this dwelling place.

         They took this valley for their toy,
(10)     They played with it in every mood,
         A cell for prayer, a hall for joy,
         They treated nature as they would.

         They coloured the ⟨whole⟩ horizon round,
         Stars flamed ⟨or⟩& faded as they bade,
(15)     All echoes hearkened for their sound,
         They made the woodlands glad or mad.

         I touch this flower of silken leaf
         Which once our childhood knew,
         Its soft leaves wound me with a grief
(20)     Whose balsam never grew.

[16₁] [six lines of erased pencil writing]

[16₂]    Hearken to yon pine-warbler,
         Singing aloft in the tree,
         Hearest thou, o traveller!
         What he singeth to me?

15 "Dirge," 13–32.
16₁ "See yonder leafless trees." Erased pencil. No differences from the ink version on p. [17]
have been discerned.
16₂ "Dirge," 33–52.

(5) Not unless God made sharp thine ear
  With sorrow such as mine,
  Out of that delicate lay couldst thou
  The heavy tale divine.

  Go, lonely man, ⟨he⟩it saith,
(10) They loved thee from their birth
  Their hands were pure, & pure their faith,
  There are no such hearts on earth.

  Ye drew one mother's milk,
  One chamber held ye all,
(15) A very tender history
  Did in your childhood fall.

  Ye cannot unlock your heart,
  The key is gone with them;
  The silent organ loudest chaunts
(20) The master's requiem.

[17] See yonder leafless trees against the sky,
  How they diffuse themselves into the air,
  And ever subdividing separate,
  Limbs into branches, branches into twigs,
(5) As if they loved the element, & hasted
  To dissipate their being into it.

↑Apr. 1829↓ ↑To E.T.E. at Philadelphia.↓
  The green grass is bowing,
  The morning wind is in it;
  Tis a tune worth thy knowing,
(10) Though it change every minute.

  Tis a tune of the spring,
  Every year plays it over,
  To the robins on the wing
  And to the pausing lover.

(15) Oer ten thousand thousand acres
  Goes light the nimble Zephyr,
  The Flowers,—tiny sect of Shakers,
  Worship him ever.

  Hark to the winning sound!
(20) They summon thee, dearest,

17 "See yonder leafless trees" (1–6); "To Ellen, at the South," 1–14 (7–20).

[18]        Saying; "We have drest for thee the ground
           'Nor yet thou appearest.

           'O hasten! tis our time,
           'Ere yet the red Summer
(5)        'Scorch our delicate prime,
           'Loved of ⟨the⟩ bee, ⟨the⟩ ↑the↓ tawny hummer.

           'O pride of thy race!
           'Sad in sooth it were to ours
           'If our brief tribe miss thy face,
(10)      'We poor New England flowers.

           '⟨Thou shalt⟩ ↑Fairest!↓ choose the fairest members
           'Of our lit⟨t⟩he society;
           'June's glories & September's
           '⟨Shall⟩ show our love & piety.

(15)      'Thou shalt command us all,
           '⟨From April's early⟩ ↑April's cowslip ⟨crocus cup violets⟩ &
               ⟨June's⟩ summer's↓ clover,
           'To the gentian in the fall
           'Blue eyed favorite of thy lover.

           'O come then quickly come,
(20)      'We are budding, we are blowing,
           'And the wind that we perfume
           'Sings a tune that's worth thy knowing.'

[19] [blank]
[20]                     Ἕν κὰι πᾶν.
                                  All things
           Are of one pattern made. Bird, beast, & plant
           Song, picture, form, space, thought, & character
           Deceive us seeming to be many things
(5)        And are but one. Beheld far off, they differ
           As God and Devil; bring them to the mind,
           They dull its edge with their monotony.
           Therefore, to know one thing, we learn another,
           And in the second reappears the first.
(10)      The specious panorama of ⟨the⟩ ↑a↓ year
           But multiplies the image of a day,—
           A belt of mirrors round a taper's flame;—
           And universal Nature through her vast
           And crowded Whole, an infinite parroquet—

18  "To Ellen, at the South," 15–36. The second "the" in line (6) is cancelled in pencil.
20  "Xenophanes," 5–19. The diacritical marks in the title are in pencil.

(15)       Repeats one tedious note.
  Concord
  1834

[21]                           21 March
                 All things ⟨are of one pattern made⟩
                 Are of one pattern made. Bird beast & plant
                 Song picture form space thought & character
                 Deceive us seeming to be many things
(5)        And are but one   ⟨Seen⟩ ↑Beheld↓ far off they differ
                 As God & Devil; bring them to the mind
                 They dull its edge with their monotony
                 Therefore to know one thing we learn another
                 And in the second reappears the first
(10)      The specious panorama of a year
                 ⟨Only repeats⟩ ↑But multiplies↓ the image of a day
                 A belt of mirrors round a candle's flame
                 And Nature through her vast & crowded whole
                 ⟨Age after age with voices numberless⟩
(15)      Like a ⟨parr⟩ silly solemn parroquet
                 Repeats one ↑tedious↓ note.

[22]     When thought is best then is there most

          ═════════

        Do that which you can do
        The world will feel its need of you.

          ═════════

        Few are free
(5)      All might be
        Tis the height
        Of the soul's flight

          ═════════

        Every thought is public
        Every nook is wide
(10)     The gossips spread each whisper
        And the gods from side to side

          ═════════

        Atom from atom yawns as far
        As moon from earth, or star from star.

          ═════════

21  "Xenophanes," 5/6, 6–16, 17/18, x, 18–19. Partially erased pencil.
22  "When thought is best" (1); "Do that which you can do" (2–3); "Few are free" (4–7); "Hush!" (8–11); "Atom from atom" (12–13). Lines (1–7) are in pencil; lines (8–11) are struck through in ink.

[23]    There is no great & no small
         To the soul that maketh all;
         And where it cometh, all things are;
         And it cometh everywhere.

               ═══

(5)     I am owner of the sphere,
         Of the Seven Stars, and the Solar Year,
         Of Caesars hand, and Plato's brain,
         Of Lord Christ's heart, and Shakspear's strain.

               ═══

         Cast the bantling on the rocks
(10)    Suckle him with the shewolf's teat
         Wintered with the hawk & fox
         Power & speed be hands & feet

[24] [blank]
[25₁]   From tree to tree ⟨flying before me⟩
         A ‖ . ⟨ . . . . ⟩ . . ⟨ . . . . . . ‖⟩
         ⟨And farther off the sparrow ‖ . . ‖⟩
         ‖ . . . . . . . . . . . . . . . ‖

[25₂]                       21 March
              It is happiness
         To bathe in this morn's soft & silvered air
         And loiter by yon loitering stream

         Sparrows far off, & nearer, yonder bird
(5)     Blue coated flying before from tree to tree
         Courageous s⟨an⟩ing a delicate overture
         To lead the tardy concert of the year

[26] [blank]
[27]       The timid it concerns to ask their way
         And fear the ambushes that round thee lay
         To make no step until the event is known,
         And ills to come as evils past bemoan;
(5)     Not so the wise; no coward watch he keeps
         To spy what danger on his pathway creeps
         Go where he will the wise man is at home,
         His ⟨house as wide as spreads⟩ ↑hearth, the earth;—his
              hall↓ the azure dome;
         Where his clear spirit leads him, there's his road

23 "There is no great" (1–4); "I am owner" (5–8); "Power" ("Cast the bantling") (9–12).
Lines (1–8) are struck through in ink; lines (9–12), in pencil, are struck through in pencil.
25₁ "Musketaquid," 16, x?, 15, x? Erased pencil.
25₂ "Musketaquid," x, 13–18. In pencil, struck through in pencil.
27 "Woodnotes, I," 99–108. Struck through in pencil.

(10)        By Gods own light illumined & foreshowed.

[28]        ⟨Dear Heart I will say to thee all I know,⟩
            ⟨Darling I love thee still;⟩
            ⟨Dearest dost hear when I speak low?⟩
            ⟨Dost thy heart my heart's thought fill?⟩

(5)         I need not hide beneath my vest
            Thy picture, the pride of art,
            ⟨For I bear it⟩ ↑Thy picture burns↓ within my breast,
            And the chain is round my heart.

            Thine eyes still shined for me, though far
(10)        I lonely roved the land or sea,
            As I behold yon evening star
            Which yet beholds not me.

            With thy high form my sleep is filled,
            Thy blazing eye wakes me at morn,
(15)        Thou dost these days with beauty gild
            Which else were trivial & forlorn.

            What arts are thine, dear maiden,
            O tell me, what arts are thine⟨?⟩,
            To teach thy name to the rippling wave,
(20)        And to the singing pine?


[29₁]       Dear Heart I ‖ . . . ‖ thee all I know
            ‖ . . . . . . . . . . . . . . ‖
            Dear love dost thou hear when I speak low
            ‖ . . . . . . . . . . . . . ‖

(5)         ‖ . . ‖ not hid beneath my vest
            Thy picture, the pride of art
            For I bear it within my breast
            And ‖ . . . ‖ round my heart

            ‖ . . . . . . . . . . ‖ far
(10)        ‖ . . . . . . . . . ‖ sea
            As I behold yon evening star
            Which yet beholds not me

            What arts are thine, dear maiden,
            O tell me what arts are thine

28 "Thine Eyes Still Shined," eight unused lines, 1–4, eight unused lines. Lines (1–4) are heavily cancelled in ink; lines (5–12) are struck through in ink. In line (7), "For I bear it" is cancelled and "Thy picture burns" inserted in pencil; in line (13), "high" is bracketed in pencil.
29₁ "Thine Eyes Still Shined," eight unused lines, 1–4, four unused lines, 5–8. Erased pencil; an erased pencil word, possibly a title, is centered at the top of the page.

(15)        To teach thy name to the rippling wave
                And to the singing pine

                This morn I climbed the misty hill
                And roamed the pastures through
                How danced thy form before my path
(20)        Amidst the deep eyed dew

[29₂]      This morn I climbed the misty hill,
                And roamed the pastures through,
                How danced thy form before my path,
                Amidst the deep eyed dew!

(5)         When the red-bird spread his sable wing
                And showed his side of flame,
                When the rosebud ripened to the rose,
                In both I read thy name.

                Why should I sing of thee?
(10)       The morning sings of thee;
                Why should I go to seek thy face?
                No face but thine I see.

[30]       When the red start spread his sable wing
                And showed his side of flame
                When the rosebud ripened to the rose
                In both I read thy name.

(5)         Why should I sing of thee
                The morning sings of thee
                Why should I go to seek thy face
                No face but thine I see

[31]       Out of the forest

                Or I be shamed when bearded men repeat
                The things I told my mother

[32] [blank]
[33]                    Van Buren.
                       ═══

                The towers that generations did combine
                To build & grace, a rat may undermine.

                    The Future.
                        ═══

                How many big events to shake the earth,
                Lie packed in silence waiting for their birth.

29₂ "Thine Eyes Still Shined," 5–12, four unused lines. Lines (1–8) are struck through in ink.
30 "Thine Eyes Still Shined," 9–12, four unused lines. Erased pencil.
31 Cf. "Hermione," 56 (1); "Or I be shamed" (2–3). In pencil.
33 "Van Buren" (1–2); "The Future" (3–4); "Heaven" (5–7).

### Heaven

(5)    O what is Heaven but the fellowship
Of minds that each can stand against the world
By its own meek and incorruptible will!

[34]          ### Webster.

Ill fits the abstemious Muse a ⟨a⟩crown to weave
For living brows; ill fits them to receive:
And yet, if Virtue abrogate the law,
One portrait,—fact or fancy—we may draw;
(5)    A form which Nature cast in the heroic mould
Of them who rescued liberty of old;
He, when the rising storm of Party roared,
Brought his great forehead to the council board,
There, while hot heads perplexed with fears the state,
(10)   Calm as the morn the manly patriot sate:
Seemed, when at last his clarion accents broke,
As if the conscience of the country spoke.
Not on its base Monadnoc surer stood,
Than he to common sense, & common good;
(15)   No mimic;—from his breast, his counsel drew,
Believed the eloquent was aye the true;
He bridged the gulf from th' alway good & wise
To that within the ⟨limits⟩vision of small eyes.
Self-centred; when he launched the genuine Word
(20)   It shook or captivated all who heard,
Ran from his mouth to mountains & the sea,
And burned in noble hearts proverb & prophecy.

[35]   Madness madness
Madness from the Gods
To every brain a several vein
Of madness from the gods
(5)    Their heads they toss ↑each one aloft↓
And shoulder each aside ↑They toss their heads with pride↓
↑Tho↓ To break free they struggle oft
And ⟨toss their heads with pride⟩ ↑shoulder each aside↓
What boots it th⟨at⟩ough their arms stretch out
(10)   And wings ⟨upon⟩ ↑behind↓ their shoulders sprout
If as at first so at last
⟨If all⟩ their ↓planted↓ feet like trees are fast
Rooted in the /slime of Fate/Sepulchre predestinate/

---

34 "Webster" ("Ill fits the abstemious Muse").
35 "The Skeptic," 1–12, 13/14, 15–28. Erased pencil.

As if their feet were ⟨‖ . . ‖feet⟩ ↑flint↓ ↑& soon↓
(15)   ↑All the trunk will grow to stone↓
Not one has surmounted
The Destiny yet
Not one has accounted
To Conscience his debt
(20) ⟨Though⟩ many in the dark have groped
⟨Or⟩ many for the dawn have hoped
And some more brave or else more blind
The freedom all desire pretend to find
Of all past men
(25) Not one has snapped the chain
All enter life each one the dupe
Of the all Deceiver Hope
[36] Each hears the siren whisper, ⟨free⟩ ↑He↓
↑Tho' first of men↓ That he shall ↑yet↓ be free
That one of their own stem
⟨Shall from their eye pluck the beam⟩
(5) ⟨And ‖ . . . ‖ ruin them redeem⟩
‖ . . . ‖ or Mohammed
   Brama or Moses
   Jove or Alcides
⟨‖ . . ‖⟩ from their eye shall pluck the beam
(10) ↑And their↓ Heart ⟨Soul⟩ from ⟨ruin shall⟩ ↑death↓ redeem
⟨Yet⟩ ↑But↓ Destiny sat still
And had her will
Know thou surely
That there is yet no prophet's ken
(15) No seer in the sons of men
Those in whom thou dost confide
Those thy love has deified
With superabundant trust
Their words are wind their forms are dust
(20) ↑O↓ Thousand blossomed ↑but↓ barren tree
Much pretending helped they thee
Merchant & statesman
Poet and craftsman
Prophet and judge
(25) Pirate and drudge
[37] /An equal fate/One fortune/ levels
Human angels human devils
For ever when a human brain
Its perfect purpose will attain

36 "The Skeptic," 29–31, 35–36, 34, 34, 33, 35–51. Erased pencil.
37 "The Skeptic," 52–61. Erased pencil.

(5)  The pitiless
   ⟨stupid with joy⟩ ↑Performance Hating↓ Nemesis
   Withdraws the world like a painted slide
   And a new world is supplied
   He that threatens is threatened
(10)  Who terrifieth is afraid

[38] [blank]

[39₁]       Shakspeare
   I see all human wits
   Are measured but a few
   Unmeasured still my Shakspeare sits
   Lone as the blessed Jew

[39₂]  I bear in youth the sad infirmities
   That use to undo the limb & sense of age:
   It hath pleased Heaven to break the dream of bliss
   Which lit my onward way with bright presage,
(5)  And my unserviceable limbs forego
   The sweet delight I found in fields & farms,
   On windy hills, whose tops with morning glow,
   And lakes, smooth mirrors of Aurora's charms.
   Yet I think on them in the silent night,
(10)  Still breaks that morn, though dim, to Memory's eye
   And the firm soul does the pale train defy
   Of grim Disease, that would her peace affright.
   Please God, I'll wrap me in mine innocence
   And bid each awful Muse drive the damned harpies hence.

 Cambridge
 1827

[40]  For this present, hard
   Is the fortune of the bard
    Born out of time:
   All his accomplishment
(5)  From Natures utmost treasure spent
    Booteth not him
   When the pine tosses its cones
   To the song of its waterfall tones
    He speeds to the woodland walks
(10)  To birds & trees he talks
   Caesar of his leafy Rome
   There the poet is at home

39₁ "Shakspeare." Erased pencil.
39₂ "Written in Sickness." "1827" is in both pencil and ink.
40 "Woodnotes, I," 1–25. In pencil, struck through in pencil.

He goes to the river side
Not hook nor line hath he
(15)    He stands in the meadows wide
Nor gun nor scythe to see
With ⟨men⟩ ↑none has↓ he ⟨has nought⟩ to do
And none seek him
Nor men below
(20)    Nor spirits dim
Sure some God his eye enchants
What he knows nobody wants
In the wood he travels glad
Without better fortune had
(25)    Melancholy without bad

[41₁]               Hard
‖ . . . . . . . . . . ‖ bard
Born out of ‖ . . . . . ‖
All his accomplishments
(5)    From Natures utmost treasure spent
Boots not
‖ . . . . ‖ the pine tosses its cones
To the song of its ‖ . . ‖ fall tones
He speeds to the woodland walks
(10)    To birds & trees he ‖ . . . ‖
And there he is ‖ . . . ‖
‖ . . . . . . . . . . . . . . ‖
‖ . . . . . . . . . . ‖ seeks
And ‖ . . . . . . . ‖ seek him
(15)    ‖ . . . . . . ‖ men below
Nor spirits dim
↑‖ . . . . . . . . ‖ plants↓
What he knows nobody wants
‖ . . . . . ‖ he travels glad
(20)    ‖ . . . . . . . . . . ‖ glad
Or ‖ . . . . . . . . ‖ sad
What he knows nobody wants
‖ . . ‖ he loves ‖ . . . . . ‖
He knows
(25)    ‖ . . . . . . ‖ wild bees settle
‖ . . . . . . . . ‖ petal
Why nature loves the number five
And why the star form she repeats

---

41₁ "Woodnotes, I," 1–10, 12, x?, x, 18–20, 26, 22/27, 23, x, x, 22/27, x, x, 33–36. Erased pencil.

[41₂]       O what would nature say?
She spared no speech today
The fungus & the bulrush spoke
Answered the pinetree & the oak
(5)     The wizard South blew down the glen
Filled the straits & filled the wide
Each maple leaf turned up its silver side
The southwind blows I leave my book
⟨I go to walk⟩
(10)    ⟨And hear his eloquent talk⟩
All things shine in his smoky ray
And all we see are pictures high
⟨&⟩Many a high hill side
Which oaks of pride
(15)    Climb to their tops
And boys run out upon their leafy ropes

      ⟨I need⟩ ↑I would↓ not bide in nature long
Could I transfer my life to song
It needs the lapsing centuries
(20)    To tell the wit of the passing breeze
And yet the landscape taunts me
Advancing then receding
⟨The⟩ ↑With↓ beauty that enchants me
Yet will not stay the reading

[42]     Planter of celestial plants
What he knows nobody wants
What he knows he hides not vaunts
Knowledge this man prizes best
(5)     Seems fantastic to the rest
⟨He studies⟩ ↑Pondering↓ shadows colors clouds
⟨The clover⟩ ⟨↑Grass↓⟩ buds, ⟨the⟩& caterpillars shrouds
⟨The⟩ boughs on which the wild bees settle
⟨The⟩ tints that spot the violets petal
(10)    Why Nature loves the number five
And why the star form she repeats
Lover of all things alive
Wonderer at all he meets
Wonderer chiefly at himself
(15)    Who can tell him what he is
Or how meet in human elf
Coming & past eternities

41₂ "Where the fungus broad & red," 10–16, 17, 17, 18–24, eight unused lines. In pencil.
42 "Woodnotes, I," 26–44, x, 44, 46/45, 46. In pencil; lines (1–20) are struck through in pencil.

And such I knew a /peasant bard/forest seer/
A minstrel like the woodland bird
(20)  of brooks &
A minstrel of the natural Year
↑Wise↓ The Almanac of times and tides vernal ides
A harp attuned to spheres & tides

[43]  It seemed that nature could not raise
A plant in any secret place
In quaking bog on snowy hill
Beneath the grass that shades the rill
(5)  Under the snow ⟨beneath⟩ between the rocks
In damp fields known to bird & fox
But he would come in the very hour
It opened in its virgin bower
As if a sunbeam showed the place
(10)  And tell its long descended race
It seemed as if the breezes brought him
It seemed as if the sparrows taught him
As if by secret sight he knew
When in far fields the orchis flowered
(15)  There are many events in the field
That are not shown to common eyes
But all her shows did Nature yield
To please & win this pilgrim wise
He saw the partridge drum in the woods
(20)  He heard the woodcocks evening hymn
He found the tawny thrush's broods
And the shy hawk did wait for him
What others did at distance hear
And guessed within the thickets gloom
(25)  Was showed to this philosopher
And at his bidding seemed to come

[44]  And such I knew a forest seer
A minstrel of the natural year
Foreteller of the vernal Ides
Wise harbinger of spheres & tides,
(5)  A lover he⟨r⟩ who knew by heart
The joys ⟨of⟩ streams mountains dales impart

[45]  You ask what guide
Through trackless thickets led
⟨I⟩ ↑Man↓ could not p⟨ei⟩ierce the desart wide

43 "Woodnotes, I," 49–74. In pencil, struck through in pencil.
44 "Woodnotes, I," 43–48. In pencil, struck through in pencil.
45 "Woodnotes, I," 131–51, x, x, 152–53. In pencil, struck through in pencil.

(Aye but) ↑I found↓ the waters bed.
(5) The watercourses were my guide
I travelled grateful by their side
Or through their channel dry
They led me thro the thicket damp
Thro brake & fern the beavers camp
(10) Thro beds of granite cut my road
And their resistless friendship showed
The waterfall sang to me
The fertile waters fed me
And brot me to the lowest land
(15) Unerring to the Ocean sand
The moss upon the forest bark
Was polestar when the night was dark
The whortle berries in the wood
Supplied me necessary food

(20) For nature ever faithful is
To them who trust her faithfulness
Keep your gift exhaust your arts
You shall not win our forest hearts
When the forest shall mislead me
(25) When the night & morning lie
[46] When sea & land refuse to feed me
Twill be time enough to die
Then will yet my mother yield
A pillow in her greenest field
(5) Nor the June flowers scorn to cover
The clay of their departed lover

[47] [blank]
[48] In unploughed Maine he sought the lumberers gang
Where from a hundred lakes young rivers sprang
He trod the unplanted forest floor whereon
The all seeing sun for ages hath not shone
(5) Where feeds the moose & walks the surly bear
And up the tall mast runs the woodpecker
And underneath dim aisles in odorous beds
The slight Linnaea hangs its twin born heads
The fragrant monument to the man of flowers
(10) Recounts his fame thro Maine's vast forest bowers
Oft in the cumbered grove at intervals

46 "Woodnotes, I," 154–59. In pencil, struck through in pencil. Above "When" in line (1) is an upper-case *W*, probably the beginning of an aborted line.
48 "Woodnotes, I," 75–92. Struck through in ink.

With sudden roar the aged pinetree falls
One crash the death hymn of the falling tree
Declares the close of its green century
(15)       Low lies the plant to whose creation went
Sweet influence from every element
Whose living ⟨f⟩towers, the years conspired to build
Whose giddy top the morning loved to gild

[49]     The brave Empedocles defying fools
Pronounced the word that mortals hate to hear
"I am divine I am not mortal made
I am superior to my human weeds"
(5)        Not sense but Reason is the Judge of truth
Reason's twofold; part human part divine
That human part may be described & taught
The other p⟨a⟩ortion language cannot speak
Degerando Vol 2 p 36

[50]             *The three Spaces.*
Room! shout the spheres when first they shined
And dived into the ample sky
Room! room! cried the new mankind
And took the oath of Liberty
(5)        Room! room! willed the opening Mind,
And found it in Variety.

[51]     Why fear to die
And let thy body lie
Under the flowers of June
Thy ⟨dust doth good⟩ ↑body food↓
(5)        ⟨The insects food⟩ ↑For the groundworm's brood↓
And thy grave smiled on by the visiting moon

Amid great Nature's halls,
Girt in by mountain walls,
And washed with waterfalls,
(10)      It would please me to die,
Where every wind that swe⟨pt⟩eps my tomb
Goes loaded with a free perfume,
Dealt out with a God's charity.

I should like to lie in sweets,
(15)      A hill's leaves for winding sheets,
And the searching sun to see

49 "The brave Empedocles." In pencil.
50 "The Three Dimensions." In pencil, struck through in pencil.
51 "Why fear to die."

That I'm laid with decency
And the commissioned wind to sing
His mighty Psalm from fall to spring
(20)    And annual tunes commemorate
Of nature's child the common fate.

---

Williamstown, Vermont:
1 June, 1831.

{52} [blank]
{53}    O fair & stately maid, whose eye
Was kindled in the upper sky
At the same torch that lighted mine;
For so I must interpret still
(5)    Thy sweet dominion o'er my will
A sympathy divine.

Ah let me blameless gaze upon
Features that seem in heart my own,
Nor fear those watchful sentinels
(10)    Which charm the more their glance forbids
Chaste-glowing underneath their lids
With fire that draws while it repels.

That wandering fire to me appears
Albeit a tiny spark
(15)    Older than the oldest spheres
That glow in the heavens dark

{54} [blank]
{55}–{56} [leaf torn out]
{57}    I ‖ . . . . . . . . . . . . . . ‖
‖ . . . . . . ‖ her knight
‖ . . . . . . . . . . . . . . . ‖
↑As noble↓ As ‖ . . . . . . . . . ‖
(5)    He ‖ . . . . . . . . . . . . . . ‖
The ‖ . . . . . . . . . . . . . ‖

{58} [blank]
{59}    The bard & mystic held me for their own
Rex.    I filled the dream of sad poetic maids
I took the friendly noble by the hand
I was the trustee of the handcartman

---

53 "To Eva" (1–12); "That wandering fire" (13–16). Lines (13–16) are in pencil.
57 Unidentified lines. Erased pencil.
59 "The bard & mystic." In pencil.

(5)        The brother of the fisher, porter, swain,—
               And these from the crowd's edge well pleased beheld
               The honor done to me as done to them.

[60] [blank]
[61] ↑My great grandfather,↓ Rev Joseph Emerson of Malden↑,↓ read the Iliad, & said, he should be sorry to think that the men & cities he read of never existed.

[62] [blank]
[63] ↑My great, great, grandfather,↓ Rev Samuel Moody of York, when somebody moved to go out during sermon, cried, "Come back you graceless sinner, come back."

[64] [blank]
[65]     I ⟨be⟩wear no badge; no ⟨‖ . . . ‖⟩tinsel star
               Glitters upon my breast;
               Nor jewelled crown nor victor's car
               Rob me of rest.

(5)        I am not poor, but I am proud
               Of one inalienable right,
               Above the envy of the crowd,—
               Thought's holy light.

               Better it is than gems or gold,
(10)       And oh! it cannot die,
               But thought will glow when the Sun grows cold,
               And mix with Deity.

182⟨1⟩3.
Boston

[66] [blank]
[67]     Goodbye proud world! I'm going home
               I am not thy friend thou art not mine
               Too long /with/thro'/ weary crowds I roam
               ↑A river ark on the ocean brine↓
(5)        Too long I am tossed like the salt sea foam

               Good bye proud world I'm going home
               Thou art not my friend: I am not thine
               Too long through weary crowds I roam
               A river ark on the ocean brine

61 "My great grandfather," is in pencil; "Rev Joseph Emerson . . . existed." is in both pencil and ink, except that the pencil comma after "Malden" is in the ink version only.

63 "My great, great, grandfather," is in pencil; "Rev Samuel Moody . . . back.' " is in both pencil and ink. See JMN 5:323.

65 "I wear no badge."

67 "Good-Bye," 1–5, 1–6. Erased pencil; lines (6–11) are struck through in pencil.

(10)      Too long I am tossed like the driven foam
          But now proud world I'm going home.

[68] [blank]
[69]     I left my dreamy page & ⟨walk⟨ed⟩ing abroad⟩ ↑sallied↓
           forth
         Received the fair inscriptions of the night
         The moon was making amber of the world
         Glittered with silver every cottage pane
(5)      The trees were rich yet ominous with gloom
                 the meadows broad
         From ferns & grasses & from folded flowers
         Sent a nocturnal fragrance
                 the harlot flies
(10)     Flashed their small fires in air or held their court
         In fairy groves of herds grass

[70]     The dreams of night on Reasons wall
         Are shadows of the thoughts of day
         And all thy fortunes as they fall
         ⟨Each⟩ ↑Some↓ secret of thy will betray

(5)      Thy dreams but trace on Reason's wall
         Shadows of the thoughts of day

[71]     Let the dreams of night recall
           Shadows of the thoughts of day
         And see thy fortunes as they fall
           Each secret of thy will betray

(5)           Roger Rain
           Come again

[72]     Twas one of the charmed days
         When the genius of God doth flow
         The wind may alter twenty ways
         A tempest cannot blow
(5)      It may blow north, it still is warm
         Or south, it still is clear
         Or east, it smells like a clover farm
         Or west, no thunder fear

         The peasant lowly great

69 "I left my dreamy page." In pencil.
70 "Memory," 1–4, 1–2. In pencil, struck through in pencil.
71 "Memory" (1–4); "Roger rain" (5–6). Lines (1–4) are in pencil, struck through in pencil; lines (5–6) are in erased pencil.
72 "Woodnotes, I," 109–20, x, 122–24, five unused lines. In pencil, struck through in pencil.

(10)    Beside the forest water sate
        The ropelike pineroots crosswise grown
        Composed the network of his throne
        Just at his feet the water was
        Burnished to a floor of glass
(15)    Painted with shadows green & proud
        Of the tree & of the cloud
        Hid in adjoining bowers the birds
        Sang their old speech older than words
        To him all creatures duly came
(20)    The red deer leaped the fishes swam

        His thought was truth his will was fate

[73]    He was the sunshine of our cause

[74]–[75] [blank]
[76]              Masque

        Love
        Asks nought his brother cannot give
        Asks nothing but does all receive

[77]            *The Skeptic*
        Madness, madness,
        Madness from the gods!
        To every brain a several vein
        Of madness from the gods!
(5)     Their heads they toss each one aloft
        They toss their heads with pride,
        Though to break free they struggle oft
        And shoulder each aside
        What boots it, though their arms stretch out,
(10)    And wings behind their shoulders sprout,
        If as at first, also at last,
        Their planted feet like trees are fast,
        Rooted in the slime of Fate,
        Sepulchre predestinate:
(15)    As if their feet were flint, & soon
        All the trunk will grow to stone.
        Not one has surmounted
        The Destiny yet:
        Not one has accounted

73 "He was the sunshine." In pencil.
76 "Love / Asks nought," 1–3. In pencil, struck through in pencil; "Masque" is also in pencil.
77 "The Skeptic," 1–26. In pencil. Lines (1–16) are struck through once in pencil, and lines (25–26) twice.

(20)  To Conscience his debt.
    Many in the dark have groped,
    Many for the dawn have hoped,
    And some more brave, or else more blind,
    The freedom all desire, pretend to find.
(25)  Of all past men
    Not one has snapped the chain
[78]  All enter life, each one the dupe
    Of the arch-deceiver Hope:
    Each hears the Siren whisper; 'he,
    Though first of men, shall yet be free;'
(5)   That one of their own stem,
    Man of Ur, or Bethlehem,
    Jove or Alcides,
    Mah⟨omet⟩ ↑moud↓ or Moses,
    From their eye shall pluck the beam
(10)  And their heart from death redeem.
    But Destiny sat still,
    And had her will.
    Know thou surely
    That there is yet no prophet's ken,
(15)  No seer in the sons of men,
    Those in whom thou dost confide,
    ⟨Those⟩ ↑Whom↓ thy love has deified,
    With a superabundant trust,—
    Their words are wind, their forms are dust.
(20)  O thousand blossomed but barren tree!
    Much-pretending, helped they thee?
    Merchant & statesman
    Poet & craftsman
    Prophet & judge
(25)  Pirate & drudge
[79]  One fortune levels
    Human angels human devils
    For ever when a human brain
    Its perfect purpose will attain
(5)   ↑Then suddenly↓ The pitiless
    Performance-hating Nemesis
    Withdraws the ⟨world⟩ ↑prize↓ like a painted slide
    And a new ⟨world⟩ ↑bauble↓ is supplied
    He that threatens is threatened
(10)  Who terrifieth is afraid

78 "The Skeptic," 27–51. In pencil; lines (1–2), (13–15), and (22–25) are struck through twice in pencil.
79 "The Skeptic," 52–61. In pencil; lines (1–2) and (9–10) are struck through twice in pencil.

[80] [blank]

[81]    Philosophers are lined with eyes within
〈Must the philosopher be a false man〉
↑And being so the sage unmakes the man↓
He is in love he cannot 〈cease〉 therefore cease his trade

(5)    Scarce the first blush has overspread his cheek
He feels it, introverts his learned eye
To catch the unconscious heart in the very act
His mother died, the only friend he had
Some tears escaped but his philosophy

(10)    Couched like a cat ↑sat watching close↓ behind 〈to watch
        his thoughts〉
And throttled all his passion. Is't not like
That devil-spider that devours her mate
Scarce freed from her embraces

[82]    Up from the burning core below
The shrill outcries of love & wo

And groined the aisles of Christian Rome
Wrought in a sad sincerity
(5)    Himself from God he could not free

[83] 10 November 1839

I like a church I like a cowl
I love a prophet of the soul
And on my heart monastic aisles
Fall like sweet 〈music〉 ↑strains↓ or 〈like〉 ↑pensive↓ smiles
(5)    Yet not for all 〈the worlds that be〉 〈↑his visions see↓〉 ↑his
        faith can see↓
Would I that cowled churchman be.
Why should the vest on him allure
Which I could not on me endure?

Not from a vain or shallow thought
(10)    His awful Jove young Phidias brought
Never from lips of cunning fell
The sublime Delphic Oracle
Out from the heart of nature rolled
The accents of the Bible old
(15)    The litanies of nations came
Like the volcano's tongue of flame
〈Profound upheaving as the sea〉

81 "Philosophers are lined." In pencil.
82 "The Problem," 17–18, 20–22. In pencil, struck through in pencil.
83 "The Problem," 1–16, x, x, 19–24. In pencil, struck through in pencil.

⟨And true as truth itself can be⟩
The hand that ⟨curved St⟩ ↑rounded↓ Peters dome
(20)    ⟨And ⟨the dread piles⟩ ↑minsters rich↓ of Christian Rome⟩
⟨Wrought in a ⟨stern⟩ ↑sad↓ sincerity⟩
⟨↑Oppressed by faith he could not free↓⟩
He builded better than he knew
The conscious stone to beauty grew

[84]    The apostles word the martyrs end
The hermits cave themselves commend
⟨Shine⟩ ↑Beam↓ still in dark & desert ages
And paint with /form/fire/ ⟨Fates iron⟩ ↑the eternal↓ pages.

(5)    Knowst thou ⟨how came⟩ ↑what wove↓ yon woodbirds nest
⟨Grass⟩ ↑Of↓ leaves & feathers from her breast
Or how the fish ↑out↓ built her shell
↑Painting↓ With ⟨tint of⟩ morn ⟨an⟩ ↑each↓ annual cell
Or how the sacred pine tree adds
(10)    To her old leaves new myriads
Such & so grew these holy piles
Whilst love & ⟨fear laid⟩ terror laid the tiles
Earth proudly wears the Parthenon
As the best gem upon her Zone
(15)    And Morning opes with haste her lids
To gaze upon the Pyramids
On Englands Abbeys bends the sky
As on its friends with kindred eye
For out of Thoughts interior sphere
(20)    These wonders ⟨grew⟩ ↑rose↓ to upper air
And Nature gladly gave them place
Adopted them into her race
And granted them an equal date
With Andes & with Aararat.

[85]    These temples grew as grows the grass
A work which Art could not surpass
⟨And as⟩ the ↑passive↓ builder lent his hand
To the vast Soul that oer him planned
(5)    ↑And↓ The ⟨self⟩same force that ⟨built⟩ ↑reared↓ the ⟨walls⟩
      ↑shrine↓
⟨Swayed⟩
/Bestrode/Inflamed/ the ⟨kneeling hosts⟩ ↑tribes that knelt↓
      within;
↑Ever↓ The ⟨unresisted⟩ ↑fiery↓ Pentecost
Binds in one flame the countless host

---

84 "The Problem," four unused lines, 25–44. In pencil, struck through in pencil.
85 "The Problem," 45–49, x, 50–68. In pencil, struck through in pencil.

(10)     Woke love & bliss through the rapt quires
         And through the priest the mind inspires

         The word unto the prophet spoken
         Was writ on tables still unbroken
         The word by seers or Sybils told
(15)     In groves of oak or fanes of gold
         Still floats upon the morning wind,
         Still whispers to the willing mind.
         One accent of the Holy Ghost
         The heedless world hath never lost
(20)     I know ⟨all that⟩ ↑what say↓ the Fathers ⟨say⟩ wise
         The book itself before me lies
         Old Chrysostom best Augustine
         And he who blent both in his line
         The younger *Golden* ⟨*Mouth*⟩ ↑*Lips*↓ or mines
(25)     Taylor the Shakspear of divines
[86]     His words are music in my ear
         I see his cowled portrait dear
         And yet for all his faith could see
         I would not the good bishop be

[87]–[90] [blank]
[91]     The sun is the statue of God

         But I a lover of Gods fables
         A pensioner at the Elysian tables

[92]     The simple people each with /basket/sack/ or tool
         Had left the young & resolute to rule
         But strange disorder in the councils crept
         Whilst they in farm & orchard toiled & slept
(5)      The farmer & the merchant missed their mart
         And no reward attends the craftsman's art
         Awaking from their lethargy they ⟨s⟩hear
         Rude words which neither land nor sea will bear
         A great concourse surrounds a single man
(10)     And waits obsequious
         Watches his words, & predicates his will
         Uprose the farmer by his apple tree
         Tarried the sailor ere he put to sea
         And who is he & who are ye he said
(15)     And what care I if ye are tail or head
         Shall I who know not of the trade of state

86 "The Problem," 69–72. In pencil, struck through in pencil.
91 "The sun is the statue" (1); "But I a lover" (2–3). In pencil.
92 "The simple people each." In pencil.

Who know not, care not for the statesmans fate
Scarce hold the name of parties & of banks
Measures or leaders, officers⁣⁣⁣ or ranks
(20)⁣⁣Shall I descend so low to ask or hear
What one man does or says with hope or fear
Follow the chance direction of his eye
Find his smile Fortune his frown poverty
God made these eyes: fear's watch they cannot keep
(25)⁣⁣God made this frame erect↑,↓ it cannot creep.

[93]⁣⁣The Dervish whined to Said
"Thou didst not tarry while I prayed;"
But Saadi answered,
The sun & moon solicit me
(5)⁣⁣Angels and Love & Destiny.
Once with manlike love & fear
I gave thee for an hour my ear,
I kept the sun & stars at bay,
And Love, for words thy tongue could say
(10)⁣⁣I cannot sell my heaven again
For all that rattles in ⟨m⟩thy brain

[94] [blank]

[95]⁣⁣⁣⁣⁣⁣⁣⁣⁣⁣⁣⁣⁣⁣⁣⁣⁣⁣⁣Lines
On being asked, Whence is the flower?

In May when sea winds pierced our solitudes
I found the fresh Rhodora in the woods,
Spreading its leafless blooms in a damp nook
To please the desert and the sluggish brook.
(5)⁣⁣The purple petals fallen in the pool
Made the black water with their beauty gay
Young Raphael might covet such a school
The lively show beguiled me from my way.
Rhodora! if the sages ask thee why
(10)⁣⁣This charm is wasted on the marsh & sky,
Tell them, dear, that if eyes were made for seeing,
Then Beauty is its own excuse for being:
Why thou wert there, O rival of the rose!
I never thought to ask, I never knew,
(15)⁣⁣But in my simple ignorance suppose
The selfsame Power that brought me there, brought you.

[96]⁣⁣On bravely through the sunshine & the showers
Time hath his work to do & we have ⟨h⟩Ours.

93 "The Dervish whined to *Said*," 1–2, 4, x, x, 5–10. In pencil.
95 "The Rhodora." Struck through in ink.
96 "On bravely through the sunshine" (1–2); "Let me go where e'er I will" (3–20).

Let me go where e'er I will
I hear a skyborn music still
(5) It sounds from all things old
It sounds from all things young
From all that's fair from all that's foul
Peals out a cheerful song
It is not only in the Rose
(10) It is not only in the bird
Not only where the Rainbow glows
Nor in the song of woman heard
But in the darkest meanest things
Theres alway alway something sings.

(15) Tis not in the high stars alone
Nor in the cups of budding flowers
Nor in the redbreast's mellow tone
Nor in the bow that smiles in showers
But in the mud & scum of things
(20) Theres alway alway something sings.

[97] Fame's a ↑'↓ sucked orange,' flattered Canning cries.

[98] Go thou to thy learned task;
I stay with the flowers of spring;
Do thou of the ages ask
What me the hours will bring.

[99] And when I am entombed in my place,
Be it remembered of a single man,
He never, though he dearly loved his race,
For fear of human eyes, swerved from his plan.

———

(5) Bard or dunce is blest, but hard
Is it to be half a bard.

———

It takes philosopher or fool
To build a fire or keep a school.

———

Tell men what they knew before

97 "Fame's a 'sucked orange.' " The added quotation mark is in pencil.
98 "Botanist."
99 "And when I am entombed" (1–4); "Bard or dunce is blest" (5–6); "It takes philosopher or fool" (7–8); "Tell men what they knew before" (9–10); "I use the knife" (11–12).

46

(10)     Paint the prospect from their door.

=====

I use the knife
To save the life.

=====

[100] [blank]

[101]    The days pass over me,
         And I am still the same;
         The aroma of my life is gone
         With the flower with which it came.

[102]    There is no evil but can speak,
         If the wheel want oil t'will creak.

[103]    This cup of life is not so shallow
             That we have drained the best,
         That all the wine at once we swallow,
             And lees make all the rest.

(5)      Maids of as soft a bloom shall marry
             As Hymen yet hath blessed:
         And fairer forms are in the quarry
             Than Phidias ⟨e'er⟩ released.

[104₁]   Little thinks in the field yon red cloaked clown
         Of ‖ . . . . . . . . . ‖ looking down
         And the ⟨cow⟩ ↑heifer↓ that lows in the distant farm
         ‖ . . . . . . ‖ lows not thy ear to charm
(5)      The ‖ . . . . . . . . . . . . . . . ‖
         ⟨Thinks⟩ ↑Dreams↓ ‖ . . . . ‖ Napoleon
         Stops ‖ . . . . . . . . . ‖ delight
         Whilst his files sweep round yon Alpine height
         Nor knowest ‖ . . . . . . . ‖ argument
(10)     ‖ . . . ‖ life ‖ . . . . . ‖ creed has lent
         All are needed ‖ . . . . . . . . . . . ‖
         Nothing is ‖ . . . . . . ‖ alone
         I thought ‖ . . . . . . . . ‖ heaven
         Singing at dawn ‖ . . . . ‖ alder bough
(15)     I brought him home in his nest at even,
         ‖ . . ‖ sings the ‖ . . . ‖ but it ‖ . . ‖ not now
         For I did not bring home the river ‖ . . . . ‖

101 "The days pass over me."
102 "There is no evil."
103 "This cup of life." In line (8), "e'er" is cancelled and boxed in pencil.
104₁ "Each and All," 1–24. Erased pencil.

‖ . . . . ‖ my ‖ . . . ‖ these sang to my eye
The delicate shells lay on the shore
(20)    The bubbles of the latest wave
Fresh pearls ‖ . . . . . ‖ enamel gave
And the bellowing of the savage sea
Greeted their safe escape to me
I wiped away the weeds & foam

[1042]    To every creature
Adam gave its name
Let each to all unmask its feature
And cognizance
(5)    Moth or bug or worm or snail
Mite or fly or atomy
Nor each nor any fail
Its lineage to proclaim
⟨Be its function & its name⟩
(10)    ⟨Publicly enrolled.⟩
Not a plant o⟨f⟩bscure
But some bright morn its flowers unfold
And tell the Universe
Its family & fame.
(15)    No fly or aphis bites the leaf
But comes a ⟨day⟩ chance

[1051]            ⟨What is Beauty?⟩
                 Each in All

Little ‖ . . . . . . . . . . . . ‖
‖ . . . . . . . . . ‖ ↑looking down↓
And ‖ . . ‖ cow in the distant farm
Lows ‖ . . . ‖ ⟨please⟩ thy ear to charm
(5)    The ⟨‖ . . ‖⟩ sexton ‖ . . . ‖ bell at noon
Thinks not that great Napoleon
⟨Napoleon⟩ stops on his march to hear
‖ . . . . . . . . . . ‖ yon Alpine height
Nor knowest thou what argument
(10)    Thy ‖ . . . . . . ‖ thy neighbors ‖ . . . . ‖
All are needed by ‖ . . . . . ‖
Nothing ‖ . . . . . . . ‖ alone
‖ . . . . . . . . . . . ‖ from heaven
‖ . . . ‖ ↑at↓ ‖ . . . . ‖ bough
(15)    I brought ‖ . . ⟨ . . . ‖ cage ‖ . . ‖ cage⟩ ↑nest↓ at even
⟨But⟩ he sings ‖ . . . ‖ song but it pleases not now

1042 "To every creature," 1–16.
1051 "Each and All," 1–23. Erased pencil, struck through several times in pencil.

For I did not bring home the river & sky
‖ . . ‖ sang to my ear these sang to my eye
‖⟨ . . . ⟩‖ lay the shells on the shore
(20) The bubbles of the retiring wave
‖ . . . . ‖ ↑Fresh↓ ‖ . . . . ‖ gave
And the ‖ . . . . . . . . . . ‖
Greeted their safe escape to me

[105₂] When egg or fretted path betray
The petty thief,
And his small malfaisance.
Many things the garden shows
(5) And pleased I stray
From tree to tree
Watching the ↑white↓ pear ⟨flowers⟩ ↑bloom↓
↑Bee↓ Infested quince or plum.
I could walk ⟨thus⟩ ↑days, years, away↓
(10) Till the slow ripening secular tree
Had reached its fruiting time
Nor think it long

Where is Skrymir? Giant Skrymir?
Come transplant the woods for me!
(15) Scoop up yonder aged ash,
Centennial pine, mahogany beech,
Oaks that grew in the dark ages
Heedful, bring them, set them straight,

[106₁] ↑I wiped away the weeds & foam↓
‖ . . . . . . . . . . . . . . ‖
‖ . . . . . . . . . ‖ things
‖ . . . . . . . . . . . . . ‖
(5) ‖ . . . . . . . . . . ‖ ↑savage roar↓
the lover
‖ . . . . . . . . ‖ peaceful maid
‖ . . . . ‖ the ‖ . . . . . . . ‖
‖ . . . . . . . . . . . . . . . ‖
(10) ‖ . . . . . . . ‖ ↑beautys↓ rich attire
‖ . . . . . . . . . . . . . . ‖ choir
But when he brought her to his /bower/hermitage/
The ‖ . . ‖ enchantment was undone
A gentle wife but ‖ . . . . . . ‖
(15) [four lines of erased pencil writing]
The ground pine ‖ . . . ‖ pretty wreath

1052 "To every creature," 17–28 (1–12); "Where is Skrymir?" 1–6 (13–18).
106₁ "Each and All," 24, 25?, 26, 27?, 28, 31, 31, 32, x?, 33–35, 37–38, four unrecovered
lines, 43–49, 50?, 51, 52?, 53. Erased pencil.

(20)　　　‖ . . . . . . . . . ‖ club moss burrs
　　　　I ‖ . . . . . . . . . . . ‖ breath
　　　　‖ . . . . . . . . . . . . . ‖ the oaks & firs
　　　　‖ . . . . . . . . . . . . . ‖ lay on the ground
　　　　‖ . . . ‖ me ‖ . . . . . . . . . . ‖
(25)　　　‖ . . . . . . . . . ‖ & of deity
　　　　‖ . . . . . . . . . . . . . . . . . ‖
　　　　‖ . . . . . . . . . ‖ morning bird
　　　　‖ . . . . . . ⟨ . . . . ⟩ ↑ . . . ↓ ‖
　　　　‖ . . . . . ‖ myself ‖ . . . . . ‖ whole.

[1062]　Can I nail the wild planet
　　　　To a place in the sky

　　　　The sea reflects the rosy sky
　　　　The sky doth marry the blue main

(5)　　　‖ . . . . . . . . . . . . . . ‖
　　　　These ‖ . . . . . . . . . . . . ‖
　　　　How fade ‖ . . . . ‖ light of ‖ . . . . ‖
　　　　In that ‖ . . . . . . . . . ‖

[1063]　In sifted soil, before my porch;
　　　　Now turn the river on their roots,
　　　　So the ↑new↓ top shall ⟨never⟩ ↑not↓ droop
　　　　His tall erected plume, nor a leaf wilt.

[1071]　I wiped away the weeds & foam
　　　　I fetched my seaborn treasures home
　　　　But the poor, unsightly noisome things
　　　　Had left their beauty on the shore
(5)　　　With the sun & the sand & the savage roar
　　　　‖ . ‖ rose ‖ . . . . . . . ‖ nor eagle are fair
　　　　‖ . . . . . . . . ⟨ . . . . ⟩ ‖ beyond compare
　　　　The lover watched his graceful maid
　　　　Amid the virgin train she strayed
(10)　　Nor knew her beautys best attire
　　　　Was woven ‖ . . . . . . . . . . ‖
　　　　At last she ‖ . . . . . . . . . ‖
　　　　‖ . . . . ⟨ . . . . ⟩ . . . . . . . . ‖
　　　　The gay ‖ . . . . . . . . . . ‖ of Day
(15)　　A gentle ‖ . . . . . . . . . . . . ‖
　　　　‖ . . . ‖ I said ‖ . . . ‖ covet truth

1062 "Can I nail the wild planet" (1–2); "The sea reflects the rosy sky" (3–4); "The Sphinx,"
69?–72? (5–8). In pencil; lines (5–8) are erased.
　1063 "Where is Skrymir?," 7–10.
　1071 "Each and All," 24–35, 36?, 37–53. Erased pencil.

Beauty is unripe childhoods cheat
I ‖ . . . ‖ leave it behind with the games of youth
As ‖ . . . . . . . . . ‖ beneath my feet
(20) The ground pine curled his pretty wreath
Running over the clubmoss burs
I inhaled the flowers breath
Around me stood the oaks & firs
Pinecones ‖ . . . . . ‖ the ground
(25) Over ‖ . ↑ . . ↓ . . . . ‖ eternal sky
Full of light and of Deity
Again I saw again I heard
The rolling river the morning bird
Beauty thro' my senses stole
(30) I yielded myself to the perfect Whole.

[1072] Have I a friend
Who is noble
I would he were nobler
Than ‖ . . . . ‖ me

[1073] The sea reflects the rosy sky,
The sky doth marry the blue main.

[108]↑ 1 ↓The Sphinx is drowsy
Her wings are furled
Her ear is heavy
She broods on the world
(5) "Who'll tell me my secret
The ages have kept?
I awaited the Seer
Whilst they slumbered & slept

↑ 2 ↓The ⟨meaning⟩ ↑fate↓ of ↑the↓ Man-⟨kind⟩↑child↓
(10) The ⟨fortune⟩ ↑meaning↓ of man
⟨The child⟩ ↑Known fruit↓ of the unknown
⟨The measureless⟩ ↑Daedalian↓ plan
Out of ⟨a⟩ sleeping a waking
Out of ⟨a⟩ waking a sleep
(15) Life death overtaking
Deep under↑neath↓ deep

Why dreameth this Mushroom
Through Ages to last
Not knowing the Future

1072 "The Sphinx," 93–96. Erased pencil.
1073 "The sea reflects the rosy sky."
108 "The Sphinx," 1–16, eight unused lines. In pencil, struck through in pencil. Stanza 2,
lines (17–24), is enclosed in parentheses at beginning and end.

(20)         How knows he the Past
And when will ⟨the⟩ ↑be↓ Foresight
⟨To⟩ his Aftersight's peer
And the hemisphere halfmind
Orb itself to a sphere.

[109]↑3↓Erect as a Sunbeam
Upspringeth the palm
The elephant browses
Undaunted & calm
(5)        In beautiful motion
The thrush plies his wings
Kind leaves of his covert
⟨To thank you⟩ ↑Your silence↓ he sings

↑4↓The waves unashamed
(10)      In difference sweet
Play glad with the breezes
Old playfellows meet
The journeying atoms
Primordial wholes
(15)      Firmly draw firmly drive
By their animate poles

↑5↓Sea earth air sound silence
Plant quadruped bird
By one music enchanted
(20)      One principle stirred
Each the other adorning
Accompany still
Night ⟨speaks to⟩ ↑veileth↓ the Morning
The ⟨mist to⟩ ↑vapor↓ the hill

[110]↑6↓The babe by its mother
Lies bathed in joy
Glide its hours uncounted
The sun is its toy
(5)        Shines the peace of all being
Without cloud in its eyes
And the sum of the world
In soft miniature lies

↑7↓But Man crouches & blushes
(10)      Absconds & conceals
He creepeth & peepeth

109 "The Sphinx," 17–40. In pencil, struck through in pencil.
110 "The Sphinx," 41–64. In pencil, struck through in pencil. In line (18), "fear" is spelled "feer."

He palters & steals
Infirm, melancholy,
Jealous glancing around
(15)   An oaf an accomplice
He poisons the ground

↑8↓ Outspoke the great Mother
Beholding his fear
At the sound of her ⟨voice⟩ ↑accents↓
(20)   Cold shuddered the sphere
Who has drugged my Boy's cup
Who has mixed my Boy's bread
Who with sadness & madness
Hath turned the manchild's head

[111]   Uprose the merry Sphinx
And crouched no more in stone
She hopped into the baby's eyes
She hopped into the moon
(5)   She spired into a yellow flame
She flowered in blossoms red
She flowed into a foaming wave
She stood Monadnoc's head

Through a thousand voices
(10)   Spoke the Universal Dame
Who telleth one of my meanings
Is monarch of all I AM

[112]   Earth & heaven in ⟨his bosom⟩ the mansoul
Converging appear
And the thought of his bosom
He sees in the sphere
(5)   The love of the damsel
All nature records
The ⟨toy of the infant⟩ ↑childs toy↓ rehearses
The laws of the ⟨Whole⟩ Lord

Eterne alternation
(10)   now follows now flies
And under pain pleasure
Under pleasure pain lies
Tides of God ebbing flowing
Part & whole whole & part

111 "The Sphinx," 121–32. In pencil, struck through in pencil.
112 "The Sphinx," eight unused lines, 97–100, four unused lines. In pencil, struck through in pencil.

(15)   And the poles of the orbit
      Unite in his heart.

[113]  ⟨In Massachusetts many noble paths⟩
      ⟨Have boun⟩

      ⟨By⟩ pride ⟨fell⟩ ↑ruined↓ the angels
      ⟨By⟩ ↑Their↓ shame the⟨y⟩m ⟨arise⟩ ↑restores↓
(5)    And the ↑joy that is↓ sweetest ⟨emotion⟩
      Lurks in stings of remorse
      Have I a ⟨friend⟩ lover
      Who is noble & free
      I would he were nobler
(10)   Than to love me

      The Demon that haunts him
      Tis the love of the Best
      Revealing the worst
      By the light of the Blest
(15)   The sleep of creation
      ⟨Lies⟩ ↑Falls↓ not on his eyes
      The Perfect has waked him

[114]↑9↓I heard a poet answer
      Aloud & cheerfully
      Say on sweet sphinx thy dirges
      Are pleasant songs to me
(5)    The sailor fears the thunder
      The planter hears it glad
      ⟨T⟩Her brothers doubt the stranger
      The maids heart leaps to the lad

      In this sour world↑, o↓ summerwind
(10)   Who taught thee sweet to blow
      ⟨Ah w⟩Who should not love me, ↑summerwind,↓
      If thou canst flatter so

   ↑1⟨1⟩o↓Earth & heaven in the mansoul
      Converging appear
(15)   And the thot of his bosom
      He sees in the Sphere
      The love of the damsel
      All natures record
      The child's toy rehearses

113 "In Massachusetts many noble paths" (1–2); "The Sphinx," 89–96, 73–74, 75?, 76, 77?–79? (3–17). In pencil; lines (3–17) and (11–17) are struck through separately in pencil.
114 "The Sphinx," 65–68, four unused lines (1–8); "In this sour world" (9–12); "The Sphinx," eight unused lines, 73–80 (13–28). In pencil, struck through in pencil; lines (13–20) are partially erased. Lines (9–12) are circled in pencil.

(20)     The laws of the lord

↑ I I ↓ The fiend that him harries
        Is the Love of the Best
        Yawns the Pit of the Dragons
        Lit by rays from the Blest
(25)    The ⟨sweet sleep⟩ ↑Lethe↓ of ⟨creation⟩ ↑nature↓
        Cannot trance him again
        His soul ⟨has⟩ see⟨n⟩s the Perfect
        Which his eyes seek in vain

[115]   Profounder profounder
        His spirit must dive
        His wheeling orb never
        At a goal will arrive
(5)     The heavens that trance him
        With sweetness untold
        ⟨He ⟨tastes⟩ ↑finds↓ them⟩ ↑Once found↓ for new heavens
        He spurneth the old

        Dull Sphinx bless thy wits
(10)    Thy sight is growing blear
        Bring Sphinx a pair of spectacles
        Her muddy eyes to clear
        The old Sphinx bit her ↑thick↓ lips
        Said, "Who taught thee me to name?
(15)    "Manchild, I am thy ⟨shadow⟩ spirit
        "Of thine eye ⟨the⟩ ↑I am↓ eyebeam

        "Thou art the unanswered question
        "Couldst ⟨thou⟩ see th⟨ine own⟩y ↑proper↓ eye
        "Alway it asketh asketh
(20)    "Every answer is a lie
        "So take thy ⟨way⟩ ↑quest↓ through nature
        "Through thousand natures ⟨f⟩ply
        "Ask on thou clothed Eternity
        "Time is the false reply."

(25)    ↑Uprose the merry Sphinx↓
        ↑And crouched no more in stone↓
                        ↑&c &c↓

[116]   I heard a poet answer
        ↑Aloud &↓ Cheerfully

115 "The Sphinx," 81–88, 105–22. In pencil, struck through in pencil.
116 "The Sphinx," 65–68, four unused lines (1–8); "Last night / She purred about me"
(9–11). In pencil; lines (1–8) are struck through in pencil.

Say on sweet Sphinx thy dirges
Announce good news to me
(5)    The ⟨culprit⟩ ↑sailor↓ fears the thunder
The ⟨farmer⟩ ↑planter↓ hears it glad
Her brothers doubt the stranger
The maid ⟨adores⟩ ↑s heart leaps to↓ the lad

⟨At⟩ ↑Last↓ night
(10)   She purred about me as I fell to sleep
And mixed herself with visions

[117]   Look danger in the eye it vanishes
Anatomize that roaring populace
⟨And⟩ big dire & overwhelming as they seem
Piecemeal ↑t'↓is nothing. Some of them scream
(5)    Fearing the ⟨rest⟩ ↑others↓ some are lookers on
One of them hectic day by day consumes
And one will die tomorrow of the flux
One of them has already changed his mind
And falls out with the ringleader ↑and one↓
(10)  ⟨One⟩Has seen his creditor amidst the crowd
And flees. And there are heavy eyes
That miss their sleep & meditate retreat.
A few malignant heads keep up the din
The rest are idle boys.

[118]   As I walked in the wood
The silence into music broke
Sang the thrush in the dark oak
I unwilling to intrude
(5)    Slink into nigh solitude
Till warned by a scout of a jay
That flying ⟨newspaper⟩ ↑courier↓ so gay
That he sees me if I ⟨dont⟩ see ↑not↓ him
His eyes are bright if mine are dim

(10)  I sat upon the ground
I leaned against an ancient pine
The pleasant breeze
Shook the forest tops like waves of ocean
I felt of the trunk the gentle motion

[119]   ⟨Econom⟨y⟩ical⟩ ↑frugal↓ Nature gave
One scent ⟨in⟩to hyson & wall flower

117 "Look danger in the eye." In pencil.
118 "As I walked in the wood" (1–9); "I sat upon the ground" (10–14). In pencil; lines (1–9) are partially erased.
119 "Xenophanes," 1–4. In pencil, struck through in pencil.

One sound ⟨in⟩to pine groves & ⟨in⟩to waterfalls
One aspect to the desert & the lake.

[120] [blank]
[121]    Good Charles the springs adorer
True worshipper of Flora
Knows't thou the gay Rhodora
    That blossoms in the May
(5)    It blooms in dark nooks
By the wood loving brooks
    And makes their twilight gay

[122] [blank]
[123]    In the deep heart of man a poet dwells
Who all the day of life his summer story tells
Scatters on every eye dust of his spells
Scent form & color to the flowers & shells
(5)    Wins the believing child with wondrous tales
Touches a cheek with colors of romance
And crowds a history into a glance
Gives beauty to the lake & fountain
Spies over sea the fires of the mountain
(10)    When thrushes ope their throat, tis he that sings
And he that paints the oriole's fiery wings
The little Shakspeare in the maidens heart
Makes Romeo of a ploughboy on his cart
⟨Crowns martyrs⟩Opens the eye to Virtues starlike meed
(15)    And gives persuasion to a gentle deed.

[124]–[125] [blank]
[126]    Announced by all the trumpets of the sky
Arrives the snow & driving o'er the fields
Seems nowhere to alight: The whited air
Hides hills & woods, the river, & the heaven,
(5)    And veils the farmhouse at the garden's end
The sled & traveller stopped, the courier's feet
Delayed, all friends shut out, the housemates sit
Around the radiant fireplace enclosed
In a tumultuous privacy of storm.
(10)    Come see the Northwinds masonry
Out of an unseen quarry evermore
Furnished with tile, the fierce artificer
Curves his white bastions with projected roof
Round every windward stake, or tree, or door.

121 "Good Charles the springs adorer." In pencil.
123 "In the deep heart of man."
126 "The Snow-Storm," 1–25. Struck through in ink.

(15)       Speeding the myriad handed his wild work
So fanciful, so savage, nought cares he
For number or proportion. Mockingly
On coop or kennel he hangs Parian wreaths;
A swan like form invests the hidden thorn;
(20)       Fills up the farmer's lane from wall to wall,
Maugre the farmers sighs, & at the gate
A tapering turret overtops the work.
And, when his hours are numbered, & the world
Is all his own, retiring, as he were not,
(25)       Leaves, when the Sun appears, astonished Art


[127₁]            The snow storm         29 Dec
Announced ‖ . . . . ‖ the trumpets of the sky
Arrives the snow ‖ . . . . . ‖ the /air/fields/
‖ . . . . . . . . . . . . . ‖ the whited air
Hides hills ‖ . . . . . . . ‖ & the heaven
(5)       And veils the ‖ . . . . . . . ‖ half a mile
The sled & traveller stopped ⟨‖ . . . . ‖ delayed⟩ ↑the couriers
    feet↓
↑Delayed↓ ‖ . . . ‖ friends shut out ‖ . . . ‖ ↑the housemates
    sit↓
⟨In a tumultuous privacy of storm⟩
Around the radiant fireplace enclosed
(10)     In a tumultuous privacy of storm
       Come see the Northwinds masonry
Out of an unseen quarry evermore
Furnished with ‖ . . . . . ‖ artificer
Curve⟨d⟩s his white bastions with projected roof
(15)     Round every windward stake or tree or door.
Speeding the myriadhanded his wild work
So fanciful so savage nought cares he
For number or proportion   Mockingly
On coop or kennel hangs Parian wreaths
(20)     A swan like form invests the hidden thorn
Fills up the farmers lane from wall to wall
Maugre the farmers sighs and at the gate
A tapering turret overtops the ⟨‖ . . . ‖⟩ work


[127₂]    To mimic in slow structures, stone by stone,
Built in an age, the mad wind's night work
The frolic Architecture of the Snow.

127₁ "The Snow-Storm," 1–7, 9, 8–22. Erased pencil.
127₂ "The Snow-Storm," 26–28. Struck through in ink.

[128]     And when his hours are numbered ‖ . . . ‖ the world
          Is all his own, retiring as ⟨if⟩ he were not,
          Leaves, when the sun appears, astonished Art
          ⟨To ape ‖ . . . . . . . . . . . . . . . ‖⟩
(5)       ‖ . . . . . . . . . . . . ‖ structures stone by stone
          Built in ⟨‖ . . . ‖⟩ an age the mad wind's night work
          The frolic Architecture of the snow
          ⟨‖ . . . . . . . . . . . . . . . . ‖⟩
          ‖ . . . . . . . . . . . . . . ‖
(10)      ‖ . . . . . . . . . ‖ wind's night work
          The ‖ . . . . . . . . . . . . ‖

[129]     O what are heroes prophets men
          But pipes through which the breath of ⟨God⟩Pan doth blow
          A momentary music. Being's tide
          Swells ⟨this way⟩ ↑hitherward↓ & ⟨at once⟩ myriads of
                    forms
(5)       Live, robed with beauty, painted by the Sun:
          ⟨Their dust pervaded by the nerves of God⟩
          Their dust pervaded by the nerves of God
          Throbs with an overmastering energy
          Knowing & doing. Ebbs the tide, they lie
(10)      White hollow shells upon the desart shore.
          But not the less the eternal wave rolls on
          To animate new millions, & exhale
          Races & ⟨worlds, as⟩ ↑planets↓ its enchanted foam.

[130] [blank]
[131]     To the sorrow stricken
          The heat of his own fire has sadness in it

          Yet sometime to the sorrow stricken
          Shall his own sorrow seem impertinent
(5)       A thing that takes no more root in the ⟨deep⟩ world
          Than doth the traveller's shadow on the rock

[132] [blank]
[133]     Go if thou wilt ambrosial Flower
          Go match thee with thy seeming peers
          I will wait Heaven's perfect hour
          Through the innumerable years

128  "The Snow-Storm," 23–25, 26, 26, 27–28, x?, x?, 27–28. Erased pencil.
129  "O what are heroes prophets men." Struck through in ink. Underlying this version is an erased pencil version, of which the following has been recovered: "momentary", inserted, in line (3); "way &" in line (4); "Live, robed" and "painted by" in line (5), which is inserted.
131  "Yet sometime to the sorrow stricken," 1–2, 1–4. In pencil.
133  "Go if thou wilt." In pencil.

[134]    In Walden wood the chickadee
Runs round the pine & maple tree,
Intent on insect slaughter:
O tufted entomologist!
(5)    Devour as many as you list,
Then drink in Walden Water.

[135]    I walked abroad
Thy work went forth to see thy work Great Soul!

[136]    ⟨With ↑his↓ two wings⟩ ↑Time↓
With his two wings black & white
Pied with the Day and Night

[137]    In Walden wood the chickadee
Runs round the pine & maple tree
Intent on insect slaughter
The tufted entomologist
(5)    May eat as many as he list
Then drink in Walden Water

[138] [blank]
[139]    Star seer Copernicus
Only could earn a curse
A slip of a fellow to show men the stars
Presum⟨ing⟩ed to discover more than they would
(5)    How dared the ⟨‖ . . ‖⟩ ↑rum↓ rascal be misunderstood
Misunderstood — Misunderstood
How dared the old graybeard be misunderstood

What a scandalous slip of a fellow was he
Presuming to show what men wished not to see

[140] [blank]
[141]                    *The Visit.*
Askest, How long thou shalt stay?
Devastator of the day!
Know, each substance & relation
In all nature's operation
(5)    Hath its unit, bound, & metre,
And every new compound
Is some product & repeater,
Some frugal product of the early found.
But the unit of the visit,

---

134 "In Walden wood the chickadee." In pencil.
135 "I walked abroad." In pencil.
136 "Compensation" ("The wings of Time"), 1, 1–2. In pencil, struck through in pencil.
137 "In Walden wood the chickadee." Erased pencil.
139 "Star seer Copernicus," 1–7, 3–4. In pencil.
141 "The Visit," 1–16, 18–26. Struck through in ink.

(10) The encounter of the wise,
   Say, what other metre is it
   Than the meeting of the eyes?
   Nature poureth into nature
   Through the channels of that feature;
(15) Horsed upon a ray of light,
   More fleet than waves or whirlwinds go,
   Hearts to hearts their meaning show,
   Sum their long experience,
   And exchange intelligence.
(20) Single look has drained the breast,
   Single moment years confessed.
   The duration of a glance
   Is the term of convenance,
   And though thy rede be Church or State,
(25) Frugal multiples of that.
[142] Speeding Nature cannot halt,
   Loiter, thou shalt rue th⟨y⟩e fault:
   If Love his moment overstay,
   Hatred's swift repulsions play.

[143] And though he dearly prized the bards of fame
   His sweetest poem was one maiden's name

[144] [blank]
[145]   You shall not love me for what daily spends
   You shall not know me in the noisy street
   Where I as others follow petty ends
   Nor when in fair saloons we chance to meet
(5) Nor when I'm jaded, sick, anxious, or mean.
   But love me then and only when you know
   Me for the channel of the river↑s↓ of God
   From deep ideal fontal heavens that flow
   Making its shores making their beauty broad,
(10) Which birds & cattle drink, drink too the roots of the grove
   And animating all it feeds with love.

[146] [blank]
[147]      Manners.

   Grace Beauty & Caprice
   Build this golden portal

142 "The Visit," 27–30. Struck through in ink.
143 "And though he dearly prized." In pencil.
145 "You shall not love me." In pencil.
147 "Manners," 1–19, 17–20. In pencil, struck through twice in pencil; lines (20–22) are separately struck through in pencil.

Graceful women chosen men
Dazzle every mortal
(5)   Their sweet & lofty /favour/countenance/
His enchanted food
He need not go to them, their forms
/Light up/Beset/ his solitude
He looketh seldom in their face,
(10)   His eyes explore the ground,
The green grass is a looking-glass
Whereon their traits are found.
Little he says to them
So dances th' heart in his breast:
(15)   Their tranquil mien bereaveth him
Of wit, of words, of rest.
Too weak to win too fond to shun
The tyrants of his doom
The too enamoured worshipper
(20)     Too weak to win too fond to shun
These tyrants of his doom
The ⟨worship-stricken mortal⟩ ↑too enamoured
worshipper↓
Scuds behind a tomb

[148] Isabel. For every thing doth hinder gratitude
As Timon's friend looked not at Timon's hand
But farther back, comparing what he gave
With that great store he drew from.
(5)  Leon.      Well, ⟨the man⟩ ↑I think ↓
↑the man↓ Was right the world owed him his bread
⟨And⟩ Timon expecting gratitude was wrong.

[149]  At last the poet spoke
The richest gifts are vain
As lightning in yon dark clouds grain
A poison in the worlds veins creeps
(5)  A devil in celestial deeps

[150] [blank]
[151]  Words of the air
Which birds of the air
Carry aloft below around
To the isles of the deep
(5)  to the snow capped steep
to thunder cloud

148 "Isabel. For every thing." In pencil.
149 "At last the poet spoke." In pencil.
151 "Where the fungus broad & red," 36–43, 43. In pencil.

to the loud bazaar
⟨To the Kings Louvre & the Kremlin of Czar⟩
↑To the haram of Sultan & Kremlin of Czar↓

[152] [blank]

[153]               *The Discontented Poet: a Masque*
              Lonely he sat, the men were strange
              The women all forbidden
              Too closely pent in narrow range
              Between two sleeps a short day's stealth
(5)           Mid many ails a brittle health
              Counts his scant stock of native wealth
              By conscience ↑sorely↓ chidden ⟨chidden⟩

              His loves were sharp sharp pains
              Outlets to his thoughts were none
(10)          A wandering fire within his veins
              His soul was smouldered & undone
              A cripple of God, half true, half formed,
              And by great sparks Promethean warmed
              Constrained by impotence to adjourn
(15)          To infinite time his eager turn,
              His lot of action from the Urn.

              He ⟨f⟩by false usage pinned about
              No breath therein, no passage out,
              Cast wishful glances at the stars
(20)          And wishful ⟨saw⟩ ↑hailed↓ the Ocean stream,
              "Merge me in the brute Universe
              Or lift to some diviner dream."

[154]         Beside him sat enduring love:
              Upon him noble eyes did rest,
              Which for the genius that there strove
              The follies bore that it invest:
(5)           They spoke not: for their earnest sense
              Outran the craft of eloquence:
              The holy lovers peaceful sate
              Through extacy inanimate
              As marble statues in a hall,
(10)          Yet was their silence musical;
              The only plaints, the sole replies,
              Were those long looks of liquid eyes.

*Chorus*   Yon waterflags, yon sighing osier,
              A drop can shake, a breath can fan

153 "The Discontented Poet: a Masque," 1–22. In pencil.
154 "The Discontented Poet: a Masque," 23–42. In pencil.

(15)         Maidens laugh & weep: Composure
                Is the pudency of man.

    *Chorus*  Means,—dear brother, ask them not;
                Soul's desire is means enow;
                Pure content is angels lot;
(20)         Thine own theatre art thou.

   [155] *Poet.*   I see your forms with deep content
                I know that ye are excellent;
                But will ye stay?
                I hear the rustle of wings
(5)          Ye meditate what to say
                When ye go to quit me forever & aye.

    *Chorus*  Brother, we are no phantom band,
                Brother accept this fatal hand
                Aches thy unbelieving heart
(10)         With the fear that we must part?
                See all we are rooted here
                By one thought to one same sphere;
                From thyself thou canst not flee,
                From thyself no more can we.

(15) Poet     Suns & stars their courses keep,
                But not angels of the deep;
                Day & night their turn observe,
                But the day of day may swerve.
                Is there warrant that the waves
(20)         Of thought from their mysterious caves
  [156]      Will heap in me their highest tide
                In me therewith beatified?
                Unsure the ebb & flow of thought,—
                The moon comes back, the spirit not.

(5)  *Chorus*  Brother, sweeter is the Law
                Than all the grace Love ever saw
                We are its suppliants. By it we
                Draw the breath of eternity:
                Serve thou it not for daily bread
(10)         Serve it for pain & fear & dread.
                Love it, though it hide its light;
                By love behold the Sun at night;
                If the Law should thee forget,
                More enamoured serve it yet:

155 "The Discontented Poet: a Masque," 43–62. In pencil.
156 "The Discontented Poet: a Masque," 63–80. In pencil.

(15)      Though it hate thee,—suffer long,—
          Put the Spirit in the wrong,—
          That were a deed to sing in Eden,
          By the waters of life to Seraphs heeding.

[157]          — — Love
          Asks nought his brother cannot give
          Asks nothing but does all receive
          Love calls not to his aid events
(5)       He to his wants can well suffice
          Asks not of others ⟨c⟩soft consents
          Nor kind Occasion without eyes
          Nor plots to ope or bolt a gate
          Nor heeds Condition's iron walls
(10)      Where he goes, goes before him Fate;
          Whom he uniteth God instals;
          Instant & perfect his access
          To the dear object of his thought,
          Though foes & lands & seas between
(15)      Himself & his love intervene.

          The sense of the world is short
          Long & various the report
          To love & be beloved
          Men & gods have not outlearned it
(20)      And how oft soeer theyve turned it
          Not to be improved

[158]      ⟨Their⟩ ↑Its↓ peace sublime his aspect kept
          His purpose woke his features slept

[159]         He walked the streets of great New York
           Full of men, the men were full of blood
          Signs of power, signs of worth,
          Yet all seemed ⟨superficial⟩ ↑trivial↓
(5)       As the cease⟨s⟩less cry
          Of the newsboys in the street
          ⟨Does not the poet remember⟩
          ⟨That the quality of the mind⟩
          ⟨Makes the name musical⟩
(10)      ⟨Memorable⟩
          Now men do not listen after
          The ⟨great⟩ voice in the breast

157 "Love / Asks nought" (1–15); "Eros" (16–21). In pencil.
158 "In Memoriam. E.B.E.," 101–2. In pencil, struck through in pencil.
159 "He walked the streets," 1–21. In pencil.

Which makes the thunder mean
But the Great God hath departed
(15)     And they listen ⟨not after God but⟩ after Scott & Byron
⟨I had no great hours⟩ ↑I met no gods—I harboured none, ↓
As I walked by noon & ⟨mid⟩night alone
The crowded ways
And yet I found in the heart of the town
(20)     A few children of God nestling in his bosom
Not detached as all the crowd appeared
[160]    each one a sutlers boat
⟨Sailing up & down⟩ ↑Cruising↓ for private gain
But these seemed undetached united
⟨Speakers for God obedient still⟩
(5)     Lovers of Love, of Truth,
And as among Indians they say
The One the One is known
So under the eaves of Wall Street
Brokers had met the Eternal
(10)     In the city of surfaces
Where I a swain became a surface
I found & worshipped Him.
Always thus ⟨nearly⟩ neighbored ⟨dwell⟩ well
The two contemporaries dwell
(15)     The World which ⟨understands the world⟩ ↑⟨wh⟩by the
         world is known↓
And Wisdom seeking still its own
I walked with men
Who seemed as if they were chairs or stools
Tables or shopwindows or champagne baskets
(20)     For these they loved & were if truly seen
I walked with others of their wisdom gave me proof
Who brought the starry heaven
As near as the house roof
[161]    The sun set but set not his hope
Stars rose his faith was earlier up
Fixed on the enormous galaxy
Deeper & older seemed his eye
(5)     ↑And↓ Matched his sufferance sublime
The taciturnity of time

The Archangel Hope
Looks to the ⟨Zenith up⟩ ↑azure cope↓
Waits through dark ages for the morn

160 "He walked the streets," 22–44. In pencil.
161 "Character," 1–6 (1–6); "The Archangel Hope" (7–10). In pencil; lines (1–6) are struck
through in pencil.

(10)       Defeated day by day but unto victory born

[162] [blank]
[163]    For nature watcheth in the rose
           And hearkens in the berry's bell
           To keep her friends to plague her foes
           And like wise God she judges well

[164]    The sinful painter drapes ‖ . . ‖ /form/goddess warm/
           Because it ⟨‖ . . . . . . ‖⟩ ↑still is naked being drest↓
           The noble sculptor ‖ . . . . . . . . . . . ‖
           Because his ‖ . . . . . . . . . . . . ‖

(5)        the ‖ . . . ‖ sculptor will not so deform
           The Idea which ‖ . . ‖ flesh itself enough invests

           The sinful painter drapes his goddess warm
           Because she still is naked, being drest;
           The God-like sculptor will not so deform
(10)       ⟨The Idea⟩ ↑Beauty↓ which limbs & flesh enough invest.

[165]    They put their finger on their lip
           The powers above
           The seas their islands clip
           The moons in Ocean dip
(5)        They love but name not love

           Far capitals, & marble courts, her eye still seemed to see,
           Minstrels, & dames, & highborn men, & of the best that be.

[166]–[167] [blank]
[168]    Where the fungus broad & red
           Lifts its head
           Like poisoned loaf of elfin bread
           Where the aster grew
(5)        With the social goldenrod
           In a chapel which the dew
           Made beautiful for God
           The maple street
           In the houseless wood
(10)       O what would nature say
           She spared no speech today
           The fungus & the bulrush spoke

**163** "Nature I," 12–15. Erased pencil.
  **164** "Painting and Sculpture," 1–3, 4?, 3–4, 1–4. In pencil; lines (1–4) and (7–10) are struck through in pencil and lines (1–6) are erased.
  **165** "Silence" (1–5); "A.H.," 3–4 (6–7). Lines (1–5) are in pencil, struck through in pencil.
  **168** "Where the fungus broad & red," 1–24 (1–24); " May Day [Invitation]," 37–47 (12–16, 19–24). In pencil. In line (22), "Which" is written "Whch".

Answered the pinetree & the oak
The wizard South blew down the glen
(15)      Filled the straits & filled the wide,
Each maple leaf turned up its silver side.
⟨The south wind blows I'll forth to walk⟩
⟨And hear his rich diurnal talk⟩
All things shine in his /damp/smoky/ ray
(20)      And all we see are pictures high
Many a high hill side
Which oaks of pride
Climb to their tops
And boys run out upon their leafy ropes

[169]   In the houseless wood
Voices followed after
Every shrub & grapeleaf
Rang with fairy laughter
(5)      I have heard them fall
Like the strain of all
King Oberons minstrelsy
    Would hear the everlasting
And know the only strong
(10)     You must ⟨go⟩ ↑worship↓ fasting
You must listen long
Words of the air
Which birds of the air
Carry aloft below around
(15)     To the isles of the deep
To the snow capped steep
To the thundercloud
To the loud bazaar
To the haram of Caliph & Kremlin of Czar
(20)     Is the verse original
Let its numbers rise & fall
As the winds do when they call
One to another

Come se⟨ek⟩arch the wood for flowers
(25)     Wild tea & wild pea
[170]   ⟨Co⟩Grape vine & succory
Coreopsis
And liatris
Flaunting in their bowers

169 "Where the fungus broad & red," 25–49. In pencil.
170 "Where the fungus broad & red," 50–65. In pencil.

(5)               Grass with greenflag halfmast high
                       Succory to match the sky
                       Columbine with horn of honey
                       Scented fern & ⟨o⟩agrimony
                       Forest full of essences
(10)             Fit for fairy presences,
                       Peppermint & sassafras
                       Sweet fern, mint, & vernal grass,
                       Panax, black birch, sugar maple,
                       Sweet & scent for Dian's table,
(15)             Elder-blow, sarsaparilla,
                       Wild-rose, lily, dry vanilla.

[171] [blank]
[172]     When Jane was absent Edgar's eye
             Roved to the door incessantly
             But when she came he went away
             For the poor youth could nothing say
(5)             Yet hated to appear unwise
             Before those beatific eyes

[173]–[175] [blank]
[176]     Though her eye seek other forms
             And a glad delight below
             Yet the love the world that warms
             Bids for me her bosom glow

(5)             She must love me till she find
             Another heart as large & true
             Her soul /like mine is unconfined/is frank as the Ocean wind/
             And the world has only two

             If Nature hold another heart
(10)             That knows a purer flame than we
             I too therein would challenge part
             And learn of love a new degree

[177] [blank]
[178]      I have found a nobler love
            Than the sordid world doth know
              Above its envy or belief

172 "When Jane was absent." In pencil.
176 "Though her eye seek other forms." In pencil.
178 "I have found a nobler love." In pencil. The erased pencil writing consists of three segments of five, four, and four lines respectively. Of the first segment nothing has been recovered; of the second, an inserted "Twins" is visible at the beginning of the third line; of the third, visible are the following: "And" and "we cannot" (first line), "In" (second line), and "Thou" and "praise" (third line).

My flames of passion glow

[thirteen lines of erased pencil writing]

[179]  It is written in keen astronomy
       It is chanted in star born songs
       Whoso belongs to ‖ . . . . . ‖
       ‖ . . . . . . . . . . . . . ‖

(5)     ‖ . . . . . . . . ‖ child
       Like a cloud over land ‖ . . ‖ sea
       If ‖ . . . . . . . . . . . ‖
       They ‖ . . . . . . . . . . ‖

       ‖ . . . . . . . . . . . . . ‖
(10)    ‖ . . . . . . . . . ‖ hours!
       ‖ . . . . . . . . . ‖ Heart!
       ‖ . . . . . . . . . . . . ‖

[180]–[181] [blank]
[182]     Fine humble bee! fine humble bee!
       Where thou art is clime for me
       Let them sail for Porto Rique
       Far off heats thro' seas to seek
(5)     I will follow thee alone
       Thou animated torrid zone!
       Zig-zag steerer, desert cheerer,
       Let me chase thy waving lines,
       Keep me nearer, me thy hearer,
(10)    Singing over shrubs & vines.
         Flower bells,
         Honied cells,
         These the tents
         Which he frequents.
(15)    Insect lover of the Sun
       Joy of thy dominion!
       Sailor of the atmosphere
       Swimmer through the waves of air
       Voyager of light & noon,
(20)    Epicurean of June,
       Wait, I prithee, till I come
       Within earshot of thy hum;
       All without is martyrdom.
         When the South wind, in May days,
(25)    With a net of shining haze,
       Silvers the horizon wall,

179 "It is written in keen astronomy." Erased pencil.
182 "The Humble-Bee," 1–26. In pencil, struck through in pencil.

[183]  And with softness touching all,
Tints the human countenance
With a color of romance,
And, infusing subtle heats,
(5)  Turns the sod to violets,
Thou in sunny solitudes,
Rover of the Underwoods,
The green silence dost displace
With thy mellow breezy bass

(10)  Hot ⟨A⟩midsummer's petted crone
Sweet to me thy drowsy tune
Telling of countless sunny hours;
Long days; and solid banks of flowers;
Of gulfs of sweetness without bound,
(15)  In Indian wildernesses found;
Of Syrian peace; immortal leisure;
Firmest cheer; and birdlike pleasure.

Aught unsavory or unclean
Hath my insect never seen:
(20)  But violets and bilberry bells
Maple sap, and daffodels,
Clover, catchfly, adderstongue,
And briar roses, dwelt among
[184]  All beside was un⟨seen⟩known waste
All was picture as he passed.

Wiser far than human seer
Yellow breeched philosopher
(5)  Seeing only what is fair
Sipping only what is sweet
Thou dost mock at fate & care
Leave the chaff & take the wheat
When the f⟨ei⟩ierce northwestern blast
(10)  Cool sea & land so far & fast
Thou already slumberest deep
Wo and want thou canst outsleep
Want and wo which torture us
Thy sleep makes ridiculous.

[185]  I reached the middle of the mount
Up which the incarnate soul doth climb

183 "The Humble-Bee," 27–49. In pencil, struck through in pencil.
184 "The Humble-Bee," 50–63. In pencil, struck through in pencil.
185 "Dirge," eight unused lines, 9–20. Erased pencil.

And paused ⟨a⟩ for them & looked around
With me who walked thro' space & time

(5)    Five rosy boys with morning light
Had leaped from one fair mother's arms
Fronted the Sun with hope as bright
And greeted God with Childhoods psalms

⟨I see the river⟩ ↑The winding Concord↓ glide↑s↓ below
(10)   Pouring as wide a flood
As when my brothers long ago
Came with me to the wood

But they are gone—the holy ones—
Who trod with me this lonely vale,
(15)   The strong, starbright companions—
Are silent, low, & pale.

My good, my noble in their prime,
Who made this world the thing it was;
Who learned with me the lore of time,
(20)   Who loved with me this ancient place.

[186]   They filled this valley with young thought
Of art & poetry & fate
The heyday of their vigour wrought
Wit grace & love in their debate

(5)    They threaded these lanes with Botany,
Garlanded them with love,
Gemmed them with keen Astronomy,
Or cheered with Song the grove.

This earth which they trod with delight
(10)   Bended to them as bendeth this grass,
Their great heart asked like yon bird from his height
Only a nestling place.

They made this valley ring
With emotion such as pleased them
(15)   They plotted schemes of glorious wing
Their hopes outsoared the Cherubim

They took this valley for their toy
They played with it in every mood
It served for business prayer or joy
(20)   They treated Nature as they would

186 "Dirge," sixteen unused lines, 21–24. In pencil; lines (1–16) are struck through several times in pencil and lines (17–20) are erased.

72

[1871] [erased pencil writing on entire page]

[1872]   ‖ . . . . . ‖ middle ‖ . . . . ‖
       Up which ‖ . . . . . . . . ‖ climb
       ‖ . . ‖ paused for them ‖ . . ‖ looked around
       With me who walked through Space & time.

(5)    Five rosy boys with morning light
       Had leaped from one fair mother's arms
       Fronted the sun with /hearts/hope/ as bright
       ‖ . . . ‖ greeted God with childhood's psalms.

       ‖ . . . . ‖ took this valley for their toy
(10)   They played with it in every mood
       A cell for prayer a hall for joy
       They managed nature as they would

       Who made ‖ . . . . . . . . . . . ‖
       Who learned with me ‖ . . . ‖ of ‖ . . . ‖
(15)   Who ‖ . . . ‖ with me this ancient place

[1873]   They coloured the whole horizon round
       Stars flamed or faded as they bade
       All Echoes hearkened for their sound
       They made the woodlands glad or mad

[1881] [approximately twenty-seven lines of erased pencil writing]

[1882]      Fine presentiments controlled him,
       As one who knew a day was great,
       And freighted with a friendly fate,
       Ere whispered news or couriers told him;
(5)    When first at morn he read the fa⟨t⟩ce
       Of Nature from his resting place
       ↑He↓ The coming day inspired
       ↑Was↓ With its ↑⟨fine⟩ rare↓ genius fired,
       And, in his bearing & his gait,
(10)   Calm expectancy did wait

[1891] [fifteen lines of erased pencil writing]

1872 "Dirge," eight unused lines, 21–24, 18–20. Erased pencil.
1873 "Dirge," 25–28. Above line (1) "Caesar's Valley" is inserted in pencil and bracketed.
1881 The erased pencil writing consists of two segments of (approximately) sixteen and eleven lines respectively. Nothing has been recovered of the first. The second, upside down at the bottom of the page, is a version of "The oriole whose note" on p. [189]; visible are "The oriole whose note" (first line), "Is" (second line), "Gifted thrush" (ninth line), and "Or" (eleventh line).
1882 "Fine presentiments."
1891 The erased pencil writing consists of two segments of one and fourteen lines respectively. Of the first segment only "Or" is visible. The second is a version of lines 11–20? and 32–35 of "The Humble-Bee"; visible are: "Insect" (first line); "With" (eighth line); "crone" (eleventh line); "⟨Of⟩", "days & solid banks", and "flowers" (fourteenth line).

[1892]  ↑‖ . . . . ‖↓ They ‖ . . . . ‖ valley for their toy
They played with it ‖ . . . . ‖ mood
It ‖ . . . . . . . . . . . . ‖ joy
They handled nature as they would.

(5)  They threaded these lanes with Botany
Garlanded them with love
Gemmed them with keen Astronomy
⟨‖ . . . ‖ them & upward strove⟩
Or ‖ . . . . . . . ‖ Song ‖ . . . . . ‖

(10)  This valley seemeth cold & dark
It ‖ . . . ⟨ . . . ⟩↑ . . ‖↓ enough before
It shook with rapture at their laugh
It ‖ . . . . . . . . ‖ flower
⟨‖ . . . . . . . . . . . . . . ‖⟩

(15)  I feel this flower of silken leaf
As ‖ . . . . ‖ this annual knew
⟨‖ . . . . ↑ . . ‖↓ me with a grief
⟨No herb ‖ . . . ‖ nature ‖ . . . ‖ grew⟩
Whose balsam never grew

[1893]  The oriole whose note
Is gay & glorious as his coat
The sparrow of the wilderness
The robin in a fatigue dress
(5)  Swallows flew in silence on.
Boblinks laughed & talked away
Gifted thrush↑es↓ who could sing
⟨Fly⟩ ↑Sail↓ like a hawk
Or fast as an ostrich walk.

[1901] [twenty-six lines of erased pencil writing]

[1902]  They knew every thing was here
Each apple & berry & bird
The ————————
They loved every month in the year

1892 "Dirge," 21–24, ten unused lines, 29–32, 32. Erased pencil.
1893 "The oriole whose note." In pencil.
1901 The erased pencil writing consists of two segments of fourteen and twelve lines respectively, corresponding roughly to lines 40–63 of "The Humble-Bee." Visible are: line (1), "of ⟨‖ . . . ‖⟩ ↑gulfs↓ of sweetness without bound"; line (2), "In tropic" and a hand sign pointing right; line (3), "Of"; line (4), "pleasure"; line (7), "never seen"; line (8) " ↑But↓ They"; line (9), "Maple sap"; line (10), "Clover" and "tongue"; line (15), "Wiser far than human seer"; line (16), "Yellow"; line (18), "Sipping"; line (20), "Leave the chaff & take the wheat"; line (22), "fast"; and line (25), "Want &".
1902 "Dirge," thirteen unused lines, 25–28, x, x. In pencil; lines (1–5) and (14–19) are struck through in pencil and lines (10–13) are erased.

(5)   They loved every month in the year

   This earth which they trod with delight
   Bended to them as bendeth this grass
   Their heart was so great they aimed at such height
   They asked nought but a dwelling place

(10)   They made the valley ring
   With emotion such as pleased them
   They plotted schemes of glorious wing
   They outsoared the singing cherubim

   They coloured the whole horizon round
(15)   Stars shone or faded as they bade
   All Echoes hearkened for their sound
   They made the valley glad or mad
    This valley which masters me with dread
    This valley which threatens me with its Dead

[191₁] [three lines of erased pencil writing]

[191₂]  I feel this flower of silky leaf
   Which once my boyhood knew
   Its soft leaves wound me with a grief
   Whose balsam never grew.
(5)   Harken to yon pine warbler
   Singing aloft in the tree
   Hearest thou O traveller
   What he singeth to me

   Not unless God had sharpened thine ears
(10)   ⟨T⟩With ⟨horror⟩sorrow ⟨dread⟩ ↑deep↓ as mine
   Out of that delicate lay couldst thou
   Such a heavy doom divine

   Go lonely man he saith
   They loved thee ⟨in⟩ ↑from↓ their ⟨heart⟩ birth
(15)   Their hands were pure & pure their faith
   There are no ⟨more⟩ ↑such hearts↓ on earth

   They would have poured their blood for thee
   Didst thou sweeten their weary lot
   They had the bitter poverty
(20)   Thou sleepest soft their graves forgot

[192]  ⟨I sauntered here for berries⟩
   ⟨With children when a child⟩

191₂ "Dirge," 29–44, four unused lines. In pencil, struck through in pencil.
 192 "Dirge," four unused lines (1–4); "always found / In the air" (5–7); "We sauntered amidst miracles" (8–18). In pencil; lines (5–7) are bracketed at the left in pencil.

⟨Each bush bore fruit like cherries⟩
⟨To babes so undefiled⟩

(5)     always found
In the air but near the ground
A selecting principle

We ⟨walked⟩ ↑sauntered↓ amidst miracles
We were the fairies in the bells
(10) The summer was our ⟨slight⟩ ↑quaint↓ bouquet
The winter eve our Milky Way
⟨And⟩ ↑We↓ played in turn with all the slides
In Natures la⟨nthorn⟩mp of ⟨many⟩ ↑suns &↓ tides
The
(15) We pierced all books with criticism
We plied with doubts the Catechism
The Christian Fold
The Bible Old

[193] Now Nature is a Funeral
Sunset
The Dawn is sad unto my eyes
The fields are solitary

(5)  This val⟨e⟩ley is all gloom
Gloomy waves the grass
The stems of the pines
Seem to remember
Their tops are looking upward out of the world

(10)   Shake before those awful Powers
Who in their ‖ . . . . . ‖ not ours

The ‖ . . . . . . . . . ‖ replenish
Let ‖ . . . . . . . . ‖ rise & fall
‖ . . . . . . ‖ do when they call
(15) ‖ . . . . . . . . . . ‖

[1941] The hours of sunshine

[1942] In the
Come seek the wood for flowers
The wild tea & the wild pea
⟨The g⟩Grapevine & succory

 193 "Now Nature is a Funeral" (1–9); "Saadi," 57–58 (10–11); "Where the fungus broad &
red," x, 45–46, x? (12–15). In pencil; lines (10–15) are erased.
 1941 Unidentified line, in pencil.
 1942 "Where the fungus broad & red," x, 48–58. In pencil.

(5)                Coreopsis
                 And liatris
       Flaunting in their savage bowers
       Grass with green flag half mast high
       Succory to match the sky
(10)       Columbine with horn of honey
       Scented fern and agrimony
       Forest full of essences      p. 249

[195]    In showers in sweeping showers the spring
       Visits the valley

       The darkest night is day to the gloom
       Of Ellangowans soul.

[196]    This world is tedious
       Shingled with lies
       Reform's as bad as vice
       Reformer as complier
(5)        And I as much a coward
       As any he I blame

[197]    And ⟨wide around⟩ the marriage of the plants
       Is sweetly solemnized

[198]    Those eyes still /followed/shined for/ me though far
       ⟨I saw those eyes however far⟩
       I lonely roved the land or sea
       As I ⟨‖ . ‖ see⟩ ↑behold↓ yon evening star
(5)        Which yet beholds not me

[199]    Those eyes still shined for me tho' far
       I lonely roved the land or sea
       As I behold yon evening star
       Which yet beholds not me

[200]    What are all the flowers
       And all the rainbows of the skies
       To the lights that rain from Eva's eyes
       She turned on me those azure orbs
(5)        And steeped me in their lavish light
       All thot, all things, that joy absorbs.

**195** "Musketaquid," 11–12 (1–2); "The darkest night is day" (3–4). In pencil; lines (1–2) are erased.
  **196** "This world is tedious." In pencil.
  **197** "Musketaquid," 20–21. Erased pencil.
  **198** "Thine Eyes Still Shined," 1, 1–4. Erased pencil.
  **199** "Thine Eyes Still Shined," 1–4. Erased pencil.
  **200** "What are all the flowers" (1–9); "I mistrust him when he sends" (10–14); "A pair of crystal eyes" (15–19). In pencil.

Yet had no hint of vain delight
⟨And⟩ ↑Yet↓ tho I spend my days in love
I never have known aught good thereof

(10)     I mistrust him when he sends
Me sweets & love & troops of friends
The day they Entertain
Create a music in the brain
Yet steal the time

(15)     A pair of crystal eyes will lead me
⟨Round⟩ ↑All↓ about the rounded globe
⟨Oft averted,⟩ ↑Averted oft,↓ if once they heed me
I will follow follow follow
To kiss the hem of her robe

[201] M prefers nettling her company to tiring them and treats inter-ested selfish people with ⟨⟨un⟩illdissembled⟩ ↑open↓ scorn. M said B. was not waywise    knew not where to stop in his talk.

[202₁] [undetermined number of lines of erased pencil writing]

[202₂] [sixteen lines of erased pencil writing]

[202₃]        *The Park.*
The prosperous, the beautiful
To me seem not to wear
The yoke of conscience masterful
Which galls me everywhere↑.↓

(5)     I cannot shake off the god↑:↓
On my neck he makes his seat↑:↓
I look at my face in the glass↑,↓
My eyes his eyeballs meet↑.↓

Enchanters! enchantresses!
(10)    Your gold makes you seem wise
The morning mist within your grounds
More proudly rolls↑,↓ more softly lies↑.↓

Yet spake yon purple mountain↑,↓
Yet said yon ancient wood↑,↓
(15)    That Night ⟨&⟩or Day, that Love or Crime
Lead all Souls to the Good.

201  In pencil.
202₁  Of this earliest layer of erased pencil writing, only "That" at the bottom of the page has been recovered.
202₂  The erased pencil writing is a version of "The Park"; no differences from the ink version by which it is overwritten have been discerned.
202₃  "The Park." Struck through in ink. The nine added punctuation marks are in pencil.

[203₁] [thirteen lines of erased pencil writing]

[203₂]                    *The Poet's Apology.*
         Think me not unkind & rude
         That I walk alone in grove & glen,
         I go to the god of the wood
         To fetch his word to men.

(5)      Tax not my sloth that I
         Fold my arms beside the brook,
         Each cloud that floated in that sky
         Writes a letter in my book.

         Chide me not, laborious band,
(10)     For the idle flowers I brought,
         Every aster in my hand
         Goes home loaded with a thought.

         There was never mystery
         But tis figured in the flowers,
(15)     Was never secret history
         But birds tell it in the bowers.

         One harvest from thy field
         Homeward brought the oxen strong,
         A second crop thine acres yield
(20)     Which I gather in a song.

[204]    Think me not unkind & rude
         That I walk alone in grove & glen
         I go to the god of the wood
         To fetch his word to men

(5)      Tax not my sloth that I
         Fold my arms beside the brook
         Each cloud that floated in the sky
         ⟨‖ . . . . . ‖ word⟩ ↑⟨‖ . . . ‖⟩ Writes a letter↓ in my book

         Chide me not laborious band
(10)     For the flowers I brought
         Every aster in my hand
         Goes home loaded with a thought

203₁ The erased pencil writing consists of three segments of four, four, and five lines respectively, versions of stanzas 1, 2, and 3 of "The Park." Visible are: line (1), "beautiful"; line (3), "yoke of"; line (4), "Which galls me everywhere"; line (5), "I cannot"; line (7), "the glass"; line (8), "⟨And I see⟩" and "↑his eyeballs meet↓"; line (9), "Enchanters"; line (10), "seem wise"; line (11), "your grounds"; and line (13), "rolls". The page is struck through in pencil.
203₂ "The Apology." Struck through in ink.
204 "The Apology," 1–12, 17–20. Erased pencil.

One harvest from thy field
Homeward brought the oxen strong
(15)    A second ‖ . . . . . ‖ yield
Which I gather ‖ . . . . . ‖

[205]    Knows he who tills this lonely field
To reap its scanty corn
What mystic fruit his acres yield
At midnight & at morn

(5)    That field by spirits bad & g⟨g⟩ood
By ⟨‖ . . ‖⟩Hell & Heaven is haunted
And every rood in the ⟨pine⟩ ↑hemlock↓ wood
I know is ground enchanted

In the long sunny afternoon
(10)    The plain was full of ghosts
I wandered up I wandered down
Beset by pensive hosts

For in those lonely grounds the sun
Shines not as on the town
(15)    In nearer arcs his journeys run
And nearer stoops the moon

There in a moment I have seen
The buried Past arise
The fields of Thessaly grew green
(20)    Old gods forsook the skies

[206]    I cannot ⟨tell in sober⟩ ↑publish in my↓ rhyme
What pranks the greenwood played
It was the Carnival of time
And Ages went or stayed

(5)    To me that spectral nook appeared
The mustering Day of doom
And round me swarmed in shadow↑y troop↓
Things past & things to come

The darkness haunteth me elsewhere
(10)    There I am full of light
In every whispering leaf I hear
More sense than sages write

There is no mystery
But tis figured in the flowers

    205 "Knows he who tills," 1–20 (1–20); "Dirge," 1–8 (1–4, 9–12). In pencil; lines (9–12) are struck through in pencil.
    206 "Knows he who tills," 21–40 (1–20); "The Apology," 13–16 (13–16). In pencil.

(15)     There is no history
         But tis calendared in the bowers

         Underwoods were full of pleasance
         All to each in kindness bend
         And every flower made obeisance
(20)     As a man unto his friend.

[207]    Far seen the river glides below
         Tossing one sparkle to the eyes
         I catch thy meaning wizard wave
         The River of my Life replies

(5)      There was never mystery
         But tis figured in the flowers
         Was never secret history
         But birds tell it in the bowers

[208] [blank]
[209]    From the stores of eldest Matter
         The deepeyed flame obedient water
         Transparent air allfeeding earth
         He took the flower of all their worth
(5)      And best with best in sweet consent
         Combined a new temperament

[210]    The sense of the world is short
         Long & various the report
         To love & be beloved
         Men & gods have not outlearned it
(5)      And how oft so eer theyve turned it
         Not to be improved

[211] [blank]
[212₁]   With thy high form my sleep is filled
         Thy blazing eye wakes me at morn
         Thou dost these days with beauty gild
         Which else were trivial & forlorn

(5)      Laid up in the eternity

[212₂]      Hear what British Merlin sung
         Of keenest eye & truest tongue

207 "Far seen the river glides below" (1–4); "Knows he who tills," 33–36 (5–8); "The Apology," 13–16 (5–8). In pencil; lines (5–8) are erased.
   209 "From the stores of eldest Matter." In pencil.
   210 "Eros." Erased pencil.
   212₁ "Thine Eyes Still Shined," four unused lines (1–4); unidentified line (5). In pencil; lines (1–4) are erased.
   212₂ "Considerations by the Way," 1–10, 11, 11, 12–16. In pencil.

Fear not, ↑that↓ they who first arrive
Usurp the seats for which all strive
(5) The /forerunners/Ancestors/ I still have found
⟨Fail to plant⟩ ↑Blinded miss↓ the vantage ground
Ever from one who comes tomorrow
Men wait their good & truth to borrow
But wilt thou measure all thy road
(10) See thou bear the lightest load
⟨Who has little most can spare⟩
Who has little to him who has less can spare
And thou beware
Ponderous gold & stuffs to bear
(15) To faint ere thou thy task fulfil
Only the light armed climb the hill
The richest of all lords is Use
[213] And country Health the loftiest Muse
Bravely feed thy heart with hope
↑So must thou have sky & scope↓
Science & Wonder are glad

(5) And where Canopus shines in May
The nations under the star are gay

⟨Fool & f⟩
⟨Love⟩ ↑Prefer↓ thine ⟨own⟩ heritage & earth
Believe God knew to fix thy birth
(10) Fool & foe may harmless roam
Loved & lovers bide at home
Of all wit's uses the main one
Is to live well with who has none
Music that can deepest reach
(15) Is the tone of cordial speech
A day for toil, an hour for sport,
But for a friend is life too short

[214] And the best gift of God
Is the love of superior souls

The potatoes in a nobleman's cellar have an aristocratic look & seem to scorn a poor mans barrels.

Stout Sparta shrined the god of Laughter
In a niche below the rafter,

213 "Considerations by the Way," 17, x, x, x, 20–21, 30, x, x, 30–31, 26–27, 22–23, 32–33. In pencil.
214 "And the best gift of God" (1–2); "Stout Sparta shrined the god" (3–6). This page is in pencil; the prose passage is erased.

(5)        Visible from every seat
            Where the young men carve their meat.

[215]                        Rome, March 22, 1833
            Alone in Rome! Why Rome is lonely too
            Besides, you need not be alone; the soul
            Shall have society of its own rank.
            Be great, be true, & all the Scipios,

(5)        The Catos, the wise patriots of Rome
            Shall flock to you, & tarry by your side,
            And comfort you with their high company.
            Virtue alone is ⟨company enough⟩ ↑sweet society↓
            It keeps the key to all heroic hearts,

(10)      And opens you a welcome in them all.
            You must be like them if you desire them
            Scorn trifles & embrace a better aim
            Than wine or sleep or ⟨other men's applause⟩ ↑praise↓
            Hunt knowledge as the lover woos a maid

(15)      And ever in the strife of your own thoughts
            Obey the nobler impulse; that is Rome
            That shall command a senate to your side
            For there is no ⟨force⟩ ↑might↓ in the Universe
            That can contend with love. It reigns forever

(20)      Wait then, sad friend, wait in majestic peace
            The hour of heaven. Generously trust
            Thy fortune's web to the beneficent hand
            That until now has put his world in fee
            To thee. He watches for thee still. His love

(25)      Broods over thee & as God lives in heaven
[216]      However long thou walkest solitary
            The hour of heaven shall come, the man appear.

[217]      Be of good cheer, brave spirit; steadfastly
            Serve that low whisper thou hast served; for know,
            God hath a select family of Sons
            Now scattered wide thro' earth, & each alone,

(5)        Who are thy spiritual kindred, & each one
            By constant service to that inward law,
            Is rearing the sublime proportions
            Of a true monarch's soul. Beauty & Strength
            The riches of a spotless memory,

(10)      The eloquence of truth, the wisdom got
            By searching of a clear & loving eye

215 "Alone in Rome!," 1–25. Lines (2–7) are bracketed and struck through in pencil; in line (18) "force" is cancelled and "might" inserted in pencil.
216 "Alone in Rome!," 26–27.
217 "Be of good cheer, brave spirit."

That seeth as God seeth     These are their gifts
And Time who keeps God's word brings on the day
To seal the marriage of these minds with thine
(15)     Thine everlasting ⟨friends⟩ lovers. Ye shall be
The salt of all the elements, world of the world

[218]–[221] [blank]
[222]     Would you know what ⟨charm⟩ ↑joy↓ is hid
In our green Musketaquid
And for travelled eyes what charms
Draw us to these meadow farms
(5)     Come & I will show you all
Makes each day a festival
Stand upon this pasture hill
Face the eastern star until
The slow eye of heaven shall show
(10)     The world above the world below

The mottled clouds like scraps of wool
Steeped in the light are beautiful
And what majestic stillness broods
Over those colored solitudes
(15)     Sleeps the vast East in pleased peace
Whilst up behind yon mountain walls
The silent ⟨streams increase⟩ ↑river ⟨upward⟩ flows↓

[223]     Tell me maiden dost thou use
Thyself thro nature to diffuse
All the angles of the coast
Were tenanted by thy sweet ghost
(5)     Bore thy colours every flower
Thine each leaf & berry bore
All wore thy badges & thy favours
In their scent or in their savours
Every moth with painted wing
(10)     Every bird in caroling
The woodboughs with thy manners waved
The rocks ⟨seemed with⟩ ↑⟨held up⟩↓ ↑uphold↓ thy name
      engraved
The sod throbbed friendly to my feet
And the sweet air with thee was sweet
(15)     The saffron cloud that floated warm
Studied thy motion, took thy form,

222 "Would you know what joy is hid," 1–10, 18–22, 23, 23. In pencil.
223 "Tell me maiden dost thou use." In pencil. In line (12), "held up" is cancelled and "uphold" inserted in ink.

And in his airy road benign
Recalled thy skill in bold design
Or seemed to use his privilege
(20) To gaze over the horizon's edge
To search where now thy beauty glowed
Or made what other purlieus proud?

[224] ⟨Would you know what we behold⟩
Would you know what charm is hid
In our green Musketaquid
And for travelled eyes what charms
(5) Draw us to these meadow farms
⟨‖ . . ‖⟩ ↑Come &↓ I will ⟨‖ . . ‖⟩ ↑show↓ you all
Makes each day a festival
Stand upon this pasture hill
⟨L⟩See the face of ‖ . . . ‖ until
(10) The slow eye of ‖ . . . . ‖ show
The world above the world below,
Out of quiet ‖ . . . ‖ cloud
Behold the miracle
Thou sawst but now the twilight sad
(15) And stood beneath the firmament
A watchman in a dark grey tent
⟨And now⟩ Waiting till God create the earth
Behold the new majestic birth
The mottled clouds like scraps of wool
(20) Steeped in the light are beautiful
⟨And⟩ what majestic Stillness broods
Over these colored solitudes
Sleeps the vast East in pleased peace
Up the far mountain walls the streams increase
(25) Inundating the heaven
⟨↑Purple & gold↓    And floating islands⟩
[225] ↑With spouting streams & waves of light↓
Which round the floating isles unite
See the world below
(5) Baptized with the pure element
A clean & glorious firmament
⟨Over the horizon battlement⟩
Touched with life by every beam

I share the good with every flower
(10) I drink the nectar of the hour
This is not the ancient earth

224 "Would you know what joy is hid," 1, 1–24. In pencil; lines (1–12) are erased.
225 "Would you know what joy is hid," 25–42. In pencil.

Whereof old chronicles ⟨record⟩ ↑relate↓
The tragic tales of crime & fate
But rather like its beads of dew
(15)    And dewbent violets fresh & new
An exhalation of the time
Oer earth heaven man is spread the morn
Tis Natures universal dawn

[226] [blank]

[227₁] Old[?]   And where is my old comrade Freeport   Is he alive
Curt. He went years ago into the country & ate apples   He turned his
mouth into ‖ . . . . ‖ his fat body became ‖ . . . . . . . . . ‖ & little ‖ . . . . .
. . ‖ or large ‖ . . . . . . . ‖ died & was buried & a fortnight ago the
sexton turned up ‖ . . . . . . . . . . . . . . . . . . . . ‖.

[227₂]    Who knows this or that
Hark in the wall to the rat
Since the world was, he has gnawed;
Of his wisdom of his fraud
(5)    What dost thou know
In the wretched little beast
Is life & heart
Child & parent
Not without relation
(10)    To fruitful field & sun & moon
What art thou? his wicked eye
Is cruel to thy cruelty

[228]               *Saadi*
Trees in groves
Kine in droves
In ocean sport the finny herds
Wedgelike cleave the air the birds
(5)    To northern lakes ⟨the⟩ fly windborne ducks
Browse the mountain sheep in flocks
Men consort in camp or town
But the poet dwells alone

God who ⟨bestowed⟩ ↑gave to him↓ the lyre
(10)    Of all mortals the desire
For all men's behoof
Straitly charged him, 'Sit aloof.'
Annexed a warning, poets say,
To the bright premium;

227₁ Unidentified prose passage in erased pencil, upside down at the bottom of the page.
227₂ "Who knows this or that." In pencil.
228 "Saadi," 1–22. In pencil.

(15) When twain together play
 The harp shall be dumb

 Many may come
 But one shall sing ↑,—↓
 Two touch the string
(20) The harp is dumb
 Though there come a million
 Wise Saadi dwells alone

[229] Yet Saadi loved the race of men
 No churl immured in cave or den
 In bower & hall
 He wants them all
(5) Nor can dispense
 With Persia for his audience
 They must give ear
 Grow red with joy & white with fear
 Yet he has no companion
(10) Come ten or come a million
 Good Saadi dwells alone

 Beware where Saadi dwells
 Wisdom of the gods is he
 Entertain it reverently
(15) Gladly round that golden lamp
 Sylvan deities encamp
 And simple maids & noble youth
 Are welcome to the man of truth
 Most welcome they who need him most
(20) They feed the spring which they exhaust
 For greater need
 Draws ⟨grea⟩better deed
 But critic spare thy vanity
[230] Nor show thy pompous parts
 To vex with odious subtlety
 The cheerer of men's hearts.

 Whispered the Muse in Saadis cot;
(5) O gentle Saadi, listen not
 Tempted by thy praise of wit
 And by thirst & appetite
 For the talents not thine own
 To sons of contradiction

229 "Saadi," 23–45. In pencil.
230 "Saadi," 46–48, 86–103. In pencil.

(10)  Never, Son of eastern morning,
    Follow falsehood follow scorning
    Denou⟨c⟩nce who will, who will deny
    And pile the hills to scale the sky
    Let theist atheist pantheist
(15)  Define & wrangle how they list
    Fierce Conserver, fierce Destroyer—
    But thou, joy giver, & enjoyer,
    Unknowing war, unknowing crime
    Gentle Saadi mind thy rhyme
(20)  Heed not what the brawlers say
    Heed thou only Saadi's lay

[231]  Let the great world bustle on
    With war & trade with camp & town
    A thousand men shall dig & eat
    ⟨A thousand↑s↓⟩ at forge & furnace↑, thousands↓ sweat
(5)   ↑And↓ Thousands sail the purple sea
    Or give or take the stroke of war
    Or crowd the market ⟨or⟩& bazaar
    Oft shall war end & peace return
    And cities rise where cities burn
(10)  Ere one man my hill shall climb
    Who can turn the golden rhyme
    Let them manage how they may
    Heed thou only Saadis lay.

      not too deep

(15)     sense of the world is short

[232]  Saadi loved the new & old
    The near & far the town & wold
    Him when Genius urged to roam
    Stronger Custom brot him home

(5)   Sadeyed Fakirs swift to say
    Dirges to ⟨the Night & Day⟩ ↑Decay↓
    ⟨Nor⟩ ↑Never↓ in the blaze of ⟨morning⟩ light
    Lose the shudder of midnight
    Who at overflowing noon
(10)  Hear wolves barking to the moon
    In the bower of dalliance sweet
    Hear the far Avenger's feet
    And shake before those Awful powers
    Who in their pride forgive not ours

231 "Saadi," 104–16, x (1–14); "Eros," 1 (15). In pencil.
232 "Saadi loved the new & old" (1–4); "Saadi," 49–58, 72–85 (5–28). In pencil.

(15)      And yet it seemeth not to me
That the high Gods love tragedy
For Saadi sat in the sun
And thanks was his contrition
For haircloth & for bloody whips
(20)      Had active hands & friendly lips
And yet his runes he rightly read
And to his folk his message sped
Sunshine in his heart transferred
Lighted each transparent word
(25)      And well could happy Persia learn
What Saadi wished to say
For Saadi's nightly stars did burn
Brighter than Dchami's day.

[233]    But when the God would teach
And lift thee to his holy mount
He sends thee from his bitter fount
Wormwood; saying Go thy ways
(5)      ⟨Leave⟩ ↑Drink not↓ the malaga of praise
⟨Do⟩ ↑Perform↓ the deed thy fellows hate
And compromise thy peaceful state
⟨Stuff thorns beneath the head⟩
Smite the white breasts which thee fed
(10)     Stuff sharp thorns beneath the head
Of those thou art bound to have comforted

[234] [blank]
[235]    How much, Preventing God! how much I owe
To the defences thou hast round me set:
Example, custom, fear, occasion slow,—
These scorned bondmen were my parapet.
(5)      I dare not peep over this parapet,
To gauge with glance the roaring gulf below,
The depths of sin to which I had descended,
Had not these me against myself defended.

Him strong Genius urged to roam
(10)     Stronger Custom brought him home

But if thou do thy best
Without remission without rest
And invite the sunbeam
And abhor to ⟨seem⟩ ↑feign or seem↓

233 "Saadi," 60–66, 68, 67–69. In pencil.
235 "Grace" (1–8); "Saadi loved the new & old," 3–4 (9–10); "But if thou do thy best" (11–21). Lines (9–21) are in pencil.

(15)       Even to those who thee shd. love
              And thy behavior approve
              If thou go in thine own likeness
              Be it health or be it sickness
              If thou go as thy fathers son
(20)       If thou wear no mask or lie
              Dealing purely & nakedly

[236]      By the rude bridge that arched the flood
              Their flag to April's breeze unfurled
              Here once the embattled farmers stood
              And fired the shot heard round the world

(5)        The foe long since in silence slept
              Alike the conqueror silent sleeps
              And Time the ruined bridge has swept
              Down the ⟨green⟩ ↑dark↓ stream which seaward creeps

              On this green bank by this soft stream
(10)       We set today a votive stone
              That memory may their deed redeem
              When like our sires our sons are gone

              ⟨O Thou⟩ ↑Spirit↓ who made those heroes dare
              To die or leave their children free
(15)       Bid Time & Nature gently spare
              The shaft we raise to them & Thee.

[237]                   Compensation.
              Why should I keep holiday
              When other men have none?
              Why but because when these ⟨were⟩are gay
              I sit and mourn alone

(5)        And why when mirth unseals all tongues
               Must mine alone be dumb?
              Ah! late I spoke to the silent throngs,
              And now their hour is come.

[238]                His jaws
              Locked with convulsion the fine nerves were tense
              As if with frost

              [six lines of erased pencil writing]

236 "Concord Fight." In pencil.
237 "Compensation" ("Why should I"). Erased pencil.
238 "I saw three blots," 4, 4, 4 (1–3); six unrecovered lines. Erased pencil. In the unrecovered segment, apparently a version of lines in "I saw three blots," the following are visible: "made those nerves[?]" (first line); "or" (fourth line); "This" (sixth line).

[239] I saw three blots on earths pleasant face
‖ . . . . . . . . . ‖ a manly form
Convulsed with lockjaw
↑Convulsion locked the jaws & froze his nerves↓

(5) His ‖ . . . . ‖ head bent backwards to his heels
⟨‖ . . ‖⟩ ↑Another↓ plagued ‖ . . . . . . . . ‖
⟨‖ . . . . ‖ whose fell poison the good⟩ ↑Foaming beneath his
　　plague the ruined↓ man
Barked at his wife & babes. The third & worst
I met a madman in my walk, his hands

(10) Held close upon his ears; and in this figure
Ragged unclean & scoffing I remembered
A peaceful & well nurtured gentleman.

[240₁] On the rude bridge that /crossed/arched/ the flood
With rustic banners ‖ . . . . . ‖ unfurled
⟨the⟩ ↑Here↓ One April morn, the farmers stood
And fired the shot heard round the world

(5) ‖ . . . . . . . . . . . . . . . ‖ slept
Alike the ‖ . . . . . . . ‖ sleep in death

Long since the foe in silence slept
Alike the conqueror silent sleeps
↑And Time↓ The ruined bridge ‖ . . . ‖ swept

(10) By the rude ‖ . . . ‖ that arched ‖ . . . . ‖
‖ . . . . . . . . ‖ breeze unfurled
‖ . . . . . . . . . . . . . ‖ farmers stood
And fired the shot heard round ‖ . . ‖ world

The ‖ . . ‖ long ‖ . . . . . . . . ‖ slept
(15) Alike the conqueror silent sleeps
And time the ruined bridge has swept
Down the green stream that seaward creeps

‖ . . . . . ‖ green bank by this soft stream
We ‖ . . . . . . . . . . . . ‖ stone
(20) ‖ . . . . . . . . . . . . . . . . ‖
When like ‖ . . . . . . . . ‖ are gone

[240₂] 　I mourn upon this battlefield
But not for those who perished here
Behold the ⟨famous⟩ river bank
Whither the angry farmers came

239 "I saw three blots." In pencil; lines (1–8) are erased.
240₁ "Concord Fight," 1–6, 5–7, 1–12. Erased pencil; lines (1–9) are struck through in
pencil.
240₂ "In Memoriam. E.B.E.," 1–17, 19, X, 20.

(5)  In sloven dress & broken rank
     Nor thought of fame.
     Their deed of blood
     All mankind praise
     Even the serene reason says
(10)  It was well done.
     The wise & ⟨‖ . ‖⟩simple have one glance
     To greet yon stern headstone
     Which more of pride than pity gave
     To mark the Britons friendless grave
(15)  Yet it is a stately tomb
     The grand return
     ⟨o⟩Of Eve & Morn
     The silver cloud
     ↑And whispering ⟨trees⟩elms↓
(20)  Might grace the dust that is most proud

[241₁] ‖ . . . . . . . . . . . . . . . . . ‖
     ‖ . . . . . . . . . . . ‖
     ‖ . . . . . . . . . ‖ gently ⟨‖ . . ‖⟩ spare
     With ‖ . . . . . . . . ‖ to them & thee

(5)  I mourn upon this battle field
     But not for them who perished here
     Behold the river bank
     Whither the angry farmers came
     In sloven dress & broken rank
(10)  Nor thought of fame
     Their deed of blood
     All mankind praise
     Even the serene Reason says
     It was well done
(15)  The wise & simple have one glance
     To greet ⟨that⟩ yon stern headstone
     Which more of pride than pity gave
     To mark the Briton's friendless grave
      Yet it is a stately tomb
(20)  The grand return
     Of Eve & morn
     The golden fringed cloud
     And washed & mirrored by the stream

     On the rude bridge that crossed the flood

241₁ "Concord Fight," x?, x?, 15–16 (1–4); "In Memoriam. E.B.E.," 1–17, 19, x (5–23); "Concord Fight," 1, 3–4, x, 4, 4 (24–29). In pencil; lines (1–4) are erased. Lines (24–29) are squeezed into the left margin beside lines (11–13). This page is reproduced in Plate 2.

(25) The poor militia stood
And promptly ⟨fired the shot⟩
At their captains word
Fired that first shot a volley heard
All round the world

[241₂] Yet not of these I muse
In this familiar place,
⟨T⟩But of a kindred face
That never joy or hope shall here diffuse.
(5) Ah Brother
I grudge not these their bed of death
↑But thine to thee who never wronged↓
↑The poorest that drew breath↓
All inborn power that could
(10) Consist with homage to the good
Flamed from his martial eye

↑His from youth↓ the leader's look
⟨Which⟩ gave the law, ⟨not⟩ ↑which others↓ took,
And never poor beseeching glance
(15) Shamed that sculptured countenance

[242] Yet not of these I muse
In this familiar place
But of a kindred face
That ⟨neither⟩ ↑never↓ joy nor hope ⟨can⟩ ↑shall↓ here
⟨again⟩ diffuse

(5) Ah brother
I grudge not these their bed of death

All inborn power that could
Consist with homage to the good
Flamed from his martial eye

(10) the Leaders look
Which gave the law not took
⟨And⟩ never ↑a↓ poor beseeching glance
Shamed that sculptured countenance

Its peace sublime his aspect kept
(15) His purpose woke, his features slept

[243] Over thy dust the endless smile
Of summer in thy Spanish isle

241₂ "In Memoriam. E.B.E.," 21–25, 32–37, 44–47. Lines (7–8) are in pencil.
242 "In Memoriam. E.B.E.," 21–25, 32, 35–37, 44–47, 101–2. In pencil; lines (1–13) are
struck through in pencil.
243 "In Memoriam. E.B.E.," 105–6, x, 73–74, x, 76, x, 103–4. In pencil. "Ah", cancelled,
appears above line (4) to the left, probably as the beginning of an aborted line.

    Not all thy breath
  ⟨Ah⟩
    I see him with superior smile
(5)   Hunted by Sorrows grisly train
    From year to year from
    With angel patience labor on
    And find his joy therein
    And yet between the spasms of pain
(10)   His genius beamed with joy again.

[244]  What he had done
    He nor commends nor grieves
    Pleads for itself the fact
    As unrepenting nature leaves
(5)    Her every act.

[245]  I cannot mask my style
    I cannot copy stale praises
    But I can well record
    The virtues in him that dwelt
(5)   The grace that over him shone
    He could not do an unhandsome act
    Beauty shaped each gesture
    Honor prompted every look
    And love & honor strove
(10)   Honor came & sat by him
    In lowly cot & painful road
    And ever the inward showed
    He should have the helmet worn
    In ⟨peaceful⟩ ↑bloodless↓ wars ⟨↑of peace↓⟩ a soldier born
(15)   Nor shall the meed be lost

[246]  ⟨Have you not heard of Dr Jewett⟩
    ⟨Who kept his oil in a glass cruet⟩
    ⟨The stopple stuck he can't undo it⟩
    ⟨Quoth I Doctor put more vigor to it⟩
(5)   ⟨Quoth he, If I break it I shall rue it⟩
    ⟨Quoth I, Really cant you do it,⟩
    ⟨And you a Doctor! Screw it! Screw it!⟩
    ⟨The Doctor screwed & quick out flew it.⟩

[247]  An ancient drop of feudal blood
    From the high line of Bulkeley-Mere

244 "In Memoriam. E.B.E.," 92–96. An erased pencil version underlies this ink version; the only visible difference is that "Pleads for" in line (3) is inserted.

245 "In Memoriam. E.B.E.," four unused lines, 51, 53/54, x, 55, x, 56–57, 58/59, x, x, x. In pencil.

246 "Have you not heard of Dr Jewett." In pencil, heavily cancelled in pencil.

247 "An ancient drop of feudal blood." In pencil.

Mixed with the democratic flood
Of sires to Yankee freedom dear.

[248]    These ⟨trees irongray⟩ trees ⟨that⟩ like tho'ts t⟨o⟩hat to
        visions congeal
    ⟨They⟩ gleamed ↑out↓ on my sight like the gleaming of steel
    These woodlands how grand & how sacred they seem
    And the air of my house but a pestilent steam

(5)    My eyes were bewitched O Nature but thou
    ⟨With thy⟩Hast with woodland perfumes disenchanted them
        now

    Words of the air
    Which birds of the air
    Carry aloft below around

(10)    To the isles of the deep
    To the snow capped steep
    To the thundercloud
    To the loud bazaar
    To the haram of Caliph & Kremlin of Czar

(15)        Is the verse original
        Let its numbers rise & fall
        As the winds do when they call
        One to another

[249]    Where the fungus broad & red
    Lifts its head
    Like poisoned loaf of elfin bread
    Where the aster grew

(5)    With the social golden rod
    In a chapel which the dew
    Made beautiful for God
        The maple street
        In the houseless wood

(10)        Voices followed after
        Every shrub & grapeleaf
        Rang with fairy laughter
        I have heard them fall
        Like the strain of all

(15)        King Oberon's minstrelsy

    Forest full of essences

248 "These trees like tho'ts" (1–6); "Where the fungus broad & red," 36–47 (7–18). In pencil.

249 "Where the fungus broad & red," 1–8, 9/25, 26–31, 58–65. In pencil. An angle bracket with "p 41" appears in the right margin with an arrow pointing below line (10); an angle bracket with "p 194" appears in the left margin below line (15).

Fit for fairy presences
Peppermint & sassafras
Sweet fern, mint, & vernal grass
(20)        Panax black birch sugar maple
Sweet & scent for Dian's table
Elderblow sarsaparilla
Wild rose lily dry vanilla

[250]      For Nature watcheth in the rose
And hearkens in the berry's bell
To keep her friends to plague her foes
And like wise God she judges well.

[251]–[252] [blank]
[253]                 *The Amulet*
Your picture smiles as first it smiled,
The ring you gave is still the same,
Your letter tells, oh changing child,
No tidings *since* it came.

(5)       Give me an amulet
That keeps intelligence with you;
Red when you love, & rosier red,
And when you love not, pale & blue.

Alas! no bonds nor vows
(10)      Can certify possession:
Torments me still the fear that love
Died in its last expression.

[254] [blank]
[255]                 Holidays
From fall to spring the russet acorn
Fruit beloved of maid & boy
Lent itself beneath the forest
To be the children's toy

(5)       Pluck it now: in vain: thou canst not;
It has shot its rootlet down'rd:
Toy no longer, it has duties,
It is anchored in the ground.

Year by year th⟨at⟩e rose-lipped maiden,
(10)      Playfellow to young & old,
Was frolic sunshine, dear to all men,
More dear to one, than mines of gold.

250 "Nature I," 12–15. In pencil.
253 "The Amulet." In pencil, struck through in pencil.
255 "Holidays." In pencil.

Where is now the lovely hoyden?
Disappeared in blessed wife,
(15)     Servant to a wooden cradle,
Living in a baby's life.

Still thou playest;—, short vacation
Fate grants each to stand aside;
Now must thou be Man & Artist;
(20)     Tis the turning of the tide.

[256]–[258] [blank]
[259]         Demure apothecary
Whose early reverend genius my young eye
With wonder followed & undoubting joy
Believing ⟨⟨in⟩that⟩ ↑that↓ cold & modest form
(5)     ↑Brooded alway↓ The Everlasting mind ⟨enshrined itself⟩
And that thou faithful didst obey the soul
So should the splendid favor of the God
⟨Shower from thy lips⟩
From thine observed lips shower words of fire
(10)    Pictures that cast ⟨upon⟩ ↑before↓ the common ⟨‖ . ‖⟩eye
I know for mine & all men know for theirs
How is the fine gold, dim; the lofty, low!
And thou reputed speaker for the soul
↑Forgoest the matchless benefit & now↓
(15)    ⟨Art a⟩ sleek deacon of the New Jerusalem
And hast defied soliciting world to be
A blind man's blind man
Was it not worth ⟨ambition to be⟩ ↑obedience to be↓
⟨To be⟩ the bard of Nature to these later times
(20)    With words like things ↑& Protean images↓
An universal speech that did present
All natural creatures as if the eye beheld
A lake a rosetree when he named their names
And better was it to cower before the phantoms
(25)    One selfdeceiving mystic drew in swarms
[260]    And legions
Whereer he flashed his visionary eye
The Caesar of his limbo
The Pluto [of] a world of ghosts
(5)     Eyes without light, men without character
Nature a cavern
And lo the young men of the land
Born to transmit with added light the torch
Received in long succession from the sires

259 "S.R.," 1–7, 8, 8, 9–24. In pencil.
260 "S.R.," x, 25, x, 26–29, x, x, 30, x, 31, 31, 32–45. In pencil.

(10)     Decline the strife of virtue, fail to be
             Redeemers of the lost degeneracy
             The bringers of glad thought, the glad & vast
             ⟨And stout revolters⟩   preferring ease
             Ease & irresolution and the smile
(15)     Of placid rich men they consent to be
             Danglers & dolls. ⟨Like⟩With these not thou ↑not thou↓
             O noble youth not thou wilt there remain
             ⟨Up⟨up⟩ward⟩   Up for thy life & for thy peoples life
             And be the sun's light & the rainbows glow
(20)     And by the power of picture to the eye
             Show wherefore it was made. Unlock the world
             Of sound to the astonished ear
             ↑And↓ Thus by thee shall man be twice a man
             Is it not better than to boast thyself
(25)     ⟨The⟩ father of fifty sons flesh of thy flesh
             Rather to live earths better bachelor
             Planting ethereal seed in souls
[261]    Spending abroad thy being in the being
             Of men whom thou dost foster & inform
             Fill with new hopes making their hearts
             Beat with more life & throb with grand desires

[262]    Who gave thee O Beauty
             The keys of this ⟨poor⟩ breast
             ⟨Who betrayed me t⟩To thy power ↑who betrayed me↓
             To be unblest or blest
(5)      In the wandering ages
             ⟨Knew⟩ ↑Met↓ I thee of old
             Or what was the service
             For which I was sold
             When first my eyes saw thee
(10)     I was thy thrall
             By magical drawings
             ⟨O subtlest of all⟩ Sweet ruler of all
             Thou intimate stranger ⟨↑Omnipresent ranger↓⟩ ↑All
                 welcomest danger↓

[263]                      *Ode to Beauty.*
             Who gave thee, Beauty
             The keys of this poor breast?
             Who ⟨put me in thy power⟩ ↑betrayed me to thy hands↓
             To be unblest or blest?

261 "S.R.," 46–47, 48, 48. In pencil.
262 "Ode to Beauty," 1–12, 15. In pencil.
263 "Ode to Beauty," 1–8, x, x, 9–11, 15–16, x, x, x, 27–33, x. In pencil; lines (1–4) are struck through in pencil. In line (21), "whom" is written "whome."

(5)       When in my wanderings
           Encountered I thee⟨;⟩ ↑of old?↓
           Or what was the service
           For which I was sold?
           Me thou never gavest birth
(10)     ⟨Nor⟩ ↑Never↓ pension in the earth
           Yet when my eyes first saw thee
           I was thy thrall
           By ⟨inmost tie⟩ ↑By magical drawings↓
           Thou intimate stranger
(15)     Thou latest & first,
           And I must ⟨escape⟩ ↑wander↓ from the world,
           Into shoreless vacancy
           Ere I can baulk or baffle thee
           Ah what avails it
(20)     To hide or ↑to↓ shun
           ⟨Thee with⟩ whom the Infinite One
           Hath ⟨shared⟩ ↑granted↓ his throne
           The Heaven high over
           Is the Deep's lover
(25)     The sun & the sea
           Ever in conspiracy
[264]    Before me run
           And draw me on,
           Yet fly me still,
           As Fate refuses
(5)       To me the ⟨maid⟩ ↑heart↓ Fate for me chooses.
           Is it that my opulent soul
           Was mingled from the generous Whole
           Sea valleys & the deep of skies
           Furnished several supplies
(10)     And now they draw me
           ⟨With native cords of man⟩ ↑Towards & forwards↓
           ⟨In several ways?⟩ ↑With mine own cords↓
           I turn the proud portfolios
           Which hold the grand designs
(15)     Of Salvator, of Guercino
           And Piranesi's lines
           Them with eager eyebeams measure
           Digger of a hidden treasure
           Or in streets or humblest places
(20)     I detect far-wandered graces
           From Olympus wide astray

264 "Ode to Beauty," 35–43, 45, x, x, 46–49, x, x, 58–61, x, x, 76–79. In pencil; lines (17–18) are struck through four times in pencil.

In lowly homes have lost their way.
↑In the great & shoreless ⟨p⟩Dark↓
↑Walk with thee as in a park↓
(25)  All ↑thats good & great↓ with thee
Pledged in deep conspiracy
Thou hast bribed the Darkness
To report of thee only
[265]  And the Morning
Itself with thoughts of thee adorning
The solitude & the square
Are in league with thy charm
(5)  The very air
Thou hast philtred for my despair
And if I ⟨fall⟩ ↑languish↓ into dreams
Again I meet the ardent beams
I dare not die
(10)  Lest I find thee in Deity.
O Beauty, if thou art God,
Give thyself to me or take myself from me.

⟨In the great & shoreless Dark⟩
⟨Walk with thee as in a park.⟩
(15)      A pair of crystal eyes will lead me
All about the rounded globe

[266]  Gliding thro the sea of forms
⟨Ever so⟩As the lightning through the storm
No feet so fleet could ever find thee
No perfect form could ever bind thee
(5)  But thou eternal fugitive
Hoverest over all that live
⟨Filling⟩
Hollow space & flower cell
Fillest with thy roses smell
(10)  But will not give the lips to taste
Of the nectar which thou hast

[267]  Gleams a charm from womans breast
A charm which cannot be caressed
Kindling torches of desire

Somewhat not to be possessed

265 "Ode to Beauty," 80–82, x, 84–88, 90, 92–93, x, x (1–14); "A pair of crystal eyes," 1–2 (15–16). In pencil.
266 "Ode to Beauty," 62–63, 66–69, 73, 72–75. In pencil.
267 "Ode to Beauty," x, 65, 71, 64–65, 70–71. Partially erased pencil.

(5)      Somewhat not to be caressed
         Skilful to inspire
         Sweet extravagant desire

[268]    To report of thee only
         Thou hast bribed the Dark
         Thro its soft immensities
         We walk in thy park
(5)      ⟨Good⟩ ↑Fruit↓ which when we go to clutch
         Floweth from the cheated touch
         Lavish lavish promiser
         /Seducing/Wiling/ Nemesis to err
         The lowliest leaf beside the pond
(10)     Thou inscribest with a bond
         In thy frolic play
         ⟨Which would bankrupt gods to pay⟩
         Would bankrupt Nature to repay

[269]–[281] [blank]
[282]                    Saadi  ↑(new)  see V 71↓
                 There are beggars in Iran and Araby
         *Said* was hungrier than all;
         Hafiz said, he was a fly
         That came to every festival.
(5)      ⟨Also⟩ he came ↑a pilgrim↓ to the mosque
         ⟨In the⟩ ↑On↓ trail of camel & caravan
         Out from Mecca to Ispahan;
         Northward, he went to snowy hills,
         At court, he sat in the grave Divan.
(10)     Was never form & never face
         So sweet to him as only grace
         Which did not slumber like a stone
         But ↑hovered↓ gleam⟨ed⟩ing ⟨in flashes⟩ & was gone.
         Beauty chased he everywhere,
(15)     In flame, in storm, in clouds of air.
[283]    He smote the lake to feed his eye
         With the precious green of the broken wave
         He flung in pebbles well to hear
         The moments music which they gave
(5)      Loved harebells nodding on a rock
         A cabin topped with curling smoke

268 "Ode to Beauty," 79, 78, four unused lines, 17–18, 21/23, 24–26, 26. In pencil; lines (1–
4) are struck through in pencil.
    282 "There are beggars," 1–6, 8–16 (1–15); "Beauty," 1–6 (10–15). In pencil.
    283 "There are beggars," 17–22, 25–26, 28, 30–32, 23–24 (1–14); "Beauty," 7–10 (1–4). In
pencil; lines (13–14) are written over, or overwritten by, six large ampersands.

And huts & tents; nor loved he less
Stately men in palaces
Fenced by form & ceremony
(10)    And more revered in mountain land
Men built with power & grace to stand
Like castles

Ring of axe or hum of wheel
or gleam which use will paint on steel

[284]    ↑Saadi added,↓ I found this,
That of goods I could not miss
If I fell into the line,
Once a member, all was mine
(5)    Houses, banquets, gardens, fountains
Fortunes /delectable/Californian/ mountains,
But if I would walk alone,
Was neither cloak nor crumb my own.

⟨and thus⟩

[285]    With beams /that stars at Christmas/like beams
      December planets/ dart
His cold eyes truth & conduct scanned,
July was in his sunny heart,
October in his liberal hand.

———

(5)    And thus the high Muse treated me
Directly never greeted me
But when she spread her dearest spells
Feigned to speak to some one else
I was ⟨welcom⟩ free to overhear
(10)    Or was welcome to forbear
But that idle word
Thus at random overheard
Was the anthem of the spheres
And proverb of a thousand years
[286]    The light with which all ⟨ages⟩ ↑planets↓ shone
The livery all events put on
It fell in rain, it grew in grain,
It wore flesh in friendly forms
(5)    ⟨It⟩ frowned in ↑my↓ foe & growled in storm
It spoke in Tullius Cicero

284 "I found this," 1–9. In pencil.
285 "S.H." (1–4); "I found this," 9–18 (5–14). In line (1), "that stars at Christmas" is circled in pencil and "like beams December planets" is in pencil; lines (5–14) are also in pencil.
286 "I found this," 19–28. In pencil.

In Milton & in Angelo
I travelled & found it in Rome
Eastward it filled all Xendom

(10)    And it lay on my hearth when I came home

[287]    Hold of the Maker, not the Made,
Sit with the cause, or grim or glad
So shalt be a crystal soul
Sphered & concentric to the whole

(5)    Try the might the Muse affords
And the balm of thotful words
↑But↓ Mask thy wisdom with delight,
Toy with the bow, yet hit the white

[288]–[291] [blank]
[292]    Hast thou named all the birds without a gun
⟨Gazed on⟩
Loved the woodrose and left it on its stalk
At rich men's tables eaten bread & pulse

(5)    Unarmed faced danger with a heart of trust
And loved so well a ⟨sweet⟩ ↑high↓ behaviour
In man or maid that thou from speech refrained
Nobility more nobly to repay
O be my friend and teach me to be thine

_____

(10)       "A new commandment," archly said the Muse,
"I give,—Thou shalt not preach, ⟨my dismal one⟩!"
Luther, Fox, Behmen, Swedenborg, grew pale,
And held their speech; and rosier clouds upbore
Hafiz & Shakspeare with their happy choirs.

_____

[293]    When thou sittest moping
Nor seeing nor hoping
Thy thought is ⟨alone⟩ ↑none↓
⟨But being freed⟩

(5)    ↑But being freed↓
↑By action & deed↓
Thy thoughts come in bands
Sisters hand in hand
Them thou canst not dispart

287 "Hold of the Maker" (1–2); "There are beggars," 54–55 (3–4); "Try the might the Muse affords," 1–2 (5–6); "Mask thy wisdom," 1–2 (7–8); "Considerations by the Way," 24–25 (7–8). In pencil.
292 "Forbearance," 1, x, 2–8 (1–9); Ἄδακρυν νέμονται Αἰῶνα" (10–14). Lines (1–9) are in pencil.
293 "When thou sittest moping." In pencil.

(10)        From the world↑s that be↓
             They reach to the stars
             From the bed of the sea.

[294] [blank]
[295]                 *Una.*
             Roving roving as it seems,
             ⟨When⟩ Una lights my clouded dreams,
             Still for journeys she is drest;
             We wander far by East & West.

(5)         In the homestead, homely thought:
             At my work, I ramble not:
             If from home, chance draw me wide,
             Half seen Una sits beside.

             In my house & garden plot,
(10)        Though beloved, I miss her not;
             But one I seek in foreign places,
             One face explore in foreign faces.

             At home a deeper thought may light
             The inward sky with chrysolite,
(15)        And I greet from far the ray
             Aurora of a de⟨eper⟩arer day.

             But if upon the seas I sail,
             Or trundle on the glowing rail,
             I am but a thought of hers,
(20)        Loveliest of travellers.

[296]     So the gentle poet's name
             To foreign parts is blown by fame;
             Seek him in his native town,
             He is hidden & unknown

[297] [blank]
[298]     Wisely said the Greek
             Be thou faithful but not fond
             To the alters foot thy friendship seek
             Not a hair beyond.

(5)          Though all fair things that fair resemble
             Though with pure passion nature tremble

             ‖ . . . . . . . . . . . . . ‖

295 "Una," 1–20. In pencil.
296 "Una," 21–24. In pencil.
298 "Pericles" (1–4); "Though all fair things," 1–2, 3?, 4–6 (5–10). In pencil; lines (7–10)
are erased.

to joy while reason is asleep
‖ . . . ‖ no fence; ‖ . . . . . ‖
(10)    Is sword ‖ . . . . . . . . ‖

[299]    ‖ . . . . ‖ feelings ‖ . . . . . . ‖
‖ . . . . . . . . . . . . ‖ side
God said, (‖ . . . . . . . . . ‖,)
‖ . . . . . . ‖ by the love of the ‖ . . ‖

(5)        It fell in the ancient periods
Which the brooding soul surveys
Or ever the wild time coined itself
Into calendar years & days

[300]–[312] [blank]
[313]    Goodbye proud world
Each & All
Humble Bee
Rhodora
Problem
Snowstorm
Wood Notes 1 & 2
Fate ["Destiny"]
Sphinx
Saadi
↑The↓ ⟨Ench⟩Park
Friendship ["Forbearance"]
⟨Pre⟩Forbearance
O fair & stately maid ["To Eva"]
Sculptor & Painter ["Painting and Sculpture"]
Suum Cuique     p. 4
The Amulet
Holidays

[314] [blank]
[315₁]      Convulsed with lockjaw
His

[315₂]      *Descriptions of Morning by the old Poets*
Aurora with the stremés of her heat
Had dried up the dew of herbés wet
      Chaucer. Tisbe of Bab[ylon].
      ["The Legend of Good Women," lines 774–75]

**299** "Though all fair things," x?, 12?, 19–20 (1–4); "Uriel," 1–4 (5–8). In pencil; lines (1–4) are erased.
**313** This list, in pencil, is of poems published in *The Western Messenger* ("Good-Bye" through "The Rhodora") and *The Dial* ("The Problem" through "Holidays"), presumably for inclusion in *Poems*, 1847, where they all appear.
**315₁** "I saw three blots," 3, 5? In pencil.
**315₂** The accents in lines (1–2) are in pencil.

The busy lark the messager of day
Saleweth in her song the morning gray
(5)    And fiery Phebus riseth up so bright
That all the orient laugheth of the sight
And with his stremes drieth in the greves
The silver dropes hanging ⟨in⟩on the leaves
        Chaucer. Knights Tale [lines 1491–96]

—————

The vapor which that fro the earthe glode
(10)   Maketh the sun to seem ruddy & brode
        [Chaucer,] Squiers Tale. [lines 393–94]

—————

See the dapple grey coursers of the morn
Beat up the light with their bright silver hoofs.
        John Marston

—————

But, look, the morn, in russet mantle clad,
Walks oer the dew of yon high eastern hill.
        Shakspear   Hamlet [1.1.166–67]

—————

[316]–[321] [blank]
[322]    When the letters loved me
        Twas high time they came
        When they ceased to love me
        Time they stopped for shame

[323]–[324] [blank]
[325] The following lines were written by my dear brother Edward
whilst sailing out of Boston harbor for Porto Rico
        1832.

Farewell ye lofty spires
That cheered the holy light
Farewell domestic fires
That broke the gloom of night
(5)    Too soon those spires are lost
Too fast we leave the bay
Too soon by Ocean tost
From hearth & home away
        Far away, far away.

(10)   Farewell the busy town
The wealthy & the wise

322 "Gifts." In pencil.
325 "The Last Farewell" (by Edward Bliss Emerson), 1–22. "But" is written to the right
below line (22) as a catchword.

Kind smile & honest frown
From bright familiar eyes
All these are fading now
(15)    Our brig hastes on her way
Her unremembering prow
Is leaping oer the Sea
        Far away, far away.

Farewell my mother fond
(20)    Too kind, too good to me
No pearl nor diamond
Would pay my debt to thee
[326]    But even thy kiss denies
Upon my cheek to stay
The winged vessel flies
And billows round her play
(5)        Far away, far away

Farewell, my brothers true,
My betters yet my peers,
How desart without you
My few & evil years!
(10)    But though aye one in heart
Together sad or gay
Rude Ocean doth us part
We separate today;
        Far away, far away.

(15)    Farewell, thou fairest one,
Unplighted yet to me;
Uncertain of thine own
I gave my heart to thee.
That untold early love
(20)    I leave untold today;
My lips in whisper move
Farewell to x x x x x !
        Far away far away.

Farewell, I breathe again
(25)    To dim New England's shore,
My heart shall beat not when
I pant for thee no more:
[327]    In yon green palmy isle
Beneath the tropic ray,

326 "The Last Farewell" (by Edward Bliss Emerson), 23–36, nine unused lines, 37–40.
327 "The Last Farewell" (by Edward Bliss Emerson), 41–45.

I murmur never while
For thee & thine I pray;
(5)                    Far away, far away.

[328]–[331] [blank]
[332]     Transcribe *The Skeptic* p. 77
              [index material omitted]

[333] [index material omitted]
[334] [blank]
[inside back cover] [blank]

332 In pencil.
333 In pencil.

# Notebook X

Notebook X was Emerson's major repository for working drafts and fair copies of poems for about six years beginning in 1845, although he seems to have used it at least as early as 1841, as the textual history of "Hermione" shows. In 1845 he committed himself to bring out a volume of his poetry, writing to William Henry Furness on 7 February that "I have been spirited up lately from several sides to collect my verses" (*Records*, p. 35). The notebook contains drafts of many of the works that first appeared in *Poems*, 1847, as well as several of the earliest translations that Emerson made of the poetry of Hafiz.

The covers of notebook X are of green and tan marbled paper over boards and measure 16.4 × 22.4 cm. The spine strip, of dark brown leather, has seven pairs of horizontal lines in gold and a gold-stamped capital "X".

Double flyleaves occur at the front and back (pp. i–iv and 265–68). Pages total 272, of which pp. i–iv and 267–68 are unlined; the rest are faintly lined with 24 lines to a page. All leaves measure 16.2 × 21.3 cm.

Eleven pages are numbered in ink, 164 in pencil, and one in pencil and ink. Ninety-six are unnumbered. Twelve pages were misnumbered by Emerson: 191 as 189, 205 as 203, 232 as 230, 243 as 241, 245 as 243, 252 as 250, 254 as 252, 256 as 254, 258 as 256, 260 as 258, and 262 as 260. Only twelve pages are blank.

The notebook contains the following enclosures:

(1) inside the front cover, four leaves of white paper containing notes in the hand of James Elliott Cabot concerning the contents of and emendations for *Poems*, 1884, and a sheet of orange paper containing notes in Cabot's hand concerning "RWE & Persian Poetry";

(2) between pp. 54–55, a sheet of white paper bearing a list in an unknown hand of the "New Members" of an unidentified Concord club: Francis Munroe, Henry A. Barrett, A. C. Collier, William R. L. Badger, Joseph Holbrook, J. M. Brown, Elijah Wood, Jr., Francis E. Bigelow, and Nathan B. Stow;

(3) inside the back cover, nine items, all of the same unlined, lightweight blue paper, once pinned together at the middle left margin. The pages, numbered 1 through 30 in an unidentified hand, each measure approximately 12.7 × 20 cm. These items consist of a single sheet ($268_a$–$268_b$), two sheets folded to make four pages each ($268_c$–$268_j$), two single sheets ($268_k$–$268_n$), and four sheets folded to make four pages each ($268_o$–$268_{dd}$).

[front cover verso][index material omitted]

[i]                                              R W Emerson

αδάκρυν νεμοῖται αἰῶνα

"It were a wrong, methought, to pass & look
On others, yet myself the while unseen."
                    Dante: Purgatory: B[ook] XIII

[ii] Nature begins with the dimple of the whirlpool, the eye of the leaf, & runs up to man. Grief & joy, Energy & durance, are web & woof but she never grieves or rejoices αδακρυν αιωνα Surprise & Casualty are the apples of her eyes

[iii]       weaned
            tanks
            creampots
            ringleader
            pharmacy
            solstice

[iv]                           Days

            Damsels of Time, the hypocritic Days,
            Muffled & dumb like barefoot dervishes,
            And marching single in an endless file,
            Bring diadems & fagots in their hands.
(5)         To each they offer gifts, after his will,
            Bread, kingdoms, stars, or sky that holds them all.
            I in my pleached garden watched the pomp,
            Forgot my morning wishes, hastily
            Took a few herbs & apples, and the Day
(10)        Turned & departed silent⟨;⟩. I, too late,
            Under his solemn fillet saw the scorn.

[1]                    ⟨Chartism⟩ ↑JANUS.↓
            Day! hast thou two faces,
            Making one place two places;
            One, by humble ⟨laborers⟩ ↑farmer↓ seen,
            Chill, & wet, ⟨unlighted,⟩ ↑uncoloured,↓ mean,

i The Greek phrase is from Pindar, Olympian Ode II, line 67: "They enjoy a life without tears"; cf. pp. [ii] and [243] below, the front cover verso of notebook Trees[A:I] (JMN 8:519), and notebook S (Salvage) p. [20]. The passage from Dante is quoted from Henry Francis Cary's translation, *The Vision; or Hell, Purgatory, and Paradise* (Philadelphia, 1822), 1:379, in Emerson's library.
ii "Surprise . . . eyes," cf. "Nature I," 7–8. For the Greek phrase, see p. [i] above. In pencil.
iii The list is in pencil.
iv "Days." Struck through in ink.
1 "The Chartist's Complaint." Struck through in ink.

(5) Useful only, ⟨long⟩ ↑triste↓ & damp,
Serving for a ⟨workman's⟩ ↑laborer's↓ lamp.
Have the same mists another side
To be the equipage of pride?
Gracing the rich man's wood & lake
(10) And park where amber mornings break,
And treacherously bright to show
His planted isle where roses glow?
O Day, & is your mightiness
A sycophant to smug success!
(15) Will the sweet sky & ocean broad
Be fine accomplices of fraud?
O sun! I ⟨hate⟩ curse thy cruel ray
Back, back to Chaos, harlot Day!

[2₁]                          Alphonso
I ‖ . . . . ‖ that things go ⟨‖ . . . . ‖⟩ ‖ . . . . ‖
Things ‖ . . . . . . ‖ of ‖ . . . ‖ kind
⟨‖ . . . . ‖⟩ ↑Lemons ‖ . . . . . . . ‖ rind↓
‖ . . . . . . . . . . . . ‖ & dies
(5) In the insufficient skies
Twill ‖ . . . ‖ longer tan
The ⟨‖ . . . ‖⟩ ↑Orange ⟨‖ . . . ‖⟩ ⟨apples⟩ cheek↓ or skin of
        man
Yon ‖ . . . . . . . . . ‖ ↑Gaunt as bitterns in the pools↓
Are no ‖ . . . . . . . . . . . ‖
(10) The ‖ . . . . . . . ‖ it ⟨Adam's blood⟩ ↑Adamhood↓
⟨‖ . . . . ‖ blot⟩ ‖ . . . . . . . . . ‖ blot
Half the Sun's disc with a spot
Puny ‖ . . . . ‖ scentless rose
Tormenting Pan to double the dose
(15) You must have ‖ . . . . ‖ debility
⟨H⟩The general sterility
Of genius the ‖ . . . . . ‖
Mighty projects countermanded
Rash ambition brokenhanded

[2₂]   Shines the last age; the next with hope is seen;
Today slinks ⟨off⟩ poorly off unmarked between:
Future or Past no ⟨d⟩richer secret folds,
O friendless Present! than thy bosom holds.

2₁ "Alphonso of Castile," 1/2, 3–4, 7–8, 11–12, 15/16, 17–18, 9–10, 25–26, 19/21, 21/22,
22–24. In pencil, struck through in pencil and erased.
2₂ "Heri, Cras, Hodie."

[3]  Use a more liberal expense
    Nor shrivel all with indigence

    Say are the old Niles dry
    Which fed ⟨nature⟩ the veins of earth & sky
(5)  That men miss the loyal heats
    Which drove them erst to social feats
    And now they vex the gods
    With blame & question pert
    With too much science hide their hurt
(10)  ↑Inquisitive↓ ↑Whether you↓
    ⟨Are ⟨‖ . . . . ‖⟩paramount⟩ ↑Are the rulers,↓ or Mildew
    ⟨To be⟩
    ⟨Gentle powers⟩ ↑Masters↓ I am in pain with you
    ⟨Gentle powers⟩ ↑Masters↓ I will be plain with you
(15)  ⟨I have⟩ in my palace of Castille
    King myself for kings can feel
    ⟨I have⟩ ↑There↓ in my thoughts I roll
    And solve & resolve the whole
    And as I am styled ↑Alphonse↓ the Wise
(20)  You shall not want for my advice
    ↑And ere you fail for rain↓
    Here is the sentiment of Spain
          either fill
    Of vital force the wasting rill
(25)  Or tumble all again in heap
    To weltering Chaos & old sleep

[4]  ⟨We⟩ ↑You↓ have tried famine no more try it
    Experiment with a full diet
    Teach us now with plenty
    For one Sun give us twenty
(5)  We must have society
    We cannot spare variety
    The plague is now too many men
    I say kill nine in every ten
    And bestow the shares of all
(10)  On the remnant decimal
    ⟨Give⟩ ↑Add↓ their nine lives to this cat
    Crowd their nine brains in his hat

[5]  I Alphonso live & learn
    ⟨I submit, things⟩ ↑Seeing nature↓ go astern

3 "Alphonso of Castile," x, x, 31–34, x, 38, 38, 37–40, x, 41–50, 27–30. In pencil, struck through in pencil and erased.
 4 "Alphonso of Castile," 51–54, 57–58, 67–72. In pencil, struck through in pencil.
 5 "Alphonso of Castile," 1–4, 6, x, 7–13, x, 15–18, 25–26, 19, 21. In pencil.

⟨Lemons r⟩Things are not good of their kind
Lemons run to leaves & rind
(5)     Hard times
Bad climes
          Spring cools & dies
In the insufficient skies
⟨Clouds⟩ ↑Imps↓ at high midsummer blot
(10)    Half the sun's disc with a spot
T'will not /longer/now avail to/ tan
Orange cheek or skin of man
Roses faint the cows are dry
Life is short weep bitterly
(15)    Yon pale fisher fools
Gaunt as bitterns in the pools
Are no brothers of my blood
They discredit Adamhood
Puny man & scentless rose
(20)    Pray Pan to double the ⟨life-⟩dose
All saints ye must have seen
The plentiful debility
[6]     The general want of head
Of Genius the sterility
Mighty projects countermanded
Rash ambition broken handed
(5)     ⟨Gods⟩ use a freer expense
Nor shrivel us with indigence
⟨Do you love⟩ ↑Rebuild or↓ ruin? either fill
Of vital force the wasting rill
Or tumble all again in heap
(10)    To weltering Chaos & old Sleep

      Say are the old Niles dry
That fed the veins of earth & sky
That men miss the loyal heats
Which drove them erst to social feats
(15)    Now with science mask their hurt
And vex the gods with question pert
⟨Inquisitive⟩ ↑Immensely curious↓ whether you
Still are rulers or Mildew

      Masters I am in pain with you
(20)    Masters I will be plain with you
⟨I⟩ in my palace of Castille
↑I↓ A king ⟨myself⟩ for kings can feel

6 "Alphonso of Castile," 21–24, x, x, 27–34, 37–44. In pencil.

[7]    There in my thoughts the matter roll
     And solve & oft resolve the whole
     And for Im styled Alphonse the Wise
     You shall not want for my advice
(5)    And ere you ⟨break⟩ ↑are bankrupt↓ for ⟨a drop of⟩ rain
     Hear the sentiment of Spain
       You have tried famine↑:↓ no more try it
     Ply us now with a full diet
     Teach your pupils now with plenty
(10)   For one sun supply us twenty
     I have thought it thoroughly over
     State of hermit state of lover
     ⟨Conclude, ↑I find↓⟩ we must have society
     We cannot spare variety
(15)   The plague is now too many men
     The cure kill nine in every ten
     And ⟨add⟩ ↑bestow↓ the shares of all
     ⟨To⟩On the remnant decimal
     Add ↑their↓ nine lives to this cat
(20)   /Crowd/Stuff/ their nine brains in his hat
     Soft you now celestial fellows
     I find you to be overzealous
     Men & gods are too extense
     Ye shall slacken & condense
[8₁]    All your overgrowth reduce
     Till your kinds abound with juice
     Earth crowded cries Too many men
     I say ‖ . . ‖ nine in every ten
(5)    And bestow ‖ . . . . ‖ shares of all
     On ‖ . . . . . . . . . ‖ decimal
     Add their nine lives to this cat
     Stuff their nine brains in his hat

     Soft you now celestial fellows
(10)   I find you ‖ . . . ‖ overzealous
     Men & gods are too extense
     You must slacken & condense
     Earth crowded ‖ . . . . . ‖ men

     ‖ . . . . . . ‖ blood ‖ . ‖ fire

7 "Alphonso of Castile," 45–58, 67–72, 59–60, 63–64. In pencil. At the end of line (14) Emerson inscribed a horizontal caret in pencil, then cancelled it in pencil; lines (15–20) are struck through three times in pencil.

8₁ "Alphonso of Castile," 65–72, 59–60, 63–64, 67, x, x, 81–82, 65–66. In pencil, struck through in pencil and erased.

(15)        Temper ‖ . . . . . ‖ with ‖ . ‖ ire

↑‖ . . . . . ‖ shall have↓ ‖ . . . ‖ of the sphere
Fit to grace the solar year
⟨If you then your growth reduce⟩
⟨Till your kinds abound with juice⟩

[8₂]   Homer
Dante
Shakspeare
Swedenborg
Goethe

Their wits & ⟨em⟩kingdoms came & went
In secular astonishment
Till Italy its matter ⟨found⟩ ↑hears↓
⟨In⟩When Dante searche⟨r⟩d the triple spheres
(5)     Then England filled all measures
Of sense of soul of thought of pleasure
And gave to ⟨th⟩Mind its emperor
⟨New scope to life⟩
And life was larger than before
(10)    And centuries broad
Nor yet attain
The sense or bound of Shakspeare's brain
Far in the North where polar night
Holds in check the frolic light
(15)    Mid snows ↑above,↓ ⟨&⟩ mines underground
The inks of Erebus he found
Transcending mortal ⟨limits⟩ goal
The Swedish ⟨seer⟩ prophet leads the soul

[9]    Clouds on clouds
↑Thro'↓ Clouds of fire & seas of mist
Burned the ⟨world⟩ globe of amethyst
⟨Eld⟩↑Old↓est forces hardly yet subside
(5)     ⟨To perfect⟩ ↑Within the↓ bound⟨s⟩ of times & tide
Saurian ⟨wizard⟩ ↑snake↓ & dragon can
Slowly ripen into man
Asia spawned its shepherd race
⟨Egypt built its⟩ ↑⟨Thebes⟩ And Nile⟨'s⟩ substructs Art's↓
granite base

8₂ "Solution," x, x, 17?, 28, 35–38, 38–39, 39–40, 43–44, 47–48, 45–46. The five names are those on which "Solution" is based. Emerson began his draft on p. [9], and continued it on p. [8] after setting off the list with a wavy line in ink.
9 "Solution," five unused lines, 6?, 8?, 9–10, x, x, 14, x, 15–16. See the note to p. [8₂].

(10)       Then war & trade & clearest clime
〈Hurried〉 ↑Precipitate↓ the 〈primal〉 man of time
And forward stepped the perfect Greek
〈Able〉 to fight to carve to paint to speak
Will, wisdom, joy had found a tongue
(15)       In the 〈new〉 ↑charmed↓ world when Homer sung

[10]               Alphonso of Castille.

       I Alphonso live & learn
Seeing Nature go astern
Things deteriorate in kind
Lemons run to leaves & rind
(5)       Meagre crop of figs & limes
Short↑er↓ 〈& evil are the〉 ↑days & harder↓ times
       Spring cools & dies
In the insufficient skies
Imps at high midsummer blot
(10)       Half the sun's disc with a spot
T'will not now avail to tan
Orange cheek or skin of man
Roses faint the goats are dry
〈Life is short〉 ↑Lisbon quakes↓ and 〈〈books〉 ↑life↓ a lie〉
       ↑the people cry↓
(15)       Yon pale fisher fools
Gaunt as bitterns in the pools
Are no brothers of my blood
They discredit Adamhood
Puny man & scentless rose
(20)       Tormenting Pan to double the dose
Eyes of gods ye must have seen
[11]       The plentiful debility
The general want of head
Of Genius the sterility
Mighty projects countermanded
(5)       Rash ambition broken handed
I pray you use a freer expense
Nor shrivel us with indigence
Rebuild or ruin: either fill
Of vital force the wasting rill
(10)       Or tumble all again in heap
To weltering Chaos & old Sleep

       Say, are the old Niles dry

10 "Alphonso of Castile," 1–18, 25–26, 19. In pencil.
11 "Alphonso of Castile," 21, 21–24, x, x, 27–34, 37–43. In pencil.

Which fed the veins of Earth & Sky,
That men now miss the loyal heats
(15)    Which drove them erst to social feats
Now with science mask their hurt
And vex the gods with question pert
Immensely curious whether you
Still are rulers or Mildew

(20)    Masters I am in pain with you
Masters I'll be plain with you
In my palace of Castille

[12₁]    A‖ . . . . . . . . ‖
As ‖ . . . . . . . . ‖
A‖ . . . . . . . . . ‖
Climbed I ‖ . . . . . . ‖

(5)    ⟨The⟩ ‖ . . . . . . . . ‖
Home ‖ . . . . . . . ‖
Below the ‖ . . . . . ‖ wind
Pathway ‖ . . . . . . ‖ wind[?]
The ‖ . . . . . . ‖ heavens hoop
(10)    And richly gemmed with towns & farms

Thousand ‖ . . . . . . . ‖ me
Our ‖ . . . . . . . . . ‖
⟨Vice ‖ . . ‖⟩ ↑In ‖ . . . . ‖↓
Virtue ‖ . . . . ‖ on the ‖ . . . ‖
(15)    Manly virtue loves the ‖ . . . . ‖

[12₂]    I a king for kings can feel
There in my thoughts the matter roll
And solve & oft resolve the whole
And for I'm styled Alphonse the Wise
(5)    Ye shall not want for my advice
If ye 'd not parch for a drop of rain
Hear the sentiment of Spain

      You have tried famine: no more try it
Ply us now with a full diet
(10)    Teach your pupils now with plenty
For one sun supply us twenty
I have tho't it thoroughly over
State of hermit state of lover
We must have society

12₁ "Monadnock," ten unused lines, 1–2, x, x. Erased pencil; lines (1–10) are struck through in pencil.
  12₂ "Alphonso of Castile," 44–60, 63–72. In pencil.

(15)        We cannot spare variety

             Hear you now celestial fellows
             Beseems not to be overzealous
             Men & gods are too extense
             Could you not slacken & condense
(20)        ⟨All⟩ your ↑rank↓ overgrowth reduce
             Till your kinds abound with juice
             Earth crowded cries, Too many men!
             My counsel is, Kill nine in ten,
             And bestow the shares of all
(25)        On the remnant decimal
             Add their nine lives to this cat
             Stuff their nine brains in his hat

[13₁]      Mow the grass & reap the grain
             [four lines of erased pencil writing]
             U‖ . . . . . . . . . . . ‖
             ‖ . . . . . . ‖ ↑old as the sun old almost as the shade↓
             ‖ . . . . . . . . . . . . ‖
             ‖ . . . . . . . . . . . . ‖
(10)        ‖ . . . . . . . . ‖ others wit
             At the ‖ . . . . . ‖ judge of fair & fit
             Nearing me ‖ . . . . . . . . ‖
             In ‖ . . . . . . . . . ‖ years
             Can ‖ . . . . . . . . . . ‖
(15)        ‖ . . . . . . . . . . . . ‖
             To ‖ . . . . . . . . . . . ‖ snow
             And tread ‖ . . . . . . . . ‖

             In ‖ . . . . . . . . . . ‖ warm
             ‖ . . . . . . . . . . . . ‖

[13₂]          Make his frame & vigor square
             With the labors he must dare
             Thatch his flesh & even his years
             With the marble which he rears
(5)         There growing slowly old at ease
             No faster than his planted trees
             He may by warrant of his age
             In schemes of broader scope engage
             So shall ye have a man of the sphere

13₁ "Monadnock," x, four unrecovered lines, 217–18, x?, x?, x, x, 230, 232, x?, x?, 220–21, x?, x? Erased pencil. Something may have been erased under lines (1–2); lines (1–17) are struck through in pencil.
13₂ "Alphonso of Castile," 73–82 (1–10); "Solution," 59, x, 61, 63, 63–68, x, x (11–22). Lines (1–10) are in pencil; in line (16), "anew" is added in pencil.

(10)      Fit to grace the solar year

                In newer days & crowded men
                In complex powers and armed states
                When Science armed & guided war
                And turbulent France
(15)            France where poet never grew
                Would ⟨cut⟩ halve the globe ↑anew↓
                Amid the roar of strife
                Calm Goethe drew the firm lines of fate & life
                And brought the Olympian wisdom down
(20)            To courts & marts villa & town
                And Time amid the deafening
                Forgets the rest to study these.

[14₁]           See p 63
                This country
                ‖ . . . . . . . . . . . . . . ‖
                ‖ . . . . . . . . . . . . . ‖
                By ‖ . . . . . . . . . . . ‖
(5)             ⟨‖ . . . ‖⟩ ↑Coarse obscene, but↓ ‖ . . . . . . . ‖
                ⟨‖ . . . . ‖⟩ ‖ . . ‖ as ‖ . . . ‖ & ‖ . . . ‖ as child
                ⟨‖ . . . ‖⟩ ‖ . . . . . . . . . . ‖ room
                ‖ . . . ‖ yet ‖ . . . . . . . . . ‖ come
                Few ‖ . . . . . . . . . . . . . ‖
(10)            ‖ . . . . . . . . ‖ hundred words
                All ‖ . . . . . . . . . . . . . ‖
                [three lines of erased pencil writing]
(15)            ⟨‖ . . . ‖⟩ ↑Ye squire↓ ‖ . . . . . ‖
                ‖ . . . . . . . . ‖ earth & ‖ . . . . . . ‖
                But is ‖ . . . . . . . . . . . ‖
                ‖ . . . . . . . . . . . . . . . ‖
                ‖ . . . . ‖ never ‖ . . . . . . . ‖
(20)            ‖ . . . . ‖ ears ↑but cause↓ ‖ . . . . ‖ jokes
                ‖ . . . . . . . . . . . . . . . ‖
                ‖ . . . . . . . . . . . . . . . ‖
                ‖ . . . . . . ‖ health and ‖ . . . . . ‖

[14₂]           Oft when I read fond pictures poets drew
                Of rural life, I thank the Power that I
                Need not this charity of paint & song.
                What all the books of ages paint I have;

14₁ "Monadnock," four unused lines?, 137–40, x?, 185–86, seven unused lines?, 202–3, x?, x?, 206. In pencil, struck through in pencil and erased.
14₂ "What all the books," x, x, x, 1–12. In pencil, struck through in pencil.

(5) What prayers & dreams of youthful genius feign
  I daily dwell in, & am not so blind
  But I can see the elastic tent of day
  Belike has wider hospitality
  Than my few needs exhaust, & beckons me
(10) Read the /devices/secrets/ on its mornings gay
  Yet Nature will not be in full possessed,
  And they who trueliest love her, heralds are
  And harbingers of a majestic race
  Who having more absorbed, more largely yield,
(15) And walk on earth as the sun walks in the sphere.

[15]  ↑Mow the grass & reap the grain↓

  O Lord I stand
  Upon this uplifted land
  Raised to draw the clouds
(5) Like an unrolled banner
  To all the dwellers /for a hundred miles/in the plains about/
  And to furnish them with sweet rivers
  And to be to them a /majestic pile/aerial isle/
  ↑Which morn & crimson eve shall paint↓
(10) For poet, for lover & for ⟨moralist[?]⟩ ↑saint↓
  The country's core
  O Lord is this all
  This dull thick ⟨‖ . . . ‖⟩ animal
  That ‖ . . . . . . . . . ‖ head
(15) Could rear & train for empire
  Sink O mountain in the ⟨sea⟩ ⟨↑pond↓⟩ ↑swamp↓
  ⟨Wither⟩ ↑Perish↓ like leaves the mountain folk
  The world is not a country joke
  ⟨Their eyes are sealed,⟩ they cannot see, unwise
(20) That which awes the ⟨traveller's⟩ ↑stranger's↓ eyes
  And drew this ⟨traveller to mount⟩ ↑moment the ⟨gazing⟩
    far-gazing youth↓
  Or else some spell or oath
  Nature lays upon their tongue
  That they shall never name or praise
(25) Their mountain for its ⟨scene⟩ ↑pictures wide↓
  Or men or dames among
[16₁] Only the seasons praise it
  Only the winds pipe

15 "Monadnock," x, 223, 221, 33–34, 35/36, 41–42, 44–46, 79, x, x, 80, 125, 127/123, 124, eight unused lines. In pencil, struck through in pencil and erased. Line (1), unerased, is set off by an angled line in pencil.

16₁ "Monadnock," x, x, x?, x?, 33?, x?, 34–36, 37?, 39, x?, 41–45. In pencil, struck through in pencil and erased.

⟨‖ . . . . . . ‖⟩
‖ . . . . . . . . . . . ‖
(5)    ‖ . . ‖ to draw the clouds
⟨‖ . . . . . . . . . . . . . . ‖⟩
Like a banner broad unrolled
To all the dwellers in the plains
Round about a hundred miles
(10)  ⟨And to⟩
Beautiful by his ↑‖ . . ‖↓ bounty
The ‖ . . . . . . . . . . . ‖
Yielded man a ⟨‖ . . . ‖⟩ ⟨sweet⟩ ↑‖ . . . . ‖↓ river
Seems to mens eyes an aerial isle
(15)  A cheerful & majestic pile
Which morn & crimson eve shall paint
For ⟨poet⟩ ↑bard for↓ lover & for saint

[16₂]         Chardon Street 1830
Dear brother, would you know the life
Please God, that I would lead?
On the first wheels that quit this weary town
Over yon western bridges I would ride
(5)  And with a cheerful benison forsake
Each street & spire & roof incontinent.
Then would I seek where God might guide my steps,
Deep in a woodland tract, a sunny farm,
Amid the mountain counties, ↑Hants↓ Franklin ⟨or⟩ Berks,
(10)  Where down the rock ravine a river ⟨pours⟩roars,
Even from a brook, & where old woods
Not tamed & cleared, cumber the ample ground
With their centennial wrecks.

[17₁]  The country's core   Inspirer ‖ . . . ‖
      ↑Wo is me for my ‖ . . . . ‖ down fall↓
‖ . . . ‖ is the ‖ . . . . . ‖ an infinity
     Lord is this all
(5)  This dull thick animal
That ‖ . . . . . . . . ‖ head
Could rear & train for nature's lead
In ‖ . . . . . . . . . ‖ stead
⟨Sink o mountain⟩
(10)  Pour in ‖ . . . . . ‖
To reach ‖ . . . . . . . . ‖

16₂ "Dear brother, would you know," 1–13. In line (9), the cancellation and addition are in pencil.
17₁ "Monadnock," 46/47, 78, x, 79, x, x, 80?, 81?, 125, x, x, 125–26, 127/123, 124, ten unused lines. In pencil, struck through in pencil and erased.

Sink o mountain in the swamp
King in thy skies thou sovereign lamp
↑Die↓ ‖ . . . ‖ like leaves the mountain folk
(15) ‖ . . . . . . . . ‖ for a tavern joke
They cannot see unwise
That which awes the strangers eyes
Drew to the mount far gazing youth
⟨Or⟩ is it that some spell or oath
(20) Nature lays upon their tongue
That they shall never name or praise
Their mountain for its pictures wide
Or men or dames among
Only the seasons praise it
(25) Only the winds pipe.

[17₂]    Find me a slope where I can feel the sun
And mark the rising of the early stars.
There will I bring my books, my household gods,
The reliquaires of my dead saint, & dwell
(5) In the sweet odor of her memory.
There, in the uncouth solitude, unlock
My ⟨slender⟩ stock of art, ⟨a⟩ ↑plant↓ dial↑s↓, in the grass,
Hang ⟨out⟩in the air a bright thermometer,
And aim a telescope at the inviolate Sun.

[18₁]    That which god aloft had set
So that men might not ‖ . . . . ‖
It ‖ . . . ‖ be their ‖ . . . ‖ ornament
And mix itself with each event
(5) Know ‖ . . . . . . . . ‖

[four lines of erased pencil writing]
(10) By ‖ . . . . . . . . . . ‖ skilled to tell
What in the ⟨enchanted⟩ ↑eternal↓ standeth well

‖ . . . . . . . . . . . . . . ‖
‖ . . . . . . . . . . . . . . ‖
Mysteries of ‖ . . . . . . ‖ laid
(15) By ‖ . . . . . . . . . . . ‖ shade
And sweet ‖ . . . . . . . . . . ‖
And change[?] ‖ . . . . . . ‖ seasons dance
‖ . . . . . . . . . . . . . . ‖ done & shown
The ‖ . . . . . . . . . . . ‖

17₂ "Dear brother, would you know," 14–22.
18₁ "Monadnock," 48–51, x?, four unrecovered lines, 90–91, x?, x?, 60–63, 67, x?, 65. In pencil, struck through in pencil and erased.

(20)  ⟨‖ . . . ‖⟩ ‖ . . . . . . . . ‖ into flowers

[18₂]  I am the Muse
Memorys daughter
I stood by Jove at the first
⟨Or no Jove had been.⟩
(5)  Take me out, & no world had been,
⟨Or a world worth little,⟩
And Chaos bare & bleak.
If life has worth, I give it.
And if all is taken, & I left,
(10)  I make amends for all.
Long I wrought to ⟨bring⟩
To ripen & refine
The stagnant craggy lump
To a brain,
(15)  And shoot it through
With electric wit
At last the snake & dragon
Shed their scales
And man was born

[19₁]  Himself it was
Who wrote
His rank upon his coat
There is no king & no state
(5)  Can fix any hero's rate
But he is there venerable
Armed and unassailable
Until he writes where all eyes rest
‖ . . . . . . . ‖ on his breast
(10)  Men go ‖ . . . . . . . . . ‖
In country and in town
With ‖ . . . . ‖ on their neck
⟨‖ . . . . ‖⟩ Judgment & a judge we seek
⟨‖ . . . . . . . . . . . . ‖ repair⟩
(15)  Nor to learned jurists chair
But they go to their peers ↑& their kinsfolk & their dears↓
In ‖ . . . . . . . . ‖ ⟨taverns⟩ instead
And louder than with speech pray
‖ . . . . . . . . . . . ‖, say
(20)  And the friend not hesitates
To assign just place & mates

18₂ "Solution," 1, x, 2, seven unused lines, 3, x, 4, x, x, x, 6, 6, x.
19₁ "Astraea," 1, 1, 2–5, x, 7–14, 15/16, x, 17–21, 22/24, 25, x. In pencil, struck through in pencil and erased.

‖ . . . . . . . . ‖ not in ↑word↓ ‖ . . . . . ‖
He is understood the better ↑He ‖ . . . . ‖ reflects the figures
    that pass↓
And every one whom he meets
(25)      In forests or in streets
[19₂]    Then was Asia
        Then was Nile
        And at last
        On the sea marge bleak
(5)       Forward stept the Perfect Greek
        That will, wit, joy, might find a tongue,
        And earth grow civil, Homer sung.
        Pleased the planet hummed the tunes
        And ⟨the⟩
(10)     And I passed into Italy
        And forbore long to sing,
        ⟨At⟩ ↑For↓ my manner is
        To sing uncalled,
        And in strange times to astonish ⟨↑appal↓⟩
(15)     Then I clothed me with vast fears
        When Dante searched the triple spheres
        I gave him my harp
        The world was all flowing into ripples of color
        Yet he wrote like Euclid

[20₁]    ⟨Reports⟩ that which he bold records
        Sentences him in his own words
        The form is his own corporal form
        And his ‖ . . . . . . . ‖ worm
(5)       ↑Ever↓ ‖ . . . . . . . . . ‖
        Loved by stars & purest ‖ . . . . ‖
        Above the passions ‖ . . . . . . ‖
        Who ‖ . . . . . . . . ‖ their state
        Who ‖ . . . . . . . . . ‖
(10)     And ⟨return⟩ ↑render↓ to ⟨‖ . . . ‖⟩ ↑an↓ ashen ⟨‖ . . . . ‖⟩ eye
        The cold ‖ . . . . . . . . ‖
        To ‖ . . . . . . . . . ‖
        It is there for benefit
        And its lakes reflect all forms
(15)     But ‖ . . . . . . . . ‖ excess
        For ‖ . . . . . . . . . ‖ storms

19₂ "Solution," 9, 11–16, x, x, 17–19, 19, 20/22, 27–28, x, 30?, x.
20₁ "Astraea," 27–34, x?, 36, x?, 38?, 39, 42, x?, 41. Erased pencil.

[20₂]    The color of his russet vest
⟨l⟩Like frozen leaves & grouse's breast
For, as the woodkinds lurk & hide,
So walks the woodman unespied

(5)    He took the color of his vest
From rabbit's coat or grouse's breast;
For, as the woodkinds lurk & hide,
So walks the woodman unespied.

---

Then I tarried long
(10)    Ere I struck my third harp
Need was to wait for a song like it
But without it the world had better not be made
Seethed in the mists of Penmanmaur
Taught by Plinlimmons bards of power
(15)    The voice of England filled all measure
Of heart & soul of strength & pleasure

[21₁]    Himself it was who wrote
His rank ‖ . . . . ‖ coat
There is ⟨‖ . ‖⟩no king ⟨& no state⟩ nor sovereign state
⟨Can⟩ ⟨Which⟩
(5)    That can fix a heroes state
But he is there venerable
‖ . . . . . . . . . . . . ‖
Until he write where all eyes rest
For ‖ . . . . . ‖ on his breast
(10)    ‖ . . . . . . . . . . . . ‖
↑I saw↓ Men go up & down
In country and in town
With this need[?] upon their necks
‖ . . . . . ‖ a judge we seek
(15)    Not to monarchs they repair
Not to learned jurists chair
But they hurry to their peers
To their kinsfolk & their dears
⟨And⟩ louder than with voices pray

20₂ "Forester," two drafts (1–8); "Solution," four unused lines, 33–36 (9–16). Lines (1–4) are in pencil.
21₁ "Astraea," 1–4, 4–5, x?, 7–8, x?, 9–22, 24. In pencil, struck through in pencil and erased. The word "Giving" appears, unerased, between lines (25–26). A few words are recoverable from a lower layer of erased pencil, apparently a draft of "Etienne de la Boéce": the word "resist" is visible below the end of line (13), "wealthy grown" below the end of line (24), and "That were a mans . . . friend's part" below line (26): cf. "Etienne . . . ," lines 10, 19, and 23.

(20)    What am I ⟨‖ . . . ‖⟩ ‖ . . . . ‖, say
And the friend not hesitates
To assign just place ‖ . . . . . . . ‖
Tho ⟨he⟩ answer⟨ing⟩ not in word or letter
‖ . . . . . . . . ‖ the better
(25)    ‖ . . . . . . . . . . ‖ that doth pass

[21₂]    *Written in a volume of Goethe*
Six ⟨happy⟩ ↑thankful↓ weeks, & let it be
A metre of prosperity,
In my coat I bore this book,
And seldom therein could I look,
(5)    For I had too much to think,
Heaven & earth to eat & drink.
Is he hapless, who can spare
In his plenty things so rare?

---

Gave to mind its emperor,
(10)    And life was larger than before,
Nor sequent centuries could hit
Orbit or sum of Shakspeare's wit
Far in the North where Polar night
Holds ⟨his⟩ ↑in↓ check the frolic light
(15)    Transcending mortal goal
The Swedish prophet leads the soul

[22₁]    Two well assorted travellers use
The highway Cupid & the Muse
They are young & strong & wise
‖ . . . . . . . . . ‖ & his
(5)    From this pair is nothing hidden
⟨Unto them⟩ ↑To this pair↓ is nought forbidden
⟨Up & down⟩ ↑Hand in hand↓ the comrades go
Every nook of ‖ . . . ‖ ⟨know⟩ through
From ‖ . . . . . . . ‖ never stray
(10)    For where they ‖ . . . . ‖ find they make their way
No joy is ‖ . . . . . . . . ‖ journeying
Land & sea ‖ . . . ‖ made for them
⟨For⟩ each ↑for↓ other they were born
Each ↑can↓ other ⟨‖ . . . . ‖⟩ ↑best↓ adorn

21₂ "Written in a Volume of Goethe" (1–8); "Solution," 37–40, 43–46 (9–16).
22₁ "Love and Thought," 1–2, x, x, 3–6, four unused lines, 7–12. Erased pencil. A few words recovered from a lower layer of erased pencil indicate a draft of "Astraea," 21–46: visible are "Therein" and "look" (first line); "book" (second line); "And" and "whom he meets" (third line); "⟨brow⟩ ↑head↓" (sixteenth line); "edge" (seventeenth line); and "Haunts also the mountain lake" (twenty-second and last line).

(15)     And the only ↑cureless↓ grief
         That has no respite or relief
         Is when by false companions crossed
         These pilgrims have each other lost

[22₂]    Thro' snows above, mines underground
         The inks of Erebus he found
         Nor scarce availed
                    Mid abysses dread
(5)      To see the glory overhead
         None near him could hear ⟨the[re]fore⟩ any sound
         But they who stood far off
         Heard the thunders as of the vault
         And feel uneathe the shaking ground
(10)     And the

[23]     ↑Their↓ Eyes look sidewise out to ⟨seek⟩ ↑watch↓
         The passing travellers life
         Then slink behind the door to ⟨fetch⟩ ↑catch↓
         The rifle & the knife

(5)      The echoes sentence him

                              ↑See p 203↓ [i.e., 205]
         Two well assorted travellers use
         The ⟨beaten road Love⟩ ↑highway Cupid↓ & the Muse
         They are young & strong & wise
         From this pair is nothing hidden
(10)     To the pair is nought forbidden
         Hand in hand the comrades go
         Every nook of nature through
         On land or sea by bank & brae
         And where they find not, make their way.
(15)     Each for other they were born
         Each can the other best adorn
         And the only cureless grief
         Past all respite or relief
         Is when by false companions crost
(20)     These pilgrims have each other lost

[24]     I have no brothers & no peers
         And the dearest interferes

22₂ "Solution," 47–48, x, x, x, 53–57.
23 "Their Eyes look sidewise" (1–4); cf. "Astraea," 28 (5); "Love and Thought," 1–2, x,
3–6, x, x, 7–12 (6–20). Lines (1–5) are in pencil; lines (6–20) are struck through in ink with
five wavy lines, one of which terminates after line (16).
24 "I have no brothers" (1–4); "Solution," 25–26, x, x, 41–42 (5–10). Lines (1–4) are in
pencil; a vertical line in ink after "say" in line (6) apparently indicates a revised line-break.

When I would spend a lonely day
Sun & moon are in my way

(5)        By thoughts I lead
Bards to say what nations need;
What ⟨↑n↓⟩ imports, what irks, & what behoves
Framed afar as Fates & Loves
    Those who lived with him became
(10)    Poets for the air was fame

[25]    What care I so ⟨that⟩ the things abide
↑Things of↓ The heavenly mind⟨ed⟩,
the rich & enriching Presences,
How long the /power to give/talent to express/ their form
(5)    Stays behind;
If they remain to me
I can spare that,
I can wait
Till the stammering fit of life is past
(10)    Till the soul its ⟨skin⟩ ↑weed↓ has cast
And led by desire of these ⟨gods or ideas⟩ ↑heavenly guides↓
I have come into a free element
And won a better instrument
They taught me a new speech
(15)    And a thousand silences
For as there is but one path for the sun
So is there ever but one word for me to say

    O blessed dream abide with me

Tented Asia columned Nile
(20)    And last by strand or rocky isle
On the ⟨sea marge⟩ windblown sea marge bleak
Forward stept

[26₁]    ‖ . . . ‖ factory of frost & rain & river
This forge of ores
land mark sea mark
‖ . . . . . . . . ‖
(5)    home cradle hunting ground & bier
for ⟨a⟩many races
And large observatory neighboring
the ‖ . . . ‖

25 "Merops," 1–2, 6, 3–4, eight unused lines, 7–8, x, 12, x, (1–18); "Solution," 11–14 (19–22). In pencil.
26₁ "Monadnock," 88, 82, x, x?, 84, 86–87, x? Erased pencil.

[26₂]  And whether I was rich & great
       Or whether I was fool & cheat
       The Muse that built the world is wise

       Pale genius roves alone
(5)    No scout can track his way
       None credits him till he have shown
       His diamonds to the day

       Not his the feaster's wine
       Nor land nor gold nor power
(10)   By want & pain God screeneth him
       To his elected hour

       Go speed the stars of thought
       On to their shining goals
       The sower scatters broad his seed
(15)   The wheat thou strew'st be souls

[27]   Genius goes alone
       No man knows his way
       None credits him till he have shown
       His jewels to the day
(5)    A thousand years they slept
       ⟨Waiting for hi⟨m⟩s⟩ ↑Whilst his slow steps↓ delay
       Ten thousand ⟨they had waited⟩ ↑their hiding kept↓
       If he had ⟨taken⟩ ↑gone↓ another way
       He misses the feasters wine
(10)   And gold & power
       So God saves him
       To his sacred ⟨days⟩ ↑hour↓

                    *Intellect*
       Rule which by obeying grows
       Knowledge which its source not knows
(15)   Wave removing whom it bears
       From the shores which he compares
       Adding wings thro things to range
       Makes him to his own blood strange

[28₁]  [three lines of erased pencil writing]
       ‖ . . . ‖ never ‖ . . . . . ‖ abreast

26₂ "And whether I was rich" (1–3); "Pale Genius roves alone" (4–15); "Intellect" ("Go, speed") (12–15). In pencil.
    27 "Pale Genius roves alone," 1–4, four unused lines, 5–8 (1–12); "Intellect" ("Rule which by obeying") (13–18). In pencil, struck through in pencil.
    28₁ "Forerunners," x?, x?, x?, 2, four unrecovered lines, 7, 9, five unrecovered lines, 19–23, x?, 25, x?, x? Erased pencil. A horizontal caret is inscribed in the left margin between lines (13–14); the last two lines are partially circled in pencil.

[four lines of erased pencil writing]
But no speed of mine || . . . ||

(10)    ↑On &↓ Away || . . . . . . . . ||
[five lines of erased pencil writing]
They || . . . . . . . . . || revellers
These had crossed them while they slept
They had || . . . . . || ↑fine[?]↓ report
In || . . . . . . . . . . . || court

(20)    ⟨|| . . . . ||⟩ ↑⟨|| . . . ||⟩ fleetest ⟨|| . . . . ||⟩ couriers alive↓ || . . . . . . ||
|| . . . . . . . . . . . . . . . . ||
|| . . . . . . . . . . . . || these returned
⟨⟨|| . . . ||⟩ ↑|| . . . . . ||↓ the || . . . . . ||⟩
|| . . . . . . . . . . . . . . . . ||

[28₂]        I stand
Upon this uplifted land
Hugely massed to draw the clouds
Like a banner unrolled
(5)    To all the dwellers ⟨o⟩in the plains
Round about a hundred miles
In his own living garment dressed
By his own bounty blessed
This constant giver
(10)    Yielding many a cheerful river
Appearing an aerial isle
A cheerful & majestic pile
Which morn & crimson eve shall paint
For bard for lover & for saint
(15)    The country's core
Inspirer prophet evermore
That which God aloft had set
So that men might it not forget
It should be their lives ornament
(20)    And mix itself with each event
Their /almanac/calendar/ & dial
Painter's pallette sorcerer's phial
Its race of plants its race of birds

[29₁] 1845   3 May   4 hours   10 m.   a m

↑Sometimes↓ || . . . . . . || they slacken
⟨↑And↓⟩ || . . . . . . . . || not overtaken

---

28₂ "Monadnock," 223, 221, 33/223, 34–36, 38–54. In pencil.
29₁ "Forerunners," 27–28, x, 29–30, x?, x?, 34–37, x?, x?, x. In pencil, all erased except the date and an insignia that follows it, consisting of two capital letters ("WF" or "MF") run together.

Some ‖ . . . . . . . . . ‖ they come near me
Their jubilant troop is near
(5) ↑Tuneful↓ ‖ . . . . . ‖ I overhear
‖ . . . . . . . . . . . . . . . ‖
‖ . . . . . . . . . . . . . . . ‖
By signs as ‖ . . . . . . . ‖ rainbows
‖ . . . . . . . . . . . . ‖ & long after
(10) ↑Listen for their ⟨‖ . . . . . . ‖⟩↓ ‖ . . . . ‖ laughter
And carry in my ‖ . . . . . . ‖ days
‖ . . . . . . . . . . . . . . ‖
‖ . . . . . . . . . . . . . ‖
And my ‖ . . . . . . . ‖ not leave me

[29₂]     Its tribe of beasts
Mysteries of colour daily laid
By the great painter light & shade
And sweet varieties of time
(5) And chance
And the mystic seasons dance
The soft succession of the hours
Thawed the snowdrift into flowers

By eldest science done & shown
(10) Much more
Their symbol & interpreter
By million changes skilled to tell
What in the Eternal standeth well

Wo is me for my hopes downfall
(15) O Lord is this all
This dull thick animal
That the ⟨austere⟩ mountain head ↑could breed↓
⟨Could rear & train for Natures lead⟩
⟨And God's high stead⟩
(20) ⟨And⟩ ↑For↓ God's vicegerency & stead

[30₁]     ⟨‖ . . . . . . . . . . ‖⟩
Virtue runs before the Muse
And defies her skill
She ‖ . ‖ rapt & doth refuse
(5) To ‖ . . ‖ a painters will

She is rapt & occupied
And she ‖ . . ‖ not bend her

292 "Monadnock," 55, 60–62, 62–65, 67, x, x, 90–91, 78–79, x, 80, x, 81, 81. In pencil.
301 "Loss and Gain." Erased pencil.

⟨↑But↓⟩ Just ‖ . . . . ‖ a poets pride
⟨‖ . . . . ‖⟩ ↑parade↓ her splendor

(10)  ↑Must↓ ⟨‖ . . . ‖⟩ ↑be↓ a bard with good intent
⟨‖ . . . . ‖⟩ No more his but hers
Throw away his pen & paint
⟨Lost among lowly⟩ ↑Worshipper with↓ worshippers

Then perchance a ⟨fiery⟩ ↑sunny↓ beam
(15)  From the heaven of fire
May ⟨replace⟩ ↑overpay↓ his ⟨perished tools⟩ ↑⟨‖ . . . ‖⟩ cost↓
And better his desire

[302]  Is all this panorama vain
Inactive on the human brain
Sink o mountain in the swamp
Hide in thy skies thou sovereign lamp
(5)  Die like leaves the mountain folk
If all is but a tavern joke
Alas they cannot see unwise
That which awes the ⟨g⟩strangers eyes
Drew to the mount far gazing youth
(10)  Is it that some spell or oath
Nature lays ⟨o⟩upon their tongue
That they shall not name or praise
Their mountain for its awe or grace
Or men or dames among
(15)  Only the seasons praise it
Only the winds pipe

[31]  Virtue runs before the muse
And defies her skill
She is rapt & doth refuse
To wait a painter's will

(5)  ⟨She is rapt &⟩ ↑Star adoring↓ occupied
⟨And she⟩ ↑Virtue↓ cannot bend her
Just to please a poets pride
To parade her splendor

The bard must be with good intent
(10)  No more his but hers
Throw away his pen & paint
⟨Worshipper⟩ ↑Kneel↓ with worshippers

Then perchance a sunny ray
From the heaven of fire

302  "Monadnock," x, x, 125–26, 127/123, 124, ten unused lines. In pencil.
31  "Loss and Gain." In pencil.

(15)        His lost tools may overpay
              And better his desire

[32₁]     The patient Destiny sits
              With roses & a shroud
              He has his way he deals his gifts
              But ours is not allowed

[32₂]     Wisely said the Greek
              Be thou faithful but not fond.
              To the altars foot thy fellow seek
              Never beyond

[33₁]     [four lines of erased pencil writing]

(5)        ‖ . . . . . . . . ‖ spring in the mind
              ‖ . . . . . . . . . . . . ‖ told
              ‖ . . . . . . . . . ‖ this throbbing heart
              A ‖ . . . . . . . . . . . . . ‖ old
              Over the winter glaciers
(10)       I see the ‖ . . . . . . ‖
              ‖ . . . . . . . . . . . ‖ snowdrift
              The ‖ . . . . . . . . . ‖

[33₂]     I serve you not if you I follow
              Shadowlike oer hill & hollow
              And bend my ⟨tho't⟩ ↑fancy↓ to your leading
              All too nimble for my treading
(5)        ⟨But⟩ when ⟨all⟩ ↑the pilgrimage↓ is done,
              And we've the landscape over run,
              I am bitter, vacant, thwarted,
              And you ↑r↓ ⟨are⟩ ↑heart is↓ unsupported
              ↑Vainly valiant↓ You have missed
(10)       The manhood that should yours resist,
              But if I could
              In grave or frolic mood
              Lead you to my altar
              ⟨There⟩ where ⟨even⟩ ↑the wisest↓ Muses falter
(15)       And worship with you the dread Life
              Which dazzles me in the dark
              ⟨And excludes the little⟩ ↑Equalizing small↓ & large
              While it doth discharge
              Its ocean in at all doors

32₁ "The World-Soul," 77–80. In pencil, struck through in pencil and erased.
32₂ "Pericles." In pencil.
33₁ Unrecovered lines (1–4); "The World-Soul," 105–12 (5–12). Erased pencil.
33₂ "Etienne de la Boéce," 1–18, x, 19–20, 23, 21–22. In pencil, struck through in pencil.

(20)        That the poor is wealthy grown
                And the hermit never alone
                That were a man's & ⟨a friend's⟩ ↑lover's↓ part
                    ↑Traveller & the road seem one↓
                    ↑With the errand to be done↓

[34]        ‖ . . . . . . . . . . ‖
                And the ‖ . . . . . . . . ‖ with mockery ↑low↓
                And the ‖ . . . . . . . . . ‖ the streets
                The ‖ . . . . . . . . . . . ‖
(5)         Into the fopperies of the town

                Bareness bareness
                Take away learning wealth & civilization
                that nature may have room to work
                The poor, she loves the poor
(10)        and by a ⟨miracle⟩ ↑marvel↓ of her own
                To strike all competition down

/[35₁]     ‖ . . . . . . . . . . . . . . ‖
                ⟨‖ . . . . . . . . . . . . ‖⟩
                The ‖ . . . . . . . ‖ clouds draw down
                The holy ‖ . . . ‖ ⟨‖ . . . ‖ streets⟩ ↑‖ . . . . . ‖ into↓ ‖ . . . ‖
(5)         ⟨‖ . . . . . . . . . . . ‖ town⟩
                The fopperies of the town

                Let ‖ . . . . . . . ‖ to town
                With[?] ‖ . . . . . . . . ‖
                And ‖ . . . . . . . . . . ‖
(10)        With railways ironed oer
                ⟨They⟩ ↑Merrily ‖ . . . ‖↓ are but sailing foam bells
                Along thought's ‖ . . . . . . ‖
                And take their ‖ . . . ‖ shape & sun color
                From him that sends the ‖ . . . ‖

(15)        ‖ . . . . . . . . . . . . ‖
                Keep firm ‖ . . . . . . . . ‖

                I ‖ . . . . ‖ willing ‖ . . . . ‖
                The ‖ . . . . . . . ‖ not like
                To give the ‖ . . . . . . ‖

[35₂]     I serve you not if you I follow
                Shadowlike ⟨or⟩oer hill & hollow

34 "The World-Soul," x?, x, x, x, 60 (1–5); "Nature I," x, x, x, 9–11 (6–11). In pencil; lines (1–5) are struck through in pencil and erased.

35₁ "The World-Soul," x?, x?, 58, 59?, 60, 60, x, x?, 67?, 68–72, x?, x, x, 73–74. In pencil, struck through in pencil and erased.

35₂ "Etienne de la Boéce," 1–18, x, 19–23. In pencil.

And bend my fancy to your leading
All too nimble for my treading
(5)    When the pilgrimage is done
And we've the landscape over run
I am bitter vacant thwarted
And your heart is unsupported
Vainly valiant you have missed
(10)   The manhood that should yours resist
Its complement. But if I could
In a grave or frolic mood
Lead you rightly to my altar
Where the wisest muses falter
(15)   And worship with you the dread Life
Which dazzles me in midnight dark
Equalizing small & large
While it doth discharge
Its ocean in at all doors
(20)   That the poor is wealthy grown
And the hermit never alone
The traveller & the road seem one
With the errand to be done
That were a man's & lover's part

[36₁]   ‖ . . . . . . . . . ‖ ↑nerves↓
           ‖ . . . . . . . . . . . . ‖

He is no ‖ . . . . . . . ‖
And his ‖ . . . ‖ are her ‖ . . . ‖
(5)   Love ‖ . . . . . . . . . ‖
‖ . . . . . . . . ‖ of Genius
And his will is not thwarted
For the ‖ . . . . . . . . ‖
Are ‖ . . . . . . ‖ his mind
(10)  And ‖ . . . . . . . . . ‖

‖ . . . . . . . . . . . . ‖
He loves ‖ . . . . . . . ‖
He ‖ . . . . . . . . . . . ‖
He ‖ . . . . . . . . ‖ the sick
(15)  And ‖ . . . . . . . . . ‖
⟨The⟩ ↑For↓ gods delight in gods
And thrust ‖ . . . . . . ‖ aside
To him who scorns ‖ . . . . . . ‖
Their ‖ . . . . ‖ fly open wide

36₁ "The World-Soul," 75, x?, 81–88, x?, 90, x?, 91–96. In pencil, struck through in pencil and erased.

[36₂]    Solar insect ↑on the wing↓
    ↑In the↓ garden murmuring
    Soothing with thy summer horn
    Swains by winter pinched & worn

(5)    the sportive sun

[37₁]    He when the world is sterile
    And the ages are effete
    Is ‖ . . . . . . . . ‖
    Will ‖ . . . . . . . ‖
(5)    He forbids to despair
    ‖ . . . . . . . . . . ‖
    And the impossible
    Has arrived at the birth

    ‖ . . . . . . . . . ‖ us
(10)    ‖ . . . . . . . . ‖ strong desire
    It whispers ‖ . . . . . ‖ rains[?]
    But leaves us in the ⟨‖ . . . ‖⟩ mire

[37₂]    Fairly fortuned   ↑Portly dozing↓
    Garden murmuring     ↑cruising↓
    Solar insect
    ⟨Consoling⟩ with the summer horn
(5)    The ⟨lads⟩ ↑swains↓ by winter pinched & worn

    Earth baking heat stone cleaving cold

    And m⟨e⟩an of wit & mark
    Repair to men of wit
    It cannot be society
(10)    In one saloon to sit.

    Samson strong at Dagon's knee
    Gropes for ⟨pillars⟩ ↑column↓ strong as he
    When his ringlets grew & curled
    Groped for axle of the world

[38]    Though I call me liberal
    And have charity for all
    Though I ⟨cherish⟩ ↑honour↓ handsome sinners
    And like rich men who give dinners

36₂ "Solar insect on the wing" (1–4); "Song of Nature," 3 (5).
37₁ "The World-Soul," 97–98, x?, x?, 101, x?, 103–4, 41–44. Erased pencil.
37₂ "Solar insect on the wing," x, 2, 1, 3–4 (1–5); "Monadnock," 57 (6); "And man of wit" (7–10); "Samson stark" (11–14). In pencil; lines (1–6) are struck through in pencil and erased.
38 "Nature I," six unused lines, 16–19, x, 20–21. In pencil.

(5)     And were I Pope should grace dispense
    To the very cocks & hens
    Yet doth much my love excel
    To the souls that never fell
    To minds that live in happiness
(10)     And do well because they please

    ↑Daring souls↓
    Who dare to fame what is unfamed
    And to do deeds ⟨as yet unnamed⟩ before they're named

[39]               Alphonso
    If I dared advise
    I submit that things are running back
    Things are not good of their kind
    Run to leaves & rind
(5)     See how summer cools & dies
    In the insufficient skies
    Puny man & scentless rose
    ⟨My counsel⟩ ↑Tormenting Pan to double the dose↓
    Do not blot
(10)     Half the suns disc with a spot
    ↑Use↓ A more liberal expense
    Nor starve the skies with indigence
    Teach us ↑now↓ with plenty
    For one sun give us twenty
(15)     I have considered the whole
    And I think
    We must have society
    We cannot spare variety
    But the plague is now too many men
(20)     I think take nine out of ten
    And add the share↑s↓ of them all
    To the /lucky/remnant/ decimal
[40]     Give ↑their↓ nine lives to this cat
    ↑Crowd their↓ Nine brains /under/in/ his hat.

    'Twill never pay to prune & patch;
    Dear Nature, make us a new batch;
(5)     We cannot forego innocence,
    Yet what boots that without good sense

39 "Alphonso of Castile," x, 3, 3–4, 7–8, 25–26, 9–10, x, x, 53–55, x, 57–58, 67–70. Partially erased pencil.

40 "Alphonso of Castile," 71–72, four unused lines, 19/21, x, 22–24. In pencil; lines (1–2) and (7–11) are erased.

You will have noticed the debility
Want of head
Of sense the sterility
(10)    Mighty projects countermanded
Rash ambition broken handed

[41₁]    ↑Oft↓ I followed happy guides
I could never ⟨‖ . . ‖⟩ ↑reach↓ their sides,
Their step is forth and ere the day
Breaks up their leaguer & away
(5)    ‖ . . . . . . ‖ I catch the scent
‖ . . . . . . . . . . . ‖
But no speed of mine avails
To hunt ‖ . . . . . ‖ ⟨‖ . . ‖⟩ ↑shining↓ trails
‖ . . . . . . . . . . . . ‖ feet
(10)    ‖ . . . . . . . . . . . . ‖ & sweet
Flowers they strew I catch the scent
Or tone of silver instrument
Leaves on the wind a ⟨‖ . . . ‖⟩ ↑melodious↓ trace
‖ . . . ‖ the ⟨‖ . . ‖⟩ never see their face
(15)    Above ‖ . . . . . . . ‖ I see their smokes
⟨Which⟩ Mixed with mist by distant lochs
‖ . . . . . . . . . . . . ‖
‖ . . . . . . . . . . . . ‖
↑They↓ ‖ . . . . . ‖ ⟨‖ . ‖⟩my ↑fine↓ revellers
(20)    ‖ . . . . . . ‖ crossed them while they slept
⟨And⟩ ↑Some↓ ‖ . . . . . . . . . ‖
In the country or the court
Fleetest couriers alive

[41₂]             either fill
Of vital force the ⟨‖ . . . ‖⟩ rill
Or throw all back to heap⟨s⟩
to chaos & sleep
(5)    Of vital force ‖ . . . . . ‖ rill
Or tumble all again in heap
To weltering chaos & old sleep

[42]    Never yet could
⟨Yet could ‖ . . . ‖⟩ ↑‖ . . ‖↓ once arrive
As they went or they returned
At the house where these sojourned.

41₁ "Forerunners," 1–4, 11, x?, 7–16, x?, x?, 19–23. In pencil, struck through in pencil and erased.

41₂ "Alphonso of Castile," 27–30, 28–30. Erased pencil; lines (1–4) are struck through in pencil.

42 "Forerunners," 24, 24–38, x, x, x. In pencil; lines (1–2) and (17–19) are erased; the second word in line (16) was heavily crossed out and then erased.

(5)        Sometimes their strong speed they slacken
                  Though they are not overtaken
                  In sleep their jubilant troop is near
                  I tuneful voices overhear
                  It may be in wood⟨s⟩ or waste⟨s⟩
(10)       At unawares 'tis come & passed
                  ⟨And⟩ their near camp my spirit knows
                  By signs gracious as rainbows
                  I thenceforward & long after
                  Listen for their harplike laughter
(15)       And carry in my heart for days
                  A ⟨‖ . . . ‖⟩ peace that hallows rudest ways
                  ⟨They ‖ . . . ‖ all the places⟩
                  ⟨The way is right⟩
                  ⟨And ‖ . . . ‖ is Light⟩

[43]       ⟨O⟩Long I followed happy guides
                  I could never reach their sides,
                  Their step is forth & ere the day
                  Break up their leaguer & away.
(5)        Keen my sense, my heart was young,
                  ⟨Hearty⟩ ⟨↑strong↓⟩ ↑Right↓ goodwill my sinews strung
                  But no speed of mine avails
                  To hunt upon their shining trails
                  On & away their hasting feet
(10)       Make the morning proud & sweet
                  Flowers they strew, I catch the scent,
                  Or tone of silver instrument
                  Leaves on the wind melodious trace
                  Yet I could never see their face.
(15)       On morning hills I see their smokes
                  Mixed with mist by distant lochs
                  I met many travellers
                  Who the road had surely kept
                  They saw not my fine revellers,
(20)       These had crossed them while they slept
                  Some had heard their fair report
                  In the Country or the Court
                  Fleetest couriers alive
                  Never yet could once arrive
                           p 42

[44]    Thanks to the morning light
          Thanks to the foaming sea

43  "Forerunners," 1–24. In pencil.
44  "The World-Soul," 1–21. In pencil.

To the bold uplands of Berkshire
To the forest rustling free
(5)    Thanks to each man of courage
To the maids of holy mind
To the boy with his games undaunted
Who never looks behind.

Cities of proud hotels,
(10)    Houses of rich & great,
A stack of smoking chimneys,
A roof of frozen slate,
It cannot conquer folly
Time & space conquering steam
(15)    And the light outspeeding telegraph
Bears nothing in its beam

The politics are base
The letters do not cheer
And tis far in the deeps of history
(20)    The voice that speaketh clear
Trade & the streets ensnare us
[45]    Our bodies are weak & worn
We plot & corrupt each other
And we despoil the unborn.

Yet there in the parlour sits
(5)    Some figure of ⟨fre⟩noble guise
Our angel in a strangers form
Or womans pleading eyes
Or only a flashing sunbeam
In at the window pane
(10)    Or music pours on mortals
Its beautiful disdain

The inevitable morning
Finds them who in cellars be
And be sure the all-loving Nature
(15)    Will smile in a factory
Yon ridge of purple landscape
Yon sky between the walls
Hold all the hidden wonders
In scanty intervals
(20)    Alas ⟨that⟩ the sprite that haunts us
Deceives our rash desire

45 "The World-Soul," 22–42. In pencil.

[46]    It whispers of the glorious gods
       And leaves us in the mire
       We cannot learn the cipher
       Thats writ upon our cell
(5)    Stars help us by a mystery
       Which we could never spell

       If but one hero knew it
       The world would blush in flame
       The sage till he hit the secret
(10)   Would hang his head for shame
       But our brothers have not ⟨s⟩read it
       Not one has found the key
       And henceforth we are comforted
       We are but such as they

(15)   Still still the secret presses
       The nearing clouds draw down
       The crimson morning flames into
       The fopperies of the town
       ↑Beneath the feigning folly↓
(20)   ↑The Fates sincerely sing↓
       ↑The Heavens themselves roll heartily↓
       ↑And share the joy they bring↓

[47]    ⟨Yet⟩ ↑And↓ what if Trade sow cities
       Like shells along the shore
       And thatch with towns the prairie broad
       With railways ironed o'er
(5)    They are but sailing foambells
       Along thoughts causing stream
       And take their shape & sun colour
       From him that sends the dream

       For Destiny does not like
(10)   To yield to men the helm
       And shoots his thought by hidden nerves
       Throughout the solid realm
       The patient Daemon sits
       With roses and a shroud
(15)   He has his way & deals his gifts
       But ours ⟨ar⟩is not allowed

       He is no churl or trifler
       And his /agents/viceroy/ are none
       Love - without - weakness

46 "The World-Soul," 43–60, x, x, 63–64. In pencil.
47 "The World-Soul," 65–86. In pencil.

(20)      Of Genius sire and son
          And his will is not thwarted
          The seeds of land & sea
[48]     Are the atoms of his body bright
          And his behest obey

          He serveth the servant
          The brave he loves amain
(5)       He kills the cripple & the sick
          And straight begins again
          For gods delight in gods
          And thrust the weak aside
          To him who scorns their charities
(10)     Their arms fly open wide

          When the old world is sterile
          And the Ages are effete
          He will from wrecks & sediment
          The fairer world complete
(15)     He forbids to despair
          His cheeks mantle with mirth
          And the unimagined good of men
          Is yeaning at the birth

          Spring still makes spring in the mind
(20)     When sixty years ⟨is⟩are told,
          Love wakes anew this throbbing heart
[49]     And we are never old.
          Over the winter glaciers
          I see the summer glow
          And through the wild-piled snowdrifts
(5)       The warm rosebuds below

[50]     Verses that ⟨Let⟩ a man may read
          With manly vigor bearing down
          Nor fear a failing verb or noun

          The sun goes down & with him takes
(5)       The ⟨gipsy maidens⟩coarseness of my poor attire
          The fair moon mounts & aye the flame
          Of gipsy beauty blazes higher

          And if I take you dames to task
          And say it frankly without guile

48 "The World-Soul," 87–107. In pencil.
49 "The World-Soul," 108–12. In pencil.
50 "Verses that a man may read" (1–3); "The Romany Girl," 1–4, 9–20 (4–19). Lines (1–3) are in pencil.

(10)        Then you are gypsies in a mask
           And I the lady all the while
           On the wild heath under the moon
           I sport & play with paler blood
           Me false on earth knoweth none
(15)        One ⟨swart⟩sallow horseman knows me good
           Rain from your cheek will wash the ⟨dye⟩
           In teeth & hair the shopmen deal
           My swarthy tint is in the grain
           The rocks & forest know it real

[51₁]      As poet to his printed book
           As lover to his maidens look
           As toilworn husband hasting home
           Climbed I Wachusett's windy dome
(5)         Pure but swift the mountain ⟨air⟩ ↑wind↓
           ⟨Blew incessant⟩ ↑Poured all day↓ its torrent blind
           Yet wheeled aloft the hawk
           His wings transparent in the sun
           Below, the roads & rivers wind
(10)        Pathways of the human kind
           The plains outspread to heaven's rim
           Glittered with lakes, with woods grew dim

           In summer many come
           To my far-appearing dome
(15)        But none in winter time
           Save the dappling shadows climb
           Under clouds my lonely head
           Old as the sun, old almost as the shade
           And comest thou
(20)        To see strange forests & new snow
           And tread uplifted land

[51₂]      My people are grim & fierce
           They are like night & day
           They are not rotten & ⟨weak⟩ false
           Every one is sounder than a king
(5)         They do not totter in the knees
           They fear not to fry or freeze

[52]       ↑And↓ ↑Wouldest thou leave thy lowland race↓
           ↑Here amid clouds to stand↓
           And wouldst be my companion
           Where I gaze

51₁ "Monadnock," twelve unused lines, 213–21. In pencil; lines (13–21) are erased.
51₂ "My people are grim." In pencil.
52 "Monadnock," 222–32, 331–32. In pencil; lines (1–11) are partially erased.

(5)        And shall gaze
               When forests fall and man is ⟨dead⟩ ↑gone↓
               Over tribes & over times
               At the burning Lyre
               Nearing me
(10)       With its stars of Northern fire
               In many thousand years

               Morning wreathes me with light scarf
               When all is fled of dun & dark
[53]       Hither comes the spruce cl⟨a⟩erk
               From square cut streets Mall & park
               From South Cove & City Wharf
               I take him up my rugged sides
(5)        Half repentent scant of breath
               Show him the dangerous granite blocks
               And /the ample map beneath/my summer snow/
               All his county sea & sand
               Dwarfed to measure of his hand
(10)       Harz Forest a tuft
               And London a toybox
               Plant his eyes on the sky hoop bounding
               See there the grim grey rounding
               Of the planet whereon thou sailest
(15)       Tumbling steep
               Down down the Bottomless deep
               He looks on that & turns pale
               Tis even so this treacherous Bullet
               Journeys eyeless on forever
(20)       He ⟨wretched pullet⟩ poor devil
               Cooped in a ship he cannot steer
               Who is the captain he knows not
[54]           Port or pilot trows not
               Then I scowl on him with grey clouds
               I chill him with my northwind
               ↑I lame him among the rocks↓
(5)        And to live he is in fear
               Then at last I let him down
               Once more into his dapper town
               To chatter frightened to his clan
               And forget me if he can

53 "Monadnock," 333, x, 334–38, 340–41, x, x, 344–45, 346/347, 348–50, 351/346, 354–57. In pencil. Slanting pencil lines through the first two words in line (2) may indicate a tentative cancellation.
54 "Monadnock," 358, 360–67. In pencil.

[55] [blank]
[56₁]    ‖ . . . . . . . . . . ‖ forests
        ‖ . . . . . ‖ by ‖ . . . . . . ‖
        In many lands ⟨the⟩ with painful steps
        ↑Ere↓ ‖ . . . . . . . ‖ find a tree

(5)        She ransacked mines & ledges
        And quarried every rock
        To choose the famous adamant
        For each eternal block

[56₂]    ↑Fine presentiments controlled him↓
        ⟨One⟩ ↑He↓ who knew a day was great
        And big with personal fate
        Before one told him
(5)        When first at morn he read the face
        Of nature from his wonted place
        The coming day inspired his speech
        And in his ↑bearing & his↓ gait
        Calm expectancy did wait

(10)     ⟨When Jove⟩ ↑Phoebus↓ his virtue to reward
        Unsealed the senses of ⟨his⟩ ↑the↓ bard

[57₁]    There is no architect
        Can build as ‖ . . . . . ‖
        She is skilful to select
        Materials for her plan
(5)        ↑‖ . . . . ‖↓ ‖ . . . . . . . ‖ use
        ‖ . . . . . . . . ‖ warily to choose
        Rafters of immortal pine
        Or c‖ . . ‖ incorruptible
        W‖ . . . . . . . . ‖ design

(10)     She lays her beams in music,
        In ‖ . . . . . . . . . ‖
        To the cad‖ . . . . . . ‖ world
        Which dances round the Sun

        ‖ . . . . . . ‖ not be displaced
(15)     B‖ . . . . . . . . . . . . ‖
        ‖ . . . . . . . . . . . . . ‖
        Out‖ . . . . . . . . . ‖ stars

56₁ "The House," 9–16. Erased pencil.
56₂ "Fine presentiments," 1–7, 9–10 (1–9); "O happy soul" (10–11). In pencil; lines (1–9) are struck through in pencil.
57₁ "The House," 1–4, x, 5–8, 17–24. Erased pencil.

[57₂]    Vain against him were hostile blows
          He did their weapons decompose
          Aimed at him the blushing blade
          Healed as fast the wounds it made
(5)      On whomsoever fell his gaze
          ⟨Him it would⟩ ↑Power it had to↓ blind & craze

          Fine presentiments controlled him
          As one who knew a day was great
          And freighted with a friendly fate
(10)    Ere whispered news or courier told him
          When first at morn he read the face
          Of nature from his rising place
          The coming day inspired
          And in his bearing & his gait
(15)    Calm expectancy did wait

[58] 20 Sept 1846
          In the turbulent beauty
          Of a /windy/gusty/ autumn day
          Poet on a sunny headland
          Sighed his soul away
(5)      Glimmered ⟨opposite⟩ ↑right in front↓ the mainmast,
          In the dark wood, of a pine
          Rolled ⟨the⟩below the stream unconscious
          Tribute to the brine
          Farms the sunny landscape dappled
(10)    Swandown clouds dappled the farms
          Cattle lowed in ⟨fair⟩ ↑russet↓ distance
          Where far oaks outstre↑t↓ched their arms
          Sudden ⟨winds⟩ ↑gusts↓ came full of meaning
          All too much to him they said
(15)    ↑South↓ Winds have long memories
          Of that be none afraid
          I cannot tell ⟨companions⟩ ↑rude listeners↓
          Half the gossip southwind said
          Twould bring ↑the↓ blushes of yon maples
(20)    To a man & to a maid

[59₁]          *The House*
          There is no architect
          Can build as the Muse can;
          She is skilful to select
          Materials for her plan;

57₂ "Vain against him" (1–7); "Fine presentiments," 1–7, 9–10 (8–16). In pencil.
58 "South Wind," 1–4, four unused lines, 5–16. In pencil.
59₁ "The House," 1–20. Erased pencil.

(5)        Slow & warily to choose
Rafters of immortal pine,
⟨Or⟩ cedar incorruptible,
Worthy her design

She threads ⟨the m‖ . . . ‖⟩ ↑dark Alpine↓ forests
(10)     ↑And↓ ⟨‖ . . . ‖⟩ ‖ . . . . . . . . ‖
In many lands with painful steps
Ere she can find a tree.

She ransacks mines & ledges
And quarries every rock,
(15)    To ⟨‖ . . . ‖⟩ ↑hew↓ the famous adamant
For each eternal block

She lays her beams in music
In music every one
To the cadence of the whirling world
(20)    Which dances round the Sun

[592] 20 Sept. 1846.
In the turbulent beauty
Of a gusty autumn day,
Poet on a sunny headland
Sighed his soul away;
(5)     Glimmered right in front the mainmast
↑(↓In the dark wood,↑)↓ of a pine;
Rolled below the stream unconscious
Tribute to the brine:
Farms the sunny landscape dappled,
(10)    Swandown clouds dappled the farms,
Cattle⟨d⟩ lowed in mellow distance
Where far oaks outstretched their arms
Sudden gusts came full of meaning,
All too much to him they said,
(15)    Southwinds have long memories,
Of that be all afraid.
I cannot tell ⟨rude⟩ ↑lewd↓ listeners
Half the telltale southwind said,
—T'would bring the blushes of yon maples
(20)    To a man & to a maid.

[60₁]    That so they shall not be displaced
By lapses or by ‖ . . . . . . ‖ wars

592 "South Wind," 1–4, four unused lines, 5–16. Lines (5–8) are struck through in ink.
60₁ "The House," 21–24. Erased pencil.

But for the ⟨‖ . . ‖⟩ ↑love↓ of happy souls
Out live the newest stars

[60₂]      What are his machines
Of steel, brass, leather, oak ↑& ivory↓
But ⟨little men,⟩ complements of his ↑perfected↓ limbs,
Dwarfs of one fixed idea, applied to him

(5)      As he applies his bending self
Unto the changing world, thus making that
A larger tool to his victorious will.
He built his mills & by his politics made
The arms of millions turn them,

(10)      New Hampshire mother of men
Sea-dented Maine, reluctant Carolina,
Must drag his car. And by ⟨the⟩ arts of peace
And in the plenitude of love & honor
Eats up the poor. ↑Much has he done already↓ He has made
        his telegraph

(15)      Propeller, car, post office, photograph,
His coast survey, vote by majority,
His life assurance, and star registry,
Preludes & hints of what he yet prepares;
Now let him make a Harp.

[61]                 *The Skeptic*                        See P. 77
Not one has surmounted
The Destiny yet;
Not one has accounted
To Conscience his debt.

(5)      Many in the dark have groped,
Many for the dawn have hoped,
And some more brave, or else more blind,
The freedom all desire, pretend to find.

Each hears the Siren whisper; he,
(10)      Though first of men, shall yet be free,
That one of their own stem,
Man of Ur or Bethlehem
Jove or Alcides,                         ↑Ignatius or Luther↓
↑Buddh↓ Mahmoud or Moses,           ↑Swedenborg Behmen↓
                                        ↑Knox Fox or Wesley↓

---

60₂ "New England Capitalist." In pencil; the cancellations and additions in lines (2–3) are in ink.

61 "The Skeptic," 17–24, 29–38, 42–43. In pencil. "See [notebook] P. 77" is set off by a wavy line in pencil; "Ignatius . . . Wesley" is added to the right of lines (13–14) and set off by a vertical line in pencil.

(15)    From their eye shall pluck the beam
And their heart from death redeem,
But Destiny sat still,
And had her will.

Those in whom thou dost confide,
(20)    Those thy love has deified

[62₁]    I can spare the college bell
And the learned lecture well
All the clergy & libraries
Academies & dictionaries
(5)    For that ⟨stoutest⟩ ↑hardy↓ English root
⟨F‖ . ‖ing⟩ ↑Thrives↓ here unvalued underfoot

[62₂]    With a superabundant trust,
Their words are wind, their forms are dust,
O thousand blossomed ⟨but⟩ barren tree
Much pretending, helped they thee?

(5)    And ever when a human brain
Its perfect purpose will attain,
The pitiless
Performance-hating Nemesis
Withdraws the world like painted slide
(10)    And a new world is ⟨still⟩ supplied.

[63₁]    Rallying round a parish steeple
The country people
Nestle warm
By hill & farm
(5)    Coarse obscene, but mild
Strong as ‖ . . . . . ‖ as child
Smoking in a ‖ . . . . . . ‖ room
Wh‖ . . . . . . . . . . . ‖
Fourscore or a hundred words
(10)    All their ⟨st‖ . . ‖⟩ ↑vocal↓ Muse affords
⟨But⟩ they ‖ . . . . . . . ‖ fashion
Than ‖ . . . . . . . . . ‖
Rude poets of the tavern hearth
Squandering your unquoted mirth
(15)    Which keeps the ground & never soars
Jake retorts & ‖ . . . ‖ roars
Tough ‖ . . . . . . . . ‖ bark

62₁ "Monadnock," 189–94. In pencil, struck through in pencil and erased.
62₂ "The Skeptic," 44–47, 54–59. In pencil.
63₁ "Monadnock," 135–36, 136, x, 137–40, 185–88, 195–206. Erased pencil.

Goes like ⟨a⟩ bullet to its mark
⟨With⟩ ↑While↓ its solid curse & jeer
(20)    Never baulks the waiting ear
To city ears keen relished jokes
On ‖ . . . ‖ & stock & farming folks
Nought the mountain yields thereof
But savage health & sinews tough

[63₂]    ⟨Loyola⟩ ↑Ignatius↓ or Luther
Swedenborg Behmen
Fox, ⟨or⟩ Knox, or Wesley

        What are his machines
(5)    Of steel brass ⟨leather⟩ ↑bullhide↓ oak ↑& ivory↓
But manikins & miniatures
Dwarfs of one ⟨fixed idea applied to⟩ ↑faculty measured
        from↓ him
As ↑nimbly↓ he applies his bending self
Unto the changing world, thus making that,
(10)    ⟨A⟩ ↑Another↓ weapon ⟨also⟩ of his conquering will.
He built his mills, & by his politics made
The arms of millions turn them.
        New Hampshire mother of men
Seadented Maine, reluctant Carolina,
(15)    Must drag his car, &, by the arts of peace,
⟨And⟩ ↑He↓ in the plenitude of love & honor
Eats up the poor. Much has he done
Has made his telegraph
Propeller, car, post office, photo⟨graph,⟩ ↑type, ↓
(20)    His coast survey, vote by majority,
His life-assurance, & star-registry,
Preludes & hints of what he ⟨yet prepares⟩ ↑next intends↓.
Now let him make a harp!

[64]–[65] [blank]
[66]    Boding
He invented occult science
And is in alliance
With sorcery
(5)    He keeps his fine ear strained
For intelligence
Out of Asia & Egypt

---

63₂ "The Skeptic," three unused lines (1–3); "New England Capitalist," 1–13, 14/15, 16–21
(4–23). Lines (1–3) are in pencil; in line (22), "next intends" was added at the bottom of facing
p. [62].
66 "The Initial Love," x, 64, x, 65?, 66, 68, six unused lines, 69, 65, x, x, 70–73. In pencil.

He can reckon
Nativities ↑Horoscope↓
(10)　Dark people ⟨sigh⟩ ↑wink↓ & beckon
And give him hints
Sortilege, sounds & tints
Coincidence
Clairvoyance
(15)　Second sight & undersong
To his ⟨domain⟩ ↑empery↓ belong
But that which touches his heart
Is /the adhesion of Fate to/When Fate by omens takes/ his
　　　part
When /omens from another/chance dropt hints from
　　　nature's/ sphere
(20)　Deeply soothe his anxious ear

[67₁]　He is read in occult science
In magic & clairvoyance
He keeps his fine ear st‖ . . . ‖
And ‖ . . . ‖ing for intelligence
(5)　And for strange coincidence
‖ . . . . . . . . . . . ‖
Things[?] ‖ . . . . . . . . ‖
‖ . . . . . . . . . . . . ‖

Se‖ . . . . . . . . . . . ‖
(10)　To ‖ . . . . ‖ curse
‖ . . . . . . . . . . . . . . . . . ‖ heart
When Fate by omens takes his part
When chance dropped hints from natures sphere
Deeply soothe his anxious ear

[67₂]　　　I am the Muse
I stood by Jove at the first

I am the bird who sung ↑alway↓
In the twilight of the first ⟨morning⟩ ↑day↓
(5)　If all is ravished & bereft
I make amends if I am left

Long I wrought
To infuse the stagnant lump with thought
Slow at last the chaos fails
(10)　Snake & dragon shed their scales

　　　The sun & planets poured amain

67₁ "The Initial Love," 64–66, 68–69, five unused lines?, 70–73. Erased pencil.
67₂ "Solution," 1–2, 1–2, x, x, 3–4, x, 6 (1–10); "Charmed from fagot," 5–7 (11–13). Lines
(11–13) are in pencil.

Like ripened seeds into his brain
There quickened to be born again

[68]     I am the Muse who sung alway
⟨I stood⟩ by Jove, at ↑dawn of↓ the first day
⟨I have a⟩ ↑Blaze of my↓ torch ⟨that eclipses⟩ ↑puts out↓ the
    sun
⟨If all else is⟩ ↑Though men of health & wealth↓ bereft
(5)     ⟨I make⟩ ↑All have↓ amends if I am left
↑Nature was blockish & brute↓
↑All was plastic but all was mute↓
Long I wrought
To ⟨animate⟩quicken the stagnant lump with thot
(10)     At last ⟨the⟩ electric ⟨fire⟩ ↑heat↓ prevails
⟨Snake & dragon shed⟩ ↑Wolves shed their fangs & snakes↓
    their scales
⟨And Man is born⟩
↑Earth smiled with flowers & man is born↓
Then Asia spawned her shepherd race
(15)     ⟨T⟩And Thebes substructs her granite base,
Tented Tartary, columned Nile,
Last ⟨by⟩ from vines on rocky isle
Or the windblown sea-marge bleak
Forward stepped the Perfect Greek
[69]     That will, wit, joy might find a tongue
And Earth grow civil, Homer sung.
Pleased the Planet hummed the tunes
⟨And found⟩ ↑Which held↓ all good beneath the moon

(5)     ⟨I passed in⟩ ↑Flown↓ to Italy, from Greece
And long ⟨forbore to sing.⟩ ↑held my peace↓
For ⟨my manner is⟩ ↑tis my wont↓
To sing uncalled,
And, in ↑days of↓ evil ⟨times,⟩ ↑plight↓
(10)     ⟨To open⟩ ↑Unlock↓ new doors of delight,
And sometimes to appal
With terrors better than hope.
⟨Then I clothed me with vast fears⟩
⟨And Dante searched the triple spheres⟩
(15)     By thoughts I lead
Bards to speak what nations need
And I clothed me with vast fears
And Dante searched the triple spheres

68 "Solution," 1–2, five unused lines, 3–6, 8, 8–14. This page is reproduced in Plate 3.
69 "Solution," 15–16, x, x, 17–19, 19–22, 24, 27–28, 25–28.

[70₁]    The heavens themselves roll heartily
        And share the joy they bring

        Bronze, bronze, pure gold never

            his tyranny
(5)    Burns up every other tie

        Wandering lodges

        though all fair things that fair resemble
        though with pure passion nature tremble

[70₂]    Hark to him yet
        Mountains roll to him like seawaves
        He deals with nature as he wills
        Nature moulds herself to him
(5)    As if he made it
        And he like a sculptor ↑his design↓
        Etches ⟨his words⟩ on Alp & Appenine

        ⟨Again was⟩ silence ↑brooded↓ in my heaven
        For seven times seventy & seven
(10)   Silence prelude of /a song/such following/
        ⟨For⟩ ↑Well worth ⟨su⟩↓ such strain ⟨need was⟩ to ⟨wait⟩
          ↑tarry↓ long
        Seethed in ⟨the⟩ mists of Penmanmaur,
        Taught by Plinlimmon's ⟨bards of⟩ ↑druid↓ Power,
        The voice of England filled all measure
(15)   Of heart & soul of strength & pleasure,
        Gave to the mind its emperor
        And life was larger than before.
        Nor sequent centuries could hit
        Orbit or sum of Shakspeares wit
(20)   The men who lived with him became
        Poets for the air was fame.

[71] Intellect is one & unifying; that is his prerogative; whilst love is
ever dualizing.
Twinborn in every paradise

        Far in the north where Polar night
        ⟨Checks⟩Holds in check the frolic light
        With dreams transcending mortal goal
        The Swedish Prophet leads the soul,

70₁ "The World-Soul," 63–64 (1–2); "Bronze, bronze" (3); "The Daemonic and the Celestial
Love," 144–45 (4–5); unidentified line (6); "Though all fair things," 1–2 (7–8). In pencil.
  70₂ "Solution," x, x, 29, 29, x, 31–32, four unused lines, 33–42.
  71 "Solution," 43–49, x, 53–56, 59–61, 63–64. The prose is in pencil.

(5) Through snows above, mines underground,
   The inks of Erebus he found
   And mid infernal wails
   To hear the Lamb's song scarce avails
   They that stood near him heard no sound
(10) But they who ⟨stood ↑far↓⟩ ↑listened far↓ aloof
   Heard thunders as of the sky roof
   And felt uneath the quaking ground

   In newer days of War & Trade
   Romance forgot & Faith decayed
(15) When science armed & guided War
   And France where poet never grew
   Halved & assigned the globe anew

[72] Many fine fancies
   A saint sometimes
   He woos with saintly homage clear
   A vestal & a mountaineer
(5) Beauty in marble walls enshrined
   ↑There↓ Would meet her as a queen
   With reverend ceremony seen

   Calm in the thunder of the strife
   Goethe ⟨drew⟩ chants the song of life
(10) And brought Olympian Wisdom down
   To court & mart↑,↓ to gown & town
   ⟨Writes with his⟩ ↑Stoop⟨s &⟩ing his↓ finger ↑wrote↓ in
    ⟨the sand⟩ ↑clay↓
   The ⟨oracle⟩ open secret of Today

   Every good below preexists above

[73] Past present future shoot
   Triple flowers from one root
   Substances at base divided
   In their summits are united

(5) By right or wrong
   Lands & goods to the strong
   Property will draw
   Still to the proprietor

   When those calm eyes opened bright

72 "Many fine fancies" (1–7); "Solution," 65, 65/66, 67–70 (8–13); "Every good below" (14). Lines (1–7) and (14) are in pencil; the comma in line (11) is in pencil. In line (1), Emerson appears to have written "fanee's".
73 "The Daemonic and the Celestial Love," 178–81, 211–14, 17–18 (1–10); "If he go apart," 1–9 (11–19). In pencil; lines (1–8) are struck through in pencil.

(10)      All were foreign in their light

If he go apart
And tear the foible from his heart
And with himself content
Live in the deed & not the event
(15)      He shall thus himself erect
Into a tower of intellect
Farseen farseeing circumspect
Star specular high & clear
And to thyself more justly dear
[74]    Than if thy heart with soft alarms
Did palpitate within his arms

Nature will not lose
In any ends she doth propose
(5)      But if thou thy debt decline
Will mulct thee with a fine
If thou refuse to bring forth men

Dear child the place
The place is with thy beauty wild
(10)     Thou spendest thyself everywhere
And flowest into waves of air

[75]       The crowning hour when bodies vie with souls
And bifold essence rushes to its poles

Plain & cold is their address
Power have they for tenderness
(5)      And so thoroughly known
Is the other by his own
They have no need of greeting
Words or forms in meeting
But they communicate
(10)     In their innermost estate

[76₁]       proud & shy

⟨They⟩ ↑There↓ need ⟨not⟩ ↑no↓ ⟨mutual⟩ vows to bind
Who not each other seek but find

What revelation in the glance

74 "If he go apart," 10–11 (1–2); "Nature will not lose" (3–7); "Dear child the place"
(8–11). In pencil. In line (1), the evidently unrelated word "Rhyme" is erased under "Than".
   75 "The crowning hour" (1–2); "The Daemonic and the Celestial Love," 225–28, 230, 229,
231–32 (3–10). In pencil; lines (3–10) are struck through in pencil.
   76₁ "The Initial Love," 88/89? (1); "The Daemonic and the Celestial Love," 219–20, four
unused lines, 17–19, x, 21–22 (2–13). In pencil.

(5)    He seemed surrounded
By many friends in strict bonds
Blood was a ⟨strict⟩ ↑tender↓ tie
When those calm eyes opened bright
All were foreign in their light
(10)   It was ever the old tale
The world old fact
Only two in the garden walked
With the twain the Godhead talked

[76₂]      I am the Muse who sung alway
By Jove, at dawn of the first day,
Blaze of my torch puts out the sun,
I soothe the sick, heal the undone
(5)    ⟨Were men⟩ ↑The world↓ of health & wealth bereft
All have amends, if I am left.
⟨Once the globe was blockish and brute⟩
⟨All was plastic but all was mute.⟩
↑Star crowned, sole sitting↓
(10)   Long I brooded, long I wrought
To fire the stagnant lump with Thought
⟨At last electric heat⟩ ↑On creeping monsters song↓ prevails
Wolves shed their fangs; & dragons, scales;
Flamed in the sky ⟨a lovelier morn⟩ ↑the sweet May morn↓
(15)   Earth smiled ⟨in⟩with flowers, & man was born
Then Asia spawn⟨ed⟩s her shepherd race
And Thebes substructs her granite base

[77₁]    They erring paint love blind
The sharpest sighted of the gods
Who bewilders all
Whom none can bewilder
(5)    He sees thro the solid Universe
Pathfinder   road builder
He can come at his own

⟨Many feet⟩ ↑Heralds nigh↓ before him run
He has ushers many a one
(10)   He touches all things with his hue
All prophesy & divine him
Shall I dare to malign him
I must ⟨him⟩ end my ⟨task⟩ ↑report↓
And report him from head to foot

76₂ "Solution," 1–2, six unused lines, 3, 3–10. Struck through in ink.
77₁ "The Daemonic and the Celestial Love," 94, 96, x, 97, 98/99, 100, x (1–7); "The Initial Love," 74–75, 77–79, 81–85, x, 86 (8–19). In pencil. In line (11), Emerson wrote "& & divine".

(15) In as far as I took note
  Trusting well his matchless power
  Of this youthful emperor
  Tyrannous & proud
  Can clear his shield from every cloud

[77₂] Tented Tartary, columned Nile;
  ⟨Last, from⟩ ↑And under↓ vines, on rocky isle,
  Or on windblown seamarge bleak,
  Forward stepped the perfect Greek.
(5) That wit & joy might find a tongue
  And earth grow civil, Homer sung.

  Flown to Italy, from Greece
  I brooded long & held my peace
  For ⟨tis my⟩ ↑I am↓ wont to sing uncalled
(10) And in days of evil plight
  ⟨To⟩ unlock doors of new delight
  And sometimes mankind I appal
  With terrors better than hope

  Then by thoughts I lead
(15) Bards to speak what nations need
  So I folded me in fears
  And Dante searched the triple spheres

[78]  Hark to him yet
  He ⟨deals with⟩ ↑moulded↓ nature /as he/at his/ will
  Tis shaped or colored, flowing or still
  And he, like sculptor, his design
(5) Etches on Alp or Appenine

  Silence brooded in my heaven
  For seven times seventy & seven
  Prelude of ⟨such⟩ ↑the↓ following song
  Well worth such strain to tarry long.

(10) Seethed in mists of Penmanmaur
  Taught by Plinlimmon's druid power
  The voice of England filled all measure
  Of heart & soul of strength & pleasure
  Gave to the mind its emperor,
(15) And life was larger than before.

[79] And as the light divided the dark

77₂ "Solution," 11–22, 24–28. Struck through in ink.
78 "Solution," x, 29–32, four unused lines, 33–38. Lines (1–5) and (10–15) are struck through in ink.
79 "And as the light" (1–4); "Solution," 39–52 (5–18). Lines (1–4) are in pencil; lines (5–18) are struck through in ink.

Thorough with living swords
So shalt thou pierce the distant age
With adamantine words.

(5)    Nor sequent centuries could hit
Orbit or sum of Shakspeare's wit;
The men who lived with him became
Poets, for the air was fame.

Far in the North, where polar night
(10)   Holds in check the frolic light,
With trances passing mortal goal,
The Swede Emanuel leads the soul.
Through snows above, mines underground,
The inks of Erebus he found.
(15)   Rehearsed to men the damned wails
Oer all the seraph song prevails
Rapt into spirit worlds alone
He walked the earth unmarked unknown

[80₁]   ‖ . . . . . . . ‖ moist & cold
[five lines of erased pencil writing]
‖ . . . . . . . . . . . ‖ turn[?]
‖ . . . . . . . . ‖ each other
[five lines of erased pencil writing]
‖ . . . . . . . . . . . ‖ eyes[?]
(15)   ‖ . . . . . . . . . . . ‖
And they glanced paradise
When they ‖ . . . . . . . ‖
But they ‖ . . . . . . . . ‖
‖ . . . . ‖ without any bound
(20)   ‖ . . . . . . . . . . . ‖ orb
‖ . . . . . . . . . ‖ of the ‖ . . . ‖
The light that ye ‖ . . . ‖ & ye ‖ . . ‖
Shall as thorough from the Willing
the Universe to the same

[80₂]       ↑Merlin↓
The Rhyme of the poet
Modulates the kings affairs
Balance loving Nature
Made all things in pairs

---

80₁ "The Daemonic and the Celestial Love," x, five unrecovered lines, x?, 29?, five unrecovered lines, 37?, x?, 40/39?, x?, x?, 42, x?, 44, 45?, 47?, 48. In pencil, struck through in pencil and erased.

80₂ "Merlin II," 1–4, 6, 5, 7–11, 16–19. Erased pencil. After line (14), the word "eyes" appears in light, unerased pencil.

(5)     Each colour ⟨‖ . . ‖⟩ ↑with↓ its counter ⟨‖ . . . ‖⟩ glowed
Each foot with antipode
Every ‖ . . . . . . . . ‖
Higher or graver
‖ . . . ‖ flavor with flavor
(10)   Leaf answers leaf upon the bough
And the paired cotyledons
Lights far furnace shines
Smelting balls & bars
Forging double stars
(15)   Glittering twins & trines

[80₃]   ⟨They⟩
The bystander caught no sound
But they who listened far aloof
Heard rendings of the sky roof
(5)     And felt beneath the quaking ground
And words in water writ became
In the next ages ⟨words of⟩ ↑living↓ flame

In newer days of war & trade
Romance forgot & faith decayed
(10)   When science armed & guided war
⟨And statesmen⟩
And clerks the Janus gates unbar
When France where poet never grew
Halved & dispart⟨ed⟩s ⟨earth⟩the globe anew
(15)   Wise Goethe raised oer joy & strife
Drew the deep lines of Fate & life
And brot olympian wisdom down
To courts & marts to town & gown.
Stooping, his finger wrote in clay
(20)   The open secret of today.

[81₁]   ‖ . . . . . . . . . . . . ‖
‖ . . . . . . . . . . . . ‖
‖ . . . . . . . . . . . ‖
‖ . . . ‖ ↑the↓ ‖ . . ‖ daemon⟨s⟩ ↑treads↓
(5)     ‖ . . . . . . . . . . . . ‖
‖ . . . . . . . . . . . . ‖
‖ . . . . . . . . ‖ . . . . . . . . ‖
‖ . . . . . . . . . ‖ Daemon
‖ . . . . . . . ‖ know the path[?] lost

80₃ "Solution," x, 53–61, x, 62–70.
81₁ "The Daemonic and the Celestial Love," eight unrecovered lines, 65/66?, x?, x?, 67?, 70, 73–76?, five unrecovered lines. In pencil, struck through in pencil and erased.

(10)      ‖ . . . . . . . . . . . . ‖
          ‖ . . . . . . . . . . . . ‖
          And ‖ . . . . . . ‖ pass to & fro.
          ‖ . . . . . . . . ‖ choir descends
          ‖ . . . . . . . . . . ‖ thoughts
(15)      ‖ . . . . . . . . . ‖ of meteors
          ‖ . . . . . . . . . . . . . ‖th
          ‖ . . . . . . . . ‖ the friction of air
          [five lines of erased pencil writing]

[81₂]                     *Merlin*
          The rhyme of the poet
          Modulates the kings affairs
          Music ‖ . . . . . . . . ‖
          Made all things in pairs
(5)       Each color has its counterpart
          And each sound & tone
          Flavor ‖ . . . ‖ with flavor
          ⟨‖ . . . ‖⟩ and the paired cotyledon
          The abyss shines
(10)      ↑Smelts ‖ . . ‖ & ‖ . . . ‖↓
          ‖ . . . . . . . . . . . . ‖
          ↑Glittering twins & trines↓
          All animals are sick ⟨with love⟩
          Lovesick with rhyme
(15)      And ‖ . . . . . . . ‖ of time
          With ‖ . . . . . . . . . ‖
          Thoughts come also ⟨‖ . . . . ‖⟩ ↑hand in hand↓
          Or in pairs mated              ↑mates↓
          Or else alternated
(20)      Each ‖ . . . . . . . . ‖
          The other ‖ . . . . . . . ‖
          B‖ . . . . . . . . . . ‖
          ‖ . . ‖ thought ‖ . . . . ‖
          Wandering thro the ‖ . . . . ‖
(25)      As ↑sad↓ bachelors
          And lonely maids
          Not ancestors

[81₃]     ⟨And these⟩
          So ⟨blooms⟩ ↑blossomed↓ the five petalled flower
          Which draws the nations to my bower
          So writ the legends that endure

81₂ "Merlin II," 1–2, x?, 4, 6–7, 9, 11, 16–17, x?, 19–23, 25–27, x?, 29?, x?, x?, 31–34.
Erased pencil.
81₃ "Solution," several trials of 71–72. Lines (1–3) are struck through in ink.

(5) So bloomed the unfading petals five
So ⟨legends⟩ shone the legends that /survive/outlive/
And these the legends
And these the lines that all outlive
   verses that all verse outlive

[82₁] Also ‖ . . . . . . ‖ the wrath
‖ . . . . . . . . . ‖ be averted
Also ‖ . . . . . . . . ‖
‖ . . . . . . . . . . . . ‖
(5) ‖ . . . . . . . . . . . . ‖
‖ . . . . ‖ is as a ‖ . . . . ‖
‖ . . . . . . ‖ he ‖ . . . . . ‖
He is ‖ . . . . . . . . ‖
‖ . . . . . . . . . . . . ‖
(10) ↑In the great eye of ‖ . . . ‖↓ ‖ . . . . . . . . . . ‖
It ‖ . . . . . . . . . . . . . . ‖ tyranny
‖ . . . . . . . . . . . . . . . . ‖ burns up other tie
‖ . . . . . . . . . . ‖
‖ . . . . . . . . ‖ & star
(15) Thou must mount for love
‖ . . . ‖ a region where the wheel
‖ . . . . . . . . . . . ‖
‖ . . . . . . . . . . . ‖
‖ . . . . . . . . ‖ revolve
(20) Where ‖ . . . . . . . . ‖
‖ . . . . . . . . ‖; and hatred
‖ . . . . . . . . . . . . ‖
‖ . . . . . . . . . . . . . ‖
To melt into one
(25) The whole creation through

[82₂] Every thought kindling with life
Sea[?] ‖ . . . . . . ‖ for its wife
As newfledged insects fly & run
To find their fellows in the sun
(5) Thoughts without ‖ . . . . . ‖ born
↑Sons↓ ↑Of Deity, unwived↓
Limp ‖ . . . . . . . . . . ‖
Wanting ‖ . . . . . . . . ‖ remembrance
And ‖ . . . . . . . . . . ‖

82₁ "The Daemonic and the Celestial Love," 88–89, 88?, seven unidentified lines, 144–45, x?, 164, 166, 169, x?, x?, 171–72, x?, x?, x?, 177, x. In pencil, struck through in pencil and erased.
82₂ "Every thought kindling." Erased pencil.

(10)    T‖ . . . . . . . . ‖ keep house
In the lovely earth
Two horses in a team
Tis but joy fully abreast
But they neigh when parted
(15)    Hearty hearted
The ‖ . . . . . . . . ‖
Rhyme of their ‖ . . . ‖ like ‖ . . . . ‖
‖ . . . . . . . . . . . . ‖
⟨And⟩ ↑Two↓ married ‖ . . . . . ‖
(20)    In ‖ . . . . . . . . ‖ society meet

[82₃]    ⟨Nor mothers⟩
And no posterity to make the earth afraid
Or keep it undecayed

[83₁]    ⟨T⟩P‖ . . . . . . . ‖ future shoot
triple blossoms from one root
Substances at base divided
In their summits are united
(5)    There quarrels cease
In the beatific peace
There ‖ . . . . . . . . ‖ rolls
‖ . . . . . . . . . . . ‖ed souls
Th‖ . . . . . ‖ sunshine of ‖ . . . . ‖
(10)    ‖ . . . . . . . . . . . . ‖
Known in part or in ‖ . . . . . ‖
‖ . . . . . . . . . . . . ‖
‖ . . . . . . . . . . . . ‖
‖ . . . . . . . . . . . . ‖
(15)    Or ‖ . . . . . . . . . ‖
Are ‖ . . . . . . . . . ‖own
‖ . . . . . . . . . . . . ‖
‖ . . . . . . ‖ Palace ‖ . . . . ‖
The circles of that sea ‖ . . . . . ‖
(20)    And ‖ . . . ‖ in ‖ . . . . . . ‖

[83₂]    The ⟨balance⟩ ↑Scale↓ of Justice is the rhyme of things
Paired as the eagle's wings
Trade & Counting use
The selfsame tuneful muse

82₃ "Merlin II," x, 35–36. Erased pencil.
83₁ "The Daemonic and the Celestial Love," 178–81, x, x, 182–83, 184?, x?, 187, x?, x?, x?, 191–92, x?, x?, 194, x? Erased pencil.
83₂ "Merlin II," 38, 37, 39–42, x, 43–46, x?, 48–49. In pencil, struck through in pencil; lines (12–14) are erased.

(5)     And Nemesis
          With even matches odd
          With thunderstroke
          Athwart space redresses
          The partial wrong
(10)    Fills the just period
          And finishes the song

          ‖ . . . . . . . . . ‖
          P‖ . . . . . ‖ of the house of life
          ↑⟨Airs⟩ Sung by↓ The ⟨‖ . . . . ‖⟩ ‖ . . . . . ‖

[84₁]   Pray for a beam
          Out of that sphere
          Thee to create & to redeem

          O what a load
(5)     Of care & toil
          By ‖ . . . ‖ use bestowed
          ⟨Falls⟩ from ‖ . . . ‖ shoulders ↑falls↓ who sees
          The true astronomy
          The period of peace
(10)    The counsel which the ages kept
          He ‖ . . . . . . . ‖ accept
          The fortunes of men
          They ‖ . . . . . . . ‖
          ‖ . . ‖ the ‖ . . . . . . ‖
(15)    ‖ . . ‖ the water ‖ . . ‖ with ‖ . . . . ‖
          By right or wrong
          Lands & goods go to the strong
          Property will draw
          Silver to silver
(20)    And kind to kind

[84₂]   Extremes of nature reconciled

          Great the art
          Great be the manners of the bard
          He shall not his brain encumber
(5)     For the he↑i↓ght of rhythm & number
          Leaving rule & pale forethought
          He must aye climb
          For his rhyme
          Pass in, pass in, the angels say

---

84₁ "The Daemonic and the Celestial Love," 196–206, 210, 210?, x?, 208?, 211–13, 215–16. Erased pencil.
84₂ "Merlin I," 52, 27–38, x, x. In pencil.

(10)    In to the upper doors
        Nor count compartments of the floors
        But mount to Paradise
        By the stairway of surprise
        The daring bard
(15)    Ever the muses will reward

[85₁]   There need no vows to bind
        Whom not each other seek but find
        They give & take no pledge ‖ . . . . ‖
        For day ‖ . . . . . . ‖ there ‖ . . . . ‖
(5)     The seer & the seen
        Are the ‖ . . . . . ‖ns

        Not with flowers
        Or perfumed gloves or gems
        Do these celebrate their loves
(10)    Not with selfish preferences
        ⟨But love maketh ‖ . . . . . ‖⟩
        Not by ribbons or by favors
        But by the ‖ . . . . . . . ‖
        B‖ . . . . . . . . ‖ strong
(15)    F‖ . . . . . . . . . . . . ‖
        And ‖ . . . . . ‖ of the times
        ‖ . . . . . . ‖ not ‖ . . . . ‖
        ‖ . . . . . . . . . . . . ‖
        ‖ . . . . . . . . . . . ‖
(20)    ‖ . . . . . . . . . . . . ‖ted
        The ‖ . . . . . . . . . . ‖
        And the ‖ . . . . . . . . ‖

[85₂]   Seek not to weave strong rhymes
        In sickly times
        Wait thy returning strength
        Merlin's mighty line
(5)     Would make a lion mild
        Bereave a tyrant of his will
        Songs can the tempest still
        Scattered on the stormy air
        Mould the year to fair increase
(10)    And lead in poetic peace

        Nor affect to hit
        /To achieve/Or compass/ that by meddling wit

85₁ "The Daemonic and the Celestial Love," 219–21, three unused lines, 235, 235–36, x, x, 238–39, nine unidentified lines. Erased pencil.
85₂ "Merlin I," 59/61, 60, 62, 51, 54, 53, 55–58, 66–71, 72/73, 74/75, 76–77. In pencil.

Which only the propitious mind
Publishes when 'tis inclined
(15)    There are open hours
When the Gods will ⟨dances⟩ ↑sallies↓ free
The /mole/dunce/ can see   ↑The fortunes of a thousand
        years↓
Then suddenly the hours shut
⟨And the⟩ ↑Nor↓ word of angels could ⟨not⟩ reveal
(20)    What they conceal

[86₁]    And they serve men austerely
After their own tendency clearly
And this is true nobility
Not to scatter bread & ⟨m⟩honey
(5)    Cloth & fuel corn & honey
But in the world to speak the truth
And dare to do the right
For he that feeds men serveth few
He serves all who ⟨speaks⟩ dares be true

[86₂]    The river knows the way
Trust the beast that carries thee

    For things more cheerly live & go
When the subtle mind
(5)    Plays aloud the tune whereto
Their pulses beat ⟨their⟩
And march their feet
And their /statures/members/ are com/bined/posed/

[87]    And this this thou must learn
That true Love hates temperance
And asks nothing. He cannot sue
But that which by him is wanted
(5)    ⟨Is in that moment granted⟩
↑Is↓ Ever on the instant granted

[88]    When devils bite
A damned parasite
Strikes at their throat & stings them home

[89]    Himself it was who wrote
His rank & quartered his own coat

86₁ "The Daemonic and the Celestial Love," 257–58, 260–61, x, 263/264, x, 267–68. Erased pencil.
86₂ "The river knows the way" (1–2); "Merlin I," 43–48 (3–8). In pencil; lines (3–8) are partially erased.
87 "The Daemonic and the Celestial Love," six unused lines. Erased pencil.
88 "When devils bite." In pencil.
89 "Astraea," 1–5, x, 7–23. In pencil.

There is no king nor sovereign state
That can fix a hero's rate
(5)    But he is there venerable
Armed unassailable
Until he write where all eyes rest
Fool or felon on his breast

I saw men go up & down
(10)    In the country & in town
With this need on their neck
Judgment & a judge we seek
Not to monarchs they repair
Nor to learned jurists chair
(15)    But they hurry to their peers
To their kinsfolk & their dears
Louder than with speech they pray
What am I? companion, say,
And the friend not hesitates
(20)    To assign just place & mates
Tho' answering not in word or letter
He is understood the better
He is to them a looking-glass
[90]    Giving the figure that doth pass
Therein the curious eye doth look
And read his fate in a true book
⟨And⟩ every passer whom he meets
(5)    /That which he/What himself/ declared repeats
⟨Sentences him in his words⟩
↑⟨That which⟩ ↑What himself↓ he confessed records↓
Sentences him in his words
The form is his own ⟨corporal⟩ form
(10)    And his mind is the penal worm

Shine forever virgin minds
Loved by stars & purest winds
↑Which↓ Above all passion high sedate
Have not ⟨c⟩hazarded their state
(15)    Baffle the searching of a spy
And render to an asking eye
The durance of a granite ledge
To those who gaze from the sea's edge
It is there for benefit
(20)    It is there for purging light
There for restoring storms

90 "Astraea," 24, x, x, 25–26, 28, 27–43. In pencil; lines (9–10) are struck through in pencil.

And its lakes reflect all comers
But it cannot exist for meanness
[91]    For tho' it is lone & unvisited
The Angel of Justice
Haunts also the mountain tarn

[92]         Good Heart that ownest all!
I ask ⟨for what is⟩ ↑a modest boon &↓ small,
Not of lands & towns the gift,
Too large a load for me to lift,
(5)    But for one proper creature
Which geographic eye
Sweeping the map of western earth
Or the ⟨Virginian⟩ ↑Atlantic↓ coast ↑from Maine↓
⟨And⟩ ↑To↓ Powhatan's domain,
(10)    Could not descry.
Is't much to ask in all thy huge creation
So ⟨miniature⟩ ↑trivial↓ a part,
A solitary heart?
Yet count me not of spirit mean
(15)    Or mine a mean demand,
[93]    For tis the concentration
And worth of all the land,
The sister of the sea,
The daughter of the strand,
(5)    Composed of air & light,
And of the swart earth-might;
So little to ⟨my⟩ ↑thy poet's↓ prayer
⟨Thou canst well⟩ ↑Thy large bounty well can↓ spare:
And yet, ↑I think↓ if she were gone,
(10)    The world were better left alone.

[94]         The worldsoul

The Master said, I will explore
If I have any unexpended store
Of colours & of harmonies.

         If there be any light upon the sea,
(5)    or on the mountains,
or in household affairs,
or in venerable morals,
So that speech may still vie with nature

---

91 "Astraea," x, 47, 46? In pencil.
92 "Lover's Petition," 1–15. Struck through in pencil.
93 "Lover's Petition," 16–25. Struck through in pencil.
94 "The worldsoul" ("The Master said"). In pencil.

[95]    I cannot leave
        My honied thought
        ⟨N⟩For the priests cant
        Or statesman's rant

(5)      If I refuse
        My study for their politic
        Which at the best is trick
        The angry muse
        Puts confusion in my brain

(10)    But who is he that prates
        Of the culture of mankind
        Or better arts & life
        Go blind worm go
        Behold the famous States
(15)    Harrying Mexico
        With rifle & with knife

        Or who with accent bolder
        D⟨i⟩are praise the freedomloving mountaineer
        I found by thee o rushing Contoocook
(20)    And in thy valleys Agiochook
 [96]   The jackals of the ⟨slave⟩↑negro↓holder

        The God who made Newhampshire
        Taunted the lofty land
        With little men
(5)      ⟨As⟩ ↑Small↓ bat & wren
        House in the oak
        If ⟨the free⟩ ↑earth↓ fire ⟨should⟩ cleave
        The ⟨mountain⟩ ↑upheaved↓ land & bury the folk
        The southern Crocodile would grieve

(10)    Virtue palters, Right is hence
        Freedom praised but hid
        Funeral eloquence
        Rattles the coffin lid

        What boots thy zeal
(15)    O glowing friend
        That would indignant rend
        The northland from the south
[97₁]   Wherefore, to what good end?
        Boston Bay & Bunker Hill

95 "Ode, Inscribed to W. H. Channing," 3–22. In pencil.
96 "Ode, Inscribed to W. H. Channing," 23–39. Erased pencil.
97₁ "Ode, Inscribed to W. H. Channing," 40–56, x, 57. In pencil; lines (5–19) are erased.

Would serve things still
Things are of the snake

(5)     The horseman serves the horse
The /farmer/neatherd/ serves the /farm/neat/
The merchant serves the purse
The ⟨devil⟩ ↑eater↓ serves ↑his↓ ⟨heaven⟩ ↑meat↓

Tis the day of the chattel
(10)    ⟨Of cotton silk & wine⟩ ↑Webs to weave & corn to grind↓
Things are in the saddle
And ride mankind

There are two laws discrete
Not reconciled
(15)    ⟨The⟩ law for ↑the↓ thing
Which ship & city builds & fleet
But it runs wild
⟨And makes man a thing⟩
It doth the man unking

[97₂]       I walk upon the deck
My thought recurs upon the uncertain sea
To what is faster than the solid land.

[98₁]       Let man serve law for man
Live for friendship live for love
For truths & harmonys behoof
⟨Let⟩ the state ↑may↓ follow ⟨the best⟩ ↑how↓ it can
(5)     As Olympus follows Jove

I do not ⟨‖ . . ‖te⟩ court
Wrinkled ⟨banker⟩ ↑shopman↓ to my ⟨woods[?]⟩ ↑sounding
          woods↓
Nor urge the unwilling ‖ . . . . . . . . . ‖
To ⟨listen⟩ when the ⟨pine ‖ . . . ‖⟩ ↑solitudes↓

(10)    Every one to his work
Things to things
Like to like
Round they roll till dark is light
Sex to sex & even to odd
(15)    The overgod
Who marries right to might
Who peoples, unpeoples,

97₂ "At Sea, September 1833," 1–3.
98₁ "Ode, Inscribed to W. H. Channing," 66–75, x, x, 78–82, x, 83. Erased pencil.

Crowds the shore & then vacates
Who exterminates

[98₂]                                     At Sea        September 1833
                            My country! can the ⟨mind⟩ ↑heart clasp↓
                        ⟨Embrace in its affection⟩ realms so vast
                        As the great oceans that wash thee enclose?
                        ↑Methinks↓ The charity ⟨is too⟩ ambitious
(5)                     That ⟨makes⟩ ↑meets↓ its arms ⟨meet⟩ ↑a↓round a continent
                        And yet, the sages say, the preference
                        Of our own cabin to ⟨a strangers wealth⟩ ↑anothers ⟨palace⟩
                            hall↓
                        The insidious love & hate that curls the lip
                        Of the frank Yankee in the tenements
(10)                    Of ducal & of royal rank abroad
                        His supercilious ignorance
                        Of ↑lordship↓ heraldry & ceremony
                        And his ↑too↓ tenacious ⟨recollection⟩ ↑memory↓
                        Amid the colored treasuries
(15)                    That deck the Louvre or the Pitti house

[99₁]       Races by stronger races
            Black by white faces
            Knows to bring honey
            Out of the lion
(5)         Grafts gentlest Scion
            On pirate & Turk.

            The Cossack eats Poland
            Like stolen fruit
            Her last noble is ruined
(10)        Last patriot mute
            Straight into double band
            The victors divide
            One half for freedom stand
            The astonished Muse finds thousands at her side

[99₂]       Of the brave steamboats puffing at New York
            Boston's halfisland & the Hadley Farms
            Washed by Connecticut ↑psalm loving stream↓
            Yea, if the ruddy Englishman speak true,

98₂ "At Sea, September 1833," 4, 4–9, 11–18. Struck through in ink. In line (2), a caret is
inscribed before the cancellation, but nothing was added.
  99₁ "Ode, Inscribed to W. H. Channing," 84–97. In pencil.
  99₂ "At Sea, September 1833," 19–28. Struck through in ink. In line (9), Emerson wrote
"His first demand, arrived in Italy," but indicated the reversal of phrases by the use of parentheses
and subscript numbers ("2" and "1").

(5)      In Rome's ⟨famed church,⟩ ↑Basilica,↓ & underneath
      The frescoed sky of its audacious dome,
      ⟨The⟩Dauntless ⟨American will⟩ ↑Kentucky chews &↓
         count↑s↓ the cost
      And build↑s↓ the shrine with dollars in his head.
      Arrived in Italy, his first demand,
(10)     "Has the starbearing squadron left Leghorn?"

[100]              Bacchus

      Pour the wine pour the wine
      As it changes to foam
      /So is its God/So the Creator/
      New & unlooked for
(5)      Rushing abroad
      In farthest & smallest
      Comes royally home

        In spider wise
      Will again geometrise
(10)     In the bee & gnat keep time
      With the annual solar chime
      The aphides like emperors
      Sprawl & play a span of hours

[101]  Comfort with a purring cat
      Prosperity in a white hat

      He who has no hands
      Perforce must use his tongue
(5)      Foxes are so cunning
      Because they are not strong

[102]     Think not thy life to me unknown
      I saw thee when thou wast alone
      Nor hills nor ‖ . . . ‖ that intervene
      Twixt ‖ . . . . . . . ‖ could screen
(5)      Tho ‖ . . . ‖ were ‖ . . . ‖ the solitude
      Than the lone ‖ . ‖ flowers in the wood
      The Angel ‖ . . . . . . . . ‖ any fate
      All day all night would roam and wait
      And on each ‖ . . . ‖ the wind would bring
(10)    ‖ . . ‖ tedious[?] ‖ . . . . ‖ journeys.
      It boots not where the body dwells
      I draw thy spirit by my spells

100 "Pour the wine!," 1–3, 5, 4, 6–13. In pencil, struck through in pencil.
101 "Comfort with a purring cat" (1–2); "Orator" (3–6). In pencil.
102 "Think not thy life," 1–18 (1–18); "I cannot find," 1–3 (19–21). Erased pencil.

Thou comest with thy burning eye
To feed my dream ‖ . . . . . . . ‖
(15)   ‖ . . . . . . . . . . ‖ thy life denied
And showing all they ‖ . . . ‖ would hide
And we would love[?] ‖ . . . . ‖ entertain
With ‖ . . . ‖, thy works thy peace thy pain

I cannot find a place so lonely
(20)   To harbour thee & me only
I cannot find a nook so deep
[103]   So sheltered may suffice to keep
The ever glowing festival
When thou & I to each are all

[104]   *At Sea, September 1833*
⟨I walk upon⟩ ↑Oft as I paced↓ the deck
My thought recur⟨s⟩red upon the uncertain sea,
To what is faster than the solid land.
My country! can the heart clasp realms so vast,
(5)   As the broad oceans that wash thee enclose?
⟨Methinks⟩ ↑Is not↓ the charity ambitious
That meets its arms around a continent;
And yet, the sages ⟨say,⟩ ↑praise↓ the preference
Of ⟨our⟩ ↑my↓ own cabin to ⟨another's⟩ ↑a baron's↓
        hall↑:↓
(10)   ↑Blame it not, then, but count it honesty,↓
The insidious love & hate that curls the lip
of the Frank Yankee in the tenements
Of ducal & of royal rank abroad,
His supercilious ignorance
[105]   Of lordship, heraldry, & ceremony,
And aye his too tenacious memory,
Amid the parti-colored treasuries
That deck the Louvre & the Pitti House,
(5)   Of the brave steamboats puffing by New York,
Boston's half island, & the Hadley Farms,
Washed by Connecticut's psalmloving stream.
Yea, if the ruddy Englishman speak true,
In Rome's basilica, & underneath
(10)   The frescoed sky of its audacious dome,
Dauntless Kentucky chews, & counts the cost,
And builds the shrine with dollars in his head.

103 "I cannot find," 4–6. Erased pencil.
104 "At Sea, September 1833," 1–14. Struck through in pencil.
105 "At Sea, September 1833," 15–28. Struck through in pencil.

Arrived in Italy, his first demand,
"Has the starbearing squadron left Leghorn?"

[106]   He loved to watch ⟨beside the lake⟩ ↑& wake↓
When the wing of the ⟨breeze⟩ ↑southwind↓ whipt the lake
And the glassy surface in ripples brake
And fled in pretty /darkness/frowns/ away

(5)   Like the flitting ⟨lights⟩ boreal lights
Rippling roses in northern nights
Or like ↑the thrill of↓ Aeolian strings
On which the ⟨wind ‖ . ‖⟩ sudden wind-god rings

He loved the windharp
(10)   With its long memory
And Merlin prisoned within
In a ⟨prison⟩ ↑dungeon↓ of air

[107]   But chiefly scorned
But he made light of all that served
His comfort & his use
And prized alone

(5)   And thot it ⟨better⟩ happier to be dead
To die for beauty than live for bread

Adoring grace & o how vain
⟨T⟩Ambition showed & ⟨lures of⟩ ↑paltering↓ gain
He thot it happier to be dead
(10)   To die for beauty than live for bread

[108]   The
The oldest

What never was not ↑& still will be↓
The old old Force
(5)   That makes & rives
⟨Dying⟩ ↑Feigns to ⟨die⟩ perish but↓ revives
↑To↓ Clings & hold ↑to bud & breed↓
And
Nor is less for being old
(10)   Never wanes by waxing old
A river that runs thro ages strong
Changes its name but the waters roll
Thro ripe & rot
Unwinding here to wind there

106 "He loved to watch" (1–8); "May-Day," 528, 531, 533, 535 (9–12); "The Harp," 49, 52,
54, 56 (9–12). Cancellations and additions in lines (2) and (7) are in pencil.
107 "Beauty," four unused lines, 25–26, 23–26. Lines (5–10) are in pencil, struck through in
pencil.
108 "What never was not," x, x, 1, 3, 7–9, x, 10, 10, four unused lines, 12.

(15)      And feeding

[109]        The gods walk in the breath of the woods,
They walk by the sounding pine,
And fill the long reach of the old seashore,
With colloquy divine

(5)      And the Poet who overhears
Each ⟨awful⟩ ↑random↓ word they say
Is the hierarch of men
⟨Whom the ages must obey⟩
⟨↑Whom the monarchs obey↓⟩

(10)     ↑Whom kings & lords obey↓

And ⟨all⟩ ↑the↓ decay↑ing↓ of the fruit
↑Forms &↓ Feeds the ⟨new &⟩ youthful root

[110]    Nineteenth day of ↑the↓ April moon
Fourth of July at Gods noon

What never was ↑not,↓ but still will be

The old old Force

(5)     ↑Sap in ⟨the⟩ oak & stars in course↓
Upholding stars in course
Which makes & rives
Feigns to perish, but revives
To bud & breed, to cling & hold,

(10)    Never wanes by waxing old
Unwinding here to wind thereon
Changing names but running on
And the decaying of the fruit
Feeds the new & youthful root

[111]    ⟨Nor less in Man controls⟩
↑And not less in human souls↓
The subtle potentate controls
Blazing from authentic eyes

(5)     The autocrat

Old Force
Lodged they say in Chaos once
Runs its never ending course

109 "The gods walk," 1–7, 8, 8, 8 (1–10); "What never was not," 11–12 (11–12). In line (12), "the" is followed by "yo" (evidently the beginning of "youthful"), which Emerson neglected to cancel.

110 "Nineteenth day of the April moon" (1–2); "What never was not," 1, 3, 2, x, 7–10, x, x, 11–12 (3–14). Lines (1–2) are in pencil.

111 "What never was not," 13/14, 13–14, x, x, 3–10. In line (9), "mooned" is probably Emerson's error for "moon &": cf. p. [113].

(10)

Filling space with mooned suns
This is that which binds & rives,
Feigns to perish but revives
To bud & breed to cling & hold
Never wanes by waxing old

[112]

Pours through man's tyrant will
The fatal ↑⟨torrent⟩ flood of empire↓ empire still
That moulded globes & races
Now to rule in milder days

(5)

The creative torrent still

[113]

What never was not, & still will be,
Weigh⟨t⟩s in sand, ⟨& sap⟩ ↑grows↓ in ⟨the⟩ tree
Burn⟨ing⟩s in fire ⟨the old old⟩ ↑primaeval↓ Force
Lodged they say in Chaos once

(5)

Shooting thence it runs its course
Filling Space with moons & suns
Now it binds, & now it rives,
Feigns to perish yet revives
To bud & breed, to cling & hold,

(10)

Never wanes by waxing old,
The decaying of the fruit
Feeding fat the younger root
Nor less in          souls
The subtle potentate controls

(15)

Pours thro mans tyrannic will
Fatal streams of empire still

[114]

How old our names are!
Tubal Cain, Vulcan, Volcano,

[115]

But ↑pealed↓ for him a deeper tone
⟨Pealed⟩ from nodding pole & ⟨rolling⟩ ↑belting↓ Zone
He heard a voice men could not hear
⟨⟨‖ . . . ‖⟩Alike in radiant⟩ ↑From centred↓ or ⟨in⟩ ↑from↓
    errant sphere

(5)

The quaking earth did quake in rhyme
And jarring chaos jarred in chime

112 "What never was not," 15–16, x, x, x. In line (2), Emerson seems to have duplicated "empire" because a transfer of ink from p. [113] partially obliterates the word as first written.
113 "What never was not."
114 "How old our names are!" In pencil.
115 "Beauty," 11–16. In pencil.

[116]        Enough is done, highminded friend, go sleep
Thou hast done a deed that bids me weep
With joy & envy at thy vestibule
And ⟨pray⟩ ↑kneel↓ to be admitted of thy school
(5)        Go sleep serene, for now thy deeds will wake
And other slumberers will rudely shake
Sleep, for thy deed will answer for thee loud
And crown thee absent to the wishful crowd
Thy genius which still drave thee as a ghost
(10)       Comes forth in actions that are uppermost
                     cheerful day
Bend henceforth loving oer thee. Go thy way
And that which ⟨was⟩ rent thee with unkindly throes
Born is more sweet than apple or the rose
(15)       Who need
In action sweat who ⟨h⟩ is father to a deed
Who ⟨cares⟩ pines or hoards who once hath won
A ⟨Blenheim⟩ frigate or a town
For now our easy faith will grant thee all
(20)       ⟨Done or⟩ undone as done thee master call

[117₁]   In thee the arts revive the spritely ⟨soul⟩ seer
That looked thro' Phidias has found a peer

For now we see the niggard cowardice
⟨Which⟩ ended so quick the inventory of arts

(5)       All the fine arts & all humanities
And still we are so poor
Our commerce is a poverty

Corn cotton iron cane wheat & vine
As these thrive or fade
(10)       The wealth of states is stablished or /decayed/unmade/
Forgetful that there is not a plant or grass
But is the keystone that will empires bind
As many arts & circles radiant
Of handmaid crafts & callings adjutant
(15)       With all their pensioners & appanage
As ↑are the↓ substances our chemistry engage

[117₂] He delighted to stand on the shore and see, when the wing of
the breeze whipt the lake, the sudden scud of ripples, which smoothed

116 "Enough is done," 1–8, 13–14, x, x, 15–16, 9–12, 17–18. In pencil, struck through in
pencil.
117₁ "Enough is done," 19–20, 29–30, 32, x, 33–42. In pencil, struck through in pencil.
117₂ Cf. JMN 14:246, and "He loved to watch." In pencil.

again and again flew like a shade and in heaven to see the pulsing &
shooting of ripples or roses

[118₁]   Seized
        The bungler seizes flowers by their heads
        He grasped them by their roots
        And taught men with surprise
(5)        The roots of words & things are the same

        We shall never fear loss of arts again
        Forgive us noble men of Judah & of Greece
        If we seem heedless of your memories
        He has reinstated man on his own heart
(10)      And we shall rightly read the life you gave
        By leaving you forgotten in your grave

[118₂]   ⟨The ringing axe the humming wheel⟩
        ↑Ring of the axe hum of the wheel↓
        And gleam which use will paint on steel

        Law solving ⟨hell ↑self↓ &⟩ passion ↑& self↓ perverse
(5)        Beamed to the bounds of the Universe

          Mid storming Passion tranquil law
        Oppressed the Universe with awe
        And oer the surging Chaos wild
        The frolic bow of Beauty smiled

[119] ————
          Why did all manly gifts in Webster fail?
        He wrote on natures grandest brow, *For Sale.*

————
        Was never form & never face
        So sweet to him as only grace
(5)        Which did not slumber like a stone
        But hovered gleaming & was gone.
        Beauty chased he everywhere
        In flame in storm in clouds of air:
        He smote the lake to feed his eye
(10)      With the precious green of the broken wave,
        He flung in pebbles well to hear
        The moment's music which they gave
        Oft pealed for him a loftier tone
        From nodding Pole & belting Zone

118₁ "Enough is done," five unused lines, 21–26. In pencil.
   118₂ "There are beggars," 23, 23–24 (1–3); "Beauty," 19?, 20, four unused lines (4–9). In pencil.
   119 "Webster" ("Why did all manly gifts") (1–2); "Beauty," 1–14 (3–16). Lines (3–16) are struck through in ink.

(15)      He heard a voice none else could hear
            From centred & from errant sphere
[120]    The quaking earth did quake in rhyme
           ⟨And weltering Chaos jarred in ch⟨y⟩ime⟩
           Seas ebbed & flowed in ⟨boisterous⟩ ↑epic↓ chime
           And yet it seemed ↑the while↓
(5)       ⟨While Music rung⟩ ↑Rung choral joy↓ from every part
           The keynote was the beating heart
           And mid the chaos, central law
           Beamed to the border ⟨of things⟩ ↑of nature↓
           And oer the surging chaos wild
(10)     The ↑frolic↓ bow of ⟨b⟩Beauty smiled
           ↑Hope sung & Beauty's rainbow smiled↓

[121] Moral of "Vestiges of Creation" was that what we call the simple characters are the most composite and good reason is for the defects & defeats & vicious streaks in great men when one sees how they are all made up of caterpillars crocodiles & centipedes & horses   This we do not like to remember & would fain kick down the ladder whereby we climbed

We are a goodnatured but brutish race, and, as the little chirping chickens run hither & thither pecking at every thing & at each other, & now & then one makes a wise pause & seems to see how pitiful it is but is ridden by chicken nature & must run & peck again so do we. Our wise people pause but can not throw off the apish chattering [122] habits, &

         Dreams but trace on Reason's wall
       Shadows of the thoughts of day
       And thy fortunes as they fall
       Each secret of the will betray

(5)      Dreams nightly trace on Memory's wall
       Shadows of the thoughts of day
       And thy fortunes as they fall
       Each bias of the will betray

        Night-dreams trace on Memory's wall
(10)    Shadows of the thoughts of day
       And thy fortunes as they fall
       Each bias of the will betray

120 "Beauty," 15–16, 16, eight unused lines. Lines (3–11) are in pencil, as is the cancellation of line (2).
121 Robert Chambers, *Vestiges of the Natural History of Creation* (New York, 1845), in Emerson's library. Emerson first read the book in late April 1845 (see L 3:283). In pencil.
122 "Memory," three drafts. Lines (1–8) and (9–12) are separately struck through in ink.

[123]      I wish that every step of yours
           be planted on adamant & not on air

           You shall plant
           Every step on adamant

(5)        Night-dreams trace on Memory's wall
           Shadows of the thoughts of day,
           And thy fortunes as they fall
           The bias of the will betray.

[124]      Enough is done highminded friend go sleep
           And leave me here                    to weep
           With joy & envy at thy vestibule
           And kneel to be admitted of thy school
(5)        Go sleep serene, for now thy deeds will wake
           And other slumberers will rudely shake
           Sleep, for thy deed will answer for thee loud
           And crown thee absent to the wishful crowd
           Actions are sons & daughters. O who need
(10)       In action sweat who's father to a deed?
           Who longer pines or hoards, that once hath won
           ⟨A brave⟩ Engine or art a frigate or a town?
           Thy genius which still drave thee as a ghost
           Comes forth in actions that are uppermost
(15)       And that which rent thee with unkindly throes
           Born is more sweet than apple or the rose
           Henceforth our easy faith will grant thee all
                Undone as done will thee the Master call
                In thee the arts revive; the spritely seer
(20)            That looked thro Phidias has found a peer
                We shall not fear the loss of arts again
                Forgive⟨s⟩ us bards of Judah & of Greece
                If we seem heedless of your memories
                He has reinstated man on his own heart
[125]           And we shall rightly read the hint you gave
                ⟨By⟩ ↑And henceforth↓ leav⟨ing⟩e your graveclothes in
                     the grave

           Cheered us with plenty
           Hencefor
(5)        For now we see the niggard cowardice
           Ended so quick the inventory of arts

123 "You shall plant," two drafts (1–4); "Memory" (5–8). Lines (1–4) are in pencil; lines
(5–8) are struck through twice in ink.
   124 "Enough is done," 1–24. In pencil.
   125 "Enough is done," 25–42. In pencil.

And six or seven branches could comprize
All the fine arts all the humanities

On a few plants & stones our commerce waits
(10) Corn cotton cane vine iron opium wheat
Hemp flax   as these grow or fade
The wealth of states is stablished or unmade
There's not a weed waves in the wind
But is the gir⟨th⟩dle that will empires bind
(15) As many arts & circles radiant
Of handmaid crafts & callings adjutant
With all their pensioners & appanage
As are the stuffs our chemistry engage

[126]      Slighted Minerva's learned tongue
But leaped with joy when, on the wind, the shell of Clio
      rung.

Chided Minerva's ⟨chiding⟩ ↑sterner↓ tongue

The Asmod⟨ea⟩aean feat is mine
(5) To spin my sand-heap into twine.

[127]   Thou shalt make thy house
The temple of a nation's vows
Spirits of a higher strain
↑Who↓ Sought thee once shall seek again
(5) I ⟨see⟩ ↑detected↓ many a god
Forth already on the road
Ancestors of beauty come
In thy breast to make a home

[128] [blank]
[129]                    Una

Roving, roving, as it seems,
⟨When⟩ Una lights my clouded dreams,
Still for journeys she is drest,
We wander far by east & west.

(5)   In the homestead, homely thought
At my work, I ramble not;
If, from home chance draw me wide,
Halfseen Una sits beside.

In my house & garden plot,

126 "Slighted Minerva's learned tongue," 1–2, 1 (1–3); "The Asmodaean feat" (4–5).
127 "Thou shalt make." In pencil.
129 "Una," 1–16.

(10)          Though beloved, I miss her not;
                But one I seek in foreign places,
                One face explore in foreign faces.

                At home, a deeper thought may light
                The inward sky with chrysolite,
(15)          And I greet from far the ray
                Aurora of a dearer day.

[130]        But if upon the seas I sail,
                Or trundle on the glowing rail,
                I am but a thought of hers,
                Loveliest of travellers.

(5)           So the gentle poet's name
                To foreign parts is b⟨r⟩lown by fame;
                Seek him in his native town,
                He is hidden & unknown.

[131]            In flint & marble beats a heart,
                The kind Earth takes her children's part
                Her cottage chamber wall & beam
                Glows with the maid↑'↓s delicious dream
(5)           The green lane is the school boys friend
                Low leaves his quarrel apprehend
                The fresh ground loves his top & ball
                The air rings jocund ⟨to⟩ ↑with↓ his call
                The snow that falls at Christmas prates
(10)          In chimney tops of sled & skates
                The youth reads omens where he goes
                And speaks all languages the rose
                The woodfly mocks with tiny noise
                The far halloo of human voice;
(15)          The perfumed berry on the spray
                Smacks of faint memories far away;
                A subtle chain of countless rings
                The next unto the farthest brings:
                And striving to be God, the worm,
(20)          Mounts thro all the spires of form.

[132]                *Initial Love*
              Venus when her son was lost
              Cried him up & down the coast

130 "Una," 17–24.
131 "May-Day," 307–8, x, x, 309–12, x, x, 315–24 (1–20); "Nature" ("A subtle chain"), 3–4, 1–2, 5–6 (11–12, 17–20). In line (4), the apostrophe is added in pencil.
132 "The Initial Love," 1–22. In pencil.

In hamlets, palaces, & parks,
And told the truant by his marks
(5) Golden curls, & quiver, & bow,—
This befel long ago:
Time & tide are strangely changed,
Men & manners much deranged
None will now find Cupid latent
(10) By this foolish antique patent
He came late along the waste
Shod like a traveller for haste
With malice dared me to proclaim him
That the maids & boys might name him

(15) Boy no more, he wears all coats,
Frocks & blouses, capes, capotes,
He bears no bow or quiver or wand
Nor chaplet on his head or hand,
You had best look at his eyes,
(20) All the rest he can disguise
In the pit of his eye is a spark
Would bring back day if it were dark
[133] And if I tell you my thought
Though I comprehend it not,
⟨Every function he absorbs⟩
In those unfathomable orbs
(5) Every function he absorbs;
He doth eat & drink & fish & shoot
And write & reason & compute
And ride, & run, & have & hold,
And whine & flatter & regret
(10) And kiss & couple & beget
By those roving eyeballs bold;
Undaunted are their courages,
Right Cossacks in their forages,
Fleeter they than any creature,
(15) They are his steeds & not his feature
Inquisitive & fierce & fasting
Restless, predatory, hasting
And they pounce on other eyes
As lions on their prey;
(20) And round their circles is writ
Plainer than the day
Beneath & within & above

133 "The Initial Love," 23–24, 26, 25–45. In pencil.

Love love love love
He lives in his eyes
[134] And doth there digest & work & spin
And buy, & sell, & lose, & win
He rolls them with delighted motion
Joy tides swell their mimic ocean
(5) And he holds them as with tortest rein
That they may seize & entertain
The glance that to their glance opposes
Like fiery honey sucked from roses.

He palmistry doth understand
(10) Inbibing virtue by his hand
As if it were a living root,
The ⟨touch⟩ ↑pulse↓ of hands will make him mute
With all his force he gathers balms
Into those wise thrilling palms

(15) He is a casuist
A mystic & a cabalist
He can your lurking thought surprise
And interpret your device
He is versed in occult science
(20) In magic & in clairvoyance
Oft he keeps his fine ear strained
And nature on her tiptoe pained
[135] For aery intelligence
And for strange coincidence
But it touches his heart
When Fate by omens takes his part
(5) And chancedropt hints from Natures sphere
Deeply soothe his anxious ear.

Heralds high before him run
He has ushers many a one
He spreads his welcome where he goes
(10) And touches all things with his rose
⟨Shall I dare to⟩All things wait for & divine him
Shall I dare to malign him
I must end my true report

Painting him from head to foot
(15) In as far as I took note
Trusting well the matchless power

134  "The Initial Love," 46–67. In pencil.
135  "The Initial Love," 68–79, 81–86, 88–90. In pencil. In the space between lines (18–19),
Emerson began an upper-case W, as if to supply line 87 of the poem.

Of this youngeyed emperor
Will clear his fame from every cloud

He is wilful mutable
(20)       Untamed inscrutable
Swifter fashioned that the faeries
[136]    Substance mixed of pure contraries
His vice some elder virtue's token
And his good is evil spoken.
Failing sometimes of his own,
(5)       He is headstrong & alone,
He affects the wood & wild
Like a flowerhunting child
Buries himself in summer waves
In trees with beasts in mines in caves
(10)      Loves nature like a horned cow
Bird or deer or caribou

Shun him, nymphs, on the fleet horses!
He has a very world of wit
O how wise are his discourses
(15)      But he is the arch hypocrite
And through all science & all art
Seeks alone his counterpart.
He is a pundit of the East
He is an augur & a priest
(20)      And his soul will melt in prayer
But word & wisdom is a snare
Corrupted by the present toy
He follows joy & only joy

[137]    There is no mask but he will wear
He invented oaths to swear
He paints he carves he chants he prays
And holds all stars in his embrace
(5)       Godlike,—but tis for his fine pelf
The social quintessence of self
Well said I he is hypocrite
And folly the end of his subtle wit
He takes a sovran privilege
(10)      Not allowed to any liege
For he does go behind all law
And right into himself does draw

136 "The Initial Love," 91–113. In pencil.
137 "The Initial Love," 114–35. In pencil. Several *t*'s are crossed in darker pencil, including, by mistake, the *l* in "sovereignly" in line (13).

For he is sovereignly allied
Heaven's oldest blood flows in his side
(15)    And interchangeably at one
With every king on every throne
That no god dare say him nay
Or see the fault or seen betray
He has the muses by the heart
(20)    And the Parcae all are of his part.

His many signs cannot be told
He has not one mode but manifold
[138]    Many fashions & addresses
Piques reproaches hurts caresses
Arguments lore poetry
Action service badinage
(5)    He will preach like a friar,
And jump like Harlequin,
He will read like a crier
And fight like a Paladin,
Immense is his memory,
(10)    Plans immense his term prolong
He is of no age
Meaning always to be young
And his wish is intimacy,
Intimater intimacy
(15)    And a stricter privacy
The impossible shall yet be done
And being two shall still be one
As the wave breaks to foam on shelves
Then runs into a wave again
(20)    These melt in one their sundered selves
Yet melted would be twain.

[139] [blank]
[140]                    *Proteus.*
Poet bred in Saadi's school
Can wind the world off any spool,
Knows the lore of more & less.
⟨Brahma⟩ ⟨filled his hand with slime⟩ ↑scooped in ⟨moist
        earth⟩ ↑dust↓ with his hand↓

138 "The Initial Love," 136–56. In pencil.
140 "Proteus," 1–19. Line (5) is in pencil at the top of the page, its position indicated by lines in pencil. As this is clearly a substitute line, Emerson must have meant to cancel all of line (4); in fact, he cancelled only "Brahma" in pencil. Line (17) occurs in erased pencil at the bottom of facing p. [141]; arrows, also erased, indicate its position.

(5)       ↑Brahma stooped from the sky↓
        & made the sun of the slime.
        He made, of a toad, an archangel,
        ⟨And, o⟩Of bats & bugs, a god as well,
        ⟨A chorus of seraphs.⟩
(10)      If he should wash your eyes with rue,
        You would remember
        How hated were the forms you clasp,
        And that once you adored the mummies,
        Trust nothing that you see
(15)      ⟨They ch⟩It changes while you look
        Do not think him a dunce ⟨who was dunce⟩
        Who wore bells & foolscap once
        He is the teacher of ages
        For there is no wise man

[141₁]               II
              The Divine
                &
          The Celestial Love

          But God said,
        I will have ‖ . ‖er gift;
        There is smoke in the flame;
        New flowerets bring, new prayers uplift,
(5)      And love without a name.
        Fond children, ye desire
        To please each other well;
        Another round, a higher,
        Ye shall climb ‖ . . ‖ the heavenly stair
(10)     And selfish preference forbear;
        And in right deserving
        And without swerving
        Each from your proper state
        Weave roses for your mate.

(15)     Deep deep are loving eyes,
        Flowed with naphtha fiery sweet,
        And the point is Paradise
        Where their glances meet
        Their gaze must yet be more profound
(20)     And ‖ . . . . . . . . ‖ bound

141₁ "The Daemonic and the Celestial Love," 23–42. Erased pencil; the title is circled in pencil. Between lines (9–10), the isolated phrase "are found" occurs.

[141₂]   Men are vascular only,
       Constructive men only,
       ⟨Cups or⟩ pipes or channels, clay or crystal
       Thro' ⟨‖ . ‖⟩ ↑them rolls↓ the stream ⟨rolls⟩ today
(5)     To roll tomorrow ⟨through others⟩ ↑otherwheres↓
       And leave these dry & mean
       As high as thy ⟨knowledge⟩ ↑perception↓ goes,
       Thou canst not overpraise the great
       Yet ⟨are there as much greater⟩ ↑grander heroes shine↓
          beyond.
(10)    ⟨Thy feet are on⟩ ↑We tread↓ the ladder's lowest round
       And before the Deity
       Thy gods are ⟨but dogs⟩ ↑pismires↓

       Flow flow the waves hated
       Accursed adored!
(15)    The waves of mutation;
       No anchorage is.
       Sleep is not, death is not,
       Who seem to die, live.

[142₁]   The axis of those eyes sun-clear
       Be the axis of the sphere;
       So shall the lights ye pour amain
       Go without check or intervals
(5)     Through from the empyrean walls
       Unto the same again.

       Close close to men,
       Like undulating layer of air,
       Right above their heads
(10)    The potent plain of Daemons spreads
       Stands to each human soul its own,
       For watch & ward, & furtherance,
       In the sn‖ . . ‖ of Nature's dance,
       And the lustre & the grace
(15)    Which fascinates each youthful heart
       Beaming from anothers part
       Translucent thro the mortal covers,
       Is the helpful[?] Daemon's form & face
       To & fro the Genius hies,
(20)    As light which plays & hovers
       Over the maiden's head,
       And dips sometimes as low as to her eyes.

**141₂** "Proteus," 20–37 (1–18); "Illusions," 1–6 (13–18). Lines (13–18) are struck through in ink.

**142₁** "The Daemonic and the Celestial Love," 43–64. Erased pencil.

[1422] House you were born in
 Friends of your youth
 Old man & young maid
 Early toil & its gains
(5) They are all vanishing
 Fleeing to fables
 Cannot be moored
 See the stars through them,
 The treacherous ⟨solids⟩ ↑marbles↓.
(10) Know, ⟨that⟩ the stars ↑yonder↓
 The ↑stars↓ everlasting ⟨stars⟩
 Are fugitive also
 And emulate, vaulted,
 The passing heat-lightning
(15) or ⟨flight of a⟩ firefly ↑s flight↓

 When thou dost return
 On the ⟨billow's⟩ ↑wave's↓ circulation
 ⟨Seeing⟩ ↑Beholding↓ the shimmer
 The wild dissipation,
(20) And out of endeavor
 To change & to flow,

[1431] Unknown, albeit lying near,
 To men the path to the Daemon sphere,
 And they that swiftly come & go
 Leave no track on the heavenly snow.
(5) Sometimes the airy homestead bends
 And the mighty Choir descends,
 And the brains of men thenceforth,
 In crowded & in still resorts
 Teem with unwonted thoughts.
(10) As when a shower of meteors
 Cross the orbit of earth
 And lit by the friction of air
 Blazes near & far
 As if the old planets bright
(15) Had slipped their sacred bars
 And wandering men at night
 Walk astonished amid stars

 Beauty of a richer vein,
 Graces of a subtler strain,

---

**142₂** "Proteus," 38–58 (1–21); "Illusions," 7–27 (1–21). Struck through in ink.
**143₁** "The Daemonic and the Celestial Love," 65–87. Erased pencil. In line (9), Emerson actually wrote "Teeem".

(20) These to men & wisdom lend,
  And the shrinking sky extend
  So is man's narrow path
  By strength & terror skirted,

[1432] The gas become solid
  And ⟨dreams⟩ ↑phantasms↓ & nothings
  Return to be things
  And endless ⟨frivolity⟩ ↑imbroglio↓
(5) Is law & the world,
  Then ⟨s⟩first shalt thou know
  That in the wild turmoil
  ↑Horsed↓ On the ⟨↑saddle-↓back of⟩ Proteus
  Only canst thou ride to power.
(10)   ↑And to Endurance.↓

  Much thou must suffer
  Be shocked & derided
  Lose faith to gain faith,
  Ah worse! must I say it?
(15) Lose thy virtue, lose thy soul,
  To gain the incorruptible.
   ⟨Know too⟩ the scale ↑in this world↓
   Of greatness ⟨in this world⟩ ↑& height↓
   Is reversed in the other.

[1441] Also (now may the wrath
  Of the Genii ⟨br⟩ be averted!)
  Also the Daemon
  Equivocally named
(5) Lord of the secret approaches
  Usurpeth & encroaches
  And cannot pass unblamed
  He is a giver of might
  Leading to no‖ . . . . . . ‖
(10) But[?] ⟨‖ . . . ‖⟩ what fate portends
  ‖ . . . . . . . . ‖s grasped[?]
  From his hearts cold chambers speaking
  He is self-seeking

  The erring painter made Love blind,
(15) Love, who shines on all,
  The radiant, sharpest sighted god,

---

1432 "Proteus," 59–77 (1–19); "Illusions," 28–37 (1–10). In line (8), "Horsed" is added, and "↑saddle-↓back of" is cancelled, in pencil. Lines (1–10) are struck through in ink.

1441 "The Daemonic and the Celestial Love," 88–89, five unused lines, 101?, x?, x?, x?, 90–91, 94–97, 99–101, 111/112, 119, x, x. In pencil; lines (1–2) and (8–13) are erased.

Whom none can bewilder,
↑The solid universe↓
Pathfinder, road-builder,
(20)    The sovereign Giver:
Love ever builds a road
Pride ever builds a wall
The daemon shy
Is Pride's ally

[1442]   Crown of power, ⟨it⟩ is ⟨made⟩ ↑fashioned↓
Of dust of abasement.

Roomy Eternity casts her schemes rarely
And ⟨a full ⟨age⟩ ↑period↓⟩ ↑an aeon vast↓ allows
(5)    For every quality & part
In the multitudinous
And many chambered heart
        ↑AZ 7↓

O happy soul beyond reward
When Jove unsealed the senses of the Bard

[1451]   Himself encloses & includes
Solitude in solitudes
↑And his love is like↓
He is an oligarch
(5)    He prizes wonder, fame, & mark
He loveth crowns
He scorneth drones
He doth elect
The beautiful, the fortunate,
(10)   And the sons of intellect,
And the souls of ample fate,
Beloved of the morning
In his prowess he exults,
And the multitude insults.
(15)   In the greatness of his strength
He looks on poor men,
And ⟨‖ . . ‖⟩ seeing his eye glare
They lose courage & despair.
He will never be gainsaid
(20)   And he will not be stayed
His hot tyranny

1442 "Proteus," 78–79 (1–2); "Roomy Eternity" (3–7); "O happy soul" (8–9). In line (4), "age" is cancelled, and "period" added, in ink; the other alterations are in pencil.

1451 "The Daemonic and the Celestial Love," 120–21, x, 123–30, 132?, 133–34, x, 135/ 136, 137, 141–48. Erased pencil.

Burns up every other tie
Therefore after a season
Is his ruthless will defied
(25)     And the dogs of Fate untied

[145₂]          ⟨There is no⟩ ↑Poet of↓ poet⟨,⟩s          ↑Corrected AZ 7↓
⟨But⟩ ↑Is↓ time the distiller
Time the inventor
↑Chemist, refiner,↓
(5)     Hath a sharp vitriol
Which can dissolve
Towns into melody.
Burn up the libraries,
Down with the colleges,
(10)     Raze the foundations,
Drive out the doctors,
Rout the philosophers,
Harry the Critics,
Men of particulars,
(15)     Narrowing niggardly,
Coming to nothing,
All their tenthousand Nays
End in the Néant.
All thro' the countryside
(20)     Rush locomotives
Prosperous grocers
Poring on newspapers
Over their shop fires
⟨Dispose of⟩ ↑Settle↓ the state

[146₁]     For the daemonic love
Is the ancestor of wars,
And the parent of remorse

Higher far
(5)     Upward, into the pure realm,
Over sun or star,
Over the flickering Daemon film,
Thou must mount for love.
Into vision which all form
(10)     In one form dissolves,

145₂ "Poet of poets," 1–2, x, 3–6, 8–24. "Corrected AZ 7" is set off by a diagonal line. Line (3) was cancelled, though the cancellation was immediately wiped; line (4) was added above line (3), the intended order being indicated by the numbers "2" and "1" in the left margin. The page is struck through twice in pencil.
146₁ "The Daemonic and the Celestial Love," 159–74, 176, x, x, x, 177–78. In pencil.

In a region where the wheel
On which all beings ride
Visibly revolves;
Where the eternal worm
(15) Girds the world with bound & term,
Where unlike things are like,
Where laugh & moan,
Hatred & love,
Pride & humility,
(20) Self & society,
Melt into one.
There Past, Present, Future, shoot

[146₂] But for the poet,
Seldom in centuries
Comes the well-tempered
Musical man.
(5) He is the waited for,
⟨He is the Hercules,⟩
⟨He shall dispose of us⟨,⟩.⟩
He is the complement
Of ⟨each⟩ ↑one↓ man & all men.
(10) ⟨Each ↑listening↓ man⟩ ⟨↑He speaks↓⟩ ↑Accosts the
         wayfarer↓
⟨Thinks the poet⟩ ↑Finds him of↓ his ⟨relation⟩ ↑kin↓
This is he that should come,
Tongue of the secret,
Key of the caskets
(15) Of Past & of Future.
Sudden the lustre
That hovered round things

[147₁] Triple flowers from one root,
Substances at base divided
In their summits are united;
There sublunar quarrels cease
(5) In the beatific peace;
There the primal essence rolls
Its river through divided souls,
And the sunny Aeon sleeps
Folding all souls in its deeps
(10) And every fair & every good
Known in part or known impure

146₂ "Poet of poets," 25–29, x, x, 30–39. Struck through in pencil.
147₁ "The Daemonic and the Celestial Love," 179–81, x, x, 182–98. In pencil.

To men below
In their archetypes endure.

(15) The race of gods
Or those we erring own,
Are shadows flitting up & down
In the still abodes.
The circles of that sea are laws,
And hides in light the nameless Cause.

(20) Pray for a beam
Out of that sphere
Thee to guide & to redeem

[147₂] Round the ⟨chamber⟩ ↑bureau↓ of Power,
Or chamber of Commerce,
Round Banks, or round beauties,
Or state-rending factions,
(5) Has quit them, & perches
Well pleased on his ⟨shoulder.⟩ ↑form.↓

⟨The⟩ ↑True↓ bard never cared
To make his welcome to the great
⟨For it⟩ costs time to live ⟨well⟩ with them
(10) Which ⟨his⟩ ↑a↓ ⟨swift⟩ genius ill supplies
Preengaged to woods & skies
⟨And he r⟩

The Poet received
Foremost of all
(15) ⟨Patent⟩ ↑Badge↓ of nobility ⟨↑rank↓⟩
⟨And freedom⟩ ↑Charter↓ of ⟨the world.⟩ ↑earth↓
↑Free of the city free of the field,↓
⟨So is he⟩ ⟨↑He is↓⟩ member of each class,
↑Knight of each order↓
(20) Fellow of monarchs,
And, what is better,
Fellow of all men.

[148₁] O what a load
of care & toil
By lying use bestowed,
From his shoulders falls who sees

**147₂** "Poet of poets," 40–50, 52?, 52, 51, 53–54, 55/56, x, 57, 59–61. The positions of lines (7–12) and (13–22) have been reversed as indicated by Emerson's numbers "2" and "1" in the left margin; lines (11–12) actually occur at the top of p. [148]. Lines (1–6) and (1–22) are struck through in pencil.

**148₁** "The Daemonic and the Celestial Love," 199–221. In pencil.

(5)     The true astronomy,
        The Universe of Peace,
        Counsel which the ages kept
        Shall the wellborn soul accept
        As the oerhanging trees
(10)    Fill the lake with images,
        As garment draws the garment's hem,
        Men their fortunes bring with them.
        By right or wrong
        Lands & goods go to the strong
(15)    Property will brutely draw
        Still to the proprietor.
        Silver to silver, creep & wind
        And kind to kind

        Nor less the eternal poles
(20)    Of tendency distribute souls
        There need no vows to bind
        Whom not each other seek but find.
        They give & take no pledge or oath,

[148₂]        But his crowning grace
        Wherefor thanks God his daily praise
        Is the purging of his eye
        To see the people of the sky.
(5)     ⟨They reach⟩ ↑Friendly hands stretch↓ forth ⟨hands⟩ to him,
        From ⟨every⟩ ↑each↓ mount & headland dim
        ⟨They⟩ him ↑they↓ beckon, ⟨&⟩ ↑him↓ advise
        Of ⟨purer⟩ ↑heavenlier↓ prosperities,
        ↑And a↓ More ⟨excellent⟩ ↑exceeding↓ grace,
(10)    And a truer bosom glow
        Than the wine fed ⟨earthworms⟩ ↑feasters↓ know
        They turn his heart from ⟨‖ . . ‖⟩lovel⟨ier⟩y maids,
        And make the darlings of the earth
        Swainish, coarse, & nothing worth.
(15)    They teach him ⟨gladly⟩ to postpone
        His pleasures to another age

[149₁]    Nature is the bond of both;
        No prayer persuades, no flattery fawns,
        Their noble meanings are their pawns.
        Plain & cold is their address,
(5)     Power have they for tenderness,
        And so thoroughly is known

**148₂** "Poet of poets," 62–65, 67, 66, 68–77.
**149₁** "The Daemonic and the Celestial Love," 222–42, x, x. In pencil.

Each other's purpose by his own,
They can parley without meeting,
Need is none of forms of greeting,
(10)    They can well communicate
⟨From⟩ ↑In↓ their innermost estate;
When each the other shall avoid
Shall each by each be most enjoyed.

Not with scarfs, or perfumed gloves,
(15)    Do these celebrate their loves;
Not by jewels, feasts, and savours,
Not by ribbons or by favours
But by the sunsparkle on the sea,
And by the cloud-shadow on the lea,
(20)    By the soothing lapse of morn to mirk,
And the cheerful round of work.
Love makes the hero strong & stark
For his task from dawn till dark

[1492]    Beyond the scope of human age
Freely as task at eve undone
Waits unblamed tomorrows sun.  ↑⟦See AZ 7↓

O patient Pan
(5)    Overpowered with sleep
Thou seemest
Yet thou dost furnish
Right music to the march of Time
This poor tooting creaking cricket.
(10)    Pan half asleep, rolling over
His great body on the grass,
Tooting, creaking,
⟨Seems⟩ ↑Feigns↓ to sleep, sleeping never
Tis his m⟨i⟩anner
(15)    Well he knows his own affair
Piling mountain chains of phlegm
On the nervous brain of man
⟨As ⟨they⟩ ↑hills↓⟩ ↑As he↓ hold↑s↓ down the central fires

[150₁]    Love makes him confident & true
There amid the mocking crew.
Love's hearts are faithful but not fond,
Bound for the just, but not beyond.

1492 "Poet of poets," 78–80 (1–3); "The patient Pan," 1, x, x, x, 5–15 (4–18). Lines (4–18) are struck through in pencil. In line (17), the ascender of the *b* in "brain" is crossed in pencil, presumably by Emerson, making it look like "train."
150₁ "The Daemonic and the Celestial Love," x, x, 251–68. In pencil.

(5)        Not glad as is the loving herd
Of self in other still preferred,
But they have heartily designed
The benefit of broad mankind

And they serve men austerely
(10)      After their own genius clearly
Not with false humility
For this is Loves nobility
Not to scatter bread & gold
Goods & raiment bought & sold
(15)      But to hold fast his simple sense
And speak the speech of innocence
And with hand & body & blood
To make his bosom-counsel good
For he that feeds men, serveth few,
(20)      He serves all who dares be true.

[150₂]   Under Alps & Andes cold.
Haply else we could not live
Life would be too wild an ode
⟨Earth & earth⟨man⟩ ↑son↓⟩ ↑Sun & planet↓ would
      explode
(5)        Ah! the poor Adamkind
Fault of sup⟨li⟩plies
From the fire fountains
We busybodies
Ever⟨more⟩ experiment
(10)      See what will come of it
Prove the quaint substances
Prove our bodies, prove our essence
Fortunes, genius, elements,
Try a foot, try a hand,
(15)      Then plunge the body in
Then our wits characters
And our gods if we can
[151]    Analysing analysing
As the chemist his new stone
Puts to azote, puts to ch⟨r⟩lorine,
Puts to vegetable blues.
(5)        Ah ⟨my dear⟩ ↑my poor↓ apothecaries,
Can ye never wiselier sit,
Meddle less & more accept,

---

150₂ "The patient Pan," 16–32. Lines (3–4) are struck through twice in ink.
   151 "The patient Pan," 33–41. In line (5), "my" is added in pencil; in line (8), "ped" is added in pencil.

With dignity not overstep⟨.⟩ped
Skies have their etiquette

[1521]    Man was made of social earth,
Child & comrade from his birth,
Tethered by a liquid cord
Of blood thro' veins of brothers poured,
(5)    Nearest seemed the ⟨household⟩ ↑fireside↓ band,
Father, Mother, sister, /brother,/stand/
These ⟨were preferred⟩ to himself ↑preferred↓
He thought virtue, devotion to them
↑Their names his dear religion stirred↓
(10)    Vice to neglect them    ↑vice↓
But Beauty abolished all ⟨relations⟩ ↑ties↓
Obliterates
From his ⟨memory⟩ ↑heart↓ the dearest traits
When those calm eyes opened bright
(15)    All were foreign in their light

[1522]    Pour the wine! Pour the wine!
As it changes to foam
So ⟨is the god⟩ ↑Demourgos↓
Rushing abroad
(5)    New & unlooked for
In furthest & smallest
Comes royally home
In spider wise
Will again geometrise
(10)    ↑Will↓ In bee & gnat keep time
With the annual solar ⟨time⟩chime
Aphides like Emperors
Sprawl & ⟨play⟩ ↑creep↓ their pair of hours
Strong Lyaeus' rosy gift
(15)    ⟨Well⟩ ↑Lightly↓ can ⟨more than⟩ ↑the↓ mountains lift
It can knit
What is done &
And what's begun
It can cancel ⟨time &⟩ bulk & time

[1531]    Man was made of social earth
Child & brother from his birth
Tethered by a liquid cord
Of blood thro veins of kindred poured

1521 "The Daemonic and the Celestial Love," 1–7, 9, 8, 9, 11, 13–14, 17–18. In pencil.
1522 "Pour the wine!," 1–3, 5, 4, 6–19. Struck through in pencil.
1531 "The Daemonic and the Celestial Love," 1–9, 11, 10, 12–14, 17–22. In pencil, struck through in pencil.

(5) ⟨Nearest seemed⟩ ↑Next his heart↓ the fireside band
 ↑Of↓ Father mother sister stand
 ⟨These e⟩Ever ⟨to⟩ ↑before↓ himself preferred
 their names his dread religion stirred
 Virtue to love, to hate them, vice
(10) Till Beauty came to snap all ties
 Till Beauty came at last
 Beauty abolishing the past
 With lotus fruit obliterates
 From his heart the dearest traits
(15) When her calm eyes opened bright
 All were foreign in their light
 It was ever the selfsame tale
 The ⟨last⟩ experience will not fail
 Only two in the garden walked
(20) And with the twain the Godhead talked

[1532] Crowds & condenses
 Into a drop a tun
 So to repeat
 No word or feat
(5) The hours an attar of ages
 Love, the Socrates of sages.

 Try the might the muse affords
 And the balm of thoughtful words

 On the seed of the first grape
(10) ↑Evermore↓ The world turns round
 As a watch on a diamond
 ⟨And⟩ out of the grapestone goes a fury
 ⟨Which⟩ makes the wheels ↑to↓ fly & burn
 And because a drop of ⟨wine⟩ the vine
(15) ⟨Is at⟩ ↑Lubricates↓ the Core,
 If thou wash thine eyes with wine,
 ⟨Thou seest⟩ ↑Thou shalt see↓ things from the centre,
 ⟨Dost⟩ ↑Shall↓ their willing essence enter,
 And canst ↑well↓ predict the path of
(20) Comets, & the fates of beauties.

[1541] Man was made of social earth

1532 "Pour the wine!," 20–25 (1–6); "Try the might the Muse affords," 1–2 (7–8); "On a raisin stone," 1–2, x, 3–5, x, 7, four unused lines (9–20). Struck through in pencil. At least the third of these entries was written before the draft of "Pour the wine!" on p. [152]: in cancelling "wine" in line (14), Emerson created an inkblot that was transferred to p. [152] when the book was closed; the verses on that page are written around the blot.
 1541 "The Daemonic and the Celestial Love," 1–7, x, 9–22. In pencil. In line (6), Emerson wrote "Mother, Father," and indicated the reversal by subscript numbers "2" and "1".

Child & brother from his birth
Tethered by a liquid cord
Of blood through veins of kindred poured
(5)    Next his heart the fireside band
↑Of↓ Mother, Father, sister, stand
Ever before himself preferred
Their names with awe & love he heard,
Virtue to love, to hate them — vice,
(10)   Till dangerous Beauty came at last
Till Beauty came to snap all ties
Beauty abolishing the past
With lotus fruit obliterates
From ⟨his⟩Memory the dearest traits
(15)   And by herself supplied
The friends whom years had closer drawn
When her calm eyes opened bright
All were foreign in their light
It was ever the selfsame tale
(20)   The old experience will not fail
Only two in the garden walked
And with the twain the Godhead talked


[1542]   Wine is the mystic centre
Wine is translated wit
Wine is a new day
Wine from the veiled secret
(5)    Tears the veil away
Wine is liquid motion

If thou wash
Monadnoc with wine
Monadnoc would exhale

(10)   ↑Swift↓ On /a/the primal/ grapestone
The wheels of nature turn
Out of it the fury comes
Wherewith the spondyls burn
And because a drop of ⟨wine⟩ ↑the vine↓
(15)   Is creation's heart
If thou wash ⟨therewith the eyne⟩ ⟨↑those eyes of thine↓⟩
    ↑thine eyes with wine↓
Nothing's hid apart.

1542 "On a raisin stone," x, 9–12, four unused lines, 1–8. Lines (10–17) are struck through in pencil. In line (16), "those eyes of thine" is added in pencil at the bottom of p. [155] and cancelled in pencil.

[155]    On ⟨the primal⟩ ↑a brown↓ grapestone
             The wheels of nature turn
             Out of it a fury comes
             Wherewith the spondyls burn

(5)       And because a drop of ⟨wine⟩the vine
             Is creation's heart
             ↑Wash with wine those eyes of thine↓
             ↑Nothing is hid, nor whole, nor part. ↓

             Today the attar is of ages
(10)     ⟨The⟩ ↑Loving↓ Heart ⟨is wiser than⟩ ↑outwits↓ the sages
             Future or Past no mightier secret holds,
             O friendless Present! than thy bosom folds.

[156]    ↑Pan's↓ Paths ⟨of Pan⟩ are wonderful,
             ⟨Who seeks to be wise shall not be.⟩
                 ↑Subtle his counsel↓
             Wisdom needs circumstance
(5)       Many concomitants:
             Goes ⟨never⟩ ↑not↓ in ⟨state⟩ ↑purple,↓
             Steals along secretly,
             Shunning the eye:
             Has the dominion
(10)     Of men & the ⟨earth,⟩ ↑planet,↓
             On this sole condition,—
             ⟨T'will⟩ ↑She shall↓ not assume it.
             When ↑first↓ the crown /touches/incloses/
             The brows of her son,
(15)     The Muse him deposes
             ↑From kingdom & throne↓
             See the spheres rushing!
             Poet that ⟨follows⟩ ↑tracks↓ them
[157]         With emulous eye,
             What lovest thou,
             Planet, or orbit?
             ⟨Lump of mars is lump of stone,⟩
(5)       ⟨All is azote or carbon.⟩
             ⟨Lovest thou⟩ ↑Whether↓ the ⟨wooden⟩ pipe?
             Or the ⟨music⟩ ↑lay↓ it discourses?

155 "On a raisin stone," 1–8 (1–8); "Pour the wine!," 24–25 (9–10); "Heri, Cras, Hodie," 3–4 (11–12). Lines (1–8) are struck through in pencil; lines (9–12) are struck through twice in pencil.

156 "Poet of poets," 81, x, 82–97. Struck through in pencil. The alterations in lines (12–13) are in pencil, and line (16) is added in pencil.

157 "Poet of poets," 98–100, x, x, 101–4, x, 105–14. Lines (1–4) and (7–20) are struck through in pencil.

In heaven up yonder,
All the⟨ir⟩ astronomy,
(10)    ⟨The mathematic show,⟩
    ↑Sun dance & star⟨shine⟩ blaze↓
Emblem is & lore of love.
Nothing's of worth
in Earth or in sky,
(15)    But ⟨thought alone.⟩ ↑Love & thot only.↓
Perish the mankind,
Bideth the thought;
Clothes itself with men & women,
Puts on a new suit
(20)    Of earth & stars.
[158]    He will come one day
Who can articulate
That which unspoken
Vaults itself over us,
(5)    Globes itself under us,
Looks out of lovers' eyes,
Dies, & is born again,—
He who can speak well.
Men hearing delighted
(10)    Shall say, That is ours,
Trees hearing shall blossom,
Rocks hearing shall tremble,
And range themselves dreamlike
In new compositions
(15)    Architecture of thought.
Then ↑'↓ twill appear
What the old centuries
[159]    Aeons were groping for,—
Times of discomfiture,
Bankrupt millenniums.

       Thought is the ⟨only⟩ price
(5)    For which I sell days,
And willing grow old,
Melting matter to pictures,
And life into law.

Cloud upon cloud

---

158 "Poet of poets," 115–31. Struck through in pencil. In line (16), the apostrophe is in pencil.

159 "Poet of poets," 132–34 (1–3); "Terminus" ("For thought"), 1/2, 3, 5, 7, 10 (4–8); "Cloud upon cloud / The world" (9–20). Lines (1–8) are struck through in pencil. Running out of room at the bottom of the page, Emerson wrote lines (19–20) along a single line.

(10)    The world is a seeming,
Feigns dying, but dies not,
Corpses rise ruddy,
Follow their funerals.
Seest thou not brother
(15)    Drops hate detachment,
And atoms disorder,
How they run into plants,
And grow into beauties.
The darkness will ⟨‖ . . ‖⟩glow,
(20)    The solitude sing

[160]          Rhyme
What care I so they stand the same
Things of the heavenly mind
How long the power to give them fame
Lingers there behind

(5)    Thus far today your favors reach
O fair appeasing presences
Ye taught my lips a single speech
And a thousand silences

Space grants beyond his fated road
(10)    No inch to the god of day
And copious language still bestowed
One word—no more—to say.

[161]          Saadi
I grieve that better souls than mine
Docile read my measured line
High destined youths & holy maids
Hallow these my orchard shades
(5)    Environ me & me baptize
With light that streams from gracious eyes
They me perfume with odorous prayers

I dare not be beloved or known
I ungrateful, I alone

[162]    Was no figure & no face
So sweet to him as only grace

160 "Merops." In pencil.
161 "I grieve that better souls," 1–6, x, 7–8. In pencil.
162 "Beauty," 1–4, 7–10 (1–8); "There are beggars," 11–14, 17–22, 25–27, 35–43 (1–22). Lines (1–8) are in pencil, struck through three times in pencil; lines (14–22) are in pencil, overwritten in ink: variations between layers occur in line (20), where the apostrophe is omitted in the pencil version, and in line (21), where, in copying, Emerson left a space between "the" and "seabird" (altered from "seabirds" in the pencil version) and later added "hardy" in pencil. The whole page is struck through in pencil.

Which did not tarry like a stone
But which gleamed & was gone
(5)    He smote the lake to feed his eye
With the precious green of the broken wave
He flung in flints that he might hear
The moments music which they gave

Loved harebells nodding on a rock
(10)    A cabin topped with curling smoke
Or hunters camp nor loved he less
Stately men in palaces
Princely women hard to please

The comrade of the snow & wind
(15)    He left each civil scale behind
Him woodgods fed with honey wild
And of his memory beguiled
In caves & hollow trees he ⟨slept⟩crept
And near the wolf & panther slept
(20)    He came to the green ocean's brim
And saw the ↑hardy↓ seabird skim
Summer & winter oer the wave

[163]    Ever find me dim regards,
Love of ladies, love of bards,
Marked forbearance, compliments,
Tokens of benevolence
(5)    What then? ⟨I⟩ can⟨not⟩ I love myself
Fame is profitless as pelf
↑Fame to ignorance allowed↓
They me ⟨revere⟩ ↑esteem↓ as I a cloud
Sailing falsely as a sphere
(10)    Hated mist if it come near

Like creature of a skiey mold
Insensible to heat or cold,
He stood beside the weltering main
By too much sympathy insane
(15)    He felt himself as if the sky walked
Or the son of the wind
A crystal soul
Sphered & concentric to the whole.

163 "Ever find me dim regards," 1–10 (1–10); "There are beggars," 44–47, 51/52, 53–55 (11–18). Lines (1–10) are in pencil; line (7) is added after line (10) with an arrow to indicate its position. Lines (11–18) are in pencil, overwritten in ink, with the following variants in the pencil layer: line (11) "mould"; line (13) "beside the main"; line (14) "Most beautiful and most insane".

[164₁]     Hoard ‖ . . . . . ‖ in ‖ . ‖ coffers
          Let ‖ . . . . . . . . ‖ riches
          Thy ⟨capital be knowledge⟩
          ↑ An easy load to bear ↓
(5)     ⟨Thou canst⟩ ‖ . . . . . . ‖ bear
          Wedges of gold & silver bars
          Let others ⟨hoard⟩ ↑ drag ↓ with care
          The devil's snares are strong
          Yet have I god in need
(10)     And if I had not god to friend
          What can the devil speed
          High heart o Hafiz though ⟨to thee⟩ ↑ not thine ↓
          ⟨F‖ . . ‖⟩ ↑ fine ↓ gold & silver ore
          More worth to thee the gift of song
(15)     And the clear insight more

[164₂]     Hoard knowledge in thy coffers
          An easy load to bear
          Wedges of gold & silver bars
          Let others drag with care.

(5)     The devil's snares are strong,
          Yet have I God in need;
          And if I had not God to friend
          What can the devil speed?

          High heart, O Hafiz! tho' not thine
(10)     Fine gold & silver ore,
          More worth to thee the gift of song,
          And the clear insight more.

[165]                              ↑ Hafiz [*Diwan*] Vol II p 22 ↓
          "Boy bring the bowl full of wine
          Bring me two bowls of the purest wine
          I take wine to be the love-potion
          This stuff for old & young, bring
(5)     Sun & moon are the wine & the glass
          In the midst of the moon bring me the sun
          How the understanding strives so earnestly
          Bring bands made of wine for the stupid head
          ⟨↑ To ↓⟩ Fan this ⟨expiring⟩ ↑ dissolving ↓ glow,
(10)     ⟨Truly⟩ ↑ That is, ↓ instead of water bring wine
          Goes the rose by, say gladly:
          Nectar of pearls & blood of the rose, bring.

**164₁** "The Poet" ("Hoard knowledge"), 1, x?, x, 2, 2, 10, 4, 5–12. Erased pencil.
**164₂** "The Poet" ("Hoard knowledge").
**165** " 'Boy bring the bowl." In pencil.

Sounds not the nightingale it is right
Sound of glass & sound of wine, bring.
(15) Mourn for nothing, since past is past
Harp⟨s⟩ & lute tones therefore bring
Only in dreams enjoy I my love
Then bring wine for wine brings sleep
Am I drunken   What is to do
(20) That I may be well drunken bring one glass more
One two cups bring to Hafiz
Be it now well or ill done, bring.

[166] Hark in the heaven what organ ↑plays↓
Steals he not the best people
Corrupts he not the best minds
Shall we let this pass in silence
(5) Ought we not to scream.

The very wind pipes rowdy songs
Drives sober people mad
Should we suffer such wrongs
And not give the alarm        [Hafiz, *Diwan*,] ↑Vol II 198↓

[167₁]           ↑Divan of Hafiz        Vol 1, 69↓
The garden of Eden is the cell of the Dervish
There shows ‖ . . . . . ‖ service of the Dervish
The treasure of ‖ . . . . . ‖ with its talisman
Is only raised by the look of the Dervish
(5) The sun lays down the crown of his ‖ . . . ‖
B‖ . . . ‖ glory ‖ . . . ‖ radiate for the Dervish
‖ . . . . . . . . ‖ palace with ‖ . . . . . ‖man
Is only a shadow of ‖ . . . . . . . ‖ the Dervish
The ‖ . . ‖ of the wise man which thro glance of the heart
(10) Turns iron into gold ‖ . . . . ‖

The army of Unright is encamped from pole to pole
But the road to victory is for the Dervish

Seekest thou the Lordship which no ruin threatens
Hear it without grudge, it is the lordship of the Dervish
(15) /Chosroes/Kaisars/ are needs & prayers Kibla
Why? They also are servants of the Dervish
O rich man boast not with thy shining & pride
Since gold & silver are a blessing of the Dervish
The treasure of Karun went to ruin in the scowl of God.

166 "The treacherous wind," 6–10, 1–4. In pencil. Overwritten by lines (6–9) are four lines of erased pencil writing; only the words "disperse" near the end of the second line and "Should" at the beginning of the third are legible.
167₁ "The garden of Eden," 1–19. In pencil; lines (2–10) are erased. Above "Chosroes" in line (15) is Emerson's bracketed notation "pl."

[1672]        Every morn a ship comes here

              Every morning brings a ship,
              Every ship brings a word,
              Well for those who have no fear,
(5)           ⟨But stand waiting⟩ ↑Looking seaward↓ well assured
              That the word the vessel brings
              Is the word they wish to hear.

[168]         As stories tell, out of the displeasure of the Dervish
              The face of the wish, for which beauties pray
              Appears in mirror before the brow of the Dervish
              I am the groom of the look, of the grand vizier of time
(5)           It has the way of the Shah the piety of the Dervish
              Hafiz desirest thou the water of Eternal life
              It flows in the dust of the door of the cell of the Dervish
              Hafiz here be discreet since the lordship of the Kingdom
              Depends on the service which thou renderest to the Dervish

[169]              [Hafiz] *Divan   Vol 1 p 61*
              Come! the palace of hope rests on its airy pillars;
              Come & bring me wine, our days are wind.
              Gladly would I yield myself as a slave to that masculine soul
              Which in the wide world all union renounces.
(5)           Should I tell thee how yesterday the Light-messenger of
                   heavenly joys
              Brought to me in the cup secret tidings.
              O highflying falcon! thou dwellest on the tree of life.
              This nook of grief seems to⟨o⟩ thee bad for a nest.
              Hearken! they call to thee down from the ⟨battlements⟩
                   ↑ramparts↓ of heaven
(10)          Truly I know not what holds thee here in a net.
              I impart to thee a counsel, mark it & keep it
              Since I have ↑received↓ the same word from the master
                   ⟨received⟩
              Seek not faith & truth in a world of lightminded girls,
              A thousand suitors ⟨has⟩ ↑counts↓ this ill-reputed bride.
(15)          Cumber thee not for the world, & my counsel forget not,
              Leave ↑behind to↓ me a wanderer ⟨back to⟩ this beloved
                   joke.
              Give thyself to that which befalls; uncover thy brow from
                   thy locks;
              Neither to me nor to thee has choice been given.
              Neither endurance nor truth belongs to the laugh of the rose

---

1672 "Letters" ("Every day"), 1, 1–6. Line (1) is in pencil.
168 "The garden of Eden," 20–28. In pencil.
169 " 'Come!—the palace of heaven," 1–14, x, 15–19. In pencil.

(20)        The loving nightingale mourns; cause enough for mourning
[170]     Why enviest thou the streaming verses of Hafiz
           Know that a god has bestowed on him eloquent speech

[171] Hafiz

          Who royally bedded
          On ermine lies
          Knows not the stone pillow
          Of the pilgrims thorn bed

(5)         Nothing suits gold so well as wine

         Desire no bread, forsake the guest hall of the earth,
         The earth is a host who murders his guests
                  [Hafiz, *Diwan*, 1] p 12

[172]            [Hafiz, *Diwan*,] ↑Vol 1. p. 79↓
         The red rose blooms
         The nightingale is drunken
         Now leave free course to drinking
         Ye reverencers of wine

(5)         The building of Sorrow it seemed /so firm/a mass/
         ⟨As if it were all of stone⟩ ↑Piled of ⟨the solid ⟨stone⟩
             ↑rock↓⟩ granite /gray/rock/↓
         O see how the crystal glass
         /Has already shattered it & broke/The pile in shivers broke/

         Bring wine; ⟨since⟩ before the Throne
(10)        Which hears our wishes
         ⟨Wise man &⟩ drunkard ↑& sage↓ are ⟨alike⟩ ↑one↓
         And prince & groom

         Since I must one day leave
         This two-ported guest house
(15)        It is all one whether my lifes course
         Be high or humble

         It is not possible without sorrow
         And without grief to live
         Since on the day of Destiny ↑was↓
(20)        Sorrow ⟨determined to us⟩ ↑assigned to us↓

[173]     For being & not-being cumber thee not
         Be ever of glad heart

170 " 'Come!—the palace of heaven," 20–21. In pencil.
171 "Who royally bedded" (1–4); "Nothing suits gold" (5); "Desire no bread" (6–7). In pencil.
172 "The red rose blooms," 1–20. In pencil.
173 "The red rose blooms," 21–36. In pencil.

The end of every excellence
Is the ⟨Néant⟩ ↑Chaos & the Night↓

(5)      Pomp, Asaph, the East-wind-horse,
The knowledge of the bird language,
Is all gone to the winds
And profits not the ⟨lord⟩ ↑king↓

⟨Swing thee⟩ ↑Mount↓ not from the straight way
(10)     In to the air with wings
The arrow flies into the air & falls
Again to earth

How can the tongue of thy quill
Thank Hafiz therefor
(15)     That thy words steadily from mouth
to mouth fly.

[174]           [Hafiz, *Diwan*,] vol 1 p 106.
Of paradise o hermit
Let us make renunciation
⟨We⟩ ↑Our names↓ are from the beginning ↑therein↓
Not inscribed
(5)     Who⟨m God love⟩ ↑out of love ⟨of⟩to God, on this earth↓
No kernel plants
⟨He⟩ ↑The same↓ is without corn also
Glad of his being.
Thee befits Mosque & rose crown
(10)     Prayer & ⟨virtue⟩ ↑orisons↓;
⟨And me⟩ ↑Mine me allows↓ the drinking house & bell-
     chime
⟨And church &⟩ ⟨↑And the nuns of the↓⟩ ↑And the pretty
     nuns'↓ cloister.
Thou pious man ⟨o⟩ withhold not
⟨Me from⟩ ↑Forbid me not the↓ ⟨w⟩vine,
(15)     On the ⟨creation⟩ ↑first↓ day was /my dust/Hafiz clay/
Kneeded with ⟨wine⟩ /it./wine/
He is no /wise man/dervise/, ⟨he⟩his /deserves/service/ not
↑Owes↓ Heavenly joys,
Who in the drinking house will not pawn
(20)     ⟨h⟩His clothes for ⟨wine⟩ ↑madeira↓,
⟨Or⟩ ↑He↓ who will let ⟨his friend's⟩ ↑the hem↓
⟨Coat⟩ ↑Of his friends garment↓ escape,
Will not rightly enjoy

174 "Ghaselle: From the Persian of Hafiz," 1–7, 7, 13–16, 9/10, 10–12, 17, x, 19, 19/20, 21,
21, x. In pencil.

[175]    Eden's bliss & the angels kisses
         Hafiz since Gods grace
         Has marked thee with favor
         Shy thou not hell & thou
(5)      Art sure of heaven

         Who lets the skirt of his friends shirt
         Escape unpledged
         Edens bliss & angels kiss
         ⟨He⟩ shall want their edge

[176]    Of paradise O hermit wise
         Let us renounce the thought
         Of old therein our names of sin
         Allah recorded not

(5)      Who dear to God neath earthly sod
         No corn-grain plants
         The same is glad that life is had
         Though corn he wants
         Thee befits mosque & cool kiosk
(10)    Fasting & orisons
         Mine me allows the drinking house
         And chase of pretty nuns
         O just fakeer with brow austere
         Forbid me not the vine
(15)    On the first day was Hafiz clay
         Kneaded with wine
         He is no dervise ne'er shall his service
         Owe heavenly ⟨meed⟩ ↑dues↓
         Who in the banquet not pawn his blanket
(20)    For Schiraz juice.

         I adjure thee By God What need hast thou of heaven
         Ask me only once what thy need of it is

[177] Hafiz
         Many our needs, yet we spare prayers
         Since thro' thy ⟨gemuth⟩ ↑nature↓ have we no need of
             praying
         ⟨Gemuth⟩ ↑The Nature↓ of my ⟨frie⟩ ↑beloved↓ is the
             world-showing mirror
         Ah it has taught me that thy need is no need

175 "Ghaselle: From the Persian of Hafiz," 23, 25–28, 21–24. In pencil. Lines (6–9) are written at the bottom of the page opposite the earlier version on p. [174].
   176 "Ghaselle: From the Persian of Hafiz," 1–8, 13–16, 9–12, 17, x, 18–20 (1–20); "Many our needs," x?, x? (21–22). In pencil.
   177 "Many our needs." In pencil.

(5)          Long time I endured the torments of the ship
                Since the pearls are mine, what do I want of the sea
                Beggar! the soul-squandering life of the beloved
                Knows thy petition. She has no need of explanation
                Prince of beauty, by God! I am burned up by love.
(10)        Ask me finally still, Have the beggars really need?
                ↑Thou↓ Importunate flee   I have nothing to do with thee
                My friends are there   Is there need of enemies
                Thy word conquers Hafiz, of itself appears virtue
                Envy & empty strife with the adversary are not needful

[178] ↑Hafiz [*Diwan*] Vol II p 344↓
                Early after the night long revel
                Took I lyre plectrum & bow↑l↓
                Bridled the horse of Reason
                Drove it with spurrs ⟨thro⟩ ↑to↓ the town of revellers

(5)          See the host flatters me
                That I fear not the blinding of Destiny
                Thou the aim of the arrow of speech
                Said the host with bows of brows

                Little profits it thee
(10)        Tho thou ⟨gir⟩ embrace me like a belt
                Spread the net for others
                Over the net the Auka soars

                Host & trusted are one
                Every difference is only a pretence
(15)        Reach us the boats of Sohra
                That we save us out of these waters

                Ah how enjoyed the Shah
                Who in himself is constantly enamoured
                All is riddle Hafiz
(20)        To explain it to us is mere talk.

[179]     Of paradise o hermit wise
                Let us renounce the thought
                Of old therein our names of sin
                Allah recorded not

(5)          Who dear to God neath earthly sod
                No corn grain plants
                The same is glad that life is had
                Though corn he wants

178 "Early after the night long revel." In pencil.
179 "Ghaselle: From the Persian of Hafiz," 1–8, 13–16, 9–12, 17–20. In pencil.

Thy mind the mosque & cool kiosk
(10)     Spare fast & orisons
Mine me allows the drinking house
And ⟨the⟩ sweet chase of ↑the↓ nuns.

O just fakeer with brow austere
Forbid me not the vine
(15)     On the first day poor Hafiz' clay
Was kneaded up with wine

He is no dervise ⟨nor⟩ heaven ⟨love⟩ ↑slights↓ his service
Who shall refuse
There in the banquet to pawn his blanket
(20)     For Schiraz juice

[180]    ⟨Suffer⟩
⟨Let⟩ ↑Who↓ his friends skirt or hem of his shirt
⟨Escape his pledge⟩ ⟨↑Shall spare to↓⟩ ⟨shall⟩ spare to pledge
↑Him↓ Edens bliss & angels kiss
(5)     Shall want their edge.

Up Hafiz ⟨the⟩ grace /of/from/ ⟨Gods⟩ high Gods face
⟨Has on thee shone⟩ ↑Beams on thee pure↓
Shy thou not hell & trust thou well
Heaven is ⟨thine own⟩ ↑secure↓

[181₁]  ↑Hafiz [*Diwan*] Vol II p 125 ↓
Drinkest thou wine ‖ . . . . . ‖ the heaven
‖ . . . . . . ‖ earth ‖ . . . ‖ diffuses
Fear no sin which
Also has its uses
(5)     Without scruple ‖ . . . . . ‖ all
All which ‖ . . . . . . . ‖
Since the murdersword of Destiny
↑Without scruple↓ Hews thee down ⟨without scruple⟩
I adjure thee o my love
(10)    B‖ . . . . . . . . . . . ‖ I crave
Come to my deathbed
Come to my grave
Ah what is heaven or hell
Angel or man
(15)    This temperence is ever
A heresy

180  "Ghaselle: From the Persian of Hafiz," x, 21–28. In pencil.
   181₁  "Drink wine, and the heaven," 1–23 (1–23); "The Builder of heaven," 2?, 2?, 3–6, 9
(17–23). In pencil, struck through in pencil, and all but "Hafiz . . . p 125" erased. Beneath this
layer is a twelve-line draft of "Ode to Beauty," in erased pencil, of which only the first line is
legible: "Who gave thee o Beauty".

Our Earth ‖ . . . . . . ‖
‖ . . . . . . . . ‖ shut in
So that no street
(20)    Leads out of it ‖ . . . ‖
On quite wonderful highways
leads wine the Understanding
The great vault stands

[181₂]                              *Rubies.*
They brought me rubies from the mine
⟨I held⟩And held them to the sun;
I said, they're drops of frozen wine
From Eden's vats that run.

(5)    I looked again; I thought them hearts
Of friends to friends unknown;
Tides that should warm each neighboring life
Are locked in sparkling stone.

But fire to thaw that ruddy snow,
(10)    To /break the winedrop's prison,/melt rubied ice/
Or /give love's scarlet tides to flow,/teach these frozen hearts
        to glow/
/That sun is yet unrisen./When shall that sun arise/

[182]        But fire to thaw that ruddy snow
To melt the ruby ice
To teach these frozen loves to glow
When shall that sun arise

[183₁]    If ‖ . . . . ‖ as ‖ . . . . . . . ‖
⟨‖ . . . . . . . ‖⟩ Beauty's not beautiful to me
‖ . . . . . . . . . . . . . . . ‖
This ch‖ . . . . . . ‖ absorbed
(5)    ‖ . . . . . . . . . . . . . . . . ‖
‖ . . . . . . . ‖ & ‖ . . . . . . . ‖
And ‖ . . . . . . . . . . . . . ‖
‖ . . . . . . . . . . . . . . . ‖
Now that Morning the mountain
(10)    ‖ . . . . . . . . . . . . . . . . ‖
‖ . . . . . . . . ‖ be
‖ . . . . . . . . . . . . ‖
‖ . . . . . . . . . . . . . . . . ‖

‖ . . . . . . . . . ‖ goes it

---

181₂ "Rubies." The variant phrasings in lines (10–12) are in pencil.
182 Rubies," 9–12. In pencil.
183₁ "Hermione," 8–9, x?, 12, four unused lines?, 19/20, x?, 22?, x?, x?, x?, 28?, 29–31, x?, x?, x? In pencil, struck through in pencil and erased.

(15)  Is it || . . . . . . . . . ||,
In thee to frame, in me to trust,
That thou to a stranger couldst belong
|| . . . . . . . || a great house
|| . . . . . . . . . || blood
(20)  || . . . . . . || they[?] come out
I || . . . . . . . . . || myself

[1832] ↑Hafiz [*Diwan*] Vol 2 p 125 ↓
If thou drink wine the heaven
Free on earth itself diffuses
Fear not sinning, which
Also has its uses

(5)  Without scruple ⟨have at⟩ ↑gather↓ all
All which is thine own
Since the murdersword of Fate
Without scruple hews thee down

I adjure thee o my love
(10)  At thy graceful feet I crave
That thou come to my deathbed
Come thou to my grave

Ah what is heaven or hell
Angel or man
(15)  This Temperance is ever
A heresy

The Builder of heaven
Has shut in the earth
So that no street
(20)  Leads out of it forth

[1841]  A priest[?] || . . . . . . || vows[?]
Ill || . . . . . . . . . ||
When thy || . . . . || glances came
|| . . . . . . . . . . . ||
(5)  And drew ⟨|| . . . . ||⟩ || . . || every trait.

Once, I || . . . . . . ||
Now I || . . . . || with all
As shepherds lamp on a hillside
Seems to the distant eye

1832 "Drink wine, and the heaven," 1–20 (1–20); "The Builder of heaven," 1–4 (17–20). In pencil.
1841 "Hermione," 34?, 35, 37, x?, 39–56. In pencil, struck through in pencil and erased.

(10)    A door into the mountain heart
So ⟨the love of thee⟩ did thy love unlock for me
‖ . . ‖ ⟨‖ . . . . ‖⟩ the highways of nature

Deceived, thou now wanderest
In strange lands unfed
(15)    And my kinsmen are come to soothe me
The southwind is my relation,
He is come with purple shades
And drugged with all spices
And in every twinkling covert
(20)    And in a hundred twilights
⟨Hovers⟩ ↑Discovers↓ ⟨over⟩thy form
Out of the heart of the forest

[1842]    On wonderful roads
Wine leads the mind forth
The vault stands unmoved
Until the Last Day

(5)    Yet *via* the Cup
Goest thou clean over all away
⟨The⟩ May the wish of pious hearts
Ever attend thee Hafiz

[1843]    Ages vainly fan their wings
Me shall keep thy love sublime

Vainly fan the air his wings
⟨If I ⟨sta⟩ rest in thy love sublime⟩
(5)    ⟨Me suffice thy loves sublime⟩
Me shall keep thy love sublime

[1851]    Thou camest yesterday
And when I sat by the brook at evening
It throbbed up from the water
‖ . . . . . . . . . . . . . ‖

(5)    The ‖ . . . . . ‖
We are thine allies,
As it is with thee, it is with her,
We are bound with thee,
We are of thy clan,

1842 "Drink wine, and the heaven," 21–28 (1–8); "The Builder of heaven," 5–6, 9–12 (1–6). In pencil.

1843 "Not yet, not yet," 43–44.

1851 "Hermione," 57–58, 60, x?, x?, 65, x, 75?, x, 66, 61/62?, 75?, 77–78. In pencil, struck through in pencil and erased.

(10)    And in hints wisdom ‖ . . . . ‖
⟨Grass⟩ ↑Lawns↓ & fire & song & darkness
She shall find thee inextricably
Follow not ‖ . . . ‖ flying ‖ . . . ‖
Come to us & she comes to thee.

[1852]    ——— ———
I am neither faint nor weary,
Fill thy will, O faultless Heart!
Here from youth to ⟨g⟩age I tarry,
Count it flight of bird or dart.
(5)    My heart at the heart of things
Heeds no longer lapse of time,

What ⟨can⟩ avail his wings
If I abide with the Cause
A hat of straw a roof of pine
(10)    Will guard my head like a castle
And I love my freedom

[186]    Thou wilt not speak as a man
Yet I never do not hear thee
Tho thou ⟨take⟩ pleas⟨ure⟩e ⟨in⟩ ↑to↓ baffl⟨ing⟩e me
In saying all pungent things
(5)    And as quietly as if nothing was said
Every word thou sayest the /universe remembers/world
        records/ & repeats
Yet thou ⟨pretendest⟩ ↑feignest↓ not to have spoken.

[1871]    If it be as they said, that she ‖ . . . . . ‖
Beauty's not beautiful
But sceptred Genius aye inorbed
⟨‖ . . . ‖⟩ ↑‖ . . . . ‖ ruled in her sphere↓
(5)    This child absorbed
The ⟨genius⟩ of ‖ . . . . . . ‖ ocean
⟨‖ . . . . . . . . . . . . . . ‖⟩
‖ . . . . . . . . . . . ‖ motion
I ask no small ‖ . . . . . ‖
(10)    ‖ . . . . . . . . . . . . . . ‖
⟨I ask⟩ ↑No↓ ‖ . . . . ‖ ringlets dead
Shorn from her comely head
Now that Morning not disdains

1852 "Not yet, not yet," 37–42, five unused lines.
186 "Thou wilt not speak." The added words in lines (6–7) are in pencil.
1871 "Hermione," 8–13, x?, 15–16, x?, 17–20, six unrecovered lines. Erased pencil. The
added material in line (4) was written on p. [186].

Mountains & the ‖ . . . . ‖ plains
[six lines of erased pencil writing]

[1872] This is he who scourged by foes
Rises straight refreshed by blows
⟨Into slavery⟩ ↑To captivity↓ they sold him,
But no prison bars would hold him
(5) Though they sealed him in a rock
Mountain walls he can unlock
Thrown to gaunt lions for their meat
The lion crouches at his feet
⟨Nor tied to⟩ ↑Him at↓ the stake ⟨would⟩ ↑no↓ flames
        assault
(10) But ⟨curved away⟩ ↑arched oer him↓ an honoring vault
This is he who is called Fate
⟨Marching by still & silent ways⟩
By secret ways & desolate

[1881] ⟨↑‖ . . . ‖↓⟩ Heedless how ⟨the⟩ the weak are strong
⟨I am at rest⟩
⟨How is it with thee⟩
Was it just
(5) In thee to frame in me to trust
Thou to ⟨a stranger⟩ ↑‖ . . . ‖↓ couldst belong
I am of a lineage
That each for ⟨every⟩ ↑each↓ doth ↑fast↓ engage
To thee as ‖ . . . ‖ I seemed
(10) ‖ . . . . . . . . . . . . . . . ‖
↑H‖ . . . ‖ vowed to b‖ . . . . . . ‖↓
‖ . . . . . . . . . . . . . . . ‖
Ill bested for gay bridegroom
↑I was by th‖ . . . . . . . . ‖ed↓
(15) When thy meteor glances came
We talked of worldly fate
And drew truly every trait

‖ . . . . . . . . . . . ‖
Now I ‖ . . . . . . . . . ‖
(20) As ‖ . . . ‖ lamp on hillside
Seems by ‖ . . . . . ‖ man espied
A door into the mountain heart
So did thy love for life unlock
Highways through ‖ . . . . ‖ rock

1872 "Worship," 1–11, x, 12. Struck through in ink.
1881 "Hermione," 27, x, x, 28–33, x?, 34, x?, 35–39, x?, 41–46. In pencil, struck through in pencil and erased.

[188₂]    But ever arrives in time
       ↑And pronounces & awards↓
       He knows thee well
       Is thy father & mother
(5)     And in another person
       Is still a joyful surprise
       He is ⟨not⟩ deaf to prayers
       But he blesses unawares
       ↑Where is He & where is he not?↓
(10)    And the riddle of the plot
       To draw the boundary line
       Betwixt the human & divine
       Betwixt his & thine

[189₁]      Deceived thou wanderest
       In strange lands unblest
       And my kinsmen come to ‖ . . . . . ‖
       Southwind is my next of blood
(5)     He is come through fragrant wood
       Drugged with all spices ↑from climates warm↓
       And in every twinkling covert
       And in ‖ . . . . . . . ‖
       ⟨Discovers⟩ ↑Unveils↓ thy form
(10)    Out of the heart of the forest dark
       The ‖ . . . . . . . . ‖
       And when I sat by the ⟨brook at evening⟩ ↑‖ . . . ‖↓
       ↑Watching the day fade↓
       It throbbed up from the /water/brook/

(15)    River & rose & crag & bird
       Frost & sun & eldest night
       ‖ . . . ‖ to me
       ↑Courage↓ We are thine allies
       And with this hint be wise
(20)    The chains of kind
       The distant bind
       ⟨As⟩ That the ‖ . . . ‖ must she ⟨ag⟩
       ⟨Against⟩ ↑Above↓ her will, be true

[189₂]    This is the oldest & best known,
       ⟨Familiar as what is⟩ ↑More near than aught thou call'st↓
         thy own,

---

188₂ "Worship," 13, x, x, x, 17–20, x, x, 21, 23, 22. Lines (3–13) are struck through in ink.
189₁ "Hermione," 47–56, x?, 58–62, 63/64?, 65–70. In pencil, struck through in pencil and erased. One or two lines of erased pencil writing beneath lines (2–3) have not been recovered.
189₂ "Worship," 15–20, x, x, 21–23. Lines (1–3) and (1–11) are struck through in ink.

Yet, beheld in another's eyes,
Is age on age a glad surprise
(5) This is he who deaf to prayers
⟨Creates⟩ ↑Makes↓ & blesses unawares.
Tell where is he. Where is he not?
Tis the riddle of the plot
To draw the mystic boundary line
(10) Severing rightly his from thine,
Which is human, which divine.

[190₁] ‖ . . . . . . . . . . . . ‖
To winds & waterfalls
A ‖ . . . . . . . ‖ festivals
‖ . . . . . ‖c & to musics thought
(5) Inextricably bound
She[?] shall find thee & be found
‖ . . . . . . . . . . . ‖ feet
[six lines of erased pencil writing]
And ‖ . . . . . . . . . ‖
[four lines of erased pencil writing]

[190₂]     Deep in the man sits fast his fate
To mould his fortunes mean or great.
Unknown to Cromwell as to me,
Was Cromwell's measure & degree,
(5) Unknown to him as to his horse
If he than grooms be better or worse.
He works, fights, plots, in rude affairs,
With boys, lords, kings, his craft compares,
Till late he learned, thro' doubt & fear,
(10) Broad England harbored not his peer,
Obeying Time, the last to own
The genius from its cloudy throne.
For, the prevision is allied
Unto the thing so signified;
(15) Or say, the foresight that awaits
Is the same Daemon that creates.

[191₁]     If it be as they said she was not fair
Beautys not beautiful to me
But sceptred Genius aye inorbed
⟨Self protected⟩ ↑Culminating↓ in her sphere.

190₁ "Hermione," x?, 72–77, eleven unrecovered lines. Erased pencil.
190₂ "Fate" ("Deep in the man"). Between "He" and "works" in line (7), "now" has been added in extremely faint pencil.
191₁ "Hermione," 8–26. Erased pencil; lines (15–16) are struck through in pencil.

(5)   This Hermione absorbed
    The lustre of the land & ocean
    Hills & islands river & tree
    In her form & motion
    I ask no bauble miniature
(10)   No ringlet dead
    Shorn from her comely head
    Now that Morning not disdains
    Mountains & the misty plains

    Her colossal portraiture
(15)   They her heralds be
    Steeped in her quality
    And singers of her fame
    Who is their Muse & dame.

    Higher, dear swallows, mind not what I say

[1912]   Delicate omens traced in air
    To him authentic witness bare
    Birds with auguries in their wings
    Chanted undeceiving things
(5)   Him to beckon, or to warn,
    Well might then the poet scorn
    To learn of scribe or courier
    Hints writ in vaster character
    And in his mind at dawn of day
(10)   Soft shadows of the evening lay.

    Already blushes in thy cheek
    The bosom thought which thou must speak;
    The bird, how far it haply roam,
    By cloud, or isle, is flying home;
(15)   And every man, in love or pride,
    Of his fate is never wide.

[1921]   Ah heedless how the weak are strong
    ↑Say↓ Was it just
    In thee to frame, in me to trust,
    Thou to the Syrian couldst belong
(5)   I am of a lineage
    That each for each doth fast engage
    To thee as ‖ . . . . . . ‖
    Hermit vowed to books & gloom
    Ill bested for gay bridegroom

1912 "Fate" ("Delicate omens"), 1–10 (1–10); "Nemesis," 1–4, 7–8 (11–16). Above line (2), Emerson entered an incomplete revision: "the lone bard to see."
1921 "Hermione," 27–46. Erased pencil.

(10)      I was by thy touch redeemed
When thy meteor glances came
We talked of worldly fate
And drew truly every trait

Once I dwelt apart
(15)      Now I live with all
As shepherds lamp on far hillside
Seems by the traveller espied
A door into the mountain heart
So didst thou quarry & unlock
(20)      Highways for me thro the rock

[192₂]      He has driven out
With real wrath the seeming rout
He will not know
Rival or foe
(5)      Makes bitter dupe
Of seeming Satan & his troop
Punishing with obscene shape
Of ass, & tadpole rat & ape
The pleasure-hunting crew
(10)      Once let the nuisance enter
With a peristaltic motion
The blue vault will shrivel & ⟨shake⟩take
Shape of scorpion or of snake
And sting the enemy to death

(15)      The blue vault will shrivel & shake
As sheds his skin the vernal snake.

[193]      Now deceived thou wanderest
In strange lands unblest

And my kinsmen come to soothe me
Southwind is my next of blood
(5)      He is come thro fragrant wood
Drugged with spice from climates warm
And in every twinkling glade
And twilight nook
Unveils thy form

(10)      Out of the forest way
⟨Thou camest⟩ ↑Forth paced it↓ yesterday
And when I sat by the water course

192₂ "Unity," sixteen unused lines.
193 "Hermione," 47–63, 65–68. Erased pencil.

Watching the daylight fade
It throbbed up from the brook

(15) River & rose & crag & bird
Frost & sun & oldest night
To me their aid preferred
Courage we are thine allies
And with this hint be wise
(20) The chains of kind
The distant bind

[1941] [four lines of erased pencil writing]
(5) ‖ . . . . . . . . . . ‖ festivals
[six or seven lines of erased pencil writing]

[1942]      Cold Bangor
Where is no summer but a thaw

[195] [blank]
[196] Hafiz [*Diwan*] Vol II p 308
The Phoenix of my heart
Has its nest in the last heaven
In the bodycage immured
 Is it long sated with life

(5) ⟨↑If↓ The Phoenix soul flies once⟩
↑When once that wild bird flies amain↓
Up out of the ashy heap
So nestles it again
In that high ⟨nest⟩ ↑keep↓

(10) ↑If he↓ Flies ⟨it⟩ up so sits ⟨it⟩he on
⟨The⟩ ↑Tuba↓ tree of Paradise
There know ⟨w⟩tis my abode
High upon the heaven ramparts

And over this world
(15) Spreads my Phoenix its wing
So rests on the whole world
The shadow of good luck

In both worlds dwells he
High over all heavens
(20) His body is of etherstuff
Yet nowhere dwells the soul

1941  Cf. "Hermione," 73 (5). Erased pencil.
1942  "Cold Bangor." In pencil.
196  "The Phoenix," 1–4, 6, 6, 5, 8, 7, 9/10, x, x, 13–14, x, 16–17, x, 19, x. In pencil.

[197] The plane of the higher world
   Is the playplace of my ⟨Phoenix⟩ ↑bird↓
   The rose bed of Paradise
   Assures him drink & food

(5)   ⟨Lost⟩ ↑Lonely↓ Hafiz ↑who↓ so long
   Thou Gods unity preachest
   ⟨Write⟩ ↑Teach↓ unity ⟨in⟩to every tongue
   Of man & genii.

[198] As the bird trims himself to the gale
   So I trim myself to the tempest of time
And I shall find something pleasant in my last throb that I am getting
out of mean polities

[199]  Everything knows everything
   Those /scowling/envious/ clouds above there know
   The smell of wine in the house below

[200]  Every house stands on foundations
   The hours of joy & pride
   ⟨Rest on⟩ neutral moods ↑do underpin↓
   ⟨Rest on⟩ grief
(5)   ⟨Rest on⟩ labor, determination,
   And the natal hour
   Heaven is no harlequin
   Tricked out in idle weeds
   Ribbons & beads
(10)  Her joys are solid flowers & fruit
   From a nocturnal root
   Which feels the acrid juice
   Of Erebus
   And turns the ⟨eternal⟩ wo of night
(15)  By natural alchemy to aye rejoicing might

[201] [blank]
[202₁] But I retire
   ⟨And hide ‖ . . . ‖ the ‖ . . . ‖⟩
   And ⟨will⟩ ↑hide myself↓ amongst my thrifty pears
   And every fault of mine ⟨hid⟩ ↑masked↓ by a growth of
    theirs

[202₂]      *Bacchus*
   Omitted verses

197 "The Phoenix," eight unused lines. In pencil.
198 "Terminus," 33–34, followed by a prose draft of unused lines (cf. p. [205₁]). In pencil.
199 "Everything knows everything." In pencil.
200 "Bacchus," ten unused lines, 7–11. In pencil.
202₁ "Terminus," four unused lines. In pencil, struck through in pencil and erased.
202₂ "Pour the wine!," 1–3, 5, 4, 6–13. In pencil.

Pour the wine pour the wine
As it changes to foam
So is its god
New & unlooked for
(5)    Rushing abroad
In farthest & smallest
Comes royally home

In spider wise
Will again geometrize
(10)    In the bee & gnat keep time
With the annual solar chime
The aphides like emperors
Sprawl & play a pair of hours

[203]    It is time to be old,
To take in sail,
The god of bounds
Who sets to seas a shore,
(5)    Who visits all in his unerring rounds
And saith to each, No More,
No farther go
A little while
Here thou shalt plan & smile
(10)    And feebly emulate
The earlier feat
And in the fault of germs
Mature the unfallen fruit
Fancy departs
(15)    ⟨Thou shalt⟩ no more invent
Curse, if thou wilt, thy sires
Bad husbands of their human stock
Who gave thee breath
But failing therewith to bequeath
(20)    The needful stark marrow to thy bones
Should second thee in thy assault
Upon the hosts of Evil & the Dark
[204₁]    But left thee ebbing veins
Raging ambition
But ⟨a⟩ ↑the↓ hand numb
Amidst the Muses deaf & dumb
(5)    ↑Would↓ ‖ . . . ‖ the worlds Crown but the hand is numb

203  "Terminus," 1–7, 19–20, x, x, 21–22, 9, 9, 23–26, 27/28, x, x. In pencil, struck through in pencil and partially erased.
204₁  "Terminus," 29, x, 32, 31–32, 6/7, 8, 10–11, x?, 12–13, x?, x?, x? In pencil, struck through in pencil and erased.

No more extend
Thy broad ambitious branches & thy roots
Arch in thy firmament
To compass of a pilgrims tent
(10)    ⟨Now ‖ . . . ‖⟩
Theres not enough for this & that
Make choice
‖ . . . . . . . . ‖
‖ . . . . . . . . . . ‖
(15)    A‖ . . . . . . . . ‖

[204₂]    True Bramin in the morning meadows wet
Expound the vedas in the violet
Or, hid in vines, peeping thro many a loop,
See the plum redden, & the beurré stoop

(5)    True Bramin in the morning meadows wet
Expound the Vedas in the violet,
Or, hid in vines, peeping thro' many a loop,
See the plum redden, & the Beurré stoop.

———

As sings the pinetree in the wind
(10)    So sings in the wind a sprig of the pine,
Her strength & soul has laughing France
Shed in each drop of wine.

———

[205₁]    I ‖ . . . ‖
⟨As the bird⟩
The voice at noon obeyed ⟨in⟩ ↑at↓ prime
As the bird trims herself to the gale
(5)    ⟨So⟩ I trim myself to the ⟨‖ . . ‖⟩ ↑storm↓ of Time
I mind the rudder reef the sail
Obey the voice at noon obeyed at prime
And it will please me at ‖ . . . . . . . . ‖
That I am escaping mean politics

(10)                Cold Bangor
Where is no summer but a thaw

[205₂]       Two well-assorted travellers use
The highway,—⟨Cupid,⟩ ↑Eros↓ & the Muse.

204₂ "Gardener," two drafts (1–8); "Nature in Leasts" (9–12). Lines (1–4) are in pencil.
205₁ "Terminus," 34?, 33, 36, 33–36, x, x (1–9); "Cold Bangor" (10–11). Erased pencil;
lines (1–9) are struck through in pencil.
205₂ "Love and Thought."

From this pair, is nothing hidden;
To the pair, is nought forbidden.

(5) Hand in hand↑,↓ the comrades go,
Every nook of nature through:
Each for other they were born,
Each can t'other best adorn;
⟨And the⟩ only ⟨cureless⟩ ↑smites a mortal↓ grief

(10) Past all ⟨respite⟩balsam or relief
⟨Is⟩ When, by false companions crossed,
The⟨se⟩ pilgrims have each other lost.

[206₁] It is time to be old
To take in sail
The god of bounds
Who sets to seas a shore

(5) Came to me in his fatal rounds
And said No more
No farther ⟨go⟩ ↑spread↓
⟨‖ . . . . . ‖ extend⟩
Thy broad ambitious branches & thy roots

(10) Contract thy firmament
To compass of a pilgrims tent
Theres not enough for this & that
Now ‖ . . . . . ‖
Economize the failing river

(15) ⟨Nor blaspheme⟩ ↑Revere↓ the giver
And solid make the few
A little while
Here plan & smile
⟨And father & mate⟩

(20) ⟨To ‖ . . . . . ‖ feat⟩
And fault of novel germs
Matures the unfallen fruit
Fancy departs
No more invent

[206₂] It is time to be old,—
To take in sail;—
The god of bounds,
Who sets to seas a shore,

(5) Came to me in his fatal rounds,
And said, "No more!
No farther spread

206₁ "Terminus," 1–7, x, 8, 10–11, 12?, 13–16, 19–20, x, x, 21–22, 9, 9. In pencil, struck
through in pencil and erased.
206₂ "Terminus," 1–9, 9–18.

Thy broad ambitious branches, & thy root;
Fancy departs,
(10)     No more invent,
Contract thy firmament
To compass of a tent,
There's not enow for this & that,
Make thy option, which of two;
(15)     Economize the failing river,
Not the less revere the Giver,
Leave the many, & hold the few.
Timely wise accept the terms,
Soften the fall with wary foot;

[2071]   Curse if thou wilt thy sires
Bad husbands of their human stock
Who gave thee breath
But failed to bequeath
(5)     The mortal sinew stark ↑as once↓
And marrow to thy bones
Should second thine assault
On Satans of the Dark
But left thee ebbing veins

(10)     Amidst the Muses left thee deaf & dumb
Raging ambition but the hands are numb

As the bird trims ‖ . . . . ‖ to the gale
I trim myself to the storm of Time
I man the rudder reef the sail
(15)     Obey the voice at eve obeyed at prime

And hide my age amidst my thrifty pears
Each fault of mine masked by a growth of theirs

[2072]   A little while
Still plan & smile,
And, fault of novel germs,
Mature the unfallen fruit.
(5)     Curse, if thou wilt, thy sires,
Bad husbands of their fires,
Who, when they gave thee breath,
Failed to bequeath
The needful sinew stark as once,
(10)     The Baresark marrow to thy bones,
But ⟨left thee⟩ ↑a legacy of↓ ebbing veins,
Inconstant heat & nerveless reins,

---

2071 "Terminus," 23–28, x, x, 29, 31–36, x, x. In pencil, struck through in pencil and erased.
2072 "Terminus," 19–36, x, x.

Amid⟨st⟩ the Muses left thee deaf & dumb,
Amid the gladiators halt & numb.

(15) As the bird trims her to the gale,
I trim myself to the storm of time,
I man the rudder, reef the sail,
Obey the voice at eve obeyed at prime,
And hide my age amidst my thrifty pears,
(20) Each fault of mine masked by a growth of theirs.

[208] It is time to be old
To take in sail
The god of bounds
Who sets to seas a shore
(5) Came to me in his fatal rounds
And said No more
No farther spread
Thy broad ambitious branches & thy root
Fancy departs
(10) No more invent
Contract thy firmament
To compass of a tent
Theres not enow for this & that
⟨Now choose⟩ ↑Make thy option↓, which of two.
(15) Economize the failing river
↑⟨Nor⟩ ↑Not the↓ less↓ Revere the Giver
⟨And solid make⟩ ↑Leave the many & hold↓ the few
↑If thou be wise accept the terms↓
↑Soften the fall with wary foot↓
(20) A little while
Still plan & smile
And fault of novel germs
Mature the unfallen fruit

[209] Curse if thou wilt thy sires
Bad husbands of their fires
Who ↑when they↓ gave thee breath
Failed to bequeath
(5) The needful sinew stark as once
⟨And⟩ ↑The Baresark↓ marrow for thy bones
But left thee ebbing veins
↑Inconstant heat↓ And nerveless reins
Amidst the muses left thee deaf & dumb

208 "Terminus," 1–9, 9–22. In pencil. Lines (18–19) were added at the bottom of the page, circled, with an arrow to indic : their position.
209 "Terminus," 23–32, 3 ͘ ͘, x, x. In pencil.

(10)        Raging ambition but the ⟨hand is⟩ ↑right arm↓ numb
           ↑Amidst the ⟨fierce⟩ gladiators did thine arm benumb↓

           As the bird trims her to the gale
           I trim myself to the storm of Time
           ⟨M⟩I man the rudder, reef the sail,
(15)        Obey the voice at eve obeyed at prime

           And hide my age amidst my thrifty pears
           Each fault of mine masked by a growth of theirs

[210]      Since the devil hopping on
           From bush to vine from man to dame
           ⟨Has⟩ Marshals temptations
           ⟨A hundred⟩ ↑A million↓ deep
(5)         And ever new beauties rise
           And with what faults soever
           The stock of illusion
           Is inexhaustible
           I meantime depreciate
(10)        Every hour in the market
           But the wares I would buy
           Are enhanced every hour
           I see no other way
           Than to run violently from the market

[211]               ↑II↓
           A ⟨king delighteth⟩ ↑queen rejoices↓ in h⟨is⟩er peers,
           ⟨For⟩ ↑And↓ wary Nature knows her own,
           By court & city, dale & down,
           And, like a lover volunteers,
(5)         And to her son will treasures more,
           And more to purpose, freely pour
           In one woodwalk, than learned men
           Will find with glass in ten times ten.

[212]               ↑I↓
           Winters know
            Easily to shed the snow
            And the untaught spring is wise
            In cowslips & anemonies.
(5)         Nature, hating art & pains,
            Baulks & baffles plotting brains,
            But she dearly loves the poor,

210 "Since the devil." In pencil.
211 "A queen rejoices." The roman numeral "II" is in pencil.
212 "Nature I," 1–6, 9–15. The roman numeral "I" is in pencil.

     And by marvels of her own
     Strikes the bald pretender down.
(10)    For nature listens in the rose
     And hearkens in the lilys bell
     To help her friends, to plague her foes,
     And, like wise God, she judges well

[213]       ↑III↓
     Delicate omens traced in air
     To him authentic witness bare;
     Birds ⟨bore⟩ with auguries on their wings
     Chanted undeceiving things
(5)     Him to beckon, him to warn,
     Well might then the poet scorn
     To learn of scribe or courier
     Hints writ in vaster character,
     And on his mind, at dawn of day,
(10)    Soft shadows of the evening lay.

  [214] [blank]
  [215]  Give all to love
     Obey thy heart
     Friends, kindred, days,
     Estate, good fame,
(5)     ⟨Yes⟩ ↑Plans, credit,↓ & the Muse;
     Nothing refuse.

     Tis a brave master
     Let it have scope
     Follow it utterly
(10)    Hope beyond hope
     It dives into noon
     With ⟨silent⟩ wing ↑unspent↓
     Nor prates beforehand ↑of its intent↓
     ⟨Of its intent⟩
(15)    But it is a god
     Knows its own path
     And the outlets of the sky

     Twas not for the mean
     It requireth courage stout
(20)    Souls above doubt
  [216₁]  Valour unbending
     Such it will reward

213  "Fate" ("Delicate omens"), 1–10. The roman numeral "III" is in pencil.
215  "Give All to Love," 1–10, 12–14, 14–20. Partially erased pencil.
216₁  "Give All to Love," 21–42. Erased pencil.

They shall return
More than they were
(5)      And ever ascending

Leave all for love;
⟨And⟩ yet hear me, yet
One word more thy heart behoved,
One pulse more of firm endeavor,
(10)      Keep thee today
⟨And⟩ tomorrow, & forever,
Free as an Arab
Of thy beloved

Cling with life to thy darling
(15)      But ⟨at⟩ ↑when↓ the first surprise
⟨Or⟩ ↑Vague↓ shadow of surmise
⟨The maiden entertains⟩ ↑Which her sunny bosom crossed↓
Of a joy apart from thee
Free be she, fancy-free,
(20)      Do not detain a ‖ . . . . ‖
Nor the least rose she ⟨flung⟩ ↑tossed↓
From her summer diadem

[216₂]            *Compensation.*

Man is the elm and Wealth the vine;
Staunch & strong the tendrils twine;
Though the frail ringlets thee deceive
None from its stock that vine can reave
(5)      Fear not then, thou child infirm,
There's no god ⟨can⟩dare wrong a worm;
Laurel crowns cleave to deserts,
And power to him who power exerts;
Hast not thy share? On winged feet
(10)      Lo! it rushes thee to meet,
And all that Nature made thy own;
Floating in air, or pent in stone,
Will rive the hills & swim the sea
And like thy shadow tend on thee.

Oversoul

(15)      Space is ample east & west,
Yet two cannot go abreast;

216₂ "Compensation" ("Man's the elm") (1–14); "Unity," 1–7 (15–21). The mottoes on pp. [216]–[221], all published in *Essays: First Series* (1847), are in the same shade of ink and were probably all entered into the notebook at the same time.

Cannot travel in it two;
Yonder masterful cuckoo
Crowds every egg out of the nest
(20)     Quick or dead except its own;
There lies a spell on sod & stone
[217]     Night & day 've been tampered with
Every quality & pith
Surcharged and sultry with a power
That works its will thro' age and hour.

        ═══

*Spiritual Laws.*
(5)     The living Heaven thy prayers respect,
House at once and architect,
Quarrying man's rejected hours,
Builds therewith eternal towers;
Sole & self-commanded works
(10)    Absolute in vital cirques,
Fears not undermining days,
Grows by decays,
And by the famous might that lurks
In reaction & recoil,
(15)    Makes flame to freeze, & ice to boil,
⟨And⟩Forging thro↑'↓ swart arms of ⟨o⟩Offence
The silver seat of Innocence.

[218₁]    I cannot spare wine
[six lines of erased pencil writing]
    ↑Sharp↓ ‖ . . . . . . . . ‖
    ‖ . . . . . . . . . . . . ‖
(10)    ‖ . . . . . . . . . . . ‖
bird, & reptile be my game
⟨‖ . . . . . . ‖⟩ Ivy ‖ . . . . ‖ fillet band
↑Blinding↓ dogwood in my hand
‖ . . . . . . . ‖ ↑me↓ in the upas boughs
(15)    ↑Where ‖ . . . . . . . ‖↓
Hemlock for my ⟨ice⟩ ⟨↑serve me↓⟩ ↑sherbet cull me↓
And prussic ⟨‖ . . . ‖⟩ ↑juice↓ to lull me
I am ‖ . . . . . . . ‖
‖ . . . . . . . . . . . ‖
(20)    I am not a ‖ . . . . . . . ‖
⟨But⟩ ↑For↓ a ‖ . . . ‖ drop of dew

**217** "Unity," 8–11 (1–4); "Spiritual Laws," 1–5, x, 6–12 (5–17). In line (16), the apostrophe is in pencil.
    **218₁** "Mithridates," 1, six unrecovered lines, 10?, x?, x?, 13–15, 18, x?, 16–17, x?, x?, x?, 21?, x?, 22, x, 25? In pencil, struck through in pencil and erased.

I am not a ‖ . . . . ‖
I will see the world    Taste it try it
I have it with me
(25)      Dark power ‖ . . ‖rry

[218₂]    Cling with life to the maid
But when the surprise
First vague shadow of surmise
Flits across her bosom young
(5)      Of a joy apart from thee
Free be she, fancy-free
Do not thou detain ‖ . . . ‖ hem
Nor the palest rose she flung
From her summer diadem

[219₁]    All virtues & mights
Hither take me use me fill me
↑Veins & arteries    Thronging bravely↓
Though it kill me    not be an owl
(5)      But ‖ . . . . . . . . ‖
in the Capitol

I cannot spare wine
I cannot spare water
Tea or tobacco
(10)      Scion of an old & wide branching stem
Every thing is kin of mine

Give me agates for my meat
⟨Chromes & drugs⟩ ↑Cantharids↓ to eat
From all kingdoms ↑‖ . . ‖↓ foods
(15)      From all Zones & altitudes

From all natures
Sharp & slimy salt & basalt
Wild & tame
‖ . . . . . . ‖ ape sealion
(20)      bird & reptile be my game

Wall ivy for my fillet band
Blinding dogwood in my hand

[219₂]              Friendship
A ruddy drop of manly blood
The moon-led sea outweighs
The world uncertain comes & goes

218₂ "Give All to Love," 34–42. Erased pencil.
219₁ "Mithridates," 26, 31–32, 32/33, 34, 34, 1, 1–2, x, 5–10, 10/11, 11–15. Erased pencil.
219₂ "Friendship" ("A ruddy drop"), 1–17. In lines (11–13), the apostrophes are in pencil.

        The lover rooted stays:
(5)      I fancied he was fled,
        And, after many a year,
        Glowed unexhausted kindliness
        Like daily sunrise there.
        My careful heart was free again,
(10)    O friend, my bosom said,
        Thro↑'↓ thee alone the sky is arched,
        Thro↑'↓ thee the rose is red;
        All things thro↑'↓ thee take nobler form,
        And look beyond the earth,
(15)    And is the mill-round of our fate
        A sun-path in thy worth;
        Me too thy nobleness has taught

[220₁]   Swing me in the Upas tree
        And vampyres when I ‖ . . . ‖ carouse

        Hemlock for my sherbet cull me
        And the prussic juice to lull me
(5)      I am imprisoned in strait & few
        I am ‖ . . . . . . ‖
        ‖ . . . . . . . . . . . ‖
        I will see the world, ‖ . . . . . . ‖
        And have it with me taste it

(10)    Dark powers & merry
        All virtues all mights
        Rights or wrongs & things allowed
        Minorities things under cloud
        Take me use me fill me
(15)    Veins & arteries though ye kill me
        Is[?] chemist ‖ . . . . . ‖
        But ‖ . . . ‖ the Appetite
        But sun me in the Capitol

[220₂]   To master my despair.
        The fountains of my hidden life
        Are through thy friendship fair.

### Art.
        Give to barrows, trays, & pans,
(5)      Grace & glimmer of romance;
        Bring the moonlight into noon
        Hid in gleaming piles of stone;

220₁ "Mithridates," 18–19, 16–17, 20, x?, x?, 22, x, 25–26, 29–32, x?, x?, 34. Erased pencil.
220₂ "Friendship" ("A ruddy drop"), 18–20 (1–3); "Art," 1–13 (4–16).

On the city's paved street
Plant gardens lined with lilac sweet;
(10)     Let spouting fountains cool the air
Singing in the sunbaked square;
Let statue, picture, park, & hall,
Ballad, flag, & festival,
The past restore, the hour adorn,
(15)     And make each morrow a new morn,
So shall the drudge in dusty frock

[221₁]     [five lines of erased pencil writing]
‖ . . . . . . . . ‖ thing

[221₂]     Spy behind the city clock
Retinues of airy kings
Skirts of angels, starry wings,
His fathers shining in bright fables,
(5)     His sons regales at heavenly tables;
Tis the privilege of Art
Thus to play its cheerful part,
Man in earth to acclimate,
And bend the exile to his fate;
(10)     And, made of the same element
With the days and the firmament,
Teach ⟨them⟩ ↑him↓ on these as stairs to climb,
And live on easy terms with time,
Whilst upper life the slender rill
(15)     Of human sense doth overfill.

[222]     I cannot spare water or wine
Tobacco leaf ↑or↓ poppy or rose
From the earthpoles to the Line
All between and all that grows
(5)     Everything is kin of mine

Give me agates for my meat
Give me cantharids to eat
From ⟨all⟩ air & ocean bring me foods
From all Zones & altitudes

(10)     From all natures sharp & slimy
Salt & basalt wild & tame
Tree & lichen ape sealion
Bird & reptile be my game

221₁ "Mithridates,"(?), cf. 5.
221₂ "Art," 14–28.
222 "Mithridates," 1–19. In pencil. Lines (1–5) are erased; lines (16–17) were added at the bottom of the page, circled, with an arrow to indicate their position.

Ivy for my fillet band
(15) Blinding dogwood in my hand
↑Hemlock for my sherbet cull me↓
↑And the prussic juice to lull me↓
Swing me in the upas boughs
⟨Ba⟩ Vampire-fanned when I carouse

[223] Hemlock for my sherbet cull me,
And the prussic juice to lull me,
⟨I am⟩ ↑Too long↓ shut in strait & few
⟨Like a moth⟩ ↑Grimly↓ Dieted on ⟨summer⟩ dew

(5) I will use the world, & sift it,
To a thousand humours shift it,
As you spin a cherry

Dark powers ↑& mad↓ & merry
All virtues, methods, mights,
(10) ⟨Organs⟩ ↑Means↓ appliances delights
↑Reputed↓ Wrongs or ↑braggart↓ rights
↑Smug routine of↓ Things allowed
Minorities, things under cloud,
Take me, use me, fill me,
(15) Vein & artery, though ye kill me
↑Lord↓ I will not be an owl
But sun me in the Capitol.

[224] ‖ . . . ‖ would say sooth
‖ . . ‖ to be its tongue
‖ . . . . . . . . . . ‖
‖ . . . . . . . . . . ‖
(5) Thou grand expressor of the present tense
Type of permanence
Amid these coward ⟨‖ . . . ‖⟩ ↑shapes of joy & grief↓
That ‖ . . . . . ‖ ↑will not bide ⟨to be seen⟩ the seeing↓
↑Good↓ ‖ . . . . . . . . ‖
(10) Without the phrases
‖ . . . . . . . . ‖
Complement to humanity
↑Who hast in ‖ . . ‖↓ ‖ . . . . . ‖ ⟨at⟩ vantage
[six lines of erased pencil writing]
(20) ‖ . . . . . . ‖ imagest ‖ . . . ‖ ⟨‖ . . . ‖⟩ ↑the stable↓
‖ . . . . . . . . . . ‖

223 "Mithridates," 16–17, 20–34. Partially erased pencil.
224 "Monadnock," x, x, x?, x?, 379–80, 382–83, 423–24, x?, 395–96, six unrecovered lines, 407, x?, x?, x? In pencil, struck through in pencil and erased.

‖ . . . . . . . . . . . . ‖
‖ . . . . . . . . . . . . ‖

[225]          ↑Mute orator↓
               Affirming affirming
               ‖ . . . . . . . . . ‖
               And seen from afar
(5)            In the horizon
               By hot ambition by the frivolous
               By vanity by spleen
               Thou maketh sane

               Ages are thy days
(10)           ‖ . . . . . . . ‖
               ‖ . . . . . . . . ‖
               ‖ . . . . . . . . ‖
               ‖ . . ‖ ↑shapes↓ of ‖ . . . ‖
               ‖ . . . . . . . ‖
(15)           ‖ . . . . . . . . ‖
               ‖ . . ‖ mixture of a ‖ . . ‖
               ‖ . . . . . . . . ‖
               But ‖ . . . . . . . . ‖
               Lover ‖ . . . . . . ‖
(20)           C‖ . . . . . . . . . ‖ the new stars
               Makes thy ‖ . . ‖ges & spars ↑‖ . . . . ‖ spars↓

[226]          Ages are thy days
               Thou grand expressor of the present tense
               And type of permanence
               Amid these coward shapes of joy & grief
(5)            That will not bide the seeing
               Mute orator
               Good to plead
               And send conviction without phrase
               Complement of human kind
(10)           Holding us at vantage still
               Our ↑⟨‖ . . . . ‖⟩ sumptuous↓ indigence
               ⟨‖ . . . . ‖ with⟩ ↑O barren mound!↓ Thy plenties fill
               We hiss & chatter
               Thou art sacred, mute
(15)           ⟨We fade & fall⟩
               Thou ↑seest↓ O watchman tall

225  "Monadnock," 423, x, 414–15, 418/420, x, 422, 378, x?, x?, x?, 382?, eight unidentified
lines. In pencil, struck through in pencil from line (1) to line (8) and erased.
226  "Monadnock," 378–80, 382–83, 423, 423–24, 395–400, 406, 405–7, x, 408, 410–11.
In pencil, struck through in pencil and erased; lines (6–8) are separately struck through in
pencil.

⟨Seest⟩ ↑Our↓ towns & races ⟨pass⟩ ↑grow & fall↓
Thou imagest the lone the stable
⟨The⟩ causal & immutable
(20)    Which we ↑all our lifetime↓ seek
And though the substance elude
In thee the shadow find

[227]    Affirming affirming
Mute orator
Good to plead
And send conviction without phrase
(5)    Thy opaker star
Seen daily from afar
In the horizon
By hot ambition
By Gain
(10)    By the frivolous
Recalleth us
And maketh sane

[228]    As in the old poetic fame
The gods are lame
And ⟨in the gods defect⟩ ↑the simular despite↓
⟨Denotes transcending force⟩ ↑Betrays abounding might↓
    ⟨↑to deepeyed intellect↓⟩
(5)    ⟨So⟩ call not ⟨thou⟩ ↑a waste↓ that barren cone
Above the floral zone
Where forests starve, ⟨a waste⟩
⟨Wrecks of⟩
Ruins of a ⟨structure⟩ style which none restore
(10)    Transporting ↑frieze or↓ architrave ⟨or frieze⟩
Of this work of the old ⟨architect⟩ ↑building Intellect↓
Does the stern style address no taste
Call it not waste

Complement of humankind
(15)    Having us at vantage still
Our sumptuous indigence
O barren mound, thy plenties fill!
We ⟨hiss⟩ ⟨↑cackle↓⟩ ↑chirp↓ & chatter
Thou art sacred, mute,
(20)    Thou seest o watchman tall

227 "Monadnock," x, 423, 423–24, 413–15, 418–22. In pencil, struck through in pencil and erased.
228 "Monadnock," 368–74, 390, 390–91, 394, x, x, 395–400, 405. Partially erased pencil.

[229] Our towns & races grow & fall
   Thou imagest the lone & stable
   Central & immutable
   Which we all our lifetime seek
(5)  And though the /thing/substance/ ↑us↓ elude
   ↑We↓ In thee the shadow find
   ↑Thou↓ In ⟨true⟩ ↑our↓ astronomy
   ⟨Thy⟩ ↑An↓ opaker star
   Seen daily from afar
(10) In the horizon
   By ambition
   By gain
   By the frivolous
   Recalleth us
(15) And maketh sane
   Mute orator
   Good to plead
   And send conviction ↑without phrase↓
   Affirming affirming
(20) Thou dost supply
   The shortness of ⟨humanity⟩ ↑rapid days↓
   And promise on the word of sooth
   A long morrow to this mortal youth


[230] Ages are thy days
   Thou grand Expressor of the present tense
   And type of permanence
   Amid these coward shapes of joy & grief
(5)  That will not bide the seeing

   As in the old poetic fame
   The gods are ⟨tame⟩ blind & lame
   And the simular despite
   Betrays the more abounding might
(10) So call not waste that barren cone
   Above the floral zone
   Where forests starve
   Nor useless hold in Thrifts balance weighed
   Gray rocks, Cyclopean blocks
(15) ↑Which↓ Who can tell what mason laid
   Ruins of a style which none restore
   ⟨Transporting⟩ ↑Replacing↓ frieze or architrave

---

229 "Monadnock," 406–7, x, 408, 410–15, 418–23, 423–24, x, 425–28. In pencil, struck through in pencil and erased.
  230 "Monadnock," 378–80, 382–83, 368–74, x, 388–91, 393–94, x. In pencil.

Of this ↑Haughty↓ work erect
Of the old building Intellect
(20)     Does the stern style address no taste

[231]    Call it not waste
It is pure use
⟨It is the Muse⟩
What ⟨harvest is like this harvest⟩ ↑sheaves like these we
     glean & bind↓
(5)     ⟨Which brings the Eternal⟩ ↑not of Ceres but the↓ ⟨hint⟩
     ↑Muse↓
↑Of a celestial Ceres & the Muse↓

Complement of human kind
Having us at vantage still
Our sumptuous indigence
(10)    O barren mound, thy plenties fill
We chirp & ⟨chatter⟩ ↑prate↓
Thou ⟨sacred⟩ art ⟨& mute⟩ ↑silent & sedate↓

Thou seest, o watchman tall,
Our towns & races grow & fall
(15)    Thou ⟨shadowest⟩ ↑imagest↓ the Lone & Stable
Central & immutable
↑For↓ Which we all our lifetime ⟨seek⟩ ↑grope↓
And tho the substance us elude
We in thee the shadow find
(20)    Thou in our astronomy
An opaker star
Seen daily from afar
In the horizon ⟨edge⟩ ↑hoop↓

[232]    By ambition
And ⟨gain⟩ errant gain
‖ . . . ‖ frivolous‖ . . . ‖
Recalleth ‖ . ‖
(5)     And ‖ . . . ‖ sane
Mute orator versed to plead
     ⟨Good to plead⟩
And send conviction without phrase
     ⟨Affirming affirming⟩
(10)    ⟨Thou to us supply⟩
     ⟨The shortness ‖ . . . . . . ‖⟩
     ⟨And ‖ . . . . . . . . ‖ word of sooth⟩

231 "Monadnock," 372, 375, x, 376–77, 377, 395–400, 405–7, x, 408, 410–15. In pencil.
The first change in line (5) was "Muse" for "hint."
232 "Monadnock," 418–23, 423–24, x, 425–28, 378–80, 382–83, 368–72. In pencil, struck
through from line (1) to line (18) five times in pencil, and the entire page erased.

⟨Long ‖ . . . . . . . . ‖ mortal youth⟩
⟨Ages are thy days⟩
(15)      ⟨Thou ‖ . . . . . . . ‖sent tense⟩
⟨And type of permanence⟩
Amid these coward shapes of joy & grief
That will ‖ . . . ‖ the seeing

As in the old poetic fame
(20)      The gods are ‖ . . . . . . ‖
And ‖ . . . . . . . ‖ despite
Betrays the more abounding might
So call not waste that barren cone
[233]    Above the floral zone
Where forests starve
Nor in Thrifts balance weighed
Reckon useless the gray rocks
(5)      Heaped in cyclopean blocks
Which who can tell what mason laid
Ruins of a style ⟨which⟩ none ↑need↓ restore
Replacing frieze or architrave
⟨Of⟩ ↑Still is↓ this haughty work erect
(10)     Of the old building Intellect.
Does the stern style address no taste.

Call it not waste
It is pure use
What sheaves like these ↑which here↓ we glean & bind
(15)     Of celestial Ceres & the Muse?

Complement of human kind
Having us at vantage still,
Our sumptuous indigence
O barren mound, thy plenties fill!
(20)     We chirp & prate
Thou are silent & sedate
Thou seest o watchman tall
[234]    Our towns & races grow & fall
⟨Thou⟩ ↑And↓ imagest the lone and stable
The Central & Immutable
For which we all our lifetime grope
(5)      And though the substance us elude
We in thee the shadow find
Thou in our astronomy

233 "Monadnock," 373–74, x, x, 388–91, 393–94, x, 372, 375–77, 395–400, 405. Erased pencil.
234 "Monadnock," 406–7, x, 408, 410–15, 418–28. In pencil.

An opaker star
Seen daily from afar
(10)     Above the horizons hoop
By circumspect ambition,
By errant Gain,
⟨By⟩ soft Lovers and the frivolous
Recalle⟨th⟩st us
(15)     And make⟨th⟩st sane
Mute orator   well skilled to plead
And send conviction without phrase
Thou dost supply
The shortness of our days
(20)     And promise on the word of sooth
Long morrow to this mortal youth.

[235]–[236] [blank]
[237] Hafiz [*Diwan*] Vol 2 p 332
Thou who with thy long hair
As with thy chains art come
Thine be opportunity
Since to ⟨w⟩ capture ⟨fools⟩ ↑slaves↓ thou comest

(5)     ⟨One hour⟩ ↑O↓ show th⟨ee⟩yself ⟨mild⟩ ↑benign↓
And ⟨a⟨l⟩fter thy custom⟩ ↑change thy mood↓
⟨Si⟩ Since they to ⟨pray⟩ ↑resign↓
Thou to ask & ⟨demand⟩ ↑claim↓ comest

Be it in peace be it in war
(10)    ⟨Ever ⟨am I⟩ to sacrifice to thee⟩ ↑To yield to thee↓ ↑⟨is⟩
↑it is↓ my doom↓
Since in every event thou art
With entran↑c↓ing kisses come

⟨Ice⟩ ↑Fire↓ & water ⟨are⟩ mingled ↑are↓
In thy swelling ruby lip
(15)    Evil eyes be far!
As a juggler thou art come

Honor to thy soft heart
And a good work wouldst thou do
Pray for all the dead
(20)    Whom thine eyelashes slew

[238]    Say what boots my virtue
Since thou intent to steal the heart's treasures

237 "Thou who with thy long hair," 1–20 (1–20); "Fair fall thy soft heart!" (17–20). In pencil.
238 "Thou who with thy long hair," 21–28. In pencil.

All drunken & confused
To my still chamber art come

(5)      See Hafis said he to me
Thy coat with spots soiled
⟨Art⟩ ↑Wert↓ thou safe from this company
⟨o⟩Once home again?

[239] *Hafiz*
Art thou wise, four things resign,—
Love, & loneness, ⟨rest⟩ ↑sloth↓, and wine.

[240]–[241] [blank]
[242₁]   Set not thy foot on graves
Hear what wine & roses say
The mountain chase, the summer waves,
The crowded town thy feet may well delay.

(5)      Set not thy foot on graves
Nor seek to unwind the ‖ . . . . ‖
Which Charitable Time
And Nature have allowed
To wrap the errors of a sage sublime

(10)     Set not thy foot on graves,
Care not to strip the dead
Of his sad ornament
‖ . . . . . . . . . . ‖,
His sheet of lead
(15)     And trophies buried
Go get them where he got them when alive
As resolutely dig or dive

[242₂]                    Nantasket.                    1841

Lobster-car, boat, or fishbasket,
Peeps, noddies, oldsquaws, or quail,
To Musketaquid what from Nantasket,
What token of greeting & hail?

(5)      Can we tie up & send you our thunder⟨?⟩,—
Pulse-beat of the sea on the shore?
Or our Rainbow, the daughter of Wonder,
Our rock-⟨ledge⟩, ⟨New England's front-⟩ ↑Massasoit's
palace-↓ door.

239 "Art thou wise."
242₁ "To J. W.," 1–12, x?, 14–17. Erased pencil.
242₂ "Nantasket." In line (8), "ledge" is cancelled in pencil.

White pebbles from Nantasket beach,
(10) Whereon to write the maiden's name;
Shells, sea-eggs, sea flowers, could they teach
Thee the fair haunts from whence they came!

---

[243] αδακρυν νεμουται αἰωνα.

"A new commandment," said the smiling Muse,
"↑I give↓ My darling son, ⟨my bard,⟩ *Thou shalt not
preach.*"
Luther, Fox, Behmen, Swedenborg grew pale,
And, on the instant, rosier clouds upbore
(5) Hafiz & Shakspeare with their happy choirs.

---

[244] ↑Hafiz [*Diwan*] Vol II p 489↓
Bring me boy the juice of the vine
Which with greatness fills us
Bring it to me who ⟨am wanting⟩ ↑at heart↓
⟨At heart⟩ ⟨↑Am wanting↓⟩ ↑Fail↓ in spirit & fulfilment
(5) Bring me the stone of the wise
Karun's treasure Noah's longevity
Come, that by thy means may open
All the doors of Luck & Life.
Bring only the liquid Fire
(10) Which seeks the *serduscht* in the dust
Bring! to me drunken 'tis allowed
To pray to the world & to Fire
Bring the wine of the glass of Jemschid
⟨Which⟩ That ⟨boasts⟩ ↑sparkles↓ therewith in the Neant
(15) Give it me that through its ⟨strengthening⟩ ↑vigor↓
I as Jemschid the world may see-thro'
Boy bring me the glass of Jemschid
Loiter not, & bring me it
Wisely said Jemschid to the Kaisar
(20) That world's not worth a barley corn
Bring me boy the nectar beaker
Since it leads to Paradise
Flute & lyre lordly speak
[245] Wine-lees outvalue crowns
Bring the veiled beauty
Who in bad houses sits
Bring her; my good name

243 "'Αδακρυν νέμονται Αἰῶνα." Three lines of erased pencil writing at the top of the page
have not been recovered.
244 "From the Persian of Hafiz," 1–16, x, x, 17–18, x, x, 19. In pencil.
245 "From the Persian of Hafiz," 20–41, x, 42. In pencil.

(5)  Give I away for wine & cup
    Bring me the fire ↑ - ↓ water
    When the lion drinks the woods burn
    Give it me that I storm heaven
    And tear the net of the wolf
(10)  Wine wherewith the Houris teach
    the Angels the customs of Paradise
    On the /glow/coals/ will I set it
    And therewith my brain perfume
    Bring me wine thro whose shimmer
(15)  Jam & Chosroes gave light
    Give me that to the flute I sing
    Where is Jam & where is Kauss
    Bring me the blessing of old times
    Bless the departed Shahs
(20)  Bring wine which spends lordship
    ↑ Of ↓ Whose purity hearts preach
    Bring it to me the Shah of hearts
    Am I even now far from the same
    Give me wine to wash me clean
[246]  of the spots of all cares
    Give & see the countenance of Luck
    Make me waste ↑ ; ↓ seek wisdoms treasure
    Whilst I dwell in Spirit garden
(5)  Why am I fettered here
    Is the glass in my hands
    ⟨Shows⟩ This mirror shows me all
    Drunken speak I of purity
    Beggar speak I of lordship
(10)  When Hafiz in riot sings
    Shouteth Sohre in her sphere
    Fear the instability of the day
    Beg of the wine life
    Since wine increases life
(15)  Opens for thee the gates of the secret
    Boy arrange the wine companions
    Since the world is to all untrue
    Let the ⟨trumpets⟩ pipes give thee remembrance
    How the crown of Kobad ⟨disappeared⟩ ↑vanished↓
(20)  Seek in ↑ red ↓ wine the heart's wish
    Without wine has it not rest
    Can the body forego the soul
    Can the heart forego wine

246 "From the Persian of Hafiz," 43–44, x, 45–46, x, 47–53, 53, x, x, 54–56, five unused lines. In pencil. In line (24), "Boy" is lightly struck through in pencil.

Boy come & fill the cup
[247]    That I to thee of Caesar speak
Boy be not sure of the world
⟨Since it will⟩ ↑Twill not shun to↓ shed thy blood
Boy be not disturbed at us
(5)    Thou art earth & not fire
Fill the glass with good wine
Without lees sweet & clear
Pour for me the sweet scented
Gold & silver have I none
(10)    Give me the ruby colored
Without falsehood without boast
Give the rosecrown, the cowl,
Only wine to mortgage
Boy be not far from the Cloister
(15)    There lies a treasure buried
Does one say to thee 'Thou shouldest not ⟨give⟩ ↑go↓
Good night; give him no answer
Bring boy the purple cup
Wh↑i↓ch rejoices heart & soul
(20)    Give me that I lose the wo
And ↑to the banquet↓ find the way↑,↓ ⟨to the feast⟩
Bring wine which nourishes the soul
Strengthens the sick heart as Ghosts do
Grant that out of the world I go
[248]    Bring the glass as moon & sun
That I in the heaven throne
Come with glasses of old wine
Gradually make me drunken
(5)    Drench thou me in purest wine
Drunken I to thee will sing
Boy, come, from thy cheeks
Exhale wine lees like the spring
Take the glass fear no sin
(10)    They drink wine in Paradise
Come I have need of wine
Take the hand with a glass
Despairing of the world-lot
Came I running to the Cloister
(15)    Give wine which maketh glad
That I my steed bestride
Run thro' the Course with Rustem

247 "From the Persian of Hafiz," x, 57–58, twenty-one unused lines. In pencil.
248 "From the Persian of Hafiz," twelve unused lines, 59–64, x, x, 65–68. In pencil.

And ⟨after⟩ ↑to↓ my hearts content gallop
Give me the ruby cup
(20)       Which opens the heart to time
That I expunge the reason
And plant banners on the worlds
That we kiss with the glass
And quench the fire of wo

[249]    Let us today drink together
Since now & then go never alike
Who has ordered the feast
Is with glad mind satisfied
(5)        Is escaped from the toils of the Diwes
Is become jealous of the dust
Who has this throne maintained?
This corner of ten days?
Ah Youth! hence in wind
(10)      Happy he who spent it well
Give wine that I may overspring
Both worlds in one
Often give me a gallon
Openly or at least in secret
(15)      Elephants carry drums
Yet the drum gives signal of march
At morn comes from the bright spheres
Houris call to my ears
Beautiful ⟨fowl⟩ bird sweet soul
(20)      Unfurl thy wing break thy cage
Sit on the roof of the seven domes
Where the souls have rest

[250]    In the time of Bisurdschimihr
Prevailed the beauty of Menutscheher
On the beaker of Nuschirvan
Wrote they once in former times
(5)        Hear from us the counsel & learn
Only a piece of the world course
Here is only a place of sorrow
Few joys are there here below
Without sorrow are we frolic
(10)      Who has nothing has no sorrow
Where is Jam & where his cup
Solomon & where his mirror
Which of the philosophers knows
When Kauss & Jam lived

---

249 "From the Persian of Hafiz," 69–73, x, x, x, 74–77, four unused lines, 78–83. In pencil.
250 "From the Persian of Hafiz," 84–91, x, 92–103, x, x, x. In pencil.

(15)    When they left this world
Left they only their names
Bind thy heart not to the earth
When thou goest come not back
Fools pour out their hearts

(20)    The confidant of the world is foreign to God
Never gives it what thou wishest
Here is not the state of joys
Boy bring the firewater
That it may quench my glow

[251]    Since my heart lies in flames
Water will I shed thereon
Boy bring me rubywater
That robs the ruby of its dye

(5)    Often give the lifewater
Fluid as the glow of the sun
A glass of wine gives thee the view
Of the five cupolas with nine steps
Without support can thereon go

(10)    Whoso can himself deny
Who is discreet is foolish
Makes himself the dust of the banquet hour
Bind thee not to the cloister of the Earth
Or thou flyest away with the dust

(15)    Give me Boy the Caesar cup
Which makes glad the heart & soul
Under wine & under cup
We signify the purest love
Youth vanishes like the lightning

(20)    Life goes by like the wind
Leave the dwelling with six doors
And the snake with nine heads
Head & gold squander freely
If thou lovest also still the Soul

[252]    Hasten into the other life
Except God all is vain
Give me boy this spirit-toy
⟨Give me⟩ physic to the wounded heart

(5)    When the cup of Jam was lost
Used the whole world it no more
Give me boy the frozen water

251 "From the Persian of Hafiz," six unused lines, 104–8, x, x, x, 109–18. In pencil.
252 "From the Persian of Hafiz," 119–21, x, 122–29, six unused lines, 130–35. In pencil.
An arrow inscribed in pencil in the left margin points to line (16). In line (17), "quickly" is
lightly struck through in pencil.

Wake the ⟨dead⟩ ↑torpid↓ heart with wine
Every ⟨c⟩lump of clay ⟨here⟩ below
(10)  Is a skull of Alexander
Seas ⟨are⟩ the blood of princes ↑are↓
Desart-sand the dust of beauties
A drunken worshipper of wine
Spake thus   the cup in his hand
(15)  The envious destiny only flatters
The stupid rejoice themselves thereon
Boy give the bitter, quickly.
Friends hand makes sweet the bitter
More than ⟨a⟩ ↑one↓ Darius was ⟨it⟩ ↑there↓
(20)  Who the whole world mastered
But when they died
Believest thou they have not been
Boy go from me to the Shah
Say to him, Shah ⟨as Jam⟩ crowned ↑like Jam↓
[253]  Seek first the heart of the poor
Since the glass so shows the worlds
Empty ⟨woes⟩ ↑sorrows↓ from this earth
↑Shah↓ Canst thou with wine expel
(5)  Now at time of pomp of thrones
This springfruit of lordship
Lord of earth   prince of times
Moon of fortune   mighty king
Whose crown's glance yields
(10)  Still rest to fishes & fowls
Heart & eyeglance of the blessed
Lord of favor lord of hearts
World commander faith nourisher
What should I say well of him
(15)  When reason is astonished before him
His power knows no limits
Powerless let I my head sink
I lift my hand to pray
Turn my face to the Creator
(20)      Lord my God by thy grace
By the secret of thy name
Thine eternal true word
By the God sent gifts
⟨Happy⟩ ↑Blessed↓ be the Lord of Earth

253  "From the Persian of Hafiz," 136–41, x, 142–45, thirteen unused lines. In pencil.

[254] ↑Hafiz [*Diwan*] Vol II 291↓
    Knowst thou the luck the friends face to see
    Rather to beg near him than a prince to bee
    Tis easy out of the soul to banish lust
    ⟨To s  The sou⟩  ⟨T⟩Not easy the friend from the soul to
(5)           thrust
    With my own heart go I like a flower
    There tear I the garment of good name
    Now kiss I secretly with the roses, as the East wind,
    Now hearken I the secrets of the nightingale
(10)    Kiss the friends lips when thou canst
(10)    Otherwise wilt thou in the lips bite full of sorrow
        Seize the chance of talking with thy friend
        Who knows if we meet again on the way.

    The Phenix of my heart has assured
    His nest in the highest heaven cope
(15)    In the body's cage immured
    Is he long weary of life's hope

    ↑If once↓ The soul phenix flew ⟨he once⟩
    Up from the heap of ashes
    So nests he again
(20)    In that high nest

    Flies he once up, he will perch
    On the tree of life
    Know, that is my home
    High on the battlements of heaven

[255]    And over this world of ours
    ⟨Spreads⟩ ↑If↓ his wings my phenix ↑spread↓
    So rests on the whole world
    Of good luck the shade

(5)    In both worlds dwells he
    ⟨High over all heaven⟩ ↑Far below the planets roll↓
    His body of ether is compact
    Yet nowhere dwells the soul

    The plane of the higher world is
(10)    The play⟨place⟩ ↑ground↓ of my Phenix plays
    The rosebed of Eden
    Assures him meat & ⟨drink⟩ ↑wine↓

    Lost Hafiz so long
    As thou Gods unity preachest

  **254** "Knowest thou the luck" (1–12); "The Phoenix," 1–4, 6, 5, 8, 7, 9–11, x (13–24). In
pencil.
  **255** "The Phoenix," 13–20, eight unused lines. In pencil.

(15)       Write unity of every leaf
          Of men & genii
                  See p 194 [i.e., 196]

[256] Hafiz [*Diwan*] II p 380
       Novice, hear me what I say
       So shalt thou be purified,
       Whilst thou dost not tread the way,
       Thou canst not be a guide.

(5)       〈There in〉 ↑Pride of↓ the gazing school,
       〈Idol of thy〉 ↑Darling of sweet↓ companions,
       Mark, hear boy, thou too shalt be
       One day the sire of sons.

       ↑Have↓ Sleep, 〈eating〉 ↑& meat↓, & drinking,
(10)      The spark of love withstood.
       Eat not, sleep not, love in thinking
       Will come rushing like a flood.

       A beam of the love of Allah
       Once fall thy soul upon,—
(15)      By God, 〈I know〉 thou then wilt be
       More 〈beauteous〉 ↑brilliant↓ than the sun.

       As learned magians do,
       Thy hand from brass withhold
       That thou in life 〈an〉 ↑true↓ alchemist
(20)      〈Become & virgin〉 ↑May turn all dross to↓ gold

[257]    From thy footsole to thy head
       A beam of God thou burnest
       So soon as without foot or head
       To the hest of God thou turnest

(5)       〈Cast thyself〉 ↑Go leap↓ into the waves,
       And have no doubt or care,
       And the flowing of the seven broad seas
       Shall never wet thy hair.

       If Allah's face on thee
(10)      Look down with love benign
       Who 〈doubts〉 ↑disbelieves↓ that thou also
       To his face turnest thine.

       Were thy form & nature
       Broken, waste, & void,

256 "Novice, hear me," 1–20. In pencil; lines (1–4) and (17–20) are struck through in pencil.
257 "Novice, hear me," 21–40 (1–20); "Faith" (5–16). In pencil.

(15)       Believe not thou also
            Art from the root destroyed
                Hast thou Hafiz in thy heart
                Hope of safety thee before
                Then wilt thou sit henceforth
(20)              In the dust of the votary's door

[258] [Hafiz, *Diwan*,] II, 358.
            Hafiz speak not of thy need
            Are not these verses thine
            Then will no nobler one concede
            Thou canst at aught repine

[259]     Heaven is alive
            Self built & quarrying itself
            Upbuilds eternal towers
            Self commanded works
(5)        In vital cirque
            By dint of being all
            Its loss is transmutation
            Fears not the craft of undermining days
            Grows by decays
(10)       And by the famous might that's lodged
            In reaction & recoil
            Makes flames to freeze & ice to boil,
            And thro' the arms of all the fiends
            Builds the firm seat of Innocence
(15)       Is no emblem to measure
            Its perfect stature, youthful power,
            Youthful urgency,
            No lapse of memory,
            Betrays the angel into unbelief
(20)       In ↑the↓ beginning has the time to come
            And on the road its home
[260]        Property is good by day
            I do not delight
            In black acres of the night
            Nor my unseasoned step disturbs
(5)        The sleeps of trees or dreams of herbs

            I am not wiser for my age,
            Nor skilful by my grief;
            Life loiters at the Book's first page,—
            Ah! could we turn the leaf!

258 "To Himself." In pencil, struck through in pencil.
259 "Spiritual Laws," 1, 3–5, x, x, x, 6–12, seven unused lines. In pencil.
260 "Parks & ponds" (1–5); "Climacteric" (6–9). Lines (1–5) are in pencil.

[261]    Samson stark at Dagon's knee
Gropes for column strong as he
When his ringlets grew & curled
Groped for axle of the world

(5)    Of all wit's uses the main one
Is to live ⟨with⟩ ↑well↓ with who has none

Sudden winds came full of meaning
All too much to him they said
Southwinds have long memories
(10)    Of that be none afraid

[262₁]    Thou ‖ . . . . . . . ‖ed
In ‖ . . . . . . . . . ‖
⟨It⟩ ↑Sole↓ ‖ . . . . . . . ‖
I‖ . . . . . . . . . ‖

(5)    ‖ . . . . . . ‖ thats spent
With[?] ba‖ . . . . . . . ‖
Twas fired ‖ . . ‖ he came into hall
Here is ‖ . . . . ‖ ↑neither charge nor ball↓
Ask not what ⟨‖ . . . . . . ‖⟩ ↑kindles↓ in his brain
(10)    ⟨‖ . . . . . ‖⟩ ↑That to whisper were profane↓
The ↑angry↓ Muse will p‖ . . . ‖ ⟨him⟩ make him blind
He cannot go back to the old store
For he is lying in wait for more

[262₂]    I am not wiser for my age
Nor skilful by my grief
Life loiters at the Books first page
And we never turn the leaf

(5)    Dark flower of Cheshire Garden
Red Evening duly dyes
Thy sombre head with rosy hues
To fix far gazing eyes
Well the planter knew how strongly
(10)    Works thy form on human thought
I muse what secret purpose had he
To draw all fancies to this spot

⟨A few miles will smooth⟩
⟨Rough Monadnoc to a gem⟩

261 "Samson stark" (1–4); "Considerations by the Way," 26–27 (5–6); "South Wind," 9–12 (7–10). In pencil; lines (5–6) and (7–10) are separately struck through in pencil.
262₁ Unidentified lines (1–4); "Scholar is a ball," 1, x?, 3–4 (5–8); "Ask not treasures," 1/3, 4, x, 1–2 (9–13). In pencil; lines (5–13) are struck through in pencil, and the entire page erased.
262₂ "Climacteric" (1–4); "Dark Flower of Cheshire garden" (5–12); "A score of airy miles," two drafts (13–16). In pencil.

(15)    A score of airy miles will smooth
        Rough Monadnoc to a gem.

[263]   To clothe the fiery thought
        In simple word succeeds
        For still the craft of genius is
        To mask a king in weeds

(5)     Scholar is a ball thats spent
        Or the barrel that it sent
        'Twas fired ere he came into hall
        Here is neither charge nor ball

        Ask not what kindles in his brain
(10)    That to whisper were profane
        Nor fragments ⟨of⟩from his ancient store
        For he lies in wait for more

――――

        Atom from atom yawns as far
        As moon from earth as star from star

――――

(15)    As sings the pinetree in the wind
        So sings in the wind a sprig of the pine.

[264₁] pursuant[?]
      music
      viceroy

        Set not thy foot on graves
        Hear what wine ‖ . . . . . . . ‖
        The mountain chase the summer waves
        The crowded town ‖ . . . . ‖ well delay

(5)     Set not thy foot on graves
        Nor seek to unwind the shroud
        Which charitable Time
        And ‖ . . ‖ have allowed
        To wrap the errors of a sage sublime

(10)    Set not thy foot on graves
        Care not to strip the dead
        Of his sad ornament
        His myrrh & wine his rings
        His sheet of lead or trophies buried

---

**263** "Poet" ("To clothe") (1–4); "Scholar is a ball" (5–8); "Ask not treasures," 1/3, 4, 1–2 (9–12); "Atom from atom" (13–14); "Nature in Leasts," 1–2 (15–16). Lines (1–12) are in pencil.
**264₁** "To J. W.," 1–13, 14/15, 16–17. In pencil, struck through in pencil and erased.

(15)       Go get them where he got them ⟨in the mine & wave⟩ ↑when
             alive↓
       Dig or dive

[264₂]    And willing to be God the worm
       Flees thro all the round of form
       Mounts thro all the spires of form

       The Dervish whined to *Said*
(5)       Thou didst not tarry while I prayed
       But Saadi answered
       Once with manlike love & fear
       I gave thee for an hour my ear
       I kept the sun & stars at bay
(10)     And love for words thy tongue could say
       I cannot sell my heaven again
       For all that rattles in thy brain

———————

       Said Saadi when I stood before
       Hassan the camel driver's door
(15)     I scorned the fame of Timour brave
       Timour to Hassan was a slave
       In every glance of Hassan's eye
       I read great years of victory
       And I who cower mean & small
(20)     In the frequent interval
       When wisdom not with me resides
       Worship toils wisdom that abides

[265₁]    Set not thy foot on graves
       Nor bark at public thieves
       nor dog the heels of the wrong doing world
       Set not thy ‖ . . . . . . ‖
(5)       Nor virtuous cynicism

       ‖ . . . . . . . ‖ waste
       ‖ . ‖ critic bark
       Quarrels or ‖ . . . . ‖
       Twill soon be dark
(10)     Up ⟨& ‖ . . . . ‖⟩ ‖ . . . ‖ ↑⟨affair⟩ aim and ‖ . . . . . ‖↓
       ‖ . . . . ‖ speed ‖ . . . . . ‖
       God bless ‖ . . . . . . ‖

264₂ "May-Day," 323–24, 324 (1–3); "Nature" ("A subtle chain"), 5–6, 6 (1–3); "The
Dervish whined to *Said*," 1–2, 4–10 (4–12); "Said Saadi,—When I stood before," 1–10 (13–22).
In pencil.
    265₁ "To J. W.," five unused lines, 18–23, 23 (1–12); "Apples of gold"(?) (13). In pencil,
struck through in pencil and erased.

Apples of ‖ . . . . . . . ‖

[265₂]  I shunned his eye the faithful man's,
I shunned the toiling Hassan's glance

————

I grieve that better souls than mine
Docile read my measured line
(5)  High destined youths & holy maids
Hallow these my orchard shades
Environ me & me baptize
With light that streams from gracious eyes,
I dare not be beloved or known,
(10)  I ungrateful, I alone.

————

Ever find me dim regards,
Love of ladies, love of bards
Marked forbearance, compliments,
Tokens of benevolence
(15)  What then   can I love myself
Fame is profitless as pelf
↑A↓ Good in nature not allowed,
They love me as I love a cloud
Sailing falsely in the sphere
(20)  Hated mist if it come near

[266]  Go thou to thy learned task
I stay with the flowers of spring,
Do thou of the ages ask
What me the hours will bring.

(5)          This cup of life is not so shallow
That we have drained the best,
          That all the wine at once we swallow
And lees make all the rest.
          Maids of as soft a bloom shall marry
(10)  As Hymen yet hath blessed,
And fairer forms are in the quarry
Than Angelo released.

[267]  Tell men what they knew before
Paint the prospect from their door

[268] [index material omitted]

2652 "Said Saadi,—When I stood before," 11–12 (1–2); "I grieve that better souls" (3–10); "Ever find me dim regards" (11–20). In pencil.
266 "Botanist" (1–4); "This cup of life is not so shallow" (5–12). Lines (1–4) are struck through in ink.
267 "Tell men what they knew before."

[268ₐ] Heartily heartily
  Nothing be false
  Men ocular jocular
  Work with the fingertips
(5) Speak no deeper than the lips
  Blow, good northwind, I grow nervous
  Good wind, blow away all trace
  Of the spectral populace.

  Poets are colorpots
(10) Dovesnecks & opaline
  Exquisite daintiness
  Vapors of wine
  Delicate gloom
  Barrel of opium
(15) Blowing simoom
  Cloud-collecting, dissipating
[268ᵦ] Brain relaxing enervating
  Put your body on your word
  Man & sonnet at accord
  Set your foot upon the scale↑s↓
(5) My foot weighs just a pound
  Said the cruel Yankee captain
  Trucking for his precious bales
  Of ermine skin & silver fur
  With the painted islander.

(10) Be of your country & house & skin
  Though you farm your ⟨own⟩ ↑proper↓ brain
  Or your own body & sweat
  For the morsel which you eat
  Cowpasture ⟨or⟩ cranberry field
(15) Stone or ice, or fisher's flakes,
  Or a shoe your labor makes
  Get your rents there
  The way to heaven is just as ⟨long⟩ ↑near↓
  F↑r↓om every cabin on the sphere.

[268ᵪ]  Be of your country & house & skin
  Though you reap nothing but your chin
  Tho you farm your body & sweat
  For the morsel that you eat

268ₐ "Heartily heartily" (1–8); "Poets are colorpots," 1–8 (9–16).
268ᵦ "Poets are colorpots," 9–17 (1–9); "Be of your country," 1–4, 6–11 (10–19). Lines (10–19) are struck through three times in ink.
268ᵪ "Be of your country," 1–18.

(5)     Ax or scythe or mallet wield
         Cedar swamp or cranberry field
         Stone, or ice, or fisher's flakes,
         Or a shoe your labor makes
         Get your rent & stipend there

(10)    Way to heaven is just as near
         From every cabin in the sphere
         Nor shun to wear
         Thy native shape & hair
         Name country tongue & times

(15)    These thy preappointed badge
         Shell & shoes of pilgrimage
         The concealments & the caves
         Where high God his heart engraves

[268d]  Fortune hateth when she sees
         A people tottering in the knees
         Settle ⟨you⟩ solidly & low
         And speak that ↑matter↓ you ⟨do⟩ know

(5)     Kingcraft ⟨has⟩ ↑is↓ the spell to bear
         ⟨All its⟩ The crownjewels everywhere.
         ⟨Carries⟩ ↑Take↓ Rome into swamp & glen
         And ⟨w⟩chalk⟨s⟩ scores with vermilion pen.

           Is Jove immortal
(10)    So is Cerberus at his portal
         Nothing but lying is mean
         ↑Never let thy banner down↓
         Rat & worm & wolverine
         Have the old dazzle of God's crown

(15)    And in the Zodiack are seen
         Health & Power become the wise
         Fill the gaps with charities
         Scatter this vetch everywhere
         It will take root in the air

(20)    But he the dreaded Fates will please
         Who has no eye or time for pease

[268e]  God having shaped him like a wedge
         And driven him to his forepledge
         Forth as from a gun.

         The dear old world is babyish
(5)     Grumble men & women wish

    **268d** "Be of your country," 19–26 (1–8); "Is Jove immortal," 1–13 (9–21). The addition and
cancellation in line (4) are in pencil.
    **268e** "Is Jove immortal," 14–16 (1–3); "Heroism," four unused lines, 7–8, 1–6, 9–10 (4–17).

In the doll house luckily none
Fondles any but his own
The hero is not fed on sweets
Daily his own heart he eats
(10) ⟨The best⟩ ↑Ruby↓ wine is drunk by knaves
Sugar spends to fatten slaves
Rose & vineleaf deck buffoons
Thunderclouds are Joves festoons
Drooping in wreaths of dread
(15) ⟨T⟩Lightning-knotted round his head
Chambers of the great are jails
And head winds right for royal sails

[268�f]    Heartily heartily sing
Ever be true in town or grove
Bears & men must have their swing
Of berries, & honey, & love.
(5) There's no ideot like the wise
And most virtue's cowardice
What each is born to let him do
Let the devil himself be true
And he has an open track
(10) And all planets at his back
↑Bare↓ Good meaning is an ass
Virtue bring⟨eth⟩s its will to pass
He is wise who marries his end
Makes heaven & earth & hell his friend
(15) Rushes to his deed
⟨And⟩Will crack nature or succeed
Values in the issue had
Tis all one
What feat is done
(20) Alike to ⟨ma⟩build an iron way
From Montreal to Boston Bay
Or make a shanty glad.

[268g]    Thank the gods thy governors
Many painful an ↑c↓estors
Wore away successive lives
To sun & ⟨maturate⟩ ↑mellow↓ a stock
(5) Which neither Rome nor Antioch
China nor Egypt could forestal
Ripe in thee now last of all.

268�f "Heartily heartily sing."
268g "Thank the gods" (1–7); "Nature I," 1–4, six unused lines, 5–6 (8–19).

Winters know
Easily to shed the snow
(10)    And the untaught Spring is wise
In cowslips and anemonies
But the wizard Solomon
And Sophroniscus' wiser son
Neither singly nor together
(15)    Could compose a sparrow's feather
Nor craft nor chemistry avails
But sparrows only make their tails
Nature hating art & pains
Mocks & baffles too much brains

[268ₕ]–[268ⱼ] [blank]
[268ₖ]    But the wizard Solomon
And Sophroniscus' wiser son
Neither singly nor together
Could compose a sparrow's feather
(5)    Nor craft nor chemistry avails
But sparrows only make their tails
Nature hating art & pains
⟨Envies⟩ ↑Mocks↓ & baffles too much brains
But she dearly loves the poor

(10)    And by a marvel of her own
To strike all competition down

For Nature listens in the rose
And hearkens in the berry's bell,
To help her friends, to plague her foes,
(15)    And like wise God she judges well.

Though I call me liberal,
And have charity for all
Tho I honor handsome sinners
And like rich men who give dinners
[268ₗ]    And were I pope should grace dispense
To the very cocks & hens
Yet doth much my love excel
To the souls that never fell,
(5)    To minds that live in happiness,
And do well because they please
Who dare to fame what is unfamed
And to do deeds before they're named

268ₖ "Nature I," six unused lines, 5–6, 9–15, four unused lines. Lines (1–8) are struck
through four times in ink.
268ₗ "Nature I," x, x, 16–21.

[268ₘ]   Our voyage is a teacup navigation
        We sail out & into port
        Be it confest
        The ethereal nation
(5)       With us have taken liberties
        We are their jest
        Only this redemption is
        We are of the makers
        As of the made
(10)     By us also the game is played
        Fear not, thou child infirm
        Theres no god dare wrong a worm.
        ⟨Strong &⟩ Staunch & strong are mine & thine
        Hast not thy share? on winged feet
(15)     ↑Crowns go to deserts↓
        ↑And power to him who power exerts↓
        Lo! it rushes thee to meet.

        If thy body pine,
        Tis the Genius's retreat
(20)     ⟨From⟩ ↑To↓ the chambers from the street,
        Magnifying the coming vaunt
[268ₙ]   Of his flowering aloe plant
        Starves the florets due today

        He has driven out
        With real wrath the seeming rout
(5)       He will not know
        Rival or foe
        But makes a bitter dupe
        Of seeming Satan & his troop
        Punishing with obscene shape
(10)     Of ass & tadpole rat & ape
        The pleasure hunting crew
        ⟨Deceives the⟩

[268ₒ]   Space is ample, east & west,
        Yet two cannot go abreast;
        Cannot travel in it two;
        Yonder masterful cuckoo
(5)       Crowds every egg out of the nest

**268ₘ** "Compensation" ("Man's the elm"), seven unused lines (1–7); "Hold of the Maker," 1–2, x (8–10); "Compensation" ("Man's the elm"), 5–6, 2, 9, 7–8, 10 (10–17); "If thy body pine," 1–4 (18–21).

**268ₙ** "If thy body pine," 5–6 (1–2); "Unity," ten unused lines (3–12). Lines (3–12) are written sideways on the page.

**268ₒ** "Unity," 1–7, x, x, 8, x, 9–11, x, x.

Except its own;
There's a juggle in the stone,
There's a treachery in the air,
⟨The mountains will not rightly sit,⟩
(10)　　Night & day've been tampered with
⟨By strong bias turned aside⟩
Every quality & pith
Surcharged & sultry with a power
Which rides & menaces the hour
(15)　　He has prepossessed all places
　　　　　　↑He has driven out↓

[268ₚ]　Once let the nuisance enter
With a peristaltic motion
The blue vault will shrivel & take
Shape of scorpion or of snake
(5)　　And sting the enemy to death
When the breath of God bloweth
All the vanes point one way
As all the needles of the earth
Tremble to the north

[268_q]　The blue vault will shrivel & shake
As sheds his skin the vernal snake.

[268ᵣ] [blank]
[268ₛ]　On the seed of the first grape
The world turns
As a watch on ⟨d⟩a diamond
And out of the grapestone goes
(5)　　A fury
Which makes the wheels fly & burn.
And because a drop of wine
Is at the core
If thou wash thine eyes with wine
(10)　　Thou seest things from the centre
Dost their essence enter
And canst predict the path of
Comets & the fates of beauties.
Wine is the mystic centre
(15)　　Wine is translated wit
Wine is a new day
Wine from the veiled secret

268ₚ "Unity," nine unused lines.
268_q "Unity," x, x.
268ₛ "On a raisin stone," 1–2, 3, 3–7, five unused lines, 9–12, x, x.

Tears the veil away.
Wine is liquid motion
(20)     Will not let us sit

[268ₜ]     If thou wash
Monadnoc with wine
Monadnoc would exhale

[268ᵤ]–[268ᵥ] [blank]
[268_w]     ⟨I⟩On a grape stone
The ⟨frame⟩ ↑wheels↓ of nature turn⟨s⟩
Out of it the fury comes
Wherewith the ⟨wheels⟩ ↑spondyls↓ burn

(5)      And because ⟨win⟩ a drop of wine
Is the ⟨heart⟩ creation's heart
If thou wash therewith the eyne
Nothing's hid apart

[268ₓ]–[268_z] [blank]
[268_aa]     To clothe the fiery thought
In simple word succee⟨e⟩ds;
For still the craft of genius is
To mask a king in weeds

(5)      I am not wiser for my age,
Nor skilful by my grief;
Life loiters at the book's first page,
And we never turn the leaf.

[268_bb] [blank]
[268_cc]     Scholar is a ball thats spent,
Or the barrel that it sent,
Twas fired ere he came into hall,
Here is neither charge nor ball.

(5)      Ask not treasures from his store,—
For he lies in wait for more;
⟨Ask not⟩ ↑Nor↓ what dawneth in his brain,—
That to whisper were profane.

[268_dd]     ⟨Value standeth in success⟩
⟨Value in the issue had⟩

268ₜ "On a raisin stone," x, x, x.
268_w "On a raisin stone," 1–8. In line (2), Emerson actually cancelled "frame of" and failed
to resupply "of."
268_aa "Poet" ("To clothe") (1–4); "Climacteric" (5–8).
268_cc "Scholar is a ball" (1–4); "Ask not treasures" (5–8).
268_dd "Heartily heartily sing," 16/17?, 17–19, 13?, 20–22 (1–8); "Heroism," 7–8, 1–6,
9–10 (9–18).

⟨Tis all one⟩
⟨What feat is done⟩
(5)    ⟨Come at your end⟩
⟨Alike to make an iron way⟩
⟨From Montreal to Boston bay⟩
⟨Or make a shanty glad⟩

The heroe is not fed on sweets
(10)    ↑ Daily ↓ His own heart he eats
The best wine is drunk by knaves
Sugar spends to fatten slaves
Rose & vineleaf deck buffoons
Thunderclouds are Joves festoons
(15)    Drooping in wreaths of dread
Lightning knotted round his head
Chambers of the great are jails
And headwinds right for royal sails

[inside back cover] [index material omitted]

# Notebook EF

Emerson began to use notebook EF extensively in 1846, although he seems to have written in it at least as early as 1841, as the textual history of "Hermione" shows. In April 1846 he purchased Joseph von Hammer-Purgstall's German edition of Hafiz's *Diwan,* translations of which fill many pages of EF; the notebook also contains quotations from the *Sháh Námeh* of Firdausi and Alexander Chodzko's *Specimens of the Popular Poetry of Persia,* both of which Emerson withdrew from the Harvard College Library on 2 September 1846. In early 1851 he used the notebook for numerous prose passages that appear in or are associated with his address on the Fugitive Slave Law delivered in Concord on 3 May. Use of the notebook seems to have continued through the middle 1850s.


The covers of notebook EF are brown leather and measure 12 × 17.9 cm. "EF" is written in black ink on the front cover. The spine, also brown leather, is blank.

Flyleaves are glued to the front and back covers (treated here as front cover verso and inside back cover). There were originally 116 pages, but the leaves bearing pp. 1–2 and 5–6 are torn out. Pages are faintly ruled on the recto and measure 12 × 18 cm.

Two pages are numbered in ink, sixty-eight are numbered in pencil, and forty-two are unnumbered. Four pages are blank.

The notebook contains one enclosure, a newspaper clipping tipped with sealing wax into the upper right corner of the inside front cover. The clipping begins, "John Randolph, in the debate upon the Missouri Question, said:" The rest of the clipping appears in the earliest level of writing on pp. 30–31.

[front cover verso] R. W. Emerson. Concord.

[table of measurements omitted]

All immoral laws are void.

[table of measurements omitted]

Tout est soldat pour vous combattre

[index material omitted]
G. H. Burleigh, Great Falls N. H.

[1]–[2] [leaf torn out]

[3₁] who can see nothing in this claim for ⟨mere sanity⟩ ↑bare human-
ity↓ & the health & honor of a Massachusetts citizen,—can see noth-
ing but canting fanaticism, sedition↑s,↓ & one idea. ⟨It seems
hopeless. I need not call names. I know they mean well    Yet so⟩
I should like to know what they would think was cause of resistance &
reasonable complaint.

[3₂]              Love creepeth where it cannot go
              And eats ⟨throu⟩ its way thro Alps of wo
              And eats through Alps to find its home
              Love creeps where else it cannot go
(5)           And eats ⟨thro Al⟩ its way thro Alps of wo
              Where way is none twill creep & wind
              And eat thro Alps its home to find

[4₁]       Empire that by serving grows

       Moore quotes "Nott's Hafiz"
Goethe the "Megadhuta"
"The inhabitants of Zinge are never afflicted with sadness or melan-
choly."—"proceeding from the influence of the star Canopus wh. rises
over them every night"
       "Seven Climates" translated by ⟨Sir⟩ W. Ouseley Esq.

---

**fcv** "All immoral laws are void" is used in "The Fugitive Slave Law" (1851), W 11:186 and
190; cf. JMN 11:350. "Tout est soldat pour vous combattre," from the *Marseillaise*, is used in
"The Fugitive Slave Law" (1854), W 11:237; see JMN 11:325 and 358. The tables of measure-
ments are in pencil. For Burleigh, see JMN 11:313.
       **3₁** "who . . . one idea" is used in "The Fugitive Slave Law" (1851), W 11:185. In pencil,
struck through in pencil; "who can . . . Yet so" is struck through with three additional pencil
lines and "It seems . . . Yet so" with six.
       **3₂** "Love," 3–4, 4, 3–4, 3–4. Lines (1–5) are struck through in ink; in line (2), "throu" is not
canceled.
       **4₁** "Intellect" ("Rule which by obeying"), 1? This page is in pencil. "Goethe . . . night' " is
struck through with a pencil line, later partially erased; the list of rhymes is struck through in
pencil. Thomas Moore, in his notes to *Lalla Rookh*, cites John Nott's translation of the odes of
Hafiz (1787) several times; the quotation from Sir William Ouseley's *Extract from a Geograph-
ical Persian Manuscript called Heft Aklim, or the Seven Climates*, is also in Moore's notes.
Goethe cites Kalidasa's lyric poem "Meghaduta" more than once.

fond
Engelond
blond
frond
Florimond
respond

[4₂]

Chasing with words fast flowing things

Thou shalt not try
To plant thy shrivelled pedantry
On the shoulders of the sky,

[5]–[6] [leaf torn out]

[7₁]   Pale Genius roves alone
No scout can track his way
None credits him till he have shown
His diamonds to the day
(5)   A thousand years they slept
The while his feet delayed
And still their hiding place had kept
If he had longer stayed
Not his the feasters wine
(10)   Nor land nor gold nor power
⟨By sacred want God saveth him⟩
⟨To his elected hour⟩
By want & pain God screeneth him
⟨Fr⟩Till his elected hour

[7₂]   Thanks to those who go & come
Who brot Hellas, ↑Thebes↓ & Rome
As near to me as is my home
Those husbands of the mind
(5)   Who keep ↑decaying↓ history good
And do not suffer ⟨Thebes⟩ ↑Tyre↓ or Troy
To know decrepitude

[8₁]   In the
I breathe freer by the pine
In cities I am ↑low &↓ mean ⟨& low⟩
The mountain waters ‖ . ‖ me clean

---

4₂ "Borrow Urania's subtle wings," 2–5.
6 Traces of pencil overwritten in ink appear on the stub of the torn leaf. Visible are, in pencil,
". . . ture" and "years", and, in ink, "new" and "bleu".
7₁ "Pale Genius roves alone," 1–4, four unused lines, 5–8, 7–8. In pencil.
7₂ "Thanks to those."
8₁ "I leave the book," x, 2–4, x, 5–6, 8 (1–8); "The civil world" (9–15). Partially erased
pencil.

(5)        ⟨Without⟩
And by the sea⟨shore⟩↑waves↓ I am strong
I hear the↑ir↓ medicinal song
Ask no physician but the wave

(10)          The world will much forgive
To bards who from its maxims live
But if the poet dare
To bend his practice to his prayer
And following his mighty heart
(15)        Shame the times & live apart
Vae solis

[8₂]     Go copy in verse one chime
Of the faery woodbells peal & cry,
Write in a book the morning's prime,
And match with words that amber sky.

[9] [Hafiz, *Diwan*,] II 438
Untruth is become the mode
And no man knows of friendship & truth
The worthy nears now the worthless
(5)    And stretch out their hands for a gift
Whoso in the world is virtuous & wise
Is no moment free from care & sorrow
On the other side the dunce lives in plenty
With gold & honour overlaid
(10)   And if a poet fluent as water
Full of heart speaking to mind & to soul
So yields him avarice no shilling
Tho his songs were worthy of Abusina
Yesterday said Reason to the Understanding
(15)   Go forth suffer & complain not
In satisfaction seek thy kingdom
And drink wine instead of other potions
Hafiz follow thou this good counsel
Then tho thy foot fall thy head shall rise

[10₁] Hafiz [*Diwan*] II 380
Novice, hear me what I say
So shalt thou be purified
Whilst thou dost not tread the way,
Thou canst not be a guide.

8₂ "My Garden," 37–40. In pencil, struck through in pencil.
9 "Untruth is become the mode." In pencil.
10₁ "Novice, hear me," 1–16. Erased pencil, struck through in pencil.

(5) Pride of the gazing school,
Lord of thy companions,
Mark, hear boy thou too shalt be
One day the sire of sons

Sleeping, eating, drinking,
(10) The spark of love withstood,
Eat not, sleep not, love in thinking
Will come rushing like a flood.

A beam of the love of Allah
Once fall thy soul upon,
(15) By God I know thou then wilt be
More brilliant than the sun.

[10₂] Future or Past no /deeper/stricter/ secret ⟨h⟩folds,
O friendless Present! than thy ⟨mantle⟩ ↑bosom↓ ⟨f⟩holds.

The wild young world unfolded
Its millionpetalled flower
(5) And in cramp form of elf & beast
↑It↓ Swathed the too much power

What made in land & sea impearled
My children all aghast
Or dreaming on the future world
(10) Or suffering from the past

[11₁] As learned magians do,
Thy hand from brass withhold,
That thou in life true alchemist
May turn all stones to gold.

(5) From thy footsole to thy head
A beam of God thou burnest,
So ‖ . . . . ‖thout foot or head
To the hest of God thou turnest

Go leap into the waves,
(10) And have no doubt or care,
And the flowing of the seven broad seas
Shall never wet thy hair.

If Allah's face on thee
Look down with love benign,

10₂ "Heri, Cras, Hodie," 3–4 (1–2); "Song of Nature," x, x, 31–32 (3–6); "What made in land & sea" (7–10). The cancellations and additions (including "stricter") in lines (1–2) are in pencil and the lines struck through in ink; lines (3–6) are in pencil.
11₁ "Novice, hear me," 17–36 (1–20); "Faith" (9–20). Partially erased pencil.

(15) Who disbelieves that thou also
   To his face turnest thine?

   And though thy form & fortune
   ⟨P⟩Were broken waste & void
   ⟨O⟩ dream not of thy eternal root
(20) A fibre is destroyed

[11₂] Already blushes in thy cheek
   The bosom thought which thou shall speak;
   The bird how far it haply roam
   By cloud or isle is flying home;
(5) And every man in love or pride
   Of his fate is never wide.

   I wrote the past in characters
   of rock & fire the scroll
   The building of the coral sea
(10) The planting of the coal

[12₁] [Hafiz, *Diwan*,] II 125
   If thou drink wine, the heaven
   Free on earth itself diffuses;
   Fear not sin ‖ . . . . . . . ‖
   Also has ‖ . . . . . . . . ‖

(5) Without scruple gather all,
   All which is thine own,
   Since the murder sword of fate
   Without scruple hews thee down.

   I beseech thee, o my ‖ . . . ‖
(10) At thy graceful ‖ . ‖ I crave
   That thou come to my deathbed
   That thou come to ‖ . ‖ grave

   The builder of heaven
   Has sundered the earth,
(15) So that no footway
   Leads out of it forth

   On turnpikes of wonder
   Wine leads the mind forth
   Forward & sideward & ‖ . ‖ward
(20) Southward & north

11₂ "Nemesis," 1–4, 7–8 (1–6); "Song of Nature," 21–24 (7–10). Lines (1–6) and (7–10) are struck through separately in ink.

12₁ "Drink wine, and the heaven," 1–12, 17–22, x, x, 23–26 (1–24); "The Builder of heaven" (13–24). Erased pencil.

The vault stands unmoved
Until the doomsday
Thee shall yet the winecup carry
Clean oer all away

[12₂] Every person of sense or humanity    is found on the freedom side
I had rather take the rope of the people than the writ of a judge
    Every thing is discredited   a work of "‖ . . . . ‖ory" is merely a green or red book

              I much prefer to speech of these
        The drip all day of rainy woods the honking of the geese

[12₃]    By consummate powers
    Gathering along the centuries
    From race on race the rarest flowers
    ⟨His rich⟩ ↑⟨T⟩My↓ wreath shall nothing miss.

(5)    And many a thousand summers
    My apples ripened well
    And light from meliorating stars
    With firmer glory fell

    And crags from satellites & rings
(10)    And broken stars I drew
    And out of spent & aged things
    I made the world anew.

[13₁] [Hafiz, *Diwan*,] II 125
    If thou drink wine the heaven
    Free on earth itself diffuses
    ‖ . . ‖ not sinning
    Also has its ‖ . . ‖

(5)    Without scruple have at all,
    All which is thine own
    Since the ‖ . . ‖ sword of fate
    Without scruple ‖ . . ‖ thee down

    ‖ . . . . . . . . ‖ love
(10)    At thy ‖ . . ‖ful feet I crave
    That ‖ . . ‖ come to my deathbed
    ‖ . . . . . . . . ‖ grave

    ‖ . . . . . . . . . . . . . . . . ‖

12₂ "I much prefer." With "Every thing is discredited," cf. "The Fugitive Slave Law" (1851), W 11:182. Erased pencil.

12₃ "Song of Nature," 13–20, 25–28. Struck through in ink.

13₁ "Drink wine, and the heaven," 1–12, 13?, 14–17, 18?, 19–20 (1–20); "The Builder of heaven," 1–4 (17–20). Erased pencil.

Angel or man
(15)    This temperance
Is a heresy

‖ . . ‖ build ‖ . . . . . ‖
‖ . . . . . . . . . . . . . . . ‖
‖ . . . . . . . . . ‖ootway
(20)    Leads out of it forth

[132] One lesson is the extreme shallowness of the leaders. No depth of thought in ⟨m⟩public men   They have no root in the world, they have no inspiration no sympathy with or re↑c↓eption of principles.   they are chiefly engaged in securing their dinner, their dividend. Judges governors presidents eminent lawyers we see what straws they are what mediocrity what slight stuff reputations are made of. Mr Boutwell succeeded in

[133]        Deep in the man sits fast his fate
To mould his fortunes mean or great
Unknown to Cromwell as to me
Was Cromwells measure & degree;
(5)    Unknown to him as to his horse,
If he than ⟨‖ . ‖⟩ ↑grooms↓ ⟨‖ . ‖⟩be better or worse.
He works, fights, plots, in rude affairs,
With boys, lords, kings, his craft compares,
Till late he learned, thro' doubt & fear,
(10)    Broad England harbored not his peer
Obeying time, the last to own
The Genius from its cloudy throne.
        For the prevision is allied
Unto the thing so signified
(15)    Or say the foresight that awaits
Is the same Daemon that creates.

[141] being insignificant tho' he ‖ . . . . . . . . ‖etts ‖ . . . . . . . . . ‖

The ⟨first⟩ crisis had the value of a sheet of lightning for illuminating power   ⟨We attained⟩
        A few persons known before as men of thought & virtue were seen to be so   The rest were punk.

132 "shallowness of the leaders," "Judges . . . they are," and "what slight . . . made of" are used in "The Fugitive Slave Law" (1851), W 11:182. George S. Boutwell was governor of Massachusetts in 1851. In pencil, struck through in pencil.
133 "Fate" ("Deep in the man").
141 "The crisis . . . illuminating power" is used in "The Fugitive Slave Law" (1851), W 11:182. Erased pencil.

[142]    I‖ . . . . . . . . ‖ forth
        The bittersweet the haunting air
        traveleth bloweth everywhere
        It preys on all
(5)     ⟨‖ . . ‖⟩ thou over all
        It
        It bites the maid with pleasing flame
        It drives the poet mad for fame
        It ⟨smites⟩ ↑stings↓ the strong with enterprise
(10)    And traveller longs for Indian skies

         I to my garden went
        To the unplanted woods
        Th
            The
(15)    More sweet than my refrain
        The first drop of April rain

[143]           ↑*Four Stories.*↓
        Over her head were the linden buds,
        And over the tree was the moon,
        And over the moon were the starry studs,
        That drop from the angels' shoon.

[151] Hafiz [*Diwan*] II 308
        My bosom's phoenix has assured
        His nest in highest heaven's cope
        In the body's cage immured
        He is weary of lifes hope
(5)     ⟨If once⟩
        ⟨Up⟩ ↑If↓ from this heap of ashes
        ⟨If⟩Once flew the bird amain
        In that high niche of heaven
        Nestles the bird again
(10)    Once flies he upward, he will perch
        On Tubas ‖ . . . . ‖ bough
        My home is on that fruited arch
        To ‖ . . . . . . . . ‖

        ‖ . . . . . . ‖ my phoenix spread
(15)    ↑How ‖ . . . ‖ falls↓ G‖ . . . ‖fully on land & sea
        ‖ . . ‖ soul refr‖ . . ‖ shade

142 "May-Day," x, 285–87, four unused lines, 289–90 (1–10); "I to my garden went" (11–12); "More sweet than," x, x, 1–2 (13–16). In pencil.
143 "Excelsior." Struck through in ink.
151 "The Phoenix," 1–4, x, 5–12, 14–16. Erased pencil.

[152] Another thing was shown that the law rests on a feeling & will be administered on that. Twenty years earlier these ju

    There are undulations of feeling, now a noble & now a sensual season, according to that will the decision be. We are in the fit of baseness, & statutes are nothing

↑In the present moment, the Senate's committee sit ridiculously, & a booby insults them.  & marshal Tukey braves the State. ↓

[16₁]    In both ‖ . . ‖ ⟨dwells⟩ ↑inhabits↓ he
        Far below the planets roll
        ⟨His⟩ Body of ether all compact
        Of Allahs own is his soul

(5)      The plane of the higher world
        Is the playground of my bird
        The rose garden of Eden
        Him meat & wine assured

        Lonely Hafiz who so long
(10)     God's unity preachest
        Still unity to every tongue
        of man & genie teach

[16₂] There is always sufficient verge & margin in any statute for the spirit of the magistrate to show itself. For instance, if Mr Sumner had heard Mr Rantoul's argument, who can doubt that the unconstitutionality of Sims's detention wd. have been affirmed.

Mr Curtis ⟨resists⟩ ↑absorbs↓ all that daylight by the plenitude of his darkness & ⟨r⟩ surrenders him.

[16₃]    For what avail
        The plough or sail,
        Or land, or life, if Freedom fail.

[17]        Fable
"If we compare the progress of the sun thro' the signs of the Zodiack

152 With "the law rests on a feeling," cf. "The Fugitive Slave Law" (1851), W 11:195; Francis Tukey, city marshal of Boston, arrested the fugitive slave Thomas Sims in 1851. In pencil, struck through in pencil.

16₁ "The Phoenix," 17–20, eight unused lines. Partially erased pencil.

16₂ With "There is . . . itself," cf. "The Fugitive Slave Law" (1851), W 11:213–14. Charles Sumner and Robert Rantoul, Jr., were prominent antislavery figures and later U.S. senators from Massachusetts; Thomas Sims was an escaped slave captured in Boston in April 1851 under the Fugitive Slave Law; George Ticknor Curtis, U.S. commissioner in Boston, ordered Sims's return to his master in Georgia. In pencil, struck through in pencil.

16₃ "Boston," 29/78, 29/78–30/79.

17 *The Shâh Nâmeh of the Persian Poet, Firdausi,* trans. and abridged by James Atkinson (London, 1832). Emerson borrowed this work from the Harvard College Library on 2 September 1846, and again on 26 July 1847. In pencil; "the signs of . . . coincidence" is struck through in ink; the "s" at the end of "others" in the "3d Labor" is not cancelled; the comma after "Dupuis" is in ink.

with the 12 labors of Hercules a striking coincidence will be observed.
1st month Leo
       1st ⟨month⟩ ↑labor↓     H[ercules] slew Nemaean lion
2d mo.  Virgo  ⟨sun enters⟩ constellation   ↑Hydra sets↓
2d labor destroys Lernaean Hydra
3d mo   Libra when Constell[ation] Centaur rises with a wineskin full
of liquor & thyrsus   Constell[ation] Boar rises in the ev[enin]g
3d Labor   Herc[ules] hospitably entertained by a Centaur slew the
other⟨s⟩ Cent[aurs]. who fought for a cask of wine—Slew the Eryman-
thean Boar, also. &c &c" Preface to Shah Nameh
"According to theory of Dupuis↑,↓ Hercules is no other than the sun
& his 12 labors a representation of the annual course of that luminary
thro the signs of the Zodiac." Preface p ix

[18₁] Firdousi born at Tus in Khorasan 950 AD
Jamschid the Binder of the Demons reigned 700 years.

---

Mr S‖ . . ‖ in the days of his reach & strength ‖ . . . . . . . . ‖ under chains
⟨nor ‖ . . . . . . . . ‖⟩ nor made the State bend. And in

[18₂]     And many a thousand summers
           My apples ripened well,
           And light from meliorating stars
           With firmer glory fell.

[19] ⟨1⟩  The crisis demonstrative
1  Who is who
2  that the Law is nothing in presence of public opinion.
3.  This last is not so bad as it appears. Webster was really once a man
of force despite the despair of his old age. This has undulations & is
now in its insanity
4. The chief lesson is individualism  By that the Southern states
conquer   They rest not on meetings but on private heats and courages

[20] Mr [John Quincy] Adams was an immense loss  He could have
made his ugly will felt. He ⟨was⟩ ↑had an↓ ugly ↑temper↓ & they were
afraid of him. [Daniel] Webster is ⟨malignant⟩ ↑hard & selfish↓, but
there is no ⟨bone⟩ ↑grit↓ in him. ⟨He never had the feeling of a⟩ ↑A↓
gentleman cows him. There is a sad story in the Charleston papers of

18₁ With "Jamschid . . . 700 years," cf. "Persian Poetry," W 8:242. This page is in pencil,
erased below the rule.
18₂ "Song of Nature," 17–20. Struck through in ink. An underlying pencil version of lines
(3–4) differs from the ink version as follows: in line (3) "of" rather than "from" and "melioriat-
ing" capitalized; in line (4) "glory" capitalized.
19 In pencil, struck through in pencil.
20 In pencil, struck through in pencil. This page is reproduced in Plate 4.

18⟨3⟩45 of the dinner accepted & eaten by him & sauced with insults to his State & to his personal friend. I wish it were the only one in his history.

[21]    ⟨Beautiful⟩ manners of boys beautiful
        There's ⟨a⟩ Bonaparte in every school
        They learn Greek easily
        It grows in them every night

(5) King.   If farmers make my land secure,
            If pedlers use their craft for me,
            How can I other than endure
            Once in a year their company

            For wary Nature knows her own
(10)        By court & city dale & down
            And like a lover volunteers
            And to her ⟨own⟩ ↑⟨minion⟩ son↓ will ↑treasures↓ more
            And more to purpose freely pour
            In one woodwalk than learned men
(15)        Will find with glass in ⟨seasons ten⟩ ↑ten times ten↓

[22₁] There is a good fortune which belonged to Hancock & Adams that the material interests of the state coincided ⟨plainly⟩ clearly with the spiritual. John Adams says Aye what all looked well ↑formerly↓ Now all looks badly; be ‖ . ‖ of the British Laws

Now unfortunately the thing in question is not our liberty, but the black mans, & the race in possession can give away that for certain supposed advantages of course the number of patriots is ‖ . . . . ‖ diminished

[22₂]       The sun goes down, & with him takes
            The coarseness of my ⟨plain⟩ ↑poor↓ attire
            The fair moon mounts, & aye the flame
            Of gipsy beauty blazes higher.
(5)         And if I take you dames to task
            And say it frankly without guile
            Then you are gipsies in a mask
            And I the lady all the while.
            On the wild heath, under the moon,
(10)        I court & play with paler blood,

21  "manners of boys" (1–4); "If farmers make" (5–8); "A queen rejoices," 2–8 (9–15). Lines (1–4) and (9–15) are in pencil; lines (5–8) are in ink over the same in pencil. The pencil version differs from the ink as follows: in line (5) "they" for "farmers" and "thy" for "my" and in line (6) "they" for "pedlers." This page is reproduced in Plate 4.
22₁  In light pencil.
22₂  "The Romany Girl," 1–4, 9–20.

Me false to mine ⟨found never one⟩ ↑dare whisper none↓
One sallow horseman knows me good.
Rain from your cheek will wash the rose
In teeth & hair the shopmen deal
(15)    My swarthy tint is in the grain
The rocks & forest know it real.

[23₁]    A poet is at home
He does not follow the old & dead
Ruins & mummies
But cities & heroes come to him
(5)    One ‖ . . ‖ will serve
As well as another
For he fills them
From his own winepress
In the village he can find.

[23₂]    Your rose is rags you city girls
You cannot live in rocks & fells

The wild air bloweth in our lungs
The keen stars sparkle in our eyes
(5)    The forest birds have taught our tongues
The panther in our dances flies

⟨The⟩ ↑Her↓ passions ⟨of⟩ the ↑shy↓ violet
From Hafiz never hides
Lovelongings of the ⟨passionate⟩ ↑raptured↓ bird
(10)    The bird to him confides

Pale northern girls we scorn your race
You captives of your parlor walls
Wear out in dress your dreary days
Exiled from the horizon halls

[24₁] The saint if he have a gold caste will get at wine were he ten times
a saint
    There is no rich man king enchanter fairy or daemon who
possesses such power as a day. The days are gods   they are omnip-
otent   They are of the least pretence & of the greatest capacity of
anything that exists,
They are made on a loom whereof ⟨P⟩the warp & woof are ↑invaria-
bly↓ two ⟨w⟩kinds of wool called past time & future time

Rule which by obeying grows
Knowledge not its fountain knows

23₁ "A poet is at home." In light pencil.
23₂ "The Romany Girl," x, x, 21–24 (1–6), 5–8 (11–14); "Hafiz" (7–10). Lines (7–10) are in
pencil.
24₁ "Intellect" ("Rule which by obeying"). This page is in pencil.

Wave removing whom it bears
From the shores which he compares
(5)       Adding wings thro things to range
Makes him to his own blood strange

[242] The sword will not cut off the giving hand.
Despise the earth, which is not worth a fly's wing.
Alms is the waking of those that sleep.
   Night takes the poor man's part, if he be bold; say the Arabs
When the belly is full, it says to the head, sing fellow.
The guest brings a benediction ⟨o⟩into your house & on departing carries away your sins.

[251]   ‖ . . . . . . . . . . . . ‖ true
      [three lines of erased pencil writing]

(5)      ‖ . . . . ‖ a heavens poor
In ‖ . . . . . . . . . ‖ dark
The suns forgotten spark

      the ‖ . . ‖
I must not borrow light
(10)     From history trite
But from friends whom God ⟨me⟩ gave
And the destiny I have

It is written on the Gate of Heaven
Wo unto him who suffers himself to be betrayed by Fate

[252]  ⟨‖ . . ‖⟩
There is always a drawback and to the immense prosperity of America, there is one, Slavery. It is needed as shade as offset ⟨or⟩as recoil

[253]   Brother, no decrepitude
Cramps the limbs of Time;
As fleet his feet, his hands as good,
His vision as sublime.
(5)     ↑As when at first Jehovah hurled↓
↑The Sun & each revolving world. ↓

The beggar ⟨is bearer of⟩ ↑begs at↓ God's command
↑And↓ Gifts awake when givers sleep

242 With "The sword will not cut off the giving hand" and "Alms is the waking of those that sleep," cf. "Alms." With "When the belly is full, it says to the head, sing fellow," cf. EL, front cover verso and "Inspiration," W 8:281.
251 Unidentified lines (1–8); "I must not borrow light" (9–12); "'Tis writ on Paradise's gate" (13–14). Erased pencil.
252 In pencil. Cf. "The Fugitive Slave Law" (1851), W 11:186.
253 "Brother, no decrepitude" (1–6); "Alms," 1–3, x, 4, 1–4, 1–4 (7–19). Lines (7–15) are struck through in ink.

Swords ⟨will⟩ ↑can↓ not cut /the/a/ giving hand
(10)  ⟨Gifts speak when you would silence ⟨keep⟩⟩
⟨Thy⟩ Nor ⟨steal⟩ ↑stab↓ the love that orphans keep.

⟨f⟩For comes the poor by Gods command
And gifts awake when givers sleep
Swords cannot cut the giving hand
(15)  Nor dies the love that orphans keep

The beggar begs at God's command,
And gifts awake when givers sleep,
Swords cannot cut a giving hand,
Nor stab the love that orphans keep

[26] As much immorality so much drawback. The greatest prosperity will in vain escape the greatest calamity. For example, there never was such a success as ⟨o⟩that of the Republic, & there never was such a mischief as ⟨the Institution of⟩ Negro slavery. ↑England has Ireland   Germany has Russia   ⟨Spain⟩ ↑Italy↓ has the Pope   And ⟨we have⟩ ↑America↓ has slavery↓

Parks & ponds are good by day
But wheres the husband doth delight
In black acres of the night
Not my unseasoned step disturbs
(5)  The sleeps of trees or dreams of herbs

[27₁][two lines of erased pencil writing]

[27₂] I transfer myself, at last, from my present local interests to my public & universal; &, since I fail as an American, I triumph as a soul. I am for education of the human race, & that Cause cannot fail. Here are many experiments to which Nature is to say Yes or No. as when a /bridge/dam/ is put across the Kennebec or Connecticutt.
You ⟨omit⟩ ⟨break⟩ ↑neglect↓ the law of fluids hydrostatic, or the frost or the wind & nothing will save you, away goes your bridge. And you neglect the natural sentiments of mankind or contravene an interest of the human race & your law is void   And all this searching is good, & proclaims the true law. This crime is a benefit, thus.

[28]     ⟨For stars also and the celestial kind⟩
⟨Their own ⟨support⟩ ↑⟨food⟩ fuel↓ are skilled to find⟩

26 "Parks & ponds." "As much . . . calamity" and "England has . . . slavery" are used in "The Fugitive Slave Law" (1851), W 11:185–86; for "England has . . . slavery," see p. [64₃] below. The prose is in pencil, with "of" in the phrase "that of the Republic" written twice; the verse is struck through in ink.
27₁ Three words are visible: at the left margin, "hearts", and at the right margin "heavens" and below it "souls".
27₂ In pencil.
28 "As Stars & the celestial Kind." The page is in pencil. The prose concludes at the bottom of p. [29].

Websters somerset

He was for liberty, for North, for Jury Trial, & against compromise. Now he is ↑for↓ the *Bill*   The explanation is in the mouth of every caucus & of every newspaper. The North has not elected him, he will try the South. The Indian came to the fort ↑said he was good Indian↓ & asked for rum; ⟨Mrs Schoolcraft told him tha⟩ ⟨& called himself good Indian.⟩ Mrs Schoolcraft told him that good Indians did not drink rum. He replied, ⟨I⟩ ↑me↓ no good Indian⟨.⟩, ⟨I⟩ ↑me↓ dam rascal.

[29]     Stars & the celestial kind
         Their own food are skilled to find

Finality

Websters pacification is instructive, that even duller than he might learn. His final settlement has ⟨stirred the⟩ dislocated the corner stones. His pacification has brought all the honesty in every house to accuse the law, & doom its downfall. It has brought the sword into the streets of Boston & chains round its Courthouse.

Mrs S[choolcraft] did not give the Indian rum or will the Union give Mr W[ebster] the desired nomination

[30₁] But the nemesis works darklier than this   It is a power that makes noon dark & eggs us on to our own undoing. And ⟨precisely⟩ its dismal ⟨performance⟩ ↑way↓ is to pillory the traitor in the moment of ⟨its⟩ ↑his↓ seeming triumph. Who has seen anything like that which is now done. The ⟨dark⟩ ⟨ominous⟩ words of John Randolph have been ringing ominously in all echoes for years,—words spoken in the ↑heat of↓ Missouri debate "We do not govern the people of the North by our black slaves, but by their own white slaves. We know

[30₂]     I found this
          That of goods I could not miss
          If I fell /within/into/ the line
          Once a member all was mine
(5)       Houses banquets gardens fountains
          Fortunes delectable mountains
          But if I would walk alone

29 "As Stars & the celestial Kind." "Websters . . . Courthouse" is used in "The Fugitive Slave Law" (1851), W 11:198–99. The page is in pencil. The prose is written above and below the verse, which is circled and struck through in pencil. "Websters . . . even duller" is struck through twice in pencil, and "than he . . . Courthouse" once. "Mrs S . . . nomination" is a continuation from p. [28].
30₁ "The Fugitive Slave Law" (1851), W 11:200. In pencil, struck through in pencil. The quotation from John Randolph of Virginia is taken from the newspaper clipping tipped onto the front cover verso.
30₂ "I found this," 1–18.

Was neither c⟨o⟩loak nor crumb my own
And thus the high mus⟨t⟩e treated me
(10)    Directly never greeted me
But when she spread her dearest spells
Feigned to speak to some one else.
I was free to overhear
Or was welcome to forbear
(15)    But that idle word
Thus at random overheard
Was the /anthem/mandate/ of the spheres
And proverb of the following years

[31₁] what we are doing. We have conquered you once & we will conquer you again. Aye we will drive you to the wall, & when we have you there once more we mean to keep you there & nail you down like base money." Those words ↑resounding ever since from California to Oregon from Cape Florida to Cape Cod↓ come down on us like the cry ⟨resounding ever since from California to Oregon⟩ of Fate on the moment when they are fulfilled. ⟨Not by them⟩ ⟨not by black but⟩ by white slaves ↑by a white↓ are we beaten, by our own White Slave Bill who looked for such ghastly ⟨vengeance⟩ ⟨for such frightful⟩ fulfill

[31₂]    ↑The↓ Light wherewith all planets shone
Livery all events put on
It fell in rain it grew in grain
It wore flesh in friendly form
(5)    It frowned in enemies
It spoke in Tullius Cicero
In Milton & in Angelo
I travelled & found it in Rome
Eastward, it filled all heathendom
(10)    And lay on my hearth when I came home.

Mask thy wisdom with delight
Toy with the bow, yet hit the white
He ⟨seemed to idle⟩ ↑loved to round a verse↓ & play
Without ⟨a⟩remoter hope or fear
(15)    ⟨Than⟩ or purpose than to please his ear
And pass the ⟨time⟩ ↑golden summer time↓
With cunning rhyme
Meantime every cunning word
Tribes & ages overheard

31₁ "The Fugitive Slave Law" (1851), W 11:200–201. In pencil, struck through in pencil.
31₂ "i found this," 19–28 (1–10); "Mask thy wisdom," 1–2, 4–12 (11–21); "Considerations by the Way," 24–25 (11–12).

(20)        T⟨o⟩hose idle catches told the laws
Holding nature to her Cause

[32₁] ment as to see what we see, our ⟨very⟩ best and proudest, the first man of the north ⟨seized⟩ ↑ stricken ↓ with irresistible madness & ⟨moving himself⟩ in the very moment of mounting the throne, taking the bit in his mouth & the collar on his neck & harnessing himself to the chariot of Southern aggression    There is a Nemesis like that of Napoleon like that of Croesus    It is a penalty on ambition that should strike mankind with horror.

[32₂]                ↑ *Spring* ↓
The wood is
Sober with a fund of joy

Winter builds
Sudden cathedrals in the wilds

(5)        Rubies are but frozen wine.

The blue vault silver-lined with hills of snow.

           Sudden winds came full of meaning
All too much to him they said.
South winds have long memories
(10)       Of that be none afraid.

[33₁] We cd. have spared the Hills & Halletts Curtises & ⟨Devenses⟩ Woodburys, but him we reckoned not for the dunghill

      To eyes that are opened by the fear of God the retribution proceeds in ⟨he that⟩ the instant of crime he puts the ⟨nec⟩ chain on ⟨the neck of⟩ the slave, & unsuspected it falls on his own neck

[33₂]               *Spring*
The ⟨air is full of whistlings⟩

"May makes the cheerful sure
May breeds & brings new blood,

---

32₁ "ment . . . aggression" is used in "The Fugitive Slave Law" (1851), W 11:201. In pencil, struck through in pencil.

32₂ "Waldeinsamkeit," 20, 19 (1–2); "May-Day," x, 112 (3–4); "Rubies," 3 (5); "The blue vault," 1 (6); "South Wind," 9–12 (7–10). Lines (1–2), (3–4), and (5) are struck through separately in ink.

33₁ "We cd. have . . . but him" is used in "The Fugitive Slave Law" (1851), W 11:201. Emerson's references are to Isaac Hill, New Hampshire politician; Benjamin Franklin Hallett, Boston Democrat and Southern sympathizer; George Ticknor Curtis, U.S. commissioner in Boston; Charles Devens, U.S. marshal for Massachusetts; and Levi Woodbury, U.S. Supreme Court justice. The page, in pencil, is struck through twice in pencil.

33₂ "May-Day," 12 (1), 278–79 (7–8); "Song of Nature," 3 (6). For the quotation from Edwards and "The sportive sun" see JMN 11:114. Lines (6–8) are struck through three times in ink.

(5)       May marcheth throughout every limb:
          May makes the merry mood."
                    Rich[ar]d Edwards   1523–1566

          The sportive sun.

          The feet which slid for months on snow
          Are glad at last to feel the ground

[34]                    *Spring*                    *Enweri*
          "In the garden ↑water↓ goes now the wind ⟨over the water.⟩
          ⟨That⟩ by filing ⟨he may⟩ ↑to↓ polish the cheeks of the pond.
          ⟨On tulips plays now the reflection of fire,⟩
          ⟨Which plays now no more in chimney & hearth.⟩
(5)       ↑And the fire put out on the household hearth↓
          ↑Rekindles now in the tulips leaf↓
          He who yesterday withdrew himself from affairs,
          Him now desire sets again in activity."

[35]                    *Spring.   Ben Jonson*
          "How comes it winter is so quite forced hence
          And locked up under ground? that every sense
          Hath several objects. Trees have got their heads
          The fields their coats that now the shining meads
(5)       Do boast the paunce, the lily, & the rose,
          And every flower doth laugh as Zephyr blows
          The seas are now more even than the land
          The river↑s↓ run as smoothed by the hand."
                    *Vision of Delight* Vol V. 334.
          ─────────

          *Ford*
          "Her youngest girl the violet breathing May
(10)      Is come to do you service
          [John Ford and Thomas Dekker, *The Sun's Darling*,
              2.1.85, 87]

[36]      "A girdle make whose buckles stretched to the length
          Shall reach from arctic to the antarctic pole
          What ground so e'er thou canst with that enclose,
          I'll give thee freely." [ibid., 2.1.224–27]

(5)       *Humor*   "Poor spring, goody herbwife"
                    *Ford.* [ibid., 2.1.213]

34 "O'er the garden water," 1–2, 4, 3, 3–4, x, x. All cancellations and additions are in pencil.
35 *The Works of Ben. Johnson* [*sic*], 6 vols. (London, 1716), in Emerson's library. The two
quotations appear in JMN 11:113–14.
36 For the quotations, see JMN 11:114.

[37]  As if Time brot a new relay
of shining virgins every May
And summer came to ripen maids
To a beauty that not fades

[38] [Hafiz, *Diwan,*] II. 54
  Lament not, o Hafiz, the distribution
Thy nature & thy verse, which flow like water, let them
   content you.

———

  Hafiz thou art from Eternity
By God created for a man
(5)  Who abhors hypocrisy
[Hafiz, *Diwan,*] I 216

———

  Hafiz since on the world
Sorrows & joys pass away
So it is better that thou ever
Of glad spirit art
[Hafiz, *Diwan,*] II 209

(10)    ↑woworth the time↓
I do not count the hours I spend
In wandering by the sounding sea
Nor those that by the wood

If then I left this delight
(15) And my thots to home rebound
I should reckon it a slight
To the /company/high cheer/ I found

[39] W[ebster]. is a spent ball. See the mouthing at Annapolis the
⟨hollowhearted⟩ maudlin about Washington
⟨At⟩ His 7 March speech is a ⟨conce⟩ measure & not a speech   It has
no merits as a speech that I remember   His genius forsook him
 There is not a memorable sentiment or ⟨fact⟩ statement   I know his
defenders will ⟨find⟩ ↑/hold/claim/↓ this ↑to be↓ praise. They are wel-
come to it ↑so↓   They would, if it were shown them that ⟨Mr⟩ Rhett
of Carolina wrote it.

37 "May-Day," 297–300. In pencil, struck through in pencil.
38 "Lament not, o Hafiz" (1–2); "Hafiz thou art" (3–5); "Hafiz since on the world" (6–9);
"Waldeinsamkeit," x, 1–2, x, 45–48 (10–17). In pencil; lines (11–17) are struck through twice
in pencil.
39 Webster's speech in the Congress on 7 March 1850, in which he declared that the Union
was more important than the slavery question, alienated many of his Northern supporters,
including Emerson; Robert Barnwell Rhett was U.S. senator from South Carolina and an early
advocate of Southern secession. In pencil.

[40] [Hafiz, *Diwan*,] I 274
⟨Give heed to the paths of song,⟩
↑O see the sonnets flight↓
Seest thou what goes fast,
A child begot in a night,
(5)    That travels ⟨a journey of years⟩ ↑a thousand years↓

Cromwell's sentence about the Gentlemen & Christians.

*Spring*
"Now the white violet is in bloom; in bloom, too, the narcissus; & in bloom the lily that frequents the hills. And now Zenophila, loved by friends, among flowers a flower in its prime, is in bloom, the sweet rose of Persuasion."
*Greek Anthology. Bohn* p. 211

[41] The persons to whom I speak need no quotation from Blackstone to ⟨prove to⟩ ↑convince↓ them that all immoral laws are void. I shall not encumber my pages with authorities which, ⟨↑by↓⟩ add↑ing↓ nothing to my conviction, can add none ⟨to those I speak to⟩ ↑to any others↓    For I do not argue, but simply say what appears true & if it does not appear true to you it will not for much speaking

[42] [Hafiz, *Diwan*,] II 298
I said to the East wind
On the tulip-enriched plain,
Of what martyrs are these the bloody corpse-cloths?
He said, Dear Hafiz, to you & me
(5)    Has no one told this.
Tell thou of wine-ruby, of silver-chin⟨s⟩,
Seize the skirt of thy friend,
Care not for the enemy,
Be God's man & fear not the Devil.

↑Spring↓
(10)    As if Time bro't a bright relay
Of shining maidens every May

When days came to ripen maids
But had no power to make them fade

40 "O mark the sonnet's flight," 1, x, x, 3–4. Lines (1–5) are in pencil; in line (3) "Seest thou" is written "Thou seest" and marked for transposition. "Cromwell's sentence" may be the quotation used in "The Fugitive Slave Law" (1854), W 11:235; see JMN 14:413. Emerson's source for the quotation about spring is *Anthologia Graeca. The Greek Anthology . . .* (London, 1852), in his library.
41 "all immoral laws are void" is used in "The Fugitive Slave Law" (1851), W 11:186 and 190; see the front cover verso above. With "The persons to . . . authorities," cf. the same address, W 11:190.
42 "I said to the East wind" (1–9); "May-Day," 297–300, 299–300 (10–15). "II 298" and lines (1–9) and (14–15) are in pencil; lines (10–15) are struck through in ink; lines (12–13) are additionally struck through twice in pencil.

And summer came to ripen maids
(15)  But to ⟨a⟩ beauty that not fades

[43₁]  Give all to love
Obey thy heart
Friends, children,
↑Estate, ↓ Good fame
(5)  ‖ . . . . ‖ & the Muse
Nothing refuse

Let it have scope
Obey it punctually
To the end
(10)  It dives into the cloud
It foretells nothing
But it is a god
Knows its own ⟨way⟩ path
And may be trusted
(15)  It was not for ↑the↓ mean
It requires ⟨great⟩ courage
And ample souls

[43₂]                    ↑Spring↓
All good birds fly low & near the earth
little shady darling & brunette

                creampots

All is seeming
death also

(5)  But o to thaw that ruddy snow
The beam to break their prison
And give the scarlet tides to flow
⟨The sun is yet unrisen⟩
The hour not struck the sun unrisen

[43₃]  I bro't a ruby from the mine
And held it to the sun,
I said, ⟨it was but⟩ ↑the gem is↓ frozen wine
From Eden's ⟨vintage⟩ ↑vats that↓ run
(5)  I looked again, I thot them hearts
Of friends to friends unknown
Tides that should warm each others life
Are locked in sparkling stone

43₁ "Give All to Love," 1–9, 12, x, 15–16, x, 18–20. Erased pencil.
43₂ "All good birds" (1–2); "All is seeming" (3–4); "Rubies," 9–12, 12 (5–9). In pencil.
43₃ "Rubies."

But fire to thaw that ruddy snow,
(10)      A beam to break their prison,
And give the scarlet tides to flow,
That sun is yet unrisen.

[441]    Such it will reward
They shall return
Other than they were
And ‖ . ‖ ascending
(5)      Abandon all for love
‖ . . . . . . . . . . . . . . . . ‖
And yet, hear me yet
One word more o noble youth
Keep ‖ . ‖self at first
(10)    ‖ . ‖ at last & forever
⟨‖ . . . . ‖do it ‖ . . ‖done⟩
‖ . . . . . ‖ of thy love

Cling with life to thy darling
But at the *earliest dream
(15)    Or shadow of surmise
‖ . ‖ maiden ‖ . . . . . ‖
Of a joy apart ‖ . ‖ thee
Free be she, fancy-free
Do not detain a hem
(20)    Nor the least rose she flung thee

[442] Hafiz [*Diwan*] Vol. 1, 316
They say that thro patience the chalk
At last becomes a ruby
Yea, true, that by the hearts blood
Twill be coloured red
(5)      The ⟨b⟩pride of my rival brings me
Into astonishment & anxiety
O Lord hinder that a beggar
In honor should be holden.
Thou high cedar art thou so stubborn
(10)    Thou boastest of thy growth
Unto which not one of my short hands
Will attain
From all sides fly up
The arrows of my prayers
(15)    Perhaps one of them ⟨wi⟩
Will yet reach something

441 "Give All to Love," 22–26, x?, 27–28, 30–31, x?, 33–36, x?, 38–41. Erased pencil.
442 "They say, through patience, chalk." In pencil.

The sill of the palace of lordship
Which thou o my moon inhabitest
Is the wor⟨s⟩kshop where out of heads
(20)     The mortar is made ready

[45₁]    Though thou loved her as thyself
As a self of purer clay
Though her parting ⟨∥ . ∥⟩ ↑dims↓ ∥ . ∥ day
And unpeoples all thy world,
(5)      Heartily know
That when the noble go
The nobler approach

[45₂]    We wish like the glass
All clean to be; who wishes it not
The East wind breathes out in scents
Spices & perfumes
(5)      Why changes not the inner mind
Violet earth into musk?

---

⟨As⟩ ↑When↓ in eternity ⟨this beauty⟩ ↑the light↓
Of thy beauty glistened, ⟨was⟩ *Love was*,
Which set the worlds on fire ⟨with fl⟩

(10)     Beams trickled from thy cheeks,
Angels saw them & remained cold
Indignant turned they then to men

See, the Understanding prayed
for a spark his light to kindle.
(15)     Jealousy was the dazzling spark

[46] Hafiz [*Diwan*] Vol 1, 328
Secretly to love & to drink, what is it↑?↓ tis a dissolute
          day's work.
I side with the ↑open↓ drunkards, be it as it may.
Loose the knots of the heart & cumber thee no farther for
          the lot
No geometer has yet disentangled this confusion.
(5)      ⟨On⟩At the trade & changes of Time wonder not;
The like enchantments keeps Destiny ready.
Hold the glass discreetly, it was put together

45₁ "Give All to Love," 43–45, x, 47–49. Erased pencil.
45₂ "We wish like the glass" (1–6); "When in eternity" (7–15). In pencil.
46 "Secretly to love & to drink," 1–14 (1–14); "Loose the knots of the heart" (3–4); "I will
be drunk" (13–14). In pencil; lines (3–4) and (13–14) are struck through in pencil; "open" in
line (3) is in parentheses, perhaps to cancel it.

Of the skulls of Jamschid, Keikobad, & Behmen,
Who teaches us where Ka↑i↓ was & Nimrod are gone
(10)    How the throne of Jamschid fell in pieces at last
See Ferhad, how he longs for the lips of Schirin
Out of the flood of tears sprang tulips before him.
Come I will be riotous & wasted by wine
⟨Since perhaps⟩ ↑Who knows but↓ I shall find treasures in a
    /desolate/wasted/decayed/ house

[47₁]          Give all to love
Obey thy heart
Friends ⟨children⟩ ⟨projects⟩ plans
Estate good fame
(5)    Yes ‖ . . . . ‖use
Nothing refuse

It is ‖ . . . . ‖
Let it have scope
Obey it punctually
(10)    To the end
It dives into the ⟨cloud⟩ height
It foretells nothing
But it is a god
Knows its own path
(15)    And may be trusted

It was not for the mean
It requires courage stout
And ⟨ample⟩ souls above doubt
Such it will reward

[47₂]    Behold the tulip it knows how trustless is the change of time
Since it gave &c &c

---

[Hafiz, *Diwan*,] Vol 1 p 332

———

This effervescing gentleman who despises a secret
Scorns me since I am riotous & enamoured,
(5)    Look at the virtues of lovers not at their faults
Since who is not virtuous himself, sees faults.

People of heart have the key to the treasure of the heart
Let none henceforth doubt of this refined truth

47₁ "Give All to Love," 1–9, x, 12, x, 14–16, x, 18–20, 22. In light pencil.
47₂ "Secretly to love & to drink," 15–16 (1–2); "This effervescing gentleman" (3–12). In pencil; lines (5–6) are struck through in pencil.

Shepherd in the vale of Rest thy wish will then be first
    fulfilled.
(10)    When thou several years hast served the Jethro of the heart
    Blood trickles from the eye of Hafiz as if he were enchanted
    When he as old man remembers the days of youth

[48₁]    They shall return
    Other than they were
    And ever ascending

    Abandon all for love
(5)    And yet, hear me, yet
    One word more, o noble youth ↑in ear behoved↓,
    Keep thyself ⟨at first⟩ today
    And ⟨at last &⟩ forever
    Free as an Arab
(10)    Of thy beloved

    Cling with life ‖ . ‖ thy darling
    But at the ‖ . . . . ‖ dream
    Or shadow of surmise
    The ‖ . . . . . . . . . ‖
(15)    Of a joy ‖ . . ‖ from thee
    Free be she, fancy-free
    Do not detain a ‖ . ‖
    Nor the least rose she flung thee
    From her ‖ . . . ‖ diadem

[48₂] I 122        Hafiz [*Diwan*]
    Stand up, that we may sacrifice ↑the soul↓
    ⟨The soul b⟩Before the pencil of the Master
    Who the picture of this world
    So masterly has painted

——————

[Hafiz, *Diwan*,] I. 314
(5)    And had Hafiz
    Ten tongues like the lily
    He wd be silent
    Like the rosebud
    While thro' love his ⟨lips are⟩ ↑mouth is↓ sealed

——————

[Hafiz, *Diwan*,] II 197
(10)    O friend blame not Hafiz,
    ⟨While he gazes after you with love⟩

48₁ "Give All to Love," 23–28, 30–36, x, 38–42. Erased pencil.
48₂ "Stand up, that we may sacrifice" (1–4); "And had Hafiz" (5–9); "O friend blame not Hafiz" (10–14). "the mole on the cheek" and "the bladder . . . the eyelash" are used in "Persian Poetry," W 8:242–43. The page is in pencil; lines (1–4) are struck through in pencil.

While his glances so follow you,
I have in him all the time
Only your friend seen.

———

the mole on the cheek, the dimple on the chin the curled hair, the
bladder in which musk is brought, the cohol, a cosmetic by which
pearls & eyebrows are indelibly stained black the rose & jasmin, the
down on the cheek, the eyelash, night is not so dark as ⟨her⟩the hair

———

The red hot horse-shoe    see [Hafiz, *Diwan,*] p 208 Vol II
nobody looks on a cypress when she is by.

[49₁]    Tho thou loved her as thyself
        ⟨↑Fairer↓⟩ As one of purer clay
        Tho her passing dims the day
        ⟨And unpeoples the town⟩
(5)       Heartily know
        That when ‖ . ‖ noble go
        The ⟨nobler approach⟩ ↑arrive↓

        Discovering
        Robbing grace from all alive

(10)      Stealing grace from all alive

[49₂] I, 129          Hafiz [*Diwan*]
        The way of love is unlimited
        The soul is there sacrificed
           There is no other way.

        Scare me not with reason
(5)       Bring wine. Since Reason as watchman
           Has nothing here to do

        When thou givest thy heart to love
        Tis good time tis a good thing
           Use no counsel first

(10)      Who smote me? Ask thine eye,
        ⟨My⟩ ↑O↓ sweet child, let this not lie
           As guilt against my Destiny

        As ⟨for⟩ the new moon needs a sharp eye
        So thou an intelligent one; not every one
(15)          Sees the ⟨mo⟩young crescent

49₁ "Give All to Love," 43–45, x, 47–49, x, 46, 46. Erased pencil.
49₂ "The way of love." In pencil. Line (10) was written "Ask thine eye, who smote me?" and
marked for transposition by superscript numbers.

Use drinking with wisdom
The way to it as to a treasure is not
   Open to every man

[50₁]   Ever is the Understanding the small coin of life
   ⟨Values⟩ it ↑counts↓ nothing by the gold of love

---

                   damp
Serving for a laborers lamp

---

(5)   His learning truly lifted Hafiz to Heaven
   But his love of thee has brot him to the dust
   [Hafiz, *Diwan*,] II 205

---

Thousand dangers of ruin has the street of love
Believe not that death frees thee from all
[Hafiz, *Diwan*,] II 205

[50₂]   Her passions the shy violet
   From Hafiz never hides
   Love longings of the raptured bird
   The bird to him confides.

---

(5)   And ever the poet *from* the land
   Steers his bark & ⟨se⟩trims his sail;
   Right out to sea his courses stand,
   New worlds to find in pinnace frail.

---

[51₁]   [approximately sixteen lines of erased pencil writing]
   And period.

It was not for the mean
It requireth courage stout
(20)   Souls above doubt
   Valour unbending
   Such ⟨it⟩ t'will reward

[51₂]   Fine days

---

Day hast ‖ . . ‖ two faces
Making ‖ . . . ‖ two places

50₁ "The understanding's copper coin" (1–2); "The Chartist's Complaint," 5–6 (3–4); "His learning truly" (5–6); "Thousand dangers" (7–8). In pencil. Lines (1–2) and (7–8) are struck through in pencil; lines (3–4) are circumscribed in pencil.

50₂ "Hafiz" (1–4); "Poet" ("Ever the poet") (5–8). The quatrains are struck through separately in ink.

51₁ "Give All to Love," sixteen unrecovered lines, x, 18–22. Erased pencil. Visible in line (6) is "brave master" (cf. line 7 of "Give All to Love"); line (21), "Valour unbending", is written at the bottom of p. [50₁] and indicated for insertion on p. [51₁] by a caret.

51₂ "The Chartist's Complaint," 1–4, 7–9, 11–16, 18, 17. The page is in light pencil, struck through in pencil; lines (8–14) are additionally struck through in pencil.

One by ‖ . . ‖ ⟨fell day⟩ seen
Chill ‖ . . . ‖ unlighted, mean

(5)    ⟨Ah one self ‖ . . . ‖⟩ ↑Have the↓ mists another side
To be the equipage of pride
Gracing the rich man's wood & lake
And treacherously to show
⟨‖ . . . . . ‖⟩His planted isle where roses glow

(10)    O day ‖ . . . . . . ‖ mightiness
A sycophant to smug success
⟨And⟩ will ‖ . ‖ sweet ↑sky↓ a ‖ . ‖ broad
⟨Blue lake⟩ be ↑fine↓ accomplices of fraud
↑Back↓ Back to Chaos harlot day

(15)    ↑O sun↓ I ‖ . . ‖ curse thy cruel ray

[5 1₃] Hafiz

O mark the Sonnets flight
⟨G⟩O follow its fleet career,
A child begot in a night,
That lives to its thousandth year.

————

(5)    Go copy in verse one chime
Of the woodbell's peal & cry;
Write in a book the mornings prime,
And match with words that amber sky.

————

The vaulters in the Circus round,
(10)    Who step from horse to horse, but never touch the ground.

————

[52₁]                    hypocrit⟨e⟩ic
[approximately ten lines of erased pencil writing]

Cling ‖ . . ‖ life ‖ . ‖ thy darling
But ‖ . ‖ the least surprise
Or shadow ‖ . ‖ surmise
(15)    Tis ‖ . . . . . . . . ‖
Of a joy apart from thee

Free be she, fancy free
Do not detain a hem

5 1₃ "O mark the sonnet's flight" (1–4); "My Garden," 37–40 (5–8); "Like vaulters in the circus round" (9–10). Lines (5–8) are struck through in ink.
52₁ "Days," 1, ten unrecovered lines (1–11); "Give All to Love," 34–36, x, 38–42 (12–20). Erased pencil. Visible in line (4) are "Bring" and "in their" (cf. line 4 of "Days").

Nor the least rose she flung
(20)    From her summer diadem

[52₂]                *Fine Days*
Day! hast thou two faces
Making one place two places
One by humble laborers seen
Chill & wet, unlighted, mean,
(5)    Useful only, long & damp
Serving for a labourers lamp
Have the same mists another side
To be the equipage of pride
Gracing the rich man's wood & lake
(10)    And
And ⟨breaking⟩ treacherously ↑bright↓ to show
His planted isle where roses g⟨ro⟩low
O day, ⟨&⟩and is your mightiness
A sycophant to smug success?
(15)    With the sweet sky & ocean broad
Be fine accomplices of fraud?
O sun! I curse thy cruel ray
Back back to Chaos harlot day!

[53₁]    Tho thou loved her as thyself
[two lines of erased pencil writing]
Tho ‖ . . . . . ‖ dims ‖ . . ‖ day
[three lines of erased pencil writing]

[53₂]    The hypocritic Days barefoot
Muffled and dumb like dervishes
Bringing fires ↑fagots↓ in their liberal hands;
Ha‖ . . . . . . ‖, towns, mountains, stars
(5)    Or sky that holds them nothing less.
I in my pleached garden watched the pomp,
Forgot my fine ambition, hastily
Took a few herbs & apples, and the Day
Turned & departed. I too late
(10)    Under his solemn fillet saw the scorn

[53₃]                Rubies.
They brot me rubies from the mine
And held them to the sun

52₂ "The Chartist's Complaint," 1–9, 11?, 11–18. In pencil.
53₁ "Give All to Love," 43, x?, x?, 45, x?, x?, x? Erased pencil.
53₂ "Days," 1/2, 2, 4, 6, 6–11. In pencil.
53₃ "Rubies." Struck through in ink; lines (1–5) are additionally struck through in ink.

I said they are drops of frozen wine
From Eden's vats that run

(5)    I looked again, I thot them hearts
Of friends to friends unknown
Tides that should warm each other life
Are locked in sparkling stone

But fire to thaw that ruddy snow,
(10)    ⟨The beam⟩ to break ⟨their⟩ ↑the winedrops↓ prison,
⟨And⟩ ↑Or↓ give ⟨the⟩ ↑love's↓ scarlet tides to flow,—
That sun is yet unrisen.

[54] [Hafiz, *Diwan*,] II 435
Bring wine release me
From care
Only with wine they drive
Sorrow away

(5)    There are no other lamps
In society
Than wine & the face
Of the handsome cupbearer

Be not proud of the Enchantment
(10)    Of thy eyelashes
Since pride profits not
Oft have I ⟨learned⟩ proved.

Master thou oft well advisest me
Not to love
(15)    But this lesson is
No law for me

Love befouls only the heart
Of great men
Since thou hast no love
(20)    Thou art excused

To a wink sacrificed I
My virtue
Ah therein is all my store
Of good works

[55]    The luck of enjoyment is there
Bating separation

54 "Bring wine release me," 1–24. In pencil; lines (17–20) are struck through in pencil.
55 "Bring wine release me," 25–28 (1–4); "Hearts secret of love" (5–8). The page is in pencil.

And the land of the heart is now
Again *urbar*   arable   fruitful
Ur = ox

---

[Hafiz, *Diwan*,] II 445
(5)           Hearts secret of love speaks
              Lutetone & song ⟨forth⟩ out
              Who purely from love goes to the ground
              Outweighs a thousand giving Hatems

---

Of what use to purse your mouth and quote St Paul, when these
Corinthian clouds, these flowers & birds say quite another matter
[R.W.E.]

[Hafiz, *Diwan*,] II 248
When the sweetheart commands out of her locks to make us a fire
girdle, then, O master, is it not permitted us to wear the frock of the
order.

[56]   Hafizs rhetoric

The robber Time that Turk of heaven

              To each they offer gifts ⟨what will he⟩ ↑after his will↓
              Bread, kingdoms, stars or sky that canopies

              Damsels of Time, the hypocritic Days
              Muffled & dumb, like barefoot dervishes
(5)           And marching single in an endless file
              Bring diadems & fagots in their hands.
              To each they offer gifts, after his will,
              Bread, kingdoms, stars, or sky that covers all
              I in my pleached garden watched the pomp
(10)          Forgot my morning wishes, hastily
              Took a few herbs & apples, & the Day
              Turned & departed silent. I, too late,
              Under his solemn fillet saw the scorn.

[57₁]         Go, speed the stars of thought
              On to their shining goals;
              The sower scatters broad the seed,
              Thy ‖ . . ‖ing be souls.

[57₂]         Daughters of Time the hypocritic Days
              Muffled & dumb, like barefoot Dervishes

---

56 "Days," 5–6, 1–11. "Hafizs . . . of heaven" and lines (1–2) are in pencil; lines (3–13) are
struck through in ink.
57₁ "Pale Genius roves alone," 9–12; "Intellect" ("Go, speed"). Erased pencil.
57₂ "Days." Struck through in ink.

And marching singly in an endless file
Bring ⟨fagots⟩ diadems & fagots in their hands
(5) Have what you will, they say, or seem to say,
Towns mountains stars or sky that holds them all.
I, in my pleached garden, watched the pomp,
Forgot my morning wishes, hastily
Took a few herbs & apples, and the Day
(10) Turned & departed silent. I, too late,
Under his solemn fillet saw the scorn.

[58₁] The living Heaven thy prayers respect
House ‖ . . ‖ once & architect
Quarrying ⟨these⟩ ↑men's↓ rejected hours
Buil‖ . ‖ therewith Eternal towers
(5) So‖ . ‖ selfcommanded works
↑Absolute↓ In ‖ . . . . . . ‖
‖ . . . . . . . . ‖ undermining days
Grows by decays,
And the famous might that lurks
(10) In reaction & recoil
⟨‖ . ‖⟩Makes flames to freeze⟨,⟩ & ice to boil,
And thro the ⟨surly⟩ arms of offence
Builds the ⟨firm⟩ seat of innocence
In ‖ . . . . . . . . ‖ all goes well
(15) No fear ‖ . . ‖ brawl no frauds compel
In the beginning ‖ . . ‖ the time to come
And on the road ‖ . ‖ home
⟨On⟩In that empire all go‖ . . . . ‖
No ⟨actions⟩ brawl no frauds compel
(20) No lapsing honor old & deaf
Betrays the saint to unbelief

[58₂]                    Villeggiatura.
Day! hast thou two faces,
Making one place two places.
One by humble farmers seen
Chill, & wet, unlighted, mean,
(5) Useful only, long & damp,
Serving for a laborer's lamp⟨;⟩.
Have the same mists another side
To be the appanage of pride,
Gracing the rich man's wood & lake
(10) ↑Where doe leads fawn when mornings wake↓

58₁ "Spiritual Laws," 1–5, x, 6–12, eight unused lines. In pencil. Lines (14–15) are bracketed
to the left.
58₂ "The Chartist's Complaint." Struck through in ink.

And treacherously bright to show
His planted isle, where ⟨g⟩roses glow.
O day! and is your mightiness
A sycophant to smug success?
(15)      Will the sweet sky, & ocean broad,
Be fine accomplices to fraud?
O Sun! I curse thy cruel ray;
Back back to Chaos harlot day!
                 Chartist.

[59] The Persians had a copyright not used with us. The writer of the Ghaselle is wont to insert his name in the last verse. We have one example in English   "The melancholy Cowley lay"   Hafiz secures his fame by this interweaving and delights in playful self assertion

[60₁]     ↑The living Heaven thy prayers respect↓
⟨Heaven⟩ ⟨It is ↑at ‖ . . . ‖hitect & house⟩
↑House at once, and architect↓
‖ . . . . . . . . . . . ‖ therewith
(5)      Self commanded works
In vital cirques.

Fears not the craft of undermining days
Grows by decays
And by the famous might that lurks
(10)     In reaction & recoil
Makes flame to freeze & ice to boil
And thro the angry armies of Offence
Builds the firm seat of Innocence
No surveyor to estimate
(15)     Its perfect figure, budding sta‖ . . ‖
Its youthful urgency
No lapse of memory old & deaf
Betrays the ⟨angel⟩ ↑saint↓ ⟨in⟩to unbelief

In the beginning sees the time to come
(20)     And on the road its home

All goes well in that Empire
No mutiny no wrath
No Tyrant ⟨w⟩rich no raging poor

[60₂]       If I should put these woods in song,
And tell what's here enjoyed,

---

59  Cf. "Persian Poetry," W 8:252. In pencil.
60₁ "Spiritual Laws," 1–2, 2, 4–5, x, 6–12, ten unused lines. In pencil, struck through twice in pencil and erased.
60₂ "My Garden," 1–4. Struck through in ink.

All men would to these gardens throng
And leave the cities void

[61₁]    Heaven is alive
⟨Self built & quarrying itself⟩
Upbuilds eternal towers
Self commanded works

(5)    In vital cirques
By dint of being all
⟨Its loss is transmutation⟩
Fears not the craft of undermining days
Grows by decays

(10)    And by the famous might that lurks
In reaction & recoil
Teach flames to freeze & ice to boil
And thro the armies of ⟨the ‖ . . . . ‖⟩
Builds the firm seat of Innocence

(15)    Is ‖ . . . . . ‖ emblem to measure
Its perfect stature youthful power
Youthful urgency
No lapse of memory
Betrays the angel into unbelief

[61₂]        The darling spring
With sudden passion languishing
Maketh all things softly smile,
Maketh pictures, mile on mile,

(5)    Holds a cup with cowslip wreathed
Whence a smokeless incense breathed
Dripping dew cold daffodillies
Making drunk with draught of lilies.
Girls are peeling the sweet willow

(10)    And the Gilead tree,
And troops of boys
Shouting with whoop & hillo
And hip, hip, three times three.

[62₁]    [fourteen lines of erased pencil writing]

[62₂]    In the beginning sees the time to come
And on the road his home

61₁ "Spiritual Laws," 1–2, 4–5, x, x, x, 6–12, five unused lines. In pencil, struck through in pencil. In line 13, "armies" is written "arms↑ies↓".

61₂ "May-Day," 1–6, x, x, 7–11.

62₁ Visible are "If" (first line), "But" (third line), "enveloped" (fourth line), "hill" (fifth line), "↑And↓ Of" (seventh line), "Since morning & mountain" (eighth line), "Or" (ninth line), "As" (tenth line), "In" (eleventh line), "There my" (twelfth line), and "In halls" (fourteenth line). The lines are an early version of "Hermione."

62₂ "Spiritual Laws," two unused lines. In pencil.

[62₃] The air is full of whistlings.
   What was that I heard
   Out of the hazy lands?
   Harp of the wind, or song of bird,
(5)  Or clapping of shepherds' hands
   A blast on ↑Oberon's↓ horn,
   Or ↑farmer's↓ cock at morn,
   Or flap of wings⟨,⟩?
   ↑It is↓ A sound, ⟨or⟩ ↑it is a↓ token
(10)  ↑That↓ The ↑marble↓ seal is broken
   ↑And↓ A change has passed on things

    When late I walked, in earlier days,
   All was stiff & stark,
   Kneedeep snows choked all the way
(15)  In the sky no spark

[63₁] [approximately five lines of erased pencil writing]

[63₂] Two well assorted travellers use
   To walk these woodlands Love & the Muse
   From this pair is nothing hidden
   Unto them is nought forbidden
(5)  Hand in hand these comrades go.
   ⟨Her that tr‖ . ‖⟩ way
   Length & breadth of Nature ‖ . . ‖
   From side to side & never stray
   For when they cannot find they make their way
(10)  No joy is like their journey known,
   Land & sea are theirs alone,
   And the only grief
   That has no respite or relief
   Is when by false companions crossed
(15)  The pilgrims have each other lost

[63₃] Winter builds
   Sudden cathedrals in the wilds.
    All the piny hosts
   Were sheeted ghosts
(5)  The forlorn icy wind
   Me from labor disinclined
   Who wd. freeze in frozen brakes

62₃ "May-Day," 12–16, x, x, 37–40, 98–101.
 63₁ Visible are "was alone" (first line), "now" (second line), "hillside" (third line), and "onto" and "mountain" (fourth line); the fifth line appears to be canceled. Cf. "Hermione," 40–42, 44.
 63₂ "Love and Thought," 1–5, x, 6, four unused lines, 9–12. In pencil.
 63₃ "May-Day," x, 112–13, 113, 115, x, 117–18, 126–27 (1–10); "I leave the book," 1–4 (11–14).

I slunk back to books & home;
Now desire of action wakes
(10)    And the wish to roam.

I leave the book, I leave the wine,
I breathe freer by the pine
In houses, I am low & mean,
Mountain waters wash me clean

[64₁]    Deceived ‖ . . ‖ wanderest
In str‖ . . . . . . . . ‖
And my ‖ . . . . ‖ come ‖ . . . ‖ me
The southwind is my next ‖ . . . ‖
(5)    He is come ‖ . . . . . . . . . ‖
And drugged with all spices
And in every twinkling covert

[64₂]    Space is ample east & west
But ‖ . . ‖ cannot go abreast
Cannot ‖ . . . . . . . ‖
Yonder masterful cuckoo
(5)    Crowds every egg out of the nest
‖ . . . . . . ‖ grow except its own
The ‖ . . . . . . . ⟨ . . . ‖⟩ & stone
Night & day ‖ . . . . . . . . ‖
Every quality & pith
(10)    Surcharged ‖ . . . . . . . . ‖
‖ . ‖ breathes one sense of

[64₃] *Retributions* One evil in all immoral acts. You borrow the succour of the devil, & he must have his fees. He was never known to abate a penny of his rents. In every nation the immorality breeds plagues. England has its Ireland: Germany ⟨its Austria⟩ ↑hatred of its people↓; Italy its Pope; & America, the most prosperous nation of the universe, has the greatest calamity in the universe, Negro slavery.

[64₄]    And by the seawaves I am strong
I hear their medicinal song,
Ask no physician but the wave.

Spring has charmed the earth
(5)    With a sunbeam from the sea.

64₁ "Hermione," 47–53. Erased pencil.
64₂ "Unity," 1–10, x. Erased pencil.
64₃ "The Fugitive Slave Law" (1851), W 8:186; for "England has . . . slavery," see p. [26] above. In pencil.
64₄ "I leave the book," 5–6, 8 (1–3); "Gentle Spring has charmed the earth," 1–2 (4–5); "May-Day," 276–79 (6–9). A rough pencil sketch of what appears to be a boat is drawn at the bottom of the page, probably inspired by lines (3–4) on facing p. [65₃].

Drug the cup, thou butler sweet,
And send the madness round
The feet that slid so long on snow,
Are glad at last to feel the ground.

[65₁]    And in a hundred sunlights,
Fear not, thou child infirm,
‖ . . ‖ no God dare wrong a worm
Laurel ‖ . . ‖ cleave to ‖ . . . ‖
(5)    Power to him who ‖ . . . . . . ‖
Not fit ‖ . . . . . . . ‖ feet
[two lines of erased pencil writing]

[65₂] It is rem‖ . . . . . ‖ & must be su‖ . . ‖ined by courses [approximately two lines of erased pencil writing]

It seeks to en‖ . . . ‖ robbery & murder ‖ . ‖ right to liberty is just as inalienable as his right to life. To take his life, is not a higher crime than to take his liberty
All the sentiments fight against it   ↑His duty is to break it↓   It introduces confusion into the statute

It demoralizes the community ⟨We cannot ‖ . . ‖ one of its⟩  A man cannot abet it without losing selfrespect & caste. It must be done by good men & must be done by bad. Capt Rhynders & Mr Hallett and men of notorious immorality must be employed

[65₃]    The maple bark is changed to red
White the lake is green again
↑Drag to the cove the hidden boat↓
↑In summer eve entranced to float↓
(5)    Fill & saturate each kind
With good according to its mind
⟨G⟩Fill each ↑kind↓ & saturate
With good according to its fate
Willow, & ⟨m⟩violet, maiden, & man.

(10)    Pour the wine, pour the wine,
Till it changes to foam.

Cup the youth that justifies
Who leaves his task to feed his eyes
Fleet the moments, fleeter.

65₁ "Compensation" ("Man's the elm"), x, 5–8, 9?, x?, x? Erased pencil.
65₂ Emerson's references are to Isaiah Rynders, New York Tammany leader, and Benjamin Franklin Hallett, Boston Democrat and Southern sympathizer. Partially erased pencil. The unrecovered erased pencil writing is prose; visible are "A" (first line) and "Of" (second line).
65₃ "May-Day," four unused lines, 280–84, eight unused lines. With lines (10–11), cf. "Pour the wine!," 1–2.

(15)  Ever to joy the cup persuades,
    Making the young girls sweeter,
    And the young men almost maids.

[66]  The bittersweet, the haunting air
    Goeth, bloweth everywhere,
    It preys on all, all prey on it.
    Blooms in beauty, thinks in wit,
(5)   Bites damsel with halfpleasing flame
    Drives the struck poet mad for fame,
    Stings the strong with enterprise
    And travellers long for Indian skies

[67₁]        Etiquette
Not persuadable obdurate whig ‖ . . . . . . . . . . . . . . . . . . . . ‖ offering
places[?]

Nature a swamp in whose purlieus we see prismatic dewdrops, but her
interiors are terrific. See what the microscope reveals unmitigated
savage, ant & insects of the drop volvox globator
As if in the preadamite world she ⟨raised⟩ bred valor only; by & by gets
on to man & then tenderness is added & thus still raises ⟨the⟩ virtue
piecemeal

[67₂]   I saw the wizard spring go forth
    Stepping daily onward north
    To greet staid ancient cavaliers
    Filing singly in stately train
(5)   And who and who are the travellers
    They were Night & Day, & Day & Night
    Pilgrims that never alight
    Short of stature they seemed, & low
    Short & bent by cold & snow.
(10)  ⟨She⟩ ↑The merry spring↓ threw wreaths on them,
    Flowerwreaths ⟨of⟩ ↑gay with↓ bud & bell,
    Many a flower & many a gem,
    They were refreshed by the smell.
    They shook the snow from hats & shoon

[68₁] [eight lines of erased pencil writing] mine If I do it, I shall know
‖ . . . ‖.

66 "May-Day," 285–88, x, x, 289–90.
 67₁ "Nature . . . terrific" and "in the preadamite . . . piecemeal" are used in "The Sovereignty
of Ethics," W 10:188; see JMN 13:450. Partially erased pencil.
 67₂ "May-Day," 325–38.
 68₁ "In its elasticity." Erased pencil. The prose, including the erased portion, is struck
through in pencil. Visible in the erased portion are "to" and "men" (first line), "mark" (second
line), "mass" (third line), "bridge" and "from" (fifth line), and "will" and "but" (seventh line).

In its elasticity
Greater temperance in ‖ . . . ‖ employ

[68₂]   They put their April raiment on
And those eternal forms
Unhurt by a thousand storms
Shot up to the height of the sky again
(5)   And danced as merrily as young men.

I saw them mask their awful glance
Meekly sidewise in gossamer lids
And to speak my thot, if none forbids
It was as if the unmeasured gods
(10)   ↑ Tired of their starry periods, ↓
Hid their majesty in cloth
Woven of tulips & painted moth

[69₁] Poem must make the poet almost as much as poet poem   a cannon with a kick
Natures even and deliberate denouement of her plot is not before-hand   keeps the children in incessant surprise   satisfies them wholly
Each man living at the waystations has muffins to get out of the millers grain and never asks whither

Our advantages are like our riches some deformity   We are monstrously good & great & not symmetrically

[69₂]   ⟨It was the day of the Vintage⟩
↑ Twas the vintage-day of field & wood ↓
When ↑ magic ↓ wine ↑ for bards ↓ is brewed ⟨for bards⟩
All in loving choirs they sat
(5)   They drunk wine never made in vat
Every tree & stem & chink
⟨Was filled with flavors⟩ ↑ Gushed with syrup ↓ to the brink
⟨And the wide⟩ ↑ The flowing ↓ air was scented still
With gums of India & Cathay
(10)   And the jungles of ⟨b⟩Brazil
In the frolic holiday
The air stole into the streets of towns
And betrayed the fund of joy
To the high school & the medalled boy
(15)   On from hall to chamber ran
To youth to maid from man to man

68₂ "May-Day," 339–50.
69₁ In pencil.
69₂ "May-Day," 358, 358-59, x, x, 360–61, four unused lines, 362–66.

[70₁]           Sweeter is the law
           Than all the grace love ever saw
           We are its suppliants  By it we
           Draw the breath of eternity
(5)           Serve thou it not for daily bread
           Serve it for fear & want & need
           Love it tho it hide its light
           By love behold the Sun at night
           Tho' the law shd thee forget
(10)         More enamoured serve it yet
           Tho it hate thee suffer long
           Put the spirit in the wrong
           That were deed & joy to sing
           By waters of light in Seraphs ring.

[70₂]       And to old eyes as well
           I see you, ⟨he⟩ ↑the old man↓ cried, ye clouds
           Airy turrets purple piled
           ⟨As ye⟩ ↑Which once↓ my infancy beguiled
(5)           Beguiling me now with the selfsame spell
           ⟨Warned I yield but know ye well⟩
           ⟨Skilful⟩ know ye ↑skilful↓ to convoy
           The total freight of hope & joy
           Into rude & homely nooks
(10)         Shed mocking lustres on shelf of books
           On farmers byre, on grassy pipes
           Or in a pool on dancing chips.
               Enchanter Enchanter!

[71] [blank]
[72]        Blame me not thou hoarse preacher
           Did not the Creator know
           Who set me on fire with this flame
           Whom I ought to love?   [R.W.E.]

---

Hafiz [*Diwan*] II, 5
(5)           Heaven aims at me every hour
           To wound me again
           "Thou, Hafiz, art not singled out
           "Many ⟨are in⟩ ↑rove↓ these ⟨desarts⟩ ↑wilds alone↓

70₁ "The Discontented Poet: a Masque," 67–80. In pencil.
   70₂ "May-Day," 367–71, x, 372–77, x. The cancellation and addition in line (2) are in pencil. With line (13), cf. "The Park," 9.
   72 "Not mine, sour priest" (1–4); "Lord my god these people," 23–28 (5–10); "Alas! till now I had not known" (11–12). In pencil; lines (11–12) are struck through in pencil.

"Many are to ruin gone."
(10)        Say I to myself again

---

[Hafiz, *Diwan*,] II 118
        Alas, ⟨that⟩ I never knew ⟨un⟩til↑1↓ now
        That my conductor & the conductor of fortune were one

---

[73]    What keeps the kinds in check

[74]–[75] [blank]
[76] [Hafiz, *Diwan*,] II 162
        I never went out of my country
        In all my life

---

[Hafiz, *Diwan*,] II 165
        For his constant dwelling place has Hafiz
        Once ⟨ch⟩for all chosen the wine-house
(5)       So chooses the lion the wood for his abode
        And the bird the plain

---

        For though her heart was well inclined
        And manners made of bounty well refined
        Yet distant capitals & ↑marble↓ courts her eye seemed still
            to see
(10)        And palaces & princes and of the best that be.

[77₁]            Compliments
[Hafiz, *Diwan*,] II 74
        Our Shah's counsel is the efflux
        Of higher light
        See thou have, if thou draw nigh him,
        Clear vision.
(5)       Take the wish for his greatness
        Into thy prayer
        Since the ear of his heart
        Converses with angels

---

        What more beautiful forms things assume
(10)        Now that the Shah comes back
            [Hafiz, *Diwan*,] II 164

73  "By kinds I keep," 1. In pencil.
76  "I never went out" (1–2); "For his constant dwelling place" (3–6); "A.H." (7–10). In pencil; lines (7–10) are struck through in pencil.
77₁  "Our Shah's counsel" (1–8); "What lovelier forms" (9–10); "Thou who with thy long hair," 17–20 (11–14); "Fair fall thy soft heart!" (11–14). In pencil; lines (9–14), partially erased, are struck through in pencil.

Compliments

[Hafiz, *Diwan*,] II, 332
⟨Honor to⟩ ↑Fair fall↓ thy soft heart
⟨And⟩ a good work wouldst thou do
↑O↓ Pray for ⟨all⟩ the dead
Whom thy eyelashes slew

[77₂]   ⟨For though⟩ ↑High was↓ her heart↑,↓ ⟨was⟩ ↑& yet was↓
        well inclined,
        Her manners made of bounty well refined
        Far capitals & marble courts her eye seemed still to see,
        ⟨K⟩Minstrels & kings & highborn dames & of the best that
        be.

[78] [blank]
[79]   Friendship

      The Tartar boy
[Hafiz, *Diwan*,] II 291
      Know⟨e⟩st thou the luck ⟨the⟩ ↑a↓ friend's face to see
      Better ⟨to⟩ beg near him than ⟨any⟩ prince to be
      Snatch the opportunity of the friend's speech
      Who knows if we meet again on the way?

[80₁]   Friendship
      If thy ⟨friend⟩ ↑darling↓ favor thee
      Both worlds thou mayest defy
      Let fortune ⟨befriend thee⟩ stand thy friend
      Armies ⟨may⟩ encamp against thee in vain

(5)      That's my ‖ . ‖ of youth ‖ . . . . ‖

      "To me is ‖ . . . . . . . . . ‖
      Thro thy friendship love" [Hafiz, *Diwan*,] II 58

      O Gods give the traveller
      Many a hundred caravans
(10)    Of hearts ‖ . . . . . . ‖ at all
      Wherever he goes, welfare! [Hafiz, *Diwan*,] II 60

77₂ "A.H." Struck through in pencil.
79 "Knowest thou the luck," 1–2, 11–12. This page is in pencil.
80₁ "If thy darling favor thee," 1–4, x?(1–5); " 'To me is" (6–7); "O Gods give the traveller"
(8–11); "Drink, hear my counsel," 5–6 (12–13); "No physician has a balsam" (14–15); "Spare
thou neither time nor blood" (16–17). In pencil. Lines (5–13) are partially erased; lines (8–13)
are struck through in pencil.

Thou learnest no secret until thou beginnest friendship
Since to the profane no heavenly tidings press in.
[Hafiz, *Diwan*,] II 71

————

(15)      No physician ha⟨d⟩s a balsam for my wo
I am only sound or sick thro my friend
[Hafiz, *Diwan*,] II 170

————

[Hafiz, *Diwan*,] II 279
Spare thou neither time nor blood for thy friend
Sacrifice also a hundred souls for one drink

————

[80₂]    Whats he that slayeth or is slain
None perishes & none destroys
Each will his life ⟨forfeit⟩ ↑destroy↓ or ⟨gain⟩ ↑kill↓
⟨⟨As⟩ ⟨↑Of↓⟩ ↑When↓ good or ill he make his choice⟩
(5)    As falls his choice on good or ill

[81] Hafiz [*Diwan*,] I. 403
It is certain that who his mind
In his friend concentered has
Has good luck to his handmaid
⟨And to his companion⟩
(5)    ⟨Far⟩ higher than the Understanding
Is the cabinet of love,
Who has his soul in his own sleeve
Kisses only the door.
The mouth of the friend perchance
(10)    Is the /seal/ring/ of Solomons hand
Which under the power of a ruby
Has the world at command
My friend has a musk down
And lips like fireglow
(15)    I will flatter the beauty finely
Who has this & that.
As long as thou art in the earth
Use ⟨opportunity⟩ occasion, work & climb
Since the Grave has a plenty
(20)    of unprofitable time.
Happy who sees the poor
Without contempt
While the first place of honour
Has many poor sitters

80₂ Cf. "Brahma," 1–2. In pencil.
81 "It is certain that who his mind," 1–24. In pencil; lines (1) and (2–12) are struck through separately in pencil.

[82]        It screens from harms body & soul
            The hearts prayer of the poor;
            Whilst he who is ashamed of the poor
            Has no good end.

_____

        *Wine*
    [Hafiz, *Diwan*,] I. 384
(5)         Who dedicates himself to the glass
            Wherein the world mirrors itself
            Lifts securely the veil
            Which separates the worlds

_____

[Hafiz, *Diwan*,] II 22,
            How the head after song so earnestly strives
(10)        Bring here bands of wine for the stupid head!

_____

    Hafiz's John Barleycorn [*Diwan*] I 429

_____            _____

                wasted with wine
        Who knows but I shall find treasure in the wasted house
                        See p. 46 supra

_____       _____

[Hafiz, *Diwan*,] II 92
            Wine resembles the Lord Jesus
            ⟨Who⟩ It wakes the dead to life

[83]        ↑Drink till the turbans are all unbound↓
            ↑Drink till the house like the world turns round↓

            ⟨For⟩ ⟨she has⟩ ↑There's↓ wealth of mornings in her year
            Of planets in her sky
(5)         But she chose the best thy youth to cheer
            Thy beauty to supply
            And many come to the stream
            To the willow & the vine
            But aye to me the happiest seem
(10)        To draw the dregs of wine

82 "It is certain that who his mind," 25–28 (1–4); "Who dedicates himself" (5–8); "To be wise the dull brain" (9–10); "I will be drunk" (11–12); "Wine resembles the Lord Jesus" (13–14). In pencil. Lines (8–10) are partially erased; lines (8–10) and (11–12) are struck through separately in pencil.
83 "Drink till the turbans" (1–2); "In my garden three ways meet," 37–44 (3–10). In pencil.

[84]  *Persian superlative*
Girl! o my girl! bunch of mint! berry of the grape!
⟨Your⟩ O beautiful girl! your name is the constellation of the pleiades.
You tie round your waist a shawl of a thousand colours,
rose faced Gouhera!
After the harvest of thy beauty the sphere of heaven itself like a poor
gleaner humbly picks up the ears of corn thou hast neglected
Heap of roses! rise up & come to me.
thou flower bed of mine!
my little apple of Ispahan
In the gulistan of thy beauty the parrot is ashamed of his feathers
roll of cinnamon,
Dance on! poise thy graceful shape to the tune of the song & let me
die for thee

[85] My Tatar girls beautiful as the waves
The very defence which /nature/the God/ has provided for the innocent
⟨is in the⟩ against cruelty is in the indignation & desire to succour it
which it awakens in ⟨the beholder⟩ ↑bosom of the beholder↓.

---

One winter at Washington is said to open the eyes. It is like Mr
Greene's lecture on gambling. Here ⟨is a contest between⟩ ↑are↓ a few
persons & parties the NY & Boston merchants Mr Webster Mr Fill-
more on the one side ⟨& the⟩ who have their own objects to carry, &
reliance is put on the personal regard to these men thro' the country to
carry them.

[86] "Do not scold me   they are guests of my eyes." Do not frown,
they want no bread, they are guests of my words" [Chodzko, *Popular
Poetry of Persia*, 1842, p. 391]
"Our dear soul is a guest in our body" [p. 392]
"Is every body our Ali whose name is Ali?" [p. 397]
"A married woman is like an orchard in autumn" [p. 403]
"A real singer will never forget what he has once learned" [p. 404]
        [[Sandal tree   arboretum]] [p. 408]
Kurrogl. p 155 "What need have I of money a dozen pounds of the
watermelon's peel in the kitchen every day is sufficient for my palate"

84 Many of these "superlatives" are from *Specimens of the Popular Poetry of Persia, as
Found in the Adventures and Improvisations of Kurroglou, the Bandit-Minstrel of Northern
Persia . . .*, trans. Alexander Chodzko (London, 1842); Emerson withdrew this volume from the
Harvard College Library on 2 September 1846. In pencil; "*Persian . . . sphere of heaven*" is
erased.
85 In pencil. "My Tatar girls . . . the beholder." is partially erased and struck through three
times in pencil.
86 In pencil. " 'Do not . . . words' ", " 'A real . . . once learned' ", "Sandal tree arboretum"
and "Kurrogl. . . . palate' " are struck through separately in pencil.

[87] Mehdum Kuly. "His heart came to its place, his tongue became an inexhaustible ⟨supp⟩ source of words full of fire & eloquence [p. 391] From a sunnito he became a sheah [p. 391] "relig & poetry constitute almost all the civilization" [p. 391]

Gouhera
Turkanna
Hellaji
Nana
Sakina
Gulam Shah
Zuleika

---

Sinai, the Written Mountain

[88] When they have offended they send elephants loaded with gold, musk, ambergris ↑camphire↓ silk & shawls ⟨We are⟩ It was Iblis that led us astray But thou art an ocean of mercy
We wait your commands; kill us;
We are the dust of your feet.

It is vain to charge the abolitionists with the new stringency of slavery in the South. Blame a ball for rebounding; or a gun for kicking; blame the air for rushing in⟨to⟩ ↑where a↓ vacuum ↑is made↓; ⟨or⟩ ↑blame↓ the boiler for exploding under the pressure of steam. these ⟨things⟩ are laws of the world water freezes at ⟨21⟩32, & boils at 212, & when ⟨a man sees reason⟩ ↑justice↓ is outraged ⟨she revolts⟩ anger begins. ↑See p 85↓

[89] [Hafiz, *Diwan*,] I 278
    So long as there's a trace
    Of wine & banquet house
    My head will lie in the dust
    Of the threshold of the winehouse
(5)    Ask thou for grace ⟨one day⟩ ↑hereafter↓
    At my gravestone
    ⟨Since⟩ that will be the pilgrim city
    Of all the drinkers of wine
    The ring of ⟨the landlor⟩ mine host hangs
(10)    Forever in my ear.
    I am; what I was

87 In pencil. " 'relig . . . the civilization' " is struck through in pencil and followed by what may be Emerson's symbol of authorship.
88 "When they . . . your feet." is in pencil. "It is . . . begins." is struck through twice in pencil; "See p 85" is in pencil.
89 "So long as there's a trace," 1–21 (1–21); "I am: what I am" (11–12). In pencil. Lines (5–16) are partially erased; lines (5–11) and (12–16) are struck through separately in pencil.

My dust will be again.
Go, blind hermit, go,
Since to thee & me alike
(15)     The secret is hidden,
And always will be.
My well beloved went
Abroad today to hunt
Whomsoever the lot had doomed
(20)     To bleed at the heart.
A place on which the sole
[90]     Of thy foot falls
Will be the resort
Of all reasonable men.
From the day when by love
(5)     I am laid (as) in the grave
Until the Judgment, my eye
Will be by thine
So long the luck of Hafiz
Will be no better
(10)     The hair of his love
Will be in the hands of another.

---

Affirmative

No seed will die.
Believe in the great & unweariable power of destiny.
No hope so bright, but is the beginning of its own fulfilment.

[91] The moral laws↑!↓—sun & rain, the frost, sleep, & death, ⟨all angels⟩ gravity, chemistry, all thoughts, all virtues, all angels & gods are on their side. Yes & the devil himself.

[92]    *Freedom*
I have read in our old Norse bible of the Edda, that the God *Freye,* or *Freedom,* had a sword so good that it would itself strew a field with carnage, whenever the owner ordered it—
Yet I think dwarves killed him once.

[93]    "It stands written on the gate of Heaven,
     'Wo *unto him who suffers himself to be betrayed by Fate!*"

[94] [Hafiz, *Diwan,*] I. 426
    To whom a glass full of red wine

90 "So long as there's a trace," 22–32. The verse is in pencil; the prose is struck through twice in ink.
91 Struck through in ink.
92 Struck through in pencil. See JMN 10:55, 11:451.
93 " 'Tis writ on Paradise's gate."
94 "To whom a glass" (1–8). The page is in pencil. With "The lot . . . nightcap," struck through in pencil, cf. "Persian Poetry," W 8:244.

Was given in the morning
To him was a place in heaven
By the Lord given.
(5)       Be no saint; look not
Too closely after drunkards
To them was on the day of lots
The love-bias given. &c

------

[Hafiz, *Diwan*,] I 113
The lot gives him only the throne of drunkenness who knows how to
prize ⟨the⟩ earthly happiness at the value of a nightcap

------

Destiny—of vines & drinkers [Hafiz, *Diwan*,] I, 45.

------

⟨The two Days [Hafiz, *Diwan*,] I, 53⟩

------

The lover's mole, ⟨her⟩ ↑my↓ eyelash is ⟨my⟩ ↑her↓ ⟨brush⟩, night is
not so dark as her hair

------

[95] The two Days [Hafiz, *Diwan*,] I. 53

"The man is a fool who deems anything ridiculous except what is bad."
Plato. Repub[lic]. B[ook] V. c[hapter] 4
"But the higher they advance in the forms of government, the more
does honour forsake them, disabled, as it were, by an asthma, from
pursuing its progress."
          [Plato,] Repub[lic]. B[ook] VIII c[hapter]. 19

[96] [Hafiz, *Diwan*,] I 434
          To him are straw and mountains alike

------

Hafiz's John Barleycorn. See [Hafiz, *Diwan*,] I. 429

          In bounding youth the night & rain
          Shut ↑toys↓ out ⟨the toys that offend⟩ ↑vex↓ the brain
                    But later, ↑dark &↓ rainy skies
(5)       Give not the cheer the sun supplies

[97] Hafiz Superlative
------

[Hafiz, *Diwan*,] I. 444
          The ninefold table of Heaven

95 "The two Days I. 53" is in pencil.
96 "To him are straw" (1); "In bounding youth" (2–5). The page is in pencil. "Hafiz's John
Barleycorn" is used in "Quotation and Originality," W 8:186.
97 "The ninefold table" (1–4); "Should I shed my tears" (5–8); "Take my heart" (9–10); "If
to the Assembly of souls," 1–4 (11–14); "Prince the ball of heaven" (15–18). The page is in
pencil; lines (9–10) are struck through in pencil.

Its gold & silver bread
Compared with the table of thy grace
Are but a morsel ⟦and the whole of that ode. p 443⟧

---

[Hafiz, *Diwan*, I,] 433
(5)    Should I shed my tears
Into the Sinderud, ⟨river⟩
Irak would in a moment
Be watered through & through

---

Take my heart in thy hand o lovely boy of Schiraz
(10)    Gladly would I give for thy mole Buchara & Samarkand
↑See [Hafiz, *Diwan*,] Vol 1 p xvii↓

---

[Hafiz, *Diwan*, I,] 370
If in world where spirits gather
The East wind thy breath shd bring
Understanding & soul would scatter
As thy locks scatter

---

[Hafiz, *Diwan*,] I 270
(15)    Prince the ball of heaven should
Under thy bat be
And the field of time of space
Should be thy playground &c &c     p 270

[98] [Hafiz, *Diwan*,] I 147
The East wind & I
Are a pair of enamoured fools
I from the spell of thine eye
He from the scent of thy hair

---

[Hafiz, *Diwan*,] II 183
(5)    Since you set no worth on the heart
Will I on the way instead of small coin
        Strew eyes.

---

The blue vault silverlined with hills of snow

When ⟨⟨the⟩ trees ↑the tints↓ in ⟨spring⟩ ↑June↓ time show⟩

98 "The roguish wind and I" (1–4); "Since you set no worth" (5–7); "The blue vault" (8);
"When trees in June," 1, 1–4 (9–13). The page is in pencil; lines (1–4) are erased.

313

(10)     ⟨The co⟩ When trees in June the colors show
         Which the autumn leaves repeat
         When the young oaks vie & glow
         With ⟨the columbines⟩ ↑pinks & slippers↓ at their feet

[99] [blank]
[100]    [R.W.E.]
         Go into the garden,
         Feed thine eyes & ears,
         And every sense;
         But do not touch a weed,
(5)      nor cut off a twig
         Be not tempted.
         If thou w⟨ont⟩ilt not be a garden tool

———————

Infamy in the air   Every thing feels the hurt.
History of it is a little too plain. Certain objects are to be had
by a few persons. Washington Winter   Party infatuation is to be the
means   It would be incredible but that we had seen *Higher Law* be-
come a gibe
⟨Pa⟩ Interest of cities, and Party: By these two means

[101]    *Hafiz* [*Diwan*]
         See for translation the odes
         Vol I, 112
            100
            110
             79 translated in X 172
         II 125
            197
            210
            268 his grave
            273 ⟨audacity⟩ heaven daring

———————

The Fug[itive Slave] Law
is contravened
  1. By ⟨M⟩ Duty
  2. By all the sentiments
  3. By all statutes because sentiments write statutes
  4. By the mischiefs it operates
  5  By the natural Nemesis

100 "Go into the garden" (1–7). With "Every thing feels the hurt" and "*Higher Law* become
a gibe" cf. "The Fugitive Slave Law" (1851), W 11:182 and 190 respectively. The page is in
pencil.
  101 With "The Fug Law is contravened" and the five outline headings, cf. "The Fugitive Slave
Law" (1851), W 11:186–201. This page is in pencil.

[102]                    *Song of the Soul.*
                 If the red slayer think he slays,
                 Or if the slain think he is slain,
                 They know not well the subtle ways
                 I keep & pass & turn again.

(5)              What is forgot to me is near,
                 ⟨And noon & midnight⟩ ↑Shadow and sunlight↓ are the
                      same,
                 Things disappeared to me appear,
                 And one to me are shame & fame.

                 They reckon ill who leave me out,
(10)             When me they fly, I am the wings,
                 I am the doubter & the doubt,
                 And I the hymn the bramin sings.

                 The wise gods pine to know my heart
                 ⟨But⟩And pine in vain the sacred seven
(15)             But thou, meek lover, ⟨trampling sense⟩ ↑scorning joy↓,
                 ⟨Cling to the right⟩ ↑/Hold/Find/ me↓ & turn thy back on
                      heaven.

   [103]   Vol I 104 Hafiz [*Diwan*]

                 Now tells the flower
                 Histories of May
                 Who fetters himself with gold
                 He is not wise.

(5)              Cheer thy heart with wine:
                 The Earth is only
                 A house to which our bones
                 Give the mortar.

                 Seek not in thy friend, truth;
(10)             Truth is dead;
                 Holy fire comes not
                 Out of Church lamps.

                 Blacken thou not my name
                 For my riot;
(15)             Who knows what the lot
                 Inscribed on the brow?

                 Turn not thy steps
                 From the grave of Hafiz,

102  "Brahma," 1–16, x.
103  "Now tells the flower." The page is in pencil; lines (17–20) are struck through in pencil.

Since though in sins sunken
(20)　　He ⟨waits for⟩ ↑expects↓ Heaven

[104]　Hafiz
　　　　Fine ode is ⟨that wh⟩ the last in [*Diwan*] Vol I

---

That he may pursue thy foes & enviers
Holds Arcturus ‖ . . ‖ morning & evening his spear

———

The lot leaps to thee as tho' it had no other aim
Tha⟨t⟩n that once thy heart should be clear thro content
(5)　　He deserves to be reckoned a hero of understanding
Who before he begins weighs the issue
Soul ⟨s⟩taste is free from bitterness
⟨While⟩
If they keep sweet thanks in the mouth
(10)　　He will enjoy the fruit of his life
Who first chooses & then enters the street
Who in good times willingly takes in hand the cup
And in time of war gladly grasps the sabre———
Goes it hard—yet turn thee not from the God's secret,
(15)　　Since the softest marrow sits in hardest bones
[105]　　Only thro temperance is sugar sweet
Therefore sat it first deep in the nest of the Cane

　　　　　x x
[Hafiz, *Diwan*, I,] p 449
See the East, he plays like a drunken lover
Now with the lips of the rose, now with the violets hair
(5)　　Thro the consent of the stuff & the manifold forms
Offers every bloom matter to a thousand tho'ts
Ever I think by myself what is the lovely Air
Which in the greying dawn heaps the dark dust
Why holds the round heaven
(10)　　Me with sorrow & woe ever fast at ⟨c⟩the centre
None learns the ⟨secr⟩ hearts secret and so is it bitter
Since the envious world seizes it by chance
Whoso is wont like the taper confided secrets to blab
Will on the tongue at last like the taper be burned.

104 "To the Shah. From Hafiz," 1–2, thirteen unused lines. In pencil. Lines (1–2) are erased; lines (1–4) and (5–15) are struck through separately in pencil.
105 "To the Shah. From Hafiz," fourteen unused lines (1–14); "Good is what goes" (15–16). The page is in pencil; lines (1–2), (7–10), and (15–16) are struck through in pencil.

⟨————⟩[Hafiz, *Diwan*,] I, 53
(15)        Good is what goes on the road of Nature
        On the straight way never yet erred man

[106] In the infancy of society, all the institutions were on a war foundation. Now they are on a peace & ⟨trade⟩ ↑commercial↓ foundation. ⟨And⟩ it is ⟨impossible⟩ affectation & anachronism to pretend the old ground.

        Could I ⟨c⟩shut in my verse one chime
        Of the sweet bells that haunt me with ring & cry
        Or ⟨in⟩ ↑copy↓ the mornings Sabbath prime
        ↑&↓ Match with words that tender sky

[107]        Cd. I win for my verse one chime
        Of the woodbells peal & cry
        Or copy the mornings Sabbath prime
        And match with words that tender sky.

(5)        Broad plains that give the shadows room
        Of skirting hills to lie,
        And
        Washed by the stream that gives & takes
        The color of the sky

[108]        *Ethical*
        *Fatal sentences*

                                               *qu vide*

[Hafiz, *Diwan*,] Vol 1 p 408
        Reach me wine   No counsel weakens the conclusion of the
             lot,
        None alters what Destiny determines for him.

———

[Hafiz, *Diwan*, I,] p. 400
        A stately bride was truly the Beauty of the Earth
        Yet none can obtain the maiden to wife.

———

[Hafiz, *Diwan*, I,] 285
(5)        The bride of the world is indeed richly drest,
        Who enjoys her must give
        His soul for ⟨a⟩the dowry.

———

106 "My Garden," 37–40. In pencil. The verse is struck through in pencil; in the prose, the ampersand before "⟨trade⟩" was accidentally canceled.
107 "My Garden," 37–40 (1–4); "Waldeinsamkeit," 5–6, x, 7–8 (5–9). In pencil; lines (1–4) and (5–9) are struck through separately in pencil.
108 "Reach me wine" (1–2); "A stately bride" (3–4); "The world is a bride" (5–7); "Has thine enemy slandered" (8–9). The page is in pencil; lines (3–4) and (5–7) are struck through separately in pencil.

[Hafiz, *Diwan*, I,] 453
        Has thine enemy slandered thy house
        He shall ⟨late feel it⟩ ↑find his sin↓ in his childs child

——

[109] [Hafiz, *Diwan*,] I 446
        Yet all comes out of this, that one door
        Opens, when another shuts.

——

[Hafiz, *Diwan*, I,] ↑421↓
        In honour dies he to whom the great seems wonderful

——

[Hafiz, *Diwan*, I,] 13
        The Earth is a host who murders his guests

——

[Hafiz, *Diwan*, I,] ↑23↓
(5)      Turn not truth from thy door. God my protector is near

——

        Hear what the glass will tell thee
        This again-married (world or fortune)
        Has had many husbands ⟨Jam & Ke⟩mighty & glorious
        Jam & Keikobad

——

(10)     There resides in the suffering    [Hafiz, *Diwan*,] II 379
        A poison which kills
        Go thou not near them
        It is dangerous

——

        Free thyself from wo        [Hafiz, *Diwan*,] II 384
(15)     Thou drinkest blood when thou enviest others their luck

——

[Hafiz, *Diwan*,] II 468
        Art thou wise & sly make renunciation on 4 things
        Rest & wine   love & solitude

[110] "Gen. Jackson stated the true doctrine when he said that every man when he takes an oath to support the Constitution means to support his understanding of it." "The Higher Law." p. 36

109 "Yet all comes out of this" (1–2); "In honour dies he" (3); "Desire no bread," 2 (4); "Turn not truth" (5); "Hear what the glass" (6–9); "There resides in the grieving" (10–13); "Free thyself from wo" (14–15); "Art thou wise" (16–17). The page is in pencil. Lines (1–4), (10–13), and (16–17) are struck through in pencil; lines (3) and (4) are additionally struck through in pencil.

110 With "All immoral laws are ipso facto void," cf. "The Fugitive Slave Law" (1851), W 11:186, 190, and the front cover verso and p. [41] above. " 'The Higher Law.' p. 36" is a reference to Ainsworth Rand Spofford, *The Higher Law Tried by Reason and Authority* (New York, 1851).

"All immoral laws are ipso facto void. Such law makes a man's duty to break it at every hazard, since man's virtue is his very self." "Higher Law" [p. 16]

[111] "Function of law is merely declaratory of the right & wrong that previously exist." [*The Higher Law,* p. 13]

For, ever the poet *from* the land
Steers his bark & trims his sail,
Right out to sea his courses stand
⟨In deepest deeps his arts prevail⟩
(5)    ⟨In new & strange his arts prevail⟩
New worlds to reach in pinnace frail

---

⟨In⟩ ↑Through↓ deepest deeps his arts prevail
New worlds to reach in pinnace frail

[112] [Hafiz, *Diwan,*] Vol 1 p 314
And had Hafiz
Ten tongues like the lily,
He would be silent
Like the rosebud,
(5)    While thro love his mouth is sealed.

⟨In⟩ ↑Oer↓ the garden water goes the wind alone
By filing to polish the cheeks of the pond
The fire is /quenched/out/ on the ⟨household⟩ ↑house↓
    hearth ↑stone↓
But it burns again in the tulips ⟨leaf⟩ ↑frond↓
(10)   Yesterday the frosty way the icy wind
⟨I⟩Me from labor disinclined
Now desire ⟨I⟩
I slunk to books & home
Now desire of action wakes
(15)   And the wish to roam.

[113]    Hafiz of his verse
[Hafiz, *Diwan,*] Vol 1 p 337
Only he despises
The verse of Hafiz

111 "The Poet" ("Ever the Poet"), 1–3, x, x, 4, x, 4. The verse is in pencil; lines (1–4) are struck through in pencil, and line (6) is erased.
112 "And had Hafiz" (1–5); "O'er the garden water," 1–4, six unused lines (6–15); "May-Day," 115, x, 126, 118, 126–27 (10–15). "Vol I p 314" and lines (1–5) are in pencil; lines (1–5) are struck through in pencil.
113 "Only he despises" (1–4); "Thy songs O Hafiz" (5–8); "I saw angels yesterday," 33–36 (9–12). The page is in pencil; lines (1–8) are struck through in pencil; "qu. vide" is circumscribed in pencil.

Who himself from nature
Is not noble

———

[Hafiz, *Diwan*, I,] p. 301        qu. vide
(5)        Thy songs O Hafiz
Are erst in Paradise
On the leaves of the jasmin
And the rose bush written

———

[Hafiz, *Diwan*, I,] p 367
No one has unveiled
(10)        Thoughts like Hafiz
Since the locks of the Word-bride
Were curled.
literally⟧   None has yet as Hafiz withdrawn the veil from the cheeks
of Thought, since the ends of the locks of the Bride of the Word were
combed.

[114]        Who compares a poem
Of others to mine
Compares gold
With ⟨pinchbeck,⟩ rush-plaits

———

[Hafiz, *Diwan*, I,] ↑15↓
(5)        Songs hast thou sung, Hafiz, & pearls hast bored
Worthy to ⟨strew⟩ ↑string↓ against the Pleiads of Heaven

———

[Hafiz, *Diwan*, I,] ↑23↓
Thy poems Hafiz shame the rose leaves
Since they breathe the praise of the rosier cheeks of thy love

———

In the kingdom of Poesy Hafiz waves like a banner
(10)        Thro' the Shah's defending favor

———

Give o Hafiz Thoughts
⟨Since thou hast⟩ these⟨,⟩ ↑are lasting joys↓
All else is only
Chatter & noise   [Hafiz, *Diwan*,] II 137

———

(15)        Where o where is the message which today
brought us tidings of joy

114 "Who compares a poem" (1–4); "Fit for the Pleiads' azure chord" (5–6); "Thy poems
Hafiz shame the rose leaves" (7–8); "In the kingdom of Poesy" (9–10); "O Hafiz, give me
thought" (11–14); "Where o where is the message" (15–18); "To Himself" (19–22). The page is
in pencil; lines (19–22) are struck through in pencil.

That instead of silver & gold I on the earth
Might strew souls.　[Hafiz, *Diwan*,] II 163

—————

(20)　　Hafiz speak not of thy need
Are not these verses thine
Then will no nobler one concede
T⟨w⟩hou canst at aught repine

—————

[Hafiz, *Diwan*,] II. 358

[115]　The fishes shed ↑their↓ pearls
Out of desire & longing
Soon as the ship of Hafiz
Swims the deep　[Hafiz, *Diwan*,] II 395

—————————

⟨Prigg's case⟩

(5)　　Oer the garden water goes the wind alone
By filing to polish the cheek of the wave
The fire is quenched on the dear hearthstone
But it burns again on the tulips brave

Oer the garden water goes the wind alone
(10)　　To rasp & to polish the cheek of the wave;
The fire is quenched on the dear hearthstone,
But it burns again on the tulips brave.

[116₁] [index material omitted]

I hung my verses in the wind
Time weather their faults might find
They were ⟨all blown⟩ ↑winnowed↓ thro & thro
Five lines lasted sound & true
(5)　　⟨For these⟩ ↑Five↓ were forged in a pot
Than the South more fierce & hot.
These the southwind could not melt
Fire their fiercer flaming felt
And the ⟨thought⟩ ↑meaning↓ was more white
(10)　　Than ↑the↓ ⟨noonday⟩ ↑days meridian↓ light
⟨So that⟩ Sun ↑shine↓ ⟨could⟩ ↑can↓ not bleach the snow
Nor unmake what ⟨I⟩ ↑poets↓ know

115 "The fishes shed" (1–4); "O'er the garden water," two drafts (5–12). Lines (1–8) and "II 395" are in pencil; lines (5–8) are struck through in ink. "Priggs case" refers to a decision by the U.S. Supreme Court in 1842 striking down a Pennsylvania conviction of Edward Prigg, who had broken a state law by returning an escaped slave to her master in Maryland.
116₁ "The Test," 1–12 (1–12); "Heri, Cras, Hodie," 3–4 (13–14). The page is in partially erased pencil.

Future or Past no stricter secret folds,
O friendless Present! than thy bosom holds.

[1162]   For comes the poor by Gods command
Gifts waken when the giver sleeps
Swords cannot cut the ⟨giving⟩ ↑liberal↓ hand
Nor dies the love the orphan keeps

[inside back cover] ⟨se⟩ ⟨hr⟩ Anka or Simorg. [Hafiz, *Diwan*,] I p. 91
[index material omitted]
[Hafiz] his grave. See [*Diwan*] Vol II p 268; and p. 267, at the top.
[index material omitted]

---

1162 "Alms." A drawing in pencil of a circle bisected by a curved line appears below the verse.
   ibc In pencil.

# Notebook EL

Notebook EL was apparently begun no later than November or early December 1849. Emerson used it throughout the 1850s and 1860s, concurrently with NP, until the publication of *May-Day* in 1867. A few entries may be later, including some revisions made during the preparation of *Selected Poems,* 1876.

The covers of notebook EL, brown, blue, and red marbled paper over boards, measure 17 × 21.5 cm. The spine strip and protective corners on the front and back covers are of brown leather; "EL" is written on the spine.

There are 296 unlined pages measuring 17.2 × 20.6 cm. The lower two-thirds of the leaf bearing pp. 75–76 is cut off, and the two leaves bearing pp. 195–98 are partly torn out, leaving curved stubs.

One hundred and twenty pages are numbered in ink, eighty-nine in pencil, and two in both ink and pencil; the rest are unnumbered. Page 215 was skipped in numbering and two pages numbered 216. Forty-eight pages are blank.

The notebook contains the following enclosures:

(1) inside the front cover, five pages of page-by-page notes on EL by Edward Emerson;

(2) between pp. 12–13, a sheet of grey letter paper measuring 20 × 25.5 cm, folded once to make four pages, all four pages inscribed in ink (here numbered $12_a$–$12_d$);

(3) between pp. 20–21, a clipping from the *Salem Gazette,* containing a poem by Lydia L. A. Very, marked in ink, and another poem by M. L. Emerson of Boxford;

(4) between pp. 102–3, a sheet of pale blue letter paper measuring 20 × 25.5 cm, folded once to make four pages, all inscribed in ink (here numbered $102_a$–$102_d$);

(5) between pp. 114–15, a half sheet of grey letter paper torn from a larger sheet to measure 17.8 × 23.1 cm, with a stationer's mark showing a sitting lion, lined on one side, and inscribed on both sides in ink (here numbered $114_a$–$114_b$);

(6) between pp. 116–17, a sheet of lined paper inscribed in ink on both sides by someone other than Emerson with four numbered verses in German, titled "Ostreichisches Volkslied, Weise von Joseph Haydn";

(7) between pp. 156–57, a half sheet of heavy lined paper torn off from a larger sheet to measure 12.9 × 20.4 cm, with a stationer's mark showing a crown with "LONDON" under it, inscribed in ink on both sides (here numbered $156_a$–$156_b$);

(8) between pp. 198–99, a sheet of blue-grey letter paper with an orb and crown watermark, torn off from a larger sheet to measure 16.3 × 20.6 cm, inscribed in ink on both sides (here numbered $198_a$–$198_b$), and a sheet of lined blue paper folded to make four pages measuring 19.7 × 25.3 cm, the rectos

numbered "5" and "6" in pencil, inscribed in ink on three pages (here numbered 198$_c$–198$_e$); and

(9) between pp. 254–55, a half sheet of blue lined paper inscribed in pencil on one side by someone other than Emerson with eight lines of verse beginning "Come brave the sea with me love" (see NP p. [301]).

[front cover verso] "When the belly is full, it says to the head, sing fellow." *Arabian Proverb*.

[index material omitted]

[1]      Try the might the Muse affords,
And the balm of thoughtful words.

———————————

           Roomy Eternity casts her schemes rarely,
And /an aeon ↑vast↓/a rounded age/ allows
(5)     ⟨For⟩ ↑To↓ each quality & part
In the multitudinous
And many-chambered heart.
↑he was as forward as a stream↓

           Roomy Eternity
(10)    Casts her schemes rarely,
And a↑n↓ ⟨rounded age⟩ ↑aeon↓ allows
To each ⟨quality⟩ ↑passion↓ & part
In the multitudinous
⟨And⟩ many-chambered heart.

[2]      Unless to thought ⟨i⟩be added will,
Apollo is an imbecile.

Confucius says,
"It is said in the Book of Poetry, 'Not disliked there, not tired of here, from day to day, & night to night ⟨will⟩ they perpetuate their praise.' " *Legge* Vol 1 p. 290[–91]

———————————

"The approaches of the spirits you cannot surmise." *Ib*. p 262

———————————

⟨To⟩What is wisdom? To give on⟨s⟩eself earnestly to the duties ⟨due⟩ to men, &, while respecting spiritual beings, to keep aloof from them,— may be called wisdom" Ib p. 55
"The wise find pleasure in water; the virtuous find pleasure in hills."
                                      56

[3]      Poet of poets
Is Time, the distiller,
Chemist, refiner:

    fcv The proverb is used in "Inspiration," W 8:281; cf. EF p. [242]. The index material is in pencil.
    1 "Try the might the Muse affords," 1–2 (1–2); "Roomy Eternity," 1/2, 3–6, x, 1–6 (3–14). Lines (3–7) are struck through three times in ink.
    2 "The comrade or the book," 3–4 (1–2). For the quotations, see James Legge, *The Chinese Classics*, 5 vols. (Hong Kong and London, 1861–1872); Emerson may have borrowed volume 1 from Charles H. Glover in October 1863 (see L 5:338).
    3 "Poet of poets," 1–16. Lines (9–16) are struck through in ink.

⟨He⟩ ↑Time↓ hath a vitriol
(5)        Which can dissolve
Towns into melody,
Rubbish to gold.
        Burn up the libraries!
        Down with the colleges!
(10)      Raze the foundations!
        Drive out the doctors!
        Rout the philosophers!
        Exile the critics!
        Men of particulars,
(15)      Narrowing niggardly
        Something to nothing.
[4]     All their ten thousand ways
End in the Néant.

        All through the countryside
Rush locomotives:
(5)        Prosperous grocers
Poring on newspapers
Over their shop fires
Settle the State.
But, for the Poet,—
(10)      Seldom in centuries
Comes the well-tempered
Musical man.
He is the waited-for,
He is the complement,
[5]     ⟨Of⟩ ⟨↑The↓⟩ one man ⟨&⟩of all men.
The random wayfarer
⟨T⟩Counts him of his kin.
This is he that should come
(5)        ↑The↓ Tongue of the secret,
↑The↓ Key of the casket⟨s.⟩,
Of Past & of Future.
Sudden the lustre
That hovered round cities,
(10)      Round ⟨the⟩ bureaus of Power,
Or Chambers of Commerce,
Round banks, or round beauties,
Or state-rending factions,
Has quit them, & perches
[6]     Well pleased on his form.

4 "Poet of poets," 17–30. Struck through in ink.
5 "Poet of poets," 31–44.
6 "Poet of poets," 45–52, 51, 53–56. In line (13), "forest" is added in pencil.

True bard never cared
To flatter the ⟨great⟩ ↑princes↓
Costs time to live with them.
(5)    Ill genius affords it,
Preengaged to the skies.
↑Foremost of all men↓
The Poet ⟨received⟩ ↑inherits↓
⟨Foremost of all⟩
(10)    Badge of nobility,
Charter of Earth;
Free of the city,
Free of the ⟨field,⟩ /meadows/forest/,
[7]    Knight of each order,
Sworn of each guild,
Fellow of monarchs,
And, what is better,
(5)    ⟨Fellow⟩ ↑Mate↓ of all men.

Pan's paths are wonderful.
Subtile his counsel.
Wisdom needs circumstance,
Many concomitants,
(10)    Goes not in purple,
Steals along secretly,
Shunning the eye;
Has the dominion
Of men & the planet,
(15)    On this sole condition,—
She shall not assume it.
When ⟨first⟩ the crown ⟨touches⟩ ↑first incloses↓
[8]    ↑When the crown first incloses↓
The brows of her son,
The Muse him deposes
From kingdom & throne.
↑————↓

(5)    See the spheres rushing,—
Poet that tracks them
With emulous eye,
What lovest thou?
Planet, or orbit?
(10)    Whether the pipe⟨r⟩,

7 "Poet of poets," 57–61, 81–92. In line (17), "first" and "touches" are circled in pencil and canceled in ink; "first incloses" is added in pencil traced over in ink.

8 "Poet of poets," 92–106, 107?, 107–9. Lines (5–19) are struck through in ink. Emerson left a space in line (15), then inserted both "Emblem" and "Science".

Or ↑the↓ lay, it discourses?
In heaven, up yonder,
All the astronomy,
Sun-dance & star blaze,
(15)　　Is ↑/Emblem/Science/↓ of love.

⟨Nothings⟩
Nought is of worth
In earth or in sky
But Love & Thought only.
[9]　　↑Fast↓ ⟨P⟩perish the mankind,
↑Firm↓ Bideth the thought,
Clothes it⟨self⟩ with Adam-kind,
Puts on a new suit
(5)　　Of earth & ↑of↓ stars.
He will come one day
Who can articulate
That which unspoken
Vaults itself over us,
(10)　　Globes itself under us,
Looks out of lovers' eyes,
Dies, & is born again;—
He who can speak well;
Men hearing delighted
(15)　　Shall say, *that is ours.*
Trees hearing shall blossom,
Rocks hearing shall tremble,
And range themselves dreamlike
[10]　　In new compositions,
Architecture of thought.
Then will appear
What the old centuries,
(5)　　Aeons were groping for,
Times of discomfiture,
Bankrupt millenniums.

Thought is the sole price
For which I sell days,
(10)　　And willing grow ⟨old,⟩ ↑aged,↓
Melting matter to pictures,
And life into law.

9 "Poet of poets," 110–27. Lines (1–5) are struck through in ink.
10 "Poet of poets," 128–34 (1–7); "Terminus" ("For thought"), 2–3, 5, 7, 10 (8–12). Lines (1–7) are struck through in ink; a vertical line is drawn in ink in the left margin beside lines (8–12).

[11]     The patient Pan,
        ⟨⟨Overpowered⟩ with sleep ↑overpowered↓⟩
        ↑Drunken with nectar↓
        ⟨Tosseth⟩ ↑Sleep⟨eth⟩s↓ or feign⟨eth⟩s slumber

(5)      ⟨And, as if he knew not, hums⟩
        ↑⟨Heedlessly⟩ ↑Drowsily↓ humming↓
        Music to the march of Time.
        This poor tooting creaking cricket,
        Pan half asleep, rolling over

(10)    His great body in the grass,
        Tooting, creaking,
        Feigns to sleep, sleeping never:
        Tis his manner,
        Well he knows his own affair,

(15)    Piling mountain-chains of phlegm
        On the nervous brain of man,
        As he holds down central fires
        Under Alps & Andes cold.

[12]     Haply else we could not live

[12ₐ]   O patient Pan
        Overpowered with sleep
        Thou seemest
        And in the wide fools dance

(5)      ⟨Cider-fed fandangoes⟩
        Of the stupid Adamkind
        Thou furnishest
        Right music
        This poor tooting creaking cricket.

(10)    Pan half asleep rolling over
        His great body on the grass
        Tooting creaking
        Seems to sleep, sleeping never;
        Tis his manner

(15)    Well he knows his own affair
        Piling mountain chains of phlegm
        On the nervous brain of man
        As they hold down the central fires
        ⟨With⟩ ↑Under↓ Alps & Andes cold

(20)    ↑Haply↓ ⟨Other percha⟩Else we could not live
        Life were to ↑o↓ wild ⟨&⟩an ode

[12ᵦ]   We should explode

---

11  "The patient Pan," 1, x, 2–3, x, 4–16.
12  "The patient Pan," 17.
12ₐ "The patient Pan," 1, four unused lines, 20, x, 5–18.
12ᵦ "The patient Pan," 19–39.

Ah restless race
Fault of ⟨rich⟩ supplies
From the fire fountains
(5) We busybodies
Evermore experiment
See what will come of it
⟨Try⟩ ↑Prove↓ the ⟨str⟩quaint substances
⟨Try⟩ ↑Prove↓ our bodies ⟨try⟩ ↑prove↓ our essence
(10) Fortunes, genius, elements
Put a foot in; then a hand in,
Then plunge the body in.
Then our wits characters
And our gods if we can
(15) Analysing analysing
As the chemist his new stone
Put to azote put to chlorine
Put to vegetable blues
Ah ⟨ye⟩ poor apothecaries
(20) Can ye never wiselier sit
Meddle less & more accept
[12c] With dignity, not overstep
Skies have their etiquette

We are faithful to time
Time measured in moments
(5) Only so many
Share of Methusalem
Share of the babe
Hundredhanded, hundredeyed,
Fussy & anxious
(10) We would so gladly
Serve an apprenticeship
Day by day faithfully
Learn the use of Adam's tools
Fire & water, azote, carbon,
(15) Gravity levity
Hatred attraction
Animals chemistry
Botany land
Have a right to our flesh
(20) Know the honest earth by heart

[12d] Do the feat of Archimedes

12c "The patient Pan," 40–59.
12d "The patient Pan," 60–79.

If the earth reject her sons
Till theyve learned her alphabeta
None but ⟨Arago & Humboldt⟩ ↑Hooke & Newton dare↓
(5)     ⟨Dare⟩ cross the threshold ↑when it thunders↓

⟨But⟩ life is all too short for farming
All too short for architecture
⟨Far⟩ ↑All↓ too short to learn the tongues
And for philosophy
(10)    Life's done ere weve begun to think.
Solid farming   haw & geeing
Driv⟨ing⟩e uphill the loaded team
⟨To⟩ bud the pear & dig potatoes
What time Lyra's in the Zenith
(15)    That is wholesome as it makes
Man as massive as ⟨a⟩the glebe
Pricks ⟨the⟩ dropsical pretension
Tames the infinite romance
Underpins the falcon turrets
(20)    High as fly falcons, fancy builds

[13]–[14] [blank]
[15] "Confucius was playing one day on a musical stone in Wei, when a man carrying a straw-basket passed the door of the house where Confucius was, & said, His heart is full who *so* beats the musical stone."
        [James] Legge. [*The Chinese Classics*, 1861–1872,] Vol. 1. p. 155

[16]     crimson
         cochineal
         cardinal
         blood red
         scarlet
                Confucius said;
"The Fung bird does not come; the river sends forth no map;—it is all over with me." *Legge.* [Ibid.,] Vol. 1. p. 83 [note 8, paraphrased].
Fung is the male Phenix, said to appear when a sage ascends the throne. In the days of Shun, they gambolled in his hall; & were heard singing on Mount Ke, in the time of Wan.
In Fu-he's time, a dragon-headed horse rose from the water, marked on the back so as to give that first of sages the idea of his diagrams.

[17]     On a brown grapestone
         The wheels of nature turn,

16 "crimson . . . red" is in pencil; "scarlet" is in pencil over the same in erased pencil.
17 "On a raisin stone," 1–8 (1–8); "Charmed from fagot," 1–2 (9–10). Lines (9–10) are in pencil.

Out of it a fury comes
Wherewith the ⟨spondyls⟩ burn.
(5)  And, because a drop of wine
Is creation's heart,
Rub with the vine those eyes of thine,
Nothing is hid, nor whole, nor part.

⟨He is⟩ charmed from fagot & ↑from↓ steel
(10)  Harvests grew upon his tongue

[18]        Pour the wine, pour the wine;
As it changes to foam⟨s⟩,
So the Creator,
New & unlooked for,
(5)  Rushing abroad,
In farthest & smallest
Comes royally home.

In spider wise
Will again geometrize,
(10)  Will in bee & gnat keep time
With the annual solar chime.
Aphides, like emperors,
Sprawl & creep their pair of hours.

[19]  Strong Lyaeus' rosy gift
Lightly can the mountains lift
⟨It can knit⟩
↑Knit↓ What is done
(5)  ⟨And⟩ ↑With↓ what's begun.
⟨It can cancel bulk & time,⟩
⟨↑Vanquish bulk & shorten time↓⟩
⟨Crowd &⟩ ↑In the vat it can↓ condense
Into a drop a tun,
(10)  So to repeat
No word or feat.
Moment is the sum of ages,
Love the Socrates of sages.
⟨Lift the mountain shorten time⟩
(15)  ⟨Span the poles & shorten time⟩
Sum your annals in a rhyme,
Span the poles & shorten time.

18 "Pour the wine!" 1–3, 5, 4, 6–13.
19 "Pour the wine!" 14–16, 16/17, 18–19, 19–25, 19, 19, x, 19 (1–17); "Sum your annals,"
2, 2, 1–2 (14–17). Lines (14–15) and all cancellations and additions are in pencil.

[20]                                *Water.*
                        The water understands
                        Civilization well
                        It wets my foot but prettily
                        It chills my life but wittily
(5)                     It is not disconcerted,
                        Rippled, but not broken-hearted
                        Well-used it decketh joy
                        Adorneth, doubleth joy;
                        Ill used it will destroy,
(10)                    In perfect time & measure,
                        With a face of golden pleasure,
                        Elegantly destroy.

[21]                            Slighted Minerva's learned tongue,
                        But ⟨heard⟩leaped with joy when on the wind the shell of
                            Clio rung.

                        ⟨Every⟩ ↑The↓ atom displaces all atoms beside,
                        ⟨Every⟩ ↑And↓ genius unspheres all souls that abide.

_____

(5)                     To transmute crime to wisdom, & to stem
                        The vice of Japhet by the thought of Shem.

_____

                        ↑*The Poet*↓
                        Like ⟨the⟩ vaulters in the circus round,
                        Who step from horse to h⟨ar⟩orse, but never touch the
                            ground.

[22₁]                   I know a song
                        Sing it never so loud
                                few few can hear
                        Hushed thousands listen in vain
(5)                             Yet they who hear it shed their age
                                And take their youth again

                                Hushed thousands wait
                                And s
                                Their ear though waiting thousands strain
(10)                            Their waiting ear tho thousands strain

                        In the heart of the music peals a strain
                        Which fewest of men can hear

20 "Water."
   21 "Slighted Minerva's learned tongue" (1–2); "The atom displaces" (3–4); "To transmute
crime" (5–6); "Like vaulters in the circus round" (7–8). The cancellations and additions in lines
(3–4) are in pencil.
   22₁ "Merlin's Song," 1–2, 9, 11–13, 11, x, 11/8, 11/8, 8, 9, 2, 9. Lines (1–10) are in pencil;
lines (1–6), (1–10), and (11–14) are struck through separately in pencil.

Sing it never so loud
Few be they can hear

[22₂]                    ↑ *Verse or Style.* ↓
A verse is not a vehicle to carry a sentence in, ⟨of⟩ as a jewel is carried
in a case. ⟨t⟩The verse must be alive & inseparable from its contents,
as the body of man carries the soul with it

[23]      I know a song
          ⟨Will calm & cheer the good⟩
          ⟨It will the bad enrage⟩
          Few
(5)       Sing it in the rushing crowd
          Good men it will ↑calm &↓ cheer
          Bad men it will enrage
          But sing it never so loud
          Few few can hear
(10)      Hushed thousands listen in vain
          Yet they who hear it shed their age
          And take their youth again

_____

See p 52

[24]              *At Sea   September 1833*

          Oft as I paced the deck,
          My thought recurred, on the uncertain sea,
          To what is faster than the solid land.

          My country! can the heart clasp realm so vast
(5)       As the broad oceans that wash thee enclose?
          Is not the charity ambitious,
          That meets its arms around a continent?
          And yet, the sages praise the preference
          Of ⟨my⟩ ↑their↓ own cabin to a baron's hall.
(10)      Chide it not, then, but count it honesty,
          The insidious love & hate that curl the lip
          Of the frank Yankee in the tenements
[25]      Of ducal ⟨&⟩ ↑or↓ of royal rank abroad,
          His supercilious ignorance
          Of lordship, heraldry, & ceremony,
          ⟨And, aye,⟩ ↑Nor less,↓ his too tenacious memory,

22₂ "Poetry and Imagination," W 8:54.
23 "Merlin's Song," 1, 6–7, 9, 5–7, 2, 9, 11–13. In pencil, struck through in pencil; lines
(8–12) are struck through additionally three times in pencil.
24 "At Sea, September 1833," 1–12. The cancellation and addition in line (9) are in pencil.
25 "At Sea, September 1833," 13–28. The cancellation and addition in line (1) are in pencil.

(5)     Amid the particolored treasuries
        That deck the Louvre, & the Pitti House,
        Of the brave steamboats puffing by New York,
        Boston's halfisland, & the Hadley Farms,
        Washed by Connecticut's psalm-loving stream.
(10)    Yea, if the ruddy Englishman speak true,
        In Rome's basilica, & underneath
        The frescoed sky of its audacious dome,
        Dauntless Kentucky chews, & counts the cost,
        And builds the shrine with dollars in his head.
(15)    Arrived in Italy, his first demand,
        "Has the star-bearing squadron left Leghorn?"

[26]    The best of life is presence of a Muse
        ⟨In secret visits⟩
        Who does not wish to wander, comes /in secret/by stealth/,
        Divulging to the heart she sets on flame
(5)     No popular tale no bauble for the mart

⟨*parvenu* an upstart⟩

        The clouds are rich & dark the air serene
        So like the soul of me, twere me
        Divine inviters
        I heed your lofty sign
(10)    What new enlargement to my dust ye give

[27]                    Adirondac
        What wilt thou restless bird
        Seeking in that ⟨pure⟩ ↑chaste↓ blue a ⟨bluer⟩ ↑chaster↓
            light
        Thirsting in that pure for a purer sky

October woods NP 163

                    That ⟨thrill⟩ ↑spark↓
(5)     Shot thro the pedestals
        Of ⟨mountains islands continents⟩ ↑Alp & Andes, isle &
            continent↓
        Urging astonished chaos with a thrill
        To be a brain

26 "Best boon of life," 1, x, 2–4 (1–5); "The Adirondacs," 213–14 (6–7); "Divine Inviters!"
1, x, x (8–10). In pencil; in line (3), "by stealth" is added in ink; lines (6–10) are struck through
in pencil.
27 "The Adirondacs," 208–10, x, 270/262, 263–65, 265, x. In pencil and, except for "Oc-
tober woods NP 163," which may have been added later, partially erased. In line (4), "thrill" is
canceled and "spark" added in ink; lines (1–3) and (4–10) are struck through separately in
pencil.

               Or to obey the brain of upstart man
(10)       And shake the slumbers of a million years

[28]             〈Shunned t〉
               Forbore the ant-hill,—shunned to tread
               In mercy, on one little head.

               He could condense cerulean ether
(5)        Into the very best sole leather

[29]             Spring, the alchemist
               And well she wist
               To slack her fire with icy mist
               She pours a deluge of sun heat
(5)        Launches an iceberg on the sea
               Melting glaciers line the coast
               Tempering the ardent sun

[30]             Th〈e〉is 〈present〉 ↑shining↓ moment is an edifice
               Which the omnipotent cannot rebuild.

               The sun athwart the cloud thought it no sin
               To use my land to put his rainbows in.

[31]               Pale Genius roves alone,
               No scout can track his way,
               None credits him till he have shown
               His diamonds to the day.

               Not his the feaster's wine,
               Nor land, nor gold, nor power,
(5)        By want & pain God screeneth him
               Till his elected hour.

               Go, speed the stars of Thought
(10)       On to their shining goals;—
               The sower scatters broad his seed,
               The wheat thou strew'st be souls.

[32]               What central ↑flowing↓ forces, say,
               Make up thy splendor matchless day!

28 "Forbore the ant hill," 1, 1–2 (1–3); "He could condense" (4–5). In line (1), "〈Shunned t〉" is in pencil, and lines (2–3) are in erased pencil overwritten in ink.

29 "May-Day," x, x, x, 242, x, x, x.

30 "Now" (1–2); "The sun athwart the cloud" (3–4).

31 "Pale Genius roves alone" (1–12); "Intellect" ("Go, speed") (9–12). Lines (9–12) are struck through in ink.

32 "What flowing central forces" (1–2); "May Day [Invitation]," 35–36 (3–4); "And the deep" (5); "The Past," 14, 17, 18/20, 19/20, 21, 6–7 (6–12). In pencil; lines (3–4), (6–10), and (1–12) are struck through separately in pencil.

The morning cobwebs mocked the storm
The robin listened for the worm

(5)        And the deep is as a ford

None can ↑re-↓enter there
⟨By⟩ Steal in by window or by hole
To bind or unbind what is packed
Insert a leaf new face or finish what is packed

(10)      ⟨↑Alter↓⟩ Or ⟨change⟩ add or change eternal Fact

Turn the key & bolt the door
Sweet is death forevermore

[33]     ↑Nor haughty hope nor swart chagrin↓
↑Nor murder⟨ous⟩↑ing↓ ⟨spite⟩ ↑hate↓ can enter in↓

The gods walk in the breath of the woods
They walk by the sounding pine

(5)        And fill the long reach of the old seashore
With colloquy divine.

And the poet who overhears
Each random word they say
Is the hierarch of men,

(10)      Whom kings & lords obey

The verdict was said
The debit was paid
My fortune was made
The furies were laid

(15)      The plague it was stayed
And the adamant door
Bolted down forevermore
All is ⟨safe⟩ now secure & fast.
Not the gods can shake the Past

[34₁]   *The Past*              See p 159
The debt ⟨was⟩ paid
The verdict said
The Furies laid

33 "The Past," 8–9 (1–2); "The gods walk," 1–8 (3–10); "The Past," 2, 1, 5, 3, 4, 12–13, 10–11 (11–19). Lines (11–15) occur in this order in the manuscript: (11, 12, 15, 13, 14), and are indicated for transposition by numbers in the left margin. Similarly, lines (18–19) are in reverse order in the manuscript, marked for transposition by "2" and "1" in the left margin. Lines (1–2), in pencil, are struck through in pencil; lines (11–19), in pencil, are struck through twice in pencil and partially erased; lines (18–19) are struck through again in pencil.

34₁ "The Past," 1–5, 10–14, 17–21, 15–16, 8–9. Lines (3–5) occur in this order in the manuscript: (3, 5, 4), and are indicated for transposition by numbers in the left margin. In pencil, struck through in pencil, and partially erased; in line (11), the cancellations and addition are in ink.

⟨The plague was staid⟩
(5) ↑⟨All⟩↓ ⟨⟨My⟩ fortune↑s↓ made⟩
All is now secure & fast
Not the gods can shake the Past
Flies-to the adamantine door
Bolted down forevermore

(10) None can reenter there
Steal in by window↑, ⟨chink,⟩↓ or ⟨by⟩ hole
To bind or unbind, add what lacked,
Insert a leaf or forge a name
New face or finish what is packed
(15) ⟨Add to⟩ ↑Alter↓ or ⟨change⟩ ↑mend↓ Eternal Fact

No thief so politic
No Satan with a kingly trick

Nor haughty hope nor swart chagrin
Nor murdering hate can enter in

| [342] | T W Parsons | Lowell |
|---|---|---|
| Mrs. ⟨E.F.⟩C E Perkins | B. Taylor | Longfellow |
| A. Adams | B. M. Watson | Mrs Stearns |
| Mrs Botta | Alger | A B Alcott |
| | ↑Sarah↓ Palfrey | E L Brown |
| | C Norton | W. G. Bryan |
| | E G Dudley | J G Whittier |
| | G B Emerson | F. R. Lowell |
| | O W Holmes | |
| | S. Johnson | |
| | C C Shackford | |

342 The names on p. [34], probably a partial list of people to whom Emerson sent copies of *May-Day and Other Pieces* in late April or early May 1867, include (first column) Mrs. Charles Elliott Perkins, a niece of J. M. Forbes, with whom Edward Emerson had stayed in Burlington, Iowa, for several months in 1866; Abel Adams, Emerson's old friend and business adviser; Anne Charlotte Lynch Botta, a writer, famous for the brilliance of her New York salon, whom Emerson had visited in 1865 and continued to correspond with; (second column) Thomas William Parsons, Boston dentist and poet; Bayard Taylor, prolific poet and travel writer; Benjamin Marston Watson, an old friend of the Emersons and husband of Waldo's teacher, Mary Russell; probably William Rounseville Alger, one of the young men who had arranged the lecture series at the Freeman Place Chapel in 1856, and author of *The Poetry of the East* (Boston, 1856); Sarah Hammond Palfrey, a poet who wrote under the pseudonym E. Foxton; Charles Eliot Norton, co-editor of the *North American Review* and a member of the Saturday Club; Elbridge G. Dudley, who had arranged Emerson's lectures to the Parker Fraternity; George Barrell Emerson, a second cousin; Oliver Wendell Holmes; Rev. Samuel Johnson of Lynn, Mass., a member of the Radical Club; Charles C. Shackford, whom Emerson had known since he taught at the Concord Academy following his graduation from Harvard in 1835; William Bull Wright, whose poetry Emerson had recommended to James T. Fields; Forceythe Willson, who had lived in Cambridge from 1864 to 1866, and whose poem "The Old Sergeant" Emerson had admired; Mrs. Caroline Wilson of Cincinnati, a sculptress, and one of the party with whom Emerson visited the Mammoth Cave in 1850; J. Peter Leslie, a Philadelphia librarian and an old friend of Emerson; Sidney George Fisher, a lawyer and author of *Winter Studies in the Country* (Philadel-

W B Wright
F. Willson
Mrs. Wilson, Cin.
J. P. Leslie
    Sidney Fisher
    B. P. Hunt
      Dunlap
      Arnold
      Forster
      Rawlins
      Bray
    Paulina Nash
    N. L Frothingham
    Laugel
Thomas ↑R↓ Gould
C. T. Brooks
E. P. Whipple
George Bancroft

[35]    Good Heart, that ownest all!
        I ask a modest boon & small:
        Not of lands & towns the gift,
        Too large a load for me to lift,
(5)      But, for one proper creature,
        Which geographic eye
        Sweeping the map of Western earth
        Or the Atlantic coast, from Maine
        To Powhatan's domain,
(10)    Could not descry.
        Is't much to ask, in all thy huge creation,
        So trivial a part,—
        A solitary heart?

---

phia, 1856), in Emerson's library; Benjamin Peter Hunt, Emerson's pupil and later a valued friend; probably W. B. Dunlap of Mattoon, Ill., who arranged a lecture there in December 1867; Matthew Arnold; either John Forster of the London *Examiner,* Landor's biographer, or William Edward Forster, a member of Parliament, both of whom Emerson met in 1848 and kept in touch with; probably Charles E. Rawlins, Jr., whom Emerson met in Liverpool and continued to correspond with; Charles Bray of Coventry, whom Emerson had met in 1848; Paulina Tucker Nash, sister of Emerson's first wife; Nathaniel L. Frothingham, Boston Unitarian minister; Auguste Laugel, French writer who had visited Boston in 1864; Thomas Ridgeway Gould, American sculptor who had visited Emerson in 1865; Charles Timothy Brooks, Unitarian clergyman and translator of German literature whom Emerson had known since 1838; Edwin Percy Whipple, critic and essayist; George Bancroft, historian and diplomat; (third column) James Russell Lowell; Henry Wadsworth Longfellow; Mary Preston Stearns of Medford, Emerson's hostess after a lecture in late 1854 or early 1855; Amos Bronson Alcott; Edwin Lee Brown of Chicago, who served as manager of Emerson's western lecture tour earlier in 1867; William G. Bryan of Batavia, N.Y., who had arranged a lecture there in 1860; John Greenleaf Whittier; and Frank Lowell. See JMN 16:56–61.

35 "Lover's Petition," 1–13. Struck through in ink.

[36]     Yet count me not of spirit mean,
          Or mine a mean demand,
          For tis the concentration
          And worth of all the land,
(5)      The Sister of the sea,
          The daughter of the strand,
          Composed of air & light,
          And of the swart earth-might.
          So little to thy poet's prayer
(10)    Thy large bounty well can spare.
          And yet, I think, if she were gone,
          The world were better left alone.
                ↑Printed by Mr Ide in "Oversongs."↓

[37]        Intellect
          Gravely broods apart on joy,
          And truth to tell, amused by pain

          As if they took tints from lands they wandered thro↑ugh↓
(5)      And warble back as
          Took ↑tints↓ from Hyblas wandered through
          And warble ⟨back⟩ of horizons blue
          Or trumpets which the angels blew

                Softened are against their will,
(10)    Take tones from groves they wandered through,
          Or flutes which passing angels blew.

                  for May Day

[38]     This is the age of ages this the hour

               *Nature.*
          Day by day for her darlings to her much she added more,
          In her hundred-gated Thebes every chamber was a door,
          A door to something grander,—loftier walls, & vaster floor.

[39]     ⟨Oft when I read fond pictures poets drew⟩
          ⟨Of rural life, I thank the Power that I⟩

---

36 "Lover's Petition," 14–25. Struck through in ink; "Printed by . . . 'Oversongs.' " is added in pencil. "Mr Ide" is probably A. M. Ide of Taunton, Mass., where *Over-Songs* was privately printed.

37 "Intellect / Gravely broods" (1–3); "May-Day," five unused lines, 457, x, x (4–11). Lines (1–3) and (9–11) are in ink over partially erased pencil; lines (4–8) are in erased pencil; in the pencil version, line (2) reads "Gravely ⟨& i⟩ broods . . .," line (3) "And ⟨‖ . . . . ‖ say⟩ ↑truth to tell↓ amused . . .," and line (9) is not indented. Two vertical lines, perhaps not Emerson's, are drawn in pencil to the left of lines (10–11).

38 "This is the age of ages" (1); "Nature" ("Day by day") (2–4). Line (1) is in pencil.

39 "What all the books," x, x, x, 1–12. Lines (1–3) are canceled with three vertical lines and enclosed in large parentheses; in line (9), the second "&" is added in pencil before the cancellation with an arrow to show its intended position in the insertion; in line (10), "the" is capitalized in pencil.

⟨Need not this charity of paint & song.⟩
What all the books of ages paint, I have.
(5)    What prayers & dreams of youthful genius feign,
I daily dwell in, & am not so blind
But I can see the elastic tent of day
Belike has wider hospitality
Than my few needs exhaust, ⟨& beckons me⟩ ↑& bids me
    read↓
(10)    ⟨Read t⟩The ↑quaint↓ devices on its mornings gay.
Yet nature will not be in full possessed,
And they who trueliest love her, heralds are
And harbingers of a majestic race,
Who, having more absorbed, more largely yield,
(15)    And walk on earth as the sun walks in the sphere.

[40]    Teach me your mood, o patient stars!
Who climb each night the ancient sky
Leaving on space no shade, no scars,
No hint of wrong, no fear to die.

[41]    And that no day of life ⟨s⟩may lack romance
The spiritual stars rise nightly, shedding down
A private beam into each several heart.
↑Daily the bending skies solicit man, ↓
(5)    ↑The Seasons chariot him from this exile, ↓
↑The rainbow Hours bedeck his glowing chair, ↓
↑The stormwinds urge the heavy weeks along, ↓
↑Suns haste to set, that so remoter lights↓
↑Beckon the wanderer to his vaster home. ↓
(10)    ↑For well we know the crowning gift↓
⟨The⟩ best ↑boon↓ of life is presence of a Muse
Who does not wish to wander, comes by stealth
Divulging to the heart she sets on flame
No popular tale or toy, ⟨no bauble for the mart⟩ ↑no cheap
    renown↓
(15)    When the wings grow that draw the gazing eyes
↑Ofttimes↓ Poor Genius flutter⟨s⟩ing near the Earth
⟨Quick⟩ ↑Is↓ wrecked upon the turrets of the town
But lifted till he meets the ⟨eternal⟩ ↑steadfast↓ gales
⟨Whic⟩ ↑Calm↓ Blowing from the ⟨eternal⟩ ↑everlasting↓
    west

40 "Teach me your mood."
41 "The Adirondacs," 221–29, ten unused lines (1–19); "Best boon of life" (11–19). In pencil, partially erased; lines (1–3) are struck through in pencil. Lines (4–10) are inscribed in pencil on p. [40], struck through and circumscribed in pencil, and indicated for insertion after line (3) on p. [41].

[42] [blank]

[43]         Leave me, Fear! thy throbs are base,
         Trembling for the body's sake.
         Come, Love! who dost the spirit ⟨w⟩raise,
         Because for others thou dost wake.

(5)         O it is beautiful in death
         To hide the shame of human nature's end
         In sweet & wary serving of a friend.
         Love is true Glory's field, where the last breath
         Expires in troops of honorable cares.

(10)         The wound of Fate ⟨he⟩ ↑the hero↓ cannot feel
         Smit with the heavenlier smart of social zeal.
         It draws immortal day
         In soot & ashes of our clay.
         It is the virtue that enchants it.

(15)         It is the face of God that haunts it.

[44] [blank]

[45]         Pay every debt, as if God wrote the bill,
         So to shut up each avenue of ill.

         I to my garden went
         To the unplanted woods

(5)         More sweet than my refrain
         Was the first drop of April rain

[46] [blank]

[47]    Has God on thee conferred
         A bodily presence mean as Paul's
         Yet made thee bearer of a word
         Which sleepy nations ↑in↓ to judgment calls?

(5)         O noble heart, accept
         With equal thanks the talent & disgrace;
         The marble town unwept,
         Nourish thy virtue in a private place.
         Think not that unattended

(10)         By heavenly powers thou steal'st to solitude,
         Nor yet ⟨i⟩on Earth all unbefriended

         Let Webster's lofty face
         Ever on thousands shine

43 "Leave me, Fear!" In line (10), "he" is canceled in pencil, and "the hero" added in pencil traced over in ink.

45 " 'Suum Cuique' " ("Wilt thou"), 2, 1 (1–2); "I to my garden went" (3–4); "More sweet than" (5–6). Lines (1–2) are struck through in ink; lines (3–6) are in pencil.

47 "Has God on thee conferred," 1–11, 13–16. Lines (12–15) are struck through in pencil with a large X.

(15)   A beacon set that Freedom's race
     Might gather omens from that radiant sign

[48] [blank]
[49]   ⟨Yet comes the poor⟩ ↑The beggar begs↓ by God's
      command,
     And gifts awake when givers sleep,
     Swords cannot cut the giving hand
     Nor stab the love that orphans keep.

[50]   The clouds are rich & dark, the air serene,
     So like the soul of me, t'were me.

     What wilt thou restless bird
     Seeking in that blue a deeper blue
(5)    And in that pure a purer sky

[51]   Wisp & meteor nightly falling
     But the stars of God remain↑.↓
     ————————

     ↑Tho'↓ Peril all round
     ⟨Touch not him⟩ all else appalling,
(5)    ⟨The⟩
     ↑Cannon in front, ⟨the⟩ ↑and↓ leaden rain,—↓
     ↑Him↓ Duty through the clarion calling
     To the front called not in vain

     Peril around, all else appalling,
(10)   Cannon in front, & leaden rain,
     Him Duty through the clarion calling
     To the front called not in vain.

[52]   I know ↑of Merlin↓ a song
     Which is both sweet & strong
     Sing it ⟨in⟩amid the rushing crowd
     Good men it will calm & cheer
(5)    ↑The↓ Bad ⟨men it will⟩ ↑to plots of hell↓ en⟨r⟩gage
     In the heart of the music peals a strain
     Which fewest of men can hear
     Sing it never so loud
     Few be they can hear

**49** "Alms."
**50** "The Adirondacs," 213–14, 208–10. In pencil; each entry is struck through in pencil; lines (3–5) and the line through them are partially erased.
**51** "Wisp & meteor" (1–2); "Voluntaries," two drafts of four lines first printed in the 1876 version (3–12). Lines (1–2) are written in ink over the same in partially erased pencil; the period is added to the ink inscription in pencil; lines (3–8), in pencil, are struck through in pencil and partially erased.
**52** "Merlin's Song," 1, 3, 5–9, 2, 9–13. In pencil, struck through in pencil and partially erased.

(10)  Whether it waken fear or rage
    Hushed ⟨thousands listen⟩ ↑myriads hark↓ in vain
    Yet they who hear it shed their age
    And take their youth again

[53]    I know of Merlin a song
    Sing it low or sing it loud
    It is mightier than the strong
    And ⟨casteth down⟩ ↑punishes↓ the proud
(5)   I sing it to the surging crowd
    Good men it will calm & cheer
    Bad men it will ↑to↓ enrage
    In the heart of the music peals a strain
    Which only angels hear
(10)  Whether it waken joy or rage
    Hushed myriads hark in vain
    ⟨Yet⟩ ↑But↓ they who hear it shed their age
    And take their youth again

    The brook sings on but sings in vain
(15)  Wanting the echo in my brain.

[54]  God The Lord save Massachusetts
    Without chivalry or slave⟨s⟩
    We are ignorant of stealing
    Quite too stupid to be knave⟨s⟩
(5)   ⟨How⟩ ↑And↓ to perjure ⟨how⟩and to poison
    Not our way our souls to save

    ↑Let↓ The heavy blue chain
    Of the boundless main
    Lock up their prison door,
(10)  And the cannon's wrath
    Forbid their path
    On ocean's azure floor.

 ↑dauntless, ceaseless, ↓
  Bad words
Fadeless tireless swerveless
 shunless

53 "Merlin's Song" (1–13); "Old Age" (14–15). In pencil; lines (1–13) are struck through in pencil.

54 "God The Lord save Massachusetts" (1–6); "The heavy blue chain" (7–12). The page was inscribed in pencil, partially erased, and lines (7–12) overwritten in ink. In the pencil version, which lacks punctuation, line (7) reads "⟨And⟩ the heavy . . .", and line (11) "⟨Shall bar⟩ ↑Forbid↓ their path"; "dauntless, ceaseless," is added in ink; and "Bad . . . shunless" is enclosed in large brackets.

[55] Be her cognizance allowed
   Her stars the very stars of heaven
   And her stripes the rivers proud

   If a cloud rest on Mount Vernon
(5)  Not a spot on Faneuil Hall

   Freely flows the Susquehanna,
   Freely flows the Illinois,
   Hudson proud with farm & manor,

   The heavy blue chain
(10) Of the boundless main
   Lock up their prison door
   And the cannon's wrath
   Forbid their path
   On Oceans azure floor.

[56]    God said, I am tired of kings
     I ⟨will⟩ ↑suffer them↓ no more
     Up to my ear the morning brings
     The outrage of the poor

(5)  Justice shall be instead
   And men have equal rights
   The proud man let him be as dead
   The ⟨poor⟩ ↑just↓ my heart delights

   ⟨There shall be no haughty noble⟩
(10) ↑I will have never a noble↓
   No ⟨tribe⟩ lineage counted great
   Fishers & choppers & plowmen
   ↑Shall↓ Constitute the state

   I will see if these poor men
(15) Can rule the land & sea
   And make just laws on earth below
   As planets faithful be

[57]    To Freedom we assign
    And make partition fair
    All space above the waterline
    All ground below the air

55 "Be her cognizance allowed" (1–8); "The heavy blue chain" (9–14). Lines (1–8) are in pencil; lines (4–5) and (6–8) are struck through separately in pencil.
56 "Boston Hymn," 5–8, four unused lines, 29, 29–32, 45–48. In pencil, struck through in pencil.
57 "Boston Hymn," twelve unused lines. In pencil.

(5)        And all the rest may slavery claim
              For her appointed share
              Within the earth to hide her shame
              Or ⟨out↑side↓ of the atmosphere⟩ ↑climb above the air↓
(10)       Upon the pole he hung the cord
              And to the tropics drew
              Along the round globe's quarter broad
              Along the welkin blue

[58]        ⟨The⟩ hills clapped hands the rivers shined
              The seas applauding roar
              The elements were of one mind
              As they had been of yore

(5)        My will ⟨be done⟩ fulfilled shall be
                  And what tho it be dark
                 My thunderbolt has eyes to see
              His way home to the mark

[59]           Columbia
              Columbia of the rocks
              Which dip their ⟨broad⟩ foot in the seas
              And soar to the ⟨cloudy⟩ ↑airborne↓ flocks
(5)        Of clouds ⟨& misty⟩ ↑& the Protean↓ fleece

              Leave out the tyrant
              Call in the poor & the slave
              None shall rule but the humble
              None but toil shall have
(10)       ⟨t⟩And only Toil possess

              Harp of victory ringing
              In the morning wind
              Windharp sounding
              Sounding funeral marches
(15)       of faery kings & ⟨knights⟩ ↑paladins↓
              Fallen in battle

[60]     None shall be slave but by choice
              Who is base a helot be
              For slavery

58 "Boston Hymn," four unused lines, 85–88. In pencil; lines (5–8) were struck through in pencil and the line erased.

59 "Boston Hymn," 21, 21–24, x, 26–28, 28 (1–10); "Harp of victory ringing" (11–16). In pencil; lines (2–5) and (6–10) are struck through separately in pencil and erased.

60 "Boston Hymn," seven unused lines (1–7). In pencil, struck through in pencil. Lines (8–15) are from a poem by Charles C. Emerson written between December 1831 and April 1832 when he was visiting his brother Edward in Puerto Rico.

(5)
I will have an equal partition
In this new world I have built
For slavery differs from freedom
as ⟨probity⟩ honor is wide from guilt

---

C.C.E    Porto Rico

---

"keen whistling winds,
Fast travellers from frozen Labrador,
(10)
Blow round thy hills, sharpening their blue profile,
Or heavy clouds snow-charged from o'er their breast
Lay their white burden down, while puffing blasts,
Partial like Fortune, pile a mountain here,
While yonder marsh has not a decent coat
(15)
For his bare sides."

[61]
God said, I am tired of kings
I suffer them no more
Up to my ear the morning brings
The ⟨grind⟩ outrage of the poor

(5)
They eat my ⟨people⟩ ↑tribes↓ as bread
I w

Think ye I made the ball
A field of blood & war
Where tyrants great or tyrants small
(10)
Might harry the weak & poor

[62]
I will have never a noble
No lineage counted great
Fishers & choppers & plowmen
Shall constitute a state

(5)
I will see if these poor men
Can rule the land & sea
And make just laws below the sun
As planets faithful be

[63]
Lo now, to Freedom I assign,
And make partition fair
All space above the waterline
All ground below the air.

(5)
And all the rest may slavery claim

61 "Boston Hymn," 5–8, x, x, 9–12. In pencil, struck through in pencil.
62 "Boston Hymn," 29–32, 45–48. In pencil, struck through in pencil.
63 "Boston Hymn," twelve unused lines. In pencil; lines (1–3) are struck through in pencil.

For her allotted share
Within the earth to hide her shame
Or climb above the air.

Firm to the pole he knots the cord,
(10)    And to the tropics drew
⟨Along⟩ ↑About↓ the round globe's quarter broad,
Along the welkin blue.

[64]    Hills clapped their hands, the rivers shined,
The seas applauding roar,
The Elements were of one mind
As they had been of yore.

(5)    O late to learn, o long betrayed,
O credulous men of toil,
Who took the traitor to your hearths,
Who came those hearths to spoil.

O much-revering Boston town,
(10)    Who let the varlet still
Recite his false insulting tale
⟨At⟩On haughty Bunker Hill

[65]    I break your bonds & mastership
And I unchain the slave
Free be his heart & hand henceforth
As mountain wind & wandering wave

(5)    O late to learn, o long betrayed,
O credulous men of toil!
Who took the scoundrel ⟨↑traitor↓⟩ to your hearths
Who came ↑those hearths↓ to ⟨defile &⟩ spoil,

O much revering Boston town
(10)    Who let the ⟨insulting crew⟩ ↑varlet still↓
⟨And tell⟩ ⟨↑To↓⟩ ↑Recite↓ their ⟨paltry⟩ ↑false↓ insulting
tale
At ⟨Faneuil Hall &⟩ ↑haughty↓ Bunker Hill

[66]    I will send men out of the North
By races or like snowflakes
They shall carry my purpose forth
It shall not fall to the ground

64 "Boston Hymn," twelve unused lines. Lines (1–4) are in pencil.
65 "Boston Hymn," 53–56, eight unused lines. In pencil; lines (1–4) are struck through in
pencil; lines (5–12) are lightly erased.
66 "Boston Hymn," 81?, 82–83, x (1–4); "The rules to men" (5–8); "Boston Hymn," 86–88
(9–11). In pencil; lines (1–4) and (9–11) are struck through in pencil.

(5)    ↑Those ⟨lines⟩ ↑rules↓ were ⟨m⟩writ in human hearts↓
    ↑By Him who ⟨made⟩ ↑built↓ the day↓
    The columns of the firmament
    Not firmer based than they

        And what though it be dark
(10)   My thunderbolt has eyes to see
    ⟨An⟩His way home to the mark

[67]       ⟨Fit to be⟩
    Worthy lord of wit & love
    Fit to make an angel of

        I uncover the land
(5)    Which I hid, of old time, in the west,
    As the sculptor uncovers the statue
    When he has wrot his design

    ↑I show↓ Columbia of the rocks
    Which dip their foot in the seas
(10)   And soar to the airborne flocks
    Of clouds & the Protean fleece

[68]       And as the flowing sea
    Infolds her every part
    So shall each noble townsman
    Carry the town in his heart

(5)    The blood of her hundred thousands
    Shall throb in his manly vein
    And the wit of all her wisest
    Make sunshine in his brain

_____

        My angel his name is Freedom
(10)   Make him for your king
    He shall cut paths east & west
    And fend you with his wing

    And each shall care for other
    And each to each shall bend
(15)   To the poor a noble brother,
    To the rich a manly friend.

[69]   O Boston city ⟨man-revering⟩ ↑lecture-hearing,↓
    O unitarian God-fearing,

67 "Boston Hymn," x, x, x, 17–24. In pencil; lines (4–11) are struck through in pencil.
68 "Boston," 3?, x, 100–101, 104–7 (1–8); "Boston Hymn," 13–16 (9–12); "Boston," 110–13 (13–16). In pencil; lines (9–12) are struck through in pencil.
69 "O Boston city." In line (7), the cancellation and addition are in pencil.

But more, I fear↑,↓ ⟨me,⟩ ↑bad↓ m⟨a⟩en-revering;
Too civil by half, thine evil guest⟨s⟩

(5) Make↑s↓ thee ⟨their⟩ ↑his↓ byword & ⟨their⟩ ↑his↓ jest,
And scorn↑s↓ the men that honeyed the pest,
⟨Winthrop & Everett⟩ ↑Piso & Atticus↓, with the rest.
⟨I fear⟩ thy ↑fault is↓ much civility,
Thy bane, respectability.

(10) And thou hadst been as wise, & wiser,
Lacking the Daily Advertiser.
Ah, gentlemen,—for you are gentle,—
And mental maids, not sentimental.

[70]           ⟨Little they loved the English King⟩
           ↑The English king they could not ⟨a⟩bide↓
Nor cared for the gold of the French
But Honor ⟨⟨came &⟩ sat ⟨beside⟩ by their side⟩ ↑sat these
           men beside↓

(5) Low on their wooden bench


                              ground
⟨Which⟩ Columbus sought & Cabot found
⟨or⟩ ↑And↓ that proud State whose north & southern horn
Pierce eastward the Atlantic sea


                    *Song of Nature*
(10) He ⟨n⟩lives not who can refuse me
All my force sa⟨ys⟩ith come & use me
A ⟨little⟩ ↑gleam of↓ sun, a little rain
And all is green again

[71]       ↑Apples of gold in silver salvers set↓

Try the ⟨might⟩ ↑balm↓ of thoughtful words,
And the might the Muse affords.


Try the might the Muse affords
(5) And the balm of thoughtful words


Befals again what once befel


What I cannot declare
Yet cannot all withhold

70 "Boston," 80, 80–83, four unused lines (1–9); "He lives not who can refuse me" (10–13). Lines (1–5), "*Song of Nature*," and lines (10–13) are in pencil.
71 "Apples of gold" (1); "Try the might the Muse affords," 1/2, 2/1 (2–5); "May-Day," 94 (6); "My Garden," 51–52 (7–8). Except for line (1), added in ink, the page is in pencil; lines (2–3) are struck through twice in pencil and lines (6–8) once; line (6) is erased.

[72₁]     Fall stream from Heaven & falling fall
          So did our braves; Heaven met them as they fell

          ↑Fall ⟨gentle⟩ stream from Heaven ↑to bless; ↓ returning
              well↓
          ↑So did our braves; Heaven met them as they fell. ↓

(5)               My garden is a forest patch
          Planted with ancient trees

          ↑_____↓

          ↑Fall, gentle stream from Heaven, & falling fill;↓
          ↑So did our dying heroes work God's will↓

          The planters they are gone
(10)      Scorning fame
          Yet I can read their name
          The wind & rain & the bird

          The deluge ploughed it
          And ⟨level⟩ laid out the terraces
(15)      ⟨Withdrawing⟩ ↑Ebbing↓ whence it flowed

[72₂]             Inscription on a well in Memory of
                      the martyrs of the war.
          _____    _____

                  Fall stream from Heaven to bless: return as well
          So did our sons; Heaven met them as they fell.

[73]      A patch of meadow & upland
          Reached by a mile of road,
          Soothed by the voice of waters,
          With birds & flowers bestowed.

(5)       This is my book of Chronicles,
          Code, Psalter, lexicon,
          My Genesis & ⟨C⟩calendar
          I read it as I run.

          It is my consolation
(10)      In mild or poignant grief,
          My park & my gymnasium,
          My out-of-door relief.

---

72₁ "Inscription on a Well in Memory of the Martyrs of the War" (1–4, 7–8); "My Garden,"
9, 10?, 17?, 19, x, 18, 13–15 (5–6, 9–15). In pencil; lines (5–6) and (9–15) are struck through
in pencil, and lines (1–2) and (5–15) erased.
   72₂ "Inscription on a Well in Memory of the Martyrs of the War." In ink over lines (9–11) of
the erased pencil layer.
   73 "A patch of meadow and upland," 1–12. Brackets, perhaps not Emerson's, are drawn in
pencil before line (5) and after line (12).

[74]    I come to it for strength,
    Which it can well supply,
    For Love draws might from terrene force
    And potences of sky.

(5)    The tremulous battery, earth,
    Responds to touch of man,
    It thrills to the antipodes,
    From Boston to Japan.

    The planets' child the planet knows
(10)    And to his joy replies;
    To the lark's trill unfolds the rose,
    Clouds flush their gayest dyes.

[75]    When Ali prayed & loved
    Where Syrian waters ⟨shine⟩roll,
    Upward the ninth heaven thrilled & moved
    At the tread of the jubilant soul.

[76]    O fairest passenger
    I know not who is thy sire
    Nor sits what mother by thy hearth
    But say securest thou dost hold
(5)    Of me more nearly in th‖

[77]    ⟨Thou didst⟩ ↑⟨Did⟩ but↓ recite↑s↓ my tho'ts to me.
    In thine eyes' salutary light
    I bathed my own where they lead right,
    The flowers peeped earlier on thy path.

[78]            ↑My Garden↓          ↑See p. 135↓
    If I should put the↑se↓ woods in song,
    And tell what's there enjoyed,
    All men would to ⟨my g⟩these gardens throng,
    And leave the cities void.

(5)    In my garden, three ways meet,
    Thrice the spot is blest,
    Hermit thrush comes there to sing,
    Carrier doves to rest.

74 "A patch of meadow and upland," 13–24.
75 "A patch of meadow and upland," 25–28. Struck through in ink. The lower two-thirds of the page is cut out.
76 "O fairest passenger." The page, in erased pencil, is cut off after the fifth line but the stub shows traces of at least seven more lines.
77 "but recites my tho'ts to me." These four lines in erased pencil are inscribed over traces of an earlier line or two, probably heavily canceled, and thoroughly erased.
78 "My Garden," 1–4 (1–4); "In my garden three ways meet," 1–8 (5–12). Lines (1–12) are struck through in pencil. "My Garden   See p. 135" is in pencil.

(10)
In my garden, oaken copse
The eager wind⟨s⟩ detain ↑s↓,
Sultry summer lingers there
When Autumn chills the plains.

[79]
The ↑wild↓ bees drove their sugar-trade,
⟨The spider spun ⟨his⟩ ↑her↓ silk,⟩
↑The cow-weed shed its milk↓
All day the wasp his paper made,
(5)   ↑*↓ ⟨The ants their cows did milk.⟩
↑The spider spun her silk↓

In cities high the careful brood
Of wo worn mortals darkling go
But in these sunny solitudes
(10)
My quiet roses blow

↑* The cow-weed shed its milk↓

[80]
See the air line wavy with heat
⟨And behold⟩ ↑One by one↓ the drop ↑trickle shed from the
      rock↓
⟨Setting⟩ ↑Starting↓ out on its way to the sea.

_____

In dreamy woods what forms abound
(5)
That elsewhere ⟨poet⟩ never poet found!
Here voices ring & pictures burn,
And grace on grace, where e'er I turn

_____

And he like me is not too proud
To be the poet of the crowd

(10)
The drops trickle down
Shed from the ⟨rock⟩ ↑boulder↓, one by one
Starting out on ⟨its⟩ ↑their↓ way to the sea

[81₁]
War is local f⟨e⟩avors waste
In a district
Benefit is wide as air
And o thou strong & virtuous Spring
(5)
⟨t⟩All visiting all hiving ⟨s⟩Spring

79 "In my garden three ways meet," six unused lines, 17–20. The asterisk before line (5), Emerson's note, and lines (7–10) are in pencil.

80 "His home / Where the pure drops," x, 2/3, 4 (1–3); "In dreamy woods" (4–7); "And he like me" (8–9); "His home / Where the pure drops," 2–4 (10–12). In pencil; lines (2–3) are struck through twice in pencil.

81₁ "May-Day," x, x, x, 268, x, 269–71, 89–90, 89–90, 272–75. In pencil; lines (1–11) and (10–16) are struck through separately in pencil.

Broad sowing Spring
Searching underneath the mould
For grains of wheat & /harvest/crop/ of gold
    for roots & fruits berries & bread

(10)    ⟨That man & all thy kinds be fed⟩
And ripening for all their bread
That man & all the kinds be fed
⟨I⟩So deep so large thy favors are
That one broad ⟨s⟩long midsummer day

(15)    Will to the planet overpay
The ravage of a year of war

[81₂]    Parks & ponds are good by day,
But where's the ⟨b⟩husband doth delight
In black acres of the night?
Not my unseasoned step disturbs

(5)    The sleeps of trees or dreams of herbs

Stars & the celestial kind
Their own food are skilled to find

[82]        Spices in the plants that run
To bring their first fruits to the sun
Earliest heats that follow frore
Nervéd leaf of hellebore

(5)    ⟨Sassafras & fern⟩
⟨And⟩ ⟨th⟩scarlet maple keys that burn
↑Above the sassafras & fern↓
⟨Winters⟩ ↑Frost-↓survivors berries red
Checkerberry   childrens bread

(10)    Silver birch & black
With the selfsame spice to find
⟨As⟩ ↑In↓ polygala's root & rind
Mouseear cowslip wintergreen
Which by their beauty may repel

(15)    The frost from harming what is well

[83]    The scarlet maple keys betray
What potent blood hath modest May

81₂ "Parks & ponds" (1–5); "As Stars & the celestial kind" (6–7).
82 "Spices in the plants," 1–4, 10 (1–5); "May-Day," 174 (6); "Spices in the plants," 10, 5, 5/6, 7–9, 12–14 (7–15). In pencil.
83 "May-Day," 174–75, 566–67, x, x, x, 568–69, x, 591 (1–11); "The Harp," 87–88, x, x, x, 89–90, x, 116 (3–11); "For Genius made his cabin wide," 1–4 (12–15). Lines (1–2) occur in reverse order in the manuscript, marked for transposition by the numbers "2" and "1" in the left margin. In pencil. Lines (1–4) and (8–9) are struck through in pencil; lines (12–13) are circumscribed in pencil; in line (13), Emerson wrote "theren", then dotted the "e".

⟨Passing⟩ ↑Pacing↓ thro' the woodland heard
Sharp queries of the sentry bird

(5)    Prayed ↑Day &↓ Night ⟨& mor⟩ to make him wise
⟨And Night & Morning made replies⟩
And each ⟨drops wisdom as he flies⟩ ↑with bounty made
        replies↓
        ↑The heavy grouses sudden whirr↓
        ↑The rattle of the kingfisher↓

(10)    ↑How the young heart can adorn↓
    ↑With grace each comrade↓
For genius made his cabin wide
And Love brought gods there ↑i↓n to bide
        ↑Better he ⟨thot⟩ ↑thought↓ no god can bring↓

(15)        ↑And basked in friendship all the days of Spring↓

[84]    ↑Put-in, drive home the sightless wedges, ↓
    ↑And split to flakes the crystal ledges↓
    ↑⟦See p 83    And tho he found his friendships meet↓
        ↑His quarrels too had somewhat sweet↓

(5)    This the creation
And the revealing
And
Nor the scholar need to look
Poring in a printed book

(10)    And weigh a greek article
When they can read ↑grammar↓ soon
In the sun & moon
↑Doctrine↓ In the tides ↑&↓ ⟨& in the trees⟩ ↑winds↓
And the wonders of the ⟨tribes⟩ ↑kinds↓

(15)    Or the wandering birds

By kinds I keep my kinds in check,
I plant the oak, the rose I deck.

[85]        ↑The new year's mien is ↑mild &↓ meek↓
⟨The year has⟩ the down of youth ↑is↓ on its cheek
                H[enry] T[horeau].

            or hark
Was it a squirrel's pettish bark
(5)          ⟨or ha⟩ ↑or hark↓
Where yon wedged line the Nestor leads

84 "Put in, drive home" (1–2); "For Genius made his cabin wide," 5–6 (3–4); "This the creation" (5–15); "By kinds I keep" (16–17). In pencil; lines (3–4) are struck through in pencil.
85 "The new year's mien" (1–2); "May-Day," 28, 27, 28–31, 30, 32–33, 35, x, 31? (3–14). In pencil; lines (2–12) and (4–12) are struck through separately in pencil, and the page partially erased.

With raucous voice clang
Thro tracts & provinces of sky
Northward steering
(10)    Each night descending
To a new landscape of romance
By lonely lakes to men unknown
By purple peaks & rosy palaces
In deep abysses of imperial sky

pass to p 132

[86]          *The Pilgrims.*
↑1↓ The word of the Lord by night
To the watching pilgrims came
As they sat by the seaside↑,↓
And filled their hearts with flame.

(5)    ↑2↓ God said, I am tired of kings,
I suffer them no more;
Up to my ear the morning brings
The outrage of the poor.

↑3↓ Think ye I made the ball
(10)    A field of havoc & war,
Where tyrants great & tyrants small
Might harry the weak & poor⟨.⟩↑?↓

[87]  ↑⟦↓ Justice shall reign instead,
And men shall have their rights;
Bring out the oppressor dead,
The meek my heart delights. ↑⟧↓

(5)    ↑7↓ I will divide my goods,
Call in the wretch & slave,
None shall rule but the humble,
And none but Toil shall have.

↑⟦↓ There shall be never a noble,
(10)    No lineage preferred,
Of kings & popes & emperors,
Henceforth speak not a word. ↑⟧↓

[88]↑8)↓ I will have never a noble,
No lineage counted great,

86 "Boston Hymn," 1–12. Struck through in pencil, except for the title; the numbers and
added punctuation are in pencil.
87 "Boston Hymn," four unused lines, 25–30, x, x. The brackets and "7" are added in pencil;
lines (5–12) are struck through in pencil.
88 "Boston Hymn," 29–44. Struck through in pencil; the numbers are added in pencil.

Fishers & choppers & plowmen
Shall constitute a state.

(5)　↑9)↓ Go cut down trees in the forest,
And trim the straightest boughs,
Cut down trees in the forest,
And build me a wooden house.

　↑10)↓ ↑Call the people together⟨—⟩,↓
(10)　　↑The young men & the sires↓
　　↑The digger in the harvest field,↓
　　↑Hireling & him that hires.↓

　↑11)↓ And here in a pine state-house
They shall cho⟨s⟩ose men to rule
(15)　In every needful faculty,
⟨The⟩In state, ⟨the⟩& church, & school.

[89]↑12↓Lo now, if these poor men
Can govern the land & sea,
And make just laws below the sun,
As planets faithful be.

(5)　↑13↓ And ye shall succor men;
Tis nobleness to serve;
Help them who cannot help again;
Beware from right to swerve.

　↑14↓ I break your bonds & masterships,
(10)　And I unchain the slave,
Free be his heart & hand henceforth
As wind & wandering wave!

[90]↑4)↓My angel,—his name is Freedom,
Choose him to be your king,
He shall cut pathways east & west,
And fend you with his wing.

(5)　↑5↓ Lo! I uncover the land
Which I hid of old time in the west,
As the sculptor uncovers the statue
When he has wrought his best.

　↑6↓ I show Columbia, of the rocks
(10)　Which dip their foot in the seas,
And soar to the air↑-↓borne flocks
Of clouds, & the /↑⟦↓Protean↑⟧↓/boreal/fleece.

---

89 "Boston Hymn," 45–56. Struck through in pencil; the numbers are added in pencil.
90 "Boston Hymn," 13–24. Struck through in pencil; the additions are in pencil.

[91]    Behold I make partition
        In this new world I have built,
        For Slavery differs from Freedom
        As honor is wide from guilt.

(5)     Lo now to Freedom I assign,
        And make partition fair,
        All space above the waterline
        All ground below the air.

        And what's beside may Slavery claim,
(10)    Her residue & share,
        Within the earth to hide her shame,
        Or climb above the air.

[92]    Firm to the pole he knots the cord,
        And to the tropics drew↑,↓
        About the round globe's quarter broad↑,↓
        Along the welkin blue.

(5)     Hills clapped their hands, the rivers shined,
        The seas applauding roar;
        The elements were of one mind,
        As they had been of yore.

        I will send men out of the North
(10)    By races↑,↓ like snowflakes,
        They shall carry my purpose forth↑,↓
        Which neither halts nor shakes.

[93]    My will fulfilled shall be,
        For in daylight or in dark
        My thunderbolt has eyes to see
        His way home to the mark.

(5) ↑1⟨6⟩5↓I cause from every creature
        His proper good to flow
        ⟨So⟩ ↑As↓ much as he is & doeth
        So much he shall bestow

    ↑1⟨5⟩6↓But laying hands on another
(10)    To coin his labor & sweat

91 "Boston Hymn," twelve unused lines.

92 "Boston Hymn," eight unused lines, 81?, 82–84. The added commas are in pencil; lines (9–12) are struck through in pencil.

93 "Boston Hymn," 85–88, 57–68. Lines (1–4) are struck through in pencil; lines (5–12), in pencil, are struck through in pencil and lines (5–8) partially erased; the numbers are added in pencil. In lines (13–16), "Today . . . unbound" is written on one line and "Lift . . . sound" on another.

He goes in pawn to his victim
For eternal years in debt

↑Today unbind the captive,↓
↑So only are ye unbound;↓
(15)      ↑Lift up a people from the dust,↓
↑Trump of their rescue, sound↓

[94]↑⟨16⟩ 17↓Pay ransom to the owner
And fill the bag to the brim
Who is the owner? The slave is owner,
And ever was. Pay him.

(5) ↑1⟨7⟩8↓O North! give him beauty for rags
And honor, o South! for his shame,
Nevada! coin thy golden crags
With Freedoms image & name

↑1⟨8⟩9↓Up! & the dusky race
(10)      That sat in darkness long,
Be swift their feet as antelopes,
And as behemoth strong.

[95]↑⟨19⟩20↓Come East, & west, & north,
⟨A⟩By races, as snowflakes,
And carry my purpose forth
Which neither halts nor shakes

(5)↑⟨22⟩21↓My will fulfilled shall be
For, in daylight, or in dark,
My thunderbolt has eyes to see
His way home to the mark

[96]                       *The Sea.*
I heard or seemed to hear the ⟨singing⟩ ↑chiding↓ sea
↑Say Pilgrim↓ 'Why so late & slow to come?
Am I not always here, thy summer home?
Is not my voice thy music?
(5)      My breath thy healthful climate in the heats?
My touch, thy /cure/antedote/? ↑⟨My ⟨wave⟩ ↑bay↓ thy
       bath⟩My bay thy bath?↓
Was ever building like my terraces?
Was ever couch magnificent as mine
Lie on my warm rock ledges, & there learn

94 "Boston Hymn," 69–80. In pencil, struck through in pencil.
95 "Boston Hymn," 81–88. In pencil, struck through in pencil.
96 "Sea-Shore," 1–9. Struck through in ink. The cancellation and additions in lines (1–2), and "antedote" in line (6), are in pencil; in line (6), "My ⟨wave⟩ . . . bath" is added in pencil and overwritten by "My bay thy bath?" in ink.

[97]  A little hut ⟨is better than⟩ ↑suffices like↓ a town.
I make your ⟨civic⟩ ↑sculptured↓ architecture vain
⟨Tis⟩ vain ↑⟨s⟩beside↓ ⟨by⟩ mine
Lo here ⟨are⟩ ↑is↓ Rome⟨s⟩ ↑&↓ Nineveh⟨s⟩ & Thebes
(5)  Karnak & Pyramid & Giants Stairs
⟨Prostrate⟩Half piled or prostrate ↑wreck of oldest realms↓

↑Where is my conqueror?↓ Behold the sea,

↑The↓ Opaline ⟨sea⟩, the plentiful, & strong,
Yet beautiful as is the rose of June,
(10)  Fresh as the trickling rainbow of July,
Sea full of food, the nourisher of ⟨men⟩ ↑kinds↓,
Purger of Earth ↑& medicine of men↓
⟨Making⟩ ↑creating↓ a sweet climate with its breath

[98]  And in ⟨its⟩ ↑my↓ mathematic ebb & flow
Giving a hint of that which changes not.
Who is rich but the sea-gods?
↑This is the mine, Karun, the gold maker,↓
(5)  ↑For↓ Every wave is wealth ↑to Daedalus↓
↑To the wise artist↓ Who can turn
This sinew to account, or find ⟨a load⟩ ⟨↑a load↓⟩
    ↑O waves↓
↑A load↓ ⟨This⟩ ↑⟨your⟩ our↓ ↑Atlas-shoulder⟨ed⟩s↓
    ⟨porter⟩ cannot ⟨carry?⟩ ↑lift↓
Lightly streams the spray from my crest
(10)  Like a woman's hair in the wind.

[99]  Chemist that melts the mountain & the rock

Battering the shore
Melt Andes into powder
Strewing my bed
(5)                    and in another age
Rebuild a continent for better men
My paths lead out
The exodus of nations
⟨And⟩ I disperse ⟨forever⟩

97 "Sea-Shore," 10–15, 17–23. Struck through in ink. In line (4), "are" is canceled in pencil; in line (6), "wreck of oldest realms" is added in pencil; "Where is my conqueror?" is added in pencil at the end of line (7) and the line marked for transposition; the cancellations and additions in lines (11–13) are in pencil.
98 "Sea-Shore," 24–26, x, 29–32, x, x. Struck through in ink. The cancellations and additions in lines (1–7) are in pencil; in line (8), Emerson first inserted "Atlas-shouldered" after "This", then canceled "This porter" and revised the line in pencil.
99 "Sea-Shore," x, 33/34?, 34–35, 35–38, 38–39, 41?, 46–48. Struck through in ink; the cancellations in line (9) are in pencil.

(10)      Men to all shores that front the hoary main.
            By my illusions
            Putting strange fruits & sunshine on my shores
            I make one & another coast ↑alluring↓
            ⟨Attractive⟩ to men who must see it or die

[100]   *Parnassus*
        Lord Herberts love-song. ⟦⟨"⟩See "the Great Lawsuit"

---

Donnes "I saw thee go
        Oer the white Alps alone"

            For though there is one water
            Yet I make it appear in
            the sunshine as gems & clouds

            Illusion dwells forever with the wave.
(5)      ⟨Give⟩ ↑Leave↓ me to deal with ⟨man⟩ ↑Daedalus↓
            With credulous imaginative man
            And though he ⟨hold⟩ ↑scoop↓ my water in his palm
            A few rods off he deems it gems & clouds

[101]         All day the waves assailed the rock,
            ⟨I heard no hourly chime;⟩
↑x↓     ↑⟨How⟩ ↑I↓ could ⟨I⟩ ↑not↓ hear the Minster's chime?↓
            The sea-beat scorns the ⟨minster⟩ ↑/doleful/chapel/↓ clock,
(5)      And breaks the glass of Time.

[102]   In cities high /thro crowds of cares/the careful brood/

            The wo-worn mortals darkling go
            But in these sunny solitudes
            My quiet roses blow

---

(5)         What creature slayeth or is slain?
            What creature saves or saved is?
            ⟨His life will each soul⟩ ↑Each soul his life will↓ lose or gain
            As he shall follow harm or bliss.

---

100 "*Parnassus* . . . Alps alone" is in pencil. Emerson published five stanzas of "An Ode upon a Question moved, Whether Love should continue for ever?" by Edward, Lord Herbert of Cherbury, in *Parnassus*, 1875, under the title "Celinda." Margaret Fuller quotes two lines of this poem in "The Great Lawsuit." Man *versus* Men. Woman *versus* Women," *The Dial* 4 (July 1843): 26. " 'I saw . . . alone' " is misquoted from John Donne, "Elegie XVI. On his Mistris," lines 52–53. Following the memorandum is "Sea-Shore," 44?, x, 45, 41–45. Lines (1–8) are struck through in ink; "man" and "hold" are canceled, and "Daedalus" and "scoop" added, in pencil.
   101 "All day the waves," 1–2, 2–4. The cancellations and additions in line (3) are in pencil.
   102 "In my garden three ways meet," 17–20 (1–4); "Brahma," 1/2?, x, x, x (5–8). In pencil; "23.15" and "20.57" are jotted in pencil at the top of the page. The rules are shaped like gull wings.

[102ₐ]  ↑Cloud upon cloud. ↓
↑Clouds after rain↓
Value standeth in success,
But the same value
(5)  Hideth in failure,
In poverty, mourning,
In solitude, crime;
The value adhesive
Sticks to them all
(10)  Refuses to sunder ⟨from⟩
From man, from man.
Differ servitude & rank
As chains ↑that↓ clank not, chains that clank

The last shall be first
(15)  The first be postponed
The latest promoted
At the end of the day
It first will appear
Who never surrendered
(20)  Who combated ⟨valiantly⟩ ↑stoutly, ↓
Where God was the while
We strutted we coxcombs
So condescendingly
Bowing & giving
(25)  Affecting to give
[102ᵦ]  Virtue is a cockney grown

[102c]  Burn your literary verses
Give us rather the glib curses
Of the truckmen in the street
Songs of the forecastle
(5)  To the caboose

The old men used their God at need
Smooth modern saints who write & read

For Lyra yet shall be the pole
And grass grow in the Capitol

(10)  The river knows its way
The current knows the way

[102d]  Poet bred in a right school

102ₐ "Cloud upon cloud. / Clouds," 1–25.
102ᵦ "Cloud upon cloud. / Clouds," 26.
102c "Burn your literary verses" (1–5); "The old men used" (6–7); "For Lyra yet shall be" (8–9); "The river knows the way," 1, 1 (10–11).
102d "Proteus," 1–2, five unused lines (1–7); "Honor bright o muse" (8–12).

362

Can wind the world off any spool
Genius nervous if you will
And the hankering to write
(5)    Is ⟨but⟩ identical
With cackling hen who must lay
The last egg of her litter

Honor bright o muse
↑Muses↓ Keep your faith with me
(10)   ⟨O⟩Give me some audacious hours
Draw to a just close
The poem ye begun

[103]   Thy ⟨old⟩ ↑dull↓ pen soaked in stagnant ink
No more of muses' fount shall drink

Beauty see VA 8

If ⟨t⟩Thought unlock⟨s⟩ her mysteries,
If love on me may smile,
(5)    I walk in marble galleries
And talk with kings the while.

The sun & planets fell amain
Like ripened seeds into his brain
There quickened to be born again.

[104]   Freedom loves not the burning zone,
The snowflakes are our banner stars,
Our stripes the streaming northern lights.

O wellaway whose happy thot
(5)    Bereaves him of all knowledge else

O wellaway for happy soul
When a music steals his memory

But best befriended of the god
Is he who in dark times
(10)   Being called to do a divine right
Forgets the evil times, seeing only
The far heaven which his deed ensures

103 "Thy dull pen soaked" (1–2); "In my garden three ways meet," 29–32 (3–6); "Charmed from fagot," 5–7 (7–9). The verses are in ink over erased pencil; "Beauty  see VA 8" is in pencil. In the ink layer, line (1), "old" is canceled and "dull" added in pencil. In the pencil layer, lines (1–2) are transposed, and line (1) begins "Thy old dull pen . . ."; line (3) reads "⟨When⟩ ↑If↓ Thought unlock⟨s⟩ . . .", line (4) "⟨When⟩ ↑If↓ love . . . ", and line (9) "There quickened to ⟨grow⟩ ↑be born↓ again".

104 "Voluntaries," x, 41–42, x, x, 75–77, 83–84, x, x, 92. Lines (1–3) are struck through in ink; lines (4–12) are in pencil, struck through in pencil.

[105]    Blessed is he knowing well
   Whoever fights, whoever falls,
   Justice conquers evermore,
   And he who fights on its side,
(5)   Though he were ten times slain,
   Is really victor;
   And his enemy
   Though he seem to prevail
   Is in the ↑dragon↓ grasp ⟨of Fate⟩
(10)   And reserved for a crueller ⟨end⟩ ↑fate↓

    ↑Shatter the firmament to motes,↓
   ↑The law will never break↓

[106]  Such another peerless queen
   Only could her mirror show

---

   O Sun! take off thy cloudy hood,
   O land! take off thy chain,
(5)   And fill the world with happy mood,
   And love from main to main.

   Ye shall not on this charter day
   Disloyally withhold
   Their household right from captive men
(10)   By pirates bought & sold

   Ah little knew the innocent
   In throes of birth forlorn,
   That wolves & foxes waited for
   Their ⟨infant⟩victim to be born.

[107]  So white a soul ⟨so b⟩
   a white soul in a swarthy skin
   the dusky children of the sun
   Who wear the livery of the sun
(5)   a candid soul a swarthy skin

   Such another peerless queen
   Only could her mirror show

[108]  Low let
   Low & mournful be the strain

  **105** "Voluntaries," 94?, 95–96, 98–99, 101–3?, 109–10, x, x. In pencil; lines (1–10) are struck through twice in pencil.
  **106** "Such another peerless queen" (1–2); "O sun! take off" (3–14).
  **107** "Voluntaries," x, x, 46, x, x (1–5); "Such another peerless queen" (6–7). In pencil; lines (6–7) are erased.
  **108** "Voluntaries," 1, 1–2, x, 3–8, x, x, 9–13, 13. In pencil, struck through in pencil; lines (15–16) are struck through again in pencil. In line (10), Emerson neglected to cancel "f".

Haughty thot be far from me
⟨Tender penitent⟩
(5) Tones of penitence & pain
Moanings of the ↑tropic↓ sea
Low & mournful in the cell
Where a captive sits in chain↑s↓.
Crooning ditties treasured well
(10) From the ⟨f⟩ burning tropic plains
⟨All that of his youth remains⟩
Only
Sole estate his sires bequeathed
Hapless sires to hapless son
(15) Was the wailing song they breathed
And the chain when life was done
What their fault
↑What↓ their crime

[109]  ⟨only⟩        ↑On the tablet↑s↓ of bamboo↓
                    ↑Read the laws of Wan & Woo↓
Virtues of their race
Gentle natures
(5) Hearts too soft & will to↑o↓ weak
⟨For the Fate⟩
To front the Fate that ⟨gloomed⟩ ↑ambushed↓ near
⟨Ill armed for the unequal fray⟩
Doves beneath the vultures beak
(10) ⟨Singing birds⟩
↑With↓ Songs ⟨per⟩↑dis↓suade the hunters spear

For Truth is shrill as a fife
And various as the voice of men

[110₁] Great men in the senate sate
Sage & hero side by side
⟨To⟩ build ↑⟨plan⟩ for posterity↓ the state
↑Which they shall rule with pride↓

(5) They /forgot/forbore/ to break the chain
↑Which bound the dusky tribe↓
↑The cunning owner scarce would deign↓

109 "On the tablets of bamboo" (1–2); "Voluntaries," 38?, x, 15, 16, 16, x, 17, x, 18, x, x (3–13). In lines (1–2), "only", in pencil, is canceled, and "On the . . . Wan & Woo" added, in ink; lines (3–13) are in pencil; lines (3–4) and (5–11) are struck through separately in pencil. In line (3), "virtues" is spelled "virtures".
110₁ "Voluntaries," 23–28, 29?, 30–32, 32, x, x, 34, four unused lines. In pencil; lines (1–14) are struck through in pencil. Emerson actually added line (7) between lines (9–10) and line (8) between lines (10–11), rather than obscure them.

↑And union was the bribe↓
Fate sat by & said
(10)     Life for life & pang for pang
Ye shall pay

---

⟨No seed shall die⟩
↑No seed shall die no root decay↓
I bring round the harvest day

(15)     Rich & rare ⟨the⟩ ↑their↓ Northern marts
Stout & strong her kings became
Filled earth with their arts
Filled the /heaven/temples/ with their shame

[110₂]     Rich & rare ⟨the⟩ ↑were↓ northern marts
Stout & strong ⟨her⟩ ↑their↓ kings became
Filled earth with their thousand arts
Filled the temples with their fame
(5)     ⟨Filled⟩ ↑Frowned↓ Jehovah at their shame.

[111]     When the glory grew
Grew

⟨It happens oft the good⟩
⟨Their passion⟩ ↑Evil men their crimes un↓bridle
(5)     The good their hopes with patience feed
And resting on their rights sit idle
While
⟨The⟩ ↑Till↓ working gods bring round the deed

When the bad their crimes unbridle
(10)     ⟨Oft⟩ just men oft on patience feed
Resting on their right sit idle
Till ⟨working⟩ gods bring round the ⟨deed⟩ ↑fatal meed↓

[112]     Eternal Rights
Victors over daily wrongs
They work in the dark
Work when men sleep—
(5)     The awful victors,—they misguide
Whom they will destroy.
They ⟨work⟩ ↑prepare↓ alike their triumph
By our victory or our ⟨defeat⟩ ↑fall↓

110₂ "Voluntaries," five unused lines. In line (2), "their" is added in pencil traced over in ink.
111 "Voluntaries," x, x, two drafts of an unused quatrain. In pencil; lines (3–8) are struck through in pencil.
112 "Voluntaries," 114–15, x, x, 116–17, 118?, 119?, x, x, x, 120, x (1–13); "Ring your bells backward" (14–15). Lines (1–13), in pencil, are struck through in pencil.

(10) They are unseen we are seen
    But the power is always hid
    Only ⟨the⟩ Effect glitters
    These are the real gods
    Not the fabled Jove & Mars

    Ring your bells backward, loyal towers!
(15) And warn the land of harm.

[113] See how Romance adheres
    To the deer, the lion,
     and every bird,
    Because they are free
(5) And have no master but Law
    On the wild ice in depths of sea
    On Alp or Andes side
    In the vast abyss of air
    The bird, the flying cloud,
(10) ↑The fire the wind the element↓
    ⟨Is sacred, has no tame manners cowed⟩
    ↑These have not manners coarse or cowed↓
    And no borrowed will
    But ⟨moves as⟩ ↑graceful as↓ cloud & flame
(15) ⟨So graceful⟩
    ⟨All decenci⟨s⟩es fulfill⟩
    All eyes with pleasure fill

[114] You are strong
    ⟨You hold the mountains & the shore⟩
    Throned in the mountains hold the shore
    ⟨All the forges of power⟩
(5) The iron caverns forge your bolts
    ⟨The plains⟩
      ↑The arsenals of power↓
    ↑Rank↓ Hemp flax & cotton grow
    To weave ⟨your⟩ ↑the↓ sails all winds shall blow
(10) Gliding
    Stemming all night the starlit sea
    From ⟨near the⟩ ↑either↓ Pole ⟨to cross the line⟩ ↑across the
     ⟨burning⟩ Line↓
    ↑From ⟨the far⟩ Andes to the Appenine↓
    Freighted with harvests of each clime
(15) With western gold &
    And webs of Indian toil    (see 288)

113 "See how Romance adheres." In pencil.
114 "You strong Republicans," 1–2, 2, x, 3, 7, 7–9, x, 10–12, x, x, x. In pencil; line (13) is
added in ink, and "the far" canceled in pencil.

[114ₐ]  The scarlet maple keys betray
       What potent blood hath modest May

       In May the caterpillar weaves
       His shining tent in appletrees

(5)             The Alchemist
               ↑Well she wist↓
       ⟨Tempers⟩ ↑To slack↓ her fire with icy mist
       She pours a deluge of sunheat
       ⟨Then⟩ launches an iceberg on the sea
(10)     Melting glaciers line the coast
       Tempering the ardent sun

            ⟨The scarlet maple keys betray⟩
            ⟨What potent blood hath modest may⟩

[114ᵦ]  For Genius made his cabin wide
       And ⟨l⟩Love led gods therein to bide

       For what need I of book or priest
       Or Sibyls from the mummied East
(5)     When every star is Bethlehem's star
       I count as many as there are
       Cinquefoils or violets in the grass;
       So many saints ⟨or⟩& saviors,
       So many high behaviors,
(10)     Salute the boy ⟨newly⟩ ⟨↑twelve years↓ alive⟩ ↑of years
           thrice five↓
       Who only sees what he doth give

       Who finds my garden is full fain
       ⟨↑To make his sojourn there↓⟩
       Never to go indoors again
(15)     ⟨But⟩ For life to harbour there

[115]  And more
       the genius of eac⟨ch⟩h race
       Their tongue their arms their arts & song
       And all these severed threads
(5)     You weave
       Into an imperial robe

---

114ₐ "May-Day," 174–75, five unused lines, 242, x, x, x, 174–75. Lines (1–2) are struck through in ink; lines (12–13) are fingerwiped.

   114ᵦ "For Genius made his cabin wide," 1–2 (1–2); "For what need I" (3–11); "My Garden," four unused lines (12–15). Lines (1–2) are struck through twice in ink.

   115 "And more / the genius" (1–9); "You strong Republicans" (10–21). Lines (1–9) are in pencil.

Which cloudlike grows & spreads
Each deephid secret to thy race
Is easily laid bare

(10)       You strong Republicans
Throned in the mountains hold the shore
The iron caverns forge your bolts
The hills are arsenals of power
Fields & prairies without end
(15)       Under your mighty ha↑r↓vest bend
The plains are arsenals of power
Rank hemp & flax & cotton grow
To weave the sails all winds shall blow
Stemming all night the starlit sea
(20)       From either pole to cross the line
From ⟨the ⟨and⟩far⟩ Andes to the Appenine

[116]     Where his name is named
The love of gold is unknown
None ⟨is⟩ ↑so↓ firm in the stirrup ⟨but⟩ ↑as↓ he
And all the realm of Albion is like a puff of air
(5)        He hung the globe in air

Will not the ridge of the

Will not the rose & tulip clim⟨e⟩b
The Alleganys crag sublime

What need of a ⟨stone arch⟩ ↑granite↓ bridge
(10)       When the river is turned to stone

[117]     ↑And↓ California smelts her golden crags
⟨For Liberty to coin her name on it⟩
That Liberty thereon may coin her name

↑And ↑rival↓ Coxcombs↓ ⟨Youth⟩ with enamored stare
(5)        Perused the mysteries of her coiled hair

———————

Love ↑shall↓ wash their swarthy features white

⟨Take not counsel of⟩ ↑Counsel not with↓ flesh & blood
⟨Go in this pass without hand or foot⟩
↑⟨Stay⟩ ↑Loiter↓ not for ⟨garment⟩ ↑cloak↓ nor food↓
(10)       ⟨The⟩ treasure of both worlds lies in the heart
Glory of Solomon ⟨treasures⟩ of Karun's gold

116 "Where his name is named." In pencil.
117 "Boston Hymn," 75?, 76?, 76? (1–3); "And rival Coxcombs" (4–5); "Voluntaries," x (6); "Freedom," two lines first printed as lines 22–23 in the 1867 version (7, 9), seven unused lines (8, 10–15). In pencil; lines (1–3) are struck through twice in pencil, and line (6) once.

Are empty nothings     food for wind
⟨We must⟩ not on ⟨our own works⟩ ↑his works may man↓
    rely
⟨We must by God's grace & help⟩
(15)    But trust the grace of God /on/so/ high

[118]        docile imitative men
With arts of kindness well ⟨supplied⟩ ↑applied↓
⟨And⟩ whose ear each captivating strain
Of Music /searches/fills/ from side to side
(5)        ⟨Who know⟩
        ⟨Except in⟩
        Save Music only, ⟨know⟩ ↑court↓ no Muse
But know by heart the scale of Use
And best of all drew from the sun
(10)    The wine of life the social joy
Simple race
Fidelity to friends
Content
And every feast imperfect were
(15)    Without their arts of joy

[119]    Music stoops
To the parrot on his perch
To the spider on his string

The warhorse loves the trumpet charge

(5)     Bring Beauty to the desolate
Hang ros⟨y⟩es on the stony Fate.

Can the eagle swim in the sea
Will the elephant yoke with the deer
Climb Lapland drifts of snow

[120]        These craggy hills that front the dawn
Manbearing granite of the north
Shall fiercer forms & races spawn
Charged with my genius forth

(5)     Freedom hates the ardent zone
The Northwind best to battle pipes
The snowflakes star our haughty flag
⟨And⟩ ↑Nights↓ northern streamers lend the stripes

118 "docile imitative men." In pencil.
119 "Music stoops" (1–4); "Try the might the Muse affords," 3–4 (5–6); "Can the eagle swim" (7–9). In pencil.
120 "Voluntaries," six unused lines, 41–42, 40–42. In pencil, struck through in pencil; lines (5–11) are struck through additionally three times in pencil.

The dark sky sheds the snow-flake down
(10)    The snow-flake is our banners star
Our stripes the boreal streamers are

[121]    up & the dusky race
That sat in darkness long
Be swift your feet as antelopes,
As Buffaloes be strong

(5)    Freedom all winged expands
Nor perches ⟨long in one ⟨place⟩ ↑region↓⟩ ↑on the pine too
    long↓
She has clung to the cold zone
Whose dark sky sheds the snowflake down
The snowflake is ⟨our⟩ ↑her↓ banners star
(10)    ⟨Our⟩ ↑⟨Its⟩ Her↓ stripes the boreal streamers are
↑Long↓ She ⟨has⟩ loved the Northman well
Now the hour has struck
She will adopt new tribes
She will ⟨love⟩ not ⟨less⟩ ↑refuse to dwell↓
(15)    ↑With↓ The children of the sun
The ⟨man⟩ ↑foundling↓ of the ⟨tropic⟩ ↑desart far↓
of the palm        sirocco
Whose heart is hot with direct rays
Inhabits the region of the summer star

[122]        With the solar blaze
His skin ⟨tinted⟩ ↑is tanned↓ with ⟨the⟩ fire
And his blood boils with love
Freedom
(5)    And he has avenues to God
⟨Not know↑n↓ to⟩ ↑Hid from↓ your ↑northern↓ ⟨wit⟩
    ↑brain↓
⟨And calmly⟩ ↑Far↓ behold↑⟨s⟩ing↓ without ⟨veil⟨s⟩⟩
    ↑cloud↓
⟨That which you toil by slow steps to attain⟩
What your slow steps with toil attain

(10)    He has avenues to God
Hid from your northern brain
Far beholding without cloud
What your slow steps with toil attain

121 "Boston Hymn," 77–80 (1–4); "Voluntaries," 35–36, 39–43, x, x, 45–48, x, 50 (5–19). In pencil, struck through in pencil; lines (1–4) are struck through twice more in pencil.
122 "Voluntaries," four unused lines, 51–54, 51–54. In pencil; lines (5–9) and (9–13) are struck through separately in pencil.

[123]    Low & mournful be the strain
          Haughty thought be far from me
          Tones of penitence & pain,
          Moanings of the tropic sea;
(5)     Low & tender in the cell
          Where a captive sits in chains,
          Crooning ditties treasured well
          From his Afric's torrid plains,
          Sole estate his sire bequeathed,
(10)    Hapless sire to hapless son,
          Was the wailing song he breathed,
          And his chain, when life was done.
          What his fault or what his crime?

[124]        Hearts too soft, & will too weak
         To front the Fate that /ambushed/crouches/ near
         Doves beneath the vultures beak
         Will song dissuade the /hunter's/thirsty/ spear

(5)         Great men in the senate sate
         Sage & hero side by side
         Build↑ing↓ ⟨for posterity⟩ ↑for ⟨their⟩ sons sons↓ the state
         Which they shall rule with pride

         They forbore to break the chain
(10)    Wh↑i↓ch bound the dusky tribe
         Checked by the owners' fierce disdain
         ⟨And⟩ lured by Union as ⟨a⟩the bribe

[125]        Destiny sat by, & said,
         Pang for pang your seed shall pay,
         ⟨Sheathe⟩ ↑Hide↓ ⟨for a⟩ in false peace your coward
           head,
         I bring round the harvest day.

---

(5)     They touch no term, they never sleep,
          In equal strength thro space abide
          Tho feigning ⟨to be⟩ dwarfs ⟨&⟩ ↑they crouch &↓ creep
          ↑The strong they slay, the swift outstride↓
         Fate's grass grows rank in valley clods
(10)    And rankly on the castled steep

123 "Voluntaries," 1–13. In pencil, struck through in pencil.
   124 "Voluntaries," 15–18, 23–30. In pencil; lines (1–4) and (5–12) are struck through separately in pencil.
   125 "Voluntaries," 31–34, six lines first printed in the 1867 version, 120–21. In pencil; lines (1–4) and (5–12) are struck through separately in pencil.

Speak it firmly, these are gods.
↑All are ghosts beside↓

[126]        The thrifty grass of ⟨R⟩Empire nods
On Turret-tops & valley clods.

Fate's grass grows rank in valley clods,
And rankly on the castled steep.

(5)        Unbound by time or space, they range,
They have no term, nor suffer change.
Unlooked for everywhere abide
Not to be bended or defied

[127₁]        Lift a people ⟨to be men⟩ from the dust
⟨Out of ignorance & dust⟩
↑From↓ ⟨Sca⟩Ignorance & self distrust,
/Scars/wales/ of whips & iron rust,

(5)        Scarred upon their manly breast
Say to the outraged exile, rest!

Her heart is wider than the North
More steadfast than the pole
⟨Ever⟩ ↑Still↓ to new ↑men↓ her love goes forth

(10)       ⟨Follows⟩
⟨The wheels of God forever roll⟩
Unstayed her axles roll

---

And pour the strength of human thot
Into his savage brain.

[127₂]    Her heart is wider than the North,
More steadfast than the pole,
Still to new ⟨men⟩ ↑/sons/souls/↓ her love goes forth,—
Unstayed her axles roll.

[128]    ⟨Dragged the boy from his mother's breast⟩
↑Torn from his mothers arms & breast↓
Displaced disfurnished here
And

126 "Voluntaries," several trials for lines first printed in the 1867 version. Struck through in ink.

127₁ "Boston Hymn," 67, five unused lines (1–6); "Her heart is wider," 1–3, 4?, 4, 4 (7–12); "And pour the strength" (13–14). In pencil; lines (1–6) are struck through in ink; lines (7–12) are erased.

127₂ "Her heart is wider."

128 "Voluntaries," 19–22 (1–6); "There went / To his cold urn" (7–18). In pencil; lines (1–6) are struck through in pencil.

(5) His wistful ⟨study⟩ toil to do his best
⟨Met⟩ ↑Chilled↓ with a ribald jeer

---

   There went
T⟨h⟩o his cold urn no ornament
Save the rich ashes which it pent
(10) ↑He asked↓ To his last labor no reward
⟨Save the⟩
But ransom of the ⟨slave⟩ ↑race↓ ⟨outlawed⟩ ↑abhorred↓
But ransom of a race ⟨outlawed⟩ ↑abhorred↓
But ↑arms of↓ stooping angels bound him
(15) When sunk his corpse
⟨Prone⟩ in the bloody clay
And ⟨said⟩ ↑⟨made⟩ changed↓ the night that shut around
   him
↑To↓ Morning ⟨was⟩ of purer day,

[129] O well for the fortunate soul
Which Music's wings enfold,
Stealing ⟨his⟩ ↑away the↓ memory
Of sorrows new & old.
(5) ⟨Better for him⟩ ↑But happier he↓ wh⟨e⟩ose inward sight,
Fixed on his guiding thought,
Shuts his sense ⟨to⟩on toys of time
To vacant bosoms brought:
But best befriended of the God
(10) ⟨Is⟩ he, who, in evil times,
Warned by an inward voice,
Heeds not the darkness & the dread,
Biding by his rule & choice,
Feeling only the fiery thread
(15) Leading over heroic ground,
Walled with mortal peril round

[130] To the aim which him allures
And the sweet Heaven his deed secures.

Stainless soldier on the walls,
Knowing this, ↑—↓ & asks no more, ↑—↓
(5) Whoever fights, whoever falls,
Justice conquers ⟨evermore⟩ ↑as of yore↓;

129 "Voluntaries," 75–90. Struck through in pencil and in ink; the cancellations and additions in lines (3), (5), and (10) are in pencil.
130 "Voluntaries," 91–103. Struck through in pencil and in ink; lines (1–2) are struck through again in pencil. All cancellations and additions are in pencil; a penciled "x" occurs below "⟨evermore⟩" in line (6).

↑Justice after ⟨&⟩as before↓
And he who battles on her side,
God, though he were ten times slain,

(10)    Crowns him victor glorified,
Victor over death & pain:
But his mistaking foe
↑Tho he fancies he prevails↓

[131]    Sleeps within the Dragon coil
↑Within↓ Reserved to a crueller fate

Blooms the laurel which belongs
To the valiant chief who fights;

(5)    I see the ⟨laurel⟩ ↑wreath↓, I hear the songs
Lauding the ⟨e⟩Eternal Rights,
Victors over daily wrongs:
Awful victors, they misguide
Whom they will destroy,

(10)    And their coming triumph hide
In our downfal, or our joy;
Speak it firmly,—these are gods,
All are ghosts beside.

[132]    Teacher of man
There is no orator
Can beckon or persuade
Like thee, the youth or maid

(5)    ↑Nor morn nor eve thy music fails↓
Thy birds thy songs thy brooks thy gales
Thy blooms thy kinds
Thy echoes in the wilderness
↑Heal Age & Pain & loves distress↓

(10)    ⟨↑And fire        & nourish minds↓⟩
↑Fire fainting Will ⟨& nourish⟩ ↑& nerve heroic↓
    minds↓

Thou fair & virtuous spring
Soothsayer of the eldest gods
Revealer of the inmost powers

(15)    Prometheus proffered, Jove denied.
Disclosing treasures more than true,
↑Or in what far tomorrow due↓
Speaking by the tongues of flowers

131 "Voluntaries," 109–21. Struck through in pencil and in ink; lines (1–2) are struck through again in pencil, and "Within" is added in pencil.

132 "May-Day," x, 628–30, x, 631–35, 635, 268, 607, 609–16. In pencil, struck through in pencil; line (12) is overwritten by lines (10–11). In line (19), a caret and "Ten Times" are added, and "ten" is canceled, in ink. This page is reproduced in Plate 5.

↑Ten times↓ By the lily's ⟨ten⟩ tongue⟨s⟩d ↑lily speaking↓
(20)    Singing by the small birds songs
↑Heart of bird the man's heart seeking↓
[133]    When clover paints the purple June

═══════════

None can like thee persuade
Making the splendor of the air
The morn & sparkling dew a snare

(5)    Who can resent
Thy genius wiles & blandishment
When ⟨crocus & ⟨the⟩ cowslip⟩ ↑↑cowslip &↓ shadflower↓ flaunt
↑To deck↓ The morning of the year
⟨Nor⟩ ↑Why↓ tinge thy lustres jubilant
(10)    With forecast or with fear

When all their blooms the meadows flaunt
⟨D⟩To deck the morning of the year
Why tinge thy lustres jubilant
With forecast or with fear?

(15)    ↑Teach me your mood, o patient stars↓
↑That climb each night the ancient sky!↓
↑Leaving on space no shade, no scars,↓
↑No trace of age, no fear to die.↓

[134]    Tired of the prison of the street
The jocund /boy roams wide the fields/stripling leaps the fence/
The air is hungry for his games
The rocks repeat the shouted names
(5)    Each fence provokes a leap
⟨Each⟩ ↑The↓ pebble ⟨freed⟩ ↑loosed↓ from winters frost
Asks of the urchin to be tossed
Each field & lane solicit him
To taste an unknown joy
(10)    The freshened fields the slopes beyond
The wooded hill the shining pond
Salute the happy boy
Sly beams shot from the musing pond

133 "May-Day," x, 623–27 (1–6); "When all their blooms," 1–4, 1–4 (7–14); "Teach me your mood," 1–4 (15–18). Lines (1–10) are in pencil; lines (2–4), (5–8), and (7–10) are struck through separately in pencil.
134 "May-Day," four unused lines, 313, 305–6, six unused lines. In pencil.

[135]     If I ⟨should⟩ ↑could↓ put my woods in song,
          And tell what's here enjoyed,
          All men wou:ld to th⟨e⟩is⟨e⟩ garden⟨s⟩ throng,
          And leave the cities void.

(5)     ↑(↓For joy & beauty planted it
          With faerie ⟨gardens⟩lustres cheered,
          And boding Fancy haunted it,
          With men & women weird.↑)↓

          In cities high, thro' crowds of cares,
(10)      The wo-worn mortals darkling go,
          But in these sunny solitudes
          My quiet roses blow.

          In my garden, three ways meet,
          Thrice the spot is blest,
(15)      Hermit thrush comes there to build,
          Carrier doves to rest.

[136]     In my garden, oaken copse
          The eager wind detains,
          Sultry summer lingers there
          When Autumn chills the plains.

(5)       ↑In my plot no tulip⟨s⟩ blow↑s↓↓
          ↑Snow loving pines & oaks instead↓
              ↑Selfsown my stately garden grows↓

          And chiefest thee, whom Genius loved,
          Daughter of sounding seas,
(10)      Whom Nature pampered in these lawns,
          And lavished all to please⟨.⟩

          ⟨She had⟩ ↑What↓ wealth of mornings in her year,
          ⟨And⟩ ↑What↓ planets in her sky,
          She chose her best thy heart to cheer,
(15)      Thy beauty to supply.

              Now younger ⟨lov‖ . . ‖⟩ ↑pilgrims↓ find the stream
              The willows & the vine,
              But aye to me the happiest seem
              To draw the dregs of wine.

135 "My Garden," 1–4 (1–4); "For joy & beauty" (5–8); "In my garden three ways meet,"
17–20, 1–4 (9–16). Lines (1–4) are struck through in ink; the cancellations and additions in
lines (1) and (3), and the parentheses around lines (5–8), are in pencil.
136 "In my garden three ways meet," 5–8 (1–4); "My Garden," 5–6 (5–6); "In my garden
three ways meet," 9, 33–44 (7–19). Lines (5–7) are in pencil; the cancellations and additions in
lines (12–13) are in pencil.

[137]      What need I holier dew
Than Waldens haunted wave
Distilled from Heaven's alembic blue
⟨And⟩ steeped in each forest cave.

(5)      In my plot no tulips blow
Snow loving pines & oaks instead

Selfsown my stately garden grows
The winds & windblown seed
Cold april rain & colder snows
(10)     My hedges plant & feed.

From mountains far, & valleys near,
The harvest brought today
Shall thrive in all weathers without fear
Wild planters, plant away!

(15)     ↑Who finds my garden is full fain↓
↑Never to go in doors again↓
↑For life to harbor there↓

[138]          Papas Blondine
Grew tall & wise
Eschewing vanities
And loved the truth
(5)      Can Truth suffice?
The years shall show:
Truth is ⟨on⟩ ↑put upon↓ its trial
Her judgment will not brook denial
↑In her large memory↓
(10)     ↑Is never fact forgotten↓
And she will know
If Truth's as true as she
In act↑ion↓ & ↑& in↓ word
If the false world can afford
(15)     That any sterling be

[139]      And if it ⟨be⟩ ↑prove↓ that things are rotten
She will frankly call them so
She who is real,
⟨And⟩ ↑She who↓ cannot aught conceal,

137 "In my garden three ways meet," 25–28 (1–4); "My Garden," 5–6 (5–6); "In my garden three ways meet," 9–16 (7–14); "My Garden," three unused lines (15–17). In pencil; lines (5–6) are struck through in pencil; in line (13), "Shall" is circled in pencil. Lines (15–17) are written vertically in the right margin.
   138 "Papas Blondine," 1–15. In pencil.
   139 "Papas Blondine," 16–30. In pencil; the cancellation and addition in line (9) are in ink.

(5)    She that hypocrisy disdains,
Never palters, never feigns,
But w⟨i⟩ell believes
⟨Thus⟩That she may dare
⟨Speak⟩ ↑Confess↓ her faith in any air
(10)   That honest meaning will not fail
⟨Oer⟩ over false⟨o⟩hood to prevail
↑↑She will↓ Launch her thought nor↓ ⟨never⟩ ⟨b⟩fear it
Speak the truth to ⟨those⟩ ↑who↓ will hear it.
But still as now
(15)   With pure good will

[140]       And Bounty sculptured on thy brow
⟨And⟩ give the ⟨passing⟩ ↑downhearted↓ world
Hints of Eternal cheer.

⟨Be of good cheer⟩
(5)    Brave ⟨girl⟩ ↑maid↓ obey thy heart
Accept what rule it shall impart
Nor heed one word of all the voices gay
Which in their manifolded quire
Stoop to ⟨the strong⟩ ↑Fashion↓ & stoop to please
(10)   ⟨And⟩ flatter worthless ease
Stoop to

[141]   In every house a welcome guest
For her good heart & ⟨her keen⟩ ↑searching↓ eye
Though she bring this sunlike test
⟨And bring⟨s⟩ not⟩ ⟨↑Instead of↓⟩ ↑In lieu of↓ a polished lie.
(5)    She can weave & embroider
Can write & draw
And like a mirror report
↑Orderly beautiful↓ All ⟨that⟩ she sees
But when she signs her name
(10)   ↑With plain verity content↓
⟨She⟩ ↑Never↓ prefixe⟨s⟩d ⟨no⟩a compliment
And ⟨where she associates⟩ ↑in whatever circle came↓
⟨She speaks none⟩
↑Never stooped to utter one↓

[142] Beauty prevails by novelty   unexpectedness. We had settled it that we knew men & women, they were all of one kind, & we could readily count the gradations from the type to any particular face &

140 "Papas Blondine," 31–40, 39. In pencil.
141 "Papas Blondine," 41–53, 53. In pencil.
142 "Papas Blondine," 54–59. In pencil. The prose at the top of the page, probably inscribed earlier, is circumscribed in pencil.

form. But here is one we had not seen or thot of, not so to be classed,
& we are forced to admire what we cannot understand

⟨One⟩ who if polite society
Did not exist, would it invent,
⟨And ⟨show⟩ by⟩ ↑By her↓ practice ↑show↓ its ⟨best⟩ laws,
Grace without compliment.

(5)   Grace that grows from pure intent
Grace that fascinates & draws

[143]   ⟨Go⟩ ↑Advance↓ ⟨through⟩ life as now
⟨Or⟩Bearer of good news
⟨Or telling ill news just the same⟩
↑Or if ⟨evil tidings⟩ ↑disaster↓ come↓

(5)   ⟨Ill⟩ ↑Evil↓ news were not allowed
⟨t⟩To dim her eye, ⟨or⟩ ↑her aspect↓ cloud ⟨her brow⟩
Or ⟨muffle⟩ ↑choke↓ her cheerful voice
⟨S⟩Tell ill news as thou tellest good
Nor ⟨mix thyself⟩ ↑mar thy quiet↓ in the broil

(10)   Adorn thy self with ⟨hardship⟩ ↑hardihood↓
With ice bath ↑fortify the blood↓, a↑r↓ctic winds ⟨about
thy sleep⟩ ↑blew round her bed↓
Hard fare & ⟨toil for⟩ charitable toil

[144]   O joyful spring could bard divine
The ⟨rede⟩ ↑lay↓ thou ⟨breathest⟩ ↑sing'st↓ to human souls
↑Murmured on all thy mountain airs↓
Where thy gentle deluge rolls

(5)   ⟨Heat marked with cold⟩
↑And winters wilderness repairs↓
Summer hid in chilling clouds
Day following day in opal shroud
Each a porter of Jove's fire

(10)   Charged to heat the willing earth
⟨With love & birth⟩
With love & impulse tilth & birth
As the ↑grey↓ cloud ⟨lies⟩ on the air
So on thy mystic element

(15)   Lie the ↑opal colored↓ days
⟨And⟩ ↑And waft↓ the miracle ⟨is wafted⟩ to man

[145]   ↑We hear no words our sense they balk.↓
⟨We⟩ see not the legs on which they wa⟨k⟩lk

143 "Papas Blondine," 60–61, 66, 62–70. In pencil.
144 "May-Day," seven unused lines, 605?, five unused lines, 604–6. In pencil, struck through in pencil.
145 "May-Day," six unused lines, 353/354, 355, 356/357, 351–52, x, 604–6. In pencil; lines (7–9), (10–15), and (12–15) are struck through separately in pencil.

⟨No feet are⟩
⟨The⟩ skirts ⟨are⟩ not lifted from
(5) the feet—of Isis, ↑reverend & sweet↓
But ↑comes↓ the mystic procession ⟨comes⟩ duly,
Every star, every god, ⟨every virtue is there,⟩ ↑each force
  amain↓
Marches duly in her train
And fainting nature ↑at her need↓ is made whole again

(10) ↑On carpets green↓ The maskers march
Under May's well-appointed arch
as the grey cloud in the air
So on thy mystic element
Sail the opal colored days
(15) And waft the miracle to man

[146] The ground pines wash their rusty green
The maple ↑tops their↓ crimson tint
↑on↓ The soft⟨ened⟩ path ⟨reports⟩ each track is seen
The girls foot leaves its neater print

(5) Blithe with the air's persuasion sweet
Today the stripling hates the street
He leaps the fence, roams wide the field.
The air is hungry for his games,
The rocks repeat the shouted names.
(10) The pebble, loosened by the frost,
Asks of the urchin to be tossed.
The brimming brook invites a leap
He dives the hollow, climbs the steep,
Pasture & lane so⟨c⟩licit him
(15) To taste an unknown joy
The nearer fields, the slopes beyond
The wood crowned cliff, the shining pond
Salute the happy boy.

[147] *Nature*
By kinds I keep my kinds in check
I plant the oak, the rose I deck.
↑Bring beauty to the desolate, ↓
↑Hang roses on the stony Fate. ↓

146 "May-Day," 301–4, five unused lines, 305–6, 313–14, five unused lines. Lines (1–4), in pencil, are struck through twice in pencil; lines (5–13) are struck through with three lines in ink, one of which extends to line (15) but is fingerwiped below line (13).
147 "By kinds I keep" (1–2); "Try the might the Muse affords," 3–4 (3–4); "May-Day," 93–97 (5–9); "My Garden," 51–52 (10–11); "And he like me" (12–13). In pencil; lines (5–9) are struck through in pencil with one line, and lines (10–11) with two.

(5)               The world rolls round mistrust it not
Befals again what once befel
All things return both sphere & mote
And I shall hear my bluebirds note
And dream the dream of Auburn dell

(10) *Nature* What I cannot declare
            Yet cannot all ⟨reveal⟩ ↑withhold↓

And he like me is not too proud
To be the poet of the crowd

[148]        ⟨Tell men⟩Try the might the Muse affords
And the balm of thoughtful words
Tell men what they knew before
Paint the prospect from ⟨their⟩your door

(5)     The asmodean feat is mine
To spin my sand heap into twine.

The sun & /moon/planets/ /shall fall/fell/ amain
Like sower's seeds into his brain,
There quickened to be born again.

(10)     Ring of ⟨the⟩ axe, ↑or↓ hum of ⟨the⟩ wheel,
And gleam which Use will paint on steel.

The gleam which Use bestows on steel.

Like vaulters ⟨of⟩ ↑in↓ the circus round,
Who ⟨leap⟩step from horse to horse, and never touch the
        ground.

[149]   For every god
Obeys the hymn    obeys the ode
Obeys the holy ode

      ⟨For⟩ ↑By↓ art, ⟨for⟩ ↑by↓ music, overthrilled
(5)     The wine⟨glass⟩ ↑cup↓ shakes, the wine is spilled.

See NP 300

148 "Try the might the Muse affords," 1–2 (1–2); "Tell men what they knew before" (3–4);
"The Asmodaean feat" (5–6); "Charmed from fagot," 5–7 (7–9); "There are beggars," 23–24,
24, (10–12); "Like vaulters in the circus round" (13–14). The words "planets" and "fell" in line
(7), and the cancellations and addition in line (10), are in pencil.
149 "For every god" (1–3); "By art, by music" (4–5); "Charmed from fagot," 1–4 (6–9);
"The Muses' hill" (10–11). Lines (1–3) and "See NP 300" are in pencil. "See NP 300" is partly
circumscribed on the right, apparently to connect it with lines (7–9) on p. [148] opposite,
another draft of which occurs in notebook NP, p. [300].

Charmed from fagot & from steel,
Harvests grew upon his tongue:
Past & Future must reveal
All their heart whilst Merlin sung.

(10)  The Muses' hill by Fear is guarded,
    A bolder foot is still rewarded.

[150]          Rome March 22  1833
    Alone in Rome! Why Rome is lonely too,
    Virtue alone is sweet society.
    It keeps the key to all heroic hearts,
    And opens you a welcome ⟨to them all.⟩ ↑when you dare. ↓
(5)   You must be like them, if you challenge them,
    Scorn trifles, & embrace a better aim
    Than wine, or sleep, or praise,
    Hunt knowledge, as the lover woos a maid,
    And ever, in the strife of your own tho'ts,
(10)  Obey the nobler impulse. That is Rome.
    That shall command a senate to your side
    For there is no force in the universe
    That can contend with love.
    Wait then, sad friend, wait in majestic peace
(15)  The hour of Heaven
           ↑See *P* 215, 216, 217. ↓

[151]    O strong & virtuous spring
    Cheerful broadsowing spring
    Searching underneath the mould
    For grains beyond the price of gold
(5)   Stirring roots & ripening bread
    That man & all the kinds be fed
    So deep & large thy bounties are
    That one broad long mid ↑-↓ summer day
    Will to the planet overpay
(10)  The ravage of a year of war

---

*Poet*
      as in a letter
   We have not better things to say,
   But surely say them better.

150 "Alone in Rome!," 1, 8–21. The cancellation and addition in line (4) are in pencil; "See *P* . . . 217." is in pencil.
 151 "May–Day," 268–71, 89–90, 272–75 (1–10); "Letters" ("The tongue"), 2–4 (11–13); "Poet of poets," 92–95 (14–17); "From Nature's beginning," 13–16 (14–17). Lines (1–10) are struck through in ink; in line (8), the hyphen in "mid-summer" is added in pencil.

(15)    If the crown once incloses
The brows of her son,
The muse him deposes
From kingdom & throne.

[152]    The land that has no song
Shall have a song today,
The granite ledge is dumb too long,
The vales have much to say:
(5)    For you can teach the lightning speech,
And round the globe your voices reach.

The rocky nook with hilltops three
Looked eastward from the farms
And twice ⟨a⟩ ↑each↓ day the flowing sea
(10)    Took Boston in its arms.
The men of yore were stout & poor
And sailed for bread to every shore

[153]    The waves that rocked them on the deep
To them their secret told,
Said the winds that sung the lads to sleep
'Like us be free & bold.'
(5)    The honest waves refuse to slaves
The empire of the ocean caves.

And where they went on trade intent
They did what freemen can,
Their dauntless ways did all men praise,
(10)    The merchant was a man,
The world was made for honest trade,
To plant & eat be none afraid.

[154]    Fair rose the planted hills behind
The good town on the Bay
And where the western slopes declined
The prairie stretched away.

[155]    *Poet*
Hold of the ⟨m⟩Maker, not the made,
Sit with the Cause, or grim or glad.

---

152 "Boston," four unused lines, 108–9, 1–6. The cancellation and addition in line (9) are in pencil.

153 "Boston," 13–18, 7–12.

154 "Boston," 39–42.

155 "Hold of the Maker" (1–2); "The comrade or the book," 1–2 (3–4); "There are beggars," 54–55 (5–6); "By art, by music" (7–8); "The comrade or the book" (9–14); "In building or in poem," x, 1–2 (15–17). Lines (3–4) are heavily canceled.

⟨The book is good⟩
⟨That puts me in a working mood.⟩

(5)　　　　↑A crystal Soul↓
　　　　↑Sphered & concentric to the Whole. ↓

⟨For⟩ ↑By↓ art↑,↓ ⟨for⟩ ↑by↓ music overthrilled↑,↓
The winecup shakes↑,↓ the wine is spilled↑.↓

The book is good
(10)　That puts me in a working mood.
　　　Unless to Thought ⟨is⟩be added Will,
　　　Apollo is an imbecile.
　　　What parts, what ⟨gems⟩ ↑truths,↓ what ⟨colors⟩ ↑fancies↓
　　　　　shine!
　　　Ah! but I ⟨lack⟩ ↑miss↓ the grand design.

————————————————————

(15)　　　　↑————he cared not for the form, ↓
　　　↑In building or in poem caught the rhyme, ↓
　　　↑And drank the wit in prayer or pantomime. ↓

[156]　　　The Doctors in the college hall⟨s⟩
　　　　　Praelect thro dreary hours
　　　　　But in each pause he heard the call
　　　　　Of robins out of doors

(5)　　The air is wise↑,↓ ⟨the⟩ the ⟨sea⟩ ↑wind↓ thinks well
　　　And all thro↑'↓ which it blows
　　　If plant⟨s⟩ or brain↑,↓ if egg or ⟨shell⟩ ↑cell↓
　　　Or bird or biped knows

　　　And oft at home mid tasks I heed↑,↓
(10)　I heed how wears the day↑;↓
　　　We must not halt while fiercely speed
　　　The spans of life away↑.↓

　　　What boots it here of Thebes or Rome
　　　Or lands of Eastern day.
(15)　In forests, I am still at home,
　　　And there I cannot stray

[156ₐ]　⟨Sixty Six⟩
　　　　⟨Shall⟩

　　　One night he dreamed of a palace fair

156 "How drearily in College hall." In line (5) "the" is canceled in pencil; the added punctuation is in pencil.
156ₐ "One night he dreamed" (1–8); "May–Day," 245 (9–13). "Sixty Six" and "Shall" are fingerwiped at the top of the page; "One night" in line (1) is heavily blotted; lines (9–13) are struck through in ink.

Next year it ⟨rose⟩ ↑stood↓ in marble strong,
⟨And⟩ sheltered ⟨a⟩ ↑nations↓ mighty
⟨There sate the fathers of the state⟩
(5)    ↑⟨The⟩ grave ⟨old⟩ Seigneurs sat in council there↓
There ⟨met the⟩ echoed Freedom's shrill debate

A thousand years it will stand the same
Enacting laws & breathing fame

Perfuming weeds with
(10)   Sweetens weeds with
Enhancing weeds with Syrian spices
Drugging grass with Sy
Drugging herbs with Syrian spices

[156ᵦ]   feathered mercury
      See Webster's dictionary *ad verbum* feathered.

---

I came in March
I passed in March the orchard through
And
I paced in March the crunching snow
(5)    Tinkled every ice clad bough
When twoscore weeks were past & gone
I came

[157]   ⟨↑⟨Stay⟩ ⟨Calm⟩ ↑Shun↓ passion, fold the hands of Thrift,↓⟩
      ⟨Sit still, & truth is near,⟩
      ⟨Suddenly it will uplift⟩
      ⟨Your eyelids to the ⟨light⟩ ↑sphere↓,⟩
      ⟨↑Wait a little,↓ And you shall see⟩
      ⟨The portraiture of things to be⟩

↑I walk in marble galleries,↓
↑And talk with kings the while.↓

Shun passion, fold the hands of thrift,
(10)   Sit still, and Truth is near;
Suddenly it will uplift
Your eye-lids to the sphere,
Wait a little, you shall see
The portraiture of things to be.

156ᵦ "May–Day," seven unused lines.
157 "Shun Passion" (1–6); "In my garden three ways meet," 31–32 (7–8); "Shun Passion" (9–14). Line (1) is added in grey ink, emended in black ink; lines (1–6) are canceled horizontally through each line and struck through vertically several times in ink.

[158]  ↑These rules were writ in human heart↓
↑By him who built the day,—↓
↑The columns of the firmament↓
↑Not ⟨firmer⟩ ↑deeper↓ based than they. ↓

(5)  Though Love ⟨shall weep,⟩ ↑repine,↓ & Reason chafe,
I hear a ⟨⟨vo⟩call⟩ ↑voice↓ without reply,
'Tis man's perdition to be safe,
When for the truth he ought to die.'

———

This shining hour is an edifice
(10)  Which the omnipotent cannot rebuild.

———

↑————————↓
↑My Garden↓
↑————————↓

Methought the sky looked scornful down
On all ⟨was⟩ ↑that's↓ base in man,
And airy tongues did taunt the town—
Achieve us, if you can.

(15)       I walk in marble galleries
And talk with kings the while

[159]        ↑Turn the key & bolt the door↓
↑Sweet is death forevermore↓
↑Nor haughty hope nor swart chagrin↓
↑Nor murdering hate can enter in↓

*The Past.*

(5)  The debt is paid,
The verdict said,
The Furies laid,
The Plague was stayed,
All fortunes made;
(10)  All is now secure & fast,
Not the gods can shake the Past,
Flies-to the adamantine door
Bolted down forevermore.

158 "The rules to men" (1–4); "Sacrifice" (5–8); "Now" (9–10); "In my garden three ways
meet," 21–24, 31–32 (11–16). Lines (5–8) are struck through in ink; "My Garden," the rules
above and below it, and lines (15–16) are in pencil. In line (11), Emerson wrote "the scornful
sky looked down", then added "⟨2⟩3" under "scornful", "1" under "sky", and "2" under
"looked".
159 "The Past," 6–9, 1–5, 10–21. Struck through in ink; lines (1–4) are added in the upper
right margin and struck through in ink.

None can reenter there,—
(15)    No thief so politic,
No Satan with a royal trick
Steal in by window, chink, or hole,
To bind or unbind, add what lacked,
Insert a leaf, or forge a name,
(20)    New-face or finish what is packed,
Alter or mend eternal Fact.

[160]    To the mizen, the main, & the fore,
Up with it once more,
The old tricolor,
The ribbon of power,
(5)    ↑The↓ White, blue, & red, which the nations adore.

It was down at half-mast
For a grief that is past,
⟨But that cannot last.⟩
↑To the emblem of glory no sorrow can last.↓
(10)    ⟨We have lost our chief⟩ ↑Our captain has perished,↓ the
loyal & strong,
But we must not mourn long,
For the flag has defenders
Three score ↑& more↓ millions
Guard Freedom's pavillions

↑'On Saturday, 14 June, 1777, Congress "resolved that the flag of the Thirteen United States be thirteen stripes alternate red & white; that the union be thirteen stars, white in a blue field, representing a new constellation" [George] *Bancroft*, [*A History of the United States . . .*, 10 vols. (Boston, 1834–1875),] Vol. IX. [1866] p. 352↓

[161]    A puff of air or dry or damp
Shall burn the town or quench the lamp
As the babe to the mothers breast
We are tied to the element
(5)    By ⟨force that⟩ ↑hands no↓ Will can⟨t prevent⟩
↑circumvent↓
⟨As the babe to the mothers breast⟩
Through the world east & west
⟨We are⟩ ↑Pupils &↓ children of the wind
Since ⟨or ever⟩ ↑our forefather↓ Adam sinned
(10)    And as sinks or mounts the song
We are ⟨feeble⟩ impotent or strong
A whiff of ⟨wind⟩ ↑air↓ will make the odds

160 "To the mizen, the main, & the fore."
161 "A puff of air." In pencil.

Between the victim & the gods
As blows from divers points the gale

(15) The man shall prosper or shall fail

[162] But for the chief, his fortune's made,
And if at height, no whit decayed.

———

Around the man who seeks a noble end
not angels but divinities attend.

———

(5) Easy to ⟨do⟩ ↑match↓ what others do,
⟨And do⟩ ↑Perform↓ the feat as well as they.
Hard to outdo ⟨the⟩ the ⟨best⟩ ↑wise↓, the true,
And find a loftier way.
The school decays, the learning spoils,

(10) Because of the sons of wine;
How
Canst ⟨rescue⟩ ↑⟨save⟩ snatch↓ the ⟨youth⟩ ↑stripling↓ from
     their toils
One ⟨ray of the beam⟩ ↑Yet can one ray of truth↓ divine
The ⟨⟨b⟩rays⟩ ↑blaze↓ of the ⟨torch⟩ ↑reveller's feasts↓
     outshine

(15) Great & beautiful power
These & justly ours
The lists are open to all feet

[163]                    In Memoriam:
                            E.B.E.
              I mourn upon this battlefield,
     But not for those who perished here
     Behold the riverbank
     Whither the angry farmers came

(5) In sloven dress & broken rank,
     Nor thought of fame.
     Their deed of blood
     All mankind praise,
     Even the serene Reason says,

(10) It was well done.
     The wise & simple have one glance
     To greet yon stern head-stone,
     Which more of pride than pity gave
     To mark the Briton's friendless grave.

162 "But for the chief" (1–2); "Around the man" (3–4); "Easy to match what others do"
(5–14); "Great & beautiful power" (15–17). Lines (5–14) are struck through in ink; in line (7),
"the" is canceled in pencil; in line (11), "save" is canceled, and "match" added, in pencil.
163 "In Memoriam. E.B.E.," 1–14. Struck through in ink.

[164]         Yet it is a stately tomb,
                The grand return
                Of Eve & Morn,
                ↑⟨The waving grass⟩The year's fresh bloom↓
(5)           The silver cloud,
                Might grace the dust that is most proud.

                Yet not of these I muse
                In this ancestral place,
                But of a kindred face
(10)       That never joy or hope shall here diffuse.

                Ah ⟨O⟩brother⟨,⟩! of the brief but blazing star,
                What hast thou to do with these
                Haunting this bank's historic trees

[165]         ↑Thou↓ Born for noblest life
                For actions ⟨strife⟩ ↑field↓, for ⟨triumphs⟩ ↑victor's↓
                    car,
                Thou living champion of the right
                ↑To these their penalty belonged,↓
(5)           I grudge not these their bed of death,
                But thine to thee, who never wronged
                The poorest that drew breath.

                All inborn power that could
                Consist with homage to the good
(10)       Flamed from his martial eye,
                He who seemed a soldier born,
                He should have the helmet worn
                All friends to fend, all foes defy,
                Fronting foes of God & man
(15)       ⟨Frowning down the evil doer⟩

[166]       Frowning down the evil doer
                ⟨And⟩ battling for the weak & poor,
                His from youth the leader's look
                Gave the law which others took,
(5)           And never poor beseeching glance
                Shamed that sculptured countenance.

---

**164** "In Memoriam. E.B.E.," 15–27. Struck through in ink. In line (4), "The waving grass", added in pencil, is overwritten by "The year's fresh bloom" in ink; in line (11), Emerson may have begun an indented line "O" and overwritten it with "Ah brother!"

**165** "In Memoriam. E.B.E.," 28–42. Struck through in ink; "Thou" in line (1) and the two short rules in mid-page are in pencil.

**166** "In Memoriam. E.B.E.," 42–49, 51–54. Struck through in ink; in line (8), "the" is canceled in both pencil and ink.

There is no record left on earth
Save on ⟨the⟩ tablets of the heart
Of the grace that on him shone
(10)    Of eloquent lips of joyful wit
He could not frame ⟨an act⟩ ↑⟨speak⟩ a word↓ unfit.
An act unworthy to be done

[167]  Persian
Teach your child to earn his meal,
Or you bring him up to steal.

———————

Only three things lengthen life,—
Fine clothes, fine house, & ⟨a beautiful⟩ ↑comely↓ wife.

(5)  ———————

For pearls, plunge in⟨to⟩ the sea
For greatness, wake all night

_____

Honor prompted every glance,
Honor came & sat beside him,
In lowly cot & painful road,
(10)    And evermore the cruel god
Cried 'Onward!' & the palm-crown showed.

[168]  Firm on his heart relie⟨e⟩d
What lot so⟨e⟩eer betide,
↑Work of his hand↓
He nor repents nor grieves,
(5)    Pleads for itself the fact;
As unrepenting Nature leaves
Her every act.

Born for success he seemed,
With grace to win, with heart to hold,
(10)    With shining gifts which took all eyes,
With budding power in College Halls.
Pledged in a future day to forge
Thunders to ⟨shake⟩fend the State or scourge
Tyrants despite their guards or walls.

[169]  On his young promise Beauty smiled,
↑Drew his free homage unbeguiled↓
And prosperous Age held out his hand,

167 "Teach your child" (1–2); "Only three things" (3–4); "For pearls, plunge in" (5–6); "In Memoriam. E.B.E.," 55–59 (7–11). The heading and lines (1–6) are in pencil; lines (7–11) are struck through in ink.

168 "In Memoriam. E.B.E.," 90–96, 60–66. Lines (1–7) and (8–14) are struck through separately in ink.

169 "In Memoriam. E.B.E.," 67–72, 97–104, 73–75. Lines (1–6) and (15–17) are struck through separately in ink; lines (7–14) are heavily canceled with vertical lines and loops in ink.

↑And richly for his future planned↓
(5) And troops ⟨fr⟩of friends enjoyed the ⟨hour,⟩ ↑tide↓
All, all was given, & only health denied.

⟨Then fell the bolt on the branching oak,⟩
⟨The rainbow of his hope was broke,⟩
⟨No craven cry, no secret tear,⟩
(10) ⟨He told no pang, he knew no fear,⟩
⟨Its peace sublime his aspect kept,⟩
⟨His purpose woke, his features slept.⟩
⟨And yet between the spasms of pain⟩
⟨His genius beamed with joy again.⟩

(15) I see him with superior smile
Hunted by Sorrow's grisly train
In lands remote, in toil & pain
[170] With angel patience labor on,
Nor lose the lofty port he wore,
When, foremost of the youthful band,
The prizes in all lists he won;
(5) Nor bate one jot of heart or hope,
And, least of all, the loyal tie
Which holds to home 'neath every sky,
The joy & pride the pilgrim feels
In ⟨those who⟩ ↑/hearts/mates/ which↓, round the hearth at
home,
(10) Keep pulse for pulse with those ⟨that⟩ ↑who↓ roam.

What generous beliefs console
The brave whom Fate denies the goal,
If others reach it, is content,
To Heaven's high will his will is bent.

[171] Fell the bolt on the branching oak,
The rainbow of his hope was broke,
No craven cry, no secret tear,
He told no pang, he knew no fear
(5) Its peace sublime his aspect kept,
His purpose woke, his features slept.
And yet between the spasms of pain
His genius beamed with joy again.

Now o'er thy dust the endless smile
(10) Of summer in thy Spanish isle.
Hints never loss or ⟨evil⟩cruel break

170 "In Memoriam. E.B.E.," 76–89. Struck through in ink.
171 "In Memoriam. E.B.E.," 97–116. Struck through in ink.

And sacrifice for love's dear sake,
Nor mourn the unalterable Days
That genius goes, Folly stays.
(15)    What matters how, or from what ground,
The freed soul its creator found?
Alike thy memory embalms
That orange grove, that isle of palms,
And these loved banks whose oakboughs bold
(20)    Root in the blood of heroes old.

[172]    Coin the daydawn into lines
In which its proper splendor shines;
Coin the moonlight into verse
Which all its marvels shall rehearse

(5)    Charmed from fagot & from steel
Harvests grew upon his tongue

———

Chasing with words fast flowing things
        Nor try
To plant thy sh⟨iv⟩rivelled pedantry
(10)    On the shoulders of the sky

[173]    Thanks to those who go & come
Bringing Hellas, Thebes, & Rome,
As near to me as is my home:
⟨Those⟩Careful husbands of the mind
(5)    Who keep decaying history good,
And do not suffer Tyre or Troy
To know decrepitude.

———

And what he knew he rightly knew
From winds discoursing as they flew
(10)    Discoursed of fortune as they flew
Dear omens filled the air
To him authentic witness bare
Birds bore auguries on their wings
Chanted undeceiving things—
(15)    He scorned
To learn of scribe & courier
Things writ in vaster character
And on his mind at dawn of day
Soft shadows of the evening lay.

172 "Coin the daydawn" (1–4); "Charmed from fagot," 1–2 (5–6); "Borrow Urania's subtile wings," 2–5 (7–10). Lines (5–6) are in pencil.
173 "Thanks to those" (1–7); "Fate" ("Delicate omens"), x, x, x, 1–4, 6–10 (8–19).

[174]          The solid solid Universe
                 Is pervious to Love,
                 With bandaged eyes he never errs
                 Around, below, above;
(5)             His blinding light
                 He flingeth white
                 On God's & Satan's brood,
                 And reconciles
                 By mystic wiles
(10)          The evil & the good.

[175] Good is Taliessin's Invocation of the wind at the door of Castle Teganwy.

"Discover thou what it is, the strong creature ⟨without⟩from before the flood, without flesh, without bone, without head, without feet. It will neither be older nor younger than at the beginning. It has no fear, nor the rude wants of created things. Great God! how the sea whitens, when it comes! Great are its gusts, when it comes from the south. Great is the exhaustion of man from its rapid motion. It is in the field, it is in the wood, without hand, without foot, without age, without season, & it is always of the same age with the five ages of ages; and likewise it is old some ages of ⟨ages⟩years. And it is of [176] equal breadth with the surface of the earth. And it was not born, & is not seen. It makes perturbation in the place where God wills, on the sea, on the land. It sees not nor is seen, and it is not fickle, it does not come when desired. it will not be advised to the contrary. It has no form, it bears no burden, for it is void of sin." &c. &c.   *Nash Taliesin & the Bards of Britain*. p. 171[-72]

[177]                 *Song of Taliesin*  ↑*(See Nash p. 167.)*↓
          ⟨Puny⟩ ↑⟨Poor⟩ Vain↓ Bards⟨,⟩↑!↓ I can ⟨declare⟩ ↑discover all,↓
          What ⟨is & what⟩ ↑befel or↓ shall befal.
          I come seeking what is lost,
          And my aim shall not be crossed.
(5)       Strong am I ⟨in⟩who this demand,
          More strong my ⟨lay⟩ ↑/tongue/word/↓ than Arthur's hand
          Three hundred ↑potent↓ songs & more
          Are hidden in the strain I pour:

174 "Cupido."
175–76 David William Nash, *Taliesin; or, The Bards and Druids of Britain, A Translation of the Remains of the Earliest Welsh Bards, and an Examination of the Bardic Mysteries* (London, 1858). See JMN 16:12–13. " 'Discover thou . . . on the land." is used, set in verse form, in "Poetry and Imagination," W 8:58. Pages [175] and [176] are each struck through in pencil with a large X.
177 "Song of Taliesin."

No foe ↑men↓ ⟨⟨shall⟩doth⟩ in ⟨my circles⟩ ↑these
    mountains↓ dwell
(10)    On whom I cannot cast a spell;
⟨Neither⟩ ↑Nor↓ stone ↑nor brass,↓ nor iron ring
Can ⟨hold⟩ ↑fetter↓ Elphin when I sing;
⟨What⟩ ↑All that↓ I seek ⟨for, that I⟩ ↑this hand can↓ find,
↑All↓ Gate↑s↓ ⟨I⟩ unbar, ⟨&⟩ ↑all↓ bonds unbind.

[178]    ⟨Ploughed he⟩ ↑He planted↓ where the deluge ploughed
His hired hands were wind & ⟨rain⟩ ↑cloud↓
His eyes detect the gods concealed
In the hummock of the field

[179] ————————

With the key of the secret he marches faster
From strength to strength, & for night brings day,
While clas↑s↓es or races too weak to master
The new conditions of life give way.

————————

(5)    If wishes would carry me over the land,
I would ride with loose bridle today,
I would greet every tree with a grasp of my hand,
I would drink of each river, & swim in each bay.

[180]        Seemed, tho' the soft sheen all enchants,
Cheers the rough crag & mournful dell,
As if on such stern forms & haunts,
A wintry storm more fitly fell.

(5)    The farthest from the root the sweetest grape.

That each should in his house abide
Therefore was the world so wide. *LM* 127

[181]    Nature saith,
I am not infinite,
But imprisoned & bound,
Tool of mind,
(5)    Tool of the being I feed & adorn.

Twas I did soothe
Thy thorny youth;
I found thee placed
In my most leafless waste;

178 "Seyd planted where the deluge ploughed." The cancellation and addition in line (2) are
in pencil.
    179 "With the key of the secret" (1–4); "If wishes would carry me" (5–8).
    180 "Seemed though the soft sheen" (1–4); "The farthest from the root" (5); "That each
should in his house abide" (6–7).
    181 "Nature saith."

(10)        I comforted thy little feet
            On the forlorn errand bound;
            I fed thee, with my mallows fed,
            On the first day of failing bread.

[182]               *Aeolian Harp.*
            I overhear the Parcae reel
            The threads of man at their humming wheel,
            The threads of life, & power & pain,
            So sweet & mournful falls the strain.

———————————

(5)      ⟨And these ↑are↓⟩ illusions ⟨all⟩ ↑like the tints of pearl,↓
            ⟨Illusions like the⟩ ↑or changing↓ colors of the sky
            Or ⟨like the⟩ ribbons of a dancing girl
            ⟨Which make her seem ⟨more⟩ ↑far↓ fairer & fanciful⟩
            Which ⟨⟨make⟨s⟩⟩ ↑show↓ her ⟨seem far⟩ fairer than she is⟩
                ↑can her beauty magnify↓
(10)                ↑Enhance her beauty to the eye↓

            Illusions like the tints of pearl,
            Or changing colors of the sky,
            Or ribbons of a dancing girl
            That mend her beauty to the eye.

[183]         If I could put my woods in song
            And tell what's here enjoyed,
            All men would to my gardens throng
            And leave the cities void.

(5)         My garden is a forest patch
            ⟨By⟩ ↑Which older↓ forests bound⟨ed⟩
            Its sides sloping to the water ↑stretch↓
            Which forests surround

            ↑Here once↓ The deluge ploughed↑,↓ ⟨it⟩
(10)         ⟨And⟩ laid ⟨out⟩ the terraces, one & one;
            Ebbing ↑⟨after,⟩ then to↓ whence it flowed
            ⟨And⟩ left them ⟨in⟩ ↑open to↓ the sun.
              The planters are ⟨gone⟩ ↑wrought &↓ fled
              The wind & the birds planted it
(15)             ⟨Scorning⟩ ↑Not for↓ fame, nor laws of ⟨man⟩ art
              The rain watered it

182 "The Harp," 99–102 (1–4); "Illusions like the tints of pearl," two versions (5–10, 11–14). Lines (5–10) are struck through three times in ink.
183 "My Garden," 1–4, 9–11, x, 13–20. Struck through in ink; in lines (10–11), "out" and "after" are canceled and "then to" added in pencil.

[184] Here was Jove
    And every god; none did refuse
    And be sure came at last Love,
    And after ⟨l⟩Love the Muse.

(5)  You may hear if you list her syllables
    ↑As if one spoke to another↓
    In every bosk & corner
    What bending boughs to boughs declare
    And ⟨secrets⟩ what the whispering grasses smother

(10)  In my plot no tulips blow
    Snowloving pines & oaks instead

    Aeolian harps in the pines
    ⟨Hermit thrush in the dark grove⟩
    ↑Murmur the song of the Fates↓
(15)  The infant Bacchus in the wild vine
    Far distant yet his chorus waits

[185] ⟨Sit not here, but⟩ come up to the mountain side
    There thou shalt know
    The elements & their ↑subtle↓ gear
    Wherewith they engineer↑,—↓
(5)  Clouds↑,↓ whirlwinds↑,↓ waterspouts,
    Frost & fire
    And ⟨mightier⟩ ↑finer↓ powers whence
    Stars draw their influence

    Canst thou copy in verse one chime
(10)  Of the wood bell's peal & cry
    Write in a book the morning's prime
    And match with words that amber sky.

    Here once the deluge ploughed,
    Laid the terraces, one & one,
(15)  Ebbing after whence it flowed
    Let them dry in the sun

[186] Can your ear catch the syllable
    As if one spake to another
    The ⟨maples⟩ ↑cedars↓ tall, untameable
    And what the whispering grasses smother

 184 "My Garden," 25–30, x, x, 32, 5–6, 33, x, 34–36. Lines (1–6), (7–9), and (10–16) are struck through separately in ink; lines (10–11) are struck through again three times in pencil.
 185 "My Garden," eight unused lines, 37–40, 13–16. The cancellations and additions in lines (1–7) are in pencil; lines (9–12) are struck through in ink with one line and lines (13–16) with two.
 186 "My Garden," 29–32, 5–8, x. Struck through in ink.

(5)   In my plot no tulips blow
      Snowloving pines & oaks instead
      And thick the savage maples grow
      From vernal ⟨crim⟩purple to autumn red

      My garden was not made today

[187]  The sowers made haste to depart
      The wind & the birds which sowed
      Not for fame nor by laws of art
      These planted the rain flowed

(5)   The yellow thunderbolt
      The storm barked

      Sit not, but climb the scarped cliff
      To know the winds
      Find the workers their subtle gear
(10)   Frost & fire & whirlwind
      Wherewith ↑al↓ they engineer
      Rocks which once the ocean rolled

[188] The seasons are his chariot to c⟨arry⟩onvey him from this exile. The hours covered with the ruddy colors of the rainbow are his couch & chair of repose which waft him over clouds & vapors to the Empyrean winds & storms the good drivers urge forward the heavy weeks suns hasten to set that more distant lights may beckon to him from his vaster home

[189]   ↑And here the bending skies solicit man,↓
      The seasons chariot him from this exile
     The rainbow hours ↑shall↓ tint his glowing chair
     The storm-winds urge the heavy weeks along
(5)   Suns haste to set, that ⟨the⟩ ↑so↓ remoter stars
     ⟨May beckon to him from his vaster home⟩
     Beckon the ⟨pilgrim⟩ ↑wanderer↓ to his vaster home

      For Nature true & like in every place
      Will hint her secret in a garden patch,
(10)   or in lone corners of a do⟨elf⟩leful heath,
      As in the Andes watched by fleets at sea
      or the sky-piercing ⟨p⟩horns of Himmaleh
      or Europe's pilgrims at Niagara
      And when I would recall the scenes I dreamed

187 "My Garden," 17–20, eight unused lines. Lines (1–4) are struck through in ink; lines (5–12) are in pencil.
188 "The Adirondacs," a prose version of lines 225–29. "The seasons . . . of repose" is struck through in ink with one line and the entire entry with a second.
189 "The Adirondacs," 224–29 (1–7); "For Nature true & like," 1–8 (8–15). Lines (1–7), in pencil, are struck through in ink and pencil.

(15)     On Adirondac steeps I know  
  [190]   ⟨I have no need of ⟨painter⟩ ↑draughtsmen↓⟩  
       ↑⟨What⟩ ↑Small↓ need have I of Turner or Daguerre, ↓  
       Assured to find the token once again  
       In silver lakes that unexhausted gleam,  
(5)      And peaceful woods ⟨that wave near my ⟨own⟩ door⟩  
         ↑⟨shade⟩ ↑beside↓ my cottage door. ↓  

         There is a force at work  
     To make best better, & the vilest good.  

      History & prophecy are alike  
      It matters little if thou read  
(10)    Backward or forth a frivolous creed  
      Alike unworthy thou hast learned  
      The world was drowned & shall be burned  
      As if man's Spirit were some cat  
      Loved its old barn to end with that  

  [191]   Nor reek in towns ⟨with⟩of beetling roofs  
       Jammed ⟨wi⟩by cartwheels & drayhorse hoofs  
       Suck cholera from a foul cigar  
       When oer you flames the morning star  
(5)      Lighting broad scented meadows nigh,  
       Uplifting hills, inviolate sky.  

      And o the wonder of the power,  
      The deeper secret of the hour—  
      Nature the supplement of man,  
(10)    His hidden sense interpret can;  
      What friend to friend cannot convey  
      Shall the dumb brute instructed say.  

  [192]   When wrath & terror changed Jove's regal port  
       And the rash leaping thunderbolt fell short  

  [193]        Aeolian Harp  
      ⟨Hark in the hall⟩ ↑For in thy voice, ↓ at summer eve,  
      I overhear the Parcae reel  
      The threads of man at their humming wheel,  
(5)      The threads of life & power & pain,  
      So sweet & mournful falls the strain.  

---

190 "For Nature true & like," 9–12 (1–5); "May-Day," x, 659/661 (6–7); "History & prophecy" (8–14). Lines (8–14) are in pencil.

191 "May Day [Invitation]," 48–50, x, 52–53 (1–6); "The Miracle," 17–22 (7–12). Lines (1–6) are in pencil.

192 "When wrath & terror."

193 "May–Day," 520, 524 (1–2); "The Harp," 41, 45, 99–102 (1–6).

[194]     She walked in flowers around my field
          As June herself around the sphere

          By purple peaks & rosy palaces
          In deep abysses of imperial sky

(5)       The bird was gone      the ghastly trees
          ↑Heard the wind sing with in the breeze↓
          Was this her funeral that I see
          Did that asking eye ask me?

[195]                    *My Garden*
                    If I coul‖
          And tell w‖
          All men w‖
          And leave ‖

(5)       In my p‖
          Snow-lov‖
          And ra‖
          From sp‖

          My ga‖
(10)      Which ‖
          ⟨Its⟩ ↑The↓ ⟨sides⟩ ↑banks↓ ‖
          Then pl‖

          Here onc‖
          Laid the ‖
(15)      Ebbing late‖
          They bleach ‖

[196]                    ‖e haste to depart,
                         ‖ds which sowed, ↑it,↓
                         ‖ rules of art,
                         ‖sts ⟨so⟩flowed it.

(5)                      ‖ my garden side
                         ‖ lawful web
                         ‖ean's⟩ ‖lar↓ tide
                         ‖od to ebb.

                         ‖e Jove,
(10)                     ‖d refuse;

194 "She walked in flowers" (1–2); "May–Day," x, 31? (3–4); "The bird was gone" (5–8). Lines (5–8) are in erased pencil.
195 "My Garden," 1–16. The leaves bearing pp. [195]–[198] are torn out, leaving stubs inscribed in ink.
196 "My Garden," 17–32.

||e Love,
|| Muse.

|| a syllable
||other
||meable,
||rasses smother.

(15)

[197]    Aeolian ||
Ring wi||
Infant ||
Far di||

(5)      Canst ||
Of the w||
Write ||
Or ma||

Wonde||
(10)    Of one ||
They ⟨si|| ↑ch||
To man ||

Ever the ||
But the p||
(15)    Seldom ||
Are unsea||

[198]

||ices in the air,
||e wold,
||not declare,
|| withhold.

(5)

|| on the lake
||pples wrote,
||ine & break,
||ught.

||ling to the ⟨water,⟩ ↑lake↓
(10)

||ok or urn,
||e later back,
|| they burn.

||s of men,
|| live today,
(15)    || who can read them,
|| answer, Stay!⟩
||lpture, Stay!

**197** "My Garden," 33–48.
**198** "My Garden," 49–64.

[198ₐ] Step in, it blows a little fresh,
But pardon
Pardon, but must superfluous flesh
Ridiculously shake & shiver
(5) Too broad an aim to Winter's quiver

[198_b] Parnassus
Garden poem   *CD* 150
Poet   see KL 214

[198_c]         J. R. Lowell      1859   Feb 22

The bard has reached the middle date:
Stars tonight that culminate
Shed beams fair & fortunate.
Go, inquire ⟨the⟩his horoscope,
(5) Half of memory, half of hope.

What said the sibyl⟨e⟩?
What was the fortune
She sung for him?
*Strength for the hour!*

(10) Man of marrow, man of mark,
Virtue lodged in sinew stark,
Rich supplies & never stinted,
More behind at need is hinted,
Never cumbered with the morrow,
(15) Never knew corroding sorrow,
Too well gifted to have found
Yet his opulence's bound;
[198_d] Most at home in mounting fun,
Resistless ⟨↑Beaming↓⟩ joke & luckiest pun,
Masking in the mantling tones
Of his rich laugh-loving voice,
(5) In speeding troops of Social joys,
And in volleys of wild mirth,
Purer metal, rarest worth,
Logic, passion, cordial zeal,
Such as bard & hero feel.

(10) Strength for the hour!
For the day sufficient power;

198ₐ "Step in, it blows."
198_b "Garden poem   *CD* 150" is in pencil.
198_c "James Russell Lowell," 34–38, 44–55. "Lowell" is in ink over "Lowell" in pencil.
198_d "James Russell Lowell," 56–74. In line (2), "Resistless" was canceled, and "Beaming" added, in ink, then both revisions were fingerwiped to cancel them.

Well-advised, too easily great
His large fleece to antedate.
But, if another temper come,
(15)    If on the sun shall creep a gloom,
A time & tide more exigent,
When the old mounds are torn & rent,
More proud, more strong competitors
Marshal the lists for emperors,
[198ₑ]    Then the pleasant bard will know
To put the frolic mask behind him,
↑Like an old summer-cloak,↓
And in sky-born mail to bind him,
(5)    And single-handed cope with Time,
And parry & deal the thunderstroke.

[199]    Pedants all
They wd be original
And in set phrase tell what they found

The mute pebble shames their wit
(5)    The Echo is ironical
And wiser silence ⟨strangles⟩ ↑smothered↓ speech
Buries itself in silence speech
As stars in space

↑These↓ The ⟨lives⟩ ↑fates↓ of men forecast
(10)    Of better men than live today
If ⟨he⟩ who can read them comes at last
He will spell in the sculpture, "Stay"

[200] Dreams are the irony of Jove

————————

Is morning clean, let him be clean.

They go & come
Lurking dumb
⟨O⟩In the chamber, on the stairs
(5)    The Lemurs & the Lars

Natures web star broidered
Of animated fibre woven

As the drop feeds its fated flower,
As find↑s↓ its Alp the snowy shower,

198ₑ "James Russell Lowell," 75–80.
199 "Pedants all" (1–8); "My Garden," 61–64 (9–12). In pencil; lines (9–12) are struck through in pencil and erased.
200 "Is morning clean" (1); "On the chamber," 3, 2, 1, 4 (2–5); "Nature's web" (6–7); "As the drop feeds" (8–12). In pencil except for "Dreams are the irony of Jove"; see NP p. [12].

(10)        Child of the omnific Need
            Hurled into life to do a deed,
            Man drinks the water, drinks the light

[201]       I leave the book, I leave the wine,
            I breathe freer by the pine:
            In houses, I am low & mean,
            Mountain waters wash me clean,
(5)         And by the seawaves I am strong,
            I hear their medicinal song,
            No balsam but the breeze I crave,
            And no physician but the wave.

            Gentle Spring has charmed the earth
(10)        Where an April sunbeam fell,
            Let no glacier from the north
            Floating by undo the spell.

[202] [blank]
[203]               In yonder city rich & old
            Where men toil much for little gold,
            In vault or garret, wharf or raft,
            At their sweat & handicraft,
(5)         One sultry morn beyond compare
            Wafted sweet teachings of the air
            Which no town walls can quite exclude,
            Nor streets of fops nor draymen rude.
            Up the High Street, in ⟨morning⟩market din,
(10)        A joyful May-Cart trundled in.
            Green boughs, with cage of singing birds,
            And rope of twisted vines, that girds
            ⟨And⟩ ↑with↓ festoons all the cart around,
            Whilst country-boys with willow pipes made all the air
                    resound

[204]       And halted mid the gathering crowd
            We Fairfield folk, he cried aloud,
            Proclaim to all who listen may
            A three days woodland holiday.
(5)         It is our annual village use
            To give Toil respite ⟨↑holiday↓⟩ & truce

            And we invite all worthy people

---

201 "I leave the book" (1–8); "Gentle Spring has charmed the earth" (9–12).
203 "May Day [Invitation]," 1–14. Lines (7–12) are struck through in pencil; the cancellation and addition in line (13) are in pencil.
204 "May Day [Invitation]," 15–26. In line (6), "holiday" is fingerwiped; the cancellation and addition in line (9) are in pencil.

To rendezvous at Fairfield steeple.
⟨We show you the way⟩ ↑up & we take you↓ to the woods,
(10)    Rich parks where yet no shop intrudes,
We guide you to the Red trout brook,
And ponds where perch swim to the hook,
[205]    Or ↑you shall↓ climb the hill with gun, & rouse
Rabbit or hare, pigeon & grouse.

This year we have a mended clime,
The Spring arrive⟨d⟩↑s↓ before its time;
(5)    The bluebird⟨s⟩ sang in February,
And now the peach blooms, & the cherry.
⟨I was up⟩ ↑We woke↓ this morn before the day,
The thrush had never so much to say,
The morning cobwebs showed no storm,
(10)    The robin listened for the worm,
The fungus & the bulrush spoke,
Answered the pine tree & the oak,
The subtle South blew down the glen
[206]    Filled the straits, & filled the wide,
The maple leaf turned up its silver side.
Lawns glimmer in the smoky ray,
And all we see are pictures high,
(5)    Valley deep & high hillside,
Which oaks of pride
Climb to their tops,
And boys run out upon their leafy ropes.

[207]    Why reek in towns ⟨wit⟩of beetling roofs
Jammed by cartwheels, & drayhorse hoofs,
Suck cholera from pavements foul,
Drink tainted water from the bowl,
(5)    When scented fields expanding nigh
Uplifted hills, inviolate sky?—
↑Invite your↓
Obey our summons, one & all,
To join our woodland festival.

(10)    The crowd cheered↑,↓ master & man
The elders nod, boys jumped & ran,
The town emptied like a prison

205 "May Day [Invitation]," 27–39 (1–13); "Where the fungus broad & red," 12–14 (11–13). The cancellations and additions are in pencil.
    206 "May Day [Invitation]," 40–47 (1–8); "Where the fungus broad & red," 15–16, 19–24 (1–8).
    207 "May Day [Invitation]," 48–63. Line (7) and the comma in line (10) are in pencil.

To the fields & broad horizon.
Age hobbled forth upon his crutch,
(15)    Uprose the porter & the drudge,
The pauper crept forth from his hutch
[208]   The baker let cool his oven,
The spinner left her web unwoven,
Nor man ↑nor maid↓ nor child would stay
From the festival of May.

[209]        I have trod this path a hundred times
With idle footsteps crooning rhymes,
I know each nest & webworm's tent,
The foxhole which the woodchucks rent,
(5)    Maple & oak, the old divan
Selfplanted twice like the banian;
I know not why I came again,
Unless to learn it ten times ten.
Wilt /learn/read/ the sense the woods impart
(10)   ⟨We⟩ ↑Thou↓ must bring the throbbing heart—
Love is the counterforce,
Terror, & Hope, & wild Remorse,
New knowledge, fiery Thought,
Duty to grand purpose wrought

[210]        Wandering yestermorn the brake
I reached ⟨this⟩ ↑the↓ heath beside the lake:
↑Then↓ Passing yonder oak, I heard
Sharp accents of ⟨the sentr⟩a woodland bird
(5)    I marked the singer with delight
↑But ⟨mark⟩ ↑hear↓ what↓    changed ↑my joy↓ to
    fright↑:—↓
        ↑↑And o↓ The wonder of the power↓
↑The deeper secret of this hour↓
↑Nature, the supplement of man,↓
(10)   ↑His hidden sense interpret can↓
↑What friend to friend cannot convey↓
↑Shall the dumb brute instructed say.↓
When that bird sang, I gave the theme,
That ⟨b⟩woodbird sang my last nights dream.
(15)   A brown wren was the Daniel
That pierced my trance its drift to spell;

208 "May Day [Invitation]," 64–67. In line (3), "nor maid" is circled in ink.
209 "The Miracle," 1–14. In line (9), "learn" is circled in ink.
210 "The Miracle," 15–16, 23–26, 17–22, 27–34. The cancellations and additions in lines (2), (3), and (6) are in pencil; lines (7–12) are inscribed on p. [211], circled, and marked for insertion following line (6).

Knew my quarrel, how & why,
Published it to sea & sky,
Told every word & syllable
(20)     In ⟨its⟩his flippant chirping babble,
  [211]   All my wrath, & all my shames,
Nay, Heaven be witness, blabbed the names.

  [212]  The coral worm beneath the sea
Mason planter spreads
Its rock vegetable threads
His colossal⟨l⟩ flowers
(5)     Foundation of the isles to be
⟨Future⟩ home of ⟨empire⟩ ↑imperial↓ powers
And nobler life

  [213]       The wild rose & the barberry↑'s↓ thorn
Hung out their summer pride
Where now ↑on↓ heated pavement worn
The feet of millions stride.

(5)     The land was rich outspread behind
The young men hungered more
On slippery deck with snowy wings
To skim the ocean floor.

The stormy billows kissed the cloud,
(10)    The wind mixed sea & sky,
The skipper⟨e⟩ steered blow soft or loud
↑And reached his port thereby↓

  [214]

———

The land that has no song
Shall have a song today,
The granite hills are dumb too long,
The vales have much to say:
(5)     For you can teach the lightning speech,
And round the ⟨world⟩earth your voices reach.

———

211 "The Miracle," 35–36.
212 "The coral worm." In pencil. Lines (4–5) occur in reverse order in the manuscript, marked for transposition by the numbers "2" and "1" in the left margin.
213 "Boston," 35–38, eight unused lines. Lines (1–4) are struck through in pencil; line (12) is added in pencil.
214 "Boston," four unused lines, 108–9.

*Trimountain.*
*Sicut cum patribus sit Deus nobis.*

The rocky nook with hill-tops three
Looked eastward from the farms,
And twice a day the flowing sea
Took Boston in its arms.
(5) The men of yore were stout & poor,
And sailed for bread to every shore.

And where they went on trade intent
They did what freemen can,
Their dauntless ways did all men praise,
(10) The merchant was a man.
The world was made for honest trade,
To plant & eat be none afraid.

[216] Old Europe groans with palaces,
Has lords enough & more,
We⟨'ll⟩ plant & build by foaming seas
A city of the poor.

(5) The noble craftsman we promote,
Disown the knave & fool,
⟨The⟩ ↑Each↓ honest man shall have his vote
⟨The⟩ ↑Each↓ child shall have his school.

We grant no dukedom to the few.
(10) We hold like rights, & shall,
Equal on Sunday in the pew,
On Monday in the mall.

[217] Fair rose ⟨the good town⟩the planted hills behind
The good town on the Bay,
And where the western slopes declined,
The prairie stretched away.

(5) Out from the many-fountained earth
The rivers gushed & foamed,
Sweet airs from every ⟨pore exhaled⟩ ↑forest forth↓
⟨Around⟩ ↑And from↓ the mountains roamed.

What rival towers majestic soar
(10) Along the stormy coast,
Penn's town, New York, & Baltimore,
If Boston knew the most!

215 "Boston," 1–12.
216 "Boston," 19–22, 25–28, 31–34.
217 "Boston," 39–42, four unused lines, 43–46.

[218]  They laughed to know the world so wide,
The mountains said, 'Good Day!
We greet you well, you Saxon men,
Up with your towns, & stay!'

(5)  ↑For you, they said, no barriers be,↓
↑For you no s⟨u⟩luggards' rest,↓
↑Each street leads downward to the sea,↓
↑Or ⟨out⟩↑land↓ward to the West.↓

⟨And they who⟩ ↑The ⟨states⟩ townsmen↓ braved the
English king
(10)  Found friendship in the French,
And Honor joined the patriot ring
Low on their wooden bench.

⟨O bounteou⟩

O bounteous seas that never fail!
(15)  O happy day remembered yet!
O happy Port, that spied /a/the/ sail
⟨That⟩Which, /furling, landed/wafted/ Lafayette!

↑Polestar of light in Europe's night↓
↑That never faltered from the right.↓

[219]  O pity that I pause,—
The song disdaining shuns
To name the noble sires, because
Of the unworthy sons.
(5)  For what avail the plough & sail,
Or ⟨life or⟩land, or life, if freedom fail?

But there was chaff within the flour,
And one was false in ten,
And reckless clerks in lust of power
(10)  Forgot the rights of men;
Cruel & blind, did file their mind,
And sell the blood of human kind.

Your town is full of gentle names
/Thy patriots/Which/ once were ⟨warcries⟩watchwords made;
(15)  Those war-cry names are muffled shames
On recreant sons mislaid.
What slave /would/shall/ dare a name to wear
Once Freedom's passport everywhere?

218 "Boston," 47–50, 53–56, 80–84, 84–89. Line (13) is fingerwiped; "happy" in line (15) and "furling, landed" in line (17) are circumscribed in ink; lines (18–19) are in pencil.
219 "Boston," four unused lines, 29/78–30/79, twelve unused lines. "Thy patriots" in line (14) and "would" in line (17) are circumscribed in ink.

[220]     O welaway! if this be so,
          And man cannot afford the right,
          And if the wage of love is woe,
          And honest-dealing yield despite⟨?⟩.
(5)       For what avail the plough & sail,
          Or ⟨life⟩land, or life, if Freedom fail?

          Hie to the woods, sleek citizen!
          Back to the sea, go, lands men! down;
          Climb the White Hills, sleek aldermen
(10)      And vacant leave the town.
          Go purge your blood in lake & wood,
          To honor born of hardihood.
                    or
          Ere these echoes be choked with snows
          Or over the roofs blue Ocean flows.

[221]         The sea returning day by day
          Restores the world-wide mart;
          So ⟨doth⟩ ↑let↓ each dweller on the Bay
          Fold Boston in his heart.
(5)       For what avail the plough & sail,
          Or land, or life, if freedom fail?

              ⟨May⟩ ↑Let↓ the blood of her hundred thousands
          Throb in each manly vein,
          And the wit of all her wisest
(10)      Make sunshine in h⟨er⟩is brain!
          A Union, then, of honest men,          ↑Changed↓
          Or union nevermore again!

          And each shall care for other,
          And each to each shall bend,
(15)      To the poor, a noble brother,
          To the good, an equal friend.

[222]         A blessing through the ages thus
          Shield all thy roofs & towers!
          *God with the fathers, so with us!*
          Thou darling town of ours.

(5)           But right is might /⟨a⟩in/thro/ all the world
          Provin[c]e to province faithful clung

220 "Boston," four unused lines, 29/78–30/79, six unused lines, 102–3. Lines (13–14) are struck through in pencil.
     221 "Boston," 98–101, 29/78–30/79, 104–7, two lines first printed in *Selected Poems*, 1876, 110–13. Lines (1–4), (5–6), (7–10), and (13–16) are struck through separately in pencil; the cancellation and addition in line (7) are in pencil; "Changed", after line (11), is in pencil.
     222 "Boston," 114–17, 94–97, x, 97, 97, x, x, 91–93. Lines (5–16) are in pencil.

Through good & ill ↑t↓he bolt was hurled
⟨Till⟩ the farmers won & peace was sung

Could honestly drink their tea
(10)    Till Freedom cheered & the ⟨joy⟩bells rung
Till Freedoms triumph the /joy bells/peace/ ⟨sun⟩rung

Wondered old nations brave
↑Amazed looked to↓
The magic force to find
(15)    That fired the little town to save
The rights of all mankind

For lines, see *Orientalist* p. 223

[223]    No castles no Bridge of Sighs
No castle no dungeon hole
But mountains & prairie
And shores of two oceans
(5)    And paths from the Gulf to the Pole

We cant live on old corn
But we
We reap the world for wheat
Each State shall build its joint of road
(10)    And girdle the earth thereby

For you, they said, no barriers be,
For you no sluggards rest,
Each street leads downward to the sea,
Or outward to the west.

(15)    The sea which was the barrier
Is n⟨ot⟩ow the world's highway

[224]    Methought the scornful sky looked down
On all that stained the ⟨(upstart)⟩ man,
And airy tongues did taunt the town
'Achieve us if you can.'

[225]    When all their blooms the meadows flaunt,
To deck the morning of the year
Why tinge ⟨thy⟩ ↑their↓ lustres jubilant
With forecast or with fear?

223 "Boston," ten unused lines, 53–56, x, x. Lines (1–10) and (15–16) are in pencil; lines (11–14) are struck through twice in pencil.
224 "In my garden three ways meet," 21–24. In pencil.
225 "When all their blooms" (1–4); "Teach me your mood" (5–8); "In my garden three ways meet," 17–20 (9–12); "How drearily in College hall," 5–7 (13–15). In pencil.

(5) Teach me your ⟨patience⟩ ↑mood, O patient stars↓
 That climb each night the ancient sky
 Leaving on space no⟨r⟩ shade nor scars
 ↑No hint of wrong, no fear to die. ↓
       ↑————↓

 In cities high thro crowds of cares
(10) The wo-worn mortals darkling go
 But in these sunny solitudes
 My quiet roses blow.

 The air is wise the wind thinks well
 And all thro which it blows
(15) If plant or brain, if egg or cell

[226] The Guru comes the Guru goes.
If I could write a poem, I would try the subject of Guru Nanac. See
[*The*] *Dabistan* [1843], II. 268

---

*continued from p 229*
came to this world, & his followers are the former inhabitants of hell.
The Guru comes & goes until all that multitude shall have found their
salvation  [*The Dabistan*, 1843, 2:269]

[227] When Guru came to Sattayog
 A crowd of Sikhs met him
 He sent a cow to the kitchen
 The roast was brought to the guests
(5) Some ate ⟨of it⟩ ↑the flesh↓ some ate it not
 The Guru prayed ⟨to⟩ Vishn⟨u⟩oo
 And the cow was restored to life
 Whole & sound as from the mountains
 And the timid fasters said
(10) Once we were afraid
 Henceforward we shall do thy behest.
 Not now, said Guru,
 But we will keep ⟨our⟩ this consent
 And we will meet in the Treta ⟨J⟩Yog
(15) The years went round without a sound
 And ⟨⟨we⟩at⟩ ↑we at↓ the Treta ⟨Jog⟩Yog ⟨‖ . ‖⟩be found

[228] The Guru ⟨c⟩goes the Guru comes and at the revolution of the
Treta Jog the Guru appeared The disciples assembled Then a
slaughtered horse was brought: Some ate, some abstained. The Guru

226 The long rule and the inscription following it are in pencil.
227 "When Guru came." In pencil except that in line (14) "Y" is in ink over "J" and in line
(16) "Yog" is in ink over "Jog".
228 In pencil; continued on p. [229] below.

prayed, & the horse was brot to life ⟨He said again⟩ Those who had been afraid now prayed, & said, we shall now obey. He replied, 'Your word & mine are engaged for the Dwapar Jog
In the Dwapar ⟨J⟩ age they bro't a slaughtered elephant into the assembly,    The same ⟨ev⟩happened as before & Guru said, "At the Kali Jog, The Guru goes the ⟨gu⟩Guru comes in the age of the Kali jog
A man was brot before the assembly    Whoever ate became free, who abstained remained subject to durance. but some of the Sikhs called Guru the Slave of God.—When Guru died

[*The Dabistan*, 1843, 2:268–69]

[229]    Albany.
   I care not where I am ⟨&⟩or go
   Or if my task be high or low,
   Work to hide or proudly show,
   Or if my mates shall be my peers,
(5)  Or only rare-met travellers,
   Whether I pace the shop-lined street,
   ⟨Oerlooking⟩ ↑Scanning↓ the city at their feet,
   With secret pride to rule the town
   And shire on which the dome looks down.

---

in the Sat yog two roads opened before hi⟨m⟩s soul    One led to heaven the other to hell    Guru chose the latter & having descended below he brot all the inhabitants out of hell. The Lord God said to him    These sinners cannot ⟨r⟩enter heaven. You must return into the world ⟨to⟩& liberate them. On that account Guru  ↑turn to p 226↓

[*The Dabistan*, 1843, 2:269]

[230] Nature said to man, Be Master: I will finish the house: be you the tenant,—not a piece of furniture, but the lord↑,↓ ⟨&⟩ ↑the↓ interpreter↑,↓ & user of all. Be thou the benefactor. Don't be scared by size. What are millions of miles? What are dreary durations to thee? Suns & atoms are alike: an atom is all; one atom like another, & a globe is only a lump of atoms. Every breath of air a carrier of the Universal mind.
   Chladni strewed on glass the sand
   Then struck the glass its music sweet
   The sand flew into symmetry
   Then with altered hand
(5)  drew discords, & the sand scatter⟨d⟩ed formless,

229 "I care not whither." The long rule and the prose following it are in pencil; "turn to p 226" is written upward in the right margin.
230 The cancellation and additions in the prose are in pencil. "Chladni strewed on glass," 1–11. In line (6), Emerson first wrote "We never come into new laws", then marked and numbered the line elements for transposition.

Into new laws we never come
We cannot find a foreign land
Tho we run along the diameter
Of sidereal space.

(10)    ↑Sing, & the rock will crystallize↓
↑Sing, & the plant will grow.↓

[231]    ⟨Have the same⟩ ↑Obey one↓ law ↑above, below,↓
light, heat, & sound, ⟨&⟩ ↑each a↓ liquid wave⟨s.⟩
⟨I gave you⟩ ↑And↓ Beauty for the ⟨Pilot⟩ ↑guide I gave↓
To lead where you should go.

(5)    The motes of the stream shall prate
Of the current that floats them on.

I understand mensuration & numbers. I have measured out to you by weight & tally the powers you need. I give you the land & sea, the forest & the mine, the elemental forces, nervous energy, & a good brain. See to it that you hold & administer the continent for mankind. I compute the curve of the rainbow, the ebb & flow of waters, ⟨the recoils of forces,⟩ the errors of planets, the e⟨c⟩llipse of the moon, the balance of attraction & recoil

[232]    ↑Is↓ The pace of nature slow?
Why not from strength to strength
From miracle to miracle
⟨&⟩And not as now with retardation

(5)    As with sprained foot

Nature always a victor, & reckons securely on our sympathy. "To the heroic," she says, "I show myself heroic."
He lives not who can refuse me,
All my force saith↑,↓ "Come & use me,"
A ⟨little⟩ ↑day of↓ sun, a ⟨little⟩ ↑summer↓ rain,
And all the zone is green again.

(10)    Diamond will burn, but law will hold

[233]    He lives not who can refuse me,
All my force saith, 'Come & use me.'

231 "Chladni strewed on glass," 12–17. Lines (1–2) occur in reverse order in the manuscript, marked for transposition by the numbers "2)" and "1)" in the left margin. The cancellations in lines (2) and (3) are in pencil and in line (1) in pencil and ink; "Obey one" (line 1), "each a" (line 2), and "And" and "I gave" (line 3) are added in pencil traced over in ink; "above, below." (line 1) is added in pencil and overwritten by "above below," in ink. The prose is copied from journal DL (JMN 15:28–29).
232 "Is The pace of nature slow?" (1–5); "He lives not who can refuse me" (6–9); "Diamond will burn" (10). In line (7), the added comma is in pencil. The first sentence of the prose entry occurs in notebook WA p. [246], and the second in journal VA (JMN 15:281).
233 "He lives not who can refuse me" (1–4); "Easy to match what others do," 1–9, 9, (5–14).

A little sun, a little rain,
And all the zone is green again

---

(5)       Easy to match what others do,
Perform the feat as well as they;
Hard to outdo the wise, the true,
And find a loftier way.
The school decays, the learning spoils,
(10)     Because of the sons of wine:—
How snatch the stripling from their toils?
Yet can one ray ↑of↓ truth divine
The ⟨blaze of revellers' feasts outshine⟩
↑The banquet's blaze outshine. ↓

[234]    ⟨Out of the world the water rolled for you⟩
⟨Out of the world ⟨your⟩ ↑died↓ heroes bold for you⟩

[235]           ↑*Arabian Ballad*↓

1  Under the rock    ↑on the↓ trail
He lies slain
In↑to↓ whose blood
No dew ⟨drops⟩ falls

(5)    2  ⟨G⟩A great load laid he on me
And died;
God knows, this load
Will I lift.

⟨2⟩3  "⟨Inherit⟩Heir of my revenge
(10)      Is my sister's son,
The ⟨martial⟩ warlike,
The irreconcileable.

4.  ⟨Stout⟩Mute sweats he poison,
As the otter sweats;
(15)     As the snake breathes ⟨poison⟩ ↑venom↓
↑Against↓ Which no enchantment avails

5.  ↑The↓ Stern /message/word/tidings/ came to us
Of the heavy woe;
The stoutest had they
(20)     Overpowered.

[236]6  Me had Destiny plundered
Striking down ⟨the⟩my friend,

235 "Arabian Ballad," 1–20. In pencil.
236 "Arabian Ballad," 21–40. In pencil.

/Whose dearest friend/him whose guest/
/Was left unhurt./was never harmed/

(5)   7  Sunshine was he
On the cold day,
And when the dogstar burned
He was shade & coolness.

   8  ⟨T⟩Dry were his ⟨hipps⟩ ↑hips↓
(10)  Not slow;
Moist his hand,
Bold & strong.

   9  With firm mind
Followed he his aim
(15)  Until he rested,
Then rested also the firm mind.

  10  The rain cloud was he
Imparting gifts;
And, wh⟨o⟩en ⟨↑h↓⟩ ⟨would⟩ he attacked,
(20)  ⟨A⟩The terrible lion.

[237] 11  Stately before men,
Black hair⟨,⟩ed↑,↓ long-robed,
When rushing on the foe
A lean wolf. _____

(5)  12  Two cups ⟨he⟩ offered he,
Honey and wormwood;
Fare of such kind
Tasted each.

  13  Terrible rode he alone;
(10)  No man accompanied him;
Like the sword of Yemen,
With ⟨notches⟩ ↑teeth↓ adorned.

  14  At noon we ⟨youths⟩ ↑young men↓ set forth
On the ⟨hostile march,⟩ ↑war trail↓
(15)  Rode all night
Like sweeping clouds   without rest

  15  ⟨On⟩ every one ↑was↓ a sword
⟨Was⟩ girt with a sword;
Out of the sheath ⟨parted⟩ ↑drawn↓
(20)  A glancing lightning

237 "Arabian Ballad," 41–64. In pencil.

16 They sipped the spirit of sleep,
   But, when they nodded their heads,
   We smote them,
   And they ⟨rallied.⟩ ↑were away↓

[238] 17 ↑Our↓ Vengeance ⟨took we fully;⟩ was complete.
   There escaped of two ⟨races⟩ ↑tribes↓
   Quite little,
   The least.

(5)  18 And ⟨whilst⟩ ↑when↓ the Hudselite
   Had ⟨to⟩ broken his lance ↑to kill his man↓
   The man with his lance ⟨Slew the Hudselite⟩
   Slew the Hudselite.

   19 On ⟨the⟩a rough resting place
(10)   They laid him,—
   On a sharp rock, where the very camels
   Broke their ⟨feet.⟩ paws.

   20 When the mo↑r↓ning greeted him there,
   The murdered, on the grim place,
(15)   Was he robbed,
   The booty carried away.

   21 But now ⟨be⟩ ↑are↓ murdered by me
   The Hudseleites with deep wounds;
   ⟨Murder⟩ ↑Pity↓ makes me not unhappy
(20)   Itself is murdered.

   22 The spear's thirst was assuaged
   With the first drink;
   To it was not denied
   Repeated drinks.

[239] 23 Now is wine again permitted
   Which first was forbidden:
   With much toil
   I won this permission.

(5)  24 To sword & spear,
   And to horse, gave I
   This favor,
   Which is now the good of all.

   25 Reach then the bowl,
(10)   O Sawab Ben Amre!

238 "Arabian Ballad," 65–88. In pencil.
239 "Arabian Ballad," 89–112. In pencil.

Since my body, at the command ⟨m⟩of my uncle
Is now one ↑great↓ wound.

26  ⟨&⟩And the cup of death
Reached we to the Hudseleites
(15)  Whose /working/operation/ is wo,
Blindness, & ruin.

27  Then laughed the hyenas
At the death of the Hudseleites;
And thou sawest the wolves
(20)  Whose faces ⟨⟨glanced⟩⟩ ↑shone.↓

28  The noblest vultures flew ⟨daher⟩ thither
They ⟨screamed⟩stepped from corpse to corpse
And from the richly prepared feast
They could not rise into the air.

[240]–[246] [blank]
[247]     On earth I dream, I die to be:
Time! shake not thy bald head at me,
I challenge thee to hurry past
Or for my turn to fly too fast,
(5)  Think me not numbed, or halt, ⟨or blind⟩with age
Or cares that earth to earth engage,
Caught with love's cord of twisted beams,
Or mired with climate's gross extremes;
I pass with yonder comet free,
(10)  Pass with the comet into space
Which mocks thy aeons to embrace ↑,↓
Aeons which ↑tardily↓ unfold
Realm beyond realm,—extent untold.
No early morn, no evening late
(15)  Self-upheld, disdaining Fate
Whose shining sons too great for Fame
Never heard thy weary name

[248]  Nor lives the tragic bard to say
How drear the part I held in one,
How lame the other limped away.

Could ever artist's pencil yield
(5)  The beauty of thy meanest field.

The moon which lights
My feet, my fancy more incites,

247 "The Nun's Aspiration," 29–36, 38–46. The added comma in line (11) is in pencil.
248 "The Nun's Aspiration," 47–49, eleven unused lines.

Nature is dear
Not for epochs, not for signs,
(10)    Not for measures of old time,
But for music more sublime
T'will never light a prosperous hour
Of earthly joy; in grander scope
I scorn, I scorn the frivolous hope

[249]        But o ↑to watch↓ these waves & leaves
When the stoic Nature grieves—
No human speech so beautiful
As their murmurs mine to lull.
(5)    On this altar God hath built
↑I↓ Lay my vanity & guilt.
Not me can hope or passion urge
Hearing ⟨thus⟩ ↑as now↓ the lofty dirge
Which blasts of northern mountains hymn
(10)    Nature's funeral high & dim;
Sable pageantry of clouds,
Mourning summer laid in shrouds.
Many a day shall dawn & die,
Many an angel wander by
(15)    And ↑glance on↓ my long sunken turf
Damped perchance by ocean surf,
Forgotten amid splendid tombs,
Or wreathed & hid by summer's blooms

[250]    A few words in my cradle tongue
Enough to use my mates among,
Enough for prayer, enough for thought
And lessons which my Bible taught

[251] [blank]
[252]          ↑E.H.↓
Almost I am tempted to begin & draw
And shall
To sympathetic eyes the portraiture
Of the fine angels that environ me
(5)    One is a Greek      in mind & face
⟨And doth⟩Who might ⟨establish⟩ ↑embody↓ to the latter
        times
The truth of those old artists who drew

249 "The Nun's Aspiration," 11–28. "To watch" in line (1), "I" in line (6), and "glance on" in line (15) are added in pencil; "glance on" is traced over in ink.
  250 "The Nun's Aspiration," four unused lines.
  252 "Elizabeth Hoar," 1, x, 2–6, 6–12, 19–20, 21/22, 22/23, 14–15. In pencil; lines (2) and (15–18) are erased.

Who drew
In marble or in bronze on vase or frieze
(10)      Those ⟨perfect⟩ forms
        forms of perfect simpleness
        And beauty never in excess
        So bright, so positive so much in itself
        Yet so adapted to the work it ⟨did⟩ wrought
(15)      ⟨So perfect in her action that it seemed⟩
        ⟨She condescended if she spoke⟩
        ⟨And ‖ . . . . ‖ she spoke ↑better than all↓⟩
        ⟨Did not speak worthy of her⟩
        And yet the best of angels live alone
(20)      She seemed to commune with herself & say
[253]   For either I will marry with a star,
      Or I will labor in a factory.
      So perfect in her action one would say,
      She condescended if she added speech.
(5)     And though she spoke
      Better than all the rest, she did not speak
      Worthy of her. She read in many books
      And loved the Greek as t'were her mother tongue.

[254]–[276] [blank]
[277]      Seer of productive forms
      The sight of youth is seminal

      O the maple, mountain maple, O the Norway pine,
      The walnut grove, the cedar swamp, with ladders of the
        vine.

[278]–[287] [blank]
[288]      Ring your bells backward, loyal towers!
      And warn the land of harm

      Throned in the mountains hold the shore
      The hills are arsenals of power
(5)     Rank hemp & ⟨cott⟩flax & cotton grow
      To weave the sails all winds shall blow
      Stemming all night the starl⟨ess⟩it sea
      From either Pole to cross the line

253  "Elizabeth Hoar," 17–24. In pencil.
277  "Seer of productive forms" (1–2); "O the maple, mountain maple" (3–4). Lines (1–2) are in pencil.
288  "Ring your bells backward" (1–2); "You strong Republicans," 2, 4, 8–12 (3–9); "Where his name is named," 4 (10). In pencil; lines (1–2) are overwritten in ink; punctuation in line (1) is in ink only.

From ⟨the far⟩ Andes to the Appenine

See supra p 114

(10)      ⟨Rank⟩ And all the realm of Albion is like a puff of air

[289]    Enchanter with his mob of dreams
         His Prospero's train
         ⟨I tire of our modern ⟨Jews⟩⟩
         ⟨dealer in shrouds⟩

(5)       ⟨nor pleases ↑us↓ in a square or street⟩
         ⟨to pass a man in winding sheet⟩

         till freedom /shone ⟨↑woke↓⟩/ordered/thundered/smiled/ &
           peace was sung

         Till freedom smiled & joy-bells rung

[290]

*Now.*

The passing moment is an edifice
Which the Omnipotent cannot rebuild.

Unless ⟨T⟩to ⟨t⟩Thought be added Will,
Apollo is an imbecile.

(5)      Around the man ⟨that⟩who seeks a noble end
         ⟨no⟩Not angels but divinities attend.

Thought is the sole price
For which I sell days,
And willing grow aged,—

(10)     Melting matter to pictures,
         And life into law.

                      Annie Congdon    San Francisco   Cal.

[291]           *Album*

No fate, save by the victim's fault, is low,
For God hath writ all dooms magnificent,
So guilt not traverses his tender will.

---

289 "Enchanter with his mob of dreams" (1–6); "Boston," 97, 97 (7–8). Lines (3–6) are heavily canceled in ink; lines (7–8) are in erased pencil.

290 "Now" (1–2); "The comrade or the book," 3–4 (3–4); "Around the man" (5–6); "Terminus" ("For thought"), 2–3, 5, 7, 10 (7–11). Lines (1–2) are struck through twice in ink; in line (6), "No" in pencil is written over "not" to capitalize it; "Annie Congdon . . . Cal." is in pencil.

291 "No fate, save by the victim's fault" (1–3); "Now" (4–5); "Sacrifice" (6–9); "If wishes would carry" (10–13). Lines (6–9) are struck through in ink.

(5)     This shining moment is an edifice
        Which the Omnipotent cannot rebuild.

        Though Love repine, & Reason chafe,
        There came a voice without reply,
        "Tis man's perdition to be safe,
        When for the truth he ought to die."

(10)        If wishes would carry me over the land,
        I would ride with free bridle today,
        I would greet every tree with a grasp of my hand,
        I would drink of each river, & swim in each bay.

[292]   Unless to thought be added will,
        Apollo is an imbecile.

            O what is Heaven but the fellowship
        Of minds that each can stand against the world
(5)     By its own meek but incorruptible will?

        A score of ⟨miles⟩airy miles will smooth
        Rough Monadnock to a gem.

[293]                   *Maia*
        Illusion works impenetrable,
        Weaving webs innumerable,
        Her gay pictures never fail,
        Crowds each on other, veil on veil,
(5)     ⟨A⟩ charmer who will be believed
        By Man who thirsts to be deceived.

[294]   Heroes are /wrought/formed/ in Freedom's wars
        As asteroids are chips from stars

        Diamond will burn but Truth will hold

            The poet spoke his instant tho't
(5)     And filled the age his fame
        As Joves bolt struck an inch of ground
        And lit the sky the flame

        The bolt struck but an inch of ground

292 "The comrade or the book," 3–4 (1–2); "Heaven" (3–5); "A score of airy miles" (6–7).
293 "Maia."
294 "Heroes are wrought" (1–2); "Diamond will burn" (3); "His instant thought," 1–4, 3 (4–8). In pencil.

[295] ⟨J.E. Dorgan, Belmont Cottage  Schooley Mountain, Morris Co. New Jersey⟩

> What he thought not what he did
> Though more than Caesar or the Cid

> Seer of productive forms      Y 129

(5)

> His instant thought a poet spoke
> And filled the age his fame
> ⟨The⟩
> ⟨One⟩ ↑An↓ inch of ground the lightni⟨g⟩ng strook
> ⟨And⟩ ↑But↓ lit the sky the flame

[296] [index material omitted]
[inside back cover] [index material omitted]

---

**295** "What he thought" (1–2); "Seer of productive forms," 1 (3); "His instant thought," 1–2, x, 3–4 (4–8). In pencil; cancellations and additions in lines (7–8) are in ink.

# Notebook Rhymer

Emerson used notebook Rhymer mainly as a repository for fair copies of poems throughout the 1850s and into the early 1860s. The last thirty pages may have been the first inscribed; they contain translations of Persian poetry, taken from German sources, with which Emerson was working in the early 1850s.

The covers of notebook Rhymer, which measure 19.5 × 27.3 cm, are of dark green leather with a gold-stamped decorative border running along all four edges, front and back. The spine strip, also of dark green leather, bears seven sets of gold bands alternating with five gold-stamped diamonds.

Single flyleaves occur at the front and back (pp. i–ii and 157–58). Pages total 160, of which pp. 1–4 and 152–56 are unlined; the rest are faintly lined with thirty-nine lines to a page. All leaves measure 19.4 × 26.4 cm.

Sixty-one pages are numbered in ink, thirty-five in pencil, and three in pencil and ink. Fifty-seven pages are unnumbered. About one-third of the pages (forty-nine in all) are blank.

The notebook contains the following enclosures:

(1) between pp. 2–3, a sheet of gray paper, 19.3 × 25.1 cm, to which the numbers $2_a$–$2_b$ have been assigned;

(2) between pp. 6–7, a clipping from the *Atlantic Monthly* 1 (November 1858): 47, bearing the poem "Days";

(3) between pp. 12–13, a proofsheet for *May-Day*, 1867, pp. 117–19 (though the pages are actually numbered 119–21);

(4) between pp. 16–17, two proofsheets, with corrections by Emerson, of "There are beggars in Iran & Araby," lines 1–32; "Beauty," lines 11–26; "I found this," lines 1–28; and "Mask thy wisdom with delight," lines 1–2, 4–6, 9–12 (reproduced in Plates 6 and 7);

(5) between pp. 20–21, a clipping from the *Independent* 24 (29 February 1872): 1, bearing the first installment of William Ellery Channing's poem "Eliot: The Outlaw of the Forest";

(6) between pp. 24–25, a slip of paper containing New Year's verses from Edith Emerson to her father, dated 1865;

(7) between pp. 50–51, a sheet of white paper, lined in blue and folded once, measuring 19.4 × 24.6 cm, to which the numbers $50_a$–$50_d$ have been assigned; a sheet of light gray paper, 12.5 × 19.6 cm, to which the numbers $50_e$–$50_f$ have been assigned; a sheet of white paper, torn at the left margin, approximately 12.5 × 19.5 cm, to which the numbers $50_g$–$50_h$ have been assigned; and a sheet of white paper, 12.8 × 20.5 cm, to which the numbers $50_i$–$50_j$ have been assigned;

(8) pasted to p. 60, three clippings from proofsheets of "James Russell Lowell," lines 34–38, 44–80, and the unused lines on John Holmes from "The Adirondacs" (reproduced in Plate 8);

(9) between pp. 60–61, a clipping from a proofsheet of "The Nun's Aspiration," lines 1–10, and all of "In my garden three ways meet" (reproduced in Plate 9);

(10) between pp. 80–81, a sheet of white paper, folded once, bearing a handwritten note on the art of poetry, signed "W.E.C." (William Ellery Channing) and dated 1838;

(11) pasted to p. 95, a clipping from an unidentified newspaper of January or February 1863, bearing the text of "Boston Hymn," with corrections by Emerson;

(12) between pp. 96–97, a sheet of blue paper, 19.4 × 25 cm, to which the numbers 96$_a$–96$_b$ have been assigned, and a sheet of white paper, lined in blue and folded once, measuring 19.4 × 24.6 cm, to which the numbers 96$_c$–96$_f$ have been assigned;

(13) pasted to p. 97, a clipping from the *Boatswain's Whistle*, no. 9 (18 October 1864), 65, bearing the poem "Sea-Shore," with Emerson's corrections;

(14) between pp. 100–101, a proofsheet for *May-Day*, 1867, pp. 114–16 (though the pages are actually numbered 116–18); and

(15) between pp. 138–39, a sheet of white paper, folded once, measuring 19.5 × 24.7 cm, containing copies in Emerson's hand of two unidentified poems ("O when to me will come" on the first and third pages and "Harvest" on the fourth) not by Emerson, within which is laid a slip of orange paper with notes in the hand of James Elliot Cabot; also a sheet of white paper, folded once, containing on the first and third pages verses dated August 1844 addressed to Emerson in the hand of William Ellery Channing, apparently meant to accompany a gift.

A printed sheet was once affixed to p. 102 with red sealing wax.

[front cover verso] [blank]
[i]–[ii] [blank]
[1]                              Rhymer.

[2] [blank]
[2ₐ]      And what he knew he rightly knew,
          From winds discoursing as they flew
          Singing of fortune as they flew
          The Muses' hill by Fear is guarded
(5)       A bolder foot is still rewarded

          ⟨He⟩ ↑Seyd↓ planted where the deluge ploughed,
          His hired hands were wind & ⟨rain⟩ ↑cloud↓
          His eyes ⟨detected the⟩ ↑could spy the↓ gods concealed
          In ⟨the⟩ ↑each↓ hummock of the field

(10)      His instant thought the Poet spoke
          And filled the age his fame;
          An inch of ⟨ground⟩ ↑earth↓ the ⟨lightning⟩ ↑wild bolt↓
              strook
          And lit the sky with flame.

          A crystal soul
(15)      Sphered & concentric to the whole.

              Like vaulters in the circus round
          Who step from horse to horse but never touch the ground

          Slighted Minerva's learned tongue
          But leaped with joy when on the wind the shell of Clio
              ⟨⟨sung⟩rung⟩ rung

(20)      When the crown first incloses
          The brows of her son,
          The Muse him deposes
          From kingdom & throne.

[2_b]      ↑Third Person↓
          The Poet
              ↑Genius made his cabin wide↓
              ↑And Love brought gods therein to bide↓
              Charmed from fagot & from steel

2ₐ "Fate" ("Delicate omens"), x, x, x (1–3); "The Muses' hill" (4–5); "Seyd planted where
the deluge ploughed" (6–9); "His instant thought" (10–13); "There are beggars," 54–55
(14–15); "Like vaulters in the circus round" (16–17); "Slighted Minerva's learned tongue" (18–
19); "Poet of poets," 92–95 (20–23).

2_b "For Genius made his cabin wide," 1–2 (1–2); "Charmed from fagot" (3–9); "For every
god" (10–12); "Pale Genius roves alone," 5–8, x, x, x (13–19); "For Genius made his cabin
wide" (20–25); "The pain of love" (26–27); "His home / Where the pure drops" (28–32). Beneath
line (21) is the phrase "then his friendships" in pencil. Lines (28–32) are written sideways in the
left margin.

(5)        Harvests grew upon his tongue,
Past & Future must reveal
All their heart whilst Merlin sung.
The sun & planets fell amain
Like ripened seed into his brain,
There quickened to be born again.

(10)      For every god
Obeys the hymn, obeys the ode,
Obeys the holy ode.

Not his the feasters wine
Nor land nor gold nor power,
(15)      By want & pain god forceneth him
Till his elected hour.
He prayed the Day,
Prayed Day & Night to make him wise,
And each with bounty made replies.

(20)      For Genius made his cabin wide
And Love brought gods therein to bide
Better he thought no god could bring
And basked in friendship all the days of Spring.
And though he found his friendships meet
(25)      His quarrels too had somewhat sweet.
    ⟨The pain⟩ ↑And pains↓ of love a better ⟨state⟩fate
    Than the body's best estate

↑His home↓
Where the pure drops trickle down
(30)      Shed from the boulder one by one
⟨Starting out on their way to the sea⟩
To find their way to the ancient sea

[3]–[4] [blank]
[5]     I love thy music, mellow bell,
I love thine iron chime,
To life or death, to heaven or hell,
Which calls the Sons of Time.

(5)      Thy voice upon the deep
The homebound sea-boy hails,
It charms his cares to sleep,
It cheers him as he sails.

To house of God & heavenly joys
(10)      Thy summons called our sires,

5 "I love thy music."

And good men thought thy sacred voice
Disarmed the thunder's fires.

And soon thy music, sad death-bell!
Shall lift its notes once more,
(15)     And mix my requiem with the wind
That sweeps my native shore.

                       1823

[6] [blank]

[7]                          Days.                        ↑printed↓
⟨Damsels⟩ ↑Daughters↓ of Time, the hypocritic Days,
Muffled & dumb like barefoot dervishes,
And marching single in an endless file,
Bring diadems & fagots in their hands.
(5)     To each they offer gifts, after his will,
Bread, kingdoms, stars, ⟨sk⟩or sky that holds them all.
I, in my pleached garden, watched the pomp,
Forgot my morning wishes, hastily
Took a few herbs & apples, and the Day
(10)    Turned & departed silent. I, too late,
Under h⟨is⟩er solemn fillet saw the scorn.

[8] [blank]

[9]      I know the appointed hour,
I greet my office well,
Never faster, never slower
Revolves the fatal wheel.

(5)     I am neither faint nor weary,—
Fill thy will, O faultless Heart!
Here from youth to age I tarry,
Count it flight of bird or dart.

My heart at the heart of things
(10)    Heeds no longer lapse of time,
⟨Rushing ages moult their wings⟩
⟨Bathing in thy day sublime.⟩
Ages vainly fan their wings,
Me shall keep thy love sublime.
             ↑See X 186.↓ [i.e., 184–85]

[10] [blank]

[11]    There are beggars in Iran and Araby,
⟨SAID⟩ ↑Seyd↓ was hungrier than all;
Hafiz said, he was a fly

---

7 "Days." The word "printed" and a wavy line to the right of the poem are in pencil.
  9 "Not yet, not yet," 25–28, 37–44, 43–44. "See X 186." is in pencil.
  11 "There are beggars," 1–20 (1–20); "Beauty," 1–10 (11–20). The cancellations and additions are in pencil.

That came to every festival.
(5)    Also he came to the mosque,
In the trail of camel & caravan;
Knew every temple & kiosk
Out from Mecca to Ispehan:
Northward, he ⟨went to⟩ ↑climbed the↓ snowy hills;
(10)   At court, he sat in the grave divan.
Was never form & never face
So sweet to him as only grace
Which did not slumber like a stone,
But hovered gleaming & was gone.
(15)   Beauty chased he everywhere,
In flame, in storm, in clouds of air.
He smote the lake to feed his eye
With the precious green of the broken wave;
He flung in pebbles, well to hear
(20)   The moment's music which they gave.
[12]   Loved harebells nodding on a rock,
A cabin topped with curling smoke,
And huts and tents; nor loved he less
Stately ⟨men⟩ ↑lords↓ in palaces
(5)    ↑Princely women hard to please,↓
Fenced by form and ceremony,
With etiquette & heraldry.


[13] [blank]
[14]         ↑*Merlin's Song.*↓               ↑printed.↓
    Of Merlin wise I learned a song,—
Sing it low, or sing it loud,
It is mightier than the strong,
And ⟨loftier than⟩ ↑punishes↓ the proud.
(5)    I sing it to the surging crowd,—
Good men it will calm & cheer,
Bad men it will ⟨enrage⟩ ↑chain & cage↓.
In the heart of the music peals a strain
Which only Angels hear;
(10)   Whether it waken joy or rage,
Hushed myriads hark in vain;
Yet they who hear it shed their age,
And take their youth again.


12 "There are beggars," 21–22, 25–29.
14 "Merlin's Song." In line (4) the cancellation is in pencil, while the addition is in pencil and ink; in line (7) the cancellation and addition are in pencil.

[15]                    ↑ *Lover's petition.* ↓                    ↑ printed ↓
                    Good Heart, that ownest all!
                    I ask a modest boon and small:
                    Not of lands & towns the gift,
                    Too large a load for me to lift,—
(5)                 But ⟨for⟩of one proper creature,
                    Which geographic eye,
                    Sweeping the map of Western earth,
                    Or th' Atlantic coast from Maine
                    To Powhatan's domain,
(10)                Could not descry.
                    Is't much to ask, in all thy huge Creation,
                    So trivial a part,—
                    A solitary heart?
                    Yet count me not of spirit mean,
(15)                Or mine a mean demand,
                    For tis the concentration
                    And worth of all the land,
                    The sister of the Sea,
                    The daughter of the strand,
[16]                Composed of air and light,
                    And of the swart earth-might.
                    So little to thy poet's prayer
                    Thy large bounty well can spare.
(5)                 And yet, I think, if she were gone,
                    The world were better left alone.

[17]–[22] [blank]
[23]                         Destiny.                    ↑ printed ↓
                    Already blushes in thy cheek
                    The bosom-thought which thou must speak,
                    The bird, how far it haply roam
                    By cloud or isle, is flying home;
(5)                 The maiden fears, & fearing runs
                    Into the charmed snare she shuns;
                    And every man, in love or pride,
                    Of his fate is never wide.

                    Will a woman's fan the ocean smooth⟨e⟩?
(10)                Or prayers the stony Parcae soothe?
                    Or coax the thunder from its mark?
                    Or tapers light the Chaos dark?
                    In spite of Virtue and the Muse,
                    Nemesis will have her dues,

15  "Lover's Petition," 1–19.
16  "Lover's Petition," 20–25.
23  "Nemesis."

(15)    And all our struggles & our toils
        Tighter wind the giant coils.

[24]                    *Fate.*                    ↑printed↓
        Deep in the man sits fast his fate
        To mould his fortunes mean or great:
        Unknown to Cromwell as to me
        Was Cromwell's measure or degree;
(5)     Unknown to him as to his horse,
        If he than his groom be better or worse.
        He works, plots, fights, in rude affairs,
        With boys, lords, kings, his craft compares,
        Till late he learned, thro' doubt & fear,
(10)    Broad England harboured not his peer;—
        Obeying Time, the last to own
        The Genius from its cloudy throne.
        For the prevision is allied
        Unto the thing so signified;
(15)    Or say, the foresight that awaits
        Is the same Genius that creates.

[25]                   *Manners.*                  ↑printed.↓
        Grace, Beauty & Caprice
        Build this golden portal;
        Graceful women, chosen men
        Dazzle every mortal.
(5)     Their sweet & lofty countenance
        His enchanted food;
        He need not go to them, their forms
        Beset his solitude.
        He looketh seldom in their face,
(10)    His eyes explore the ground,
        The green grass is a looking-glass
        Whereon their traits are found.
        Little he says to them,
        So dances his heart in his breast;
(15)    Their tranquil mien bereaveth him
        Of wit, of words, of rest.
        Too weak to win, too fond to shun
        The tyrants of his doom,
        The much-deceived Endymion
(20)    ⟨Scuds⟩ ↑Slips↓ behind a tomb.

24  "Fate" ("Deep in the man").
25  "Manners."

[26]               *The Chartist's Complaint.*               ↑printed↓
                Day! hast thou two faces,
                Making one place two places?
                One by humble farmer seen,
                Chill & wet, unlighted, mean,
(5)             Useful only, ⟨ch⟩triste and damp,
                Serving for a laborer's lamp?
                Have the same mists another side,
                To be the appanage of pride,
                Gracing the rich man's ⟨wood⟩ ↑lawn↓ & lake,
(10)            His park where amber mornings break,
                And treacherously bright to show
                His planted isle where roses g⟨row⟩low?
                O Day! and is your mightiness
                A sycophant to smug success?
(15)            Will the sweet sky & Ocean broad
                Be fine accomplices of fraud?
                O Sun! I curse thy cruel ray:
                Back, back to Chaos, harlot Day!


[27]                      *Rubies.*                      ↑printed↓
                They brought me rubies from the mine,
                And held them to the sun,
                I said, they are drops of frozen wine
                From Eden's vats that run.

(5)             I looked again.—I thought them hearts
                Of friends to friends unknown;
                Tides that should warm each neighboring life
                Are locked in sparkling stone.

                But fire to thaw that ruddy snow,
(10)            To break ⟨the winedrop's prison,⟩ ↑⟨rubied ice⟩
                     enchanted ice,↓
                And give love's scarlet tides to flow—
                ⟨That sun is yet unrisen.⟩
                ↑When shall that Sun arise?↓

[28] [blank]
[29]                      *Memory.*                      ↑printed.↓
                Night-dreams trace on Memory's wall
                Shadows of the thoughts of day;

26 "The Chartist's Complaint."
27 "Rubies." The cancellations and additions are in pencil and ink.
29 "Memory" (1–4); "Fate" ("Her planted eye") (5–8). In line (4) the cancellation and addi-
tion are in pencil.

432

And thy fortunes, as they fall,
⟨Each⟩ ↑The↓ bias of the will betray.

*Fate.*              ↑printed↓

(5)       Her planted eye Today controls,
Is in the Morrow most at home,
And sternly calls to Being souls
That curse her when they come.

[30] [blank]
[31]      ⟨⟨*Naturalist.*⟩ ↑*Botanist.*↓⟩ ↑*Botanist.*↓    ↑printed.↓
Go thou to thy learned task,—
I stay with the flowers of Spring;
Do thou of the Ages ask
What me the Hours will bring.

*Forester.*          ↑printed.↓

(5)       He took the color of his vest
From rabbit's coat or grouse's breast,
For, as the woodkinds lurk & hide,
So walks the woodman unespied.

*Gardener.*          ↑printed↓
True Bramin, in the morning meadows wet,
(10)     Expound the Vedas of the violet,
Or, hid in vines, peeping thro' many a loop,
See the plum redden, & the beurré stoop.

[32]      True Bramin, in the morning meadows wet,
Expound the Vedas in the violet,
Or, hid in vines, peeping through many a loop,
See the plum redden, and the beurré stoop.

[33]            *S. H.*          ↑printed.↓
With beams ⟨that stars at Christmas⟩ ↑December
    planets↓ dart,
His cold eyes truth and conduct scanned;
July was in his sunny heart,
October in his liberal hand.

*A. H.*          ↑printed.↓
(5)       High was her heart, & yet was well-inclined,
Her manners made of bounty well refined,

31 "Botanist" (1–4); "Forester" (5–8); "Gardener" (9–12). "*Naturalist.*" was canceled and "*Botanist.*" added in ink; both titles were then circled and canceled in pencil and "Botanist." written in pencil above.
32 "Gardener." Struck through four times in pencil.
33 "S. H." (1–4); "A. H." (5–8). The cancellation and addition in line (1) are in pencil.

Far capitals & marble courts her eye still seemed to see,
Minstrels, & kings, & highborn dames, & of the best
        that be.

[34]     The Yesterday doth never smile,
         Today goes drudging through the while,
         Yet, in the name of Godhead, I
         The Morrow front, and can defy:
(5)      Though I am weak, yet God, when prayed,
         ⟨Will⟩Cannot withhold his conquering aid.
         Ah me! it was my childhood's thought,
         If He should make my ⟨life⟩web a blot
         On life's fair picture of delight,
(10)     My heart's content would find it right.

[35]                    *Love & Thought.*                    ↑printed.↓
              Two well-assorted travellers use
         The highway, Eros and the Muse.
         From this pair is nothing hidden,
         To the ⟨pair⟩ ↑twins↓ is nought forbidden,
(5)      Hand in hand the comrades go
         Every nook of nature through:
         Each for other they were born,
         Each can ⟨t'⟩ other best adorn,
         Every nook of nature through:
                    ↑mortal↓ grief
(10)     Past all balsam or relief,
         ⟨Is,⟩ when by false companions crossed,
         The pilgrims have each other lost.

[36] [blank]
[37]                    *Climacteric.*                    ↑printed↓
         I am not wiser for my age,
         Nor skilful by my grief;
         Life loiters at the Book's first page,
         Ah! could we turn the leaf.

[38] [blank]
[39]              αδακρυν νεμονται αἰωνα                    ↑printed↓
         "A new commandment," said the smiling Muse,
         "I give my darling son, *Thou shalt not preach.*"

34 "The Nun's Aspiration," 1–10.
35 "Love and Thought." In line (3) "this pair" was canceled in pencil and "the twins" added
in pencil; finally the entire change was erased. In line (9) "mortal" is in pencil.
37 "Climacteric."
39 "'Αδακρυν νέμονται Αἰῶνα."

434

Luther, Fox, Behmen, Swedenborg, grew pale,
And, on the instant, rosier clouds upbore
(5)      Hafiz and Shakspeare with their happy choirs.

[40]    And many a thousand summers
My apples ripened well,
And light from meliorating stars
With firmer lustre fell.

[41]              *Natura in minimis.*       ↑printed↓
As sings the pinetree in the wind,
So sings in the wind a sprig of the pine:
↑⟨The strength & joy of laughing France⟩Her strength &
    soul has laughing France↓
↑⟨Are shed into its wine.⟩Shed in each drop of wine. ↓

(5)    A score of airy miles will smooth
Rough Monadnock to a gem.

[42]                 *Shakspeare.*      ↑printed. ↓
I see all human wits
Are measured but a few;
Unmeasured still my Shakspeare sits,
Lone as the blessed Jew.

               *Preraphaelite.*      ↑printed↓
(5)    Go copy in verse one chime
Of the wood-bell's peal & cry;
Write in a book the morning's prime,
And match with words that amber sky.

[43]    Of all wit's uses, the main one
Is to live well with who has none.

[44]    I stood silent

                  *Letters.*
Every day brings a ship,
Every ship brings a word;
Well for those who have no fear,
(5)    Looking seaward, well assured
That the word the vessel brings

40 "Song of Nature," 17–20. In pencil, struck through in pencil.
41 "Nature in Leasts" (1–4); "A score of airy miles" (5–6). In line (2) the upper dot of the colon was supplied in pencil. In lines (3–4) "The strength . . . France" and "Are . . . wine." are added in pencil, overwritten by the revised lines in ink.
42 "Shakspeare" (1–4); "My Garden," 37–40 (5–8). Lines (5–8) are struck through in pencil.
43 "Considerations by the Way," 26–27.
44 Unidentified line (1); "Letters" ("Every day") (2–7). "I stood silent" is in pencil. Lines (2–7) are struck through in ink.

Is the word they wish to hear.

[45]     Yet there will come

I stood

All things rehearse
The meaning of the universe

(5)     The cup of life is not so shallow
That we have drained the best,
That all the wine at once we swallow,
And lees make all the rest.

Maids of as soft a bloom shall marry
(10)    As Hymen yet hath blessed,
And fairer forms are in the quarry
Than Angelo released.

[46]         You shall not love me for what daily spends,
You shall not know me in the noisy street
Where I as others follow petty ends,
Nor when in fair saloons we chance to meet,
(5)     Nor when I'm jaded, sick, ⟨anxious⟩ ↑perplexed↓, or mean:
But love me then & only when you know
Me for the channel of the rivers of God,
From deep, ideal, fontal heavens that flow,
Making the shores, making their beauty broad,
(10)    Which birds & cattle drink, ↑drink too the roots of the
        grove,↓
And animating all it feeds with love.

[47]             *Webster.*
Why did all manly gifts in Webster fail?
He wrote on Nature's grandest brow, *For Sale.*

            *Economy.*                    ↑printed↓
Pay every debt,—as if God wrote the bill,—
So to shut up the avenues of ill.

[48]             *Poet.*                   ↑printed↓
To clothe the fiery thought
In simple word succeeds,
For still the craft of genius is
To mask a king in weeds.

45 Unidentified lines (1–2); "All things rehearse" (3–4); "The cup of life is not so shallow"
(5–12). Lines (1–4) are in pencil.
46 "You shall not love me."
47 "Webster" ("Why did all manly gifts") (1–2); " 'Suum Cuique' " ("Wilt thou"), 2, 1 (3–4).
48 "Poet" ("To clothe") (1–4); "Casella" (5–8).

*Poet.*  ↑printed↓

(5) Test of the Poet is knowledge of love,
For Eros is older than Saturn or Jove;
Never was poet, of late or of yore,
Who was not tremulous with love-lore.

[49]  *Orator.*  ↑printed↓
He who has no hands
Perforce must use his tongue;
Foxes are so cunning,
Because they are not strong.

[50]  *Friendship.*  ↑printed↓
↑Well and↓ Wisely spoke the Greek,
Be thou faithful, but not fond;
To the Altar's foot thy fellow seek,—
The Furies wake beyond.

Sacrifice.  ↑printed↓
(5) Though Love repine, and Reason chafe,
I hear a voice without reply,
'Tis man's perdition to be safe,
When for the truth he ought to die.'

[50ₐ] Third Person  *Poet*
The atom displaces all atoms beside
And Genius unspheres all souls that abide

Forbore the ant hill, shunned to tread,
In mercy, on one little head

(5) The gods walk in the breath of the woods
They walk by the sounding pine,
And fill the long reach of the old seashore
With colloquy divine
And the poet who overhears
(10) Each random word they say
Is the ⟨/hierarch/monarch/ of men⟩ ↑prophet without peers↓
Whom kings & lords obey.

What flowing central forces, say,
Make up thy splendor, matchless day!

49 "Orator."
50 "Pericles" (1–4); "Sacrifice" (5–8).
50ₐ "The atom displaces" (1–2); "Forbore the ant hill" (3–4); "The gods walk," 1–8 (5–12);
"What flowing central forces" (13–14); "As Stars & the celestial Kind" (15–16). "Third person"
is set off by an angled line in ink.

(15)        As Stars & the celestial Kind
               Their own food are skilled to find

[50ᵦ]      By art, by music, overthrilled
               The wine cup shakes, the wine is spilled

               In building or in poem caught the rhyme
                   And drank the wit in prayer or pantomime

(5)         ↑Doth not↓ The Rock of Ages melt⟨s a⟨way⟩lway⟩
               Into the mineral air,
               To /yield/be/ the quarry whence is built
               Thought, & its mansion fair.

               The Understanding's copper coin
(10)        Counts not with the gold of Love,
               The strengths & skills the Titans join
               Melt before the glance of Jove.

[50ᵤ]      A queen rejoices in her peers,
               And wary Nature knows her own
               By court or city, dale or down,
               And like a lover volunteers,
(5)         And to her son will treasures more
               And more to purpose freely pour
               In one wood-walk than learned men
               Will find with glass in ten times ten.

                  Delicate omens traced in air
(10)        To him authentic witness bare;
               Birds with auguries on their wings
               Chanted undeceiving things
               Him to beckon, him to warn,—
               Well might then the poet scorn
(15)        To learn of scribe or courier
               Hints writ in vaster character;
               ⟨&⟩And in his mind at dawn of day
               Soft shadows of the evening lay.

[50ᵤ]      By thought, by music, overfilled
               The wine cup shakes, the wine is spilled.

               The best of life is presence of a muse
               Who does not wish to wander, comes by stealth,

50ᵦ "By art, by music" (1–2); "In building or in poem" (3–4); "Ever the Rock of Ages melts" (5–8); "The understanding's copper coin," 1–2, x, x (9–12).
    50ᵤ "A queen rejoices" (1–8); "Fate" ("Delicate omens"), 1–10 (9–18).
    50ᵤ "By art, by music" (1–2); "Best boon of life" (3–11).

(5)        Divulging to the heart she sets a flame
            No popular tale, no bauble for the mart⟨,⟩.
            When the wings grow that draw the ⟨c⟩gazing ⟨eyes⟩
                    ↑crowd↓,
            Ofttimes poor Genius fluttering near the earth
            Is wrecked upon the turrets of the town:
(10)      But, lifted till he meets the steadfast gales
            Calm blowing from the Everlasting West

[50ₑ]           Second Person
            Rules to the bard made evident
            By Him who built the day,
            The columns of the firmament
            Not deeper based than they.
(5)        ↑The brook sings on, but sings in vain↓
            ↑Wanting the echo in thy brain↓
            Shun Passion, fold the hands of Thrift,
            Sit still, & Truth is near;
            Suddenly it will uplift
(10)      Your eyelids to the sphere.
            Wait a little, you shall see
            The portraiture of things to be;
            ⟨Shall⟩ ↑And↓ overhear the Parcae reel
            Threads of Man at their humming wheel,
(15)      Threads of life & power & pain,
            So sweet & mournful falls the strain
            ↑————————↓
            ↑See Also *NP* 284, 129,↓

[50f]      ↑Sum your annals in a rhyme↓
            ↑Span the poles & shorten time↓
            Try the might the Muse affords,
            And the balm of thoughtful words:
(5)        Hold of the Maker, not the Made,
            Sit with the Cause, or grim, or glad,
            Bring beauty to the desolate,
            Hang roses on the stony Fate,
            Coin ⟨the⟩ ↑common↓ daylight into lines
(10)      In which its proper splendor shines;
            Coin the moonlight into verse
            Which all its ⟨splendor⟩ ↑magic↓ shall rehearse.

50ₑ "The rules to men" (1–4); "Old Age" (5–6); "Shun Passion" (7–12); "The Harp," 99–102 (13–16). "See . . . 129," and the preceding short rule are in pencil.

50f "Sum your annals" (1–2); "Try the might the Muse affords," 1–2 (3–4); "Hold of the Maker" (5–6); "Try the might the Muse affords," 3–4 (7–8); "Coin the daydawn" (9–12); "Tell men what they knew before" (13–14); "There are beggars," 23–24 (15–16); "The Asmodaean feat" (17–18); "Borrow Urania's subtile wings" (19–23).

Tell men what they knew before,
Paint the prospect from their door,
(15) The ring of axe, the hum of wheel,
And gleam which Use will paint on steel.
The Asmodean feat be thine
To spin the sand-heap into twine.
↑Borrow Urania's subtile wings↓
(20) Chasing with words fast-flowing things:
Cling to the sacred fact, nor try
To plant thy shrivelled pedantry
On the shoulders of the sky.

[50g] ⟨↑Ever↓⟩ ↑Doth not↓ The ⟨r⟩Rock of ages melt⟨s alway⟩
Into the mineral air
⟨To ⟨yield⟩be the⟩ ↑To be the ⟨unspent⟩↓ quarry whence is
built
Thought & its mansion fair

_____          _____

(5) Teach me your mood o patient stars
Who climb each night the ancient sky
Leaving on space no shade, no scars,
No trace of age, no fear to die.

_____

Brother no decrepitude
(10) Cramps the ⟨wing⟩ limbs of Time
As fleet his feet his hands as good
His vision as sublime

Teach me your mood
Teach

[50h] ⟨Poetry & Criticism.⟩ *unread*

[50i]       Slighting Minervas learned tongue
But heard with joy when on the wind the shell of Clio rung

[50j] _____

No fate, save by the victim's fault, is low,
For God hath writ all dooms magnificent,
So Guilt not traverses his tender will.

50g "Ever the Rock of Ages melts" (1–4); "Teach me your mood" (5–8); "Brother, no decrep-
itude" (9–12); "Teach me your mood," 1, 1 (13–14).
50h "Poetry and Criticism" is the title of a lecture given by Emerson on 19 October 1868 in
Boston; it also served as the working title for the long first chapter of *Letters and Social Aims*,
1876. The entry is written sideways in the left margin.
50i "Slighted Minerva's learned tongue."
50j "No fate, save by the victim's fault" (1–3); "Terminus" ("For thought"), 2–3, 5, 7, 10
(4–8).

Thought is the sole price
(5)      For which we ⟨gr⟩sell days,
And willing grow aged,
Melting matter to pictures,
And life into law.

[51]                ↑Artist.↓                       ↑printed↓
Quit the hut, frequent the palace,
Reck not what the people say;
For still where e'er the trees grow biggest,
Huntsmen find the easiest way.

                                                      ↑printed↓

(5)      Visions of the night recall
         Shadows of the thoughts of day,
And thy fortunes, as they fall,
         Each secret of the Will betray.

[52]          Thus the high ⟨m⟩Muse treated me
Directly never greeted me
                 &c
              See NO 65

[53]              ↑Nativity.↓                  ↑printed↓
Ere he was born, the stars of fate
Plotted to make him rich and great:
When from the womb the babe was loosed,
The gate of gifts behind him closed.

[54] [blank]
[55]          *Written in a Volume of Goethe.*
Six thankful weeks,—& let it be
A metre of prosperity,—
In my coat I bore this book,
And seldom therein could I look,
(5)      ⟨For I had⟩ ↑Each morning brought↓ too much to think,
Heaven & earth to eat & drink.
Is he hapless, who can spare
In his plenty things so rare?

51 "Artist" (1–4); "Memory" (5–8). The title "Artist." and lines (5–8) are in pencil.
52 "I found this," 9–10.
53 "Horoscope."
55 "Written in a Volume of Goethe." In line (5) the cancellation and addition are in pencil
and ink.

[56] [ . . . ]

[57]                     *Freedom.*                    ↑printed↓

Once I wished I might rehearse
Freedom's paean in my verse,
That the slave who caught the strain
Should throb until he snapt ⟨the⟩his chain.

(5)      But the Spirit said, "Not so;
Speak it not, or speak it low;
Name not lightly to be said,
Gift too precious to be prayed,
Passion not to be exprest

(10)     But by heaving of the breast:
Yet,—would'st thou the mountain find
Where this deity is shrined,
Who gives to seas and sunset skies
Their unspent beauty of surprise,

(15)     And, when it lists him, waken can
Brute & savage into man;
Or, if in thy heart he shine,
Blends the starry fates with thine,
Draws angels nigh to dwell with thee,

(20)     And makes thy thoughts archangels be;
↑Counsel not with flesh & blood,↓
↑Loiter not for cloak or food,↓
Freedom's secret would'st thou know?—
Right thou feelest, ⟨rashly⟩ ↑/instant/swiftly/↓ do."

[58] [blank]

[59]                   ↑South wind.↓              ↑printed in Channing's
                                                  Life of Thoreau.↓

In the turbulent beauty
Of a gusty autumn day,
Poet in a wood-crowned headland
Sighed his soul away.

(5)      Farms the sunny landscape dappled,
Swan-down clouds dappled the farms,
Cattle lowed in hazy distance
Where far oaks outstretched their arms.
Sudden gusts came full of meaning,

(10)     All too much to him they said;—
Southwinds have long memories,
Of that be none afraid.

57 "Freedom," 1–20, two lines first printed in the 1867 version, 21–22. Lines (21–22) are written at the bottom of p. [56], circled, and their position indicated by a caret on p. [57]. In line (24) the cancellation and additions are in pencil.
59 "South Wind." The title is in pencil and ink.

I cannot tell rude listeners
Half the telltale Southwind said,
(15)   T'would bring the blushes of yon maples
To a man and to a maid.

[60] [ . . . ]
[61]                        Northman.                        ↑printed↓
The gale that wrecked you on the sand,
It helped my rowers to row;
The storm is my best galley-hand,
And drives me where I go.

                        From *Alcuin*.                        ↑printed. ↓
(5)        The sea is the road of the bold,
Frontier of the wheatsown plains,
The pit wherein all ⟨rivers⟩ ↑streams are↓ rolled,
And fountain of the rains.

[62] [blank]
[63]                        *Hush!*                        ↑printed↓
Every thought is public,
Every nook is wide,
The gossips spread each whisper,
And the gods from side to side.

(5)        Atom from atom yawns as far
As moon from earth, or star from star.

[64] [blank]
[65]                ↑*Nature.* ↓                        ↑printed. ↓
Boon Nature yields each day a brag which we now first
        behold,
And trains us on to slight the new, as if it were the old;
And blest is he, who playing deep, yet haply asks not why,
Too busied with the crowded hour to ⟨as⟩fear to live or die.

[66]                        Hafiz.                        ↑printed↓
Her passions the shy violet
From Hafiz never hides;
Love-longings of the raptured bird
The bird to him confides.

60 Three clippings from proofsheets are pasted on the page; see the descriptive headnote at
the beginning of this notebook.
61 "Northman" (1–4); "From Alcuin" (5–8).
63 "Hush!" (1–4); "Atom from atom" (5–6).
65 "Nature" ("Boon Nature").
66 "Hafiz."

[67]                  Poet.               ↑printed↓

⟨And⟩ ever the poet *from* the land
Steers his bark, & trims his sail,
Right out to sea his courses stand,
New worlds to find in pinnace frail.

[68]             Borrowing.               ↑printed↓
—— ↑ *Translated from the French.* ↓

Some of your hurts you have cured,
And the sharpest you still have survived;
But what torments of wo you endured
From evils that never arrived!

——

[69]         ↑ *Heri, Cras, Hodie.* ↓         ↑printed↓

Shines the last age; the next with hope is seen;
Today slinks poorly off unmarked between:
↑Future or Past no ⟨stricter⟩ ↑richer↓ secret folds, ↓
↑O friendless Present! than thy bosom holds. ↓

[70] [blank]
[71]             *Gypsy's Song.*            ↑printed↓
    The sun goes down, & with him takes
The coarseness of my poor attire;
The fair moon mounts, & aye the flame
Of gypsy beauty blazes higher.

(5)    Pale northern girls! You scorn our race,
You, captives of your air-tight halls,
Wear out in-doors your sickly days,
But leave us ⟨o⟩the horizon walls.

And if I take you, dames, to task,
(10)   And say it frankly without guile,
Then you are gypsies in a mask,
And I the lady all the while.

If on the heath, ⟨under⟩ ↑below↓ the moon,
I court & play with paler blood,
(15)   Me false to mine dare whisper none,
↑—↓One sallow horse-man knows me good.

Go, keep your cheek's rose from the rain,
For teeth & hair with shopmen deal,

67  "Poet" ("Ever the Poet"). All in pencil except "printed".
68  "Borrowing. From the French." All in pencil except "printed".
69  "Heri, Cras, Hodie." Lines (1–2) are struck through twice in pencil.
71  "The Romany Girl," 1–18. The word "printed" and a curving line to the right of the verses are in pencil.

[72] My swarthy tint is in the grain,
   The rocks & forest know it real.

   The wild air bloweth in our lungs,
   The keen stars twinkle in our eyes,
(5)  The birds gave us our wily tongues,
   The panther in our dances flies.

   You doubt we read the stars on high,
   ↑—↓Nathless, we read your fortunes true;
   The stars may hide in the upper sky,
(10)  But without glass we fathom you.

  [73]    *Una.*
   Roving, roving, as it seems,
   Una lights my clouded dreams,
   Still for journeys she is drest,
   We wander far by east & west.

(5)  In the homestead, homely thought;
   At my work I ramble not;
   If from home chance draw me wide,
   Half seen Una sits beside.

   In my house & garden plot,
(10)  Though beloved, I miss her not;
   But one I seek in foreign places,
   One face explore in foreign faces.

   At home a deeper thought may light
   The inward sky with chrysolite,
(15)  And I greet from far the ray,
   Aurora of a dearer day.

   But if upon the seas I sail,
   Or trundle on the glowing rail,
   I am but a thought of hers,
(20)  Loveliest of travellers.

   So the gentle poet's name
   To foreign parts is blown by fame,
   Seek him in his native town,
   He is hidden & unknown.

 [74] [blank]
 [75]    ↑Spring Winds↓
   The April winds are magical
   And thrill our tuneful frames,

---

72 "The Romany Girl," 19–28.
73 "Una."
75 "April." The title is in pencil.

The garden walks are passional
To bachelors & dames.
(5)      The hedge is gemmed with diamonds
The air with cupids full,
The clues of fairy Rosamonds
Guide lovers to the pool.
Each dimple in the water,
(10)    Each leaf that shades the rock
Can cozen, pique, & flatter,
Can parley & provoke.
Puck, Robin, & the goblins
Know more than all the books;
(15)    Down with your dol⟨l⟩eful problems,
Come court the sunny brooks.
The south winds are quick-witted,
The schools are sad & slow;
The masters quite omitted
(20)    The lore we care to know.

   [76] [blank]
   [77]              *Two Rivers.*             ↑printed↓
Thy summer voice, Musketaquit,
Repeats the music of the rain;
But sweeter rivers pulsing flit
Through thee, as thou through Concord plain.

(5)    Thou in thy narrow banks art pent,—
The stream I love unbounded goes
Through flood, & sea, & firmament,
Through light, through life, it forward flows.

I see the inundation sweet,
(10)    I hear the spending of the stream,
Through years, through men, through nature fleet,
Thro' passion, thought, thro' power, & dream.

Musketaquit, a goblin strong,
Of shard & flint makes jewels gay,
(15)    They lose their grief who hear his song,
And where he winds is the day of day.

So forth & brighter fares my stream,—
Who drink it, shall not thirst again;
No darkness stains its equal gleam,
(20)    And ages drop in it like rain.

77 "Two Rivers." The word "printed" and a curving line to the right of the verses are in pencil.

[78]–[80] [blank]

[81]                              *Purging.*                    ↑printed↓

    ↑⟨*Phoebus Apollo*⟩ ↑Musa↓ *loquitur.* ↓
    I hung my verses in the wind,
    Time & tide their faults may find.
    ⟨They⟩All were ⟨all⟩ winnowed through & through;
    Five lines lasted sound & true;

(5)    Five were smelted in a pot
    Than the south more fierce & hot.
    These the ⟨southwind⟩ ↑siroc↓ could not melt,
    Fire their fiercer flaming felt,
    And the meaning was more white

(10)   Than July's meridian light.
    Sunshine cannot bleach the snow,
    Nor Time unmake what poets know.
    Have you eyes to find the five
    Which five hundred did survive?

[82]                         *Song of Nature.*                 ↑printed. ↓

    Mine are the night & morning,
    The pits of air, the gulf of Space,
    The sportive sun, the gibbous moon,
    The innumerable days.

(5)    I hide in the solar glory,
    I lurk in the pealing song,
    I rest on the pitch of the torrent,
    No less in death am strong.

    No numbers have counted my tallies,
(10)   No tribes my house can fill,
    I sit by the shining Fount of life,
    And pour the deluge still.

[83]   And ever by delicate powers
    Gathering along the centuries
    From race on race the rarest flowers,
    My wreath shall nothing miss.

(5)    And many a thousand summers
    My apples ripened well,
    And light from meliorating stars
    With firmer glory fell.

81 "The Test."
82 "Song of Nature," 1–12.
83 "Song of Nature," 13–28.

(10)
I wrote the past in characters
Of rock & fire the scroll,
The building in the coral sea,
The planting of the coal.

(15)
And thefts from satellites & ⟨suns⟩ ↑rings,↓
And broken stars I drew,
And out of spent & aged things
I formed the world anew.

[84]
What time the gods kept carnival
Tricked out in star & flower,
And in cramp elf & saurian forms
They swathed their too much power.

(5)
Time & Thought were my surveyors,
They laid their courses well,
They boiled the sea & baked the layers
Of granite, marl, & shell.

(10)
But he, the manchild glorious,
Where tarries he the while⟨,⟩?
The rainbow shines his harbinger,
The sunset gleams his smile.

(15)
My boreal lights ⟨gleam⟩leap upward,
Forthright my planets roll,
⟨But he⟩And still the manchild is not born,
The summit of the whole.

[85]
Must time & tide forever run?
Will never my winds go sleep in the west?
Will never my wheels which whirl the sun
And satellites, have rest?

(5)
Too much of donning & doffing,
Too slow the rainbow fades,
I weary of my robe of snow,
My leaves, & my cascades;

(10)
I tire of globes & races,
Too long the game is played;
What without him is summer's pomp,
Or winter's frozen shade?

I travail in pain for him,
My creatures travail & wait,

84 "Song of Nature," 29–44.
85 "Song of Nature," 45–64.

(15)      His couriers come by squadrons,
     He comes not to the gate.

     Twice I have moulded an image,
     And thrice outstretched my hand,
     Made one of day, & one of night,
(20)      And one of the salt sea sand.

[86]      One in a Judaean manger,
     And one by Avon stream,
     One over against the mouths of Nile,
     And one in the Academe.

(5)      I moulded kings & saviours,
     And bards o'er kings to rule;
     But fell the starry influence short,
     The cup was never full.

     Yet whirl the glowing wheels once more,
(10)      And mix the bowl again;
     Seethe, Fate! the ancient elements,
     Heat, cold, dry, wet, & peace & pain.

     Let war & trade & creeds & song
     Blend, ripen race on race,
(15)      The sunburnt world a man shall breed
     Of all the zones, & countless days.

[87]      No ray is dimmed, no atom worn,
     My oldest force is good as new,
     And the fresh rose on yonder thorn
     Gives back the bending heavens in dew.

[88]          *The Titmouse.*             ↑printed↓
     You shall not be overbold
     When you deal with arctic cold,
     As late I found my lukewarm blood
     Chilled wading in the snow-choked wood.
(5)      How should I fight? my foeman fine
     Has million arms to one of mine:
     East, west, for aid I looked in vain,
     East, west, north, south, are his domain.
     Miles off, three dangerous miles is home,
(10)      Must borrow his winds who there would come.
     Up & away for life! be fleet!—
     The frost-king ties my fumbling feet,

86  "Song of Nature," four lines first printed in the 1867 version, 65–76.
87  "Song of Nature," 77–80.
88  "The Titmouse," 1–16.

Sings in my ears,—my hands are stones,—
Curdles the blood to the marble bones,
(15)   Tugs at the heart-strings, numbs the sense,
And hems in life with narrowing fence.

[89]   Well, in this broad bed lie & sleep,
The punctual stars will vigil keep,
Embalmed by purifying cold,
The winds shall sing their deadmarch old,
(5)   The snow is no ignoble shroud,
The moon thy mourner, & the cloud.

Softly,—but this way fate was pointing,
T'was coming fast to such anointing,
When piped a tiny voice hard by,
(10)   Gay & polite, a cheerful cry,
*Chic-chicadee-dee!* fancy note
Out of sound heart & merry throat,
As if it said, Good day, good sir!
Fine afternoon, old passenger!
(15)   Happy to meet you in these places,
Where January brings few men's faces.

This poet, though he live apart,
Moved by his hospitable heart,
[90]   Sped, when I passed his sylvan fort
To do the honors of his court,
As fits a feathered lord of land,—
Flew near, with soft wing grazed my hand,
(5)   Hopped on the bough, then, darting low,
Prints his small impress on the snow,
Shows feats of his gymnastic play,
Head downward, clinging to the spray.

Here was this atom in full breath,
(10)   Hurling defiance at vast death,
This scrap of valor just for play
Fronts the northwind in waistcoat gray,
As if to shame my weak behaviour;
I greeted loud my little saviour,
(15)   "You pet! What dost here? & what for?
In these woods, thy small Labrador,
At this pinch, wee San Salvador!
[91]   What fire burns in that little chest,

89 "The Titmouse," 17–34.
90 "The Titmouse," 35–51.
91 "The Titmouse," 52–71.

So frolic, stout, & self-possest?—
↑ Didst steal⟨t⟩ the glow which lights the west? ↓
Henceforth I wear no stripe but thine,
(5)     Ashes & ⟨black⟩ ↑jet↓ all hues outshine.
Why are not diamonds black & gray
To ape thy daredevil array?
And I affirm, the spacious North
Exists to draw thy virtue forth.
(10)    I think no virtue ⟨grows⟩goes with size,
The reason of all cowardice
Is, that men are overgrown,
And, to be valiant, must come down
To the titmouse dimension.

(15)        Tis goodwill makes intelligence,
And I began to catch the sense
Of my bird's song; 'Live out of doors
In the great woods, on prairie floors.
I dine in the sun; when he sinks in the sea,
(20)   I too have a hole in a hollow tree,
[92]   And I like less when summer beats
With stifling beams on these retreats,
Than noontide twilights which snow makes
With tempest of the blinding flakes.'
(5)       ↑ For well the soul, if stout within, ↓
       ↑ Can arm impregnably the skin; ↓
       ↑ And polar frost my frame defied ↓
       ↑ Made of the air that blows outside. ↓
       With glad remembrance of my debt,
(10)   I homeward turn; Farewell, my pet!
When here again thy pilgrim comes,
He shall bring store of seeds & crumbs.
Henceforth I prize thy wiry chant
O'er all that mass ⟨or⟩& minster vaunt;
(15)   For men mis-hear thy call in spring,
As t'would accost some frivolous wing,
Crying out of the hazel copse, *Phe-be!*
And, in winter, *Chic-a-dee-dee!*
I think old Caesar must have heard
(20)   In northern Gaul my dauntless bird,
And, echoed in some frosty wold,
Borrowed thy battle-numbers bold.
[93]   And I will write our annals new,

92 "The Titmouse," 72–93. Lines (5–8) are added in the space left between verse paragraphs.
93 "The Titmouse," 94–99.

And thank thee for a better clew,
I, who dreamed not when I came here
To find the antidote of fear,

(5)       Now hear thee say in Roman key,
       *Paean! Veni, vidi, vici.*

[94] [blank]
[95] [ . . . ]
[96] [blank]
[96ₐ]                    S. R.
             Demure apothecary

Whose early reverend genius my young eye
With wonder followed, & undoubting joy,
Believing in that cold & modest form

(5)       Brooded alway the everlasting mind.
And that thou faithful didst obey the ⟨God⟩soul,
So should the splendid favour of the God
From thine observed lips shower words of fire,
Pictures that cast before the common eye,

(10)      I know ⟨n⟩for mine, & all men know for theirs.
How is the fine gold dim! the lofty low!
And thou, reputed speaker for the soul,
Forgoest the matchless benefit, & now,
Sleek deacon of the New Jerusalem,

(15)      Thou hast defied the offering world to be
A blind man's blind man.
Was it not worth ambition
To be the bard of nature to these times
With words like things,

(20)      An universal speech that did present
All natural creatures, and the eye beheld
A lake, a rose tree, when he named their names?

[96ᵦ]          And better was it to cower before the phantoms
One self deceiving mystic drew in swarms
Wherever rolled his visionary eye,

95 Pasted on the page is a clipping of an unidentified newspaper reprint of "Boston Hymn," identical in wording to the *Atlantic Monthly* text. Emerson wrote "Boston Hymn." above the clipping and numbered the stanzas consecutively to 16, at which point he wrote "Insert a Stanza" to the left, and, to the right, the number "(17)" and the following: "Today unbind the captive, / So only are ye unbound; / Lift up a people from the dust, / Trump of their rescue, sound!" The remaining stanzas are numbered 18–22. In line 19 "his" is canceled and "the" added; in line 59 "So" is canceled and "As" added; in line 61 "his" is canceled. All in pencil except "1" in ink beside the first stanza.

96ₐ "S. R.," 1–22.
96ᵦ "S. R.," 23–48.

The ⟨som⟨p⟩bre⟩ ↑Swedish↓ Pluto of a world of ghosts,
(5)    Eyes without light, men without character,
Nature a cave⟨rn⟩ of theologions?————

And lo! the young men of the land
Decline the strife of virtue, fail to be
The bringers of glad thought, preferring Ease
(10)   Ease & irresolution & the ⟨smile of placid rich⟩wine
Of placid rich men, they consent to be
Danglers & dolls. With these, not thou, not thou,
O noblest youth, not thou wilt there remain!
Up! for thy life, & for thy people's life!
(15)   And be the sun's light & the rainbow's glow,
And by the power of picture, to the eye
Show wherefore it was made. Unlock
The world of sound to the astonished ear,
And thus by thee shall man be twice a man.
(20)   Were it not better than to boast thyself
Father of fifty sons, flesh of thy flesh,
Rather to live earth's better bachelor
Planting ethereal seed in souls,
Spreading abroad thy being in the being
(25)   Of men whom thou dost foster & inform,
Fill with new hopes, & shake with grand desire?

[96c]                   Poet
First Person
    ⟨If Thought unlock her Mysteries,⟩
    ⟨If Love on me may smile,⟩
    ⟨I walk in marble galleries,⟩
    ⟨And talk with kings the while.⟩

(5)    The comrade or the book is good
That puts me in a working mood:
⟨T⟩Unless to thought be added will,
Apollo is an imbecile.
What parts, what truth, what fancies shine!
(10)   ↑—↓Ah! but I miss the just design.

⟨When⟩If Pindar pour⟨ed⟩ to Jove his hymn
I mark⟨ed⟩ the mountain range dislimn;
I ⟨saw⟩ ↑see↓ the rose & tulip climb
The Allegany's crag sublime.

(15)   The pain of love a better fate
Than the body's best estate

96c "In my garden three ways meet," 29–32 (1–4); "The comrade or the book" (5–10); "In my garden three ways meet," four unused lines (11–14); "The pain of love" (15–16); "The sun athwart the cloud" (17–18). Lines (1–4) are struck through three times in ink.

The sun athwart the cloud tho't it no sin
To use my land to put his rainbows in

[96_d] Thought is the sole price
For which I ⟨sell days⟩ am sold
And willing grow ⟨aged⟩ old
Melting matter to pictures
(5) And life into law.

————

The brook sings on, but sings in vain
Wanting the echo in my brain.

————

Nature ⟨said⟩ By kinds I keep my kinds in check
I plant the oak, the rose I deck.

————

(10) All day the waves assailed the rock
I could not hear the minster's chime
The sea-beat scorns the sexton's clock
And breaks the glass of Time.

————

In cities high ⟨thro crowds of cares⟩ ↑the careful brood↓
(15) ⟨The⟩Of wo-worn mortals darkling go,
But in these sunny solitudes
My quiet roses blow.

If Thought unlock her mysteries,
If Love on me may smile,
(20) I walk in marble galleries
And talk with kings the while.

If Pindar pour to Jove his hymn, &c
I mark

[96_e] The air is wise, the wind thinks well,
And all through which it blows,
If plant or brain, if egg or cell,
⟨Or bird or biped knows⟩ ↑To joyful beauty grows.↓

96_d "Terminus" ("For thought"), 2–3, 5, 7, 10 (1–5); "Old Age" (6–7); "By kinds I keep" (8–9); "All day the waves" (10–13); "In my garden three ways meet," 17–20, 29–32, x, x (14–23). In line (8) "Nature" is set off by a large square bracket to the right. Lines (8–9) are struck through in ink.

96_e "How drearily in College hall," 5–16 (1–12); "In my garden three ways meet," 21–24 (13–16); "Teach me your mood" (17–20). In line (6) Emerson wrote "Iheed", canceled the "I" and wrote it further out in the margin; in line (11) he neglected to cancel the word "am".

(5)    And oft at home 'mid tasks I heed
      ↑I↓ ⟨I⟩heed how wears the day—
    We must not halt while fiercely speed
    The spans of life away.

    ⟨What boots it⟩ ↑Who asketh↓ here of Thebes or Rome
(10)   Or lands of eastern day?
    In forests ⟨I am⟩ ↑joy is↓ still at home,
    And there I cannot stray.

    Methought the sky looked scornful down
    On all was base in man
(15)   And airy tongues did taunt the town
    'Achieve us if you can!'

    Teach me your mood, o patient stars,
    That climb each night the ancient sky,
    Leaving on space no shade, no scars,
(20)   No ⟨sore⟩ ↑sad↓ mischance, no fear to die.

[96f]    I care not wh⟨ere⟩ither I may go,
    Or if my task be high or low,
    Work to hide or proudly show,
    Or if my mates shall be my peers
(5)    Or only rare-met travellers,
    Whether I pace the shop-lined street
    ↑And↓ Scan⟨ning⟩ the city at my feet
    With secret pride to rule the town
    And shire on which the dome looks down.

[97] [ . . . ]
[98]           *Nature.*             ↑printed↓
    She is gamesome & good,
    But of mutable mood,
    No dreary repeater now & again,
    She will be all things to all men.
(5)    She who is old, but nowise feeble,
    Pours her power into the people,
    Merry & manifold without bar,
    Makes & moulds them what they are,
    And what they call their city way

96f "I care not whither."

97 A clipping of the poem "Sea-Shore" from the *Boatswain's Whistle*, no. 9 (18 October 1864), 65, is pasted on the page, which carries the following inscriptions by Emerson: "Printed" in ink at the top; "I carve the coastwise mountains into caves" in pencil to the right of lines 10–11; "Washing out harms & griefs from memory," in pencil to the right of line 23, with an arrow indicating insertion after that line; in line 42 the misprint "shells" is corrected in pencil to "spells".

98 "Nature II," 1–18. In line (14) "are" is circled and canceled in pencil.

(10)       Is not their way but hers,
                And what, they say, they made today,
                They learned of the oaks & firs.
                She spawneth men as mallows fresh,
                Hero⟨es⟩ & maiden⟨s are⟩ flesh of her flesh.
(15)       She drugs her water & her wheat
                With the flavors she finds meet,
                And gives them what to drink & eat,
                And having thus their bread & growth,
[99]       They do her bidding nothing lo⟨a⟩th.
                What⟨'⟩↑i↓s most theirs is not their own,
                But borrowed in atoms from iron & stone,
                And in their vaunted works of Art
(5)        The masterstroke is still her part.

[100]          *Terminus.*                ↑Printed↓
                It is time to be old,
                To take in sail:—
                The god of bounds,
                Who sets to seas a shore,
(5)        Came to me in his fatal rounds,
                And said, "No more!
                No farther ⟨spread⟩ ↑shoot↓
                Thy broad ambitious branches, & thy root,
                Fancy departs: no more invent,
(10)       Contract thy firmament
                To compass of a tent.
                There's not enow for this & that,
                Make thy option which of two;
                Economize the failing river,
(15)       Not the less revere the Giver,
                Leave the many, & hold the few.
                Timely wise accept the terms,
                Soften the fall with wary foot;
[101]     A little while
                Still plan & smile,
                And, fault of n⟨ew⟩ovel germs,
                Mature the unfallen fruit.
(5)        Curse, if thou wilt, thy sires,
                Bad husbands of their fires,
                Who, when they gave thee breath,
                Failed to bequeath

**99** "Nature II," 19–23.
**100** "Terminus," 1–18.
**101** "Terminus," 19–36, x, x. Lines (19–20), bracketed to the left, are struck through three times in ink.

(10)    The needful sinew stark as once,
The Baresark marrow to thy bones,
But left a legacy of ebbing veins,
Inconstant heat & nerveless reins,
Amid the Muses, left thee deaf and dumb,
Amid the gladiators, halt and numb.

(15)    As the bird trims her to the gale,
I trim myself to the storm of time,
I man the rudder, reef the sail,
Obey the voice at eve obeyed at prime,
⟨And hide my age amidst my thrifty pears,⟩
(20)    ⟨Each fault of mine masked by a growth of theirs.⟩

[102]    Lowly faithful, banish fear;
Right onward drive unharmed,
The port, well worth the cruise, is near,
And every wave is charmed.

———

[103]    They reach no term, they never sleep,
In equal strength through space abide,
Though, feigning dwarfs, they crouch & creep,
The strong they slay, the swift outstride:
(5)    Fate's grass grows rank in valley clods,
And rankly on the castled steep,
Speak it firmly, these are gods,
All are ghosts beside.

[104]                  Now.
                    ———

This ⟨passing⟩ ↑shining↓ moment is an edifice
Which the Omnipotent cannot rebuild.

═══

*Inscription on Mrs Forbes's Spring.*
Fall stream from Heaven to bless,—return as well,—
So did our braves; Heaven met them as they fell.
                  ↑See *E.L* 72.↓

[105]              *Cupido.*
The solid solid Universe
Is pervious to Love,

102  "Terminus," 37–40. In line (1) the upper dot of the semicolon is in pencil.
103  "Voluntaries," six lines first printed in the 1867 version, 120–21. In pencil.
104  "Now" (1–2); "Inscription on a Well in Memory of the Martyrs of the War" (3–4). "See *E.L* 72." is in pencil.
105  "Cupido."

With bandaged eyes he never errs,
Around, below, above,
(5)        His blinding light
He flingeth white
On God's & Satan's brood,
And reconciles
By mystic wiles
(10)      The evil and the good.

[106]    No fate, save by the victim's fault, is low,
For God hath writ all dooms magnificent,
So guilt not traverses his tender will.

Slight⟨ed⟩ing Minerva's learned tongue,
(5)        But heard with joy when on the wind the shell of Clio rung.

[107]–[112] [blank]
[113] There is nothing in all the periodical literature of this country that a boy might not wipe out with his hand. I once heard of a Man confined in the lunatic asylum who wrote incessantly for the ‖ . . . . . ‖ but dipped his pen in slop ‖ . . . . . ‖ no syllable remained. ‖ . . . . . . . ‖ this age not with those shallow ‖ . . . ‖ ages of the Charleses and Queen Annes but with the great & grave times of Egyhptian

[114]–[115] [blank]
[116]    Doth not the *Rock of Ages* melt
Into the mineral air,
To be the quarry whence is built
Thought, & its mansion fair?

[117]    Every atom displaces
All atoms beside,
Every genius unspheres
All souls in its pride.

[118] [blank]
[119]                *Brahma.*
If the red slayer think he slays,
Or if the slain think he is slain,
They know not well the subtle ways
I keep, & pass, & turn again.

(5)        Far or forgot to me is near,
Shadow & sunlight are the same,

106  "No fate, save by the victim's fault" (1–3); "Slighted Minerva's learned tongue" (4–5).
113  The entry is in erased pencil upside down at the bottom of the page.
116  "Ever the Rock of Ages melts." "*Rock of Ages*" is underlined twice.
117  "The atom displaces."
119  "Brahma."

The vanished gods to me appear,
And one to me are shame & fame.

(10) They reckon ill who leave me out,
When me they fly, I am the wings;
I am the doubter & the doubt,
And I the hymn the bramin sings.

The strong gods pine for my abode,
And pine in vain—the sacred Seven;
(15) But thou, meek lover of the good!
Find me, & turn thy back on heaven.

[120] [blank]
[121]      *Seid Nimetollah of Kuhistan.*
          The Solar Dance of the Dervish.
          ————                                    ↑printed↓

          Spin the ball! I reel, I burn,
Nor head from foot can I discern,
Nor my heart from love of mine,
Nor the winecup from the wine.
(5) All my doing, all my leaving,
Reaches not to my perceiving;
Lost in whirl of spheres I rove,
And know only—that I love.

          I am seeker of the stone,
(10) Living gem of Solomon.
From the shore of souls arrived,
In the sea of sense I dived.
But what is land, or what is wave,
To me who only jewels crave?
(15) Love is the air-fed fire intense;
↑and↓ My heart ⟨is⟩ the frankincense.
[122] Ah! I flame as aloes do,
Yet the censer cannot know.
I'm all knowing, yet unknowing,
Stand not, pause not, in my going.

(5) Ask not me, as Muftis can,
To recite the Alcoran;
Well I love the meaning sweet,—
I tread the book beneath my feet.

          Lo, the God's love blazes higher,
(10) Till all difference expire!

121 "Song of Seid Nimetollah of Kuhistan," 1–16.
122 "Song of Seid Nimetollah of Kuhistan," 17–34.

What are Moslems? What are Giaours?
All are Love's, and all are ours.
I embrace the true believers,
But I reck not of deceivers.
(15)    Firm to heaven my bosom clings,
Heedless of inferior things.
⟨And⟩Down on earth there, underfoot,
What men chatter, know I not.

[123]                                                            Hafiz
                      The Exile.                           ↑printed↓
In Farsistan, the violet spreads
Its leaves to the rival sky;
I ask how far is the Tigris flood,
And the vine that grows thereby?

(5)    Except the amber morning wind,
Not one saluted me here,
There is no ⟨man⟩ ↑lover↓ in ali Bagdat
To offer the exile cheer.

I know that thou, O morning wind,
(10)    O'er Kernan's meadow blowest;
And thou, heart-warming nightingale,
My father's orchard knowest.

O why did partial Fortune
From that bright land banish me?
(15)    So long as I wait in Bagdat,
The Tigris is all I see.

[124]    The merchant hath stuffs of price,
And gems from ⟨each⟩ ↑the↓ sea-washed strand,
And princes offer me grace
To stay in the Syrian land.

(5)    But what is gold for, but for gifts?
And dark, without love, is the day;
And all that I see in Bagdat
Is the Tigris to float me away.

[125] ↑Omar Chiam↓                             ↑printed↓
        Unbar the door, since thou the Opener art,
        Show me the forward way, since thou art guide,

123 "The Exile," 1–16. Angled lines in pencil before line (13) and after line (16) set this stanza off.
    124 "The Exile," 17–24.
    125 "Unbar the door."

I put no faith in pilot or in chart,
Since they are transient, & thou do⟨es⟩st abide.

[126] [blank]
[127] ↑Ibn Jemin.↓                                    ↑printed↓
        Two things thou shalt not long for, if thou love a mind
           serene,
        A woman to thy wife, though she were a crowned queen;
        And, the second, borrowed money, tho' the smiling lender
           say,
        That he will not demand the debt, until the Judgment Day.

[128]                                                  ↑printed↓
        On prince or bride no diamond stone
        Half so gracious ever shone,
        As the light of enterprize
        Beaming from a young man's eyes.

(5)      In thy holiday of life,
        Use occasion, work & climb,
        The sepulchre has overmuch
        Unprofitable time.

[129] ↑Hafiz↓                                          ↑Printed↓
        ====

        O Hafiz, speak not of thy need,
        Are not these verses thine?
        Then, all the Poets are agreed,
        No man can less repine.
        ====

(5)      I truly have no treasure,                      ↑printed↓
        Yet have I rich content;
        The first from Allah to the Shah,
        The last to Hafiz went.
        ====

(10)     Fit for the Pleiads' a⟨s⟩zure cord,              ↑printed↓
        The songs I sung, the pearls I bored.
        ====

[130]   O mark the Sonnet's flight,
        O follow its fleet career,
        A child begot in a night
        That lives to its thousandth year.

127 "From Ibn Jemin."
128 "On prince or bride" (1–4); "In thy holiday of life" (5–8). "printed" is in pencil.
129 "To Himself" (1–4); "I have no hoarded treasure" (5–8); "Fit for the Pleiads' azure chord"
(9–10). The word "printed" is in each instance in pencil.
130 "O mark the sonnet's flight."

[131]                              *The Phoenix.*                    ↑printed↓
My ⟨bosom's⟩ phoenix ⟨has assured⟩ ↑long ago secured↓
His nest in the sky-vault's cope;
In the body's cage immured
He is weary of life's hope.

(5)         Round & round this heap of ashes
            Now flies the bird amain;
            But in that odorous niche of heaven
            Nestles the bird again.

            Once flies he upward, he will perch
(10)        On ↑*↓Tuba's golden bough;
            His home is on that fruited arch
            Which cools the blest below.

            If over this world of ours
            His wings my phoenix spread,
(15)        How gracious falls on land & sea
            The soul-refreshing shade!

            Either world inhabits he,
            Sees oft below him planets roll;
            His body is all of air compact,
(20)        Of Allah's love his soul.

[132] ↑Hafiz↓                                        ↑printed↓

                              ═══

            Hoard knowledge in thy coffers,—
            An easy load to bear,—
            ⟨Ingots⟩Wedges of gold, & ⟨diamonds⟩silver bars
            Let others drag with care.

(5)         The devil's snares are strong,
            Yet have I God in need;
            And, if I had not God to friend,
            What can the devil speed?

            ⟨⟨Courage⟩High heart, o Hafiz, though not thine⟩
(10)        ↑And what tho' not to thee belong↓
            ↑Fine↓ ⟨Gold↑,↓ wedge⟩ ↑pearls↓ & silver ore,

131 "The Phoenix." The asterisk in line (10) refers to Emerson's inserted notation "*The Tree of Life" at the bottom of the page. The word "printed" is in pencil, as are the cancellations and addition in line (1), the asterisk, and the footnote.
132 "The Poet" ("Hoard knowledge"), 1–2, 3/10, 4–9, x, 10–12. Line (9) is canceled, and line (10) is added, in pencil. In line (11) Emerson first wrote "Gold wedge" then added "Fine" and the comma and canceled "wedge"; finally, in pencil, he canceled "Gold," and added "pearls". The word "printed" and brackets to the right of lines (1–4) and (9–13) are also in pencil.

More worth to thee the gift of song,
And the clear insight more. ↑printed↓

—————

[133] ↑Hafiz↓ ↑printed↓
There resides in the grieving
A poison to kill;
Beware to go near them,
Tis pestilent still.

[134] *Hilali.* ↑printed↓
Hark what, now loud, now low, the pining flute complains,
Without tongue, yellow-cheeked, full of winds that wail &
    sigh,
Saying, sweet heart, the old mystery remains,
If I am I; thou, thou; or thou art I.

[135] *Songs are for heroes.* ↑printed↓
Thou foolish Hafiz! say, do churls
Know the worth of Oman's pearls?
Give the gem which dims the moon
To the noblest, or to none.

[136] [blank]
[137] Enweri ↑printed↓
Not in their houses stand the stars,
But oer the pinnacles of thine!

↑printed↓
By thy worth & weight, the stars gravitate,
And the equipoise of heaven is thy house's equipoise.

Hafiz. ↑printed↓
(5) Thy foes to hunt, thy enviers to strike down,
Poises Arcturus aloft, morning & evening, his spear.

[138] Hafiz ↑printed↓
Fair fall thy soft heart!
A good work wilt thou do?

133 "There resides in the grieving." The word "printed" and a curving line to the right of the
verses are in pencil.
134 "The Flute." The word "printed" is in pencil.
135 "Friendship" ("Thou foolish Hafiz!"). The word "printed" is in pencil.
137 "To the Shah. From Enweri" ("Not in their houses") (1–2); "To the Shah. From Enweri"
("From thy worth") (3–4); "To the Shah. From Hafiz" (5–6). The word "printed" is in each
instance in pencil.
138 "Thou who with thy long hair," 17–20 (1–4); "Fair fall thy soft heart!" (1–4); "The
roguish wind" (5–8). The word "printed" is in pencil, as is a curving line to the right of lines
(1–4).

O pray for the dead
Whom thine eyelashes slew.

(5)    The roguish wind and I
Are truly an amorous pair;
Me burns the sparkle of thine eye,
He fans thy scented hair.

[139] Hafiz.
The treacherous wind pipes a lewd song,
Makes saints perverse, & angels bad;
Shall we sit & see such wrong,
And not cry out like mad!
(5)    Fie! what flute pants in the North?
What viol in the west?
Steals Virtue not from men of worth?
Corrupts he not the best?
Shall this pass in silence by?
(10)   Shall we not make hue & cry?

[140]                               *Hafiz.*
I said to heaven that glowed above,
O hide yon sun-filled zone,
Hide all the stars you boast!
For, in the world of love,
(5)    And estimation true,
The heaped-up harvest of the moon
Is worth one barleycorn at most,—
The Pleiads' sheaf but two.

————

*Alms.*                           *Hafiz.*
The beggar comes by God's command;
(10)   Gifts waken when the giver sleeps;
Swords cannot cut the liberal hand;
Nor dies the love the orphan keeps.

————

[141]                        ↑printed↓
He who has a thousand friends has not a friend to spare,
And he who has one enemy will meet him everywhere.

[142] [blank]
[143] Ibn Jemin
For two rewards, & nought beside,
A prudent man the world would ride;

139 "The treacherous wind."
140 "From Hafiz" (1–8); "Alms" (9–12).
141 "He who has a thousand friends." The word "printed" is in pencil.
143 "For two rewards."

His friend with benefits to crown,
And put his adversary down.

[144] Hafiz                    *Epitaph.*                    ↑Printed↓
    Bethink, poor heart, what bitter kind of jest
    Mad Destiny this tender stripling played;—
    For a warm breast of ivory to his breast,
    It laid a slab of marble on his head.

[145] Hafiz                                              ↑printed↓
    'Tis writ on Paradise's gate,
    Wo to the dupe that yields to Fate!

    Omar-Chiam                                   ↑printed↓
    In Earth's wide thoroughfares below,
    Two only men contented go;—
(5)    Who knows what's right, & what's forbid,
    And he from whom is knowledge hid.

[146] Hafiz
    We would do nought but good,
    Else shall dishonor come
    On the day when the flying soul
    Hies backward to its home.

    ———

                                               ↑printed↓
(5)    I batter the wheel of heaven,
    When it rolls not rightly by;
    I am not one of the snivellers
    Who fall on it & die.

    ———

[147] Hafiz                                              ↑printed↓
    They say, through patience, chalk
    Becomes a ruby stone;
    Ah! yes, but by the true heart's blood
    The chalk is crimson grown.

    ═══

    Hafiz.                                       ↑printed↓
(5)    ⟨Dear friend,⟩ ↑Dearest,↓ where thy shadow falls,
    Beauty sits, and Music calls;

144 "Epitaph." The word "Printed" and a curving line to the right of the verses are in pencil.
145 "'Tis writ on Paradise's gate" (1–2); "On earth's wide thoroughfares below" (3–6). The repeated word "printed" and curving lines to the right of each verse are in pencil.
146 "We would do nought but good" (1–4); "I batter the wheel of heaven" (5–8). The word "printed" is in pencil, as is a curving line to the right of lines (5–8).
147 "They say, through patience, chalk" (1–4); "Dearest, where thy shadow falls" (5–8). The repeated word "printed" and curving lines to the right of each verse are in pencil.

Where thy form & favor come,
All good creatures have their home.

[148] Hafiz.

Lo! where from Heaven's high roof
Misfortune staggers down;
We, just from harm to stand aloof,
Will to the wineshop run.

[149] Hafiz

Drink wine, and the heaven
New lustre diffuses,
And doubt not that sinning
Has also its uses.

(5) The builder of Heaven      ↑printed↓
Has sundered the earth,
So that no footway
Leads out of it forth:

On turnpikes of wonder
(10) Wine leads the mind forth,
Straight, sidewise & upward
Southward and north.

Stands the vault adamantine
Until the last day;
(15) The wine-cup shall ferry
Thee o'er it away.

[150] Around the man who seeks a noble end
Not angels but divinities attend.

No fate, save by the victim's fault, is low,
For God hath writ all dooms magnificent,
(5) So guilt not traverses his tender will.

[151]             ↑printed↓
On two days, 'tis needless to run from thy grave,
⟨On the day God has set,⟩ ↑The appointed↓ and the
unappointed day;

148 "Lo! where from Heaven's high roof."
149 "Drink wine, and the heaven," 1–4, 17–22, x, x, 23–26 (1–16); "The Builder of heaven"
(5–16). The word "printed" and a curving line to the right of lines (5–16) are in pencil.
150 "Around the man" (1–2); "No fate, save by the victim's fault" (3–5).
151 "On two days" (1–4); "Humility" (5–8). The word "printed" is in both instances in
pencil.

On the first, neither balm nor physician can save,
Nor thee, on the second, the Universe slay.

(5)       On the Last Day, men will wear       ↑printed↓
On their heads the dust,
As ensign & as diadem
Of their lowly trust.

{152]–[155] [blank]
{156]–[157] [index material omitted]
{158] [blank]
[inside back cover] [blank]

# Notebook NP

Notebook NP was certainly in use by the spring of 1857, although a few entries may be a year or two earlier; it continued in heavy use until at least 1868. A number of pages contain prose passages for Emerson's talk on Robert Burns in Boston in January 1859. Emerson returned to the notebook for a few poems published in *Selected Poems* in 1876.

The covers of notebook NP, gray, black, orange, and yellow marbled paper over boards, measure 17.3 × 21.3 cm. The spine strip and protective corners on the front and back covers are of brown leather. "NP" is written on the spine and upper front corner.

There are 304 unlined pages measuring 17.3 × 20.8 cm. The seven leaves bearing pp. 49–52, 85–88, 107–10, and 287–88 are torn or cut out, leaving narrow stubs.

Ninety pages are numbered in pencil, 133 in ink, and four in ink over pencil; the rest are unnumbered. The two pages following pp. 146–47 were skipped in the numbering; they are designated 148.1 and 149.1, while the subsequent two pages are designated 148.2 and 149.2. Pages 68 and 89 are misnumbered 66 and 85 respectively; p. 136 is misnumbered and corrected. Twenty-two pages are blank.

The notebook contains the following six enclosures, the first five inside the front cover:

(1) a sheet of blue paper, lined on one side, 20 × 25.2 cm, inscribed on both sides, then folded to form four pages and inscribed on the first two at right angles to the earlier inscription (here numbered front cover verso$_{a-d}$);

(2) a sheet of letter paper torn off from a folded sheet to measure 17.6 × 22.7 cm, lightly lined on the verso, numbered "23" in pencil and inscribed on the recto (here numbered front cover verso$_e$);

(3) a sheet of blue paper lined in blue on both sides, 19.7 × 25.3 cm, numbered "2" in pencil and inscribed on one side (here numbered front cover verso$_f$);

(4) a sheet of unlined paper, 12.3 × 19.4 cm, inscribed on one side (here numbered front cover verso$_g$);

(5) a printed invitation to "Inauguration of the Halleck Statue" dated New York, 1 May 1877, made out to "R W Emerson Esq", inscribed on the back with a list of German words and definitions (here numbered front cover verso$_h$); and

(6) between pp. 148.2–149.2, a sheet of thin gray letter paper, 12.8 × 20.3 cm, torn off at the left and inscribed on one side (here numbered 148.2$_a$).

In addition, inside the front cover are seventeen sheets of notes on NP and copies of poems, most of them by Edward Emerson; between pp. 180–81 a sheet with Edward Emerson's copy of the lines on Stillman; and between pp. 122–23 a single oak leaf.

[front cover]                                                    NP

[front cover verso] [blank]
[front cover verso<sub>a</sub>]

        From the beginning
        Sin blunders & brags
        ⟨Best⟩ ↑True↓ making↑,↓ ⟨&⟩ ↑true↓ winning
        Go hid⟨ing⟩↑den↓ in rags.

(5)      Wit has the creation
        Of worlds & their fame
        On one stipulation—
        ⟨Of yielding its claim⟩ ↑Renouncing the same.↓

        Choose the strain it discourses
(10)    Or ⟨the ivory⟩ ↑⟨Nestylis'⟩ the sycamore↓ pipe ↑reed↓
        Hold the mystical forces
        Or the skies they ⟨create⟩ made ripe. ↑breed↓

        When the crown first incloses
        The brows of her son,
(15)    The Muse him deposes
        From kingdom & throne.

[front cover verso<sub>b</sub>]

        Delicate omens ⟨filled the⟩ ↑traced in↓ air
        To him authentic witness bare
        Birds ⟨bore⟩ ↑with↓ auguries on their wings
        Chant⟨ing⟩ed undeceiving things
(5)      Him to beckon   him to warn
        Well might then the poet scorn
        To learn of scribe or courier
        ⟨Facts⟩ ↑Hints↓ writ in vaster character
        And on his mind at dawn of day
(10)    Soft shadows of the evening lay.

[front cover verso<sub>c</sub>]

        Poet
        Hold of the Maker, not the Made
        Sit with the Cause or grim or glad

        a crystal soul
        Sphered & concentric to the Whole

fcv<sub>a</sub> "From Nature's beginning," 1–8, 11–12, 9–10, 13–16 (1–16); "Poet of poets," 88–95
(5–8, 13–16). In pencil, partially overwritten by "Charmed by fagot" (fcv<sub>d</sub> below). In line (3),
the cancellations and insertions are in ink. In line (10), "Nestylis' " is canceled, and "the syca-
more" and "reed" are added, in ink. In line (12), "breed" is in ink.
   fcv<sub>b</sub> "Fate" ("Delicate omens"), 1–10.
   fcv<sub>c</sub> "Hold of the Maker" (1–2); "There are beggars," 54–55 (3–4); "By art, by music" (5–6);
"Try the might the Muse affords," 1–2 (7–8); "There are beggars," 23–24 (9–10).

(5)        For art, for music overthrilled,
        The wine cup shakes, the wine is spilled.

        Try the might the Muse affords,
        And the balm of thoughtful Words

        Ring of axe, or hum of wheel,
(10)      And gleam which use will paint on steel

[front cover verso$_d$]
        Charmed from fagot & from steel
        Harvests grew upon his tongue
        Past & Future must reveal
        All their heart whilst Saadi sung
(5)        The sun & moon must fall amain
        Like sowers seeds into his brain
        There quickened to be born again

[front cover verso$_e$]
        ⟦I leave the book, ⟨I⟩ leave ↑thou↓ the wine
        I breathe freer by the pine.
        In houses, I am low & mean,
        Mountain waters wash me clean
(5)        And by the seawaves I am strong
        I hear their medicinal song
        No balsam but the breeze I crave
        And no physician but the wave⟧

[front cover verso$_f$]
        The yesterday doth never smile,
        Today goes drudging through the while,
        Yet, in the name of Godhead, I
        The Morrow front, & can defy:
(5)        Though I am weak, yet God, when prayed,
        Cannot withhold his conquering aid.
        Ah me! it was my childhood's thought,
        If he should make my web a blot
        On life's fair picture of delight,
(10)      My heart's content would find it right.

[front cover verso$_g$]        ↑*Refrains.*↓

⟨Ere these echoes be checked by snows⟩

fcv$_d$  "Charmed from fagot."
fcv$_e$  "I leave the book." "23" is written in pencil in the upper right corner.
fcv$_f$  "The Nun's Aspiration," 1–10. "2" is written in pencil in the upper right corner.
fcv$_g$  "Boston," 102, four unused lines, 11/51–12/52, six unused lines, two lines first printed in *Selected Poems*, 1876, 108–9. Lines ⟨6–7⟩ are struck through in ink.

The false and blind may file their mind
And sell the blood of human kind

————

(5)    For never will die the captive's cry
On the echoes of God till ⟨r⟩Right draws nigh.

————

⟨The world was made for honest trade⟩
⟨To plant & eat be none afraid⟩

————

16

What slave would dare a name to wear
Once freedom's watchword everywhere

————

(10)    For power and place they sell their race
And kissed the hands of courtiers base

————

What slave shall dare a name to wear
Once Freedom's passport everywhere

————

22

A union then of honest men
(15)    Or union nevermore again

————

⟨For you can teach the lightning speech⟩
⟨And round the earth your voices reach⟩

[front cover verso_h]
Beweismittel   proof
nothfall   case of necessity
unshadlich   harmless
↑behulflich   helpful↓
furst   prince
erlassen   permitted
erwahnen,   mention
*hauptsache,   main point*
↑unselig   unblessed↓
↑Auftrag   commission↓
↑tauschen   deceived↓
↑bereit   prepared↓
↑dienst   service↓
↑eroffnen   open↓
entledigen   acquit yourself
Ihnen   to you
Spiel   plays

**fcv_h**  In pencil.

ruhmlich   agreeable
erfreulich   joyful
gezogen   drawn
Mittheil⟨eneng⟩ungen   communicated
Malerin   a painter
absicht   design
alsdan   then
Anspruche   claim
geltend   to influence
beweismittel   proof
Schwarz   black
Nothfall   ↑case of↓ necessity
unschadlich   harmless
Furst   prince

[1]                                          ———

   Slighting Minerva's learned tongue,
 But heard with joy when on the wind the shell of Clio rung.

[2] ———                                      ═══

  Though Love repine, & Reason chafe,
  I heard a voice without reply,—
  'Tis man's perdition to be safe,
  When for the truth he ought to die.'

  ———                              ———

(5)  Dearest, where thy shadow falls,
  Beauty sits & Music calls;
  Where thy form & favor come,
  All good creatures have their home.

  ———                              ———

  Night-dreams trace on Memory's wall
(10) Shadows of the thoughts of day,
  And thy fortunes, as they fall,
  The bias of the will betray.

  ———                              ———

  Go thou to thy learned task,
  I stay with the flowers of spring;
(15) Do thou of the ages ask
  What me the hours will bring.

       ———

1 "Slighted Minerva's learned tongue."
2 "Sacrifice" (1–4); "Dearest, where thy shadow falls" (5–8); "Memory" (9–12); "Botanist" (13–16); "Poet" ("To clothe") (17–20).

To clothe the fiery thought
In simple words succeeds;
For still the craft of genius is
(20)    To mask a king in weeds.

———

[3] ↑*Suum Cuique.*↓
Wilt thou seal up the avenues of ill?
Pay every debt, as if God wrote the bill.

———————

Shines the ⟨p⟩last age; the next with hope is seen;
Today slinks poorly ⟨of⟩off unmarked between:
(5)    Future or past no richer secret folds,
O friendless Present! than thy bosom holds.
                   ↑See "Quatrains" below, p. 132↓

When wrath & terror changed Jove's regal port,
And the rashleaping thunderbolt fell short.

[4]    Softens the air so cold & rude
What can the heart do less?
If Earth puts off her savage mood,
We should learn gentleness.

[5] 1825
      Not frolic Beauty weaving wanton nets
From her soft ambush peeps with radiant eye;
Tis safer when the curled syren frowns.

———

No fate, save by the victim's fault, is low,
(5)    For God hath writ all dooms magnificent,
So guilt not traverses his tender will.

———

Shalt be affianced to a heavenlier bride
For I see glory ⟨la⟩hasting to thy side.

———

When Ali prayed & loved
(10)    Where Syrian waters roll,
A⟨f⟩loft the ninth heaven glowed & moved
At the tread of the jubilant soul

   3  " 'Suum Cuique' " ("Wilt thou") (1–2); "Heri, Cras, Hodie" (3–6); "When wrath & terror" (7–8). Lines (1–2) are crowded in at the top of the page and may have been added. Lines (3–6) are struck through, and "See . . . 132" added, in pencil.
   4  "Softens the air."
   5  "Not frolic Beauty" (1–3); "No fate, save by the victim's fault" (4–6); "Shalt be affianced" (7–8); "A patch of meadow & upland," 25–28 (9–12). Lines (9–12) are struck through once in ink.

[6] Letter to M F on Spring    see S 270
     description R 72.
     hymen *CL* 38

         Hold of the Maker, not the made,
         Sit with the Cause, or grim, or glad,

[7]         The darling Spring
         With sudden passion languishing
         Maketh all things softly smile
         Maketh pictures mile on mile ↑,↓
(5)       Holds a cup with cowslips wreathed
         Whence a smokeless incense breathed
         Dripping dew cold daffadillies
         Making drunk with draught of lilies
         Girls are peeling the sweetwillow,
(10)      And the Gilead tree,
         And troops of boys
         Shouting with whoop & hilloa,
         And hip, hip, three times three

[8] [blank]
[9]         The air is full of whistlings ↑clear↓
         What was that I heard
         Out of the hazy lands
         Harp of the wind, or song of bird,
(5)       Or clapping of shepherd's hands⟨.⟩?
         Or a blast on Oberons horn⟨?⟩,
         Or a farmers cock at morn,
         Or flap of wings?—
         It is a sound, it i⟨t⟩s a token,
(10)      That the marble sleep is broken,
         And a change has passed on things

         When late I walked in earlier days
         All was stiff & stark
         Kneedeep snows choked all the ways
(15)      In the sky no spark

6 Part of the letter to Margaret Fuller (L 2:254–55), versified in "April," is copied in note-book S (Salvage), pp. [270]–[271], followed by "See a descriptive passage. R 72" and a line later used in "May–Day"; the passages cited in journal R, p. [72], and CL, p. [38], are also developed in "May–Day." Following the memorandum is "Hold of the Maker." "Letter . . . CL 38" is in pencil.

7 "May–Day," 1–6, x, x, 7–11. Struck through in ink.

9 "May–Day," 12–16, x, x, 37?, 38–40, 98–101. In line (1), "clear" is added in pencil. Struck through in ink.

[10]      When summer winds are dashed with East
          And frost with famine checks the feast
          And half the year he shrouds in snow
          Where off the gulf the southwinds blow

(5)              ⟨The careful brood⟩
          In cities high through crowds of cares
          The wo-worn mortals darkling go
          But in these sunny solitudes
          My quiet roses grow.

[11]           Winter builds
          Sudden cathedrals in the wilds

                ⟨All⟩ the piny hosts were sheeted ghosts
          The forlorn icy wind
(5)       Me from ⟨labor⟩ ↑ranging↓ disinclined
          Who would freeze in frozen brakes?
          I shrunk back to books & home ↑;↓
          Now, desire of action wakes⟨,⟩
          And the wish to roam.

(10)      I leave the book ↑,↓ I leave the wine ↑,↓
          I breathe freer by the pine ↑;↓
          In houses ↑,↓ I am low & mean,
          Mountain waters wash me clean ↑,↓

[12]      On the chamber, on the stairs,
             Lurking dumb,
             Go & come
          Lemurs and Lars.

Dreams are the irony of Jove
Night's⟨'⟩ dreams are satires ⟨of⟩on the day

(5)       O pedant of the Holy Ghost

[13]      And by the sea⟨waves⟩ I am strong,
          I hear their medicinal song,

10  "When summer winds" (1–4); "In my garden three ways meet," 17, 17–20 (5–9). Lines
(1–4) are in pencil.
    11  "May–Day," x, 112–13, 115, x, 117–18, 126–27 (1–9); "I leave the book," 1–4 (10–13).
Lines (1–9) are struck through in ink.
    12  "On the chamber" (1–4); "O pedant of the Holy Ghost" (5). With the two lines of prose
following the quatrain, cf. "Memory," 1. "Dreams are the irony of Jove" also occurs in EL
p. [200].
    13  "I leave the book," 5–8, x (1–5); "Gentle Spring has charmed the earth," 1–2, 2–4 (6–10);
"May–Day," 276–79, four unused lines (11–18). In line (1), the cancellation is in blue pencil,
perhaps not by Emerson. Lines (3) and (5), the added period in line (4), and "Gentle" in line (6)
are in pencil; lines (5) and (18) are canceled in pencil. Lines (11–14) are struck through in ink.

↑No balsam but the breeze I crave↓
⟨Ask⟩ ↑And↓ no physician but the wave↑.↓
(5)    ⟨↑No temple but the windy cave↓⟩

↑Gentle↓ Spring has charmed the earth
⟨With a sunbeam from the sea,⟩
↑Where an april sunbeam fell↓
Let no glacier from the north
(10)   Floating by undo the spell.

Drug the cup, thou butler sweet,
And send the madness round;
The feet that slid so long ⟨i⟩on snow
Are glad at last to feel the ground.

(15)   The maple bark is changed to red
White↑st↓ ⟨the⟩ lake↑s↓ ⟨is⟩ ↑are↓ green again
Drag↑ged↓ to the cove the hidden boat
⟨In summer eve an⟨c⟩trancd to float⟩
[14]   Wherein our summer Muse shall float

[15]   Fill & saturate each kind
With good according to its mind,
Fill each kind, & saturate
With good according to its fate,
(5)    Willow & violet, maiden, & man.

Pour the wine, pour the wine,
Till it changes to foam:
Cup the youth that justifies
Who leaves his task to feed his eyes.

(10)   Fleet the moments, fleeter;
Ever to joy the cup persuades,
Making the young girls sweeter,
And the young men almost maids.

[16] [ . . . ]
[17]     The bittersweet, the haunting air
Goeth, bloweth, everywhere,
It preys on all, all prey on it,
Blooms in beauty, thinks in wit,

14 "May–Day," x.

15 "May–Day," 280–84, eight unused lines; cf. "Pour the wine!," 1–2 (6–7). Lines (1–5) are struck through in ink.

17 "May–Day," 285–88, x, x, 289–94, 297–300, 325–27. Struck through in ink. Lines (9–16) are inscribed, headed "A", on p. [16], struck through twice in ink, enclosed on the left by a large ink bracket, and indicated for insertion by a caret on p. [17] and the notation "Insert A" in brackets.

(5)       Bites damsel⟨f⟩ with halfpleasing flame,
           Drives the struck poet mad for fame,
           ↑It↓ Stin⟨s⟩gs the strong with enterprise,
           And travellers long for Indian skies.
           ↑And, where it comes, this courier fleet↓
(10)     ↑⟨Wakes⟩ Fans in all hearts expectance sweet↓
               ↑As if Tomorrow ⟨would⟩ ↑should↓ redeem↓
               ↑The ⟨rose & star⟩ ↑vanished roses↓ of ⟨mid⟩nights
                   dream↓

               ↑As if Time bro't a new relay, ↓
           ↑Of shining ⟨maidens⟩ ↑virgins↓ every may, ↓
(15)     ↑And summer came to ripen maids↓
           ↑To a beauty that not fades. ↓

           I saw the wizard spring go forth
           Stepping daily onward north
           To greet staid ancient cavaliers,

[18] [blank]
[19]     Filing singly in stately train;—
           And who, and who are the travellers?
           They were Night & Day, & Day & Night,
           Pilgrims wight that never alight.
(5)       Short ⟨of stature⟩ ↑as dwarfs↓ they seemed, & low,
           Short & bent by cold & snow,
           The merry Spring threw wreaths on them
           Flower-wreath↑s↓ gay with bud & bell,
           Many a flower, & many a gem,
(10)     They were refreshed by the smell,
           They shook the snow from hats & shoon,
           They put their April raiment on,

[20]         Pedants all
           They would be original
           The mute pebble shames their wit
           The echo is ironical
(5)       And wiser silence swallows speech

[21]     And those eternal forms
           Unhurt by a thousand storms,
           Shot up to the height of the sky again,
           And danced as merrily as young men.

19 "May–Day," 328–31, 332?, 333–39. Struck through in ink. The cancellation and inser-
tion in line (5) are in pencil.
   20 "Pedants all," 1–2, 4–6.
   21 "May–Day," 340–50. Struck through in ink.

(5)        I saw them mask their awful glance
            Meekly sidewise in gossamer lids,
            And to speak my tho't if none forbids,
            It was as if the unmeasured Gods,
            Tired of their starry periods,
(10)       Hid their majesty in cloth
            Woven of tulips & painted moth.

[22] [blank]
[23]      Twas the vintage-day of field & wood
            When magic wine for bards is brewed,
            ⟨All in loving choirs they sat,⟩
            ⟨They drunk wine never made in vat,⟩
(5)        Every tree & stem & chink
            Gushed with syrup to the brink
            The flowing air was scented still
            With ⟨g⟨e⟩ums⟩ ↑gums↓ of India & Cathay,
            And the jungles of Brazil.
(10)       In the frolic holiday,
            The air stole into the streets of towns
            And betrayed the fund of joy
            To the high school & medalled boy,

[24] [blank]
[25]      On from hall to chamber ran,
            To youth & maid, from man to man,
            To babes, and to old eyes as well.
            I see you, the old man cried, ye clouds,
(5)        Airy turrets, purple piled,
            Which once my infancy beguiled,
            Beguiling now with the selfsame spell;
            I know ye skilful to convoy
            The total freight of hope & joy
(10)       Into rude & homely nooks,
            Shed mocking lustres on shelf of books,
            On farmers byre, on grassy pipes,
            Or in a pool of dancing chips

[26]         The healthy youth distils
            Westwind & rocks & lake to joy
            To grace of maids
            To kings & ⟨paladins⟩ signors of romance
(5)        In listed fields who poise the lance

23 "May–Day," 358–59, x, x, 360–61, four unused lines, 362–64. Struck through in ink. The cancellation and addition in line (8) are in pencil.
   25 "May–Day," 365–77. Struck through in ink.
   26 "The healthy youth distils." In pencil.

And, looking oer the country fields,
Which melting streams of spring have flowed
Sees realms of history again
Such as he read in "Ville de Rome,"
(10)    And "Champions of Christendom,"
And erst in Amadis de Gaul,
Or painful Bunyan's Holy War.

[27]    Enchanter Enchanter

Ah not to me these dreams belong
A better voice peals through my song

[28]    Spices in the plants that run
To bring their firstfruits to the sun
Earliest heats that follow frore
Nerved leaf of hellebore
(5)    Sweet willow, checkerber⟨y⟩ry red,
With its savory leaf for bread
Silver birch & black
With the selfsame spice
Found in polygala root & rind
(10)    Sassafras & fern
Benzoin
Mouse ear cowslip wintergreen
Which by ⟨beauty⟩ ↑aroma↓ may ⟨repel⟩compel
The frost ⟨from harming⟩ ↑to spare↓ what scents so well

[29]    With searching hands
Searching under↑neath↓ the mould
For grains of wheat & more than gold
So rich thy well-doings are
(5)    One midsummer day
Will overpay
The ravage of ten years of war

The scarlet maple-keys of ⟨m⟩May

———

For Genius made his cabin wide
(10)    And Love led gods therein to bide
[30]    ↑See p 42↓
The ⟨blithe may⟩ ↑April↓ winds are magical

27 "May–Day," x (1); "Ah! not to me" (2–3). With line (1), cf. "The Park," 9.
28 "Spices in the plants." In pencil; "compel" in line (13) and the cancellation and addition in line (14) are in ink.
29 "May–Day," x, 270–71, 272?, 273–75, 174 (1–8); "For Genius made her cabin wide," 1–2 (9–10). In pencil; lines (1–8) are struck through in pencil.
30 "April," 1–11, 11/12, 13, x, 14–20. In pencil, struck through three times in pencil to form two X's.

And thrill our tuneful frames
The garden ⟨days⟩ ↑walks↓ are passional
To bachelors & dames
(5)    The ⟨lawn⟩ ↑hedge↓ is ⟨thick⟩gemmed with diamonds
The air with cupids full
The cobweb clue of Rosamonds
⟨Half seen by lake⟩ & ↑Lures lovers to the↓ pool
And every ⟨pool of⟩ ↑dimpling↓ water
(10)    Each leaf that shades the rock
⟨Knows to⟩ ↑Can↓ cozen ⟨& to⟩ ↑snare &↓ flatter
⟨To pique⟩ ↑Can parley↓ & ⟨to⟩ provoke
                    ↑Puck & goblin↓
O they have secret lessons
(15)    ⟨That are not⟩ ↑Know more than all↓ in your books
Forsake your ⟨greybeard pedants⟩ ↑mournful problems↓
And court the sunny brooks
The southwinds are quickwitted
The colleges are slow
(20)    The masters quite omitted
The lore we care to know


[31]         ⟨Spring⟩ ↑The blithe ⟨m⟩May-↓winds are magical
And thrill our tuneful frames
⟨These are the days of⟩ ↑The garden days are↓ passion↑al↓
↑To bachelors & dames↓
(5)    The air with cupids full
For the eyes that are young
And eyesparkles
down the dell from the pool
And every pool of water
(10)    And every ⟨dancing⟩ leaf ↑that shades the rock↓
⟨Seems⟩ ↑Knows↓ to cozen & to flatter
To /pique & to provoke/parley & to mock/
O they have secret lessons
That are not in your books
(15)    The writers quite omitted
All that we care to know
[32]    The southwinds are quickwitted
The ⟨colleges are⟩ ↑schools are sad &↓ slow,

31 "April," 1–4, 6, x, x, 8?, 9?, 10–11, 11/12, x, 14, 19–20. The cancellations and additions in lines (1), (3–4), and (10–11) are in pencil; in line (15) the t's in "omitted" are crossed in pencil. Struck through in pencil; lines (15–16) are struck through separately in pencil.

32 "April," 17–20 (1–4); "She paints with white & red" (5–6); "October woods, wherein," 2?, 2, x, 3?, x, 8, x (7–13). The cancellation and addition in line (2), "See p. 42", lines (7–13), and "See p. 163" are in pencil; lines (1–4) are struck through twice in pencil.

The masters quite omitted
The lore we care to know.
↑See p 42↓

(5)      She paints with white & red the moors
To draw the nations out of doors

Autumn brings to pass
The dream of boy
⟨And his⟩ he is a king in the ⟨wood⟩ ↑wold↓
(10)   In pomp of purple & gold
Passing all that can be told
From pavilion to pavilion
⟨P⟩Marches proud       ↑See p. 163↓

[33]   Mallows
first sign celestial natures show
Of sympathy with ours below

Spring ⟨with⟩ cold with dropping rain
(5)   Willows & lilacs brings again
The whistling of unnumbered birds
And trumpet lowing of the herds

The force that
What fiery force the earth renews
(10)  ⟨In⟩ The tribes of form the flush of hues;
⟨The⟩ joy ⟨that⟩ shed⟨s⟩↑ding↓ rosy waves abroad,
Flows from the heart of Love, the lord,

marriage of plants
wedding of birds
(15)  pairing of all kinds
the very frog & his mate a gayer coat

[34]   For what need I of book or priest
⟨Or /creed/scroll/ from the mysterious East⟩
⟨Or saint or sibyl from the⟩
↑Or↓ Sibyl ⟨or saint⟩ from the mummied East
(5)  ⟨Saint or Messiah from the East⟩
When every star is Bethlehem star
⟨And Ive⟩ ↑I count↓ as many as there are
/Lilies/cinquefoils/ or violets in the grass

So many saints & saviors
(10)  So many high behaviors

33 "May–Day," three unused lines, 170–73, 176?, 176–79, three unused lines, 230. Struck through in ink.
34 "For what need I." The cancellations and additions in lines (2–5) and (7) are in pencil.

⟨To him⟩ ↑Salute the bard↓ who is ⟨/himself./well/⟩ ↑alive↓
And only sees what he doth give

[35]    Her passions the shy violet
From Hafiz never hides
Lovelongings of the raptured bird
The bird to him confides.

(5)    Ill not receive her in my doors
Nor ⟨sweep for her my⟩ ↑Spread for her my carpet floors↓
But in the hills appoint a meeting
In fields will pay my loyal greeting
I quench my fire
(10)    And to the ⟨woodlands fare⟩ ↑wilderness repair↓
The ⟨mighty festival⟩ ↑vernal jubilee↓ to share
My house is open for mankind
The gods I harbour in my mind
But when the puissant ⟨ha⟩ semigod

[36]    The spring comes up from the South
And Earth & air are overflowed
Earth with the melted ice
And air with love infusion
(5)    There is no house ⟨to hold the power⟩ ↑or hall↓
Can hold her festival
We will go to the /mighty/haughty/ woods
↑Fronting the liberated floods↓
We will go to relenting mountains
(10)    And listen to the uproar of joy
And see the sparkle of the delivered rivers
And mark the rivers of sap
Mounting in the pipes of the trees
And see the colors of love in birds
(15)    And in frogs & lizards
And in human cheeks
in the song of birds
& songs of men
We will hear the tiny roar
(20)    Of the insects evermore

[37]    Test of the poet his knowledge of love
The knowledge is older than Saturn or Jove,

35 "Hafiz" (1–4); "May–Day," 213?, 214?, eight unused lines (5–14). Lines (5–14) are in pencil; lines (1–4) and (5–10) are struck through separately in pencil.
36 "May–Day," four unused lines, 215–18, x, 220, 222, 221?/223, 224, 228, 230, x, 615?, x, 232–33. In pencil.
37 "Casella," 1–4, 1–4 (1–8); "May–Day," x, x, 242, x, x, x (9–14). Lines (9–14) are in pencil; lines (1–4) are struck through in ink.

Never was poet of late or of yore
Who was not tremulous with love-lore

(5)     Test of the poet ⟨h⟩is knowledge of love,
For Eros is older than Saturn or Jove,
Never was poet of late or of yore
Who was not tremulous with love-lore.

The      A chemist
(10)    ⟨Who⟩ tempers her fire with ic⟨e⟩↑y mist↓
Pours in a deluge of sunheat
And launches an iceberg on the sea
↑Melting↓ Icebergs ⟨floating⟩ line the coast
Tempering ⟨well⟩ the ardent sun

[38]    The millionhanded sculptor mould
⟨All⟩ quaint ⟨shapes of bud & plant⟩
↑Quaint bud & blossom↑s↓ ⟨millio⟩ myriadfold↓
To fit the soil to fend ⟨the⟩ cold ↑airs↓
(5)     And ⟨hide⟩ ↑mask↓ the glory she prepares
The million handed painter pours
⟨Her⟩ opal ⟨⟨h⟩colors⟩ ↑hues↓ on earth & sky
On the new creatures
The calving cow the
(10)    By farmhouse
By houses lies a fresher green
On men & maids a fresher mien
As if Time brot a new relay

Turn swiftlier round, o tardy ball,
(15)    And sun this frozen side,
Bring hither back the robin's call,
Bring back the tulip's pride.

[39]    ↑Put in drive home the sightless wedges↓
↑And split to chips the crystal ledges↓

But never yet the man was found
Who could the mystery expound
(5)     Tho' Adam born when oaks were young
⟨And lived⟩ ↑Endured↓, the Bible says, as long,
But when at last the patriarch died
The Gordian ⟨knot⟩ ↑noose↓ was ⟨still⟩ ↑not↓ untied.

38 "May–Day," 252–53, 253, x, x, 254–55, x, x, x, 295–97, 51–54. In pencil; lines (1–9), (10–15), and (14–17) are struck through separately in pencil.
    39 "Put in, drive home" (1–2); "But never yet" (3–10); "May–Day," x, x (11–12). Lines (1–2) and (11–12) are in pencil.

He left, though goodly centuries old,
(10)         Meek natures secret still untold.

↑In May↓ The caterpillar weaves
H⟨s⟩is shining tent in apple-trees

[40]       Like an inundation of the sea
Rolling over continents mountaintops
And faster flowing oer the plains
Whi⟨th⟩
(5)        With a white edge to the running silver
So goes the deluge of the heat
From the south over the land
With invisible flood
Painting Paradises
(10)        infusing fires which glow
in tulips & azalea & laurel
Climbing the northern Zones
Where a thousands towns
Lay like cockles on the be⟨e⟩ach
(15)        Or like tents on a plain

[41]       The quaking earth did quake in rhyme
Seas ebbed & flowed with clanging chime

I go to behold
The millionhanded sculptor mould
(5)        Quaint buds & blossoms ⟨million⟩ ↑myriad↓ fold
To fit the soil to fend cold airs
And mask the glory he prepares
The millionhanded painter pours
Opal hues ⟨on earth & sky⟩ ↑& purple dye↓
(10)        Flush with tulips region floors
Softer tints run up the sky

Spring   *TU* 69 70, *V* 143   *S* 270
Von Hammer [*Geschichte,*] p 259

[42]       The April winds are magical,
And thrill our tuneful frames,
The garden walks are passional
To bachelors & dames.
(5)        The hedge is gemmed with diamonds,

40 "May–Day," 236?, 237?, 239, x, 240/241, 242–43, x, 244, 246, x, 248–51. In pencil.
41 "Beauty," 15–16 (1–2); "May–Day," x, 252–53, x, x, 254–57 (3–11). Lines (3–11) are in pencil; lines (1–2) are struck through in ink. With "*V* 143 . . . p 259" cf. JMN 11:114; for "*S* 270" see p. [6] above.
42 "April." Except for the cancellation in line (8), all cancellations and additions are in pencil; those in line (15) are traced over in ink.

The air with cupids full,
The ⟨cobweb⟩ clues of ↑fairy↓ Rosamonds
/Lure⟨s⟩/Guide/ lovers to the pool,
⟨And every dimpling⟩ ↑Each dimple in the↓ water,
(10)    And leaf that shades the rock,
Can cozen, pique, & flatter,
Can parley & provoke.
Goodfellow, Puck, & goblin↑s↓,
Know more than all the books,
(15)    ⟨Forsake⟩ ↑Down with↓ your ⟨mournful⟩ ↑doleful↓
        problems
↑Come↓ And court the sunny brooks.
The southwinds are quickwitted,
The schools are sad & slow,
The masters quite omitted
(20)    The lore we care to know.

[43]

Hold of the Maker, not the Made,
Sit with the Cause or grim or glad.

You must not be overbo⟨d⟩ld
When you fight with arctic cold
(5)    How should I fight? my foeman fine
Has million arms to one of mine
In vain I toss my limbs about
And thump my sides to keep him out
In vain I ru⟨n⟩b & ru⟨b⟩n & shout
(10)    East west ⟨for shelter strain⟩ ↑I turn in vain↓
East west south north are his domain
Miles off, ⟨two⟩three dangerous miles is home
↑I must borrow his winds to come there↓
Too happy could I thither come
(15)    ⟨↑No↓ Nonsense, speed⟩ ↑Up & away↓ with flying feet
Alas the foe is far more fleet
Near is the war the aid is far

[44]    Sings in my ears my hands are stones
The blood is marbling to my bones
              my marble bones

43 "Hold of the Maker" (1–2); "The Titmouse," 1–2, 5–6, 7?, x, 7?, 7–10, 10?, 11, x, 7? (3–17). Lines (7–9) are struck through once, and lines (3–17) twice, in ink.
44 "The Titmouse," 13–14, 14–15, x, 17–18, x, 21, 22, 20, 19. Struck through in ink.

Tugs at the heartstrings      numbs the sense
(5)      Crushes with his omnipotence
Well in this broadbed lie down to sleep
The punctual stars will vigil keep
Not
The snow is no ignoble shroud
(10)      The moon for mourner & the cloud
The winds shall sing their deadmarch old
Honest the purifying cold

[45]      She had wealth of mornings in her year,
And planets in her sky,
She chose the best thy heart to cheer
Thy beauty to supply.

(5)      Now younger lovers find the stream
The willow ↑s↓ & the vine,
But aye to me the happiest seem
To draw the dregs of wine.

        Birds
These the fables she esteems
(10)      Reality most like to dreams
Welcome back you little nations
Far traveled in the south plantations
And your enchanting manners bring
And your autumnal gathering
(5)      Exchange in conclave federal
Greetings kind to each & all
Consc[i]ous each ⟨d⟩of duty done
& unstained as the Sun

[46]      We had not brot it to this point
But ⟨w⟩it was coming so far
When I heard a tiny voice hard by
a cheerful voice friendly & polite
(5)      Which seemed to say Good Day
Glad to see you in these places
⟨Where⟩ few come ⟨to see us⟩ ↑so far↓ in January
Chickadee dee      cheerful note
Out of warm heart & merry throat
(10)      The little esquimaux in gray
Frisked at his ease from /stem to spray/the icy sprays/

45 "In my garden three ways meet," 37–44 (1–8); "The Titmouse," ten unused lines (9–18); "May-Day," 416/418? (13). The added "s" in line (6), "Birds", and lines (9–18) are in pencil. Lines (9–18) are crowded in at the bottom of the page, lines (9–11) run in on two lines and lines (14–18) on three, with the beginnings of lines indicated by capitalization.

46 "The Titmouse," x, 24?, 25–26, 29, 31–32, 27–28, 46?, 42?, 43–46, 49?, x, 50? In pencil.

Here was this atomy in full breath
Hurling defiance at vast death
This scrap of ⟨life⟩ ↑feathers↓ just for play

(15)    Fronts the northwind in waistcoat gray
⟨Y⟩I said you small wonder   ↑What ar[e] you for↓
    Arctic navigator      fore
Of Baffins Bay & Labrador

[47₁]    The Muses' hill by fear is guarded
A bolder foot is still rewarded

The men who lived with him became
Poets, for the air was fame.

[47₂]    What fire ⟨is⟩burns in that little chest
So frolic strong & selfpossest
And I declared the spacious North
Exists to draw thy virtue forth

(5)    Why are not diamonds black & gray
To ape thy ⟨matchless⟩ ⟨perilous⟩ ↑daredevil↓ array
/There are no colors good/Henceforth I wear no stripe/ but
    thine
↑Ashes &↓ Black ⟨& gray⟩ all hues outshine
I think no virtue goes with size

(10)    The reason of all cowardice
Is that men are overgrown
And ⟨if⟩ to be brave we must come down
To the titmouse dimension
Thou scrap of valor

[48]        There to shame my weak behavior
I hailed aloud my little saviour
↑↑And I ha↓ little thought in coming here↓
↑To find an antidote to fear↓

(5)        Step in but it blows a little fresh
Step in but thy superfluous flesh
↑Ridiculously↓ Doth shake & shiver
Too large a
Too broad an aim to winter's quiver

(10)    The minion warrior in his hold
Scorn⟨ing⟩ed to lose ⟨his⟩ play for snow or cold
His note is now my organ piece

47₁ "The Muses' hill" (1–2); "Solution," 41–42 (3–4). Lines (3–4) are in pencil, the later draft of "The Titmouse" written around but not over them.
47₂ "The Titmouse," 52–53, 59–60, 57–58, 55–56, 61–65, 45. In pencil.
48 "The Titmouse," 47–48, 96–97, nine unused lines, 88/89, 98–99. In pencil.

Which I prefer to all German ↑s↓
Chickadee dee Phebe
(15)    A triumphal march in ⟨grandest⟩ ↑Roman↓ key
Paean Veni Vidi Vici

[49]–[52] [two leaves torn out]
[53]    For joy & beauty planted it
With faerie gardens cheered,
And boding fancy haunted it
With men & women weird.

---

(5)    What fire burns in that little chest
So frolic, stout, & self possest?
Didst steal the glow that lights the west?
I maintain the spacious North
Exists to draw thy Virtue forth
(10)    Henceforth I wear no stripe but thine
Ashes & black all hues outshine
Why are not diamonds black & gray
To ape thy daredevil array
[54]    I think no virtue goes with size
The reason of all cowardice
Is that men are overgrown
And to be ⟨brave⟩valiant must come down
(5)    To the titmouse dimension

The minion warrior in his hold
Scorned to lose play for snow or cold
His note is now my organ /piece/vaunt/
Which I prefer to cathedral chanting
(10)    Chickadee dee ⟨cheerful⟩ ↑saucy↓ note
Out of sound heart & merry throat
Men mis⟨called⟩write thy call in spring
Phe—be      some frivolous wing
And in winter    Chick a dee dee
[55]    ↑I think old Caesar must have heard↓
↑In northern Gaul my dauntless bird↓

49–52 The stubs of these leaves indicate that pp. [50]–[52] were inscribed in ink, apparently with a draft of "The Titmouse"; visible a fifth of the way down on p. [50] are the ends of lines 4–15 and on p. [51] the beginnings of lines 17–18, followed by four lines, the first three numbered "3", "4", and "2". Offset on p. [53] indicates that the last six lines on p. [52] were struck through in ink.
53 "For joy & beauty" (1–4); "The Titmouse," 52–54, 59–60, 55–58 (5–13). Lines (5–13) are struck through in ink.
54 "The Titmouse," 61–65, four unused lines, 27–28, 86, 87/88, 89. Struck through in ink. Lines (6–7) are enclosed in large ink parentheses.
55 "The Titmouse," 90–91, 92?, x, 93, 93 (1–6); "O sun! take off," 9–12 (7–10); "The Titmouse," 94–99 (11–16). Lines (1–6) and (11–16) are struck through separately in ink.

Ju⟨il⟩lius in some northern wold
Caught from thy
(5)            thy battle-/numbers/burden/ bold
Borrowed thy short song's burden bold

---

Ah! little knew the innocent
In throes of birth forlorn
That wolves & foxes waited for
(10)    Their victim to be born.

---

But ⟨I aye hear⟩we must write our annals new
And thank thee for a better clew
Who little thot when I came here
To find the antidote of fear
(15)    Henceforth I hear thee say in Roman key
Paean! Veni Vidi Vici.

[56]        Round him ⟨the⟩ ↑lift↓ glittering thundertops
And he will run between the drops
Of the great shower of glory
         ⟨↑the pretty savage Pequot↓⟩
(5)          Live out of doors
In the great woods & airy moors
I dine in the sun
When he sinks in the sea
I have a hole in a hollow tree
(10)    ⟨Step in⟩ ↑This air↓ it blows a little fresh
⟨Step in⟩ ↑No more↓,—but thy superfluous flesh
Ridiculously shakes & shivers
Too broad an aim to winters quiver

[57] binocular vision

        When stifling summer beats
With too hot nights on these retreats

The courage that can last
Is not the courage that makes haste
(5)          When noontide
The noontide twilight which snow makes
With tempest of the falling flakes
the dimple in the snow

56 "The Titmouse," four unused lines, 68–70, 70–71, four unused lines. Lines (1–4) are in pencil; lines (5–13) are struck through in ink.

57 "The Titmouse," 72–73, x, x, 74, 74–75, 40?, x, 78–79. The phrase "binocular vision" and lines (3–11) are in pencil. Lines (1–2) are struck through in ink; lines (6–7) are struck through twice in pencil, and lines (10–11) once.

The heroes are the tender men

(10)    And easily the blast defied
Made of the air that blows outside

[58]    I am what is   was   & will be & my skirt none has
lifted
In flow & rushing I abide
I march by still & silent ways

The sportive sun the gibbous moon
(5)    the pits of air the gulf of space
the washing sea     the winnowing wind

Not in silver & gold
Not in thunder & light
Not in Age or in Power
(10)    ⟨Does⟩ ↑Is↓ Jove↑s beatitude↓
But wisdom & good

What happened to the Pyth⟨ia⟩oness who would prophesy when not
inspired   Plut[arch's Morals, London, 1718,] IV p 59

[59] His memory was an immense museum    the mind ⟨a⟩ receptacle
of forms

p     The pits of air
the gulf of space
My sleep is short I wake alway
the gaudy Bacchus
(5)    Minerva     I came from myself

The crocodile which hath no tongue
The field of truth the river of time

I hide in the light
I am dumb in ⟨sound⟩ song
(10)    I rest in the flowing
In need I abound

[60]    Doubt not, so long as earth has bread,
Thou first & foremost shalt be fed.
The providence that is most large
Takes hearts like thine in special charge,

58 "Song of Nature," x, x, x, 3, 2, six unused lines. In pencil. With line (1), cf. unused lines
for "May–Day" in notebook EL p. [145] above, and KL[A] p. [55] below.
59 "Song of Nature," 2, 2, five unused lines, 5–7, x. In pencil.
60 "The Titmouse," six lines first printed as lines 83–88 in the 1867 version (1–6); "Letters"
("The tongue") (7–10). Lines (1–6) are struck through in ink. In lines (7–8), "⟨My⟩ ↑The↓
tongue . . . for" is written in ink over "My tongue . . . for" in pencil.

(5)         Helps ⟨those⟩ ↑who↓ for their own need are strong,
         And the sky doats on cheerful song.

           ———

         ↑⟨My⟩ ↑The↓ tongue is prone to lose the way, ↓
         ↑Not so the pen, for↓ in a letter
         We have not better things to say,
(10)       But surely say them better.

           ———

[61]      From Nature's beginning
         Sin blunders & brags,
         True making, true winning
         Go hidden in rags.

(5)         Wit has the creation
         Of worlds & their fame
         On one stipulation,
         —Renouncing the same.

         What wilt thou? the Forces?
(10)       Or skies which they breed?
         The strain it discourses
         Or Pan ↑?↓ ⟨&⟩or his reed?

         If the crown once incloses
         The brows of her son,
(15)       The Muse him deposes
         From kingdom & throne

[62] [blank]
[63]      Sit still, the truth is near
         Suddenly it will uplift
         Your eyelids to the light,
         And you shall see
(5)         The portra ↑i↓ ture of things to be.

         The pain of love a better fate
         Than the body's best estate

---

         Your wars
         And your autumnal gatherings
(10)       When ⟨the⟩ summers work is past & done
         And you meet in conclave general
         /Consult/Exchange/ in conclave federal
         On greetings ⟨fa⟩ kind to each & all

  61  "From Nature's beginning" (1–16); "Poet of poets," 88–95 (5–8, 13–16). Lines (9–12) are struck through in pencil.
  63  "Shun Passion," 2–6 (1–5); "The pain of love" (6–7); "May–Day," nine unused lines, 421–22 (8–18).

Conscious of each of duty done
(15)    ⟨Each as stainless as the sun⟩
Each unstained as is the sun
                    condescend
To man as to a lubber friend
[64]    And ↑generous↓ teach our aukward race
Courage probity & grace

                My birds

They seem a toy
(5)     Darlings of /children/⟨poets⟩/ & of ⟨men⟩ ↑bard⟨s⟩↓
Perfect ⟨creatures⟩ kinds by vice unmarred
All of worth & beauty set
Gems in Natures cabinet

These the fables she esteems
(10)    ↑Reality↓ Most like to ⟨poetry &⟩ dreams
Far travelled in the south plantations
Come back you little nations

Bring your music & rhythmic flight
↑Your colors          for the eyes delight↓
(15)    Nestle in our roof
Weave your chamber weatherproof
Your enchanting manners bring
Courage grace

[65]    By consummate powers
Gathering along the centuries
From race on race the rarest flowers
My wreath shall nothing miss.
(5)     And many a thousand summers
My apples ripened well,
And light from meliorating stars
Wi⟨h⟩th firmer glory fell.
I wrote the past in characters
(10)    Of rock & fire the scroll
The building ⟨of⟩ ↑in↓ the coral sea,
The planting ⟨the p⟩of the coal.
And thefts from satellites & rings
And broken stars I drew,
(15)    And out of spent & aged things
I made the world anew.

64 "May–Day," 423–24, 416?, x, 415, 416?, x, 413, four unused lines, 417–20, 416/418?, 424 (1–18). In pencil. Lines (1–2) are struck through three times in pencil, and lines (4–18) once.

65 "Song of Nature," 13–28. Struck through in ink.

[66]       How all the gods kept carnival
Tricked out in star & flower
And in cramp form of elf & beast
They swathed their too much power
(5)       The wild young world unfolded
Its million petalled flower

Time & thought the high surveyors
⟨They⟩ ↑Have↓ laid their courses well
Tapped the sea & heaved the layers
(10)      Of coal & marble shell

           There is power supreme oer powers
         And when will Jove allow
         My lights to quench my seas to ebb

[67₁]    I made the wind
fire
rain
Then I made man

(5)       His tongue was ⟨armed with⟩ ↑framed to↓ music
And his hand was armed with skill
And his face ⟨was armed with⟩ ↑the mould of↓ beauty
And his heart ⟨was armed with⟩ ↑the throne of↓ will

But ah my leaves have lost their charm
(10)      I weary of my pilgrimage
I tire to be clothed again with snows
Anon in garlands & cascades

If there be a power
O when will Jove allow

[67₂]         I framed his tongue to music
       I armed his hands with skill
I moulded his face to beauty
And his heart the throne of Will.

[68]     My lights to quench
My tides to ebb
My wheels which whirl the sun & satellite ↑to rest↓

66 "Song of Nature," 29–32, x, x, 33–36, x, x, x. Lines (1–5) and (7–10) are struck through separately in ink, but the first mark is fingerwiped below line (4); lines (11–13) are in pencil.
67₁ "Song of Nature," eight unused lines, 52?, 51?, 51?, 52?, x, x (1–14); "Power" ("His tongue") (5–8). In pencil; lines (1–8) and (9–12) are struck through separately in pencil.
67₂ "Power" ("His tongue"). With line (3), cf. "Song of Nature," 65.
68 "Song of Nature," x, x, 47/48, 45–48, 53, x, x, x, 52?, x, 51–52. In pencil, struck through in pencil. "Laura Johnson" is written to the right of line (2) in ink.

(5)  Will ⟨never⟩ time & tide ⟨be never done⟩ ↑forever run↓
    ↑Will never↓ My winds ⟨to⟩ ↑go↓ sleep in the West
    ↑Will never↓ My ⟨winds⟩ ↑wheels↓ which whirl the sun
And satellite ⟨to⟩ ↑have↓ rest?

    I tire of globes & ages
Of water & of flame
(10)  /Of still/My book's/ returning pages
⟨A n⟩Thro' endless times the same

My leaves have lost their charm
My wandering clouds their grace
I tire of my robe of snows
(15)  My leaves & my cascades

[69]    ↑I tire of globes & ages,↓
    ↑Too long the game is played↓
↑⟨For⟩ what ⟨to me⟩ are to me springs sunlit leaves↓
    ↑Or winter's starlit shades?↓
          ↑See p 77↓

(5)    Winters know
Easily to shed the snow,
And the untaught spring is wise
In cowslips & anemonies.
Nature hating art & pains,
(10)  Baulks & baffles plotting brains,
    ↑Casualty & Surprise↓
    ↑Are the apples of her eyes,↓
But she dearly loves ⟨her own⟩ ↑the poor↓,
And by marvels of her own
(15)  Strikes the bold pretender down
For nature listens in the rose
And hearkens in the lily's bell
To help her friends, to plague her foes,
And, like wise God, she judges well

[70]    A queen rejoices in her peers,
And wary Nature knows her own,
By court & city, dale & down,
And like a lover volunteers,
(5)    And to her son will treasures more
And more to purpose freely pour

---

69  "Song of Nature," 53–54, 55?, 56 (1–4); "Nature I," 1–15 (5–19). Lines (1–4) and "See p 77" are in pencil. Lines (11–12), in ink over the pencil inscription on p. [68], are circled and struck through twice in ink, and their intended position shown by an arrow; lines (5–10) and (12–19) are struck through in ink.
70  "A queen rejoices."

In one woodwalk than learned men
Will find with glass in ten times ten.

[71]        ↑Omens ⟨*Fate*⟩↓
Delicate omens traced in air
To him authentic witness bare;
Birds with auguries on their wings
Chanted undeceiving things
(5)    Him to beckon, him to warn,
Well might then the poet scorn
To learn of scribe or courier
Hints writ in vaster character;
And on his mind at dawn of day
(10)   Soft shadows of the evening lay.

Apples of gold in silver salvers set

I have an arrow that ⟨will⟩can find its mark
A mastiff that will bite without a bark

[72]  ↑*Nature*↓
By kinds I keep my kinds in check,
I plant the oak, the rose I deck.

The Rock of Ages melt↑s↓ alway
Into the mineral air,
(5)    To yield the quarry whence is built
Thought, & its mansion fair.

But Nature whistled with all her winds,
Did as she pleased, & went her way.

Teach me your mood, o patient stars!
(10)   Who climb each night ⟨your⟩the ancient sky,
Leaving on space no shade, no scars,
No trace of age, no fear to die.

[73]        ↑Fate↓
Deep in the man sits fast his fate⟨,⟩
To mould his fortunes mean or great.
Unknown to Cromwell, as to me,
Was Cromwell's measure & degree;
(5)    Unknown to him as to his horse
If he than grooms be better or worse.
He works, fights, plots, in rude affairs,

71 "Fate" ("Delicate omens"), 1–10 (1–10); "Apples of gold" (11); "I have an arrow" (12–13). "Omens ⟨Fate⟩" is in light pencil; lines (1–10) are struck through in ink.
72 "By kinds I keep" (1–2); "Ever the Rock of Ages melts" (3–6); "But Nature whistled" (7–8); "Teach me your mood" (9–12).
73 "Fate" ("Deep in the man"). Struck through in ink; "Fate" is added in pencil.

With boys, lords, kings, his craft compares,
Till late he learned, thro doubt & fear,
(10)      Broad England harboured not his peer,
Obeying Time, the last to own
The genius from its cloudy throne.
For the prevision is allied
Unto the thing so signified;
(15)      Or say, the foresight that awaits
Is the same Daemon that creates.

[74]      ↑See p 255↓
Already blushes in thy cheek
The bosom thought which thou must speak
The bird, how far it haply roam,
By cloud or isle, is flying home;
(5)      And every man, in love or pride,
Of his fate is never wide.

The maiden fears, & fearing runs
Into the /ambush which/ambuscade/ she shuns

[75]      In flint & marble beats a heart,
The kind earth takes her children's part;
⟨In⟩Her cottage chamber, wall & beam
Glows with the maid's delicious dream;
(5)      The green lane is the schoolboy's friend,
Low leaves his quarrel apprehend;
The fresh ground loves his top & ball,
The air rings jocund with his call.
The snow that falls at Christmas prates
(10)      In chimney-tops of sled & skates;
The youth reads omens where he goes,
And speaks all languages the rose.
The wood-fly mocks with tiny noise
The far halloo of human voice;
(15)      The perfumed berry on the spray
Smacks of faint memories far away.

[76]      A subtle chain of countless rings
The next unto the farthest brings,

74 "Nemesis," 1–4, 7–8, 5–6. Struck through once in ink and once in pencil. "See p 255" and "ambuscade" in line (8) are in pencil.

75 "May–Day," 307–8, x, x, 309–12, x, x, 315–20 (1–16); "Nature" ("A subtle chain"), 3–4 (11–12). Lines (1–8) and (11–16) are struck through separately in ink, and lines (11–12) twice in pencil.

76 "May–Day," 321–24 (1–4); "Nature" ("A subtle chain"), 1–2, 5–6 (1–4); "Song of Nature," 51?, 50–52 (5–8). Lines (5–8) are in pencil; lines (1–4) are struck through in ink, and lines (6–8) in pencil.

And, striving to be ⟨God⟩ ↑man↓, the worm
Mounts thro' all the spires of form.

(5)        I tire

Too soon the sunset fades
I ⟨tire⟩ will no more my robe of snows
My leaves & my cascades

[77]    I tire of globes & races
Too long the game is played
I tire of seas & mountain coasts
My leaves & my cascades

(5)      ⟨Enough of times & seasons⟩
↑Too much of donning & doffing,↓
Too slow the rainbow fades,
I love no more my robe of snows,
My leaves, & my cascades.

(10)    And what must be the splendor of that Soul
Buried in Anna's beauty for its tomb?

---

See *Iamblichus* p. 171

[78]    And roll the river where it will,
Towns on its banks will rise.

---

Dear are the pleasant memories
Of unreturning years,
(5)    And griefs recalled delight not less,—
Youth's terrors & its tears

---

A train of gay & clouded days
Dappled with joy, & grief, & praise,
Beauty to fire us, saints to save,
(10)    Escort us to a little grave.

[79]    He took the color of his vest
From rabbit's coat or grouse's ⟨ves⟩breast,
For, as the woodkinds lurk & hide,
So walks the woodman unespied.

---

77 "Song of Nature," 53–54, x, 52, x, 49–52 (1–9); "Then what must be the splendor" (10–11). Lines (1–4) are in pencil; lines (1–9) are struck through in ink.

78 "And roll the river" (1–2); "Dear are the pleasant memories" (3–6); "Life" (7–10).

79 "Forester" (1–4); "Life" (5–8); "The genial spark" (9–12). Lines (5–12) are in pencil; in line (5), the addition is in ink. In line (9) "spark" is written over an erased word; "spark" was also written above it and erased. Lines (1–4) are struck through in pencil.

(5)        ⟨A train of ↑gay & clouded↓ days⟩
              ⟨Dappled with joy & grief & praise⟩
              ⟨↑Beauty to fire us, saints to save↓⟩
              ⟨Escort us to a little grave.⟩

---

              The genial ⟨‖ . ‖⟩spark the poet felt
(10)        ↑Flamed↓ Till every barrier melt,
              He poured his heart out like a bird,
              And as he spoke, so was he heard.

---

[80]–[81] [blank]
[82]       And walked in flowers around my field
          As June herself around the Sphere.

[83]       Go copy in verse one chime
          Of the woodbell's peal & cry
          Write in ⟨thy⟩a book the morning's prime
          And match with words that amber sky.

---

        The poor Poet's praise.—
(5)        If bright the sun, he tarries;
          All day his song is heard;
          And when he goes, he carries
          No more baggage than a bird.

[84] feathered Mercury    See Websters Dictionary

                    ‖*ad verbum*
                    ‖feathered

        I came in March

        I tell you sirs,
        ⟨For⟩ this ⟨poor weed of⟩ root plebeian
        Had its head in the empyrean

[85]–[88] [two leaves cut out]
[89]       One night he dreamed of a palace fair,—
          Next year, it stood in marble strong,
          Sheltered a nation's proudest throne,

---

82 "She walked in flowers."
83 "My Garden," 37–40 (1–4); "If bright the sun" (5–8). Lines (1–4) are struck through in pencil.
84 "May–Day," x (1); "I tell you sirs" (2–4). Lines (2–4) are in pencil. For the reference to "feathered Mercury," see notebook EL p. [156ᵦ] above.
86 The stub shows traces of five lines in ink beginning a fifth of the way down the page, probably "Song of Nature," 31–35.
88 The stub shows only a comma in ink at the end of one line near the top of the page.
89 "One night he dreamed."

(5)
    There sate the fathers of the state,
    There echoed freedom's shrill debate
    A thousand years it will stand the same
    Enacting laws & breathing Fame.

[90]        cusped

[91]    Thanks to those who go & come,
    Who brot Hellas, Thebes, & Rome,
    As near to me as is my home;—
    Those careful husbands of the mind
(5)    Who keep decaying history good,
    And do not suffer Tyre or Troy
    To know decrepitude

[92]      ↑Good sir↓ Take us along with you
    We also prize the mountain view
    But more we prize the honoring
    ⟨The⟩ eye, voice, ↑&↓ counsel, of the /bard/guard/

(5)      The low December vault in June be ↑up-↓lifted high
    And largest clouds be flakes of down in that enormous sky.

[93] [blank]
[94]      As the bird trims her to the gale
    I trim myself to the storm of time
    I man the rudder, reef the sail,
    Obey the voice in age, obeyed at prime,
(5)    ⟨When⟩ ↑Darker↓ the sky ⟨darkens at my side⟩ ↑nearer will
      stand↓
    The pilot ⟨draws⟩ ↑great↓ /to guide my hand/close at hand/
    Whispering me to banish fear
    Right onward drive unharmed
    The port well worth the cruise is near
(10)    And every wave is charmed.
    Is the sky dark? ↑it saith,↓ more near will stand
    The pilot ⟨⟨true⟩ ↑chief↓ to guide thy⟩ ↑with unerring↓
      hand
    ⟨Be thou steadfast⟩ banish fear
    Right onward drive unharmed
(15)    The port well worth the cruise is near,
    And every wave is charmed.

90 In pencil.
91 "Thanks to those."
92 "Good sir Take us along" (1–4); "The low December vault" (5–6). Lines (1–4) are in pencil.
94 "Terminus," 33–36, x, x, 37–40, x, x, 37–40. The page is struck through three times, and lines (13–16) twice more, in ink.

[95]–[97] [blank]
[98]     With the key of the secret he marches faster
       From strength to strength, & for night brings day,
       While classes or tribes too weak to master
       The flowing conditions of life, give way.
              See XO 68

[99] [Jones] V[ery]. could read the song of a bobolink into English
sentences   but that is easier he could look at an apple tree in bloom &
tell you accurately what it said to you & you wd listen & ponder &
confess that he had said what you felt.

[100]    Rules will never fabricate
       The ⟨hero⟩ ↑semigod whom↓ we await,
       He must be musical,
       Tremulous, impressional,
(5)      Alive to ⟨every⟩ ↑gentle↓ influence
       Of landscape, or of sky,
       And tender to the ↑spirit-↓touch
       Of every human eye:
       Yet to his native centre ⟨firm⟩ ↑fast↓
(10)    ↑Can Jovelike↓
       ↑Can fluent fates in /new mould/adamant/ cast↓

[101]     Brother, no decrepitude
       Cramps the limbs of Time;
       As fleet his feet, his hands as good,
       His vision as sublime.

(5)      The vaulters in the circus round,
       Who step from horse to horse but never touch the ground.

[102]    Love on his errand bound to go,
       Can swim the ⟨sea,⟩ ↑flood,↓ & wade thro' snow;
       Where way is none, ⟨t'will⟩ ↑can↓ creep & wind,
       And eat through Alps ⟨its⟩ ↑his↓ home to find.

(5)      ⟨If my old spyglass could⟩ ↑Could my old telescope↓ retain
       All pictures it hath spied
       When peeping through the cottage pane
       Or palace windows wide
       I went to Venice, went to France

---

98 "With the key of the secret."
99 In pencil.
  100 "Culture," 1?, 2–9, x, 11. Lines (10–11) and all cancellations and additions are in pencil;
lines (1–9) are struck through in ink.
    101 "Brother, no decrepitude" (1–4); "Like vaulters in the circus round" (5–6).
    102 "Love" (1–4); "Could my old telescope" (5–16). Lines (1–4) are struck through in ink.
Lines (13–16) and the cancellation and addition in line (1) are in pencil.

(10)    And Genoa's golden street
〈I〉 ↑At Naples↓ saw the Carnival
And Arqua's monument
If yonder mirror knew
All it beheld before
(15)    What rosy blushes painted it
Groups, solos, tête a têtes

[103]    ↑↑The↓ Pain of love's a better fate↓
↑Than the body's best estate↓

Love on his errand bound to go
Can swim the sea & wade the snow

(5)    Love creepeth where it cannot go,
〈And eats its way thro Alps of snow,〉
〈↑Swims thro waves & wades thro snow↓〉
Where way is none, t'will creep & wind,
And eat thro Alps its home to find.

(10)    And swims the sea & wades the snow

Love on his quest is bound to go,
And swims the sea & wades the snow,
Where way is none, twill creep & wind,
And eat thro' Alps its home to find

[104]    What need I holier dew
Than Walden's haunted wave
Distilled from heavens alembic blue
〈I〉Stored in Earths secret cave
(5)    Steeped in each forest cave

[105]    ↑Ah me can maxims educate↓
Rules will never fabricate
The semigod whom we await;
He must be musical,
(5)    Tremulous, impressional,
Alive to gentle influence
Of landscape or of sky,
And tender to the spirit-touch
Of 〈the human〉 ↑man's or maiden's↓ eye;
(10)    Yet to his native centre fast↑,↓

103 "The pain of love" (1–2); "Love," 1–2, 3?, 4/2, 2–4, 2, 1–4 (3–14). Lines (3–4), (7), and (10–14) and the cancellations in lines (6–7) are in pencil. Lines (3–10) are struck through three times in pencil and lines (11–14) once.

104 "In my garden three ways meet," 25–27, 28?, 28. In pencil.

105 "Culture," 1, 1?, 2–9, x, 11. Lines (1) and (11) and the comma in line (10) are in pencil; in line (12), "can" is canceled and "re-" added in pencil. Lines (2–12) are struck through in ink.

↑New laws to history dispense↓
And the worlds flowing fates in his own ⟨pattern⟩ ↑mould
⟨can⟩ ↑re-↓ ↓cast

[106]     In my garden, three ways meet,
Thrice the spot is blest,
Hermit thrush comes there to sing,
Carrier doves to rest.

(5)     In my garden, oaken copse
The eager wind detains
Sultry summer lingers there
When Autumn chills the plains.

The bees were in their sugar house
(10)     The spider spun his silk
The wasp made paper all the day
The ants their cows did milk

If I should put the woods in song
And tell whats here enjoyed
(15)     All men would to these gardens throng
And leave the cities void

[107]–[110] [two leaves torn out]
[111]     And what avail
The plough & sail,
Or ⟨lif⟩land or life, if freedom fail?

The heavy blue chain
(5)     Of the boundless main
Didst thou, ⟨o just man⟩ ↑Malone↓, endure.

↑For↓ ⟨Y⟩you can teach
The lightning speech
And round the world your white arm reach

(10)     For ne⟨'er⟩ver will die the captive's cry
On the echoes of God, till Right draws nigh

---

106 "In my garden three ways meet," 1–8, four unused lines (1–12); "My Garden," 1–4 (13–16). Lines (9–12) are in pencil; lines (13–16) are struck through in ink.

107 Surviving letters and words on the stub show "Mu" at the top of the page, in pencil and with a horizontal pencil line below it, followed by an ink version of "The Test."

108 The stub shows traces of seven lines in ink, possibly prose, filling the upper two-thirds of the page.

109 The stub shows traces of four lines of prose in ink, beginning at mid-page.

110 The stub shows a trace of pencil three or four lines down from the top of the page.

111 "Boston," 29/78, 29/78, 30/79 (1–3); "The heavy blue chain," 1–2, x (4–6); "Boston," 108, 108–9, x, x (7–11). Lines (7–9) and the cancellation and addition in line (6) are in pencil. Lines (1–3) are struck through in ink; two vertical lines are drawn in pencil in the left margin beside lines (10–11).

[112]      The world was made
             For honest trade
             To plant & eat be none afraid

             The honest waves
(5)        Refuse to slaves
             The empire of the ⟨sea⟩ ↑ocean caves↓

             I bade the sabre work & eat
             Commands the sword to work & eat

[113] I know a song which is more hurtful than strychnine, or the kiss of the asp. It blasts those who hear it, changes their color & shape, & dissipates their substance. It is called Time.

I know a song, which, tho' it be sung never so loud, few can hear;— only six or seven persons: yet they who hear it, though they were old, become young again; when it is sung, [114] the stars twinkle & change color, & the moon bends nearer the earth.

I know where to find songs, new & better than any I have heard.

[115]       Fate
             Power
             Wealth
             Culture

             Aloft in secret veins of air
             Blows the sweet breath of song,
             Ah! few to scale those uplands dare,
             Though they to all belong.

             Behavior
              Wo⟨sh⟩rship

[116]       In the ⟨a⟩Arctic circle felt
             Streaming from the Equator's belt
             Shod with light the selfsame power
             Drives the birds to Labrador
(5)        Puts in↑,↓ drives home the sightless wedges
             Exploding bur↑s↓ts the crystal ledges
             Uncurls the downy northern fern
             Makes hot gulfstreams the iceberg burn
             Unborn unspent in every hour

112 "Boston," 11/51, 11/51, 12/52, 17, 17–18, x, x. In pencil.
113–14 Cf. JMN 13:171, 14:73–74, and "Merlin's Song."
115 "Waldeinsamkeit," 37–40. Lines (1–4) are struck through in pencil. The titles, in pencil, refer to the first six essays in *The Conduct of Life*, 1860.
116 "May–Day," ten unused lines (1–10); "Put in, drive home" (5–6). In pencil; the comma in line (5) is in ink.

(10)         Works untired thro' seasons four

[117]    Roomy Eternity casts her schemes rarely,
          And ⟨a full period⟩ ↑an aeon↓ allows
          For ⟨every⟩ ↑each↓ quality & part
          In the multitudinous
(5)        ⟨M⟩And many-chambered heart.

[118] [blank]

[119]    Boon Nature yields each day a brag, which we now first
              behold,
          And trains us on to slight the new, as if it were the old;
          But blest is he who, playing deep, yet haply asks not why,
          Too busied with the crowded day to fear to live or die.

(5)             I said to ⟨the⟩ heaven that glowed above,
          O hide yon sun-filled zone,
          Hide all the stars you boast!
          For, in the world of love,
          And estimation true,
(10)        The heaped-up harvest of the moon
          Is worth one barley corn, at most,
          The Pleiads' sheaf but two.

[120] [blank]

[121]    At Plymouth in the friendly crowd
          Mamma was ⟨once⟩ ↑not↓ a ⟨t⟩little proud
          To see her ⟨silver⟩ ↑beaming↓ candlesticks
          Almost outshine their lighted wicks
(5)        Why not? since shafts of solid silver
          ⟨Would⟩
          Might tempt the Plymouth saints to pilfer
          But ⟨cruel⟩ Time, a more ⟨ta⟩relentless thief
          Betrayed Mamma & these to grief
(10)        He stole the silver grain by grain
          ⟨Till nought was left but shameless copper⟩
          ↑Nothing but copper would remain↓
          But ⟨now⟩ ↑when↓ Aladdin came to town
          ⟨With⟩ ↑Hiding↓ his famed lamp ⟨hid⟩ in his gown
(15)        Touched the old sticks with fingers new
          ⟨Put⟩ ↑As if with↓ starshine ⟨in the red & blue⟩ ↑riddled
              through ⟨& through⟩↓
          And now they beam like her own feats
          Of mercy in the Concord streets.

117 "Roomy Eternity," 1/2, 3–6.
119 "Nature" ("Boon Nature") (1–4); "I said to heaven" (5–12). Struck through in ink; lines
(1–4) are also struck through in pencil; the cancellation in line (5) is in pencil.
121 "At Plymouth in the friendly crowd." In pencil.

[122]        for gentle harp to gentle hearts
The secret of the world imparts
And not today nor ↑yet↓ tomorrow
Can spend its wealth of hope & sorrow.

(5)        But onward ⟨ever still⟩ to the practised ear
Unfolds new sense & tender cheer

I've come to live with you, sweet friends,

―――――

Many & subtle are my lays
The latest better than the first
(10)      For I can mend the happiest days
And ⟨heal⟩ ↑charm↓ the anguish of the worst

[123]      Soft & softlier hold me friends
Thanks ⟨for⟩ ↑if your↓ tender care
Unbinds & gives me to the air
⟨Not for fingers⟩ ↑Keep your↓ lips or finger tips
(5)        For flute⟨s⟩ & ⟨pianos⟩ ↑or spinnet's↓ dancing chips
⟨But give me to⟩ ↑I await↓ a tenderer touch
I ask more or not so much
Give me to the atmosphere
Where is the wind my brother ↑—↓ where?
(10)     ⟨Ope the window⟩
Lift the sash, ⟨put⟩ ↑lay↓ me within
Now ⟨hearken⟩ lend your ears & I begin
For gentle harp to gentle hearts
The secret of the world imparts
(15)     And not today & not tomorrow
Can spend its wealth of hope & sorrow
But ever more to practised ear
Unlocks new sense & subtler cheer

[124]      ↑Tis↓ Mine to ⟨se⟩ watch the sun at work
⟨And⟩ ↑Or↓ if he hide in clouds & shirk
⟨To⟩ ↑I↓ keep the pitcoal to the mark
And test the force of wood & bark
(5)        ↑Upon my wise enamelled scales↓
↑the learned numbers never fail↓
From sixty up to seventy one

    122 "Maiden Speech of the Aeolian Harp," 12–18, 20–23. In pencil; the addition in line (3) is in ink.
    123 "Maiden Speech of the Aeolian Harp," 1–9, 10?, 10–17. In pencil, struck through in pencil.
    124 "Thermometer," 1–2, 4, 3, 5–10, 13, x, 14, x, 15–16. Line (6) is added at the top of the page and a line drawn to show its intended position. Erased pencil, struck through in pencil with a large X.

The grades of household comfort run
If they climb a hairsbreadth higher
(10)    ⟨Open⟩ ↑Fling wide↓ the door ⟨& quench⟩ ↑put out↓ the
        fire

Twice I dive twenty below zero
⟨Twice in the year⟩
⟨And thrice⟩ ↑Thrice ⟨‖ . . . ‖ to⟩ climb↓ to heat would
      blacken Nero
But much prefer the temperate
(15)    Health & heart will prosper man
At the mean point of 54

[125]            ↑*Thermometer*↓
Mine to watch the sun at work
Or if he hide in clouds & shirk
I test the force of wood & bark,
And keep the pitcoal to the mark
(5)    On my white enamelled scale
The warning numbers never fail
From sixty up to seventy one
The grades of household comfort run
If they climb a hairsbreadth higher
(10)    Fling wide the door, put out the fire,
Each year will have its holidays
Which I report nor blame nor praise
Twice I dive twenty below zero
Twice climb to heat would blacken Nero
(15)    But health & heart will prosper more
At the mean point of 54

[126]    Dear Ellen
E must have
      They say you need a muff
And surely you must have one
(5)    Of warm /& gay &/arctic squirrel/ stuff
And let it be a brave one
Mamma ⟨will add⟩ ↑of course↓ a ⟨cap⟩ ↑will add↓
But nobody knows but you
What ↑sort of↓ cap the angels ⟨wear⟩ ↑clad↓
(10)    So here's the ↑bank↓ paper ⟨cheque⟩ ↑due↓

How the best angels heads are clad

125 "Thermometer." In pencil.
126 "Dear Ellen must have a muff," 1, 1, 1–8, 7. In pencil. In line (7), "will add" is canceled
and "of course" added, as is "bank" in line (10), in purple pencil.

[127]    Dear Ellen must have a muff
        Such as ⟨A⟩best angels /wear/have one/
        But nobody knows b

        Mamma must add a cap
(5)      But nobody knows but you
        What is the style of angels
        So here is the Concord Bank

    [128] One of M.M.E.'s contemplations of Nature almost ran into
rhyme, & might be easily rendered thus.
        But oh these waves & leaves
        When ⟨the⟩ ↑haply↓ Stoic Nature grieves—
        No human speech so beautiful
        As their murmurs mine to lull.
(5)      On this altar God hath built
        I lay my vanity & guilt,
        Nor me can Hope or Passion urge
        ↑⟨While⟩ I↓ Hear⟨ing⟩ /thus/as now/ the lofty dirge
        ⟨When⟩ ↑Which↓ blasts of northern mountains hymn
(10)    Nature's funeral high & dim,
        Sable pageantry of clouds,
        Mourning summer laid in shrouds.
        Many a day shall dawn & die,
        Many an angel wander by,
(15)    ⟨In this vale⟩ ↑⟨Light as they pass⟩ And passing, light↓ my
            sunken turf,
        ⟨Damped⟩ ↑Moist↓ perchance by Ocean surf,
        Forgotten amid splendid tombs,
        Yet wreathed & hid by summer's blooms.
  See [notebook] MME [4] p. 114     ↑Copied in *ETE*↓ p. 100,

[129] or this—    ↑Copied in *ETE* p 102↓
        ⟨Time th⟩ ⟨s⟩Shake not thy bald head↑, Time!↓ at me:
        I challenge thee to hurry past
        Or for my turn to fly too fast.
        Think me not numbed or halt with age,
(5)      Or cares that earth to earth engage,—
        ⟨Caught⟩ ↑Snared↓ with Love's cord of twisted beams
        Or mired with Climate's gross extremes,
        I pass with yonder comet free,—

127 "Dear Ellen must have a muff," 1–2, 6, 5–8. In pencil.
128 "The Nun's Aspiration," 11–28. All cancellations and additions are in pencil. Struck
through once in pencil from "rendered thus." to the bottom of the page, and again in very light
pencil through lines (1–14).
129 "The Nun's Aspiration," 30–36, 38–46, 48–49. The additions at the top and bottom
and the cancellation and addition in line (6) are in pencil. Struck through in pencil.

Pass with the comet into space
(10)    Which mocks thy aeons to embrace,
↑Elastic↓ Aeons which unfold
Realm beyond realm—extent un⟨ol⟩told,
No early morn, no evening late,—
Vast, self-upheld disdaining Fate
(15)    Whose shining sons too great for fame
Never heard thy weary name.
—How drear the part I held in one!
How lame the other limped away!
↑See↓

[130]    Could ever artist's pencil yield
The beauty of thy meanest field.

How drear the part I held in one,
How lame the other limped away.

(5)    The moon which lights
My feet my fancy more incites.
Nature is dear
Not for epochs, not for signs,
Not for measures of old time,
(10)    But for music more sublime.
T↑'↓ will never light a prosperous hour
Of earthly joy: in grander scope
I scorn, I scorn, the frivolous hope

A few words in my cradle tongue
(15)    Enough to use my mates among,
Enough for prayer, enough for thought,
And lessons which my Bible taught

[131]    ═══
Quatrains.
═══

[132]    ⟨Usque ad aras.⟩
*Pericles.*
Well & wisely said the Greek,
'Be thou faithful, but not fond;
To the altar's foot thy fellow seek,
The Furies wake beyond.

130 "The Nun's Aspiration," x, x, 48–49, thirteen unused lines. The apostrophe in line (11) is in pencil.

132 "Pericles" (1–4); "Climacteric" (5–8); "Botanist" (9–12). Struck through in ink; "Botanist" is enclosed in a rectangle in ink.

Climacteric.

(5)
I am not wiser for my age,
Nor skilful by my grief;
Life loiters at the book's first page,
Ah! could we turn the leaf.—

⟨Naturalist.⟩ ↑Botanist.↓
Go thou to thy learned task;
(10)
I stay with the flowers of spring;
Do thou of the Ages ask
What me the Hours will bring.

[133]                    *Memory.*
Nightdreams trace on Memory's wall
Shadows of the thoughts of day,
And thy fortunes, as they fall,
The bias of the will betray.

⟨Nativity⟩Horoscope.

(5)
Ere he was born, the stars of fate
Plotted to make him rich & great:
When from the womb the babe was loosed,
The gate of gifts behind him closed.

*Cras, Heri, Hodie.*
Shines the ⟨p⟩last Age, the next with hope is seen,
(10)
Today slinks poorly off unmarked between;
Future or Past no richer secret folds,
O friendless Present! than thy bosom holds.

*Fate.*
Her planted eye Today controls,
Is in the morrow most at home,
(15)
And ⟨call⟩sternly calls to being souls
That curse her when they come.

[134]                    *Forester.*
He took the color of his vest
From rabbit's coat or grouse's breast,
For, as the woodkinds lurk & hide,
So walks the woodman unespied.

133 "Memory" (1–4); "Horoscope" (5–8); "Heri, Cras, Hodie" (9–12); "Fate" ("Her planted eye") (13–16). Struck through in ink.
134 "Forester" (1–4); "Gardener" (5–8); "Northman" (9–12); "From Alcuin" (13–16). Struck through in ink.

*Gardener.*

(5) True Bramin in the morning meadows wet,
Expound the Vedas of the violet,
Or, hid in vines, peeping through many a loop,
See the plum redden, & the beurré stoop.

*Northman.*

The gale that wrecked you on the sand
(10) It helped my rowers to row,
The storm is my best galley hand
And drives me where I go.

*From Alcuin.*

The sea is the road of the bold,
Frontier of the wheatsown plains,
(15) The pit wherein the streams are rolled,
And fountain of the rains.

[135]     *Poet.*
⟨t⟩To clothe the fiery thought
In simple word succeeds,
For still the craft of genius is
To mask a king in weeds.

*Orator.*

(5) He who has no hands
Perforce must use his tongue;
Foxes are so cunning
Because they are not strong.

*Artist.*

Quit the hut, frequent the palace,
(10) Reck not what the people say;
For still, wher↑e↓e'er the trees grow biggest,
Huntsmen find the easiest way.

[136]     ———

*Poet.*

Ever the poet *from* the land
Steers his bark, & trims his sail,
Right out to sea his courses stand,
New worlds to find in pinnace frail.

     ———

*Shakspeare.*

(5) I see all human wits
Are measured but a few,

135 "Poet" ("To clothe") (1–4); "Orator" (5–8); "Artist" (9–12). Struck through in ink.
136 "Poet" ("Ever the poet") (1–4); "Shakspeare" (5–8); "Hafiz" (9–12). Struck through in ink.

Unmeasured still my Shakspeare sits
Lone as the blessed Jew.

———

Hafiz.
Her passions the shy violet
(10)    From Hafiz never hides,
Love-longings of the raptured bird
The bird to him confides.

[137]             S.H.
With beams December planets dart
His cold eye truth & conduct scanned,
July was in his sunny heart,
October in his liberal hand.

A.H.
(5)    High was her heart, & yet was well-inclined,
Her manners made of bounty well-refined,
Far capitals, & marble courts, her eye seemed still to see,
Minstrels, & kings, & highborn dames, & of the best that
      be.

[138]
———
↑Don't you wish you could?↓

———

↑*Preraphaelite.*↓
Go, copy in verse one chime
Of the wood bell's peal & cry;
Write in a book the morning's prime,
(5)    And match with words that amber sky.

———

*Poet.*
Test of the Poet is knowledge of love,
For Eros is older than Saturn or Jove;
Never was Poet of late, or of yore,
⟨But he was⟩↑Who was not↓ tremulous with love-lore.

[139]            ———
*Hush*!
Every /crypt/thought/ is public,
Every nook is wide,
Thy gossips spread /the/each/ whisper,
And the gods from sid⟨d⟩e to side.

———

137 "S. H." (1–4); "A. H." (5–8). Struck through in ink.
   138 "My Garden," 1?, 37–40 (1–5); "Casella" (6–9). *"Preraphaelite."* and lines (2–9) are
struck through in ink.
   139 "Hush!" (1–4); "Nature in Leasts" (5–8); "Nature" ("Boon Nature") (9–12). The words
"thought" in line (1) and "each" in line (3) are in pencil. Struck through in ink.

*Natura in minimis.*

(5) As sings the pinetree in the wind
So sings in the wind a sprig of the pine;
Her strength & soul has laughing France
Shed in each drop of wine.

---

*Nature.*

Boon Nature yields each day a brag which we now first
behold
(10) And trains us on to slight the new, as if it were the old:
But blest is he, who, playing deep, yet haply asks not why,
Too busied with the crowded hour to fear to live or die!

[140]

---

*Borrowing.*

Some of your hurts you have cured,
And the sharpest you still have survived,
But what torments of wo you endured
From evils that never arrived!

---

*Fate.*

(5) ⟨Ere he was born, the stars of fate⟩
⟨Plotted to make him rich & great;⟩
⟨When from the womb the babe was loosed,⟩
⟨The gate of gifts behind him closed.⟩

*Love*

Love on his errand bound to go,
(10) Can swim the flood, & wade through snow;
Where way is none, t'will creep & wind,
And eat through Alps ⟨his⟩ its home to find.

[141] Ever the Rock of Ages melts
Into the mineral air,
To be the quarry whence is built
Thought & its mansion fair.

---

Excelsior,
*a song of degrees.*

(5) Over her head were the linden buds,
And over the tree was the moon,

140 "Borrowing. From the French" (1–4); "Horoscope" (5–8); "Love" (9–12). Lines (1–8)
are struck through in ink with a fine pen; the page is struck through in heavier ink, the mark
fingerwiped down to line (5).
141 "Ever the Rock of Ages melts" (1–4); "Excelsior" (5–8). "Excelsior . . . *degrees.*" and
lines (5–8) are struck through in ink.

And over the moon the starry studs
That drop from the angels' shoon.

———

[142]     If not so good
         Yet such as I could

[143]–[145] [blank]
 [146]    With a troop of friends
         All good & wise men
         I crossed Champlain
         And went up the ⟨banks⟩ ↑Forks↓
(5)      Of the Ausable River ↑to explore↓
         ⟨To⟩ the Adirondac Lakes
         First to the Saranac
         There we took boats,
         ⟨Every⟩ ↑Each↓ man a boat & ⟨a⟩ guide,
(10)    Ten    men ten guides
         ⟨S[t]arted up⟩ ⟨↑Rowed↓⟩ ↑Next morn we ⟨rowed⟩ swept
             with oars↓ the Saranac
         Into Round Lake
         Where all the mountains drew around us
         Tahawus  Seward  Macintyre  Baldhead
(15)    Crowned not with wreaths but mountains
 [147]    ↑Cheered at heart by the ⟨gay⟩ mor bright morn↓
         ⟨On⟩ the gay flotilla went
         ⟨Through summer rushes⟩
         Through the tall summer bullrushes
(5)      Through purple beds of pickerel flower
         Through banks of lilies white & gold
         Where the deer feeds at night
         On through Upper Saranac
         And up the Raquette stream
(10)    To a small crooked inlet
         Winding thro grass in & out
         Two miles of flags ↑& pads↓ & sponge
         To Follansbee's Water the lake of loons
         ↑Northward↓ Two miles up this lake we rowed
(15)    ⟨An⟩ Under low mountains
         Which composed the shore
         Clothed in the virgin forest

  142 "If not so good." In pencil.
  146 "The Adirondacs," 1, motto 1?, 1–4, 7, 5, 5–10, 13. In pencil, struck through in pencil
and partially erased.
  147 "The Adirondacs," 16, 16, 17/24?, 17/24?, 18–21, 21/22, 22–27, 28?, 28? In pencil,
partially erased.

[148.1] U
   Near the lakes head
   ⟨Where⟩ ↑Eastward↓ a ⟨little⟩ bay makes in ⟨eastward⟩ to
    the land
   Between two rocky arms
(5)  We climbed the bank
   And in the depth of forest twilight
   ⟨Laid⟩ ↑Wield↓ the first axe these echoes ever heard
   ⟨We barked the⟩
   We cut young trees to make the camp poles
(10)  ⟨Cut a re⟩
   Laid a rear wall of logs
   And built a light supporting frame
   Then barked the spruce to cover the camp
   Then made a light, & kindled the camp fire

[149.1] The wood was ⟨thick⟩ ↑rich↓ with various trees
   Spruce cedar maple poplar beech & fir
   Three pines, white, pitch, & Norway,
   five-leaved, three-leaved, & two leaved, grew thereby
(5)  And the ⟨white⟩ pine was fifteen feet in girth,
   The maple ⟨seven or eight,⟩ ↑measured eight↓

[148.2] Ten men wonted to lie warm & soft
   In wellhung chambers
   Lay here on hemlock boughs like Indians
   They fancied the light air
(5)  Long shut out that circled round them
   Made them boys again.
   More pleasing was it
   To leave their duties beyond the mountains
   Here no doorbell announced /an idle visiter/a fop/
(10)  Here no mailbag or express waited them
   Here no letter came or went
   Nothing here was ploughed or reaped ↑or bought or sold↓
   The frost could blight no rose
   The rain could spoil no clothes
(15)  For all were drest for mountains
  Nature attempted nothing she could not perform

[148.2ₐ] Dark Flower of Cheshire garden

148.1 "The Adirondacs," x, 29–31, 31–33, 35, 34, x, x, x, 35–36. In pencil, partially erased.
149.1 "The Adirondacs," 37–38, 40–43. In pencil, partially erased.
148.2 "The Adirondacs," 50–52, 59, 60?, 61, x, 62?, 65–66, 66–69, 71, 71/72. In pencil, struck through in pencil and partially erased.
148.2ₐ "Dark Flower of Cheshire garden" (1–8); "The Earth" (9–12). The cancellation and additions in line (11) are in pencil.

Red Evening duly dyes
Thy sombre head with rosy hues
To fix fargazing eyes.
(5)   Well the planter knew how strongly
Works thy form on human thought:
I muse what secret purpose had he
To draw all fancies to this spot.

---

### The Earth.

⟨The⟩ ↑Our↓ eyeless bark sails free
(10)   ↑Tho'↓ ⟨R⟩rough with boom & spar
—Andes↑,↓ Alp⟨s⟩ ↑or↓ Himmalee,—
Strikes never moon or star

[149.2]   In Adirondac lakes
The guide rows without his hat
A blue flannel shirt & grey trowsers
Make all his dress.
(5)   In the rain or at night he dons a coat,
At morning he doffs it;
A paddle in one hand, or an oar,
In the other, a rifle,
Are his needful arms
(10)   All day we swept the lake with oars
From Camp Maple to Osprey Bay
Watching when the dogs should drive in the deer
Or whipping its surface for trout
Or diving from the rock for a bath at noon
(15)   Or waking the long echoes by guns & cries
[150]   Or listening to the laughter of the loons
or in the evening twilight
beholding the procession of the pines
And later still with lighted jack
(5)   in the bows of the boat
Stealing with paddle ⟨on⟩ to the feeding grounds of the
      ↑red↓ deer to aim a shot at the buck,
↑Hark what is that 'tis a tree falling in the forest↓
as he stands astonished at the meteor light, then turns to
      bound away a moment too late.
Or we tried our rifles at a mark

149.2 "The Adirondacs," 73–75, 75/76?, 76/77, 77–79, 79, 108–13. In pencil, struck through in pencil and partially erased.

150 "The Adirondacs," 114–18, 119/120, 121/122, 123/124, 125–29, 130/133. In pencil, struck through in pencil and partially erased.

(10) Six rods, ⟨ten rods⟩ twenty, forty,
   Or we tried our wits at sharp jokes, the sally & retort,
   with laughter like the crack of rifle
   Or we climbed the near heights
   To ⟨explore for a lake⟩ ↑seek a reputed lake↓ which we
     never found.

[151] We admired the stature of our guides
   Their strength & suppleness & skill,
   Skill to row, to swim, to shoot, to build a camp,
   to climb a stem without boughs
(5) fifty feet
   courage to face any foe in the forest
   & wit to find & vanquish him
   healthy men frolic & innocent
   lumberers in winter in summer guides
(10) ⟨They can⟩
   Their strong arms can pull ↑at↓ the oar 30 000 ⟨times⟩
    ↑strokes↓ in a day.
   They can kill the catamount the wolf & the bear

[152]  The bald eagle flew over us
   The osprey screamed
   The ravens croaked, owls hooted,
   The woodpecker hammered,
(5) And the heron rose in the swamp

   How went the day
   Two doctors in the camp
   Dissected warily the ⟨fresh⟩ newkilled deer
   Weighed the trout's brain
(10) Captured ⟨mice,⟩ ↑the↓ lizard, salamander, ⟨crab⟩ ↑shrew↓
   ↑Crab—↓ snail & dragonfly minnow & moth
   Nought came amiss to scoopnet
   And one pot of alcohol
   Furnished a safe sepulchre for all.
(15) Others sought plants, the gentian,
   & the fern, the long whip-scirpus
   ⟨the⟩ rosy polygonum, pride of the lake bank, the cardinal
[153] the gentian pickerel the harebell by the gorge of Ausable

   We scoffed at the distant city
   At its ⟨trivial⟩ timorous ways

 151 "The Adirondacs," 80–88, x, 89/90, 85. In pencil, struck through in pencil and partially erased.
 152 "The Adirondacs," 146, 146–47, 147/148, 148, 107?, 133–34, 134–36, 138–43. In pencil, struck through in pencil.
 153 "The Adirondacs," 142/145, 160–61, 161, 161/162, 163/164, x, x, 170, 171?/172?, 173–75. In pencil, struck through in pencil.

Magnifying trifles

(5) And we thought how shall we build our rooftree sure here
And come hither with our sons hereafter.
Then we rejoiced in our protectors
Which before this we disparaged
And called by many spiteful nam⟨in⟩es

(10) For who are our protectors from the cockneys of New York
& Boston
Who but the midges, the musquitoes, and the black flies?
Which torment the tender cit
But which we drive away

[154] with a smudge or at worst
Fend off with a veil
Ale was on our table, ale drunk from tin pans, and a little
wine.
We were fed on venison & trout on pork and potatoes &
beans & ⟨good⟩ new ⟨made flour⟩ ↑wheat-↓⟨f⟩bread
(5) And all ate heartily & laughed heartily whilst they ate
And Stillman the wise captain of the party, our pious
Aeneas, said with a firm voice
"No chronic dyspepsia ever came from eating indigestible
food." And some of the party murmured; others saw
that he spoke the truth.

[155] The midge the black fly & musquito
adorned our necks with a red necklace
and our hand with red wristbands
and our ankles with rosy bands
(5) But after a day we heeded them not

We fly away from cities but we bring
The best of cities with us
these learned classifiers
men knowing what they seek
(10) eyes which nought escapes
armed eyes of experts
We praise the guide we praise the forest life
But will we yield our dearbought lore
of Books & trained experiment
(15) or think the ⟨In⟩ ↑Sioux↓ a match for Cuvier
O no, not we; witness the shout that shook
The wild echoes of the Tupper Lake

154 "The Adirondacs," 175–76, 177/178, 179, 180/182?, 183/184, 185/186/187. Erased
pencil.
155 "The Adirondacs," 166–67, 167, 167–68, 302–3, 303–4, 304?, 304–10. Erased pencil.

[156]    when first
We passed from boat to boat the tidings
of ⟨ocean⟩ ↑the wire↓ cable laid across the sea
And landed on this coast

(5)    Or witness the mute allhail
The traveller gives when on the verge
Of the wilderness he hears in rude loghouse
a tune well played on the piano
Well done⟨,⟩! he cries, the wolf is kept outside, the bear the
    rattlesnake the rain & snow,

(10)    All the fierce enemies hunger & cold, this thin spruce roof
    this sturdy log wall and this

[157]    rank plantation will suffice to stave off once for all
Now cast off fright
⟨And⟩ ↑Now↓ speed the gay celerities of art
What was impossible in all this waste

(5)    Within ⟨this⟩ four walls is possible again
Culture & books secrets of skill
the fame of masters and eager ↑strife↓
Strife of competing pupils
    together or alone

(10)        to outdo each other
    and extort applause
↑Genius is born once more↓
Twirl the old wheels
Time makes fresh start again

(15)    On for a thousand years of genius more

[158]    Best is the poor save only that he craves
Riches

    That thrill
Shot thro' the ⟨base⟩ pedestals

(5)    of mountains, islands, continents,
Urg⟨ed⟩ing astonished Chaos with a thrill
To be a brain
Or to obey the brain of upstart man
And shake the slumbers of a million years

(10)    A spasm throbbing through the pedestals
Of mountain, island, continent, & main,
Urging astonished Chaos with a thrill

156 "The Adirondacs," x, 242, 239–40, 310–11, 312/313, 314, 315/316, 317/318/319.
Erased pencil.
   157 "The Adirondacs," 319, x, 320–25, 325–26, 326, x, 328, 328–29. Erased pencil.
   158 "Best is the poor" (1–2); "The Adirondacs," x, 262–65, 265, x, 262–65, 265–66, x,
267–70 (3–20). Lines (1–9) are in pencil; lines (10–20) are struck through in ink.

To be a brain, or to obey the brain
Of upstart Man

(15)    The lightning has gone loafing it too long
In all the idle past
He must to school & learn his verb & noun
And teach his nimbleness to work for man
Spelling with guided tongue man's messages

(20)    Shot thro the weltering pit of the salt sea

[159]    O mark the day
When our three boats
Entering Big Tupper bound for the white falls
at the lake's head encountered

(5)    Two ⟨boats⟩ of our friends returning to the camp
They held a printed Journal waving high
⟨Won from a traveller new arriv⟨ing⟩ed⟩
Won from a new arriving traveller
⟨And⟩ Big with great news & told us ⟨& the echoes⟩ the
        /tidings/bulletin/

(10)    ⟨The wires were laid & Europe joined to us⟩
for which the /nations/world had/ waited,
Of the wire cable laid across the sea,
And landed on our coast.
            Loud the ⟨cries of joy⟩ exulting cries

(15)    from boat to boat & to the echoes round
We have few moments in the longest life

[160]    of such pure joy & wonder
And suiting well the ⟨place⟩ ↑solitudes↓
A burst of joy as if we told the fact
To ears intelligent, as if gray rock

(5)    And cedar grove ⟨&⟩ hill & lake could know
The triumph of mankind.
As if we men were talking in a vein
⟨In⟩Of sympathy so large that ours was theirs
And a prime end of the most subtle element

(10)    Were fairly reached at last.
↑Bend nearer moon↓    Yon thundertops
Let them hear well, tis theirs as much as ours
And yet I marked even in the manly joy

[161]    Of our great hearted Doctor in his boat
Perhaps I erred, a shade of ⟨shame⟩ ↑discontent↓
Or was it for man ↑kind↓ a generous shame
As of a luck not quite legitimate

159 "The Adirondacs," 230–32, x, 234–36, 236–37, 239, 238–42, 249. In pencil.
160 "The Adirondacs," 250–61, 271. In pencil.
161 "The Adirondacs," 272–87. In pencil.

(5) Since fortune snatched from wit the lions part?
Was it a college pique of town & gown?
As one in whose memory it burned
That not ⟨the doctors⟩ ↑professors↓ but /the/some/
  vagabonds
⟨Had⟩ found ↑ten years since↓ the Californian gold
(10) And now again a hungry company
Led by determined sons of trade
Borrowing from the shop the tools
Of scien⟨s⟩ce not from masters of the art
Had won the brightest laurel of all time
(15) Twas always thus the hand & head
Are ever rivals but tho' this is swift

[162] And that is slow, this Prometheus
And that the Jove yet however hid
It was from Jove the other stole his fire
And without Jove the good had never been
(5) Tis not mohawks or cannibals
But ever the white race
the whites instructed by the whitest
Who do the feat
Let not him mourn who best entitled was
(10) Nay let him mourn least
Yea plant the tree that bears best apples, plant
And water, nor ⟨look⟩ ↑watch↓ thou askance
Wheth⟨y⟩er thy sons or strangers eat the fruit
Enough that men eat it & are refreshed

[163] October woods, wherein
The boy's dream comes to pass,
And nature ⟨crowns him⟩ ↑squanders↓ on the boy her pomp
And crowns him with a more than royal crown
(5) And unimagined splendor waits ⟨on⟩ his steps
The ⟨humble pilgrim⟩ ↑⟨gazing⟩ urchin↓ walks thro tents of
  gold
Thro crimson chambers porphyry & pearl
Pavilion on pavilion garlanded
Incensed & starred with lights & airs & shapes
(10) And sounds, music
Beyond the best conceit of pomp or power

[164] ⟨bird⟩ What wilt thou ↑restless↓ bird?
Seeking in that pure blue a bluer light

162 "The Adirondacs," 288–301. In pencil.
163 "October woods, wherein." In pencil.
164 "The Adirondacs," 208–10, nine unused lines. In pencil.

Thirsting in that pure for a purer sky
The
(5)         Every one pauses passing thro' the pines
To hear the sealike harmonies
the fall of water or the hum of seas
Or seeing the moon is touched & privately
as if he heard himself privately accosted
(10)       or when birds sing recalls his hours of youth
or in a mountain echo's voice regains
Arcad⟨ia⟩y Merlin

[165]   Your rank is all reversed.
Now let the men of cloth
Bow to the stalwart ⟨do⟩guides in overalls;
They are the doctors of the wilderness,
(5)      And we the lowprized laymen.
In sooth ⟨blue⟩ ↑red↓ flannel is a saucy test
Wh ↑i↓ ch few can stand

The sallow knows the basketmaker's thumb
The oar the guide's

(10)     Stumbling through vast selfsimilar woods
To find by night the nearest way to camp

[166]      Welcome! the woodgods cried,
Welcome, though late.

For Nature wonts her children,
Tho' late returning, to her primitive ways.
(5)      Off soundings, seamen do not suffer cold,
And, in the forest, delicate men
Sleep on the ⟨ground⟩ ↑hemlock boughs↓ ⟨nor fear
     rheumatic pain⟩ ↑as on down beds↓

[167]   As water poured through hollows of the hills
To fill this chain of lakes & rivulets
So nature shed forth beauty lavishly
From her abundant horn

(5)      What can stay
The flower, bird, wave or cloud
Each from its several perfectness

165 "The Adirondacs," 93, 93–98, 101–2, 105–6. Struck through in ink.
166 "The Adirondacs," 44–45, 54?, 55–58. In line (7), the cancellations and "as on down beds" are in pencil. Struck through in ink.
167 "The Adirondacs," 149–52, x, x, x, 46–49. Lines (1–7) are struck through in ink, the mark fingerwiped below line (4); lines (1–4) are struck through once more in ink, and lines (8–11) twice.

The stars peeped thro our maple boughs
Which o'er hung, like a cloud, our camping fire
(10)      And old decaying trunks the forest floor
Lit with phosphoric crumbs.

[168]    Wise & polite

And if I ⟨should draw⟩ drew
Their several portraits you would own
Chaucer had no such worthy crew
(5)      ⟨And less⟩ ↑Nor↓ Boccac⟨io⟩e in Decameron

The Doctor with whose fame
Both worlds are filled, whom France
⟨Covets⟩ ↑Grudges↓ to us ⟨as once⟩ ↑/as long she/more than/↓
    she ⟨coveted⟩ ↑pined↓
↑Long time↓ ↑For↓ Canada ↑once↓ and Acadie,
(10)      But lost like those

[169]    *Hoar*
The keenest wit, the Judge,
⟨The man of⟩ many weapons ↑can he draw↓
A champion in the state
A giant in the law

(5)      Both worlds are filled
Whose ⟨glory⟩ ↑lustre↓ France
By her envy doth enhance
Grudging to
Grudg⟨ed⟩ing to the New World more than she
(10)     ⟨Canada once & Acadie⟩
↑Once↓ Grudged Quebec ⟨once⟩ & Acadie

[170]    *Holmes*   ↑see 190↓
⟨There was a humorist⟩
↑With these there came a humorist↓
Kindhearted ↑gentle gay↓
⟨Nourishing⟩ ↑Caressing↓ his infirmities
(5)      ⟨With which he still did⟩ ↑As cossets for his↓ play
As ⟨f⟩gentle as a ⟨girl⟩ ↑maid↓
Yet with a ⟨rude⟩ ↑bold↓ address
Which still surprised to lead
Such masked tenderness
(10)     And he contrived to give

168 "The Adirondacs," motto (1–5), five unused lines (6–10). In pencil. In line (9), "once" is
added, and circled, in pencil.
169 "The Adirondacs," eleven unused lines. In pencil.
170 "The Adirondacs," sixteen unused lines. In pencil, struck through in pencil.

⟨Importance⟩ to his ⟨razor⟩ ↑walkingstick↓ or ⟨his⟩ chair
  ↑Or to his least affair↓
    A price superlative
He was born to ⟨give⟩ ↑lend↓ a grace

(15)  To a rude & savage place,
⟨And⟩ such his proper merits shone

[171₁]    That it needed not be ⟨told⟩ ↑known↓
He was brother ⟨to the man⟩ ↑in mind & blood↓
  ↑To the man of merr⟨y⟩iest mood↓
Of keen ↑est↓ point & edge

(5)  Who fills all ↑Saxon↓ minds
With his redundant fancy & his wit

That it needed not be known
He was twin in mind & blood
To the man of merriest mood

(10)  Of keenest point & edge
And of the Muse's privilege,
Who fills all Saxon minds
With his redundant fancy & his wit

[171₂]  Homer
Dante
Shakspeare
Milton
Goethe

[172]    ↑Prophet & Bard↓
Highborn Hoel
⟨High⟩ ↑Well↓born Lowell
⟨Then for Lowell⟩

(5)  What said the Sibyl
What was the fortune
She sung for him
"Strength for the hour"
Man of marrow ↑& of mark↓

(10)  Rich supplies & never stinted
⟨Plenty⟩ more behind ↑at need↓ is hinted
Never cumbered with the morrow
Not yet apprised of sorrow
⟨Or⟩ ⟨Entertained⟩ ↑Well contented↓ with today

(15)  ⟨In the opulence he shows⟩

171₁ "The Adirondacs," thirteen unused lines. In pencil. Lines (1–6) and (1–13) are struck through separately in pencil.

171₂ For Homer, Dante, Shakespeare, and Goethe, see "Solution," 16, 28, 40, and 65.

172 "James Russell Lowell," 40, 42–43, x, 44–48, 50–53, x, x, 54–57. In pencil, struck through in pencil.

⟨Too opulent⟩ ↑Quite too affluent↓ to have found
⟨Once⟩ ↑Yet↓ his opulences bound
⟨Yet⟩ ⟨Totally present in the fun⟩ ↑Most at home in
    mounting fun↓
⟨Best of all in joke⟩ ↑Broadest joke & luck[i]est pun↓

[1731]   ⟨Hiding⟩ ↑Masking↓ in the mantling tones
Of his rich voice
⟨& present wit⟩ ↑Speeding troops of social joys↓
↑And in the volleys of his mirth↓

(5)   The resources of a mind
logic passion generous zeal
such as bard & martyr feel
Strength for the hour
⟨For the present, present power⟩

(10)   For the day sufficient power
But if another temper come
A time more exigent
⟨C⟩Higher competitors
A race of Emperors

(15)   he will know
to put this /gay/frolic/ masque behind him
As an old cloak
And in sky born mail to bind him
And single handed cope with Time

(20)   ⟨For⟩ ↑And parry & deal↓ the thunderstroke

[1732]   Homer
Dante                Bach
Shakspeare     Beethoven
Milton             Handel
⟨Burns⟩          Haydn
Goethe            Mozart

[174]             *Wyman*
Science & sense
Without pretence
He did what he essayed
His level gun will hit ⟨the⟩ ⟨its mark⟩ ↑white↓

(5)   ↑His cautious tongue will speak the right↓
↑Of that be none afraid↓

1731 "James Russell Lowell," 58–61, x, 63–65, 66?, 66, 69, 71, 73–80. In pencil, struck through in pencil.

1732 The right-hand column is in pencil. For Homer, Dante, Shakespeare, and Goethe, see "Solution," 16, 28, 40, and 65.

174 "The Adirondacs," six unused lines. In pencil.

[175]       Eve

[176]       *Woodman*

Man of affairs

Harmonizing oddest pairs

↑With a passion to unite↓

Who can marry oil & water ↑if he might↓

(5)       ⟨Mind & matter⟩

↑Loves each ⟨alone⟩ ↑in turn↓ but looks beyond↓

↑Every merit has his vote↓

↑In spite of class or nation↓

Gentle mind outrageous matter

(10)      Filled with Shakspeare down to Choate

His catholic admiration

⟨Worships⟩

⟨Admiring⟩ ↑Adoring↓ Jesus can excuse Iscariot

We that know him

(15)      Much we owe him

Skilled to work

In the age of Bronze

[177]      Loves to turn it to account

Of ⟨the⟩ helpless callow brood

From the Muses mount

Skill to reconcile

(5)       Scientific feud

↑Alien elements↓

With ⟨a heart to⟩ open heart & hand

⟨Court⟩ ↑Comes to succor↓ the neglected

Till it blush to be respected

(10)             Fond of merit runs the scale

of genial approbation

Filled

↑Skilled was he to reconcile↓

↑Scientific feud↓

(15)      To pacify the injured heart

And mollify the rude

⟨Comes to succor the neglected⟩

And whilst genius he respected

Hastes to succor the neglected

(20)      ↑and was founder of the Club↓

↑Most modest in the famous Hub↓

175  In pencil.
176  "The Adirondacs," seventeen unused lines. In pencil.
177  "The Adirondacs," twenty-five unused lines. In pencil; lines (22–25) are written vertically in the left margin.

↑Man of anecdote & character↓
↑Too witty to annoy↓
↑And every feast imperfect were↓
(25)    ↑Without his arts of joy↓

[178]                     *Howe*
↑Not in vain did Fate dispense↓
↑Generous heart & solid sense↓
⟨Strong sense⟩Skilful to build ↑Force to be↓ leader sage
Staff on which the orphan leans
(5)    ⟨Wise Conductor Leader⟩
↑Force to make a leader sage↓
⟨Stuff by which⟩ ↑On such stuff as he↓ society
Stands from age to age
⟨Hono⟩ ⟨self honored &⟩
(10)        In honor & self honoring
Where thou art, society
Still will live & best will be
Who does easily & well
What costs the rest expense of brain
(15)    Ancestral merits richly dwell
↑And the lost remain↓
And in th⟨is⟩y life the honored sire
Will fill ⟨his unfilled cup⟩ ↑the stinted chalice higher↓
[179]    ⟨And fill the gap⟩
↑And fate repair↓
↑The world's mishap↓
⟨In that hasty loss⟩
(5)    ↑And fill the gap↓
By the completed virtues of the heir.

Skilled to marry ends to means

---

As on the wide air sleeps the haze
So on thy broad mystic van
(10)    Sail the opal-colored days
And waft the miracle to man.

[180]    Stillman
            gallant artist, head & hand

178 "The Adirondacs," eighteen unused lines. In pencil.
179 "The Adirondacs," seven unused lines (1–7); "May–Day," 603–6 (8–11). In pencil.
180 "The Adirondacs," twenty-nine unused lines. In pencil; "peace & amity" in line (9) and the cancellation in line (10) are in ink. "Admiral of all the lakes / Of the new plantation" is added to the right of a bracket after "Easily chief" in line (11), then overwritten by lines (13–17). Line (20) is inserted above the end of line (19) and partly circumscribed. Line (21) is inscribed at the bottom of the page, circled, and connected by a line to line (20). Lines (22–23) are inscribed at the bottom of p. [181], partly circumscribed and connected to line (21).

Adopted of Tahawus grand
↑In the wild domesticated↓
↑man & mountain rightly mated↓
(5) ↑Like forest child the forest ranged↓
↑As one↓ Who had exchanged
After old Indian ⟨rites⟩ ↑mode↓
⟨His name⟩ ↑Totem↓ & ⟨arms⟩ ↑bow & spear↓
In sign of ⟨friendship⟩peace & ⟨amity⟩ ↑brotherhood↓
(10) With his Indian ⟨friend⟩ ↑peer↓
Easily chief  ⟨↑Admiral of all the lakes↓⟩
⟨↑Of the new plantation↓⟩
↑Can hunt & fish & rule & row↓
↑And outshoot each in his own bow↓
(15) ↑& paint & plant & execute↓
⟨↑Till he saw each blossom fruit↓⟩
↑Till ⟨he⟩ each blossom became fruit↓
Who ⟨had⟩ ↑held↓
The key of ⟨the situation⟩ ↑each occasion↓
(20) ↑Earning richly for his share↓
↑The Governor's chair↓
↑Bore the day's duties in his head↓
↑And with living method sped↓
↑⟨Earning well the⟩ Admiral of the designed plantation↓
(25) ⟨Carried⟩ ↑Bore↓ the days duties in his head
With living method sped
↑Firm↓ Unperplexed
Inspiring trust
↑unvexed↓
[181] ⟨And only ruling⟩
And only ⟨ordering⟩ ↑dictating↓ because he must

And all he carried in his heart
He could ⟨express⟩ ↑⟨utter⟩ ↑publish↓ & define↓
(5) Orderly line by line
On canvass by his art

I could wish
So wor[t]hy a master worthier pupils had;
The best were bad

(10) Earning ⟨well⟩ richly for his share
The Governor's chair
In ⟨the⟩ our designed plantation

[182] ↑In the wild↓ domesticated
Man & mountain rightly mated

181 "The Adirondacs," twelve unused lines. In pencil.
182 "The Adirondacs," eight unused lines. In pencil.

Can ⟨row &⟩ shoot & fish & rule & row
And outshoot each in his own bow
(5)        And ⟨e⟩paint & plan & execute
An

Firm unperplexed
By no flaws of temper vexed

[183]       Can teach the lightning speech
He has gone loafing it too long
⟨He must to school & learn his verb & noun⟩
↑In all the idle past↓
(5)        Scattering his fire broadcast
through the sky
He must to school & learn his verb & noun
↑Lay the track & build the town↓
And teach his nimbleness to work for man
(10)      Spelling with guided tongue mans messages
Shot thro the weltering pit of the salt sea

[184] A ⟨clinging⟩ ↑dread↓ charm clings to the name of Fate, as of a beautiful snake which we fear & admire, and all our Science has not availed to ⟨remove it dissipate⟩ disenchant us. ⟨We shall try to name⟩ ↑When we watch↓ the colors of the talisman & ⟨be just to⟩ ↑we must find↓ the secret virtues which they betray

[185] A man cannot escape his fate; he runs to it by the efforts he makes to escape it.

A man carries good omen into one house. he does not less carry, in spite of himself, a /withering/baleful/ look & influence into other company.

Fate is the name for half of Nature,—for nature resisted. When Nature is intelligently conspired with, all is righted.
↑transferred to *EO* p. 62.↓

[186] Everybody carries a charmed life

Men believe in right of might but also in the might of right

the artist who painted his wife before he ever saw her.

---

183 "Boston," 108 (1); "The Adirondacs," 266?, 266?, 267, x, x, x, 267, x, 268–70 (1–11). In pencil, struck through twice in pencil and partially erased.

184 In pencil. The entry also occurs in notebook EO p. [61].

185 "A man cannot . . . escape it." is in pencil overwritten in ink; "A man carries . . . company." is in pencil. "Fate is the name . . . conspired with" is in pencil overwritten in ink, while "all is righted." is only in ink; the comma after "Nature" is in pencil. The phrase "transferred to *EO* p. 62." is in pencil, set off from what precedes it by a curved line. The page is struck through in pencil.

186 "Everybody . . . of right" is in pencil; "the artist . . . saw her." is struck through in pencil.

And Montaigne & Etienne, when they first met, ran into each other's arms as if long acquainted.

R[owse]. said, God made him because ⟨it was necessary⟩ he could not help it & therefore he did not care for God, but for the necessity, or that [187] which is. ⟨R⟩I replied, 'you say God made you; *no*, it was that necessity, which is the true God, & you must care for that, & do it homage, because you are of it, & it is immense & indispensable. You put the name of God on the wrong party.

Lidian told Rowse, she thought, if he would paint in oils, it must take a long time to learn to use the colors. He replied, "If I have any thing to learn, I shall not try them."

[188]    ⟨The use which pra⟩
       The gleam which Practice paints on steel
       The lustre which Use paints on steel

His was a good horse, nothing suits him so well as to go fast; & the faster he goes, the better he is pleased; nay, he can never go fast enough to suit him

[189]    Wise and polite. And if I drew
       Their several portraits, you would own
       Chaucer had no such worthy crew,
       Nor Boccace in Decameron.

[190]             *J. Holmes*
       With these there came a humorist
       Kind-hearted, gentle, gay,
       Caressing his infirmities
       As cossets for his play
(5)      As gentle as a maid
       Yet with a bold address
       Which still surprised to lead
       Such masked tenderness
       And he ⟨contrived⟩ ↑had ⟨grace⟩ skill↓ to give
(10)    To his walking stick or chair
       Or to his least affair,
       A price superlative
       He was born to lend a grace
       To a rude & savage place
[191]    Such his proper merits shone

187 "Lidian told . . . try them.' " is in pencil overwritten in ink. Samuel Worcester Rowse (1822–1901) made a crayon sketch of Emerson in June 1858; see L 5:114.
  188 "There are beggars," 24, 24, 24 (1–3). In pencil.
  189 "The Adirondacs," motto. In pencil, struck through in pencil.
  190 "The Adirondacs," fourteen unused lines. In pencil.
  191 "The Adirondacs," nine unused lines. In pencil.

That it needed not be known
He was twin in mind & blood
To the man of merriest mood
(5)      And of keenest point & edge
And of the Muses privilege
↑Skilled to show the fair & fit↓
Who fills all Saxon minds
With his redundant fancy & his wit

[192] [blank]
[193]                ↑*Lowell*↓
Prophet & Bard
Highborn Hoel
Wellborn Lowell
What said the Sibyl
(5)      What was the fortune
She sung for him?—
'*Strength for the hour.*'

Man of marrow, man of mark
Virtue lodged in sinew stark
(10)    Rich supplies & never stinted
More behind at need is hinted
Never cumbered with the morrow,
Never ⟨yet⟩ knew corro⟨sive⟩ding sorrow,
Well contented with today
(15)    ⟨Quite t⟩Too ↑well-↓gifted to have found
Yet his opulence's bound
[194]   Most at home in mounting fun
Broadest joke & luckiest pun
Masking in the mantling tones
⟨Of ↑his↓ rich laugh⟨ter⟩-loving voice⟩
(5)      Of his rich laugh-loving voice
In speeding troops of social joys
And in volleys of ⟨his⟩ ↑wild↓ mirth
Purer metal, rarest worth
Logic, passion, generous zeal
(10)    Such as bard & martyr feel.

Strength for the hour;
For the day, sufficient power;
⟨Nor will⟩ ↑Well advised↓
And quite too easily great
(15)    His large fate to antedate

193 "James Russell Lowell," 40, 42–53, x, 54–55. In pencil.
194 "James Russell Lowell," 56–59, 59–67, 67–68. In pencil.

[195]    But if another temper come
〈And〉 ↑If↓ on the sun shall creep a gloom
A time & tide more exigent
More proud, more strong competitors,
(5)    Challenge a race for emperors
Then the pleasant bard will know
To put this frolic masque behind him
〈As〉 ↑Like↓ an old summer cloak
And in skyborn mail to bind him
(10)    And single-handed cope with Time
And parry & deal the thunderstroke

[196]    The Rock of Ages melts alway
Into the mineral air
The unspent quarry whence to build
Thought & its mansion fair

(5)    〈Ever the〉 ↑Doth not the↓ rock of ages melt〈s〉
Into the mineral air,
To be the quarry whence 〈ascends〉 ↑is built↓
Thought & its mansion fair.

[197]    If I should put the woods in song,
And tell what's here enjoyed,
All men would to these gardens throng,
And leave the cities void.

(5)    The bees were in their sugar house
The spider spun his silk
The wasp made paper all the day
〈Asclepias shed its milk〉
The cow-weed shed its milk

[198]    How drearily in College hall
The Doctor stretched the hours!
But in each pause 〈I〉 ↑we↓ hear↑d↓ the call
Of robins out of doors.

———

(5)    It is not 〈clemency〉 ↑favor↓ we ask or give
〈But honest /dealing/trade/ whereby all men live〉
↑By honest trade shall all men live.↓

**195** "James Russell Lowell," 69–71, 73–80. In pencil.
**196** "Ever the Rock of Ages melts," 1–4, 1–4. Lines (1–4) are in pencil.
**197** "My Garden," 1–4 (1–4); "In my garden three ways meet," five unused lines (5–9). In pencil.
   **198** "How drearily in College hall," 1–4 (1–4); "Boston," x, 11/51?, 11/51? (5–7); "Try the might the Muse affords," 3–4 (8–9). In pencil.

Bring Beauty to the desolate
Hang roses on the stony Fate

[199]    And hither came the puritan
⟨The⟩ With speech & manners plain
To do

———

A gleam of sunshine on the wall
(5)    To him imparted more than all
The revels of the carnival

———

If curses be the wage of love
Hide in thy skies thou fruitless Jove
↑Not be be named↓
(10)    It is clear
Why the gods will not appear
They are ashamed

———

[200]    The land that has no song
Shall have a song today
The hills the rocks are dumb too long
The vales have much to say

(5)    /Hearts/Meek/ of flesh & not of stone,
Not too good to love their own,
Quitting English homes & cheer
To fast in rock & forest here

Out from the many fountained earth
(10)    The rivers gushed & foamed
Sweet airs from every pore exhaled
Around the mountains roamed

[201]    The land that has no song
Shall have a song today
The granite bed is dumb too long
⟨The stone is rolled away⟩
(5)    ↑And Earth a word to say↓
For you can teach the lightning speech
And round the earth your voice↑es↓ reach

The rocky nook wi[t]h hilltops three
Looked eastward from the farms,
(10)    And twice a day the flowing sea

199 "Boston," three unused lines (1–3); "May–Day," 435–37 (4–6); "If curses be the wage
of love" (7–12). In pencil; lines (4–6) are struck through in pencil.
    200 "Boston," twelve unused lines. Lines (1–4) and (9–12) are in pencil.
    201 "Boston," five unused lines, 108–9, 1–6. In pencil.

Took Boston in its arms
The youth of yore were stout & poor
And sailed for bread to every shore

[202]  The waves that rocked him on the deep
    ↑To him their secret told↓
  Bade him be uncontrolled
  The winds that sung the boy to sleep
(5)  Bade him be free & bold
  The honest waves refuse to slaves
  The Empire of the Ocean caves

    And where they went on trade intent
    They /carried all their thought/did what freemen can/
(10)    Their dauntless ways did all men praise
    The merchant was a man
  The world was made for honest trade
  To plant & eat be none afraid

[203]  Your town is full of gentle names
  By patriots once were watchwords made
  Those warcry names are muffled shames
  On /coward/recreant/ sons ⟨decayed⟩ mislaid
(5)  ⟨But who⟩ ↑⟨Sla⟩What slave↓ would dare, a name to ⟨wear⟩
    ↑bear↓
  ⟨Disowned by freedom everywhere⟩
  ⟨Is⟩ ↑Once↓ freedoms watchword everywhere

  Nor take your fathers names in vain

  O happy town beside the sea,
(10)  Whose roads lead everywhere to all;
  Than thine no deeper ⟨ditch⟩ ↑moat↓ can be,
  No steeper fence, no better wall.

  O bounteous seas that never fail,
  O happy day remembered yet,
(15)  O happy port that spied a sail,
  Which, furling, landed Lafayette.

[204]  Hie to the woods, sleek citizen,
  To the deep sea go, landsmen, down;
  ⟨Off to the⟩ ↑Climb the white↓ hills, ye aldermen,
  And empty leave the town;
(5)  Go purge your blood in lake & wood
  To honor born of hardihood

---

202  "Boston," 13–14, x, 15–18, 7–10, 11/51–12/52. In pencil; line (2) is in ink.
203  "Boston," eight unused lines, 57–60, 84–87. Lines (1–8) are in pencil.
204  "Boston," six unused lines (1–6); "Boston Hymn," 41?, x (7–8). In pencil.

⟨From⟩ their pine ⟨cap⟩ ↑shingle↓ statehouse held the sea &
    land,
The past they pondered, & the future planned

[205]    For what avail the plough & sail
Or land, or life, if freedom fail?

        The very same the men of fame
        did file their mind ⟨& sell⟩
(5)       And sell the blood of human kind

For power & place they sell their race
And /locked their hands with smiling knaves/kissed the
    hands of statesmen base/

        ————

        Ere these echoes be choked by snows
        And these echoes were choked with snows

[206]    Nature is good
Not rude
But of mutable mood
⟨Nor stiffly the same⟩ ↑No ⟨selfsame⟩ ↑dreary↓ monotone↓
    now & again
(5)    ⟨But⟩ she is all things to all men
She pours her power into the people
She who is not old or feeble
And makes & moulds them such as they are
And what they call their city ways
(10)   Are not their ⟨ways⟩ ↑own↓ no but hers
And what they invented yesterday
They learned of the oaks & firs
Though they know it not
And men learn manners of oaks & firs
(15)   God wot
[207]    For she ⟨makes them⟩ ↑sheds men↓ as mallows fresh
And ⟨they⟩ ↑their nations↓ are flesh of her flesh
She feeds them
She drugs her water & her wheat
(5)    And feeds them thence to eat
And having thus their breed & growth
They do her bidding nothing loth
And their culture comes from Nile

205 "Boston," 29/78–30/79, five unused lines, 102, 102. In pencil; in line (7), "kissed . . .
base" is in ink. Lines (1–2) and (8–9) are struck through in ink.
   206 "Nature II," 1?, x, 2–4, 6, 5, 8–10, 11?, 12, x, 12?, x. In pencil; in line (4), "selfsame" is
canceled, and "dreary" added, in ink. Struck through in pencil.
   207 "Nature II," 13–14, x, 15, 17?, 18–19, x, x, 20–23. In pencil, struck through in pencil;
lines (8–9) are struck through twice more in pencil.

And from the crocodile
(10)      What/s most their own/they call theirs/ is not their own
But is borrowed from earth & stone

And in their vaunted Art
The masterstroke is still her part

[208₁] Burns an exceptional fame, ⟨a b⟩ has the charm of a childs prattle which the mother & children think divine. Only everybody in the street is of his family, & he the wild darling of them all. Gods bairns are ‖ . . ‖ to ‖ . ‖.
Burns alone made a language classic. He
His sapphic ‖ . . . . ‖
his motherwit
his commonsense
his love of nature which was the love of bleak leagues of land &

[208₂]                    Nature.
⟨Nature⟩ ↑She↓ is gamesome & good
But of mutable mood,
No ⟨grinding monotone⟩ ↑dreary repeater↓ now & again,
⟨She is⟩ ↑Like Paul will be↓ all things to all men.
(5)      She who is old, but nowise feeble,
Pours her power into the people,
Merry & manifold without bar,
⟨And⟩ makes & moulds them ⟨⟨such⟩ ↑all↓ as⟩ ↑what↓ they are,
And what they call their city way,
(10)    Is not their ⟨⟨way⟩own at all,⟩ ↑way↓ but hers,
And what, they say, they made today,
They learned of the oaks & firs.

[209₁] of snow choked brooks
of birds & hares & ⟨mice⟩fieldmice & thistle & heather which he knew daily
He   Every man in the street thinks of the Poets God help them and of Robert Burns

His satire & grand plain sense connect him with Cervantes and Aesop & Rabelais & Shakspeare & Carlyle & Butler

———————

Poet of the middle class of grey hodden of linsey woolsey of the blouse

208₁ Cf. "Robert Burns, Speech Delivered at the Celebration of the Burns Centenary, Boston, January 25, 1859," W 11:439–43. In pencil, struck through in pencil.
208₂ "Nature II," 1–12. The cancellation and addition in line (4) are in pencil; "such" in line (8) and "at all," in line (10) are canceled in both pencil and ink. Struck through in ink.
209₁ Cf. "Robert Burns," W 11:439–43. In pencil.

[2092]　⟨For⟩ she ⟨sheds⟩ ↑spawneth↓ men as mallows fresh
　　　　⟨And their⟩ ↑Heroes &↓ nations are flesh of her flesh

　　　　She drugs her water & her wheat
　　　　↑With what flavors she finds meet↓
(5)　　And ⟨feeds⟩ gives them ↑what↓ to drink & ⟨to⟩ eat,
　　　　And having thus their breed & growth,
　　　　They do her bidding nothing loath.

　　　　Whats most theirs is not their own,
　　　　But ⟨is⟩ borrowed in atoms from iron & stone,

(10)　　And in their vaunted works of Art
　　　　The masterstroke is still her part,

[210] this day is an uprising of the Saxon people to do him honor

　　　　Her name is Fate her vision rolls
　　　　In the Future most at home
　　　　And ↑sternly↓ calls ⟨into existence⟩ ↑to being↓ souls
　　　　That curse her when they come

(5)　　⟨Her⟩ ↑Fate's↓ planted eye ⟨the⟩ ↑To↓Day controls,
　　　　In the Morrow most at home,
　　　　And sternly calls to Being souls
　　　　That curse her when they come

[211₁]　　Fate

　　　　Her name is Fate who /all/today/ controls
　　　　in the /future/Morrow/ sits at home
　　　　And sternly calls to being souls
　　　　That curse her when they come

(5)　　⟨The past she made t⟩
　　　　Fate made the past, today controls
　　　　In the Morrow sits at home
　　　　And sternly calls to being, souls
　　　　That curse her when they come

[211₂]　What are his machines
　　　　Of steel, brass, ⟨leather⟩ ↑bullhide↓, oak, & ivory,
　　　　But complements of his perfected limbs,

2092 "Nature II," 13–23. The cancellations and additions in lines (1–2) are in pencil. Struck through in ink.
210 Following the conclusion of the notes for "Robert Burns" (W 11:439–43) is "Fate" ("Her planted eye"), x, 2–4, 1–4. In pencil, the verse struck through in pencil; lines (1–4) and (5–8) are struck through again separately in pencil.
211₁ "Fate" ("Her planted eye"), 1–4, x, 1–4. In pencil, struck through in pencil. In line (1), "all" is circled in pencil.
211₂ "New England Capitalist," 1–2, x, 4–13, 14/15, 17–20.

Dwarfs of one fixed idea applied to him,
(5)     As ↑nimbly↓ he applies his binding self
Unto the ⟨changing⟩ ↑rounding↓ world, thus making that
A larger tool to his victorious will?
He built his mills, &, by his politics, made
The arms of millions turn them.
(10)   New Hampshire, mother of men,
Sea-dented Maine, reluctant Carolina,
Must drag his car, &, by the arts of peace,
⟨And⟩ ↑He↓ in the plenitude of love & honor,
Eats up the poor. Much has he done already

(15)   Propeller, car, postoffice, photo/graph/type/,
His coast-survey, vote-by-majority,
His life-assurance, & star-registry,
Preludes & hints of what he yet prepares

[212] At the sudden naming from I know not whom that the 25 ↑Jan↓ was the centennial anniversary a sudden consent animated the great English race ⟨ev⟩ in all its colonies & ⟨gov⟩ states all over the world to keep the day. We are here to hold our parliament of love & poesy as men were wont to do in the Middle Ages   And we with the best reason. I can only ⟨express⟩ explain this ⟨consent⟩ singular unanimity in a race which [213] rarely acts together but otherwise each for himself, by the fact that Robert Burns the poet of the Middle Class represents in the mind of this race today that great uprising of the Middle Class against the armed & titled minorities which worked politically in the American & French Revolutions & which not in govts so much as in social order has changed the face of the world

[214] His birth breeding & fortunes were for this great destiny low
His sentiment was ⟨the last self trust⟩ absolute independence   a life of labor
His doctrine was Commonsense joyful aggressive irresistible

[215] Not Luther struck more telling blows against ⟨Superstition⟩ ↑False Religion↓ than did this brave singer
He too had his flights to Eisleben his escapes from Church & excommunication
His satire has lost none of its edge his musical arrows yet sing through the world
His grand plain sense is strangely identical with that of Rabelais Shakspeare ↑in Comedy↓ Cervantes Butler Burns   & ⟨I find the like⟩ if I should add another name I should find it only in a ⟨coun⟩ living countryman of Burns

212–17 In pencil; cf. "Robert Burns," W 11:439–42. On p. [212], "ev" is not canceled.

[216] Yes but in him it was Poetry. He has endeared the farm & the farmhouse & the cottage   all the details of their life   the patch & the poverty   the homely food   the fear of debt   the hardship   the dear society there of brothers & sisters proud of each other   knowing so few & finding amends for poverty in books & thought

He is the poet of ⟨th⟩poor men of grey hodden   of ⟨satinette⟩ & guernsey coat   linsey wolsey & blouse

[217] What a love of nature! and, shall I say it? of middle class nature, not of Ocean & starry firmament & tropical scenery
but of the homely nature which the poor see around them   of bleak leagues of pasture ⟨l⟩ & stubble   of ice & sleet & snow choked brooks   of birds & hares & field mice & thistles & heather which he daily knew

[218]      ↑A howling wolf that by Potomac ran↓
       ⟨This wolf will⟩ ↑Would↓ sharper bite than shark or tiger can,
       And every drop of his blood he stole from a different man.

————

The land was all electric
(5)        There was no need of trumpets
           ↑As they float by coast & crag↓
       There was no need of banners
       Every zephyr was a bugle
       Every maple was a flag
(10)       Each steeple was a rallying sign
       The tocsin was its bell
       Sharp steel was the lieutenant
       And powder was his men.

       The mountain echoes ⟨spoke⟩ ↑roar,↓
(15)       Every crutch became a pike,
       The woods & meadows murmured war,
       And the valleys shouted, Strike!

[219] He is an exceptional man   The people who care nothing for literature & poetry care for Burns   It was indifferent, they thot who saw him, whether he wrote verses or not   he mt have done any thing else as well

218 "A howling wolf that by Potomac ran" (1–3); "The land was all electric" (4–17). In line (2), the cancellation is in both ink and pencil, and the addition in pencil; line (6) is in pencil. In line (14), the cancellation and addition are in pencil traced over in ink.
219 "Robert Burns," W 11:441. In pencil.

[220]     Terminus
          —————

          For thought & not praise;
          Thought is the wages
          For which I sell days,
          Will gladly sell ages,
(5)       And willing grow old,
          Deaf, & dumb, & blind, & cold,
          Melting matter into dreams,
          Panoramas which I saw
          And whatever glows or seems
(10)      Into substance into Law

     [221] And yet how true a poet is he   he has given voice to all the
experiences of common life   to the   show me the
 He has written the liturgy for the farmer & the citizen ↑how many
Bonny Doons↓ the John Anderson my Joe John the Auld Lang Syne
the ⟨songs of⟩ love songs of Burns still woo & melt thousands of maids
to their farmer of today
the farm work the country holiday every fishing coble

[222] [blank]
[223]     As if a fleet should sail
          Sportive before the morning gale
          And armies force their march ⟨to chase⟩ ↑in chase↓
          The gliding ⟨vision⟩ ↑convoy↓ to ⟨oppose⟩ ↑destroy↓
(5)       When it shall ⟨please⟩ ↑deign↓ to touch the coast
          And disembark its pent up ho⟨a⟩st
          ⟨As if⟩ ↑Or a↓ pursuing child should strain
          After the summer bow along the plain

[224] The ⟨health⟩ Memory of Burns
I am afraid it is not left us to say much of it   The west winds are
murmuring it. Open the windows & hearken for the incoming tide &
see what the waves say of it   The doves perching allways on the
e⟨v⟩aves of the stone church opposite may know something about
it   Every name in Middle Scotland keeps his name bright
Memory of Burns! Every boys & girls & mans memory carries
snatches of his songs and can say them by heart, &, what is strangest
of all, though he [225] never learned them. ⟨the bells ring them⟩ the
wind whispers them ⟨the river⟩ birds whistle them, the corn & barley
& bulrushes   the handorgans in ⟨the⟩ all cities   the music boxes at
Geneva   the chime of bells

220 "Terminus" ("For thought").
221 "Robert Burns," W 11:441–42. In pencil.
223 "As if a fleet should sail." In pencil.
224–25, 227–28 In pencil; used in "Robert Burns," W 11:442–43.

They are the property & the solace of mankind

And as we are only men

[226] [blank]
[227] And as he was thus poet of the poor anxious cheerful working humanity   so he had the language of ⟨a⟩ low life. He grew up in a rural Scottish district speaking a homely patois unintelligible to all but natives, and he has made that lowland Scotch a Doric dialect of fame,   ⟨He⟩It is the only example in history of a language made classic by the genius of a single man. But more than this [228] he had that great secret of ⟨literature⟩ ↑genius↓, to draw from the bottom of society the strength of its speech & ⟨by the beauty of his genius⟩ astonish the ears of the polite with these artless words better than art, & ⟨ma⟩ filtered of all offence thro his beauty   He knew where to g  H  It seemed odious to Luther that the Devil should ⟨all⟩ have all the best tunes, he would bring them into the churches; and Burns knew how to [229] to take from fairs & gypsies & blacksmith & drover the speech of the market & street & clothe it with melody.

> Fate.
> Her planted eye Today controls,
> Is in the Morrow most at home,
> And sternly calls to Being souls
> That curse her when they come.

[230] [blank]
[231] ↑1859.   22 Feby↓
> As I left my door,
> The Muse came by,
> Said, whither away?
> I well-pleased to praise myself,
(5) And in this presence raise myself,
> Replied,—To keep thy bard's birthday.
> ↑—↓"O happy morn! O happy eve!"
> Rejoined the Muse, "⟨&⟩And dost thou weave
> For noble night a noble rhyme,
(10) And up to Song through friendship climb?
> For every guest,
> Ere he can rest,
> Plucks for my son or flower or fruit,
> In sign of Nature's glad salute."

---

**229** "to take . . . gypsies", in pencil, and "& blacksmith . . . melody.", in ink, are used in "Robert Burns," W 11:442. Following the prose is "Fate" ("Her planted eye"), struck through three times in ink.
**231** "James Russell Lowell," 1–16.

(15)           Alas! thou knows't
          Dearest muse, I cannot boast
[232]        Of any grace from thee.
To thy spare bounty, Queen, thou ow'st—
No verse will flow from me.
Beside, the bard himself profuse
(5)    In thy accomplishment
Does Comedy & lyric use,
And to thy sisters all too dear,
Too gifted, than that he can chuse
⟨To⟩ ↑But↓ raise an eyebrow's hint severe
(10)  On the toiling good intention
Of ill-equipped inapprehension.

"The bard is loyal,"
Said the queen,
With haughtier mien,
(15) "And hear thou this, my mandate royal.
[233] Instant to the Sibyl's chair,
To the Delphic Maid repair:
He has reached the middle date,
Stars tonight that culminate
(5)   Shed beams fair & fortunate.
Go inquire his horoscope,
Half of memory, half of hope.

———

From Pâques to Noel,
Prophets & bards,
(10) Merlin, Llewellyn,
Highborn Hoel,
Well born Lowell,
What said the Sibyl,
What was the fortune
(15) She sung for him?
*Strength for the Hour.*

[234₁]      Said Wards my friend
And like the shuttle thro the loom
Or holy ghost shoots from the tomb
Or Apollo rushing from the womb
(5)   I passed clear

232 "James Russell Lowell," 17–31. The cancellation and addition in line (9) are in pencil.
233 "James Russell Lowell," 32–47.
234₁ "Said, 'Wards my friend.'" In pencil.

[2342]  Man of marrow, man of mark,
        Virtue lodged in sinew stark,
        Rich supplies, & never stinted,—
        More behind at need is hinted:
(5)     Never cumbered with the Morrow,
        Never knew corroding sorrow;
        Too well-gifted to have found
        Yet his opulence's bound;
        Most at home in mounting fun,
(10)    Broadest joke, & luckiest pun,
        Masking in the mantling tones
        Of a rich laugh-loving voice,
        In speeding troops of social joys,
        And in volleys of wild mirth,
(15)    Purer metal, rarest worth,
[235]   Logic, passion, cordial Zeal,
        Such as bard & martyr feel.

            Strength for the hour.
        For the day sufficient power,
(5)     Well-advised, too easily great
        His large fleece to antedate.
        But, if another temper come,
        If on the sun shall creep a gloom,
        A time & tide more exigent,
(10)    When the old mounds are torn & rent,
        More proud, more strong competitors
        Marshal the lists for emperors,—
        Then the pleasant bard will know
        To put this frolic masque behind him
(15)    Like an old /summer/familiar/ cloak,
[236]       And in sky-born mail to bind him,
        And single-handed cope with ⟨t⟩Time,
        And parry & deal the thunderstroke,

[237]   Two arts he had to live & grow
        In case of need to utter ⟨nay,⟩ ↑Nay,↓
        And to hold his tongue forever & aye;
        And those his nayword might distress
(5)     So well he spoke neer loved him less

2342 "James Russell Lowell," 48–62.
235 "James Russell Lowell," 63–77. In line (15), "familiar" is in pencil.
236 "James Russell Lowell," 78–80.
237 "Two arts he had" (1–5); two unidentified lines (6–7); "Said, 'Wards my friend' " (8–12); "May–Day," 273, 274/275 (13–14). In pencil; lines (2–3) are overwritten, and lines (6–7) added, in ink; in line (2), the pencil inscription reads "If need were to utter nay".

↑When the stern old Calvinist↓
↑Doubled religion in his fist↓

    Said, 'Wards my friend,'
And like the shuttle ⟨from⟩ ↑thro'↓ the loom

(10)    Or saint soul rising from the tomb
Or Phebus ⟨sh⟩ rushing from the womb
    I passed clear

One shining day
Offsets the ruin of Ten years of war

[238]    Securely by that anchoring cord
       the /mystic/finest/anchoring/ cord

⟨The⟩ ↑How↓ body to the soul is moored
If once again that mystic string

(5)    As erst it wont would ⟨tap⟩ ↑thrill↓ & ring

I never knew but one immortal girl.

[239]    A patch of meadow & upland
⟨A mile along the road⟩
Reached by a mile of road
↑Soothe↑d↓ by the voice of waters↓

(5)    With birds & flowers ⟨&⟩ bestowed

This is my ⟨historybook⟩book of Chronicles
My Bible ⟨lawbook⟩ ↑code &↓ lexicon
My genesis & ⟨daybook⟩ ↑calendar↓
I read it as I run

(10)    It is my consolation
In ⟨less or graver⟩ ↑mild or poignant↓ grief
My park & my gymnasium
My out of door relief

[240]    Hither I come for the strength
Which well it can supply
I draw it from the ⟨power⟩ ↑strength↓ of earth
And ⟨from powers of the⟩ ↑potencies of↓ sky

(5)    The tremulous battery earth
Replies to ⟨electric⟩ ↑touch of↓ man

238 "May–Day," x, x, 579–81 (1–5); "The Harp," 104–6 (3–5); "I never knew but one immortal girl" (6). Lines (1–5) are in pencil. Lines (2–5) are struck through in pencil; the three variants in line (2) are also struck through diagonally in pencil, perhaps to cancel them.
239 "A patch of meadow & upland," 1–2, 2–12. In pencil.
240 "A patch of meadow & upland," 13–20, x, 21–24. In pencil.

It thrills to the antipodes
I draw it from Japan

(10) ⟨I come in joy & well it knows⟩
↑The planets child the planet knows↓
⟨The jubilant earth⟩ ↑And to his joy↓ replies
⟨The⟩ ↑To↓ thrushes trill ⟨the⟩ unfolds the rose
⟨↑Nor↓⟩ Clouds ⟨hang out⟩ ↑flush↓ their gayest dyes.

[241] When Ali prayed & loved
⟨The dervish told⟩ ↑Where Syrian waters roll↓
↑Upward↓ The ninth heaven ⟨m⟩thrilled & moved
At the tread of the jubilant soul

[242]       A patch of meadow & upland
Reached by a mile of road,
Soothed by the voice of waters,
With birds & flowers bestowed;

(5) This is my book of Chronicles,
⟨My bible,⟩ code, ↑psalter,↓ ⟨&⟩ lexicon,
My Genesis & calendar,
I read it as I run.

It is my consolation
(10) In mild or poignant grief;
My park & my gymnasium,
My out-of-door relief.

[243] ⟨Hither⟩ I come ↑to it↓ for ⟨the⟩ strength
Which it can well supply,
⟨I draw it from the⟩ ↑For Love draws might from terrene↓
force↑,↓ ⟨of earth,⟩
And potences of sky.

(5) The tremulous /battery,/pulsing/ earth,
⟨Replies⟩ ↑Responds↓ to touch of man;
It thrills to the antipodes,
From Boston to Japan.

The planets' child the planet⟨s⟩ know↑s↓,
(10) And to his joy replies;
To the lark's trill unfolds the rose,
Clouds flush their gayest dies

[244] When Ali prayed & loved

241 "A patch of meadow & upland," 25–28. In pencil.
242 "A patch of meadow & upland," 1–12. Lines (5–12) are struck through twice in pencil.
243 "A patch of meadow & upland," 13–24.
244 "A patch of meadow & upland," 25–28. Struck through twice in ink.

Where Syrian waters roll,
Upward the ninth heaven thrilled ↑& moved↓
At the tread of the jubilant soul.

[245] ↑Old Age↓
    The brook sings on the selfsame strain
    But finds no echo in my brain

[246] See [notebook] MME ↑II↓ p [151–]152
*To the Clock*
    Hail requiem of departed time
    Never was ⟨incumbents⟩ ↑richman's↓ funeral
    Followed ⟨by the ⟨eager⟩ heir↑'s eager feet↓⟩ ↑behind
        the pall↓
    ↑By the heir's eager feet,↓

(5)    With resignation more complete
    Yet not his hope is mine

    Thou diggst the grave of each day
    Not mine, Dig it thou shalt;
    I defy thee to forbear it

[247]    O Time thou loiterer
    Thou whose might
    Laid low ⟨the Titan↑s↓⟩ ↑Enceladus & crushed the moth↓
    Rest on thy hoary throne ⟨heedless⟩ forgetting

(5)    ↑Alike↓ Thy agitations & thy graves

    Ara[c]hnean webs decoying & destroying
    Webs whereat ↑the↓ Gorgons ply
    But lo! thy web's motheaten
    The shuttles ⟨s⟩quiver as the loom's beams are shaken

[248]    Nature says
    I am not infinite
    But imprisoned & bound
    Tool of mind

(5)    ⟨Even⟩ ↑Tool↓ of the being I feed & adorn
    Twas I ⟨that soot⟩ did sooth
    Thy thorny youth
    I found thee placed
    In my most leafless waste

(10)    I comforted thy little feet
    On the forlorn errand bound

245 "Old Age."
246 "To the Clock," 1–9. In pencil.
247 "To the Clock," 10–18. In pencil.
248 "Nature saith." In pencil.

I fed thee with my mallows fed
On the first day of failing bread

[249] ↑MME II p 170↓
 The clouds are rich & dark, the air serene;
So like the soul of me, 'twere me
Is sadness on me at the retrospect
Or at the foresight of obscurer years
(5) Like yonder sailing cloud
Whereon the purple iris dwells in beauty
Superior to all its gaudy skirts.

[250]  The idle centuries draw from air
↑The ⟨awful⟩ grand Pacific groves↓
The Californian giant woods
These /in turn in ages doff/the leaves of ages spare/
(5) Their ⟨annual leaves to clothe the rock⟩
↑To clothe the ⟨vast rock⟩ ↑granite↓ bleak & bare↓
What smiths & in what furnace ⟨forged⟩ ↑rolled↓
(In dizzy ⟨distances of time⟩ ↑aeons dim & mute↓
⟨Make the⟩ ↑The reeling↓ brain /reel to ⟨think of⟩/cannot
  compute/)
(10) The iron copper & the gold
And oldest stars can ill recall
What races throve & /ended/died/ to ⟨make⟩ ↑pave↓
↑The planet with↓ the floor of lime
What /plants/flowers & ferns & palms/ were pressed
(15) In the herbal of the coal
[251] And ⟨all⟩ th⟨is⟩e stupefying flight
Of ages is as the fleeting of a night
In which the mallows ripen

She sheds her years as flakes of snow
(5) ↑as freely↓ She sheds a myriad years
As ⟨the⟩ freely as the flakes
That fill the air on a winter day
For the ⟨mighty⟩ ↑patient↓ Pan
Hath no stint of time or room
(10) But sweep & margin for his plan
Before all dates beyond all doom
Older than worlds outlives all doom

But when her heaps are piled
Tis vain until

249 "The Adirondacs," 213–14, 216–20. In pencil.
250 "Wealth," 13, x, x, 15–16, 16, 18–24, 26, 28. In pencil. In line (9), "brain" is also partly canceled.
251 "Wealth," twelve unused lines, 29–31, x. In pencil.

(15)    The   Arrives the will
        To ↑choose & to↓ combine

[252]        Alas the while
    That yesterday should never smile
    That grinning masks in memory
    ↑Fair homes↓ Deform & mortify

(5)    To think & think down stars & suns

    East & west are both alluring
    ↑Law & Thought for Aye enduring↓

        Winter
    May come in snow or curdling cold

[253]    Thus passing to the /earth/sod/ ↑from whence we came↓
    Where fairer laws dissolve than those that knit this frame

---

    And out of chaos & slime
    To draw the in measure & design
(5)    The threads of good & fit & fair
    And lo thro them thrills
    The electric thrills of law
    That bind the ores of nature wild
    With the /religion/conscience/ of the child

[254]    The Yesterday does never smile,
    Today goes drudging thro' the while,
    Yet, in the name of Godhead, I
    The Morrow front, & can defy;
(5)    Though I am weak, yet God, when prayed,
    Cannot withhold his conquering aid.

    Ah me! it was my childhood's tho('t,)ught,
    If he should make my web a blot
    On life's fair picture of delight,
(10)    My heart's content would find it right.
            ↑Copied in *ETE* 173↓

[255]
            ↑*Fate.*↓
    Already blushes in thy cheek
    The bosom thought which thou must speak;

252 "The Nun's Aspiration," 2?, 1, seven unused lines (1–9); "Wealth," 4? (5). In pencil.
253 "The Nun's Aspiration," x, x, (1–2); "Wealth," 32–33, 33, 46/47, 47–49 (1–9). In pencil.
254 "The Nun's Aspiration," 1–10. Struck through in pencil. "Copied in *ETE* 173" is in pencil.
255 "Nemesis." Lines (13–14) are in reverse order in the manuscript, marked for transposition by "2)" and "1)" in pencil in the left margin. Struck through in ink.

The bird, how far it haply roam,
By cloud or isle, is flying home;
(5) The maiden fears, & fearing runs
Into the charmed snare she shuns;
And every man, in love or pride,
Of his fate is never wide.
Will a woman's fan the ocean smoothe?
(10) Or prayer the stony Parcae sooth?
Or coax the thunder from its mark?
Or tapers light Hell's bowels dark?
In spite of Virtue & the Muse;
⟨Savage Fate⟩ ↑Nemesis↓ will have her dues,
(15) And all our struggles & our toils
Tighter wind the giant coils.

[256] Song of Nature

↑1↓

Mine are the night & morning,
The pits of air, the /⟨gulf of⟩/swallowing/ space,
The sportive sun, the gibbous moon,
The innumerable days.

↑2↓

(5) I hide in the /blinding/solar/ ⟨light⟩ ↑glory↓,
I ⟨am dumb⟩ ↑lurk↓ in the pealing song,
I rest on the pitch of the torrent,
In ⟨slumber, I am⟩ ↑death, newborn &↓ strong.

↑3↓

No numbers have counted my tallies,
(10) No tribes my house can fill,
I sit by the shining Fount of Life,
And pour the deluge still.

[257]                    ↑4↓ ⟨First of May.⟩
⟨↑1↓⟩ ↑And↓ By consummate powers
Gathering along the centuries
From race ⟨to⟩on race the rarest flowers
My wreath shall nothing miss.

⟨↑2.↓⟩                    ↑5↓
(5) And many a thousand summers
My apples ⟨u⟩ripened well,

256 "Song of Nature," 1–12. Struck through in ink.
257 "Song of Nature," 13–26. Struck through in ink; lines (2–4) are struck through additionally in ink.

And light from meliorating stars
With firmer glory fell.

⟨↑3.↓⟩                          ↑6↓
                I wrote the past in characters
(10)            Of rock & fire the scroll,
                The building in the coral sea,
                The planting of the coal.

⟨↑4↓⟩                          ↑7↓
                And thefts from satellites & rings
                And broken stars I drew,
[258]           And out of spent & aged things
                I formed the world anew.

                              ↑8.↓
⟨↑5↓⟩ What time the gods kept carnival,
                Tricked out in star & flower,
(5)             And in cramp ⟨form of⟩elf & Saurian forms
                They swathed their too much power.

                              ↑9.↓
⟨↑6↓⟩ Time & thought were my surveyors,
                They laid their courses well;
                They boiled the sea, & baked the layers
(10)            Of granite, marl, & shell.

                          ↑10.↓
↑7↓ But he, the manchild glorious,
                Where tarries he the while?
                The rainbow is his harbinger,
                The sunset is his smile.

[259]                         ↑11↓
⟨↑8↓⟩ My boreal lights stream upward,
                For⟨ward⟩↑thright↓ my planets roll,
                And still the manchild is not born,
                The summit of the whole.

                          ↑13.↓
(5) ⟨↑10.↓⟩ Too much of donning & doffing,
                Too slow the rainbow fades,
                I weary of my robe of snow,
                My leaves, & my cascades.

258 "Song of Nature," 27–40. Struck through in ink.
259 "Song of Nature," 41–44, 49–60. Following line (4), horizontal carets are drawn in ink in the left and right margins to indicate the insertion of stanza 12 from p. [261]. Struck through in ink.

↑14.↓
⟨↑11.↓⟩ I tire of globes & races,
(10)      Too long the game is played;
      What, without him, is summers pomp,
      Or winter's frozen shade?

↑15.↓
⟨↑12.↓⟩ I /go/travail/ in pain for him,
      My creatures travail & wait,
(15)      His courier↑s↓ come by thousands,
      He comes not to the gate.

[260]          ↑16↓
⟨↑13↓⟩ Twice I have moulded an image,
      And thrice outstretched my hand,
      Made one of day, & one of night,
      And one of the salt-sea-sand.

↑17↓
(5) ⟨↑14↓⟩ One in a Judaean manger,
      And one by Avon stream,
      One over against the mouths of N⟨u⟩ile
      And one in the Academe.

↑18↓
⟨↑15↓⟩ I ⟨have made tuneful poets,⟩ ↑moulded kings & saviours,↓
(10)      And ⟨captains born⟩ ↑bards o'er kings↓ to rule,
      But fell the starry influence short
      The cup was never full.

[261]          ↑12↓
⟨↑9.↓⟩ Must time & tide forever run?
      Will never my winds go sleep in the West?
      Will never my wheels which whirl⟨e⟩ the sun
      And satellites, have rest?

[262]          ↑19.↓
      Yet whirl the wheels once more,
      And mix the bowl again,
      Seethe↑,↓ Fate! the ancient elements,
      Heat, cold, wet, dry, & peace, & pain.

↑20.↓
(5)      Let war, & trade, & creeds, & song,
      Blend, ripen race on race,

    260 "Song of Nature," 61–64, four lines first printed in the 1867 version, 65–68. Struck through in ink.
    261 "Song of Nature," 45–48. The lines are circumscribed in ink.
    262 "Song of Nature," 69–80. The comma in line (3) is in pencil. Struck through twice in ink.

The sunburnt world a man shall breed
Of all the Zones, & countless days.

↑21.↓
No ray is dimmed, no atom worn,
(10) My oldest force is good as new,
And the fresh rose on yonder thorn
Gives back the bending heavens in dew.

[263]  Who saw the hid beginnings
When Chaos & Order strove?
⟨N⟩Or who can date the morning ↑prime↓
And purple flame of love?

(5) I saw the hid beginnings
When Chaos & Order strove,
And I can date the morning ↑prime↓
And purple flame of Love.

Song breathed from all the forest,
(10) The total air was fame;
It seemed the world was all torches
That suddenly caught the flame.

[264] Is there never a retroscope mirror
In the realms & corners of space,
That can give us a glimpse of the battle
And the soldiers face to face?

(5) Sit here on the basalt ranges,
Where twisted hills betray
The feet of the world-old Forces
Who wrestled here on a day.

[265] When the purple flame shoots up,
And Love ascends his throne,
I cannot hear your songs, o birds,
For the witchery of my own.

(5) And every human heart
Still keeps that golden day,
And rings the bells of jubilee
On its own First of May.

[266]  ↑Verses accompanying an Aeolian harp
given to W.H. & E.E. Forbes. 1 Jan.y 1868↓

263 "Who saw the hid beginnings," 1–12. In lines (3) and (7), "prime" is in pencil.
264 "Who saw the hid beginnings," 13–20.
265 "Who saw the hid beginnings," 21–28.
266 "Maiden Speech of the Aeolian Harp," 1–20.

Soft & softlier hold me, friends!
Thanks if your genial care
Unbind & give me to the air
Keep your lips or finger-tips
(5)      For flute or spinnet's dancing chips;
I await a tenderer touch,
I ask more or not so much:
Give me to the atmosphere,—
Where is the Wind my brother,—where?
(10)    Lift the sash, lay me within,
Lend ↑me↓ your ears, & I begin.
For gentle harp to gentle hearts
The secret of the world imparts;
And not today, & not tomorrow
(15)    Can dra↑i↓n its wealth of hope & sorrow,
But day by day to loving ear
Unlocks new sense & loftier cheer.
        I've come to live with you, sweet friends,
This home my minstrel-journeying ends.
(20)    Many & subtle are my lays,
[267]   The latest better than the first,
For I can mend the happiest days,
And charm the anguish of the Worst.

[268] [blank]
[269]   The bees were in their sugar house
The spider spun his silk
The wasp made paper all the day
The cow weed shed its milk

————

(5)   ↑X↓ In cities high ⟨thro crowds of cares⟩ ↑with varied moods↓
The wo worn mortals darkling go
But in these sunny solitudes
My quiet roses grow

————

[270]          ⟨Walden⟩
      In my garden three ways meet
Thrice the spot is blessed
Hermit thrush comes there to build
Carrier doves to rest

267 "Maiden Speech of the Aeolian Harp," 21–23.
269 "In my garden three ways meet," four unused lines, 17–20. In pencil.
270 "In my garden three ways meet," 1–8 (1–8); "For joy & beauty" (9–12); "My Garden,"
5–6 (13–14). Lines (1–12), in pencil, are struck through twice in pencil; lines (9–12) are struck
through twice more in pencil. Lines (13–14) are struck through twice in ink.

(5)        In my garden oaken copse
The eager wind detains
Sultry summer lingers there
When Autumn chills the plains

For joy & beauty planted it
(10)      With faerie gardens cheered
And boding fancy haunted it
With men & women weird

In my plot no tulips blow
Snowloving pines & oaks instead

[271]                 ↑Walden↓
⟨If I should⟩ ↑Should Hafiz↓ put my woods in song
And tell what's here enjoyed
All men would to th⟨ese⟩is garden⟨s⟩ throng
And leave the cities void

(5)        For joy & beauty planted it
With faerie lustres cheered
And boding Fancy haunted it
With men & women weird

↑☞ p. 269 verses↓                        ↑Insert X p. 269↓
In my garden three ways meet
(10)      Thrice the spot is blest
Hermit thrush comes there to build
Carrier doves to rest

In my garden oaken copse
The eager wind detains
(15)      Sultry summer lingers there
When Autumn chills the plains

[272]      And chiefest ⟨her⟩ ↑thee↓ whom ⟨Nature⟩ ↑Genius↓ loved
⟨The maid of whom Genius graced⟩
↑Daughter of sounding seas↓
⟨Whom Nature wood⟩
(5)        Whom Nature pampered in these lawns
And lavished all to please

She had wealth of mornings in her year,
And planets in her sky,

---

271 "My Garden," 1–4 (1–4); "For joy & beauty" (5–8); "In my garden three ways meet,"
1–8 (9–16). In pencil; the addition in the left margin following line (8) is in ink. Lines (1–4) are
struck through in pencil.
272 "In my garden three ways meet," 33, x, 34, x, 35–44, 25–28. In pencil.

She chose her best thy heart to cheer,
(10)    Thy beauty to supply.

Now younger lovers find the stream
The willows & the vine
But aye to me the happiest seem
To draw the dregs of wine

(15)    What need I holier dew
Than Waldens haunted wave,
Distilled from heaven's alembic blue,
Steeped in each forest cave.

[273]      The idle centuries draw from air
The grand Pacific grove
These must the leaves of ages spare
To clothe the granite bleak & bare
(5)    Ere /harvests/wheat & vines can/ wave above
What smiths, & in what furnace, rolled
In dizzy aeons dim & mute,
Which reeling brain ⟨fails to⟩ ↑can ill↓ compute,
The iron, copper, lead, & gold.
(10)    Nor oldest star ⟨c⟩record or save
Kingdoms of races dead to pave
The planet with a floor of lime
[274]      ⟨T⟩Dust is their pyramid & mole
or knows what flowers ferns & palms were pressed
↑Under toppling mountain's breast↓
In the safe herbal of the coal.
(5)    To Him who rules oer us & ours
The stupefying flight
Of ages is as a vernal night
In which the tender mallows blow
Or morning mushroom learns to grow
(10)    He sheds his years as flakes that play
T⟨r⟩hrough the long winter day
The patient Pan
Knows no stint of time or room
[275]      But sweep & margin for his plan
Before all birth beyond all doom
      But when the quarried means are piled
All is in vain until

273 "Wealth," 13, x, 15–24. Struck through in ink.
274 "Wealth," 25–28, nine unused lines. Lines (1–4) are scribbled through five times in pencil; lines (5–13) are struck through in ink.
275 "Wealth," x, x, 29, 30?, 31?, 31?, 32/33, x, 33, 46?, 47–49. Lines (1–2) and (3–13) are struck through separately in ink.

(5)        Arrives the man arrives the will
                To choose & to combine
                And wit from slime & chaos draw
                All in measure & design
                The threads of good & fit & fair

(10)       And through these shoot
                Electric thrills of law
                That binds the strengths of nature wild
                With the conscience of a child.

[276]                      Michel Angelo's
                          First Sonnet.
/The sculptor never dreamed a form/Never did sculptors
              dream unfold/
⟨Which the⟩ ↑A form which↓ marble doth not hold
In its white block, yet it therein shall find
Only the unerring hand & bold,

(5)        Which still obeys the mind.
                So ⟨bide⟩ ↑hide↓ in thee, thou heavenly dame!
The ill I shun, the good I claim;
I, alas, no more alive,
Miss the aim whereto I strive

(10)           Not love, nor beauty's pride,
Nor fortune, nor thy coldness, can I chide,
If, whilst within thy heart abide
Both death & pity, my unequal skill
⟨Cannot carve out the life, but⟩ ↑Fails of the life, but draws
           the↓ death I sculpture still.

[277]   Sweet, sweet, is sleep,—Ah! sweeter, to be stone,
        Whilst wrong & shame exist & grow;
        Not to see, not to feel, is a boon;
        ⟨S⟩Then, not to wake me, pray speak low!
                    ↑M. Angelo↓

[278] The coil of space, the frontier the chasm, the abysm, topless &
bottomless, cones of shooting light, sidereal spaces, & where they end
⟨they⟩ begin again. And the worlds of God are a dot on its border,
worlds upon worlds can add nothing to him; & ⟨the thought swims⟩
worlds have room to swim on its outer limb
        Ah waste & ⟨sea⟩ ↑ocean↓ fold ⟨up⟩on fold
        And doubled ever by the thought
        Which nothing bounds↑,↓ which all can hold

276 "Sonnet of Michel Angelo Buonaroti." Except for the title, struck through in ink.
277 "Sweet, sweet, is sleep."
278 "The coil of space," 6–8. The cancellations and additions in lines (1) and (3) of the verse
are in pencil.

[279] ⟨Ah⟩O elastic heaven, devouring bounds, budding & bour-
geoning into distances which light nor electricity nor possibility of
creation can measure or fill, mocking God himself. Yet law fills it, &
my thought penetrates its uttermost corner & newest starting-point

The coil of space the cones of light
Starry orbits
Where they end, begin & enlarge
And the worlds of God
(5)      Are a dot on its marge

Ah waste & ocean, fold on fold,
And doubled ever ↑more↓ by Thought
Which nothing bounds which all can hold

[280]    I moulded kings & saviours
And bards who monarchs rule
And bards who kings might rule

detonating   culminating
festal  balsam  cordial  virtuous

I moulded kings & saviours,
(5)      And bards o'er kings to rule,
Yet fell the starry influence short
The cup was never full.

[281]    I moulded kings & saviours
And bards by song to rule
But fell the starry influence short
The cup was never full

[282]    Have ye seen the caterpillar
Foully warking in his nest?
Tis the poor man getting siller,
Without cleanness, without rest.

(5)      Have you seen the butterfly
In ⟨rags⟩ braw claithing drest?
Tis the poor man gotten rich,
In rings & painted vest.

The poor man crawls in web of rags,
(10)    And sore bested with woes,

279 "The coil of space." The verse is in pencil.
280 "Song of Nature," 65–66, 66, 65–68. The words between lines (3) and (4) are in pencil.
Lines (1–3) are struck through in ink twice and lines (4–7) once.
281 "Song of Nature," 65–68. In pencil, struck through in pencil.
282 "Have ye seen the caterpillar."

But when he flees on riches' wings,
He laugheth at his foes.


[283] [blank]
[284]    For Fancys gift
Can mountains lift;
The Muse can knit
What ↑i↓s past & ⟨done⟩ ↑what is done↓
(5)    With ⟨what's⟩ ↑the web that's just↓ begun,
⟨It makes⟩ ↑Making↓ ⟨light of⟩ ↑free with↓ time ⟨or⟩& size,
Dwindles here, there magnifies
⟨Into a drop⟩ ↑Swells a rain-drop ⟨in⟩to↓ a tun;
So to repeat
(10)    No word or feat,
Crowds in a day the ⟨otto⟩ ↑sum↓ of ages,
And blushing Love outwits the sages.


[285]    Pour the wine! pour the wine!
As it changes to foam,
So flashes the day-god
Rushing abroad,
(5)    Ever new & unlooked for,
In furthest & smallest
Comes royally home.
In spider wise
Will again geometrize,
(10)    Will in bee & gnat keep time
With the annual solar chime;
Aphides like emperors
Sprawl & play their pair of hours


[286]        Better held ⟨b⟩
↑To↓ Hold him by his eyes & ears
Than by his belly or his fears
Stories of Ptolemy & Cyrus
(5)    From every book & ⟨each⟩ ↑old↓ papyrus
The balance of the world is kept
And dewdrop & haze & the pencil of light
Are as ↑old &↓ longlived as Chaos & Night


    **284** "Pour the wine!," 14–25. In line (6), "It makes" is canceled, and "Making" added, in pencil; the cancellation and addition in line (11) are in pencil.
    **285** "Pour the wine!," 1–13.
    **286** "Better held." In pencil.

[287]–[288] [leaf torn out]
[289]     Travel is the office of a wheel

Only light armed climb the hill
I found they left the best places

Science & wonder are glad
(5)     ↑Where↓ The star Canopus shines
⟨↑All↓⟩ the tribes are never sad
Spartans shrined the laughters god
In every ⟨din⟩ banquet hall
But ah for friendship lifes too short
(10)     With him we are easily great

Masking wisdom with delight
Toy with the bow yet hit the white

Debt standing at my door
Held out his thousand hands

[290]     ↑And hungry Debt with thousand hands↓
↑Stood at my door & held them out↓
Was never form & never face
So sweet to Seyd as only grace
(5)     Which did not slumber like a stone
But hovered gleaming, & was gone.
Beauty chased he everywhere
In flame, in storm, in clouds ⟨in⟩of air,
He smote the lake to feed his eye
(10)     With the precious green of the broken wave,
He flung in pebbles well to hear
The moment's music which they gave.
Loved hare-bells nodding on a rock,
A cabin topped with curling smoke,
(15)     And huts & tents, nor loved he less
Stately men in palaces,
[291]     Princely women hard to please,
Fenced ⟨with⟩ ↑by↓ form & ceremony
With etiquette & hera⟨dl⟩ldry.

---

287–88 Initial letters surviving on the recto of the stub and letters and punctuation at the ends of lines on the verso indicate that both pages were fully inscribed in ink, probably with a near-final draft of "Worship."
289 "Considerations by the Way," x, 15, x, x, 20–21, four unused lines, 24–25 (1–12); "Stout Sparta shrined the god," 1–2 (7–8); "Mask thy wisdom," 1–2 (11–12); "And hungry Debt" (13–14). Lines (1–12) are in pencil; lines (11–12) are struck through in pencil.
290 "And hungry Debt" (1–2); "There are beggars," 11–22, 25–26 (3–16); "Beauty," 1–10 (3–12). Lines (3–12) are struck through in ink three times and lines (3–16) once.
291 "There are beggars," 27–29 (1–3); "These craggy hills" (4–7).

Nature says,
These craggy hills that front the dawn
(5)     Man-bearing granite of the North
Shall fiercer forms & races spawn
Charged with my genius forth

[292]   Freedom hates the ardent Zone
The ⟨patriot⟩ ↑north↓ wind ⟨a war tune⟩ ↑best to battle↓
    pipes,
The snow-flakes star our haughty flag,
And northern streamers lend ⟨us⟩ ↑the↓ stripes.

---

↑Poet↓
(5)     Shun Passion, fold the hands of Thrift,
Sit still, & Truth is near;
Suddenly it will uplift
Your eyelids to the sphere;
Wait a little, you shall see
(10)    The portraiture of things to be.

---

The rules to men made evident
By Him who built the day,
The columns of the firmament
Not firmer based than they.

[293]   Eve roved in Paradise we heard
With no more baggage than a bird
Exiled she soon found necessary
More garments than she liked to carry
(5)     Adam invented trunk & sack
And boot & tray the weeds to pack
But when the hatbox was complete
She thot /even outside/the outworld/ /nature/the garden/
    sweet
And transmits to her /daughter/Ellen/ dear
(10)    to Ellen this cunning cube ↑of leather↓ here

[294]       Too late the anxious fire came
The Express had mounted his pot of flame
No gift tho' urged by Ediths voice
No bugler can the rider bring
(5)     Only this paper scrap can make amends

292 "Voluntaries," x, x, 41?–42? (1–4); "Shun Passion" (5–10); "The rules to men" (11–14).
293 "Eve roved in Paradise," 1–7, 10–12 (1–10); "If bright the sun," 4 (2). In pencil. In lines
(9–10), "daughter" is partly circled and "to Ellen" is circled.
294 "Too late the anxious fire came." In pencil.

Tomorrow rides with equal fire
And brings the haughty horseman home
He well can wait
This horse forever bounds
(10)    This horn to fancy ever sounds
The warcloud hints what bursts behind

[295] ↑*Poet.*↓
The Muses' hill by Fear is guarded,
A bolder foot is still rewarded.

———

Like vaulters of the circus round,
Who step from horse to horse, & never touch the ground.

———

(5)    For every god
Obeys the hymn, obeys the ode,
Obeys the holy ode.

———

⟨An⟩His instant thought a poet spoke ↑,↓
And filled the ⟨sk⟩age his fame;
(10)    An inch of ground the ⟨lightning⟩ ⟨↑wild bolt↓⟩ ↑lightning↓
        strook
But ⟨fille⟩lit the sky /the/with/ flame.

———

Delicate omens trac↑e↓d in air, &c     *supra* 7⟨3⟩1 ↑71↓

———

Poet of poets     *EL* 3, 18,

[296₁]    Up & the dusky race
That sat in darkness long
Be swift your feet as antelopes
As buffaloes be strong

       *Poet*
(5)    Try the might the Muse affords,
And the balm of thoughtful words.
Bring music to the desolate
Hang roses on the stony fate

═══

295 "The Muses' hill" (1–2); "Like vaulters in the circus round" (3–4); "For every god,"
1–2, 2 (5–7); "His instant thought" (8–11); "Fate" ("Delicate omens"), 1 (12); "Poet of poets,"
1 (13). The rules following lines (2) and (4) and the comma in line (8) are in pencil; in lines
(10–11), "wild bolt" is canceled, and "lightning" and "with" added, in pencil. In line (12), "73"
is corrected to "71", and "71" added below it, in pencil.
296₁ "Boston Hymn," 77–80 (1–4); "Try the might the Muse affords" (5–8); "Charmed from
fagot," 5–7 (9–11). Lines (1–4) are in pencil, struck through in pencil.

560

(10)
The sun & moon shall fall amain
Like sowers seeds into his brain,
There quickened to be born again.

[296₂]
The Asmodean feat is thine
To spin the sandheap into twine

[297]
From the beginning
Sin blunders & brags,
True making, true winning
Go hidden in rags.

(5)
Wit has the creation
Of worlds & their fame
On one stipulation,—
Renouncing the same.

(10)
Which wilt thou have?
Have the mystical forces,
Or skies which they breed?
The strain it discourses,
Or the sycamore reed?

(15)
When the crown first encloses
The brows of her son,
The Muse him deposes
From kingdom & throne

[298] ↑*Poet.*↓
⟨a⟩A crystal soul
Sphered & concentric to the Whole.

(5)
Charmed from fagot & from steel,
Harvests grew upon his tongue;
Past & Future must reveal
All their heart whilst Saadi sung
⟨The⟩ sun & moon must fall amain,
Like sower↑'↓s⟨'⟩ seeds into his brain,
There quickened to be born again.

[299] ↑*Poet.*↓
Ring of axe, & hum of wheel,
And gleam which use will paint on steel.

296₂ "The Asmodaean feat."
297 "From Nature's beginning," 1–9, 9, 10–16 (1–17); "Poet of poets," 88–95 (5–8, 14–17). Lines (10–11) and (12–13) occur in reverse order in the manuscript, marked for transposition by brackets around each pair of lines and the numbers "2" and "1" in the left margin.
298 "There are beggars," 54–55 (1–2); "Charmed from fagot" (3–9).
299 "There are beggars," 23–24 (1–2); "By art, by music" (3–4); "Hold of the Maker" (5–6); "The comrade or the book," 3–4 (7–8).

For art, for Music, overthrilled,
The winecup shakes, the wine is spilled.

(5)      Hold of the Maker, not the made,
Sit with the cause, or grim or glad,

Unless to ⟨t⟩Thought be added Will,
Apollo is an imbecile.

[300]    For art, for music, overthrilled,
The wine cup shakes, the wine is spilled

——

The sun & moon shall fall amain
Like sower ↑'↓ s⟨'⟩ seeds into his brain
(5)      There quickened to be born again

——

Saadi held the Muse in awe
She was his mistress & his law
A twelvemonth he could silence hold
Nor ran to speak till she him told
(10)    He felt the flame, the fanning wings,
Nor offered words till they were things.
Glad when the solid mountain swims
/In/To/ Music & uplifting ⟨rhymes⟩ ↑hymns↓

————

a crystal soul
(15)    Sphered & concentric to the Whole.
↑see *EL* 148↓

————

No song so tuneful, ⟨said⟩ ↑quoth↓ the fox,
As the rich crowing of the cocks.

[301] Suoni la tromba
"Come brave the sea with me, love
The Empire of the free, love
There shalt thou dwell with me, love,
My blessing & my pride.

(5)      Tho fair the earth may be, love
It is not like the sea, love
Where soars the eagle free, love
As oer its waves we glide."

————

300 "By art, by music" (1–2); "Charmed from fagot," 5–7 (3–5); "Saadi held the Muse in awe" (6–13); "There are beggars," 54–55 (14–15); "No song so tuneful" (16–17). Lines (1–15) and "See *EL* 148" are in pencil; the cancellation and addition in line (13) are in ink.

301 Following the quotation (see the ninth insert in EL, described on p. 324 above) is "The comrade or the book" (9–14). "Suoni la tromba" (Italian: "Let the trumpet sound") and lines (1–8) are in pencil.

Th⟨e⟩at book is good
(10)     That puts me in a working mood
Unless to Thought is added Will,
Apollo is an imbecile.
What parts, what gems, what colors shine!—
Ah! but I miss the grand design.

[302] [index material omitted]
[inside back cover] [index material omitted]

# Notebook KL[A]

Notebook KL[A] contains a fair copy of about four-fifths of a late stage of "May–Day," along with a few related fragments. It was probably written after journal KL was begun in the spring or summer of 1864 or during the spring of 1865.

Notebook KL[A] occupies pp. 223–78 of journal KL, but is written upside down and back to front relative to that journal and appears to be a separate entity. Journal KL was published in JMN 15:414–80; see that volume for a bibliographical description.

Emerson paginated the notebook in pencil, beginning with p. 1 on p. 278 of KL and running to p. 51 on p. 223; p. 3 is misnumbered 2 and corrected; pp. 2 and 52–56 are unnumbered. Nine of the 56 pages that comprise the notebook are blank.

[1]                    Io paean! the darling Spring
                With sudden passion languishing,
                Maketh all things softly smile,
                Painteth pictures mile on mile,
(5)             Holds a cup with cowslips wreathed,
                Whence a smokeless incense breathed

                Dripping dew cold daffadillies,
                Making drunk with wine of lilies,
                Girls are peeling the sweet willow,
(10)            Poplar white & Gilead tree,
                And troops of boys
                Shouting with whoop & hilloa,
                And hip, hip, three times three

[2] [blank]
[3]             The air is full of whistlings bland,—

                What was that I heard
                Out of the hazy land?
                Harp of the wind, or noise of bird,
(5)             Or clapping of shepherds' hands;
                Or vagrant booming ⟨of⟩in the air,
                Voice of a meteor lost in day,—
                Such tidings of the starry space
                Can this elastic air convey:
(10)            Or, haply, twas the cannonade
                Of the pent & darkened lake,
                Cooled by the pendent mountain's shade,
                Whose deeps, till beams of noonday break,
[4]             Afflicted moan, & latest hold
                ⟨Even i⟩Into ↑mid-↓ May the iceberg cold.
                Was it a squirrel's pettish bark?
                Or clarionet of jay? or, hark,
(5)             Where yon wedged line the Nestor leads,
                Steering north with raucous cry
                Through tracts & provinces of sky,
                Every night alighting down
                In new landscapes of romance,
(10)            Where darkling feed the clamorous clans
                By lonely lakes to men unknown

1 "May–Day," 1–6, x, x, 7–11. Struck through in ink.
3 "May–Day," 12–24. Struck through in ink.
4 "May–Day," 25–35. Struck through in ink. In line (2), the cancellation and revision are in ink over pencil.

[5]            Come the tumult whence it will,
            Voice of sport, or rush of wings,
            It is a sound, it is a token,
            That the marble sleep is broken,
(5)            And a change has passed on things.

            Beneath the calm, within the light,
            A ⟨restless⟩ ↑hid unruly↓ appetite
            Of ⟨larger⟩ ↑swifter↓ life, a surer hope
            ⟨Prompts⟩ ↑Strains↓ every sense to ⟨utmost⟩ ↑larger↓ scope
(10)           ⟨Would drain the bowl⟩ ↑Rash to anticipate↓
                    ↑halting steps of aged Fate↓
            ↑Slow grows the palm, ↑too↓ slow⟨er⟩ the pearl,↓
            ↑When↓ Nature ⟨dotes &⟩ falters, ⟨zeal⟩ ↑fain↓ would
                ⟨fain⟩ ↑zeal↓
            Grasp the Spondyls of her wheel
(15)           And grasping give the tires another whirl
            Ripen slow palm   perfect the pearl

[6]            Turn swiftlier round, o tardy ball
            And sun this frozen side.
            Bring hither back the robin's call,
            Bring back the tulip's pride.

[7]            Why chidest thou the tardy Spring?
            The hardy bunting does not chide,
            The blackbirds make the maples ring⟨,⟩
            With social cheer & jubilee;
(5)            The redwing flutes his O-ka-lee,
            The robins know the melting snow,
            And song sparrow, prophetic-eyed,
            Its nest ⟨by⟩ ↑beside↓ ⟨o⟩the ⟨old⟩ snowdrift weaves,
            Secure the osiers yet will hide
(10)           Its callow brood in mantling leaves.
            And thou, by science all undone,
            Why only must thy reason fail
            To see the southing of the sun?

[8]            The world rolls round, mistrust it not—
            Befals again what once befel,
            All things return, both sphere & mote,
            And I shall hear my bluebird's note,
(5)            And dream the dream of Auburn dell.

5 "May–Day," 36–50, 47. Struck through in ink. The cancellation and addition in line (8), "larger" in line (9), and lines (10–11) and (13–16) are in pencil.
  6 "May–Day," 51–54. Struck through in ink, and the mark fingerwiped.
  7 "May–Day," 55–67. Struck through in ink.
  8 "May–Day," 93–97. Struck through in ink.

[9]     When late I walked, in earlier days,
All was stiff & stark,
Kneedeep snows choked all the ways,
In the sky no spark.
(5)     Firm-braced, I sought my ancient woods,
Struggling through the drifted ⟨wood⟩roads;
The whited desert knew me not,
Snow-ridges masked each darling spot,
The summer dells, by genius haunted,
(10)    One arctic moon had disenchanted.
All the sweet secrets ⟨F⟩therein hid
By Fancy, ghastly spells undid!
Eldest mason, Frost, had piled,
With wicked ingenuity,
(15)    Swift cathedrals in the wild;
The piny hosts were sheeted ghosts,
[10]        In the starlit minster aisled,
I found no joy. the icy wind
Might rule the forest to his mind:
Who would freeze in frozen brakes?—
(5)     Back to books & sheltered home,
And woodfire flickering on the walls,
To hear, when, 'mid our talk & games,
Without the baffled northwind calls.

        A happier hour! A longer day!—
(10)    Now the sun leads in the May,
Now desire of action wakes,
And the wish to roam.

[11]        The caged linnet in the spring
Hearkens for the choral glee,
When his fellows on the wing
Migrate from the Southern sea.
(5)     When trellised grapes their flowers unmask,
And the newborn tendrils twine,
The old wine darkling in the cask
Feels the bloom on the living ⟨w⟩vine,
And bursts the hoops at hint of Spring.
(10)    And so perchance in Adams race
Of Eden some memorial trace
Survived the Fall   survived the Flood

9 "May–Day," 98–113. Struck through in ink.
10 "May–Day," 114–21, 124–27. Struck through in ink.
11 "May–Day," 128–39, 140?–141? Lines (1–9) are struck through in ink; lines (10–14) and
"*FOR* 1⟨5⟩6" are in pencil.

⟨And⟩ in newborn boy the passion glows
To see the Garden

FOR 1⟨5⟩6

[12]     Or was it that ⟨o⟩in Adam's race
Of Eden's bower some dreamlike trace
Survived the Flight & swam the Flood
And ↑throbs↓ in the ⟨latest-born abode⟩ ↑youngest blood↓
(5)     To tread the forfeit Paradise
And feed once more the exiled eyes
But when the happy child
In May beheld the blooming wild ↑e↓
And heard what strains the bluebirds sing
(10)     Thought Eden knew no balmier spring

[13]     Not for a regiment's parade,
Nor evil laws or rulers made,
Blue Walden rolls its cannonade,
But for a lofty sign
(5)     Which the Zodiack threw,
That the bondage days are told,
And waters free as winds shall flow.
Lo! how all the tribes combine
⟨t⟩To rout the flying foe.
(10)     See, every patriot oakleaf throws
His elfin length upon the snows,
Not idle, since the pet all day
Draws to the spot the solar ray,
Ere sunset quarrying inches down,
(15)     And halfway to the mosses brown,
While the grass beneath the rime
[14]     Has hints of the propitious time,
And upward pries & perforates
Through the cold slab a thousand gates,
Till green lances peering through
(5)     Bend happy in the welkin blue.

The Grecian worshipped where he found
The sun-drawn mallows rive the ground
First sign celestial natures show
Of sympathy with ours below.
(10)     April cold with dropping rain
Willows & lilacs brings again,

12 "May–Day," 137–45, 148. In pencil.
13 "May–Day," 149–64. Struck through in ink.
14 "May–Day," 165–69, four unused lines, 170–73. Struck through in ink.

The whistle of returning birds,
And trumpet-lowing of the herds.

[15]  　　　What fiery force the earth renews?
The wealth of forms, the flush of hues⟨,⟩?
Joy shed in rosy waves abroad
Flows from the heart of Love, the Lord.

(5)  　　　Hitherward rolls the storm of heat,
I feel its ⟨welcome⟩finer billows beat,
Like a sea which me infolds;
Heat, the formless former strong.
⟨Sculptor⟩ ↑⟨Lord⟩ To whom the embryo worlds belong↓
(10)  ⟨Which⟩ ↑Heat↓ with viewless fingers moulds,
Swells, & mellows, & matures,
Paints, & flavors, & allures,
Bird & ⟨willow⟩ ↑briar↓ inly warms,
Still enriches & ⟨informs⟩transforms,
[16]  Gives the ⟨grass⟩ ↑reed↓ & lily length,
Adds to oak & oxen strength,
Boils the world in tepid lakes,
Burns the world, yet, burnt, remakes,
(5)  Enveloping heat, enchanted robe,
Wraps the daisy & the globe,
Transforming what it doth enfold,
Life out of death, new out of old,
Painting fawns' & leopards' fells,
(10)  Seethes the gulf-encrimsoning shells,
Fires gardens with a joyful blaze
Of tulips, in the morning's rays:
The dead log touched bursts into leaf,
The wheat-blade w⟨a⟩hispers of the sheaf.
[17]  What god is this ↑⟦↓Vulcanian↑⟧↓ heat,
Earth's prime secret, sculpture's seat,
Doth it bear hidden in its heart,
Waterline patterns of all art,
(5)  All figures, organs, hues, & graces⟨.⟩?

Is it Daedalus? is it Love?
Or walks in mask almighty Jove,

15 "May–Day," 176–82, 183?, x, 183–87. Struck through in ink. In line (5), "ward" (in "Hitherward") is circled in pencil.
16 "May–Day," 188–201. Struck through in ink. The cancellation and addition in line (1) are in pencil.
17 "May–Day," 202–10, four unused lines. Struck through in ink. The brackets in line (1) and the question mark in line (5) are in pencil.

And drops from Power's redundant horn
All seeds of beauty to be born?

(10)          He comes, the puissant semigod,
And earth & air are overflowed,
Earth with waters, air with juices
That infuriate love infuses.

[18]          No spacious house nor monarch's hall
Suffice to hold the festival:
Up & away! where haughty woods
Front the liberated floods,
(5)          We will climb the broadbacked hills,
Hear the uproar of their joy;
We will mark the leaps & gleams
Of the new-delivered streams,
And the murmuring rivers of sap
(10)          Mount in the pipes of the trees,
Giddy with day to the topmost spire,
Which for a spike of tender green
Bartered its powdery cap.

[19]          And the colors of joy in the bird,
And the love in his carol heard,
⟨And the⟩ frog & lizard in holiday coats,
And ⟨the⟩ turtle brave in his golden spots.
(5)          We will hear the tiny roar
Of the insects evermore,
While cheerful cries of crag & plain
Reply to the thunder of river & main.

            As poured the flood of the ancient sea,
(10)          Spilling over mountain-chains,
Bending forests as bends the sedge,
Faster flowing o'er the plains,
A world-wide wave with a foaming edge
[20]          That rims the running silver sheet
So pours the deluge of the heat
Broad northward oer the land,
Painting artless Paradises

(5)          Fanning secret fires which glow
In columbine & clover-blow,
Climbing the northern zones,
Where a thousand pallid towns

18 "May–Day," 215–27. Lines (1–2) and (3–13) are struck through separately in ink.
19 "May–Day," 228–40. Struck through in ink.
20 "May–Day," 241–44, 246–53. Struck through in ink.

Lie like cockles on a beach,
(10)  Or like tents upon a plain.

[21]

The million ↑ - ↓ handed sculptor moulds
Quaintest bud & blossom folds,
The million-handed painter pours
Opal hues & purple dye;
Flush with ⟨tulips⟩ island floors,
And the tints of heaven reply.

(5)

Wreath⟨es⟩s to the May! for happy Spring
Doth today her dowry bring,
The love of kind, the joy, the grace,
Hymen of element & race,
Knowing well to celebrate
(10)  With song, & hue, & star, & state,
With tender light, & youthful cheer,
The spousals of the newborn year.
Lo! love's inundation poured
Over space & race abroad!

[22] [blank]
[23]

Drug the cup, thou butler sweet,
And send the madness round;
The feet that slid so long on sleet
Are glad to feel the ground.
(5)  Fill and saturate each kind,
With good according to its mind;
Fill each kind, & saturate
With good agreeing with its fate,
Willow & violet, maiden & man.

(10)

The bittersweet, the haunting air
Goeth, bloweth everywhere;
It preys on all, all prey on it,
Blooms in beauty, thinks in wit,
[24]  Stings the strong with enterprize,
Makes travellers long for Indian skies,
Bites damsels with half-pleasing flame,
Drives the struck poet mad for fame.
(5)  And, where it comes, this courier fleet
Fans in all hearts expectance sweet,
As if tomorrow should redeem

21 "May–Day," 254–67. Struck through in ink. The cancellation in line (3) is in pencil.
23 "May–Day," 276–88. Struck through in ink.
24 "May–Day," 289–90, x, x, 291–300. Struck through in ink.

The vanished rose of evening's dream⟨,⟩.
By houses lies a fresher green,
(10)    On men & maids a ruddier mien,
As if Time brought a new relay
Of shining virgins, every May,
And summer came to ripen maids
To a beauty that not fades.

[25]        I saw the wizard Spring go forth
Stepping daily onward north,
To greet staid ancient cavaliers
Filing singly in stately train;—
(5)    And who, and who are the travellers?
They were Night & Day, & Day & Night,
Pilgrims wight ↑(↓that never alight.↑)↓
I saw the Days deformed & low,
Short & bent by cold & snow,—
(10)    The merry Spring threw wreaths on them,—
Flower wreaths gay with bud & bell,—
Many a flower, & many a gem,
[26]    They were refreshed by the smell,
They shook the snow from hats & shoon,
They put their April raiment on,
And those eternal forms,
(5)    Unhurt by a thousand storms,
Shot up to the height of the sky again,
And danced as merrily as young men.
I saw them mask their awful glance
Sidewise meek in gossamer lids,
(10)    And to speak my thought, if none forbids,
It was as if the eternal gods,
Tired of their starry periods,
Hid their majesty in cloth
Woven of tulips & painted moth.

[27]        ↑〚Insert seven lines beginning
(On carpets green the maskers march)〛↓
'Twas the vintage-day of field & wood
When magic wine for bards is brewed,
Every tree & stem & chink
Gushed with syrup to the brink.
(5)    The air stole into the streets of towns,

25 "May–Day," 325–36. Struck through in ink. The parentheses in line (7) are in pencil.
26 "May–Day," 337–50. Struck through in ink.
27 "May–Day," 358–70. Struck through in ink. "〚Insert . . . march)〛," a reference to p. [55],
is in pencil.

And betrayed the fund of joy
To the high-school, & medalled boy,
On from hall to chamber ran,
From youth to maid, from boy to man,
(10)    To babes, & to old eyes, as well;
'Once more,' the old man cried, 'ye clouds,
Airy turrets, purple-piled,
Which once my infancy beguiled,
[28]    Beguile me with the selfsame spell:
I know ye skilful to convoy
The total freight of hope & joy
Into rude & homely nooks,
(5)    Shed mocking lustres on shelf of books,
On farmer's byre, on ⟨d⟩ grassy pipes,
Or on a pool of dancing chips.

[29]    I care not if the ⟨things⟩ ↑pomps↓ you show
Be what they ↑soothfast↓ appear
And if it be to you allowed
To ⟨make⟩ fool me with a sh⟨ing⟩ining cloud,
(5)    So only new griefs are consoled
By new delights, as old by old,
Frankly I ⟨yield myself⟩ ↑will be↓ your guest,
Count your change & cheer the best.
The world hath overmuch of pain,—
(10)    If Nature give me joy again,
Of such deceit I'll not complain.

[30] [blank]
[31]    Ah well I mind the calendar
Faithful ⟨an⟩thro' a thousand years
Of the ↑painted↓ race of flowers,
Exact to days, exact to hours,
(5)    Counted on the spacious dial
Yon broidered Zodiack girds.
I know the pretty almanac
Of the punctual coming-back,
On their due days, of the birds.
(10)    I marked them yestermorn,—
A flock of finches darting
[32]    Beneath the crystal arch,

28 "May–Day," 371–77. Struck through in ink.
29 "May–Day," 378–79, 382–90. Struck through in ink, the mark fingerwiped below line (1); lines (1–3) are separately struck through.
31 "May–Day," 391–401. Struck through in ink with a large X. Emerson left a space in line (3), then inserted "painted" in pencil.
32 "May–Day," 402–10. Struck through in ink.

Piping, as they flew, a march,
Belike the one they used in parting,
Last year, from yon oak or larch.
(5)    Dusky sparrows in a crowd,
Diving, darting⟨,⟩ northward free,
Suddenly betook them all,
Every one to his hole in the wall,
Or to his niche in the appletree

[33]        Poets praise that hidden wine
Hid in milk we drew
At the barrier of Time,
When our life was new.
(5)    We had eaten fairy fruit,
We were quick from head to foot,
↑⟦↓All our nerves were viol strings,
At our shoulder budded wings, ↑⟧↓
All the forms we looked on shone
(10)   As with diamond dews thereon.
What cared we for costly joys,
The Museum's far-fetched toys?
Gleam of sunshine on the wall
[34]   ⟨Imparted⟩ ↑Yielded↓ deeper cheer than all
The revels of the Carnival⟨;⟩:
We a pine grove did prefer
To a marble theatre,
(5)    Could with gods on mallows dine,
Nor cared for spices, nor for wine;
Wreaths of mist & rainbows spanned
Arch on arch the grimmest land,
↑⟦↓Low moor, bare downs, & ragged hills;
Our orators were upland rills;
Open sense was ours, & keen,
To sound & color, shade & sheen. ↑⟧↓

[35]   Whistle of a woodland bird
Made the pulses dance,
Note of horn in valleys heard
Filled the region with romance.

(5)       None can tell how sweet
How virtuous the morning air:

33  "May–Day," 425–30, x, x, 431–35. Lines (1–5) and (1–13) are struck through separately in ink. In lines (7–8), the brackets are added, and "All" mended, in pencil.
34  "May–Day," 436–43, four unused lines. Struck through in ink. The cancellation and addition in line (1), and the brackets in lines (9) and (12), are in pencil.
35  "May–Day," 444–54. Lines (1–4) and (5–11) are struck through separately in ink.

Every accent vibrates well,—
Not alone the woodbird's call,
Or shouting boys that chase their ball,
(10)    Pass the minstrel's art,
But the plowman's thoughtless cry
[36]    Lowing oxen, sheep that bleat,
And the joiner's hammer-beat,
Softened are above their will,
Warble back as passed thro' heaven
(5)    All grating discords melt,
No dissonant note is dealt
To hurt the halcyon tide.
And though thy voice be shrill
Like rasping file on steel
(10)    Such is the temper of the air,
Echo waits with art & care
    ↑And will↓ The faults of song ⟨will she⟩ repair.

[37]    So by remote Superior Lake,
And by resounding Mackinac,
When northern storms the forest shake,
And billows on the long beach break,
(5)    The artful air doth separate
Note by note all sounds that grate,
Smothering in her ample breast
All but godlike words,
Reporting to the happy ear
(10)    Only purified accords.
⟨‖ . . . . ‖⟩Wondrous music daunts the Indian brave,
Convent chanting, which the child
[38]    ↑Hears↓ Pealing from the panther's cave
And the impenetrable wild.
Hushed the awestruck Indian hear,
And deems his father's spirit near,
      ↑See S p 145↓

[39]    One musician is sure,
His wisdom will not fail,
He has not tasted wine impure,

36 "May–Day," 455–57, x, 458–59, x, 460–64. Struck through in ink.
37 "May–Day," 465–74, 476–77. Struck through in ink.
38 "May–Day," 478–79, x, x. Struck through in ink. "See S p 145" is in pencil. The entry in notebook S (Salvage) p. [145] reads in part: "Tis because Nature is an instrument so thoroughly musical, that the most aukward hand cannot draw a discord from it. A devil struck the chords in defiance, & his spite was punished by a sweeter melody than the angels made."
39 "May–Day," 480–92 (1–13); "The Harp," 1–13 (1–13). Struck through in ink.

Nor bent to passion frail:
(5)  Age cannot c⟨ol⟩loud his memory,
Nor ⟨years⟩ ↑grief↓ untune his voice,
Ranging ⟨along⟩ ↑down↓ the ruled scale,
From tone of joy to inward wail,
Tempering the pitch of all
(10)  In his windy cave.
He all the fables knows,
And in their ⟨voices⟩causes tells,
Knows Natures rarest moods,
[40]  Ever on her secret broods.
The Muse of men is coy,
Oft-courted will not come,
In palaces & market squares,
(5)  Entreated, she is dumb.
But my minstrel knows & tells
The counsel of the gods,
Knows the spell of Holy Book,
Knows the law of Night & Day,
(10)  And the heart of girls & boys,
The tragic & the gay.
And what is writ on Round Table
[41]  Of Arthur & his peers,
What sea & land discoursing say
In sidereal years,
He renders all his lore
(5)  In numbers wild as dreams,
⟨Tempered yet in⟩ ↑Modulating↓ all extremes⟨,⟩:
⟨He⟩ knows what the spangled meadow saith
To the children who have faith;
Only to children children sing,
(10)  Only to youth will ⟨be⟩spring be spring


[42]  ↑Who is the Bard thus magnified?↓
⟨This minstrel that I praise⟩
⟨↑⟨Minstrel⟩ ↑Chief of song↓ where ⟨sacred⟩ poets feast↓⟩
↑Chief of song where poets feast↓
(5)  Is the windharp which thou seest
In the casement at my side.

40 "May–Day," 493–504 (1–12); "The Harp," 14–25 (1–12). Struck through in ink.
41 "May–Day," 505–14 (1–10); "The Harp," 26–35 (1–10). Struck through in ink. In line (7), "knows" is circled in pencil.
42 "May–Day," 515, x, 517, 517–25 (1–12); "The Harp," 36, x, 38, 38–46 (1–12). Lines (1–6) and (7–12) are struck through separately in ink. Line (1) is in pencil.

Aeolian Harp!
How strangely wise thy strain!
Gay for youth, gay for youth,

(10)    Sweet is art, but sweeter truth,
In the hall, at summer eve,
Deep life, deep beauty, skilled to weave.

[43]    From the eager opening strings
Rung loud & bold the song.
Who loved not the windharp's note?
We did doat

(5)    On its mystic song,
With its primaeval memory,
Reporting what old minstrels said
Of Merlin ⟨prisoned⟩ ↑locked↓ the harp within,
Merlin paying the pain of sin,

(10)    Pent in a dungeon made of air,
And some attain his voice to hear,
Words of fate & cries of fear,
But pillowed all on melody,
As fits the griefs of ⟨the wise⟩ ↑bards↓ to be.

[44] [blank]

[45]    Nor less the golden time
Spoke to the eye, with optic chime,
By the hillbound woodland lake,
When flaws of wind the water whipt

(5)    Into fleets of ripples gay,
The swift slight spiritual drift,
More like northern meteors' play
Than any spectacle of day.

How easily doth youth persuade

(10)    Its children to delight!
What happy fools an image made,
A sounding verse, a ballad right.

[46] [blank]

[47]    Methought, thus listening, at my side⟨,⟩
A window rose, &, to say sooth,
I looked forth on the fields of youth;
⟨I saw⟩ ↑I saw fair↓ boys ⟨↑I saw↓⟩ bestriding steeds,

43 "May–Day," 526–39 (1–14); "The Harp," 47–60 (1–14). Struck through in ink. In line (8), the cancellation is in pencil.
45 "May–Day," twelve unused lines. Struck through in ink.
47 "May–Day," 583–92, 595, 593–95 (1–14); "The Harp," 108–17, 120, 118–20 (1–14). Struck through four times in ink. Lines (9–10) occur in reverse order in the manuscript, marked for transposition by "2)" and "1)" in the left margin.

(5)      I knew their forms in fancy weeds,
Long long ⟨unseen⟩ ↑concealed↓ ⟨thro' adverse⟩ ↑by
    sundering↓ fates,
Mates of my youth, ↑—↓ yet not my mates,
Stronger & bolder far than I,
With grace with genius ⟨them⟩ ↑well↓ attired,

(10)    And then as now ↑from far↓ admired ⟨afar⟩
⟨And loved with passion cold & shy⟩
Followed with love
They know not of,
With passion cold & shy.

[48] [blank]

[49]     O fair and virtuous Spring!
Soothsayer of the eldest gods,
Revealer of the inmost powers
Prometheus pr⟨omised⟩offered, Jove denied;

(5)     Disclosing treasures more than true,
Or in what far tomorrow ⟨V⟩due;
Speaking by the tongues of flowers,
By the ten-tongued lily speaking,
Singing by the oriole songs,

(10)    Heart of bird the man's heart seeking
Recorder of man's pristine might
Prophet of mere rich delight

[50] [blank]

[51]     Whispering hints of treasure hid
Under ⟨Earth's⟩ ↑morn's↓ unlifted lid,
⟨Regions⟩ ↑Islands↓ looming just beyond
⟨Far⟩ ↑Yon↓ horizon's shining bound;

(5)     Who can like thee our /rags/sin/ upbraid,
Or taunt us with our hope decayed,
Or who like thee persuade,
Making the splendor of the air,
The morn & sparkling dew a snare,

(10)    Or who resent
Thy genius, wiles, & blandishment

[52] [blank]

[53]         ↑⟦↓ O joyful Spring! could bard repeat
The lay thou sing'st to human ⟨sols⟩souls

---

**49** "May–Day," 268?, 607, 609–16, x, x. Struck through five times in ink. Line (12) is struck through four times in pencil, probably to cancel it.

**51** "May–Day," 617–27. Struck through in ink with a large X.

**53** "May–Day," ten unused lines, 603–6. Lines (1–10) are bracketed and struck through in pencil.

Murmured on thy mountain airs,
Where thy gentle deluge rolls,
(5) And winter's wilderness repairs;
Summer hid in chilling clouds,
Day following day in lucent shrouds,
Each a porter of Jove's fire,
Charged to burn the willing earth
(10) With love & impulse, tilth & birth. ↑〛↓
Soft on the south wind sleeps the haze,
So on thy broad mystic van
Lie the opal-colored days,
And waft the miracle to man

[54] [blank]
[55] We hear no words, our sense they balk,
See not the legs on which they walk,
Skirts are not lifted from the feet
Of Isis reverend & sweet,
(5) But comes the high procession duly,
↑〚↓ On carpets green the maskers march
Below May's well-appointed arch,
Each star, each god, each grace amain,
Every joy & virtue speed,
(10) Marching duly in her train,
And fainting Nature at her need
Is made whole again. ↑〛↓

[56] It is not a mile of rosetrees
It is not a ⟨a⟩concert
Nor the popes choir
That we ⟨require⟩ ↑desire↓
(5) But one beam to penetrate

Hafiz
Its passion the ⟨wild⟩ ↑shy↓ violet
From Hafiz never hides
Lovelongings of the raptured bird
The bird to him confides

---

55 "May–Day," five unused lines, 351–57. Struck through three times in ink. The brackets in lines (6) and (12) are in ink over pencil; see p. [27].
56 "It is not a mile of rosetrees" (1–5); "Hafiz" (6–9). In pencil.

# Notebook ETE Verses

Notebook ETE Verses contains fair copies of poems written in the 1850s and 1860s, many of them copied here in 1867 or later, perhaps as late as 1875 when it was used in planning *Selected Poems,* published in 1876. The notebook itself may have been begun much earlier to gather Emerson's memories of his first wife, Ellen Tucker Emerson; the month and year of her birth are entered on the flyleaf, and prose passages about her on pp. 11–12 and 23 are copied from an 1839 journal and an 1833 letter. "Verses" was added separately below "ETE" on the front cover, probably when Emerson began to use the notebook for poetry, but he usually referred to the notebook simply as "ETE."

The covers of notebook ETE Verses, blue paper over boards, measure 15.7 × 20 cm. The spine strip is of maroon leather, stamped with six pairs of gold bands. "ETE" and "Verses" are written on the front cover, set off by rules above and below.

The inside front cover, front and back flyleaves (pp. i–ii, 179–80) and inside back cover are blue paper. The 184 pages measure 15.3 × 19.3 cm, of which pp. 1–4 and 175–78 are unlined; the rest are lined with twenty-five lines to the page.

One hundred and twenty-two pages are numbered in pencil, and two in both pencil and ink; the rest are unnumbered. Emerson repeated page numbers 50 and 51. Fifty-two pages are misnumbered, usually by two, and corrected in pencil: 24, 42, 82, 92, 102–5, 110–16 (misnumbered as 190–96), 118, 120, 122, 124–26 (misnumbered as 198, 200, 202, 204–6), 132, 134–35, 142–44, 146, 148–58, 160–62, 164, 166, 168, 170, 172–76, and 178. Page 126 is also corrected in ink; p. 159 is misnumbered 157 and not corrected. One hundred and twenty pages are blank.

The notebook contains the following enclosures in Emerson's hand:

(1) between pp. 30–31, a sheet of white letter paper folded to make four pages measuring 12.3 × 19.4 cm, inscribed with a tentative table of contents for *Selected Poems* (here numbered 30ₐ–30_d); pasted to the bottom of p. 30_d is a half sheet, once folded, measuring 12.8 × 12.8 cm, inscribed on one side with titles of "Questionable" poems for *Selected Poems* (here numbered 30ₑ);

(2) between pp. 32–33, a slip of white paper torn off from a larger sheet to measure 10 × 13.2 cm, once folded, inscribed on one side with "*Proposed Additions*" to the contents of *Selected Poems* (here numbered 32ₐ);

(3) and (4) between pp. 56–57, a sheet of white letter paper folded to make four pages measuring 12.2 × 19.5 cm, inscribed on both rectos (here numbered 56ₐ–56_b), and a sheet of white paper, lined in blue on the recto, torn off along a fold at the left to measure 19.4 × 24.5 cm, with a stationer's mark ("L.L.B & P" enclosed in an ornate rectangle) in the upper left corner, numbered "7" in pencil and inscribed on both sides (here numbered 56_c–56_d);

(5) between pp. 74–75, a slip of white laid paper torn off from a larger sheet at the right side and bottom to measure 10.1 × 12.6 cm, once folded, inscribed on the recto (here numbered 74$_a$);

(6) between pp. 78–79, a sheet of white letter paper torn off at a fold at the left to measure 12.2 × 19.5 cm, inscribed on the verso (here numbered 78$_a$);

(7) and (8) between pp. 104–5, a sheet of the same white letter paper as p. 78$_a$, inscribed on both sides (here numbered 104$_a$–104$_b$), and a sheet of blue laid letter paper torn off at the right to measure 13.2 × 20.8 cm, once folded in three and again in the middle, inscribed on both sides (here numbered 104$_c$–104$_d$).

A scrap of paper inscribed "Broom" and "Ironing sheet," possibly by Emerson, on the Houghton photocopy of this notebook between pp. 18–19, has not been found.

A number of materials not in Emerson's hand are laid in at several points: between pp. 52–53 a sheet of white paper bearing copies of "Teach me your mood," "Voluntaries" lines 93–96, "The Exile," "Ah! not to me," "I found this" lines 9–18, and "Eros"; between pp. 62–63 a proofsheet of "The Last Farewell" by Emerson's brother Edward for *May–Day*, 1867; between pp. 68–69 a newspaper clipping about the "semi-centennial" in 1839 of the inauguration of Washington, quoting an ode by William Cullen Bryant; and between pp. 142–43 a sheet of white paper bearing a copy of "Maiden Speech of the Aeolian Harp."

[front cover]

ETE

↑══════↓
↑Verses.↓
↑══════↓

[front cover verso] [blank]
[i] E. T. E.

[ii]          Catalogue of poems. p. 2

          June 1811

[1]                                              R. W. Emerson.

[2] 1  Sphinx
    2  Each & All
    3  Problem
    4  Visit
    5  Uriel
    6  Rhea
    7  World Soul
    8  Alphonzo
    9  Mithridates
   10  Saadi
   ⟨11⟩ ↑10½↓  May Day
   ⟨10¾  The Harp⟩
   11  Rhodora
   12  Humble Bee
   13  Titmouse
   14  Snowstorm
   15  Forerunners
   16  Hamatreya
   17  Brahma
   18  Astraea
   19  Etienne de la Boece
   20  Forbearance
   21  Letters
   22  Sursum Corda
   23  Ode to Beauty
   24  Give All to Love
   25  Romany Girl
   26  Fate

ii In pencil.
  2 The list of poems, in almost the order printed in *Selected Poems*, 1876, is in lightly erased pencil in three columns beginning 1, 28, and 53. Earlier lists appear on pp. [30ₐ]–[30ₑ] below and in Poems folder 31.

27 Guy
28 To Eva
29 Amulet
↑29½ Harp↓
30 Hermione
31 Initial Daemonic & Celestial Love
32 Sea-Shore
33 Merlin
34 Bacchus
35 ⟨Woodnotes⟩The Harp
↑36 Woodnotes↓
36↑½↓ ⟨‖ . . . ‖⟩Monadnoc
37 Mountain & Squirrel
37½ Two Rivers
38 Waldeinsamkeit
39 Song of Nature
    Harp
40 Xenophanes
41 Musketaquid
42 Day's Ration
43 Experience
↑44 Days↓
↑45 My Garden↓
46 Aeolian Harp, Maiden Speech
47 Friendship
48 Beauty
49 Manners
50 Eros
51 Art
52 Worship
53 ⟨Aspiration⟩
52½ The Nun's Prayer
54 Terminus
55 Ordination Hymn
56 Concord Hymn
57 Boston Hymn
58 Fourth July
59 Voluntaries
60 Dirge
61 Threnody
62 Boston

3 "Fate" ("That you are fair"), 40–41, 40. "Nor wh" is in erased pencil. Lines (1–2) are struck through twice in ink; line (3) is in pencil.

[3] *Corrections of New Edition of Poems*

"Fate." 1st Vol. p. 47 ⟨Nor wh⟩
> Nor whether your name is baser or braver
> Nor for the fashion of your behavior

> Whether your name's renowned or low

[4]–[6] [blank]

[7]       ⟨Ever⟩ ↑Doth not↓ the *Rock of Ages* melt⟨s⟩
> Into the liquid air,
> To be the quarry whence is built
> Thought & its mansion fair.

———

(5)       No ⟨F⟩fate save by the victim's fault is low,
> For God hath writ all dooms magnificent,
> So guilt not traverses his tender will.

———

[8]                          *Life.*
> A train of gay and clouded days
> Dappled with joy and grief & praise,
> Beauty to ↑/fire/burn/↓ us, saints to save,
> Escort us to a little grave.

[9]       The sun athwart the cloud thought it no sin
> To use my land to put his rainbow in.

[10] [blank]

[11]            Letter from C.C. Emerson to Elizabeth Hoar.

7 Dec 1833. I said I left the miniature for your Sunday's study; Yes—and it was a life that was like a serene Sabbath that gave to its beautiful Original that rare grace of form & manners & character. You will not be displeased that I dwell so fondly on the image that is in my mind of Ellen. It is an Ideal that, if ⟨w⟩I were a Platonist, I should believe to have been one of the Forms of Beauty in the Universal Mind. She moved ever in an atmosphere of her own, a crystal sphere, & nothing vulgar in neighboring persons & circumstances touched her. Light fell on her from heaven where her conversation was; she was nursed in solitude, & she brought away from it what it scarcely ever fails to bestow on fine minds, a self collected temper of Soul, an unstudied dignity of mien & air, which, without violating the law [12] of love, repels too near an approach.

---

7 "Ever the Rock of Ages melts" (1–4); "No fate, save by the victim's fault" (5–7). Lines (5–7) are in pencil.

8 "Life." In line (3), Emerson left a space after "Beauty to" and added both "fire" and "burn" in pencil.

9 "The sun athwart the cloud."

[13]–[14] [blank]

[15]                       *April.*

The April winds are magical
And thrill our tuneful frames ↑ ; ↓
The garden walks are passional
To bachelors and dames.

(5)      The hedge is gemmed with diamonds,
The air with Cupids full,
The clues of fairy Rosamonds
Guide lovers to the pool.
Each dimple in the water,

(10)    Each leaf that shades the ⟨brook⟩rock
Can cozen, pique, and flatter,
Can parley & provoke.
Goodfellow, Puck, & goblins
Know more than any book,

(15)    Down with your doleful problems,
And court the sunny brook.
The south winds are quick-witted,
The schools are sad & slow,
The masters quite omitted

(20)    The lore we care to know.

[16]                 ⟨*Cupido.*⟩ ↑ Eros. ↓

The solid solid Universe
Is pervious to Love,
With bandaged eyes he never errs
Around, below, above.

(5)      His blinding light
He flingeth white
On God's and Satan's brood,
And reconciles
By mystic wiles

(10)    The evil and the good.

[17]–[18] [blank]

[19]                 *Aeolian Harp.*

Soft & soft⟨er⟩lier hold me, friends,—
Thanks if your genial care
Unbind and give me to the air.
Keep your lips or finger-tips

(5)      For flute or spinnet's dancing chips;
I await a tenderer touch,

15  "April." In line (2), the semicolon is in pencil.
16  "Cupido." "*Cupido.*" is canceled, and "Eros." added, in pencil.
19  "Maiden Speech of the Aeolian Harp."

I ask more, or not so much:
Give me to the atmosphere,—
Where is the wind my brother,—where?
(10) Lift the sash, lay me within,
Lend me your ears, and I begin.
For gentle harp to gentle hearts
The secret of the world imparts;
And not today, & not tomorrow,
(15) Can drain its wealth of hope and sorrow,
But day by day to loving ear
Unlocks new sense and loftier cheer.
I've come to live with you, sweet friends;
This home my minstrel-journeying ends.
(20) Many & subtle are my lays,
The latest better than the first,
For I can mend the happiest days,
And charm the anguish of the worst.

[20]                         *Water.*
The Water understands
Civilization well—
It wets my foot, but prettily,
It chills my life, but wittily,
(5) It is not disconcerted,
It is not broken-hearted,
Well used, it decketh joy,
Adorneth, doubleth joy;
Ill-used it will destroy
(10) In perfect time and measure,
With a face of golden pleasure,
Elegantly destroy.

[21]                 Inscription on a Well in Memory
                    of the Martyrs of the War.

───────

Fall stream from Heaven to bless: return as well;
So did our sons; Heaven met them as they fell.

───────

[22] [blank]
    [23] Ellen was never alone. I could not imagine her poor & solitary.
She was like a tree in flower. So much soft budding informing beauty

20 "Water."
21 "Inscription on a Well in Memory of the Martyrs of the War."
23 See JMN 7:168.

586

was society for itself, & she taught the eye that beheld her, why Beauty was ever painted with loves & graces attending her steps.
Feb. 1839.

[24]–[26] [blank]
[27] ======

> Ah! not to me these dreams belong,
> A better voice sings through my song.

======

> Thus the high Muse treated me—
> Directly never greeted me,
(5)
> But when she spread her dearest spells,
> Feigned to speak to some one else;
> I was free to overhear,
> Or I might at will forbear;
> Not the less that casual word,
(10)
> Thus at random overheard,
> Was the symphony of spheres,
> And proverb of a thousand years.

======

> Quoth Saadi, when I stood before
> Hassan the camel-driver's door,
(15)
> I scorned the fame of Timour brave,—
> Timour to Hassan was a slave.
> In every glance of Hassan's eye
> I read great years of victory;
> And I, who cower mean and small
(20)
> In the frequent interval
> When Wisdom not with me resides,
> Worship toil's wisdom that abides;
> I shunned his eye,—the faithful man's,
> I shunned the toiling Hassan's glance.

======

[28] [blank]
[29]
> On the chamber, on the stairs,
> Lurking dumb,
> Go and come
> ↑The↓ Lemurs and ↑the↓ Lars.

(5)
> I have an arrow that can find its mark,
> A mastiff that will bite without a bark.

27 "Ah! not to me" (1–2); "I found this," 9–18 (3–12); "Said Saadi,—When I stood before" (13–24).
29 "On the chamber" (1–4); "I have an arrow" (5–6).

[30]     "Success shall be in thy courser tall
         Success in thyself which is best of all—"
                         Svend Vonved

         From high to higher forces
         The scale of power uprears,
(5)      The heroes on their horses,
         The gods upon the spheres.

[30ₐ]          *Selected Poems*
         The Sphinx      I. ↑p. 7↓
         The Problem     I. ↑17↓
         Each and All    I. ↑14↓
         To Rhea         I. ↑21↓
         The Visit    ↑25↓
         Uriel        ↑27↓
         ↑(↓Hamatrya↑)      53↓
         Rhodora   ↑59↓
         Humble Bee   ↑60↓
         Snow-storm   ↑65↓
         Etienne de la Boéce    ↑126↓
         Forbearance            ↑130↓
         Forerunners            ↑133↓
         Sursum Corda           ↑135↓
         Ode to Beauty          ↑136↓
         Give all to Love       ↑141↓
         To Eva                 ↑147↓
         Hermione               ↑151↓
[30ᵦ] ———
         Initial, Daemonic,
         and Celestial Love.   ↑156↓
         ———
         Saadi                 ↑197↓
         Musketaquid           ↑227↓
         Dirge                 ↑232↓
         Threnody              ↑236↓
         Hymn at Concord Monument   ↑250↓

30 " 'Success shall . . . Vonved" is in pencil; the lines are from "Svend Vonved," translated by George Borrow in *Romantic Ballads, translated from the Danish; and Miscellaneous Pieces* (London, 1826), p. 64, and are used in "Success," W 7:287. See JMN 13:380 and 14:257. Following the quotation is "From high to higher forces" (3–6).

30ₐ The list of poems laid in between pp. [30]–[31] is probably the earliest of three such lists for *Selected Poems*, 1876; another headed "For reprinting" (Poems folder 31) is followed by the near-final table of contents on p. [2] above. The additions, in pencil, give the page numbers of these poems in *Poems*, 1847 ("I").

30ᵦ The additions, page numbers in *Poems*, 1847, and *May–Day*, 1867 ("Vol II"), are in pencil.

Vol II     Brahma     ↑65↓
        ⟨Ode⟩Fourth of July Ode in Concord    ↑72↓
        Boston Hymn    ↑75↓
        Voluntaries    ↑81↓
        Lover's Petition        ↑90↓
        Letters            ↑94↓
        Romany Girl       ↑109↓
        Days              ↑111↓
        ⟨Two⟩

[30c]     The Titmouse       ↑II 119↓
        Seashore          ↑II ⟨119⟩125↓
        Song of Nature     ↑II 128↓
        Two Rivers         ↑II 134↓
        Terminus          ↑II 146↓
Search for Beauty       ↑II 168↓
        Manners          ↑II 170↓
        Art               ↑II 172↓
        Worship           ↑II 176↓
        Friendship         ↑II. 166↓
        Compensation      ↑II 159↓
        Boston          ↑Atlantic↓
        Cupido          ⟨↑Atlantic↓⟩
        ↑Guy↓

           1827
             37
             47
             57
            6⟨6⟩7
             76

[30d] [arithmetic omitted]

[30e]           *Questionable*
        The World Soul       I. 30
        Alphonso of Castille.    I. 36
        Mithridates    I. 41
        Fate       ⟨2⟩I. 45
↑1↓     Guy          I. 48
        Wood Notes, I & II   I. 67
        Monadnoc       I. 94

30c The additions are in pencil; the numbers refer to pages in *May–Day,* 1867. "Friendship" was inscribed below "Cupido," circled in pencil, and a line drawn to indicate its placement between "Worship" and "Compensation." Beside "Cupido," "Atlantic" is erased.

30d In pencil.

30e "1," added in pencil in the left margin, may refer to either "Fate" or "Guy." Following "Wood Notes," "I & II" is circled in ink.

Fable ———squirrel I. 115,
Astraea             I. 123,
Compensation   ⟨2⟩II 159
Amulet              I. 148
Hymn⟨e⟩ at Second Church,

[31]–[32] [blank]
[32ₐ] *Proposed Additions*
    April    15
    Amita

    May Day ↑Invitation↓
    The Miracle   154   ETE
    The Nun's Prayer (Amita)   102 E

[33]    Roomy Eternity
    Casts her schemes rarely,
    And an aeon allows
    For each quality and part
(5)    In the multitudinous
    And many-chambered heart.

    ══════

    The passing moment is an edifice
    Which the Omnipotent cannot rebuild.

    ══════

[34] [blank]
[35]          May.
    When all their blooms the meadows flaunt
    To deck the morning of the year,
    Why tinge thy lustres jubilant
    With forecast or with fear?

(5)    Softens the air so sharp and rude,
    What can the heart do less?
    If Earth put off her savage mood,
    Let us learn gentleness.

    The purple flame all bosoms girds,
(10)    And Love ascends his throne;
    I cannot hear your songs, O birds!
    For the witchery of my own.

32ₐ In pencil, except for "The Nun's Prayer," which is in ink. All the proposed additions are in notebook ETE, "April" on p. [15] above, "Amita" ("The Nun's Aspiration") and "May Day [Invitation]" on pp. [102] and [148] below.
   33 "Roomy Eternity" (1–6); "Now" (7–8).
   35 "When all their blooms" (1–4); "Softens the air" (5–8); "Who saw the hid beginnings," 21–28 (9–16).

Each human heart this tide makes free
To keep the golden day,
(15)    And ring the bells of jubilee
On its own First of May.

[36] [blank]
[37]          Fortune and Hope! I've made my port,
Farewell ye twin deceivers!
You've trained me many a weary chase,
Go cozen new believers.

[38]–[40] [blank]
[41]    The sun & moon shall fall amain
Like sower's seeds into his brain,
There quickened to be born again.

[42] [blank]
[43]          *Letters.*
The tongue is prone to lose the way,
Not so the pen, for in a letter
We have not better things to say,
But surely say them better.

(5)    All day the waves assailed the rock,
I heard no church-bell chime;
The sea-beat scorns the minster clock,
And breaks the glass of Time.

[44] [blank]
[45]    The beggar begs by God's command,
And gifts awake when givers sleep,
Swords cannot cut the giving hand,
Nor stab the love that orphans keep.

(5)    These rules were writ in human heart
By Him who built the day,—
The columns of the firmament
Not deeper ⟨fenced⟩based than they.

Methought the sky looked scornful down
(10)    On all was base in man,
And airy tongues did taunt the town
'Achieve us if you can.'

[46]    If bright the sun, he tarries;

37 "Fortune & Hope."
41 "Charmed from fagot," 5–7. In pencil.
43 "Letters" ("The tongue") (1–4); "All day the waves" (5–8).
45 "Alms" (1–4); "The rules to men" (5–8); "In my garden three ways meet," 21–24 (9–12).
46 "If bright the sun."

All day his song is heard;
And when he goes, he carries
No more baggage than a bird.

[47]–[56] [twelve pages blank]
[56ₐ]    Peril around all else appalling,
Cannon in front, and leaden rain,
Him Duty through the clarion calling
To the van ↑called↓ not ⟨called⟩ in vain.

[56ᵦ]          *Eros.*
The solid solid Universe
Is pervious to Love,
With bandaged eyes he never errs
Around, below, above:
(5)    His blinding light
He flingeth white
On God's and Satans brood,
And reconciles
By mystic wiles
(10)    The evil and the good.

[56ᵪ]       ↑J↑.↓ H↑olmes.↓↓
With these there came a humorist
Kind hearted, gentle, gay,
Caressing his infirmities
As cossets for his play;
(5)    As gentle as a maid
Yet with a bold address
Which still surprised to lead
Such maskéd tenderness.
And he had skill to give
(10)    To his walking-stick or chair,
Or to his least affair,
A price superlative.
He was ⟨b⟩ there to lend a grace
To a rude & savage place;
(15)    Such his proper merits shone,
That it needed not be known
[56_d]    He was twin in mind & blood
To the man of merriest mood,

56ₐ "Voluntaries," four lines first printed in the 1876 version.
56ᵦ "Cupido."
56ᵪ "The Adirondacs," sixteen unused lines. In the title, "J H" is in pencil, expanded in ink
with a fine pen. Written in the upper right corner is "7".
56_d "The Adirondacs," seven unused lines.

And of keenest point & edge,
And of the muses' privilege,—
(5)  Skilled to show the fair & fit,
Who fills all Saxon minds
With his redundant fancy & his wit.

[57]–[58] [blank]
[59]   They strew in the path of kings & czars
        Jewels & pearls of price,
      But for thy head I will pluck down stars,
        And pave thy way with eyes.

(5)    I have sought for thee a costlier dome
        Than Mahmoud's palace high,
      And thou returned shall find thy home
        In the apple of love's eye.

[60]–[74] [blank]
[74ₐ]   Amer[ica]
        Ocean a sieve

––––––

Saucy independence shines in all eyes so that even the lawlessness of
the Celts is good as a check. I have great trust in the immense force
with which interests gravitate   Elements of crime are in every body
yet the ⟨inn⟩ streets are full of innocent people & only now & then an
outrage.

[75]–[78] [blank]
[78ₐ]   Teach me your mood, O patient stars!
      Who climb each night the ancient sky,
      Leaving on space no shade, no scars,
      No trace of age, no fear to die.

[79]   With the key of the secret he marches faster
      From strength to strength, and for night brings day,
      While classes or tribes too weak to master
      The flowing conditions of life, give way.

[80]–[99] [blank]
[100]        But oh! these waves & leaves↑,—↓
      When haply stoic Nature grieves—
      No human speech so beautiful
      As their murmurs mine to lull.

59 "They strew in the path of kings and czars."
74ₐ In pencil.
78ₐ "Teach me your mood."
79 "With the key of the secret."
100 "The Nun's Aspiration," 11–28. The added punctuation in line (1) is in pencil.

593

(5)        On this altar God hath built
                I lay my vanity and guilt,
                Nor me can Hope or Passion urge
                Hearing as now the lofty dirge
                Which blasts of Northern mountains hymn,
(10)      Nature's funeral high and dim,—
                Sable pageantry of clouds,
                Mourning summer laid in shrouds.
                      Many a day shall dawn & die,
                Many an Angel wander by,
(15)      And passing, light my sunken turf
                Moist perhaps by Ocean surf,
                Forgotten amid splendid tombs,
                Yet wreathed & hid by summer's blooms.

[101] [blank]
[102]          ⟨Amita.⟩   ↑Aspiration↓
                On earth I dream—I die to be:
                Time! shake not thy bald head at me.
                I challenge thee to ⟨fly too fast⟩hurry past,
                Or for my turn to fly too fast.
(5)        Think me not numbed, or halt with age,
                Or cares that earth to earth engage,
                Caught with love's cord of twisted beams,
                Or mired ⟨with⟩by climate's gross extremes:
                I tire of shadows, I rush to ⟨be⟩Be,—
(10)      I pass with yonder comet free;
                Pass with the comet into space
                Which mocks thy aeons to embrace;
                Aeons which tardily unfold
                Realm beyond realm, extent untold.
(15)      No early morn, no evening late,
                ↑Realm↓ Self up-held, disdaining Fate,
                Whose shining sons, too great for fame,
                Never heard thy weary name:
                Nor lives the tragic bard to say
(20)      How drear⟨y⟩ the part I held in one,
                How lame the other limped away.

[103]     ↑See also *NP* 130,↓

                The Yesterday doth never smile;
                Today goes drudging through, the while.

102  "The Nun's Aspiration," 29–49. In line (16), "Realm" is added in pencil.
103  "The Nun's Aspiration," 1–10, four unused lines. "See also *NP* 130," is added in pencil.
In line (13), Emerson left a space after "Paved for my" and later added "soul" in pencil.

Yet in the name of Godhead, I
The morrow front, and can defy:
(5)    Though I am weak, yet God, when prayed,
Cannot withhold his conquering aid.
Ah me! it was my childhood's thought,
If He should make my web a blot
On life's fair picture of delight,
(10)   My hearts content would find it right.

One balm remained, "It was foreknown";
Betide what might, that thought alone
Paved for my ↑soul↓ the dreary past
With gems more rich than kings amassed.

[104]   Easy to match what others do,
Perform the feat as well as they;
Hard to outdo the wise, the true,
And find a loftier way:
(5)    The School decays, the learning spoils
Because of the suns of wine;
How snatch the stripling from their toils?—
Yet can one ray of truth divine
The blaze of reveller's feasts outshine.

[104a]  The yesterday doth never smile,
Today goes drudging through the while,
Yet, in the name of Godhead, I
The morrow front & can defy:
(5)    Though I am weak, yet God, when prayed,
Cannot withhold his conquering aid.
Ah me! it was my childhood's thought
If he should make my web a blot
On life's fair picture of delight,
(10)   My heart's content would find it right.

[104b]  And the air echoes more than mortal love

*ML*    IV. p 131    148   218

[104c]  Around the man who seeks a noble end
Not angels but divinities attend.

---

104 "Easy to match what others do."
104a "The Nun's Aspiration," 1–10.
104b "And the air echoes more." In pencil.
104c "Around the man" (1–2); "Now" (3–4); "No fate, save by the victim's fault" (5–7);
"Heaven" (8–10); "His instant thought," 1–4, 1 (11–15).

This passing moment is an edifice
Which the Omnipotent cannot rebuild

————

(5)       No fate, save by the victim's fault, is low,
For God hath writ all dooms magnificent,
So guilt not traverses his tender will.

————

O what is Heaven but the fellowship
Of minds that each can stand against the world
(10)     By its own meek but incorruptible will?

————

The poet spoke his instant thought
And filled the Age his fame,
As Jove's bolt struck an inch of ground
And lit the sky with flame

————

(15)     ⟨His instant thought a poet spoke⟩

[104ᵈ]      18 Jan     Sir Andrew Burton     Hunt *DO* 67

[105]–[106] [blank]
[107]   Its passion the shy violet
From Hafiz never hides,
Love-longings of the raptured bird
The bird to him confides.
                *Hafiz.*

[108]–[111] [blank]
[112]   O sun! take off thy hood of clouds,
O land! take off thy chain,
And fill the world with happy mood
And love from main to main.

(5)       Ye shall not on this charter day
Disloyally wit↑h↓hold
Their household rights from captive men
By pirates bought & sold.

Ah little knew the innocent
(10)     In throes of birth forlorn,
That wolves & foxes waited for
Their victim to be born.

104ᵈ "Sir Andrew . . . 67" is inscribed in pencil at the bottom of the page, upside down with respect to "18 Jan."
107 "Hafiz."
112 "O sun! take off."

[113]–[131] [blank]

[132]         I care not where I am or go,
Or if my task be high or low,
Work to hide, or proudly show,
Or if my mates shall be my peers,
(5)         Or only rare-met travellers;
Whether I pace the shop-lined street,
Or lofty square where statesmen meet
Eyeing the city at their feet,
With secret pride to rule the town
(10)      And shire on which the dome looks down.

[133]–[134] [blank]

[135]     With the key of the secret he marches faster
From strength to strength, and for night brings day,
While classes or tribes too weak to master
The flowing conditions of life give way.

[136] [blank]

[137]                   ↑ *Refrains.* ↓

———

Go purge your blood in lake & wood
To honor born of hardihood.

———

For never will die the captive's cry
On the echoes of God, till right draws nigh.

———

(5)     Ring your bells backward, loyal towers!
And warn the land of harm.

———

What slave shall dare a name to wear
Once Freedom's passport everywhere?

———

An union then of honest men
(10)   Or union never more again.

———

Go purge your blood in lake & wood
To ⟨h⟩Honor born of hardihood.

———

For power & place they sell their race,
And kiss the hands of statesmen base.

———

132 "I care not whither," 1–6, x, 7–9.
135 "With the key of the secret."
137 "Boston," four unused lines (1–4); "Ring your bells backward" (5–6); "Boston," x, x, two lines first printed in *Selected Poems,* 1876, four unused lines, 108–9 (7–16). "*Refrains.*" is added in pencil.

(15)     For you can teach the lightning speech
         And round the globe your voices reach.

         ⟨Wh⟩

[138]–[141] [blank]
[142]              ⟨Wind⟩Aeolian Harp.                    1 Jan. 1868.
                   Soft & softlier hold me, friends!
         Thanks if your genial care
         Unbind and give me to the air.
         Keep your lips or finger-tips
(5)      For flute or spinnet's dancing chips;
         I await a tenderer touch,
         I ask more or not so much:
         Give me to the atmosphere,—
         Where is the Wind my brother, ↑—↓ where?
(10)     Lift the sash, lay me within,
         Lend me your ears, and I begin.
         For gentle harp to gentle hearts
         The secret of the world imparts;
         And not today, and not tomorrow
(15)     Can drain its wealth of hope & sorrow,
         But day by day to loving ear
         Unlocks new sense & loftier cheer.
              I've come to live with you, sweet friends;
         This home my minstrel journeying ends.
(20)     Many and subtle are my lays,
         The latest better than the first,
         For I can mend the happiest days,
         And charm the anguish of the worst.

[143]–[144] [blank]
[145]         My tongue is prone to lose the way,
         Not so my pen, for in a letter
         We have not better things to say,
         But surely put them better.

[146] [blank]
[147]                   May Day.
         When all their blooms the meadows flaunt
         To deck the morning of the year
         Why tinge thy lustres jubilant
         With forecast or with fear?
(5)      Softens the air so sharp and rude,

142 "Maiden Speech of the Aeolian Harp."
145 "Letters" ("The tongue").
147 "When all their blooms" (1–4); "Softens the air" (5–8); "Who saw the hid beginnings,"
21–28 (9–16).

What can the heart do less?
If ⟨e⟩Earth put off her savage mood,
Let us learn gentleness.

(10)    The purple flame all bosoms girds
And Love ascends his throne,—
I cannot hear your songs, O birds!
For the witchery of my own.

Each human heart this tide makes free
To keep the golden day,
(15)    And ring the bells of jubilee
On its own First of May.

---

[148]               *May-Day.*
In yonder city rich and old
Where men toil much for little gold,
In vault or garret, wharf or raft,
At their sweat & handicraft,
(5)    One sultry morn beyond compare
Wafted sweet teachings of the air,
Which no town-walls can qu⟨i⟩ite exclude,
Nor streets of fops, nor draymen rude.
Up the High Street in market din
(10)    A joyful May-cart trundled in;
Green boughs with cage of singing birds,
And rope of twisted vines that girds
With festoons all the cart around,
Whilst country boys with willow pipes made all the air
        resound.

(15)    It hal⟨e⟩ted mid the gathering crowd;—
"We Fairfield folk," one cried aloud,
"Proclaim to all who listen may
A three days↑'↓ woodland holiday;
It is our annual village use
(20)    To give toil amnesty and truce,
And we invite all worthy people
To rendezvous at Fairfield steeple

[149]    Up! and we take you to the woods,
Parks where no shop or mill intrudes:
We guide you to the Red-Trout brook,
And ponds where perch swim to the hook;

**148**  "May Day [Invitation]," 1–22. In line (18), the added apostrophe is in pencil.
  **149**  "May Day [Invitation]," 23–42; "Where the fungus broad & red," 12–16, 19 (15–20).
The added punctuation in lines (6), (12–15), (17), and (19) is in pencil.

(5)        Or you shall climb the hill, & rouse
Rabbit or hare ↑ , ↓ pigeon or grouse ↑ — ↓
This year we have a mended clime,
The Spring arrived before its time;
The blue-birds sang in February,

(10)     And now the peach blooms, & the cherry⟨,⟩.
We woke this morn before the day,
The thrush had never so much to say ↑ ; ↓
The morning cobwebs showed no storm ↑ , ↓
The robin listened for the worm ↑ , ↓

(15)     The fungus & the bulrush spoke ↑ , — ↓
Answered the pine-tree & the oak;
The subtle South blew down the glen ↑ , ↓
Filled the straits, & filled the wide,
The maple-leaf turned up its silver side ↑ : ↓

(20)     Lawns glimmer in the smoky ray
[150]    And all we see are pictures high,
Valley deep, & steep hill-side,
Which oaks of pride
Climb to their tops,

(5)        And boys run out upon their leafy ropes.

Why reek in towns of beetling roofs
Jammed by cart-wheels & dray-horse hoofs,
Suck cholera from pavements foul,
Drink tainted water from the ⟨lo⟩bowl

(10)     When scented fields expanding nigh,
Uplifted hills, inviolate sky,
Invite ↑ you to their revelry. ↓

Obey our summons, one and all,
To join our woodland festival."

(15)     —The crowd cheered Master and Man;
The elders nod,—boys jumped & ran;
The town emptied like a prison
To the fields & broad horizon;
Age hobbled forth upon his crutch,

(20)     Uprose the porter, & the drudge,
The pauper crept out from his hutch;
[151]    The baker's boy let cool his oven,
The spinner left h⟨is⟩er web unwoven,
Nor man nor maid, nor child would stay
From the Festival of May.

150 "May Day [Invitation]," 43–63; "Where the fungus broad & red," 20–24 (1–5). The addition in line (12) is in pencil overwritten in ink; the period is only in ink.
151 "May Day [Invitation]," 64–67.

[152]                    ↑ James R. ↓ Lowell

Verses read by me at the Saturday Club ↑, on the
Anniversary of ↓ Lowell's birth-day 1859, February 22.

The bard has reached the middle date:
Stars tonight that culminate
Shed beams fair and fortunate.
Go, inquire his horoscope,—
(5)      Half of Memory, half of hope.
                What said the Sibyl?
                What was the fortune
                She sung for him?—
                *Strength for the hour!*

(10)     Man of marrow, man of mark,
Virtue lodged in sinew stark,
Rich supplies, and never stinted,
More behind at need is hinted,—
Never cumbered with the morrow,
(15)     Never knew corroding sorrow,
Too well gifted to have found
Yet his opulence's bound;
Most at home in mounting fun,
Beaming joke and luckiest pun,
(20)     Masking in the mantling tones
Of his rich laugh-loving voice,
[153]    In speeding troops of social joys,
And in volleys of wild mirth,
Purer metal, rarest worth,
Logic, passion, cordial zeal,
(5)      Such as bard and hero feel.

*Strength for the hour!*
For the day sufficient power;
Well-advised, too easily great
His large fleece to antedate.
(10)     But, if another temper come,
If on the sun shall creep a gloom,
A time and tide more exigent,
When the old mounds are torn and rent,
More proud, more strong competitors
(15)     Marshal the lists for emperors,—
↑ — ↓ Then the pleasant bard will know

152 "James Russell Lowell," 34–38, 44–59.
153 "James Russell Lowell," 60–80.

To put the frolic mask behind him,
Like an old summer cloak,
And in sky-born mail to bind him,
(20)      And single-handed cope with Time,
And parry and deal the thunderstroke.

[154]         *The Miracle.*
I have trod this path a hundred times
With idle footsteps, crooning rhymes,
I know each nest & web-worms tent;
The fox-hole which the woodchucks rent
(5)      Maple & oak, the old "divan,"
Self-planted twice like the banian;
I know not why I came again
Unless to learn it ten times ten⟨,⟩.
To read the sense the woods impart,
(10)     You must bring the throbbing heart;
Love is aye the counterforce,
Terror, & Hope, & wild ⟨r⟩Remorse.
Newest knowledge, fiery thought,
Or Duty to grand purpose wrought.

(15)         Wandering yester-morn the brake,
I reached the margin of the lake,
And oh! the wonder of the power,
The deeper secret of the hour!—
[155]    Nature, the supplement of Man,
His hidden sense interpret can,—
What friend to friend cannot convey
Shall the dumb bird instructed say.
(5)      Passing yonder oak, I heard
Sharp accents of my woodland bird,—
I watched the singer with delight,—
But mark what changed my joy to fright,
When that bird sang, I gave the theme,—
(10)     That wood-bird sa⟨w⟩ng my last night's dream,
A brown wren was the Daniel
That pierced my trance its drift to tell;
↑It↓ Knew my quarrel, how and why,
Published it to lake and sky,—
(15)     Told every word and syllable
In his flippant chirping babble,
All my wrath, & all my shames,
Nay, Heaven be witness,—gave the names.

154 "The Miracle," 1–18.
155 "The Miracle," 19–36.

[156]          ↑*Adirondacs*↓
⟨And if⟩ ↑Wise & polite, & if I drew↓
Their several portraits, you would own
Chaucer had no such worthy crew,
Nor Boccace in Decameron

              J *Stillman.*
(5)     Gallant artist, head & hand,
        Adopted of Tahàwas grand,
        In the wild domesticated,
        Man and mountain rightly mated,
        Like forest child the forest ranged,
(10)    Or, as one who had exchanged,
        After ↑the↓ old Indian mode,
        Totem, ⟨&⟩and bow, and spear,
        In sign of peace & brotherhood,
        With some Indian peer.
(15)    Easily chief↑, needs no relief,↓
        Can hunt, and fish, & rule, & row,
        And outshoot each in his own bow,
[157]   And paint, and plan, and execute.

        Easily chief, who held
        The key of each occasion,
        Earning richly for his share,
(5)     Of our band the Governor's chair,
        In our designed plantation.
        Bore the day's duties in his head,
        And with living method sped.
        Firm, unperplexed,
(10)    By no flaws of temper vexed,
        Inspiring trust,
        And only dictating because he must.
        All ↑forms↓ he carried in his heart
        He could publish and define
(15)    Orderly, and line by line,
        On canvas, by his art.
            I could wish
        So worthy master worthier pupils had,
        I doubt the best were bad

[158] [blank]
[159]   The sun athwart the cloud thought it no sin
        To use my land to put his rainbows in

156 "The Adirondacs," motto (1–4), thirteen unused lines (5–17). "*Adirondacs . . .*
Decameron" and the addition in line (15) are in pencil.
    157 "The Adirondacs," nineteen unused lines.
    159 "The sun athwart the cloud." Erased pencil, struck through in pencil.

[160]–[165] [blank]

[166]                    ↑John Holmes↓
                      ↑———————↓

With these there came a humorist
Kind hearted, gentle, gay,

Caressing his infirmities
As cossets for his play;
(5)         As gentle as a maid,
Yet with a bold address
Which still surprised to lead
Such maskèd tenderness.
And he had skill to give
(10)        To his walking-stick or chair
Or to his least affair
A price superlative.
He was there to lend a grace
To a rude and savage place;
(15)        Such his proper merits shone
That it needed not be known
He was twin in mind & blood
To the man of merriest mood;
And of keenest point & edge,
[167]       And of the Muses' privilege,
Skilled to show the fair and fit,
Who feeds all Saxon minds
With his redundant fancy & his wit.

[168] [blank]
[169]                    Wyman
Science & sense
Without pretence,
He did what he essayed,
His level gun will hit the white,
(5)         His cautious tongue will speak the right,
Of that be none afraid.

[170]       Around the man who seeks a noble end
Not angels but divinities attend.

The sun & moon shall fall amain
Like sowers seeds into his brain,
(5)         There quickened to be born again.

166 "The Adirondacs," nineteen unused lines. "John Holmes" and the rule below it are in pencil.
167 "The Adirondacs," four unused lines.
169 "The Adirondacs," six unused lines. In pencil.
170 "Around the man" (1–2); "Charmed from fagot," 5–7 (3–5). Lines (3–5) are in pencil.

[171]  Peril around all else appalling,
Cannon in front, and leaden rain,
Him Duty through the clarion calling
To the front, ⟨not⟩ called ↑not↓ in vain.

(5)  The heavy blue chain
Of the boundless main
Lock up their prison door,
And the cannon's wrath
Forbid their path
(10)  On Ocean's azure floor.

Ring your bells backward, loyal towers!
And warn the land of harm.

[172]  Atom from atom yawns as far
As moon from earth, ⟨—⟩or star from star.

---

### Birds

[173]  The Yesterday doth never smile,
Today goes drudging through the while,
Yet in the name of Godhead, I
The Morrow front, & can defy;
(5)  Though I am weak, yet God, when prayed,
Cannot withhold his conquering aid.

Ah me! it was my childhood's thought,
If He should make my web a blot
On life's fair picture of delight,
(10)  My heart's content would find it right.

[174]                    *Now.*
This shining moment is an edifice
Which the Omnipotent cannot rebuild.

---

*Heaven.*
↑11↓ Oh what is Heaven but the fellowship
Of minds that each can stand against the world
(5)  By its own meek but incorruptible will?

---

⟨No fate save by the victims fault is low⟩

171 "Voluntaries," four lines first printed in the 1876 version (1–4); "The heavy blue chain"
(5–10); "Ring your bells backward" (11–12).
172 "Atom from atom yawns as far."
173 "The Nun's Aspiration," 1–10.
174 "Now" (1–2); "Heaven" (3–5); "No fate, save by the victim's fault," 1 (6). Single vertical
lines are drawn in pencil in the left margin beside lines (1–2) and (3–5); beside line (3), "11,"
added in pencil, is overwritten by the vertical line. Line (6) is heavily canceled with swirls in ink.

[175]                    ↑*Suum Cuique.*↓
              Wilt thou seal up the avenues of ill⟨,⟩?
              Pay every debt, as if God wrote the bill.
                        (Printed in "May Day," &c)

              ───────

              ↑The↓ Pain of love's a better fate
              Than the body's best estate.

              ───────

(5)           Future or Past no richer secret folds,
              O friendless Present! than thy bosom holds.

              ───────

              Teach me your mood, O patient stars!
              Who climb each night the ancient sky,
              Leaving on space no shade, no scars,
(10)          No trace of age, no fear to die.

              That each should in his house abide,
              Therefore was the world so wide

[176]         ↑"↓No fate, save by the victim's fault, is low,
              For God hath writ all dooms magnificent,
              So guilt not traverses ⟨h⟩His tender will.

──────────────

              Though Love repine, and Reason chafe,
(5)           I heard a voice without reply,—
              'Tis man's perdition to be safe,
              When for the truth he ought to die.'
                        ↑Printed in May Day↓

         ──────

              Shines the last Age; the next with hope is seen,
              Today slinks poorly off unmarked between;
(10)          Future or Past no richer secret folds,
              O friendless Present! than thy bosom holds.
                        ↑Printed in May Day ↑volume↓ ↓

         ──────

[177] [blank]
[178]–[179] [index material omitted]
[180] [blank]
[inside back cover] [blank]

175 " 'Suum Cuique' " ("Wilt thou") (1–2); "The pain of love" (3–4); "Heri, Cras, Hodie,"
3–4 (5–6); "Teach me your mood" (7–10); "That each should in his house abide" (11–12). In
the left margin, a bracket is drawn beside lines (1–2); two red pencil lines, possibly not Emer-
son's, are drawn beside lines (5–6); and a black pencil line is drawn beside lines (7–10). "Printed
in 'May Day,' &c" is partly circumscribed in ink.
176 "No fate, save by the victim's fault" (1–3); "Sacrifice" (4–7); "Heri, Cras, Hodie"
(8–11). The quotation mark in line (1) is in pencil. The additions following lines (7) and (11)
are circumscribed in ink.
178–79 These pages are reproduced in Plate 10.

# Additional Manuscripts

This section prints selected manuscripts of textual significance in the Poems folders in the Houghton Library, in other holdings in Houghton, and in individual libraries throughout the United States. Each text has been verified against the manuscripts with two exceptions, "Eve roved in Paradise" in Poems folder 172 and "Terminus" in the Yale University Library, which have been read against photocopy only.

Treatment of the manuscripts is the same as for the poetry notebooks, except that pagination is made consecutive within manuscripts, disregarding blank pages and Emerson's own page numbers, which sometimes derive from different stages of the text. (Emerson's page numbers are, however, given in the notes.)

When more than one manuscript is printed from a Poems folder, the order followed is that of presumed sequence of composition rather than of location in the folder, which is usually of no significance.

## "The Adirondacs" (Poems folder 24)

[1]                  ↑E. H.↓
         Not in vain did Fate dispense
         Generous heart & solid sense
         Staff on which the orphan leans
         /Force to ⟨make⟩ ↑build↓/Skilful to find means/ a leader sage
(5)       ⟨Stuff by which⟩ ↑on such stuff as he↓ ⟨society⟩
              ↑fraternity↓
         Stands from age to age
         In honor & self honoring
         Where ⟨thou art,⟩ ↑he dwells,↓ society
         Still will live & best will be.
(10)      One who does easily & well
         What costs the rest expense of brain
         In ⟨thee⟩ ↑him↓ ancestral merits dwell
         ↑And the cost remain↓
         And in ⟨thy⟩ ↑his↓ life ⟨the honored⟩ ↑his virtuous↓ sire
(15)      Will fill the stinted chalice higher
         And Fate repair
         The world's mishap
         And fill the gap
         By the completed virtues of the heir

(20)      ↑Skilled to adapt to ends the means↓

## "The Adirondacs" (Poems folder 40)

[1]                  H. W.
         Man of affairs
         Harmonizing oddest pairs
         With a passion to unite
         Oil & water if he might:
(5)       Fond of books, of genius fond,
         Loves each in turn, but looks beyond:
         Every merit has his vote
         In spite of class or nation;
         Filled with Shakspeare down to Choate,

1 "The Adirondacs," twenty unused lines. The title "E. H." and "remain" in line (13) are in pencil; before "Not" in line (1) is written "One", probably the beginning of an abortive line; in line (5), "Stuff by which" was canceled in ink, then "which society" canceled in pencil and "fraternity" written in pencil.

1 "The Adirondacs," eighteen unused lines. The period in line (17) is in pencil.

(10)       His catholic admiration
           Adoring Jesus can excuse Iscariot.
           We that know him
           Much we owe him
           Skilled to work in the Age of Bronze

(15)       Loves to turn it to account
           Of the helpless callow brood
           From the Muses' mount ↑.↓
           Skilled was he to reconcile
 [2]     Scientific feud,
           To pacify the wounded heart,
           And mollify the rude.
           Comes to ⟨n⟩succor the neglected
(5)        Till they blush to be respected,
           And was founder of the Club
           Most modest in the famous Hub.

           ↑ Man of anecdote & character ↓
           ↑ Too witty to annoy ↓
(10)       ↑ And every feast imperfect were ↓
           ↑ Without his arts of joy. ↓

## "The Adirondacs" (Houghton, Harvard)

[1]               Adirondac.
 ↑——↓Wise and polite,—and if I drew
           Their several portraits, you would own
           Chaucer had no such worthy crew,
           Nor Boccace in Decameron.

[2]        The Adirondacs.           August, 1858.

           We crossed Champlain to Keeseville with our friends,
           Thence, in strong country carts, rode up the forks
           Of the Ausable stream, intent to reach
           The Adirondac lakes. At Martin's beach,
(5)        We chose our boats, each man a boat & guide,
           Ten men, ten guides.

           Next morn, we swept with oars the Saranac,
           With skies of benediction, to Round Lake,
           Where all the sacred mountains drew around us,

---

2 "The Adirondacs," eleven unused lines. Lines (8–11) are in pencil.
1 "The Adirondacs," motto. Written below the last line to the right and canceled is "Ms".
2 "The Adirondacs," 1–15. "1" is written in ink in the upper right corner.

(10)        Taháwus, Seaward, Macintyre, Baldhead,
           And other Titans without Muse or name.
           Pleased with these grand companions, we glide on,
           Instead of flowers, crowned with a wreath of hills,
           And made our distance wider, boat from boat,
(15)        As each would hear the oracle alone.

[3]        By the bright morn the gay flotilla slid
           Through files of flags that gleamed like bayonets,
           Through purple beds of pickerel flower,
           Through scented banks of lilies white & gold,
(5)        Where the deer feeds at night,
           On through the Upper Saranac, & up
           Père Raquette stream, to a small tortuous pass
           Winding through grassy shallows in & out,
           Two creeping miles of rushes, pads, & sponge,
(10)        To Follansbee Water, & the Lake of Loons.

           Northward the length of Follansbee we rowed,
           Under low mountains, whose unbroken ridge
           Ponderous with beechen forest sloped the shore.
           A pause & council: then, where near the head
(15)        On the east, a bay makes inward to the land
           Between two rocky arms, we climb the bank
           And in the twilight of the forest noon
[4]        Wield the first axe these echoes ever heard.
           We cut young trees to make our poles & thwarts,
           Barked the white spruce to weatherfend the roof,
           Then struck a light, & kindled the camp-fire.

(5)          The wood was sovran with centennial trees
           Oak, cedar, maple, poplar, beech, & fir,
           Linden & spruce. In strict society
           Three conifers, white, pitch, & Norway pine,
           Five-leaved three-leaved & two-leaved grew thereby.
(10)        Our patron pine was fifteen feet in girth
           The maple measured eight.—

           "Welcome!" the wood god murmured through the leaves,
           "Welcome, though late, unknowing, yet known to me."
           Evening drew on, stars peeped through maple boughs,
(15)         Which o'erhung, like a cloud, our camping fire.
            Decayed millennial trunks, like moonlight flecks,
           Lit with phosphoric crumbs the forest floor.

3 "The Adirondacs," 16–32.
4 "The Adirondacs," 33–49.

[5]           Ten scholars wonted to lie warm & soft
In well-hung chambers daintily bestowed,
Lie here on hemlock boughs, like Sacs & Sioux,
And greet unanimous the joyful change.
(5)          So fast will Nature acclimate her sons,
Though late returning to her pristine ways.
Off soundings, seamen do not suffer cold,
And, in the forest, delicate clerks, unbrowned,
Sleep on the ⟨hemlock boughs⟩ ↑fragrant brush↓, as on
          down beds.
(10)       Up with the dawn, they fancied the light air
That circled freshly in their forest dress
Made them to boys again. Happier that they
Slipped of[f] their pack of duties, leagues behind,
At the first mounting of the giant stairs.
(15)       No placard on these rocks warned to the polls,
No doorbell heralded a visiter,
No courier waits, no letter came or went,
Nothing was ploughed, or reaped, or bought, or sold;
[6]           The frost might glitter, it would blight no crop,
The falling rain will spoil no holiday.
We were made freemen of the forest laws,
All drest, like Nature, fit for her own ends,
(5)          Essaying nothing she cannot perform.

                 In Adirondac lakes,
At morn or noon, the guide rows bareheaded:
Shoes, flannel shirt, & kersey trowsers make
His brief toilette: At night, or in the rain,
(10)       He dons a surcoat which he doffs at morn:
A paddle in the right hand, or an oar,
And, in the left, a gun, his needful arms.
By turns we praised the stature of our guides,
Their rival strength & suppleness, their skill
(15)       To row, to swim, to shoot, to build a camp,
To climb a lofty stem, clean without boughs
[7]           Full fifty feet, & bring the eaglet down:
Temper to face wolf, bear, ⟨&⟩or catamount,
And wit to trap or take him in his lair.
Sound ruddy men, frolic & innocent,
(5)          In winter, lumberers; in summer, guides;
Their sinewy arms pull at the oar untired
Three times ten thousand strokes, from morn to ev[e]

5 "The Adirondacs," 50–67. "4" is written in pencil and ink in the upper left corner.
6 "The Adirondacs," 68–83. "5" is written in pencil in the upper right corner.
7 "The Adirondacs," 84–102. "6" is written in ink in the upper left corner.

Look to yourselves, ye polished gentlemen.
No city airs or arts pass current here.
(10)    Your rank is all reversed: ⟨L⟩let men of cloth
Bow to the stalwart churls in overalls.
*They* are the doctors of the wilderness,
And we the low-prized laymen.
In sooth, red flannel is a saucy test
(15)    Which few can put on with impunity.
What make you, master, fumbling at the oar
Will you catch crabs? ↑Truth pricks all bubbles he[re]↓
The sallow knows the basket-maker's thumb,
The oar, the guide's. Dare you accept the tasks
[8]    ⟨He shall impose—to find a spring,⟩
He('ll set you,⟩ ↑shall impose, to↓ find a spring, trap foxes,
Tell ⟨⟨time⟩ ↑hours↓ by the sun,⟩ ↑the sun's time,↓ ⟨point⟩
    ↑determine↓ the true north,
    ↑Or↓ Stumbling ↑rush↓ through vast self-similar woods
(5)    To ⟨find⟩ ⟨↑thread↓⟩ ⟨↑grope↓⟩ ↑thread↓ by night the
    nearest way to camp?

Ask you, how went the hours?
All day we swept the lake↑,↓ ⟨with oars⟩ ↑searched every
    cove,↓
North from Camp Maple, ⟨S⟩south to Osprey Bay,
Watching when the loud dogs should drive in deer,
(10)    Or whipping its rough surface for a trout;
Or bathers, diving from the rock at noon;
Challenging Echo by our guns & cries;
Or listening to the laughter of the loon;
Or, in the evening twilight's latest red,
(15)    Beholding the procession of the Pines;
[9]    Or, later yet, beneath a lighted jack,
In the ↑boat's↓ bows↑,↓ ⟨of the boat,⟩ a silent night-hunter
Stealing with paddle to the feeding grounds
Of the red deer, to aim at a square mist.
(5)    Hark to that muffled roar! a tree in the wood[s]
Is fallen: but hush! it has not scared the buck
Who stands astonished at the meteor light,
Then turns to bound away,—is it too late?

Sometimes we tried our rifles at ↑a↓ mark,
(10)    Six rods, sixteen, twenty, or forty five;

8 "The Adirondacs," 103, 103–16. In line (4), "Or" and "rush" are in pencil. "7" is written in ink in the upper right corner.
    9 "The Adirondacs," 117–33. In line (17), "ne'er" is canceled and "not" inserted in pencil. "8" is written in ink in the upper left corner.

Sometimes our wits at sally & retort,
With laughter sudden as the crack of rifle;
Or parties scaled the near declivities
⟨To seek⟩ ↑Competing seekers of↓ a rumored lake,
(15)    Whose unauthenticated waves we named
Lake Probability,— our carbuncle,
Long sought, ⟨ne'er⟩ ↑not↓ found. ⟨Tw⟩

[10]          Two Doctors in the camp
Dissect the new-killed deer, weighed the trout's brain,
Captured the lizard, salamander, shrew,
Crab, mice, snail, dragonfly, minnow, & moth;
(5)    Insatiate skill in water or in air
Waved the scoop net, & nothing came amiss;
The while, a leaden pot of alcohol
Gave ⟨one⟩ ↑an↓ impartial tomb to all the kinds.
Not less the ambitious botanist sought plants,
(10)    Orchis & gentian, fern, & long whip-scirpus,
Rosy polygonum, lake-margin's pride,
Hypnum, & hydnum, mushroom, sponge, & moss,
Or harebell nodding in the gorge of falls.
Above, the eagle flew, the osprey screamed,
(15)    The raven croaked, owls hoot⟨ed⟩, the woodpecker
Hammered, & the heron rose in the swamp.
As water poured through hollows of the hills
[11]    To ⟨fill⟩ ↑feed↓ this ⟨chain⟩ ↑wealth↓ of lakes & rivulets,
So Nature shed all beauty lavishly
From her redundant horn.

          Masters of this green empire
(5)    Bounded by dawn & sunset, & the day
Rounded by hours where each outdid the last
In miracles of pomp, we must be proud,
As if associates of the sylvan gods.
We seemed the dwellers of the Zodiack,
(10)    So pure the ↑Alpine↓ element we breathed,
So light, so lofty pictures came & went.
We trode on air, contemned the distant Town,
Its timorous ways, big trifles, & we planned
That we should build a rooftree in the woods,
(15)    And how we should come hither with our sons,
Hereafter,—willing they, & more adroit.
[12]    Hard⟨f⟩ fare, hard bed, & comic misery,—

10 "The Adirondacs," 133–49. "9" is written in ink in the upper right corner.
11 "The Adirondacs," 150–64. "10" is written in ink in the upper left corner.
12 "The Adirondacs," 165–80. "11" is written in ink in the upper right corner.

The midge, the blue fly, & the musquito
Painted our necks, hands, ankles, with red bands:
But, on the second day, we heed them not,
(5)    Nay, we saluted them Auxiliaries,
Whom earlier we had chid with spiteful names.
For who defends our leafy tabernacle
From bold intrusion of the travelling crowd,
Who but the midge, musquito, & the fly,
(10)   Which past endurance sting the tender cit,
But which we learn to scatter with a smudge,
Or baffle with a veil⟨?⟩↑, or slight by scorn?↓

Our foaming ale we drunk from hunters' pans,
Ale, & a sup of wine. Our steward gave
(15)   Venison & trout, potatoes, beans, wheat-bread;
All ate like abbots, &, if any missed
[13]   Their wonted convenance, ↑⟨f⟩cheerly↓ hid the loss
With hunters' appetite, & peals of mirth.
And Stillman, our guides' Guide, & Commodore,
Crusoe, Crusader, Pius Aeneas, said aloud,
(5)    "Chronic dyspepsia never came from eating
Food indi⟨spensib⟩gestible":—then murmured some,
Others applauded him who spoke the truth.

[14]    Nor doubt but ↑visitings of↓ graver thought
Checked in these souls the turbulent heyday
Mid all the hints & glories of the home.
For who can tell what sudden privacies
(5)    Were sought & found, amid the hue & cry
Of scholars furloughed from their tasks, & let
Into this Oreads' ↑fended↓ Paradise,
As chapels in the city; thoroughfares,
Whither gaunt Labor slips to wipe his brow,
(10)   And meditate a moment on Heaven's rest.
Judge with what sweet surprises Nature spoke
To each apart, ⟨turning⟩ ↑lifting↓ her lovely shows
To spiritual lessons pointed home.
[15]    And as through dreams in watches of the night
⟨By⟩ So through all creatures in their form & ways
Some mystic hint accosts ⟨us⟩ ↑the vigilant,↓
Not clearly voiced, but waking a new sense

13  "The Adirondacs," 181–87. In line (4), "Pius Æneas," is written above "Pius Aeneas," to clarify it. "12" is written in ink in the upper left corner.
   14  "The Adirondacs," 188–200. In line (1), "of" is written over a canceled "of". "13" is written in ink in the upper right corner.
   15  "The Adirondacs," 201–10. In line (3), "us" is canceled and "the vigilant," inserted in ink. "14" is written in ink in the upper left corner.

(5)        Inviting to new knowledge, one with ⟨the⟩ old.
Hark to that petulant chirp! what ails the warbler?
Mark his capricious ways ⟨as if⟩ to draw the eye.
Now soar again. What wilt thou, restless bird,
Seeking in that chaste blue a bluer light,
(10)      Thirsting in that pure for a purer sky?

[16]        And presently the sky is changed; O world!
What pictures & what harmonies are thine!
The clouds are rich & dark, the air serene,
So like the soul of me, ↑what if↓ 'twere me?
(5)        A melancholy better than all mirth⟨,⟩↑.↓
⟨Sometimes restoring heavy youthful days.⟩
Comes the sweet sadness at the retrospect,
Or at the foresight of obscurer years?
Like yon⟨der⟩ ↑slow-↓sailing cloudy promontory,
(10)      Whereon the purple iris dwells in beauty
Superior to all its gaudy skirts—

[17]        And, that no day of life may lack romance,
The spiritual stars rise nightly, shedding down
A private beam into each several heart.
Daily the bending skies solicit man,
(5)        The Seasons chariot him from this exile,
The rainbow Hours bedeck his glowing chair,
The storm winds urge the heavy weeks along,
Suns haste to set, that so remoter lights
Beckon the wanderer to his vaster home.
(10)      For well we know, the crowning gift
The best of life, is presence of a muse
Who does not wish to wander, comes by stealth,
Divulging to the heart she sets on flame
No popular tale or toy, no cheap renown,
(15)      When the wings grow that draw ↑the↓ gazing eyes
⟨Unbalanced⟩ ↑Ofttimes poor↓ Genius fluttering near the
        earth
Is wrecked upon the turrets of the town:
But lifted till he meets the steadfast gales
Calm blowing from the Everlasting West.

[18]        With a vermilion pencil mark the day
When of our little fleet three cruising skiffs
Entering Big Tupper, bound for the foaming Falls
⟨o⟩Of loud Bog River, suddenly confront

16 "The Adirondacs," 211–15, x, 216–20. "15" is written in pencil in the upper right corner.
17 "The Adirondacs," 221–29, ten unused lines (1–19); "Best boon of life" (11–19). Lines
(10–19) are struck through in ink. "16" is written in pencil in the upper right corner.
18 "The Adirondacs," 230–45. "17" is written in ink in the upper right corner.

(5) Two of our mates returning with swift oars.
 One held a printed journal waving high
 ⟨Bi⟩Caught from a late-arriving traveller,
 Big with great news, & shouted the report
 For which the world had waited, now firm fact,
(10) Of the wire-cable laid beneath the sea,
 And landed on ⟨the⟩our coast, & pulsating
 With ductile fire. Loud exulting cries
 From boat to boat, & to the echoes round,
 Greet the glad miracle. Thought's new found path
(15) Shall supplement henceforth all trodden ways,
 Match God's equator with a zone of art,
[19] And lift man's public action to ⟨the⟩a height
 Worthy the enormous cloud of witnesses
 ⟨He summons to assist him.⟩
 ↑When linked ⟨continents⟩hemispheres attest his deed. ↓

(5) We have few moments in the longest life
 Of such delight & wonder as ⟨were ours,⟩ ↑the⟨n⟩re grew. ↓
 Nor yet unsuited to that solitude:
 A burst of joy as if we told the fact
 To ears intelligent, as if gray rock,
(10) And cedar grove, & cliff, & lake should know
 The triumph of mankind, this day of days ↑, ↓
 As if we men were talking in a vein
 Of sympathy so large, that ours was theirs,
 And a prime end of the most subtle element
(15) Were fairly reached at last. Wake echoing caves!
 Bend nearer, faint day-moon! Yon thundertops,
 Let them hear well! tis theirs as much as ours.

[20] A spasm throbbing through the pedestals
 Of Alp & Andes, isle & continent,
 Urging astonished Chaos with a thrill
 To be a brain, or serve the brain of man.
(5) The lightning has run masterless too long,
 He must to school, & learn his verb & noun,
 And teach his nimbleness to earn his wage,
 Spelling with guided tongue man's messages
 Shot through the weltering pit of the salt sea

[21] And yet I marked, even in the manly joy

19 "The Adirondacs," 246–47, x, 248–61. In line (11), the comma after "days" is in pencil.
"18" is written in ink in the upper left corner.
 20 "The Adirondacs," 262–70. "19" is written in ink in the upper right corner.
 21 "The Adirondacs," 271–85. The hyphen in line (2) and the comma in line (4) are in pencil.
"21" is written in ink in the upper right corner.

Of our great ↑-↓ hearted Doctor in his boat,
(Perchance I erred,) a shade of discontent,
Or was it for mankind a generous shame ↑,↓

(5) As of a luck not quite legitimate,
Since fortune snatched from wit the lion's part?
Was it a college pique of town & gown,
As one within whose memory it burned
That not academicians, but some lout

(10) Found ten years since the California gold.
And now, again, a hungry company
Of traders, led by corporate sons of trade,
↑Perversely↓ Borrowing from the shop the tools
Of science, not from ↑the↓ philosophers,

(15) Had won the brightest laurel of all time.


[22] T'⟨⟨was⟩is⟩was always thus, ↑& will be↓; ⟨the⟩ hand & head
Are ever rivals: but, tho' this be swift,
The other slow,— this the Prometheus,
And that the Jove,—yet, howsoever hid,

(5) It was from Jove the other stole his fire,
And, without Jove, the good had never been.
It is not Iroquois or Cannibals ↑,↓
But ever the free ⟨wise⟩ race with front sublime
And these instructed by their wisest too

(10) Who do the feat. ⟨— —⟩ ↑& lift humanity.↓
Let not him mourn who best entitled was,
Nay mourn not one: ⟨L⟩let him exult,
Yea, plant the tree that bears best apples, plant,
And water it with wine, nor watch askance

(15) Whether thy sons or strangers eat the fruit:
Enough that mankind eat, & are refreshed.

[23]                    [white line.]

We flee away from cities, but we bring
The best of cities with us, these learned classifiers,
Men knowing what they seek, armed eyes of experts.
We praise the guide, we praise the forest life;

(5 But will we sacrifice our dearbought lore
(5) Of books, & ⟨trained experiment⟩arts & trained experiment,
Or count the Sioux a match for Agassiz
O no, not we! witness the shout that shook
Wild Tupper lake; Witness the mute all-hail

(10) The joyful traveller gives, when on the verge

22 "The Adirondacs," 286–301. In line (1), "the" is canceled in pencil; the comma in line (7) is in pencil.
23 "The Adirondacs," 302–13, x, 314–16.

Of Indian wilderness he hears
From a log-cabin stream Beethoven's notes
⟨Masterly played.⟩
On the piano, ⟨heedless of the wolf⟩ ↑played with master's
    hand↓.

(15)  "Well done!" he cries, "the bear is kept at bay,
The lynx, the rattlesnake, the flood, the fire,

[24]  All the fierce enemies, ↑ague,↓ hunger, ⟨&⟩ cold,
This thin spruce roof, this clayed log-wall,
This wild plantation will suffice to chase.
Now speed the gay celerities of Art,

(5)  What in the desert was impossible
Within four walls is possible again,—
Culture & libraries, mysteries of skill,
Traditioned fame of masters, eager strife
Of keen competing youths, joined or alone

(10)  To outdo each other, & extort applause.
Genius is born once more. Twirl the old wheels
Time makes fresh start again
On for a thousand years of genius more,

[25]  The holidays were fruitful, but must end,
One August evening had a cooler breath,
Into each mind intruding duties crept;
⟨For had we not left truest friends at home⟩

(5)  ↑Burned in each heart remembrances of home;↓
Nay, letters found us in our paradise;
So in the gladness of the new event
We struck our camp, & ⟨quit⟩ ↑left↓ the happy hills.
The fortunate star that rose on us sank not;

(10)  The prodigal sunshine rested on the land,
The rivers gambolled onward to the sea,
And Nature, the inscrutable & mute,
Permitted on her infinite repose
Almost a smile to steal to cheer her sons,

(15)  As if one riddle of the Sphinx were guessed
                R. W. Emerson

## "Alphonso of Castile" (Houghton, Harvard)

[1]                *Alphonso of Castille.*

I Alphonso live & learn,
Seeing nature go astern,

24 "The Adirondacs," 317–29.
25 "The Adirondacs," 330–32, x, 333–43. "Conclusion of 'Adirondacs.'" is written in the
upper left corner and "22" in the upper right corner.
1 "Alphonso of Castile," 1–20.

Things deteriorate in kind,
Lemons run to leaves & rind,
(5)      Meagre crop of figs & limes,
Shorter days, & harder times.
⟨The year's first quarter⟩ ↑Flowering April↓ cools & dies
In the insufficient skies;
Imps at high midsummer blot
(10)     Half the sun's disc with a spot;
Twill not now avail to tan
Orange cheek or skin of man.
Roses bleach, the goats are dry,
Lisbon quakes, the people cry:
(15)     Yon pale fisher fools,
Gaunt as bitterns in the pools,
Are no brothers of my blood,
They discredit Adamhood.
Eyes of gods! ye must have seen,
(20)     Oer your ramparts as ye lean,
[2]      The general debility,
Of genius the sterility,
Mighty projects countermanded,
Rash ambition broken-handed,
(5)      Puny man & scentless rose
Tormenting Pan to double the dose.
Rebuild or ruin: either fill
Of vital force the wasted rill,
Or tumble all again in heap
(10)     To weltering Chaos & to sleep.

Say are the old Niles dry,
Which fed the veins of earth & sky,
That mortals miss the loyal heats
Which drove them erst to social feats,
(15)     And now to savage selfness grown
Think nature barely serves for one⟨?⟩.
With science poorly mask their hurt,
And vex the gods with question pert,
Immensely curious whether you
(20)     Still are rulers, or mildew.

Masters! I am in pain with you,
Masters! I'll be plain with you.
[3]      In my palace of Castille,
I, a king, for kings can feel;

2 "Alphonso of Castile," 21–42.
3 "Alphonso of Castile," 43–67.

There my thoughts the matter roll,
And solve & oft resolve the whole;
(5)  And, for I'm styled Alphonse the Wise,
Y⟨o⟩e shall not fail for sound advice;
Before ye want a drop of rain,
Hear the sentiment of Spain.

You have tried famine: no more try it:
(10)  Ply us now with a full diet;
Teach your pupils now with plenty,
For one sun supply us twenty,
I have thought it thoroughly over,
State of hermit, state of lover;
(15)  We must have society,
We cannot spare variety.
Hear you, then, celestial fellows!
Fits not to be overzealous,
Steads not to work upon the jump,
(20)  Nor wine nor brains perpetual pump.
Men & gods are too extense;—
Could you slacken & condense?
Your rank overgrowths reduce
Till your kinds abound with juice.
(25)  Earth crowded cries, 'Too many men!'
[4]  My counsel is, kill nine in ten,
And bestow the shares of all
On the remnant decimal.
Add their nine lives to this cat,
(5)  Stuff their nine brains in his hat,
Make his frame & forces square
With the labors he must dare.
Nerve his arm & even his years
With the marble which he rears.
(10)  ⟨And⟩ ↑There↓ grow↑ing↓ slowly old at ease
No faster than his planted trees
⟨That⟩ he ↑may↓ by warrant of his age
In schemes of broader scope engage;
So shall ye have a man of the sphere,
(15)  Fit to grace the solar year.

## "April" (Poems folder 63)

[1]  ↑O southwinds have long memories↓

---

4 "Alphonso of Castile," 68–82.
1 "April," x, 1–2, 3?, 6, x, x, 8?, 9–12, x, 14, 19–20. In pencil. Line (1) is written after the last line and indicated for transposition by an asterisk and a hand sign next to it and an asterisk to the right above "Spring winds are magical."

Spring winds are magical
And thrill our tuneful frames
These are the days of passion
(5)    The air with Cupids full
For the eyes that are young
And sparkles
⟨From⟩ Down the dell from the pool
And every pool of water
(10)    And every dancing leaf
Seems to cozen & to flatter
To pique & to /provoke/mock/
O they have secret lessons
That are not in your books
(15)    They quite omitted
All we care to know


## "At Sea, September 1833" (Poems folder 64)

{1}        Oft as I paced the deck,
My thought recurred on the uncertain sea
To what is faster than the solid land.
My Country! can the heart clasp realm so vast
(5)    As the broad oceans that wash thee inclose?
Is not the charity ambitious
That meets its arms about a continent?
And yet the sages praise the preference
Of my own cabin to a baron's hall.
(10)    Chide it not then, but count it honesty
The insidious love & hate that curl the lip
Of the frank Yankee in the tenements
Of ducal & of royal rank abroad;
His super⟨stit⟩cilious ignorance
(15)    Of lordship, heraldry, & ceremony;
{2}    Nor less, his too tenacious memory,
Amid the particolor⟨ored⟩ed treasuries
That deck the Louvre & the Pitti House,
Of the brave steamboats puffing by New York,
(5)    Boston's half-island, & the Hadley Farms⟨,⟩
Washed by Connecticut's psalm-loving stream.
Yea, if the ruddy Englishman speak true,
In Rome's basilica, and underneath
The frescoed sky of its audacious dome,
(10)    Dauntless Kentucky chews, & counts the cost,

1 "At Sea, September 1833," 1–15.
2 "At Sea, September 1833," 16–28.

And builds the shrine with dollars in his head.
Arrived in Italy, his first demand,—
'Has the star-bearing squadron left Leghorn?'

## "Boston" (Poems folder 31)

[1]    [list of poems omitted]

[2]    Ring your bells backward, loyal towers!
        And warn the land of harm.

[3]    ↑Let↓ ⟨T⟩the heavy blue chain
        Of the boundless main
        Lock up their prison door,
        And the cannons wrath
(5)    Forbid their path
        On ocean's azure floor.

        Peril around all else appalling
        Cannon in front and leaden rain,
        Him Duty through the clarion calling
(10)    To the front called not in vain—

                ⟨Ring your⟩

        ⟨Let the heavy blue chain⟩
        ⟨Of the boundless main⟩
        ⟨Lock up their prison door⟩
(15)    ⟨And the cannons wrath⟩
        ⟨Forbid their path⟩
        ⟨On ocean's azure floor⟩

[4]    Softened are above their will
        Take tones from groves they wandered through
        Or /trumpets/flutes/ which ⟨the⟩ ↑passing↓ angels blew

        Peril around all else appalling
(5)    Cannon in front & leaden rain
        Him Duty through the clarion calling
        To the front ⟨not⟩called not in vain

1  See ETE pp. [2] and [30ₐ]–[30ₑ].
2  "Ring your bells backward."
3  "The heavy blue chain" (1–6); "Voluntaries," four lines first printed in the 1876 version (7–10); "Ring your bells backward," 1 (11); "The heavy blue chain" (12–17).
4  "May-Day," 457, x, x (1–3); "Voluntaries," four lines first printed in the 1876 version (4–7); "Boston," x, x, 108–9, four unused lines (8–15). Lines (8–9) and (14–15) and "*NP* 205," are in pencil; lines (8–9), (10–11), (12–13), and (14–15) are separately struck through in pencil. Emerson's three "Remainders" are "Boston," "Maiden Speech of the Aeolian Harp," and "Hymn Sung at the Second Church, Boston, at the Ordination of Rev. Chandler Robbins."

Remainders

Boston Tea Party
Aeolian Harp
Second Church

Go purge your blood in lake & wood
To honor born of hardihood

(10)    For you can teach the lightning speech
And round the world your white arms reach

For never will die the captive's cry
On the echoes of God, till Right draws nigh.

*NP* 205, For power ⟨& place they⟩ sell their race
(15)    And ⟨locked their hands⟩ kissed the hands of statesmen base


## "Boston" (Poems folder 32)

[1]    For you can teach the lightning speech,
And round the globe your voices reach,

What slave shall dare a name to wear
Once freedom's passport everywhere?

(5)    A union then of honest men,
Or union never more again.

But right is might thro all the world
Province to province bravely clung;
Thro' good & ill the bolt was hurled,
(10)    Till the farmers ⟨won⟩ ↑cheered↓, & peace was sung.
Till Freedom      & the joybells rung

For Power & place they sell their race
And locked their hands with statesmen base

For never will die the captive's cry
(15)    On the echoes of God, till Right draws nigh.

1 "Boston," 108–9, x, x, two lines first printed in *Selected Poems*, 1876, 94–97, 97, four unused lines. Lines (7–10) are struck through in ink; vertical lines are drawn in ink to the left of lines (1–2), (3–4), (5–6), and (12–13).

[2]      Go purge your blood in lake & wood
            To honor born of hardihood

———

            For never will die the captives cry
            On the echoes of God till Right draws nigh

———

(5)      For power & place they sell their race
            And kiss the hands of statesmen base

———

[3]      Hear what British Merlin sung
                *Conduct of Life*, p. 213

            Tou⟨t⟩s sont soldat↑s↓ pour vous combattre
            S'ils tombent, nos jeune⟨'⟩s heros,
            La terre ⟨pr⟩ en produire de nouveax
(5)      Contre vous tous ⟨con⟩prètes à se battre

[4]      A union the[mutilated]
            Or union ne[mutilated]

———

            What slave s[mutilated]
            Once Freedom'[mutilated]

## "Boston" (Poems folder 88, manuscript 1)

[1]      ⟨The world is full of palaces⟩
            ↑Old Europe crushed with palaces↓
            ⟨We have⟩ ↑Has lords↓ enough & more
            We plant & build ⟨too by the⟩by foaming seas
(5)      A city of the poor

            An union then of honest men
            Or union nevermore again

            The heavy blue chain of the boundless main
            ⟨Didst thou⟩
(10)    Was bound about the man of Pain

2 "Boston," six unused lines. Six lines in faint pencil, apparently a version of "Boston," 90–93, are overwritten by lines (1–5); visible are "The" (second line), "To see the secret force" (third line), "Which" (fourth line), "Where" (fifth line), and "To [unrecovered] of all mankind" (sixth line).

3 "Considerations by the Way," 1 (1); *Marseillaise* (Claude Joseph Rouget de Lisle) (2–5). Lines (2–5) are in pencil and upside down.

4 "Boston," two lines first printed in *Selected Poems*, 1876, x, x. In pencil.

1 "Boston," 19, 19–22, two lines first printed in *Selected Poems*, 1876 (1–7); "The heavy blue chain," 1/2, x, x (8–10); "Boston," five unused lines, 102–3 (11–17). Lines (1–5) are struck through in ink.

Cruel & blind did file their mind
And sell the blood of human kind

---

Signed & sealed with ⟨traitor b⟩smiling face
For power & place they sell their race
(15)      Locked ↑their↓ hands with traitors base

Ere these echoes be choked with snows
Or over the town blue ocean flows

[2]     ⟨We love the living Patriot⟩
     ↑The noble workman we promote↓
     ⟨And what if once the man miswrote⟩
     ⟨Or children played the fool,⟩
(5)      ↑⟨And we⟩ disown the knave & fool↓
     The honest man shall have his vote,
     The child shall have his school.

We give no lordship to the few,
We hold like rights & shall,
(10)     Equal on Sunday in the pew,
     On Monday in the Mall.

New days will shed new lights around,
⟨The father & the⟩ ↑⟨Tomorrow,⟩ Next morn shall sire and↓
     child⟨,⟩
⟨↑Shall↓⟩ Come ⟨home⟩ ↑back↓ to reason with a bound
(15)     That they were once beguiled.

## "Boston" (Poems folder 88, manuscript 2)

[1]     Old Europe groans with palaces,
     Has lords enough & more;
     We plant & build by foaming seas
     A city of the poor.

## "Boston" (Poems folder 88, manuscript 3)

[1]     The wild rose & the barberry thorn
     Hung out their summer pride
     Where now on heated pavement worn
     The feet of millions stride.

2 "Boston," x, 25, x, x, 26–28, 31–34, four unused lines.
1 "Boston," 19–22. Struck through in ink.
1 "Boston," 35–38, seven unused lines. Lines (1–4) are struck through in pencil.

(5)        The land ⟨was⟩ ↑lay↓ rich outspread behind
               The young men hungered more
               On slippery deck with snowy wings
               To skim the ocean floor.

               The stormy billow kissed the cloud,
(10)       The wind mixed sea & sky,
               The skipper steered,—blow soft or loud,

## "Boston" (Poems folder 88, manuscript 4)

[1]            Little they loved the English King

               The English king they could not bide
               Nor cared for the gold of the French,
               ⟨But⟩ ↑With↓ Honor ⟨came & sat⟩ ↑sitting↓ by their side
(5)        Low on their wooden bench.

               The blood of her hundred thousands
               Shall throb in his manly vein
               And the wit of all her wisest
               Make sunshine in his brain

(10)       And each shall care for other
               And each to each can bend
               To the poor a noble brother
               To the rich a manly friend

## "Boston" (Poems folder 88, manuscript 5)

[1]            The sea returning day by day
               Restores the worldwide mart;
               So shall each dweller on the Bay
               Fold Boston in his heart.
(5)        For what avail the plough or sail,
               Or land or life, if freedom fail?

               A blessing through the ages thus
               Shield all thy roofs & towers,
               'God with the fathers, so with us!'
(10)       Thou darling town of ours!

[2]            But there was chaff within the flour
               And one was false in ten

1 "Boston," 80, 80–83, 104–7, 110–13. Lines (1–5) are struck through in ink.
1 "Boston," 98–101, 29/78–30/79, 114–17.
2 "Boston," six unused lines, 25–28, 31.

And reckless clerks in lust of power
Forgot the rights of men
(5) Cruel & blind did file their mind
And sell the blood of human kind

The noble craftsman we promote,
Disown the knave & fool,
Each honest man ↑shall have his vote,↓
(10) Each child shall have ⟨its⟩his school.

We grant no dukedom to the few

## "Boston" (Poems folder 88, manuscript 6)

[1] Hie to the woods, sleek citizen,
To the deep sea, go, landsmen, down;
Climb the White hills, ⟨ye⟩ ↑fat↓ aldermen,
And vacant leave the town;
(5) Go purge your blood in lake & wood,
To honor born of hardihood.

[2] Ere these echoes be choked by snows
Or over the roofs blue ocean flows

## "Boston" (Poems folder 88, manuscript 7)

[1] Trimountain.

The land that has no song
Shall have a song today,
The granite ledge is dumb ↑too↓ long
The vales ⟨m⟩have much to say.
(5) For you can teach the lightning speech
And round the globe your voices reach.

The rocky nook with hill⟨s⟩tops three
Looked eastward from the farms,
And twice a day the flowing sea
(10) Took Boston in its arms.
The men of yore were stout & poor,
And sailed for bread to every shore.

[2] The waves that rocked them on the deep
To them their secret told

1 "Boston," six unused lines.
2 "Boston," 102–3.
1 "Boston," four unused lines, 108–9, 1–6.
2 "Boston," 13–18, 7–12.

⟨The⟩Said the winds that sung the lads to sleep,
"Like us be free & bold";
(5)        The honest waves refuse to slaves
The empire of the ocean caves.

And where they went on trade intent
They did what freemen can;
Their dauntless ways did all men praise
(10)      The merchant was a man
The world was made for honest trade
To plant & eat be none afraid

[3]      They laughed to know the world so wide
The mountains said, Good day!
We greet you well, you Saxon men,
Here build your towns & stay.
(5)        The world was made for honest trade
To plant & eat be none afraid.

Your town is full of gentle names
By patriots once were watchwords made
These warcry names are muffled shames
(10)      On recreant sons mislaid
Shall a slave dare a name to bear
Once vowed to Freedom everywhere?

[4]      O pity that I pause,—
The ⟨muse⟩ ↑song↓ disdaining shuns
To name the noble sires because
Of /the unworthy/undeserving/ sons

(5)        O welaway if this be so
And man cannot afford the right
And if the wage of love be wo↑e↓,
And honest dealing yield despite,
For what avail &c.

(10)      Hie to the woods, sleek citizen,
Back to the sea go landmen down
Climb the White Hills, sleek aldermen
And vacant leave the town
Go purge your blood in lake & wood
(15)      To honor born of hardihood.
or Ere these echoes be choked
Or over the roofs blue Ocean

3  "Boston," 47–52, six unused lines.
4  "Boston," eight unused lines, 29/78, six unused lines, 102–3.

## "Boston" (Poems folder 88, manuscript 8)

[1]     The rocky nook with hilltops three
        Looked eastward from the farms,
        And twice a day the flowing sea
        Took Boston in its arms.
(5)     The men of yore were stout & poor,
        And sailed for bread to every shore

        The waves that rocked them on the deep
        To them their secret told,
        Said the winds that sung the lads to sleep,
(10)    'Like us be free & bold.'
        The honest waves refuse to slaves
        The empire of the ocean ⟨w⟩caves.

[2]     And where they went on trade intent
        They did what freemen can,
        Their dauntless ways did all men praise,
        The merchant was a man.
(5)     The world was made for honest trade,
        To plant & eat be none afraid.

        Fair rose the planted hills behind
        The good town on the Bay,
        And where the western slopes declined
(10)    The prairie stretched away.

[3]     From /healthy/sparkling/ springs that never failed
        The rivers ⟨ru⟩gushed & ⟨roared⟩foamed
        Sweet airs from every pore exhaled
        Around the mountains roamed.

(5)     What rival tow⟨ns⟩ers majestic soar⟨ed⟩
        Along the stormy coast!
        Penn's town, New York, & Baltimore,
        ⟨But⟩If Boston knew the most!

[4]         They laughed to know the world so wide
        The mountains said, Good day!
        We greet you well, you Saxon men,
        Up with your towns, & stay.

(5)     ⟨What⟩And they who braved the English King
        Found friendship in the French

1  "Boston," 1–6, 13–18.
2  "Boston," 7–12, 39–42.
3  "Boston," four unused lines, 43–46.
4  "Boston," 47–50, 80–83, 57–60.

And Honor joined the patriot ring
On their poor wooden bench

(10)
O happy town beside the sea!
Whose roads lead everywhere to all,
Than thine no deeper moat can be,
No steeper fence, no better wall.

[5]
↑Old Europe groans with palaces,↓
↑Has lords enough & more,↓
↑We plant & build by foaming seas↓
↑A city of the poor.↓

(5)
The noble craftsman we promote,
Disown the knave & fool;
The honest man shall have his vote,
The child shall have his school.

(10)
We ⟨give n⟩grant no dukedom to the few,
We hold like rights & shall,
Equal on Sunday in the pew,
On Monday in the Mall.

[6]
But there was chaff ↑within the flour,↓
And /nine/one/ were false in ten,
And reckless clerks in lust of power
Forgot the rights of men:
(5)
Cruel & blind did file their mind,
To sell the blood of human kind.

[7]
O bounteous seas that never fail!
O happy day remembered yet!
O happy port, that spied the sail
Which, furling, landed Lafayette!

(5)
O pity that I pause!
The song disdaining shuns
To name the noble sires, because
Of the unworthy sons.
For what avail the plough & sail,
(10)
Or land, or life, if freedom fail?

Your town is full of gentle names
By patriots once were watchwords made.
Those war-cry names are muffled shames
On recreant sons mislaid.

5 "Boston," 19–22, 25–28, 31–34.
6 "Boston," six unused lines.
7 "Boston," 84–87, four unused lines, 29/78–30/79, six unused lines.

(15) What slave would dare a name to wear
   Once Freedom's passport everywhere.

[8] O welaway! if this be so,
   And man cannot afford the right;
   And if the wage of love is wo,
   And honest dealing yield despite.
(5) For what avail the plough & sail
   Or land, or life, if freedom fail?

   Hie to the woods, sleek citizen;
   ↑Back↓ To the ⟨deep⟩ sea, go ⟨landsmen⟩ down;
   Climb the White Hills, fat aldermen,
(10) And vacant leave the town.
  Go purge your blood in lake & wood
  To honor born of hardihood

     <u>or</u>

  Ere these echoes be choked with snows,
  Or over the roofs blue Ocean flows.

[9] The sea returning day by day
   Restores the worldwide mart,
   So ⟨doth⟩ ↑shall↓ each dweller on the Bay
   Fold Boston in his heart.
(5) For what avail the plough & sail
   Or land, or life, if freedom fail.

   ⟨A blessing thro' the ages thus⟩
   ⟨Shield all thy roofs & towers!⟩
   ⟨God with the fathers, so with us!⟩
(10) ⟨Thou darling town of ours!⟩

[10] The blood of ⟨her hundred thousands⟩ ↑/each/the/ pilgrim
    sires↓
   Throb in ⟨‖ . ‖⟩each manly vein
   And ⟨the⟩ ↑Franklins↓ wit ⟨of all her wisest⟩ ↑& Adams'
    fire↓
   Make sunshine in his brain

(5) And each shall care for other,
   And each to each shall bend,
   To the poor, a noble brother,
   To the good, an equal friend.

8 "Boston," four unused lines, 29/78–30/79, six unused lines, 102–3.
9 "Boston," 98–101, 29/78–30/79, 114–17.
10 "Boston," 104–7, 110–17. "Terminus" is written upside down at the bottom center of the page.

A blessing through the ages thus
(10)    Shield all thy roofs & towers
God with the ⟨F⟩fathers so with us!
Thou darling town of ours!

## "Boston" (Poems folder 88, manuscript 9)

[1]          ↑ *Trimountain.* ↓

↑ *Sicut cum patribus sit Deus nobis.* ↓

The land that has no song
⟨T⟩Shall have a song today,
The granite ledge is dumb too long,
The vales have much to say.
(5)    ⟨For⟩
Its men can teach the lightning speech,
And round the globe their voices reach.

————

↑ I. ↓
The rocky Nook with hilltops three
Looked eastward from the farms,
(10)    And twice a day the flowing sea
Took Boston in its arms:
The men of yore were ⟨proud⟩stout & poor,
And sailed for bread to every shore.

↑ II. ↓
The waves that rocked them on the deep
(15)    To them their secret told,
Said the winds that sung the lads to sleep,
"Like us be free & bold.
The honest waves refuse to slaves
The empire of the Ocean caves."

[2]          Trimountain

=

Sicut cum patribus, sit Deus nobis.

————

⟨The rocky nook with hilltops three⟩
⟨Looked eastward from the farms,⟩
⟨And twice a day the flowing sea⟩
⟨Took Boston in its arms.⟩

1 "Boston," four unused lines, x, 108–9, 1–6, 13–18.
2 "Boston," 1–12. The title, motto, and short rules are left over from an earlier stage of the poem.

(5) ⟨The men of yore were ⟨proud⟩stout & poor,⟩
⟨And sailed for bread to every shore.⟩

↑III.↓

And where they went, on trade intent,
They did what freemen can;
Their dauntless ways did all men praise,
(10) The merchant was a man.
The world was made for honest trade,
To plant & eat be none afraid.

[3] Old Europe groans with palaces
Has lords enough & more
We plant & build by foaming seas
A city of the poor.
(5) For what avail the plough & sail,
Or land, or life, if freedom fail?

The noble craftsman we promote,
Disown the knave & fool;
Each honest man shall have his vote,
(10) Each child shall have his school.

We grant no dukedoms to the few,
We hold like rights & shall,
Equal on Sunday in the pew,
On Monday in the mall.

[4] Fair rose the planted hills behind
The good town on the Bay,
And where the western slopes declined
The ⟨r⟩prairie stretched away.

(5) Out from the many-fountained earth
The rivers gushed & foamed,
Sweet airs from every forest forth
Around the mountains roamed.

What rival towers majestic soar
(10) Along the stormy coast,—
Penn's town, New York, & Baltimore,
If Boston knew the most!

[5] They laughed to know the world so wide,
The mountains said, "Good-day!
We greet you well, you Saxon men,
Up with your towns, & stay."

3 "Boston," 19–22, 29/78–30/79, 25–28, 31–34.
4 "Boston," 39–42, four unused lines, 43–46.
5 "Boston," 47–50, 53–56, 80–83.

(5)       "For you," they said, "no barriers be,
            For you no sluggard's rest;
            Each street leads downward to the Sea,
            Or land-ward to the West."

            The townsmen braved the English King,
(10)     Found friendship in the French,
            And Honor joined the patriot ring
            Low on their wooden bench.

[6]      O bounteous seas that never fail!
            O day remembered yet!
            O happy port that spied the sail
            Which wafted Lafayette!
(5)            Abdiel bright, in Europe's night,
                That never faltered from the right.

            O pity that I pause,—
            The song disdaining shuns
            To name the noble sires, because
(10)     Of the unworthy sons:
            For what avail the plough & sail,
            Or land, or life, if freedom fail?

            But there was chaff within the flour,
            And one was false in ten;
(15)     And reckless clerks in lust of power
            Forgot the rights of men;
             Cruel & blind did file their mind,
            And sell the blood of human kind.

[7]      Your town is full of gentle names
            /By patriots/Which/ once were watchwords made;
            Those war-cry names are muffled shames
            On recreant sons mislaid.
(5)            What slave shall dare a name to wear
            Once Freedom's passport everywhere?

            O welaway! if this be so,
            And man cannot afford the right,
            And if the wage of love is woe,
(10)     And honest dealing yield despite.
               For what avail the plough & sail,
               Or land, or life, if freedom fail?

6 "Boston," 84–89, four unused lines, 29/78–30/79, six unused lines.

7 "Boston," ten unused lines, 29/78–30/79, four unused lines, 102–3. In line (2), "By patriots" is bracketed in ink and "Which" is in pencil.

Hie to the woods, sleek citizen!
Back to the sea, go landsmen down!
(15) Climb the White Hills, sleek aldermen,
And vacant leave the town:
Ere these echoes be choked with snows,
Or over the roofs blue Ocean flows.

[8] The sea returning day by day
Restores the world-wide mart,
So let each dweller on the Bay
Fold Boston in his heart.
(5) For what avail the plough & sail,
Or land or life, if freedom fail?

Let the blood of her hundred thousands
Throb in each manly vein
And the wit of all her wisest
(10) Make sunshine in his brain.
A union then of honest men,
Or Union nevermore again.

And each shall care for other,
And each to each shall bend,
(15) To the poor a noble brother,
To the good an equal friend.

A blessing through the ages thus
Shield all thy roofs & towers!
*God with the fathers, So with us!*
(20) Thou darling town of ours!

## "Boston" (Poems folder 88, manuscript 10)

[1]                    Trimountain

1. The rocky nook with hilltops three
Looked eastward from the farms,
And twice each day the flowing sea
Took Boston in its arms.
(5)        The men of yore were stout & poor,
And sailed for bread to every shore.

2. And where they went on trade intent
They did what freemen can;
Their dauntless ways did all men praise,

---

8 "Boston," 98–101, 29/78–30/79, 104–7, two lines first printed in *Selected Poems*, 1876, 110–17.
1 "Boston," 1–12.

(10)        The merchant was a man.
             The world was made for honest trade,
             To plant & eat be none afraid.

[2]    3 Old Europe groans with palaces
             Has lords enough & more
             We plant & build by foaming seas
             A city of the poor.

(5)        ⟨Th⟩
         4 The noble craftsman we promote,
             Disown the knave & fool,
             Each honest man shall have his vote,
             Each child shall have his school.

(10)     5 We grant no dukedom to the few,
             We hold like rights, & shall,
             Equal on Sunday in the pew,
             On Monday in the Mall.

[3]    6 Fair rose the planted hills behind
             The good town on the Bay,
             And where the western hills declined,
             The prairie stretched away.

(5)       7 Out from the many-fountained earth
             The rivers gushed & foamed,
             Sweet airs from every forest forth
             And from the mountains roamed.

         8 What rival towers majestic ⟨rose⟩soar
(10)        Along the stormy coast,
             Penn's town, New York, & Baltimore,
             —⟨B⟩If Boston knew the most!

[4]    They laughed to know the world so wide,—
             The mountains cried, 'Good day!
             We greet you well, you Saxon men
             Up with your towns, & stay!'

(5)       For you,' they said, 'no barriers be,
             For you no sluggard's nest,
             Each street leads downward to the sea
             Or landward to the West.'

         The townsmen braved the English King,
(10)        Found friendship with the French,

2 "Boston," 19–22, x, 25–28, 31–34.
3 "Boston," 39–42, four unused lines, 43–46.
4 "Boston," 47–50, 53–56, 80–83.

And Honor joined the patriot ring
Low on their wooden bench.

[5]    12. O bounteous seas that never fail
O day remembered yet
O happy port that spied the sail
Which wafted Lafayette!
(5)            ⟨Pillar⟩Polestar of light in Europe's night,
That never faltered from the right.

13 O pity that I pause,—
The song disdaining shuns
To name the noble sires, because
(10)    Of the unworthy sons.
For what avail the plough & sail
Or land, or life, if Freedom fail?

14 But there was chaff within the flour,
And one was false in ten,
(15)    And reckless clerks in lust of power
Forgot the rights of men,
Cruel & blind did file their mind,
And sell the blood of human kind.

[6]    15 Your town is full of gentle names
Which once were watchwords made;
Those war-cry names are muffled shames
On recreant sons mislaid.
(5)            ⟨↑For never will die the captives cry↓⟩
⟨↑On the echoes of God till Right draws nigh↓⟩
What slave shall dare a name to wear
Once Freedom's pass-port everywhere!

16 O welaway! if this be so,
(10)    And man cannot afford the right,
And if the wage of love is wo,
And honest dealing yield despite,
For what avail the plough & sail,
Or land, or life, if freedom fail.
(15)    ↑For never will die the captive's cry↓
↑On the echoes of God till Right draws nigh↓

17 Hie to the woods, sleek citizen,
Back to the sea go landsmen down,
Climb the White Hills, smooth aldermen,

5 "Boston," 84–89, four unused lines, 29/78–30/79, six unused lines.
6 "Boston," twelve unused lines, 29/78–30/79, eight unused lines, 102–3. Lines (5–6), (15–16), and (23–24) are in pencil; lines (5–6) are canceled in pencil; a bracket is drawn in pencil to the left of lines (13–14).

(20)     And vacant leave the town.
                Go purge your blood in lake & wood
                To honor born of hardihood.
                ↑or Ere these echoes be choked in snows↓
                    ↑⟨And⟩ ↑Or↓ over the roofs rude Ocean flows↓

[7]   18 The sea returning, day by day,
                Restores the world-wide mart,
                So let each dweller on the Bay
                Fold Boston in his heart;
(5)                 For what avail the plough & sail,
                    Or land, or life, if Freedom fail?

        19 Let the blood of her hundred thousands
                Throb in each manly vein
                And the wit of all her wisest
(10)            Make sunshine in his brain:
                    ⟨A⟩ A union then of honest men,
                    Or Union nevermore again.

        20 And each shall care for other,
                And each to each shall bend,
(15)            To the poor, a noble brother,
                To the good, an equal friend.

[8]   18      A blessing through the Ages thus
                Shield all thy roofs & towers!
                *God with the fathers, so with us,*
                Thou darling town of ours!


## "Boston" (Poems folder 88, manuscript 11)

[1]    1 The land that has no song
                Shall have a song today
                The granite ledge is dumb too long
                The vales have much to say;
(5)                 For you can teach the lightning speech
                    And round the globe your voices reach.

        2 The rocky nook with hill-tops three
                    Looked eastward from the farms,
                And twice a day the flowing sea
(10)            Took Boston in its arms;

7 "Boston," 98–101, 29/78–30/79, 104–7, two lines first printed in *Selected Poems*, 1876, 110–13.
8 "Boston," 114–17.
1 "Boston," four unused lines, 108–9, 1–12.

The men of yore were stout & poor,
And sailed for bread to every shore.

3 And where they went on trade intent
They did what freemen can,
(15)  Their dauntless ways did all men praise,
The merchant was a man:
The world was made for honest trade,
To plant & eat be none afraid.

[2]  4  The waves that rocked them on the deep
To them their secret told,
Said the winds that sung the lads to sleep,
'Like us, be free & bold;
(5)  The honest waves refuse to slaves
The empire of the ocean waves.

⟨5⟩ ⟨And where they went on trade intent,⟩
⟨They did what freemen can;⟩
⟨Their dauntless ways did all men praise,⟩
(10)  ⟨The merchant was a man.⟩
⟨The world was made for honest trade,⟩
⟨To plant & eat be none afraid.⟩

⟨6⟩5 Old Europe groans with palaces,—
Has lords enough, & more;
(15)  We plant & build by foaming seas
A city of the poor.

⟨7⟩6 The noble craftsman we promote,
Disown the knave & fool;
Each honest man shall have his vote,
(20)  Each child shall have his school.
↑For what avail the plough or sail↓
↑Or land or life, if freedom fail?↓

[3]  ⟨8⟩7 We grant no dukedoms to the few,
We hold like rights, & shall,—
Equal on Sunday in the pew,
On Monday, in the mall.
(5)  ↑Till these echoes be choked with snows,↓
↑Or over the town blue ocean flows.↓

⟨9⟩8 The wild rose & the barberry thorn
Hung out their summer pride,

2 "Boston," 13–18, 7–12, 19–22, 25–30. In line (21), "For what" is in pencil and "avail" is
in pencil and ink.
3 "Boston," 31–34, 102–3, 35–42, four unused lines. In line (5), "Till these echoes" is in
pencil; a bracket is drawn in pencil to the left of line (15).

Where now on heated pavements worn
(10)     The feet of millions stride.

⟨10⟩9 Fair rose the planted hills behind
The good town on the Bay,
And where the western slopes declined,
The prairie stretched away.

(15) ⟨11⟩10 Out from the many-fountained earth
The rivers gushed & foamed,
Sweet airs from every forest forth
And from the mountains roamed.

[4] ⟨12⟩ ↑11↓   What rival towers majestic soar
Along the stormy coast,—
Penn's town, New York, & Baltimore,
If Boston knew the most!
(5)        For you can teach the lightning speech,
And round the globe your voices reach.

⟨13⟩12 They laughed to know the world so wide,—
The mountains said, "Good day!
We greet you well, you Saxon men,
(10)      Up with your towns, & stay!"
The world was made for honest trade,
To plant & ⟨build⟩eat be none afraid.

⟨14⟩13 For you, they said, no barriers be;
For you, no sluggard's rest;
(15)     Each street leads downward to the sea,
Or land-ward to the west.

⟨15⟩14 O happy town beside the Sea!
Whose roads lead everywhere to all!
Than thine no deeper moat can be,
(20)     No steeper fence, no better wall.

[5] ⟨18⟩ ↑17↓   The townsmen braved the English King
Found friendship ⟨wi⟩in the French,
And Honor joined the patriot ring
Low on their wooden bench.

(5) ⟨19⟩18 O bounteous seas that never fail!
O day remembered yet,!
O happy port that spied the sail
Which wafted Lafayette,

4 "Boston," 43–46, 108–9, 47–60.
5 "Boston," 80–89.

(10)     Polestar of light, in Europe's night,
        That never faltered from the right

[6]  20 The sea returning day by day
      Restores the world wide mart
      So let each dweller on the Bay
      Fold Boston in his heart
(5)      For what avail the plough & sail,
      Or land, or life, if Freedom fail?

    21 Let the blood of her hundred thousands
      Throb in each manly vein,
      And the wit of all her wisest
(10)     Make sunshine in h⟨is⟩er brain;
      A union then of honest men
      Or union nevermore again.

    22 And each shall care for other,
      And each to each shall bend,
(15)     To the poor a noble brother,
      To the good an equal friend.

[7]  23 A blessing through the ages thus
      Shield all thy roofs & towers!
      *God with the fathers, so with us*⟨,⟩!
      Thou darling town of ours.

## "Boston" (Poems folder 88, manuscript 12)

[1]   Bad news from ↑George on↓ the English throne
     You are thriving well, said he,
     By these presents be it known
     You pay us a tax on Tea.
(5)     Tis very small, no ⟨thing⟩ ↑load↓ at all
     Honor enough that we sent the call

    "Not so," said Boston, "Good my lord,
    We pay your governors here,
    ⟨By these presents, be it known,⟩Richly for their bed &
      board
(10)   Six thousand pounds a year.
     Millions for home government
     But for tribute not one cent.

6 "Boston," 98–101, 28/78–30/79, 104–7, two lines first printed in *Selected Poems,* 1876,
110–13.
 7 "Boston," 114–17.
 1 "Boston," 61–70, 72–73. Struck through in pencil.

## "Boston" (Poems folder 88, manuscript 13)

[1] *Refrains.*

——————

An union then of honest men
Or union nevermore again

——————

Cruel & blind did file their mind
And sell the blood of human kind

——————

(5)    For power & place they sell their race
And locked their hands with traitors base

——————

⟨Ere⟩ ↑Till↓ these echoes be choked with snows
Or over the town blue ocean flows

——————

For what avail the plough or sail
(10)   Or land or life if freedom fail

——————

For day by day could Boston Bay
Their honest ⟨toil could⟩ labor overpay

——————

The world was made for honest trade
To plant & eat be none afraid

——————

(15)   The honest waves refuse to slaves
The empire of the ocean caves

——————

The men of yore were stout & poor
And sailed for bread to every shore

——————

⟨Ere these echoes be choked by snows⟩
(20)   ⟨Or over ⟨the⟩ our roofs blue ocean flows⟩

——————

[2]    For you can teach the lightning speech,
And round the globe your voices reach.

——————

What slave shall dare a name to bear
Once pledged to Freedom everywhere

——————

1 "Boston," two lines first printed in *Selected Poems*, 1876, four unused lines, 102–3, 29/78–30/79, 23–24, 11/51–12/52, 17–18, 5–6, 102–3. Lines (3–4), (13–14), (15–16), (17–18), and (19–20) are each struck through once in pencil; lines (11–12) are struck through twice in pencil; in line (7), "Ere" is canceled and "Till" inserted in pencil; and a large X is drawn in pencil to the left of lines (9–10).

2 "Boston," 108–9, x, x, 23–24, five unused lines.

(5)   ⟨For day by day could Boston Bay⟩
     ⟨Their honest labor overpay.⟩

———

     ⟨Shall a slave dare⟩
     Go purge your blood in lake & wood,
     To honor born of hardihood

———

(10)   ⟨Cruel & blind did file their mind⟩
     ⟨And sell the blood of human kind.⟩

———

## "Boston" (Poems folder 110)

[1]   For what avail the plough & sail
     or land or life if freedom fail

     For neer will die the captive's cry
     On the echoes of God, till /Right draws nigh./God reply./

## "Boston" (Cambridge Public Library)

[1]   Wondered old nations brave
     Nations looked on amazed
     The secret force to find
     Which fired the little town to ⟨guard⟩ save
(5)   The rights of all mankind
       Kings stared & empires brave
     ⟨Old states &⟩ ↑Wondered old↓ empires brave
     The secret force to find
     Which fired the pretty town to save
(10)   The rights of all mankind

[2]   But right is might in all the world
     And province to province faithful /clung /stood/
     ⟨Till⟩ At last ↑Until↓
     Thro good & ill till peace
(5)   Till the farmers won & peace was sung

——————

     Could honestly buy & drink their tea

1 "Boston," 29/78–30/79, x, x. Struck through in pencil.
1 "Boston," 90, 90–93, 90, 90–93. Lines (2–5) are in pencil except for "save" in line (4).
2 "Boston," 94–95, 97, 96–97, x. In pencil except for "At last" and "Until" in line (3).

## "Boston" (Massachusetts Historical Society)

[1]                     *Boston.*

1.    The rocky nook with hilltops three
Looked eastward from the farms,
And twice each day the flowing sea
Took Boston in its arms.

(5)         The men of yore were stout & poor,
And sailed for bread to every shore.

———

2. And where they went on trade intent
They did what freemen can;
Their dauntless ways did all men praise,
(10)       The merchant was a man.
The world was made for honest trade,
To plant & eat be none afraid.

———

3. The waves that rocked them on the deep
To them their secret told;
(15)      Said the winds that sung the lads to sleep,
Like us, be free & bold:
The honest waves refuse to slaves
The empire of the Ocean ⟨w⟩caves.

———

[2]    4. Old Europe groans with palaces,
Has lords enough, & more;—
We plant & build by foaming seas
A city of the poor.
(5)        ↑For day by day could Boston Bay ↓
↑Their honest labor overpay. ↓

5. The noble craftsman we promote,
Disown the knave & fool;
Each honest man shall have his vote,
(10)      Each child shall have his school.
For what avail the plough or sail,
Or land or life, if freedom fail?

———

6. We grant no dukedoms to the few,
We hold like rights, & shall,—
(15)      Equal on Sunday in the pew,
On Monday in the mall;
⟨Till these echoes be choked with snows,⟩
⟨⟨And⟩Or over the town blue Ocean flows.⟩

———

1 "Boston," 1–18.
2 "Boston," 19–34, 102–3, 35–38.

↑7. The wild rose & the barberry thorn↓
(20)         ↑Hung out their summer pride,↓
             ↑Where now on heated pavements worn↓
             ↑The feet of millions stride. ↓

[3]     8 Fair rose the planted hills behind
             The good town on the Bay;
             And where the western slopes declined
             The prairie stretched away.
(5)          ⟨Go purge your blood in lake & wood,⟩
             ⟨To honor born of hardihood.⟩

        ⟨9 Out from the many-fountained earth⟩
             ⟨The rivers gushed & foamed;⟩
             ⟨Sweet airs from every forest forth⟩
(10)         ⟨And from the mountains roamed.⟩

⟨10⟩ ↑9↓ What rival towers majestic soar
             Along the stormy coast,—
             Penn's town, New York, & Baltimore,
             If Boston knew the most!

(15) ⟨11⟩ ↑10↓ They laughed to know the world so wide,
             The Mountains said, "Good day!
             We greet you well, you Saxon men,
             Up with your towns, & stay!"
             The world was made for honest trade,
(20)         To plant & eat be none afraid.

[4] 1⟨2⟩1 For you, they said, no barriers be,
             For you no sluggard rest;
             Each street leads downward to the sea,
             Or land-ward to the West.

(5)     1⟨3⟩2 O happy town beside the sea,
             Whose roads lead everywhere to all,
             Than thine no deeper moat can be,
             No steeper fence, no better wall!
             ↑For what avail↓

        1⟨4⟩3 Bad news from George on the English throne—
(10)         "You are thriving well," said he,
             "Now by these presents, be it known,
             "You shall pay us a tax on tea;
             "Tis very small, no load at all,
             "Honor enough that we send the call."

3  "Boston," 39–42, six unused lines, 43–52.
4  "Boston," 53–60, 29/78, 61–66. Line (9) is in pencil.

[5] 1⟨5⟩4 "Not so," said Boston, "Good my lord,
⟨Abundant for⟩We pay your Governors here
Abundant for their bed & board,
Ten thousand pounds a year,
(5)        (Your Highness knows our rule)
*Millions for home ⟨g⟩Government*
*But for tribute never a cent.*

1⟨6⟩5 *The cargo came!* And who could blame
If Indians s⟨ie⟩eized the tea,
(10)     And, chest by chest, let down the same
Into the laughing sea?
For what avail the plough or sail,
Or land, or life, if freedom fail?

[6] 1⟨7⟩6 The townsmen braved the English king,—
Found friendship in the French,
And Honor joined the patriot ring
Low on their wooden bench.

(5)    1⟨8⟩7 O bounteous seas that never fail⟨;⟩!
O day remembered yet!
O happy port that spied the sail
Which wafted Lafayette⟨,⟩!
Polestar of light in Europe's night,
(10)     That never faltered from the right.

⟨19 The sea returning day by day⟩
⟨Restores the world-wide mart,⟩
⟨So let each dweller on the Bay⟩
⟨Fold Boston in his heart:⟩
(15)     ⟨⟨For what avail the plough or sail,⟩⟩
⟨⟨Or land, or life, if freedom fail?⟩⟩

[7]    18 Kings ⟨stared, &⟩ ↑Shook with fear, Old↓ Empires ⟨brave⟩
↑crave↓
The secret force to find
Which fired the little state to save
The rights of all mankind.

(5)    19 ↑But right is might through all the world↓
↑Province to Province faithful stood↓
↑Through good & ill the war bolt hurled↓
↑Till Freedom triumphed & Peace was sung↓

———

5 "Boston," 67–79.
6 "Boston," 80–89, 98–101, 29/78–30/79. A hand sign pointing right and an American flag are drawn in the left margin between lines (10–11).
7 "Boston," 90–103.

20 The sea returning day by day
(10) Restores the worldwide mart;
 So let each dweller in the Bay
 Fold Boston in his heart;
  Till these echoes be choked with snows
  ⟨And⟩Or over ⟨our town⟩ ↑Trimount↓ blue Ocean flows.

[8] 2⟨0⟩1 Let the blood of her hundred thousands
 Throb in each manly vein,
 And the wit of all her wisest
 Make sunshine in h⟨is⟩er brain:
(5)  ⟨A union then of honest men,⟩
  ⟨Or Union never more again.⟩

2⟨1⟩2 And each shall care for other,
 And each to each shall bend,
 To the poor a noble brother,
(10) To the good an equal friend.

2⟨2⟩3 A blessing through the ages thus
 Shield all thy roofs & towers!
 *God ⟨for⟩with the fathers, so with us,*
 Thou darling town of ours!


## "Boston Hymn" (Poems folder 38)

[1] Hang out your ensign to the sun,
 Open your mouth to drink the breath
 Which the Lord sends to those
 Whom he calls to a penal death.
(5) He hath honored you overmuch
 Far above your right
 You shall go to early graves
 Without funeral without dirge
 Men shall say Where was the Avenger
(10) Why was not he alert
 They should have been harried
 They have not their desert

[2]  These craggy hills that front the dawn
 Man-bearing granite of the north,

---

8 "Boston," 104–7, two lines first printed in *Selected Poems*, 1876, 110–17.
1 Unidentified lines. Upside down at the bottom of the page is a large R with two rules below it.
2 "These craggy hills" (1–4); "And hungry Debt" (5–6, 7–8); "Boston Hymn," 49, 49–52, 49–52 (9–17).

Shall fiercer forms & races spawn
Charged with my genius forth.

(5) And hungry Debt beseiged my door
And still held out his hundred hands

And hungry Debt with ⟨thousand⟩ ↑his hundred↓ hands
⟨Stood at⟩ ↑Beseiged↓ my door & held them out
I charge you well to comfort men

(10) I charge you to ⟨serve⟩ ↑/comfort/succor/↓ men
Your honor & ⟨high⟩ place is to serve
To ⟨merit well of ⟨all⟩ ↑humble↓ men⟩ ↑give those who
  cannot give again↓
⟨A⟩Never from right to swerve
I charge you  to succor men

(15) Tis nobleness to serve
Help ⟨those⟩ them who cannot help again
Nor from the right to swerve

[3]    the book is good
That puts /me/the soul/ in a working mood

The pain of love a better fate
Than the body's best estate

(5) Of the Maker not the Made
Dwell with the Cause or grim or glad

Count it unmanly not to vote

[4] A union then of honest men
Or union nevermore again

Here was a force no king could bind
And nations watched

(5) And watched

Across the Ocean wave

Rough hemp & flax & cotton grow
To weave the sails all winds shall blow

Stemming all night the starlit sea
(10) From either Pole across the Line
Freighted ⟨with⟩ from all ⟨ports⟩ ↑climes↓ that be

3 "The comrade or the book," 1–2 (1–2); "The pain of love" (3–4); "Hold of the Maker" (5–6); unidentified line (7). Lines (3–4) and (5–6) are struck through separately in ink.
4 "Boston," two lines first printed in *Selected Poems*, 1876, 90?, 90?, 90?, unused lines. Lines (3–6) are in pencil.

From Andes to the Appenine
Rank hemp & flax & cotten grow
To weave the sails all winds shall blow

[5] Do like the best of Physicians said Beckford heal the disease by
doing nothing      Bancroft VI 79
        Indian speech p. 86
Hutchinson obtained a grant of £200 from the King
        Here was force King cd not bind

    They
        A town to guard the
            To guard the rights of all mankind

16000 pop. of Boston
In 1770 410 wives in Boston agreed to renounce tea    p. 333

(5)         The little town taught Parliament
            How to defend ⟨t⟩ the rights


## "Brahma" (Poems folder 12)

[1]                     Brahma.

                        ———

            If the red slayer think he slays,
            Or if the slain think he is slain,
            ⟨He knows⟩ ↑They know↓ not yet the subtle ways
            I keep & ⟨tur⟩pass & turn again

(5)         Far or forgot to me is near
            Shadow & sunlight are the same
            The vanished gods not less appear
            And one to me is shame & fame

            They reckon ill who leave me out
(10)        When me they fly, I am the wings
            I am the doubter & the doubt
            And I the hymn the Bramin sings.

            The strong gods pine for my abode
            And pine in vain the sacred seven
(15)        But thou, meek lover of the good,
            Find me, & turn thy back on heaven

5 "Boston," 90?, x, 92–93, x, 93. This page is in pencil. The prose references are to George
Bancroft's *A History of the United States*, vol. 6 (1854), in Emerson's library.
    1 "Brahma." In pencil. Several horizontal lines are drawn in pencil above, through, and under
the title.

## "The civil world will much forgive" (Poems folder 17)

[1]       The civil world will much forgive
           To bards who from its maxims live
           But if, grown bold, the poet dare
           Bend his practice to his prayer,
(5)      And, following his mighty heart
           Shame the time, & live apart,
           *Vae solis!*
           I found this ↑,—↓
           That of goods I could not miss
(10)     If I fell within the line,
           Once a member, all was mine,
           Houses, banquets, gardens, fountains,
           Fortune's delectable mountains;
           But if I would walk alone ↑,↓
(15)     Was neither cloak nor crumb my own ↑.↓

## "Compensation" ("The wings of Time") (Poems folder 58)

[1]                Motto to *"Compensation."*
1841    The wings of Time are black & white
           Pied with ⟨day⟩ ↑morning↓ & with night
           Mountain tall & ocean deep
           Trembling balance duly keep
(5)      In changing moon in tidal wave
           Glows the feud of Want & Have
           ⟨In sign⟩ ⟨↑Metre↓⟩ ↑Gauge↓ of ⟨m⟩More ⟨or⟩& Less thro'
               space
           Electric star or pencil plays:
           The lonely Earth amid the balls
(10)     That hurry through the eternal halls
           A makeweight flying to the void,
           A supplemental asteroid,
           A compensatory spark,
           Shoots athwart the neutral Dark.

## "The Daemonic and the Celestial Love" (Houghton, Harvard)

[1]       He is an oligarch
           He prizes wonder, fame, & mark;

1 "The civil world" (1–7); "I found this," 1–8 (8–15). In line (8), the comma and dash are in pencil, as are the comma in line (14) and the period in line (15).

1 "Compensation" ("The wings of Time"). Struck through in ink.

1 "The Daemonic and the Celestial Love," 123–30, 132?, 133–37, 141–48, 159–61. "5" is written in ink at the top center.

He loveth crowns,
And scorneth drones.
(5)    He doth elect
The beautiful, the fortunate,
And the sons of intellect,
And the soul of ample fate,
Beloved of the morning.
(10)    In his prowess he exults,
And the multitude insults.
↑In the greatness of his strength↓
He looks on poor men,
And seeing his ⟨fierceness⟩ ↑eye glare↓
(15)    They lose heart & ⟨sink,⟩ despair.
He will never be gainsaid,
And he will not be stayed.
His hot tyranny
Burns up every other tie,
(20)    Therefore, after a season,
Is his cold will defied,
And the dogs of Fate untied.
For the demoni⟨acal⟩c love
Is the ⟨seed⟩↑ancestor↓ of wars ⟨& remorse⟩,
(25)    And the parent of remorse.


[2]    Higher far,
Upward, into the pure realm,
Over sun or star,
Over the flickering Daemon film,
(5)    Thou must mount for Love
Into vision which all forms
In one form dissolves;
In a region where the wheel,
On which all beings ride,
(10)    Visibly revolves.
Where the eternal worm
Girds the world with bound & term,
Where unlike things are like,
Where laugh & moan,
(15)    Hatred & love,
Pride & humility,
Self & society,
Melt into one.

2 "The Daemonic and the Celestial Love," 162–74, 176, x, x, x, 177–81. "6" is written in ink at the top center.

> There Past, Present, Future, shoot
(20) Triple flowers from one root;
> Substances at base divided
> In their summits are united:
[3] There sublunar quarrels cease
> In the beatific peace.
> There the primal essence rolls
> Its river through divided souls,
(5) And the sunny Aeon sleeps
> Folding all souls in its deeps;
> And every fair & every good
> Known in part or known impure
> To men below,
(10) In their archetypes endure.

> The race of gods,
> Or those we erring own,
> Are shadows flitting up & down
> In the still abodes.
(15) The circles of that sea are laws
> And hides in light the nameless Cause

> Pray for a beam
> Out of that sphere
> Thee to guide & to redeem.
(20) O what a load
> Of care and toil
[4] By lying use bestowed
> From his shoulders falls who sees
> The true astronomy,
> The Universe of Peace.
(5) Counsel which the ages kept
> Shall the wellborn soul accept
> As the oerhanging trees
> Fill the lake with images
> As garment draws the garments hem
(10) Men their fortunes bring with them.

> By right or wrong
> Lands & goods go to the strong
> Property will brutely draw
> Still to the proprietor

3 "The Daemonic and the Celestial Love," x, x, 182–200. "7" is written in ink at the top center.

4 "The Daemonic and the Celestial Love," 201–18. "8" is written in ink in the upper left corner.

(15)    Silver to silver
         And kind to kind.

         Not less the eternal poles
         Of tendency distribute souls

[5]    There need no vows to bind
         Whom not each other seek but find.
         They give & take no pledge or oath
         Nature is the bond of both.
(5)    No prayer persuades, no flattery fawns,
         Their noble meanings are their pawns
         Plain & cold is their address
         Power have they for tenderness
         And so thoroughly is known
(10)   Each others purpose by his own,
         They can parley without meeting
         Need is none of forms of greeting
         They can well communicate
         In their innermost estate
(15)   When each the other shall avoid,
         Shall each by each be most enjoyed.

         Not with scarfs or perfumed gloves
         Do these celebrate their loves,
         Not by jewels, feasts or savours,
(20)   Not by ribbons or by favours,
         But by the sun-sparkle on the sea,
         And by the cloud-shadow on the lea,
         By the soothing lapse of morn to mirk
         And by the cheerful round of work
[6]    Love makes the hero strong & stark
         For his task from dawn till dark;
         Love makes him confident & true
         There amid the mocking crew.
(5)    Loves hearts are faithful, but not fond,
         Bound for the just, but not beyond:
         Not glad as is the loving herd
         Of self in other still preferred,
         But they have heartily adopted
(10)   The weal of broad mankind.

         ⟨But th⟩And they serve men austerely,
         After their own genius clearly,

---

5 "The Daemonic and the Celestial Love," 219–42. "9" is written in ink at the top center.
6 "The Daemonic and the Celestial Love," four unused lines, 251–68. "10" is written in ink at the top center.

Not with false humility:
For this is Love's nobility
(15)    Not to scatter bread & gold
Goods & raiment, bought & sold
But to hold fast his simple sense
And speak the speech of innocence
And with hand & body & blood
(20)    To make his bosom-counsel good.
For he that feeds men, serveth few,
He serveth all who dares be true.

## "Day by day returns" (Poems folder 19)

{1} 1831 Day by day returns
The everlasting sun
Replenishing material urns
With God's unspared donation
(5)    But the day of day
The orb within the mind
⟨That maketh⟩ ↑Creating↓ fair & good alway
Shines not as once it shined.

Brothers, no decrepitude
(10)   ⟨Chills⟩ ↑Cramps↓ the limbs of Time
As fleet his feet, his hands as good,
His ⟨workings⟩ ↑vision↓ as sublime;
On nature's wheels there is no rust
Nor less on man's enchanted dust
(15)   Beauty & Force alight

Vast the realm of Being is
In the waste one nook is his
What soever hap befals
In his visions narrow walls
(20)   He is there to testify

## "Dear brother, would you know the life" (Poems folder 22)

{1}            Lines written in 1831.    Boston,
————

Dear brother, would you know the life
Please God that I would lead?

1 "Day by day returns" (1–20); "Brother, no decrepitude" (9–12). In line (12), "vision" is in both pencil and ink.
1 "Dear brother, would you know," 1–16, 16.

On the first wheels that quit this weary town,
Over yon western bridges I would speed
(5)    And with a cheerful benison forsake
Each street & spire & suburb, known from birth
Then following where the impatient Genius leads
Deep in a woodland seek a sunny farm
Amid the mountain counties, Franklin, Berks,
(10)   Where down the steep ravine a river roars
Even from a brook, & where old woods,
Spared by the ax, cumber the ample ground
With their centennial wrecks.
Find me a slope where I can feel the sun,
(15)   And mark the rising of the early stars
There will I bring my books & make my home
With pious care my household gods will bring
[2]    The dear remembrance of now ruined days
⟨Will bring⟩The relics of my dead & dwell again
In the sweet odor of her memory.
There, in the uncouth solitude, unlock
(5)    My slender stock of art,
⟨I will⟩ adjust my dial ⟨in the grass,⟩ ↑on a grassy mound,↓
Hang in the air a bright thermometer,
And aim a telescope at Uranus

## "The Dervish whined to *Said*" (Poems folder 79)

[1]      The Dervish whined to *Said,*
"Thou didst not tarry while I prayed."
↑Beware the fires which Eblis burned. ↓
But Saadi coldly thus returned,
(5)    "Once, with manlike love & fear,
I gave thee for an hour my ear,
I kept the sun & stars at bay,
And love, for words thy tongue could say;
I cannot sell my heaven again
(10)   For all that rattles in thy brain.

## "The Discontented Poet: a Masque" (Poems folder 73)

[1]    Lonely he sat: the men were strange,
The women all forbidden,

2 "Dear brother, would you know," x, 17–20, 20, 21–22.
1 "The Dervish whined to *Said.*"
1 "The Discontented Poet: a Masque," 1–22. Lines (1–16) and (8–22) are struck through separately in ink; single vertical lines are drawn in pencil to the left of lines (4–5) and (12–15). "Poet" and "9" are written in pencil in the upper left corner.

Too closely pent in narrow range
Between two sleeps a short day's stealth
(5)    'Mid many ails a brittle health
Counts his scant stock of native wealth
By conscience chidden, chidden.

His loves were sharp sharp pains;
Outlets to his thoughts were none;
(10)   A wandering fire within his veins
His soul was smouldered & undone:
A cripple of God, half-true, half formed,
And by great sparks Promethean warmed,
Constrained by impotence to adjourn
(15)   To infinite time his eager turn,
His lot of action from the Urn.

He by false usage pinned about,
No breath therein, no passage out,
Cast wishful glances at the stars,
(20)   And wishful saw the Ocean stream,
"Merge me in the brute Universe,
Or lift to some diviner dream."

[2]   Beside him sat enduring love
Upon him noble eyes did rest
Which for the ⟨beauty⟩ ↑genius↓ that there strove
The follies bore that it invest
(5)   They spoke not: for their earnest sense
Outran the craft of eloquence
The holy lovers peaceful sate
Thro ecstasy inanimate
As marble statues in a hall
(10)   Yet was their silence musical
The only plaints the sole replies
Were those long looks of liquid eyes

## "The Discontented Poet: a Masque" (Houghton, Harvard)

[1]   Lonely he sat: the men were strange,
The women all forbidden:
Too closely pent in narrow range,
Between two sleeps a short day's stealth,

---

2 "The Discontented Poet: a Masque," 23–34. Lines (1–12) are struck through twice in ink;
a vertical line is drawn in pencil to the left of lines (1–6).
1 "The Discontented Poet: a Masque," 1–11, x, 12–19.

(5) Mid many ails a brittle health,
    Counts his scant stock of native wealth,
    By conscience chidden chidden

    His loves were sharp sharp pains,
    Outlets to his thoughts were none,
(10) A wandering fire within his veins
    His soul was smouldered & undone;
    The joy of life a bitter groan.
    A cripple of God, half true, half formed,
    And by great sparks Promethean warmed,
(15) Constrained by impotence to adjourn
    To infinite time his eager turn,
    His lot of action from the Urn.
    He by false usage pinned about—
    No breath therein, no passage out,
(20) Cast wishful glances at the stars,
[2]  And wishful saw the Ocean stream,—
    'Merge me in the brute universe,
    Or lift to some diviner dream!'

    Beside him sat enduring love
(5) Upon him noble eyes did rest
    Which for the genius that there strove
    The follies bore that it invest.
    They spoke not: for their earnest sense
    Outran the craft of eloquence
(10) The holy lovers peaceful sate
    Through extacy inanimate
    As marble statues in a hall
    Yet was their silence musical
    The only plaints the sole replies
(15) Were those long looks of liquid eyes.

First they signified to him that he should be calm: and this was their sense—

    Yon waterflags, yon sighing osier,
    A drop can shake, a breath can fan,
    Maidens laugh & weep: Composure
    Is the pudency of Man.

[3] Then when he lamented his want of powers & aids they taught thus—

2 "The Discontented Poet: a Masque," 20–38. "First they signified . . . sense—" is in pencil.
3 "The Discontented Poet: a Masque," 39–56. "Then when he . . . thus—" is in pencil.

Means,—dear brother, ask them not:
Soul's desire is means enow:
Pure content is angels' lot:
Thine own theatre art thou.

———

Then he said

———

(5)      I see your forms with deep content
I know that ye are excellent
But will ye stay?
I hear the rustle of wings
Ye meditate what to say
(10)     When ye go to quit me forever & aye

———

And they answered

———

Brother we are no phantom band
Brother accept this fatal hand
Aches thy unbelieving heart
With the fear that we must part?
(15)     See! all we are rooted here
By one thought to one same sphere:
From thyself thou canst not flee
From thyself no more can we.

[4] Then he said

———

Sun & stars their courses keep
But not angels of the deep:
Day & night their turn observe
But the day of day may swerve:
(5)      Is there warrant that the waves
Of thought from their mysterious caves
Will heap in me their highest tide
In me therewith beatified?
Unsure the ebb & flood of thought,
(10)     The moon comes back, the Spirit not.

They answered

———

Brother, sweeter is the Law
Than all the grace Love ever saw,
We are its suppliants. By it we
Draw the breath of Eternity.

4 "The Discontented Poet: a Masque," 57–80.

(15)      Serve thou it not for daily bread
             Serve it for pain & fear & dread.
             Love it though it hide its light.
             By love behold the Sun at night
             If the Law should thee forget,
(20)      All enamoured, serve it yet:
             Though it hate thee, suffer long,
             Put the Spirit in the wrong.
             That were a deed to sing in Eden
             By the waters of life to seraphs heeding.

## "Divine Inviters! I accept" (Poems folder 73)

[1]      Divine Inviters! I accept
             The courtesy ye have shown & kept
             From ancient ages for the bard,
             To modulate
(5)       With finer fate
             A fortune ⟨cold⟩harsh & hard.
             With aim like yours
             I watch your course,
             ↑Who never break your lawful dance↓
(10)      ↑By error or intemperance.↓
             O birds of ether without wings!
             O heavenly ships without a sail!
             O fire of fire! o best of things!
             O mariners who never fail!
(15)      Sail swiftly through your amber vault
             An animated law, a presence to exalt

## "Easy to match what others do" (Houghton, Harvard)

[1]      Easy to do what others do
             ⟨And ⟨just⟩do⟩ ↑Perform the feat↓ as well as they
             Hard to outdo the best the true
             And ⟨tread a⟩ find a loftier way

(5)       The ⟨college⟩ ↑school↓ decays the learning spoils
             Because of the sons of wine;—
             ⟨How to⟩ ↑For youth What↓ rescue ⟨the youth⟩ from their
                 toils?

    1 "Divine Inviters! I accept." Lines (9–10) are written at the bottom of the page and their place of insertion indicated by an arrow. "Poet" and "7" are written in pencil in the upper left corner.
    1 "Easy to match what others do," 1–8, 8/9?, 9, 8?, 8?

One ray of ⟨the⟩ truth divine.
⟨The ray to burn the⟩
(10)    The rays that burn outshine
    ↑What Redantor divine↓
    ↑What panoply divine?↓


## "Elizabeth Hoar" (Poems folder 26)

[1]               ↑*Elizabeth Hoar.*↓
    Almost I am tempted to ⟨begin⟩ essay
    For sympathetic eyes the portraiture
    Of the good angels that environ me.
    ⟨One⟩My sister is a Greek in mind & face
(5)    And well embodies to these latest years
    The truth of those ⟨old artists⟩ high sculptors old who drew
    In marble or in bronze, on vase or frieze
    The perfect forms of Pallas or the Muse;
    Forms in simplicity complete
(10)    And beauty of the ⟨disdain⟩soul disdaining art.
    So bright, so positive, so much itself,
    Yet so adapted to the work it wrought
    It drew true love, but was complete alone.
    ⟨And yet the best of angels live alone.⟩
(15)    She seemed to commune with herself, & say,
    ↑I cannot stoop to custom & the crowd,↓
    For either I will marry with a star,
    Or I will pick threads in a factory.
    So perfect in her action, one would say,
(20)    She condescended if she added speech.
    Her look was sympathy, & though she spoke
    Better than all the rest, she did not speak
    Worthy of her. She read in many books,
    And loved the Greek as t'were her mother tongue
[2]    She knew the value of the passing day
    Thought it no mark of virtue to be scornful
    Or cry for better company, but held
    Each day a solid good; never mistook
(5)    The fashionable judgment for her own.
    So keen perception that no judge or scribe
    Could vie with her unerring estimate.
    When through much silence & delay she spoke,
    It was the Mind's own oracle, through joy

1 "Elizabeth Hoar," 1–24. The title is in pencil; line (14) is canceled in pencil.
2 "Elizabeth Hoar," 25–35.

(10)       And love of truth or beauty so perceived:
              Never a poor return on self.

## "Eve roved in Paradise" (Poems folder 172)

[1]           Eve roved in Paradise, I've heard,
              With no more baggage than a bird;
              Exiled, she soon found necessary
              More garments than she liked to carry;
(5)         Adam devised valise & sack,
              And trunk & tray her weeds to pack,
              But when the hatbox ⟨was⟩ ↑he↓ invented,
              Dear Eve declared herself contented;
              Eden was well—Angels prefer it—
(10)        She thought the outworld had its merit;
              And now transmits to Ellen dear
              This sable cube of comfort here.

## "Ever find me dim regards" (Goethe's *Werke,* 1828–1833, vol. 50)

[1] Hel.  Ever find me dim regards
              Love of ladies love of bards
              Marked forbearance compliments
              Tokens of benevolence
(5)         What boots it! I cannot love myself

              They love me as I love th[e] cloud
              Sailing falsely as a sphere
              Hated mist could it draw near

## "Fate" ("That you are fair") (University of Virginia)

[1] You shall have the rest of my thought on Festus, which lies by me in numbers somewhat rude, I own, for the topic.—

              That you are fair or wise is vain,
              Or strong, or rich, or generous,
              You must have also the untaught strain
              That sheds beauty on the rose.

    1 "Eve roved in Paradise." In pencil. The date "1864." is written in ink below the poem, probably not in Emerson's hand.
    1 "Ever find me dim regards," 1–5, 8–10. In pencil. In line (6), "th" may be canceled.
    1 "Fate" ("That you are fair"), 1–22.

(5)      There is a melody born of melody
         Which melts the world into a sea.
         Toil could never compass it,
         Art its height could never hit,
         It came never out of wit,
(10)     But a music music-born
         Well may Jove & Juno scorn.
         Thy beauty, if it lack the fire
         Which drives me mad with sweet desire,
         What boots it? What the soldier's mail,
(15)     Unless he conquer & prevail?
         What all the goods thy pride which lift
         If thou pine for another's gift?
         Alas that one is born in blight,
         Victim of perpetual slight:—
(20)     When thou lookest in his face,
         Thy heart saith, Brother! go thy ways:
         None shall ever ask what thou doest,
[2]       Or care an apple for what thou knowest,
         Or listen when thou repliest,
         Or remember where thou liest,
         Or how thy supper is sodden,—
(5)      And another is born
         To make the sun forgotten.
         Surely he carries a talisman
         Under his tongue,
         Broad are his shoulders, & strong,
(10)     And his eye is scornful,
         Threatening, & young.
         I hold it of little matter
         Whether your jewel be of pure water,
         A rose diamond, or a white,—
(15)     But whether it dazzle me with light.
         I care not how you are drest
         In the coarsest or in the best,
         Nor whether your name is base or brave,
         Nor for the fashion of your behaviour,
(20)     But whether you charm me,
         Bid my bread feed, & my fire warm me,
         And dress up nature in your favors.
         Only one thing is forever good,
         And that is success,—
(25)     Dear to the Eumenides,

2 "Fate" ("That you are fair"), 23–50.

And dear to all the heavenly brood.
He carries the eagles,—victorious lord,—
Who bides at home, nor looks abroad.

## "For Genius made his cabin wide" (Poems folder 78)

[1]      He basked in friendships all the days of spring

for better mates, he thought, no god could bring,
And basked in friendships all the days of spring.

And though he found his friendships meet,
(5)      His quarrels too had somewhat sweet

For genius made his cabin wide
And Love led gods therein to bide

How the young heart can adorn
With grace each comrade
(10)    Better he tho't no god could bring
And basks in friendship all the days of spring

## "Forth to encounter thy affianced doom" (Poems folder 34)

[1]      Forth to encounter thy affianced doom
And art affianced to a noble doom
Shalt be affianced to a heavenlier bride
For I see ⟨g⟩Glory hasting to thy side;
(5)      Not frolic Beauty weaving wanton nets
⟨Lies in⟩ ↑From her↓ soft ambush peeps with radiant eye
Tis safer when the curled Syren frowns
No fate, save by the victim's fault, is low
For God hath writ all dooms magnificent
(10)    So guilt not traverses his tender will.
I make ye witness prophesying Stars
And by the light of prophesying Stars
And men whose faces were a history
Be of thine Age the priceless ornament.
(15)    Outface the brass browed slanders of the time
Trust not the words of ruby lips suspect those rolling eyes
Those rosy wreaths hide scorpion whips

Are these bare trees
The orchestra whence all that music rang

1 "For Genius made his cabin wide," 4, 3–6, 1–2, x, x, 3–4. Line (1) is struck through in pencil four times and lines (2–3) twice; "for" and "mates" in line (3) are circled in pencil.
   1 "Forth to encounter" (1–21); "Shalt be affianced" (3–4); "Not frolic Beauty" (5–7); "No fate, save by the victim's fault" (8–10).

(20)   Nor all the rich elixirs of the world
     Can bring the life that's sped.


## "From the Persian of Hafiz" (Berg, New York Public Library)

[1]         ↑From the Persian of Hafiz.↓
       ↑————————————————↓

  ↑The poems of Hafiz are held by the Persians to be mystical & allegor-
ical. The following Ode, notwithstanding its anacreontic style, is re-
garded by his German editor, Von Hammer, as one of those which
earned for Hafiz among his countrymen the title of 'Tongue of the
Secret.'↓

     Butler, fetch the ruby wine
     Which with sudden greatness fills us;
     Pour for me who in my spirit
     Fail in ⟨perf⟩courage & performance.
(5)    Bring the philosophic stone,
     Karun's treasure, Noah's life;
     Haste, that by thy means I open
     All the doors of luck & life.
     Bring me, boy, the fire-water,
(10)   Zoroaster sought in dust.
     To Hafiz revelling tis allowed
     To pray to Matter and to Fire.
     Bring the wine of Jamschid's glass
     That shone, ere time was, in the Néant.
(15)   Give it me that through its virtue
     I, as Jamschid, see through worlds.
     W⟨ell⟩isely said ⟨Jamschid to⟩ the Kaiser Jamschid,
     This world's not worth a barleycorn.
     Bring me, boy, the nectar cup
(20)   Since it leads to Paradise
 [2]   Flute & lyre lordly speak
     Lees of wine outvalue crowns.
     ↑Hither↓ Bring ⟨me, boy,⟩ the veiled beauty
     Who in ill-famed houses sits:
(5)    ⟨Bring⟩ ↑Lead↓ her forth: my honest name
     Freely barter I for wine.
     Bring me, boy, the firewater,
     ↑—↓Drinks the lion⟨,⟩—the woods burn.
     Give it me, that I storm heaven,

 1 "From the Persian of Hafiz," 1–18, x, x. "1" and "190" are written in ink in the upper right corner.
 2 "From the Persian of Hafiz," 19–38, 41–46. "2" and "191" are written in ink in the upper left corner.

|        |                                                      |
|--------|------------------------------------------------------|
| (10)   | Tear the net ⟨of⟩ ↑from↓ the Arch-wolf.              |
|        | Wine, wherewith the Houris teach                     |
|        | Angels the ways of Paradise.                         |
|        | On the glowing coals I'll set it,                    |
|        | And therewith my brain perfume.                      |
| (15)   | Bring me wine, through whose effulgence              |
|        | Jam & Chosroes yielded light:                        |
|        | ⟨Bring⟩Wine, that to the flute I sing                |
|        | Where is Jam, & where is Kauss.                      |
|        | Bring the blessing of old times;                     |
| (20)   | Bless the old departed Shahs;                        |
|        | Bring it me, the Shah of hearts.                     |
|        | Bring me wine to wash me clean                       |
|        | Of the weatherstains of care,                        |
|        | See the countenance of luck.                         |
| (25)   | While I dwell in spirit-gardens,                     |
|        | Wherefore sit I shackled here?                       |
| [3]    | ⟨Drunk⟩ ↑Lo↓, this mirror shows me all.             |
|        | Drunk, I speak of purity;                            |
|        | Beggar, I of lordship speak.                         |
|        | When Hafiz in his revel sings,                       |
| (5)    | Shouteth Sohra in her sphere.                        |
|        |                                                      |
|        | Fear the changes of a day:                           |
|        | Bring wine which increases life,                     |
|        | Since the world is all untrue,                       |
|        | Let the trumpets thee remind                         |
| (10)   | How the crown of Kobad vanished.                     |
|        | ⟨Seek in wine the heart's desire⟩                    |
|        | ⟨Without wine there is not rest⟩                     |
|        | Be not certain of the world;                         |
|        | T'will not spare to shed thy blood.                  |
| (15)   | Desperate of the world's affair,                     |
|        | Came I running to the wine-house.                    |
|        | Give me wine which maketh glad,                      |
|        | That I may my steed bestride,                        |
|        | Through the course career with Rustem,               |
| (20)   | Gallop to my heart's content.                        |
|        | Give me, boy, the ruby cup                           |
|        | Which unlocks the heart with wine,                   |
|        | That I reason quite renounce,                        |
|        | And plant banners on the worlds.                     |
| (25)   | ⟨That⟩ Let us make our glasses kiss,                 |

3 "From the Persian of Hafiz," 47–56, x, x, 57–64, x, x, 65–68. "Hafiz" is written in ink in the upper left corner, and "⟨3⟩" and "192" in the upper right corner.

Let us quench the sorrow-cinders:
[4]    Today let us drink together.
Whoso has a ⟨feast announced,⟩ ↑banquet dressed,↓
Is with glad mind satisfied,
Scaping from the snares of Dews.

(5)    Alas for youth! tis gone in wind,—
Happy he who spent it well.
Give me wine, that I o'erleap
Both worlds at a single spring.
Stole at dawn from glowing spheres
(10)    Call of Houris to mine ear;
'O happy bird! delicious soul!
'Spread thy pinion, break the cage;
'Sit on the roof of the seven domes,
'Where the spirits take repose.'

(15)    In the time of Bisurdschimihr,
Menutscheher's beauty shined.
On the beaker of Nushirvan,
Wrote they once in elder times,
'Hear the counsel, learn from us
(20)    'Sample of the course of things;
[5]    ⟨'Sample of the course of things;⟩
'Earth, it is a place of sorrow,
'Scanty joys are here below,
'Who has nothing, has no sorrow."

(5)    Where is Jam, & where his cup?
Solomon, & his mirror where?
Which of the wise masters knows
What time Kauss & Jam existed?
When those heroes left this world,
(10)    Left they nothing but their names.
Bind thy heart not to the earth,
When thou goest, come not back.
Fools squander on the world their hearts,
⟨There at home & remote from heaven.⟩
(15)    ↑League with it, is feud with heaven;↓
Never gives it what thou wishest.

A cup of wine imparts the sight
Of the five heaven-domes with nine steps;
Whoso can himself renounce,

4 "From the Persian of Hafiz," 69, 71–89. "4" and "193" are written in ink in the upper left corner.

5 "From the Persian of Hafiz," 89–101, x, 102–12. "Hafiz" is written in ink in the upper left corner, and "⟨5⟩" and "194" in the upper right corner.

(20)    Without support ⟨can⟩ ↑shall↓ walk thereon.
        Who ⟨is⟩ discreet ↑is,↓ is not wise.
        Give me, boy, the Kaisar cup
        Which rejoices heart & soul;
        Under ⟨wine⟩ type of wine & cup
(25)    Signify we purest love.
[6]     Youth like lightning disappears,
        Life goes by us as the wind;
        Leave the dwelling with six doors,
        And the serpent with nine heads;
(5)     Life & silver spend thou freely,
        If thou ⟨lovest well⟩ ↑honourest↓ the soul.
        Haste into the other life;
        All is nought save God alone.
        Give me, boy, this toy of daemons.
(10)    When the cup of Jam was lost,
        Him availed the world no more.
        Fetch the wineglass made of ice,
        Wake the torpid heart with wine.
        Every clod of loam below us
(15)    Is a skull of Alexander;
        Oceans are the blood of princes;
        Desart sands the dust of beauties.
        More than one Darius was there
        Who the whole world overcame;
(20)    But since these gave up the ghost,
        Thinkest thou they never were?

[7]     Boy, go from me to the Shah,
        Say to him; Shah crowned as Jam,
        ⟨Seek⟩ ↑Win↓ thou first the poor man's heart,
        Then the glass; so know the world.
(5)     Empty sorrows from this earth
        Canst thou drive away with wine.
        Now in thy throne's recent beauty,
        In the flowing tide of power,
        ⟨Lord of earth, & prince of times,⟩
(10)    Moon of fortune, mighty king,
        Whose tiara sheddeth lustre,
        Peace secure to fish & fowl,
        Heart & eye-sparkle to saints;
        Shoreless is the sea of praise,—

6 "From the Persian of Hafiz," 113–33. "⟨6⟩" and "195" are written in ink in the upper left corner.

7 "From the Persian of Hafiz," 134–41, x, 142–55. "⟨7⟩" and "196" are written in the upper right corner.

(15)     I content me with a prayer.
            From Nisami's poet-works,
            Highest ornament of Speech,
            ↑Here a↓ Verse⟨s three⟩ will I recite,
            Verse⟨s⟩ ↑as↓ beautiful as pearls:
(20)     "More kingdoms ⟨mayst thou subdue⟩ ↑wait thy diadem,↓
            "Than ⟨thyself canst think⟩ ↑are known to thee by name;↓
            "May the sovran destiny
            "Grant a victory every morn!"

## "The gods walk in the breath of the woods" (Poems folder 73)

[1]     The gods talk in the breath of the woods
            They talk in the shaken pine,
            And fill the long reach of the old seashore
            With dialogue divine
(5)     And the poet who overhears
            Some random word they say
            Is the fated man of men
            Whom the ages must obey
            One who having nectar drank
(10)    Into blissful orgies sank;
            He takes no mark of night or day,
            He cannot go, but cannot stay,
            He would, yet would not, counsel keep,
            But like a walker in his sleep
(15)    With staring eye that seeth none
            Ridiculously up & down
            Seeks how he may fitly tell
            The heart o'erlading miracle.

## "Grace" (*A Selection from . . . John Milton,* 1826, vol. 1)

[1]     How much, preventing God! how much I owe
            To the ↑de↓fences thou hast round me set
            Example Custom Fear Occasion slow
            ⟨Were props to my tottering Conscience⟩
(5)     ⟨Hedged in my soul from Satans creeping net⟩
            These scorned bondmen were my parapet
            I dare not peep over this parapet
            To gage with glance the roaring gulf below
            The depths of sin to which I had descended
(10)    Had not these me against myself defended

1  "The gods walk." "Poet" and "4" are written in pencil in the upper left corner.
1  "Grace," 1–3, x, x, 4–8. In pencil. In line (8), "gage" may be "gauge."

## "Has God on thee conferred" (Poems folder 19)

[1] 1831 On thee has God conferred
⟨n⟩bodily presence mean as Paul's
Yet made thee bearer of a word
That sleepy nations as with trumpet calls

(5) O noble heart accept
With equal thanks the talent & disgrace
The splendid town unwept
Nourish thy power in a private place.

Think not that unattended
(10) By heavenly Powers thou steal'st to solitude
Nor even on earth all unbefriended
Tho no sweet rabble shouts on thee intrude

Let Webster's lofty face
Ever on thousands shine
(15) A beacon set that Freedoms race
Might gather omens from that radiant sign.


## "I found this" (Poems folder 5)

[1] And thus the high muse treated me
Directly never greeted me
But when she spread her dearest spells
Feigned to speak to some one else.
(5) I was free to overhear
⟨Or was welcome to forbear⟩
Or I might at will forbear↑;↓
⟨But⟩ ↑Yet↓, /mark me well, that idle/that incoherent/ word
Thus at random overheard
(10) Was the ⟨anthem⟩ ↑symphony↓ of ⟨the⟩ spheres
And proverb of the following years
The light wherewith all planets shone
⟨And⟩ ↑The↓ livery all events put on,
It fell in rain, it grew in grain,
(15) It put on flesh in friendly form
It frowned in enemies
It spoke in Tullius Cicero

1 "Has God on thee conferred."
1 "I found this," 9–14, 14–25. In line (7), the semicolon is in pencil; in line (8), "But" is canceled and "Yet" inserted in pencil and parentheses are drawn around "mark me well, that idle"; and in line (13), "And" is canceled and "The" inserted in pencil.

    In Milton & in Angelo
[2]   I travelled & found it at Rome
    Eastward it filled all heathendom
    And it lay on my hearth when I came home.


## "I found this" (Poems folder 23)

[1]   And thus the high muse treated ⟨me⟩ ↑him↓,
    Directly never greeted ⟨me,⟩ ↑him,↓
    And, when she spread her dearest spells,
    Feigned to speak to some one else.
(5)   But that incoherent word
    Thus at random overheard,
    Was the symphony of spheres,
    And proverb of a thousand years,
    A beam with which all planets shone,
(10)   A livery all events put on.
    It spoke in Tullius Cicero,
    In Milton, and in Angelo,
    ⟨I⟩He travelled & found it at Rome,
    Eastward it filled all heathendom,
(15)   And it lay in ⟨my⟩ ↑his↓ hearth when ⟨I⟩he came home.


## "I found this" (Poems folder 78)

[1]    Saadi answered, I found this,
      ⟨‖ . ‖⟩That of goods I could not miss,
    If I fell into the line,
    Once a member, all was mine,
(5)    Houses, banquets, gardens, fountains,
    Fortune's delectable mountains,
    But, if I would walk alone,
    Was neither cloak nor crumb my own.

    And thus the high muse treated me,—
(10)   Directly never greeted me,
    But, when she spread her dearest spells,
    Feigned to speak to some one else;
    I was free to overhear,
    Or was welcome to forbear;
(15)   But that idle word

2 "I found this," 26–28.
1 "I found this," 9–12, 15–20, 24–28.
1 "I found this," 1–18. In line (1), "Saadi answered," is circled in pencil.

Thus at random overheard
Was the anthem of the spheres,
And proverb of a thousand years;
[2] The light with which all planets shone,
The livery all events put on,
It fell in rain, it grew in grain,
It wore flesh in friendly form,
(5) It frowned in ⟨enemies,⟩ ↑foes, & growled in storm;↓
It spoke in Tullius Cicero,
In Milton & in Angelo,
I travelled, & found it ⟨at⟩ ↑in↓ Rome,
Eastward it filled all Christendom
(10) And it lay on my hearth when I came home.


## "I leave the book, leave thou the wine" (Poems folder 23)

[1] He ↑freelier↓ breathed ⟨freelier by⟩ ↑beside↓ the pine
In cities he was low & mean
The mountain waters washed him clean
And by the seawaves he was strong
(5) He heard their medicinal song
Asked no physician but the wave
↑No ⟨dwelling⟩ ↑palace↓ but his sea-beat cave. ↓


## "I love thy music, mellow bell" (Poems folder 44)

[1] 1823
I love thy music, mellow bell,
I love thine iron chime,
To life or death, to heaven or hell,
Which calls the sons of Time.

(5) Thy voice upon the deep
The homebound seaboy hails,
It charms his cares to sleep,
It cheers him as he sails.

To ⟨merry hall or house of God⟩ ↑house of God & heavenly
joys↓
(10) Thy summons called our sires,
And good men thought thy sacred voice
Disarmed the thunder's fires.

2 "I found this," 19–28.
1 "I leave the book, " 2–6, 8, x.
1 "I love thy music."

And from thy music, sad Death bell!
Shall lift its notes once more
(15)    And mix my requiem with ↑the↓ wind
That sweeps my native shore.
1823

## "In my garden three ways meet" (Poems folder 48, manuscript 1)

[1]    ⟨If Thought unlock her mysteries⟩
⟨If ⟨Love⟩ ↑friendship↓ on me smile⟩
⟨I walk in marble galleries⟩
⟨And talk with kings the while⟩

(5)    ⟨In cities high the careful brood⟩
⟨Of woworn mortals darkling go⟩
⟨But in these sunny solitudes⟩
⟨My quiet roses blow⟩

In my garden three ways meet,
(10)    Thrice the spot is blest,
Hermit thrush comes there to build,
Carrier doves to rest.

/In my garden oaken copse/The alder copse the haughty
    pine/
The eager wind detain⟨s⟩,
(15)    ↑There↓ Sultry summer lingers there,
When Autumn chills the plains.

In my plot no tulips blow,
Snowloving pines & oaks instead,

[2]    Selfsown my stately garden grows,
The winds & wind-blown seed,
Cold April rain & colder snows
My hedges plant & feed.

(5)    From mountains far & valleys near
The harvest brought today
Thrive in all weathers without fear;
Wild planters! plant away,

1 "In my garden three ways meet," 29–32, 17–20, 1–8 (1–16); "My Garden," 5–6 (17–18).
In line (13), "The alder copse the haughty pine" is in pencil; in line (14), the "s" in "detains" is
canceled in pencil; in line (15), "There" is in pencil; lines (17–18) are struck through twice in
ink.
2 "In my garden three ways meet," 9–16, 25–28, 17–24.

(10)    What need I holier dew
Than Walden's haunted wave,
Distilled from heaven's alembic blue,
Steeped in each forest cave?

In cities high, the careful crowds
Of woworn mortals darkling go,
(15)    But in these sunny solitudes
My quiet roses blow.

↑Methought the sky looked scornful down↓
↑On all was base in man;↓
↑And airy tongues did taunt the town,↓
↑Achieve ⟨us if you can⟩ ↑⟨our⟩ ↑Our↓ peace who can!↓ ↓

[3]    If Thought unlock her mysteries,
If Friendship on me smile,
I walk in marble galleries,
And talk with kings the while.

(5)    But chiefest thou, whom Genius loved,
Daughter of sounding seas,
Whom Nature pampered in these lawns,
And lavished all to please:

What wealth of mornings in her year,
(10)    What planets in her sky!
She chose her best thy heart to cheer,
Thy beauty to supply.

Now younger pilgrims find the stream,
The willows & the vine,
(15)    But aye to me the happiest seem
To draw the dregs of wine.

[4]    The mystic lake ⟨with⟩ ↑obeys a↓ private ⟨laws⟩ ↑code↓
Not blent with natures general web
Not twice a day its /ebb/fall/ & flood
Five years, men say, its flood & ebb

(5)    The tides that wash my garden-side
Keep
Play not in Natures lawful web
Heed not the ⟨sea⟩ oceans daily tide
Five years from flood to ebb

3  "In my garden three ways meet," 29–44.
4  "My Garden," 21–24, 21, x, 22–24. In pencil.

"In my garden three ways meet" (Poems folder 48, manuscript 2)

[1]       In my garden three ways meet
Thrice the spot is blest
Hermit thrush comes there to build
Carrier doves to rest

(5)     There broad armed oaks the copses maze
The ⟨eager⟩ ↑cold sea-↓wind detain↑;↓
⟨Oft⟩ ↑Here↓ sultry summer overstays
When Autumn chills the plain

Self-sown my stately garden grows,
(10)    The winds & wind-blown seed,
Cold April rain, & colder snows
My hedges plant & feed.

From mountains ↑far↓ & valleys near
The harvests ⟨brought⟩ ↑sown↓ today
(15)    Thrive in all weathers without fear,—
Wild planters plant away!

[2]       In cities high the careful crowds
Of wo worn mortals darkling go
But in these sunny solitudes
My quiet roses blow.

(5)     Methought the sky looked scornful down
On all was base in man,
And airy tongues did taunt the town,
'Achieve our peace who can!

⟨If Thought unlock her mysteries⟩
(10)    What need I holier dew
Than Walden's haunted wave
Distilled from heaven's alembic blue,
Steeped in each forest cave.

⟨Let⟩ ↑If↓ Thought unlock her mysteries
(15)    ⟨Let⟩ ↑If↓ Friendship on me smile,
I walk in marble galleries,
I talk with kings the while.

[3]      And chiefest thou, whom Genius loved,
Daughter of sounding seas,
Whom Nature pampered in these groves,
And lavished all to please.

1 "In my garden three ways meet," 1–16. In line (6), "eager" is canceled and "cold sea-" and the semicolon inserted in pencil; in line (7), "Oft" is canceled and "Here" inserted in pencil. "3" is written in pencil in the upper right corner.
   2 "In my garden three ways meet," 17–24, 29, 25–32.
   3 "In my garden three ways meet," 33–44 (1–12); "My Garden," 49–52 (13–16). Lines (13–16) are in pencil, struck through in pencil. "4" is written in pencil in the upper right corner.

(5)    What wealth of mornings in her year,
        What planets in her sky!
        She chose her best thy heart to cheer,
        Thy beauty to supply.

        Now younger pilgrims find the stream,
(10)    The willows & the vine,
        But aye to me the happiest seem
        To draw the dregs of wine.

          ⟨Oft rings in the air⟩ ↑I have heard voices in the air↓
        ⟨Oft⟩ ↑And↓ murmurs in the wold
(15)    ↑That ⟨say⟩ ↑speak↓ ↓ What I cannot declare
        Yet cannot all withhold

[4]     But the meanings cling to the water
        ⟨They are not current in towns⟩ ↑Stay here till you return↓
        Go back to the house you cannot carry them
        And when you return ↑hither↓
(5)    ⟨They burn again on all waves & hedges⟩
        On waves & hedges still they burn
        Cannot be carried in any urn

        But the meanings cling to the water
        Cannot be carried in book or urn
(10)    When you came back hither
        On waves & hedges still they burn

        Yet they tell the fortunes of men
        And of better men than live today
        And of higher worlds
(15)    And when one comes who can comprehend them
        They will say to him, stay!

        ⟨With cholera in your foul cigar⟩
        Nor reek in towns with beetling roofs
        When the ↑fresh scented↓ meads are nigh
(20)    With /fragrant/the freeborn hills/ & the inviolate sky

## "James Russell Lowell" (Poems folder 86, manuscript 1)

[1]               ↑J. R. L.↓

        What said the Sibyl?
        What was the fortune

4 "My Garden," 57, 59, 58–60, 60, 58, 57–62, x, 63–64 (1–16); "May Day [Invitation],"
50?, 48, 52–53 (17–20). Lines (7–17) are in pencil; in lines (4), (19), and (20), "hither", "fresh
scented", and "the freeborn hills" are in pencil; line (5) is canceled in pencil; the page is struck
through twice in ink.
  1 "James Russell Lowell," 44–60. The title is in pencil; in line (14), "Broadest" is canceled
and "Beaming" inserted in pencil.

She sung for him?
Strength for the hour.

(5)     Man of marrow, man of mark,
Virtue lodged in sinew stark,
Rich supplies & never stinted,
More behind at need is hinted;
Never cumbered with the morrow,
(10)    Never knew corroding sorrow,
Too well-gifted to have found
Yet his opulence's bound;
Most at home in mounting fun,
(Broadest) ↑Beaming↓ joke & luckiest pun,
(15)    Masking in the mantling tones
Of a rich laugh-loving voice,
In speeding troops of social joys

[2]    And in volleys of wild mirth
Purer metal, rarest worth,
Logic, passion, cordial zeal,
Such as bard & martyr feel.
(5)        Strength for the hour;
For the day sufficient Power,
Well advised, too easily great,
His large fame to antedate.
But, if another temper come,—
(10)    If on the sun shall creep a gloom,
A time & tide more exigent,
When the old mounds are torn & rent;
More proud, more strong competitors
Marshal the lists for Emperors;—
(15)    Then, the pleasant bard will know
To put the frolic mask behind him,
Like an old summer cloak,
And in sky-born mail to bind him
And single-handed cope with Time,
(20)    And parry & deal the thunderstroke.

## "James Russell Lowell" (Poems folder 86, manuscript 2)

[1]    As I left my door
The Muse came by
Said "Whither away?"

2 "James Russell Lowell," 61–80.
1 "James Russell Lowell," 1–17.

I, well-pleased to praise myself,
(5)    And in such presence raise myself,
Replied—'To keep thy bard's birthday.'
"O happy Morn! o happy eve!"
The Muse rejoined, "And dost thou weave
For noble night a noble rhyme,
(10)   And up to song through friendship climb?
For every guest,
Ere he can rest,
⟨Piles⟩ ↑Plucks↓ for my son or flower⟨s⟩ or fruit,
In sign of Nature's glad salute."

(15)   ↑—↓'Alas! thou know'st,
Dearest Muse, I cannot boast
Of any grace from thee:
[2]    ↑To↓ Thy spar⟨ing⟩e bounty, queen, thou ⟨knowst⟩ ↑owest↓
No verse will flow from me.
Beside, the bard himself profuse
In thy accomplishment,
(5)    Does Comedy & ⟨Ode⟩ lyric use
And to thy sisters all too dear,
Too gifted, than that he can choose
To raise an eyebrow too severe
On the toiling good intention
(10)   Of ill-equipped incomprehension

"The bard is loyal,"
Said the Queen
With haughtier mien,
⟨And see thou keep⟩ ↑"↑And↓ Hear thou this↓ my mandate
    royal:
(15)   Instant to the Sibyl's chair,
To the Delphic maid repair;
He has reached the middle date:
[3]    Stars tonight that culminate
Shed beams fair & fortunate,
Go & ask the horoscope,
Half of memory, half of hope.

———

(5)    ⟨From Pâques to Noel⟩
⟨Prophets & Bards,⟩

2 "James Russell Lowell," 18–34.
3 "James Russell Lowell," 35–53.

677

⟨Merlin, Llewellyn,⟩
⟨Highborn Hoel⟩
⟨Well-born Lowell,—⟩
(10)    What said the Sibyl⟨e⟩
What was the fortune
She sung for him?—
*Strength for the hour.*

Man of marrow, man of mark,
(15)    Virtue lodged in sinew stark,
Rich supplies & never stinted,
More behind at need is hinted,
Never cumbered with the morrow,
Never knew corroding sorrow,
[4]    Too well gifted to have found
Yet his opulence's bound;
Most at home in mounting fun,
⟨Broadest⟩ ↑Beaming↓ joke and luckiest pun;
(5)    Masking in the mantling tones
Of his rich laugh-loving voice,
In speeding troops of social joys,
And in volleys of wild mirth,
Purer metal, rarest worth,
(10)    Logic, passion, cordial zeal,
Such as bard & hero feel.

*Strength for the hour.*
For the day sufficient power,
Well-advised, too easily great
(15)    His large fleece to antedate.

But, if another temper come,
If on the sun shall creep a gloom,
A time & tide more exigent,
When the old ⟨bounds⟩ mounds are torn & rent,
[5]    More proud, more strong competitors,
Marshal the lists for Emperors,
Then the pleasant bard will know
To put this frolic masque behind him,
(5)    Like an old summer cloak,
And in sky-born mail to bind him,
And single-handed cope with Time,
And parry & deal the thunderstroke.

4 "James Russell Lowell," 54–72. In line (4), "Broadest" is canceled and "Beaming" inserted in pencil.
5 "James Russell Lowell," 73–80.

## "James Russell Lowell" (Poems folder 87)

[1]                              Lowell

> From Paques to Noel
> Prophets & Bards,
> Merlin, Llewellyn,
> Highborn Hoel,
(5)
> Well born Lowell,
> 'What said the Sibyl?
> 'What was the fortune
> She sung for him?'
> *Strength for the hour.*

(10)
> Man of marrow, man of mark,
> Virtue lodged in sinew stark,
> Rich supplies, & never stinted,
> More behind at need is hinted
> Never cumbered with the morrow
(15)
> Never knew corroding sorrow,
> Too well gifted to have found
> Yet his opulence's bound;
> Most at home in mounting fun,
> Broadest joke & luckiest pun,
(20)
> Masking in the mantling tones
> Of a rich laugh-loving voice,
> In speeding troops of social joys,
[2]
> And in volleys of wild mirth,
> Purer metal, rarest worth,
> Logic, passion, cordial zeal,
> Such as bard & martyr feel.

(5)
> *Strength for the hour,*
> For the day sufficient power;
> Well advised, too easily great
> His large fleece to antedate;
> But, if another temper come,
(10)
> If on the sun shall creep a gloom,
> A time & tide more exigent,
> When the old mounds are torn & rent,—
> More proud, more strong competitors
> Marshal the lists for emperors,
(15)
> Then the pleasant bard will know
> To put this frolic masque behind him,

---

1 "James Russell Lowell," 39–60.
2 "James Russell Lowell," 61–76, 78–80.

And in sky-born mail to bind him,
And single-handed cope with Time,
And parry & deal the thunderstroke

## "Leave me, Fear! thy throbs are base" (Poems folder 53)

[1] 1831 Leave me, Fear! thy throbs are base
Trembling for the body's sake;
O Love! thou dost the spirit raise,
Since for others thou dost wake.
(5)      O it is beautiful in death
To hide the shame of human nature's end
In sweet & wary servings of a friend.
Love is true Glory's field, where the last breath
Expires in troops of honorable cares.

(10)          The wound of Fate he cannot feel
Smit with the heavenlier smart of social zeal

## "Mask thy wisdom with delight" (Poems folder 5)

[1]       And thou
Mask thy wisdom with delight
Toy with the bow yet hit the white
As ⟨the old Omar knew,⟩ ↑Dchelaleddin↓ old & gray
(5)      He seemed to bask ↑to dream↓ & play
Without remoter hope or fear
⟨Or purpose⟩ than ⟨to please⟩ ↑still to entertain↓ his ear
And pass the burning summer time
In the palmgrove with a rhyme
(10)     ⟨Meantime⟩ ↑Heedless that↓ /every/each/ cunning word
Tribes & ages overheard
Those idle catches told the laws
Holding nature to her cause

## "Mask thy wisdom with delight" (Poems folder 78)

[1]       Mask thy wisdom with delight,
Toy with the bow, yet hit the white.

1 "Leave me, Fear!," 1–11.
1 "Mask thy wisdom," x, 1–12 (1–13); "Considerations by the Way," 24–25 (2–3). In line (5), "to dream" is in pencil; in line (10), "Meantime" is canceled and "Heedless that" and "each" added in pencil.
1 "Mask thy wisdom," 1–2, x, x, 4–12 (1–13); "Considerations by the Way," 24–25 (1–2).

The lesson which the Muses say
Was sweet to hear & to obey.
(5) He loved to round a verse, & play,
Without remoter hope, or fear,
Or purpose, than to please his ear.
And ⟨pass⟩ ↑all↓ the golden summer-time
⟨Ringing⟩ ↑Rung out↓ the hours with happy rhyme.
(10) Meantime every cunning word
Tribes & ages overheard:
Those idle catches told the laws
Holding nature to her Cause.

## "May–Day" (Poems folder 15)

[1] By remote Superior Lake
And far resounding Mackinac
When Northwinds smite ↑the ↑lonely↓ few↓
In that lone world the artful air
(5) Plays discreet the chorister
Note from note to separate
Smothering in her ample breast
All discords that invade & grate
Sings aloft the golden words,
(10) Showers discreetly all the rest,
Reporting to the happy ear
Only purified accords.

Angels' music
Awe-struck
(15) Spirit⟨-voices⟩s scare the ⟨Indian⟩ ↑painted↓ brave
↑Tis↓ Convent-music ⟨daunts⟩ ↑cries↓ the child
Sounding from the panther's cave
And the impenetrable wild

## "May–Day" (Poems folder 49)

[1] ↑In the Arctic circle felt↓
↑Streaming from the Equator's belt↓

↑Shod with light,↓ The selfsame Power
Drives the fowl to Labrador
(5) ⟨⟨Streaming⟩Soft uncurls the downy fern⟩

1 "May–Day," 465–67, 469, x, 469/470, 471, x, x, x, 473–74, x, x, 476–79. In line (15), "Indian" is canceled in pencil and ink and "painted" is encircled in pencil.
1 "May–Day," seventeen unused lines, 652–55.

⟨Tropic fires the iceberg burn⟩
⟨Streaming from Equator's belt⟩
⟨Is in Arctic circles felt⟩
⟨Soft uncurls the downy fern⟩
(10)   Uncurls the downy northern fern
The gulf's hot waves the iceberg burn
Works not alone in seasons four
But still renewed in every hour
Toils without stint, snaps every bond,
(15)   ⟨From⟩ ↑Climbs↓ highest height to gaze beyond
And from attainment forth will grope
Instructed to a larger hope.
Under gentle types↑,↓ ⟨of⟩ ↑my↓ Spring
Masks the Might of Nature's King,
(20)   An energy that searches thorough
From Chaos to the dawning Morrow

[2]   If wisest prophets truly teach,
Deeper ⟨yet⟩ ↑far↓ its virtues reach
Into all our human plight,
⟨To⟩ the soul's pilgrimage & flight,
(5)   Steeps with ⟨its will⟩ ↑grace↓ the elements,
⟨And present Ill to Good⟩ ↑Bane to benefit↓ ferments.

Where angry demons plot & ⟨work⟩lurk,
Wakes redeeming Force to work
On city or on solitude,
(10)   Step by step, lifts bad to good;
Without halting, without rest,
Lifting ⟨be⟩Better up to Best,
Planting seeds of harvest pure,
⟨When lies perish⟩Perish lies, but truths endure

[3]   Put in, drive home the sightless wedges,
Exploding burst the crystal ledges.


## "May Day [Invitation]" (Poems folder 55, manuscript 1)

[1]   In yonder city rich & old
Where men toil much for little gold,
In vault, or shop, or wharf, or raft
At their sweat & handicraft,

2 "May–Day," x, x, 656–57, four unused lines, 658–63. Lines (7–8) are in parentheses and struck through in ink, probably to cancel them.
3 "Put in, drive home."
1 "May Day [Invitation]," 1–14. "⟨29⟩39" is written in the upper right corner, "29" in pencil and "39" in ink.

(5)        One ↑sultry↓ morn
Wafted sweet teachings of the air
Which no town walls can quite exclude,
Nor streets of fops nor drayman rude,
Up the High street in morning din
(10)      A joyful Maycart trundled in;
Green boughs, with cage of singing birds,
And rope of twisted vines that girds
And festoons all the cart around,
While country boys ↑(↓with pipes made all the air
     resound↑)↓

[2]       Proclaim⟨ing⟩ed to all who listen may
A threedays woodland holiday
It is our village use
To give      respite & truce

(5)        We show you the way to the woods,
Rich parks where yet no man intrudes,
We ⟨show⟩ ↑guide↓ you ↑to↓ the red trout brook,
And ponds where perch swim to the hook,
⟨And who will⟩ ↑Or↓ climb the hill ↑with gun↓ & rouse
(10)      Rabbit ⟨or⟩ ↑&↓ hare, pigeon ⟨or⟩ ↑&↓ grouse.

The town emptied like a prison
For the fields & broad horizon
Age limped out on his crutch
Uprose the porter & the drudge
(15)      The pauper crept /out/forth/ from his hutch,
Not man nor child would stay
From the festival of May


## "May Day [Invitation]" (Poems folder 55, manuscript 2)

[1]       In yonder City rich & old,
Where men toil much for little gold,
In vault, or garret, wharf, or raft
At their ⟨shop⟩sweat & handicraft
(5)        One sultry morn beyond compare
Wafted sweet teachings of the air
Which no town walls can quite exclude,
Nor streets of fops nor draymen rude.
Up the High street in market din
(10)      A joyful May-cart trundled in.

2 "May Day [Invitation]," 17–20, 23–28, 59–63, 66–67.
1 "May Day [Invitation]," 1–14, x, x.

Green boughs with cage of singing birds
And rope of twisted vines that girds
And festoons all the cart around
Six country boys made all the air resound
(15)   An older farmer forward stood
With friendly face & earnest mood
[2]   And halted mid the gathering crowd
We Fairfield folks, he cried aloud,
Proclaim to all who listen may
A three days' woodland holiday
(5)   It is our annual village use
To give our hands respite & truce
And we invite all decent people
To rendezvous at Fairfield steeple

We show you the way to the woods
(10)   Rich parks where yet ↑no house intrudes↓
We guide you to the red trout brook
And ponds where perch swim to the hook
Or climb the hill with gun, & rouse
Rabbit ⟨or⟩& hare, pigeon & grouse

(15)   But more the spring is antedated
      ↑the bluebirds came in February↓
The spring has come before its time
⟨The rye⟩ ↑Today↓ ↑The peach ⟨is⟩ bloom⟨ing⟩s & the
      cherry↓
I was up this morn before the day
(20)   ⟨Nature⟩ ↑The pastures had↓ had never so much to say

[3]   Why reek in towns with beetling roofs
Jammed by cartwheels & drayhorse hoofs
Suck cholera from ⟨alleys⟩ ↑pavements↓ foul
⟨And⟩ drink the ↑tainted↓ water from ⟨your drains⟩ ↑the
      bowl.↓
(5)   When scented fields expanding nigh
Uplifted hills inviolate sky
⟨Through us invite you⟩ ↑Obey our summons↓ one & all
To join our woodland festival

The crowd cheered master & man
(10)   The elders ⟨w⟩nod boys jumped & ran

The town emptied like a prison
To the fields & broad horizon

2 "May Day [Invitation]," 15–28, 30–31, 30, 32–34. Lines (15–20) are struck through twice in ink.
3 "May Day [Invitation]," 48–53, 54/55, 56–64, 66–67.

Age ho⟨f⟩bbled forth upon his crutch
Uprose the porter & the drudge
(15)    The ⟨porter⟩pauper crept forth from his hutch
The baker let cool his oven
Nor man nor child would stay
From the festival of May

[4]    This year we have an ⟨altered⟩ ↑a mended↓ clime
The spring arrived before its time
The bluebirds ⟨came⟩ ↑sang↓ in February
⟨Today⟩ ↑And now↓ the peach blooms & the cherry
(5)    I was up ⟨today⟩this morn before the day
⟨⟨Robin⟩The⟩ ↑The Thrush⟨es⟩↓ had never so much to say
The morning cobwebs ⟨mocked⟩ ↑showed no↓ the storm
The robin listened for the worm
The fungus & the bulrush spoke
(10)    Answered the pinetree & the oak
The subtle South blew down the glen
Filled the straits & filled the wide,
The maple leaf turned up its silver side
Lawns glimmer in the smoky ray
(15)    And all we see are pictures ⟨high⟩gay,
Valley deep & high hillside,
Which oaks of pride
Climb to their tops,
And boys run out upon the leafy ropes

[5]    We summon you come one come all
And join the woodland festival.

The town emptied like a prison
To the fields & broad horizon
(5)    Age hobbled out upon his crutch
Uprose the porter & the drudge
The pauper crept forth from his hutch
Nor man nor child would stay
From the festival of May.

## "May Day [Invitation]" (Poems folder 55, manuscript 3)

[1]                *May–day.*
In yonder city, rich & old,
Where men toil much for little gold,

4 "May Day [Invitation]," 29–47 (1–19); "Where the fungus broad & red," 12–16, 19–24 (9–19).
5 "May Day [Invitation]," 55–56, 59–63, 66–67. Struck through twice in ink.
1 "May Day [Invitation]," 1–14.

In vault or garret, wharf or raft,
At their sweat & handicraft,
(5)       One sultry morn beyond compare
Wafted sweet teachings of the air,
Which no town-walls can quite exclude,
Nor streets of fops, nor draymen rude;
Up the High street in market din
(10)      A joyful May-cart trundled in;
Green boughs, with cage of singing birds,
And rope of twisted vines, that girds
With festoons all the cart around,
Whilst country boys with willow pipes made all the air
           resound.

[2]     It halted mid the gathering crowd:—
"We Fairfield folk," ⟨he⟩ ↑one↓ cried aloud,
"Proclaim to all who listen may
A three days' woodland holiday:
(5)       It is our annual village use
To give ↑toil↓ amnesty & truce,
And we invite all worthy people
To rendezvous at Fairfield steeple.

         Up! & we take you to the woods,
(10)      ⟨Rich⟩ parks where ⟨yet⟩ no shop ↑or hut↓ intrudes;
We guide you to ⟨R⟩the Red Trout brook,
And ponds where perch swim to the hook;
Or you shall climb the hill, & rouse
Rabbit or hare, pigeon & grouse.

[3]       This year we have a mended clime:—
The spring arrived before its time,—
The bluebirds sang in February,
And now, the peach blooms & the cherry:
(5)       I woke this morn before the day,
The thrush had never so much to say;
The morning cobwebs showed no storm,
The robin listened for the worm,
The fungus & the bulrush spoke,—
(10)      Answered the pine-tree & the oak;
The subtle South blew down the glen,—
Filled the straits & filled the wide;—
The maple-leaf turned up its silver side;

---

2 "May Day [Invitation]," 15–28. In line (2), "he" is canceled and "one" inserted in pencil.
3 "May Day [Invitation]," 29–43 (1–15); "Where the fungus broad & red," 12–16, 19–20 (9–15).

Lawns glimmer in the smoky ray,
(15)    And all we see are pictures high,
  [4]    Valley deep & ⟨high⟩ ↑steep↓ hill-side,
Which oaks of pride
Climb to their tops,
And boys run out upon their leafy ropes.

(5)      Why reek in town ↑s↓ of beetling roofs
Jammed by cart-wheels & drayhorse hoofs,
Suck cholera from pavements fowl,
Drink tainted water from the bowl,
When scented fields expanding nigh
(10)    Uplifted hills, inviolate sky,
Invite
Obey our summons one & all
To join our woodland festival.

  [5]    The crowd cheered master & man,
The elder(')s nod,—boys jumped & ran,
The town emptied like a prison
To the fields & broad horizon,
(5)     Age hobbled forth upon his crutch
Uprose the porter & the drudge.
The pauper crept out from his hutch
The baker's boy let cool ⟨the⟩his oven,
The spinner left her web unwoven,
(10)    Nor man nor maid nor child would stay
From the festival of May.

---

⟨All my wrath, & all my shames,⟩
⟨Nay, Heaven be witness, blabbed the names.⟩

## "Merlin I" (Houghton, Harvard)

[1]              Merlin.

I.

Thy trivial harp will never please
Or fill my craving ear
Its chords should ring as blows the breeze,
Free, peremptory, clear.

4 "May Day [Invitation]," 44–56 (1–13); "Where the fungus broad & red," 21–24 (1–4). In line (1), "high" is canceled and "steep" inserted in pencil; after line (13) is a rule, the inserted catchphrase "The crowd cheered", and a hand sign pointing to the next page; "Miracle" is written upside down in the lower right corner.

5 "May Day [Invitation]," 57–67 (1–11); "The Miracle," 35–36 (12–13).

1 "Merlin I," 1–17.

(5)        No jingling serenader's art  
               Nor tinkle of piano strings  
               Can make the wild blood start  
               In its mystic springs.  
               The kingly bard  
(10)      Must smite the chords rudely & hard  
               As with hammer or with mace  
               That they may render back  
               Artful thunder that conveys  
               Secrets of the solar track,  
(15)      ⟨Laws⟩Sparks of the supersolar blaze.  
               Merlin's blows are strokes of fate  
               Chiming with the forest tone  
[2]        When boughs buffet boughs in the wood,  
               Chiming with the gasp & moan  
               Of the ice-imprisoned flood  
               With the pulse of manly hearts  
(5)        With the voice of orators  
               With the din of city arts  
               With the cannonade of wars  
               With the marches of the brave  
               And prayers of might from martyrs' cave  

(10)            Great is the art,  
               Great be the manners of the bard  
               He shall not his brain encumber  
               With the coil of rhythm & number,  
               But leaving rule & pale forethought,  
(15)      He shall aye climb  
               For his rhyme.  
               Pass in, pass in! the angels say,  
               In to the upper ⟨floors⟩doors,  
               Nor count compartments of the floors,  
(20)      But mount to Paradise  
               By the stairway of surprise.  

[3]        Things more cheerly live & go  
               What time the subtle mind  
               Plays aloud the tune whereto  
               Their pulses beat  
(5)        And march their feet,  
               And their members are combined.  

               By sybarites beguiled  
               He shall no task decline;

2 "Merlin I," 18–38.  
3 "Merlin I," 43–56, 55, 57–60.

Merlin's mighty line
(10)    Extremes of nature reconciled,
Bereaved a tyrant of his will,
And made the lion mild.
Songs can the tempest still
Scattered on the stormy air,
(15)    ⟨Songs can the tempest still⟩
Mould the year to fair increase,
And bring in poetic peace.

He shall not seek to weave
In weak unhappy times
[4]    Efficacious rhymes.—
Wait thy returning ⟨rhymes⟩strength—
The soaring orbit of the muse ↑exceeds the comets length↓

Nor affect to hit
(5)    Or compass that by meddling wit
Which only the propitious mind
Publishes when tis inclined.
There are open hours
When the God's will sallies free
(10)    And the dull ideot might see
The flowing fortunes of a thousand years,
Then shut the doors, at unawares,
Nor sword of angels could reveal
What they conceal.


## "The Miracle" (Poems folder 56, manuscript 1)

[1]    I have trod this path a hundred times
With idle footsteps crooning rhymes
I know every stock & stone
Maple & oak, the old divan
(5)    Selfplanted twice like the banian
I know not why I came again

↑B.↓    —Ah but the wood must signify
Today they will not signify
↑A.↓    And how & when will they signify?

(10)↑B.↓    The woods are well enough
Nature is sound & hickory tough,

---

4 "Merlin I," 61–62, 65–73, 74/75, 76–77.
1 "The Miracle," 1–3, 5–7, seven unused lines, 11–16, 23–24. "47" is written in ink in the upper right corner.

My friend, the covenant needs two;
The Muse requires both *What* & *Who*.
Love is the counter⟨part⟩ ↑force↓
(15)  Terror & Hope & ↑wild↓ Remorse,
New knowledge, fiery thought
Duty to grand purpose ⟨br⟩wrought
↑Wandering yestermorn the brake↓
⟨I came out to⟩ ↑I reached↓ this heath ⟨by⟩ ↑beside↓ the lake
(20)  ⟨Wandering⟩ yestermorn I heard
Sharp ⟨pierces of the sentry⟩ ↑accents of a woodland↓ bird
[2]  The bird sang as if I gave the theme
The bird sang my last nights dream
A brown wren was the Daniel
That pierced my trance its drift to spell
(5)  Knew my /secret/quarrel/, how & why,
Published it to sea & sky,
Told every word & syllable,
In his flippant chirping babble,
All my /doubts/wrath/ & all my shames,
(10)  Nay, God is witness, babbled the names.


## "The Miracle" (Poems folder 56, manuscript 2)

[1]  I have trod this path a ⟨thousand⟩ ↑hundred↓ times
With idle footsteps crooning rhymes,
I know /every ⟨stock⟩ ↑shrub↓/each nest/ & ⟨stone⟩ ↑& webworm's tent↓
The fox⟨es'⟩ hole ⟨now⟩ ↑which↓ the woodchuck's ⟨own⟩ ↑rent↓
(5)  Maple & oak, the old divan
Self-planted twice like the banian,
I know not why I came again
Unless to learn it ten times ten
⟨If we would make⟩ ↑Wilt have the⟨ir⟩ sense↓ the woods impart
(10)  ⟨We⟩ ↑Thou↓ must bring the throbbing heart.
Love  is    the counterforce,—
Terror, & Hope, & wild remorse,
New knowledge, fiery thought,
Duty to grand purpose wrought.

2 "The Miracle," 27–36. "48" is written in pencil in the upper right corner.
1 "The Miracle," 1–16. In line (8), "he" is written above "learn", probably as an incomplete alternative.

(15)    Wandering yestermorn the brake
        I reached this heath beside the lake
  [2]   ⟨Idly sauntering⟩ ↑⟨When I reached yon⟩ ↑Passing yonder ↓
              oak ↓ I heard
        Sharp accents of a woodland bird
        ↑I marked the singer with delight ↓
        ↑Which presently was changed to fright ↓
(5)     The bird sang as if I gave the theme,
        Th⟨e⟩at ⟨bird⟩ woodbird sang my last nights dream;
        A brown wren was the Daniel
        That pierced my trance its drift to tell,
        Knew my quarrel, how & why,
(10)    Published it to sea & sky,
        Told every word & syllable
        In his flippant chirping babble,
        All my wrath, & all my shames,
        Nay, Heaven be witness, blabbed the names.


## "The Miracle" (Poems folder 56, manuscript 3)

  [1]                   *The Miracle.*
              I have trod this path a hundred times,
        With idle footsteps, crooning rhymes,
        I know each nest & web-worm's tent,
        The fox-hole which the woodchucks rent,
(5)     Maple & oak, the old divan
        Self-planted twice, like the banian;
        I know not why I came again
        Unless to learn it ten times ten.
        ⟨Wilt ↑you↓⟩ ↑To↓ read the sense the woods impart?
(10)    ⟨We⟩ ↑You↓ must bring the throbbing heart.
              Love is the counterforce,—
        Terror, & Hope, & wild Remorse,
        Newest knowledge, fiery thought,
        ↑or↓ Duty to grand purpose wrought.

  [2]         Wandering yestermorn the brake,
        I reached this heath beside the lake,
        ⟨↑And↓ Passing yonder oak, I heard⟩
        ⟨Sharp accents of ⟨my⟩ ↑a↓ woodland bird,⟩
(5)     ⟨I watched the singer with delight,⟩

2 "The Miracle," 23–36.
1 "The Miracle," 1–14.
2 "The Miracle," 15–16, 23–26, 17–36. In the bottom right corner "Introduction" is written upside down and in pencil, overwritten by the last lines of the poem.

⟨But mark what changed my joy to fright,⟩
And o the wonder of the ⟨hour⟩Power,—
The deeper secret of the hour,—
Nature the supplement of Man
(10) His hidden sense interpret can,—
What friend to friend cannot convey
Shall the ⟨dumb⟩ brute ↑bird↓ instructed say.
Passing yonder oak I heard
Sharp accents of my woodland bird,—
(15) I ⟨mar⟩watched the singer with delight,—
But mark what changed my joy to fright,—
When that bird sang, I gave the theme,—
That woodbird sang my last night's dream,
A brown wren was the Daniel
(20) That pierced my trance its drift to tell,
Knew my quarrel, how & why,
Published it to ⟨sea⟩ ↑lake↓ & sky,
Told every word & syllable,
In his flippant, chirping babble,
(25) ↑All my wrath, & all my shames,↓
↑Nay & God is witness, gave the names.↓

## "Monadnock" (Poems folder 59)

[1] The mountain utters the same sense
Unchanged in its intelligence
For ages sheds its walnut leaves
One joy it joys, one grief it grieves

=====

(5) By consummate powers
Gathering along the centuries
From race on race the rarest flowers
His rich wreath shall nothing miss

Ascending thorough just degrees
(10) To a consummate holiness
⟨Like⟩ ↑As↓ angel blind to trespass done
And bleaching all ⟨souls⟩ ↑stains↓ like the sun

## "New England Capitalist" (Poems folder 60)

[1]                    *New England Capitalist.*
What are his machines

---

1 "Monadnock," 401–4 (1–4); "Song of Nature," 13–16, four unused lines (5–12). Lines (1–4) and (5–8) are separately struck through in ink.
1 "New England Capitalist," 1–17. "Stalwart" in line (10) is in pencil; brackets are drawn at the beginning of line (1) and the end of line (7).

Of steel, brass, leather, oak, & ivory,
But manikins & miniatures,
Dwarfs of one faculty, measured from him,
(5)    As nimbly he applies his bending self
Unto the changing world, thus making that
Another weapon of his conquering will?
He built the mills, & by his polities, made
The arms of millions turn them.

(10)        ↑Stalwart↓ New Hampshire, mother of men,
Sea-dented Maine, reluctant Carolina,
Must drag his coach, & by ⟨the⟩ arts of peace
He, in the plenitude of love & honor,
Eats up the poor,—⟨both⟩poor citizen ⟨&⟩ ↑poor↓ state.
(15)        Much has he done,
Has made his telegraph,
Propeller, car, postoffice, phototype,
[2]    His coast survey, vote by majority,
His life assurance, & star registry,
Preludes & hints of what he /meditates;—/ventures next,/
Now let him make a harp!

## "Not yet, not yet" (Poems folder 73)

[1]    Not yet, not yet
Impatient friend,—
A little while attend,—
Not yet I sing: but I must wait
(5)    My hand upon the silent string
Fully until the end.

I see the coming light
I see the scattered gleams
Aloft beneath on left & right
(10)    The star↑-↓sown ether beams:
These are but seeds of days
Not yet a steadfast morn
An intermittent blaze
An embryo God unborn
(15)    How all things sparkle
The dust is alive
⟨The moment is miracle⟩
To the birth they arrive
I snuff the breath of my morning afar

2 "New England Capitalist," 18–21. In line (3), "ventures next," is in pencil.
1 "Not yet, not yet," 1–28. "Poet" and "5" are written in the upper left corner.

(20)  I see the pale lustres condense to a star
    The fading colours fix,
    The vanishing are seen,
    And the world that shall be
    Twins the world that has been.

(25)  I know the appointed hour,
    I greet my office well,
    Never faster, never slower,
    Revolves the fatal wheel.

[2]  The Fairest enchants me
    The Mighty commands me
    ⟨O child⟩ ↑Saying↓ stand in thy place
    Up & eastward turn thy face

(5)  As mountains for the morning wait
    Coming early coming late
    So thou attend the enriching Fate
    Which none can ⟨hold⟩ ↑stay,↓ & none accelerate↑.↓
    I am neither faint nor weary↑,↓

(10)  Fill thy will↑,↓ o faultless heart↑!↓
    Here from youth to age I tarry↑,—↓
    Count it flight of bird or dart
    My heart at the heart of things
    Heeds no longer lapse of time

(15)  Rushing ages moult their wings
    Bathing in thy day sublime.

        1843

## "The Nun's Aspiration" (Poems folder 62)

[1]       ↑The Nun's Prayer.↓
        ——————

    On earth I dream;—I die to be:
    Time! shake not thy bald head at me
    I challenge thee to hurry past,
    Or for my turn to fly too fast.

(5)  Think me not numbed or halt with age,
    Or cares that earth to earth engage,
    Caught with love's cord of twisted beams,
    Or mired by Climate's gross extremes⟨;⟩.
    ⟨I pass with⟩I tire of ⟨shadows,⟩ ↑shams,↓ I rush to *Be*,—

(10)  I pass with yonder comet free;
    Pass with the comet into space

  2 "Not yet, not yet," 29–44. The punctuation in lines (8–11) is in pencil.
  1 "The Nun's Aspiration," 29–49. "The Nun's Prayer.", "But" and "Realms" in line (16), and "See also *ETE* 100, 173" are in pencil. "53 1/2" is written in pencil in the upper left corner.

Which mocks thy aeons to embrace;
Aeons which tardily unfold
Realm beyond realm,—extent untold.
(15)    No early morn, no evening late,—
↑/But/Realms/↓ Self-upheld, disdaining Fate,
Whose sh⟨iver⟩ining sons, too great for fame,
Never heard thy weary name;
Nor lives the tragic bard to say
(20)    How drear the part I held in one,
How lame the other limped away.
↑See also *ETE* 100, 173 ↓

## "On a raisin stone" (Poems folder 67)

[1]    On a raisin stone
The wheels of nature turn,
Out of it the fury comes
Wherewith the spondyls burn.
(5)    And, because the seed of the vine
Is creation's heart,
Wash with wine those eyes of thine
To know the hidden part.

Wine is translated wit,
(10)    Wine is the day of day,
Wine from the veiled secret
Tears the veil away.

## "A pair of crystal eyes will lead him" (Poems folder 2)

[1]    A pair of crystal eyes will lead him
All about the rounded globe
Oft ⟨averted, if⟩ ↑averse, if↓ once they heed him
He will follow, follow, follow,
(5)    To kiss the hem of the maiden's robe.

## "The Phoenix" (Poems folder 36)

[1]        The Phoenix.              Hafiz
My phoenix long ago secured
His nest in the sky-vault's cope;

1  "On a raisin stone."
1  "A pair of crystal eyes."
1  "The Phoenix," 1–4, x, 5–20.

In the body's cage immured,
⟨He is weary of life's hope.⟩
(5)    ↑Fell his plumes, & pined his hope.↓

Round & round this heap of ashes
Now flies the bird amain,
Till in that odorous niche of heaven
He nestle close again.

(10)    Once flies he upward, he will perch
On Tuba's golden bough;
His home is on that fruited arch
Which cools the blest below.

If, over this world of ours
(15)    His wings my phoenix spread,
How gracious falls on land & sea
The soul-refreshing shade!

Either world inhabits he,
Sees oft below him planets roll;—
(20)    His body is all of air compact,
Of Allah's love his soul.


## "The Pilgrims" (Poems folder 88)

[1]                The Pilgrims.

[2]       ⟨I will have an equal partition⟩
          ⟨I will have a just⟩ ↑⟨Hark now,⟩ ↑Behold↓ I make↓
            partition
          In this new world I have built,
          For slavery differs from freedom
(5)      As honor is wide from guilt.

[3]       Lo now to Freedom I assign
          And make partition fair,
          All space above the waterline
          All ground below the air.

(5)      And ⟨all⟩ ↑what's↓ beside may slavery claim
          Her residue & share,
          Within the earth to hide her shame,
          Or climb above the air.

[4]            Firm to the pole he knots the cord,

2 "The Pilgrims," 1, 1–4. In line (2), "Hark now," is canceled and "Behold" inserted in pencil. "7" is written in ink in the upper right corner.
   3 "The Pilgrims," 5–12. "8" is written in ink in the upper right corner.
   4 "The Pilgrims," 13–20. "9" is written in ink in the upper right corner.

And to the tropics drew,
About the round globe's quarter broad,
Along the welkin blue.

(5)      Hills clapped their hands, the rivers shined,
The seas applauding roar,
The elements were of one mind,
As they had been of yore.

## "Saadi" (Berg, New York Public Library)

[1]                      Saadi.

Trees in groves,
Kine in droves,
In ocean sport the ⟨finny⟩ ↑scaly↓ herds,
Wedgelike cleave the air the birds,
(5)      To northern lakes fly wind-borne ducks,
Browse the mountain sheep in flocks,
Men consort in camp & town,
But the poet dwells alone.

God who gave to him the lyre,
(10)     Of all mortals the desire,
For all ↑breathing↓ men's behoof,
Straitly charged him, 'Sit aloof;'
Annexed a warning, poets say,
To the bright premium,—
(15)     ↑Ever↓ ⟨w⟩When twain together play,
Shall the harp be dumb.

[2]      Many may come
But one shall sing
Two touch the string
The harp is dumb
(5)      Though there come a million
Wise Saadi dwells alone.

Yet Saadi loved the race of men,—
No churl immured in cave or den,—
In bower & hall
(10)     He wants them all,
Nor can dispense
With Persia for his audience,

1 "Saadi," 1–16.
2 "Saadi," 17–35.

They must give ear,
Grow red with joy, & white with fear,
(15)     Yet he has no companion,
Come ten, or come a million,
Good Saadi dwells alone.

Be thou ware where Saadi dwells⟨,⟩.
⟨Wisdom of the gods is he,⟩
[3]     ⟨Entertain it reverently⟩
Gladly round that golden lamp
Sylvan deities encamp,
And simple maids & noble youth
(5)     Are welcome to the man of truth.
Most welcome they who need him most,
They feed the spring which they exhaust:
For greater need
Draws better deed:
(10)     But, critic, spare thy vanity,
Nor show thy pompous parts,
To vex with odious subtlety
The cheerer of men's hearts.

Sad eyed Fakirs swiftly say
(15)     Endless dirges to decay,
⟨Who n⟩Never in the blaze of light
Lose the shudder of midnight;
⟨Who,⟩ ↑And↓ at overflowing noon,
Hear wolves barking at the moon;
[4]     In the bower of dalliance sweet
Hear the far Avenger's feet;
And shake before those awful Powers
Who in their pride forgive not ours.
(5)     Thus the sad eyed Fakirs preach;
'Bard, when thee would Allah teach,
And lift thee to his holy mount,
He sends thee from his bitter fount,
Wormwood; saying, Go thy ways,
(10)     Drink not the malaga of praise,
But do the deed thy fellows hate,
And compromise thy peaceful state.
Smite the white breasts which thee fed,
Stuff sharp thorns beneath the head
(15)     Of them thou shouldst have comforted.
For out of wo & out of crime

3 "Saadi," 36–54.
4 "Saadi," 55–75.

Draws the heart a lore sublime.'
And yet it seemeth not to me
That the high gods love tragedy;
(20)    For Saadi sat in the sun,
And thanks was his contrition;
[5]    For haircloth & for bloody whips,
Had active hands & smiling lips;
And yet his runes he rightly read,
And to his folk his message sped.
(5)    Sunshine in his heart transferred
Lighted each transparent word;
And well could honoring Persia learn
What Saadi wished to say;
For Saadi's nightly stars did burn
(10)    Brighter than Dschami's day.

Whispered the Muse in Saadi's cot;
O gentle Saadi, listen not,
Tempted by thy praise of wit,
Or by thirst & appetite
(15)    For the talents not thine own,
To sons of contradiction.
Never, son of eastern morning,
Follow falsehood, follow scorning,
[6]    Denounce who will, who will, deny,
And pile the hills to scale the sky;
Let theist, atheist, pantheist,
Define & wrangle how they list,—
(5)    Fierce conserver, fierce destroyer,—
But thou joy-giver & enjoyer,
Unknowing war, unknowing crime,
Gentle Saadi, mind thy rhyme.
Heed not what the brawlers say,
(10)    Heed thou only Saadi's lay.

Let the great world bustle on
With war & trade, with camp & town,
A thousand men shall dig & eat
At forge & furnace thousands sweat,
(15)    And thousands sail the purple sea,
And give or take the stroke of war,
Or crowd the market & bazaar,
Oft shall war end, & peace return,
And cities rise where cities burn,
(20)    Ere one man my hill shall climb,

5 "Saadi," 76–93. "Saadi 2)" is written in the upper left corner.
6 "Saadi," 94–114.

Who can turn the golden rhyme;
[7] ⟨Masking wisdom with delight,⟩
⟨Toy with the bow, yet hit the white.⟩
Let them manage how they may,
Heed thou only Saadi's lay.
(5) Seek the living among the dead:
Man in man is imprisonèd.
Barefooted Dervish is not poor,
If fate unlock his bosom's door,
So that what his eye hath seen
(10) His tongue can paint, as bright, as keen,
And what his tender heart hath felt,
With equal fire thy heart shall melt.
⟨Now his memory is a den,⟩
⟨Sealed tomb ⟨from⟩ ↑to↓ gods & men,⟩
(15) ⟨Whose rich secrets not transpire;⟩
⟨Speech should be like air & fire;⟩
⟨But to speak when he assays,⟩
⟨His voice is bestial & base,⟩
⟨Himself he heareth hiss & hoot,⟩
(20) ⟨And crimson shame him maketh mute.⟩
⟨But⟩ ↑For,↓ whom the muses shine upon,
And touch with soft persuasion,
His words like a storm-wind can bring
[8] Terror & beauty on their wing;
In his every syllable
Lurketh nature veritable;
And though he speak in midnight dark,
(5) In heaven, no star; on earth, no spark;
Yet before the listener's eye
Swims the world in ecstasy,
The forest waves, the morning breaks,
The pastures sleep, ripple the lakes,
(10) Leaves twinkle, flowers like persons be,
And life pulsates in rock or tree.
Saadi! so far thy words shall reach;
Suns rise & set in Saadi's speech.

And thus to Saadi said the Muse;
(15) Eat thou the bread which men refuse;
Flee from the goods which from thee flee;
Seek nothing; Fortune seeketh thee.

7 "Saadi," x, x, 115–35 (1–23); "Considerations by the Way," 24–25 (1–2); "Mask thy wisdom," 1–2 (1–2).
8 "Saadi," 136–55.

(20)

[9]

(5)

(10)

(15)

(20)

[10]

(5)

Nor mount, nor dive; all good things keep
The midway of the eternal deep;
Wish not to fill the isles with eyes
To fetch thee birds of paradise;
O⟨r⟩n thine orchard's edge belong,
All the brags of plume & song;
Wise Ali's sunbright sayings pass
For proverbs in the market place;
Through mountains bored by regal art
Toil whistles as he drives his cart.
Nor scour the seas, nor sift mankind,
A poet or a friend to find;
Behold, he watches at the door,
Behold his shadow on the floor.
Open innumerable doors
The heaven where unveiled Allah pours
The flood of truth, the flood of good,
The seraph's & the cherub's food;
Those doors are men; the Pariah hind
Admits thee to the perfect Mind.
Seek not beyond thy cottage wall
Redeemers that can yield thee all.
While thou sittest at thy door,
On the desart's yellow floor,
Listening to the grayhaired crones,
Foolish gossips, ancient drones,—
Saadi, see, they rise in stature
To the height of mighty Nature,
And the secret stands revealed
Fraudulent Time in vain concealed,
That blessed gods in servile masks
Plied for thee thy household tasks.

## "Said Saadi,—When I stood before" (Poems folder 23)

[1]

(5)

Said Saadi, when I stood before
Hassan the camel-driver's door,
I scorned the fame of Timour brave,
Timour to Hassan was a slave.
In every glance of Hassan's eye
I read great years of victory
And I who cower mean & small

9 "Saadi," 156–77. "Saadi 3)" is written in the upper left corner.
10 "Saadi," 178–84.
1 "Said Saadi,—When I stood before," 1–10.

                    In the frequent interval
                    When wisdom not with me resides
(10)                Worship ⟨the⟩ toil's wisdom that abides
   [2]              ⟨I shunned his glance⟩
                    I shunned his eye, the faithful man's,
                    I shunned the ⟨noble⟩ ↑toiling↓ Hassan's glance.


## "Terminus" (Poems folder 9)

   [1] Autob.
                    As goes the bark's mast through the gale,
                    So I trim myself to the storm of time
                    I man the rudder, ⟨trim⟩reef the sail,
                    Obey the voice in age obeyed in prime,
(5)                 And hide my years among my budding pears,
                    Each fault of mine masked by a growth of theirs.


## "Terminus" (Poems folder 18)

   [1]                          Climacteric.

                    It is time to be old,—
                    To take in sail:—
                    The god of bounds,
                    Who sets to seas a shore,
(5)                 Came to me in his fatal rounds,
                    And said, "no more⟨.⟩!
                    No farther ⟨spread⟩ ↑shoot↓
                    Thy broad ambitious branches, ↑& thy root: ↓
                    Fancy departs;
(10)                No more invent,
                    Contract thy firmament
                    To compass of a tent.
                    There's not enow for this & that,
                    Make thy option, which of two;
(15)                Economize the failing river;
                    Not the less revere the Giver,
                    Leave the many, & hold the few.
   [2]              Timely wise, accept the terms,
                    Check thy fall with wary foot,

2  "Said Saadi,—When I stood before," 11/12, 11–12.
1  "Terminus," 33–36, x, x.
1  "Terminus," 1–9, 9–16.
2  "Terminus," 17–28, 31, 32?, 32.

A little while,
Still plan & smile,
(5) And, fault of novel germs,
Mature the unfallen fruit.
⟨Curse⟩ ↑Chide↓, if thou wilt, thy sires,
Bad husbands of their fires,
Who, when they gave thee breath,
(10) Failed to bequeath
The stalwart sinew, stark as once,
The ⟨old Norse⟩ ↑Norseland↓ marrow to thy bones,
Amid the singers, left thee dumb,
⟨And early winter made thy right arm numb."⟩
(15) Amid the athletes, made thy right arm numb.

[3] As the bird trims her to the gale,
I trim myself to the storm of time,
I man the rudder, reef the sail,
Obey the voice ⟨in⟩at eve obeyed at prime,
(5) And hide my age amidst my thrifty pears,
Each fault of mine masked by a growth of theirs.

Lowly faithful, banish fear,
Right onward sail unharmed;
The port, well worth the cruise, is near,
(10) And every wave is charmed.
R. Waldo Emerson

## "Terminus" (Yale)

[1]                    Terminus.

It is time to be old,
To take in sail:—
The god of bounds,
Who sets to seas a shore,
(5) Came to me in his fatal rounds,
And said, 'No more!
No farther spread
Thy broad ambitious branches, & thy root;
Fancy departs: no more invent,
(10) Contract thy firmament
To compass of a tent.
There's not enow for this & that,
Make thy option which of two;
Economize the failing river,

3 "Terminus," 33–36, x, x, 37–40.
1 "Terminus," 1–17.

(15)        Not the less adore the Giver,
           Leave the many, & hold the few.
           Timely wise accept the terms,
[2]        Soften the fall with wary foot;
           A little while
           Still plan & smile,
           And, fault of novel germs,
(5)         Mature the unfallen fruit.

           Curse, if thou wilt, thy sires,
           Bad husbands of their fires,
           Who, when they gave thee breath,
           Failed to bequeath
(10)        The needful sinew stark as once,
           The Baresark marrow ⟨for⟩to thy bones,
           But left a legacy of ebbing veins,
           Inconstant heat & nerveless reins;
           Amid the Muses, left thee deaf & dumb,
(15)        Amid the gladiators, halt and numb.'

           As the bird trims her to the gale,
           I trim myself to the storm of time,
           I man the rudder, reef the sail,
           Obey the voice at eve, obeyed at prime;
[3]        'Is the sky dark?' it saith, 'more near will stand
           The pilot's Pilot to thy hand.
           Lowly faithful, banish fear,
           Right onward drive unharmed,
(5)         The port, well worth the cruise, is near,
           And every wave is charmed.
                       R. W. Emerson

## "There are beggars in Iran & Araby" (Poems folder 79, manuscript 1)

[1]           There are beggars in Iran & Araby,
           Seyd was hungrier than all;
           Hafiz said, he was a fly
           That came to every festival.
(5)         He came a pilgrim to the mosque
           On trail of camel & caravan,
           Knew every temple & kiosk

2 "Terminus," 18–36.
3 "Terminus," x, x, 37–40.
1 "There are beggars," 1–19 (1–19); "Beauty," 1–9 (11–19). "9" is written in pencil in the upper right corner.

Out from Mecca to Ispahan:
Northward he went to the snowy hills,
(10)    At court, he sat in the grave Divan.
Was never form & never face
So sweet to him as only grace
Which did not slumber like a stone,
But hovered gleaming & was gone.
(15)    Beauty chased he everywhere
In flame, in storm, in clouds of air.
He smote the lake to feed his eye
With the beryl beam of the broken wave,
He flung in pebbles well to hear
[2]    The moment's music which they gave;

Loved harebells nodding on a rock,
A cabin topped with curling smoke,
Ring of axe, or hum of wheel,
(5)    Or gleam which Use will paint on steel.
And huts & tents; nor loved he less
Stately dukes in palaces,
↑Princely women hard to please,↓
Fenced by form & ceremony,
(10)    With etiquette & heraldry.
And more revered in mountain land
Men built with power & grace to stand
Like castles

## "There are beggars in Iran & Araby" (Poems folder 79, manuscript 2)

[1]    There are beggars in Iran & Araby,
*Said* was hungrier than all;
Hafiz said, he was a fly
That came to every festival:
(5)    Also he came to the mosque,
In the trail of camel & caravan,
⟨N⟩Knew every temple & kiosk
Out from Mecca to Ispahan;
Northward he went to the snowy hills
(10)    At court he sat in the grave Divan
Was never form & never face
So sweet to him as only grace
Which did not slumber like a stone,

2  "There are beggars," 20–32 (1–13); "Beauty," 10 (1). "10" is written in pencil in the upper right corner.
  1  "There are beggars," 1–15 (1–15); "Beauty," 1–5 (11–15).

But hovered gleaming & was gone.
(15)    Beauty chased he everywhere
[2]    In flame, in storm, in clouds of air.
He smote the lake to feed his eye
With the /precious green/beryl beam/ of the broken wave;
He flung in pebbles, well to hear
(5)    The moment's music which they gave.
Loved harebells nodding on a rock,
A cabin topped with curling smoke,
And huts & tents, nor loved he less
Stately men in palaces,
(10)    Fenced by form & ceremony.

Decked by courtly rites & dress
And etiquette of gentilesse
⟨The comrade⟩ ↑But when the mate↓ of ⟨the⟩ snow & wind
He left each civil scale behind
(15)    Him woodgods fed with honey wild
And of his memory beguiled
In caves & hollow trees he ⟨slept⟩ crept
And near the wolf & panther ⟨crept⟩ slept
[3]      He came to the green oceans brim
And saw the ↑wheeling↓ seabird⟨s⟩ skim
Summer & winter oer the wave

Like creature of a skiey mould
(5)    Impassible to heat or cold
He stood before the ↑tumbling↓ main
⟨Participant & yet insane⟩
↑With joy too tense for sober brain↓
He shared the life of the element
(10)    The tie of blood & shame was rent
He felt himself
As if in him the welkin walked,
The winds took flesh, ⟨&⟩ the mountain talked.
And he the bard, a crystal soul,
(15)    Sphered & concentric to the whole.

## "There are beggars in Iran & Araby" (Poems folder 79, manuscript 3)

[1]    Comrade of the snow & wind
He left each civil scale behind

2 "There are beggars," 16–22, 25–26, 28, 33–40 (1–18); "Beauty," 6–10 (1–5). In line (3), "beryl beam" is in pencil.
3 "There are beggars," 41–55. In line (2), "wheeling" is in pencil.
1 "There are beggars," 35–45, x, x, 46–47, 51/52, x, x, x.

⟨The⟩ ↑Him↓ woodgods fed ⟨him⟩ with honey wild
And ⟨him⟩ of ↑his↓ memory beguiled
(5)    In caves & hollow trees he crept
And near the wolf & panther slept
He came to the ⟨sea⟩ ↑green ocean's rim↓
And saw the sea birds skim
Summer & winter oer the wave
(10)   Like creatures made of skiey mould
Impassible to heat or cold.
⟨He walked along the shore⟩
⟨Then into the drifting snow⟩
He stood ⟨in the scene⟩ ↑beside the main↓
(15)   Beautiful but insane
He felt himself as if the sky walked
Or the son of the wind
There was no man near
To mete himself withal


## "There resides in the grieving" (Poems folder 36)

[1]    ↑There resides ↑in↓ the grieving↓           *Hafiz.*
↑A poison to kill;↓
↑Beware to go near them,↓
↑Tis pestilent still.↓

(5)    The builder of Heaven
Hath sundered the earth,
So that no footway
Leads out of it forth.

On turnpikes of wonder
(10)   Wine leads the mind forth,
Straight, sidewise, & upward,
East, southward, & north.

Stands the vault adamantine
Until the Last Day;—
(15)   The wine-cup shall ferry
Thee o'er it away.


## "The Titmouse" (Houghton, Harvard)

[1]       *The Titmouse.*

You shall not be overbold
When you deal with arctic cold,

1 "There resides in the grieving" (1–4); "The Builder of heaven" (5–16).
1 "The Titmouse," 1–10. "1" is written in ink in the upper right corner.

As late I found my lukewarm blood
Chilled wading in the snow-choked wood.

(5)       How should I fight? my foeman fine
Has million arms to one of mine:
East, west, for aid I looked in vain,
East, west, north, south, are his domain.
Miles off, three dangerous miles is home,
(10)     Must borrow his winds who there would come.
[2]     Up & away for life! be fleet!
⟨Alas! he⟩ ↑The frost-king↓ ties my fumbling feet.
⟨All aid remote, the foe is nigh,⟩
⟨Shoots from the ground, drops from the sky,⟩
(5)       Sings in my ears, my hands are stones,
Curdles the blood to the marble bones,
Tugs at the heartstrings, numbs the sense,
Hems in the life with narrowing fence.
    Well, in this broad bed lie & sleep,
(10)     The punctual stars will vigil keep,
Embalmed ⟨in⟩by purifying cold,
The winds shall sing their dead march old,
The snow is no ignoble shroud,
The moon thy mourner, & the cloud.

[3]     Softly,—but this way fate was pointing,
Twas coming fast to such anointing,
When piped a tiny voice hard by,
Gay, & polite, a cheerful cry,
(5)       Chicadeedee! saucy note,
Out of sound heart & merry throat
As if it said, 'Good day, good sir!
Fine afternoon, old passenger!
Happy to meet you in these places,
(10)     Where January brings few men's faces.

[4] [blank]
[5]     This hermit, though he live apart,
⟨Lodges⟩ ↑Moved by↓ a hospitable heart,
Hastes, when ⟨you⟩ ↑I↓ pass his sylvan fort,
To do the honors of his court,
(5)       As fits a feathered lord of the land,
Flies near, with soft wing sweeps ⟨your⟩ ↑my↓ hand
Hops on the bough, then, darting low,

2  "The Titmouse," 11–12, x, x, 13–22. Brackets are drawn in pencil around lines (3–4).
3  "The Titmouse," 23–32. "2" is written in ink in the upper right corner.
5  "The Titmouse," 33–42. "3" is written in ink in the upper right corner.

Prints his small impress on the snow,
Shows feats of his gymnastic play
(10)        Head downward, clinging to the spray

[6] [blank]
[7]        ⟨The little Esquimaux in gray⟩
        ⟨Mounted at ease each icy spray.⟩
        Here was this atom in full breath
        Hurling defiance at vast death,
(5)        This scrap of valor just for play
        Fronts the northwind in waistcoat gray
        As if to shame my weak behavior:
        I greeted loud my little savior,
        'You pet! what dost here? & what for?
(10)        In these woods, thy small Labrador,
        At this pinch wee San Salvador!
        What fire burns in that little chest,
        So frolic, stout, & selfpossest?
        Didst steal the glow that lights the west

[8] [blank]
[9]        Henceforth I wear no stripe but thine
        Ashes & black all hues outshine.
        Why are not diamonds black & gray
        To ape thy daredevil array?
(5)        And I affirm the spacious north
        Exists to draw thy Virtue forth.
        I think no virtue goes with size,
        The reason of all cowardice
        Is, that men are overgrown,
(10)        And, to be valiant, must come down
        To the titmouse dimension.

[10] [blank]
[11]        Tis goodwill makes intelligence,
        And I began to catch the sense
        Of my birds song; "Live out of doors
        In the great woods, & prairie floors;
(5)        I dine in the sun; when he sinks in the sea,
        I too have a hole in a hollow tree.
        And I like less when summer beats
        With stifling beams on these retreats
        Than noontide twilights which snow makes
(10)        With tempest of the blinding flakes.

7 "The Titmouse," x, x, 43–54. "4" is written in ink in the upper right corner.
9 "The Titmouse," 55–65. "5" is written in ink in the upper right corner.
11 "The Titmouse," 66–79. "6" is written in ink in the upper right corner.

For well the soul, if stout within,
Can arm impregnably the skin
And polar frost my frame defied
Made of the air that blows outside

[12] [blank]
[13]    With glad remembrance of my debt,
    I homeward turn; Farewell, my pet!
    When here again thy pilgrim comes
    He shall bring store of seeds & crumbs
(5)    ⟨Nor doubt, so long as earth yields bread,⟩
    ⟨Thou first & foremost shalt be fed.⟩
    ⟨The Providence that is most large⟩
    ⟨Takes hearts like thine in special charge⟩
    ⟨Helps who for their own need are strong⟩
(10)    ⟨And God & man love cheerful song.⟩

[14] [blank]
[15]    Henceforth I prize thy wiry chant
    Oer all that mass or minster vaunt.
    For men mis-hear thy call in spring
    As ⟨if it⟩ ↑t'↓ would accost some frivolous wing
(5)    Crying out of the copse, Phe—be!
    And, in winter, chic a dee dee!
    I think old Caesar must have heard
    In Northern Gaul my dauntless bird,
    And, echoed in some frosty wold,
(10)    Borrowed thy battle numbers bold.
    ⟨But⟩ ↑And↓ I shall write our annals new,
    And thank thee for a better clew,
    I who dreamed not, when I came here
    To find the antidote of fear,
(15)    Now hear thee say in Roman key
    Paean! Ve-ni Vi↑-↓di, Vi-ci.


## "To Ellen, at the South" (Poems folder 85)

[1]               To Eva at the South.

The green grass is bowing,
The morning wind is in it,
Tis a tune worth thy knowing,

13 "The Titmouse," 80–83, six lines first printed in the 1867 version. "7" is written in ink in the upper right corner.
15 "The Titmouse," 84–99. "8" is written in ink in the upper right corner.
1 "To Ellen, at the South," 1–22. "1" is written in ink in the upper right corner.

Though it change every minute.

(5)    Tis a tune of the spring,
Every year plays it over
To the robins on the wing,
And to the pausing lover.

O'er ten thousand thousand acres
(10)  Goes light the nimble Zephyr,
The Flowers,—tiny sect of Shakers,
Worship him ever.

Hark to the winning sound!
They summon thee, dearest,
(15)  Saying, "We have drest for thee the ground,
Nor yet thou appearest.

O hasten! tis our time,
Ere yet the red Summer
Scorch our delicate prime
(20)  Loved of the bee,—the tawny hummer.

O pride of thy race!
Sad in sooth it were to ours,
[2]   If our brief tribe miss thy face,—
We poor New England flowers.

Thou shalt choose the fairest members
Of our lithe society,
(5)   June's glories & September's
Shall show our love & piety.

Thou shalt command us all,
From Aprils early clover
To the gentian in the fall,
(10)  Blue eyed favorite of thy lover.

O come, then, quickly come,
We are budding, we are blowing,
And the wind that we perfume,
Sings a tune thats worth the knowing."

## "Uriel" (Houghton, Harvard)

[1] You have heard news from Saadi, that the most baleful heresy has been broached in heaven at some Epoch not fixed. It seems some body

2 "To Ellen, at the South," 23–36. "Eva", with short rules above and below it, is written sideways in the lower left corner.
1 "Uriel," 1–12.

said words like these, that Geometers might say what they pleased, but in Uranometry there was no right line. But here you have it at large.

> It fell in the ancient periods
> Which the brooding soul surveys
> Or ever the wild Time coined itself
> Into calendar years & days.

(5)
> This was the lapse of Uriel
> Which in Paradise befel:
> Once among the Pleiads walking
> SAID overheard the young gods talking,
> And the treason too long pent

(10)
> To his ears was evident.
> The young deities discussed
> Laws of form & metre just

[2]
> Orb, quintessence, & sunbeams,
> What subsisteth, & what seems.
> One with low tones that decide,
> And doubt & reverend use defied,

(5)
> With a look that shook the sphere,
> And stirred the devils everywhere,
> Gave his sentiment divine
> Against the being of a line;
> "Line in nature is not found,

(10)
> Unit & universe are round;
> In vain produced, all ⟨br⟩rays return,
> Evil will bless, and ice will burn."
> As Uriel spoke with piercing eye
> A shudder ran around the sky,

(15)
> The stern old war-gods shook their heads
> The seraphs frowned from myrtle beds,
> Seemed to the holy festival
> The rash word boded ill to all,
> The balance-beam of Fate was bent,

(20)
> The bounds of good & ill were rent,

[3]
> Strong Hades could not keep its own,
> But all slid to confusion.

> A sad self-knowledge withering fell
> On the beauty of Uriel,

(5)
> In heaven once eminent the god
> Withdrew that hour into his cloud,
> Whether doomed to long gyration

2 "Uriel," 13–32.
3 "Uriel," 33–51.

In the sea of generation,
Or by knowledge grown too bright
(10)      To hit the nerve of feebler sight.
Straightway a forgetting wind
Stole over the celestial kind,
And their lips the secret kept,
If in ashes the live coal slept.
(15)      But now & then truth speaking things
Shamed the angels' veiling wings,
And shrilling from the solar course,
Or from fruit of chemic force,
Procession of a soul in matter,
[4]       Or the speeding change of water,
Or out of good of evil born,
Came Uriel's voice of godlike scorn,
And a blush tinged the upper sky,
(5)       And the gods start the[y] scarce knew why.

## "Wachusett" (Poems folder 90)

[1]                     Wachusett.

                       ———

⟨From the shoulder of Wachusett⟩
⟨To ⟨m⟩Mexico the eagle flew.⟩

When the day broke,
Wachusett spoke to Monadnoc.
(5)       "I water six counties,
I feed a hundred towns,
I am seen by a million men,
And by never a soldier.
My streams turn papermills,
(10)      Cornmills, cotton mills, & forges.
Up hither comes the railroad whistle
Asking for chestnut sleepers,
Asking for pine & oak,
Stout knees of shiptimber,
(15)      Promising towns & cities instead;
But the lives of men
None asketh. ⟨The young eagle is gone,⟩
⟨The old eagle starved.⟩

4 "Uriel," 52–56.
1 "Wachusett." In lines (17–18), "The young . . . starved." is canceled in pencil.

                    I feel the feet of men on my sides,
(20)            As I feel the feet of birds,
                    Or the snow-flakes alighting.
                    But when one comes whose heart beats
                    To behold thee, o Monadnoc!
                    Whose roots touch my roots,
(25)            I also feel the pulse."

⟨Princeton, Apr 3. 1845⟩


## "When all their blooms the meadows flaunt" (Poems folder 92)

[1]            ↑When all their blooms the meadows flaunt↓
                    ↑To deck the morning of the year,↓
                    ↑Why tinge thy lustres jubilant↓
                    ↑With forecast or with fear?↓

(5)                    Softens the air so sharp & rude,
                    What can the heart do less?
                    If earth put off her savage mood,
                    Let us learn gentleness.

                    The purple flame ⟨shoots up for all,⟩ ↑all ⟨kindreds⟩bosoms
                        girds↓
(10)            And Love ascends his throne,
                    I cannot hear your songs, o birds!
                    For the witchery of my own.
                    ⟨And every⟩ ↑Each↓ human heart ↑this tide makes free↓
                    ⟨Still⟩ ↑To↓ keep⟨s⟩ that golden day,
(15)            And ring⟨s⟩ the bells of jubilee
                    On its own First of May.


## "Who saw the hid beginnings" (Poems folder 78)

[1]                    Who saw the hid beginnings
                    When Chaos & Order strove?
                    Or who can date the morning
                    The purple flaming of love?
(5)                    I saw the hid beginnings
                    When chaos & order strove,
                    And I can date the morning,
                    The purple flame of love.

1 "When all their blooms" (1–4); "Softens the air" (5–8); "Who saw the hid beginnings,"
21–28 (9–16). In line (13), "And every" is canceled in pencil and ink.
1 "Who saw the hid beginnings," 1–12.

Song breathed from all the forest,
(10)   The total air was fame,
It seemed the world was all torches
That suddenly caught the flame.

[2]   Is there never a retroscope mirror
In the realms & corners of space,
That can give us a glimpse of the battle
And the soldiers face to face?

(5)   Sit here on the basalt ranges
Where twisted hills betray
The feet of the world-old forces
⟨That⟩ ↑Who↓ wrestled here on a day.

When the purple flame shoots up
(10)   And love ascends his throne,
I cannot hear your songs, o birds,
For the witchery of my own.
       And every human heart
       Still keeps that golden day
(15)   And rings the bells of ⟨joy⟩ jubilee
On its own First of May.


## "Whoso alas is young" (Poems folder 94)

{1}           Whoso alas is young
              And being young is wise
              And deaf to saws of gray advice
              Hath listened when the Muses sung
(5)   And heard with joy when on the wind the shell of Clio rung

              In tender youth if he was proud
              Nor would his gentle soul profane
              And loathed the arts of gain
              Assorted with the rabble crowd
(10)   But shared his soul with few, or sauntered lone & proud


## "The World-Soul" (Houghton, Harvard)

{1}           Thanks to the morning light,
              Thanks to the foaming sea,

2 "Who saw the hid beginnings," 13–28.
1 "Whoso alas is young" (1–10); "Slighted Minerva's learned tongue" (4–5). Lines (7–8) are
in reverse order in the manuscript, marked for transposition by "2" and "1" in the left margin.
1 "The World-Soul," 1–20.

To the bold uplands of Berkshire,
To the forest rustling free,
(5) Thanks to each man of courage,
To the maids of holy mind,
To the boy with his games undaunted
Who never looks behind.

Cities of proud hotels
(10) Houses of rich & great,—
A stack of smoking chimneys,
A roof of frozen slate.
It cannot conquer folly
Time-&-space-conquering steam
(15) And the light-outspeeding telegraph
Bears nothing on its beam.

The politics are base
The letters do not cheer
And tis far in the deeps of history
(20) The voice that speaketh clear
[2] Trade & the streets ensnare us,
Our bodies are weak & worn,
We plot & corrupt each other,
And we despoil the unborn.

(5) Yet there in the parlour sits
Some figure of noble guise,
Our angel in a stranger's form,
Or woman's pleading eyes;
Or only a flashing sunbeam
(10) In at the windowpane,
Or music pours on mortals
Its beautiful disdain.

The inevitable Morning
Finds them who in cellars be,
(15) And be sure the all-loving Nature
Will smile in a factory.
Yon ridge of purple landscape,
Yon sky between the walls
Hold all the hidden wonders
(20) In scanty intervals.

Alas! the sprite that haunts us
Deceives our rash desire,

2 "The World-Soul," 21–42.

[3] It whispers of the glorious gods,
And leaves us in the mire.
We cannot learn the cipher
That's writ upon our cell,
(5) Stars help us by a mystery
Which we could never spell.

If but one hero knew it,
The world would blush in flame;
The sage till he hit the secret
(10) Would hang his head for shame.
But our brothers have not read it,
Not one has found the key,
And henceforth we are comforted,
We are but such as they.

(15) Still, still the secret presses,
The nearing clouds draw down,
The crimson morning flames into
The fopperies of the town.

[4] Yet what if Trade sow cities
Like shells along the shore
And thatch with towns the prairie broad
With railways ironed o'er?
(5) They are but sailing foam-bells
Along Thought's causing stream,
And take their shape & sun-colour
From him that sends the dream.

For Destiny does not like
(10) To yield to men the helm,
And shoots his thought by hidden nerves
Throughout the solid realm.
The patient Daemon sits
With roses and a shroud,
(15) He has his way, & deals his gifts,—
But ours is not allowed.

He is no churl or trifler,
And his agents—they are none,—
Love without weakness,
(20) Of ⟨g⟩Genius sire and son.
⟨He kills the cripple & the sick⟩And his will is not thwarted,
⟨And straight begins again⟩The seeds of land & sea

3 "The World-Soul," 43–60.
4 "The World-Soul," 65–88. In line (23), "bright" is in pencil.

717

Are the atoms of his body ↑bright↓
And his behest obey.

## "Written in a Volume of Goethe" (Goethe's *Werke*, 1828–1833, vol. 50)

[1]    Let it be
    A ⟨measure⟩ meter of prosperity
    In my coat I bore this book
    And ⟨never⟩ ↑seldom↓ therein could I look
(5)    Now I had too much to think
    Heaven & earth to eat & drink

    Is he hapless who can spare
    In his plenty things so rare

## "You fast at feasts and oft invited shun" (Poems folder 96)

[1]    ⟨I⟩ ↑You↓ fast at ⟨home⟩ ↑feasts↓ and oft invited shun
    The pleasant morsel & oft provoked
    Amid the wiles of talk to egotism
    ⟨I⟩You turn ⟨aside the b⟩ ↑the↓ bait aside & ⟨talk⟩ speak of others
(5)    Or smarting under ⟨censure⟩ unjust blame, ↑make gentle answer. ↓
    To what good end? Were it not better done
    As oft ⟨I⟩ ↑you↓ think & do, to let things go
    Even as they will down the swallowing stream
    Of universal custom than to resist
(10)    And make those sharp encounters which perhaps
    Shall presently be as they had never been
    Be of good cheer, brave spirit! Steadfastly
    Serve that low whisper thou hast served, for know
    God hath a select family of sons
(15)    Now scattered wide thro' earth, & each one alone,
    Who are thy spiritual kindred, & each one
    By constant service to that inward law
    Is rearing up the bright proportions
    Of his majestic mind. Beauty; & Strength;
(20)    The riches of a spotless Memory;
    The eloquence of truth; ⟨&⟩ the ⟨stable⟩ Wisdom got

1 "Written in a Volume of Goethe." In pencil.
1 "You fast at feasts," 1–29 (1–29); "Be of good cheer, brave spirit" (12–27). A wavy horizontal line is drawn across the top of the page; lines (10–11) are struck through in ink.

⟨Of⟩By a purged & benevolent eye
That seeth as God seeth. These are their gifts
And time who keeps Gods word brings in the day

(25) ⟨To seal the marriage of these minds with thine⟩
Thine everlasting friends   Ye shall be
The salt of things   The church of the first born
A constellation of sweet influence
To all that live.

[2]                         They and you
Shall have delight ⟨↑‖ . . . ‖↓⟩ ⟨in⟩ each ↑in the↓ other's
        worth
And ⟨exercise⟩ ↑breathe↓ your virtues in an emulous love
Tasking the monumental strength of truth

(5) And love in ages grown to act for ⟨ever⟩ aye.

2 "You fast at feasts," 30–34.

# Analysis of Poems

Each poem, poetic fragment, and translation in Emerson's poetry notebooks is discussed below. The purpose is to order all of the available information to present a coherent picture of the poem or fragment from its earliest, often incomplete appearance to its first published (or final unpublished) form. Full titles of published poems are given, as are complete first lines (from the latest text) of unpublished poems and fragments. Except for short, isolated units of verse that exist in unique versions, each analysis is divided into three categories:

(1) Texts. All known holograph texts are noted, whether in the poetry notebooks, the JMN, unpublished Emerson notebooks, individual manuscripts, letters, or elsewhere, such as other people's autograph albums or the pages of printed books. The relationship of the various drafts, when it can be determined, is given in order to present a history of the poem in all its manuscript versions.

References to Poems folders 1–172 are to the large file of Emerson poetry manuscripts in the Houghton Library, MS Am1280.235(1–172). The Houghton also contains poetry manuscripts in other files.

Notebooks by Emerson not published in this volume or in the JMN will appear in whole or in part in the forthcoming *Topical Notebooks of Ralph Waldo Emerson,* to be published by the University of Missouri Press. This edition will print all of the poetry in those notebooks.

Separate manuscripts, if of sufficient textual importance, are printed in the Additional Manuscripts section above; other manuscripts in the Houghton Library or elsewhere are noted in individual analyses, where any substantive variants they may contain are given.

Line numbers of published poems cited here are always those of first publication. When this is *Poems, 1847,* the Boston edition rather than the London one (which omits some lines and adds others) is followed.

(2) Dates. The time of composition of each poem, as well as the probable date of later drafts, is given if it can be determined. All available evidence, internal or external, in the poems themselves and in documents by Emerson and others, is used to establish the probable dates. Conjectures as to dates by James Elliot Cabot, Edward Emerson, and Carl Strauch are also noted.

However, since Emerson often used several poetry notebooks concurrently and did not follow a pattern of orderly inscription in individual notebooks, dates of successive drafts cannot be established with absolute certainty. Also, in the regular journals Emerson frequently wrote drafts on blank pages, then wrote around the drafts days or weeks later, so that nearby dates may be significantly later than the actual date of inscription.

(3) Publication. First publication of each poem by Emerson in periodicals, gift annuals, or elsewhere is noted, as is its first appearance in his own poetry collections and (in the case of mottoes and translations) in his essay collections. Other periodical or book publication during his lifetime is mentioned if significant; normally, however, such appearances merely copy one of the published texts without further revision by Emerson.

Always noted is the appearance of a poem in any or all of the following: *Poems*, 1847, Boston and London editions; *May–Day*, 1867; *Selected Poems*, 1876; *Poems*, 1884 (the Riverside Edition, edited by James Elliot Cabot); and the Centenary Edition (W), 1903–1904, edited by Edward Emerson.

If a poem was not published during Emerson's lifetime, its subsequent publication by James Elliot Cabot, Edward Emerson, Ralph L. Rusk, Carl Strauch, or in the JMN is noted. If a poem has never been published, that of course is also mentioned.

The section titled "See Also" gives other relevant references. These include especially Edward Emerson's notes to the Centenary Edition, his edition of the journals, Ralph L. Rusk's life of Emerson and his edition of Emerson's letters, Carl Strauch's dissertation and the various articles drawn from it, and related poems or prose passages by Emerson.

## "A. H."

*Texts:* The earliest draft of any part of this quatrain is the incomplete pencil version of lines 3–4 in journal NO (JMN 13:407), overwritten by an ink entry. The full quatrain, lines 3–4 drawn from the NO text, occurs in pencil in EF p. 76 and in a revised ink version in EF p. 77. Lines 3–4 of this version occur with further changes in NO (JMN 13:420), where they follow a related prose passage. Emerson copied this entire entry in notebook L Camadeva p. 72, while lines 3–4 were copied separately in P p. 165. A version of lines 3–4, different from any of these but possibly intermediate between the NO drafts, occurs in Emerson's letter of 27 April 1855 to Caroline Sturgis Tappan in New York preparing to go to Europe: "I went the other day to see your sister [Anne Sturgis Hooper], who received me with great kindness. Her manners & beauty will serve to vindicate America to you in England & Italy, and, whilst she stays at home, I shall reckon securely on your return. / Far capitals & marble courts her eye seemed still to see, / Minstrels, & dames, & highborn men, the princeliest that be" (MS in the Tappan Papers, Houghton). The full quatrain in the EF p. 77 text occurs in two titled ink fair copies in Rhymer p. 33 (with the notation "printed") and NP p. 137.

*Date:* Journal NO, in which lines 3–4 first appear, was used between February and August 1855. Emerson's letter suggests composition in the spring of that year. The idea of the quatrain may be distantly derived from a collection of notes in NO: "Manners rare & powerful as beauty, / keys to palaces, / know the ceremonies. / Contrivance of wise men" (JMN 13:394). The first of these notes refers to a statement by a "Mrs H." that "Manners [are] as rare & as powerful as beauty" (JMN 13:96 and 381). In February 1855, Emerson wrote the lecture "Beauty" or, as Cabot gives the title, "Beauty and Manners" (see Cabot, *Memoir,* 2:759 and L 4:494–95). "Mrs H." and "A. H." would thus appear to be Anne (or Anna) Hooper, wife of Samuel Hooper and sister of Caroline Sturgis Tappan.

*Publication: May–Day,* 1867, p. 181; reprinted in *Poems,* 1884, p. 238, and W 9:291.

## "'Άδακρυν νέμονται Αἰῶνα"

*Texts:* The order of the drafts is as follows: journal O (JMN 9:396–97), where the text is marked "Printed"; P p. 292; X p. 243 (the first titled draft); and Rhymer p. 39 (which, though not quite identical to the published form, also carries the notation "printed").

*Date:* The draft in O must have been written between April 1846 and February 1847, the period of use of that journal. The poem seems to reflect Emerson's recent reading of Hafiz, whose *Diwan* he had purchased in April 1846. The title, from Pindar, Olympian Ode II, line 67, occurs in notebook Trees [A:I] (JMN 8:519), probably from 1843; it occurs also in X pp. i and ii (truncated), and in notebook S (Salvage) p. 20. In S (Salvage) the phrase occurs as the heading to a passage that includes the following: "the most devout persons are the freest speakers in reference to divine things, as Luther, Melancthon, More, Fuller, Herbert, Milton,—whose words are an offence to the pursed mouths which make formal prayers; and they are freethinkers also" (the passage is drawn from JMN 4:350). The poem is thematically related to prose meditations of April or May 1846 in JMN 9:405–8, and to the "Ode, Inscribed to W. H. Channing," written in June.

*Publication: May–Day,* 1867, p. 191; reprinted in *Poems,* 1884, p. 244, and W 9:297.

## "The Adirondacs"

*Texts:* The earliest text of Emerson's verse narrative of his Adirondack camping trip in August 1858 is the partially erased pencil draft in NP pp. 146–

62, which, though out of order and incomplete, takes the poem through line 329. It draws on two earlier prose accounts, the first in journal DO (JMN 13:34–35 and 55–56), written while Emerson was still at the camp, the second in notebook WA pp. 93–99, written after his return. A note on pines in WA p. 91 is the source of lines 40–41, and a list of birds in WA p. 92 the source of lines 146–48.

To fill out the first draft, Emerson returned to WA and versified sections of the prose account: lines 93–98 on p. 92; two unused lines, intended for the section on the guides, on p. 94; and lines 44–45, 54, 56–58, 149–52, three unused lines, 46–49, and 101–2 on pp. 98–100. (In addition, the phrase "laughter of the loon" in a collection of single lines in WA p. 46 echoes line 114.) These lines he copied and expanded in ink in NP: lines 93–98 and 101–2 on p. 165 (together with a draft of lines 105–6); lines 44–45 and 54–58 on p. 166; and lines 149–52, the three unused lines, and lines 46–49 on p. 167.

Emerson continued in pencil in NP with the first draft of the four-line motto on p. 168 (copied in pencil in NP p. 189, ETE p. 156, and notebook OP Gulistan p. ii, and in ink in an autograph copy titled "Friends at Follansbee Lake" in the University of Virginia Library), followed by verse biographies, not used in the poem, of eight of his companions: Louis Agassiz on pp. 168–69; Ebenezer Rockwood Hoar on p. 169; John Holmes on pp. 170–71 (revised in NP pp. 190–91 and copied in ETE pp. 56$_c$–56$_d$ and 166–67); James Russell Lowell on pp. 172–73 (revised on pp. 193–95 and later used in "James Russell Lowell"); Jeffries Wyman on p. 174 (copied in ETE p. 169); Horatio Woodman on pp. 176–77 (revised in Poems folder 40); Estes Howe on pp. 178–79 (revised in Poems folder 24); and William James Stillman on pp. 180–82 (revised in ETE pp. 156–57). For the texts in folders 24 and 40, see Additional Manuscripts.

The first draft of lines 266–70 follows the biographies on NP p. 183, and is copied, along with lines 262–65, on p. 158. The first draft of lines 208–10, in NP p. 164, is revised in EL p. 27 (headed "Adirondac") and again in EL p. 50, both EL drafts being struck through and erased. Also in EL p. 27 are a note, "October woods NP 163" (which may indicate that Emerson intended using the eleven-line fragment beginning "October woods, wherein" in "The Adirondacs"), and lines 262–65, revised from NP p. 158.

Lines 213–14 and 216–20 occur in NP p. 249, both versified from passages by Mary Moody Emerson in notebook MME 2. Lines 213–14 derive from p. 170: "The clouds are rich & dark,—air serene,—so like the soul of me, t'were me," and lines 216–20 from p. 181: "Is sadness on me at retrospection?—or at prospect of darker years, like the cloud on which the purple iris dwells in beauty,—superior to its gaudy colors?" (both of these passages are struck through). Lines 213–14 also occur in EL pp. 26 (following the first draft of "Best boon of life") and 50. Lines 221–23 occur in a pencil draft in EL p. 41 (followed by a draft of "Best boon of life"); lines 224–29, versified in EL p. 189 from a prose passage on the preceding page, are copied in EL

p. 40 and marked for insertion on p. 41. Line 215 may have been supplied later, suggested by "Sadness is better than walking, talking, acting somnambulism" in MME 2 p. 180, or "the same solitary joy will go with me" in MME 2 p. 182. Line 70 was apparently suggested by two lines in journal V (JMN 9:167). For "Taháwus" (line 10), see JMN 15:361.

The only complete text is the printer's copy for *May–Day* in the Houghton Library, revisions in which indicate Emerson was still working with the text until press time (see Additional Manuscripts). Following line 329 is a note by the printer, "Twelve lines are to be added here" (see L 5:511); Emerson subsequently supplied the last fourteen lines of the poem on a sheet of blue paper. Ten unused lines follow line 229, the last nine a draft of "Best boon of life" apparently taken from EL p. 41. A proofsheet of the unused lines on John Holmes is pasted to Rhymer p. 60; see Plate 8.

*Date:* The earliest draft in NP pp. 146–62 and the prose and verse in notebook WA may be as early as September 1858; directly after the WA entries Emerson began notes and a long draft of his talk "The Man with the Hoe," given at the Cattle Show in Concord on 29 September 1858. The sketches of individuals in NP pp. 168–82 cannot be later than 22 February 1859 since they include the first draft of "James Russell Lowell," read to the Saturday Club on that date, and may have been written before the start of a heavy lecture season in November. The lines in EL and NP derived from MME 2, none of which appear in the pencil draft in NP, cannot be earlier than January 1859, when Emerson began that notebook. The poem was in proof in March or early April 1867. Emerson apparently read some form of it to the Ladies Social Club on 27 March 1865; he noted "E. P. Whipple's read 'Adirondac' " opposite that date in Pocket Diary 16 (JMN 15:527).

*Publication:* First published in *May–Day*, 1867, pp. 41–62; reprinted in *Poems*, 1884, pp. 159–70, and W 9:182–94. Lines 224–29 are also printed in *Poems*, 1884, p. 278, as the first fragment on Nature. Though a cut proof of the lines on John Holmes is pasted into Rhymer p. 60, along with proofs of "James Russell Lowell," the lines were never published. Edward Emerson printed the biographical verses on Woodman, Stillman, Lowell, Howe, and Wyman in *The Early Years of the Saturday Club* (Boston and New York, 1918), pp. 125, 175–76, 200–202, 283, and 424, along with selected lines from the poem on pp. 170–76.

*See Also:* (1) "Best boon of life," (2) "James Russell Lowell," (3) "October woods, wherein," (4) Strauch diss., pp. 419–44 (text) and 655–79 (notes), and (5) Paul F. Jamieson, "Emerson in the Adirondacks," *New York History* 39 (July 1958): 215–37, and the same author's "A Note on Emerson's 'Adirondacs,' " *NEQ* 31 (March 1958): 88–90.

## "Ah! not to me these dreams belong"

*Texts:* The first draft of this couplet occurs with the prose source in journal ST (JMN 16:243). This is followed by fair copies in ETE p. 27, notebook Phi

Beta, front cover verso and p. 205, and notebook PY p. 224 (the last two cite ST), and a variant draft in NP p. 27.

*Date:* The first draft in ST was written in 1871 or 1872.

*Publication:* Unpublished by Emerson. First published in *Poems,* 1884, p. 277, from the NP text, and reprinted in W 9:333.

## "Ah strange strange strange"

*Text:* This fragment occurs in pencil in P p. 13, where the first line is over-written by the last line of an ink fair copy of "Each and All."

*Date:* The fragment was written between 1834, when P was begun, and February 1839, when "Each and All" was published.

*Publication:* Unpublished.

## "Alas! till now I had not known"

*Texts:* The version of lines 7–8 of Hafiz, Book XX, Ode I (*Diwan* 2:118) in EF p. 72 probably precedes the draft of lines 1–12 (beginning "Safe home, pure wine, true friend") in notebook Orientalist p. 176. Another version of lines 7–8 in Orientalist p. 57 is apparently later; it was copied into Poems folder 36.

*Date:* Undetermined.

*Publication:* The couplet was published in the Orientalist p. 57 form in "Persian Poetry," 1858, p. 726, and in the essay as collected in *Letters and Social Aims,* 1876, p. 221, and W 8:245. It also occurs in "Fate," *Conduct of Life,* 1860, p. 34, and W 6:40.

## "All day the waves assailed the rock"

*Texts:* The first two drafts, in journal VS (JMN 13:188), relate to prose passages there and in JMN 13:169. The poem was further revised in EL p. 101 and in variant fair copies in Rhymer p. 96_d and ETE p. 43.

*Date:* On 20 July 1853, Emerson and Bronson Alcott traveled to the beach at Nahant, passing through the Lynn depot. Emerson miscalculated the time and had to hurry to catch the return train, missing an opportunity to visit with the Abel Adamses, who were vacationing nearby (see L 4:375–76). The entries in VS, including the first two drafts of the poem, relate directly to this experience and must have been composed very shortly afterward. The revision in EL may have been done several years later, since that draft seems related to lines on the preceding page used in "Sea-Shore."

*Publication:* Unpublished by Emerson. First published from the ETE text in *Poems,* 1884, p. 284; reprinted with the nonauthorial title "Nahant" in W 9:345.

*See Also:* JMN 16:104.

## "All good birds fly low & near the earth"

*Text:* The only occurrence of this two-line fragment is in EF p. 43. The heading "Spring" added above it indicates a relation to materials, probably intended for use in "May–Day," so headed on previous pages. The lines have not been found elsewhere in Emerson's published or unpublished writings.

## "All is seeming"

*Text:* This two-line fragment occurs in EF p. 43. It has not been found elsewhere in Emerson's published or unpublished writings.

## "All the great & good"

*Texts:* An ink draft in Blotting Book III (JMN 3:289–90) is the source of the ink fair copy in CSA p. 43.

*Date:* Both the Blotting Book III and CSA texts bear the date "6 July 1831."

*Publication:* Unpublished by Emerson. First published in J 2:394 from the Blotting Book III text.

## "All things rehearse"

*Text:* The only occurrence of this couplet is in Rhymer p. 45. The lines are, perhaps accidentally, reminiscent of "Woodnotes, II," lines 197–98.

*Date:* Undetermined.

*Publication:* Unpublished.

## "Alms"

*Texts:* In EF p. 24 is a list of Oriental proverbs, among which are versions of lines 2 and 3 of "Alms." An ink draft of the poem at EF p. 116 probably precedes the three ink drafts in EF p. 25 and another at EL p. 49. A fair copy, with the title "Alms" and an ascription to Hafiz, occurs in Rhymer p. 140. A late copy in ETE p. 45 is the source of the identical version in Poems folder 62.

*Date:* The material in EF p. 24 is written over a prose source for "Days," while the three drafts on EF p. 25 are written over material relating to "The Fugitive Slave Law" (1851). "Alms" was therefore written in 1851 or later.

*Publication:* First published in *Sketches and Reminiscences of the Radical Club,* ed. Mrs. John T. Sargent (Boston, 1880), p. 398. Collected in *Poems,* 1884, p. 289, and reprinted in W 9:350. The quatrain has never been printed with the title that Emerson gave it in Rhymer p. 140.

## "Alone in Rome! Why Rome is lonely too"

*Texts:* The earliest draft of this poem is in journal Q (JMN 4:71). This is the source of the ink version in P pp. 215–16, where lines 2–7 are bracketed and struck through. A condensed ink version in EL p. 150, consisting of lines 1 and 8–20 and the first half of line 21, is taken from the version in P.

*Date:* Both the P and EL texts have the notation "Rome, March 22, 1833." However, Emerson did not arrive in Rome until 26 March. In transcribing the poem into P, Emerson mistakenly took the date of 22 March from the prose passage that immediately precedes it in Q. He left Rome on 23 April.

*Publication:* Unpublished by Emerson. First published, from the P text, in *Poems,* 1884, pp. 301–2, with the title "Written at Rome, 1833"; reprinted in W 9:396–97, with the title "Written at Rome" and the appended date "1833." In J 3:75–76 the poem is printed from the P text and dated "*March* 27 [1833]."

*See Also:* Strauch diss., pp. 332–33 (text) and 505–8 (notes).

## "Alphonso of Castile"

*Texts:* The first four drafts of "Alphonso" are all in notebook X in the following order of inscription: pp. 39–41, 2–4, 5–8, and 10–13. Even the last of these is a rough draft, so that one or more intermediate versions, now lost, must have preceded the fair copy in Houghton (see Additional Manuscripts) and the printer's copy for the London edition of *Poems*, 1847, also in Houghton.

*Date:* Emerson's letter of 27 July 1846 to Elizabeth Hoar (L 3:341) shows that he had only recently completed the poem. "Alphonso" develops an entry in journal O of May 1846 (JMN 9:427), which is in turn related to the erased entry reported in JMN 9:437, n. 260. Other pertinent passages also date from the period May through July: "American debility" (JMN 9:384), "Double the dose" (JMN 9:388), the reference to Alphonso of Castile (JMN 9:397), and two passages on "omissions" (JMN 9:397). The text at X p. 13 is written over an erased draft of "Monadnock." Edward Emerson (W 9:413) incorrectly dated the poem to the summer of 1847.

*Publication: Poems*, 1847, pp. 36–40 (Boston) and pp. 26–29 (London); reprinted in *Selected Poems*, 1876, pp. 29–31, *Poems*, 1884, pp. 27–29, and W 9:25–28.

## "always found / In the air . . . "

*Text:* These two and a half lines occur in pencil in P p. 192, set off by a large bracket from the lines of "Dirge" that precede them. They have not been found elsewhere in Emerson's published or unpublished writings.

## "The Amulet"

*Texts:* A draft of stanzas 2 and 3 occurs in erased pencil in journal Books Small (JMN 8:469); three erased pencil versions of stanza 1 and one of stanza 2 occur in notebook Dialling, as does an ink version (mutilated) of stanza 2 (JMN 8:515–16). A pencil fair copy, with title, occurs in P p. 253. Printer's copy for the London edition of *Poems*, 1847, is at Yale.

*Date:* Composed between April and June 1842. In journal K, just before an entry for 3 April, occurs the source of lines 11–12: "The inconvenience of love is that we are always tormented by the fear that it expired in the last expression of it" (JMN 8:219).

*Publication: The Dial* 3 (July 1842): 73–74; collected in *Poems*, 1847, p. 148 (Boston) and pp. 117–18 (London); reprinted in *Selected Poems*, 1876, p. 93, *Poems*, 1884, p. 88, and W 9:98–99.

## "An ancient drop of feudal blood"

*Text:* The only text of this quatrain, which refers to Emerson's descent from Peter Bulkeley, the founder of Concord, is in pencil in P p. 247. Possibly related to "In Memoriam. E. B. E.," it has not been found elsewhere in Emerson's published or unpublished writings.

## "An ancient lady who dwelt in Rome"

*Text:* The sole draft is an ink fair copy in CSA p. 39.

*Date:* No date can be assigned to this fragment concerning the sale of the Sibylline books to the Roman king Tarquin the Proud, although content and style suggest Emerson's college years, 1817–1821.

*Publication:* Unpublished.

## "And as the light divided the dark"

*Text:* The only manuscript version of this quatrain is the pencil draft in X p. 79. The poem seems to be related to lines 57–58 of "Solution," an early version of which appears, erased, in X p. 80. As the ink draft of "Solution" in X pp. 76–81 is interrupted by the draft of "And as the light," the quatrain was evidently set down first.

*Date:* Undetermined.

*Publication:* Unpublished by Emerson. First published in W 9:330.

## "And had Hafiz"

*Text:* These five lines, a translation of Hafiz, Book VIII, Ode LXXIV, lines 25–28 (*Diwan* 1:314), occur in pencil in EF pp. 48 and 112. They have not been found elsewhere in Emerson's published or unpublished writings.

## "And he like me is not too proud"

*Texts:* Two identical texts of the couplet occur in EL pp. 80 and 147.

*Date:* Undetermined. Lines for "My Garden" preceding the couplet in EL p. 147 were written no earlier than 1863.

*Publication:* Unpublished.

## "And hungry Debt with his hundred hands"

*Texts:* The first draft of this couplet is in NP p. 289, revised on p. 290. The latest version occurs in Poems folder 38 (see Additional Manuscripts under "Boston Hymn").

*Date:* The first draft is written after a motto published in *The Conduct of Life,* 1860; the version in Poems folder 38 was inscribed before December 1862.

*Publication:* Unpublished.

## "And man of wit & mark"

*Text:* This quatrain occurs in pencil in X p. 37.

*Date:* The text was probably inscribed in 1845 (see "Solar insect on the wing").

*Publication:* Unpublished.

## "And more / The genius of each race"

*Text:* The only text of these nine lines is in pencil in EL p. 115. They appear to have been written at the same time as the pencil draft of "You strong Republicans" on p. 114, and may be a continuation of it.

*Date:* In his notes on this notebook, Edward Emerson speculates that pp. 115–31 are "More preparation for *Voluntaries* apparently of early date, perhaps before the war." The next few pages of EL mix lines for "Voluntaries" and "Boston Hymn" probably written in late 1862 or early 1863.

*Publication:* Unpublished.

## "And pour the strength of human tho[ugh]t"

*Text:* These two lines occur only in pencil in EL p. 127, separated by a rule from a draft of lines which include one used in "Boston Hymn."

*Date:* Late December 1862, if written at the same time as the "Boston Hymn" draft above it, or no later than 7 September 1863, if written, like the surrounding drafts, during the composition of "Voluntaries."

*Publication:* Unpublished.

## "And rival Coxcombs with enamored stare"

*Text:* This couplet occurs in pencil in EL p. 117. It has not been found elsewhere in Emerson's published or unpublished writings.

## "And roll the river where it will"

*Text:* The only text of this two-line fragment occurs in NP p. 78. It has not been found elsewhere in Emerson's published or unpublished writings.

## "And the air echoes more than mortal love"

*Text:* The only text of this line, versified from notebook MME 4 p. 255 ("The very air is the echo of more than mortal love"), is in ETE p. 104ᵦ.

*Date:* Probably late February 1869, if, as seems likely, the references that follow the line, all to quotations from Mary Moody Emerson in notebooks ML pp. 148 and 218 and MME 4 p. 131, were gathered for "Amita," Emerson's lecture on his aunt, given in Boston 1 March 1869.

*Publication:* Unpublished.

## "And the best gift of God"

*Text:* This two-line fragment occurs in pencil in P p. 214. It has not been found elsewhere in Emerson's published or unpublished writings.

## "And the deep is as a ford"

*Text:* This single line occurs in pencil in EL p. 32.

*Date:* After 1863, the earliest possible date for "What flowing central forces," which precedes it on the page.

*Publication:* Unpublished.

## "And though he dearly prized the bards of fame"

*Texts:* Two texts exist, one in pencil in P p. 143, and another in ink in notebook L Camadeva p. 111.

*Date:* Undetermined. Laid in with the text in P is a strip of paper with Edward Emerson's notation, "To E[llen] T[ucker] E[merson] at Phil-[adelphia]." The evidence for this identification is unknown, but if it is accurate, the poem dates from April or May 1830.

*Publication:* Unpublished.


## "And when I am entombed in my place"

*Text:* The only text is an ink fair copy in P p. 99, referred to in the index as "Epitaph."

*Date:* Undetermined, though the other fragments on P p. 99 seem to date from the mid-1830s.

*Publication:* Unpublished by Emerson. First published in W 9:395.


## "And whether I was rich & great"

*Text:* This three-line fragment occurs in X p. 26, written over an erased draft of "Monadnock" in a lighter shade of pencil than the apparently unrelated lines of "Pale Genius roves alone" that follow it.

*Date:* Since composition falls between "Monadnock" and "Pale Genius roves alone," the fragment must date from 1845–1847.

*Publication:* Unpublished.


## "Ann is spotless"

*Texts:* The couplet is in pencil in P p. 13. Cf. "This is spotless / That is not less" in journal B (JMN 5:147).

*Date:* The entry in journal B is dated 27 March 1836. Since the version in P occurs with two other pencil entries that seem to be in the same handwriting, one of which ("Ah strange strange strange") must be before February 1839, its composition falls between those two dates.

*Publication:* Unpublished.


## "The Apology"

*Texts:* An erased pencil version of this poem, untitled and lacking stanza 4, occurs in P p. 204. Stanza 4 occurs in erased pencil on p. 207, having been revised from p. 206, where it is part of "Knows he who tills this lonely field." The complete poem, in an ink fair copy with the title "The Poet's Apology," occurs on p. 203, written over an erased draft of "The Park." Printer's copy for the London edition of *Poems, 1847,* is in Poems folder 8.

*Date:* After 1841, the apparent date of "The Park." Emerson sent the poem along with "Dirge" in a letter of 12 March 1844 to William H. Furness, editor of *The Gift* (see *Records,* pp. 31–32). Edward Emerson's note to the poem (W 9:440) asserts that it "belongs to the early period of its author's Concord life."

*Publication: The Gift: A Christmas, New Year, and Birthday Present* (Philadelphia, 1845), p. 77, with the P title. Collected in *Poems, 1847,* pp. 178–79 (Boston) and pp. 142–43 (London), with the title "The Apology"; reprinted in *Poems, 1884,* pp. 105–6, and W 9:119.

*See Also:* "Knows he who tills this lonely field."

## "Apples of gold in silver salvers set"

*Texts:* This single line, a metrical rendition of Proverbs 25:11, appears in journal AB (JMN 10:8), EL p. 71, NP p. 71, and, possibly, in erased pencil in X p. 265.

*Date:* The AB text, not necessarily the first, was written between February and April 1847, the period of use of that journal.

*Publication:* Unpublished by Emerson. First published, as a quotation, in J 7:244.

## "April"

*Texts:* The first draft, in Poems folder 63 (see Additional Manuscripts), was followed by a second in NP pp. 31–32, a third in NP p. 30, and a fourth in NP p. 42, with some revision back and forth among the drafts. The fair copy in Rhymer p. 75, with the added title "Spring Winds," precedes the final copy, titled "April," in ETE p. 15.

*Date:* The source of the poem is a paragraph from Emerson's letter of 21 February 1840 to Margaret Fuller (L 2:255): "These spring winds are magical in their operation on our attuned frames. These are the days of passion when the air is full of cupids & devils for eyes that are still young; and every pool of water & every dry leaf & refuse straw seems to flatter, provoke, mock, or pique us. I who am not young have not yet forgot the enchantment,

& still occasionally see dead leaves & wizards that peep & mutter. Let us surrender ourselves for fifteen minutes to the slightest of these nameless influences—these nymphs or imps of wood & flood of pasture & roadside, and we shall quickly find out what an ignorant pretending old Dummy is Literature who has quite omitted all that we care to know—all that we have not said ourselves." Emerson copied this paragraph into notebook S (Salvage) p. 270 and might have returned to it at any time. The only clues as to when he did return are to be found in NP. At the bottom of p. 41 is a collection of cross references to materials on the theme of "Spring"; "S 270" is among them. These references were copied from notebook TU (JMN 11:114), where they had been entered in the spring or summer of 1849. On p. 6 of NP is another reference to "S 270" that may be as late as 1859.

*Publication:* First published in *Selected Poems,* 1876, p. 125, from the ETE fair copy; reprinted with an editorial change in line 7 ("The cobweb clues of Rosamond" for "The clews of fairy Rosamonds") in *Poems,* 1884, p. 219, and W 9:255.

*See Also:* Carl F. Strauch, "Emerson as a Creator of Vignettes," *MLN* 70 (April 1955): 274–78.


## "Arabian Ballad"


*Text:* This translation of an untitled ballad with numbered stanzas in Goethe's *Noten und Abhandlungen zu besserem Verständnis des West-östlichen Divans* in Emerson's edition of *Goethe's Werke,* 55 vols. (Stuttgart and Tübingen, 1828–1833), 6:12–17, occurs in pencil in EL pp. 235–39. It has not been found elsewhere in Emerson's published or unpublished writings.


## "The Archangel Hope"


*Text:* The only text is a pencil draft in P p. 161.

*Date:* Probably composed between 1842 and 1844. The prose source is a passage in journal K that ends with the sentence, "I am *Defeated* all the time; yet to Victory I am born" (JMN 8:227–28). The passage occurs between entries made 6 and 10 April 1842. The P text follows, and is possibly related to, a draft of the opening lines of "Character," first published in 1844.

*Publication:* Unpublished by Emerson. First published in *Poems,* 1884, p. 296, and reprinted in W 9:354.

# "Around the man who seeks a noble end"

*Texts:* The earliest draft of this couplet occurs in notebook Encyclopedia (JMN 6:231), where Emerson included it, followed by his symbol of authorship, among "Passages that awaken the feeling of the moral Sublime." Later drafts occur in EL pp. 162 and 290, Rhymer p. 150, and ETE pp. 104c and 170.

*Date:* On 29 June 1831, Emerson wrote in Blotting Book III: "'Tis a noble but a true word of Bacon [in *De Augmentis Scientiarum*]—If once the mind has chosen noble ends, then not virtues but Divinities encompass it—'Si animus semel generosos fines optaverit, statim non modo virtutes circumstant, sed et Numina' " (JMN 3:266–67). The Latin was repeated in a different form in a journal entry of 21 July 1831 (JMN 3:274), in which Emerson noted its evocation of the feeling of the "moral sublime." In sermon no. 127, first delivered on 18 September 1831, Emerson wrote: "And from one good action a man finds his way open & easy to many so that it was anciently said 'When once a man has chosen noble ends then not virtues but divinities throng around him.' " A similar idea, as Edward Emerson noted (W 9:509), occurs in "The Divinity School Address" (W 1:124), in a passage based on a journal entry for 10 December 1836 (JMN 5:266). The versification in Encyclopedia was probably set down soon after the inscription of the source entries in Blotting Book III, though in any event before 1836, when Emerson ceased to use Encyclopedia.

*Publication:* Unpublished by Emerson. First published in *Poems,* 1884, p. 288, and reprinted in W 9:349.

*See Also:* Kenneth Walter Cameron, "Emerson and the Motif That 'Spirits Associate,' " *ESQ,* no. 12 (3d quarter 1958): 45–46.

# "Art"

*Text:* The only surviving manuscript text of this motto is an ink fair copy in X pp. 220–21.

*Date:* The poem was probably inscribed in 1847, since it belongs to a group of fair copies of mottoes for the 1847 edition of *Essays: First Series.* It is written over an erased draft of "Mithridates" composed in 1846.

*Publication: Essays: First Series,* 1847, p. 315; collected in *May–Day,* 1867, pp. 172–73, and reprinted in *Selected Poems,* 1876, pp. 181–82, *Poems,* 1884, p. 235, and W 9:277–78.

## "Art thou wise, four things resign"

*Texts:* The couplet translates Hafiz, Book XXVII, Ode LXXVII, lines 21–22 (*Diwan* 2:468). The first draft in EF p. 109 is revised in X p. 239.

*Date:* Undetermined.

*Publication:* Unpublished.

## "Artist"

*Texts:* A draft of lines 3–4 occurs in journal AB (JMN 10:33), while the first draft of the entire quatrain occurs in journal GO (JMN 13:80–81), with the title "To an Artist." Rhymer p. 51 and NP p. 135 contain fair copies.

*Date:* A number of possible prose sources, none very close, are nevertheless worth mentioning: Edward Emerson (W 9:497) calls attention to a journal entry for 1850 (JMN 11:240), and elsewhere (W 7:407) suggests that a passage from the essay "Books" provides a parallel (cf. JMN 11:48, an entry for November 1848). The journal entry immediately preceding the first complete text (JMN 13:80) may have a bearing, as also might a sentence from *Nature*, 1836: "The poet, the orator, bred in the woods, whose senses have been nourished by their fair and appeasing changes, year after year, without design and without heed,—shall not lose their lesson altogether, in the roar of cities or the broil of politics" (W 1:31). Lines 3–4 were apparently written in late March or early April 1847, while the GO text certainly dates to August 1852.

*Publication: The Dial* (Cincinnati) 1 (March 1860): 195; collected in *May–Day,* 1867, p. 183, and reprinted in *Poems,* 1884, p. 239, and W 9:291.

## "As I walked in the wood"

*Text:* This nine-line fragment occurs in partially erased pencil in P p. 118. It may be related to "I sat upon the ground," though it has not been found elsewhere in Emerson's published or unpublished writings.

## "As if a fleet should sail"

*Text:* The only text of this eight-line fragment occurs in pencil in NP p. 223. It has not been found elsewhere in Emerson's published or unpublished writings.

## "As Stars & the celestial Kind"

*Texts:* The first two drafts are in EF pp. 28 and 29, where a draft of "The Fugitive Slave Law" (1851) is written around them. Later copies are in EL p. 81, journal DO (JMN 13:9), and Rhymer p. 50$_a$.

*Date:* The EF drafts were done before the spring of 1851. The copy in journal DO is probably not earlier than March 1852.

*Publication:* Unpublished by Emerson. First published in JMN 13.

## "As the drop feeds its fated flower"

*Text:* This poem occurs only in pencil in EL p. 200.

*Date:* Undetermined.

*Publication:* Unpublished by Emerson. First published in *Poems,* 1884, p. 295, and reprinted in W 9:355.

## "Ask not treasures from his store"

*Texts:* An erased pencil draft occurs in X p. 262, followed by a pencil draft in X p. 263 and a copy in ink in X p. 268$_{cc}$.

*Date:* Undetermined, though the insert, X pp. 268$_a$-268$_{dd}$, seems to date from about 1847.

*Publication:* Unpublished.

## "The Asmodaean feat be mine"

*Texts:* The first draft is probably X p. 126, followed by journal IO p. 61 (JMN 13:314). Later inscriptions occur in IO p. i (JMN 13:291), EL p. 148, Rhymer p. 50$_f$, and NP p. 296. In the last three instances the couplet occurs together with other brief fragments.

*Date:* In the first two drafts the couplet is associated with a reference to Minerva, and was probably inscribed in both locations at about the same time: May 1854. Reference to the devil Asmodaeus occurs as early in Emerson's writings as 21 July 1836 (see JMN 5:186). In a letter to Emerson of 16

February 1845, Carlyle refers to "Michael Scott setting the devil to twist ropes of sand" (*The Correspondence of Emerson and Carlyle,* ed. Joseph Slater, New York and London, 1964, p. 377).

*Publication:* Unpublished by Emerson. First published in *Poems,* 1884, p. 277, and reprinted in W 9:334.

*See Also:* W 8:393 and 9:507.

## "Astraea"

*Texts:* Emerson wrote a draft of the poem in X pp. 19–20 and revised it on pp. 21–22. What appears to be a version of line 28 occurs in X p. 23. He revised the poem once more in X pp. 89–91, and then erased the earlier drafts. Printer's copy for the London edition of *Poems,* 1847, is in the Huntington Library; in it, "spot" is canceled for "grot" in line 45.

*Date:* Since the passage in X p. 21 is written over a draft of "Etienne de la Boéce," "Astraea" must have been written sometime between late 1843 and 1846. No evidence has been discovered to support Edward Emerson's statement (W 9:428) that Emerson contemplated "ΓΝΩΘΙ ΣΕΑΥΤΟΝ" as a title.

*Publication: Poems,* 1847, pp. 123–25 (Boston) and pp. 96–98 (London); reprinted in *Selected Poems,* 1876, pp. 74–75, *Poems,* 1884, pp. 75–76, and W 9:80–81.

## "At last the poet spoke"

*Texts:* This five-line fragment occurs in pencil in P p. 149 and was copied in ink in Poems folder 73 with the last line changed to "A devil hides in heavenly deeps."

*Date:* The earlier text was probably written in 1840 or 1841, contemporary with "The Discontented Poet: a Masque," a draft of which occurs in P pp. 153–56. The fragment recurs in the manuscripts that Emerson assembled in 1842–1843 for the purposes of expanding the "Masque."

*Publication:* Unpublished.

## "At Plymouth in the friendly crowd"

*Text:* The only text of this gift poem for Lidian Emerson is in NP p. 121.

*Date:* The verses were probably written in late December 1867 to accompany a New Year's gift. They immediately precede a draft of "Maiden Speech of the Aeolian Harp," written at that time.

*Publication:* Unpublished.

## "At Sea, September 1833"

*Texts:* Notebook Sea 1833 (JMN 4:240–42) contains the earliest version of the poem. The first 29 lines of this rough draft in ink were much later revised and given a title in the ink version in X pp. 98–99, which is inscribed over erased lines used in the "Ode, Inscribed to W. H. Channing." In X p. 97 occurs a three-line passage identical to added lines in Sea 1833 (JMN 4:242); these became lines 1–3 in the next draft in X pp. 104–5. A copy of the verses, with a few revisions, occurs in EL pp. 24–25, followed (as the revision of line 16 indicates) by an untitled fair copy in Poems folder 64 (see Additional Manuscripts).

*Date:* The first draft was written between 16 and 22 September 1833, while Emerson was returning from his first trip to Europe. The second draft could not have been done before June 1846, the date of the "Ode." The date of the three-line introductory passage cannot be determined, since priority between the X and Sea 1833 texts of these lines is uncertain. If the X text was written first, it could not be earlier than 1846; otherwise it would date from between 1833 and 1846. Its source appears to be a remark of Samuel Johnson's on the sea as "the only terra firma," recorded by Emerson and commented on in an entry in journal IO in 1854 (JMN 13:370–71); it is likely, however, that Emerson had encountered Johnson's remark much earlier.

*Publication:* Unpublished by Emerson. First published in J 3:206–7 from the Sea 1833 text.

## "The atom displaces all atoms beside"

*Texts:* The draft of the couplet (in quatrain form) in Rhymer p. 117 is probably the earliest, followed by the revision in EL p. 21 and the fair copy in Rhymer p. 50$_a$.

*Date:* The prose source for this couplet is an entry in notebook BO Conduct: "Every atom displaces every other atom; & every soul unspheres every soul but itself See CO 208" (JMN 12:585); it also occurs in slightly different form in journal AC (JMN 14:217). The reference to journal CO (JMN 11:428) is evidently an error, though it seems to be insisted upon: the page contains a letter from Caroline Sturgis, written in 1845, but apparently transcribed by Emerson in 1851, the date also of the entry in BO Conduct.

*Publication:* Unpublished by Emerson. First published in *Poems*, 1884, p. 275, from the Rhymer p. 50ₐ text, and reprinted in W 9:331.

## "Atom from atom yawns as far"

*Texts:* Eight manuscript texts exist: one in pencil in journal Books Small (JMN 8:470), one in ink in journal K (JMN 8:246), three ink fair copies in P p. 22, X p. 263, and Rhymer p. 63, two more in Poems folder 28, and another in ETE p. 172. All texts are identical in wording except for those in K and X, which have "as" for "or" in line 2.

*Date:* The prose source is the statement in journal K, "this new molecular philosophy goes to show that there are astronomical interspaces betwixt atom & atom" (JMN 8:246), written in the first week of May 1842. Since the couplet follows on the facing manuscript page, it was presumably written about the same time.

*Publication:* Unpublished by Emerson. First published in *Poems*, 1884, p. 280, and reprinted in W 9:339.

## "Awed I behold once more"

*Text:* The only text is an ink fair copy in CSA pp. 19–21.

*Date:* Emerson notes the place and date of the poem in CSA p. 19: "Concord, Mass— / June 1827," when he returned from his trip to Charleston, South Carolina, and St. Augustine, Florida.

*Publication:* Unpublished by Emerson. First published in W 9:385–87 with the nonauthorial title "The River." In J 2:208–9 the lines appear with the nonauthorial title "At the Old Manse."

## "Bacchus"

*Texts:* All that survives of Emerson's rough drafts is a passage in pencil in X p. 200 consisting of ten unused lines and a version of lines 7–11. Printer's copy for the London edition of *Poems*, 1847, is in the Berg Collection, New York Public Library; in it, "Of that whose" is changed to "Whose ample" in line 15.

*Date:* Emerson listed "Bacchus" as among the poems that he "wrote lately" in a letter of 27 July 1846 to Elizabeth Hoar (L 3:341). The source of the poem is an entry in journal O written between 27 June and 24 July 1846 (JMN 9:441).

*Publication: Poems,* 1847, pp. 188–91 (Boston) and pp. 149–52 (London); reprinted in *Selected Poems,* 1876, pp. 117–19, *Poems,* 1884, pp. 111–13, and W 9:125–27.

*See Also:* (1) "Pour the wine!," (2) W 9:443–45, and (3) Bernard J. Paris, "Emerson's 'Bacchus,' " *MLQ* 23 (1962): 150–59.


## "The bard & mystic held me for their own"

*Text:* The poem occurs in pencil in P p. 59, with "Rex." written in the left margin beside line 2.

*Date:* Undetermined.

*Publication:* Unpublished by Emerson. Published without title in *Poems,* 1884, p. 297, and reprinted in W 9:357 with the title "Rex." In both places "service" replaces "honor" in the last line. It is not certain that Emerson intended "Rex" as the title.


## "Bard or dunce is blest, but hard"

*Texts:* Three slightly different versions exist: in journal B (JMN 5:45), in a letter of 14 March 1836 to Frederic Henry Hedge (L 2:7), and in an ink fair copy in P p. 99, with the index reference "Proverb."

*Date:* The entry in B is dated 29 May 1835.

*Publication:* Unpublished by Emerson. First published in J 3:486.

*See Also:* "Woodnotes, I," lines 1–6.


## "Be her cognizance allowed"

*Text:* This fragment, perhaps rejected from "Boston" or "Boston Hymn," occurs in a pencil draft in EL p. 55. It has not been found elsewhere in Emerson's published or unpublished writings.

## "Be of good cheer, brave spirit; steadfastly"

*Texts:* These sixteen lines occur in a fair copy in P p. 217. They are revised from a longer poem of 34 lines, of which they constitute lines 12–27, in Poems folder 96 (see Additional Manuscripts under "You fast at feasts and oft invited shun").

*Date:* Undetermined, though judging from the handwriting, the longer version must belong to the period 1821–1829.

*Publication:* Unpublished by Emerson. First published in *Poems,* 1884, p. 291, and reprinted in W 9:381–82.

## "Be of your country & house & skin"

*Texts:* Two successive versions occur in X: one of ten lines on p. 268$_b$, followed by one of twenty-six lines on pp. 268$_c$–268$_d$.

*Date:* The poem's appearance in the X insert, which contains several fair copies of mottoes for the 1847 edition of *Essays: First Series,* suggests a date of composition in 1846 or 1847.

*Publication:* Unpublished.

## "Beauty"

*Texts:* The first ten and the last sixteen lines of this poem developed separately. For the history of the first section, see "There are beggars," an unfinished sequel to "Saadi" begun in 1844 or 1845. The earliest part of the later, concluding section is represented in three identical drafts of lines 15–16, which occur in journal VO (JMN 14:202), notebook PY p. 201, and NP p. 41. One or more of these precede the rough draft of lines 11–16 in X p. 115, which is in turn followed on X pp. 119–20 by a draft of lines 1–16 and eight unused lines. Lines 19–20 were recovered from an otherwise rejected passage in X p. 118, while X p. 107 contains rough drafts of lines 23–26. A complete copy of lines 11–26 occurs in Poems folder 79 along with two drafts of "There are beggars," which, as noted above, includes lines 1–10 of "Beauty." A proofsheet of the folder 79 text of lines 11–26 is laid in between pp. 16–17 of Rhymer; see Plates 6 and 7.

*Date:* The first section appears in the earliest form of "There are beggars," dating from between May 1844 and March 1845. The couplet that became lines 15–16 was inscribed in VO between 20 February and 11 May 1858, although the text in NP may conceivably be earlier. The evidence, then, suggests that the second section was written and joined to the first section between 1858 and 1860, the date of publication.

*Publication: The Conduct of Life,* 1860, p. 245; collected in *May–Day,* 1867, pp. 168–69, and reprinted in *Selected Poems,* 1876, p. 178, *Poems,* 1884, pp. 233–34, and W 9:275–76.

*See Also:* "There are beggars."

## "Best boon of life is Presence of a Muse"

*Texts:* The first draft of the verse is in EL p. 26, followed by the drafts in Rhymer p. 50$_d$ and EL p. 41, which show evidence of mutual influence. Poems folder 62 contains a fair copy that descends from the EL revision, with the additional change of "Who" to "That" in line 2. The poem also occurs between lines 229–30 of a copy of "The Adirondacs" in the Houghton Library (see Additional Manuscripts under that poem).

*Date:* This unfinished poem is a versification of a passage in prose by Mary Moody Emerson, drawn by Emerson from his notebook of transcriptions, MME 4 pp. 236–37: "The ideal of existence is the company of a Muse who don't wish to wander, whose visits are in secret, who divulges things not to be made popular. Soon as the wings grow, which bring the gazing eyes, even a Young & a Cowper flutter too near the earth." Emerson probably came into possession of his aunt's diaries when she stayed with him briefly in the summer of 1858 (see Strauch diss., p. 104). MME 4 was begun on 3 September 1860, as indicated by a note on the inside front cover.

*Publication:* Unpublished by Emerson. First published in *Poems,* 1884, p. 278, from the Poems folder 62 text; here it is followed by a row of asterisks apparently indicating omitted material, though none appears in the manuscripts. The poem was not reprinted in W 9.

## "Best is the poor save only that he craves"

*Text:* The only text of this one-and-a-half line fragment is in NP p. 158.

*Date:* Since it interrupts, and therefore antedates, a draft of "The Adirondacs," the fragment must be 1858 or earlier.

*Publication:* Unpublished.

## "Better held"

*Text:* These eight lines, indexed "Eloquence," occur only in a pencil draft in NP p. 286. Possibly they are not to be considered as parts of a single poem. They have not been found elsewhere in Emerson's published or unpublished writings.

## "The bird was gone the ghastly trees"

*Text:* This poem occurs in erased pencil in EL p. 194. It has not been found elsewhere in Emerson's published or unpublished writings.

## "The blue vault silver-lined with hills of snow"

*Texts:* This single line occurs in EF pp. 32 and 98, and in Poems folder 78.

*Date:* The verses in EF p. 32, several of which are copied from journal V (JMN 9:169), are written over a pencil passage used in "The Fugitive Slave Law" (1851). The copy in Poems folder 78 follows verses used in "My Garden" that were written no earlier than 1861.

*Publication:* Unpublished.

## "Borrow Urania's subtile wings"

*Texts:* Lines 2 and 3–5 appear together, though as discrete fragments, in Poems folder 79 and EF p. 4. In EL p. 172 they occur as a single four-line poem with a short second line ("Nor try"). In Rhymer p. 50f line 1 is added for the rhyme, the short line is filled out, and the poem is joined with other fugitive verses on the Poet.

*Date:* Undetermined.

*Publication:* Unpublished by Emerson. Lines 3–5 were first published, from the Poems folder 79 text, in *Poems,* 1884, p. 276. In W 9:333 lines 2–5 were published from the EL p. 172 text in an editorially created three-line format.

*See Also:* "Coin the daydawn."

## "Borrowing. From the French"

*Texts:* In journal DO (JMN 13:18) Emerson entered the four lines of verse in French of which this poem is a translation, and followed it on the same page with the first draft of the quatrain. A revised text, with the title "Borrowing," appears later in DO (JMN 13:52); this was copied into Rhymer p. 68 and NP p. 140.

*Date:* The first draft was composed in April 1852.

*Publication:* First published in "Considerations by the Way" in *The Conduct of Life,* 1860, p. 233, with "griefs" in line 1, "pain" in line 3, and "that" in line 4. The text published in *May–Day,* 1867, p. 186, has "hurts" in line 1, "grief" in line 3, and "which" in line 4. The *May–Day* text was reprinted in *Poems,* 1884, p. 241, and W 9:294.

## "Boston"

*Texts:* This poem, which bore the title "Trimountain" in its early phases, exists in many drafts in the notebooks and in a number of separate manuscripts, testifying to the difficulty Emerson had in bringing it to a satisfactory conclusion. Intent on writing a paean to his home town, Emerson nevertheless felt compelled to include a section on Boston's failure to confront the issue of slavery, yet this impulse warred with the overall positive tenor of the poem. In addition, Emerson felt that each of the stanzas should end with a refrain, yet he was never able to write a sufficient number of different ones for this purpose, and often experimented by attaching different refrains to different stanzas. (One indication of this difficulty is the seven separate collections of refrains that Emerson compiled at various times, in NP front cover verso$_g$, NP pp. 111–12, ETE p. 137, and Poems folders 31, 32, 88, and 110; for the last four, see Additional Manuscripts.) In light of the troubled history of this poem the sequence of manuscript texts is not always clear, but the main line of succession is summarized below. (In this discussion, the thirteen texts in Poems folder 88, which, with the exception of the last, a collection of refrains, are printed in Additional Manuscripts in the approximate order of composition, are identified as ms. 1, ms. 2, etc.; unused stanzas are referred to by the first words of their opening lines.)

The main text in the notebooks occurs in EL pp. 215–22, which consists of the title "Trimountain," the Latin motto of Boston, and twenty-one stanzas (often lacking refrains) in the following order: 1–2, 4–6, 8, "Out from," 9–10, 11 (inserted), 16–17, "O pity," "But there," "Your town," "O welaway," "Hie to," and 20–23. Stanza 11 is brought in from p. 223, where it is derived from notebook Orientalist p. 213. To this main text Emerson added an epigraph stanza ("The land that has no song") at the beginning on p. 214, and on p. 222 he scribbled stanzas 19 and 18, perhaps at a much later time. A note at the end of p. 222, "For lines, see *Orientalist* p. 223" led to the transfer of three stanzas (7, "The land was rich," and "The stormy billows") from there to p. 213 via ms. 3.

Numerous texts anterior to the main one in EL survive. The most significant is ms. 8, which consists of stanzas 1, 3, 2, 8, "Out from," 9–10, 16, 12, 4–6, "But there," 17, "O pity," "Your town," "O welaway," "Hie to," 20, 23, and 21–23. Prior to that is ms. 7, which is titled "Trimountain" and has the epigraph and stanzas 1, 3, 2, 10, "Your town," "O pity," "O welaway," and "Hie to." Still earlier separate manuscripts of different stanzas are ms. 1 (stanzas 4–6 and "New days"); ms. 2 (stanza 4); ms. 4 (stanzas 16, 21, and 22); ms. 5 (stanzas 20, 23, "But there," and 5); and ms. 6 (stanza "Hie to"). In the notebooks, prior texts are in EL pp. 68 (stanzas 20–22), 70 (stanza 16), and 152–54 (the epigraph and stanzas 1, 3, 2, and 8), and in NP pp. 200–4 (the epigraph, stanzas "/Hearts/Meek/ of flesh" and "Out from," the epigraph, and stanzas 1, 3, 2, "Your town," 12, 17, and "Hie to"); see also several unused lines and refrains on pp. 198–99 and 205.

The very earliest texts are of individual refrains: lines 29–30 (which double as lines 78–79) in journal SO (JMN 14:99), and lines 29–30, 11–12, 17–18, and one beginning "An union then" (eventually published as lines 35–36 in *Selected Poems*, 1876) in notebook WO Liberty (JMN 14:424). Somewhat later is the text of stanzas "Hie to," "Your town," 1, 3, 1, 3, "O once," and the epigraph in journal AC (JMN 14:271–72), and later yet the text of stanzas 12 and 17 in journal KL (JMN 15:455; for the source of lines 59–60 see 15:270 and 448). Lines 29–30 also occur in EF p. 16, line 108 occurs in NP p. 183 with lines from "The Adirondacs," and lines 88–89 occur in Emerson's Index Major.

Emerson made a number of further attempts to bring the poem to a satisfactory conclusion. Two of these attempts, ms. 9 and ms. 10, retain the stanzas on slavery, while a third, ms. 11 (presumably written after the Civil War, when the question had become moot), does not. When Emerson decided to adapt the poem for the centenary of the Boston Tea Party in December 1873, he wrote three stanzas about that event (13, 14, and 15); only one text of 13 and 14 exists, in ms. 12. A draft of stanzas 18 and 19, the source of the late added lines in EL p. 222, is in the Cambridge Public Library, a gift of Thomas Wentworth Higginson in 1895; yet earlier trials of stanza 18 are in Poems folder 38. A manuscript of the poem in the Massachusetts Historical Society, presented by Edward Emerson in 1918, is possibly the one from which Emerson read; it has the title "Boston" and a number of additions, deletions, and variant readings. (For the last three texts, see Additional Manuscripts.)

Two fair copies following the *Selected Poems* text are in the Houghton Library and Lilly Library of Indiana University. In the first, which has the title and Latin motto but not the headnote, lines 35–36, 45–48, and 76–81 are added, as is "stouter" in line 62, and "his" is changed to "her" in line 109. The second fair copy has the title, the Latin motto, and the headnote "Read in Faneuil Hall ⟨Bosto⟩on the Centennial Anniversary of the Tea Party. Dec. 16, 1873", is missing lines 35–36, and has the following variant readings: "What rival towns majestic soar" for line 45, "No steeper fence no better wall!" for line 62, "me" canceled for "us" in line 66, "with" instead of "in" in line 83, "are" instead of "be" in line 104, and "And" instead of "Or" in line 105. (Line numbers in this paragraph follow the *Selected Poems* text.)

*Date:* The passages in SO, WO Liberty, AC, and KL date from 1856, 1857, 1859, and 1864 respectively; since the main text in EL pp. 215–22 includes lines from all four sources, it presumably was written no earlier than the latest year. Texts that omit the stanzas about slavery (from ms. 11 on) must date from after the Civil War, while the stanzas about the Boston Tea Party itself (13, 14, and 15) presumably date from shortly before Emerson read the poem on 16 December 1873.

*Publication:* First published in the *Atlantic Monthly* 37 (February 1876): 195–97; see L 6:254–55 for the circumstances surrounding this appearance. Reprinted with revisions and the addition of a refrain (as lines 35–36) in *Selected Poems*, 1876, pp. 214–18, *Poems*, 1884, pp. 182–86 (with a postscript giving six of the unused stanzas), and W 9:212–17 (with four of the unused stanzas given in a note on pp. 473–74). The first six stanzas as printed in *Selected Poems* were published in *Sketches and Reminiscences of the Radical Club* (Boston, 1880), pp. 294–95.

*See Also:* (1) "Be her cognizance allowed," (2) "Boston Hymn," and (3) "O Boston city."

## "Boston Hymn"

*Texts:* (In what follows, line numbers refer to the poem as printed in *May–Day*, 1867, since earlier published versions inadvertently omitted lines 65–68 [stanza 17].)

Three major drafts of this poem, written to celebrate the coming into force of the Emancipation Proclamation on 1 January 1863, occur in EL pp. 56–60, 61–68, and 86–95. The first (and earliest) one consists of lines 5–8, 29–32, 45–48, 85–88, and 21–28 (stanzas 2, 8, 12, 22, and 6–7), plus seven additional stanzas later dropped; the second consists of lines 5–12, 29–32, 45–48, 53–56, 81–88, 17–24, and 13–16 (stanzas 2–3, 8, 12, 14, 21–22, 5–6, and 4), plus seven stanzas later dropped (including some from the first draft and others that are new); the third draft, which is entitled "The Pilgrims," consists of all the published stanzas, though not in the final order, and six of the total of ten rejected stanzas. At some point intermediate between the second and third drafts, Emerson excerpted five of the rejected stanzas and made of them a separate poem called "The Pilgrims" (manuscript in Poems folder 88; see Additional Manuscripts). This poem was then reintegrated into the third draft and the title appropriated for it.

Other draft fragments occur as follows. Two preliminary versions of lines 49–52 (stanza 13) occur in Poems folder 38 (see Additional Manuscripts). An early trial of lines 75–76 appears in EL p. 117, and one of lines 77–80 (stanza 20), drawn from NP p. 296, is in EL p. 121. Lines 81–84 (stanza 21) may be derived from NP p. 291 (see "These craggy hills"). The source for lines 5–6 is in journal CL (JMN 14:356), and a draft passage containing line 67 is in EL p. 127. A separate titled manuscript in Poems folder 11 contains lines 1–12, with no variants from the published text, while lines 57–60 (stanza 15) were copied into journal GL (JMN 15:158) on 23 January 1863.

Two manuscripts containing the entire text exist: the first, in the Houghton Library, is actually a composite of two manuscripts, one (undoubtedly the one read from at the Boston Music Hall) on blue paper with numbered pages, and another, on white lined paper without page numbers. According to the diary of John Weiss, the original (blue) manuscript was separated at the celebratory gathering at the home of Mrs. George L. Stearns on the evening of 1 January; Samuel Longfellow received all but the last "page" (more likely the last sheet), which Weiss got and which is now with his diary in the Massachusetts Historical Society. The provenance of the manuscript on white sheets is not known. This Houghton manuscript, taken as a whole, differs from the first published text as follows: "the statue" for "his statue" in line 19; "In state, & church," for "In church and state," in line 44; "laying hands" for "laying his hands" in line 61; "into pawn to the victim" for "in pawn to his victim" in line 63; "That lay" for "That sat" in line 78; "Rise" canceled for "Come" in line 81; "like" for "as" in line 82; "Ye shall carry" for "And carry" in line 83; and "Its" for "His" in line 88. The Weiss copy of p. 7 has "I will send men out of the North" canceled for "Rise East, & west & north" in line 81; "like" for "as" in line 82; and "They" for "And" in line 83.

The second manuscript, in the Lilly Library, Indiana University, is part of an album compiled by Mrs. Stearns entitled "John Brown Album. Emancipation Evening 1863" for which she requested an autographed copy of the poem. It differs from the first published text in having "the statue" for "his statue" in line 19, "As much" for "So much" in line 59, and "laying hands" for "laying his hands" in line 61. It is probable that three other manuscript copies once existed: those for the two first periodical publications, and one prepared for Rebecca Duncan (see L 5:303). Finally, a corrected clipping of a newspaper reprinting of the poem occurs at Rhymer p. 95.

*Date:* Emerson was asked by John S. Dwight to provide a prefatory poem for the musical celebration on 1 January. Always hard-pressed to write verses on demand, Emerson had to report to Dwight on 19 December that although he had "made some rude experiments at verses" on the previous night (probably the first, perhaps the first and second drafts in EL), he was still uncertain whether the poem would be finished in time. In a letter dated only "Tuesday P.M." (most probably 23 December), he wrote again to say that he had not yet been able to complete the poem, and asked that his name be omitted from the program. "Still," he went on, "I flatter myself that if I should have a good sleep tonight (for I am a bad sleeper lately) I may even yet, at the eleventh hour, pray to be admitted. But it is too slight a chance to be at all waited for . . ." (both letters quoted in George W. Cooke, *John Sullivan Dwight* [Boston, 1898], pp. 190–91; the second letter was re-edited by Kenneth Cameron in the article cited below). In a letter to Mrs. Stearns on the 28th, Emerson noted that "the verses are still not written" (letter quoted by Strauch in the article cited below). Emerson thus must have finished the poem (presumably in the third draft, EL pp. 86–95) between 28 December and the morning of 1 January, since the ceremony began at 3 p.m.

*Publication:* First published, with lines 65–68 omitted, in an account of the public celebration in *Dwight's Journal of Music* 22 (24 January 1863): 337, and almost simultaneously in the *Atlantic Monthly* 11 (February 1863): 227–28. That the lines were not omitted by design is made clear in Emerson's letter to Mrs. George L. Stearns of 10 December 1863 accompanying the copy for the John Brown Album: "I have supplied in this transcript a stanza which was read on the 1 January, but was accidentally dropt out, when I sent a copy to the printer" (quoted in the article by Strauch cited below). Emerson evidently derived the printer's copy not from the manuscript he read from— which had passed out of his possession—but from the third draft in EL, in which the seventeenth stanza is not numbered. The poem was reprinted by the New England Loyal Publication Society of Boston in a single sheet titled "Emerson's New England Hymn" (no. 108, c. August 1863); as "American Hymn" in *Pitman's Popular Lecturer and Reader*, n. s., vol. 8 (August 1863), 252–54; and in *Lyrics of Loyalty*, ed. Frank Moore (New York, 1864), pp. 253–56. The missing lines were restored when the poem was collected in *May–Day*, 1867, pp. 75–80; reprinted in *Selected Poems*, 1876, pp. 203–6, *Poems*, 1884, pp. 174–77, and W 9:201–4.

*See Also:* (1) "Be her cognizance allowed," (2) "Boston," (3) "Harp of victory ringing," (4) Carl F. Strauch, "The Background for Emerson's 'Boston Hymn,'" AL 14 (March 1942): 36–47, (5) Strauch diss., pp. 445–52 (text) and 680–700 (notes), and (6) Kenneth W. Cameron, "The First Appearance of Emerson's 'Boston Hymn,'" ESQ, no. 22 (1st quarter 1961), 97–101.

## "Botanist"

*Texts:* Six texts exist, all in ink, all identical in wording: in P p. 98, untitled; in X p. 266, untitled and struck through; in Rhymer p. 31, with the heading "Naturalist." canceled by "Botanist." and the notation "printed."; in NP p. 2, untitled; in NP p. 132, with the heading "Botanist" and struck through; and in a signed fair copy in the Chicago Historical Society.

*Date:* Undetermined, though its appearance in P would suggest a composition before 1845.

*Publication: The Dial* (Cincinnati) 1 (February 1860): 131. Reprinted in *May–Day,* 1867, p. 184, with "flowers" for "hours" in the last line. Both *Poems,* 1884, p. 239, and W 9:292 revert to the "hours" version. A text given by Channing in *Thoreau,* p. 135, reads in the last line: "What to me the Hours will bring."

## " 'Boy bring the bowl full of wine"

*Text:* The only text of this translation of Hafiz, Book IX, Ode XIII (*Diwan* 2:22–23), is in pencil in X p. 165. The translation of lines 7–8 ("To be wise the dull brain") in EF p. 82 appears to be a separate undertaking.

*Date:* Not earlier than April 1846, when Emerson acquired his copy of the *Diwan.* Since the poem occurs at the beginning of a section of X devoted to translations from Hafiz—a section including "Ghaselle: From the Persian of Hafiz," published in *Poems,* 1847—it is probable that the present translation dates to 1846.

*Publication:* Unpublished.

## "Brahma"

*Texts:* An early four-line version of the poem on the last page of journal Y (JMN 9:354) was revised in EF p. 80 and again in EL p. 102. The later and much longer draft entitled "Song of the Soul" in journal SO (JMN 14:102–3) represents a fresh conception. Working simultaneously with this and a second draft, also so titled, in EF p. 102, Emerson made his revisions. On a sheet laid in at p. 6 of notebook Parnassus is a transcription of a rough draft, complete with revisions, but not in Emerson's hand. Likewise, on a sheet laid in at p. 118 of notebook L Camadeva is a transcription of lines 9–10, also not in Emerson's hand. Fair copies occur in Poems folder 12 (see Additional Manuscripts), notebook Orientalist pp. 141 and 161, and Rhymer p. 119.

*Date:* The germ of the poem (and the immediate source of the short version) is a passage from *The Vishnu Purana* copied by Emerson into journal Y in

1845: "What living creature slays or is slain? What living creature preserves or is preserved? Each is his own destroyer or preserver, as he follows evil or good" (JMN 9:319). Since the EF text of the short version is written over translations from Hafiz, it would appear to have been set down some time after April 1846, when Emerson acquired his copy of the *Diwan*. The Y text of the verse is out of the chronological sequence of that journal, so that it is quite possible that it and the EF text were written in 1847 when Emerson copied the prose source from Y into journal AB (JMN 10:36–37). (At some point Emerson also copied a very similar passage from Charles Wilkins's translation of *The Bhagvat-Geeta* [London, 1785], pp. 37–38, in Orientalist p. 256.) The longer version of the poem was evidently inspired by Emerson's reading in the summer of 1856 of Thoreau's copy of *The Upanishads* (see L 5:70–71). The draft in SO, composed between 23 July and 8 August 1856, appears in the context of notes taken from that book.

*Publication: Atlantic Monthly* 1 (November 1857): 48; collected in *May–Day*, 1867, pp. 65–66; reprinted in *Selected Poems*, 1876, p. 73, *Poems*, 1884, pp. 170–71, and W 9:195. The Y text of the short version was published by Edward Emerson in his note to "Brahma" in W 9:465.

*See Also:* (1) Strauch diss., pp. 400–2 (text) and 607–9 (notes) and (2) Leyla Goren, "Elements of Brahminism in the Transcendentalism of Emerson," *ESQ*, no. 34 (1st quarter 1964), supplement, esp. pp. 34ff.

## "The brave Empedocles defying fools"

*Text:* The only manuscript text occurs in pencil in P p. 49, with the notation "Degerando Vol 2 p 36".

*Date:* Emerson acquired Marie Joseph de Gérando's *Histoire Comparée des Systèmes de Philosophie*, 4 vols. (Paris, 1822–1823), in the summer of 1830 (L 1:306). Although he quoted extensively from volume 1 in Blotting Book IV, beginning on 27 October (JMN 3:360–70), no excerpts from or references to volume 2 have been discovered in any of Emerson's journals or notebooks. It is therefore impossible to determine when he might have written these verses, though 1830 or 1831 seems likely. The passage in de Gérando that Emerson versified reads as follows: "On accuse Empédocle de l'orgueil le plus ridicule, parce qu'il s'était lui-même comparé à un Dieu: 'Je suis un dieu, dit-il dans les vers conservés par Sextus; je ne suis point sujet à la mort, je suis supérieur aux choses humaines' . . . . 'Suivant le témoignage de plusieurs,' dit ailleurs Sextus, . . . 'Empédocle attribuait non aux sens, mais à la droite raison, la prérogative de juger de la vérité. La droite raison est en partie divine, en partie humaine; la seconde peut être exprimée, mais aucun langage ne peut traduire la première.'" The passages that are the sources of lines 3, 4, 7, and 8 are marked in the margin with pencil lines in Emerson's copy. See also journal B between 16 and 19 April 1835 (JMN 5:31): "Empedocles said bravely 'I am God; I am immortal; I contemn human affairs'; & all men hated him."

*Publication:* Unpublished by Emerson. First published in W 9:353.

*See Also:* (1) Carl F. Strauch, "Gérando: A Source for Emerson," *MLN* 58 (January 1943): 64–67, and (2) Strauch diss., pp. 299 (text) and 479–83 (notes).

## "Bring wine release me"

*Text:* This poem, which translates Hafiz, Book XXVII, Ode LII, lines 1–28 (*Diwan* 2:435–437), occurs in a pencil draft in EF pp. 54–55. It has not been found elsewhere in Emerson's published or unpublished writings.

## "Bronze, bronze, pure gold never"

*Text:* This single line occurs in pencil in X p. 70.

*Date:* The context of the other verses on the page suggests a date of about 1843.

*Publication:* Unpublished.

## "Brother, no decrepitude"

*Texts:* The earliest manuscript containing this quatrain is a copy of a poem beginning "Day by day returns" in Poems folder 19, where "Brother, no decrepitude" occurs as the first four lines of a seven-line second stanza (see Additional Manuscripts under "Day by day returns"). Emerson added this entire stanza to a manuscript in Poems folder 73, which contains the abandoned drafts of the expanded version of "The Discontented Poet: a Masque"; this version has "Brother" in line 1, "Chills" in line 2, and "vision" in line 4. However, having thus broken up the text of "Day by day returns," Emerson seems thereafter to have regarded "Brother, no decrepitude" as a separate poem, and copies occur in EF p. 25 (lengthened by the addition of two lines), Rhymer p. 50$_g$, and NP p. 101.

*Date:* The Poems folder 19 manuscript of "Day by day returns" carries the date "1831," but since journal sources dating from 10 August 1834 (JMN 4:309) and 5 March 1836 (JMN 5:135) lie behind portions not included in

"Brother, no decrepitude," the inscribed date must be wrong. This error in itself, together with the evidence of the journal sources, suggests that the manuscript is a later copy of a poem first written in the mid to late 1830s. Emerson assembled the manuscripts in Poems folder 73 not earlier than April 1842.

*Publication:* Unpublished by Emerson. First published as lines 294–97 of "The Poet," a work concocted by James Elliot Cabot from the Poems folder 73 manuscripts and published in *Poems,* 1884, pp. 253–63 (the lines occur on p. 263). "Day by day returns" was also first published in *Poems,* 1884, pp. 291–92, where the omission of lines 9–15 was indicated by a row of asterisks; it was reprinted in W 9:392.

*See Also:* "The Discontented Poet: a Masque."

## "The Builder of heaven"

*Texts:* This poem translates Hafiz, Book XXI, Ode II, lines 17–26 (*Diwan* 2:126). Though published by Emerson in this form, it belongs in fact to the longer translation "Drink wine, and the heaven," of which it forms lines 17–26 (with two additional lines). Drafts of the longer version occur in X pp. 181 and 183–84, EF pp. 12 and 13, and, in a shorter version that still includes the present verses, in notebook Orientalist pp. 52–53 and 83, Rhymer p. 149, and Poems folder 36. In the Rhymer text the stanzas corresponding to "The Builder of heaven" are marked "printed"; the folder 36 text consists of the present poem preceded by "There resides in the grieving" (see Additional Manuscripts under that title).

*Date:* Since the EF text is overwritten by material used in "The Fugitive Slave Law" (1851), composition must have occurred between April 1846, when Emerson acquired his copy of the *Diwan,* and 1851.

*Publication:* First published in "Persian Poetry," 1858, p. 727, in a text slightly different from any of the manuscripts, but evidently deriving from Rhymer. The poem appears in the essay as collected in *Letters and Social Aims,* 1876, pp. 221–22, and in W 8:246–47.

## "Burn your literary verses"

*Text:* This five-line fragment appears in EL p. 102$_c$.

*Date:* Two other fragments on the same page develop prose sources written in 1846.

*Publication:* Unpublished.

753

## "But for the chief, his fortune's made"

*Text:* This couplet occurs in EL p. 162. It has not been found elsewhere in Emerson's published or unpublished writings.

## "But I a lover of Gods fables"

*Text:* This couplet appears in pencil in P p. 91. It has not been found elsewhere in Emerson's published or unpublished writings.

## "But if thou do thy best"

*Texts:* A pencil draft in journal Books Small (JMN 8:464) is revised in P p. 235.

*Date:* In Books Small the verses immediately follow a draft of lines 72–79 of "Saadi" in the same light pencil. Strauch (diss., p. 639) assumes a connection between the two passages, a hypothesis supported by the appearance in P pp. 228–33 of lines actually used in "Saadi." A date of 1840 to 1842 thus seems likely.

*Publication:* Unpublished by Emerson. First published in *Poems*, 1884, p. 296, with a final row of asterisks to indicate that the verses are unfinished; reprinted in W 9:356.

*See Also:* Strauch diss., pp. 65–66 and 639.

## "But Nature whistled with all her winds"

*Texts:* In notebook BL p. 185, Emerson wrote "We can't make half a bow, & say, I honor & despise you. But Nature can: she whistles with all her winds, & does as she pleases." The first draft of the couplet occurs in pencil below this and is copied in ink in NP p. 72.

*Date:* Emerson dated notebook BL 1859–1860. Edward Emerson reprinted the passage from BL, which he called "Journal, 1860," in W 9:509.

*Publication:* Unpublished by Emerson. First published in *Poems*, 1884, p. 287, and reprinted in W 9:348.

## "But never yet the man was found"

*Texts:* The first draft, in pencil and with several trials of various lines, is in notebook PY pp. 202–3; an ink fair copy is in NP p. 39. Though a revision of lines 5–6, probably made later than the NP text, follows lines 7–8 in PY p. 203, Emerson did not necessarily intend to reverse the couplets.

*Date:* Undetermined, though the verses are perhaps related to others concerning Adam written in journal FOR (JMN 15:318–19) for "May–Day" in 1863. Notebook PY dates from no earlier than the 1860s.

*Publication:* Unpublished by Emerson. First published in *Poems,* 1884, p. 280, from the NP text, and reprinted in W 9:339.

## "but recites my tho'ts to me"

*Text:* These four lines occur in erased pencil in EL p. 77. They have not been found elsewhere in Emerson's published or unpublished writings.

## "By art, by music overthrilled"

*Texts:* A prose entry in journal CL (JMN 14:308–9) concerns "the beatitude of intellect": "It is too great for feeble souls, and they are overexcited. The wineglass shakes, & the wine is spilled." These sentences are versified in the two drafts that immediately follow. Other drafts occur in EL pp. 149 and 155, on an insert inside the front cover of NP, in NP pp. 299 and 300, and in Rhymer pp. 50_b and 50_d. While the Rhymer drafts appear to be the latest, the precise order cannot be determined.

*Date:* The first draft seems to have been written, with the prose entry from which it derives, between 16 and 20 August 1859.

*Publication:* Unpublished by Emerson. First published in *Poems,* 1884, p. 274, from one of the NP texts, with "For art, for music" in line 1. The revisions in EL and the texts in Rhymer suggest that "By art, by music" was the later form. The couplet was reprinted in W 9:330.

## "By kinds I keep my kinds in check"

*Texts:* A draft in journal DL (JMN 15:28) may have been inspired by the immediately preceding prose passage. In EF p. 73, in the midst of a series of translations from Hafiz, is the single line, "What keeps the kinds in check". Other drafts, in undetermined order, are in EL pp. 84 and 147, Rhymer p. 96$_d$, NP p. 72, and Poems folder 14.

*Date:* Undetermined, though the DL draft was written in 1863.

*Publication:* Unpublished by Emerson. First published in JMN 15.

## "Can I nail the wild planet"

*Text:* These two lines occur in pencil in P p. 106. They have not been found elsewhere in Emerson's published or unpublished writings.

## "Can the eagle swim in the sea"

*Text:* These three lines occur in a series of fragments, all in pencil, in EL p. 119. They have not been found elsewhere in Emerson's published or unpublished writings.

## "Casella"

*Texts:* The first three drafts occur in journal VO (JMN 14:188). The text in notebook PY p. 201 is a pencil fair copy of the second of the VO drafts, while notebook L Camadeva p. 2 contains a text deriving from the third VO draft. The two versions in NP p. 37 represent copies of the unrevised and revised forms, respectively, of the L Camadeva text; the second of these was copied into NP p. 138 and again into Rhymer p. 48. The last two texts carry the heading "Poet."

*Date:* The prose source for this quatrain is an entry in journal O dating from the summer of 1846 (JMN 9:442): "Metre of the Poet again, is his science of love. Does he know that lore? Never was poet who was not tremulous with love-lore." Eleven years later, in late 1857, Emerson versified these sentences in the three VO drafts. Probably his attention was drawn to the germinal sentences in the course of preparing his lecture on "Success," the basis for the essay of the same title, where the idea reappears (see W 7:302–3). The text in PY follows on the same page two couplets copied from VO sometime after May 1858 (JMN 14:202).

*Publication: May–Day,* 1867, p. 190, where the title "Casella" first appears; reprinted in *Poems,* 1884, p. 243, and W 9:296.

## "Character"

*Texts:* Two drafts of the first six lines, identical in wording, occur in P p. 161 and Poems folder 73. No manuscript text of the last four lines has been found.

*Date:* Line 6 is drawn from an entry in journal F 2 (JMN 7:546), which was probably written in February 1841. Emerson assembled the manuscripts in Poems folder 73 in 1842 and 1843, hoping to expand "The Discontented Poet: a Masque," though by 1844 he seems to have given up the project.

*Publication: Essays: Second Series,* 1844, p. 89; collected in *May–Day,* 1867, p. 164, and reprinted in *Poems,* 1884, p. 231, and W 9:273. In *Poems,* 1884, p. 257, the first six lines were printed from the text in Poems folder 73 as lines 134–39 of the editorially constructed work called "The Poet."

## "Charmed from fagot and from steel"

*Texts:* The first four and the last three lines of this seven-line poem developed separately. Line 2 appears for the first time (as "Harvests grow on his tongue") among notes that Emerson made on *The Vishnu Purana,* probably in 1845, and which he is known to have reviewed in 1859 (Poems folder 95). Lines 1–2 appear first in EL p. 17, then in EL p. 172, which probably precedes the draft of lines 1–4 in EL p. 149. The source of lines 5–7 is ultimately a journal entry of 11 May 1838 (JMN 5:496–97), which concludes: "I sow the sun & moon for seeds." While this phrasing is substantially repeated in an entry for 17 January 1841 (JMN 7:412; see also 7:415), an entry for 9 October 1838 (JMN 7:102) is a more immediate source: "I thought I saw the sun & moon fall into his head, as seeds fall into the ground, that they might quicken & bring forth new worlds to fill nature." This sentence was revised and versified in notebook XO p. 101. The XO version reappears in ETE pp. 41 and 170, NP pp. 296 and 300, and EL p. 148. The text at EL p. 148 was revised and copied in EL p. 103, which, in turn, seems to be the source of the text at X p. 67. The manuscript of the motto for "Culture," submitted as printer's copy for *The Conduct of Life* in 1860, ends with five canceled lines, of which the first three are the XO form of lines 5–7; the other two lines read "And Art's & Wisdoms garnered power / Spring from his hand a fresh-blown flower." Texts of the whole poem occur in NP on an insert inside the front cover and on p. 298 (the XO form of lines 5–7), and in Rhymer p. 2_b (text descending from EL p. 103).

*Date:* While the sources go back to 1838 and line 2 may be as early as 1845, probably neither section of the poem is much earlier than 1859. Notebook

XO was used throughout the 1850s and 1860s. The "Culture" manuscript suggests that the two sections of the poem were not joined until some time after 1860. This is consistent with the generally late date of the Rhymer insert (pp. 2$_a$-2$_b$), with the somewhat mystifying reference to journal VA (1862–1863) at EL p. 103, and with the fact that the draft of lines 5–7 in X p. 67 was inscribed after the lines of "Solution" on that page.

*Publication:* Unpublished by Emerson. First published as lines 30–36 of the editorially concocted poem beginning "Mask thy wisdom" in W 9:326. There is no evidence that Emerson authorized the joining of "Charmed from fagot" with the other fragments gathered by Cabot and Edward Emerson in "Mask thy wisdom."

*See Also:* (1) "The Poet," line 32 (W 9:310), and (2) "Worship."

## "The Chartist's Complaint"

*Texts:* The first draft, an eight-line version in journal AB (JMN 10:49), is revised in pencil in EF pp. 50–51, where it carries the title "Fine days." This is followed by a third draft, similarly titled, in EF p. 52, written over the first draft of "Days." The fourth draft, in ink over a draft of "Spiritual Laws," occurs in EF p. 58 with the title "Villeggiatura" and the appended notation "Chartist" at the bottom of the page. The final revision of the poem, with the title "Janus" replacing "Chartism," occurs in X p. 1. Rhymer p. 26 contains a fair copy with the title as published. Another fair copy is owned by St. John's Seminary, Camarillo, California; it is identical in wording to the Rhymer text as revised except for "wood" rather than "lawn" in line 9 and "to" rather than "of" in line 16.

*Date:* The first draft in AB was written between 25 March and 5 April 1847. The EF drafts, in their physical relation to the drafts of "Days," show that Emerson regarded the two poems as companion pieces, as, indeed, their publication histories also suggest. It is therefore quite likely that the EF drafts were done in 1851, shortly after the completion of "Days."

*Publication: Atlantic Monthly* 1 (November 1857): 47; collected in *May-Day*, 1867, pp. 112–13, and reprinted in *Poems*, 1884, p. 197, and W 9:232.

*See Also:* Carl F. Strauch, "The MS Relationships of Emerson's 'Days,' " PQ 29 (April 1950): 199–208.

## "Chladni strewed on glass the sand"

*Text:* These seventeen lines of verse, part of an inscription in prose and verse treating the relation of mind and nature, occur in EL pp. 230–31.

*Date:* The prose source in journal AZ (JMN 11:203), from the winter of 1849–1850, describes the experiment of Ernst Florens Friedrich Chladni (1756–1827).

*Publication:* Unpublished.

## "The civil world will much forgive"

*Texts:* A draft of lines 1–6 in light pencil in journal Books Small (JMN 8:476) was copied and partially erased in EF p. 8, where "Vae solis" appears as a seventh line. A revised draft occurs in Poems folder 17, combined with the first eight lines of "I found this" (see Additional Manuscripts).

*Date:* The first draft may be as early as 1840–1843, the main period of use of Books Small, although it is written over an earlier inscription. The EF draft is earlier than the mid-1850s, when the ink inscription of lines 37–40 of "My Garden" was written over the erased pencil layer in which "The civil world" appears.

*Publication:* Unpublished by Emerson. First published in combination with "I found this" in *Poems,* 1884, p. 266, and reprinted in W 9:323.

## "Climacteric"

*Texts:* Three identical drafts of this quatrain give an early form of line 4: X pp. 262 and 268$_{aa}$ and a copy in Poems folder 42. Four identical texts give the final form of line 4: X p. 260, the titled fair copies in Rhymer p. 37 and NP p. 132, and the copy included in Emerson's letter of 14 April 1853 to Caroline Sturgis Tappan (Houghton, Tappan Papers).

*Date:* The draft in X p. 268$_{aa}$ may be as early as 1847, since among the poems in this insert are several fair copies of mottoes used in the 1847 edition of *Essays: First Series.* The letter to Mrs. Tappan shows that the final form of the poem had been arrived at by 1853.

*Publication: The Dial* (Cincinnati) 1 (February 1860): 131; collected in *May–Day,* 1867, p. 188, and reprinted in *Poems,* 1884, p. 242, and W 9:295.

## "Cloud upon cloud. / Clouds"

*Text:* The poem occurs in EL pp. 102$_a$-102$_b$. The first two lines, which are added, may derive from the poem discussed in the following entry ("Cloud upon cloud / The world"); however, cf. the first line of the draft of "Solution" in X p. 9.

*Date:* Undetermined.

*Publication:* Unpublished.

## "Cloud upon cloud / The world"

*Text:* The only text of this twelve-line poem is in X p. 159. Line 1 may derive distantly from a draft of "Solution" in X p. 9.

*Date:* The poem, as Carl F. Strauch has argued (diss., pp. 576–83), evidently is related to the entire cluster of texts (generally on the theme of "illusion") inscribed in X pp. 140–159. Part of this cluster, not including "Cloud upon cloud," was revised in journal AZ in November or December 1849 (see "Roomy Eternity").

*Publication:* Unpublished.

## "The coil of space the cones of light"

*Texts:* The prose source of lines 1–5, in ink in NP p. 278, shifts into verse for three lines (lines 6–8), then back into prose on p. 279, followed by an eight-line draft of the poem in pencil. In his notes on NP, Edward Emerson suggests Mary Moody Emerson as the source of these lines, but no relevant passage has been discovered in Emerson's MME notebooks.

*Date:* Undetermined. The ink inscription in NP pp. 278–79 appears to have been made at the same time as the lines for "Song of Nature" on the following page, probably late in 1859.

*Publication:* Unpublished.

## "Coin the daydawn into lines"

*Texts:* These four lines occur as an independent poem in EL p. 172 and, in Rhymer p. 50f, as part of a pastiche in which Emerson attempted to bring together many of his fragments on the Poet.

*Date:* Undetermined.

*Publication:* Unpublished by Emerson. First published in W 9:333 from the EL text. Edward Emerson evidently took all of EL p. 172 as a single poem, omitted "Charmed from fagot," which had already appeared as lines 30–31 of "Mask thy wisdom" (W 9:326), and conflated the four lines of "Borrow Urania's subtile wings" into three, accounting for the excessively long first line as published.

## "Cold Bangor"

*Texts:* The two lines in erased pencil in X p. 205 are repeated in X p. 194. The lines are a versification of an entry in journal V (JMN 9:132): "In Maine they have not a summer but a thaw."

*Date:* The entry in V belongs to 1844 or 1845, though the verses were probably written in early October 1846, when Emerson was lecturing in Bangor and doing last-minute revisions for his first book of poems (see L 3:353–57, which also indicate that the weather was bad).

*Publication:* Unpublished.

## " 'Come!—the palace of heaven rests on aëry pillars"

*Texts:* The first draft, in pencil in X pp. 169–170, is revised in ink in note-book Orientalist pp. 158–59. The poem translates Hafiz, Book III, Ode XIII (*Diwan* 1:61–62). In Orientalist p. 160 Emerson copied out a translation of the first fifteen lines of this poem from Herman Bicknell, *Hafiz of Shiraz: Selections from His Poems* (London, 1875), p. 50, a volume he owned. Bicknell's translation seems to have been heavily influenced by Emerson's as printed in 1858.

*Date:* The first draft was probably written between 1846 and 1850, since it follows immediately after lines from "The garden of Eden," also taken from Book III of the *Diwan*.

*Publication:* A version differing in several places from either draft appears in "Persian Poetry," 1858, p. 730, in the essay as reprinted in *Letters and Social Aims*, 1876, p. 230, and in W 8:256.

## "Comfort with a purring cat"

*Text:* This couplet occurs in pencil in X p. 101. It has not been found elsewhere in Emerson's published or unpublished writings.

## "Compensation" ("Man's the elm")

*Texts:* A portion of the early version of the poem in X p. 268ₘ is revised in the erased pencil draft in EF p. 65, which precedes the late, titled version in X p. 216.

*Date:* The poem's manuscript relation to "Unity," its origin in the insert in X (which dates from 1847), and the date of its publication suggest composition in 1847. As Edward Emerson suggests (W 9:494–95), the last six lines recall a journal entry for 25 September 1840 (JMN 7:400).

*Publication:* First published as the second of two mottoes to "Compensation" in the 1847 edition of *Essays: First Series,* p. 82. These mottoes were brought together in *May–Day,* 1867, pp. 159–60, under the title "Compensation" and assigned roman numerals I and II.

*See Also:* "Compensation" ("The wings of Time").

## "Compensation" ("The wings of Time")

*Texts:* The only evidence of a preliminary draft is the version of lines 1–2 in P p. 136. The complete text exists in pencil with the title "Motto to 'Compensation' " in Poems folder 58 (see Additional Manuscripts).

*Date:* The manuscript in Poems folder 58 is dated 1841.

*Publication:* First published as the first of two mottoes to "Compensation" in the 1847 edition of *Essays: First Series,* p. 81. These mottoes were brought together in *May–Day,* 1867, pp. 159–60, under the title "Compensation" and assigned roman numerals I and II.

*See Also:* "Compensation" ("Man's the elm").

## "Compensation" ("Why should I")

*Texts:* The earliest text is a pencil draft, with the title written twice, in journal A (JMN 4:347). Two versions, also titled, occur in P: one in erased pencil on p. 237, and an ink fair copy on p. 9 with the notation "New York Nov. 1834." Margaret Fuller transcribed the poem, with some inaccuracies, in her letter of 18 June 1837 to Caroline Sturgis (see *The Letters of Margaret Fuller,* ed. Robert N. Hudspeth, 1 [Ithaca and London, 1983], 285). An unlocated copy was offered in Anderson sale no. 1449, 25 November 1919.

*Date:* The pencil draft in A is partially overwritten by an entry of 1 December 1834, lending support to Emerson's date of November in P. He was in

New York from 17 October through early November as a supply minister, and gave a lecture in Brooklyn on 3 November. Line 4 probably reflects his sadness at the news of his brother Edward's death in Puerto Rico, which reached him on 18 October. Journal entries for 5 November (JMN 4:332–33) give Emerson's impression of the raucous elections in New York.

*Publication: Poems,* 1847, p. 129 (Boston) and p. 101 (London); reprinted in *Poems,* 1884, p. 77, and W 9:83.

*See Also:* Strauch diss., pp. 61–62.

## "The comrade or the book is good"

*Texts:* The first draft of lines 3–4 occurs in notebook TO p. 276: "If thought is not conjoined with will / ⟨Then Plato⟩ ↑Apollo↓ ⟨will be⟩ ↑is an↓ imbecile". Later drafts, all identical, occur in NP p. 299 and in EL pp. 2, 290, and 292. Lines 1–2 occur first in Poems folder 38 (see Additional Manuscripts under "Boston Hymn"), then in EL p. 155, which also contains the first draft of the entire poem. The copy in NP p. 301 was made before the version in EL p. 155 was revised. The copy in Rhymer p. 96c is the latest.

*Date:* Undetermined. Edward Emerson pointed to a source for this poem in "Intellect" (W 2:336): "The thought of genius is spontaneous; but the power of picture or expression . . . implies a mixture of will, a certain control over the spontaneous states, without which no production is possible." A later parallel, also suggested by Edward Emerson, is closer to the phrasings of the poem: "To a great genius there must be a great will. If the thought is not a lamp to the will, does not proceed to an act, the wise are imbecile" ("Natural History of Intellect," W 12:46). The difference between the earlier and later statements of this idea is probably due to Emerson's having read Pierre Lanfrey, *L'Eglise et les philosophes au dix-huitième siècle* (Paris, 1855); in 1856 Emerson copied into his journal Lanfrey's remark that "Avec un grand génie, il faut une grande volonté" (JMN 14:94), and recopied it in 1859 (JMN 14:222).

*Publication:* Unpublished by Emerson. First published from the NP text in *Poems,* 1884, p. 274, and reprinted in W 9:331.

## "Concord Fight"

*Texts:* The earliest draft of the poem occurs in erased pencil in P pp. 240–41: three versions of the first stanza appear, two of the second, and one each of the third and fourth. (Page 241 is reproduced in Plate 2.) A pencil fair copy of the entire poem occurs in P p. 236. Another, later version occurs in journal RO (JMN 14:34–35), where, however, the first line is a version of the ninth. Lines 1–2 and 9 occur in Pocket Diary 26, kept in 1875 (JMN 16:474), no doubt jotted down in connection with the remarks Emerson was to make at the dedication of the Minuteman statue at the North Bridge on 19 April 1876. Printer's copy for the London edition of *Poems,* 1847, is in the Sterling Library, University of London. A fair copy of the poem, which Emerson wrote in the autograph album of Mrs. James T. Fields, is in the Morgan Library; this has "hath" for "has" in line 7 and "and" for "or" in line 14. (The manuscript appears in facsimile in *American Literary Autographs from Washington Irving to Henry James,* ed. Herbert Cahoon et al. [New York, 1977].) Another copy, in the original broadside version, including the title "Original Hymn," has not been located, though a photocopy is in the Houghton Library. Two other fair copies exist: one in the Lilly Library, Indiana University, entitled "Concord Fight," and another, in the Boston Public Library, written out at the request of Mellen Chamberlain, the librarian, in 1880; both have "and" for "or" in line 14. A facsimile of the first stanza, from an unidentified manuscript, appears in Charles Hamilton, *The Signature of America: A Fresh Look at Famous Handwriting* (New York, 1979), p. 81. Another copy of the first stanza, dated 2 March 1874, is reported in *ESQ,* no. 13 (4th quarter 1958), 40. A copy of the complete poem, signed by Emerson but not in his hand, is in the University of Virginia Library.

*Date:* The occasion of the poem was the dedication of the monument at the site of the battle of Concord, originally to be held on 19 April 1836. Because of delays, however, the celebration was actually held on 4 July 1837. The poem was composed not long before, for in a letter of 27 June, Emerson's mother wrote his brother William that "Waldo, has written a hymn, to be sung to the tune of old hundred" (L 2:85, n. 121). The hymn was sung by the assembled townspeople, but Emerson was not among them; on that day he was in Plymouth with Lidian.

*Publication:* The poem was first published as a broadside at the time of the celebration, and appeared in both the *Concord Freeman* and the *Yeoman's Gazette* of 8 July. It was printed in *Poems,* 1847, pp. 250–51 (Boston) and p. 200 (London), with slight revision of the wording and with the title "Hymn: Sung at the Completion of the Concord Monument, April 19, 1836." The 1836 date was retained in the editions published during Emerson's lifetime and in *Poems,* 1884, but was changed to 4 July 1837 by Edward Emerson in W 9:158 on the basis of the incontrovertible evidence (W 9:454). In *Selected Poems,* 1876, p. 202, the main title was changed to "Concord Fight"; in *Poems,* 1884, p. 139, it became, for the first time, "Concord Hymn."

*See Also:* (1) Rusk, *Life,* pp. 273–74, and (2) Strauch diss., pp. 355–56 (text) and 551–54 (notes).

## "Considerations by the Way"

*Texts:* The first draft occurs in P pp. 212–13, lacking lines 18–19, 24–25, and 28–29, and containing five lines not in the poem as published. Lines 15 and 20–21 are in NP p. 289 in a collection of fragments, as are lines 24–25, which are drawn from the abandoned poem "Mask thy wisdom with delight." Lines 24–25 also occur in P p. 287, Poems folder 23 (with "Masking wisdom" for "Mask thy wisdom"), and, canceled, between lines 114–15 of the printer's copy of "Saadi" for the London edition of *Poems,* 1847 (see Additional Manuscripts under "Saadi"). Lines 26–27 occur separately in X p. 261 and Rhymer p. 43. Another copy of these lines, signed and dated "Concord: Feb 1849", was offered for sale by Books With a Past, Concord, Mass., in October 1984; this text has "have" for "has" in line 28. In Poems folder 32 is the notation "Hear what British Merlin sung *Conduct of Life,* p. 213" (see Additional Manuscripts under "Boston").

*Date:* Undetermined. A series of articles by Kenneth W. Cameron (see below) has examined the sources of the poem in Emerson's reading, but none of these helps to determine the date of composition. Line 15, for example, is an adaptation of a Zoroastrian fragment, "Things divine are not obtainable by mortals who understand body, but only as many as are lightly armed arrive at the summit"; Emerson may have found this in any one of three sources published before 1835. "Cyndyllan" (or Cynddylan) figures in an elegy by the Welsh poet Llywarch Hen that Emerson quoted in an 1835 lecture, "Permanent Traits of the English National Genius" (*Early Lectures* 1:240). (Note, however, that as the drafts indicate, the Celtic motif was a late addition to Emerson's poem.) Lines 26–27 are a verse translation of a sentence by Voltaire that Emerson copied into his journal as early as 1826 (JMN 3:51). The evidence would thus indicate a date in the late 1830s for the bulk of the poem, with some individual lines either earlier or later.

*Publication:* Published as the motto to "Considerations by the Way" in *The Conduct of Life,* 1860, pp. 213–14 (the only printing in Emerson's lifetime). Lines 1–27 were reprinted in W 9:218–19 as part II of "Merlin's Song," a decision evidently made by Edward Emerson. Lines 26–27 were published as an independent couplet in *Poems,* 1884, p. 289, and reprinted in W 9:351.

*See Also:* (1) "Mask thy wisdom," (2) "Merlin's Song," (3) Kenneth W. Cameron, "The Significance of Emerson's Second Merlin Song," *ESQ,* no. 2 (1st quarter 1956), 2–7, (4) Cameron, "A Further Note on Emerson's 'Second Merlin Song,'" *ESQ,* no. 6 (1st quarter 1957), 10–11, and (5) Cameron, "Emerson's *Second Merlin Song* and Economist H. C. Carey," *ESQ,* no. 13 (1st quarter 1958), 65–83.

## "The coral worm beneath the sea"

*Text:* This seven-line fragment occurs in a pencil draft in EL p. 212. It has not been found elsewhere in Emerson's published or unpublished writings.

## "Could my old telescope retain"

*Text:* The only text of this twelve-line poem occurs in NP p. 102. It has not been found elsewhere in Emerson's published or unpublished writings.

## "The crowning hour when bodies vie with souls"

*Texts:* The couplet occurs first in journal Books Small (JMN 8:446) and was copied in X p. 75. In both locations it is loosely associated with material used in "The Daemonic and the Celestial Love," and is probably the basis for lines 217–18 of that poem.

*Date:* Between 1840 and 1843.

*Publication:* Unpublished by Emerson. First published in JMN 8.

## "Culture"

*Texts:* The first draft of this motto in NP p. 100 is revised on p. 105. The final manuscript text, in printer's copy for the essay "Culture" in the Huntington Library, is followed by five canceled lines: lines 5–7 of "Charmed from fagot" and two unused lines, "And Art's & Wisdoms garnered power / Spring from his hand a fresh-blown flower."

*Date:* Undetermined.

*Publication: The Conduct of Life*, 1860, p. 111, and subsequent editions, including W 6:129; reprinted in *May–Day*, 1867, p. 165, *Poems*, 1884, p. 232, and W 9:273.

*See Also:* "Poet of poets," lines 28–29, which closely resemble lines 2–3 of "Culture."

## "Cupido"

*Texts:* The first draft, in journal Z[A] p. 74 (JMN 8:345), is written over an erased draft of "Una." A false start of the poem occurs in Z[A] p. 72, where it is also associated with "Una." A nearly identical draft occurs in notebook L Camadeva p. 45, of which a fair copy appears on p. 140 with the canceled title "Eros." Additional fair copies occur in EL p. 174 (untitled), Rhymer p. 105 ("Cupido"), ETE pp. 16 (with the title "Eros" replacing "Cupido") and 56ᵦ ("Eros"), and in Poems folder 87 (untitled, in the same manuscript with a fair copy of "James Russell Lowell"). In the draft contents of the 1876 *Selected Poems* (see ETE p. 2), the title is still "Eros."

*Date:* The first draft appears to belong to March 1843, as Edward Emerson suggested (W 9:492). The earliest date for the Poems folder 87 text would be 1859, the year Lowell turned forty, and 1863 for the ETE p. 56ᵦ text, which follows lines used in "Voluntaries."

*Publication: Selected Poems,* 1876, p. 180; reprinted in *Poems,* 1884, p. 221, and W 9:257.

## "The Daemonic and the Celestial Love"

*Texts:* The manuscript history of this poem shows that it was conceived separately from "The Initial Love" and that it was written as a unit. The earliest substantial draft is represented in an incomplete manuscript in ink (pp. 5–10 only) in the Houghton Library, where the text begins at line 123 (see Additional Manuscripts). This draft collects and revises a number of earlier fragments (including, presumably, all or most of the lines before line 123) occurring in notebook X: p. 70 (lines 144–45); p. 73 (lines 178–81 [from an erased pencil draft on p. 83], 211–14, 17–18]); p. 75 (lines 225–32); p. 76 (lines 219–20 [which occur first in JMN 8:462], 17–19, 21–22); p. 77 (lines 94, 96–100); p. 80 (a partially recovered passage evidently consisting of lines 29–48); p. 81 (a 22-line passage including lines 65–67, 70, 73–76); p. 82 (a 25-line passage including lines 88–89, 144–45, 164, 166, 169, 171–72, 177); p. 83 (lines 178–84, 187, 191–92, 194); p. 84 (lines 196–206, 208, 210–13, 215–16); p. 85 (lines 219–21, 235–36, and 238–39, among other incompletely recovered lines); p. 86 (lines 257–58, 260–61, 263, 267–68); and p. 87 (six unused lines). Lines 233–34 first appear in journal Books Small (JMN 8:474–75), where they may have belonged to an early draft of "Threnody." The couplet also occurs in journal G (JMN 8:30) and notebook L Camadeva p. 41, where it carries the notation "printed". Probably this refers to its having been quoted in "Character," *Essays: Second Series,* 1844, p. 122. Lines 61–64 first occur in journal V (JMN 9:95). What may or may not be line 94 is reported as partially erased pencil writing in JMN 8:417, n. 232. The Houghton manuscript was the source of the pencil draft, later partly erased, entitled "II / The Divine / & / The Celestial Love" in X pp. 141–50. This text, following a nearly complete draft of "Initial Love" on X pp. 132–38, begins with line 23. A portion of this text was further revised in pencil, later erased, in journal Y pp. 135–38 (JMN 9:305–7), producing a version of lines 49–101 and 120–32. Lines 82–91 were still further revised in pencil in Y p. 138 (JMN 9:308). Three successive drafts of an introductory section (lines 1–22) occur in X pp. 152–54. No other manuscripts have been located between these and the printer's copy for the London edition of *Poems*, 1847, which is in the Houghton Library. In the printer's copy, lines 77–80 (English lineation here and below) originally read "As if the old planets bright / Had slipped their sacred bars, / And wandering men at night / Walk amid the seeming stars" but were changed to the published version; in line 115 "Poured" is changed to "Born"; line 132 is written twice but the second inscription canceled; in line 240 "By the" is changed to "The"; in line 245 "Have" is changed to "Yield"; and in line 252 "as is the loving herd" is changed to "as the low-loving herd".

*Date:* A prose source for the concluding couplet (lines 267–68) occurs in journal G: "He who serves some, shall be served by some: he who serves all, shall be served by all" (JMN 8:39, between 31 August and 4 September 1841). Another version, closer to the poetic form, occurs in journal Books Small (JMN 8:445–46). The draft in Y (which comes late in the process of composition) is overwritten by notes that Emerson took from *The Vishnu Purana*, a book he first read in the summer of 1845 (see L 3:293). Journal Y appears to have been used between September 1845 and March 1846. The poem was probably composed, in the main, in 1845.

*Publication: Poems*, 1847, pp. 164–77 (Boston) and pp. 130–41 (London). In the Boston edition, "The Daemonic and the Celestial Love" is the title given collectively to the second and third parts of "Initial, Daemonic, and Celestial Love." In the London edition it is the second part of "Ode," and is further divided with the subheadings "Daemonic Love" (p. 130) and "Celestial Love" (p. 137). The London edition also omits line 10 (as in the printer's copy) and makes a number of changes in words and phrasing. The poem was further revised, as Edward Emerson noted (W 9:437), in the *Selected Poems*, 1876, by displacing lines 23–48 from the "Daemonic" into the "Celestial" section and omitting lines 123–26, among other less significant changes. This revised text was reprinted in W 9:109–18.

*See Also:* (1) "The Initial Love," (2) "If he go apart," (3) "Nature will not lose," (4) "The crowning hour," and (5) John S. Harrison, *The Teachers of Emerson* (New York, 1910), pp. 146–57 (sources).

## "Dark Flower of Cheshire garden"

*Texts:* The pencil version in X p. 262 is presumably the source of the identical ink text in NP p. 148.2ₐ.

*Date:* Before 1851. The evidence of X p. 262 suggests that the poem was written at the same time as or earlier than "A score of airy miles," which was written in 1851 or earlier.

*Publication:* Unpublished by Emerson. First published in *Poems,* 1884, p. 310, with the nonauthorial title "Monadnoc from Afar"; reprinted with the supplied title in W 9:361.

## "The darkest night is day to the gloom"

*Text:* This fragment occurs in faint pencil in P p. 195. It has not been found elsewhere in Emerson's published or unpublished writings. Godfrey Bertram, Laird of Ellangowan, is a character in Sir Walter Scott's *Guy Mannering* (1815).

## "Days"

*Texts:* The four earliest drafts, all in EF, occur on pp. 52, 53, 57, and 56. These are followed, among the notebook drafts, by X p. iv and Rhymer p. 7, both titled fair copies. There are several independent manuscript copies: (1) one in Houghton (called the Storrer MS by Strauch), (2) Poems folder 20, (3) Poems folder 21, (4) one in the Morgan Library (the Fields MS, possibly printer's copy for *May–Day*), and (5) a copy made for George W. Childs in 1876, in the University of Virginia Library (see L 6:290). These texts differ from the first published version as follows: (1) and (2) "Damsels" for "Daughters" in line 1 and "his" for "her" in line 11; (3) "Children" as an alternate for "Daughters" in line 1, "and" for "or" in line 6, and "his" changed to "her" in line 11; (4) "Damsels" in line 1 and "and" in line 6; and (5) "and" in line 6. Several more manuscripts may be in private hands, as suggested by the evidence of sale catalogues: see *ESQ*, no. 6 (1st quarter 1957), 26, and no. 13 (4th quarter 1958), 40.

*Date:* The date of composition is to be inferred from Emerson's entry in journal DO: "Thus I have written within a twelvemonth verses ('Days') . . ." (JMN 13:10). Strauch claims that the entry dates from January 1852. A better conjecture might be February or March, thus pointing to composition in the spring or summer of 1851. The fact that it precedes a draft of lines from "Give All to Love" in the erased pencil layer in EF p. 52 suggests, however, that it may be as early as 1846. Emerson had entertained the premise of "Days" as early as 1822 (see the poem "Idealism" in JMN 1:81). In January 1825 he wrote: "Days that come dancing on fraught with delights / Dash our blown hopes as they limp heavily by" (JMN 2:405). Parallel prose statements may be found in JMN 5:253 (28 November 1836)—a passage used in "Doctrine of the Hands," *Early Lectures* 2:235; in letters of 1840 and 1841 to Margaret Fuller (L 2:342, 463); and in a letter to Mary Moody Emerson in 1843 (L 3:232). F. O. Matthiessen (*American Renaissance*, 1941, pp. 59–60, n. 7) argued that Shakespeare's *Troilus and Cressida*, 3.3.145–46, might have been a source: there is corroboration for this view in Emerson's letter of 3 September 1846 to Lidian (L 3:344). In an entry in journal CD (24 May 1847) Emerson also uses the central image of the poem: "The days come & go like muffled & veiled figures sent from a distant friendly party, but they say nothing, & if we do not use the gifts they bring, they carry them as silently away" (JMN 10:61). This passage and others are indexed and amplified at JMN 10:379–80 and indexed again, in October 1848, in JMN 11:21, suggesting that Emerson may have thought of writing an essay or lecture on the subject. (Much of this material was in fact eventually used in "Works and Days," first given as a lecture in 1857: see W 7:395–96.) See also JMN 11:102–3, 154, and EF p. 24.

*Publication: Atlantic Monthly* 1 (November 1857): 47. Evidently the text submitted to the *Atlantic* read "hypocritical" in line 1: see Emerson's letter to Francis Underwood, 24 September 1857, in Bliss Perry, *Park-Street Papers* (Boston and New York, 1908), p. 245, which invites J. R. Lowell to make the correction to "hypocritic." The poem was reprinted, with a different error in line 1 ("Damsels" for "Daughters"), in *May–Day*, 1867, p. 111 (see L 5:518 concerning this error), and again, corrected, in *Selected Poems*, 1876, p. 172, in *Poems*, 1884, p. 196, and in W 9:228.

*See Also:* (1) Frederick I. Carpenter, *Emerson and Asia*, 1930, p. 187, (2) Matthiessen, *American Renaissance*, 1941, pp. 55–64, (3) Egbert S. Oliver, "Emerson's 'Days,' " *NEQ* 19 (December 1946): 518–24, (4) Nelson F. Adkins, "Emerson's 'Days' and Edward Young," *MLN* 63 (April 1948): 269–71, (5) Carl F. Strauch, "The MS Relationships of Emerson's 'Days,' " *PQ* 29 (April 1950): 199–208, (6) Mario D'Avanzo, "Emerson's 'Days' and Proverbs," *ATQ* 1 (1969): 83–85, and (7) Strauch diss., pp. 394–95 (text) and 584–90 (notes).

## "The days pass over me"

*Texts:* Two texts exist, both in ink: in journal Blotting Book Psi (JMN 3:260), with "Like" in line 4, and in P p. 101, with "With" in line 4.

*Date:* The version in Blotting Book Psi occurs between entries of 20 and 25 June 1831, several months after the death of Emerson's first wife.

*Publication:* Unpublished by Emerson. First published in W 9:395 from the P text, with the incorrect date "1833."

*See Also:* "My days roll by me" (JMN 3:36).

## "Dear are the pleasant memories"

*Text:* The only text of this quatrain occurs in NP p. 78. It has not been found elsewhere in Emerson's published or unpublished writings.

## "Dear brother, would you know the life"

*Texts:* The first draft is a single-sheet manuscript in Poems folder 22, where the verses are headed "Lines written in 1831. Boston" (see Additional Manuscripts). The poem was revised in X pp. 16–17, where the heading was changed to "Chardon Street 1830."

*Date:* Ellen Tucker Emerson died at the Chardon Street house on 8 February 1831, and the poem was written shortly thereafter. The date in X is an obvious error, suggesting that Emerson was working either from memory or from a lost, undated, intermediate manuscript. The draft in X is written over lines used in "Monadnock," and must therefore have been set down in 1845 or later.

*Publication:* Unpublished by Emerson. First published from the X text with several minor errors and the nonauthorial title "A Letter" in W 9:391–92.

## "Dear child the place"

*Text:* This four-line fragment occurs in pencil in X p. 74. It has not been found elsewhere in Emerson's published or unpublished writings.

## "Dear Ellen, many a golden year"

*Text:* An ink fair copy is in CSA p. 25.

*Date:* CSA bears the notation "Pepperell [Massachusetts] Sept. 1829—". In that month Emerson and Ellen Tucker, with her mother and sister, were making a tour of Massachusetts and Connecticut prior to their marriage on 30 September. They evidently stopped at Pepperell, briefly, on 11 September (see L 1:282–84).

*Publication:* Unpublished by Emerson. First published in J 2:265–66.

*See Also:* (1) "I call her beautiful;—she says" and (2) *One First Love*, p. 101.

## "Dear Ellen must have a muff"

*Texts:* The only texts of this gift poem for Emerson's daughter Ellen are two pencil drafts in NP pp. 126 and 127.

*Date:* The verses were probably written in late December 1867 to accompany a New Year's gift. Three other gift poems, including "Maiden Speech of the Aeolian Harp," written at that time, occur on the preceding pages in NP.

*Publication:* Unpublished.

## "Dearest, where thy shadow falls"

*Texts:* The source for this translation from Hafiz has not been located; the earliest draft is probably notebook Orientalist p. 26 (where the revised text begins "Mirza!") or, possibly, journal LM (JMN 10:341), where, however, the text may have been quoted as a comment on the preceding prose. The unrevised Orientalist text was in any event copied into Rhymer p. 147 at the same time that "They say, through patience, chalk" was copied from the same page. The revision in the Rhymer text is reflected in the fair copies in NP p. 2 and notebook L Camadeva p. 79.

*Date:* The LM draft was written in July 1848.

*Publication:* First published from the revised Orientalist text in "Persian Poetry," 1858, p. 728, though the verses do not appear in the essay as reprinted. Published again, from the text as revised in Rhymer, in *May–Day,* 1867, p. 199, and reprinted in *Poems,* 1884, p. 247, and W 9:301.

*See Also:* (1) "They say, through patience, chalk" and (2) J. D. Yohannan, "Emerson's Translations of Persian Poetry from German Sources," *AL* 14 (January 1943): 419.

## "The Dervish whined to *Said*"

*Text:* The five texts of the poem were composed in the following order: a pencil draft in notebook Dialling, among many verses eventually used in "Saadi" (JMN 8:513); a pencil version in P p. 93; pencil versions in X p. 264 (written over an erased draft of "To J. W.") and Poems folder 23, both of which drop the fourth and fifth lines of the first draft; and a final version in pencil in Poems folder 79 (see Additional Manuscripts).

*Date:* The draft in Dialling, a notebook Emerson used heavily after becoming editor of *The Dial* in April 1842, strongly suggests composition in the summer of that year. This is made even more likely by its presence among lines of "Saadi," published in *The Dial* in October 1842. Edward Emerson (W 9:505) suggests a prose source in journal J in June 1842, a passage about Sunday preachers (JMN 8:181), but the resemblance is slight and can be matched by other passages in a similar vein (e.g., JMN 8:179 and 186). Emerson's avoidance of church drew comment from W. H. Furness in 1840 (*Records,* p. 13) and from Hawthorne in 1842 (*American Notebooks,* 1972, p. 343).

*Publication:* Unpublished by Emerson. First published in W 9:322–23, from the Poems folder 79 text.

*See Also:* "Saadi."

## "Desire no bread, forsake the guest hall of the earth"

*Texts:* The couplet appears in X p. 171, while line 2 is given by itself in notebook Orientalist p. 57 and EF p. 109. The verses translate Hafiz, Book I, Ode VII, lines 17–18 (*Diwan* 1:12).

*Date:* Undetermined.

*Publication:* Line 2 was quoted in "Persian Poetry," 1858, p. 726, in the essay as reprinted in *Letters and Social Aims,* 1876, p. 220, and in W 8:245.

## "Diamond will burn but Truth will hold"

*Texts:* This single line occurs in slightly different versions in EL pp. 232 (ink) and 294 (pencil).

*Date:* The version on p. 232 follows verses written no earlier than 1867.

*Publication:* Unpublished.

## "Dirge"

*Texts:* The initial draft of this poem, in pencil, occurs in P pp. 185–87 and 189–92; possibly related lines occur on pp. 192–93. (In the following analysis, unpublished stanzas are referred to by the first words of their opening lines.) P p. 185: stanzas "I reached," "Five rosy boys," 3, 4, 5; p. 186: "They filled," "They threaded," "This earth," "They made," 6; p. 187: "I reached,"

"Five rosy boys," 6, 5 (underlying layer), 7 (overlying layer), with "Caesar's Valley" (bracketed) at the top of the page; p. 189: 6, "They threaded," "This valley," 8; p. 190: "They knew," "This earth," "They made," 7; p. 191: 8, 9, 10, 11, "They would have"; p. 192: "I sauntered," three unrelated lines, eleven lines possibly related but in varying meter and with a different rhyme scheme; p. 193: nine possibly related lines but in varying meter and unrhymed. On p. 205, stanzas 1 and 2 appear with stanzas from another poem, "Knows he who tills this lonely field." An ink fair copy, titled, occurs in P pp. 14–16; it consists of the poem as printed preceded by stanzas "I reached" and "Five rosy boys." An additional copy of "I reached," identical to the P p. 14 text, is included in Emerson's letter to W. H. Furness of 12 March 1844 (see below). Printer's copy for the London edition of *Poems*, 1847, is in the Berg Collection, New York Public Library; in it, "whole" is canceled before "horizon" in line 25, "or" is changed to "and" in line 26, "merry" is canceled for "glad" in line 28, "be" is changed to "it" in line 41, and "best doth" is changed to "loudest" in line 51.

*Date:* Edward Emerson died on 1 October 1834, Charles Emerson on 9 May 1836. The draft at P pp. 14–16 carries the notation "*1838*", as does the London printer's copy, a reference in each case to the date of composition rather than inscription. Stanzas 1 and 2, however, were written between 1840 and 1844 (see "Knows he who tills this lonely field"). When Emerson sent the poem to Furness on 12 March 1844 for publication, he noted that it "was composed or rather hummed by me one afternoon, years ago, as I walked in the woods & on the narrow plain through which our Concord River flows, not far from my grandfather's house, and remembered my brothers Edward & Charles . . . . At the time of this walk, I was thirtyfive years old . . ." (MS in the Furness Papers, Van Pelt Library, University of Pennsylvania, quoted with some errors in *Records*, pp. 30–31). Emerson turned 35 on 25 May 1838. His age is reflected in lines 1–2 of stanza "I reached," which recall the opening lines of Dante's *Divine Comedy*: "Nel mezzo del cammin di nostra vita . . . ." The letter to Furness further indicates that Emerson rejected the original opening because he had inadvertently switched form from the long to the regular hymnal stanza.

*Publication:* First published in *The Gift: A Christmas, New Year, and Birthday Present* (Philadelphia, 1845), pp. 94–96, and collected in *Poems*, 1847, pp. 232–35 (Boston) and pp. 185–87 (London). The text published in *Memory and Hope* (Boston, 1851), pp. 237–39, appears to have been set from the unrevised *Gift* text, for it retains the reading "lonely" in line 14. Reprinted in *Selected Poems*, 1876, pp. 188–89. In *Poems*, 1884, pp. 127–29, the poem is subtitled "Concord, 1838," and stanzas "I reached" and "Five rosy boys" are printed as a preface. Both changes are retained in W 9:145–47.

*See Also:* (1) "Knows he who tills this lonely field," (2) "Now Nature is a Funeral," (3) "We sauntered amidst miracles," and (4) W 9:451–52.

# "The Discontented Poet: a Masque"

*Texts:* Of the three surviving fair copies the earliest is an untitled manuscript in ink in the Tappan Papers, Houghton Library; next come an untitled fragment in ink consisting of the first 34 lines in Poems folder 73, and the complete titled version in pencil in P pp. 153–56. (For the texts in Houghton and Poems folder 73, see Additional Manuscripts). The only surviving partial drafts are of the concluding lines: a canceled draft of lines 67–74 occurs on a half sheet used to record an insert in the introductory lecture to "The Present Age" series (*Early Lectures* 3:453); this text was revised and amplified in the pencil draft of lines 67–80 in EF p. 70. The same lines, evidently drawn from the P text, with "want" for "fear" in line 72, occur in an ink fair copy in the Yale University Library.

*Date:* The draft of lines 67–74 in the lecture insert probably represents the beginning of composition. The lecture itself was written in late November or early December 1839, though the insert may belong to 1840. In November 1840 Emerson wrote an entry in journal F 2 (JMN 7:529) that was to become the source of lines 57–66 and 75–80: "The moon keeps its appointment— Will not the good Spirit? Wherefore have we labored & fasted, say we, & thou takest no note? Let him not take note, if he please to hide,—then it were sublime beyond a poet's dreams still to labor & abstain & obey, &, if thou canst, *to put the good Spirit in the wrong.* That were a feat to sing in Elysium, on Olympus, by the waters of life in the New Jerusalem." Two manuscript pages later—also in November 1840—is the prose source for lines 37–38. Various parallels and analogues are to be found in other writings of this period, notably in two letters to Caroline Sturgis, of 18 September 1840 (L 2:326–27, where the conjectural date is in error) and 25 September 1840 (L 2:337–38), as well as in the essay "Friendship" (W 2:191–217), composed about the same time, and in the lecture "The Poet" (*Early Lectures* 3:348–65), dating from the fall of 1841. "The Discontented Poet" was therefore most likely composed between the fall of 1840 and April 1842, when Emerson wrote the first draft (JMN 8:226–27) of verses used in an attempt to expand the poem. During 1842 and 1843 he composed numerous fragments on the same general theme, and seems to have tried halfheartedly to combine them. (These manuscripts, discovered together at the time of Emerson's death, were the basis for the text created by James Elliot Cabot and published as "The Poet" in *Poems,* 1884. The manuscripts are now in Poems folder 73.) Although the expanded version was well along by 24 August 1842, when Margaret Fuller examined the manuscripts and copied several lines (see Joel Myerson, "Margaret Fuller's 1842 Journal," *HLB* 21 [1973]: 326), Emerson was still using the original title of the poem as late as March 1843, when he seems to have thought of publishing it (JMN 8:529–30 and n. 39). Confusion about the date and character of "The Discontented Poet" was fostered by

Cabot's note to "The Poet" in *Poems*, 1884, p. 253: "This poem was begun as early as 1831, probably earlier, and received additions for more than twenty years, but was never completed. In its early form it was entitled, The Discontented Poet, A Masque." In fact no more than four years passed between the poem's inception and the abandonment of the expanded form, during which time (probably in the first year) the only finished form was arrived at. Edward Emerson fared no better in dating the poem (W 9:500–1, 504–5), having been misled not only by Cabot but also by the erroneous date of 1831 appearing with an early manuscript of "Brother, no decrepitude"—a fragment arbitrarily printed as part of "The Poet" in 1884, but never belonging to "The Discontented Poet."

*Publication:* Unpublished by Emerson. Portions of the poem appear as lines 182–201, 222–25, 250–53, and 258–93 of "The Poet," *Poems*, 1884, pp. 253–63, reprinted in W 9:309–20.

## "Divine Inviters! I accept"

*Texts:* The only complete draft occurs in Poems folder 73 (see Additional Manuscripts). Lines 9–10 occur in a manuscript dated 1841 (Poems folder 58), containing, among other fragments, a draft of the motto for "Compensation"; the couplet, with the revision of "By" for "With" in line 10, was copied at the bottom of the Poems folder 73 manuscript and indicated for insertion in the text. Three lines beginning "Divine inviters" in EL p. 26 may represent an unsuccessful attempt to make use of these lines in a draft of "The Adirondacs."

*Date:* The source of these lines is a journal entry for 6 June 1841 about an evening's boating with Thoreau (JMN 7:454–55); the poem was probably written in that year.

*Publication:* Unpublished by Emerson. First published as lines 149–64 of "The Poet" (a work assembled by Cabot) in *Poems*, 1884, p. 258, and reprinted in W 9:314–15.

## "Do that which you can do"

*Texts:* This couplet occurs in pencil in notebook Delta (JMN 12:260) and in P p. 22.

*Date:* The Delta text occurs among notes for the lecture "Doctrine of the Hands," written shortly before its first delivery on 13 December 1837. The phrasing of line 1 occurs in a canceled portion of the lecture (*Early Lectures* 2:449).

*Publication:* Unpublished by Emerson. First published in JMN 12.

## "docile imitative men"

*Text:* This fragment occurs in pencil in EL p. 118; above it, Edward Emerson identified the subject as "The negro." At points it trails off into notes and may be related to "Voluntaries," parts of which Emerson drafted in the same section of EL. It has not been found elsewhere in Emerson's published or unpublished writings.

## "Drink, hear my counsel, my son, that the world fret thee not"

*Texts:* The poem, which translates Hafiz, Book XII, Ode X, lines 7–12 (*Diwan* 2:71), occurs in journal IO (JMN 13:304–5). A version of lines 5–6 also appears in EF p. 80.

*Date:* The IO text falls between entries of May 1854.

*Publication:* Lines 5–6 were published in a prose version in "Persian Poetry," 1858, p. 731, and in the essay as reprinted in *Letters and Social Aims*, 1876, p. 232, and W 8:258. Lines 1 and 3–6 (omitting the canceled second line) were quoted from IO by Edward Emerson in his notes to "Persian Poetry" (W 8:422).

## "Drink till the turbans are all unbound"

*Text:* This couplet, possibly from Hafiz, occurs in pencil in EF p. 83. It has not been found elsewhere in Emerson's published or unpublished writings.

## "Drink wine, and the heaven"

*Texts:* The order of the eight drafts of this translation from Hafiz appears to be as follows: (1) a 23-line version in erased pencil in X p. 181, under a draft of "Rubies"; (2) a 28-line version in pencil in X pp. 183–84, over an erased draft of "Hermione"; (3) and (4) two erased pencil drafts in EF pp. 12–13, overwritten with lines used in "Song of Nature," a draft of "Fate" ("Deep in the man"), and prose fragments used in "The Fugitive Slave Law" (1851); (5) a 16-line version in ink, corrected in pencil, in notebook Orientalist pp. 52–53; (6) a further revised 16-line version in Orientalist p. 83; (7) a fair copy of the 16-line version in Rhymer p. 149, where the last three stanzas are marked "printed"; and (8) another fair copy, in Poems folder 36, which supplies to these three stanzas a new beginning: lines 1–4 of "There resides in the grieving" (see Additional Manuscripts under that title). The poem, in its 28-line form, is a translation of Hafiz, Book XXI, Ode II (*Diwan* 2:125–26). Line numbers refer to the fullest version, in X pp. 183–84.

*Date:* The relation of the EF drafts to the prose material used in "The Fugitive Slave Law" points to a period of composition between 1846 and 1851.

*Publication:* Unpublished except for lines 17–26, which appeared in "Persian Poetry," 1858 (see "The Builder of heaven").

## "Each and All"

*Texts:* The first draft of the poem is in erased pencil in P pp. 105–6; this was revised (and later erased) on pp. 104 and 107. An ink fair copy drawn from the latter two pages occurs in P pp. 11–13. Printer's copy for the London edition of *Poems*, 1847, is in the Yale University Library; it has "lists" for the misprint "lifts" in line 7 and "of" canceled before "deity" in line 49.

*Date:* Journal A contains several prose entries closely paralleling passages in this poem: one of 16 May 1834, about sea shells (lines 19–28), used in lectures of 1834 and 1835 (*Early Lectures* 1:73–74 and 317); one written between 12 and 15 July about Napoleon (lines 5–8); and one between 26 November and 1 December about "the shepherd . . . in his red cloak" (lines 1–2) (JMN 4:291, 304, 345–46). A lengthy entry of 3 May expresses the general idea and some of the specific details of the poem (JMN 4:287–89). It is worth noting that these entries all pertain to the first 28 lines of the poem— the matter on p. 105—and would seem to point to composition toward the close of 1834. Since the poem was not published until February 1839, how-ever, any time between 1834 and 1838 is possible. Several apparently perti-nent journal entries seem to imply a date later than 1834: one in journal B for 28 March 1835 ("Nothing is beautiful alone") resembles line 12 (JMN 5:26, cf. 6:201). A passage in journal C between 12 and 16 April 1837 (JMN 5:297) that has parallels to the loss of "gay enchantment" in marriage (lines 31–38) suggests that while the poem may have been begun as early as 1834, this section at least is not earlier than the spring of 1837.

*Publication: Western Messenger* 6 (February 1839): 229–30. The text pub-lished by Longfellow in *The Waif: A Collection of Poems* (Cambridge, 1845), pp. 73–75, omits lines 29–38, a passage which includes the lines apparently suggested by the latest journal source (see L 3:364n). This would seem to imply a manuscript form of the poem as it might have existed between 1835 and 1837, though how Longfellow would have come upon such a manuscript is not known. The reading of "club-moss burrs" in line 41 of the *Waif* text is represented in the notebook drafts, but not in the poem as previously published. Reprinted from the *Messenger* text, but omitting lines 29–30, in *Poems,* 1847, pp. 14–16 (Boston) and pp. 7–9 (London); *Selected Poems,* 1876, pp. 12–13; *Poems,* 1884, pp. 14–15; and W 9:4–6.

*See Also:* Carl F. Strauch, "The Year of Emerson's Poetic Maturity: 1834," PQ 34 (October 1955): 369–73.

## "Early after the night long revel"

*Text:* The poem, which translates Hafiz, Book XXVI, Ode IX (*Diwan* 2:344–45), occurs in a pencil fair copy in X p. 178.

*Date:* Probably 1846, since it appears to have been inscribed before the third draft of "Ghaselle: From the Persian of Hafiz" on X pp. 179–80; that poem was published in *Poems,* 1847.

*Publication:* Unpublished.

## "The Earth"

*Text:* The only text of this quatrain is a titled ink draft on an inserted sheet, NP p. 148.2$_a$.

*Date:* Undetermined.

*Publication:* Unpublished by Emerson. First published in *Poems,* 1884, p. 282, and reprinted in W 9:341. In his note in W 9:508, Edward Emerson erroneously associates the quatrain with "Monadnock."

## "Easy to match what others do"

*Texts:* The first draft occurs in a single-sheet manuscript in the Houghton Library (see Additional Manuscripts). This was revised in EL p. 162 and copied in EL p. 233 and ETE p. 104. A version in Poems folder 62 is drawn from the ETE text, except that it has "sons" for the incorrect "suns" in line 6 and the last line reads "The blaze of the revellers' feasts outshine." The revision of the last line in EL p. 233 is not reflected in the other texts, though the fact is not sufficient in itself to show that this draft is the latest.

*Date:* Undetermined.

*Publication:* Unpublished by Emerson. First published in *Poems,* 1884, p. 289, and reprinted in W 9:351.

## "Elizabeth Hoar"

*Texts:* The poem, a character sketch of the family friend and companion who lived with the Emersons after her fiance, Charles Emerson, died, developed through six partial drafts before reaching its final form. The prose source of lines 17–18, apparently a statement by Elizabeth, occurs in journal Books Small, and is versified later in that journal (JMN 8:452, 475). Lines 1–12, 14–15, and 17–24 occur in journal RO (JMN 14:6–8); this draft is revised in EL pp. 252–53. A later draft in notebook OP Gulistan, pp. 50–51, derived from RO, contains lines 14–15, 17–24, and 26–35; lines 26–35 also occur in notebook QL pp. 32–33. The entire poem occurs in Poems folder 26 (see Additional Manuscripts).

*Date:* The first draft of lines 17–18 is probably from 1842–1843, while the partial draft in RO is from 1855. Emerson noted the source for line 14, Emanuel Swedenborg, *A Treatise Concerning Heaven . . . and . . . Hell,* 1823, in several journals and notebooks from the early 1840s or before up to 1855 (JMN 6:315, 13:8 and 44, and 14:14).

*Publication:* Unpublished by Emerson. The first eighteen lines of the OP Gulistan text were published (from a transcription not in Emerson's hand) in Elizabeth Maxfield-Miller, "Emerson and Elizabeth of Concord," *HLB* 19 (July 1971): 300.

## "Enchanter with his mob of dreams"

*Text:* The poem occurs in EL p. 289 in a draft in which lines 3–6 are canceled in ink; it is possible that these lines are a commentary upon the beginning couplet or a separate fragment. The poem has not been found elsewhere in Emerson's published or unpublished writings.

## "Enough is done highminded friend go sleep"

*Texts:* The latest text of this unfinished elegy is in X pp. 124–25. This is preceded by drafts in X pp. 116–18.

*Date:* Undetermined. The draft at X p. 117 is overwritten by material dating to 1859.

*Publication:* Unpublished.

## "Epitaph"

*Texts:* This quatrain translates Hafiz, Fragment XLII (misnumbered LXII) (*Diwan* 2:573). A first draft in pencil is followed by a second in ink, both in notebook Orientalist p. 110. The titled fair copy in Rhymer p. 144 was made before pencil revisions were entered in the second Orientalist text. The copy in Poems folder 36 is identical to the Rhymer text.

*Date:* Undetermined.

*Publication:* First published in "Persian Poetry," 1858, p. 730, from the Rhymer text. The poem does not appear in later reprintings of this essay. Published separately, with the title as above, in *May–Day,* 1867, p. 198, with the change of "maiden" for "ivory" in line 3, reflecting the late revisions in Orientalist p. 110. This text was reprinted in *Poems,* 1884, p. 246, and W 9:300.

## "Eros"

*Texts:* The earliest occurrence of any part of this poem appears to be the fragment "sense of the world is short" in P p. 231. An erased draft of the poem occurs in P p. 210, transcribed in P p. 157. An ink fair copy, untitled, in notebook L Camadeva p. 21 precedes the ink fair copy, with the title "Love," in Poems folder 58; both have the wording of the first published text.

*Date:* Undetermined.

*Publication:* The Dial 4 (January 1844): 401, with the title "Eros"; collected in *Poems,* 1847, p. 150 (Boston) and p. 118 (London). The text in *Poems,* 1884, p. 89, with a reading in line 6 found only in the P drafts, was reprinted in W 9:100.

## "Etienne de la Boéce"

*Texts:* There are evidences of a first draft (only lines 10, 19, and 23 are identifiable) in X p. 21, erased under a layer (also erased) of "Astraea." A revised draft, in pencil, appears on X p. 33, written over an erased draft of

"The World-Soul"; this is followed by a fair copy, again in pencil, on X p. 35. In each case the last line is lacking. A couplet incorporated as lines 21–22 first occurs in journal Books Small (JMN 8:463). Printer's copy for the London edition of *Poems*, 1847, is in the Huntington Library; it has "yours" for the incorrect "your's" in line 10; "In a grave or frolic mood" is changed to "In severe or cordial mood" in line 12; "And" is inserted at the beginning of line 15; and lines 23–24 appear reversed and are marked for transposition.

*Date:* Edward Emerson suggests (W 9:429) that "Etienne" was written in 1833, on the basis of a journal entry he ascribes to that year, but which was actually written in the spring of 1843 (JMN 8:375). In September of that year Emerson read Montaigne's *Journey into Italy* in the younger Hazlitt's 1842 edition of *The Complete Works*. In journal U he remarks: "Then what a treasure, to enlarge my knowledge of his friend by his narrative of the last days & the death of Etienne de la Boetie" (JMN 9:28; cf. Emerson's letters to Margaret Fuller, 10? October 1843 [L 3:212], and to Thoreau, 25 October 1843, in *The Atlantic Monthly* 69 [May 1892]: 596). The couplet in journal Books Small occurs among draft passages used in "Cosmos" and must have been written in 1846 (cf. JMN 8:462, n. 67). Thus the draft of "Etienne" on X p. 33 (where the couplet is added) was written earlier, perhaps in 1843 or 1844, and the draft on X p. 35 dates to 1846.

*Publication: Poems*, 1847, pp. 126–27 (Boston) and pp. 99–100 (London); reprinted in *Selected Poems*, 1876, p. 76, *Poems*, 1884, pp. 76–77, and W 9:82.

## "Eve roved in Paradise, I've heard"

*Text:* The first draft of this gift poem, identified by Edward Emerson in notes to NP as "New Years poem to E.T.E. [Emerson's daughter Ellen] with trunk," occurs in pencil in NP p. 293. A photocopy of an unlocated manuscript, probably the one that accompanied the gift, is in Poems folder 172 (see Additional Manuscripts).

*Date:* The text in the photocopy carries the date "1864," though the handwriting is probably not Emerson's.

*Publication:* Unpublished.

*See Also:* "If bright the sun."

## "Ever find me dim regards"

*Texts:* Emerson composed the first draft in pencil on the rear flyleaf of his copy of Goethe's *Werke* (Stuttgart and Tübingen, 1828–1833), vol. 50, which is vol. 10 of *Goethes Nachgelassene Werke* (see Additional Manuscripts), and revised it in X p. 163. Fair copies occur in X p. 265 and Poems folder 23; in the latter "They" is canceled for "These" in line 8. In the last two locations the poem follows immediately after "I grieve that better souls," while in X p. 163 it follows one page later.

*Date:* About 1837 (see "Written in a Volume of Goethe").

*Publication:* Unpublished by Emerson. First published, as a part of "I grieve that better souls," in *Poems,* 1884, p. 270; the combination was reprinted in W 9:327.

*See Also:* "I grieve that better souls."

## "Ever the Rock of Ages melts"

*Texts:* The first two drafts of the quatrain occur in journal VO (JMN 14:183 and 185). The most likely transmission of the text from this point is to the version in NP p. 72 and the first trial in NP p. 196; between this and the other draft on the same page are interposed the two drafts in the insert in Rhymer (pp. 50$_b$ and 50$_g$). After the second trial in NP the draft in Rhymer p. 116 seems to follow, then ETE p. 7, NP p. 141, and notebook BL p. 203.

*Date:* Many prose passages in the journals and elsewhere bear on the idea of this quatrain, as, for example, an entry of 10 April 1837 on the capacity of love to melt "boundary mountains . . . into air" (JMN 5:294) or another of 24 June 1840 on the moral significance of molecular motility in heat (JMN 7:375), or this, from April 1846 (JMN 9:357): "Nature may be cooked into all shapes, & not recognized. Mountains & oceans we think we understand;—yes, so long as they are contented to be such, and are safe with the geologist; but when they are melted in Promethean alembics, & come out men; & then, melted again, come out words, without any abatement but with an exaltation of power—!" In December 1856 Emerson entered in journal SO the single sentence, "The Rock of Ages is diffused into the mineral air," immediately after a notation that trees get nineteen-twentieths of their nourishment from the air (JMN 14:46). Five months later, in May 1857, he wrote: "The Rock of Ages dissolves himself into the mineral air, & thus becomes the foundation of mortal frames" (JMN 14:142). The first drafts of the quatrain, in journal VO, were written between May and December 1857. While the verse drafts were being evolved, Emerson worked up the idea in an oration entitled "The Man with the Hoe," delivered at the Middlesex Cattle Show in Concord on 29 September 1858. This was the precursor of the essay "Farming" (see W 7:143–45). The idea appears also in the essay "Perpetual Forces," mainly written in 1862 (see W 10:70).

*Publication:* Unpublished by Emerson. First published in *Poems,* 1884, p. 295, and reprinted in W 9:355.

*See Also:* EL p. 99 for evidence of a relationship between this poem and "Sea-Shore."

## "Every good below preexists above"

*Text:* This single line occurs in pencil in X p. 72. It has not been found elsewhere in Emerson's published or unpublished writings.

## "Every thought kindling with life"

*Text:* This fragment occurs in erased pencil in X p. 82, and is perhaps related to "Merlin II." Lines 19–20, in any event, resemble lines 14–15 of that poem.

*Date:* The lines are written over an erased draft of "The Daemonic and the Celestial Love" and under a draft of two lines used in "Merlin II," which suggests a period of composition between 1843 and 1846.

*Publication:* Unpublished.

## "Everything knows everything"

*Text:* This three-line fragment occurs in pencil in X p. 199. It has not been found elsewhere in Emerson's published or unpublished writings.

## "Excelsior"

*Texts:* The first draft is in journal C, just before an entry of 1 May 1838 (JMN 5:483). This draft was revised and given the title "Four Stories" in EF p. 14; this in turn was copied into NP p. 141 with the omission of one word and given the title "Excelsior, *a song of degrees.*" Poems folder 172 contains a photostat of a fair copy signed and dated "Concord— / May, 1859."; this untitled text is identical in wording to the EF version.

*Date:* Early 1838. The version in EF was written no earlier than the mid-1850s.

*Publication:* First published in a text slightly different from any of the manuscripts in *May–Day,* 1867, p. 185; reprinted in *Poems,* 1884, p. 240, and W 9:293.

## "The Exile"

*Texts:* This poem translates and conflates at least two sources, and includes material (lines 21–24) that is probably original with Emerson. The first draft is in notebook Orientalist p. 100, where a translation of two lines attributed to Hafiz (source undetermined) is developed on p. 102 into lines 5–8; also on p. 100 is a draft translation of the source in Kermani (*Geschichte,* p. 248) in eight lines (lines 9–16). Orientalist p. 116 contains (1) a translation of Hafiz, Book XXIV, Ode IV, lines 21–28 (*Diwan* 2:282), of which the last four become lines 1–4 of "The Exile," and (2) a revision of the Kermani lines, separated by a rule. Orientalist p. 130 contains a further revision of lines 9–16, to which is added a version of lines 21–24, drawn from notebook PY p. 31, where the first two drafts of these lines occur (see JMN 13:357 for another copy of lines 23–24). The disparate elements come together in the drafts in Orientalist pp. 144–45 (lines 5–24) and 146–47 (lines 5–24 and 1–4, numbered to place the last, added stanza in first position). Titled fair copies are in Rhymer pp. 123–24 and Poems folder 36, both of which assign the poem to Hafiz; the former differs from the latter in that it has "wind" for "breeze" in line 5, cancels "man" for "lover" in line 7, and cancels "each" for "the" in line 18; the latter changes "offered" to "offer" in line 19 and changes "strand" to "land" in line 20.

*Date:* Undetermined. Emerson copied lines 23–24 into journal IO (JMN 13:357) in September 1854.

*Publication:* First published in "Persian Poetry," 1858, p. 732, where it is attributed to Kermani; it does not appear in later reprintings of this essay. When the poem was collected in *May–Day,* 1867, pp. 196–97, lines 13–16 were dropped. This shortened version was reprinted in *Poems,* 1884, pp. 245–46, and W 9:298–99.

*See Also:* J. D. Yohannan, "Emerson's Translations of Persian Poetry from German Sources," *AL* 14 (January 1943): 413–14.

## "Fair fall thy soft heart!"

*Texts:* This quatrain, from Hafiz, Book XXVI, Ode I, lines 17–20 (*Diwan* 2:333), occurs with the translation of the entire ode ("Thou who with thy long hair") in X pp. 237–38, and was revised separately in EF p. 77, where it is overwritten by a draft of "A. H." Copies of the quatrain occur in notebook Orientalist p. 54, Rhymer p. 138, and Poems folder 37.

*Date:* The EF text must have been written before the spring of 1855, the apparent date of composition of lines 3–4 of "A. H."

*Publication:* "Persian Poetry," 1858, p. 731, and in the essay as reprinted in *Letters and Social Aims,* 1876, p. 233, and W 8:260.

*See Also:* "Thou who with thy long hair."

## "Faith"

*Texts:* This twelve-line poem translates Hafiz, Book XXVII, Ode XVI, lines 25–36 (*Diwan* 2:381–82); it was published by Emerson in this form and with this title, though in fact it belongs to the longer translation, "Novice, hear me," of which it forms stanzas 7–9. The first draft of the longer version is in X pp. 256–57, copied and revised in EF pp. 10–11, where it is erased under drafts of "Heri, Cras, Hodie," "Song of Nature," and "Nemesis." Emerson wrote out a copy of the first stanza of "Faith" for Lucretia Mott, to whom he sent it in a letter of 18 April 1850: "Go, leap into the waves, / And have no doubt, nor care,— / And the flowing of the seven broad seas / Shall never wet thy hair." (MS in the University of Virginia Library, Barrett Collection). Shortly afterward Emerson separately revised the three stanzas and supplied the title "Faith" in notebook Orientalist p. 23. Printer's copy for *The Liberty Bell,* endorsed by its editor, Edmund Quincy, is in the University of Texas Library.

*Date:* The Mott copy of April 1850 was clearly written after the X and EF drafts and before the Orientalist draft. L 4:229 apparently refers to Quincy's request for a contribution, and suggests that Emerson had not decided, by mid-September 1850, what he would offer. He finally sent the poem, with several others, in October (see *The Liberty Bell,* p. 81).

*Publication: The Liberty Bell* (Boston, 1851), pp. 79–80; reprinted in *Uncollected Writings,* 1912, p. 187. The first two stanzas appear by themselves in revised form in "Persian Poetry," 1858, p. 732, and in the essay as reprinted in *Letters and Social Aims,* 1876, p. 234, and W 8:261.

*See Also:* "Novice, hear me."

## "Fame"

*Texts:* A draft of the first stanza appears in notebook No. XVI (JMN 2:407–8), followed by stanzas 1–4 in journal 1826 (JMN 3:11). Stanza 5 appears in journal 1826–1828 (JMN 3:90), while an ink fair copy of the whole appears in P pp. 1–2 with the title "Fame" and the date "1826."

*Date:* The editors of JMN 2 date the first stanza to 1825 on the basis of the large handwriting, a compensation for Emerson's eye trouble in that year. The draft of stanzas 1–4 was written between January and March 1826. The fifth stanza occurs among journal entries for 1827, although it may have been entered earlier.

*Publication:* "Fame" shares the honor, with "William Rufus and the Jew," of being Emerson's first published poem. It appeared in *The Offering for 1829* [ed. Andrews Norton] (Cambridge, 1829), pp. 52–53, from the text in journals 1826 and 1826–1828. Emerson did not reprint the poem during his lifetime. The P text, however, was printed in *Poems,* 1884, pp. 311–12. In J 2:80–81 and 210 the 1826/1826–1828 text is printed with the comment, "These verses [were] never published by [Emerson]" (p. 80n); the last two lines of the P text are given in a note (p. 210n). W 9:383–84 reprints the 1884 version, including the erroneous date of "1824."

*See Also:* Ralph Thompson, "Emerson and *The Offering for 1829,*" AL 6 (May 1934): 151–57.

## "Fame's a 'sucked orange,' flattered Canning cries"

*Text:* This single line occurs in ink in P p. 97. It has not been found elsewhere in Emerson's published or unpublished writings. The reference is presumably to George Canning (1770–1827), who had a long and distinguished career as a member of Parliament.

## "Far seen the river glides below"

*Texts:* Texts occur in pencil in Poems folder 29, with "Genius" in the last line, and P p. 207, with "River" in the last line.

*Date:* The surrounding texts in P indicate a date somewhere between 1838 and 1844.

*Publication:* Unpublished by Emerson. This quatrain appears (in the P text form) as the final stanza of "Peter's Field" ("Knows he who tills this lonely field") in *Poems,* 1884, p. 303, and W 9:364. It was taken to be the conclusion of that poem because it appears directly after it in P. However, the somewhat different handwriting, the fact that the subject is not truly congruent, and the appearance of the quatrain by itself in folder 29 argue for its being an independent composition.

*See Also:* (1) "Knows he who tills this lonely field" and (2) "The Apology."

"The farthest from the root the sweetest grape"

*Texts:* This single line appears in slightly different forms in journal LM (JMN 10:347) and EL p. 180, both times in association with the couplet "That each should in his house abide." It is incorrectly linked with the entry that precedes it in JMN 10:347.

*Date:* The LM draft dates from late July or early August 1848, shortly after Emerson's return from England on 27 July.

*Publication:* Unpublished by Emerson. First published in JMN 10.

## "Fate" ("Deep in the man")

*Texts:* The first draft, in pencil in notebook EO p. 139, consists of lines 1–12 followed by two lines eventually used as "Nemesis," lines 13–14. This draft is headed "Hutchinson", evidently a reference to the *Memoirs of the Life of Colonel Hutchinson . . . Written by His Widow*, 2 vols. (London, 1822), in Emerson's library. The second draft (lines 1–12), also in pencil, is in EO p. 138. Drafts of lines 15–16 and 13–16 occur in EO on the front cover verso and on pp. 140–41 respectively. The next draft (of the entire 16-line poem) occurs in EF p. 13, followed by two nearly identical drafts in X p. 190 and NP p. 73. The titled fair copy in Rhymer p. 24 is the source of the published text.

*Date:* Emerson read Lucy Hutchinson's *Memoirs* between April and July 1855 and took notes (JMN 13:427). The poem was completed by 1860.

*Publication:* Lines 13–16 were detached and published as lines 11–14 of "Fate" ("Delicate omens") in *The Conduct of Life*, 1860, p. xi. They were restored to their original place at the conclusion of the present poem in its first printing in *May–Day*, 1867, p. 69. This text was reprinted in *Poems*, 1884, p. 171, and W 9:197.

## "Fate" ("Delicate omens")

*Texts:* The first draft, in EL p. 173, consists of three unused lines followed by lines 1–4 and 6–10. The unused lines are repeated in Rhymer p. 2$_a$, where Emerson attempted to join them with other fragments. NP front cover verso$_b$ contains a draft of lines 1–10. The very similar drafts at X pp. 191 and 213 are intermediate between those in NP front cover verso$_b$ and p. 71, where, in the last instance, the verses belong to a series of three poems the sequence of which was determined in X pp. 211–13. Another draft, probably the last inscribed, is in Rhymer p. 50c. None of these contains the last four lines of the motto as first printed: these were taken from "Fate" ("Deep in the man") shortly before publication.

*Date:* Undetermined, though the 14-line version probably did not exist much before 1860.

*Publication: The Conduct of Life,* 1860, p. xi. A version of this poem, of undetermined derivation, was printed as lines 39–48 of "Mask thy wisdom" as published in *Poems,* 1884, p. 268, and W 9:326.

*See Also:* NP p. 295.

## "Fate" ("Her planted eye")

*Texts:* The first four drafts occur in NP pp. 210–11; those on p. 211 (the second and third drafts) are overwritten by the third draft of "New England Capitalist." Copies of the poem, titled, occur in NP pp. 229 and 133 and in Rhymer p. 29, in the last two instances among collections of quatrains.

*Date:* Undetermined. The copy in NP p. 229 follows notes that Emerson made for his address to the Burns Club on 25 January 1859. A list of quatrain titles in notebook HT (JMN 15:489) includes "Fate"; the notebook was used in 1864 for notes on Thoreau.

*Publication: May–Day,* 1867, p. 187, reprinted in *Poems,* 1884, p. 241, and W 9:294.

## "Fate" ("That you are fair")

*Texts:* Two complete texts of this poem exist. One, in the University of Virginia library, was apparently included in a letter, since it has the headnote "You shall have the rest of my thought on Festus, which lies by me in numbers somewhat rude, I own, for the topic" (see Additional Manuscripts). The second, printer's copy for the London edition of *Poems,* 1847, is in the Huntington Library; in it, "an apple" and an inserted "acorn" are canceled for "a rush" in line 23, and "whether" is canceled for "how" in line 38. In ETE p. 3, Emerson listed possible corrections of lines 40–41, probably for *Selected Poems,* 1876.

*Date:* The University of Virginia manuscript is dated 27 June 1841 by someone other than Emerson; in a letter of 17 June 1841, he mentions having a copy of Philip James Bailey's *Festus* by him (L 2:405–6). The recipient may have been Margaret Fuller, then editor of *The Dial,* although the manuscript did not serve as printer's copy for the publication of the poem in that magazine.

*Publication:* First published, with the title "Fate," in *The Dial* 2 (October 1841): 205–6; reprinted in *Poems,* 1847, pp. 45–47 (Boston) and pp. 33–35 (London) and in *Selected Poems,* 1876, pp. 88–89. The poem appeared under the nonauthorial title "Destiny" in *Poems,* 1884, pp. 32–33, and W 9:31–32. Lines 45–50 were printed as a motto to "Success" in W 7:281.


## "Few are free"


*Texts:* The two couplets that make up this poem occur in pencil in P p. 22. The first appears twice as prose, in Blotting Book Psi between entries of 19 and 29 November 1830 (JMN 3:212, cf. 3:258), and in Pocket Diary 1, perhaps also from 1830 (JMN 3:343). The second couplet seems to be an adaptation of Wordsworth's "And the most difficult of tasks to *keep* / Heights which the soul is competent to gain" (*Excursion* 4.138–39), which Emerson quoted many times: in journal Q on 17 September 1833 (JMN 4:87); in journal A on 12 April 1834 (JMN 4:274); in journal K on 1 May 1842 (JMN 8:242); in journal V in 1844 or 1845 (JMN 9:123); and in other places.

*Date:* Undetermined, but probably in the 1830s.

*Publication:* Unpublished.


## "Fine presentiments controlled him"


*Texts:* The earliest text is a pencil draft in X p. 56, revised on facing p. 57. An ink version, with additional revisions and a lacking line supplied, occurs in P p. 188.

*Date:* Undetermined.

*Publication:* Unpublished by Emerson. First published in W 9:415 in the notes to "Guy" with the comment, "In one of the earlier verse-books [X p. 57], on the same page with ['Vain against him'], are [these] lines, apparently destined for this poem." In point of fact, however, "Guy" as published in *Poems,* 1847, does not include "Vain against him," which indeed first appears as part of that poem in the posthumous edition of 1884. No evidence exists, in other words, to suggest that either "Fine presentiments" *or* "Vain against him" were ever "destined" for inclusion in "Guy." The two sets of verses on X p. 57 are in different shades of pencil and were evidently written at different times.

## "The fishes shed their pearls"

*Text:* The poem, translating Hafiz, Book XXVII, Ode XXVI, lines 37–40 (*Diwan* 2:395), occurs in EF p. 115.

*Date:* Undetermined.

*Publication:* First published in a prose version in "Persian Poetry," 1858, p. 729; reprinted with the essay in *Letters and Social Aims,* 1876, p. 227, and W 8:252.

## "Fit for the Pleiads' azure chord"

*Texts:* The first draft of this translation from Hafiz, Book I, Ode VIII, lines 17–18 (*Diwan* 1:15), is in EF p. 114. This text is revised in the two drafts in notebook Orientalist p. 24, followed by fair copies in Orientalist p. 25, Rhymer p. 129, and Poems folder 36. The source in Hafiz is referred to by von Hammer-Purgstall in a passage from his Introduction to the *Diwan* (1:xxxv) that Emerson translated in Orientalist p. 201.

*Date:* As with other translations in the early pages of Orientalist that were copied into Rhymer, this was probably written in 1850.

*Publication:* "Persian Poetry," 1858, p. 729, and in the essay as reprinted in *Letters and Social Aims,* 1876, p. 228, and W 8:253.

## "The Flute"

*Texts:* This quatrain translates the first half of each caesura-divided line of "Proben aus dem Breviere der Derwische" by Jalaluddin [i.e., Mewlana Dschelaleddin] Rumi from *Geschichte,* p. 197. The first draft, which translates more of the poem, occurs in notebook Orientalist p. 19 with the title "The Soul." On p. 18 are two drafts, in pencil, of the four lines that Emerson would finally use. These are followed by drafts on pp. 122 and 132, and fair copies in Rhymer p. 134 and Poems folder 36 (titled "Flute" and with "Hark" canceled for "Hear" in line 1).

*Date:* As with other translations in the early pages of Orientalist that were copied into Rhymer, this was probably written in 1850.

*Publication:* In "Persian Poetry," 1858, p. 733, the lines are introduced as "A stanza of Hilali on a Flute." (The error of attribution is traceable to Orientalist p. 122.) Excluded from the essay as reprinted, the poem was published again in *May–Day,* 1867, p. 202, with the title "The Flute. From Hilali." Reprinted in *Poems,* 1884, p. 248, and W 9:303.

## "For every god"

*Texts:* The first draft of this three-line poem is in ink in notebook ML p. 138, followed by copies in EL p. 149, Rhymer p. 2ᵦ, and NP p. 295.

*Date:* Undetermined, though most of the material in the Rhymer insert (pp. 2ₐ–2ᵦ) dates from the early to mid 1860s.

*Publication:* Unpublished by Emerson. Lines 1–2 were published in *Poems,* 1884, p. 274, and reprinted in W 9:330.

## "For Genius made his cabin wide"

*Texts:* The earliest draft of this six-line fragment is probably EL p. 83, where the opening four lines belong to a draft of "The Harp" at a time when "The Harp" was still a part of "May–Day"; EL p. 84 contains lines 5–6. The drafts of lines 1–2 in EL p. 114ᵦ and NP p. 29 have "led" for "brought" in line 2. A draft of all six lines, not in order and with different versions of several lines, occurs in Poems folder 78 (see Additional Manuscripts), while the poem arrives at its most finished form (along with an additional draft of lines 1–2) in Rhymer p. 2ᵦ. Line 4 occurs by itself in journal GL (JMN 15:140).

*Date:* "The Harp" seems to have been written (originally as part of "May–Day") not earlier than 1861, which is also the date of the entry of line 4 in journal GL. The Rhymer insert (pp. 2ₐ–2ᵦ) contains lines written in the early to mid 1860s.

*Publication:* Unpublished by Emerson. Lines 1–2 were published in *Poems,* 1884, p. 275, and reprinted in W 9:331.

## "For his constant dwelling place has Hafiz"

*Text:* The quatrain, translating Hafiz, Book XXIII, Ode X, lines 37–40 (*Diwan* 2:165), occurs in EF p. 76. It has not been found elsewhere in Emerson's published or unpublished writings.

## "For joy & beauty planted it"

*Texts:* The first two drafts of this quatrain are in journal VO (JMN 14:136 and 181), in the second instance in a draft of "Waldeinsamkeit." The transmission of the text from this point is probably to the ink draft in NP p. 53, and from there to NP pp. 270 and 271, where the quatrain appears as part of a longer draft of "In my garden three ways meet." This longer draft, including "For joy and beauty," was revised in EL p. 135.

*Date:* The VO drafts date from 1857. The second must have been written after 18 August, the date of Emerson's trip to the Forbes estate at Naushon, which inspired "Waldeinsamkeit"; it is overwritten by a prose entry used in "Country Life," first given as a lecture in March 1858. The copy in NP p. 53 interrupts, and was thus written before, the surrounding lines of "The Titmouse," written in 1862.

*Publication:* Unpublished by Emerson. First published in *Poems*, 1884, p. 281, and reprinted in W 9:340.

## "For Lyra yet shall be the pole"

*Text:* This couplet occurs in EL p. 102$_c$. It has not been found elsewhere in Emerson's published or unpublished writings.

## "For Nature true & like in every place"

*Text:* This poem occurs in ink in EL pp. 189–90 following a pencil draft of lines used in "The Adirondacs."

*Date:* After August 1858, when Emerson traveled to the Adirondacks with friends from the Saturday Club.

*Publication:* Unpublished by Emerson. First published, with the omission of line 6, in *Poems*, 1884, p. 279, and reprinted in W 9:338.

## "For pearls, plunge in the sea"

*Text:* The couplet occurs in EL p. 167 under the heading "Persian."

*Date:* The prose source, from Sir John Chardin, *Voyages du Chevalier Chardin, en Perse, et Autres Lieux de l'Orient* . . . , ed. L. Langlès, 10 vols. (Paris,

1811), 5:26, is translated by Emerson in journal FOR (JMN 15:374). He borrowed this volume from the Boston Athenaeum from 16 to 31 October 1863.

*Publication:* Unpublished.

## "For two rewards & nought beside"

*Texts:* In notebook Orientalist p. 92 the first draft, of ten lines, is followed by a revision of the first four lines. A revised copy of the four lines is in Rhymer p. 143. The poem translates the opening of "Esberai du dschis dschujid u bes" by Emir Mahmud Ben Jemin Ferjumendi (Ibn Jemin), from *Geschichte,* p. 238.

*Date:* Undetermined.

*Publication:* Unpublished.

## "For what need I of book or priest"

*Texts:* The first draft in journal SO (JMN 14:67) is revised and expanded in NP p. 34 and copied with further revisions into EL p. 114$_b$.

*Date:* The first draft, possibly rejected from "Two Rivers," was written in March or April 1856.

*Publication:* Unpublished by Emerson. First published from the NP text in *Poems,* 1884, p. 276, and reprinted in W 9:333.

## "Forbearance"

*Text:* A pencil fair copy is in P p. 292.

*Date:* Undetermined.

*Publication: The Dial* 2 (January 1842): 373; collected in *Poems,* 1847, p. 130 (Boston) and p. 102 (London). Reprinted in *Selected Poems,* 1876, p. 77, *Poems,* 1884, p. 78, and W 9:83.

## "Forbore the ant hill, shunned to tread"

*Texts:* Two substantially identical copies of this couplet occur in EL p. 28 and Rhymer p. 50$_a$.

*Date:* Undetermined, though in EL p. 28 the couplet immediately precedes "He could condense," written in 1859.

*Publication:* Unpublished by Emerson. First published in *Poems,* 1884, p. 275, and reprinted in W 9:332.

## "Forerunners"

*Texts:* The first draft occurs in erased pencil in X pp. 28–29, beneath drafts of "Monadnock." The poem was revised on pp. 41–42, and lines 1–24 again on p. 43. By writing "p 42" at the end of this partial draft, Emerson in effect joined it to the second half of the poem's second draft. He then erased the material on p. 41 as well as the first two and last three lines on p. 42 to produce a complete text. This draft is referred to in the index to X as "Guides". Printer's copy for *The Diadem* is in Poems folder 33, and for the London edition of *Poems,* 1847, in the University of Virginia Library. In the latter, "morni[ng]" is canceled for "eastern" in line 15.

*Date:* The draft in X p. 29 is headed "1845 3 May 4 hours 10 m. a m". Emerson sent the poem (along with "A Fable" and "Loss and Gain") to William Henry Furness on 9 May for publication in Furness's annual *The Diadem* (*Records,* p. 39). These poems were inspired by one or more recent trips to Mt. Wachusett, one on 1–3 April and another in the first week of May (mentioned under the date of 9 May in the MS account book for 1845–1849). Edward Emerson recalled his father having said that "Forerunners" "came to him as he walked home from Wachusett" (W 9:430).

*Publication: The Diadem for MDCCCXLVI* (Philadelphia, 1846), pp. 95–96, with the title "The Fore-Runners." Emerson acknowledged receipt of his copy on 15 October 1845 (*Records,* p. 44). The poem was collected in *Poems,* 1847, pp. 133–34 (Boston) and pp. 104–5 (London), and reprinted in *Selected Poems,* 1876, pp. 68–69, *Poems,* 1884, pp. 79–80, and W 9:85–86.

## "Forester"

*Texts:* The earliest text of this quatrain is the pencil version in X p. 20, revised in ink on the same page (both written over the erased first draft of "Astraea"). NP pp. 79 and 134 as well as Rhymer p. 31 contain fair copies, of which the last two give the title.

*Date:* Undetermined.

*Publication: The Dial* (Cincinnati) 1 (February 1860): 131; collected in *May–Day,* 1867, p. 184, and reprinted in *Poems,* 1884, p. 240, and W 9:292.

## "Fortune & Hope no more beguile"

*Texts:* Two versions of this quatrain, a translation of two lines by Prudentius quoted in Robert Burton's *The Anatomy of Melancholy,* part 2, section 3, member 6, occur in journal NO (JMN 13:389–90), one in ink, the other in ink over erased pencil; Emerson copied the first version in ETE p. 37. In notebook NQ p. 61, he entered the original lines: "Inveni portum; spes et Fortuna valete; / Nil mihi vobiscum, ludite nunc alios," and followed them with a different version of the quatrain: "Fortune & Hope no more beguile, / Farewell, ye gay deceivers; / You've led me many a weary mile, / Go flatter young believers." (Burton's own translation is "Mine haven's found, fortune and hope, adieu! / Mock others now, for I have done with you.")

*Date:* The NO drafts date from February 1855; notebook NQ was used in the 1860s and 1870s.

*Publication:* Unpublished by Emerson. The second version in NO was published in J 8:518.

## "Free thyself from wo"

*Text:* This translation of Hafiz, Book XXVII, Ode XIX, lines 1–2 (*Diwan* 2:384), appears in EF p. 109. It has not been found elsewhere in Emerson's published or unpublished writings.

## "Freedom"

*Texts:* The first four drafts occur in journal HO (JMN 13:229–32). The fifth, titled, is in Rhymer p. 57, where two lines from a draft passage in EL p. 117 were added between lines 20–21 some time after first publication.

*Date:* The poem was composed between 7 August 1853, when Julia Griffiths wrote to Emerson for a contribution to a projected antislavery volume, and 24 October, when he sent the poem (MS of the letter in the University of Virginia Library, Barrett Collection). Despite the date of 1854 on the title-page, the volume was intended for sale in December 1853 to benefit the Rochester Anti-Slavery Society.

*Publication:* First published with the title "On Freedom" in *Autographs for Freedom,* ed. Julia Griffiths (Auburn and Rochester, 1854), pp. 235–36, in the original 22-line version. The 24-line version (lines added between lines 21–22), titled as above, appears in *May–Day,* 1867, pp. 70–71, and was reprinted in *Poems,* 1884, p. 172 and W 9:198.

## "Friendship" ("A ruddy drop")

*Text:* The only surviving version of this motto is an ink fair copy in X pp. 219–20.

*Date:* The text was probably inscribed in 1847, since it belongs to a group of fair copies of mottoes for the 1847 edition of *Essays: First Series*. It was written over an erased draft of "Mithridates," which was composed in 1846.

*Publication: Essays: First Series,* 1847, p. 173; collected in *May–Day,* 1867, pp. 166–67, with an alteration in line 15, and reprinted in *Selected Poems,* 1876, p. 177, *Poems,* 1884, pp. 232–33, and W 9:274.

## "Friendship" ("Thou foolish Hafiz!")

*Texts:* In journal IO p. 1792 (JMN 13:349–350) Emerson translated Hafiz, Book XIII, Ode I, lines 25–32 (*Diwan* 2:91). The first four lines became "The chemist of love," published in "Persian Poetry," 1858, p. 731. The second four lines were revised separately on the same page of IO, producing a text from which the version in notebook OP Gulistan p. i and Rhymer p. 135 both descend. The OP Gulistan text differs only in having "Reckless Hafiz," in line 1 and "that" in line 3; the Rhymer text is titled "Songs are for heroes."

*Date:* The IO draft appears to date from the summer of 1854.

*Publication:* First published in "Persian Poetry," 1858, p. 729, without title. The lines do not occur in later reprintings of this essay. Published again, with the title "Friendship," in *May–Day,* 1867, p. 199; reprinted in *Poems,* 1884, p. 247, and W 9:300.

## "From Alcuin"

*Texts:* The first draft of the poem occurs in journal VS immediately after the prose source (JMN 13:180). A titled fair copy is in Rhymer p. 61, followed by another copy, corrected, in NP p. 134. An untitled copy, signed and dated "Staten Island 20 May 1857", is in the John D. Batchelder Collection in the Library of Congress; it follows the Rhymer text as corrected.

*Date:* Emerson's note in journal VS is "Alcuin called the Sea, the road of the bold; the frontier of the land; the hostelry of the rivers; & the source of the rains." The poem was probably written in mid-June 1853, since the prose and the verse draft occur in the midst of notes taken from Augustine Thierry,

*History of the Conquest of England by the Normans* (London, 1841), which Emerson borrowed from the Boston Athenaeum on 13 June. The VS draft is followed immediately by a journal entry for 14 June.

*Publication: The Dial* (Cincinnati) 1 (March 1860): 195; collected in *May–Day,* 1867, p. 185, and reprinted in *Poems,* 1884, p. 240, and W 9:293.

*See Also:* "Northman."

## "From Hafiz"

*Texts:* In notebook L Camadeva p. 133, Emerson gives a prose translation of Hafiz, Book XXV, Ode X, lines 9–10 (*Diwan* 2:327); the first four drafts of the poem occur on pp. 132–34. The copies in Rhymer p. 140 and NP p. 119 are nearly identical, though possibly that in NP came first. All the drafts are untitled.

*Date:* Undetermined.

*Publication: May–Day,* 1867, p. 197, with the title as above; reprinted in *Poems,* 1884, p. 246, and W 9:299.

## "From high to higher forces"

*Texts:* Two identical texts occur in journal VO (JMN 14:130) and ETE p. 30.

*Date:* The entry in VO was written in 1857, probably in March or April.

*Publication:* Unpublished by Emerson. First published in *Poems,* 1884, p. 288, and reprinted in W 9:349. The poem is also used as the second motto to "Progress of Culture," W 8:206.

## "From Ibn Jemin"

*Texts:* The poem translates "Merdi asade bibajed neküned meili dü tschis" by Ibn Jemin (Emir Mahmud Ben Jemin Ferjumendi) from *Geschichte,* p. 239. Identical fair copies of the poem occur in notebook Orientalist p. 98, Rhymer p. 127, and Poems folder 46.

*Date:* Undetermined.

*Publication:* First published in "Persian Poetry," 1858, p. 726, though it does not appear in later reprintings of this essay. Published again, with the title as above, in *May–Day,* 1867, p. 201, and reprinted in *Poems,* 1884, p. 248, and W 9:302.

## "From Nature's beginning"

*Texts:* The first draft, on a sheet of paper laid inside the front cover of NP, is revised first on a sheet laid in at the end of journal CD (JMN 10:122–23), then in NP p. 297, and finally in NP p. 61. Lines 5–8 and 13–16 were drawn from "Poet of poets," where they comprise lines 88–95.

*Date:* Undetermined. The lines that derive from "Poet of poets" were composed between 1846 and 1849.

*Publication:* Unpublished by Emerson. First published in JMN 10.

*See Also:* "Poet of poets."

## "From the Persian of Hafiz"

*Texts:* The pencil draft in X pp. 244–53 translates "Sakiname, das Buch der Schenken," lines 1–238, by Hafiz (*Diwan* 2:489–502). Printer's copy for the London edition of *Poems,* 1847, in the Berg Collection, New York Public Library, has numerous revisions (see Additional Manuscripts).

*Date:* Between April 1846, when Emerson acquired his copy of the *Diwan,* and October, when he sent the manuscripts for *Poems,* 1847, to the publishers.

*Publication:* Two significantly different versions of this translation were published in *Poems,* 1847, pp. 209–16 (Boston) and pp. 166–72 (London). In addition to 36 differences in wording, the Boston edition has three lines not in the London edition, and the London edition has four lines not in the Boston edition; the line totals are 155 and 156 respectively. The translation was omitted from all later collections.

## "From the stores of eldest Matter"

*Texts:* A pencil draft of the first three lines of this six-line fragment occurs in journal R p. 135, and is transcribed in pencil on p. 134 (JMN 8:418, 417). All six lines occur in a fair copy in P p. 209.

*Date:* The two pencil texts in R occur between entries of 20 May and 10 June 1843.

*Publication:* Unpublished by Emerson. First published in *Poems,* 1884, pp. 296–97, and reprinted in W 9:356.

## "The Future"

*Texts:* This couplet appears, untitled, in journal A, overwritten by an entry of late November 1834 (JMN 4:345); it was copied in revised form several pages earlier, between entries of 5 and 15 November (JMN 4:334). An ink fair copy, titled, occurs in P p. 33.

*Date:* Presumably November 1834. If, as the editor of JMN 4 speculates (p. 334, n. 241), the couplet is Emerson's adaptation of *Othello* 1.3.377, "There are many events in the womb of time, which will be delivered," then an entry in journal A of 16 August is pertinent: "The remarkable sentences of Lear, Hamlet, Othello, Macbeth, might as naturally have been composed in 1834 as in 1600" (JMN 4:311).

*Publication:* Unpublished by Emerson. First published in J 3:359, from the revised A text.

## "The garden of Eden is the cell of the Dervish"

*Text:* The poem translates Hafiz, Book III, Ode XVII (*Diwan* 1:69–70). The only text is a partially erased pencil draft in X pp. 167–68. Lines 11–12 were quoted as prose in journal AZ (JMN 11:233) and again in notebook Morals p. 282. This prose was used, somewhat altered, in Emerson's "The Fugitive Slave Law" of 1854 (W 11:235).

*Date:* The likelihood is that the verse translation precedes the prose quotation, which dates from 1850. The translations from Hafiz in X include a series from Book III of the *Diwan*, one of which, "Ghaselle: From the Persian of Hafiz," was published in *Poems*, 1847.

*Publication:* Unpublished.

## "Gardener"

*Texts:* An entry in journal E written between 26 and 31 July 1840 includes the first draft of lines 1–2 (JMN 7:386). Nine years later, in journal TU, Emerson added lines 3–4 (see JMN 11:158). Of the copies in the poetry notebooks, the two in X p. 204—one in pencil and the other in ink—are probably the earliest. Fair copies also occur in Rhymer pp. 31 and 32 and in NP p. 134. The X copies are written over a draft of "Terminus."

*Date:* The source for the quatrain is suggested in Emerson's letter to Samuel Gray Ward of 18 July or, more probably, 28 July 1840 (see L 2:314 concerning the discrepancy): "In the sleep of the great heats there was nothing for me but to read the Vedas, the bible of the tropics, which I find I come back upon every three or four years. It is sublime as heat and night and a breathless ocean. It contains every religious sentiment, all the grand ethics which visit in turn each noble and poetic mind, and nothing is easier than to separate what must have been the primeval inspiration from the endless ceremonial nonsense which caricatures and contradicts it through every chapter. It is of no use to put away the book: if I trust myself in the woods or in a boat upon the pond, nature makes a Bramin of me presently: eternal necessity, eternal compensation, unfathomable power, unbroken silence,—this is her creed. Peace, she saith to me, and purity and absolute abandonment—these penances expiate all sin and bring you to the beatitude of the 'Eight Gods.' " (*Letters from Ralph Waldo Emerson to a Friend*, ed. Charles Eliot Norton [Boston, 1899], pp. 28–29). Lines 1–2 were written in the last week of July 1840; the poem as a whole dates from September 1849.

*Publication: The Dial* (Cincinnati) 1 (March 1860): 195; collected in *May–Day*, 1867, p. 184, and reprinted in *Poems*, 1884, p. 239, and W 9:292.

*See Also:* Carl F. Strauch, "The Date of Emerson's 'Terminus,' " *PMLA* 65 (June 1950): 361.

## "The genial spark the poet felt"

*Text:* The only text of this quatrain occurs in pencil in NP p. 79. It has not been found elsewhere in Emerson's published or unpublished writings.

## "Gentle Spring has charmed the earth"

*Texts:* This quatrain, possibly rejected either from "May–Day" or "I leave the book," occurs as a couplet in EF p. 64 and is revised and expanded in NP p. 13. The NP version is copied in EL p. 201.

*Date:* Undetermined.

*Publication:* Unpublished.

## "Ghaselle: From the Persian of Hafiz"

*Texts:* Three successive drafts occur in X pp. 174–75, 176, and 179–80. Printer's copy for the London edition of *Poems*, 1847, is in the Berg Collection, New York Public Library; this has "friend's skirt" for the misprint "friend's shirt" in line 21. The poem translates Hafiz, Book III, Ode XL (*Diwan* 1:106–7).

*Date:* Between April 1846, when Emerson acquired his copy of the *Diwan*, and October, when he sent the manuscripts for *Poems*, 1847, to the publishers.

*Publication: Poems*, 1847, pp. 217–18 (Boston) and pp. 173–74 (London); in the latter, the title is simply "From the Persian of Hafiz" and stanzas 3 and 4 are reversed. The poem was omitted from all later collections.

## "Gifts"

*Texts:* Two identical pencil drafts of this quatrain exist, in notebook Dialling (JMN 8:514) and in P p. 322; in both the subject is "letters."

*Date:* The version in Dialling must have been inscribed in 1842: it is followed by related verses that develop a journal entry of c. 20 March of that year.

*Publication:* First published as the motto to "Gifts" in *Essays: Second Series*, 1844, p. 171, with several revisions, including "Gifts" for "letters" in line 1. Reprinted in W 3:157 and 9:283.

## "Give All to Love"

*Texts:* Of the four drafts of the poem, all in erased pencil, the first three occur in EF pp. 43–45, 47–49, and 51–53. The fourth draft is in X pp. 215–16, the material on p. 216 being overwritten by a fair copy of "Compensation" ("Man's the elm"). The last nine lines on X p. 216 are revised on p. 218, written over an erased draft of "Mithridates."

*Date:* "Give All to Love" and "Hermione" are the only poems originating in EF to be published in *Poems*, 1847. Although these are clearly among the earliest entries in EF, it cannot be determined how long before publication either of these poems was begun. The revisions in X p. 218, however, must date to the summer or early fall of 1846, between July, when "Mithridates" was written, and early October, when the manuscript was sent to the publishers.

*Publication: Poems*, 1847, pp. 141–43 (Boston) and pp. 111–13 (London); reprinted in *Selected Poems*, 1876, pp. 84–85, *Poems*, 1884, pp. 84–85, and W 9:90–92.

## "Go if thou wilt ambrosial Flower"

*Text:* The only draft is in pencil in P p. 133.

*Date:* Undetermined.

*Publication:* Unpublished by Emerson. First published in *Poems,* 1884, p. 294, and reprinted in W 9:355.

## "Go into the garden"

*Text:* The poem appears only in a pencil draft in EF p. 100, with Emerson's symbol of authorship above it.

*Date:* Since a passage used in "The Fugitive Slave Law" (1851) begins below the verse on p. 100, the poem was written no later than that year.

*Publication:* Unpublished.

## "God the Lord save Massachusetts"

*Text:* This six-line poem occurs in EL p. 54 in partially erased pencil. It has not been found elsewhere in Emerson's published or unpublished writings.

## "The gods walk in the breath of the woods"

*Texts:* The first surviving draft is in journal Books Small (JMN 8:475), revised in journal R (JMN 8:412–13). Poems folder 73 contains a fair copy of the R text (see Additional Manuscripts). In these drafts the first line reads: "The gods talk . . . ." Lines 1–8 (beginning "The gods walk . . .") were revised as a separate poem in X p. 109, from which the texts at EL p. 33 and Rhymer p. 50ₐ both descend.

*Date:* The revision in journal R of the longer, 18-line version was done in May or June 1843. The short version may have been done any time thereafter.

*Publication:* Unpublished by Emerson. The longer version was first published (from the Poems folder 73 copy) as lines 73–90 of "The Poet" (a piece assembled by Cabot) in *Poems,* 1884, pp. 255–56, and reprinted in that format in W 9:311–12.

## "Good-Bye"

*Texts:* The earliest version of the poem, in two roughly equal sections, occurs in Wide World XIII (JMN 2:223–24 and 243). The first is an ink draft of lines 1–16, the second an ink fair copy of lines 15–30. These are the source of the ink fair copy in CSA pp. 37–38, which in turn is the source of the ink fair copy in P pp. 5–6. Unhappy with the first stanza, Emerson revised it in pencil on P p. 67, where the line "A river ark on the ocean brine" first appears as an insert. A pencil fair copy follows this draft; it is struck through in pencil and both versions are erased. The new line was subsequently inserted in the fair copy on P pp. 5–6. Printer's copy for *The Western Messenger* is in the Houghton Library, together with Emerson's letter of transmittal to James Freeman Clarke; the printer's copy has "the pride" for "pride" in line 27. A copy of the last stanza, not in Emerson's hand but signed by him and bearing his notation "Concord, May 3, 1878" is in the University of Rochester Library.

*Date:* The first portion of the Wide World XIII text appears between entries dated 22 February and March 1824, the second between entries of 18 April and 2 May. When Emerson sent the manuscript to Clarke on 27 February 1839, he noted that the poem was written "sixteen [actually fifteen] years ago, when I kept school in Boston, and lived in a corner of Roxbury called Canterbury" (Holmes, *Emerson,* p. 129); the CSA text is headed "Canterbury." Relevant to the idea of the poem is Shakespeare's *Romeo and Juliet* 5.1.72: "The world is not thy friend, nor the world's law," quoted in Wide World 9 on 13 March 1823 (JMN 2:101).

*Publication:* First published in *The Western Messenger* 6 (April 1839): 402, with the title "Good-Bye, Proud World!"; collected in *Poems,* 1847, pp. 57–58 (Boston) and pp. 42–43 (London) as "Good-Bye." Emerson later came to dislike the poem as juvenile and omitted it from *Selected Poems,* 1876, but it was included in *Poems,* 1884, pp. 37–38, and Edward Emerson made it the opening poem of the Centenary Edition, W 9:3–4, in place of "The Sphinx."

*See Also:* (1) W 9:403–4, and (2) Kendall B. Taft, "The Byronic Background of Emerson's 'Good-Bye,'" *NEQ* 27 (December 1954): 525–27.

## "Good Charles the springs adorer"

*Text:* The only draft is in pencil in P p. 121.

*Date:* Undetermined. Strauch, diss., p. 521, noting a resemblance of phrasing between this fragment and "The Rhodora," suggests that they may have been composed about the same time—that is, in May 1834. "Charles" is undoubtedly Emerson's brother Charles Chauncy Emerson, who died in May 1836.

*Publication:* Unpublished.

## "Good is what goes on the road of Nature"

*Text:* This translation of the first two lines of Hafiz, Book III, Ode IX (*Diwan* 1:53), occurs in EF p. 105.

*Date:* Undetermined.

*Publication:* Published in prose form in "Persian Poetry," 1858, p. 726, and in the essay as reprinted in *Letters and Social Aims,* 1876, p. 220, and W 8:245.

## "Good sir Take us along with you"

*Text:* The only text of this quatrain occurs in pencil in NP p. 92. It has not been found elsewhere in Emerson's published or unpublished writings.

## "Grace"

*Texts:* The earliest draft of this poem, first noticed by G. R. Elliott in 1928, occurs in faint pencil on the inside front cover of volume 1 of Emerson's copy of *A Selection from the English Prose Works of John Milton* (Boston, 1826), now in the Houghton Library (see Additional Manuscripts). An ink fair copy that omits the fourth and fifth lines of the earlier draft (struck through in the Milton volume) occurs in P p. 235.

*Date:* The date has been variously conjectured. C. P. Hotson (1928) dated it between September and 25 December 1832, on the assumption that the poem was inspired by Sampson Reed's anonymous article, "External Restraint," in the *New Jerusalem Magazine* (see Emerson's comment on the article in JMN 4:45–46); G. R. Elliott (1929) discussed the influence of Milton on the poem and, citing a journal entry for 13 March 1833 (JMN 4:68–69), argued for a date of composition toward the end of the period 1831 to 1833; Strauch opted for "late 1828 to late 1833, with a strong possibility that it was written in the autumn, 1833" (diss., pp. 510–11); J. C. Broderick (1958) agreed with N. A. Brittin (1936) that the poem was probably influenced by Herbert's "Sinne" and noted that Emerson very likely read that poem in late December 1829 in Coleridge's *Aids to Reflection*, ed. James Marsh (Burlington, Vt., 1829), pp. 255–56. This view is supported by the fact that Emerson quoted "Sinne" in his sermon no. 63, delivered 24 January 1830 and again on 4 September 1831.

*Publication:* First published, with the title "Grace," in *The Dial* 2 (January 1842): 373; reprinted, untitled and unattributed, as a motto to chapter 7 of *Memoirs of Margaret Fuller Ossoli* (Boston, 1852), 2:117, of which Emerson was a co-author. On this printing see W 9:510 and L 4:267. Not collected in Emerson's lifetime, "Grace" appeared in *Poems,* 1884, p. 299, and W 9:359.

*See Also:* (1) C. P. Hotson, "A Background for Emerson's Poem 'Grace,' " *NEQ* 1 (April 1928): 124–32; (2) G. R. Elliott, "On Emerson's 'Grace' and 'Self-Reliance,' " *NEQ* 2 (January 1929): 93–104; (3) N. A. Brittin, "Emerson and the Metaphysical Poets," *AL* 8 (March 1936): 1–21; (4) Strauch diss., pp. 63, 65–66, 334 (text) and 509–20 (notes); and (5) J. C. Broderick, "The Date and Source of Emerson's 'Grace,' " *MLN* 73 (February 1958): 91–95.

## "Great & beautiful power"

*Text:* These three lines occur in EL p. 162. They have not been found elsewhere in Emerson's published or unpublished writings.

## "Hafiz"

*Text:* The draft in EF p. 23 was inscribed earlier than, and therefore interrupts, a draft of "The Romany Girl" written between 1855 and 1857. This is probably the earliest version of the quatrain, followed by the version in journal NO (JMN 13:423), which has "Saadi" for "Hafiz" in line 2, and EF p. 50, a fair copy. Other drafts, some with slight variations, occur in notebook PY p. 241, Rhymer p. 66, NP pp. 35 and 136, KL[A] p. 56, KL (JMN 15:464–65), and ETE p. 107.

*Date:* The context of the drafts in NO and EF points to a date of composition of 1855; the KL draft was inscribed in 1865.

*Publication: May–Day,* 1867, p. 190; reprinted in *Poems,* 1884, p. 243, and W 9:296.

*See Also:* (1) J. D. Yohannan, "Emerson's Translations of Persian Poetry from German Sources," *AL* 14 (January 1943): 415–16, and (2) "Poet" ("Ever the Poet").

## "Hafiz since on the world"

*Text:* These lines, which translate Hafiz, Book XXIII, Ode XXXIV, lines 25–28 (*Diwan* 2:209), occur in EF p. 38. They have not been found elsewhere in Emerson's published or unpublished writings.

## "Hafiz thou art from Eternity"

*Text:* These three lines, which translate Hafiz, Book VIII, Ode VII, lines 34–36 (*Diwan* 1:216), occur in EF p. 38. They have not been found elsewhere in Emerson's published or unpublished writings.

## "The Harp"

*Texts:* (Note: This poem was originally conceived and published as a part of "May–Day." Line numbers in the following discussion refer to the first separate form of "The Harp" as given in *Selected Poems*, 1876, though the reader should bear in mind that all drafts before 1867, such as those in KL[A], are in fact drafts of "May–Day.") A fragment consisting of lines 49, 52, 54, and 56 occurs in X p. 106, where it is related to, and probably was written at the same time as, the immediately preceding draft of "He loved to watch" (1859). Lines 99–102 are also very likely earlier in composition than the remainder of the poem, though they were the last to be added. They occur as an independent unit in EL p. 182 (with the title "Aeolian Harp"), in Rhymer p. 50e, where they are part of a cento of Emerson's own verses (including "Old Age," which dates to 1861), and, with a version of lines 41 and 45, in EL p. 193, where Emerson is apparently trying, some time after 1867, to incorporate the lines into "The Harp." Drafts of the greater part of the verses that became "The Harp" occur in KL[A]: of lines 1–60 on pp. 39–43, and of lines 108–20 on p. 47. Apart from the single line 81 in notebook ML p. 278 ("Scott, crowned bard of generous boys"), lines 104–6 in NP p. 238, and lines 87–90 and 116 in EL p. 83, these are all the surviving drafts: no manuscripts containing lines 61–80, 82–86, 91–98, 103, 107, or 121–27 have been discovered.

*Date:* In February or March 1861 Emerson entered in journal GL a meditation on the Aeolian harp and the "delicious sensibility of youth" (JMN 15:118). This appears to be the principal source for the poem, though a few lines are certainly earlier. The fragment in X p. 106, for example, seems to date from 1859; lines 99–102 are perhaps as early, though the third draft of these lines was probably done after 1867. The KL[A] drafts were written in late 1866 (see the analysis of "May–Day").

*Publication:* First published, without lines 99–102, as lines 480–602 of "May–Day" in *May–Day,* 1867, pp. 29–36. These lines were excerpted, and, with the addition of lines 99–102, printed for the first time as "The Harp" in *Selected Poems,* 1876, pp. 120–24. The poem was reprinted in *Poems,* 1884, pp. 203–7, and W 9:237–41.

*See Also:* "He loved to watch."

## "Harp of victory ringing"

*Text:* These lines, possibly rejected from "Boston Hymn," occur in EL p. 59 surrounded by a draft of that poem. They have not been found elsewhere in Emerson's published or unpublished writings.

## "Has God on thee conferred"

*Texts:* Two variant ink fair copies exist: one in Poems folder 19 (see Additional Manuscripts) and another, which omits the twelfth line and with the final stanza struck through, in EL p. 47.

*Date:* The Poems folder 19 text is dated 1831, though the actual inscription of this fair copy probably occurred much later.

*Publication:* Unpublished by Emerson. A conflated text of lines 1–11 was published in *Poems,* 1884, p. 293; lines 12–15 were first published in W 9:398.

*See Also:* W 9:518.

## "Has thine enemy slandered thy house"

*Text:* This two-line fragment, a translation of Hafiz, Book VIII, Ode CLXVII, lines 81–82 (*Diwan* 1:453), occurs in EF p. 108 in a list of entries headed "Ethical" and "Fatal sentences." It has not been found elsewhere in Emerson's published or unpublished writings.

## "Have ye seen the caterpillar"

*Text:* The poem occurs in two fair copies, one in journal No. XV (JMN 2:339), and another, with slight revisions, in NP p. 282.

*Date:* The earlier text dates from 1825.

*Publication:* Unpublished by Emerson. First published in W 9:374 with the nonauthorial title "Riches."

## "Have you not heard of Dr Jewett"

*Text:* The only text of this eight-line jape about an unidentified Dr. Jewett is in pencil in P p. 246, thoroughly canceled by many swirling lines. It has not been found elsewhere in Emerson's published or unpublished writings.

## "He could condense cerulean ether"

*Texts:* Identical texts of this couplet occur in journal CL (JMN 14:325) and EL p. 28.

*Date:* The CL draft occurs among entries for September 1859. The prose source, drawn from the S'wétás'watara Upanishad in Thoreau's copy of *The Taittariya, Aitaréya, . . . Upanishads,* trans. E. Röer (Calcutta, 1853), volume 15 of *Bibliotheca Indica,* p. 68 (see L 5:71), was recorded in journal SO (JMN 14:101) in July 1856.

*Publication:* Unpublished by Emerson. First published in W 9:332.

## "He lives not who can refuse me"

*Texts:* The first draft of this quatrain appears in journal LN with the heading "Song of Nature" (JMN 16:61–62). A slightly revised version of this draft was copied, with the heading, in EL p. 70 and revised further. Another form of the LN draft was copied and revised in EL pp. 232 and 233.

*Date:* The first draft dates from the spring of 1867; it develops a source in journal VA from July 1862: "What was it Goethe said of Nature's tilth? 'This field has been reaped for a thousand years, but lo! a little sun & rain and all is green again' " (JMN 15:274).

*Publication:* Unpublished by Emerson. First published from the EL p. 70 text in *Poems,* 1884, p. 286; published again, in a composite text, in W 9:347.

## "He loved to watch & wake"

*Text:* The only manuscript text of this poem is in X p. 106, indexed "Ripples." The lines that follow on the page, used in "The Harp," are related thematically and were probably written at the same time.

*Date:* The source of the lines is a prose passage in X p. 117, which derives from an 1859 entry in journal AC headed "Ripple Pond": "The rippling of the pond under a gusty south wind . . . gives the like delight to the eye, as the fitful play of the same wind on the Aeolian harp to the ear. Or the darting & scud of ripples is like the auroral shootings in the night heaven" (JMN 14:246; cf. 7:491). A version of this entry was used in "Inspiration" (W 8:288). Probably the verses were written in 1859.

*Publication:* Unpublished by Emerson. First published in *Poems,* 1884, p. 264, and reprinted in W 9:321–22, as, in both instances, lines 35–42 of "There are beggars." In no surviving manuscript, however, are these lines associated with a draft of that unfinished poem: the assumption must be that they were interpolated by Cabot.

*See Also:* W 8:426–27.

## "He must have / Droll fancies"

*Texts:* The full text of this poem is an ink fair copy in CSA pp. 3–7. The first fifty-five lines appear in ink in journal 1826–1828 (JMN 3:84–85) and are clearly the source of the corresponding lines in CSA.

*Date:* At the bottom of CSA p. 5 Emerson wrote "Charleston S.C. 1826" (corrected from "1827"), implying a date after 7 December when he arrived in that city. However, because this date falls in the middle of a sentence (between lines 60–61), it is unclear whether it is to be taken as referring to the first fifty-five or the first sixty-six lines. The date "16 Aug." at the beginning of line 67 indicates that the remainder of the poem was written the following summer.

*Publication:* Unpublished by Emerson. First published from the CSA text in J 2:197–201.

*See Also:* Strauch diss., pp. 56–57.

## "He walked the streets of great New York"

*Text:* The only text is a pencil draft in P pp. 159–60.

*Date:* The verses derive from Emerson's lecture trip to New York from 25 February to 15 March 1842 and were probably written shortly after his return to Concord. See his letters of this period (L 3:17–30) and the entry in journal K between 20 and 23 March (JMN 8:204) for similarities of language and idea. In journal W, kept from March to September 1845, Emerson wrote retrospectively, "Like to like, or, as I wrote in New-York, —⟨I met no gods,— I harboured none.)" (JMN 9:206).

*Publication:* Unpublished.

## "He was the sunshine of our cause"

*Text:* This single line appears in pencil in P p. 73. It has not been found elsewhere in Emerson's published or unpublished writings. Possibly it was intended for "Woodnotes, I," a passage of which, also in pencil, occurs on the preceding page.

## "He who has a thousand friends has not a friend to spare"

*Texts:* In journal NO Emerson quoted the prose source (attributed to Ali Ben Abi Taleb, though the source has not been identified) and versified it in two drafts (JMN 13:425–26). The result was copied, with one word change, into Rhymer p. 141 and Poems folder 36.

*Date:* An entry in journal TU (JMN 11:100) shows that Emerson knew the prose form as early as 1849, though his versification in NO dates to April or May 1855. A year later he was planning to use this material in "Considerations by the Way" (JMN 14:56).

*Publication:* First published in "Persian Poetry," 1858, p. 726, though it does not appear in later reprintings of this essay. Published again in "Considerations by the Way," *Conduct of Life*, 1860, p. 240 (see W 6:273), and collected in *May–Day*, 1867, p. 200. Reprinted in *Poems*, 1884, p. 248, and W 9:302.

*See Also:* JMN 16:51.

## "The healthy youth distils"

*Text:* The only text of this twelve-line fragment occurs in pencil in NP p. 26; it may be related to "May–Day," lines from which occur on many of the preceding and following pages. It has not been found elsewhere in Emerson's published or unpublished writings.

## "Hear what the glass will tell thee"

*Text:* This four-line fragment, a translation of Hafiz, Book XXIII, Ode X, lines 29–32 (*Diwan* 2:165), occurs in EF p. 109. It has not been found elsewhere in Emerson's published or unpublished writings.

## "Heartily heartily"

*Text:* The only text is in ink in X p. 268$_a$. The relationship of this fragment to those that follow in this lengthy insert is undetermined.

*Date:* The poems in the insert appear to belong to the period 1846–1847.

*Publication:* Unpublished.

## "Heartily heartily sing"

*Texts:* An eight-line draft fragment occurs in ink, canceled in ink, in X p. 268$_{dd}$. The entire poem occurs in ink in X p. 268$_f$.

*Date:* The poems in this insert appear to belong to the period 1846–1847. Rail service between Boston and Montreal opened in 1851 (see lines 20–21).

*Publication:* Unpublished.

## "Hearts secret of love speaks"

*Text:* These four lines, a translation of Hafiz, Book XXVII, Ode LX, lines 9–12 (*Diwan* 2:445), occur in EF p. 55. They have not been found elsewhere in Emerson's published or unpublished writings.

## "Heaven"

*Texts:* The earliest version of this three-line verse occurs, untitled, in Poems folder 96, where it is accompanied by a rejected fourth line: "Each doth suffice unto itself". The poem was copied in journal A (JMN 4:341) between entries of 19 and 21 November 1834 (untitled); in P p. 33 (titled, with "and" for "but" in line 3); in EL p. 292 (untitled); in ETE pp. 104$_c$ (untitled) and 174 (titled); and in notebook Parnassus p. 82 (untitled). Three late transcriptions occur in Pocket Diaries: see JMN 16:468 (1874), 497 (1877), and 507 (1878). A signed, undated fair copy is in the Houghton Library.

*Date:* The journal A draft of November 1834 supplies the only reliable evidence as to date, though the Poems folder 96 draft, to judge by context and handwriting, may have been inscribed as much as ten years earlier.

*Publication:* Unpublished by Emerson. First published, untitled, in *Poems,* 1884, p. 297, from the P text, as the "and" in line 3 makes clear. Reprinted in W 9:395 and in J 3:368 (from the A text) with the note "When some friend asked Mr. Emerson to write something in an album, he often wrote these lines."

## "The heavy blue chain"

*Texts:* This poem descends from a prose source in journal DO (JMN 13:32) in two versions that produce almost distinct poems. The first stage includes a versification of the source in NP p. 111, with "o just man" in line 3 canceled for "Malone" (unidentified); a copy of the unrevised version in notebook PY p. 200; and a repetition of the prose source in notebook WO Liberty, with a different verse rendition and two succeeding lines that may be an attempt to continue the poem (JMN 14:423). The second stage begins with an erased pencil draft in EL p. 54 in which line 3 is different and the poem is extended to six lines; this version was copied on p. 55 and then recopied, with "Let" added to the beginning of line 1, over the pencil draft on p. 54. Texts in ETE p. 171 and Poems folder 62 follow the second EL version ("The heavy . . ."), while texts in folder 31 (two examples, the second canceled; see Additional Manuscripts under "Boston") and on an enclosure between pp. 122–23 of notebook QL follow the third ("Let the heavy . . ."). Poems folder 88 contains yet another version that was not further developed: "The heavy blue chain of the boundless main / ⟨Didst thou⟩ / Was bound about the man of Pain" (see Additional Manuscripts under "Boston," manuscript 1).

*Date:* The source is a prose translation of the "Preiddeu Annwn" ("Spoils of the Deep") of Taliesin in Edward Davies, *The Mythology and Rites of the British Druids* (London, 1809), p. 515, which Emerson borrowed from the Boston Athenaeum from 8 to 17 July 1852. The text in WO Liberty dates from 1857; it is evidently related in that location to a draft of "Ode. Sung in . . . Concord, 4 July 1857." The poem usually appears in association with lines used in "Boston" and "Voluntaries." The draft in Poems folder 88 may have been an attempt to adapt the first two lines into a refrain for "Boston."

*Publication:* Unpublished by Emerson. First published, in the unrevised NP version, in *Poems,* 1884, p. 315 with the nonauthorial title "The Exile (After Taliessin)" and reprinted in W 9:376. Emerson used the prose source in "Poetry and Imagination," *Letters and Social Aims,* 1876, p. 52, and later reprintings including W 8:59.

## "Her heart is wider than the North"

*Texts:* The first draft of this quatrain is in erased pencil in EL p. 127, over-written by a revised copy in ink. It has not been found elsewhere in Emerson's published or unpublished writings.

## "Heri, Cras, Hodie"

*Texts:* Lines 3–4 were evidently worked over several times before being joined to the first couplet to make the quatrain. The sequence of these reworkings cannot be established, though the draft in EF p. 10 may be the earliest. Other versions of lines 3–4 occur in Poems folder 79 ("Of mystery no stricter hold / Friendless Present than thy fold"), notebook PY p. 241, journal NO (JMN 13:413), X p. 155, EF p. 116, and ETE p. 175. At X p. 155 Emerson added the couplet to lines 22–23 of "Pour the wine!," while at EF p. 116 it follows an early draft of "The Test." Probably the earliest versions of the quatrain as a whole are those in journal NO (JMN 13:418 and 453), followed by drafts in Rhymer p. 69 (where the title and the last two lines were added to a draft of lines 1–2), X p. 2, NP pp. 3 and 133, and ETE p. 176. The last five are substantially identical to the published text. A signed copy of lines 3–4 is in an autograph album begun by John Endicott Peabody, now in the Houghton Library.

*Date:* The proximity of the several stages of composition in journal NO strongly suggests that the poem arrived quickly at its final form and that it was the work of the spring and summer of 1855. (On the significance of EF p. 116, see "The Test," below.) The title comes from an anecdote copied into journal IO from the *Memoirs of Samuel Pepys* (London, 1825), 1:179, between 11 September and 14 October 1854 (see JMN 13:361). An unlocated prose source, perhaps based on a passage from "Self-Reliance" (see W 2:67), was copied and revised in journal AC (JMN 14:211).

*Publication: The Dial* (Cincinnati) 1 (February 1860): 131, with the title "Cras, heri, hodie"; reprinted with the corrected title in *May–Day,* 1867, p. 188, *Poems,* 1884, p. 242, and W 9:295.

## "Hermione"

*Texts:* The earliest draft, in erased pencil in EF pp. 62–63, is revised in three successive erased drafts in X pp. 183–85, 187–90, and 191–94. Each text begins with line 8. The phrase "Out of the forest", possibly a version of line 56, occurs in pencil in P p. 31. The unlocated printer's copy for the London edition of *Poems,* 1847, was listed in sale catalogue no. 346 issued by Maggs Brothers of London in 1916 and the first page (lines 1–20) reproduced in facsimile; the manuscript was again offered for sale by Maggs Brothers in 1923.

*Date:* The text in X p. 185 is overwritten in ink by the first draft of a portion of "Not yet, not yet" that Emerson quoted in second draft form in a letter to

Lidian of 14 June 1841 (L 2:404–5). Also in 1841 Emerson used the name "Hermione" to refer to Caroline Sturgis (JMN 8:51).

*Publication: Poems,* 1847, pp. 151–55 (Boston) and pp. 119–22 (London). Reprinted in *Selected Poems,* 1876, pp. 94–96, *Poems,* 1884, pp. 89–92, and W 9:100–103.

## "Heroes are /wrought/formed/ in Freedom's wars"

*Text:* This couplet occurs in pencil in EL p. 294. It has not been found elsewhere in Emerson's published or unpublished writings.

## "Heroism"

*Texts:* The earliest surviving text, in X p. 268$_{dd}$, is revised and expanded by the addition of four unused lines in X p. 268$_e$.

*Date:* The first of the unused lines recalls an entry in journal V of 1844 or 1845, "Society is babyish" (JMN 9:108), though the poem was evidently written in 1846–1847, the date of the X insert.

*Publication:* First published as the motto to "Heroism" in *Essays: First Series,* 1847, p. 221, and included in later editions and reprintings including W 2:243. Collected in *May–Day,* 1867, p. 163, and reprinted in *Poems,* 1884, p. 231, and W 9:272.

## "His home / Where the pure drops trickle down"

*Texts:* The first two drafts of this fragment occur in EL p. 80, followed by a third in Rhymer p. 2$_b$.

*Date:* Undetermined, though the material in the Rhymer insert (pp. 2$_a$–2$_b$) seems to date from the early to mid 1860s.

*Publication:* Unpublished.

## "His instant thought the Poet spoke"

*Texts:* The first draft of the verse, in journal LN p. 117 (JMN 16:36), was revised on p. 22 (JMN 16:9–10); further revisions followed in ETE p. 104$_c$, EL pp. 294 and 295, NP p. 295, and Rhymer p. 2$_a$.

*Date:* The prose source of this quatrain is in an entry in journal KL (JMN 15:460): "The thunderbolt /falls/strikes/ ⟨but in⟩ on an inch of ground, but the light of it fills the horizon." This became more explicitly a metaphor for thought in the revised version entered in notebook JK (JMN 10:368). The prose dates to 1865; the first verse draft occurs between entries dated 31 August and 13 September 1866.

*Publication:* Unpublished by Emerson. First published in *Poems*, 1884, p. 277, apparently from the NP text, and reprinted in W 9:334.

## "His learning truly lifted Hafiz to Heaven"

*Text:* This two-line fragment, translating Hafiz, Book XXIII, Ode XXXII, lines 15–16 (*Diwan* 2:205), occurs only in EF p. 50. It is overwritten by the second draft of "Hafiz."

*Date:* Between 1851, the probable date of the preceding lines from "The Chartist's Complaint," and 1855, the date of "Hafiz."

*Publication:* Unpublished.

## "History & prophecy are alike"

*Text:* This seven-line fragment occurs in pencil in EL p. 190.

*Date:* After August 1858, the earliest possible date of composition of "For Nature true & like," which precedes it on the page.

*Publication:* Unpublished.

## "Hold of the Maker, not the Made"

*Texts:* Numerous texts of this couplet exist, in four forms: (1) "Hold of the Maker, not the Made, / Sit with the Cause, or grim or glad": P p. 287, Rhymer p. 50$_f$, NP front cover verso$_c$ and pp. 6, 43, and 299, EL p. 155, and notebook PY p. 204; (2) "I hold of the Maker not of the Made, / I sit with the Cause or grim or glad": journal AC (JMN 14:241); (3) "Of the Maker not the Made / Dwell with the Cause or grim or glad": Poems folder 38 (see Additional Manuscripts under "Boston Hymn"); and (4) "We are of the makers / As of the made / By us also the game is played": X p. 268$_m$. The versions in NP pp. i and 299 and EL p. 155 carry the subject heading "Poet."

*Date:* Undetermined, though presumably in the early 1840s. The two lines of the couplet have different prose sources in journal E. The first occurs in an entry written between 13 and 19 April 1841: "I am of the Maker not of the Made" (JMN 7:428–29); these words also occur on a loose sheet laid in at this point. (A variant version occurs in "Fate," W 6:26.) The second occurs in an entry of 7 October 1840: "I sit at home with the cause grim or glad" (JMN 7:404), used in "Self-Reliance" (W 2:71). The two sentences occur on facing manuscript pages in notebook Index Minor (JMN 12:524), where their proximity may have suggested to Emerson that he combine them; the entries were made in late 1843. The X insert associates the lines with an early draft of "Compensation" ("Man's the elm"), written in 1846 or 1847. The text of the couplet in AC dates from the period February-May 1859, when this journal was in use.

*Publication:* Unpublished by Emerson. First published in *Poems,* 1884, p. 274, and reprinted in W 9:331.

*See Also:* W 12:46.

## "Holidays"

*Texts:* A pencil fair copy, with title, occurs in P p. 255. Printer's copy for the London edition of *Poems,* 1847, is in the Berg Collection, New York Public Library; this has "to" canceled for "in" in line 8 and "Where is now" canceled for "Whither went" in line 13.

*Date:* Between April 1841 and June 1842. An entry in journal E, between 24 April and 4 May 1841, is clearly the source of stanzas 1–2: "We must play sometimes. Six months, from October to April or May, the acorn lends itself as a plaything to the children; but now, in May, its game is over: would you lift the pretty fruit from the ground? behold, it is anchored to the spot by a stout & strenuous root of six inches or more & is already no acorn but an oak" (JMN 7:440). Stanzas 3–4 may have been suggested by journal entries for 12 and 16 April 1837 (JMN 5:297–98). The poem was published in July 1842.

*Publication: The Dial* 3 (July 1842): 73; collected, with revisions, in *Poems,* 1847, pp. 206–7 (Boston) and pp. 164–65 (London), and reprinted in *Poems,* 1884, pp. 119–20, and W 9:136.

*See Also:* "Each and All," lines 29–36, for similarities to stanzas 3–4.

## "Honor bright o muse"

*Text:* This five-line fragment occurs in EL p. 102$_d$. It has not been found elsewhere in Emerson's published or unpublished writings.

## "Horoscope"

*Texts:* The first draft of the poem occurs in notebook Orientalist p. 22, where, though it follows a translation of "The Phoenix," it is signed "R. W. E." to indicate that it is an original composition. Later copies, all substantially identical, occur in NP pp. 133 (with the title "Nativity" canceled and "Horoscope" added) and 140 (with the title "Fate"), Rhymer p. 53 (with the title "Nativity"), and in notebook EO p. 59 (untitled).

*Date:* The prose source for lines 3–4 occurs in journal AB (JMN 10:34) under the heading "Horoscope": "When he comes forth from his mother's womb, the gate of gifts closes behind him" (used in "Fate," W 6:10–11). This passage was written between 25 March and 5 April 1847, while the Orientalist draft is probably no earlier than 1850, the apparent date of "The Phoenix." Although Edward Emerson claimed there was an Oriental source for the poem (W 9:498), none has been located. Possibly he was misled by the occurrence of the first draft in Orientalist.

*Publication:* May–Day, 1867, p. 187; reprinted in *Poems*, 1884, p. 241, and W 9:294.

## "The House"

*Texts:* The earliest draft is that in erased pencil in X pp. 57 (lines 1–8 and 17–24) and 56 (lines 9–16). The whole poem, with title, was then written out in pencil on pp. 59–60 and subsequently erased; this version is indexed in X as "Building Muse." Printer's copy for the London edition of *Poems*, 1847, is in the Berg Collection, New York Public Library.

*Date:* Undetermined.

*Publication:* Poems, 1847, pp. 195–96 (Boston) and pp. 155–56 (London). Excluded from *Selected Poems*, 1876, and *Poems*, 1884, "The House" was reprinted in W 9:128–29.

## "How drearily in College hall"

*Texts:* This unfinished 16-line poem was rejected from "Waldeinsamkeit" and revised separately. The first drafts are in journal VO (JMN 14:181–83 and 186–87, where the lines in question are noted as having been used in "Walden"; see, however, the *Publication* note, below). The next draft, in EL p. 156, organizes and revises all four stanzas. Lines 1–4 were then separately revised in NP p. 198, and the remainder in Rhymer p. 96ₑ after lines 5–7 had first been revised in EL p. 225.

*Date:* The VO drafts, from which "Waldeinsamkeit" emerged, were written in the summer of 1857. Lines 5–8 have their source in a journal entry for 1857: "But 'tis the Northwind that thinks, & whatever it blows through,— is it pinewood or biped,—thinks rightly & beautifully" (JMN 14:139).

*Publication:* Unpublished by Emerson. First published in W 9:372, where Edward Emerson printed the lines as a new ending to a poem ("In my garden three ways meet") to which Cabot, in *Poems,* 1884, pp. 307–9, had given the nonauthorial title "Walden."

*See Also:* (1) "In my garden three ways meet," (2) "My Garden," and (3) "Waldeinsamkeit."

## "How old our names are!"

*Text:* The only text of these two lines occurs in X p. 114. In "Poetry and Imagination" Emerson wrote, "See how tenacious we are of the old names" (W 8:25).

*Date:* Undetermined.

*Publication:* Unpublished.

## "A howling wolf that by Potomac ran"

*Text:* The only text of this tercet occurs in NP p. 218.

*Date:* In his notes on NP, Edward Emerson lists p. 218 as "a trial for a war poem." The fragment is, however, closely related to "The land was all electric," a poem about John Brown which follows on the same page. Both poems were undoubtedly written shortly after Brown's arrest at Harpers Ferry on 18 October 1859.

*Publication:* Unpublished.

*See Also:* "The land was all electric."

## "The Humble-Bee"

*Texts:* Traces of a rough draft occur in erased pencil in P pp. 189–90, and possibly on p. 188, though nothing has been recovered from the latter page.

A pencil fair copy, untitled, occurs in P pp. 182–84. The manuscript that Emerson sent to James Freeman Clarke in a letter of 7 December 1838 for publication in *The Western Messenger* survives in the Houghton Library. What may be printer's copy for the London edition of *Poems*, 1847, is also in Houghton; this has lines 11–14 of the *Western Messenger* text canceled, "Portly" canceled for "Burly" in line 1, and "summer" canceled for "sunny" in line 28 (*Poems* lineation). Another copy, in the Manuscript Division, New York Public Library, was written out for R. H. Stoddard in October 1858 (see L 5:120); it follows the American *Poems* text. A signed fair copy of lines 1–6, with the revised form of line 1 and "zoul" for "zone" in line 6, is in the Duke University Library.

*Date:* In a journal entry for 9 May 1837, Emerson wrote, "Yesterday in the woods I followed the fine humble bee with rhymes & fancies fine" (JMN 5:327). On 14 May he wrote, "The humblebee & the pine warbler seem to me the proper objects of attention in these disastrous times" (JMN 5:327).

*Publication: The Western Messenger* 6 (February 1839): 239–41, with the title "To the Humble-Bee." When Emerson reprinted the poem in *Poems*, 1847, pp. 60–63 (Boston) and pp. 45–47 (London), he changed the title to "The Humble-Bee" and made several revisions. These include the rewriting of line 1, the elimination of four lines at the beginning of the second stanza, and the addition, in the middle of the fifth stanza, of four lines taken from his uncompleted poem "Where the fungus broad & red."

*See Also:* Strauch diss., pp. 66–67.

## "Humility"

*Texts:* Identical drafts of this translation from Hafiz occur in ink in notebook Orientalist p. 8 and notebook Morals p. 40. The draft in Orientalist was revised in pencil, and the result copied into Rhymer p. 151, where it is noted as "printed." The Orientalist draft gives the title as above, and notes the source as "I 196" (i.e., Hafiz, *Diwan* 1:196), though in fact it matches nothing at that location.

*Date:* Its occurrence so early in Orientalist suggests a date before 1850.

*Publication:* First published, in a text differing slightly from any of the manuscripts, in "Worship," *The Conduct of Life*, 1860, p. 204, and in subsequent editions and printings including W 6:234.

## "Hush!"

*Texts:* Eight manuscript texts exist: (1) two in light pencil, untitled, in journal Books Small (JMN 8:466–67); (2) an ink fair copy, untitled, in P p. 22, an amalgam of the Books Small texts; (3) an ink fair copy, following the P text, with title and the notation "printed", in Rhymer p. 63; (4) an ink fair copy, with title and variants, in NP p. 139; and (5) three ink versions in Poems folder 28, all following the P text except for line 2 of one version, which reads "Through the world so wide".

*Date:* Undetermined, but possibly 1842. The quatrain is followed in P, Rhymer, and Poems folder 28 (twice) by the couplet "Atom from atom," and in Books Small only eleven pages separate the two. Since the couplet dates from early May 1842, this may also be the time of composition of the quatrain. The relation of this poem to prose sources is highly problematical since no passage by itself provides a convincing parallel. In August 1837, Emerson received an invitation to speak at the Salem Lyceum, "provided no allusions are made to religious controversy, or other exciting topics upon which the public mind is honestly divided." Emerson declined the invitation, and, concluding his discussion of the matter in journal C, quoted an epigram: "The motto on all palace gates is *Hush*" (JMN 5:376). Writing in "Compensation" on public censorship, Emerson noted that "every suppressed or expunged word reverberates through the earth from side to side" (W 2:120). Some of the humor of the tone and phrasing may derive from a different source: in "The Over-Soul" he wrote, "I feel [that] . . . in my trivial conversation with my neighbors, . . . somewhat higher in each of us overlooks this by-play, and Jove nods to Jove from behind each of us" (W 2:278, cf. JMN 7:413–14, an entry for 20 January 1841).

*Publication: May–Day,* 1867, p. 182; reprinted in *Poems,* 1884, p. 238, and W 9:291.

*See Also:* "Atom from atom."

## "I am owner of the sphere"

*Texts:* This quatrain occurs in notebook F No. 1 (JMN 12:144) and in an ink fair copy in P p. 23. The first has "Jesus" in the last line and the second "Lord Christ", the reading in the published version.

*Date:* Since F No. 1, an index notebook, was used between 1836 and 1840, and since the quatrain occurs following entries inscribed in 1839, composition in 1839 or 1840 is likely. An entry in journal D, written between 19 and 21 June 1838 (JMN 7:26), may be relevant: certainly Emerson read the passage when compiling the index in F No. 1. The prose immediately preceding the draft in F No. 1 has its source in journal C, March 1838 (JMN 5:470).

*Publication:* This quatrain and the one that precedes it in P p. 23 ("There is no great and no small") appear as mottoes to "History" in *Essays: First*

*Series*, 1841, pp. 2 and 1 respectively, and in subsequent editions and reprintings. They do not appear in any collection of Emerson's poetry in his lifetime nor in *Poems*, 1884. In W 9:282 they are gathered as parts II and I of "The Informing Spirit," a nonauthorial title.

*See Also:* "There is no great and no small."

## "I am: what I am"

*Text:* These two lines occur as lines 11–12 in a translation ("So long as there's a trace") of Hafiz, Book VIII, Ode L (*Diwan* 1:278–79), in EF pp. 89–90.

*Date:* Since lines 21–24 of the longer translation occur in journal CD (JMN 10:68), apparently in 1847, the first draft must have been composed either in 1846, when Emerson acquired his copy of the *Diwan*, or 1847.

*Publication:* "Persian Poetry," 1858, p. 728, and in the essay as collected in *Letters and Social Aims*, 1876, p. 225, and reprinted in W 8:250.

## "I batter the wheel of heaven"

*Texts:* The quatrain translates Hafiz, Book XXI, Ode I, lines 21–24 (*Diwan* 2:125). Three successive drafts are in notebook Orientalist p. 177, Rhymer p. 146, and journal VO (JMN 14:131).

*Date:* Only the third draft can be dated: it was written in March or April 1857.

*Publication:* "Persian Poetry," 1858, p. 726, and in the essay as reprinted in *Letters and Social Aims*, 1876, p. 220, and W 8:244–45.

## "I call her beautiful;—she says"

*Text:* An ink fair copy is in CSA p. 26.

*Date:* CSA bears the notation "Pepperell, [Massachusetts] Sept. 1829—". In that month Emerson and Ellen Tucker, with her mother and sister, were making a tour of Massachusetts and Connecticut prior to their marriage on 30 September. They evidently stopped at Pepperell, briefly, on 11 September (see L 1:282–84).

*Publication:* Unpublished by Emerson. First published in J 2:266.

*See Also:* (1) "Dear Ellen, many a golden year" and (2) *One First Love*, p. 102.

## "I cannot find a place so lonely"

*Text:* The first and second verse drafts are in notebook Dialling (JMN 8:514 and 491), transcribed in pencil in X pp. 102–3 and erased.

*Date:* The source of the poem is an entry in journal K, "I cannot get into a sufficiently private place, I cannot get enough alone to write a letter to one whom I love" (JMN 8:204, used in "Society and Solitude," W 7:4). This entry falls between others of 20 and 23 March 1842. Emerson used Dialling in 1841 and 1842.

*Publication:* Unpublished by Emerson. First published in JMN 8.

## "I care not whither I may go"

*Texts:* The first draft is in journal DL (JMN 15:11). This is followed by fair copies in EL p. 229 and ETE p. 132, and a revised version, descending from the EL text, in Rhymer p. 96ᶠ.

*Date:* The first draft appears to have been done in 1860 or 1861. The EL draft is headed "Albany"; Emerson was in Albany, N.Y., on 26 December 1862 and on three or four occasions in 1865 (12–14 January, 10 February, 30 November, and possibly 7 December).

*Publication:* Unpublished by Emerson. First published in JMN 15.

## "I found this"

*Texts:* The first draft of this poem, a work that Emerson never brought to final form, occurs in pencil in journal V (JMN 9:169–70), broken into two segments of eight and twenty lines respectively. The first segment was copied in pencil in P p. 284 and in ink in Poems folder 17, where it is preceded by a six-and-a-half line fragment ("The civil world") that first appears in a pencil draft in journal Books Small (JMN 8:476) and also in erased pencil in EF p. 8 (see Additional Manuscripts under "The civil world"). The journal V draft of the whole poem was revised in ink in EF pp. 30–31, where it is written, without a break into segments, over a passage of "The Fugitive Slave Law" (1851); this draft was in turn revised in Poems folder 78 (see Additional Manuscripts), producing a version of the second segment that was copied, with slight revisions, in P pp. 285–86. (A proofsheet of the text in folder 78, with several corrections in ink and "heart" for "hearth" in line 28, is laid in between pp. 16–17 of Rhymer; see Plate 7.) In P the poem is associated with

823

the second draft of the first segment, from which it is separated only by a draft of "S. H." on p. 285. Later drafts of the second segment occur by themselves: first in Poems folder 5, in ink with pencil revisions, and in Poems folder 23, lacking five lines (see Additional Manuscripts for both texts); in journal IO (JMN 13:353), lacking three lines and headed "Quotation"; in ink in journal NO p. 65 (JMN 13:402–3), lacking the final ten lines and called "one of my Saadi scraps of verse"; and, finally, in ETE p. 27, again lacking the final ten lines. The first two lines of the second segment also occur in pencil in Rhymer p. 52 as a cross reference with the notation "see NO 65".

*Date:* The pencil draft in V must have been composed between May 1844 and March 1845, the period of use of this journal. Probably the first segment was entered in P p. 284 shortly thereafter, since at any later date Emerson's tendency would have been to put it in X. The text of the second segment in P pp. 285–86 is later than that of the first segment, as evidenced by the fact that it is in a darker shade of pencil and that a draft of "S. H." (written not earlier than 1852) intervenes. The fragment that Emerson experimentally prefixed to the first segment in Poems folder 17 ("The civil world") dates from 1840–1843, the period of primary use of journal Books Small, in which a first draft appears. The EF draft of the entire poem (without prefix) was done in 1851 or later since it is written over "Fugitive Slave Law" material. The IO and NO drafts of the second segment date from 1854 and 1855, respectively. As Edward Emerson suggested (W 2:444), a passage in "Art" from *Essays: First Series* (W 2:361–62) may have been a source for the conclusion of the poem (cf. JMN 7:222–23).

*Publication:* Unpublished by Emerson. First published in *Poems,* 1884, pp. 266–67, with the prefatory six-and-a-half lines from Poems folder 17, which Cabot evidently regarded as the intended preface to the entire poem. His text of the second segment is a conflation of the P and Poems folder 5 texts. Cabot's text of 1884 was reprinted in W 9:323–24.

## "I grieve that better souls than mine"

*Texts:* The first two drafts—a ten- and a nine-line version—occur among passages relating to "Saadi" in notebook Dialling (JMN 8:514–15). A couplet resembling lines 5–6 occurs in journal Books Small p. 59 (JMN 8:459). The nine-line draft at X p. 161, with the heading "Saadi," precedes the eight-line version in X p. 265. The last copy, an eight-line version in ink, occurs in Poems folder 23; it is the same as the X p. 265 version except that "and" is canceled for "or" in line 7. The poem is associated in most of these locations with other "Saadi" fragments including "Said Saadi,—When I stood before" and "The Dervish whined to *Said*" as well as the non-"Saadi" poem "Ever find me dim regards."

*Date:* The "Saadi" fragments in Dialling were written in the spring or summer of 1842.

*Publication:* Unpublished by Emerson. First published in *Poems*, 1884, p. 270, along with "Ever find me dim regards." This combination was reprinted in W 9:327.

## "I have an arrow that can find its mark"

*Texts:* The first line is written as prose in journal VO, with the second line added in pencil (JMN 14:134). Two versions in verse form occur in NP p. 71 and ETE p. 29.

*Date:* The entry in journal VO was written in 1857, probably in April.

*Publication:* Unpublished by Emerson. First published in *Poems*, 1884, p. 315, and reprinted in W 9:376.

## "I have found a nobler love"

*Text:* This quatrain appears in pencil in P p. 178. It has not been found elsewhere in Emerson's published or unpublished writings.

## "I have no brothers & no peers"

*Text:* The only manuscript text is a pencil fair copy in X p. 24.

*Date:* Early 1845. The source of lines 3–4 is a sentence in journal V: "The sun & moon are in my way when I would be solitary" (JMN 9:131); the entry follows immediately after notes copied from a book borrowed from the Boston Athenaeum from 16 January to 11 February 1845.

*Publication:* Unpublished by Emerson. First published in *Poems*, 1884, p. 275, with supplied punctuation, and reprinted in W 9:332.

## "I have no hoarded treasure"

*Texts:* The quatrain first appears as lines 13–16 of a translation of Hafiz, Book VIII, Ode LV, lines 1–24 (*Diwan* 1:285), in journal CD (JMN 10:67–

68). Identically revised versions of these four lines occur in notebook Orientalist p. 25 and Rhymer p. 129, though the context shows that the quatrain was copied into, rather than from, Rhymer. Printer's copy for *The Liberty Bell* is in the University of Texas Library.

*Date:* Although the draft of the entire ode in CD was done in 1847, many of the translations in the early pages of Orientalist can be dated to 1850, especially those that were copied into Rhymer. This fact, together with the date of "October, 1850" appearing with the *Liberty Bell* contributions (p. 81), points to its separation and revision in that year.

*Publication: The Liberty Bell* (Boston, 1851), p. 81, follows the manuscript in the reading "I truly have no treasure" for line 1, but erroneously adds the quatrain to the end of "The Poet" ("Hoard knowledge"), ignoring Emerson's short double rules above and below the lines. When the quatrain was published in "Persian Poetry," 1858, p. 729, the first line read as given above. This text appears in the essay as reprinted in *Letters and Social Aims*, 1876, p. 228, and W 8:253. The *Liberty Bell* text was reprinted in *Uncollected Writings*, 1912, p. 188.

*See Also:* "The world is a bride," which translates lines 17–19 of the same ode.

## "I leave the book, I leave the wine"

*Texts:* The first draft, consisting of lines 2–6 and 8, occurs in partially erased pencil in EF p. 8. A revised version in ink occurs in EF pp. 63–64 in the midst of an extended sequence of lines (pp. 61–70) intended for "May–Day." This entire sequence was revised in ink in NP pp. 7–27, in which "I leave the book," lengthened to eight lines, falls on pp. 11 and 13. A seven-line version revised into third person and past tense for use with some Saadi fragments appears in Poems folder 23 (see Additional Manuscripts). The NP text appears in fair copies in NP front cover verso$_e$ (with a variant in line 1) and EL p. 201. In three instances (EF pp. 63–64, NP pp. 11 and 13, and EL p. 201) the poem precedes "Gentle Spring has charmed the earth."

*Date:* The second draft, written over a passage from "The Fugitive Slave Law" (1851), must be from that year or later. A source for the poem, and for line 3 in particular, occurs in an entry in journal D for 25 November 1838 (JMN 7:158–59).

*Publication:* Unpublished by Emerson. The Poems folder 23 text was published in *Poems*, 1884, p. 267, where it appears as lines 15–21 of an editorially joined series of fragments beginning with "Mask thy wisdom"; this combination was reprinted in W 9:324–26.

## "I left my dreamy page & sallied forth"

*Text:* The only manuscript text occurs in pencil in P p. 69.

*Date:* Emerson no doubt wrote the poem on or about 10 June 1838. A prose passage in journal D of that date (JMN 7:10) is the source of the poem.

*Publication:* Unpublished by Emerson. First published in W 9:346–47 with a number of erroneous readings, supplied punctuation, and the nonauthorial title "Night in June," which, however, resembles the heading in D, "Night: Progress, or, a Ladder of four steps," and the index reference in D and P: "Night."

*See Also:* Strauch diss., pp. 68–71.

## "I love thy music, mellow bell"

*Texts:* The first draft, in notebook No. XVIII (JMN 1:301–2), gives a version of lines 1–8 together with several unused lines. In journal Wide World 8 (JMN 2:54) is the canceled first draft of lines 9–16. A fair copy of the entire poem occurs with the date "1823" on the preceding page of Wide World 8 (JMN 2:53–54). Copies bearing the same date are in Rhymer p. 5 and Poems folder 44 (see Additional Manuscripts).

*Date:* The date of 1823 refers to the second draft and the actual completion of the poem; the first draft falls between journal entries dated 21 October 1821 and 21 February 1822.

*Publication:* Unpublished by Emerson. First published in W 9:379 with the nonauthorial title "The Bell."

## "I mistrust him when he sends"

*Texts:* These five lines occur in pencil in journal Books Small with "What are all the flowers" and lines from "Saadi" (JMN 8:460), and, revised, in pencil in P p. 200.

*Date:* The draft in Books Small must have been written before October 1842, when "Saadi" was published, and probably in that year.

*Publication:* Unpublished by Emerson. First published in JMN 8.

## "I much prefer to speech of these"

*Text:* These two lines occur in erased pencil in EF p. 12, following a passage associated with "The Fugitive Slave Law" (1851), upon which they may comment.

*Date:* Probably composed in the spring of 1851, when Emerson inscribed the passage on the Fugitive Slave Law.

*Publication:* Unpublished.

## "I must not borrow light"

*Text:* This four-line fragment occurs in erased pencil in EF p. 25.

*Date:* The text appears to have been inscribed at the same time as the preceding unidentified lines, also erased, which are overwritten by a passage used in "The Fugitive Slave Law" (1851).

*Publication:* Unpublished.

## "I never knew but one immortal girl"

*Text:* This single line occurs in NP p. 238. A similar line ("I never knew but one") begins a six-line poetic fragment in journal SO (JMN 14:70).

*Date:* Undetermined. The fragment in SO dates from 1856.

*Publication:* Unpublished.

## "I never went out of my country"

*Text:* These two lines, a translation of Hafiz, Book XXIII, Ode IX, lines 21–22 (*Diwan* 2:162), occur in EF p. 76. They have not been found elsewhere in Emerson's published or unpublished writings.

## "I said to the East wind"

*Text:* These lines, which translate Hafiz, Book XXIV, Ode XVI, lines 19–27 (*Diwan* 2:298), occur in pencil in EF p. 42. They have not been found elsewhere in Emerson's published or unpublished writings.

## "I sat upon the ground"

*Text:* This five-line fragment occurs in pencil in P p. 118. It may be related to "As I walked in the wood," which occurs directly above it. It has not been found elsewhere in Emerson's published or unpublished writings.

## "I saw angels yesterday"

*Texts:* The poem, which translates Hafiz, Book VIII, Ode CIX (*Diwan* 1:366–68), appears in three drafts. The first, of lines 33–36, is in EF p. 113 in a series headed "Hafiz of his verse"; below it Emerson translated von Hammer-Purgstall's literal translation of the quatrain from the Farsi. The entire poem occurs in notebook Orientalist pp. 153–54, with lines 1–20 revised on p. 152.

*Date:* Undetermined.

*Publication:* A prose version of lines 33–36 was published in "Persian Poetry," 1858, p. 729, and in the essay as reprinted in *Letters and Social Aims,* 1876, p. 227, and W 8:253.

## "I saw three blots on earths pleasant face"

*Texts:* The fullest version of these verses, with all but the last four lines erased, occurs in pencil in P p. 239. Two short fragments occur on pp. 238 (in erased pencil) and 315 (in unerased pencil); the second is overwritten by extracts from Chaucer, probably made in connection with Emerson's lecture on Chaucer, first given on 26 November 1835.

*Date:* December 1834, or some time in 1835. The first two "blots" seen by the speaker occur in an entry of 2 December 1834 in journal A: "A lockjaw which bended a man's head backward to his heels, and that beastly hydrophobia which makes him bark at his wife & children,—what explains these?" (JMN 4:349; used in "Heroism," W 2:249).

*Publication:* Unpublished.

## "I spread my gorgeous sail"

*Texts:* Two ink fair copies exist, an early one in notebook No. XVIII (JMN 1:328–29) and one in CSA p. 33 drawn from it.

*Date:* The CSA text bears the date "1822," which would agree with the period of use of No. XVIII.

*Publication:* Unpublished by Emerson. First published in JMN 1.

## "I tell you sirs"

*Text:* The only text of this three-line fragment occurs in pencil in NP p. 84. It has not been found elsewhere in Emerson's published or unpublished writings.

## "I to my garden went"

*Texts:* These lines, which may be unused lines from an early draft of "May–Day," occur in EF p. 14 and EL p. 45; in both cases they precede "More sweet than my refrain." The EF draft is written over a passage from "The Fugitive Slave Law" (1851), and is in turn overwritten by a draft of "Excelsior."

*Date:* Between 1851, the date of the "Fugitive Slave Law" passage, and 1859, the latest probable date for the copy of "Excelsior."

*Publication:* Unpublished.

## "I use the knife"

*Text:* This couplet appears in ink in P p. 99, with the index reference "Proverb."

*Date:* Undetermined, though Emerson wrote several similar proverbs during the period 1834–1837. See, for example, JMN 5:278.

*Publication:* Unpublished.

## "I walked abroad"

*Text:* This two-line fragment appears in pencil in P p. 135. It has not been found elsewhere in Emerson's published or unpublished writings.

## "I wear no badge; no tinsel star"

*Texts:* The earliest version, in ink, occurs in journal Wide World 12 (JMN 2:196), where for reasons unknown the first seven lines are struck through with a curving line. Two slightly revised ink versions appear in CSA p. 36 and P p. 65.

*Date:* The Wide World 12 text is dated "Dec. 31. 1823." The copied P text has the notation "1823. Boston." Emerson was actually living in the town of Roxbury in December of that year, though he was teaching in Boston.

*Publication:* Unpublished by Emerson. The second and third stanzas were published from the P text in W 9:380 with the nonauthorial title "Thought." All three stanzas appear in J 1:305.

*See Also:* Strauch diss., pp. 291 (text) and 453–61 (notes).

## "I will be drunk and down with wine"

*Texts:* These two lines, which translate Hafiz, Book VIII, Ode LXXXIV, lines 13–14 (*Diwan* 1:329), appear in a longer translation of the ode ("Secretly to love & to drink") in EF p. 46, and, separately, in revised form, in EF p. 82 and notebook Orientalist p. 53.

*Date:* The first draft was written between April 1846, when Emerson acquired his copy of the *Diwan*, and the spring of 1847, when a portion of the longer draft (see "Loose the knots of the heart") was quoted in a prose entry in journal CD (JMN 10:68).

*Publication:* "Persian Poetry," 1858, p. 727, and in the essay as collected in *Letters and Social Aims*, 1876, p. 221, and W 8:246.

## "If bright the sun, he tarries"

*Texts:* In the first draft in journal AC (JMN 14:278), lines 3–4 were written first at the top of the page, and "Poverty's praise" added above them. Then follows the quatrain in darker ink, the only draft showing revision. Fair copies occur in NP p. 83, headed "The poor Poet's praise.—", and in ETE p. 46. In NP p. 293, line 4 is adapted as line 2 of the gift poem "Eve roved in Paradise."

*Date:* The draft in journal AC was written in the spring of 1859.

*Publication:* Unpublished by Emerson. First published in *Poems*, 1884, p. 277, and reprinted in W 9:334.

## "If curses be the wage of love"

*Text:* The only text of this six-line poem occurs in pencil in NP p. 199.

*Date:* Undetermined.

*Publication:* Unpublished by Emerson. First published in *Poems*, 1884, p. 298, and reprinted in W 9:358.

## "If farmers make my land secure"

*Text:* This quatrain occurs only in EF p. 21, where a pencil draft is overwritten by a slightly revised ink version; the word "King." is written before the first line in both texts (see Plate 4). The quatrain has not been found elsewhere in Emerson's published or unpublished writings.

## "If he go apart"

*Text:* This eleven-line fragment, possibly intended for "The Daemonic and the Celestial Love," occurs in pencil in X pp. 73–74. It has not been found elsewhere in Emerson's published or unpublished writings.

## "If not so good"

*Text:* The only text of this couplet occurs in pencil in NP p. 142. It has not been found elsewhere in Emerson's published or unpublished writings.

## "If thy body pine"

*Text:* This six-line fragment occurs in ink in X pp. $268_m$–$268_n$. It has not been found elsewhere in Emerson's published or unpublished writings.

## "If thy darling favor thee"

*Text:* This four-line fragment, translated from an unidentified source in Hafiz, occurs in pencil in EF p. 80. It has not been found elsewhere in Emerson's published or unpublished writings.

## "If to the Assembly of souls"

*Texts:* This poem, which translates Hafiz, Book VIII, Ode CX, lines 33–44 (*Diwan* 1:370), occurs in two drafts. Lines 1–4 appear in EF p. 97 in a series of entries headed "Hafiz superlative"; the twelve-line version occurs in notebook Orientalist p. 234.

*Date:* Undetermined.

*Publication:* Unpublished.

## "If wishes would carry me over the land"

*Texts:* This quatrain occurs in EL p. 179 and is copied with the revision of a single word on p. 291.

*Date:* The first EL text is preceded by the second draft of "With the key of the secret," written no earlier than 1856.

*Publication:* Unpublished.

## "Illusions"

*Texts:* The only notebook draft occurs in ink in X pp. 141–43, where the verses comprise lines 32–68 of "Proteus," from which they were taken to serve as a motto to the essay "Illusions." Printer's copy for *The Conduct of Life* is in the University of Virginia Library; it has "passing" in line 20 rather than the printed "lambent".

*Date:* Undetermined, but see "Proteus."

*Publication:* First published in *The Conduct of Life*, 1860, pp. 271–72, reprinted in subsequent editions including W 6:307–8, and collected in W 9:287–88.

## "Illusions like the tints of pearl"

*Texts:* This quatrain occurs in a heavily revised first draft in EL p. 182, followed on the same page by a revised fair copy.

*Date:* Undetermined. The drafts are preceded on the page by "The Harp," lines 99–102, probably written in the early 1860s.

*Publication:* Unpublished by Emerson. First published in *Poems,* 1884, p. 286, and reprinted in W 9:348.

## "In bounding youth the night & rain"

*Text:* These four lines, possibly from Hafiz, appear in pencil in EF p. 96; they have not been found elsewhere in Emerson's published or unpublished writings.

## "In building or in poem caught the rhyme"

*Texts:* This fragment occurs in pencil in journal F 2 (JMN 7:489), where it appears to be a comment on Jones Very's poetry. It was copied into EL p. 155, and into Rhymer p. 50ᵦ with the omission of an imperfect first line.

*Date:* The F 2 draft was inscribed on 28 or 29 March 1840.

*Publication:* Unpublished by Emerson. First published in JMN 7.

## "In dreamy woods what forms abound"

*Text:* The only draft of the quatrain is in pencil in EL p. 80.

*Date:* The poem occurs between the first and second drafts of "His home / Where the pure drops," the third draft of which appears in an insert in Rhymer dating from the early to mid 1860s. The couplet immediately following ("And he like me") appears likewise to have been written in the early to mid 1860s.

*Publication:* Unpublished.

## "In honour dies he to whom the great seems wonderful"

*Text:* This single line, a translation of Hafiz, Book VIII, Ode CXLV, line 7 (*Diwan* 1:421), occurs in EF p. 109.

*Date:* Undetermined.

*Publication:* Published as prose in "Persian Poetry," 1858, p. 726, and in the essay as reprinted in *Letters and Social Aims,* 1876, p. 220, and W 8:245.

## "In its elasticity"

*Text:* This two-line fragment in erased pencil, only partially recovered, occurs in EF p. 68, and may be either verse or prose. It has not been found elsewhere in Emerson's published or unpublished writings.

## "In Massachusetts many noble paths"

*Text:* This fragment, only a line and a half long, occurs in pencil in P p. 113, deleted by swirling horizontal lines. It has not been found elsewhere in Emerson's published or unpublished writings.

## "In Memoriam. E. B. E."

*Texts:* The earliest drafts of this poem occur in P pp. 240–45, as follows: lines 1–19 (lacking line 18) in pencil on p. 241, transcribed and revised in ink with the addition of line 20 on p. 240; lines 21–25, 32, 35–37, and 44–47 in pencil on p. 242, transcribed and revised in ink on p. 241, with lines 33–34 added in pencil; lines 101–2 in pencil on p. 242, transcribed from a pencil version on p. 158, which is in turn drawn from an earlier version in journal D (JMN 7:176); lines 105–6, 73–74, 76, and 103–4 in pencil on p. 243; lines 92–96 in pencil, written over in ink, on p. 244; and lines 51, 53–59 in pencil on p. 245, with a number of rejected lines. (Page 241 is reproduced in Plate 2.) From these drafts was drawn an ink version, with title, in EL pp. 163–71, as follows: lines 1–59 (lacking line 50) on pp. 163–67; lines 90–96 and 60–66 on p. 168; lines 67–72, 97–104 (canceled) and 73–75 on p. 169; lines 76–89 on p. 170; and lines 97–116 on p. 171. All entries in EL except the canceled lines on p. 169 are struck through in ink. A copy, in Margaret Fuller's hand, of lines 46–47 and 92–96 appear on the same manuscript as a copy, also in Fuller's hand, of Emerson's letter to Ezra Weston of late May 1836; the lines read "Never poor beseeching glance / Shamed that sculptured countenance; / What he had done / He nor ⟨repents⟩ ↑commends↓ nor grieves, / Pleads for itself the fact, / As unrepenting Nature leaves / Her every act." The text of a separate manuscript draft of lines 35–37 and 41–47, inserted inside the front cover of journal ST, is given in JMN 16:202.

*Date:* Undetermined. Emerson's brother Edward died 1 October 1834; the first version of lines 101–2 in journal D occurs between entries of 10 and 13 March 1839. The draft of the poem in P is written over an erased draft of "Concord Fight," written in the spring of 1837.

*Publication:* Lines 92–96 were first published as the second of two mottoes to "Character," *Essays: Second Series,* 1844, p. 96. The poem as a whole was first published in *May–Day,* 1867, pp. 148–54, reprinted in *Poems,* 1884, pp. 224–27, and W 9:261–65.

## "In my garden three ways meet"

*Texts:* This poem evolved in loose relation with "My Garden," stanzas of which appear with certain of the drafts. The two latest drafts, in Poems folder 48, were composed before the attendant stanzas of "My Garden" had been perfected and published in December 1866. There seem to be two main lines of development in the poem's composition:

1. The first draft of an unused stanza on bees occurs in notebook WA p. 176; this is revised and joined to "My Garden," lines 1–4, in NP p. 197, which is in turn the source of the draft in NP p. 106 of lines 1–8, the bees stanza, and "My Garden," lines 1–4. This is reordered and revised in the draft (headed "My Garden") in EL pp. 78–79, where lines 17–20 are added. (Lines 17–20 exist in separate drafts in EL pp. 102 and 225, NP p. 10, and notebook RT p. 53, though the order of composition is uncertain.) The draft in EL pp. 78–79 is again revised and reorganized in NP pp. 269–71, where an attempt was made to incorporate "For joy & beauty" and "My Garden," lines 5–6, first composed in 1857 and 1861 respectively. This draft was extended, on p. 272, by the addition of the first draft of lines 33–36, a copy of lines 37–44 (drawn from NP p. 45 and the first draft at EF p. 83), and a copy of lines 25–28, drawn from NP p. 104. All of this material, with the exception of the now abandoned bees stanza, was copied and revised in the draft at EL pp. 135–37, where lines 9–16 were added from the first draft in journal FOR (JMN 15:342). This occurred not earlier than 28 April 1863, the date of the FOR draft. Ignoring material not finally used in the poem, this draft now included lines 17–20 and 1–4 (p. 135), 5–9 and 33–44 (p. 136), and 25–28 and 9–16 (p. 137).

2. In 1849 Emerson wrote in journal TU (JMN 11:109): "The sky looks indignantly on all that is doubtful & obscure in man." Ten years later he copied this sentence into journal CL (JMN 14:296) and versified it, producing the first two drafts of lines 21–24. This was further revised in EL p. 158, again in EL p. 224, and once more in Rhymer p. 96$_e$. (Still later, and apparently apart from the development of "In my garden three ways meet," Emerson copied the stanza into ETE p. 45 and from there into Poems folder 62.) The material in the Rhymer insert at p. 96 was gathered mainly from sources in EL. Lines 29–32 on pp. 96$_c$ and 96$_d$ came from the first full draft in EL p. 103, where lines 31–32 had been drawn from EL pp. 157 and 158. Lines 17–20 on p. 96$_d$ were probably drawn from NP p. 10, while lines 21–24 on p. 96$_e$, as already noted, came from EL p. 224. The prose source for the second

of the unused lines ("If Pindar pour") on pp. 96$_c$ and 96$_d$ occurs in journal AC (JMN 14:228).

Even at this point the poem is obviously in a chaotic state, though in fact all the stanzas appear, each in nearly final form, either in EL pp. 135–37 or Rhymer pp. 96$_c$-96$_e$. The first text in Poems folder 48 is a selection of these, while the second text is a final arrangement (see Additional Manuscripts for both texts). The proofsheet "Supplenda," inserted in Rhymer between pp. 60 and 61, faithfully reproduces the wording of the second folder 48 text as corrected, with two further substantive revisions: "There" to "The" in line 5, and "Here" to "And" in line 7 (see Plate 9). It follows, on the same sheet, lines 1–10 of "The Nun's Aspiration."

*Date:* Lines 21–24 were composed in journal CL in 1859. The rejected stanza on bees from WA and "If Pindar pour" likewise date to 1859. The draft at EL pp. 135–37, however, incorporates lines 9–16, first composed in April 1863. The presence of rough draft lines of "My Garden" in the second text in Poems folder 48 shows that the last version was done before December 1866, the date of publication of "My Garden."

*Publication:* Unpublished by Emerson. First published from the second Poems folder 48 text with the nonauthorial title "Walden" (possibly drawn from NP p. 271) in *Poems*, 1884, pp. 307–9, with a slightly misleading note by Cabot: "This poem represents the early form of *My Garden*, which, in years, grew from this beginning." When the poem was published in W 9:370–72, lines 29–32 were placed in brackets, lines 33–44 were dropped, and four new stanzas were added from EL p. 156 ("How drearily in College hall").

*See Also:* (1) "My Garden" and (2) "How drearily in College hall."

## "In the deep heart of man a poet dwells"

*Text:* An ink fair copy of this fifteen-line poem occurs in P p. 123, with the index reference "The Muse."

*Date:* Undetermined.

*Publication:* Unpublished by Emerson. First published in *Poems*, 1884, p. 313, with the nonauthorial title "The Enchanter," and reprinted in W 9:372–73.

## "In the kingdom of Poesy Hafiz waves like a banner"

*Text:* This two-line fragment, translated from an unlocated source in Hafiz, occurs in EF p. 114 in a series of entries headed "Hafiz of his verse." It has not been found elsewhere in Emerson's published or unpublished writings.

## "In this sour world, o summerwind"

*Text:* This quatrain occurs in pencil in P p. 114, set off from the lines of "The Sphinx" that surround it by a circle drawn in pencil.

*Date:* Since the quatrain was clearly inscribed before the lines of "The Sphinx," it must have been written before the summer of 1840.

*Publication:* Unpublished.

## "In thy holiday of life"

*Texts:* The source of this translation from Hafiz has not been identified. The text in notebook Orientalist p. 17 is the source of that in Rhymer p. 128.

*Date:* The poem was probably written in 1850 (see "On prince or bride," which occurs with both texts).

*Publication:* Unpublished.

## "In Walden wood the chickadee"

*Text:* An erased pencil draft appears in P p. 137; an unerased copy, slightly revised, is in P p. 134.

*Date:* Undetermined.

*Publication:* Unpublished by Emerson. First published in W 9:342.

## "The Initial Love"

*Texts:* Only a small portion of the poem is represented in draft fragments, and these come late in the process of composition. In X p. 66 is a pencil draft of what became lines 64–73; this was revised in pencil on p. 67 and later erased. A draft of lines 74–86 (lacking lines 76 and 80) occurs in X p. 77. The single phrase "proud & shy" in pencil on p. 76 suggests lines 88–89, and may or may not imply an attempt to continue the text from p. 77. A draft of the entire poem in the Houghton Library is followed by the pencil fair copy in X pp. 132–38, from which it differs as follows: lines 62–63 are missing; four lines found in an earlier form in X pp. 66–67 ("Magic numbers he can reckon, / See(s stones) ↑ walls ↓ & pavements wink & beckon: / Second sight

& undersong / To his empery belong;") are canceled after line 69; line 77 reads "And touches all with hue of rose"; in line 105, "And" is canceled for "But"; and in line 137, "and" is canceled before "hurts." Printer's copy for the London edition of *Poems*, 1847, is also in the Houghton Library; it differs from the published text as follows: line 21 reads "In the pit of his eye's a spark" instead of the incorrect "In the pit of his eyes a spark"; "He is" is canceled for "Mainly" in line 64; "joy" is canceled for "toy" in line 112; and "sovereignly" is changed to "sovranly" in line 126. The fact that lines 1–59 and 87–156 are already, with very few exceptions, in final form in their earliest manuscript appearance suggests not only that a number of prior manuscripts have been lost, but also that lines 60–86 were the last to be completed.

*Date:* The poem appears to have been written some time between 1840 and 1845, before "The Daemonic and the Celestial Love." Lines 11–12 have their source in a passage in journal E (JMN 7:406), written in October 1840.

*Publication: Poems*, 1847, pp. 156–64 (Boston) and pp. 123–29 (London). In the Boston edition the poem forms part I of "Initial, Daemonic, and Celestial Love"; in the London edition it is part I of "Ode" and lacks line 138. Reprinted with the omission of lines 118–21 and 138–39 in *Selected Poems*, 1876, pp. 97–102, *Poems*, 1884, pp. 92–97, and W 9:103–9.

*See Also:* Carl F. Strauch, "Emerson's Adaptation of Myth in 'The Initial Love,'" *ATQ* 25 (1975): 51–65.

# "Inscription on a Well in Memory of the Martyrs of the War"

*Texts:* The first three drafts occur in pencil (of which two are erased) in EL p. 72, overwritten by a fair copy, titled, in ink. Additional fair copies occur in Rhymer p. 104, ETE p. 21, and journal ST (JMN 16:240). Still another copy, in Poems folder 51, bears the heading "Inscription for Mrs Forbes's Memorial Fountain" and follows the Rhymer text; it has long been associated with Emerson's letter of 17 April 1870 to Sarah Swain Forbes, who commissioned the inscription; the poem is not, however, referred to in the letter (L 6:113–14).

*Date:* The poem was inscribed on the side of a well built in 1866 on the estate of Mrs. Forbes in Milton, Massachusetts (see L 6:113n). Since the first drafts in EL p. 72 occur with lines of "My Garden," published in December 1866, the "Inscription" very probably dates to that year as well.

*Publication:* Unpublished by Emerson. First published in *Poems*, 1884, p. 315, and reprinted in W 9:376.

## "Intellect" ("Go, speed")

*Texts:* The first draft is in erased pencil in EF p. 57. A slightly revised form of this text became the last stanza of "Pale Genius roves alone" in the pencil draft in X p. 26. The text of this poem was copied in ink in EL p. 31, where the last stanza was struck through in ink, evidently at the time of its separate publication.

*Date:* Probably between 1845 and 1847, since the X text is written over erased lines of "Monadnock" written in 1845.

*Publication:* First published as the motto to "Intellect" in the 1847 edition of *Essays: First Series*, p. 293, and included in later editions and reprintings, including W 2:323. The EL text of "Pale Genius roves alone" was published in *Poems*, 1884, pp. 268–69, and reprinted in W 9:326–27.

## "Intellect" ("Rule which by obeying")

*Texts:* The first draft occurs in pencil, untitled, in notebook S (Salvage) p. 168, possibly preceded by a draft of line 1 in EF p. 4. A revised version in pencil in X p. 27 carries the title "Intellect." The third draft, which revises line 2, is in pencil, untitled, in EF p. 24.

*Date:* A source for line 1 may be found in journal J: "That the Intellect grows by moral obedience, seems to me the Judgment Day" (JMN 8:177), an entry written in June 1842. A source for line 6 occurs twice in journal O: "Intellect makes him strange among his house-mates" (JMN 9:357 and 363), written in April 1846. Notebook S (Salvage) was used throughout the 1840s and 1850s. The third draft, in EF, is overwritten by the prose source for "Alms" and was therefore inscribed no later than 1851.

*Publication:* Unpublished by Emerson. First published from the S (Salvage) text in W 9:360, with the nonauthorial title "Insight."

## "Intellect / Gravely broods apart on joy"

*Text:* The fragment, written and revised in pencil in EL p. 37, was partially erased and a final version written in ink over it.

*Date:* The probable prose source in journal Books Small (JMN 8:444) was expanded in journal N (JMN 8:283) between entries of 12 and 15 October 1842. The drafts in EF may have been written years later.

*Publication:* Unpublished by Emerson. First published in W 9:375 with the nonauthorial title "Intellect" and a first line beginning "Gravely it broods . . . ."

## "Is Jove immortal"

*Text:* The only text of this sixteen-line poem is in ink in X pp. 268<sub>d</sub>–268<sub>e</sub>. It follows "Be of your country," to which it may be related.

*Date:* The context of the poem in the X insert suggests a date of composition in 1846 or 1847.

*Publication:* Unpublished.

## "Is morning clean, let him be clean"

*Text:* This single line occurs in EL p. 200. It has not been found elsewhere in Emerson's published or unpublished writings.

## "Is The pace of nature slow?"

*Text:* The poem occurs only in EL p. 232.

*Date:* The prose source is an 1859 entry in journal CL: "The pace of nature is so slow. Why not from strength to strength, from miracle to miracle, & not as now with this retardation, as if Nature had sprained her foot, & makes plenteous stopping at little stations" (JMN 14:310–11). Emerson sprained his foot on an excursion to Mt. Wachusett in late July or early August 1859 (see JMN 14:311).

*Publication:* Unpublished.

## "Isabel. For every thing doth hinder gratitude"

*Text:* This seven-line interchange between "Isabel" and "Leon" occurs in pencil in P p. 148. It has not been found elsewhere in Emerson's published or unpublished writings.

## "It is certain that who his mind"

*Text:* This poem, which translates Hafiz, Book VIII, Ode CXXXII, lines 1–28 (*Diwan* 1:403–4), occurs in EF pp. 81–82. It has not been found elsewhere in Emerson's published or unpublished writings.

## "It is not a mile of rosetrees"

*Text:* This five-line fragment occurs in pencil in KL[A] p. 56, and was probably written in 1864 or 1865, after the "May–Day" material in that notebook. It has not been found elsewhere in Emerson's published or unpublished writings.

## "It is written in keen astronomy"

*Text:* The only text of this twelve-line poem is in erased pencil in P p. 179. It has not been found elsewhere in Emerson's published or unpublished writings.

## "It takes philosopher or fool"

*Texts:* Two slightly different texts exist, in notebook Encyclopedia (JMN 6:142) and in P p. 99, with the index reference "Proverb."

*Date:* Undetermined. Emerson last kept a school in October 1826.

*Publication:* Unpublished by Emerson. First published in Rusk, *Life*, p. 91, from the P text.

## "James Russell Lowell"

*Texts:* Ten partial or complete manuscripts of this poem exist. The first draft, in NP pp. 172–73, among unused biographical sketches written for "The Adirondacs," begins with line 40 (though the first three lines on the page may have been added above the canceled line "Then for Lowell") and lacks lines 41, 49, 62, 67–68, 70, and 72. The second draft, in NP pp. 193–95, also begins with line 40 and lacks lines 41 and 72. These are followed by two manuscripts in Poems folder 86: the first is a text of lines 44–80 with the title "J. R. L." added in pencil, and the second, untitled, is a complete eighty-line text, but with lines 39–43 canceled. Another complete text occurs in NP pp. 231–36, while a copy of lines 39–80, in Poems folder 87, lacks line 77. (For the texts in folders 86 and 87, see Additional Manuscripts.) Three almost identical texts, all beginning with a variant of line 34 and lacking lines 39–43, occur in EL pp. 198$_c$–198$_e$, ETE pp. 152–53, and notebook QL pp. 49–51; in the last, titled "James Russell Lowell," the verses are noted as having been read on Lowell's *fiftieth* birthday. (A proofsheet of this version of the poem, following the ETE text, is pasted to Rhymer p. 60; see Plate 8.) An untitled fair copy of the complete text in the New York Public Library, Berg Collection, is inscribed by Lowell "Autograph of Emerson's poem on my 40*th* birthday, 1859," and was probably the copy Emerson read from. It appears to be taken from the complete text in folder 86 as revised, except that lines 39–43 are not canceled and four lines have slight variants: line 25 ("To raise an eyebrow's hint severe"), line 37 ("Go inquire his horoscope,"), line 57 ("Broadest joke, & luckiest pun,"), and line 71 ("A time & tide too exigent").

*Date:* The first two drafts in NP were probably written between Emerson's return from the Adirondack trip (which included Lowell) in late August 1858 and the start of a heavy lecture schedule in November and December of that year. He reworked it, nearly doubling its length with an invocation, in time to read it at the Saturday Club on 22 February 1859, then cut the invocation in some of the later versions.

*Publication:* Unpublished by Emerson. First published by Charles Eliot Norton from the Lowell manuscript, with the nonauthorial title "To Lowell, on his Fortieth Birthday," in *The Century Magazine* 47 (November 1893): 3–4, with "wight" for "night" in line 9; reprinted in Edward Waldo Emerson, *The Early Years of the Saturday Club* (Boston and New York, 1918), pp. 200–202.

*See Also:* (1) "The Adirondacs," and (2) Strauch diss., pp. 668–70.

## "Knowest thou the luck a friend's face to see"

*Texts:* Emerson translated Hafiz, Book XXIV, Ode XII, lines 1–12 (*Diwan* 2:291) in a pencil draft in X p. 254, and revised lines 1–2 and 11–12 as a separate poem in EF p. 79.

*Date:* Between April 1846, when Emerson acquired his copy of the *Diwan*, and October 1850, the latest possible date for "The Phoenix," the second draft of which follows the present poem in X p. 254. Since these in turn follow the long translation "From the Persian of Hafiz" published in *Poems,* 1847, composition in the early part of this period is most likely.

*Publication:* Unpublished.

## "Knows he who tills this lonely field"

*Text:* This poem, which Emerson apparently never brought to completion, occurs in pencil in P pp. 205–6, with the third stanza struck through in pencil. Emerson used three stanzas in two other poems: the first and third became stanzas 1 and 2 of "Dirge," and the ninth, after being transcribed and then erased on p. 207, became stanza 4 of "The Apology."

*Date:* The source of the fifth stanza is a prose passage written between 19 June and 16 August 1840, in journal F 2: "Once in the fields with the lowing cattle, the birds, the trees, the waters & satisfying outlines of the landscape, and I cannot tell whether this is /Tempe/Thessaly/ and Enna, or Concord & Acton" (JMN 7:505). Since the ninth stanza became part of "The Apology" no earlier than 1841, and since "Dirge," into which stanzas 1 and 3 were transferred, was sent to W. H. Furness on 12 March 1844, for publication, this poem was obviously written in the intervening years.

*Publication:* Unpublished by Emerson. First published in *Poems,* 1884, pp. 302–3, with the nonauthorial title "Peter's Field," taken from Emerson's index reference in P. This version omits stanza 9, brackets stanzas 1 and 3, and adds as a final stanza the quatrain at the top of P p. 207, which was taken to be part of the poem. An appended note reads: "This poem on the memories and associations of the field by the Concord River where Mr. Emerson and his brothers walked in their youth, is probably of earlier date than *The Dirge,* with which it has two verses in common." When this version was reprinted in W 9:363–64, the same note was included (pp. 511–12), but with "is probably" changed to "must be."

*See Also:* "Far seen the river glides below."

## "Lament not, o Hafiz, the distribution"

*Text:* These two lines, translating Hafiz, Book XI, Ode VI, lines 15–16 (*Diwan* 2:54), occur in pencil in EF p. 38. They have not been found elsewhere in Emerson's published or unpublished writings.

## "The land was all electric"

*Texts:* The first draft of this poem, in journal CL (JMN 14:332), is revised in NP p. 218.

*Date:* The poem was clearly inspired by John Brown's raid on Harpers Ferry, which is the subject of the surrounding prose commentary in CL. It was composed shortly after Brown's arrest on 18 October 1859.

*Publication:* Unpublished by Emerson. The CL text was first published in J 9:246 with the nonauthorial title "War."

*See Also:* "A howling wolf that by Potomac ran."

## "Last night / She purred about me as I fell to sleep"

*Text:* This three-line fragment occurs in pencil in P p. 116, at the end of many pages devoted to "The Sphinx" and perhaps suggested by it. It has not been found elsewhere in Emerson's published or unpublished writings.

## "Leave me, Fear! thy throbs are base"

*Texts:* A version of this poem in fifteen lines occurs in EL p. 43; the first eleven lines were copied in notebook L Camadeva p. 118. A slightly different version of lines 1–11 occurs in an ink fair copy in Poems folder 53 (see Additional Manuscripts).

*Date:* The Poems folder 53 text carries the date 1831.

*Publication:* Unpublished by Emerson. Published in *Poems*, 1884, p. 292, from the EL text, but not reprinted in W 9.

## "Let me go where e'er I will"

*Text:* An untitled ink fair copy is in P p. 96.

*Date:* Undetermined.

*Publication:* Unpublished by Emerson. First published in *Poems*, 1884, pp. 272–73, and reprinted in W 9:365 with the nonauthorial title "Music," perhaps drawn from Emerson's index reference in P: "Music everywhere."

*See Also:* (1) Strauch diss., pp. 357 (text) and 555–58 (notes) and (2) W 9:512.

## "Letters" ("Every day")

*Texts:* The first draft of "Letters" is in X p. 167 among drafts of translations from Hafiz, though it appears to be an original composition. A fair copy, titled, is in Rhymer p. 44. A number of loose manuscript fair copies exist, all identical in wording to the Rhymer and *May–Day* texts: one at the University of Texas, another at the University of Virginia, a third and fourth in Poems folders 27 and 172 (a photocopy of an unlocated manuscript), and a fifth, a copy made for Oliver Wendell Holmes, Jr., in the Houghton Library.

*Date:* Undetermined. The Holmes copy, dated "March 1862," was enclosed in a letter (still with the manuscript) dated at Concord on 23 March 1862.

*Publication:* First published in *May–Day,* 1867, p. 94, and reprinted in *Selected Poems,* 1876, p. 78, *Poems,* 1884, p. 188, and W 9:217.

## "Letters" ("The tongue")

*Texts:* The first draft, in EL p. 151, headed "Poet," includes part of line 2 and lines 3–4; it is expanded into a quatrain in NP p. 60. This version was copied in ETE p. 43, where the title "Letters" appears. A slightly different fair copy occurs in ETE p. 145.

*Date:* The NP draft appears on the page below lines composed in 1862 for the first draft of "The Titmouse." The idea of the poem was an old one with Emerson; prose parallels occur in "Friendship" (W 2:191–92 and 211) in passages based on journal entries of 1835 and 1841 respectively (JMN 5:34 and 7:370).

*Publication:* Unpublished by Emerson. First published, untitled, from the ETE p. 43 text in *Poems,* 1884, p. 290, and reprinted in W 9:351.

## "Life"

*Texts:* The first draft of this quatrain occurs in pencil, heavily canceled, in NP p. 79, followed by a fair copy on p. 78; another, titled "Life," is in ETE p. 8, with a variant showing that Emerson was still dissatisfied with line 3.

*Date:* Undetermined.

*Publication:* Unpublished by Emerson. First published, with the title, from the NP text in *Poems,* 1884, p. 287, and reprinted in W 9:349.

## "Like vaulters in the circus round"

*Texts:* No certain sequence of composition can be inferred from the minor differences among the drafts, which occur in journal W (JMN 9:232), EF

p. 51, EL pp. 21 (headed "The Poet") and 148, Rhymer p. 2ₐ, NP pp. 101 and 295 (headed "Poet"), and in the manuscript (though not the published text) of *Representative Men*. This text reads: "Poets, like vaulters in the circus round, / ⟨Can⟩May step from horse to horse, but never touch the ground." (Buffalo and Erie County Public Library.)

*Date:* Possibly the source of the couplet was Emerson's attendance with his son Waldo at a circus between 25 and 28 May 1840, where he saw "a man ride standing on the back of two galloping horses, a third horse being interposed between the two . . ." (JMN 7:358, repeated in JMN 10:403–4). The image is closely related to a prose passage of 17 May 1840 (JMN 7:351). The couplet, therefore, was written between May 1840, the period of the sources, and June 1845, the date of the journal W text. The EF draft is written over an erased draft of "The Chartist's Complaint," which would date it to 1851 or later. The Rhymer draft follows on the same page as a fragment ("His instant thought") composed in 1866.

*Publication:* Unpublished by Emerson. First published in *Poems,* 1884, p. 275, and reprinted in W 9:331.

*See Also:* (1) W 7:350 and (2) John Q. Anderson, "Emerson's 'Horses of Thought,'" *ESQ,* no. 5 (4th quarter 1956), 1–2.

## "Lo! where from Heaven's high roof"

*Texts:* This quatrain, which translates Hafiz, Book XXIII, Ode XXIII, lines 29–32 (*Diwan* 2:188), occurs in two drafts in notebook Orientalist p. 9; the second of these was copied into Rhymer p. 148. The lines have not been found elsewhere in Emerson's published or unpublished writings.

*Date:* Undetermined.

*Publication:* Unpublished.

## "Look danger in the eye it vanishes"

*Text:* This fourteen-line description of a mob scene occurs in pencil in P p. 117. It has not been found elsewhere in Emerson's published or unpublished writings.

## "Loose the knots of the heart; never think on thy fate"

*Texts:* These two lines from Hafiz, Book VIII, Ode LXXXIV, lines 3–4 (*Diwan* 1:328), occur in a longer translation of the ode ("Secretly to love & to drink") in EF p. 46, and, separately, in revised form, in notebook EO p. i.

*Date:* Undetermined. In the spring of 1847, Emerson quoted part of line 1 in a prose entry in journal CD (JMN 10:68).

*Publication:* Both the verse and a portion of the prose entry including line 1 were published in "Persian Poetry," 1858, p. 727, and in the essay as collected in *Letters and Social Aims,* 1876, pp. 221 and 222; reprinted in W 8:246 and 247.

## "Lord my god these people"

*Texts:* This 28-line poem, which translates Hafiz, Book IX, Ode II, lines 9–36 (*Diwan* 2:4–5), occurs in six drafts, five of them partial. The full poem appears in notebook Orientalist pp. 127–28, followed by successive pencil drafts of lines 9–28 in the same notebook on pp. 168–69, 169–70, and 171; lines 5–12 occur in a final draft on p. 173. A separate translation of lines 23–28 occurs in EF p. 72.

*Date:* Undetermined.

*Publication:* Lines 5–12 ("If my darling should depart") were published in "Persian Poetry," 1858, p. 732, but do not appear in the essay as reprinted. Collected in *May–Day,* 1867, p. 198, these lines were reprinted in *Poems,* 1884, p. 246, and W 9:300.

## "Loss and Gain"

*Texts:* The first draft, in pencil in X p. 30, was copied and revised on p. 31 before being erased. The poem is referred to in the index to X as "Virtue & Art."

*Date:* Since this poem was among the three that Emerson sent to W. H. Furness on 9 May 1845 for publication in *The Diadem* (see "Forerunners"), it may have been written, like the others, shortly before this date. Carl F. Strauch, however, relates the poem to "Painting and Sculpture" and to sources dating from 1840 and 1841. The index reference is perhaps further evidence for Strauch's view.

*Publication: The Diadem for MDCCCXLVI* (Philadelphia, 1846), p. 9. Emerson acknowledged receipt of his copy of the book on 15 October 1845 (Furness, *Records,* p. 44). The poem was reprinted in *Poems,* 1847, pp. 192–93 (Boston) and p. 153 (London), but was excluded from all subsequent collections.

*See Also:* Carl F. Strauch, "Hatred's Swift Repulsions: Emerson, Margaret Fuller, and Others," *SRom* 7 (Winter 1968): 79–80.

## "Love"

*Texts:* Lines 3–4 of this quatrain developed through a series of trials in EF p. 3; the entire quatrain appears in several forms in NP p. 103, is revised on p. 102, and is transcribed in a fair copy on p. 140.

*Date:* In late 1827 Emerson quoted the germ of line 3 from *Golden Remains of the Ever Memorable Mr. John Hales, of Eton College* (London, 1673) in notebook Encyclopedia (JMN 6:180): "Love will creep where it cannot go"; cf. JMN 7:398, L 3:131, and Shakespeare, *The Two Gentlemen of Verona* 4.2.19–20. The sentence is repeated in notebook L Camadeva p. 35, while a prose version of line 4, "Love eats his way through Alps of opposition," occurs in journal VO (JMN 14:191) and L Camadeva p. 137. The EF draft is written over passages for "The Fugitive Slave Law" (1851) and is therefore later than that year. The VO source suggests composition in 1857 or later, a period consistent with Emerson's use of L Camadeva.

*Publication:* First published in *May–Day,* 1867, p. 189; reprinted in *Poems,* 1884, p. 242, and W 9:295.

## "Love and Thought"

*Texts:* The first draft is in pencil in EF p. 63; the second, in erased pencil, is in X p. 22, while a third and fourth occur in X pp. 23 and 205. All are untitled. The text in Rhymer p. 35, with title and the notation "printed", was evidently the source of the *May–Day* text, though it shows signs of having been revised still further following publication. There seems to be a relation between this poem and "Unity," a draft of which is in EF p. 64 (cf. especially lines 1–3 of "Unity").

*Date:* Undetermined.

*Publication:* *May–Day,* 1867, p. 89. Excluded from *Poems,* 1884, the poem was restored in W 9:210.

*See Also:* (1) "Their Eyes look sidewise" and (2) *Letters from Ralph Waldo Emerson to a Friend,* ed. Charles Eliot Norton (Boston, 1899), p. 48.

## "Love / Asks nought his brother cannot give"

*Texts:* The full text of this poem, in pencil in P p. 157, is preceded by two three-line draft fragments, one in pencil in P p. 76, and another, in erased pencil, in journal F 2 (JMN 7:533). The single word "Masque" in pencil at the top of P p. 76 is possibly a reference to "The Discontented Poet: a Masque."

*Date:* The fragment in journal F 2 appears to have been written in November 1840, a date consistent with the possible reference to "The Discontented Poet" and coincident with Emerson's debate with Margaret Fuller and Caroline Sturgis on love and friendship.

*Publication:* Unpublished by Emerson. First published in *Poems*, 1884, p. 294, and reprinted in W 9:353.

## "Lover's Petition"

*Texts:* The first two drafts, untitled, occur in pencil in journal Y (JMN 9:277–78 and 283–84); the second was indexed as "Lover's Prayer." The poem was revised again, in ink, in X pp. 92–93, where it is indexed as "Good Heart." There are two fair copies: one in EL pp. 35–36 and another in Rhymer pp. 15–16. The Rhymer text is indexed as "Love's Petition," though the title as published was later added at the head of the verses; the EL copy appears to be the source of the printed text.

*Date:* The first two drafts date to the fall of 1845.

*Publication:* First printed in *Over-Songs* (Cambridge, Mass., 1864), on the rectos of unnumbered leaves 10 and 11. This was an edition of five copies, issued to celebrate the marriage of Henry Morton Lovering and Isabel Francelia Morse, 28 June 1864. Other contributors included Bayard Taylor, G. W. Curtis, and Lucy Larcom. The poem was reprinted in *May–Day*, 1867, pp. 90–91, but was excluded from all subsequent collections.

## "The low December vault in June be uplifted high"

*Text:* The only text of this couplet occurs in NP p. 92.

*Date:* Undetermined.

*Publication:* Unpublished by Emerson. First published in *Poems*, 1884, p. 283, with "lifted" for "uplifted" in line 1, and reprinted in W 9:342.

## "Maia"

*Text:* A titled fair copy of this six-line poem occurs in EL p. 293.

*Date:* Undetermined.

*Publication:* Unpublished by Emerson. First published in W 9:348.

# "Maiden Speech of the Aeolian Harp"

*Texts:* The earliest surviving text of this gift poem, with two versions of lines 12–17 but lacking line 19, occurs in pencil in NP pp. 122–23. Fair copies of the finished poem occur in NP pp. 266–67 and ETE pp. 19 and 142, and in a photostat of an unlocated manuscript in Poems folder 167. This last, perhaps the copy that accompanied Emerson's gift to his daughter Edith and her husband, follows the NP fair copy except for four variants: line 3 has "Unbinds" and "gives" for "Unbind" and "give"; line 9 has "Lend your ears" for "Lend me your ears"; and line 19 has "house" for "home".

*Date:* Presumably the poem was written shortly before 2 January 1868, when the gift was presented. Emerson noted that he "arrived [from a western lecture tour] at my daughter's house in Milton on the *2nd* & found they had postponed New Year's one day for my sake" (L 6:3).

*Publication:* First published in *Selected Poems,* 1876, p. 176; reprinted in *Poems,* 1884, p. 220, and W 9:256.

# "Manners"

*Texts:* A pencil draft occurs in journal F 2 (JMN 7:511), a revised pencil version, titled, in P p. 147, and an ink fair copy in Rhymer p. 25 with the notation "printed."

*Date:* The draft in F 2 is dated 18 August 1840. It is a versification of a passage of the same date on the facing manuscript page, after which Emerson wrote many years later, "turned in a verse and printed."

*Publication: Conduct of Life,* 1860, p. 145, as the motto to "Behavior." Collected in *May–Day,* 1867, pp. 170–71, with the title as above, and reprinted in *Selected Poems,* 1876, p. 179, *Poems,* 1884, p. 234, and W 9:276–77.

*See Also:* (1) W 9:496 and (2) *Letters from Ralph Waldo Emerson to a Friend,* ed. Charles Eliot Norton (Boston, 1899), p. 32.

# "manners of boys beautiful"

*Text:* These four lines, which may be notes as easily as an attempt at a quatrain, appear in pencil in EF p. 21; see Plate 4. They have not been found elsewhere in Emerson's published or unpublished writings.

## "Many fine fancies"

*Text:* The only text of this seven-line fragment is in pencil in X p. 72. It has not been found elsewhere in Emerson's published or unpublished writings.

## "Many our needs, yet we spare prayers"

*Text:* The only text of this fourteen-line translation from Hafiz (source un-located) occurs in pencil in X pp. 176–77. It has not been found elsewhere in Emerson's published or unpublished writings.

## "Mask thy wisdom with delight"

*Texts:* This poem, more or less closely associated with "I found this" in each of its manuscript occurrences, exists in four principal drafts, the order of which is partly inferred from the transmission of the companion text. The earliest version is almost certainly the eleven-line ink draft in EF p. 31 (lack-ing line 3), which follows a draft of "I found this" on pp. 30–31. (It is possible that an earlier draft was written on the missing leaf in journal V, JMN 9:170, which follows the first draft of "I found this.") Next is the nine-line version that immediately follows "I found this" in Poems folder 78; it is identical in wording to the EF text as revised except that lines 7–8 are omitted. (A proofsheet of this nine-line version, with "sages" for "ages" in line 10, is laid in between pp. 16–17 of Rhymer; see Plate 7.) Another draft in folder 78 contains a revised version of lines 7–8 and two new lines between lines 2 and 4. The fourth draft, which drops the new lines but adds line 3 and the prefatory statement "And thou", is in Poems folder 5. (See Additional Man-uscripts for the last two texts.) Lines 1–2 appear by themselves in P p. 287, NP p. 289, Poems folder 23, and, canceled, between lines 114–15 of a text of "Saadi" in the Berg Collection, New York Public Library (see Additional Manuscripts under "Saadi"). Emerson used them as lines 24–25 of the motto to the essay "Considerations by the Way," 1860.

*Date:* The EF draft was written over erased passages from "The Fugitive Slave Law" (1851), indicating inscription in that year or later. If the first draft was inscribed on the missing leaf in V, the poem would have been composed in 1844 or 1845.

*Publication:* Except for lines 1–2, printed in the motto to "Considerations by the Way," *Conduct of Life*, 1860, p. 213, this poem was unpublished by

Emerson. First published from the Poems folder 5 text in *Poems,* 1884, p. 267, in connection with several other fragments not closely related in the notebooks, and reprinted in W 9:324–25.

*See Also:* "Considerations by the Way."

## "May–Day"

*Texts:* The major draft of this poem, about four-fifths of the whole, occurs in notebook KL[A]. This draft assembles materials inscribed in numerous journals and notebooks over many years. Except for three substantial partial drafts in journal Z and notebooks EF and NP, discussed directly below, analysis of the poem is based on the KL[A] draft in terms of the thirty-one verse paragraphs that comprised the poem on its first publication.

A pencil draft in notebook Z (JMN 6:296–97) provides an early, partial text of lines 1–4 and 325–77. This was revised and expanded in EF pp. 61–70, where a number of additional lines are drawn from journal V (JMN 9:169) via EF pp. 32–33, while yet other lines come from EF pp. 14 and 112. This draft includes lines 1–16, 37–40, 98–101, 112–13, 115, 117–18, 126–27, 276–90, 325–50, and 358–77. It was revised on the recto pages in NP from pp. 7 to 25. Lines 297–300, which occur first in Pocket Diary 5 and then in journals IO and NO (JMN 13:492, 318, and 411) were copied in EF pp. 37 and 42 and then transferred to NP p. 16 for insertion on p. 17. These materials occur in the main KL[A] draft on pp. 1, 3, 5, 9–10, and 23–28.

In the KL[A] draft, the first verse paragraph, lines 1–40, in addition to the lines drawn from the partial drafts mentioned above, takes line 27 from notebook WA p. 46 and lines 27–35 from EL p. 85 via a revision in journal FOR (JMN 15:341); cf. also EL p. 194. The draft in KL[A] is on pp. 1 and 3–5. The second verse paragraph (lines 41–54) occurs in KL[A] pp. 5–6, with an earlier draft of lines 51–54 in NP p. 38. The prose source for the third verse paragraph (lines 55–67) occurs in journal VA (JMN 15:249–50), versified in KL[A] p. 7.

The prose source of lines 85–86 of the fourth verse paragraph (lines 68–92) is in journal FOR (JMN 15:406), while drafts of lines 89–90 occur in EL pp. 81 and 151 as part of a different section of the poem (see discussion of lines 268–75); the verse paragraph does not occur in KL[A]. The short fifth verse paragraph (lines 93–97) was drafted in EL p. 147, which drew line 94 from trials in journal VA (JMN 15:308) and EL p. 71, while lines 96–97 are derived from a prose passage in journal GL (JMN 15:118); the draft in KL[A] is on p. 8. Sources for the sixth verse paragraph (lines 98–127), which occurs in KL[A] pp. 9–10, are drawn from the drafts discussed in the second paragraph above. Verse paragraph seven (lines 128–48) is in KL[A] pp. 11–12 and draws lines 137–38 from fragmentary trials and the prose source in journal FOR (JMN 15:318–19 and 322); lines 146–47 do not appear in the KL[A] draft.

The first three lines of verse paragraph eight (lines 149–69) grow out of a prose passage in journal SO (JMN 14:62) that was altered and then versified in notebook WA p. 41; a later revision of the lines is in journal GL (JMN 15:124). Lines 164–69 derive from a prose passage in journal CL (JMN 14:336). The verse paragraph occurs in KL[A] pp. 13–14. The first four lines of verse paragraph nine (lines 170–79) derive from a first draft in journal AC (JMN 14:245), revised and expanded in NP p. 33, where only lines 174–75 are lacking. These two lines originate in a trial line in NP p. 29 that is revised in EL p. 82, expanded in EL p. 83, and copied twice in EL p. 114a. In KL[A] the verse paragraph, minus lines 174–75, is on pp. 14–15. Verse paragraph ten (lines 180–210) occurs solely in KL[A] pp. 15–17.

In the eleventh verse paragraph (lines 211–35), a trial of lines 213–14 is in NP p. 35, and trials of lines 215–24, 228–30, and 232–33 are in NP p. 36; line 230 is also in NP p. 33. Lines 215–35 occur in KL[A] pp. 18–19; no manuscript text has been located for lines 211–12. Verse paragraph twelve (lines 236–57) was largely drafted in NP pp. 40–41. Trials of an unused passage including line 242 occur in NP p. 37 and in successive revisions in EL pp. 114a and 29. An earlier draft of lines 252–55 occurs in NP p. 38. Only line 245 does not appear in the draft in KL[A] pp. 19–21, but it occurs in five trials in EL p. 156a. The only text of verse paragraph thirteen (lines 258–67) is in KL[A] p. 21.

The fourteenth verse paragraph (lines 268–75) does not appear in KL[A]. These lines, however, do occur in a fragmentary draft in NP p. 237, revised and expanded successively in NP p. 29 and EL p. 81; they reach nearly final form in EL p. 151. In the latter two texts they incorporate lines 89–90. A version of line 268 occurs in EL p. 132 with lines that appear near the end of the poem as published; in this context it also appears in KL[A] p. 49. Verse paragraphs fifteen and sixteen (lines 276–84 and 285–300), which occur in KL[A] pp. 23–24, contain materials from the partial drafts discussed in the second paragraph above as well as a draft of lines 295–97 in NP p. 38.

Verse paragraph seventeen (lines 301–24) does not occur in the KL[A] draft, but was constructed from materials in two notebooks. The first four lines occur in EL p. 146, a page which also contains a revision of an earlier draft of lines 305–6 and 313–14 in EL p. 134. The prose source for lines 308–12 occurs in journal RS (JMN 11:61–62). Lines 307–12 and 315–24 are drafted in NP pp. 75–76, drawn from X p. 131; lines 323–24 derive from three trials in journal V (JMN 9:219 and 163) and X p. 264. Lines 315–16 and 321–24 were adapted as the headnote to *Nature* in 1849; see "Nature" ("A subtle chain"). Much of the material in verse paragraphs eighteen and nineteen (lines 325–57 and 358–90) descends from the partial drafts in notebooks Z, EF, and NP described in the second paragraph above. Lines 329–64 also occur in Poems folder 6, where "shoes" is canceled for "shoon" in line 338, "April" is canceled for "eternal" in line 340, and line 354 is inserted. Lines 351–57 occur in an earlier draft in EL p. 145; they appear at the end of the KL[A] draft on p. 55, while all the other lines except lines

380–81 occur on pp. 25–29. No manuscript texts of lines 380–81 have been located.

Only the first twenty lines of verse paragraph twenty (lines 391–424) occur in the KL[A] draft, on pp. 31–32. Parts of the remainder occur in a series of drafts in NP: the germ of lines 416/418 occurs on p. 45, and versions of lines 413–24 are in NP pp. 63–64. The draft of verse paragraph twenty-one (lines 425–47) in KL[A] pp. 33–35 draws lines 435–37 from NP p. 199. The twenty-second verse paragraph (lines 448–64) occurs in KL[A] pp. 35–36; line 457 is drawn from EL p. 37 (see also Additional Manuscripts under "Boston," Poems folder 31). The prose source for verse paragraph twenty-three (lines 465–79) occurs in journal LN (JMN 16:46); an early draft of the lines is in Poems folder 15 (see Additional Manuscripts), and in KL[A] the lines appear on pp. 37–38, omitting line 475. The twenty-fourth verse paragraph (lines 480–514) occurs in KL[A] pp. 39–41, and the twenty-fifth and twenty-sixth (lines 515–16 and 517–19) on KL[A] p. 42, omitting line 516; no other drafts of these lines have been discovered.

Only the first twenty lines of verse paragraph twenty-seven (lines 520–81) occur in KL[A], on pp. 42–43. Of these lines, lines 520 and 524 occur in EL p. 193, and lines 528, 531, 533, and 535 are in X p. 106. Of the lines not in KL[A], lines 566–69 occur in EL p. 83 and lines 579–81 are in NP p. 238. Of the twenty-eighth verse paragraph (lines 582–602), lines 583–95 occur in KL[A] p. 47. Lines 582–86 descend from a prose passage in journal GL (JMN 15:118), which may have served as the germ for verse paragraphs twenty-four through twenty-eight (see the discussion of "The Harp" in the *Publication* section below). A version of line 560 occurs in notebook ML p. 278, and line 591 is in EL p. 83. Verse paragraph twenty-nine (lines 603–27) occurs in two parts in KL[A]: lines 603–6 are on p. 53, descending from two successive versions in EL pp. 144–45, and lines 607–27 are on pp. 49 and 51, descending from drafts of lines 607, 609–16, and 623–27 in EL pp. 132–33; cf. also NP p. 36. The short thirtieth verse paragraph (lines 628–35) occurs only in EL p. 132 (see Plate 5). The only drafts located for lines of verse paragraph thirty-one (lines 636–63) are of lines 636–37 and 658–63, which occur in notebook WA pp. 228–30 and are revised and expanded in Poems folder 49 (see Additional Manuscripts).

Many of these drafts contain lines not used in the published poem; see especially EF pp. 14, 65, 69; EL pp. 29, 37, 114a, 134, 144–46, 194; NP pp. 13, 15, 23, 33, 35–38, 63–64; WA pp. 228–30; Poems folder 49; and KL[A] pp. 14, 17, 34, 45, 53, 55.

In none of the manuscript texts does the poem bear the title "May–Day"; Emerson usually referred to it in his indexes as "Spring." The title was presumably appropriated at a very late stage from the unpublished poem called in this edition "May Day [Invitation]."

The gaps and unused lines in the KL[A] text of the poem suggest that further composition occurred in unlocated drafts, which may have been used and then discarded in the extensive recastings of the poem in 1876 and 1884.

*Date:* The main draft of the poem in notebook KL[A] dates from late 1866, as a letter of Emerson's of 25 February 1867 indicates: "I began in the autumn to collect my own scattered verses not hitherto published in a book, & added of quite unpublished verses about half the volume & . . . it was all in type about the 1 December" (L 5:506–7). The date is corroborated by the appearance in KL[A] of lines 465–79, the prose source of which in journal LN dates from September or October 1866. The earliest appearance of any part of the poem, in notebook Z, may be as early as 1838, while the genesis of lines 323–24 in journal V dates from 1844 or 1845 and the germ of lines 308–12 in journal RS is from 1848. The drafts in EF pp. 61–70 and NP pp. 7–25 are apparently from the mid 1850s, since the EF draft is in part written over passages used in the address on "The Fugitive Slave Law" (1851) and the NP draft incorporates materials from Emerson's 1854 pocket diary and journals IO and NO, in use in 1854 and 1855. Some lines in the EF draft also occur in EF pp. 32–37, among materials that derive from journals TU and AZ, in use in 1849 and 1850. The germ of line 416/418 on NP p. 45 occurs in the midst of the first draft of "The Titmouse," written in January 1862. The source of lines 149–51 in journal SO is dated 5 April 1856. Materials drawn from notebook WA date from 1856–1857, while those from journals AC and CL are from 1859. The prose germ for much of the section later detached as "The Harp" (lines 480–602) in journal GL is from 1861, while materials from journal FOR and the prose source of lines 56–67 in journal VA date from 1863. Fragmentary drafts in EL and NP that appear with lines used in "Boston" and "Voluntaries" probably date from 1863 and 1864.

*Publication:* First published in *May–Day,* 1867, pp. 3–39. Reprinted, with extensive rearrangement and revision, including the omission of 147 lines and the addition of two others (after lines 283 and 362) in *Selected Poems,* 1876, pp. 40–57. The bulk of the omitted lines (lines 480–602) were printed separately on pp. 120–24 as "The Harp"; see the analysis of that poem. James Elliot Cabot further rearranged "May–Day" in *Poems,* 1884, pp. 143–59, restoring some lines, omitting or transposing others, and adding two lines after line 457 from EL p. 37, where they are marked "for May Day" by Emerson; this text was reprinted in W 9:163–81.

## "May Day [Invitation]"

*Texts:* The first rough draft of this poem, 27 lines in partially erased pencil in journal KL (JMN 15:462–63), includes only lines 1–11, 17–18, 59–63, and 66–67 of the final text. This is followed by two untitled drafts in Poems folder 55, the earlier and shorter one made up of lines 1–14, 17–20, 23–28, 59–63, and 66–67. The second draft in folder 55 consists of the following segments: (1) lines 1–28 with two unused lines after line 14; (2) the first draft of lines 30–34; (3) lines 48–53 from a draft in EL p. 191, revised and expanded there from an earlier four-line draft in Poems folder 48 (see Additional Manuscripts under "In my garden"); (4) the first draft of lines 54–58; and (5) a revision of lines 59–64 and 66–67. On the next page of this manuscript Emerson revised lines 29–34 and incorporated two earlier fragments: a couplet inscribed in pencil in EL p. 32, revised to become lines 35–36, and eleven lines, originally lines 12–16 and 19–24 of "Where the fungus broad & red," taken from the text in P p. 168 to become lines 37–47. This is followed by a revision of lines 55–56 and a fair copy of lines 59–63 and 66–67. (For the two texts in folder 55, see Additional Manuscripts.)

There are three complete texts of 67 lines, their order determined by slight revisions: in EL pp. 203–8, untitled but indexed under "May cart"; a third manuscript in Poems folder 55, titled "May–day" (see Additional Manuscripts), and lastly in ETE pp. 148–51, titled "May–Day" and indexed under that heading. Emerson appropriated the title for the long title poem of *May–Day*, 1867, which had been indexed under "Spring" during its composition and was still untitled in the KL[A] text. The title "May Day [Invitation]" used in this edition derives from a list of "Proposed Additions" to the contents of *Selected Poems*, 1876, in ETE p. 32ₐ, which includes "May Day ↑Invitation↓". In several locations texts of "May Day [Invitation]" precede drafts of "The Miracle," which may have been conceived as a continuation or companion piece. "The Miracle" follows immediately after "May Day ↑Invitation↓" in the list of "Proposed Additions."

*Date:* The first draft in journal KL dates from April 1865, though the sections taken from P p. 168 and EL pp. 32 and 191 were all written earlier.

*Publication:* Unpublished.

*See Also:* (1) "The Miracle" and (2) "Where the fungus broad & red."

### "Memory"

*Texts:* Numerous texts of this quatrain exist. By following the pattern of revisions, their order through six notebooks can be determined with some certainty.

1. Journal F 2 contains the earliest drafts, all in pencil: two of five lines each, of which the second is the earlier, and one of four lines on the preceding manuscript page (JMN 7:509, 508); all three versions are struck through in pencil.

2. In P pp. 70 and 71 occur two further pencil drafts, the first of which is followed by an experimental revision of the first two lines; these drafts are struck through in pencil.

3. Notebook X pp. 122–23 contains four drafts, all in ink, in which the final form of the quatrain emerges, as the successive changes in the first line

show: from "Dreams but trace on Reason's wall" to "Dreams nightly trace on Memory's wall" to "Night-dreams trace on Memory's wall." Each of the four versions is struck through in ink.

4. Rhymer contains two drafts: one in ink on p. 29, in which the title "Memory" appears for the first time, and one in pencil on p. 51, which recovers some of the wording of the earliest drafts, though it is a late copy. Both drafts have "printed" written beside them.

5. Two versions in ink in NP pp. 2 and 133 are in final form; the first lacks the title and the second is struck though. Also in NP, on p. 12, occur two lines of prose that echo the first line of the quatrain and that are related, both here and in notebook Phi Beta p. 153, to "On the chamber" (see also EL p. 200).

6. The quatrain appears in ink in final form but untitled in notebook EO p. 59, struck through in ink.

A signed ink fair copy in the Manuscript Division, New York Public Library, was removed from the library's copy of *May–Day*.

*Date:* The three pencil drafts in journal F 2 occur directly before an entry of 16 August 1840, and presumably date from that time. Among several prose sources in the journals, the closest is an entry for 16 October 1837: "Culture inspects our dreams also. The pictures of the night will always bear some proportion to the visions of the day" (JMN 5:398, cf. 5:285).

*Publication:* May–Day, 1867, p. 188; reprinted in *Poems*, 1884, p. 242, and W 9:295.

## "Merlin I"

*Texts:* The very rough draft of lines 1–25 in journal V (JMN 9:167–68) appears to be continued in X pp. 84–86. It is equally possible, however, that the two drafts were conceived independently and brought together later as an afterthought. A manuscript of "Merlin I" and "Merlin II" in the Houghton Library contains a version of the poem in ink still lacking lines 39–42 and 63–64 (see Additional Manuscripts). Printer's copy for the London edition of *Poems*, 1847, is in the Huntington Library (lines 1–40) and the Berg Collection, New York Public Library (lines 41–77).

*Date:* The journal V draft, which, as Edward Emerson suggested (W 9:440), probably dates to 1845, appears to be a working out of the prose source in journal D (JMN 7:219), written on 27 June 1839. Emerson wrote on 27 July 1846 that he had lately completed a number of poems, including "Merlin" (L 3:341), undoubtedly referring to "Merlin I" and "Merlin II" together. The relation between the drafts in X of "Merlin I" (pp. 84–86) and "Merlin II" (pp. 81–83, with an additional draft of the opening lines on p. 80) is difficult to assess. The index reference in X to "Merlin" is to p. 81. It is probable that

"Merlin II" was written first (the Houghton manuscript proves at least that it was perfected first), and that the verses on pp. 84–86 were part of an abortive attempt to enlarge the poem.

*Publication:* Poems, 1847, pp. 180–84 (Boston) and pp. 143–46 (London). Reprinted in *Poems,* 1884, pp. 106–9, and W 9:120–22.

*See Also:* (1) "The river knows the way" and (2) "Merlin II."

## "Merlin II"

*Texts:* The first draft of "Merlin II" occurs in X pp. 81–83, where the lines carry the title (and index reference) "Merlin." An additional draft of the opening lines occurs in erased pencil on p. 80. A fair copy in ink is in the Houghton Library; in it, line 14 reads "Two married sides" rather than the published "Eldest rite, two married sides" and "Ea[ch]" is overwritten by "One" in line 29. In this manuscript the poem follows an imperfect fair copy (lacking lines 39–42 and 63–64) of "Merlin I." Printer's copy for the London edition of *Poems,* 1847, is in the Berg Collection, New York Public Library; in it, "Are coeval" is canceled for "In one body" in line 13, "Eldest rite," is added to the beginning of line 14, and "While" is canceled for "As" in line 52.

*Date:* Emerson wrote on 27 July 1846 that he had lately completed a number of poems, including "Merlin" (L 3:341), undoubtedly referring to "Merlin I" and "II" together. Of the two, "Merlin II" arrived first at final form, as shown by the Houghton fair copy. The title given to the draft in X as well as its position relative to the draft of the latter portions of "Merlin I" on X pp. 84–86 suggest that of the two it was begun first—probably in 1845. Lines 24–25 seem to derive from a couplet rejected from "Saadi" in 1842 (JMN 7:480). Line 50 bears a similar relation to line 10 of "Water."

*Publication:* Poems, 1847, pp. 185–87 (Boston) and pp. 147–49 (London). Reprinted in *Poems,* 1884, pp. 109–10, and W 9:123–24.

*See Also:* (1) "Every thought kindling" and (2) "Merlin I."

## "Merlin's Song"

*Texts:* Lines 12–13 were the first written: they occur in pencil in journal SO (JMN 14:74), following versions of the prose source on the same and preceding manuscript pages. The first two drafts of the poem as a whole occur in EL pp. 22 and 23. The poem was revised in the partially erased draft in EL p. 52 and copied with further revisions into EL p. 53 (pencil) and Rhymer p. 14 (ink), where the poem, titled, carries the notation "printed."

*Date:* The prose source, written in SO in April 1856 and copied into NP pp. 113–14, is an imitation of stanzas 149–57 of "The Runic Chapter" in Paul Henri Mallet, *Northern Antiquities* (London, 1847), pp. 371–72, parts of which Emerson had copied into journal VS in 1853 (JMN 13:171). He knew this poem as early as 1820 when he copied into his notebook passages quoted in William Godwin's *Life of Geoffrey Chaucer* (JMN 1:371). The poem could have been written at any time between 1856 and its publication in 1867.

*Publication: May–Day,* 1867, p. 96. Omitted from *Selected Poems,* 1876, and *Poems,* 1884, it was reprinted in W 9:218 as part I of "Merlin's Song," editorially enlarged by the addition of "Considerations by the Way" as an untitled part II (see W 9:475–76).

*See Also:* Kenneth W. Cameron, "The Potent Song in Emerson's Merlin Poems," *PQ* 32 (January 1953): 22–28.

## "Merops"

*Texts:* The earliest draft, in pencil, is in X p. 25. A pencil fair copy in X p. 160 carries the title "Rhyme."

*Date:* Undetermined.

*Publication: Poems,* 1847, p. 194 (Boston) and p. 154 (London). Lines 5–8 were quoted by William Ellery Channing in *Thoreau,* p. 119. The poem was reprinted in *Poems,* 1884, p. 113, and W 9:127–28. The draft at X p. 25 was published with several errors in the note to "Merops" in W 9:445–46.

## "The Miracle"

*Texts:* A partial first draft of the poem occurs in journal KL (JMN 15:463–64). This was revised in two successive drafts in Poems folder 56. Further revision occurred in EL pp. 209–11, where lines 17–22 are drawn from EL p. 191. A fair copy, slightly revised, is in Poems folder 56, while the final fair copy is in ETE pp. 154–55. (For the three texts in Poems folder 56, see Additional Manuscripts; see also a canceled version of lines 35–36 in the third text of "May Day [Invitation]" in Poems folder 55 in Additional Manuscripts.)

*Date:* The first draft in KL dates from 1864–1865. Drafts of this poem are usually associated with "May Day [Invitation]."

*Publication:* Unpublished by Emerson. First published in *Poems,* 1884, pp. 305–6, and reprinted in W 9:368–69.

## "Mithridates"

*Texts:* Drafts of the poem occur in erased pencil in X pp. 218–19, 219–20, and, partially erased, in X pp. 222–23. Only one word has been recovered from the short erased pencil passage on p. 221, which may be a revision of the opening lines. An ink fair copy in the Houghton Library is identical in wording to the first published text.

*Date:* In Emerson's letter of 27 July 1846 to Elizabeth Hoar, he mentions "Mithridates" as among the poems he "wrote lately" (L 3:341).

*Publication:* Poems, 1847, pp. 41–42 (Boston) and pp. 30–31 (London). The last two lines were omitted when the poem was reprinted in *Selected Poems,* 1876, pp. 32–33, and thereafter in *Poems,* 1884, pp. 30–31, and W 9:28–29.

## "Monadnock"

*Texts:* The history of the composition of this poem is complex and in places doubtful. No complete manuscript draft exists, and for certain portions of the poem (e.g., lines 92–123 and 233–330) there is no manuscript authority at all. The available evidence, however, points to at least two stages of composition.

1. In its earliest form the poem was called "Wachusett," as shown by the index designation of two fragments in X pp. 13 and 51 (but see p. 12 also for traces of the opening lines on p. 51). These fragments bear a close relationship to an unfinished poem in Poems folder 90 that Emerson wrote and dated 3 April 1845 at Princeton, Massachusetts, a town lying at the foot of Mt. Wachusett (see Additional Manuscripts under "Wachusett"). It would seem that Emerson's purpose in these early fragments was to supply an introductory frame and a human speaker to "Wachusett" (in which the mountain is imagined as addressing its neighbor, Monadnock); this effort grew progressively longer and may at last have simply swamped the original conception. (In a preliminary list of contents for the London edition of *Poems,* 1847, Emerson included "Wachusett," but struck it out, almost certainly because by October 1846 "Monadnock" had come to replace it; see L 3:358n.) The earliest drafts are in X pp. 12–13, which are revised on pp. 51–52. The material on X p. 14 is revised on p. 63—which revision probably inspired the new lines on p. 62. The material from p. 15 is revised on pp. 16–17; the material from p. 16 is in turn revised on p. 28, while the lines from pp. 17–18 are revised on pp. 29–30. The revisions done on pp. 28–30 seem in turn to have prompted the new lines composed on p. 26. Lines 331–67, an unusually long and coherent passage, appear on pp. 52–54, bringing the first stage of composition to a close.

2. On 27 June 1846, Emerson noted in journal O (JMN 9:432–33): "We had conversation today concerning the poet & his problem. He is there to see the type & truly interpret it; O mountain what would your highness say? thou grand expressor of the present tense; of permanence; yet is there also a taunt at the mutables from old Sitfast. If the poet could only forget himself in his theme, be the tongue of the mountain, his egotism would subside and that firm line which he had drawn would remain like the names of discoverers of planets, written in the sky in letters which could never be obliterated." The passage is directly the source of the lines with which the draft in X pp. 224–25 begins. This draft of the last sixty lines of the poem was revised four times: on pp. 226–27, 228–29, 231–32, and once more on 233–34. X p. 230 contains a draft of the opening of this section as well as two new transitional passages. Lines 401–4 were evidently a late addition to the poem; a version of these lines occurs in a manuscript in Poems folder 59 (see Additional Manuscripts). Line 57 occurs isolated from the drafts both in JMN 9:169 and X p. 37.

*Date:* Ralph L. Rusk thought the germ of the poem was to be found in Emerson's letter of 3 September 1839 to Margaret Fuller (L 2:220 and note); yet while attitudes expressed in that letter (and the one following) certainly found their way into the poem, "Monadnock" was unquestionably written in 1845 and 1846. Edward Emerson (W 9:424) argued for 1845 on the basis of the date ("1845 3 May 4 hours 10 m. a m") written in X p. 29. A careful examination of this page of the notebook reveals, however, that the date belongs not to the "Monadnock" draft, but instead to the largely erased lower layer, a draft of "Forerunners." Thus while the "Wachusett" poem is dated 3 April, the early "Monadnock" fragments could not have been inscribed for more than a month afterward. The second stage of composition belongs to the period between 27 June 1846 and September of that year, when, according to a letter in the possession of Eleanor Tilton, Emerson sent a copy of the poem to Caroline Sturgis.

*Publication:* First published with the title "Monadnoc" in *Poems,* 1847, pp. 94–114 (Boston) and (with a number of variants and the omission of line 35) pp. 73–90 (London); reprinted, with the title as given above, in *Selected Poems,* 1876, pp. 141–54, and, with the earlier title, in *Poems,* 1884, pp. 58–70, and W 9:60–75. Lines 401–4 were published separately from the Poems folder 59 text in *Poems,* 1884, p. 282, and again in W 1:409 among the notes to "Nature," but not in W 9.

*See Also:* "My people are grim."

## "More sweet than my refrain"

*Text:* This couplet occurs in EF p. 14 and EL p. 45, both times in association with "I to my garden went."

*Date:* Between 1851 and 1859 (see "I to my garden went").

*Publication:* Unpublished.

## "The Muses' hill by Fear is guarded"

*Texts:* Four identical drafts of this couplet exist, set down in indeterminate order in EL p. 149, NP pp. 47 and 295, and Rhymer p. 2ₐ, where it is joined with lines rejected from "Fate" ("Delicate omens").

*Date:* The EL text follows on the same manuscript page verses ("By art, by music") that could not have been written before August 1859. The text at NP p. 47 interrupts, and therefore antedates, a draft of "The Titmouse" inscribed in 1862. The contextual association of "The Muses' hill" with "Fate" ("Delicate omens") both in Rhymer p. 2ₐ and NP p. 295 suggests a date of composition in late 1859.

*Publication:* Unpublished by Emerson. First published in *Poems*, 1884, p. 277, and reprinted in W 9:334.

## "Music stoops"

*Text:* These lines occur in pencil in EL p. 119. They have not been found elsewhere in Emerson's published or unpublished writings.

## "Musketaquid"

*Texts:* Drafts of approximately half the poem survive. Probably the earliest of the fragments are in P: versions of lines 13–18, dated "21 March," are on p. 25, while drafts of lines 11–12 and 20–21 occur in erased pencil on pp. 195 and 197 respectively. In journal Books Small (JMN 8:458, 465, 466) are pencil drafts of lines 24–25, 1–8, and 68–74, respectively. In notebook Phi are four versions of all or part of lines 26–34 (JMN 12:279–80, 284). Printer's copy for the London edition of *Poems*, 1847, is in the Berg Collection, New York Public Library; in it, "pitying," is inserted and "rock-like" canceled for "solitary" in line 9, and "Thus" and "they hint" are canceled for "And" and "disclose" in line 46 (English lineation).

*Date:* The first indication of Emerson's desire to write a poem on the Musketaquid, or Concord, River occurs in a letter to Lydia Jackson in early March 1835: "I have promised him a song . . . whenever the tardy, callow muse shall new moult her feathers. River large & inkstand little, deep & deep would blend their voices" (L 1:440); the following paragraph contains the prose source of lines 24–25. The latest of the four draft passages in notebook Phi follows on the same manuscript page index entries set down in 1842 (see JMN 12:283–84, n. 25). The phrase "the sannup and the squaw" occurs both in line 28 (part of the passage in Phi) and in a letter of 19 July 1843 (L 3:187). No entry in journal Books Small can be shown to be of an earlier date than 1840. On 30 October 1846, when Emerson sent the poem to John Chapman for publication, he spoke of it as having been completed considerably earlier: it "has declined very much in my good graces by keeping" (L 3:359). The fragments in P may be early, but the poem as a whole probably dates to 1843 or 1844.

*Publication: Poems,* 1847, pp. 227–31 (Boston) and (with a number of variants, the omission of line 73, and the substitution of two entirely different lines for lines 26–31) pp. 181–84 (London); reprinted in *Selected Poems,* 1876, pp. 164–66, *Poems,* 1884, pp. 124–27, and W 9:141–44.

*See Also:* W 9:450–51.

## "My Garden"

*Texts:* The principal texts of this poem were inscribed in EL: a rough draft on pp. 183–87 (the first forty lines only), and the fair copy of the entire poem on pp. 195–98 (which, however, were torn out). These drafts incorporate many fragments that had been developed elsewhere. Lines 1–4 occur in EF p. 60, EL p. 78, and NP pp. 106, 197, and 271. Lines 5–6 turn up first in a draft in journal GL (JMN 15:123) and were copied into NP p. 270. These six lines belonged first to drafts of "In my garden three ways meet," and can be found so connected in drafts of that poem in EL pp. 135–37 and in Poems folder 48 (see Additional Manuscripts under "In my garden"). The second of these drafts also includes trials of lines 21–24, 49–52, and 57–64. An additional draft of lines 5–6 with two rejected lines to fill out the quatrain is in Poems folder 78 ("In my plot no tulips blow, / Snowloving pines & oaks instead, / The lemons hide the glass below, / The pines can wade in the snow"). A draft of lines 9–10, 13–15, and 17–19 occurs in erased pencil in EL p. 72 in the midst of several trials of "Inscription on a Well." Lines 37–40, which exist in twelve drafts and fair copies as an independent quatrain, are probably the oldest portion of the poem, though neither the date of composition nor the order of the drafts can be positively determined. The drafts occur in EF pp. 8, 51, 106, and 107, in Rhymer p. 42, and in NP pp. 83 and 138. Still other drafts are in notebook Z and journal NO (JMN 6:298–99, 13:423) and in notebook PY p. 240. The two drafts in JMN 13 are perhaps a revision done under the inspiration of a remark about English painters that Emerson quoted from the *Life of Benjamin Robert Haydon* (London, 1853). The fair copies in Rhymer and NP p. 138 carry the title "Preraphaelite," and probably therefore date to 1854 or 1855. Lines 51–52 occur in journal VA (JMN 15:308) and were probably copied into (rather than from) EL pp. 71 and 147. They next appear joined with lines 49–50 in the draft of "In my garden three ways meet" in Poems folder 48, mentioned above. Lines 61–64 were revised from the Poems folder 48 text in an erased pencil draft in EL p. 199, apparently immediately before the composition of the ink fair copy of the whole poem in EL pp. 195–98. What appears to be an unused quatrain occurs in EL p. 114ᵦ. Printer's copy for *May–Day* is in the Huntington Library; in it, an "s" is canceled at the end of "side" in line 21, "chant" is written over "sing" in line 43, and "who" is written over "he" in line 63. A marginal notation shows that the poem was being set in type on 12 November 1866. The title of the poem appears to have been first intended for "In my garden three ways meet": see EL p. 158.

*Date:* Lines 37–40 existed as a separate quatrain by the mid-1850s; lines 5–6 were written in GL in March 1861, and lines 51–52 in VA in the late winter of 1863. Nevertheless, the draft fragment in EL p. 72, written at the same time as the "Inscription on a Well," and clearly prior to the two principal texts of "My Garden," shows that the poem as a whole was composed in 1866.

*Publication: Atlantic Monthly* 18 (December 1866): 665–66; collected in *May–Day*, 1867, pp. 114–18, and reprinted in *Poems*, 1884, pp. 197–200, and W 9:229–31.

## "My people are grim & fierce"

*Text:* The only text of this six-line fragment is in pencil in X p. 51, written over an erased pencil draft of "Monadnock," and perhaps suggested by or related to it.

*Date:* After 3 May 1845, the earliest possible date for the "Monadnock" passage.

*Publication:* Unpublished.

## "Nantasket"

*Texts:* The earliest surviving draft occurs in ink in journal G (JMN 8:20). This was copied, revised, and given the title "Nantasket" in X p. 242.

*Date:* The G text occurs among notations set down in July 1841. Emerson stayed at Worrock's Hotel, Nantasket Beach, for two weeks beginning 8 July (see L 2:416–33). The X text is dated 1841, but it was Emerson's practice to give subsequent drafts the date of composition rather than of inscription, so that while 1841 seems a likely date for the revised text, it might be later.

*Publication:* Unpublished by Emerson. First published in J 6:13–14.

## "Nature" ("A subtle chain")

*Texts:* This motto to the 1849 revised edition of *Nature* is a borrowing from "May–Day": the lines correspond to lines 321–22, 315–16, 323–24 of the longer and later-published poem. A seven-line poetic fragment in journal W (JMN 9:219) contains verses that eventually became lines 5–6 of "Nature"; this couplet was revised separately in journal V (JMN 9:163) and again in X p. 264. In X p. 131 is a draft of "May–Day," lines 307–324; this includes the lines that comprise the motto. The entire passage is repeated with a few revisions in NP pp. 75–76.

*Date:* Lines 5–6 were composed in journal W in 1845. The prose source for the passage in X p. 131 is an entry for December 1848 in journal RS (JMN 11:61–62). The motto was therefore written, as a motto, in the first six months of 1849.

*Publication:* First published in September 1849 in *Nature; Addresses, and Lectures,* 1849, p. vii, and, three months later, on the title page of *Nature,* 1849. In W 9:281 the poem is the first of two under the title "Nature": the second is the wholly unrelated motto to the essay "Nature" in *Essays: Second Series,* 1844, a poem for which no drafts exist in the poetry notebooks (see, however, JMN 8:462).

*See Also:* (1) Journal AB p. 71 (JMN 10:32), and (2) Richard Lee Francis, "Completing the Sphere: Emerson's Revisions of the Mottoes of *Nature,*" *Studies in the American Renaissance,* 1979, pp. 231–37.

## "Nature" ("Boon Nature")

*Texts:* The first three drafts of this quatrain occur in journal TU (JMN 11:118–19). Probably the next drafts are those in notebook WA pp. i and (with the lines divided into tetrameters) 271. Other drafts occur in NP pp. 119 and 139 and in Rhymer p. 65; the latter two bear the title "Nature."

*Date:* The TU drafts were composed in June 1849.

*Publication:* First published in *The Dial* (Cincinnati) 1 (March 1860): 195, in a text that does not exactly match any of the manuscripts (having "yields" in line 1 and "see" in line 2). The text published in *May–Day,* 1867, p. 186, matching the NP p. 139 and Rhymer fair copies, was reprinted in *Poems,* 1884, p. 241, and W 9:294. William Ellery Channing's text in *Thoreau,* p. 182, reads "day" for "hour" in line 4, and must therefore derive from Emerson's manuscript, probably from WA p. i.

## "Nature" ("Day by day")

*Texts:* The poem occurs in two almost identical titled drafts in EL p. 38 and journal NY (JMN 16:124).

*Date:* The draft in NY dates from 1868. A prose source for the image of "hundred-gated Thebes" occurs in an 1849 passage in journal TU (JMN 11:158).

*Publication:* Unpublished by Emerson. First published, without title, in *Poems,* 1884, p. 281, and reprinted in W 9:341.

## "Nature I"

*Texts:* The first substantial draft of the poem occurs in ink in X pp. 268$_g$ and 268$_k$–268$_l$: it consists of lines 1–4, a passage of six unused lines (here designated "A"), 5–6, passage "A" repeated, 5–6, 9–15, another passage of six unused lines (here designated "B"), and 16–21. The last 12 lines of this draft have their origin in an entry in journal Books Small (JMN 8:446), consisting of "B" and lines 16–17. This passage was revised in X p. 38 and expanded by the addition of lines 18–21 before being copied into X pp. 268$_k$–268$_l$. Lines 12–15 were actually the first to be written, and were originally regarded by Emerson as a separate quatrain: they occur in an erased pencil draft in P p. 163, in pencil in P p. 250, and in ink with the prefatory word "Beware!" on the verso of a leaf used for an insert in the lecture "Humanity of Science" (*Early Lectures* 2:382). Another copy of these lines, signed and dated "Concord: Feb 1849", was offered for sale by Books With a Past, Concord, Massachusetts, in October 1984; it is identical in wording to the "Humanity of Science" text (including "Beware!") except for "plague" instead of "hurt" in line 14. Lines 9–11 first occur in X p. 34, where they may originally have been part of a draft of "The World-Soul." Passages "A" and "B" were dropped in the next draft in X p. 212, which consists of lines 1–6 and 9–15 only. Emerson added a roman numeral "I" above the lines to make them part of a sequence with "A queen rejoices" on p. 211, marked "II," and "Fate" ("Delicate omens") on p. 213, marked "III." Some time after he copied the poems in the indicated sequence in NP pp. 69–71, he added lines 7–8 to

"Nature I" (NP p. 69). The prose source of lines 7–8 may be either X p. ii or an entry in journal JK (JMN 10:383). No complete manuscript of the poem is known.

*Date:* The "Humanity of Science" lecture was first delivered on 22 December 1836, though the insert and the inscription of the quatrain are likely to be somewhat later. The origin of these verses in P, however, is evidence of an early date. The draft in the X insert after p. 268 was probably composed in 1846 or 1847, as these pages contain drafts of three different mottoes for the 1847 edition of *Essays: First Series.* Such a date is consistent also with the presumption that lines 9–11 originally belonged to a draft of "The World-Soul." The later drafts cannot be dated.

*Publication: May–Day,* 1867, pp. 105–6; reprinted in *Poems,* 1884, p. 193, and W 9:225.

## "Nature II"

*Texts:* The first draft in pencil in NP pp. 206–7 is revised in ink on pp. 208–9. An ink fair copy, marked "printed," is in Rhymer pp. 98–99.

*Date:* The second draft is written over passages used in "Robert Burns," a speech that Emerson delivered on 25 January 1859.

*Publication: May–Day,* 1867, pp. 107–8; reprinted in *Poems,* 1884, p. 194, and W 9:226.

## "Nature in Leasts"

*Texts:* Lines 1–2 of this quatrain, which are considerably older than the poem as a whole, appear in final form in the earliest text in journal K (JMN 8:241). The lines also appear in X p. 263 and Rhymer p. 41, where they were given the title "Natura in minimis." Possibly the earliest surviving draft of the whole quatrain is a signed fair copy in ink on a slip of paper inserted between pp. 12 and 13 of notebook Morals. The third line of this draft ("The life & strength & soul of France") becomes "The strength & joy of laughing France" in the revision in journal GO (JMN 13:101), with which it otherwise verbally agrees. This text of lines 3–4 was added in pencil to the ink drafts of lines 1–2 in Rhymer p. 41 and was then revised in ink to final form. Texts at X p. 204 and NP p. 139—the first untitled, the second carrying the title "Natura in minimis"—are fair copies. A separate signed fair copy is in the University of Virginia Library. A copy of lines 1–2 in the Houghton Library Autograph File was written out for John Mills in Manchester, England, on 2

March 1848; another copy in the Brown University Library is signed and dated 26 January 1859; another is slipped into the front of journal NY (JMN 16:97). The earlier title derives from a quotation attributed to Malpighi in JMN 9:410: "Cum tota in minimis existat natura" (cf. JMN 15:7, where "Natura in minimis existit" is attributed to Aristotle). The final title appears for the first time in the *May–Day* printing.

*Date:* Lines 1–2 seem to have been written in journal K between 22 and 30 April 1842. In X p. 263 they follow "Atom from atom," another couplet composed in that month. The draft of the whole in journal GO (presumably the second draft of the quatrain) dates to October 1852.

*Publication: The Dial* (Cincinnati) 1 (March 1860): 195, with the title "*Natura in minimis.*" The only substantive alteration in the next printing, in *May–Day*, 1867, p. 191, was the change of title to "Nature in Leasts." The quatrain was reprinted in *Poems*, 1884, p. 244, and W 9:297.

## "Nature saith"

*Texts:* The first draft of this thirteen-line fragment occurs in pencil in NP p. 248, followed by a fair copy in ink in EL p. 181. It is Emerson's versification of a passage by Mary Moody Emerson in notebook MME 2, pp. 148–49: "I am not infinite, nor have I power or will, but, bound & imprisoned, the tool of mind, even of the beings I feed & adorn. Vital I feel not,—active,—but passive; and cannot aid the creatures which seem my progeny,—my self! But you are ingrate to tire of me, now you want to look beyond: twas I who soothed your thorny childhood, though you knew me not. And you were placed in my most leafless waste; yet I comforted thee when going on the daily errand,—fed thee with my mallows on the first young day of bread · failing."

*Date:* Undetermined.

*Publication:* Unpublished.

*See Also:* "These craggy hills," which is introduced by the phrase "Nature says."

## "Nature will not lose"

*Text:* The only text of this five-line fragment is in pencil in X p. 74, where it may be related to "If he go apart," which precedes it. The verses have not been found elsewhere in Emerson's published or unpublished writings.

## "Nature's web star-broidered"

*Texts:* These lines occur in pencil overwritten in ink in Poems folder 58; the pencil text has "wove" for "woven" in line 2. Another pencil draft, identical in wording to the ink version, is in EL p. 200.

*Date:* The folder 58 text is on a page dated 1841. In the left margin is a list of nine essays in *Essays: First Series,* suggesting Emerson may have used the page when considering mottoes for the 1847 edition of that book.

*Publication:* Unpublished.

## "Nemesis"

*Texts:* The two stanzas of this poem developed separately. Drafts of the first occur as follows: in EF p. 11 is a version of lines 1–4 and 7–8 written over a partially erased draft of "Novice, hear me"; this was copied with the change of a single word into X p. 191, where it follows on the same page a draft of "Fate" ("Delicate omens"). This was in turn copied into NP p. 74, where lines 5–6 were added. The second stanza, apparently at first a quite separate conception, has for its source a quotation from Aeschylus's *The Supplicants* in notebook EO p. 36: "Whatever is fated, that will take place. The great immense mind of Jove is not to be transgressed. O mighty Jove, defend me from the nuptials of the sons of AEgyptus. That indeed would be best: but you would soothe a deity not to be soothed" (*The Seven Tragedies of Aeschylus,* 3d ed. [Oxford, 1843], p. 280). In EO p. 37 is the pencil first draft of the second stanza, drawing lines 13 and 14 from EO p. 95. Lines 15–16 were revised in EO p. 106 and lines 13–14 in EO p. 139 before the entire stanza was written out in a pencil draft in EO p. 38. Fair copies of the whole poem occur in Rhymer p. 23 (with the title "Destiny") and in NP p. 255 (with the title "Fate").

*Date:* Undetermined. The copy of Aeschylus that Emerson purchased in England in 1848 (see JMN 10:336) is the source of the quotation in EO.

*Publication:* First published in *May–Day,* 1867, pp. 67–68, and reprinted in W 9:196.

## "New England Capitalist"

*Texts:* Five manuscript drafts of the poem are known, composed in the following order: (1) Notebook Trees [A:I], in pencil (JMN 8:524–25); (2) X

p. 60, in pencil, where the first few lines are written over the erased last stanza of "The House"; (3) NP p. 211, in ink, written over erased drafts of "Fate" ("Her planted eye"); (4) X p. 63, in ink, written over erased lines used in "Monadnock"; and (5) a draft in ink, with title, in Poems folder 60 (see Additional Manuscripts).

*Date:* Notebook Trees was first used in 1843, the same year in which, as Carl F. Strauch has pointed out, Emerson became acquainted with the recently invented telegraph (line 16). Strauch conjectures that the poem may have been written while Emerson was engaged with his lecture series on New England delivered in Baltimore, Philadelphia, and New York between 10 January and 22 February 1843. If the first draft is indeed as early as this, the revisions must have been done over a number of years, since the fourth draft (X p. 63) is written over lines composed in 1845. The idea of the poem may be traced back to a journal entry for 6 February 1841 (JMN 7:420), and that of lines 1–7 to JMN 7:426.

*Publication:* Unpublished by Emerson. First published, with commentary, in Carl F. Strauch, "Emerson's 'New England Capitalist,' " *HLB* 10 (1956): 245–53, where manuscripts 1 and 5 above are reproduced.

## "The new year's mien is mild & meek"

*Text:* This couplet, in partially erased pencil, occurs in EL p. 85; the notation "H T." written below it may indicate it is a versification of a sentence from Thoreau. The couplet has not been found elsewhere in Emerson's published or unpublished writings.

## "The ninefold table of Heaven"

*Text:* This quatrain, in EF p. 97, a page headed "Hafiz superlative," translates Hafiz, Book VIII, Ode CLXIV, lines 21–24 (*Diwan* 1:444–45). It has not been found elsewhere in Emerson's published or unpublished writings.

## "Nineteenth day of the April moon"

*Text:* This couplet is in pencil in X p. 110. It has not been found elsewhere in Emerson's published or unpublished writings.

## "No fate, save by the victim's fault, is low"

*Texts:* These three lines were originally lines 8–10 of a poem beginning "Forth to encounter thy affianced doom" in Poems folder 34 (see Additional Manuscripts under that title). Emerson made many copies of the shorter poem, including, apparently, copies for autograph-seekers. Versions occur in EL p. 291, Rhymer pp. 50ⱼ, 106, and 150, NP p. 5, ETE pp. 7, 104c, and 176 (cf. p. 174), Poems folder 14 (with "blessed" canceled for "tender" in line 3), Pocket Diaries 28 and 29 (JMN 16:497 and 507), and in a manuscript in the Duke University Library, dated 29 August 1877. Another, dated 21 March 1870, was reported for sale in *ESQ*, no. 6 (1st quarter 1957), 26.

*Date:* "Forth to encounter thy affianced doom" is a very early poem, to judge from the handwriting in the undated manuscript in Poems folder 34. The copy in NP p. 5 (which occurs with two other excerpts from this poem) supplies the date "1825"; this is probably a guess on Emerson's part and the verses may be even older. The copy in Poems folder 14 seems to date to 1841, while the copies in the Pocket Diaries were inscribed in 1878 and 1879.

*Publication:* Unpublished by Emerson. First published in *Poems,* 1884, p. 288, and reprinted in W 9:349.

*See Also:* "Not frolic Beauty" and "Shalt be affianced," which derive from the same poem.

## "No physician has a balsam for my wo"

*Text:* These lines, which translate Hafiz, Book XXIII, Ode XIV, lines 9–10 (*Diwan* 2:170), occur in EF p. 80. They have not been found elsewhere in Emerson's published or unpublished writings.

## "No song so tuneful, quoth the fox"

*Texts:* The first draft of this couplet occurs in pencil above its prose source in journal FOR (JMN 15:386); it is revised in NP p. 300.

*Date:* The draft in FOR occurs shortly before an entry of 2 November 1863.

*Publication:* Unpublished by Emerson. First published in JMN 15.

## "Northman"

*Texts:* The first four drafts of this quatrain occur in journal IO (JMN 13:360 and 356), followed by fair copies in journal DO (JMN 13:19), Rhymer p. 61, and NP p. 134. The latter two bear the title.

*Date:* Among the remoter sources for this quatrain is the line from Butler's *Hudibras,* "We only row we're steered by fate," which Emerson quoted in journal B (JMN 5:33) in 1835, and the statement by Gibbon that "The winds & waves are always on the side of the ablest navigators," quoted in the same journal (JMN 5:108) and used in "Nature" (W 1:20). The immediate source, however, is Augustin Thierry, *History of the Conquest of England by the Normans* (London, 1841), p. 21, a passage quoted by Emerson in journal VS (JMN 13:172): " 'The force of the storm,' [the Vikings] would sing, 'is a help to the arm of our rowers; the hurricane is in our service; it carries us the way we would go.' " Emerson withdrew Thierry's *History* from the Boston Athenaeum in June 1853 and made his notes in June or July. The first drafts in IO, however, occur among notes from Pepys's *Memoirs,* which he borrowed from the Athenaeum in September and October 1854.

*Publication: The Dial* (Cincinnati) 1 (March 1860): 195; reprinted in *May–Day,* 1867, p. 185, *Poems,* 1884, p. 240, and W 9:293.

*See Also:* "From Alcuin."

## "Not frolic Beauty weaving wanton nets"

*Texts:* These three lines were originally lines 5–7 of "Forth to encounter thy affianced doom" in Poems folder 34 (see Additional Manuscripts under that title). The only text of the three-line version occurs in NP p. 5 with two other short excerpts from that poem.

*Date:* Undetermined. Emerson dated NP p. 5 "1825," probably from memory.

*Publication:* Unpublished.

*See Also:* "No fate, save by the victim's fault" and "Shalt be affianced."

## "Not mine, sour priest, not mine the blame"

*Texts:* This poem, possibly a translation from Hafiz, occurs in four drafts. The first, in EF p. 72, is followed by Emerson's symbol of authorship; however, ink fair copies in notebooks EO p. 93 and L Camadeva p. 66 carry attributions to Hafiz. The latter copy is struck through three times in ink and, on the same page, revised into a rhymed quatrain: "Not mine, sour priest, not mine the blame, / Did not wise god approve / Who lit in me this quenchless flame / What maiden I should love?"

*Date:* Undetermined.

*Publication:* Unpublished.

## "Not yet, not yet"

*Texts:* The earliest draft is a fragment in X p. 185 (lines 37–42, followed by five unused lines), written in ink over an erased draft of "Hermione." This was followed soon after by the extensive draft in notebook Dialling (JMN 8:506–7); line 1 occurs separately four manuscript pages later. A fair copy of the entire fragment occurs in Poems folder 73 (see Additional Manuscripts). From this Emerson extracted lines 25–28 and 37–44 as a separate poem of three stanzas in Rhymer p. 9, the last two lines of which he revised in X p. 184 and then transcribed back into the Rhymer text.

*Date:* The second draft (Dialling) can be dated from Emerson's letter to Lidian of 14 June 1841, in which he quoted lines 37–44 as "verses that I find scribbled in a latest page" (L 2:404–5). The "hat of straw" mentioned in the third of the unused lines in X p. 185 appears in JMN 8:5 in an entry written perhaps a few weeks later. The fair copy in Poems folder 73 is dated 1843. The revision in X p. 184 (and of course the addition to the Rhymer text) must have been done after April 1846, the earliest possible date for "Drink wine, and the heaven," which occurs in pencil in X p. 184.

*Publication:* Unpublished by Emerson. The long version was published as lines 91–133 of "The Poet" (a piece assembled by Cabot) in *Poems,* 1884, pp. 256–57, and reprinted in W 9:312–13.

## "Nothing suits gold so well as wine"

*Text:* This single line, undoubtedly from Hafiz, occurs with other translations in X p. 171. It has not been found elsewhere in Emerson's published or unpublished writings.

## "Novice, hear me what I say"

*Texts:* The poem translates Hafiz, Book XXVII, Ode XVI (*Diwan* 2:380–82). The first draft is in pencil in X pp. 256–57; the second, lacking lines 37–40, is in erased pencil in EF pp. 10–11. Lines 25–36 were separately revised in notebook Orientalist p. 23 and given the title "Faith."

*Date:* Between 1846, when Emerson acquired his copy of the *Diwan,* and 1850, when "Faith" was published. The revision in Orientalist was probably done in 1850.

*Publication:* Unpublished, except as follows: lines 25–36, with the title "Faith," were published in *The Liberty Bell* (Boston, 1851), pp. 79–80, reprinted in *Uncollected Writings,* 1912, p. 187. Lines 25–32, slightly revised and without title, appear again in "Persian Poetry," 1858, p. 732.

*See Also:* "Faith."

## "Now"

*Texts:* Emerson's special fondness for this couplet, which he gave six different openings, is evinced by the number of times he inscribed it. The lines occur in the published journals as follows: JMN 5:127 and 145, n. 435; 12:206; 14:56, 124, and 211; 16:185, 497, and 507. In the poetry notebooks they occur in EL pp. 30, 158, 290, and 291, Rhymer p. 104 (with the title "Now"), and ETE pp. 33, 104c, and 174 (with the title "Now"). They are also inscribed, beginning "This shining moment", in Emerson's correction copy of *Society and Solitude,* 1870, p. 139 (the half-title page for "Works and Days").

*Date:* The source of the couplet is probably the erased pencil text referred to in the footnote to JMN 5:145, which evidently prompted the draft set down between 28 February and 4 March 1836 in journal B (JMN 5:127). The last recorded inscription (JMN 16:507) dates to 1878.

*Publication:* Unpublished by Emerson. First published in *Poems,* 1884, p. 288, untitled, with "passing" in line 1, and reprinted as a motto to "Works and Days," W 7:156; published also in W 9:350, untitled, with "shining" in line 1.

## "Now Nature is a Funeral"

*Text:* These lines occur in pencil in P p. 193, and, though they lack meter and rhyme scheme, are probably related to "Dirge," drafts of which occupy the preceding pages. The lines have not been found elsewhere in Emerson's published or unpublished writings.

## "Now tells the flower"

*Text:* This poem, a translation of Hafiz, Book III, Ode XXXIX, lines 9–28 (*Diwan* 1:104–5), occurs in pencil in EF p. 103. It has not been found elsewhere in Emerson's published or unpublished writings.

## "The Nun's Aspiration"

*Texts:* The poem was written in three distinct sections, and as much as a decade passed between its inception and completion.

An early form of lines 1–2 with additional unused lines in NP pp. 252–53 is followed by a draft of lines 1–10 in notebook BL p. 196 (in ink, lines 7–10 over erased pencil). The sources for these lines occur in notebook MME 2 in which, beginning in January 1859, Emerson copied passages from the "almanacks" or diaries of his aunt Mary Moody Emerson. On p. 7 is the source for lines 1–6: "The yesterday does never smile, as I would; yet, in the name of the shepherd of mankind, I defy tomorrow. God himself cannot withdraw himself. Health feeble, alone, most alone, but I defy tomorrow." On pp. 13–14 is the source for lines 7–10: "And the simple principle which made me say in youth & laborious poverty, that, should He make me a blot on the fair face of his creation, I should rejoice in His will, has never been equaled,—though it returns in the long life of destitution, like an Angel." (Emerson's note, keyed to the word "equaled," reads: "She means, that was the highwater mark in her history. R.W.E.") The BL draft was copied into MME 1 p. 7, NP p. 254, and later, as the notation in NP indicates, into ETE p. 173. Other copies occur in Rhymer p. 34, NP front cover verso$_e$, and ETE pp. 103 and 104$_a$. A single-sheet fair copy of lines 1–10, struck through four times in ink, is in the University of Virginia Library, where it is associated with *May–Day* printer's copy for "Solution."

The remainder of the poem had its origin also in Aunt Mary's diaries. In EL p. 249 Emerson versified a passage from MME 4 pp. 110–13: "Oh these mystic scenes of Autumn, when her solemn stole encircles us, it seems but a moment when the veil will be raised. Already the sublime dirge of Nature's funeral is hymned by the blasts of the mountains, & the sable pageantry of clouds is mourning the fallen beauty of the summer. How well do the emblems of sorrow in Nature correspond to that element of man's constitution. . . . These waves, these leaves tell their own tale of their Maker—if not, I feel unworthy to give them voice. No human language is so beautiful as their murmurs. But of these indefinable emotions so dear—too dear perhaps—of reasonings too nothing,—if the divine power of conscience is disregarded. On its altar hallowed by God's own erection, let every pleasure be sacrificed. Time enough for other pleasures, when this is secured in the immediate fruition of virtue. . . . A dull walk to see Mrs Thacher x x x, &, in the darker recollections of returning, what pleasure Byron gave me. And when '*my dust is as it should be,*' when the long sunken turf is forgotten amid splendid tombs, then, o then, where the recollections of my pigmy life will be? How peculiar the power to exert on the future,—to look at the present through the vista of ages." Emerson's versification of this in EL p. 249 was revised in NP p. 128 and copied in ETE p. 100 (this would eventually become lines 11–28 of the complete poem).

In NP p. 129, Emerson versified another passage, this one from MME 4 pp. 41–42: "Shake not thy bald head at me, I defy thee to go too fast. Am I furry in sight,—fettered by age,—mired by climate—I wander beyond thee. I pass with the comet into space which mocks thy gnomons—which will exist by travellers who never heard thy earthly fugitive name. The frivolous now deny thee, and thy native home old space, any being. But I respect both—with them for modes of account or existence I shall unravel their labyrinths and explore their birth places. Neither shall I spurn them, I think, when able to look through all their boasted possessions—and remembering how drear the part I hold in the one—how tedious, how wasting the other." Emerson's versification in NP p. 129 was copied and revised in EL pp. 247–48, in a manuscript in Poems folder 62 (see Additional Manuscripts), and in ETE p. 102, where it was at first entitled "Amita," then "Aspiration" (this would eventually become lines 29–49 of the completed poem). Related verses appear in NP p. 130, copied into EL pp. 248 and 250.

The arrangement and location of the various drafts suggest strongly that Emerson composed and revised the last two segments (in NP and EL) without a clear intention of joining them with lines 1–10. The idea of making a single poem of the verses collected in ETE pp. 100–103 first becomes manifest in the third draft of the final section (the Poems folder 62 manuscript), where the title "The Nun's Prayer" and the notation "See also *ETE* 100, 173" are added in pencil. A fair copy of the entire poem, titled "The Nun's Aspiration," possibly printer's copy, is in the Lehigh University Library.

*Date:* Lines 1–10 were almost certainly composed in 1859: notebook MME 2 was written out in January 1859; the draft in NP pp. 252–53 was inscribed before the lines used in the motto to "Wealth," published in *The Conduct of Life*, 1860; notebook BL was used in 1859 and 1860. Lines 11–49 probably date to 1869 when Emerson was preparing an account of his aunt's life to be read (on 1 March) before the New England Women's Club in Boston. According to Edward Emerson (W 10:596), this account was entitled "Amita." The proofsheet "Supplenda," inserted in Rhymer between pp. 60 and 61, has a text of lines 1–10 and may be a preliminary effort for the first printing in 1876 (see Plate 9).

*Publication:* First published in *Selected Poems*, 1876, pp. 184–85, with the misreading "happy" for "haply" in line 12. Reprinted in *Poems*, 1884, pp. 217–18, and W 9:253–54.

*See Also:* Strauch diss., pp. 102–11.

## "O Boston city lecture-hearing"

*Text:* The poem occurs only in an ink draft in EL p. 69.

*Date:* Undetermined. Emerson's mortification at the passive behavior of Boston's leading citizens in the face of Southern intransigence on the slavery question is reflected in the early version of the poem "Boston" and in several passages in his journals; see, for instance, an entry for 1855 in notebook WO Liberty (JMN 14:404–5) that has several parallels with this poem.

*Publication:* Unpublished by Emerson. First published by Edward Emerson in his notes to "Boston," W 9:474.

## "O fairest passenger"

*Text:* These lines occur in erased pencil in EL p. 76. The page was cut out of the notebook after line 5; the stub shows traces of at least seven more lines. The poem has not been found elsewhere in Emerson's published or unpublished writings.

## "O friend blame not Hafiz"

*Text:* This quatrain, which translates Hafiz, Book XXIII, Ode XXVII, lines 37–40 (*Diwan* 2:197), occurs in pencil in EF p. 48. It has not been found elsewhere in Emerson's published or unpublished writings.

## "O Gods give the traveller"

*Text:* These four lines, which translate Hafiz, Book XII, Ode III, lines 17–20 (*Diwan* 2:60), occur in EF p. 80; they have not been found elsewhere in Emerson's published or unpublished writings. The German text for the partially undeciphered line is "Der Herzen folgen, gieb ihm stets."

## "O Hafiz, give me thought"

*Texts:* This quatrain, which translates Hafiz, Book XXII, Ode IV, lines 37–40 (*Diwan* 2:137), occurs in EF p. 114, in three drafts in journal VO p. 77, and in a fair copy in VO p. i (JMN 14:139–40, 120). The EF draft is sufficiently different from those in VO to suggest that it was translated independently.

*Date:* The VO drafts were written in May 1857.

*Publication:* Unpublished by Emerson. First published in JMN 14.

## "O happy soul beyond reward"

*Texts:* The first draft of this couplet occurs in pencil in X p. 56; a revised version in ink occurs in X p. 144.

*Date:* The date of the first draft cannot be determined; the second, however, was probably not written before November 1849, the earliest possible date for the draft of "Roomy Eternity" that precedes it in X p. 144.

*Publication:* Unpublished.

## "O mark the sonnet's flight"

*Texts:* The first draft, in EF p. 40, is followed by revisions in journal NO (JMN 13:423) and EF p. 51. The text in Rhymer p. 130 is a copy from EF p. 51, while the version in Poems folder 36, in which line 2 reads "Follow who can its fleet career," seems to be a late improvement. The quatrain translates Hafiz, Book VIII, Ode XLVI, lines 13–16 (*Diwan* 1:274).

*Date:* The NO draft was done in 1855.

*Publication:* Unpublished by Emerson. First published in J 8:542 from the NO draft.

## "O pedant of the Holy Ghost"

*Text:* This single line occurs in NP p. 12.

*Date:* A sentence of 1844 or 1845 in journal V may have some relevance to this line: "The aim of writers is to tame the Holy Ghost, & produce it as a show to the city" (JMN 9:163). The immediately following prose entry in V is the source of "On the chamber," the second draft of which is also in NP p. 12.

*Publication:* Unpublished.

## "O sun! take off thy hood of clouds"

*Texts:* The first draft, consisting of the first stanza and three trials of the second stanza, occurs in notebook WO Liberty (JMN 14:427–28), at the end of the first draft of "Ode. Sung in the Town Hall, Concord, July 4, 1857," for which the lines were evidently intended (the first stanza is separated from the trials of the second by a draft of the tenth stanza of the "Ode"). Rejected from the "Ode," the lines were revised and extended in a separate second draft in journal VO (JMN 14:153). Ink fair copies of the full three-stanza form are in EL p. 106 and ETE p. 112. Lines 9–12 occur separately in ink in NP p. 55.

*Date:* The draft in WO Liberty dates from the first half of 1857, and probably shortly before 4 July; the draft in VO occurs between entries dated 9 June and 8 July 1857.

*Publication:* Unpublished by Emerson. First published in JMN 14.

## "O the maple, mountain maple, O the Norway pine"

*Text:* This couplet occurs in journal H (JMN 8:98) and EL p. 277.

*Date:* The text in H dates from September or October 1841.

*Publication:* Unpublished by Emerson. First published in JMN 8.

## "O what are heroes prophets men"

*Texts:* An erased pencil draft and an ink fair copy are in P p. 129.

*Date:* Undetermined. The central image of the poem apparently comes from a temperance lecture by George Bancroft as Emerson remembered it in an entry of 20 February 1824 in journal Wide World XIII: "the representation of the body as the corruptible & perishable 'channel, thro' which flow for a season the streams of immortal thought' " (JMN 2:221). Similar references occur in notebooks No. XVIII[A] and No. XVI (JMN 2:389 and 402) and, most notably, in journal B for 15 October 1835: "To him who by God's grace has seen that by being a mere tunnel or pipe through which the divine Will flows, he becomes great, & becomes a Man,—the future wears an eternal smile . . ." (JMN 5:96). A similar entry for 28 October (JMN 5:103) was used in the lecture "The School," given on 19 December 1838 (*Early Lectures* 3:36).

*Publication:* Unpublished by Emerson. First published in *Poems*, 1884, p. 309, with the nonauthorial title "Pan," probably suggested by Emerson's index reference in P, "Pantheos." Reprinted in W 9:360. The evidence for Edward Emerson's statement in W 9:511 that Emerson considered the title "Divine Afflatus" for these lines is not apparent.

*See Also:* B. Bernard Cohen, "Emerson's Poem 'Pan,' " *MLN* 70 (January 1955): 32–33.

## "October woods, wherein"

*Texts:* A rudimentary draft in pencil in NP p. 32 precedes the revised draft on p. 163.

*Date:* The poem was almost certainly written in 1858, and presumably in October of that year. The second draft in NP interrupts, and therefore ante-dates, a draft of "The Adirondacs" composed in the fall of 1858. A cross reference to "October woods NP 163" occurs in EL p. 27 in the midst of another draft of "The Adirondacs." A prose parallel to the poem is in the essay "Success" (W 7:298), based on a lecture of the same name delivered at Hartford, Connecticut, on 14 December 1858.

*Publication:* Unpublished by Emerson. First published by Edward Emerson in a note to the essay "Success" (W 7:440) and in W 9:362.

## "Ode, Inscribed to W. H. Channing"

*Texts:* A draft of lines 3–57, 66–75, and 78–97 occurs in pencil, partially erased, in X pp. 95–99. Printer's copy for the London edition of *Poems*, 1847, is in the Berg Collection, New York Public Library; it has "sand" (line 61) and "glebe" (line 63) for the London misreadings "land" and "globe", and in line 81 "He who" is overwritten by "Who".

*Date:* The printer's copy bears the canceled notation "Monadnoc, June 1846". There are numerous journal sources: a passage on the poet's relation to government (JMN 9:393–94, 1846?, cf. lines 1–11); "In New Hampshire the dignity of the landscape made more obvious the meanness of the tavern-haunting men" (JMN 7:236, 5 September 1839, cf. lines 24–26); "Many a farmer is but a horse's horse or a pig's pig" (JMN 8:278, 8 October 1842, cf. lines 44–45); "If a man live in the saddle the saddle somehow will come to live in him" (JMN 7:102, 9 October 1838, cf. lines 50–51); "Each race of man . . . kills the weaker races . . . but his doom . . . overtakes him at last . . ." (JMN 7:90, 28 September 1838, repeated in JMN 10:404, cf. lines 83–87); and a passage on the Russians and Poles (JMN 9:383, May or June 1846, cf. lines 90–97).

*Publication:* *Poems*, 1847, pp. 117–22 (Boston) and pp. 92–96 (London); reprinted in *Poems*, 1884, pp. 71–74, and W 9:76–79.

*See Also:* (1) George Arms, "Emerson's 'Ode Inscribed to W. H. Channing,'" *College English* 22 (March 1961): 407–9, and (2) Carl F. Strauch, "The Background and Meaning of the 'Ode Inscribed to W. H. Channing," *ESQ* 42 (1st quarter 1966): supplement, 4–14.

## "Ode to Beauty"

*Texts:* The principal text of this poem occurs in pencil, titled, in P pp. 263–65, a draft consisting of lines 1–11, 15–16, 27–33, 35–43, 45–49, 58–61, 76–82, 84–88, 90, and 92–93, with a number of rejected lines. Additional segments of the poem occur in pencil in P on p. 266 (lines 62–63, 66–69, and 72–75), p. 267 (lines 64–65 and 70–71, with a rejected line), and p. 268 (lines 78–79, 17–18, 21/23, and 24–26, with four rejected lines). On p. 262 is a revision in pencil of lines 1–12 and 15. Two draft fragments represent revisions done after the poem's first publication: in notebook Trees [A:I] (JMN 8:527) is a version of lines 1–4, and in journal U (JMN 9:26) a version of lines 13–16 continues with an early draft of four succeeding lines first published in *Poems,* 1847. Lines 54–57 first appear, canceled, in the manuscript of the lecture "Modern Aspects of Letters" (*Early Lectures* 1:534). An erased passage of twelve lines in X p. 181 begins with the second-draft (or final) form of line 1, and may have been inscribed after first publication. A manuscript of the whole poem in the Berg Collection, New York Public Library, agrees closely with the London edition of *Poems,* 1847, and may have been printer's copy, though it lacks the usual inscribed page numbers.

*Date:* Undetermined. Probably lines 54–57 are the oldest part of the poem. The lecture from which they were canceled was first delivered on 14 January 1836. These lines were probably influenced in their form by *Paradise Regained* 4.361–62, quoted by Emerson in "John Milton" (*Early Lectures* 1:162) less than a year earlier; the more direct source, however, is an entry in journal A for 1 February 1834: "Some thoughts always find us young, and keep us so" (JMN 4:260), a passage also used in "The Over-Soul" (W 2:272). The source of lines 46–49 is an entry in journal D for 8 June 1838: "I pleased myself in seeing the pictures brought in her portfolio by S[arah]. M[argaret]. F[uller].; Guercino, Piranesi, Leyden &c." (JMN 7:6, cf. W 7:359). The draft of lines 13–16 and of the additional lines in journal U occurs after an entry of 26 September 1843, and represents a revision of the *Dial* text; Emerson probably did this in response to Thoreau's criticism in a letter of 17 October 1843, which cites line 14 in particular as "stereotyped." The draft in notebook Trees [A:I] likewise falls between the *Dial* publication and the preparation of *Poems,* 1847.

*Publication: The Dial* 4 (October 1843): 257–59; reprinted, with revisions and the addition of six lines, in *Poems,* 1847, pp. 136–40 (Boston) and pp. 107–11 (London). Reprinted in *Selected Poems,* 1876, pp. 80–83, *Poems,* 1884, pp. 81–84, and W 9:87–90. Lines 54–57 were used as the second of two mottoes to "The Poet," *Essays: Second Series,* 1844, p. 2. The London edition of this work has "keeps" in the last line, an error of which Emerson complained in a letter to Chapman (L 3:274).

## "O'er the garden water goes the wind alone"

*Texts:* Emerson's translation of Enweri, "Kasside zum Lobe Nassireddin Taher's, und Beschreibung des Frühlings," lines 8–10 (*Geschichte*, p. 96), provided a quatrain published in "Persian Poetry," as well as several lines used in "May–Day." The earliest drafts, of six lines, are in journal AZ (JMN 11:238) and notebook Orientalist p. 63, where identical texts show similar revisions in line 2; next is the revision in EF p. 34. All three of these drafts are headed "Spring," implying an intention to use the lines in "May–Day." A further revision in EF p. 112 modifies the wording of the first four lines (the quatrain) but expands the last two into six lines, of which lines 5 and 7–10 correspond to "May–Day," lines 115, 126, 118, and 126–27. The quatrain was revised to final form in two drafts in EF p. 115 and one in Orientalist p. 63.

*Date:* The AZ draft dates from 1850; the final form of the quatrain preceded the publication of "Persian Poetry" in 1858.

*Publication:* The quatrain appeared in "Persian Poetry," 1858, p. 731, in the essay as reprinted in *Letters and Social Aims,* 1876, p. 232, and in subsequent editions including W 8:258. For the history of the lines used in "May–Day," see the analysis of that poem.

## "Oil & Wine"

*Texts:* An ink version, partially revised, occurs in journal Sermons and Journal (JMN 3:157); it is presumably the source of the ink fair copy in CSA p. 35. The editors of JMN 3 speculate that two lines adjacent to the text may originally have been part of the poem; while this is unlikely in terms of stanzaic form, the thought of the couplet is consistent with the theme of the poem.

*Date:* The Sermons and Journal text appears, apparently out of sequence, at the very end of the journal, which Emerson kept from March 1828 to July 1829. Thus it could have been written at any time during that period.

*Publication:* Unpublished by Emerson. First published in JMN 3.

## "Old Age"

*Texts:* The first draft of this couplet occurs in journal GL (JMN 15:135) among notes for the lecture "Old Age." Other drafts appear in EL p. 53,

Rhymer pp. 50$_e$ (joined with other verses) and 96$_d$, and, in a slightly different version, in NP p. 245. The heading or title "Old Age" appears with the text in GL and NP.

*Date:* The GL first draft dates to 1861 and probably to April of that year. The lecture "Old Age," published in January 1862, was evidently written during the preceding summer (see W 7:446).

*Publication:* Unpublished by Emerson. First published, without title, in *Poems,* 1884, p. 276, and reprinted in W 9:332.

## "The old men used their God at need"

*Text:* This couplet occurs only in EL p. 102$_c$. It has not been found elsewhere in Emerson's published or unpublished writings.

## "On a raisin stone"

*Texts:* The earliest draft, in ink in X pp. 268$_s$–268$_t$, is revised in ink in X pp. 153–54. The lines on p. 153, struck through in pencil, are revised again on p. 268$_w$, producing the first complete draft of lines 1–8; this segment is further revised in two drafts on pp. 154–55, and once more in EL p. 17. A fair copy of the entire twelve-line poem is in Poems folder 67 (see Additional Manuscripts).

*Date:* The drafts in X pp. 153–55 and in EL are closely related to the third and fourth drafts of "Pour the wine!" and may have belonged to that poem in the early stages of its own development. Since the poem originates in the X insert, which includes several mottoes for the 1847 edition of *Essays: First Series,* that year is a likely date of composition.

*Publication:* Unpublished by Emerson. The first eight lines were published by Edward Emerson in a note to "Persian Poetry" (W 8:419–20), while the entire poem first appears in a note to "Bacchus" (W 9:444–45) with a version of "Pour the wine!"

## "On bravely through the sunshine & the showers"

*Texts:* Two texts exist, both in ink: in journal Q (JMN 4:73) and P p. 96.

*Date:* The couplet occurs in Q between entries of 18 and 25 May 1833. It is a versification of a sentence from Alessandro Manzoni's *I Promessi Sposi,* "Il tempo il suo mestiere, ed io il mio," which occurs on the same manuscript page.

*Publication:* Unpublished by Emerson. First published in *Poems*, 1884, p. 276, and reprinted in W 9:358. It also appears as the motto for "The Man of Letters" in W 10:239.

## "On earth's wide thoroughfares below"

*Texts:* In notebook Orientalist pp. 29–30 Emerson translated 28 lines of Omar Khayyam from *Geschichte,* pp. 81–82. Lines 25–28 of this translation were revised on p. 31 and copied into Rhymer p. 145.

*Date:* Undetermined.

*Publication:* "Persian Poetry," 1858, p. 726, and in the essay as reprinted in *Letters and Social Aims,* 1876, p. 219, and W 8:244. Also published in Channing, *Thoreau,* p. 266, where the text begins "In earth's . . ." and thus appears to derive from Emerson's manuscript. The poem was not otherwise collected.

*See Also:* "Each spot where tulips" ("Persian Poetry," 1858, p. 731) and "Unbar the door," which, with the present poem, all derive from the same first draft.

## "On prince or bride no diamond stone"

*Texts:* The poem translates line 4 of Enweri's "Sich selbst zum Rathe," from *Geschichte,* p. 91. Notebook Orientalist p. 16 has two drafts of a two-line version, followed by a draft in ink over pencil of the final four-line version, which carries (in the pencil version only) the title "Enterprize." The copy in Rhymer p. 128 is identical to the Orientalist text, but is not titled.

*Date:* Emerson gives a prose translation close in wording to the second two-line version in an entry in journal BO (JMN 11:310), written probably in November or December 1850. It is likely that the verse drafts were composed shortly thereafter.

*Publication:* First published in "Persian Poetry," 1858, p. 726, though it does not appear in later reprintings of the essay. Published again in *May–Day,* 1867, p. 200, and collected in *Poems*, 1884, p. 247, and W 9:301.

## "On the chamber, on the stairs"

*Texts:* The first draft is in pencil in EL p. 200, followed by an ink version in NP p. 12. This was copied with other material on the same page into notebook Phi Beta p. 153. The ink version in ETE p. 29 probably descends independently from NP p. 12.

*Date:* In 1844 or 1845 Emerson wrote in journal V (JMN 9:163), "The Daemons lurk & are dumb: they hate the newspapers." The single line "O pedant of the Holy Ghost" in NP p. 12 derives from a prose entry on the same page of journal V. In an entry in journal ST dating from the early 1870s, Emerson wrote "The Lars & lemurs are angry & threaten me" (JMN 16:225).

*Publication:* Unpublished by Emerson. First published in *Poems,* 1884, p. 289, from the NP text with the first line beginning "In the chamber . . . ," and reprinted in W 9:350.


## "On the tablets of bamboo"

*Text:* The only text of this couplet is in EL p. 109.

*Date:* Emerson's source, a translation from Confucius in James Legge, *The Chinese Classics* . . ., 5 vols. (Hong Kong and London, 1861–1872), 1: prolegomena, is as follows: " 'The government of Wan and Wu,' he said, 'is displayed in the records,—the tablets of wood and bamboo.' " The first volume of Legge was in Emerson's hands in October 1863 (see L 5:338). Wen Wang and Wu Wang, father and son, founded the Chou dynasty in the twelfth century B.C.

*Publication:* Unpublished.


## "On two days, it steads not to run from thy grave"

*Texts:* The quatrain is a translation of lines by Pindar of Rei in Kuhistan given in *Geschichte,* p. 43. The first draft is probably that in journal TU (JMN 11:103), followed by a slight revision in notebook Orientalist p. 11 and a more significant revision in Orientalist p. 117. This text was copied and revised in Rhymer p. 151.

*Date:* The first draft was written in May 1849.

*Publication:* First published with the wording of the first line as above in "Fate," *The Conduct of Life,* 1860, p. 3 (see W 6:5). Collected in *May–Day,* 1867, p. 201, and reprinted in *Poems,* 1884, p. 248, and W 9:302.

*See Also:* EF pp. 94–95.

## "One night he dreamed of a palace fair"

*Texts:* A first draft occurs in EL p. 156ₐ, a loose sheet inserted between pp. 156–57; a fair copy is in NP p. 89. The poem has not been found elsewhere in Emerson's published or unpublished writings.

## "Only he despises"

*Text:* This four-line fragment, which translates Hafiz, Book VIII, Ode XC, lines 49–52 (*Diwan* 1:337), occurs in EF p. 113 in a series of entries headed "Hafiz of his verse."

*Date:* Undetermined.

*Publication:* Published in a prose version in "Persian Poetry," 1858, p. 729, and in the essay as collected in *Letters and Social Aims,* 1876, p. 227, and reprinted in W 8:253.

## "Only three things lengthen life"

*Text:* This couplet occurs only in EL p. 167.

*Date:* The prose source is an aphorism Emerson translated in journal FOR (JMN 15:373) from Sir John Chardin, *Voyages du Chevalier Chardin, en Perse, et Autres Lieux de l'Orient . . .,* ed. L. Langlès, 10 vols. (Paris, 1811), 5:21. He borrowed this volume from the Boston Athenaeum from 16 to 31 October 1863.

*Publication:* Unpublished.

## "Or I be shamed when bearded men repeat"

*Text:* This two-line fragment occurs in pencil in P p. 31. It has not been found elsewhere in Emerson's published or unpublished writings.

## "Orator"

*Texts:* There are six manuscript texts of this quatrain, all substantially identical. Probably the first drafts are the two in journal O (JMN 9:443), one in erased pencil, the other a copy in ink. Other texts are in X p. 101, Rhymer p. 49 (titled), NP p. 135 (titled), and journal IO (JMN 13:332).

*Date:* The journal O drafts appear to have been composed in June or July 1846. The context includes much speculation about eloquence and oratory; a suggestive entry occurs in O p. 199: "To every creature its own weapon, however skilfully concealed" (JMN 9:413). This follows immediately an entry in which Emerson invokes the fox as the traditional symbol of cunning. The IO draft was inscribed in 1854.

*Publication:* First published in *The Dial* (Cincinnati) 1 (March 1860): 195; collected in *May–Day*, 1867, p. 182, and reprinted in *Poems*, 1884, p. 238, and W 9:291.

## "The oriole whose note"

*Texts:* These nine lines occur in erased pencil, upside down, in P p. 188, and in pencil on the facing page, p. 189.

*Date:* The proximity of these drafts to the first draft of "The Humble-Bee" suggests that the material on p. 188 may have been composed at the same time—on or about 8 May 1837 (see the note on the dating of "The Humble-Bee"). The material on p. 189 is written over erased lines of "Dirge" and must have been inscribed in 1838 or later.

*Publication:* Unpublished.

## "Our Shah's counsel is the efflux"

*Text:* The poem, translating Hafiz, Book XII, Ode XII, lines 25–32 (*Diwan* 2:74), occurs under the heading "Compliments" in EF p. 77. It has not been found elsewhere in Emerson's published or unpublished writings.

## "The pain of love's a better fate"

*Texts:* Seven drafts of this couplet have been noted: the first, in journal FOR (JMN 15:384), is followed by others in Rhymer pp. 2$_b$ and 96$_c$, NP pp. 63 and 103, ETE p. 175, and Poems folder 38 (see Additional Manuscripts under "Boston Hymn"). The couplet is a translation from Saadi (see *Geschichte*, p. 212).

*Date:* The first draft was written in late 1863.

*Publication:* First published in J 9:545, from the FOR text.

## "Painting and Sculpture"

*Texts:* An erased pencil draft occurs in P p. 164, followed immediately by a revised pencil version. Neither is titled; Emerson's index reference to p. 164 is "Sculptor."

*Date:* Carl F. Strauch argues persuasively that the poem reflects an interest in painting and sculpture kindled by Margaret Fuller and Samuel Gray Ward in 1838–1841 and by the opening of the Athenaeum sculpture gallery in July 1840. A closely related journal entry (JMN 8:109) seems to have been written shortly after the poem was published. The article on "Painting and Sculpture" in *The Dial* for July 1841 (which may have influenced Emerson's choice of title) was written by Sophia Dana Ripley.

*Publication: The Dial* 2 (October 1841): 205; reprinted in *Poems,* 1847, p. 208 (Boston) and p. 165 (London). It was not included in *Poems,* 1884, or W 9.

*See Also:* Carl F. Strauch, "Hatred's Swift Repulsions: Emerson, Margaret Fuller, and Others," *SRom* 7 (Winter 1968): 79–80.

## "A pair of crystal eyes will lead him"

*Texts:* The order of the several drafts cannot be determined with certainty. It is possible that lines 1–2, which appear in the midst of drafts of "Ode to Beauty" in P p. 265, were written first. This supposition would help to account for the reading "Beauty's robe" in line 5 of the pencil draft in notebook L Camadeva p. 69. Other drafts are in journal Books Small (JMN 8:466), P p. 200, and Poems folder 2 (see Additional Manuscripts); only the last is in ink.

*Date:* The Books Small text occurs in the same light pencil as the two drafts of "Hush!" that follow on the same manuscript page. Since "Hush!" appears to have been written in 1842, the present poem may date from the same year. The other verses in P p. 200, likewise copied and revised from Books Small, also appear to date from 1842. Lines 1–2, on the evidence of their association with "Ode to Beauty," would in any event have been written before the publication of that poem in *The Dial* for October 1843.

*Publication:* Unpublished by Emerson. First published in JMN 8.

## "Pale Genius roves alone"

*Texts:* The earliest draft occurs in pencil in X p. 27, a version of the first and second stanzas, with a rejected stanza between them. This text was revised in pencil in EF p. 7. The earliest draft of the third stanza occurs in pencil in EF p. 57; this stanza was joined to the first two in X p. 26 (written over erased lines used in "Monadnock") and EL p. 31, where the presence of punctuation suggests a final draft. The attempt, at Rhymer p. 2ᵦ, to develop the second stanza as a separate poem was undertaken many years later.

*Date:* The poem arrived at its finished, three-stanza form between 1845 (the date of the "Monadnock" passage) and 1847 (when the third stanza was published as the motto for "Intellect" in the 1847 edition of *Essays: First Series,* p. 293). The material in the Rhymer insert (pp. 2ₐ–2ᵦ) was inscribed in the early to mid 1860s.

*Publication:* Apart from lines 9–12, as noted above, the poem was unpublished during Emerson's lifetime. It was first published from the EL text in *Poems,* 1884, pp. 268–69, and reprinted in W 9:326–27.

*See Also:* "Intellect" ("Go, speed").

## "Papas Blondine"

*Texts:* A full text of this poem to Ellen Emerson occurs in pencil in EL pp. 138–43. Poems folder 158 contains a typescript, prepared under the direction of Edward Emerson, of an earlier, shorter version titled "To Ellen" with the handwritten subtitle "on her birth day." This version, consisting of lines 1–8, 11–12, 14–20, 22/23, 24–29, 30/31, 32–33, x, and 34–40, reads as follows: "Papa's little girl / Grew tall and wise / Eschewing vanities / And loved the truth. / Can it suffice? / The years shall show us / Truth is on its trial / Her judgment will not brook denial / And she will know / If Truth's as true as she, / If the false world can afford / That any sterling sterling be. / And if the things are rotten / She will frankly call them so / She that is real / And cannot aught conceal / She that scorns hypocrisy / And well believes that she may dare / Speak out her faith in any air / And honest meaning will not fail / O'er any falsehood to prevail. / Aye, do not fear it / Speak the truth to those who will hear it. / But still as now / With pure good will sculptured on thy brow / And give us in the passing world / Hint of eternal cheer. / Fear not / Be of good cheer, / Brave darling, mind thy heart / Dare do all it shall impart / Nor heed one word of all the voices gay / Which in their manifold choir / Aim no higher than to please / And flatter comfortable ease."

*Date:* Edward Emerson noted on the typescript, "This, I feel sure was a birthday or a New Years poem, written by Father to Ellen in her early teens." If this surmise is correct, the poem dates from 1852–1856.

*Publication:* Unpublished.

## "The Park"

*Texts:* An erased pencil version of lines 1–12 in P p. 203 precedes the erased pencil version of the entire poem in P p. 202, which is overwritten by a titled fair copy in ink. An ink fair copy of lines 1–12, untitled, in the Houghton Library, is probably intermediate between the first and second of the erased pencil drafts in P; it is identical in wording to the second P text except for "eyebeams" instead of "eyeballs" in line 8 and "Enchanters!" instead of "enchantresses!" in line 9. The reading in line 9 links it to a draft of "Manners" in journal F 2 (JMN 7:510) and to a draft of "May–Day" in EF p. 70; see also NP p. 27. Printer's copy for the London edition of *Poems,* 1847, is in the Berg Collection, New York Public Library.

*Date:* Edward Emerson proposed two sources (see W 2:414 and 9:430): first, a paragraph in "Friendship" (W 2:195–96), of which the journal source (JMN 5:162), written in May 1836, had been used in two lectures before finding its way into "Friendship," and, second, a letter of 1 March 1841 to Samuel Gray Ward (*Letters from Ralph Waldo Emerson to a Friend,* ed. Charles Eliot Norton [Boston, 1899], p. 32). A parallel perhaps closer than either of these, however, may be found in an entry in journal E for 6 June 1841: "The chief is the chief all the world over, & not his hat or his shoes, his land, his title or his purse. He who knows the most,—he who knows what sweets & virtues are in the ground beneath him, the waters before him, the plants around him, the heavens above him,—he is the enchanter, he is the rich & the royal man" (JMN 7:454). Line 9 occurs as early as 18 August 1840 with the F 2 draft of "Manners," a poem on a similar theme.

*Publication: The Dial* 2 (January 1842): 373. Collected in *Poems,* 1847, pp. 131–32 (Boston) and p. 103 (London), and reprinted in *Poems,* 1884, p. 78, and W 9:84.

## "Parks & ponds are good by day"

*Texts:* The first draft is in pencil in X p. 260. This is followed by a revised ink fair copy in EF p. 26 and another, which differs only in having punctuation, in EL p. 81.

*Date:* The copy in EF was inscribed in 1851 or later, after the prose entry used in "The Fugitive Slave Law" of that year. Possibly there is a connection between this poem and a fragment written in 1843 (JMN 8:333): "The husband has the nearest acres / The poet has the far."

*Publication:* Unpublished by Emerson. First published in *Poems,* 1884, p. 283, in a text that conflates the first and second versions, and reprinted in W 9:342.

## "The Past"

*Texts:* This poem occurs in three drafts, all in EL. The first two are in partially erased pencil on pp. 32–33 and p. 34; the third, in ink, is on p. 159. In none of the drafts is the order of the lines that of the printed version.

*Date:* Undetermined.

*Publication:* First published in *May–Day,* 1867, pp. 143–44; reprinted in *Poems,* 1884, pp. 221–22, and W 9:257–58.

## "A patch of meadow & upland"

*Texts:* The first draft, in pencil in NP pp. 239–41, is followed immediately by a revised ink draft on pp. 242–44. Lines 25–28 occur in slightly different form in NP p. 5. An ink fair copy is in EL pp. 73–75.

*Date:* Undetermined.

*Publication:* Unpublished by Emerson. Lines 1–4 and 13–20 were first published in *Poems,* 1884, p. 307, with the nonauthorial title "The Waterfall." This version has variants in lines 1, 16, and 18, readings from the first draft in lines 13–14, and a row of asterisks at the end to indicate omitted stanzas. It was reprinted, with the addition of lines 21–28, in W 9:369–70.

## "The patient Pan"

*Texts:* This unfinished poem exists in an 82-line first draft in EL pp. 12$_a$–12$_d$, followed by two shorter revisions: the first, in X pp. 149–51, revises the first 44 lines in a 41-line draft; the second, in EL pp. 11–12, revises the first 17 lines of the X text. Line numbers in this edition, therefore, follow EL pp. 11–12 for lines 1–17, X pp. 150–51 for lines 18–41, and EL pp. 12$_c$–12$_d$ for lines 42–79. The line "The patient Pan" is also found among unused lines from "Wealth" (see NP pp. 251 and 274). In W 9:507–8 Edward Emerson quoted a pertinent passage from "Natural History of Intellect" (W 12:36).

*Date:* The X text was inscribed after the draft of "Poet of poets" (see X p. 149), and is still loosely associated with that poem in EL. This would suggest that "The patient Pan" was probably written during the winter of 1849–1850.

*Publication:* Unpublished by Emerson. Lines 1–18 (taken by Cabot from EL pp. 11–12, with the addition of the eighteenth line from X p. 150, where it is struck through) were published in *Poems,* 1884, pp. 279–80, and W 9:335.

## "Pedants all"

*Texts:* The poem occurs in two versions, an eight-line pencil draft in EL p. 199 and a five-line ink version in NP p. 20 omitting lines 3 and 7–8. It has not been found elsewhere in Emerson's published or unpublished writings.

## "Pericles"

*Texts:* The earliest draft, untitled, occurs in light pencil in journal Books Small (JMN 8:473). This is the source of the pencil version in P p. 298, which in turn is the source of the revised pencil version in X p. 32. An ink version in Rhymer p. 50 is further revised and bears both the title "Friendship" and the notation "printed". A yet later ink version, struck through in ink, is in NP p. 132, with the title "Pericles" after the canceled title "*Usque ad aras.*"

*Date:* The first draft probably dates to the spring of 1843, as do the draft fragments of "To Rhea" and "Threnody" that occur immediately before and after it in Books Small. The draft in X p. 32 is written over erased lines of "The World-Soul" that in turn were apparently written in 1844. In W 9:499, Edward Emerson explained that a "Latin rendering of a Greek saying was spoken of by Mr. Emerson as the source of the quatrain. One asks a neighbor, 'But are you not then my friend?' '*Usque ad aras,*' is the reply—*As far as the altars.*" Emerson recorded the phrase—attributed to Pericles by Plutarch—in Blotting Book I in 1826 (JMN 6:34).

*Publication: May–Day,* 1867, p. 189; reprinted in *Poems,* 1884, p. 243, and W 9:296.

## "Philosophers are lined with eyes within"

*Text:* The only text is in pencil in P p. 81.

*Date:* Undetermined.

*Publication:* Unpublished by Emerson. First published in *Poems,* 1884, p. 314, with the nonauthorial title "Philosopher," taken from Emerson's index reference in P. Reprinted in W 9:374–75.

## "The Phoenix"

*Texts:* The pencil draft in X pp. 196–97 is the earliest. It is revised in X pp. 254–55, and again in the erased pencil draft in EF pp. 15–16. Rhymer p. 131

contains a fair copy that was the source of the manuscript, now at the University of Texas Library, sent to Edmund Quincy for publication in *The Liberty Bell*. This manuscript has "cage" for the printed misreading "eye" in line 3, "In both worlds" is canceled for "Either world" in line 17, and "them" is overwritten by "him" in line 18. Another fair copy in Poems folder 36, which has several variant readings, seems to be later than any of these (see Additional Manuscripts). The poem loosely translates Hafiz, Book XXIV, Ode XXIV (*Diwan* 2:308–9). The first three drafts are of the entire 28-line poem, while the others, including the published versions, are of the first 20 lines only. In Emerson's copy of the *Diwan*, penciled X's occur at the head of the poem and after line 17.

*Date:* Between April 1846, when Emerson acquired his copy of the *Diwan*, and October 1850, when he sent the manuscript to Quincy for publication (see *The Liberty Bell,* p. 81).

*Publication:* First published in the antislavery album *The Liberty Bell* (Boston, 1851), pp. 78–79. Published again, without title and with the first line as altered in the Rhymer text, in "Persian Poetry," 1858, p. 730. Lines 13–20 appear with the change of "o'er" for "falls on" in line 15 in Channing, *Thoreau,* p. 149. When "Persian Poetry" was reprinted in *Letters and Social Aims,* 1876, "is" in line 4 was changed to "was", an alteration maintained in later editions. Finally, the poem was reprinted from *The Liberty Bell* in *Uncollected Writings,* 1912, pp. 186–87, repeating the original printer's error in line 3.

*See Also:* Richard Tuerk, "Emerson as Translator—'The Phoenix,'" *ESQ* 63 (Spring 1971): 24–26.

## "Poet" ("Ever the Poet")

*Texts:* The poem originates in a four-line pencil draft in EF p. 111. This was revised in two drafts in journal NO (*JMN* 13:410–12), followed by additional revisions of line 4 in EF p. 111. Identical ink fair copies occur in EF p. 50, notebook PY p. 240, and Rhymer p. 67. In the last two of these "And" in line 1 was later canceled, a revision reflected in the fair copy in NP p. 136 and in the manuscript copy in the Morgan Library signed by Emerson and dated "Concord, Jany 1860." A pencil fair copy in notebook IT p. 117 combines the latest form of line 1 with an early form of line 4, so that its place in the evolution of the text cannot be determined.

*Date:* The early transmission of the text of this poem nearly duplicates that of the quatrain "Hafiz," which likewise originated in EF and subsequently appeared in EF p. 50, journal NO, PY p. 241, Rhymer p. 66, and NP p. 136.

The context in NO and the poem's relation to "Hafiz" indicate that it was written in April 1855.

*Publication: May–Day,* 1867, p. 183; reprinted in *Poems,* 1884, p. 239, and W 9:292.

## "The Poet" ("Hoard knowledge")

*Texts:* The earliest draft, in pencil in X p. 164, was erased after being copied into notebook Orientalist p. 13, then revised again in Rhymer p. 132. Revisions made in the Rhymer text are reflected in the ink fair copy in X p. 164, written over the erased first draft. Printer's copy for *The Liberty Bell* printing is in the University of Texas library. The poem is a translation of Hafiz, Book XXIII, Ode LI, lines 33–44 (*Diwan* 2:234–35).

*Date:* In October 1850 Emerson submitted this and several other translations from Hafiz to Edmund Quincy for publication in *The Liberty Bell,* an anti-slavery collection. The printer's copy, which bears Quincy's initials, derives from the Rhymer draft before it was revised, showing that Emerson continued to work on the poem between 1850 and 1858.

*Publication: The Liberty Bell* (Boston, 1851), pp. 80–81. The third stanza was quoted in final revised form in "Persian Poetry," 1858, p. 729, and in the essay as reprinted in *Letters and Social Aims,* 1876, p. 228, and W 8:253. A slightly different version of the same stanza appears in Channing, *Thoreau,* p. 149. The poem was reprinted from *The Liberty Bell* in *Uncollected Writings,* 1912, p. 188. In both of these locations the poem is joined with the quatrain "I truly have no treasure"; in the original printer's copy, however, the quatrain is in fact set off by Emerson's characteristic two short rules, which were simply overlooked.

*See Also:* "I truly have no treasure."

## "Poet" ("To clothe")

*Texts:* The pencil draft in X p. 263 is the earliest, followed by virtually identical drafts in ink in X p. 268$_{aa}$, Rhymer p. 48 (titled, with the notation "printed"), Poems folder 84, and NP p. 135 (titled). A version in NP p. 2 is the only one that gives the later form of line 2 ("words" for "word").

*Date:* The appearance of the second draft in the X insert suggests a date of composition no later than 1847. The text at NP p. 2 was probably inscribed between 1860 and 1867.

*Publication: The Dial* (Cincinnati) 1 (March 1860): 195, with "word" in line 2; collected in *May–Day*, 1867, p. 183, with "words" in line 2. Reprinted in *Poems*, 1884, p. 239, and W 9:292. The quatrain also appears without title and with the earlier form of line 2 in Channing, *Thoreau*, p. 127.

## "A poet is at home"

*Text:* This nine-line fragment occurs in pencil in EF p. 23, overwritten by what is probably the first draft of "Hafiz" and a revised draft of parts of "The Romany Girl."

*Date:* Before 1855, the apparent date of "Hafiz."

*Publication:* Unpublished.

## "Poet of poets"

*Texts:* The first draft of the poem occurs in X pp. 145–49 and was revised in journal AZ (JMN 11:185–86, 190–91, 193). The first 61 lines of this second draft were further revised in EL pp. 3–7, where they are joined with another long passage (EL pp. 7–10), the first draft of which occurs in X pp. 156–59. The line numbering for this unfinished poem therefore follows EL for lines 1–61 and 81–134, and AZ for lines 62–80. Lines 92–95 also appear separately in EL p. 151 and Rhymer p. 2$_a$, prior to their use, along with lines 88–91, in "From Nature's beginning."

This system of line numbering does not result in or imply an authoritative text, but is simply a means of accounting for all the lines demonstrably belonging to the poem. Carl F. Strauch has argued that the poem should be regarded as part of a larger poem consisting of the following: "Roomy Eternity," "Poet of poets," "Terminus" ("For thought"), and "Cloud upon cloud / The world." In the absence of unequivocal evidence as to Emerson's final intention, the present editors have chosen to treat these texts separately, indicating where appropriate their relationship to "Poet of poets." An inscription in NP p. 295—"Poet of poets *EL* 3, 18"—provides some grounds for excluding "Roomy Eternity" and additionally suggests a relationship of "Poet of poets" to "Pour the wine!"

*Date:* Line 35, "The Tongue of the secret," is an allusion to Hafiz (see the headnote to "From the Persian of Hafiz" in *Poems*, 1847, p. 209 of the Boston edition), suggesting that the poem is not earlier than 1846. The second draft, in AZ—which presumably followed shortly after the first—dates to late November or early December 1849. It follows an entry for 17 November, and part of the text, on AZ p. 18, is written in ink over a list of people to whom

Emerson proposed to send copies of *Representative Men*. He actually began to send these copies in late December 1849.

*Publication:* Unpublished by Emerson. Only lines 62–80 appeared in print before the AZ text was published in J 8:66–68; these appeared in *Poems*, 1884, pp. 271–72, and were reprinted in W 9:329.

*See Also:* (1) "From Nature's beginning" and (2) Strauch diss., pp. 383–93 (text) and 576–83 (notes), for the more inclusive version of the poem to which he gave the title "Eternity."

## "Poets are colorpots"

*Text:* This seventeen-line fragment occurs in ink in X pp. 268ₐ–268_b. It has not been found elsewhere in Emerson's published or unpublished writings.

## "Pour the wine!"

*Texts:* The first draft occurs in pencil in X p. 100. These lines were copied, with the change of "pair" for "span" in the last line, in X p. 202. In both locations the verses carry the title "Bacchus," though the further notation "Omitted verses" appears with the second draft. In X pp. 152–53 Emerson made further revisions and extended the poem by twelve lines, including lines 24–25, which are revised from a draft on p. 155. This longer poem was further revised in EL pp. 18–19. The last of the manuscript drafts is in NP pp. 285 and 284, where, among other revisions, the fourth and fifth lines are reversed. The twelve lines added in the third draft (X pp. 152–53) appear here on p. 284, and while it is possible that Emerson meant by this to detach them from the poem, it is more likely that he simply chose to write on a blank p. 284 in preference to an already inscribed p. 286. The appearance of lines 1–2 among lines used in "May–Day" in EF p. 65 and NP p. 15 may precede the first draft of "Pour the wine!" but more likely they were borrowed at some later period.

*Date:* The relation of the poem to "Bacchus" is suggested not only by the titles given to the first two drafts, but also by the proximity of the second draft to a fragment of "Bacchus" in X p. 200. "Bacchus" was written in 1846. The "May–Day" drafts in EF pp. 60–71 date from between 1845 and 1851. There is perhaps a parallel between lines 15 and 19 (especially in the EL draft) and the following sentence from "Fate": "[Steam] could be used to lift away, chain and compel other devils far more reluctant and dangerous, namely, cubic miles of earth, mountains . . . time he shall lengthen, and shorten space" (W 6:33–34).

*Publication:* Unpublished by Emerson. First published, from X pp. 152–53, in W 9:444 (part of Edward Emerson's note to "Bacchus"), to which was further added an early version of "On a raisin stone." The NP version of lines 14–25 was printed as a motto to "Poetry and Imagination," W 8:2, and in W 9:328.

## "Power" ("Cast the bantling")

*Text:* This quatrain occurs in pencil in P p. 23.

*Date:* The source of the poem appears to be a paragraph from the lecture "The Poet" (1841): "You may find [poetic genius], though rarely, in Senates, when the forest has cast out some wild, black-browed bantling, some great boy, to show the same energy in the crowd of officials, which he had learned in driving cattle to the hills, or in scrambling through thickets in a winter forest, or through the swamp and river for his game. In the folds of his brow, in the majesty of his mien, nature shall vindicate her son; and even in that strange and perhaps unworthy place and company, remind you of the lessons taught him in earlier days by the torrent, in the gloom of the pine woods, when he was the companion of crows and jays and foxes, and a hunter of the bear" (*Early Lectures* 3:362).

*Publication:* This quatrain appears as the motto to "Self-Reliance" in *Essays: First Series,* 1841, p. 36, and in subsequent reprintings, including W 2:44. It was collected in *May–Day,* 1867, p. 187, with the title as above, and reprinted in *Poems,* 1884, p. 242, and W 9:295.

## "Power" ("His tongue")

*Texts:* The earliest text of this quatrain occurs in NP p. 67 as part of a pencil draft of "Song of Nature." This draft is overwritten by a later version of the quatrain in ink, rewritten in the first person.

*Date:* The first draft was composed in 1859, the date of "Song of Nature"; the second may be later than 1860.

*Publication:* The first version was published as the motto to "Power" in *Conduct of Life,* 1860, p. 43 (see W 6:51), and reprinted in W 9:284. The second was published in *Poems,* 1884, p. 274, and reprinted in W 9:330.

## "Prince the ball of heaven should"

*Text:* This quatrain, which translates Hafiz, Book VIII, Ode XLIII, lines 1–4 (*Diwan* 1:270), occurs in EF p. 97 in a series of entries headed "Hafiz superlative." It has not been found elsewhere in Emerson's published or unpublished writings.

## "The Problem"

*Texts:* A complete pencil draft, untitled, occurs in P pp. 83–86, dated "10 November 1839." Revisions of lines 17–18 and 20–22 occur in pencil on p. 82, and at the top of p. 84 are four lines that do not appear in the poem as published. Printer's copy for the London edition of *Poems,* 1847, is in the University of Texas library; in it, "her" is canceled for "its" in lines 27 and 38, and "flames" is overwritten by "fanes" in line 58.

*Date:* The prose source of this poem is a passage in journal D dated 28 August 1838: "It is very grateful to me to go into an English Church & hear the liturgy read. Yet nothing would induce me to be the English priest. I find an unpleasant dilemma in this, nearer home. I dislike to be a clergyman & refuse to be one. Yet how rich a music would be to me a holy clergyman in my town. It seems to me he cannot be a man, quite & whole. Yet how plain is the need of one, & how high yes highest is the function. Here is Division of labor that I like not. A man must sacrifice his manhood for the social good. Something is wrong I see not what" (JMN 7:60). A prose source for lines 31–32 is to be found in a sentence added to a journal entry for 20 September 1836: "Love & fear laid the stones in their own order"—said of a cathedral (JMN 5:196). Emerson's own date for the poem of 10 November 1839 is striking evidence of his ability to return to a passage over a year later and versify it. "It is also remarkable in this," says Edward Emerson (W 9:405), "that it would almost seem, like Athene, to have sprung matured and perfect from its author's brain. No fragments, no trials remain; much fewer verbal changes than is usual appear in the manuscript book of poetry, and not one since the poem saw light in the first number of the *Dial* in July, 1840." Curiously, Emerson wrote to Margaret Fuller on 14 November 1839 to say that he was "preparing to rhyme with might & main. Not possibly can I promise a syllable for the next century" (L 2:234). By 12 December, however, he was ready to mention the poem to Fuller: "I wrote some verses for [*The Dial*] one Sunday lately at church: the better place not always the better poetry: I cannot send them today, for I let Henry Thoreau carry them away lately when he brought me poetry" (L 2:242–43). Thoreau copied the poem into his commonplace book (now in the Morgan Library), adding, "Suggested, and at least partially written in Church, Nov. 10th — 39."

*Publication: The Dial* 1 (July 1840): 122–23, with a few revisions of the P text. This text was reprinted in *The Estray,* ed. H. W. Longfellow (Boston, 1847), pp. 54–57. (Although Longfellow wrote to Emerson for a corrected copy [see L 3:365n], evidently no substantive corrections were offered: *The*

*Estray* reproduces the *Dial* text with only a slight styling of accidentals.) The poem was collected in *Poems*, 1847, pp. 17–20 (Boston) and pp. 9–12 (London), and reprinted in *Poems*, 1884, pp. 15–17, and W 9:6–9. Edward Emerson, on the basis of Emerson's index reference in P, claimed that "at first [he] called it 'The Priest' " (W 9:405), but it is not clear that this is to be taken as a title.

*See Also:* (1) Strauch diss., pp. 138–40 and 363–67, (2) Conrad Wright, "Emerson, Barzillai Frost, and the Divinity School Address," *Harvard Theological Review* 49 (January 1956): 19–43, (3) Kenneth W. Cameron, "Emerson, Thoreau, Parson Frost and 'The Problem,' " *ESQ*, no. 6 (1st quarter 1957), 16, (4) Curtis Dahl, "A Parallel to Emerson's 'Conscious Stone,' " *ESQ*, no. 19 (2d quarter 1960), 18–19, and (5) Kenneth W. Cameron, "Early Background for Emerson's 'The Problem,' " *ESQ*, no. 27 (2d quarter 1962), 37–46.

## "Proteus"

*Texts:* The principal draft is in ink in X pp. 140–44. Of this 79-line poem, lines 32–68 became, with a few changes, the motto for "Illusions" in *The Conduct of Life*, 1860. A fragment in EL p. 102$_d$ consists of lines 1–2 and five unused lines; it is unclear whether this precedes or follows the draft in X.

*Date:* The poem was written no earlier than 1845, the earliest possible date for the erased draft of "The Daemonic and the Celestial Love" overwritten by the present poem in X pp. 141–44. The source for line 2 seems to be an entry in journal Books Small (JMN 8:447), expanded in an 1846 entry in journal O, "The world, the universe may be reeled off from any Idea, like a ball of yarn" (JMN 9:387). References to Proteus in Emerson's writings are most frequent in the mid-1840s and become quite rare thereafter.

*Publication:* Lines 32–68 were published as "Illusions" in *The Conduct of Life*, 1860, pp. 271–72, reprinted in subsequent editions of that work including W 6:307–8, and collected in W 9:287–88.

## "A puff of air or dry or damp"

*Text:* This poem occurs in pencil in EL p. 161. It has not been found elsewhere in Emerson's published or unpublished writings.

## "Put in, drive home the sightless wedges"

*Texts:* This couplet, closely associated with the composition of "May–Day," occurs in four drafts. Two different pencil versions occur in EL p. 84 and NP

p. 39. A third version occurs in ink in Poems folder 49 after a preliminary draft of lines associated with "May–Day" (see Additional Manuscripts under that title). A fourth version is in NP p. 116, integrated into the opening lines of the rejected passage in folder 49.

*Date:* The lines probably date from the early 1860s. The EL text is followed by lines of "For Genius made his cabin wide," written not earlier than 1861, and the NP p. 39 text is followed by "But never yet," perhaps from 1863.

*Publication:* Unpublished by Emerson. First published in the EL version in *Poems,* 1884, p. 287, and reprinted in W 9:347. Cf. "Sea-Shore," line 12.

## "A queen rejoices in her peers"

*Texts:* A pencil draft of lines 2–8 occurs in EF p. 21 (see Plate 4), copied and revised with the addition of line 1 in ink in X p. 211. Here Emerson later added in pencil a roman numeral "II," thereby making the poem part of a sequence with "Nature I" and "Fate" ("Delicate omens") on pp. 212 and 213. X p. 211 is indexed as "Studies of Nature," a reference, evidently, to the entire sequence. The three poems were copied out in the indicated order in NP, where "A queen rejoices" falls on p. 70. The text at Rhymer p. 50c is identical to the NP text and precedes "Fate" ("Delicate omens") on the same page.

*Date:* Undetermined.

*Publication:* Unpublished by Emerson. First published with the nonauthorial title "The Walk" in *Poems,* 1884, p. 304, and reprinted in W 9:366.

## "Reach me wine No counsel weakens the conclusion of the lot"

*Text:* These two lines, translating Hafiz, Book VIII, Ode CXXXVI, lines 5–6 (*Diwan* 1:408), occur in EF p. 108 under the headings "Ethical" and "Fatal sentences." They have not been found elsewhere in Emerson's published or unpublished writings.

## "The red rose blooms"

*Texts:* The principal draft is that in X pp. 172–73, a translation of Hafiz, Book III, Ode XXIV (*Diwan* 1:79–82). A different version of the third stanza appears in notebook Orientalist p. 204 and notebook TO p. 59. This is the version, printed as prose, that is quoted in "Persian Poetry," 1858, p. 728, and in the essay as collected in *Letters and Social Aims,* 1876, p. 225, and W 8:250.

*Date:* The first draft was probably composed shortly after Emerson acquired his copy of the *Diwan* in April 1846. Notebook X contains a series of translations from Book III, one of which, the "Ghaselle: From the Persian of Hafiz," was published in *Poems,* 1847.

*Publication:* Apart from the third stanza, as noted above, the poem is unpublished.

## "The Rhodora"

*Texts:* The earliest surviving text is a pencil fair copy, untitled, in CSA p. 23. This presumably is the source of the revised ink fair copy in P p. 95, which bears the title "Lines / On being asked, Whence is the flower?" Printer's copy for the *Western Messenger,* with this title, is in the Houghton Library; in it, line 11 begins "Tell them, dear," as do all the other manuscript texts, rather than the "Dear, tell them," of the magazine version. Printer's copy for the London edition of *Poems,* 1847, is in the Berg Collection, New York Public Library. A copy, signed by Emerson but not in his hand, is in the University of Virginia Library.

*Date:* The CSA text bears the notation "Newton 1834," and the month, as the first line indicates, is May. At the time Emerson was visiting his maternal aunt Mary Haskins Ladd and her husband William, and spending much time speculating, as his journal shows, on the competing botanical ideas of Linnaeus and Goethe.

*Publication: The Western Messenger* 7 (July 1839): 166, with the title "The Rhodora. Lines on Being Asked, Whence is the Flower?" Collected in *Poems,* 1847, p. 59 (Boston) and p. 44 (London), with a new version of lines 7–8; reprinted in *Selected Poems,* 1876, p. 58, *Poems,* 1884, p. 39, and W 9:37–38.

*See Also:* (1) "Good Charles the springs adorer," which has similar phrasing, (2) Holmes, *Emerson,* pp. 129–31, (3) Strauch diss., pp. 335–36 (text) and 521–26 (notes), and (4) Carl F. Strauch, "The Year of Emerson's Poetic Maturity: 1834," *NEQ* 34 (October 1955): 361–65.

## "Ring your bells backward, loyal towers!"

*Texts:* Six texts of these two lines exist, all identical in wording. The first is in journal VO (JMN 14:191), where it is preceded on the page by the prose source: "They [not specified] ring their bells backward when there is a fire." Other copies are in EL pp. 112 and 288, in ETE p. 137 in a collection of "Refrains," in Poems folder 31 (see Additional Manuscripts under "Boston"), and in notebook QL on a sheet laid in between pp. 122–23.

*Date:* The prose source and first draft in VO are from 1857. The EL and QL copies are associated with "Voluntaries," while the ETE copy was apparently part of Emerson's search of the notebooks for refrains for "Boston."

*Publication:* Unpublished by Emerson. First published in JMN 14.


## "The river knows the way"


*Text:* The two versions of the first line in EL p. 102₍c₎ probably precede the two-line form that occurs in pencil in X p. 86, written over an erased draft of "The Daemonic and the Celestial Love"; it appears to have been inscribed at the same time as the lines of "Merlin I" that follow.

*Date:* The verses have their source in a phrase in journal O, pp. 202 and 203: "the current knows the way" (JMN 9:414), written in May 1846. This would be consistent with the supposed date of "Merlin I."

*Publication:* Unpublished.


## "Roger Rain"


*Texts:* An ink draft occurs in journal A (JMN 4:283), a pencil draft in P p. 13, and an erased pencil draft in P p. 71.

*Date:* The two lines were composed on or directly after 26 April 1834, when Emerson noted in his journal, "Rain rain. The good rain like a bad preacher does not know when to leave off" (JMN 4:281). The journal A draft occurs between entries for 26 and 28 April.

*Publication:* Unpublished by Emerson. First published in JMN 4.

*See Also:* "Suum Cuique" ("The rain has spoiled").


## "The roguish wind and I"


*Texts:* The poem translates Hafiz, Book III, Ode LXVII, lines 21–24 (*Diwan* 1:146–47). The first draft is in erased pencil in EF p. 98, followed by three revised versions in notebook Orientalist pp. 54–55, and a fair copy in Rhymer p. 138.

*Date:* Undetermined.

*Publication:* Unpublished.

## "The Romany Girl"

*Texts:* The immediate source of the poem is a one-sentence entry in journal NO p. 43: "The sun goes down, & with it the coarseness of my attire: the moon rises, and with it the power of my beauty" (JMN 13:396). Emerson versified the sentence in a quatrain on NO p. 44 and revised it on p. 45. Next follows the draft in NO p. 20 of lines 1–4 and 9–20, though the nearly identical text in X p. 50 might possibly have preceded it. These lines (from the NO text) are revised in EF p. 22, followed, on p. 23, by a draft of lines 21–24 and 5–8, which are written around the quatrain "Hafiz." What is perhaps an early draft of the last stanza appears on a slip of paper inserted into Emerson's Account Book 6 in the accounts for March 1857: "We bide by market & moors / Fortunes we can spae & spell / We know life's taste tho' not indoors / Pale men's fortunes reading well." Otherwise this stanza appears only in the fair copy of the whole poem in Rhymer pp. 71–72 (which bears the title "Gypsy's Song") and in the manuscript copy sent to J. R. Lowell for publication in *The Atlantic Monthly,* which is now in the Houghton Library Autograph file.

*Date:* The drafts in journal NO occur among entries for February 1855. The second stanza appears late in the process of composition even though the source for line 5 ("Pales filles du nord! vous n'êtes pas mes soeurs") can be traced back as far as 1840 (see JMN 7:536; cf. 13:268). A source for the association of Gypsy women and the horizon (line 8) is in journal Z[A] (JMN 8:345), written over an erased draft of "Una" and apparently dating to 1843. The poem may have been completed at any time between 1855 and 1857, though the latter date seems more probable.

*Publication: The Atlantic Monthly* 1 (November 1857): 46–47, with the title "The Rommany Girl," following Emerson's misspelling in the printer's copy. Emerson returned proof for this printing on 24 September 1857, rejecting Lowell's proposed emendation in line 13: "beneath the moon" (see Bliss Perry, *Park-Street Papers* [Boston, 1908], p. 245). The spelling of the title was corrected in *May–Day,* 1867, where the poem appears, with a different emendation in line 13 ("below the moon"), on pp. 109–10. It was reprinted in *Selected Poems,* 1876, pp. 86–87, *Poems,* 1884, pp. 195–96, and W 9:227–28.

## "Roomy Eternity"

*Texts:* The first draft in X p. 144 was revised in journal AZ (JMN 11:185), as the notation "AZ 7" in X indicates. Carl F. Strauch has argued that "Roomy Eternity" is in fact the opening lines of a long poem he calls "Eternity" that consists also of "Poet of poets," "Terminus" ("For thought"), and "Cloud upon cloud / The world." While there is certainly some relation among these fragments, and while they were certainly all written at about the same time, there is no clear indication that Emerson arrived at a final intention regarding them. The present editors have therefore chosen to represent them as fragments, indicating where appropriate their interrelationships. The precise sequence of the remaining drafts of "Roomy Eternity" is likewise uncertain: two ink drafts occur in EL p. 1, another in NP p. 117, and an ink fair copy in ETE p. 33.

*Date:* The second draft, in AZ, was written in November or early December 1849 and was probably followed quickly by the next two or three versions.

*Publication:* Unpublished by Emerson. First published in *Poems*, 1884, p. 288, and reprinted in W 9:350.

*See Also:* Strauch diss., pp. 383–93 (text) and 576–83 (notes), for the more inclusive version of the poem to which he gave the title "Eternity."

## "Rubies"

*Texts:* The earliest partial draft is the pencil version of lines 9–12 in EF p. 43. This is revised in ink lower down on the page, and an ink draft of lines 1–8, added later above it, is written over the first (pencil) draft of lines 9–12. Subsequent drafts of the poem occur in the following order: EF p. 53, X p. 181 (with an additional draft of lines 9–12 on p. 182), and Rhymer p. 27, which was the source, after revision, of the first printing. A fair copy in Poems folder 74 differs from the *May–Day* version in having "in" for "to" in line 2, "were" for "are" in line 3, and "melt the rubied ice" for "break enchanted ice" in line 10. A version of lines 5–8 was inscribed, probably from memory, in Emerson's pocket diary for 1855 (JMN 13:507).

*Date:* The central conceit of the poem may be traced back to a couplet set down in journal V in 1844 or 1845 and copied into notebook L Camadeva p. 111: "Friends to me are frozen wine / I wait the sun shall on them shine" (JMN 9:165), and to the single phrase "frozen wine" several pages later in journal V (JMN 9:169). In EF p. 32 Emerson expanded the phrase to "Rubies are but frozen wine." In 1848 he wrote that "All the gems are fossil wine"

(JMN 10:434). The text of "Rubies" at EF p. 53 is written over a draft of "Days" and so could not be earlier than 1851.

*Publication: May–Day,* 1867, p. 95; reprinted in *Poems,* 1884, p. 188, and W 9:217–18.

## "The rules to men made evident"

*Texts:* The evidence of the draft at EL p. 66 suggests that in its earliest form this quatrain was a stanza rejected from "Boston Hymn." The lines were slightly revised in EL p. 158 and copied, successively, into ETE p. 45 and Poems folder 62. These drafts all preserve the rhyme scheme of "Boston Hymn" (xaxa). A second phase of the poem's evolution occurred when, in revisions in NP p. 292 and Rhymer p. $50_e$, the first line was altered to produce a quatrain rhyme scheme (abab). Emerson was perhaps influenced in making this change by the presence in EL p. 157 of the poem "Shun Passion," which was copied and revised with "The rules to men" in both NP and Rhymer. Quite possibly the Rhymer draft is the latest, but because it seems to have been specially adapted to the theme of the Poet (see line 1), and because it is joined with other fragments, this draft has not been taken by the editors as representing Emerson's final intention.

*Date:* The relation of the poem to "Boston Hymn" and the fact that it appears in Rhymer p. $50_e$ with other fragments written not earlier than 1861 point to a date of 1862–1863.

*Publication:* Unpublished by Emerson. First published, from the NP text, in *Poems,* 1884, p. 273, and reprinted in W 9:358. A version differing from the manuscripts was published as a motto to "The Sovereignty of Ethics," *Lectures and Biographical Sketches,* 1884, p. 175, and W 10:181.

## "S. H."

*Texts:* The earliest appearance of this quatrain, untitled, is in ink in journal GO (JMN 13:105). It also occurs in P p. 285, untitled, and in Rhymer p. 33, titled and with the notation "printed"; in each place the first line is emended. An ink fair copy, titled and with the revised first line, occurs in NP p. 137. Two texts of this poem are in the Houghton Library, each with a draft of a letter to George F. Hoar of 19 April 1877; one of these texts, which has a variant in line 3 ("shined" for "was"), is printed in L 6:304. The letter and poem as sent are in the George F. Hoar Papers, Massachusetts Historical Society; here the text of the poem is identical in wording to the NP copy. As Edward Emerson noted (W 9:498), "This quatrain is Mr. Emerson's tribute to the upright citizen and lawyer, Samuel Hoar, the 'Squire' of Concord, and father of his friends, Judge E. R. Hoar and Miss Elizabeth Hoar."

*Date:* The first draft in GO is among entries of October 1852.

*Publication:* First published in "Character of Samuel Hoar," *Monthly Religious Magazine* 17 (January 1857): 9, collected in *May–Day*, 1867, p. 181, and reprinted in *Poems,* 1884, p. 240, and W 9:293. Reprinted also with the essay in W 10:448.

## "S. R."

*Texts:* An untitled pencil draft in P pp. 259–61 is the source of the titled fair copy in ink in Rhymer pp. 96ₐ–96_b.

*Date:* Undetermined, though Carl F. Strauch, in "Emerson Rejects Reed and Hails Thoreau," *HLB* 16 (1968): 272, speculates that Emerson wrote the poem in the summer of 1838, on the evidence of a rift between Emerson and his former mentor, Swedenborgian Sampson Reed, in that year (see JMN 7:31 for an entry of 22 June 1838 that is hostile to Reed).

*Publication:* Unpublished by Emerson. First published by Strauch on pp. 258–59 of the article cited above, from the Rhymer text with several minor misreadings. Previously, lines 1–6 had been quoted by Edward Emerson in the notes to *Representative Men* (W 4:295), lines 23–28 in the annotations to "Historic Notes of Life and Letters in New England" (W 10:574), and lines 1–3 by Rusk in *Life*, p. 118.

*See Also:* Strauch diss., pp. 358–60 (text) and 559–63 (notes).

## "Saadi"

*Texts:* Emerson brought the poem through three principal drafts to a length of 113 lines. Scattered texts for most of the remainder of the poem, an additional 71 lines, are extant, but no complete manuscript version of the poem exists apart from printer's copy for the London edition of *Poems,* 1847, in the Berg Collection, New York Public Library. This is a revised version of the first printing in *The Dial,* and was misread in several places by the English printers; see Additional Manuscripts.

The earliest draft is in notebook Dialling pp. 79–82 (JMN 8:508–10) and consists of lines 1–2, 5–8, 21–22, 25–26, 29–48, and 87–103. This was revised and expanded in the second draft in Dialling pp. 83–87 (JMN 8:510–13), consisting of lines 1–22, 25–48, 87–108, and 110–16. Lines 82–85, first composed in Dialling p. 67, probably as an autonomous quatrain, were revised and added to the end of the second draft at p. 88 (JMN 8:503, 513–14). Lines 72–79, first composed in journal Books Small p. 67, were revised in Dialling p. 77 (JMN 8:464, 508). The third draft (which, like the first two, is in pencil) occurs in P pp. 228–33, and consists of lines 1–116, lacking only lines 59 and 70–71. In this draft Emerson drew lines 57–58 from P p. 193, and lines 60–69 from journal Books Small p. 61 (JMN 8:460).

For the latter portion of the poem, Emerson drew mainly on an early draft of "Where the fungus broad & red" in journal E (JMN 7:479–80), where one finds the first versions of lines 119–25, 127–28, 131–32, 135–36, 143–48, 175, 177–80, and 183–84. Lines 153–58 occur in an early version in Books Small p. 82 (JMN 8:469); a reference to the first line of this fragment ("not too deep") occurs in P p. 231. Finally, what may be a version of lines 133–36 occurs in pencil in notebook Parnassus p. 1: "—Deathless powers to verse belong, / And they like demigods are strong / On whom the Muses smile".

*Date:* None of the manuscript texts can be specifically dated. However, the passages in E cannot be earlier than October 1839, when the journal was begun, and neither Books Small nor Dialling is earlier than 1840. Since the poem was first published in October 1842, the time of composition must be between late 1839 and the summer of 1842. The first draft of lines 82–85 was evidently written before the lines of "Woodnotes, II" on the same page; this would indicate that the quatrain was composed before October 1841.

*Publication:* The Dial 3 (October 1842): 265–69; collected in *Poems,* 1847, pp. 197–205 (Boston) and pp. 156–63 (London), with several revisions and the omission of lines 125–32 in the American edition and lines 35–36 and 125–32 in the English edition. Reprinted in *Selected Poems,* 1876, pp. 34–39, *Poems,* 1884, pp. 114–19, and W 9:129–35.

*See Also:* (1) "Saadi loved the new & old" and (2) "When thou sittest moping."

## "Saadi held the Muse in awe"

*Text:* The only text of this eight-line fragment occurs in pencil in NP p. 300.

*Date:* Undetermined, but no earlier than 16–20 August 1859, the date of composition of "By art, by music," the first couplet in NP p. 300.

*Publication:* Unpublished by Emerson. First published in *Poems,* 1884, pp. 267–68, and reprinted in W 9:325.

## "Saadi loved the new & old"

*Texts:* These four lines occur in pencil at the top of P p. 232, in the midst of a draft of "Saadi," but, as the smaller handwriting and lighter shade of pencil suggest, not a part of it. Lines 3–4 appear separately, in pencil, on P p. 235, where they follow a copy in ink of "Grace," which may in fact have inspired the couplet.

*Date:* Undetermined, though the copy of "Grace" may have been made in connection with its publication in *The Dial* for January 1842. Since the four-line version appears to interrupt a draft of "Saadi," a poem published in October 1842, a date of 1841 or 1842 seems a reasonable conjecture.

*Publication:* Unpublished by Emerson. Lines 3–4 were published in *Poems,* 1884, p. 295, and reprinted in W 9:354.

## "Sacrifice"

*Texts:* The draft in EL p. 158 is the source of the titled fair copy in Rhymer p. 50. The texts at ETE p. 176 and NP p. 2, which have "I heard" in line 2, probably precede those in EL p. 291, journal KL (JMN 15:438), the Houghton manuscript headed "Concord," and the signed fair copy in Poems folder 83, all of which have the published reading ("There came"). A copy of the poem, signed and dated by Emerson "Concord— September, 1867." but possibly not in his hand, is in the John D. Batchelder Collection in the Library of Congress.

*Date:* Lines 3–4 appear as a prose quotation in journal VO (JMN 14:191), apparently entered in December 1857. Edward Emerson, W 9:499, gives their source as "a sermon by Caleb Vines, a Puritan, on 'Caleb's integrity in following the Lord fully,' preached at St. Margaret's, Westminster, before the Honourable House of Commons, November 30, 1642." The first draft of the quatrain, however, follows on the same manuscript page the second draft of "The rules to men," suggesting a composition not earlier than 1862–1863. The KL draft falls between entries of 24 September and 9 October 1864. The poem was quoted in, and was perhaps written for, the lecture on "Character," first delivered on 1 January 1865; it was published with that lecture in the following year.

*Publication:* First published in "Character," *North American Review* 102 (April 1866): 359, and in the essay as reprinted in W 10:96. It was collected in *May–Day,* 1867, p. 189, and reprinted in *Poems,* 1884, p. 243, and W 9:296.

## "Said Saadi,—When I stood before"

*Texts:* The first draft is in pencil in notebook Dialling (JMN 8:513). The second, which works out the concluding lines, is in Poems folder 23 (see

Additional Manuscripts) and is followed by texts in X pp. 264–65 and ETE p. 27, a late fair copy with an altered first line. In all locations except the last, the poem is associated with "The Dervish whined to Said."

*Date:* The pencil draft in Dialling, a notebook Emerson used heavily after becoming editor of *The Dial* in April 1842, strongly suggests composition in the summer of that year. This is made even more likely by its presence among lines of "Saadi," published in *The Dial* for October 1842. A possibly relevant passage in "Man the Reformer" (W 1:236–38), cited by Edward Emerson (W 9:506), has for its source an 1840 journal entry (JMN 7:525–26). Edward Emerson's note also identifies "Hassan" as Edmund Hosmer, a Concord farmer.

*Publication:* First published in Channing, *Thoreau*, p. 167, with "rich" for "great" in line 6. Published again in *Poems*, 1884, pp. 265–66, and reprinted in W 9:323.

## "Said, 'Wards my friend' "

*Texts:* Two texts of this five-line fragment about Samuel Gray Ward occur in pencil in NP pp. 234 and 237.

*Date:* Undetermined. The draft in NP p. 234 is overwritten by part of a fair copy of "James Russell Lowell," written in early 1859.

*Publication:* Unpublished.

## "St. Augustine"

*Texts:* Four draft fragments exist: one of lines 1–3, 5–16, and 20–25 in journal 1826–1828 (JMN 3:89), and three others in journal Sermons and Journal as follows: (1) lines 26–27 and 31–35 (JMN 3:124), (2) lines 43–45, 47–49, 51, 53, 55–56, and 59–72 (JMN 3:151), and (3) lines 73–75 and 77–83 (JMN 3:123–24). These were brought together, revised, and extended in the ink fair copy in CSA pp. 11–15. (Page 11 is reproduced in Plate 1.) More of the poem existed at one time, as Emerson indicated by his notation in CSA p. 14: "(Here is a chasm very much to be regretted in the original manuscript.)" Line 4, inscribed in pencil on CSA p. 10, may have been intended as an alternate for line 3, as Edward Emerson has suggested (J 2:149); nevertheless it is clearly marked for insertion *after* that line, and none of the usual indications are given (such as parentheses) that would signal an intentionally alternate or variant line.

*Date:* Emerson noted "Written at St Augustine in 1826" in Sermons and Journal (JMN 3:151), but he did not arrive in that city until the middle of

January 1827, staying until 28 March. The texts in *Sermons and Journal* are evidently revisions of the lost original, and were done in 1828 and 1829.

*Publication:* Unpublished by Emerson. The first 72 lines (minus line 4) were printed from the CSA text in J 2:149–51. The entire poem was published—in scrambled order, however, and with several misreadings—by Mrs. Henry L. Richmond in "Ralph Waldo Emerson in Florida," *Florida Historical Quarterly* 18 (October 1939): 74–93. A facsimile of CSA p. 15 occurs on p. 74 of this article.

*See Also: One First Love*, p. 62.

## "Samson stark at Dagon's knee"

*Texts:* The pencil draft in X p. 37 is revised in pencil in X p. 261.

*Date:* Since the earlier draft is written over an erased segment of "The World-Soul," it could not have been set down before 1844. The source of the poem is Judges 16:23–30.

*Publication:* Unpublished by Emerson. First published in *Poems*, 1884, p. 281, and reprinted in W 9:348.

## "Scholar is a ball thats spent"

*Texts:* Three drafts occur, all in X: in erased pencil on p. 262, in pencil on p. 263, and in ink on p. 268$_{cc}$.

*Date:* Undetermined, though the insert, X pp. 268$_a$–268$_{dd}$, seems to date from about 1847.

*Publication:* Unpublished.

## "A score of airy miles will smooth"

*Texts:* The first and second drafts are in X p. 262; fair copies are in EL p. 292 and Rhymer p. 41. A fair copy, evidently given to an autograph seeker, is now in the University of Virginia Library; it is inscribed "R. W. Emerson / Pittsburgh, Apr. 1851". Another, signed but not dated, is unlocated, though a photocopy is preserved in Poems folder 172. All of the texts except Rhymer and EL read "Monadnoc" rather than "Monadnock" in line 2.

*Date:* Before April 1851. Emerson left Pittsburgh on 1 or 2 April after concluding a lecture series.

*Publication:* Unpublished by Emerson. First published in *Poems,* 1884, p. 282, and reprinted in W 9:341.


## "The sea reflects the rosy sky"


*Texts:* The two lines occur in pencil in P p. 106, and in ink (with punctuation) in P p. 107.

*Date:* The text on p. 107 is written over a draft of "The Sphinx," while the version on p. 106 lies under a draft of "Where is Skrymir?" This would imply composition between 1841 and 1847.

*Publication:* Unpublished.


## "Sea-Shore"


*Texts:* The earliest text is in EL pp. 96–100; a later draft of lines 26–31 occurs in journal KL (JMN 15:454). Printer's copy for first publication in *The Boatswain's Whistle* is in the University of Virginia Library; in it, line 4 is changed from "Is not thy voice my cradle song?" to "Is not my voice thy music, morn & eve?," "like" is canceled for "as" in line 8, "but" is canceled for "and" in line 15, "your" is canceled for "thy" in line 16, "my" and "thy" are canceled for "the" and "my" in line 37, "my" is canceled before "arts" in line 40, and "spells" occurs in line 42 rather than the misprint "shells." A clipping of the poem as printed in *The Boatswain's Whistle* is attached to Rhymer p. 97; two additional lines used in the 1867 version (after lines 12 and 23 respectively) are written in pencil to the right of it, and "shells" is corrected to "spells." Poems folder 171 contains a photostat of a titled fair copy of lines 1–17 (*May–Day* version); the original manuscript is in the Hall of Fame, New York City.

*Date:* The source of the poem is a prose passage dated 23 July 1856 in journal SO (JMN 14:100–101); cf. also a later passage in SO (JMN 14:108) and an earlier one in journal CD (JMN 10:62). Edward Emerson gives an account of the origin of the poem in a note (W 9:484–85), but mistakenly says the year was 1857, not 1856 (cf. L 5:23–24).

*Publication: The Boatswain's Whistle,* 9 (18 October 1864), 65. Reprinted with revisions and the addition of two lines in *May–Day,* 1867, pp. 125–27, *Selected Poems,* 1876, pp. 112–13, *Poems,* 1884, pp. 207–9, and W 9:242–43.

*See Also:* Strauch diss., pp. 403–9.

## "Secretly to love & to drink, what is it? tis a dissolute day's work"

*Texts:* The poem, which translates Hafiz, Book VIII, Ode LXXXIV, lines 1–16 (*Diwan* 1:328–29), occurs in EF pp. 46–47. Lines 3–4, struck through in pencil, occur in revised form in notebook EO p. i (see "Loose the knots of the heart"); lines 13–14, also struck through in pencil, are revised and copied in EF p. 82, and again in notebook Orientalist p. 53 (see "I will be drunk").

*Date:* Emerson quoted the first part of line 3 in a prose entry in journal CD (JMN 10:68) dating from 1847. The translation in EF was probably composed therefore between April 1846, when Emerson acquired his copy of the *Diwan,* and the end of July 1847, when he stopped using journal CD.

*Publication:* Unpublished except for lines 3–4 and 13–14, which appear in "Persian Poetry," 1858, p. 727; reprinted in *Letters and Social Aims,* 1876, p. 220, and W 8:246.

## "See how Romance adheres"

*Text:* The only draft of these lines occurs in pencil in EL p. 113. They have not been found elsewhere in Emerson's published or unpublished writings.

## "See yonder leafless trees against the sky"

*Text:* A pencil draft of this six-line text was erased on P p. 16 after being copied in ink on p. 17.

*Date:* Undetermined, though the erased pencil draft is overwritten by an ink fair copy of "Dirge," which may have been inscribed as early as 1838.

*Publication:* Unpublished by Emerson. First published without title in *Poems,* 1884, p. 282; reprinted in W 9:342 with the nonauthorial title "Transition."

## "Seemed though the soft sheen all enchants"

*Texts:* This quatrain occurs in three nearly identical texts: in ink in EL p. 180, in pencil in notebook ML p. 143, and in ink in notebook QL on a sheet laid in between pp. 122–23. The QL inscription, which has "form" for "storm" in line 3, appears with two other quatrains that are cross-referenced to EL p. 225.

*Date:* Undetermined.

*Publication:* Unpublished by Emerson. First published in *Poems*, 1884, p. 286, with "Seems" for "Seemed" in line 1, and reprinted in W 9:347.

## "Seer of productive forms"

*Texts:* These two lines, which are arguably not verse, occur in pencil in EL p. 277. A note on p. 295 refers to the prose source in journal Y (JMN 9:303).

*Date:* The passage in Y dates from late 1845.

*Publication:* Unpublished by Emerson. First published, as prose, in JMN 9.

## "Seyd planted where the deluge ploughed"

*Texts:* The first version, in EL p. 178, is revised in Rhymer p. 2$_a$. Line 1 evidently influenced "My Garden," line 13 (see EL p. 183).

*Date:* Edward Emerson (W 7:354) pointed out a prose parallel to lines 1–2 in "Civilization" (W 7:28), based on a lecture first given in April 1861. The apparent journal source, however (JMN 15:184), dates to 1862, so that the passage in question must be a late addition to the text. The year 1862 is in any event generally consistent with the date of the other entries in the Rhymer insert.

*Publication:* Unpublished by Emerson. First published from the EL text in *Poems*, 1884, p. 276, and reprinted in W 9:332.

## "Shakspeare"

*Texts:* Five texts exist, all with identical wording: one in erased pencil, titled, in P p. 39, followed by three titled ink fair copies in P p. 7, Rhymer p. 42, and NP p. 136, and, finally, by a text, in pencil and untitled, in notebook LI p. i. The P texts are undoubtedly the earliest.

*Date:* Undetermined, but possibly in 1838. Emerson read *King Lear* and *Hamlet* on 8–9 November of that year, and, in journal D, between 10 and 12 November, noted that "Shakspeare fills us with wonder the first time we approach him . . . . Then . . . we lose sight of him for [a] period of years. By & by we return, & there he stands immeasureable as at first" (JMN 7:143, cf. 147).

*Publication:* *May–Day*, 1867, p. 190. Reprinted in *Poems*, 1884, p. 243, and W 9:296.

## "Shalt be affianced to a heavenlier bride"

*Texts:* This couplet was originally lines 3–4 of "Forth to encounter thy affianced doom" in Poems folder 34 (see Additional Manuscripts under that title). The only text of the couplet as a separate entity occurs in NP p. 5 with two other short excerpts from that poem.

*Date:* Undetermined. Emerson dated NP p. 5 "1825," probably from memory.

*Publication:* Unpublished.

*See Also:* "No fate, save by the victim's fault" and "Not frolic Beauty."

## "She paints with white & red the moors"

*Texts:* Two identical texts of this couplet, beginning "And paints . . . ," occur in journal VO (JMN 14:127 and 182); an ink version beginning as above is in NP p. 32.

*Date:* The date of the drafts in VO is 1857.

*Publication:* Unpublished by Emerson. First published in the NP version in *Poems*, 1884, p. 282, and reprinted in W 9:341. A variant form is used in "Country Life," first published in W 12:133–67 (see p. 151) from a lecture delivered in December 1857.

## "She walked in flowers around my field"

*Texts:* These two lines occur in pencil in journal AC (JMN 14:252), in ink in EL p. 194, and in ink in NP p. 82, where "She" is replaced by "And" in line 1.

*Date:* The draft in AC dates from 1859.

*Publication:* Unpublished by Emerson. First published, in the AC and EL form, in *Poems*, 1884, p. 290, and reprinted in W 9:351.

## "Should I shed my tears"

*Text:* This quatrain, which translates Hafiz, Book VIII, Ode CLVI, lines 13–16 (*Diwan* 1:433), occurs in EF p. 97 in a series of entries headed "Hafiz superlative." It has not been found elsewhere in Emerson's published or unpublished writings.

## "Shun Passion, fold the hands of Thrift"

*Texts:* The first draft is the short, five-line version in NP p. 63, followed by the two drafts in EL p. 157 and the copies, associated with "The rules to men," in NP p. 292 and Rhymer p. 50ₑ, where the lines are joined with yet other verses.

*Date:* The manuscript relation between this poem and "The rules to men" suggests a date of composition about 1862–1863.

*Publication:* Unpublished by Emerson. First published in *Poems,* 1884, p. 273, and reprinted in W 9:358.

## "Silence"

*Text:* The only text is in pencil in P p. 165.

*Date:* The poem was probably written in 1838. An entry in journal D for 9 October of that year is the source of lines 1–2: "They put their finger on their lip—the Powers above,—" (JMN 7:98).

*Publication:* First published with the title as above in *The Dial* 1 (October 1840): 158. Omitted from *Poems,* 1847, it was collected in *Poems,* 1884, p. 300, with the nonauthorial title "Eros," and reprinted in W 9:362.

## "The simple people each with /basket/sack/ or tool"

*Text:* The only text is in pencil in P p. 92.

*Date:* Undetermined. Carl Strauch, influenced by the notation "ΦBK?" written in pencil by Edward Emerson above the lines in P, conjectured that these 25 lines are a preliminary draft of the long passage on Lafayette in Emerson's Phi Beta Kappa poem of 1834, and thus to be dated in that year (see Strauch, "Emerson's Phi Beta Kappa Poem," *NEQ* 23 [March 1950]: 75–76, 85–87). Although lines 12–13 appear as lines 143–44 of the poem (or vice versa), the resemblance is otherwise negligible.

*Publication:* Unpublished by Emerson. First published in Strauch, "Emerson's Phi Beta Kappa Poem," p. 76.

## "Since the devil hopping on"

*Text:* This fourteen-line fragment occurs in pencil in X p. 210. It has not been found elsewhere in Emerson's published or unpublished writings.

## "Since you set no worth on the heart"

*Text:* These lines, which translate Hafiz, Book XXIII, Ode XXI, lines 7–9 (*Diwan* 2:183), occur in EF p. 98. They have not been found elsewhere in Emerson's published or unpublished writings.

## "The Skeptic"

*Texts:* The earliest version of this poem occurs in pencil in journal K (JMN 8:244–45). This is the source of the erased pencil version in P pp. 35–37, which in turn was transcribed and revised in P pp. 77–79, where the title first appears. Eventually about half the lines in this version were struck through, while the remainder were copied, with the title, into X pp. 61–63 and further revised. The text in P pp. 77–79 seems to have undergone some slight further revision, but Emerson never achieved a satisfactory final version of the text.

*Date:* Begun between February and May 1842, as the K draft shows, this poem underwent revision during a period of at least three years. The X draft is written over lines used in "Monadnock," a poem begun in 1845.

*Publication:* Unpublished by Emerson. First published by Carl F. Strauch in "The Importance of Emerson's Skeptical Mood," *HLB* 11 (Winter 1957): 117–39, from the P pp. 77–79 text, with accompanying analysis and several plates.

*See Also:* Strauch diss., pp. 369–73 (text).

## "Slighted Minerva's learned tongue"

*Texts:* The couplet, in a somewhat different form, was originally lines 4–5 of an early unpublished poem, "Whoso alas is young." A draft of the first stanza of this poem occurs together with an unused first line of the second stanza in journal 1826 (JMN 3:7). A fair copy of the complete poem, in Emerson's early handwriting, is in Poems folder 94 (see Additional Manuscripts). The couplet was detached and revised a number of times in later years: first in X p. 126 (with an additional draft of line 1), then, in no certain order, in EL p. 21, Rhymer pp. 2ₐ, 50ᵢ, and 106, and NP p. 1.

*Date:* The first stanza of "Whoso alas is young" was written between January and March 1826. The X text was probably inscribed along with "The Asmodaean feat" in May 1854 or shortly thereafter. The allusion to Minerva in line 1 was apparently inspired by the prose source for "The Asmodaean feat" at JMN 13:314.

*Publication:* Emerson quoted the couplet in "Inspiration," *Letters and Social Aims,* 1876, p. 257, reprinted in W 8:287. It was first collected in *Poems,* 1884, p. 278, and reprinted in W 9:334.

## "The Snow-Storm"

*Texts:* The initial version of this poem, in run-on form, but with verse lines occasionally indicated by capitalization, appears in pencil in notebook 1833, used in the years 1833–1836 (JMN 6:246). A revised version appears in erased pencil in P pp. 127–28 with the heading "The snow storm 29 Dec", while an untitled ink fair copy, taken from this, is in P pp. 126–27. Printer's copy for the London edition of *Poems,* 1847, is in the Berg Collection, New York Public Library; this has "sled" in line 6 for the misreading "steed" of the printed text.

*Date:* On 27 December 1834, Emerson wrote in journal A, "Snow & moonlight make all landscapes alike. Every thing may be painted, every thing sung, but to be poetized its feet must be just lifted from the ground" (JMN 4:377). On 28 December, Emerson wrote of the "mute music" of the landscape. The reference to "29 Dec" in P p. 127 links the poem to an entry of 29 December 1834: "To the music of the surly storm that thickens the darkness of the night abroad & rocks the walls & fans my cheek through the chinks & cracks I would sing my strain though hoarse & small" (JMN 4:382). Another entry of the same night or the next day refers to a "great willowtree over my roof" as "the trumpet . . . of the storm" (JMN 4:384). Presumably the poem was written shortly after the storm.

*Publication: The Dial* 1 (January 1841): 339. Collected in *Poems,* 1847, pp. 65–66 (Boston) and pp. 49–50 (London); reprinted in *Selected Poems,* 1876, pp. 66–67, *Poems,* 1884, pp. 42–43, and W 9:41–42.

*See Also:* (1) Strauch diss., pp. 140–46, 351–53 (text), and 545–46 (notes), and (2) Strauch, "The Year of Emerson's Poetic Maturity: 1834," *PQ* 34 (October 1955): 354–56, 373–77.

## "So long as there's a trace"

*Text:* This poem, which translates Hafiz, Book VIII, Ode L (*Diwan* 1:278–79), occurs in a pencil draft in EF pp. 89–90. An earlier version of lines 21–24 is in journal CD (JMN 10:68).

*Date:* The CD draft was probably written in the late spring of 1847.

*Publication:* A version of lines 11–12 was published in "Persian Poetry," 1858, p. 728, and in the essay as collected in *Letters and Social Aims,* 1876, p. 225, and W 8:250.

*See Also:* "I am: what I am."

## "Softens the air so sharp and rude"

*Texts:* This quatrain occurs by itself in NP p. 4. Revised, it is combined with another quatrain, "When all their blooms," and lines 21–28 of "Who saw the hid beginnings," in Poems folder 92 (see Additional Manuscripts under "When all their blooms"). This is followed by fair copies in ETE p. 35, titled "May," and ETE p. 147, titled "May Day." The four-stanza poem may have been intended as a preamble to "May Day [Invitation]," a text of which, titled "May–Day," follows in ETE pp. 148–51; the ETE index lists "May Day 148, 147, 35" together.

*Date:* Undetermined.

*Publication:* Unpublished.

## "Solar insect on the wing"

*Texts:* An erased pencil draft in X p. 37 is revised in ink on p. 36.

*Date:* The only evidence as to the date of the poem is its context in notebook X. The phrase "the sportive sun" on p. 36, which became line 3 of "Song of Nature," first appears in journal Y (JMN 9:292), which dates to 1845. On X p. 37 the erased text precedes the phrase "Earth baking heat stone cleaving cold", evidently erased at the same time: this is line 57 of "Monadnock," which seems also to have been written in 1845. Both drafts of "Solar insect" were written over an erased draft of "The World-Soul," which is probably no earlier than 1844.

*Publication:* Unpublished by Emerson. First published in *Poems,* 1884, p. 283, and reprinted in W 9:343.

## "Solution"

*Texts:* Four principal drafts of the poem exist, all in ink and all in notebook X. The earliest is on pp. 8–9, where Emerson wrote out (on p. 8) the list of the five poets to be commemorated, began the verses on p. 9, and continued them on p. 8; running out of room there, he concluded on p. 13. The first revision begins on p. 18 and continues to p. 22 over erased fragments of several poems that were first published in *Poems,* 1847. This text is interrupted by unerased texts of "Forester" and "Written in a Volume of Goethe." In X p. 24, a six-line fragment contributes four lines not found in earlier drafts (lines 25–26 and 41–42). Of these the last two are taken from journal Books Small (JMN 8:463), and also appear separately in NP p. 47, where lines from "The Titmouse" are written around them. In X p. 25 are three and a half lines revised from p. 19 that seem to be intermediate between the second draft and the third, on pp. 67–72. (Page 68 is reproduced in Plate 3.) The poem was revised once more on pp. 76–81. Printer's copy for *May–Day,* 1867, is in the University of Virginia Library; in it, "With" is overwritten by "Bring" in line 24, "town & gown" is changed to "gown & town" in line 68, and "bloomed" rather than "bloom" appears in line 71.

*Date:* On 14 November 1860, Emerson wrote to J. R. Lowell enclosing "The Test" for publication in *The Atlantic Monthly,* saying, "If you choose to print it, I can put my solution into rhyme in another number" (L 5:230; with the names given in this letter compare the lists in NP pp. 171 and 173). "The Test" appeared in the January 1861 issue, but its sequel, "Solution," was not forthcoming. Carl Strauch theorized on the basis of the four drafts that Emerson had unusual difficulty with this poem and that he may not have completed it much before its publication in 1867 (diss., p. 80). Undoubtedly the first drafts belong to 1860 or early 1861. The text in NP p. 47 was written before 1862.

*Publication:* First published in *May–Day,* 1867, pp. 98–102; reprinted in *Poems,* 1884, pp. 189–91, and W 9:220–23. Texts from X pp. 9 and 18–19 were reproduced in Edward Emerson's note to the poem in W 9:476–77. The fragment in X p. 24 was published separately in *Poems,* 1884, p. 273, and reprinted with the omission of the last two lines in W 9:330.

*See Also:* (1) "And as the light" and (2) "The Test."

## "Song of Nature"

*Texts:* This poem developed out of a series of unrelated phrases and lines over a number of years, and was at one point a shorter poem entitled "First of May."

The phrase "the sportive sun" (line 3) occurs in several locations: journals Y and TU (JMN 9:292 and 11:114), X p. 36, and EF p. 33, and was eventually expanded into lines 2–3 and 5–7 in NP pp. 58–59. A version of lines 13–16 occurs in Poems folder 59 as the first half of a two-stanza poem (see

Additional Manuscripts under "Monadnock"). Lines 17–20 appear in journal NO (JMN 13:422–23) and were incorporated into a version of lines 13–28 and 31–32 in EF pp. 10–12; they appear again in EF p. 18, and, with one variant, in Rhymer p. 40. Lines 17–18 also appear in Poems folder 58 in a gathering of fragments. The germ for line 33 occurs in journal VO (JMN 14:182) and notebook PY p. 201, while a first draft of lines 37–44 and 57–60 occurs in journal Books Small (JMN 8:464–65).

A first consolidation of several of these elements occurs in NP pp. 65–69, which contains lines 13–36, 45–48, and 51–56; lines 49–54 are further developed on pp. 76–77. A subsequent consolidation occurs in notebook BL pp. 199–204, which contains lines 13–44 and 53–68, plus an additional stanza after line 64 that persists through all the remaining manuscript versions but was omitted from the poem as first published. The poem reached what Emerson temporarily considered final form in NP pp. 257–61, where the poem consisted, in order, of lines 13–44, 49–64, the stanza later dropped, 65–68, and 45–48. Emerson titled this poem "First of May" and numbered the stanzas 1–8, 10–15, and 9.

Sometime in the summer or fall of 1859 Emerson made a fair copy of the lines on NP pp. 257–61 (the "First of May" version, but with line 13 omitted and lines 45–48 in their proper place), titled them "A fragment of the Song of Nature," and sent them to his brother William with a query at the end, "Shall I send you the remainder." This copy, in Poems folder 77, follows the NP text as revised except for line 57, which has "travail" for the alternates "go" and "travail"; line 58, which has "mourn" for "travail"; and lines 65–66, which are unrevised. William's response to the poem was favorable, and on 23 October Emerson wrote him that "I finished the 'Song of Nature' . . . by writing six more quatrains, & sent it to Lowell" (L 5:178). Three of the added stanzas, which Emerson numbered 1, 2, and 3, were inscribed on NP p. 256; he then renumbered stanzas 1–8, 10–15, 9 as 4–11, 13–18, 12 and added three stanzas at the end, numbering them 19, 20, and 21. Lines 65–68 (stanza 17) were revised further on pp. 280–81. A fair copy of the entire poem was made in Rhymer pp. 82–87.

Printer's copy for the *Atlantic Monthly* is in the Houghton Library with the notation "Send back Manuscript to me J[ames]. R[ussell]. L[owell]." It includes the omitted stanza after line 64 and differs from the printed text as follows: line 8 reads "Nor less in death am strong.", "thousands," is canceled for "squadrons," in line 59, and lines 65–66 read "I moulded tuneful poets, / And captains born to rule;".

*Date:* The fragments in journals Y, NO, and VO date from 1845, 1855, and 1857 respectively. The EF drafts are, in part, written over material from "The Fugitive Slave Law" (1851). Lines 45–48 (stanza 12) and 49–52 (stanza 13) in NP pp. 67–68 are drawn from passages by Mary Moody Emerson that Emerson copied into notebook MME 2 in 1859: "Oh if there be a Power superior to me, (& that there is, my own dread fetters proclaim,) when will he let my lights go out,—my tides cease to an eternal ebb,—my wheels which whirl this ceaseless rotation of suns & satellites stop the great chariot of their maker in mid career?" (p. 147) and "Even these leaves you use to think my better emblems—have lost their charm on me too, & I weary of my pilgrimage,—tired that I must again be clothed in the grandeurs of winter, and anon be bedizened in flowers & cascades" (pp. 146–47). The poem was included in a letter to Lowell of mid-October 1859; in the letter Emerson noted that he "hope[d] to mend the poem in printing" (L 5:178).

*Publication:* First published in the *Atlantic Monthly* 5 (January 1860): 18–20. Reprinted, with the omitted stanza after line 64 added, in *May–Day*, 1867, pp. 128–33, *Selected Poems*, 1876, pp. 159–62, *Poems*, 1884, pp. 209–12, and W 9:244–47.

*See Also:* (1) "Power" ("His tongue"), (2) Carl F. Strauch, "The Sources of Emerson's 'Song of Nature,'" *HLB* 9 (Autumn 1955): 300–334, and (3) Strauch diss., pp. 410–18 (text) and 631–45 (notes).

## "Song of Seid Nimetollah of Kuhistan"

*Texts:* The "Song" translates the first of two "Mystische Gasele" from *Geschichte*, p. 223. Notebook Orientalist pp. 41–50 contains four complete drafts as well as several drafts of sections of the poem; on p. 40 is a draft of the introductory remarks that accompanied the poem on its first publication. The fair copy in Rhymer pp. 121–22 probably precedes the manuscript, signed and dated December 1853, in the Brown University Library, which may have been printer's copy for the Cincinnati *Dial;* it differs from that text only in having "Yet" for "But" in line 18 and "difference" for "differences" in line 26. The revision of line 16 in the Rhymer text first appears in print in *May–Day.*

*Date:* Undetermined. As early as 1842 Emerson mentioned "A dance which represented the seasons & the solar system" (JMN 8:458, cf. 9:452 and 11:17). On 16 November 1859, Moncure D. Conway wrote to Emerson for permission to publish this poem, which had "so long been in my treasury" (L 5:181). Conway had visited Concord in 1853 and perhaps brought away the Brown University copy.

*Publication:* First published without title in "Persian Poetry," 1858, pp. 733–34, though it does not appear in the essay as reprinted; published again in Conway's *The Dial* (Cincinnati) 1 (January 1860): 37, with the title "The Sacred Dance. / [From the Persian.]" and a headnote probably written by Conway from information supplied by Emerson. The poem was collected in *May–Day*, 1867, pp. 203–4, with the title as given above and a headnote revised from "Persian Poetry"; reprinted in *Poems*, 1884, pp. 249–50, and W 9:304–5.

## "Song of Taliesin"

*Text:* The poem occurs, heavily revised, in EL p. 177.

*Date:* Emerson adapted, with numerous changes and omissions, an English translation of a Welsh poem of Taliesin that appeared in David William Nash, *Taliesin; or, the Bards and Druids of Britain* . . . (London, 1858), p. 164. Emerson was reading Nash's work in June 1866, as quotations in journal LN (JMN 16:12–13) make clear.

*Publication:* Unpublished.

## "Sonnet of Michel Angelo Buonaroti"

*Texts:* Four successive drafts of this translation of Sonetto I from *Rime di Michelangelo Buonarroti* . . . (Paris, 1821), in Emerson's library, occur in journal AC (JMN 14:220–21, 221, 223, and 222–23), followed by another revision in NP p. 276. Emerson mentions the poem in lecture notes in journals CL (JMN 14:321) and DL (JMN 15:9).

*Date:* The drafts in AC imply a date of late 1858 or early 1859.

*Publication: May–Day,* 1867, p. 195; reprinted in *Poems,* 1884, pp. 244–45, and W 9:298. Lines 1–5 were reprinted as an epigraph to "Michel Angelo" in *Natural History of Intellect,* 1893, p. 97, and W 12:213.

## "South Wind"

*Texts:* The quatrain comprising lines 9–12 seems to be older than the rest of the poem: it appears separately in pencil in X p. 261 and in EF p. 32 among scraps of verses headed "Spring." Texts of the complete poem occur in X pp. 58 (with an additional stanza) and 59 (where the stanza is struck through). A fair copy in ink appears in Rhymer p. 59, where the title "South wind" and the notation "printed in Channing's Life of Thoreau" were added later.

*Date:* Most of the verse fragments in EF pp. 32–33, though not the "South Wind" quatrain, were revised from journal V (JMN 9:169), where they seem to date from the spring of 1845; Emerson noted the remarkable thaws of that spring earlier in journal V (JMN 9:149–50). The earliest complete drafts (X pp. 58–59) carry the date "20 Sept. 1846." On that day, a Sunday, Emerson went boating with Ellery Channing (JMN 9:455), who is perhaps referred to in line 3. Lines 13–14 have their immediate source in a letter from Margaret Fuller of 3 May 1840: "I cannot write down what the Southern gales have whispered" (*The Letters of Margaret Fuller,* ed. Robert N. Hudspeth, 2 [Ithaca and London, 1983]: 135; here she is evidently responding to the language of Emerson's letter of 15 April: see L 2:282).

*Publication:* First published, without title, in Channing, *Thoreau,* p. 183. Lines 9–16 were published in *Poems,* 1884, p. 310, with the title "The South Wind." The entire poem appears in W 9:361–62 with the title "September," drawn from the index reference in X.

*See Also:* Carl F. Strauch, "Hatred's Swift Repulsions: Emerson, Margaret Fuller, and Others," *SRom* 7 (Winter 1968): 75.


## "Spare thou neither time nor blood for thy friend"


*Text:* These lines, which translate Hafiz, Book XXIV, Ode II, lines 13–15 (*Diwan* 2:279), occur in EF p. 80. They have not been found elsewhere in Emerson's published or unpublished writings.


## "The Sphinx"


*Texts:* The earliest version of the poem, an erased draft of all or parts of stanzas 1–8 and 16–17, occurs in journal E (JMN 5:354–57). The second draft, in pencil in P pp. 108–11, adds the second half of the second stanza (lines 9–12) and reverses the order of the sixth and seventh stanzas. Emerson then numbered stanzas 1–8, but not 16 and 17, indicating he knew that additional intermediate stanzas were needed. On pp. 112–15 he provided these as follows: on p. 112, a rejected stanza and stanza 13, the second half of which (lines 69–72) was later replaced with verses the first draft of which occurs in erased pencil on p. 106; on p. 113, stanza 12 and an early version of stanza 10; on p. 114, stanza 9 (and so marked by Emerson), the second half of which was later replaced, a copy (subsequently erased) of the rejected stanza from p. 112 (marked "10" by Emerson), and a revision of stanza 10 from p. 113 (marked "11"); on p. 115, stanzas 11, 14, and 15, and the first two lines of stanza 16. The presence of these two lines and the notation "&c &c" after them indicate that Emerson intended to link up with the conclusion as written on p. 111. The first draft of stanza 9 as it appears on p. 114 occurs on p. 116, and an early version of the second half of stanza 12 (lines 93–96) appears in erased pencil on p. 107. All material relating to "The Sphinx" on pp. 108–16 is struck through in pencil.

*Date:* The erased pencil version in E is overwritten by material of late May 1840. In a letter to Margaret Fuller on 21 July of that year, Emerson wrote, "The 'Sphinx' has fourteen verses & only wants one to complete it, but that is unluckily in the middle & like Aladdin's window" (L 2:317). It is not clear which "verse" or stanza Emerson is referring to, if any, since the poem as published has seventeen, not fourteen stanzas. Four months later the poem was still not quite complete. When he sent it to Fuller for inclusion in *The Dial,* he requested proofsheets, indicating that he had "not quite settled two or three words in the piece" (L 2:361). The prose source for lines 93–96 (in stanza 12) is an entry in journal E between 10 and 17 May 1840: "The love of me accuses the other party. I wish he were nobler than to love me" (JMN 7:349). This passage was used in "Circles" (W 2:307), which Emerson was writing in September. The last two lines of the rejected stanza on pp. 112 and 114 have their source in a passage from "The Divinity School Address" (W 1:121).

*Publication: The Dial* 1 (January 1841): 348–50; collected as the first item in *Poems,* 1847, pp. 7–13 (Boston) and pp. 1–6 (London). Reprinted in *Selected Poems,* 1876, pp. 7–11, and *Poems,* 1884, pp. 9–13. In the Centenary edition, Edward Emerson gave first position to "Good-Bye" on the grounds that the "Sphinx has no doubt cut off, in the very portal, readers who would have found good and joyful words for themselves, had not her riddle been beyond their powers" (W 9:403). "The Sphinx" appears in W 9:20–25.

## "Spices in the plants that run"

*Texts:* These lines, almost certainly rejected from "May–Day," occur in two drafts. The first, in pencil in EL p. 82, includes a line later used in that poem; the second, with some added lines, is in NP p. 28.

*Date:* Undetermined.

*Publication:* Unpublished by Emerson. First published from the NP text in W 9:336, combined with other fragments, and from the EL text in a note to "May–Day," W 9:459.

## "Spiritual Laws"

*Texts:* Seven drafts of this 12-line motto have been noted, all composed within about a year, and with a certain amount of revising back and forth among the drafts. The apparent sequence of composition is as follows: the first two drafts are in journal O (JMN 9:437–38 and 442–43), the third in X p. 259, the fourth through the sixth in EF in pencil on pp. 61–62, 60 (erased), and 58. The last text, a titled fair copy in ink with an unused line, is in X p. 217.

*Date:* The drafts in O date from midsummer 1846. The fair copy in X seems to have been written in 1847, since it appears with a series of mottoes for the 1847 edition of *Essays: First Series.*

*Publication:* First published as the motto to "Spiritual Laws" in *Essays: First Series,* 1847, p. 115. Collected in *May–Day,* 1867, p. 174, and reprinted in *Poems,* 1884, p. 236, and W 9:275. Edward Emerson published lines 1–14 of the text at X p. 259 in his note to the poem in W 9:495–96.

## "Stand up, that we may sacrifice the soul"

*Text:* These lines, which translate Hafiz, Book III, Ode L, lines 17–20 (*Diwan* 1:122–23), occur in EF p. 48. They have not been found elsewhere in Emerson's published or unpublished writings.

## "Star seer Copernicus"

*Text:* This seven-line fragment, followed by a revised version of lines 3–4, occurs in pencil in P p. 139. It has not been found elsewhere in Emerson's published or unpublished writings.

## "A stately bride is the shining world"

*Texts:* These two lines, which translate Hafiz, Book VIII, Ode CXXIX, lines 13–14 (*Diwan* 1:400), occur in EF p. 108 under the headings "Ethical" and "Fatal sentences," and are revised in notebook Orientalist p. 57.

*Date:* Undetermined. The version in Orientalist is the first of five entries on the page, of which the other four were published in "Persian Poetry," 1858.

*Publication:* Unpublished.

## "Step in, it blows a little fresh"

*Text:* This five-line fragment occurs on a sheet inserted between EL pp. 198–99; the sheet also bears two notes headed "Parnassus." The fragment has not been found elsewhere in Emerson's published or unpublished writings.

## "Stout Sparta shrined the god of Laughter"

*Texts:* The full text of this quatrain occurs in pencil in P p. 214; another version of lines 1–2 occurs in pencil in NP p. 289. The quatrain has not been found elsewhere in Emerson's published or unpublished writings.

## "Such another peerless queen"

*Texts:* These two lines were inscribed in pencil in EL p. 107, then erased after being copied in ink on p. 106.

*Date:* Undetermined.

*Publication:* Unpublished by Emerson. First published in *Poems*, 1884, p. 290, and reprinted in W 9:350.

## "Sum your annals in a rhyme"

*Texts:* This couplet appears twice: once in EL p. 19 as an adaptation of lines which, revised a different way, appear in "Pour the wine!," and once as a supplied introduction to a collection of verse fragments on the Poet in Rhymer p. 50f.

*Date:* No earlier than 1846, the apparent date of "Pour the wine!"

*Publication:* Unpublished.

## "The sun athwart the cloud thought it no sin"

*Texts:* Drafts of this couplet occur in journal VO (JMN 14:202), EL p. 30, Rhymer p. 96c, ETE pp. 9 and 159, and notebook PY p. 201 (twice). The texts are all substantially identical except for those in PY, which, as their context indicates, were revised from the VO text.

*Date:* The VO copy, which is not necessarily the first, was written in May 1858. The copy in ETE p. 159 occurs in the midst of "Adirondacs" fragments, which would also suggest a date of 1858.

*Publication:* Unpublished by Emerson. First published in *Poems,* 1884, p. 281, and reprinted in W 9:340.

## "The sun is the statue of God"

*Text:* This single line appears in pencil in P p. 91. It has not been found elsewhere in Emerson's published or unpublished writings.

## "Suum Cuique" ("The rain has spoiled")

*Texts:* Two texts exist, both untitled: an ink fair copy in P p. 4, dated "Newton, 1834," and an ink version in journal B (JMN 5:194), between entries of 13 and 20 September 1836. The texts differ slightly in wording and the latter lacks all punctuation but a final period.

*Date:* Sometime between April and October 1834, when Emerson was living in Newton. An entry for 26 April 1834 in journal A (JMN 4:281) is suggestive: "Rain rain. The good rain like a bad preacher does not know when to leave off."

*Publication:* Emerson quoted the poem from the B text in his lecture "Tragedy," given 23 January 1839 (*Early Lectures* 3:116), but the poem was omitted when the lecture was printed as "The Tragic" in *The Dial* 4 (April 1844): 515–21. By then it had been published, from the P text, in *The Dial* 1 (January 1841): 347, with the title "Suum Cuique"; later it was collected in *Poems,* 1847, p. 128 (Boston) and p. 100 (London). It was not reprinted in *Selected Poems,* 1876, *Poems,* 1884, or W 9. In J 4:85 the poem was printed from the B text.

*See Also:* "Roger Rain."

## " 'Suum Cuique' " ("Wilt thou")

*Texts:* The first form of the couplet is represented by the draft in EL p. 45 and the fair copy in Rhymer p. 47, titled "Economy." In journal CL (JMN

14:324–25) the poem is revised in three stages to its second form, represented by titled fair copies in NP p. 3 and ETE p. 175, both with the title "*Suum Cuique.*"

*Date:* Emerson entertained the idea of this couplet a long while before composing it: see JMN 5:476 and 7:144–45. These journal entries are associated in the index list in JMN 12:290, and the second was used in "Compensation" in a passage that, as Edward Emerson pointed out (W 2:400), foreshadows the present poem. The revision of the couplet in CL was done in September 1859.

*Publication: May–Day,* 1867, p. 182; reprinted in *Poems,* 1884, p. 238, and, with the omission of the quotation marks around the title, in W 9:357.

## "Sweet, sweet, is sleep,—Ah! sweeter, to be stone"

*Texts:* Two drafts of this quatrain, Emerson's translation of Michelangelo's "Riposta, In Persona della Notte" in *Rime di Michelangelo Buonarroti . . .* (Paris, 1821), in Emerson's library, occur in journal AC (JMN 14:224); a revision is in NP p. 277.

*Date:* The drafts in AC date from early 1859.

*Publication:* Unpublished by Emerson. First published, from the second AC text, in J 9:171.

## "Take my heart in thy hand, O beautiful boy of Schiraz"

*Texts:* These two lines translate Hafiz, Book I, Ode VIII, lines 1–2 (*Diwan* 1:13), though as the note accompanying the first draft in EF p. 97 indicates, Emerson encountered the lines in an anecdote recounted by von Hammer-Purgstall in the foreword (*Diwan* 1:xvii). The lines were revised in notebook Orientalist p. 58.

*Date:* Undetermined.

*Publication:* First published from the Orientalist text as part of the anecdote from von Hammer-Purgstall in "Persian Poetry," 1858, p. 728, and in the essay as collected in *Letters and Social Aims,* 1876, p. 226, and W 8:251.

## "Teach me your mood, O patient stars!"

*Texts:* The first draft of the quatrain occurs in EL p. 225 among stanzas of "In my garden three ways meet," for which it was perhaps intended, along with "When all their blooms," which precedes it on the same page. Other copies are in EL pp. 40 and 133, Rhymer pp. 50$_g$ (with two additional partial drafts of line 1) and 96$_e$, NP p. 72, ETE pp. 78$_a$ and 175, an enclosure in notebook QL pp. 122–23, and (in the ETE form) in an autograph album once owned by John Endicott Peabody and now in the Houghton Library.

*Date:* Although the quatrain is of considerably later composition, its germ appears to be a passage in *Nature,* 1836: "The moral influence of nature upon every individual is that amount of truth which it illustrates to him. Who can estimate this? Who can guess how much firmness the sea-beaten rock has taught the fisherman? how much tranquillity has been reflected to man from the azure sky, over whose unspotted deeps the winds forevermore drive flocks of stormy clouds, and leave no wrinkle or stain?" (W 1:42). The relation of the drafts in EL p. 225 and Rhymer 96$_e$ to draft fragments of "In my garden three ways meet" indicates composition in 1859 or shortly thereafter.

*Publication:* Unpublished by Emerson. First published in *Poems,* 1884, p. 277; also published as lines 5–8 of "When all their blooms" in W 9:340. The authority for this latter combination is of course the first draft at EL p. 225 and the text at EL p. 133; neither can be construed, however, as representing Emerson's final intention.

## "Teach your child to earn his meal"

*Text:* This couplet occurs only in EL p. 167.

*Date:* The prose source, an aphorism translated by Emerson from Sir John Chardin, *Voyages du Chevalier Chardin, en Perse, et Autres Lieux de l'Orient . . .*, ed. L. Langlès, 10 vols. (Paris, 1811), 5:22, occurs twice in journal FOR (JMN 15:373 and 392). Emerson borrowed the volume from the Boston Athenaeum from 16 to 31 October 1863.

*Publication:* Unpublished.

## "Tell me maiden dost thou use"

*Texts:* An erased pencil draft in journal V (JMN 9:143–44) is presumably the source of the pencil fair copy, slightly revised, in P p. 223.

*Date:* Sometime between May 1844, when Emerson began using journal V, and the end of that year. The draft in V is overwritten by notes made by Emerson in January 1845 from Louis Antoine Fauvelet de Bourrienne, *Private Memoirs of Napoleon Bonaparte,* 4 vols. (London, 1830).

*Publication:* Unpublished by Emerson. First published in W 9:387–88 with the nonauthorial title "Lines to Ellen" and the date "1829." In the absence of texts prior to that in V, both of these notations must be regarded as highly speculative.

## "Tell men what they knew before"

*Texts:* Six texts exist, of which the first four have the reading "their door" in line 2: in P p. 99, X p. 267, Rhymer p. 50₁ (in combination with other couplets), and notebook RT p. 24 (which bears the title "*Nobil Volgar eloquenza*"). In the text at EL p. 148, which is combined with another couplet, "their" is overwritten by "your", while RT p. 126 has "your door". The P text has the index reference "Proverb."

*Date:* Undetermined, though the other "Proverbs" inscribed in P p. 99 seem to date from the mid 1830s. For the title in RT, see an entry in journal TU for 1849 (JMN 11:133–34).

*Publication:* Unpublished by Emerson. First published in *Poems,* 1884, p. 294, with "their door," and reprinted in W 9:354.

## "Terminus"

*Texts:* There are four successive drafts of the poem in X, all untitled. The first, as Carl Strauch has demonstrated, actually begins with lines 33–34 on p. 198, includes the unused lines on p. 202, and continues with the main sequence of the draft on pp. 203–5. The second draft, in erased pencil, occupies pp. 206–7, and is indexed as "Tis time to be old." The third is in pencil on pp. 208–9, and the fourth, in ink, is written over the erased second draft on pp. 206–7. None of these drafts extends beyond line 36: a draft of the end of the poem occurs in NP p. 94. Rhymer pp. 100–102 is a titled fair copy of the entire poem and the source of the text as published, though a fair copy in the Yale University Library is probably earlier, since it retains the unused lines about the Pilot, which originate in the NP text. Another copy (location unknown) was reported in a letter of 23 October 1944 from Mrs. Frederick Peterson to Blanche Prichard McCrum, now owned by Eleanor Tilton: this manuscript is reputed to have contained a different version of the Pilot lines, "Is the sky dark? the pilot saith, / More near shall stand / The Pilot to thy hand." A fourth fair copy, signed, and with the title "Climacteric," occurs in Poems folder 18; this seems on the evidence of lines 7, 19, 24, and 28–29 to carry revision beyond the latest published state of the poem. A fragmentary draft in Poems folder 9, headed "Autob.", gives a version of lines 33–36 and two unused lines ("And hide . . . of theirs"), but seems not to belong to the development of the poem. (For the texts in folders 9 and 18 and the Yale University Library, see Additional Manuscripts.)

*Date:* In *Emerson in Concord* (Boston, 1889), pp. 183 and 257, Edward Emerson strongly hinted that the poem was written in 1866, and repeated the hint in the notes in W 9:489–90. Carl F. Strauch argued that the first draft at least was most likely written in 1850–1851. The fact that this first draft begins with lines 33–34 is significant because it suggests the possibility that the translation from Hafiz ("The Phoenix") on the two preceding pages may have influenced the poem at its very inception. Since "The Phoenix" appears to have been written in 1850, the connection favors Strauch's conclusion. The fact that the draft on p. 202 is underneath a draft of "Pour the wine!," however, implies a still earlier date, as does a journal entry for April 1846, overlooked by Strauch: "I grow old, I accept conditions;—thus far—no farther;—to learn that we are not the first born, but the latest born; that we have no wings; that the sins of our predecessors are on us like a mountain of obstruction" (JMN 9:363). Strauch further argues that the reference to politics in the first draft is most consistent with what we know of Emerson's reaction to the Fugitive Slave Law, but the "Ode, Inscribed to W. H. Channing," written in June 1846, is no more friendly to politics than the first draft of "Terminus." An entry in journal LM in 1848 connects the idea of a dislike of politics with "thrifty trees": "I am struck with the unimportance of our American politics. We prosper with such vigour that like thrifty trees . . . we do not suffer from the profligate gang who fatten on us" (JMN 10:345). But it is impossible to tell whether this is an anticipation or a reminiscence of the poem. The same may be said of Emerson's letter of 1 April 1847, in which, after discussing the purchase of the Warren lot and his intention of planting fruit trees, he says, "This year I am as resolute as ever Falstaff was to live within bounds. And I am taking in sail; and shall break out of slavery, if I can" (L 3:390). The date of the first draft has to be regarded as uncertain, though the probability that it was written between April 1846 and the end of 1851 is very high. The draft of the ending in NP is probably much later which might explain why the poem was not published until 1867.

*Publication: The Atlantic Monthly* 19 (January 1867): 111–12; collected in *May–Day*, 1867, pp. 140–42, and reprinted in *Poems*, 1884, pp. 216–17, and W 9:251–52.

*See Also:* (1) Carl F. Strauch, "The Date of Emerson's 'Terminus,' " *PMLA* 65 (June 1950): 360–70, and (2) JMN 9:414, 418.


## "Terminus" ("For thought")


*Texts:* The poem exists in two versions, of which the shorter five-line one is earlier. The first draft of this is in X p. 159, where it may represent an impromptu on lines from "Poet of poets" on p. 157 ("Nothing's of worth / in Earth or in sky, / But ⟨thought alone.⟩ ↑Love & thot only.↓ "). Other drafts of the short version are in Rhymer pp. 50ⱼ and 96_d, and EL pp. 10 and 290. The EL texts are indexed "Terminus" though they, like those in Rhymer, lack titles. The longer ten-line version is in NP p. 220, where it carries the title "Terminus."

*Date:* A quotation from Plato entered in journal CD may be a source for both the "Poet of poets" passage and "Terminus": "The true coin for which all else ought to be changeable is a right understanding of what is good" (JMN 10:114). Whether the first draft derives from "Poet of poets" or not, it was clearly inscribed after that poem, and could therefore not have been written before December 1849.

*Publication:* Unpublished by Emerson. First published, from the NP text, in *Poems*, 1884, pp. 270–71, and reprinted in W 9:328.


## "The Test"


*Texts:* The first and second drafts occur in pencil in notebook Z (JMN 6:298–99), the third, partially erased, in EF p. 116. These drafts all lack the last two lines, which, however, are present in the ink versions in Rhymer p. 81 (titled "Purging") and NP p. 107, where only the stub of the leaf remains. Printer's copy for *May–Day*, 1867, is in the Boston Public Library.

*Date:* Undetermined. The drafts of "May–Day" and "My Garden" that appear with the poem in Z seem to date from between 1851 and 1855. The version sent to J. R. Lowell for publication on 14 November 1860 (L 5:230) was evidently not derived from the Rhymer text, which has the *May–Day* form of line 14.

*Publication: The Atlantic Monthly* 7 (January 1861): 85. Collected, with a revised line 14, in *May–Day,* 1867, p. 97, and reprinted in *Poems,* 1884, p. 189, and W 9:220.

*See Also:* "Solution."

## "Thank the gods thy governors"

*Text:* The only text of this seven-line poem is in ink in X p. 268$_g$.

*Date:* The X insert, which contains several fair copies of mottoes for the 1847 edition of *Essays: First Series,* dates from 1846–1847.

*Publication:* Unpublished.

## "Thanks to those who go & come"

*Texts:* The first draft of the poem is in EF p. 7, the second occurs in NP p. 91, and the third, with minor revisions, is in EL p. 173.

*Date:* The EF draft is written over an early version of "Pale Genius roves alone," and so must be later than 1845.

*Publication:* Unpublished.

## "That each should in his house abide"

*Texts:* This couplet first appears in journal LM (JMN 10:347), where the first line is added above and below a prose entry beginning "Therefore was the world so wide . . . ." (The JMN text mistakenly shows the first line added to the next entry, from which it is entirely separate.) The couplet also appears in EL p. 180 and ETE p. 175.

*Date:* The prose version was written between Emerson's return from England on 27 July 1848 and 6 August of that year, the next dated entry in LM.

*Publication:* Unpublished by Emerson. First published in *Poems,* 1884, p. 298, and reprinted in W 9:354. The couplet also appears as one of two headnotes to "Society and Solitude," W 7:2.


## "That wandering fire to me appears"


*Text:* This quatrain occurs in pencil in P p. 53, apparently as a comment on the verses "To Eva" that precede it on the page. It has not been found elsewhere in Emerson's published or unpublished writings.


## "Their Eyes look sidewise out to watch"


*Text:* The only text of this fragment is in pencil in X p. 23.

*Date:* Undetermined, though if the succeeding line is in fact a preliminary version of "Astraea," line 28, these verses would be earlier than 1846. The reference to "passing travellers" suggests a relation between this fragment and "Love and Thought," a later ink draft of which occurs on the same page.

*Publication:* Unpublished.


## "Then what must be the splendor of that soul"


*Texts:* The first draft of this couplet occurs in journal VO (JMN 14:131), a versification of a passage in *Iamblichus on the Mysteries of the Egyptians, Chaldeans, and Assyrians* (Chiswick, 1821), in Emerson's library. Emerson copied both couplet and citation into NP p. 77, then returned to VO some time later and revised that draft.

*Date:* The entry in VO dates from early 1857.

*Publication:* Unpublished by Emerson. First published in JMN 14.


## "There are beggars in Iran & Araby"


*Texts:* Two major segments of this uncompleted poem can be distinguished. The first ("There are beggars in Iran & Araby . . . like castles") is found in six principal manuscript versions, and the second segment ("But when the mate of snow & wind . . . Sphered & concentric to the whole") in three; each segment has numerous subsidiary drafts. Of the principal texts of the first segment the earliest is a 26-line pencil draft in journal V (JMN 9:130). The next, which is marked "see V 71" and bears the heading "Saadi (new)," occurs in pencil in P pp. 282–83, and consists of 27 lines followed by an additional couplet intended for insertion. The third draft is in ink in Rhymer pp. 11–12, followed by two drafts in Poems folder 79, the second somewhat longer than the first. (A proofsheet of the first version in folder 79, with corrections in ink, is laid in between pp. 16–17 of Rhymer; see Plate 6.) Finally, a late text of the first section, apparently drawn from the version in V, appears in notebook QL, pp. 81–82, headed "Saadi Again." The principal texts for the second segment are a preliminary version of 19 lines in folder 79, a 17-line version in X pp. 162–63, and the full version of 21 lines in folder 79, attached to the first segment by the transitional lines "Decked by courtly rites & dress / And etiquette of gentilesse." (For all the folder 79 texts, see Additional Manuscripts). Line numbers in the notes and below follow the fuller version of each segment in folder 79 (lines 1–32 and 35–55), plus the transitional couplet (lines 33–34).

The following texts are subsidiary to the main ones: a first draft of lines 11–14 and 17–20, in pencil, in X p. 162, which precedes the first draft of the first segment, mentioned above, in journal V; a draft of lines 11–22 and 25–29 in NP pp. 290–91; and a later version of lines 21–22 and 25–27 in X p. 162. Lines 23–24, which were introduced in the second principal draft, have a separate history. Line 24 was apparently first worked out in NP p. 188 and joined to line 23 at X p. 118. The couplet was revised in EL p. 148 before being added to the draft in P. The couplet also subsequently appears in Rhymer p. 50$_f$ (with other verses), on an insert inside the front cover of NP, in NP p. 299, and, finally, in considerably revised form, in journal VA (JMN 15:236). Lines 54–55 likewise have a separate history, appearing first as the conclusion of an unrelated poem in journal Z[A] (JMN 8:329), then with other verses in P p. 287. A truncated version of the lines occurs in EL p. 155, Rhymer p. 2$_a$, on an insert inside the front cover of NP, and in NP pp. 298 and 300.

Lines 11–20 of this poem were eventually combined with a passage in Poems folder 79 ("Oft pealed for him . . . bread") to form the motto to "Beauty" in *The Conduct of Life,* 1860, p. 245.

*Date:* The pencil draft of the first segment in V follows an entry dated 15 October 1844 and immediately precedes notes that Emerson took from books borrowed from the Boston Athenaeum in January 1845; the draft of the last two lines of the second segment in journal Z[A] must have been written between November 1842 and March 1843, the inclusive dates of use of the journal. The various revisions of both segments in different notebooks and in folder 79 were apparently made over a period of many years. Notebook QL was used in the 1870s.

*Publication:* Unpublished by Emerson. The main text of the poem, omitting the lines that became part of the motto to "Beauty," was combined with two other passages and published in *Poems,* 1884, pp. 263–65; this combination was reprinted in W 9:320–22. Lines 21–28, 33–40, 46, 48–50, and 52–55, preceded by two lines not otherwise associated with the poem, are used as one of two headnotes to "Society and Solitude," W 7:1.

*See Also:* "Beauty."

## "There is no evil but can speak"

*Text:* The only text is in ink in P p. 102.

*Date:* Undetermined. The first line of this couplet is an adaptation of "There is no ill thing in Spain but that which can speak," a Spanish proverb Emerson found in Vicesimus Knox's *Elegant Extracts . . . in Prose,* 7th ed., 2 vols. (London, 1797), 2:1035. On 12 May 1832, Emerson transcribed it and many other proverbs in journal Q (JMN 4:17). On 10 September 1833, while in Liverpool, he wrote in journal Q: "I have heard the proverb that there is no evil but can speak" (JMN 4:85). The second line of the couplet is also, of course, proverbial.

*Publication:* Unpublished.

## "There is no great & no small"

*Text:* The only text is an ink fair copy in P p. 23.

*Date:* The first edition of *Essays: First Series* contains only three original verse mottoes, and all were drawn from P p. 23, suggesting that their inscription, if not their composition, dates from late 1840.

*Publication:* This quatrain and the one that follows it in P p. 23 ("I am owner of the sphere") appear as mottoes to "History" in *Essays: First Series,* 1841, pp. 1 and 2 respectively, and in subsequent editions and reprintings including W 2:1–2. They do not appear in any collection of Emerson's poetry in his lifetime nor in *Poems*, 1884. In W 9:282 they appear as parts I and II of "The Informing Spirit," a nonauthorial title.

*See Also:* (1) "I am owner of the sphere" and (2) "Power."

## "There resides in the grieving"

*Texts:* The first draft is in EF p. 109, followed by a revision in notebook Orientalist p. 51; this text was copied in ink into Rhymer p. 133, where it carries the notation "printed." The text of the two fair copies in Poems folder 36 is identical to that of Rhymer; one of them serves as an experimental beginning to "The Builder of heaven" (see Additional Manuscripts). The poem translates Hafiz, Book XXVII, Ode XV, lines 5–8 (*Diwan* 2:379).

*Date:* Undetermined.

*Publication:* "Persian Poetry," 1858, p. 727, and in the essay as collected in *Letters and Social Aims*, 1876, p. 221, and W 8:246.

## "There went / To his cold urn"

*Text:* These lines, which occur only in a pencil draft in EL p. 128, are probably a tribute to Robert Gould Shaw, the Bostonian who led a regiment of black soldiers in the Civil War. They were apparently rejected from "Voluntaries," lines from which occur on the surrounding pages.

*Date:* The poem was written between 18 July 1863, when Shaw was killed in an assault on Fort Wagner, S.C., and October, when "Voluntaries" was published.

*Publication:* Unpublished.

## "Thermometer"

*Texts:* The first draft of this gift poem occurs in erased pencil in NP p. 124; a titled fair copy follows on p. 125. A photostat of an unlocated manuscript, probably the copy that accompanied the gift, is in Poems folder 167; in it, "seventytwo" is changed to "seventyone" in line 7, line 11 reads "Weather hath sprees & holidays," and lines 15–16 read "But wit & beauty prosper more / At the safe point of fifty-four."

*Date:* The verses were probably written in late December 1867 to accompany a New Year's gift. In NP they follow a draft of "Maiden Speech of the Aeolian Harp," written at that time.

*Publication:* Unpublished.

## "These craggy hills that front the dawn"

*Text:* This quatrain, introduced by the phrase "Nature says," occurs in NP p. 291 and Poems folder 38 (see Additional Manuscripts under "Boston Hymn").

*Date:* The source for line 2 first occurs in journal CO in 1851 (JMN 11:420), and again in two locations in journal GL in 1861 (JMN 15:121 and 123). A general similarity between this quatrain and "Boston Hymn," lines 77–80, suggests composition in the early 1860s.

*Publication:* Unpublished.

*See Also:* "Nature saith."

## "These trees like tho'ts that to visions congeal"

*Text:* The only text of this six-line fragment is in pencil in P p. 248. It has not been found elsewhere in Emerson's published or unpublished writings.

## "They say, through patience, chalk"

*Texts:* In EF p. 44 is a 20-line draft translation of Hafiz, Book VIII, Ode LXXVI, lines 5–24 (*Diwan* 1:316–17), of which the first four lines were revised in notebook Orientalist p. 26 and copied into Rhymer p. 147, where the verses are marked "printed."

*Date:* Because the poem is followed in Orientalist and Rhymer by "Dearest, where thy shadow falls," composition probably occurred in the summer of 1848. The draft in EF p. 44 must in any event have been composed before May 1849 because in that month Emerson copied two unrelated lines from EF p. 45 into journal TU (JMN 11:107) and mistakenly gave as their source that of the present poem as inscribed on p. 44.

*Publication:* First published from the Rhymer text in "Persian Poetry," 1858, p. 731, though it does not appear in later reprintings of this essay. It was collected in *May–Day*, 1867, p. 199, and reprinted in *Poems*, 1884, p. 247, and W 9:300.

*See Also:* "Dearest, where thy shadow falls."

## "They strew in the path of kings and czars"

*Texts:* The first three drafts of this translation of Hafiz, Book XXIII, Ode XXV, lines 5–12 (*Diwan* 2:192) occur in journal VO (JMN 14:152–53), two in erased pencil and one in ink; the ink version was copied into ETE p. 59.

*Date:* The date of the drafts in VO is 1857.

*Publication:* First published in "Persian Poetry," 1858, p. 731; reprinted in the essay as collected in *Letters and Social Aims*, 1876, p. 234, and in subsequent editions including W 8:260.

## "Thine Eyes Still Shined"

*Texts:* The latest and fullest of the notebook drafts—an ink fair copy in P pp. 28–29—has eight stanzas, though the poem as published consists only of the third, sixth, and seventh of these. The third stanza (i.e., lines 1–4 of the poem as published) occurs in erased pencil in P p. 198; it was transcribed on p. 199 and subsequently erased. A draft of the entire poem, lacking only the ultimately unused fourth stanza, was written in pencil in P pp. 29–30. This fourth stanza was then written in pencil in P p. 212 and erased along with the draft on pp. 29–30 when the ink fair copy was made on pp. 28–29. The first of the eight stanzas was heavily canceled and the second, third, sixth, and seventh were struck through. The untitled printer's copy for the London edition of *Poems*, 1847, is in the Berg Collection, New York Public Library.

*Date:* The poem, dealing as it does with separation from Ellen Emerson, presumably dates either from the period of their courtship and engagement in 1828 and 1829 or, if after their marriage, from the time of Ellen's stay in Philadelphia from 1 April to mid-May 1830. The Centenary edition suggests it "was probably written during Mrs. Emerson's absence in the South, either in the Spring before or following her marriage" (W 9:436); Edith W. Gregg says it "must have been written early [in the] summer [of 1829]" (*One First Love*, p. 47), but gives no evidence; Henry F. Pommer, in *Emerson's First Marriage* (Carbondale, Ill., 1967), p. 40, conjectures that it was written in April 1830.

*Publication: Poems,* 1847, p. 149 (Boston) and p. 117 (London). In the London edition the title occurs only in the table of contents. All but the first of the rejected stanzas were published in the notes to the Centenary edition (W 9:436).

## "Think not thy life to me unknown"

*Text:* The only text of this eighteen-line fragment occurs in erased pencil in X p. 102.

*Date:* The poem was probably inscribed at the same time as "I cannot find" in X pp. 102–3; evidence suggests that the latter poem was written no earlier than 1842, and probably in that year.

*Publication:* Unpublished.

## "This cup of life is not so shallow"

*Texts:* Nine texts of all or part of this poem exist. The earliest is an ink draft of the second stanza in journal 1826–1828 (JMN 3:83), in the midst of other verses written at different times during those years. All the other texts are ink fair copies. One, of the entire poem, and another, of the first stanza, occur in notebook XVI (JMN 2:410 and 411, n. 26, respectively); the first is followed by a single line that may be the opening of a projected third stanza, "And Time will yet reveal such treasures", and the page on which the second occurs has its lower half torn off. Another occurs in CSA p. 1, and yet another of the first stanza, joined with unrelated lines, is in journal Sermons and Journal (JMN 3:154). Later than any of these is the one in P p. 103 with the cancellation in pencil of "e'er" in the last line, and later still the one in X p. 266, where "Phidias" in the last line has become "Angelo." The versions in Rhymer p. 45 and Poems folder 81 are identical with the X text.

*Date:* The fact that this poem is the first one copied into CSA, a notebook that bears the initial notation "Charleston South Carolina. / Saint Augustine, Florida.", indicates strongly that it was written during Emerson's stay in one of those two cities, from December 1826 to April 1827. This is corroborated by the appearance of a draft of the second stanza in journal 1826–1828, which Emerson is known to have taken with him on his Southern trip.

*Publication:* Unpublished by Emerson. First published by William Ellery Channing in *Thoreau,* p. 132. Published again in W 9:387 with the nonauthorial title "Good Hope" and dated "in December, 1827, [when] the young minister . . . first saw Ellen Tucker . . ." (p. 516). Also printed in J 2:132 with the nonauthorial title "Song" between entries of November and December 1826, and again in J 2:219–20 as "Song" before a letter of 20 November 1827, with the comment "These verses appear to have been written earlier in the year,—it is impossible to tell just when . . . ."

*See Also:* Strauch diss., pp. 46–56.

## "This effervescing gentleman who despises a secret"

*Text:* This poem, which translates Hafiz, Book VIII, Ode LXXXVII, lines 1–4 and 9–14 (*Diwan* 1:332–33), occurs in EF p. 47. It has not been found elsewhere in Emerson's published or unpublished writings.

## "This is the age of ages this the hour"

*Text:* This single line, in pencil in EL p. 38, may bear some relation to the heading "The Age, & the Hour" and the sentence following it, written in 1864, in journal KL (JMN 15:449). The line has not been found elsewhere in Emerson's published or unpublished writings.

## "This the creation"

*Text:* This eleven-line fragment occurs in pencil in EL p. 84, surrounded by verses written in the 1860s. It has not been found elsewhere in Emerson's published or unpublished writings.

## "This world is tedious"

*Text:* These six lines occur in pencil in P p. 196. They have not been found elsewhere in Emerson's published or unpublished writings.

## "Thou shalt make thy house"

*Text:* The only manuscript text is in X p. 127.

*Date:* Undetermined.

*Publication:* Unpublished by Emerson. First published in *Poems*, 1884, p. 295, and reprinted in W 9:354.

## "Thou who with thy long hair"

*Texts:* The poem translates Hafiz, Book XXVI, Ode I (*Diwan* 2:332–33). The principal draft occurs in X pp. 237–38. Emerson revised the fifth stanza ("Fair fall thy soft heart!") in pencil in EF p. 77, where it is overwritten with a draft of the quatrain "A. H." This stanza, with "wilt" for "wouldst" in line 18, also occurs in notebook Orientalist p. 54, Rhymer p. 138, and Poems folder 37.

*Date:* Undetermined, though before the spring of 1855, the apparent date of composition of lines 3–4 of "A. H."

*Publication:* Unpublished, except for stanza 5, which appears in "Persian Poetry," 1858, p. 731, and in the essay as collected in *Letters and Social Aims,* 1876, p. 233, and W 8:260.

*See Also:* "Fair fall thy soft heart!"

## "Thou wilt not speak as a man"

*Text:* The only text of this fragment is in ink in X p. 186. It has not been found elsewhere in Emerson's published or unpublished writings.

## "Though all fair things that fair resemble"

*Texts:* A 23-line first draft of this poem occurs in pencil in journal Books Small (JMN 8:473–75). The first six, possibly the twelfth, and the nineteenth and twentieth lines of this draft were revised in pencil in P pp. 298–99, where everything after the second line was erased. Lines 1–2, all that Emerson finally wished to save, occur again in pencil in X p. 70, overwritten with a draft of "Solution."

*Date:* The first draft was probably written in the spring of 1843, as suggested by the fact that parts of it were subsequently incorporated into "Threnody" and "The Daemonic and the Celestial Love." The revision in P was probably made at the same time that "Pericles" (also in P p. 298) was revised from the preceding page in Books Small, a text which in turn immediately follows a draft of "To Rhea" done in May 1843.

*Publication:* Unpublished by Emerson. First published in JMN 8.

## "Though her eye seek other forms"

*Text:* The only text is in pencil in P p. 176.

*Date:* Edward Emerson assigned to these lines a date of 1829 (W 9:389) on the assumption that they related to Emerson's courtship of Ellen Tucker.

*Publication:* Unpublished by Emerson. First published in W 9:388–89 with the nonauthorial title "Security."

## "Thousand dangers of ruin has the street of love"

*Text:* This two-line fragment, translating Hafiz, Book XXIII, Ode XXXII, lines 9–10 (*Diwan* 2:205), occurs only in EF p. 50. On the same page are two other translations from the *Diwan,* including one of lines 15–16 of the same ode ("His learning truly"), and two lines from "The Chartist's Complaint."

*Date:* Since the second draft of the quatrain entitled "Hafiz," dating from 1855, is written over the companion couplet from Ode XXXII, both sets of verses were probably inscribed between 1851, the apparent date of the EF drafts of "The Chartist's Complaint," and 1855, the date of the "Hafiz" draft.

*Publication:* Unpublished.

## "The Three Dimensions"

*Texts:* Two texts exist, with differing first lines: one in ink in journal R entitled "The three Dimensions" (JMN 8:431), and one in pencil in P p. 50 entitled "The three Spaces." The R text is presumably earlier since it follows a prose entry entitled "Variety" that conveys the same idea.

*Date:* The text in R occurs between entries of 22 June and 8 July 1843.

*Publication: The Dial* 4 (October 1843): 226, with a first line different from either of the manuscript versions. Emerson did not reprint the poem in his lifetime, nor does it appear in *Poems,* 1884, or W 9; its first book publication was in *The Poems of Ralph Waldo Emerson* (London and Newcastle-on-Tyne, 1886), volume 30 of *The Canterbury Poets,* p. 59. It is also printed in J 6:419, from the R text.

## "Thy dull pen soaked in stagnant ink"

*Text:* The first draft of this couplet, in pencil, is overwritten by the second draft in ink in EL p. 103. The couplet has not been found elsewhere in Emerson's published or unpublished writings.

## "Thy poems Hafiz shame the rose leaves"

*Text:* This translation of Hafiz, Book I, Ode XIII, lines 15–16 (*Diwan* 1:23), occurs in EF p. 114 in a series of entries headed "Hafiz of his verse." It has not been found elsewhere in Emerson's published or unpublished writings.

## "Thy songs O Hafiz"

*Text:* This translation of Hafiz, Book VIII, Ode LXIV, lines 37–40 (*Diwan* 1:301), occurs in EF p. 113 in a series of entries headed "Hafiz of his verse." It has not been found elsewhere in Emerson's published or unpublished writings.

## " 'Tis writ on Paradise's gate"

*Texts:* These two lines are a translation of Hafiz, Book XXVII, Ode XX, lines 15–16 (*Diwan* 2:386). Probably the earliest draft is that in journal AB (JMN 10:55), where Emerson indicated that he had transcribed the lines into notebook EO p. 177. He also copied the lines into EF p. 93 (as the prose copied at the same time from the same page in AB into EF p. 92 makes clear), and revised them in pencil in EF p. 25, erasing them there after making a copy in notebook Orientalist p. 57. This was revised into final form in Orientalist p. 56, and copied into EO p. i and Rhymer p. 145. Another version occurs in notebook L Camadeva p. 99: "It stands written on the Gate of Heaven / Wo to him who allows himself to be betrayed by Fate!"

*Date:* The first draft (in AB) dates to April or May 1847. In notebook BO Conduct, used in October 1851 to collect material for "Fate," Emerson indexed the AB draft (JMN 12:585).

*Publication:* First published in "Persian Poetry," 1858, p. 727, and in the essay as collected in *Letters and Social Aims*, 1876, p. 221, and W 8:245. A prose version evidently drawn from Orientalist p. 57 is quoted in "Fate" in *The Conduct of Life*, 1860, p. 24 (see W 6:29). The poem was not otherwise collected.

## "The Titmouse"

*Texts:* The first draft occurs in pencil in NP pp. 45–48, where it carries the title "Birds." The ink draft in NP pp. 43–44, confined to the first twenty-two lines, supplies a new opening. These texts were brought together and revised in the ink draft in NP pp. 50–57. The next draft portion, confined to lines 33–42, 80–83, and the first two of the six lines added after line 83 in the *May-Day* printing, occurs in journal VA (JMN 15:242–43) immediately after its prose source: "A chicadee came out to greet me, flew about within reach of my hands, perched on the nearest bough, flew down into the snow, rested there two seconds, then up again, just over my head, & busied himself on the dead bark. I whistled to him through my teeth, and, (I think, in response,) he began at once to whistle. I promised him crumbs, & must not go again to these woods without them." Line 78 was borrowed from an unused scrap of verse in journal GL (JMN 15:123), written in 1861. A fair copy of the entire poem is in Rhymer pp. 88–93. The six lines on NP p. 60, deriving from two unused lines in the VA draft, appear, canceled, in the printer's copy for the *Atlantic Monthly* in the Houghton Library (see Additional Manuscripts). Printer's copy for *May–Day*, dated "Nov 12" by the compositor, is in the Morgan Library. It omits line 54, as the *May–Day* text does, but also omits lines 76–79 and the six-line addition after line 83, both of which *May–Day* prints; in addition, in line 65 "dimension" is written over "proportion".

*Date:* A date of January or February 1862 for all the drafts and fragments in NP except the one on p. 60 is supported by Emerson's letter of 19 February 1862 to Margaret Perkins Forbes: "I have a little neighbor who, I am sure, is also a neighbor of yours, the black-capped titmouse . . . . If I can get my poem to him fairly copied out, I will send it to you with this: if not, soon" (manuscript in the Special Collections, Columbia University Library). The prose journal entry in GL recording Emerson's encounter with the chicadee (or titmouse) in Walden woods is dated March 3. Emerson completed his revisions shortly thereafter, since his account book for 1859–1865 shows that he was paid for the poem on March 14. In an undated letter to James T. Fields, probably about 1 April, Emerson made some final minor changes in the text and approved two additional alterations suggested by Fields (see *Harper's* 68 [February 1884]: 462).

*Publication: The Atlantic Monthly* 9 (May 1862): 585–87. Its first book publication was in James T. Fields, ed., *Good Company for Every Day in the Year* (Boston, 1866), pp. 284–87. Collected in *May–Day*, 1867, pp. 119–24, with the omission of line 54 and the addition of six lines after what thus became line 82. Reprinted in *Poems*, 1884, pp. 200–203, and W 9:233–36.


## "To be wise the dull brain so earnestly throbs"


*Texts:* These two lines, which translate Hafiz, Book IX, Ode XIII, lines 7–8 (*Diwan* 2:22), occur in EF p. 82 in a partially erased pencil draft; a revision appears in notebook Orientalist p. 53. The translation of the entire ode in X p. 165 (" 'Boy bring the bowl'") appears to be a separate undertaking.

*Date:* Undetermined.

*Publication:* First published in "Persian Poetry," 1858, p. 727; reprinted in the essay as collected in *Letters and Social Aims*, 1876, p. 221, and W 8:246.

## "To Ellen, at the South"

*Texts:* Two texts exist, an ink fair copy with several later revisions in P pp. 17–18, with the title "To E.T.E. at Philadelphia" and the date "Apr. 1829", and one in Poems folder 85 taken from it with the title "To Eva at the South" (see Additional Manuscripts).

*Date:* The date of April 1829 in P p. 17 is clearly an error for April 1830. The editors of the Centenary edition, misled by the 1829 date, were moved to explain that since Emerson and Ellen were not married until September of that year, "the initials should have been E.L.T." (W 9:435). Carl Strauch, diss., p. 64, accepts the 1829 date on the basis of Emerson's letter of 25 April 1829 to his brother William (L 1:270) in which he speaks of Ellen "& mother & sisters [going on] a journey," but this journey was only to Worcester, Massachusetts, Hartford, Connecticut, and Concord, New Hampshire; see *One First Love*, p. 18. Emerson and Ellen took a trip to Philadelphia in mid-March of 1830, arriving on the 20th; he departed alone for Boston about 1 April, returning to pick her up in mid-May (L 1:296, 299, 302).

*Publication: The Dial* 3 (January 1843): 327–28, from the Poems folder 85 text, with the title "To Eva at the South." Collected in *Poems*, 1847, pp. 144–46 (Boston) and pp. 114–15 (London), with the revisions in P and the title "To Ellen, at the South"; reprinted in *Poems*, 1884, pp. 86–87, and W 9:93–94.

*See Also: One First Love*, pp. 128–31.

## "To Eva"

*Text:* The only manuscript version is an ink fair copy, untitled, in P p. 53. An unlocated copy was offered at Anderson sale no. 1449, 25 November 1919.

*Date:* This romantic address to a "fair & stately maid" would seem to date from the period of Emerson's courtship of and engagement to Ellen Tucker, 25 December 1827 to 29 September 1829.

*Publication: The Dial* 1 (July 1840): 84, with the title "To \*\*\*\*." Collected in *Poems*, 1847, p. 147 (Boston) and p. 116 (London), with the present title; reprinted in *Poems*, 1884, p. 87, and W 9:95.

## "To every creature"

*Texts:* The earliest draft of these lines, heavily revised, occurs in pencil in journal CD (JMN 10:81–82). This is the source of the ink version at the end of CD (JMN 10:121–22). An intermediate pencil version of the first ten lines occurs several manuscript pages before this (JMN 10:119). A later version, in ink, occurs in P pp. 104–5, without the last five lines.

*Date:* The initial pencil draft in CD occurs among entries of June 1847 and reflects several prose observations in that journal about orchards, insects, and gardening. Each occurrence of the full poem is followed by "Where is Skrymir? Giant Skrymir?"

*Publication:* Unpublished by Emerson. The last nine lines of the P text were published in W 9:343 with the nonauthorial title "The Garden."

*See Also:* EL p. 198ᵦ.

## "To him are straw and mountains alike"

*Text:* This single line, a translation of Hafiz, Book VIII, Ode CLVII, line 5 (*Diwan* 1:434), occurs in EF p. 96. It has not been found elsewhere in Emerson's published or unpublished writings.

## "To Himself"

*Texts:* The quatrain translates Hafiz, Book XXVII, Ode II, lines 29–32 (*Diwan* 2:358). Identical pencil versions in X p. 258 and EF p. 114 precede the ink draft in notebook Orientalist p. 24, which is the source of the *Liberty Bell* printing and, after the revision of line 4, of the fair copy in Rhymer p. 129. Printer's copy for *The Liberty Bell* is in the University of Texas Library.

*Date:* Between 1846 and 1850; the Orientalist draft was probably written in 1850 (cf. "Faith," which was inscribed in 1850 in Orientalist p. 23). Emerson's contributions to *The Liberty Bell* conclude with the notation "Concord, October, 1850."

*Publication:* First published in *The Liberty Bell* (Boston, 1851), p. 81, from the unrevised Orientalist text; reprinted in *Uncollected Writings,* 1912, p. 189. Printed again, from the Rhymer text, in "Persian Poetry," 1858, p. 729, and in the essay as collected in *Letters and Social Aims,* 1876, p. 228, and W 8:254.

## "To J. W."

*Texts:* The first draft occurs in erased pencil in X pp. 264–65, while the second, revising only the lines from p. 264, occurs in erased pencil in X p. 242. Three lines of unrecovered erased pencil writing at the top of p. 243, however, may also belong to this draft.

*Date:* In his note to the poem in W 9:414, Edward Emerson identified "J. W." as the "Rev. John Weiss, a young clergyman and an able writer, who had seemed to Mr. Emerson to dwell overmuch on Goethe's failings." An entry in journal E written at the end of December 1840 seems to refer to this: "If you criticize a fine genius as Burns or Goethe, the odds are that you are quite out of your reckoning, and are only whipping your own false portrait of the man" (JMN 7:410); in the remainder of the entry Emerson turns this caution on himself. Five journal pages later is an entry that seems to suggest line 16 of the poem: "He did not get it from books but where the bookmaker got it" (JMN 7:412). In late July or early August 1842, Emerson advised himself to "husband your criticism on J. W. for a few days & he will have demonstrated his insufficiency to all men's eyes & give you no farther trouble" (JMN 8:192–93). In his note to "Goethe; or, the Writer" in *Representative Men* (W 4:371–72), Edward Emerson quotes a journal passage (see JMN 9:145–46) that he implies is the source of the poem. Reference to the original passage shows that the name excised from the beginning is not John Weiss, however, but George Putnam. In the journals and letters of the 1840s there are many indications of Emerson's annoyance at what he called "that local *prestige* against Goethe" (L 3:286). While the poem could have been written at any time between 1841 and 1846, its association with John Weiss suggests a composition earlier rather than later in this period. The fact that the draft at X p. 242 is overwritten by a fair copy of "Nantasket" dated 1841 is probably not significant (see "Nantasket").

*Publication:* Poems, 1847, pp. 43–44 (Boston) and pp. 32–33 (London); reprinted in *Poems,* 1884, pp. 31–32, and W 9:29–30.

## " 'To me is ‖ . . . . . . . . . ‖"

*Text:* These two lines, translating Hafiz, Book XII, Ode II, lines 19–20 (*Diwan* 2:58), occur in partially erased pencil in EF p. 80. They have not been found elsewhere in Emerson's published or unpublished writings. The German text for the partially undeciphered line is "Mir ist's im Innern des Gemüths."

## "To the Clock"

*Texts:* The only text of this poem occurs in pencil in NP pp. 246–47. It is Emerson's versification of three prose passages by Mary Moody Emerson in notebook MME 2:

"Hail, requiem of departed Time! Never was incumbent's funeral followed by expectant heir with more satisfaction. Yet not his hope is mine. In thy weary womb are prolific numbers of the same sad hour,—colored by the memory of defeats in virtue, by the prophecy of others more dreary, blind & sickly. Yet He who formed thy web, who stretched thy warp, from long ages, has graciously given man to throw his little shuttle, or feel he does, & irrigate the filling woof with many a flowery rainbow—labours—rather evanescent efforts, which will wear like flowerets in riper soils,—hast attuned his mind in such unison with the harp of the universe that he is never without some chord of hope's music" (pp. 151–52).

"In all thy limbo lumber, old Time, take this on to that ending. O, thou diggest the grave of every coming day,—not mine. But wilt.—I defy thee to do otherwise" (p. 155).

"O time, thou loiterer, and I too loiter, &, epicurean-like, enjoy without health to make the effort to renounce a meter (?) or even send for my little Madge. But thou, whose might has laid low the vastest & crushed the worm, restest on thy hoary throne with like potency over thy agitations & thy graves. O when will thy routines give way to higher & lasting institutions?—when thy trophies, and thy name, & all its wizard forms, be lost by the genius of Eternity? Often more tremendous in her hereditary power,—but often more glorious, no deceitful promises, no fantastic illusions, no riddles concealed by thy shrouds, none of thy Arachnean webs which decoy & destroy. Hasten to finish thy motley work, on which frightful gorgons are at play, spite of holy ghosts—tis already motheaten, & its shuttles quaver as the beams of the loom are shaken" (pp. 142–44).

The poem has not been found elsewhere in Emerson's published or unpublished writings.

## "To the mizen, the main, & the fore"

*Texts:* The first draft is in erased pencil in notebook ML pp. 128–29; a revised and expanded draft in ink occurs in EL p. 160.

*Date:* The draft in ML was presumably written shortly after the assassination of "our chief," Abraham Lincoln, on 15 April 1865.

*Publication:* Unpublished.


## "To the Shah. From Enweri" ("From thy worth")


*Texts:* The first draft in notebook Orientalist p. 16 is revised on p. 87 and followed on the same page by a fair copy. Other copies are in Rhymer p. 137 and Poems folder 36. The two lines are a loose translation from "An den Dichter Schedschaai" by Enweri in *Geschichte,* p. 91.

*Date:* Probably written in 1850: see the following entry.

*Publication:* "Persian Poetry," 1858, p. 728, but not in the essay as reprinted. Collected in *May–Day,* 1867, p. 203, and reprinted in *Poems,* 1884, p. 249, and W 9:303.


## "To the Shah. From Enweri" ("Not in their houses")


*Texts:* The first draft in notebook Orientalist p. 31 is revised on p. 87 and followed by a fair copy on the same page. Later texts are in Rhymer p. 137 and Poems folder 36. The two lines are a translation of line 5 of "Kasside, zum Lobe Amadeddin Firusschahs" by Enweri, from *Geschichte,* p. 94.

*Date:* Journal AZ (JMN 11:251) contains a reference to Emerson's translation of a poem by Enweri (*Geschichte,* pp. 92–93) done in Orientalist pp. 33–35. Appearances strongly suggest that both translations were done at the same time, in 1850.

*Publication:* "Persian Poetry," 1858, p. 728, but not in the essay as reprinted. Collected in *May–Day,* 1867, p. 202; reprinted in Channing, *Thoreau,* p. 135, in *Poems,* 1884, p. 249, and in W 9:303.

*See Also:* JMN 14:196.


## "To the Shah. From Hafiz"


*Texts:* The first draft, in EF pp. 104–5, is a 28-line translation from Hafiz, Book VIII, Ode CLXVII (*Diwan* 1:452, 453, 449). The first two lines of this draft (corresponding to lines 53–54 of the ode) were copied and revised in notebook Orientalist p. 58. Fair copies then occur in Orientalist p. 87, Rhymer p. 137, and Poems folder 36; in line 1 of the last, "hunt" is written over "strike" and "enemies" occurs in place of "enviers", the term in the other manuscripts and the printed texts.

*Date:* Between 1850 and 1858. Of the three brief poems "To the Shah," this was evidently the last to be translated, since it was inscribed after the other two in Orientalist p. 87.

*Publication:* "Persian Poetry," 1858, p. 728, and in the essay as collected in *Letters and Social Aims,* 1876, p. 226, and W 8:251. The lines were published again in *May–Day,* 1867, p. 202, and reprinted in *Poems,* 1884, p. 249, and W 9:303.

## "To transmute crime to wisdom, & to stem"

*Texts:* The first text of this couplet, in erased pencil in journal O, is followed immediately by a copy in ink (JMN 9:384). An identical fair copy occurs in EL p. 21, and a variant fair copy is in notebook Orientalist p. 1.

*Date:* The texts in journal O probably date from May or June 1846.

*Publication:* Unpublished by Emerson. First published in the EL form in *Poems,* 1884, p. 275, with "&" changed to "so" in line 1, and reprinted in W 9:332. The Orientalist form was published as the motto to "Persian Poetry" in W 8:235.

## "To whom a glass full of red wine"

*Text:* The poem, which translates Hafiz, Book VIII, Ode CLI, lines 1–8 (*Diwan* 1:426–27), occurs in EF p. 94. It has not been found elsewhere in Emerson's published or unpublished writings.

## "Too late the anxious fire came"

*Text:* The only text of this gift poem occurs in pencil in NP p. 294.

*Date:* A note by Edward Emerson identifies the poem as "New Year's Poem to E[dward] W[aldo] E[merson] with Wm Hunt's *Bugler*"—i.e., a lithograph of William Morris Hunt's painting *The Bugle Call,* 1861.

*Publication:* Unpublished.

## "The treacherous wind pipes a lewd song"

*Texts:* Nearly identical texts occur in X p. 166 (pencil) and notebook Orientalist p. 15 (ink). The Orientalist text was revised in ink, then copied in pencil on p. 14 and revised further. This was in turn copied in Orientalist p. 78, where the stanzas were reversed. The final copy in Rhymer p. 139 seems to combine elements from several preceding drafts. The source of the poem is Hafiz, Book XXIII, Ode XXVIII, lines 13–16 (*Diwan* 2:198).

*Date:* Undetermined.

*Publication:* Unpublished.

## "Try the might the Muse affords"

*Texts:* The only complete text of this quatrain is in NP p. 296, with the heading "Poet." The first two lines occur in P p. 287, X p. 153, Rhymer p. 50f, NP on an insert inside the front cover, EL pp. 1, 71 (twice, the reversed first version struck through in pencil), and 148, and in journal FOR (JMN 15:344). The second two lines occur in Rhymer p. 50f, NP p. 198, and EL pp. 119 and 147; in these versions "beauty" appears for the "music" of the quatrain.

*Date:* Undetermined. The FOR version dates from 1863.

*Publication:* Unpublished by Emerson. First published in *Poems*, 1884, p. 271, and reprinted in W 9:329.

## "Turn not truth from thy door. God my protector is near"

*Text:* This single line, translating Hafiz, Book I, Ode XIII, line 6 (*Diwan* 1:23), occurs in EF p. 109. It has not been found elsewhere in Emerson's published or unpublished writings.

## "Two arts he had to live & grow"

*Text:* The only text of this five-line fragment occurs in pencil in NP p. 237, with lines 2–3 revised in ink. It has not been found elsewhere in Emerson's published or unpublished writings.

## "Two Rivers"

*Texts:* The first draft of the poem (lines 1–16 only) begins in journal SO p. 87 and is continued on p. 90 (JMN 14:65–67); an additional revision of lines 1–8 occurs on p. 194 (JMN 14:94). In journal VO p. 78 is a further revision in ink of lines 1–16, with a preceding pencil draft of lines 13–16 and two versions of lines 17–20 on p. 79 (JMN 14:140–41). A fair copy of the whole poem is in Rhymer p. 77, and a titled copy anterior to it is in the Houghton Library. The latter is identical in wording to the Rhymer text except that "silent" is canceled for "pulsing" in line 3, "stream" is canceled for "flood," in line 7, "I hear" is inserted and "eternal" is canceled before "spending" in line 10, "like" is canceled for "a" in line 13, "the" is inserted in line 16, "So &" is canceled for "So forth &" in line 17, and "Fed by the falling stars" is canceled for "And ages drop in it" in line 20. A manuscript copy of the third stanza, signed and dated "Concord, Massachusetts—December 10, 1878" is in the Concord Public Library; it appeared in facsimile in *ESQ* 32 (3d quarter 1963): pt. 3, p. 1.

*Date:* Lines 5–8 seem to have their ultimate source in an 1840 journal entry: "We see the river glide below us but we see not the river that glides over us & envelopes us in its floods" (JMN 7:499; cf. "Far seen the river glides below"). The first drafts, in journal SO, date from 1856. The first full draft, in journal VO, was composed between May and October 1857; it is partially overwritten by a paragraph on the financial panic of October of that year. The Rhymer fair copy was obviously inscribed before the VO draft was overwritten.

*Publication: The Atlantic Monthly* 1 (January 1858): 311; collected in *May–Day,* 1867, pp. 134–35; reprinted in *Selected Poems,* 1876, p. 156 (with an altered twelfth line), *Poems,* 1884, p. 213, and W 9:248.

## "Una"

*Texts:* Three successive erased pencil drafts, the second and third titled, occur in journal Z[A] pp. 78 and 76, 74 and 72, and 58–57 (JMN 8:343–48, including notes 105 and 108). A pencil fair copy is in P pp. 295–96, and ink fair copies are in X pp. 129–30 and Rhymer p. 73.

*Date:* The drafts in Z[A] were written between November 1842 and March 1843, the period of use of this journal, or, more probably, given the travel imagery of the poem, from early January to early March of the latter year, when Emerson was on a lecture tour.

*Publication:* First published in *May–Day,* 1867, pp. 92–93; omitted from *Poems,* 1884, the poem was reprinted in W 9:210–11.

## "Unbar the door, since thou the Opener art"

*Texts:* This quatrain translates lines 3–4 of a selection from Omar Khayyam in *Geschichte*, p. 81. Much of this selection is translated in the first draft in notebook Orientalist pp. 29–30; the beginning (including the quatrain) is revised on p. 64. In Orientalist p. 77 the quatrain occurs separately, added to the end of verses beginning "In Senahar I lost my son" (see *Geschichte*, p. 218). A fair copy of "Unbar the door" occurs in Rhymer p. 125; another, with the same wording and dated "Concord. 15 April, 1852" is in the Morgan Library.

*Date:* Before 15 April 1852.

*Publication:* Although the Rhymer text is marked "printed," no publication has been noted before W 9:301.

*See Also:* "Each spot where tulips" ("Persian Poetry," 1858, p. 731), and "On earth's wide thoroughfares," which, with the present poem, all derive from the same first draft.

## "The understanding's copper coin"

*Texts:* The two lines translate Hafiz, Book IX, Ode I, lines 17–18 (*Diwan* 2:3). The first draft in EF p. 50 is followed by the revision in notebook TO p. 193 and the ink fair copy in notebook Orientalist p. 7. To this copy Emerson added in pencil two more lines (evidently not a translation) to make a quatrain, then wrote and revised an additional two lines in separate ink and pencil drafts as an alternate conclusion. A version of the second ending appears in the fair copy in Rhymer p. 50$_b$.

*Date:* The first draft was written between 1846 and 1851, the apparent date of the lines for "The Chartist's Complaint" on EF p. 50.

*Publication:* Published in the two-line form in "Persian Poetry," 1858, p. 727, and in the essay as collected in *Letters and Social Aims*, 1876, p. 221, and W 8:245. Neither of the two sets of concluding lines was published.

## "Unity"

*Texts:* The earliest surviving draft is in ink in X p. 268$_o$, revised in the erased pencil draft in EF p. 64. An ink fair copy occurs with the heading "Oversoul" in X pp. 216–17. The inscription at X p. 268$_o$ shows that at some point Emerson thought of adding a passage on X p. 268$_n$ ("He has driven out"), and possibly of continuing with the lines on pp. 268$_p$–268$_q$. These two passages are in fact joined together and revised in X p. 192, though it is possible that they are no longer, at this point, to be associated with "Unity."

*Date:* The poem's origin in the large X insert suggests composition in the latter half of 1846 or the first half of 1847, which is also the most probable date of the fair copy in X pp. 216–17. (Note that the lines from "Give All to Love" on p. 216 were erased after the revision on p. 218; this must have occurred after July 1846 because the lines are there inscribed over a draft of "Mithridates," written in that month.)

*Publication:* First published as the untitled motto for "The Over-Soul" in the 1847 edition of *Essays: First Series,* p. 241, and reprinted with that essay in subsequent editions including W 2:265. Collected, with the title "Unity," in *May–Day,* 1867, p. 175, and reprinted in *Poems,* 1884, p. 236, and W 9:279.

*See Also:* "Love and Thought."

## "Untruth is become the mode"

*Text:* This poem, which translates Hafiz, Book XXVII, Ode LIV (*Diwan* 2:438), occurs in EF p. 9. It has not been found elsewhere in Emerson's published or unpublished writings.

## "Uriel"

*Texts:* Two complete manuscript texts exist, one in the Tappan Papers, Houghton, and another, printer's copy for the London edition of *Poems,* 1847, in the Huntington Library. The Tappan manuscript, probably sent to Caroline Sturgis (later married to William A. Tappan), has a headnote and several variant readings (see Additional Manuscripts). The printer's copy has "bounds" for the printed misreading "bonds" in line 32 and "godlike" canceled for "cherub" in line 54. Lines 1–4 occur in pencil in journal Books Small (JMN 8:463), and, again in pencil, in P p. 299. An early version of lines 27 and 39–56 occurs in erased pencil in journal V (JMN 9:170–71).

*Date:* The version of lines 1–4 in Books Small must have been inscribed in 1840–1843, and lines 27 and 39–56 in V between May 1844 and March 1845, the periods of use, respectively, of those journals. With line 21, "Line in nature is not found," and the Tappan headnote cf. journal Z[A], February 1843: "There is no line that does not return; I suppose the mathematicians will tell us that . . . straight lines are lines with long curves, but that there is no straight line in nature" (JMN 8:339); journal R, May 1843: "Extremes meet: there is no straight line" (JMN 8:397); and numerous other places.

*Publication: Poems,* 1847, pp. 27–29 (Boston) and pp. 18–20 (London); reprinted in *Selected Poems,* 1876, pp. 19–20, *Poems,* 1884, pp. 21–23, and W 9:13–15.

*See Also:* Strauch diss., pp. 377–80 (text).

## "Vain against him were hostile blows"

*Text:* The only text of this six-line fragment is in pencil in X p. 57, written over an erased draft of "The House."

*Date:* "The House" was published in *Poems,* 1847. "Vain against him" was written some time before the draft of "Fine presentiments" that follows in pencil on the same page. The fact that the latter poem exists in a later ink version in P, a notebook rarely used after 1845, would suggest a date of composition in the early to mid 1840s.

*Publication:* Unpublished by Emerson. The fragment, with an altered first line, was inserted into "Guy" after line 16 in *Poems,* 1884, p. 34, on what authority is not known. This form of the poem was reprinted in W 9:33–34. Edward Emerson (W 9:415) interpreted the evidence of X p. 57 as implying that "Fine presentiments" had been "destined" for use in "Guy" because he erroneously believed that "Vain against him" was in actuality a draft fragment of the original form of "Guy."

*See Also:* "Fine presentiments."

## "Van Buren"

*Texts:* This couplet, which occurs in an ink fair copy in P p. 33, was taken from Emerson's Phi Beta Kappa poem of 1834, where it figures as lines 269–70. The manuscript of the whole poem is in the Houghton Library.

*Date:* The full poem was delivered on 28 August 1834 and was apparently written in that month (see JMN 4:314–15). At this time Martin Van Buren was vice president under Andrew Jackson; he served as president from 1837 to 1841.

*Publication:* Unpublished by Emerson. First published as part of the original Phi Beta Kappa poem in Carl F. Strauch, "Emerson's Phi Beta Kappa Poem," *NEQ* 23 (March 1950): 65–90.

*See Also:* "Webster" ("Ill fits the abstemious Muse").

## "Verses that a man may read"

*Text:* This three-line fragment occurs in pencil in X p. 50. It has not been found elsewhere in Emerson's published or unpublished writings.

## "The Visit"

*Texts:* The earliest draft of the poem occurs in ink in journal U (JMN 9:12). The first few verses are in run-on form, but lines are indicated by capitalization. A revised version occurs in erased pencil on the facing manuscript page (JMN 9:12, n. 21). A later version, with title, occurs in partially erased pencil further on in U; it lacks lines 25–26, which are provided in erased pencil on the facing manuscript page (JMN 9:73–75). This is the source of the ink fair copy, titled and lacking line 17, that occurs in P pp. 141–42. Printer's copy for the London edition of *Poems*, 1847, is in the Huntington Library.

*Date:* The first two drafts in U, between entries of 25 August and 3 September 1843, were probably inspired by Caroline Sturgis's week-long visit that began on 28 August (L 3:203). The third draft appears to have been written in February 1844. A passage in a letter to Margaret Fuller of 12 October 1838 may have influenced lines 29–30: "We are armed all over with these subtle antagonisms which as soon as we meet begin to play . . ." (L 2:168). Needing this sentence to "fill up a bad hole" in his essay on "Friendship" (W 2:199), Emerson asked Fuller in June and July 1840 for the return of the letter (L 2:306 and 314).

*Publication: The Dial* 4 (April 1844): 528. Collected in *Poems*, 1847, pp. 25–26 (Boston) and pp. 16–17 (London). Reprinted in *Selected Poems*, 1876, pp. 17–18, *Poems*, 1884, pp. 20–21, and W 9:12–13.

*See Also:* Carl F. Strauch, "Hatred's Swift Repulsions: Emerson, Margaret Fuller, and Others," *SRom* 7 (Winter 1968): 93–94.

## "Voluntaries"

*Texts:* The poem was composed in two discontinuous partial drafts in EL, the earlier on pp. 104–12 and the later on pp. 120–31. Neither draft includes lines 14, 37, 44, 49, 55–74, or 104–8, but the later draft includes six lines not printed in the first published appearance and restored after line 119 in 1867; these lines also occur in Rhymer p. 103, along with lines 120–21. The prose germ for lines 39–42 occurs in journals WAR and VA (JMN 15:178, 246, and 250), while a trial versification of these lines appears in NP p. 292.

Four lines that were added after line 92 in 1876 first occur in EL p. 51 (two drafts) and also in ETE pp. 56ₐ and 171, Poems folders 31 (two drafts; see Additional Manuscripts under "Boston") and 62, and notebook QL on an enclosure between pp. 122–23; all these versions except ETE p. 56ₐ have "front" for "van" (the published reading) in the fourth line.

Printer's copy for first publication in *The Atlantic Monthly* was donated by James T. Fields to the Mississippi Valley Sanitation Fair, held 7–8 October 1864; it is now in the Rutherford B. Hayes Library, Fremont, Ohio, together with a letter to Fields commenting on proof corrections. It differs from the published text as follows: line 14 is missing (although a space is left for it); "wing" occurs for "van" in line 37; "Long she clung" is canceled for "Clinging" in line 39; "Unknown to" is canceled for "Hid from" in line 52; "give" occurs for "drain" in line 58; "To put aside" occurs for "Break sharply off" in line 63; "To leave" occurs for "Forsake" in line 64; "To" occurs for "And" in line 65; "& fine" occurs for "benign" in line 67; "of" is canceled for "in" in line 70; "Fixed" and "guiding" are canceled for "Stayed" and "subtile" in line 80; "as of yore" is canceled for "evermore" in line 96; "But his mistaking" is canceled for "Forever: but his erring" in line 102; the line "Though he fancies he prevails," is canceled before line 103; "crueller" occurs for "speechless" in line 110; two lines, "Sleeps within the dragon coil / Reserved to a crueller fate", are canceled after line 110; and "&" is canceled for "or" in line 119.

Emerson also prepared a copy of the poem for Francis George Shaw, the father of Robert Gould Shaw; this manuscript, which has not been traced, was sent on 10 September 1863 (see L 5:336).

*Date:* While the germ of lines 39–42 dates from 1862, the poem was composed within about a month of the death of Robert Gould Shaw on 18 July 1863. Emerson received proofs for the *Atlantic* printing on 4 September and returned them on the 7th, intending to send "a pair of closing lines" later (letter to Fields mentioned above).

*Publication:* First published in *The Atlantic Monthly* 12 (October 1863): 504–6, and again, from the manuscript sent to Francis George Shaw, in *Memorial R[obert] G[ould] S[haw]* (Cambridge, Mass., 1864), pp. 161–64; in *May–Day,* 1867, pp. 81–88, where six lines from EL p. 125 are added after line 119; and in *Selected Poems,* 1876, pp. 209–14, where an additional four lines are added after line 92. This enhanced version (but with lines 106–14 in the 1876 lineation omitted) appears in *Poems,* 1884, pp. 178–82, and W 9:205–9. Parts 2 and 3 of the poem in the *Atlantic Monthly* form were printed separately as broadsides by the New England Loyal Publication Society of Boston, no. 126 (10 October 1863) and no. 134 (31 October 1863). Part of the poem was also reprinted in *Cloud Crystals; A Snow-Flake Album. Collected and Edited by a Lady* (New York, 1864), p. 156.

## "Waldeinsamkeit"

*Texts:* The main draft of this poem is in pencil in journal VO pp. 226–41 (JMN 14:180–87). Incomplete, out of sequence, and interspersed with passages from other poems, it nevertheless contains all but lines 29–32 and 49–50. Earlier draft fragments are lines 19–20 in journal V (JMN 9:169) and lines 1–2 and 41–44, each preceded by their prose sources, in VO pp. 93 and 153 (JMN 14:145–46 and 161). The prose source of lines 33–36 is in VO p. 158 (JMN 14:162). Other texts of lines occur as follows: lines 1–2, 5–8, 19–20, and 45–48 in EF pp. 38, 107, 32, and 38 respectively, and lines 37–40 in NP p. 115. The source of line 26 is Hafiz, Book XXIII, Ode XXVIII, line 17 (*Diwan* 2:198), a translation of which occurs in "Persian Poetry," 1858, p. 726; cf. notebook Orientalist, pp. 60 and 61. No fair copy of the poem has been located, although Emerson wrote the poem in the visitors' album at the Naushon Island estate of his father-in-law, John Murray Forbes, in September 1858 (L 5:118–19).

*Date:* The main draft in VO probably dates from the late summer of 1857. This is corroborated by a comment Emerson made in a letter to Mrs. Forbes of 18 September 1858: "I am not sure that the first sketch of [the verses] did not originate at Naushon, a year ago" (L 5:118). The first appearance of lines 19–20 in journal V, however, dates from 1844 or 1845.

*Publication:* First published, without Emerson's knowledge (as he says in his letter to Mrs. Forbes), in *The Atlantic Monthly* 2 (October 1858): 550–51. Reprinted in *May–Day*, 1867, pp. 136–39, and, with the omission of lines 45–48, in *Selected Poems*, 1876, pp. 157–58, *Poems*, 1884, pp. 214–15, and W 9:249–51.

## "Water"

*Texts:* Three copies of this poem exist: one in journal H (JMN 8:111–12) and two, titled, in EL p. 20 and ETE p. 20. Line 10 was subsequently used as line 50 of "Merlin II."

*Date:* The text in journal H occurs between entries of 16 and 24 October 1841.

*Publication:* Unpublished by Emerson. First published from the ETE text in *Poems*, 1884, p. 284, and reprinted in W 9:344.

## "The way of love is unlimited"

*Text:* This poem, which translates Hafiz, Book III, Ode LV, lines 1–18 (*Diwan* 1:129–30), occurs in pencil in EF p. 49. It has not been found elsewhere in Emerson's published or unpublished writings.

## "We sauntered amidst miracles"

*Text:* These lines, which occur in pencil in P p. 192, are probably related to "Dirge," drafts of which occupy the preceding pages. While generally in the same meter, they do not, however, have the same rhyme scheme.

*Date:* Undetermined.

*Publication:* Unpublished by Emerson. The lines were first published in Edward Emerson's notes to the concocted poem "Peter's Field" as "another account of the [Emerson] brothers' joys" (W 9:512).

## "We wish like the glass"

*Texts:* The full poem, which translates Hafiz, Book VIII, Ode LXXXII, lines 27–32 (*Diwan* 1:326), occurs in EF p. 45. Lines 5–6 of the translation are quoted in an entry in journal TU (JMN 11:106–7) and again in a prose version in journal NO (JMN 13:414).

*Date:* The full translation evidently precedes the quotation in TU in 1849. The NO version dates from 1855.

*Publication:* Unpublished except for the prose version of lines 5–6 in "Poetry and Imagination," *Letters and Social Aims,* 1876, p. 16, reprinted in W 8:18.

## "We would do nought but good"

*Text:* The only manuscript text of this quatrain, a translation of an unlocated passage from Hafiz, is an ink fair copy in Rhymer p. 146.

*Date:* Undetermined.

*Publication:* A prose version was published in "Persian Poetry," 1858, pp. 727–28, and in the essay as collected in *Letters and Social Aims,* 1876, pp. 223–24, and W 8:249.

## "Wealth"

*Texts:* The first draft of this motto, in pencil in NP pp. 250–51 and 253, includes lines 13, 15–16, 18–24, 26, 28–33, and 46–49; this was revised and expanded in ink to include lines 13, 15–33, and 46–49 in NP pp. 273–75.

Lines 30–33 were further revised in journal CL (JMN 14:325). What may be an early form of line 4 appears in NP p. 252; it is an exact quotation from Mary Moody Emerson as transcribed in notebook MME 2 p. 5. Printer's copy for *The Conduct of Life* is in the Princeton University Library; in it, line 34 reads "Then rose fair temples, towns, & marts," "might" is canceled for "slaves" in line 40, and "wires" occurs for "wire" in line 41.

*Date:* Undetermined. The revision in CL dates from 1859.

*Publication:* First published in *The Conduct of Life*, 1860, pp. 71–72, and subsequent editions including W 6:83–84; reprinted in W 9:285–86.

## "Webster" ("Ill fits the abstemious Muse")

*Text:* These lines, which occur in an ink fair copy in P p. 34, were copied from Emerson's Phi Beta Kappa poem of 1834, where they figure as lines 241–62. The manuscript of the whole poem is in the Houghton Library.

*Date:* The full poem was delivered on 28 August 1834 and was apparently written in that month (see JMN 4:314–15). Daniel Webster was U.S. Senator from Massachusetts from 1827 to 1841.

*Publication:* Unpublished by Emerson. First published separately in *Poems*, 1884, p. 312, and reprinted in W 9:398–99. Published as part of the original Phi Beta Kappa poem in Carl F. Strauch, "Emerson's Phi Beta Kappa Poem," *NEQ* 23 (March 1950): 65–90.

*See Also:* "Van Buren."

## "Webster" ("Why did all manly gifts")

*Texts:* The first drafts are in journal GO (JMN 13:76). Fair copies are in X p. 119 (untitled) and Rhymer p. 47, with the title "Webster."

*Date:* The GO drafts appear to have been written between 22 July 1852, when Emerson heard Webster praised by Robert C. Winthrop, and 1 August, the date of a subsequent entry. Edward Emerson assigned the couplet a date of 1854 and added that it "was written sadly after Webster's death" (W 9:518). Webster died on 24 October 1852.

*Publication:* Unpublished by Emerson. First published in W 9:399.

# "What all the books of ages paint, I have"

*Texts:* This poem occurs first in X p. 14, written over an erased passage from "Monadnock," and then, slightly revised and with the first three lines canceled, in EL p. 39.

*Date:* Not before 1845, the date of the "Monadnock" passage.

*Publication:* Unpublished by Emerson. First published in *Poems,* 1884, p. 280, and reprinted in W 9:339.

# "What are all the flowers"

*Texts:* These nine lines occur in pencil in journal Books Small in the midst of other verses (JMN 8:459–60) and, revised, in pencil in P p. 200.

*Date:* Journal Books Small was used between 1840 and 1843.

*Publication:* Unpublished by Emerson. First published in JMN 8.

# "What flowing central forces, say"

*Texts:* The prose source and the first draft occur together in journal FOR (JMN 15:316). The couplet was copied into EL p. 32 and revised slightly in Rhymer p. 50ₐ.

*Date:* The first draft dates to March or April 1863.

*Publication:* Unpublished by Emerson. First published in *Poems,* 1884, p. 281, in the FOR and EL form; reprinted in W 9:340 and used as the motto for "Perpetual Forces" (W 10:67).

# "What he thought not what he did"

*Text:* This couplet occurs in pencil in EL p. 295. It has not been found elsewhere in Emerson's published or unpublished writings.

# "What lovelier forms things wear"

*Texts:* These two lines, which translate Hafiz, Book XXIII, Ode X, lines 13–14 (*Diwan* 2:164), occur in EF p. 77 in partially erased pencil; they are revised in notebook Orientalist p. 58.

*Date:* The EF draft is overwritten by the third draft of "A. H.," which dates from 1855.

*Publication:* Published in "Persian Poetry," 1858, p. 728, and in the essay as collected in *Letters and Social Aims,* 1876, p. 226, and W 8:251.

## "What made in land & sea impearled"

*Text:* This quatrain occurs only in EF p. 10, preceded by an early partial draft of "Heri, Cras, Hodie" and lines 31–32 of "Song of Nature."

*Date:* Probably 1855, the apparent date of the lines used in "Heri, Cras, Hodie."

*Publication:* Unpublished.

## "What never was not, & still will be"

*Texts:* The first draft of the poem occurs in X p. 108, followed at the bottom of facing p. 109 by a version of lines 11–12. A second draft occurs on pp. 110–11, followed on p. 111 by a separate draft of lines 3–10. On p. 112 is a trial conclusion for the poem including three unused lines. A third and last draft occurs on p. 113.

*Date:* Undetermined.

*Publication:* Unpublished.

## "When all their blooms the meadows flaunt"

*Texts:* The first version of this quatrain, in pencil in EL p. 133, is part of a draft of "May–Day"; it is revised on the same page and copied in EL p. 225, where it is followed by the first draft of the quatrain "Teach me your mood" and lines used in "In my garden three ways meet." A later form of "Teach me your mood" is added in EL p. 133, and both quatrains copied on a sheet inserted between pp. 122–23 of notebook QL. A revision in line 3 in EL p. 225 may be later, and occurs only in that text.

   The quatrain also occurs in Poems folder 55 following lines perhaps intended for "May Day [Invitation]" and is added in Poems folder 92 above the quatrain "Softens the air" and lines 21–28 of "Who saw the hid beginnings" (see Additional Manuscripts for the folder 92 text). These sixteen lines, copied in ETE p. 35 under the title "May" and in ETE p. 147 under the title "May–Day," may have been intended to accompany "May Day [Invitation]," a text of which follows on pp. 148–51 under the same title.

*Date:* The association of the draft in EL p. 225 with "In my garden three ways meet" points to a date of 1859 or later. The four texts associated with "May Day [Invitation]" were probably written between 10 April 1865, the date of the first draft of that poem in journal KL, and 1867, when the title was appropriated for the title poem of *May–Day.*

*Publication:* Unpublished by Emerson. First published, combined with "Teach me your mood," in W 9:340.

## "When devils bite"

*Text:* This three-line fragment is in pencil in X p. 88. It has not been found elsewhere in Emerson's published or unpublished writings.

## "When Guru came to Sattayog"

*Text:* This sixteen-line fragment in EL p. 227 is a versification of a prose passage from *The Dabistan, or School of Manners,* trans. David Shea and Anthony Troyer, 3 vols. (Paris, 1843), 2:268–69; the passage surrounds the verse in EL pp. 226 and 228–29.

*Date:* Emerson cited volume 2 of *The Dabistan* in notebook ML p. 82 after January 1865 and in journal NY (JMN 16:152) in 1869.

*Publication:* Unpublished.

## "When in eternity the light"

*Texts:* These lines, a translation of Hafiz, Book VIII, Ode LXXII, lines 1–9 (*Diwan* 1:310–11), occur in EF p. 45. The entire ode of twenty-one lines appears in what is apparently an independent translation in notebook OS pp. 82–83. No other texts of either version have been found elsewhere in Emerson's published or unpublished writings.

## "When Jane was absent Edgar's eye"

*Text:* These six lines occur in pencil in P p. 172. They have not been found elsewhere in Emerson's published or unpublished writings.

## "When summer winds are dashed with East"

*Text:* The only text of this four-line fragment occurs in pencil in NP p. 10. It has not been found elsewhere in Emerson's published or unpublished writings.

## "When thou sittest moping"

*Texts:* These lines first occur in pencil in journal E (JMN 7:480), where they belong to an early draft of "Saadi." Emerson copied them, revised, into P p. 293.

*Date:* Between October 1839, when E was begun, and October 1842, when "Saadi" was published in *The Dial.*

*Publication:* Unpublished by Emerson. First published in JMN 7.

## "When thought is best then is there most"

*Text:* This single line, which is arguably not verse, occurs in pencil in P p. 22. Emerson used it in a letter to Carlyle of 31 July 1846 (*The Correspondence of Emerson and Carlyle,* ed. Joseph Slater, New York and London: 1964, p. 407). Otherwise it has not been found in Emerson's published or unpublished writings.

## "When trees in June the colors show"

*Text:* This quatrain (preceded by a draft of line 1) occurs in pencil in EF p. 98. It has not been found elsewhere in Emerson's published or unpublished writings.

## "When wrath & terror changed Jove's regal port"

*Texts:* The first draft of this couplet, in erased pencil with two versions of line 2, and the second draft, in ink, occur in journal NO (JMN 13:413); fair copies are in EL p. 192 and NP p. 3.

*Date:* Journal NO was used between February and August 1855.

*Publication:* Unpublished by Emerson. First published in *Poems,* 1884, p. 298, and reprinted in W 9:358.

## "Where his name is named"

*Texts:* This ten-line fragment occurs in pencil in EL p. 116; line 4 is repeated in EL p. 288 following the second draft of "You strong Republicans." The fragment has not been found elsewhere in Emerson's published or unpublished writings.

## "Where is Skrymir? Giant Skrymir?"

*Texts:* The earliest draft of these lines occurs in pencil in journal CD (JMN 10:82). This is the source of the ink version at the end of CD (JMN 10:122), which in turn is the source of the ink version in P pp. 105–6.

*Date:* The initial pencil draft in CD occurs among entries of June 1847 and reflects Emerson's horticultural interests as expressed several times in that journal; cf. especially an entry about Captain Abel Moore, Emerson's neighbor, who "danced a thousand tons of gravel from yonder blowing sandheap on to the bog meadow beneath us where now the English grass is waving over countless acres" (JMN 10:101). Skrymir is a giant in Norse mythology whom Emerson read about in *The Prose or Younger Edda Commonly Ascribed to Snorri Sturluson,* trans. George Webbe Dasent (London, 1842); numerous references to this work occur in CD, including one of 18 July mentioning Skrymir (JMN 10:116). All three manuscript occurrences of this poem follow "To every creature," which is likewise concerned with horticulture.

*Publication:* First published in Channing, *Thoreau,* p. 147, in a text slightly different from any of the surviving manuscripts.

## "Where o where is the message which today"

*Text:* This four-line fragment, a translation of Hafiz, Book XXIII, Ode X, lines 5–8 (*Diwan* 2:163), occurs in EF p. 114 in a series of entries headed "Hafiz of his verse." It has not been found elsewhere in Emerson's published or unpublished writings.

## "Where the fungus broad & red"

*Texts:* The lines grouped under this heading appear to be an attempt at a poem on nature that Emerson never completed. In what follows, the text used for purposes of line numbering is that in P pp. 168–70, where the disparate elements are brought together. All versions are in pencil unless otherwise noted.

Three stages of the poem may be discerned. The first consists of scattered drafts of groups of lines, as follows: (1) lines 10–24 occur in journal E (JMN 7:478–79), followed by 48 other lines in like vein, many of which Emerson eventually used in "Saadi"; (2) an early version of what appear to be lines 1–9 and 25–35 occurs, erased, in journal Books Small (JMN 8:444–45); (3) also in Books Small are lines 58–65, and three additional lines (JMN 8:470, cf. 8:451 for lines 60–61); (4) P p. 41 contains lines 10–24, drawn from journal E, followed by eight further lines, six of which appear in the additional segment in E (JMN 7:479–80); (5) P p. 151 contains lines 36–43; (6) P p. 193 contains lines 45–46; and (7) P p. 194 contains lines 48–58, followed by the note "[P] p. 249."

The second stage of the poem is a preliminary arrangement in P pp. 248–49, which consists of, in order: (1) lines 36–47 from P pp. 151 and 193; (2) lines 1–9 and 25–31 from Books Small, with the notation "[P] p 41" to indicate the insertion of lines 10–24 from that page; and (3) lines 58–65 from Books Small, preceded by the notation "[P] p 194" to show the intended insertion of lines 48–57 from that page, possibly written to bridge an awkward gap. The verses are preceded on p. 248 by "These trees like tho'ts," which, despite different meter, may have been intended as an introduction.

The third stage is the version in P pp. 168–70, which consists of all of the lines in P pp. 248–49 (with intended insertions) in final order, and with the restoration of lines 32–35 from Books Small (JMN 8:445).

In his index to P Emerson listed p. 168 under the general term "Woods." Additionally, lines 12–16 and 19–24 occur, in ink, in the unpublished poem "May–Day" (called "May Day [Invitation]" in this edition) in three locations: EL pp. 205–6, Poems folder 55 (see Additional Manuscripts under "May Day [Invitation]," second and third texts), and ETE pp. 149–50. The absence of lines 17–18 implies that these appearances are later than that in P p. 168, where the lines occur but are canceled.

*Date:* Lines 10–24 appear out of chronological sequence in journal E, and could have been written at any time between the start of that journal (October 1839) and the appearance of "Saadi" (with which the lines are associated) in *The Dial* for October 1842. Lines 1–9 and 25–35 appear in Books Small overwritten by entries that date from the spring and summer of 1843. Lines 58–65 in Books Small must have been written after mid-April 1842, when Emerson first learned of the plant "rattlesnake's master" (cited in a rejected line) from Chester Dewey's *Report on the Herbaceous Flowering Plants of Massachusetts* . . . (Cambridge, 1840) (JMN 8:232). This meager information allows us to date the various segments of the poem from (possibly) 1839 to 1842 and later.

*Publication:* Lines 54–57 were inserted into "The Humble-Bee" after the forty-third line of the *Poems,* 1847, text, though no other part of the poem was published during Emerson's lifetime. In W 9:337–38, "Fragment on Nature, III" corresponds to lines 1–7, 10–16, 19–24, 8, 9/25, and 26–41 of the final P text of "Where the fungus broad & red"; in W 9:335–36, "Fragment on Nature, II," lines 1–18 correspond to lines 48–65 of the final P text.

*See Also:* "May–Day [Invitation]."

## "Who compares a poem"

*Text:* This poem, which translates Hafiz, Book III, Ode XXX, lines 21–24 (*Diwan* 1:91), occurs in EF p. 114 in a series of entries headed "Hafiz of his verse." It has not been found elsewhere in Emerson's published or unpublished writings.

## "Who dedicates himself to the glass"

*Text:* These four lines, which translate Hafiz, Book VIII, Ode CXX, lines 9–12 (*Diwan* 1:384), occur in EF p. 82. They have not been found elsewhere in Emerson's published or unpublished writings.

## "Who knows this or that"

*Text:* The only manuscript text is in pencil in P p. 227.

*Date:* The similarity of the first five lines to a passage in "History" (W 2:39–40), first pointed out by Edward Emerson in W 9:514, led Carl Strauch (diss., p. 547) to assign the lines to the period 1836–1839. However, the overlooked source of the "History" passage occurs in journal F 2 (JMN 7:544) between entries for 20 December 1840 and 30 January 1841. The poem, then, was probably written in late 1840 or in 1841.

*Publication:* Unpublished by Emerson. First printed in *Poems,* 1884, p. 314, with the nonauthorial title "Limits," and reprinted in W 9:375.

*See Also:* Strauch diss., pp. 354 (text) and 547–50 (notes).

## "Who royally bedded"

*Text:* These four lines, a translation from an unlocated source in Hafiz, occur in pencil in X p. 171. They have not been found elsewhere in Emerson's published or unpublished writings.

## "Who saw the hid beginnings"

*Texts:* The earliest draft, lacking the second stanza, is scattered over several pages in journal Books Small (JMN 8:462–64 and 466–67) in the same very dark pencil as drafts for "Song of Nature." Next is the pencil fair copy in notebook BL pp. 205–7, which, although reversing stanzas 4 and 5 and putting them at the end, otherwise follows the order of the stanzas as inscribed in Books Small. Two later revisions in the BL draft perfect rhymes, but are not reflected in subsequent manuscript texts. Stanza 2 first appears in the version in Poems folder 78, in which the final order of the stanzas is determined (see Additional Manuscripts). This manuscript, marked "Supplenda," is apparently the source of the final fair copy in NP pp. 263–65. As with the Books Small draft, the texts in BL and NP are associated with "Song of Nature." In Poems folder 92, lines 21–28 are further revised and combined with two quatrains, "When all their blooms" and "Softens the air," to make a 16-line poem, fair copies of which occur in ETE pp. 35 (titled "May") and 147 (titled "May Day") (see Additional Manuscripts under "When all their blooms"). The second ETE text is followed on the next page by the final draft of "May Day [Invitation]" and may have been intended as a preamble to it.

*Date:* Probably 1840–1843, the major period of use of Books Small, although Carl Strauch assigns a conjectural date of 1846 or 1847 to these drafts.

*Publication:* Unpublished by Emerson. First published, apparently from the NP text, in *Poems,* 1884, pp. 304–5, with the nonauthorial title "May Morning" and a row of asterisks after stanzas 3 and 5 that correspond to page breaks in the text in NP. Reprinted in W 9:366–67 with the nonauthorial title "Cosmos."

*See Also:* Carl F. Strauch, "The Sources of Emerson's 'Song of Nature,' " *HLB* 9 (Autumn 1955): 300–334.

## "Why fear to die"

*Texts:* The earliest version of the poem, dated "Williamstown Vt. 1 June, 1831," occurs in ink in Blotting Book Psi (JMN 3:231); on the previous manuscript page is a series of lines beginning "Why fear to die" that have a similar theme. An ink fair copy appears in P p. 51 with several revisions and the same notation of place and time of composition.

*Date:* 1 June 1831, while Emerson was on his way to Burlington, Vermont, with his brother Charles (see L 1:323). A recollection of this trip is contained in an entry for 19 December 1831 in Blotting Book III: "Following my own thoughts, especially as sometimes they have moved me in the country, (as in the Gulf-Road in Vermont,) I should lie down in the lap of earth as trustingly as ever on my bed" (JMN 3:312).

*Publication:* Unpublished by Emerson. First published in W 9:390–91 from the P text under the title "A Mountain Grave," derived from Emerson's index reference in P: "↑Gr[een].↓ Mountain grave." Printed in J 2:383 (P version) under the heading "Written at Williamstown, Vermont / June 1, 1831" and listed as "Lines on *Death*" in the table of contents, p. xii.

*See Also:* Strauch diss., pp. 306–7 (text) and 485–86 (notes).

## "The winds are cold, the days are dark"

*Text:* The only manuscript text is an ink fair copy with added pencil punctuation in CSA p. 45.

*Date:* Undetermined, though Carl Strauch conjectures that the poem was written in the autumn or winter of 1827.

*Publication:* Unpublished.

*See Also:* Strauch diss., p. 292 (text), where the lines are given the nonauthorial title "This Iron Soil," and pp. 462–63 (notes).

## "Wine resembles the Lord Jesus"

*Text:* These two lines, translating Hafiz, Book XIII, Ode II, lines 5–6 (*Diwan* 2:92), occur in EF p. 82. They have not been found elsewhere in Emerson's published or unpublished writings.

## "Wisp & meteor nightly falling"

*Text:* These two lines occur in EL p. 51 in pencil overwritten in ink.

*Date:* Undetermined.

*Publication:* Unpublished by Emerson. First published with the nonauthorial title "The Heavens" in W 9:341.

## "With the key of the secret he marches faster"

*Texts:* The source for lines 3–4, a statement by Karl Marx first copied in journal GO (JMN 13:127), is paraphrased in notebook XO p. 68, and the first draft of the quatrain written below it. Emerson apparently copied this version in EL p. 179, then revised the draft in XO; three fair copies of the revised version occur in NP p. 98 and ETE pp. 79 and 135.

*Date:* Undetermined. Journal GO was used in 1852–1853; notebook XO was begun in 1856. Lewis S. Feuer gives the source of Marx's statement as his article "Forced Emigration" in the *New York Daily Tribune,* 22 March 1853, but the attribution is highly conjectural. The central idea of the poem had occurred often in Emerson's writing; see for example JMN 7:90, 10:357 and 404, 11:23 and 31, and "Ode, Inscribed to W. H. Channing."

*Publication:* Unpublished by Emerson. First published in *Poems,* 1884, p. 297, and reprinted in W 9:357.

*See Also:* (1) Rusk, *Life,* pp. 370–71, and (2) Lewis S. Feuer, "Ralph Waldo Emerson's Reference to Karl Marx," *NEQ* 33 (September 1960): 378–79.

## "Woodnotes, I"

*Texts:* Lines 1–2 occur first in an entry for 29 May 1835 in journal B (JMN 5:45), and, revised, in a letter of 14 March 1836, to Frederic Henry Hedge (L 2:7). The first substantial draft of the poem occurs in erased pencil in P p. 41, a rough and incomplete version of lines 1–36. The second draft, in pencil, begins on P p. 40 (lines 1–25), continues on p. 42 (lines 26–42), and concludes on p. 43 (lines 49–74). Additional verses on p. 42, a rough draft of lines 43–46, are in a slightly lighter shade of pencil and were probably interpolated after the main sequence was inscribed. These verses are revised and expanded in pencil on p. 44 (lines 43–48). On pp. 45–46 is a pencil draft of lines 131–59, with two rejected lines after line 151. Three other portions of the poem occur elsewhere in P: lines 99–108 on p. 27, lines 75–92 on p. 48 (separated from the main draft by a blank p. 47), and a draft of lines 109–24, with additional rejected lines, on p. 72. Printer's copy for the London edition of *Poems,* 1847, is in the Berg Collection, New York Public Library; it has "moose" in line 79 and "gild" in line 92 for the misreadings "mouse" and "guild" of the printed text, "falling tree" canceled for "perfect tree" in line 87, and "may" canceled for "can" in line 100.

*Date:* The manuscripts may give incidental support to the Emerson family tradition that "a part of this picture [of the 'forest seer'] was drawn before [Emerson] knew Thoreau's gifts and experiences" (W 9:420). The occurrence of lines 1–2 in documents of 1835 and 1836 coincides in time with the source for lines 35–36 in journal B, an entry for 15 May 1835: "Why am I more curious to know the reason why the star form is so oft repeated in botany or why the number five is such a favorite with nature . . ." (JMN 5:42). Lines 77–78 were taken from Emerson's Phi Beta Kappa poem of 1834, lines 95–96 (see Carl F. Strauch, "Emerson's Phi Beta Kappa Poem," *NEQ* 23 [March 1950]: 84). The idea of line 105 is contained in a Spanish proverb quoted in journal Q (JMN 4:17) in 1832, and loosely paraphrased in journal E (JMN 7:332) during the last week of December 1839. Emerson may have been sufficiently acquainted with Thoreau to have written the interpolated lines in P pp. 42 and 44 by 1836, or, more probably, by 1837 (Rusk, *Life*, p. 254).

*Publication: The Dial* 1 (October 1840): 242–45. Collected in *Poems,* 1847, pp. 67–74 (Boston) and (with several variants and the omission of line 135) pp. 50–56 (London). The poem was shortened for *Selected Poems,* 1876, pp. 126–29, by the omission of lines 1–6, 17–20, 26–28, and 75–108 (the entire third section). In *Poems,* 1884, pp. 43–47, lines 75–108 were restored; this text was reprinted in W 9:43–48, while the original lines 1–6 and 17–28 were given in the notes (W 9:419–20).

## "The world is a bride superbly dressed"

*Text:* An early version of this couplet appears in a translation of Hafiz, Book VIII, Ode LV, lines 1–24 (*Diwan* 1:285) in journal CD (JMN 10:67–68); a revision reducing the four German lines (17–20) to three occurs in EF p. 108 under the headings "Ethical" and "Fatal sentences"; this is revised into two lines in notebook Orientalist p. 57.

*Date:* The first draft was written in 1847.

*Publication:* First published in "Persian Poetry," 1858, p. 727, and reprinted with the essay in *Letters and Social Aims,* 1876, p. 221, and W 8:246.

*See Also:* "I have no hoarded treasure," which translates lines 13–16 of the same ode.

## "The World-Soul"

*Texts:* The drafts of the earlier parts of the poem are apparently lost. In X pp. 32–37 are erased pencil drafts, some with unused lines, as follows: on p. 32, lines 77–80; on p. 33, lines 105–12; on p. 34, line 60; on p. 35, lines

58–60 and 67–72; on p. 36, lines 75 and 81–96; and on p. 37, lines 97–104 and 41–44. The material on pp. 33 and 35 is overwritten with lines of "Etienne de la Boéce." Emerson then made an ink fair copy, of which the surviving pages (in the Tappan Papers, Houghton Library) contain lines 1–60 and 65–88, with a space left for the missing half-stanza (see Additional Manuscripts). This was copied in pencil with very few revisions in X pp. 44–49, where Emerson again left a space to accommodate lines 61–64, the last two lines of which were supplied from a draft in X p. 70. None of the drafts is titled, though X p. 44 is indexed as "Morning." Printer's copy for *The Diadem* is in the Furness Papers, Van Pelt Library, University of Pennsylvania; see Furness, *Records,* pp. 55–59, for a transcription that omits only one verbal detail: the cancellation of "chimneys" for "chambers" in line 11. Printer's copy for the London edition of *Poems,* 1847, is in the Houghton Library; it has "pleading" written over "weeping" in line 28.

*Date:* Evidence as to the date of composition is of several sorts. The reference to the telegraph in line 15 indicates a date after January 1843, when Emerson first became aware of the invention (L 3:120). It was not until 24 May 1844, however, that the first public messages were actually conveyed by telegraph. Edward Emerson (W 1:458) suggested that "the last part of the 'World-Soul' . . . is a rendering . . . in verse" of a certain passage in "The Young American" (W 1:373); the source of the passage is an entry in journal R written between 10 and 17 April 1843 (JMN 8:384). On 19 June 1845, Margaret Fuller quoted lines 9–32 in "Asylum for Discharged Female Convicts," *New-York Daily Tribune,* p. 1, in a text substantially coinciding with the Tappan and X fair copies. Nearly a year later, on 10 June 1846, Emerson sent the poem to William H. Furness for publication in the annual *The Diadem.* He wrote: "I enclose a piece, which, for want of a better name, I call 'the World Soul.' *Anima Mundi* was the name, but we are bound at least in poetry to speak English. I had the poem when I wrote before [22 May], but in the smallness of my portfolio of new pieces, dared not send away one of so many lines, until you tell me that I may print it in my new book, if I have one, in spite of you. . . . I have heard that Margaret Fuller printed a verse or two of this piece once in the Tribune, but I never saw them. She printed if she printed, from a copy I had lent to Elizabeth Hoar. I am almost tempted to send you another copy of the same piece, that you may select your own reading from the *Variorum.* But . . . I will only say, that in the copy from which I now transcribe this, the 8th stanza has only one quatrain, and I have just added four lines to make it complete. And now it strikes me that the poem was a little more intelligible before. If you think so, leave out the quatrain." (The manuscript of this letter is still with the *Diadem* printer's copy in the Van Pelt Library; it was published in Furness, *Records,* pp. 54–55). The conclusions to be drawn are (1) that the draft fragments in X pp. 32–37, judging from their relation to the "Etienne" passages, were inscribed between late 1843 and early 1845, (2) that the Tappan manuscript—very likely the source of Margaret Fuller's text—represents the state of the poem at a point not later than June 1845, and (3) that lines 61–64 were added to complete the poem very shortly before 10 June 1846.

*Publication:* Lines 9–32 were published by Margaret Fuller, as noted above, on 19 June 1845. The entire poem first appeared in *The Diadem for MDCCCXLVII* (Philadelphia, 1847 [i.e., October 1846]), pp. 76–78, and three months later in *Poems,* 1847, pp. 30–35 (Boston) and pp. 21–25 (London). It was reprinted in *Selected Poems,* 1876, pp. 24–28, *Poems,* 1884, pp. 23–27, and W 9:15–19.

## "The worldsoul" ("The Master said")

*Text:* This unfinished eight-line poem occurs in pencil in X p. 94. It has not been found elsewhere in Emerson's published or unpublished writings.

## "Worship"

*Texts:* A draft of the poem occurs in ink over an erased draft of "Hermione" in X pp. 187–88, together with a second draft of lines 15–23 on X p. 189. Evidences of a late draft in ink occur on the stub of a leaf (pp. 287–88) torn out of NP. In 1864 Emerson wrote out a fair copy that was reproduced in facsimile in *Autograph Leaves of Our Country's Authors* (Baltimore, 1864), pp. 132–33 (see L 5:353); this manuscript is now in the University of Texas Library.

*Date:* A principal source of the poem is *The Vishnu Purana* and the notes that Emerson took from p. 267 of the H. H. Wilson translation (London, 1840). These notes, preserved in Poems folder 95, were partly copied into journal CL (JMN 14:297–98). A favorite line from *The Iliad* served as a source for line 15 (see JMN 9:94 and 220). The date of composition is unclear, with some evidence pointing to 1845—the source for line 15 and Emerson's reading of *The Vishnu Purana* (see L 3:293 and JMN 9:312)—and other evidence pointing to 1859—the composition of the essay "Worship" and the probability that the notes were copied in preparation for that essay. Given Emerson's general practice of writing mottoes near the time of publication, however, and the fact that the earlier sources remained available, 1859 would seem to be the more likely time of composition.

*Publication: The Conduct of Life,* 1860, p. 173; collected in *May–Day,* 1867, pp. 176–77, and reprinted in *Selected Poems,* 1876, p. 183, *Poems,* 1884, p. 237, and W 9:279–80.

## "Would you know what joy is hid"

*Texts:* The principal draft of this poem, which Emerson abandoned during revision, occurs in pencil in P pp. 224–25. The first eleven lines (plus the canceled draft of the first line) were erased after the passage was revised on p. 222. The last seven lines on p. 224 were also revised on p. 222, but not erased.

*Date:* Undetermined. In his note to the poem in W 9:509, Edward Emerson speculated that "These verses were probably written while Mr. Emerson was visiting Dr. Ezra Ripley . . . at the Manse, after [Emerson's] return from Europe in 1833. Opposite the house is a pasture-hill giving a fine view of the great meadows to the eastward, and, on the western horizon, of some of the mountains on the New Hampshire line." Although journal sources dating to 1835 and 1838 have been proposed (JMN 5:13 and 7:33), they do not present convincing parallels. Emerson's use of p. 222 for revision suggests that "Tell me maiden dost thou use" was already inscribed on p. 223. If so, the present poem would not be earlier than 1844.

*Publication:* Unpublished by Emerson. A synthetic text composed of the segments at the top of p. 222, at the bottom of p. 224, and on p. 225 (less the last two lines, with the omission indicated by asterisks) was published in *Poems*, 1884, pp. 285–86, with the nonauthorial title "Sunrise" (Emerson's index reference to p. 224 is "Musketaquid"). This text was reprinted in W 9:345–46.

*See Also:* "Tell me maiden dost thou use."

## "Written in a Volume of Goethe"

*Texts:* The first draft occurs in pencil on the inside front cover of Emerson's copy of vol. 50 of Goethe's *Werke* (Stuttgart and Tübingen, 1828–1833), which is vol. 10 of *Goethe's Nachgelassene Werke* (see Additional Manuscripts). The second (titled) occurs in X p. 21, and the third (also titled) is in Rhymer p. 55.

*Date:* Probably 1837. Emerson acquired *Goethe's Nachgelassene Werke* in the first week of August 1836, and as he reported to his brother William on 8 August, he had "read little else than [these] books lately" (L 2:32–33). He translated portions of vol. 10 of the *Nachgelassene Werke* in 1837 (see JMN 6:289–91 and 299–303). On 21 April 1840, he wrote to Carlyle: "You asked me if I read German . . . . I have contrived to read almost every volume of Goethe, and I have 55 but I have read nothing else: but I have not now looked even into Goethe for a long time" (*The Correspondence of Emerson and Carlyle*, ed. Joseph Slater [New York, 1964], p. 269).

*Publication:* Unpublished by Emerson. First published in *Poems,* 1884, p. 313, and reprinted in W 4:371 and W 9:373.

## "Written in Naples, March, 1833"

*Texts:* The first draft of this poem occurs in pencil in journal Sicily (JMN 4:130), between entries written during Emerson's stay in Catania, 1–3 March 1833. It was copied and revised in journal Q (JMN 4:69–70) between entries of 13–22 March, when he was in Naples. An ink fair copy, revised from the Q text, appears in P p. 3 with the present title; in his index to P Emerson listed the page under the notation "Ellen."

*Date:* Between 1 and 22 March 1833.

*Publication:* Unpublished by Emerson. First published in *Poems,* 1884, pp. 300–301, from the P text, and reprinted in W 9:395–96. In J 3:64–65 the poem was reprinted from W 9 with a few slight changes and given the title "At Naples."

*See Also:* Strauch diss., pp. 329–31 (text) and 502–4 (notes).

## "Written in Sickness"

*Texts:* The earliest text is an ink fair copy with the title "Sonnet / Written in sickness" in journal 1826–1828 (JMN 3:87); this is apparently the source of the ink fair copy with the title "Written in Sickness" in CSA p. 31, which in turn is the source of the untitled ink fair copy in P p. 39.

*Date:* The 1826–1828 text bears the notation "Cambridge, D[ivinity]. H[all]. 7 Dec. 1827.—", during a return of the ill health that had sent Emerson to the South the previous winter.

*Publication:* Unpublished by Emerson. First published from the P text in *Poems,* 1884, pp. 290–91, and reprinted in W 9:381. Another version, a conflation of the 1826–1828 and CSA texts, appears in J 2:217–18.

*See Also:* Strauch diss., pp. 295–96 (text) and 473–75 (notes).

## "Xenophanes"

*Texts:* A pencil version of lines 5–19, partially erased and dated "21 March," occurs in P p. 21; it is the source of a revised ink fair copy of the same lines in P p. 20 that bears the title "'Εν κὰι πᾶν." and the notation "Concord 1834." A pencil draft of lines 1–4 occurs in P p. 119. Printer's copy for the London edition of *Poems,* 1847, is in the Berg Collection, New York Public Library; in it, "we" is canceled before "explore" in line 12, and "tedious" is canceled for "cricket" in line 19.

*Date:* Although Emerson's notations on P pp. 20–21 clearly imply that lines 5–19 were written in Concord on 21 March 1834, he was actually in New Bedford lecturing that day. Edward Emerson (W 9:449) and Carl Strauch ("The Year of Emerson's Poetic Maturity: 1834," *PQ* 34 [October 1955]: 353–77) accept 1834 as the year of composition on the basis of internal evidence. Some credence is given to the supposition that the year may actually be 1836 by a number of references in journal B: the appearance of the Greek phrase in a series of quotations from Goethe (JMN 5:128); a reference to Xenophanes (with whom the phrase is associated) in an entry of 11 March (JMN 5:136); and an entry of—significantly—21 March in which Emerson reports finding a sentence in Goethe that is "a comment and consent to my speculations on the All in Each in Nature this last week" (JMN 5:138). It is not known at what point before publication lines 1–4 on P p. 119 were written and connected to the poem.

*Publication: Poems,* 1847, pp. 219–20 (Boston) and p. 175 (London); reprinted in *Selected Poems,* 1876, p. 163, *Poems,* 1884, pp. 120–21, and W 9:137. In the London edition of *Poems,* 1847, the last line reads: "Repeats one cricket note." This language reflects a last-minute emendation in the manuscript that Emerson sent to England, a change almost certainly, if remotely, influenced by a passage rejected from the 1841 lecture "The Poet" (see *Early Lectures* 3:514). On 29 December 1846, Emerson wrote to Chapman, his English publisher, requesting that this line be changed to conform to the text of the American edition (manuscript letter in the Chapman Papers, Sterling Library, University of London).

## "Yet all comes out of this, that one door"

*Text:* These two lines, which translate Hafiz, Book VIII, Ode CLXV, lines 21–22 (*Diwan* 1:446), occur in EF p. 109.

*Date:* Undetermined.

*Publication:* A prose version, "Here is the sum, that, when one door opens, another shuts," was published in "Persian Poetry," 1858, p. 726, and in the essay as collected in *Letters and Social Aims,* 1876, p. 220, and W 8:245.

## "Yet sometime to the sorrow stricken"

*Texts:* A draft of lines 1–2 precedes a draft of the four lines of the poem, all in pencil, in P p. 131.

*Date:* Undetermined, though perhaps in the late summer or fall of 1838. The source of lines 3–4 appears to be an entry for 16 September 1838 in journal D (JMN 7:73).

*Publication:* Unpublished by Emerson. First published in *Poems*, 1884, p. 296, where the first words are misread as "Yes, sometimes . . ."; reprinted in W 9:355.

## "You shall not love me for what daily spends"

*Texts:* An erased pencil draft occurs in notebook Dialling (JMN 8:502–3, where several lines are incorrectly transcribed). A pencil version, apparently drawn from this, occurs in P p. 145. Two ink fair copies exist, in Rhymer p. 46 and notebook L Camadeva p. 37.

*Date:* The pencil draft in Dialling cannot be later than the summer of 1842, for it is overwritten in ink by notes on the death of James Pierrepont Greaves on 11 March, used in Emerson's essay "English Reformers" in *The Dial* for October. Sources for the phrase "the channel of the rivers of God" are discussed in the entry for "O what are heroes prophets men."

*Publication:* Unpublished by Emerson. The first eight lines were published in *Poems*, 1884, p. 293, and reprinted in W 9:352.

## "You shall plant"

*Texts:* The two-line first draft in X p. 123 is revised on the same page into a couplet. The verses have not been found elsewhere in Emerson's published or unpublished writings.

## "You strong Republicans"

*Texts:* The first incomplete draft, in pencil in EL p. 114, is revised in pencil in EL p. 288, where it is followed by line 4 of "Where his name is named." This version was then copied and further revised in EL p. 115.

*Date:* Undetermined.

*Publication:* Unpublished.

# APPENDIX

## Emerson's Indexes

This index combines Emerson's own indexes to his poetry notebooks, which occur on P pp. 332 and 333; X front cover verso, p. 268, and the inside back cover; EF front cover verso and the inside back cover; EL front cover verso, p. 296, and the inside back cover; Rhymer pp. 156 and 157; NP p. 302 and the inside back cover; and ETE pp. 178 and 179. Of these, the ones on EL inside back cover, Rhymer p. 157, and ETE p. 178 are finished (alphabetical and in ink) and the others are preliminary (not alphabetical and usually in pencil). ETE pp. 178–79 are reproduced in Plate 10.

Entry headings that are highly similar have been combined. These include Adirondac and Adirondacs; C.C.E. and C.C.E's; Cup of life and The cup of life; Holmes and J. Holmes; Lowell, Lowell, J.R., and Lowell, Mr.; Muse and The Muse; and War-song and Warsong.

Page numbers that Emerson struck through or wrote over to correct are set in cancellation brackets. Incorrect or missing page references are followed by the correct page number in editorial brackets. A word added to an index heading is set in insert arrows. No attempt is made to indicate cancellation of entries in a preliminary index when it was superseded by a finished index, or to show which page numbers were added to entries at a later time than the first inscription of an index.

Adirondacs, EL 27, ⟨50⟩; NP 164; ETE 154 [156]
Aeolian Harp, X 106; EL 193; ETE 19
Air, EL 161
Albany, EL 229
Album, X 164; EL 174, 291; Rhymer 150; NP 5
Alcuin, Rhymer 61
Alms, Rhymer 140
Alphonso, X 5
Amita, ETE 100, 102, 171, 173
Apothecary, P 259
April, ETE 15
Arabian Ballad, EL 235
Artist, Rhymer 51
As sings the pinetree, Rhymer 41
Aspiration, ETE 102
At sea, X 104
Atom, Rhymer 117

Bacchus, X 100, 200
Beauty, P 263; EL 106, 142

Bells, EL [112, 288]
Blooms the laurel, EL 131
Borrowing, Rhymer 68
Boston, EL 64, 152, 216; NP 200
Boston Hymn, Rhymer 95
Boston song, EL 152
Botanist, P 43; Rhymer 31
Bramah, Rhymer 119
Bramin, Rhymer 32
Brothers, P 187
Building Muse, X ⟨57⟩59

Catalogue, ETE 2
C.C.E., EL 60; ETE 11
Celestial Love, X 141
Chain, ETE 171
Chartist's Complaint, Rhymer 26
Chicadee, NP ⟨43⟩, ⟨46⟩, 60
Climacteric, Rhymer 37
Compensation, P 9
Concord Fight, P 240
Concord Monument, P 237 [236]

Confucius, EL 2, 15
Conscience, P 202
Coral, EL 212
Cras, hodie, heri, Rhymer 69
Criticism, EL 148
Cromwell, NP 73
Culture, NP 105
Cup of life, Rhymer 45
Cupido, EL 174; Rhymer 105; ETE 16

Daniel, EL 209
Days, Rhymer 7
The Dervish, X 167
Destiny, Rhymer 23; NP 211
Dirge, P 14
Drink wine, & the heaven, Rhymer 149

Each in All, P 11, ⟨105⟩
"Easy to do," EL 162
E.B.E., P 240, 325; EL 163
Edwards Farewell, P ⟨325⟩
E H, EL 252
Ellen, P 3; ETE 23
Eloquence, NP 286
Εν και παν, P ⟨21⟩20
Enchanters, P 202
Enough is said, X ⟨116⟩, 124
Epitaph, P 99
Eros and Muse, Rhymer 35
E.T.E., EL 138, ⟨163⟩
Eternity, ETE 33
Exile, Rhymer 123

Fable, EF 17
Fame, P 1
Fate, X 190, EL ⟨183⟩182, 193; Rhymer 24,
    29; NP 73, 184, 211, 229, 255; ETE 176
Fine Days, EF 52
Flag, EL 160; NP 292
Forest, P 48
Forester, Rhymer 31
Fortune & Hope, ETE 37
Fourth of July, Rhymer 79
Freedom, EL 117, 127; Rhymer 57; NP 111
Friendship, P 292; Rhymer 50, 141
↑From↓ Hafiz, Rhymer 129

Garden, EL 135, 158, 183, 195
Gardener, Rhymer 31
Genius goes alone, X 27
Give all to Love, X 213 [215]
Goethe, Rhymer 55
Good Heart, X 92
Good Heart that ownest all, X 92; EL 35
↑Gr.↓ Mountain grave, P 51
Guru, EL 228
Guides, X ⟨41⟩43

Gypsy, X 50
Gypsy Song, Rhymer 71

Hafiz, Rhymer 66, 135, 137, 140; NP 119,
    ⟨134⟩136; ETE 59
Hafiz—Allah, EF 96
Hafiz—Compliments, EF 77
Hafiz—Copyright, EF 59
Hafiz, Dervish, X 167
Hafiz—Fatal & Ethical Sentences, EF 108
Hafiz—friendship, EF 80, 81
Hafiz—his life, EF 76
Hafiz—his nature, EF 38
Hafiz—his philosophy, EF 42, 72
Hafiz—his phoenix-soul, X 194 [196]; EF 15
Hafiz, If thou drink wine, X 183
Hafiz—love, EF 48, 49, 50, 55
Hafiz, Ode, X 169
Hafiz—odes, EF 101
Hafiz of his Verse, EF 113
Hafiz, "Of Paradise," X 178 [179]
Hafiz, Phoenix, X 194 [196]
Hafiz, Red rose, X 172
Hafiz—Rhetoric, EF 56
Hafiz—Sentences, EF 104
Hafiz—Superlative, EF 84, 86, 97
Hafiz, The long ode, X 242 [244]
Hafiz—The two Days, EF 95
Hafiz—wine, EF 82
Harp, EL 193; NP 266
Heaven, X 256 [259]; ETE 172 [174]
Heroics, ETE [no page]
Hilali, Rhymer 134
Himself it was who wrote, X 89
Hoar, E., EL 252
Holmes, J, Rhymer 60; ETE 166
Humble Bee, P ⟨189⟩182
Hush!, Rhymer 63

I cannot leave, X 95
I care not where, ETE 132
I know a song, EL ⟨23⟩, ⟨52⟩, 53
I know the appointed hour, Rhymer 9
I serve you not if you I follow, X 35
Ibn Jemin, Rhymer 127
If thou drink wine, X 183
Initial Love, X 132
Inscription, ETE 21
Inscription for a Well, ETE 21
Inspiration, NP 27
It is time to be old, X 206

Lars, NP [12]
Lemurs, ETE 29
Lemurs & Lars, EL 200
Letters, Rhymer 44; ETE 43, 145
Life, ETE 8

List of Names, EL 34
Lost at Sea, by J. O Rockwell, P 197
Love, Rhymer 46, 105; NP 103, 119; ETE 16
Loves petition, Rhymer 15
Lowell, J.R., Rhymer 60; NP 231; ETE 152
Lowell's birthday, ETE 152

Machines, X 60
Madness, P ⟨85⟩77
Maia, EL 182, 293
Manners, P 147; Rhymer 25
Masque, P ⟨176⟩153
May, ETE 35
May cart, EL 203
May Day, ETE 35, 147, 148
Memory, Rhymer 29
Merlin, P 212; X 81; EL 53; NP 289
Merlin's Song, Rhymer 14
Michel Angelo, NP 276
Miracle, ETE ⟨153⟩152 [154]
Mirror, EL 106
Mithridates, X 220
M.M.E., EL 181, 247; Rhymer 34; NP 128, 152, 182 [notebook MME 2 p. 182?], 246, 248, ⟨254⟩252, 254; ETE 100, 102, 173
Moment, ETE 33
Morals, EL 158
Morning, X 44
"Morning," P ⟨315⟩
Mottoes, X 214 [215]; ETE 172, 174, 176
Motto to Beauty, X 119
Motto to Worship, X 186
Mud sill, EL 61
The Muse, P 123; ETE 27
Music everywhere, P 96
Musketaquid, P 224
My Garden, EL ⟨78⟩, 135, 158, 183, ⟨193⟩195
My walk, EL 73

Nantasket, X 240 [242]
Nativity, Rhymer 53
Nature, EL 38, 103, 147, 181, 189, 201, 230; Rhymer 65, 98; NP 69
Nature is good, NP 206
Nature, Song of, Rhymer 82
New Commandment, Rhymer 39
Night, P 69
Northman, Rhymer 61
Not beautiful, X ⟨183⟩189 [183, 191]
Now, Rhymer 104; ETE 172 [174]
Nun's Prayer, ETE 100, 102

Of paradise o hermit wise, X 178 [179]
Oft when I read fond pictures poets drew, X 14

Old Age, NP 245
Omens, NP 71
Orator, Rhymer 49
Ordeal, NP 107

Pantheos, P 129
Parnassus, EL 100
Past, EL ⟨32⟩34, 159
Peasant, P 72
Pen, ETE 145
Peril, EL 51; ETE 171
Peters field, P 204 [205–206]
Phenixes, EL 16
Philosopher, P 81
Phoenix, EL 16; Rhymer 131
Pilgrims, EL 86
Poet, EL 148, 155, 172, 294; Rhymer 48, 67; NP 27, 284, ⟨200⟩300
The poetic gift, NP 284, 300
Poetry, EL 1, 71
Poet's apology, P 203
Pour the wine, NP 285
Preraphaelite, Rhymer 42
↑Present↓ Hour, ETE 33
The priest, P 83
Proverbs, P 99
Purging, Rhymer 81

Quatrains, NP 132

Rainbow, ETE 9
Refrains, NP 111, 112, 284; ETE 137
Rhodora, P 95
Rhyme, X 79, 160
Ripples, X 106
Rock, ETE 7
Rock of Ages, Rhymer 116
Rome, EL 150
Rowse, NP 186
Rubies, X ⟨161⟩181; Rhymer 27, 147

S R, P 260
S W, P 260
Saadi, P 93, 228; Rhymer 11; NP 290, 298, 300; ETE 27
Saadi—New, P 282
Sculptor, P 164
Sea, EL 24, 96
Sea-Shore, Rhymer 97
Seasons, EL 189
September, X 59
Set not thy foot on graves, X 240 [242]
Shakspeare, Rhymer 42
The Skeptic, P 77; X 61
Sky, NP 92
Slave, ETE 112
Slavery, EL 106

Snowstorm, P 126
Solar Dance, Rhymer 121
Solution, X ⟨8⟩, ⟨9⟩, ⟨13⟩, ⟨18⟩, 68; EL 103
Song, NP 113
Song of Nature, EL 230; NP ⟨65⟩, 85, 255
    [256?], 257
Soul, EF 102
Southwind, Rhymer 59
Sphinx, P 108
Spring, EF 32, 33, 34, 35, 36, 40; EL 81,
    103, 132, 134, 144; NP 7, 116
Spring-winds, Rhymer 75
Stars, EL 41, 189, 225; NP 72; ETE 175
Stillman, NP 180; ETE 156
Studies of Nature, X 211
Suum Cuique, ETE 173 [175]

Taliesin, EL 175, 177
Telegraph, NP 158
Temperament, P 209
Terminus, EL 10; Rhymer 100; NP 94
Tho' I call me liberal, X 38
Time, NP 247
Tis time to be old, X 206
Titmouse, Rhymer 88; NP 60 "and Vol 9
    Atlantic"
To A.H., Rhymer 33
To S.H., Rhymer 33
Today, ETE 173
Tongue & Pen, ETE 145
Trimountain, EL 215 [216.1]

Truth, EL 157
Two Rivers, Rhymer 77

Una, P 295; X [129–130], Rhymer 73

Verse or Style, EL 22
Very, NP 99
Vestiges of Creation, X 120 [121]
Vines, EL 158
Virtue & Art, X 31
Visit, P 141
Voluntaries, EL 40, 125, 127, 128; Rhymer
    102 [103]; ETE 171

Wachusett, X ⟨13⟩ 51
Walden, NP ⟨45⟩, ⟨53⟩, ⟨106⟩, ⟨197⟩, 270
Walk, EL 73
War-song, EL 104, [no page]
Water, EL 20, 72; Rhymer 104; ETE 20
Wealth, NP 273
Webster, P 34, Rhymer 47
Well, ETE 21
What care I so things abide, X 25
Wind, EL 161
Wishes, EL 179
Woodman, NP 176
Woods, P 168; EF 38
Wyman, ETE 169
Worm, NP 76
Worship, NP 287

Xenien, ETE 7, 172, ⟨173⟩, 174, 175

# Index

This index contains the following kinds of entries:

(1) names of individuals mentioned in prose passages or lists in the text of Emerson's poetry notebooks, in headnotes and footnotes, and in the analyses of individual poems when the reference is more than passing;

(2) titles of books, poems, essays, and other writings by individuals other than Emerson;

(3) titles of books, lectures, essays, and addresses by Emerson;

(4) titles of poems by Emerson which do not appear in the poetry notebooks but are mentioned in the analyses or printed in the Additional Manuscripts section;

(5) nonauthorial titles given to Emerson's poems or fragments by James Elliot Cabot, Edward W. Emerson, or Carl F. Strauch.

The poems, fragments, and translations in the poetry notebooks are not indexed; they may be found in alphabetical order in the Analysis of Poems section. Individuals, places, works of literature, and other references within the poems themselves are also not indexed.

Adams, Abel, 338, 726
Adams, John, 275
Adams, John Quincy, 274
Aeschylus, *The Supplicants,* 870
Agassiz, Louis, 723
Alcott, Amos Bronson, 338, 725
Alcuin, 797
Alger, William Rounseville (?), 338
Ali Ben Abi Taleb, 811
Alphonso X of Castile, 727-28
"Amita" (lecture), 731, 877
*Anthologia Graeca. The Greek Anthology,* 284
Aristotle, 869
Arnold, Matthew, 339
"Art" (essay), 824
"At Naples" (nonauthorial title), 977
"At the Old Manse" (nonauthorial title), 740

Bach, Johann Sebastian, 524
Bacon, Francis, *De Augmentis Scientiarum,* 735
Badger, William R. L., 109
Bailey, Philip James, *Festus,* 789
Bancroft, George, 339, 880; *A History of the United States,* 388, 649n
Bangor, Me., 761
Barrett, Henry A., 109
"Beauty" (essay), 936-37; (lecture), 722

Beethoven, Ludwig van, 524
"Behavior" (essay), 503, 851
"The Bell" (nonauthorial title), 827
*The Bhagvat-Geeta,* 751
Bible: *Judges,* 911; *Proverbs,* 733
Bicknell, Herman, *Hafiz of Shiraz: Selections from his Poems,* 761
Bigelow, Francis E., 109
Bonaparte, Napoleon, 778
"Books" (essay), 736
Borrow, George, *Romantic Ballads,* 588n
Boston, Mass., 745-47, 877-78
Botta, Anne Charlotte Lynch, 338
Bourrienne, Louis Antoine Fauvelet de, *Private Memoirs of Napoleon Bonaparte,* 931
Boutwell, George S., 271
Bray, Charles, 339
Brooks, Charles Timothy, 339
Brown, Edwin Lee, 338
Brown, J. M., 109
Brown, John, 819, 845
Bryan, William G., 338
Bryant, William Cullen, 581; "The Antiquity of Freedom," 16
Bulkeley, Peter, 728
Burleigh, G. H., 265
Burlington, Vt., 971
Burns, Robert, 524, 535-40
Burton, Andrew, 596

Burton, Robert, *The Anatomy of Melancholy*, 796
Butler, Samuel, *Hudibras*, 873

Canning, George, 787
Carlyle, Thomas, 738, 966, 976
Chamberlain, Mellen, 764
Chambers, Robert, *Vestiges of the Natural History of Creation*, 178
Channing, William Ellery, 425, 923; "Eliot: The Outlaw of the Forest," 424
Chapman, John, 864, 882, 978
"Character" (essay), 767, 836, 909
"Character of Samuel Hoar" (essay), 907
Chardin, John, *Voyages . . . en Perse, et Autres Lieux de l'Orient*, 793, 887, 930
Chaucer, Geoffrey, 829; "The Knight's Tale," 106; "The Legend of Good Women," 105; "The Squire's Tale," 106
"Chaucer" (lecture), 829
Childs, George W., 769
*The Chinese Classics*, 325, 331, 886
Chladni, Ernst Florens Friedrich, 758-59
Chodzko, Alexander, *Specimens of the Popular Poetry of Persia*, 264, 309-10
"Circles" (essay), 925
"Civilization" (essay), 914
Clarke, James Freeman, 804, 820
Coleridge, Samuel Taylor, *Aids to Reflection*, 806
Collier, A. C., 109
"Come brave the sea with me love" (unidentified poem), 324, 562
"Compensation" (essay), 762, 776, 821, 929
Concord, Mass., 763-64
"Concord Hymn" (nonauthorial title), 764
Concord River, 863
Confucius, 325, 331, 886
Congdon, Annie, 421
"Considerations by the Way" (essay), 745, 765, 811, 852
Conway, Moncure D., 922
"Cosmos" (nonauthorial title), 970
"Country Life" (lecture), 793, 915
Cowley, Abraham, "The Complaint," 297
Cromwell, Oliver, 284
"Culture" (essay), 503, 757-58, 766
Curtis, George Ticknor, 273, 281

*The Dabistan, or School of Manners*, 412-13, 965
Dante Alighieri, 115, 523, 524; *The Divine Comedy*, 110, 774
Davies, Edward, *The Mythology and Rites of the British Druids*, 813
"Day by day returns" (poem), 654
Dekker, Thomas, and John Ford, *The Sun's Darling*, 282

"Destiny" (nonauthorial title), 790
Devens, Charles, 281
Dewey, Chester, *Report on the Herbaceous Flowering Plants of Massachusetts*, 969
"The Divinity School Address," 735, 925
"Doctrine of the Hands" (lecture), 770, 776
Donne, John, "Elegie XVI. On his Mistris," 361n
Dorgan, J. E., 423
Dudley, Elbridge G., 338
Duncan, Rebecca, 748
Dunlap, W. B. (?), 339
Dwight, John Sullivan, 748

Edwards, Richard, 282
Emancipation Proclamation, 747
Emerson, Charles Chauncy (brother), 346n, 347, 584, 774, 780, 805, 971
Emerson, Edith (daughter), 424, 851
Emerson, Edward Bliss (brother), 346n, 746, 763, 774, 835; "The Last Farewell," 106-8, 581
Emerson, Edward Waldo (son), 952
Emerson, Ellen Tucker (daughter), 772, 782, 890
Emerson, Ellen Tucker (wife), 580, 584, 586, 732, 770-71, 822, 940-41, 944, 947
Emerson, George Barrell, 338
Emerson, Joseph, 38
Emerson, Lidian (wife), 529, 738, 770, 815, 863, 874
Emerson, M. L., 323
Emerson, Mary Moody (aunt), 723, 731, 743, 760, 770, 869, 876-77, 921, 950, 962
Emerson, Ruth Haskins (mother), 764
Emerson, Waldo (son), 847
Emerson, William (brother), 764, 921, 947, 976
Empedocles, 751-52
"The Enchanter" (nonauthorial title), 837
"English Reformers" (essay), 979
Enweri, 883, 885, 951
"Eros" (nonauthorial title), 916
"Eternity" (nonauthorial title), 897, 905
"Ethnical Scriptures. Hermes Trismegistus" (article), 16
"The Exile (After Taliessin)" (nonauthorial title), 813

"Farming" (essay), 783, 945
"Fate" (essay), 503, 725, 817-18, 886, 897, 945
Fields, James T., 946, 959
Fields, Mrs. James T., 764
Fillmore, Millard, 309
Firdausi, *The Sháh Námeh*, 264, 273n, 274
Fisher, Sidney George, 339

Forbes, Edith Emerson. *See* Emerson, Edith
Forbes, John Murray, 960
Forbes, Margaret Perkins, 946
Forbes, Mrs. John Murray, 839, 960
Ford, John, and Thomas Dekker, *The Sun's Darling*, 282
Forster, John (?), 339
Forster, William Edward (?), 339
"Forth to encounter thy affianced doom" (poem), 663-64
"Fragment on Nature, II" (nonauthorial title), 969
"Fragment on Nature, III" (nonauthorial title), 969
"Friendship" (essay), 775, 846, 891, 958
Frothingham, Nathaniel L., 339
"The Fugitive Slave Law" (1851) (address), 264, 265n, 270n, 271n, 273n, 277n-281n, 284n, 300n, 314n, 318n
"The Fugitive Slave Law" (1854) (address), 265n, 284n, 800
Fuller, Margaret, 474, 733, 762, 770, 775, 782, 790, 835, 850, 862, 882, 889, 899, 923, 925, 958; "Asylum for Discharged Female Convicts," 974; "The Great Lawsuit," 361; *Memoirs of Margaret Fuller Ossoli*, 806
Furness, William Henry, 109, 733, 773-74, 795, 844, 848, 974

"The Garden" (nonauthorial title), 948
Gérando, Marie Joseph de, *Histoire Comparée des Systèmes de Philosophie*, 751
*Geschichte der schönen Redekünste Persiens*, 484, 785, 791, 794, 798, 883, 885-86, 888, 922, 951, 955
Gibbon, Edward, 873
"Gifts" (essay), 802
Glover, Charles H., 325n
Godwin, William, *Life of Geoffrey Chaucer*, 860
Goethe, Johann Wolfgang von, 115, 265, 523-24, 809, 902, 949, 978; *Nachgelassene Werke*, 783, 976; *Noten und Abhandlungen zu besserem Verständnis des West-östlichen Divans*, 734; *Werke*, 734, 782, 976
"Goethe; or, the Writer" (essay), 949
"Good Hope" (nonauthorial title), 941
Gould, Thomas Ridgeway, 339
Greaves, James Pierrepont, 979
Greene, Mr., 309
Griffiths, Julia, 796
"Guy" (poem), 790, 957

Hafiz, 265, 297, 727, 772, 777, 785, 806, 832, 834, 837-38, 852, 873-74, 896, 961,
970; *Diwan*, 264, 290, 295, 308, 312, 314, 316, 322, 722, 725, 729, 736, 750, 752-53, 761, 773, 777-79, 781, 785-86, 791-92, 796-800, 802, 805, 807-8, 811-12, 816, 820, 822-23, 825, 829, 831, 833-34, 842-44, 847-48, 871-72, 874-75, 878-79, 887-88, 894-95, 898, 901, 903, 913, 915, 917-18, 924, 926, 929, 938-40, 942-46, 948-49, 951-53, 955-56, 960-61, 963, 965, 967, 969, 971, 973, 978. *See also* Bicknell, Herman
Hales, John, *Golden Remains*, 849
Halleck, Fitz-Greene, 468
Hallett, Benjamin Franklin, 281, 301
Hancock, John, 275
Handel, George Frederick, 524
"Harvest" (unidentified poem), 425
Hawthorne, Nathaniel, 773
Haydn, Franz Joseph, 323, 524
Haydon, Benjamin Robert, *Life*, 865
"The Heavens" (nonauthorial title), 972
Hedge, Frederic Henry, 741, 972
Herbert, Edward, of Cherbury, "An Ode upon a Question moved . . . ," 361n
Herbert, George, "Sinne," 805-6
"Heroism" (essay), 815, 829
Higginson, Thomas Wentworth, 746
Hill, Isaac, 281
"Historic Notes of Life and Letters in New England" (essay), 907
"History" (essay), 821, 937, 969
Hoar, Ebenezer Rockwood, 723
Hoar, Elizabeth, 584, 728, 741, 780, 861, 974
Hoar, George F., 906
Hoar, Samuel, 906
Holbrook, Joseph, 109
Holmes, John, 723-24
Holmes, Oliver Wendell, 338
Holmes, Oliver Wendell, Jr., 846
Homer, 115, 523-24; *Iliad*, 38, 975
Hooper, Anne Sturgis, 721-22
Hosmer, Edmund, 910
Howe, Estes, 723-24
"Humanity of Science" (lecture), 867-68
Hunt, Benjamin Peter, 339
Hunt, Thomas Sterry, 596
Hunt, William Morris, *The Bugle Call* (painting), 952
Hutchinson, Lucy, *Memoirs of the Life of Colonel Hutchinson*, 788

*Iamblichus on the Mysteries of the Egyptians, Chaldeans, and Assyrians*, 497, 935
Ibn Jemin, 794, 798
Ide, A. M. (?), 340
"Idealism" (poem), 769

987

"Illusions" (essay), 833, 900
"The Informing Spirit" (nonauthorial title), 822, 938
"Insight" (nonauthorial title), 840
"Inspiration" (essay), 277n, 918
"Intellect" (essay), 763, 840, 890; (nonauthorial title), 841

Jackson, Lydia. *See* Emerson, Lidian
Jalaluddin Rumi, 791
Jewett, Dr., 809
"John Milton" (lecture), 882
Johnson, Laura, 493n
Jonson, Ben, "Vision of Delight," 282
Johnson, Samuel, 739
Johnson, Rev. Samuel, 338

Kalidasa, "Meghaduta," 265
Kermani, 785
Knox, Vicesimus, *Elegant Extracts . . . in Prose,* 937

Ladd, Mary Haskins, 902
Ladd, William, 902
Lafayette, Marie Joseph, marquis de, 916
Lanfrey, Pierre, *L'Eglise et les philosophes au dix-huitième siècle,* 763
Laugel, Auguste, 339
Legge, James, *The Chinese Classics,* 325, 331, 886
Leslie, J. Peter, 339
"A Letter" (nonauthorial title), 771
"Limits" (nonauthorial title), 969
Lincoln, Abraham, 951
"Lines to Ellen" (nonauthorial title), 931
Linnaeus, Carolus, 902
Llywarch Hen, 765
Longfellow, Henry Wadsworth, 338, 778-79, 899
Longfellow, Samuel, 748
Lowell, Frank, 338
Lowell, James Russell, 338, 723-24, 770, 842-43, 904, 920-22, 934

Mallet, Paul Henri, *Northern Antiquities,* 860
Malone (unidentified), 813
Malpighi, Marcello, 869
"The Man of Letters" (address), 885
"Man the Reformer" (lecture), 910
"The Man with the Hoe" (address), 724, 783
Manzoni, Alessandro, *I Promessi Sposi,* 884
Marston, John, 106
Marx, Karl, 972; "Forced Emigration," 972
*May-Day and Other Pieces,* recipients of, 338-39
"May Morning" (nonauthorial title), 970

McCrum, Blanche Prichard, 932
*Memoirs of Margaret Fuller Ossoli* (book), 806
"Michel Angelo" (lecture), 923
Michelangelo: *Rime,* 923, 929; "Riposta, In Persona della Notte," 929; "Sonetto I," 923
Mills, John, 868
Milton, John, 523-24; *Paradise Regained,* 882; *A Selection from . . . the English Prose Works,* 805
Mississippi Valley Sanitation Fair, 959
"Modern Aspects of Letters" (lecture), 882
"Monadnock from Afar" (nonauthorial title), 769
Monadnock, Mount, 861-62
Montaigne, Michel Eyquem de, 529; *Journey into Italy,* 782
Moody, Samuel, 38
Moore, Abel, 967
Moore, Thomas, *Lalla Rookh,* 265n
Mott, Lucretia, 786
"A Mountain Grave" (nonauthorial title), 971
Mozart, Wolfgang Amadeus, 524
Munroe, Francis, 109
"Music" (nonauthorial title), 845

Nahant, Mass., 725
"Nahant" (nonauthorial title), 726
Nantasket Beach, Mass., 865
Naples, Italy, 977
Napoleon. *See* Bonaparte, Napoleon
Nash, David William, *Taliesin; or, the Bards and Druids of Britain,* 394, 923
Nash, Paulina Tucker, 339
"Natural History of Intellect" (lecture), 763, 892
*Nature* (book), 736, 854, 866, 930
"Nature" (essay), 862, 866, 873
Naushon Island, Mass., 793, 960
New York, N.Y., 763, 810-11
"Night in June" (nonauthorial title), 827
Norton, Charles Eliot, 338
Nott, John, 265

"O when to me will come" (unidentified poem), 425
"Old Age" (lecture), 883-84
Omar Khayyam, 885, 955
Ouseley, William, *Extract from . . . Heft Aklim, or the Seven Climates,* 265
"The Over-Soul" (essay), 821, 882, 956

Palfrey, Sarah Hammond, 338
"Pan" (nonauthorial title), 880
*Parnassus* (poetry anthology), 361, 402
Parsons, Thomas Williams, 338

Peabody, John Endicott, 814, 930
Pepperell, Mass., 771, 822
Pepys, Samuel, *Memoirs,* 814
Pericles, 893
Perkins, Mrs. Charles Elliot, 338
"Permanent Traits of the English National Genius" (lecture), 765
"Perpetual Forces" (essay), 783, 963
"Persian Poetry" (essay), 274n, 289n, 297n, 311n, 725, 753, 761, 772-73, 777-78, 781, 785-86, 791-92, 797-98, 805, 811, 822, 826, 829, 831, 834, 848, 875, 883-85, 887, 894-95, 902, 913, 919, 922, 926, 929, 938, 940, 943, 945, 947, 949, 951-52, 955, 960-61, 964, 973, 978
"Peter's Field" (nonauthorial title), 787, 844, 961
Peterson, Mrs. Frederick, 932
Phi Beta Kappa Poem, 916, 957, 962, 973
"Philosopher" (nonauthorial title), 893
"The Pilgrims" (poem), 696-97, 747-48
Pindar, "Olympian Ode II," 110n, 722
Pindar of Rei in Kuhistan, 886
Plato, 933; *Republic,* 312
Plutarch, 893; *Morals,* 490
"The Poet" (essay), 882; (lecture), 775, 898, 978; (nonauthorial title), 753, 757, 775-76, 803, 874
"Poetry and Criticism" (lecture), 440
"Poetry and Imagination" (essay), 813, 819, 898, 961
"Power" (essay), 503, 898
"The Present Age" (lecture series), 775
"The Priest" (nonauthorial title), 900
Prigg, Edward, 321
"Progress of Culture" (essay), 798
Prudentius, 796
Putnam, George, 949

Quincy, Edmund, 786, 894-95
"Quotation and Originality" (essay), 312n

Randolph, John, 264, 279
Rantoul, Robert, Jr., 273
Rawlins, Charles E., Jr. (?), 339
Reed, Sampson, 907; "External Restraint," 805
*Representative Men* (book), 847, 907
"Rex" (nonauthorial title), 741
Rhett, Robert Barnwell, 283
"Riches" (nonauthorial title), 809
Ripley, Sophia Dana, "Painting and Sculpture," 889
"The River" (nonauthorial title), 740
"Robert Burns" (address), 535n-540n
Rochester (N.Y.) Anti-Slavery Society, 796
Rockwell, James Otis, "The Lost at Sea," 16

Rome, Italy, 727
Rouget de Lisle, Claude Joseph, *Marseillaise,* 265n, 624n
Rowse, Samuel Worcester, 529
Rynders, Isaiah, 301

Saadi (Said, Seyd), 772, 824, 888, 907-9, 914, 936
Said. *See* Saadi
St. Augustine, Fla., 910
Salem, Mass., 821
"The School" (lecture), 880
Schoolcraft, Mrs., 279
Scott, Walter, *Guy Mannering,* 769
"Security" (nonauthorial title), 944
Seid Nimetollah of Kuhistan, 922
*Selected Poems,* list of poems for, 582-83, 588-90
"Self-Reliance" (essay), 814, 817, 898
"September" (nonauthorial title), 924
Sermon no. 63, 806
Sermon no. 127, 735
Seyd. *See* Saadi
Shakespeare, William, 115, 523-24, 914; *Hamlet,* 106, 914; *King Lear,* 914; *Othello,* 800; *Romeo and Juliet,* 804; *Troilus and Cressida,* 770; *The Two Gentlemen of Verona,* 849
Shaw, Francis George, 959
Shaw, Robert Gould, 938, 959
Shackford, Charles C., 338
Sims, Thomas, 273
"S[lowly?] with measured tread" (unidentified poem), 16
Snorri Sturluson, *The Prose or Younger Edda,* 967
"Society and Solitude" (essay), 823, 935, 937
"Song" (nonauthorial title), 942
"The Sovereignty of Ethics" (essay), 302n, 906
"Spiritual Laws" (essay), 926
Spofford, Ainsworth Rand, *The Higher Law Tried by Reason and Authority,* 318-19
Stearns, Mrs. George L., 748-49
Stearns, Mary Preston, 338
Stillman, William James, 723-24
Stoddard, Richard Henry, 820
Stow, Nathan B., 109
Sturgis, Caroline. *See* Tappan, Caroline Sturgis
"Success" (essay), 588n, 790; (lecture), 756
Sumner, Charles, 273
"Sunrise" (nonauthorial title), 976
"Svend Vonved," 588
Swedenborg, Emanuel, 115; *A Treatise Concerning Heaven . . . and . . . Hell,* 780
*S'wétás'watara Upanishad,* 809

*The Taittariya, Aitaréya, . . . Upanishads,* 809

Taliesin, 394, 923; "Preiddeu Annwn," 813. *See also* Davies, Edward *and* Nash, David William

Tappan, Caroline Sturgis, 721, 739, 759, 762, 775, 815, 850, 862, 956, 958

Tarquin the Proud, 729

Taylor, Bayard, 338

Thierry, Augustine, *History of the Conquest of England by the Normans,* 797-98, 873

"This Iron Soil" (nonauthorial title), 971

Thoreau, Henry, 335, 751, 776, 782, 809, 871, 882, 899, 973

"Thought" (nonauthorial title), 831

"To Lowell, on his Fortieth Birthday" (nonauthorial title), 843

"Tragedy," "The Tragic" (lecture), 928

"Transition" (nonauthorial title), 913

Tucker, Ellen. *See* Emerson, Ellen Tucker (wife)

Tukey, Francis, 273

Underwood, Francis, 770

*The Upanishads,* 751

Van Buren, Martin, 957

Very, Jones, 500, 834

Very, Lydia L. A., 323

Vines, Caleb, 909

*The Vishnu Purana,* 750, 757, 768, 975

Voltaire (François Marie Arouet), 765

Wachusett, Mount, 795, 841, 861

"Wachusett" (poem), 713-14, 861

"Walden" (nonauthorial title), 819, 837

"The Walk" (nonauthorial title), 901

"War" (nonauthorial title), 845

Ward, Samuel Gray, 800, 889, 891, 910

"The Waterfall" (nonauthorial title), 892

Watson, Benjamin Marston, 338

"Wealth" (essay), 503

Webster, Daniel, 274, 279, 283, 309, 962

Webster, Noah, *An American Dictionary of the English Language,* 386, 498

Weiss, John, 748, 949

Weston, Ezra, 835

Whipple, Edwin Percy, 339, 724

Whittier, John Greenleaf, 338

"Whoso alas is young" (poem), 715

"William Rufus and the Jew" (poem), 787

Willson, Forceythe, 339

Wilson, Caroline, 339

Winthrop, Robert C., 962

Wood, Elijah, Jr., 109

Woodbury, Levi, 281

Woodman, Horatio, 723-24

Wordsworth, William, *The Excursion,* 790

"Works and Days" (essay), 770, 875

"Worship" (essay), 503, 820, 975

Wright, William Bull, 339

"Written at Rome, 1833" (nonauthorial title), 727

"Written at Williamstown, Vermont" (nonauthorial title), 971

Wyman, Jeffries, 723-24

Xenophanes, 977-78

"You fast at feasts and oft invited shun" (poem), 718-19

"The Young American" (lecture), 974

Zoroaster, 765